AN ANTHOLOGY OF QUR'ANIC COMMENTARIES

VOLUME II
ON WOMEN

Building on the success of *An Anthology of Qur'anic Commentaries, Volume I: On the Nature of the Divine*, this second volume in the series focuses on a critical and contentious theme: Women in the Qur'an and traditional Qur'anic commentaries. It comprises analyses of the female subject in the Qur'an, annotated translations of Qur'anic commentaries spanning twelve centuries, interviews with contemporary Muslim scholars and extensive introductory materials, which frame the work throughout and render these technically complex materials accessible to the reader. *On Women* begins with a critical introduction to the study of women and gender in the genre of Qur'anic commentaries. A unique prolegomenon then follows key Qur'anic terms in a chronological sequence, showing how the Qur'an's worldview on women developed from the earliest Meccan revelations, when women were addressed only implicitly as a part of households or in the course of anti-pagan polemic, to the period of the final revelations in Medina, when women were addressed directly as pious and social subjects. The remainder of the volume translates, critically annotates and analyses interpretations of six select Qur'anic verses on women. These verses, chosen because of their relevance to women's lived experience, speak of the creation of humankind beginning with a single soul (Q. 4:1); the exemplary figure of Mary, the mother of Jesus (Q. 3:35–6); women's status in marriage (Q. 4:34); 'veiling' as it relates to Qur'anic norms of modesty (Q. 24:31); and women's legal testimony, and hence legal capacity, (Q. 2:282). While highlighting variation, continuity, and plurality in the genre of Qur'anic commentaries, Volume II goes beyond medieval interpretive paradigms to include perspectives marginalised by that tradition, such as the voices of women themselves.

KAREN BAUER is a Senior Research Associate at the Institute of Ismaili Studies, London. She is the author of *Gender Hierarchy in the Qur'ān: Medieval Interpretations, Modern Responses* (Cambridge, 2015) and editor of *Aims, Methods and Contexts of Qur'anic Exegesis (2nd/8th–9th/15th C.)* (Oxford, 2013). She has also published on the history of Qur'anic interpretation, on women's status as judges and witnesses in Islamic law, and on the history of emotions in Islam.

FERAS HAMZA is Head of the School of the Humanities and Social Sciences at the University of Wollongong in Dubai, UAE, and is also a Research Fellow in the Qur'anic Studies Unit at the Institute of Ismaili Studies, London. He co-edited (with Sajjad Rizvi and Farhana Mayer) *An Anthology of Qur'anic Commentaries, Volume I: On the Nature of the Divine* (Oxford, 2008) and is the general series editor for the multi-volume Anthology of Qur'anic Commentaries. He has authored several historical articles on the early Muslim community, as well as articles on the epistemological and methodological approaches in Qur'anic and *tafsīr* studies. He is currently working on a hermeneutics-based project entitled *Time and Narrative in the Qur'an*.

The Institute of Ismaili Studies

Qur'anic Studies Series 20

Series editor, Omar Alí-de-Unzaga

Previously published titles:

1. Suha Taji-Farouki, editor, *Modern Muslim Intellectuals and the Qur'an* (2004; Paperback 2006)
2. Abdullah Saeed, editor, *Approaches to the Qur'an in Contemporary Indonesia* (2005)
3. Annabel Keeler *Sufi Hermeneutics: The Qur'an Commentary of Rashīd al-Dīn Maybudī* (2006; Paperback 2017)
4. Fahmida Suleman, editor, *Word of God, Art of Man: The Qur'an and its Creative Expressions* (2007; Paperback 2010)
5. Feras Hamza and Sajjad Rizvi, editors, with Farhana Mayer, *An Anthology of Qur'anic Commentaries, Volume I: On the Nature of the Divine* (2008; Paperback 2010)
6. Toby Mayer, translator, *Keys to the Arcana: Shahrastānī's Esoteric Commentary on the Qur'an* (2009; Paperback 2019)
7. Travis Zadeh *The Vernacular Qur'an: Translation and the Rise of Persian Exegesis* (2012)
8. Martin Nguyen *Sufi Master and Qur'an Scholar: Abū'l-Qāsim al-Qushayrī and the Laṭā'if al-ishārāt* (2012)
9. Karen Bauer, editor *Aims, Methods and Contexts of Qur'anic Exegesis (2nd/8th–9th/15th C.)* (2013)
10. Angelika Neuwirth *Scripture, Poetry and the Making of a Community: Reading the Qur'an as a Literary Text* (2014)
11. M. Brett Wilson *Translating the Qur'an in an Age of Nationalism: Print Culture and Modern Islam in Turkey* (2014)
12. Andreas Görke and Johanna Pink, editors, *Tafsīr and Islamic Intellectual History: Exploring the Boundaries of a Genre* (2014)
13. S.R. Burge, editor, *The Meaning of the Word: Lexicology and Qur'anic Exegesis* (2015)
14. Suha Taji-Farouki, editor, *The Qur'an and Its Readers Worldwide: Contemporary Commentaries and Translations* (2015)
15. Annabel Keeler and Sajjad Rizvi, editors, *The Spirit and the Letter: Approaches to the Esoteric Interpretation of the Qur'an* (2016)

16. Nuha Alshaar, editor, *The Qur'an and Adab: The Shaping of Literary Traditions in Classical Islam* (2017)

17. Asma Hilali *The Sanaa Palimpsest: The Transmission of the Qur'an in the First Centuries AH* (2017)

18. Alessandro Cancian, editor, *Approaches to the Qur'an in Contemporary Iran* (2019)

19. Zulfikar Hirji, editor, *Approaches to the Qur'an in Sub-Saharan Africa* (2019)

An Anthology of Qur'anic Commentaries

VOLUME II
On Women

EDITED BY

Karen Bauer and Feras Hamza

OXFORD
UNIVERSITY PRESS

in association with

THE INSTITUTE OF ISMAILI STUDIES
LONDON

OXFORD
UNIVERSITY PRESS

Great Clarendon Street, Oxford OX2 6DP
Oxford University Press is a department of the University of Oxford.
It furthers the University's objective of excellence in research, scholarship,
and education by publishing worldwide in
Oxford New York
Auckland Cape Town Dar es Salaam Hong Kong Karachi
Kuala Lumpur Madrid Melbourne Mexico City Nairobi
New Delhi Shanghai Taipei Toronto

With offices in

Argentina Austria Brazil Chile Czech Republic France Greece
Guatemala Hungary Italy Japan Poland Portugal Singapore
South Korea Switzerland Thailand Turkey Ukraine Vietnam

Oxford is a registered trade mark of Oxford University Press
in the UK and in certain other countries

Published in the United States
by Oxford University Press Inc., New York

First published 2021

British Library Cataloguing in Publication Data
Data available

Library of Congress Cataloging in Publication Data
Data available

Cover photograph: Detached album folio showing a woman with a spray of flowers. From Iran,
Safavid period, *c.* 1575.
Arthur M. Sackler Gallery, Smithsonian Institution, Washington, DC:
Purchase – Smithsonian. Unrestricted Trust Funds, Smithsonian Collections Acquisition
Program, and Dr. Arthur M. Sackler,
S1986.296
Map: From *An Anthology of Qur'anic Commentaries, Volume I: On the Nature of the Divine*
(Oxford, 2008), p. 20.
Arabic verses: Typography by Tom Milo using DecoType ACE
Cover design: RefineCatch

Index by Kirsty Adegboro, Professional Member, Society of Indexers
Typeset by RefineCatch Ltd, Bungay, Suffolk
Printed in Great Britain on acid-free paper by
TJ Books Ltd, Padstow, Cornwall

ISBN 978-0-19284285-5

The Institute of Ismaili Studies

The Institute of Ismaili Studies was established in 1977 with the objectives of promoting scholarship and learning on Islam, in historical as well as contemporary contexts, and fostering better understanding of Islam's relationship with other societies and faiths.

The Institute's programmes encourage a perspective which is not confined to the theological and religious heritage of Islam, but seeks to explore the relationship of religious ideas to broader dimensions of society and culture. The programmes thus *encourage* an interdisciplinary approach to Islamic history and thought. Particular attention is given to the issues of modernity that arise as Muslims seek to relate their heritage to the contemporary situation.

Within the Islamic tradition, the Institute promotes research on those areas which have, to date, received relatively little attention from scholars. These include the intellectual and literary expressions of Shiʿism in general and Ismailism in particular.

The Institute's objectives are realised through concrete programmes and activities organised by various departments of the Institute, at times in collaboration with other institutions of learning. These programmes and activities are informed by the full range of cultures in which Islam is practised today. From the Middle East, South and Central Asia, and Africa to the industrialised societies in the West, they consider the variety of contexts which shape the ideals, beliefs and practices of the faith.

In facilitating the *Qur'anic Studies Series* and other publications, the Institute's sole purpose is to encourage original research and analysis of relevant issues, which often leads to diverse views and interpretations. While every effort is made to ensure that the publications are of a high academic standard, the opinions expressed in these publications must be understood as belonging to their authors alone.

QUR'ANIC STUDIES SERIES

THE QUR'AN has been an inexhaustible source of intellectual and spiritual reflection in Islamic history, giving rise to ever-proliferating commentaries and interpretations. Many of these have remained a realm for specialists due to their scholarly demands. Others, more widely read, remain untranslated from the primary language of their composition. This series aims to make some of these materials from a broad chronological range – the formative centuries of Islam to the present day – available to a wider readership through translation and publication in English, accompanied where necessary by introductory or explanatory materials. The series will also include contextual-analytical and survey studies of these primary materials.

Throughout this series and others like it which may appear in the future, the aim is to allow the materials to speak for themselves. Not surprisingly, in the Muslim world where its scriptural sources continue to command passionate interest and commitment, the Qur'an has been subject to contending, often antithetical ideas and interpretations. The series takes no sides in these debates. The aim rather is to place on the record the rich diversity and plurality of approaches and opinions which have appealed to the Qur'an throughout history (and even more so today). The breadth of this range, however partisan or controversial individual presentations within it may be, is instructive in itself. While there is always room in such matters for personal preferences, commitment to particular traditions of belief, and scholarly evaluations, much is to be gained by a simple appreciation, not always evident today, of the enormous wealth of intellectual effort that has been devoted to the Qur'an from the earliest times. It is hoped that through this objective, this series will prove of use to scholars and students in Qur'anic Studies as well as other allied and relevant fields.

Contents

Foreword

The Anthology of Qur'anic Commentaries aims to make the reception and interpretation of the Qur'an accessible to anyone interested in cultural and religious studies, rather than it remaining the province of those specialising in Islamic studies. With this in mind, the main research question underlying the Anthology is: how do historical, intellectual and social circumstances affect interpretation?

The multiple volumes of the Anthology will, collectively, emphasise the historicity of *tafsīr*, the fact that each commentator – and commentary – is a product of his own time. The volumes are designed as a standard reference work and textbook for university courses, but they also contribute towards a 'mapping' of how ideas, concepts, dogmas and fields of knowledge have evolved along a fluid history to the present time. The Anthology is a reflection of the plurality of meanings that the Qur'an itself allows for, and which have produced a vast and venerable tradition of diverse interpretations.

Each volume in the Anthology of Qur'anic Commentaries will focus on a group of Qur'anic verses organised thematically, and present the commentary on, and interpretation of, each verse by a selection of commentators representing various schools of thought. The selected commentaries will extend across a broad chronological range, from the first commentaries to the present day, and reflect linguistic and cultural variations in the field of *tafsīr*. The choice of themes for the volumes is informed by three main concerns: the topics covered in the Qur'an itself; the various subjects that have preoccupied commentators throughout history, which change over time in a variety of ways; and those issues relevant to today's world and to the contemporary scholarly understanding of the intellectual history of Islam and its heritage.

This multi-volume work hopes to add to our understanding of the evolutionary and context-dependent character of many Islamic religious and theological concepts, and to the Muslim community's conception of its own intellectual history. Such an approach calls for an examination of Islamic thought as an evolving phenomenon which responded, and continues to respond, to the circumstances of each period. This research supports the conception of Islam as a fluid intellectual civilisation with internal variety, in contrast to the view of Islam as a rigid, monolithic and unchanging community and set of norms.

Omar Alí-de-Unzaga
Academic Co-ordinator, Qur'anic Studies
The Institute of Ismaili Studies

Acknowledgements

This project has been many years in the making, and many people have helped us along the way. First and foremost, we must extend our gratitude to our in-house team at the Institute of Ismaili Studies, who have been instrumental in facilitating this project. They include the director of the Department of Academic Research and Publications Dr Farhad Daftary; the Academic Coordinator of Qur'anic Studies, Omar Alí-de-Unzaga, to whom we return below; our generous and unfailing Qur'anic Studies administrator Naushin Shariff, who has helped with all things from the technical parts of interviews to the Index of Qur'anic Citations; the entire Qur'anic Studies team, who have cheered us along with both academic and social support throughout; and, especially, the in-house Institute editors who have helped us in many ways, big and small: our main editor Lisa Morgan for her dedication, care and patience with this overwhelmingly large project, Tara Woolnough for showing great wisdom in her general editorial oversight, Russell Harris for his help with the Prosopographical Appendix, and Eleanor Payton for proofreading the entire volume.

We would also like to extend our thanks to the helpful and lovely staff at the Aga Khan Library, who supported this project in innumerable ways, and who even sent a number of books to us when we had no library access due to the Covid lockdown. We are particularly grateful to Walid Ghali, Pedro Sanchez and Alex Leach.

Special thanks to our colleagues Nicolai Sinai and Shehnaz Haqqani for their helpful feedback on the Prolegomenon. Part of that piece is published here; the full version has ended up becoming its own volume on women in the Qur'ān.

Many of our colleagues were incredibly generous and helpful with their time and resources. The following have helped us along the way by giving us feedback, their own published and unpublished work or their scanned textual sources. Their generosity was particularly welcome in times of Covid when we had limited library access. They include Kecia Ali, Yasmin Amin, Omar Anchassi, Helen Blatherwick, Emran El-Badawi, Ash Geissinger, Fârès Gillon, Paul Gledhill, Celine Ibrahim, Joseph E. Lowry, Toby Mayer, Tahera Qutbuddin, Sajjad Rizvi and Devin Stewart. Particular thanks goes to Abdeali Qutbuddin for, long ago, introducing Karen to the interpretations of Mu'ayyad fī'l-Dīn al-Shīrāzī and Qāḍī al-Nuʿmān.

We would like to thank all of our interview subjects: those whose interviews took place in Iran a decade ago in 2011; and amina wadud and Sa'diyya Shaikh, whose interviews took place over Zoom in 2020. Karen Bauer's 2011 interviews in Iran were supported by a British Academy small grant and by the support of the Institute of Ismaili Studies, including Dr Daftary, whose letter endorsed the trip and who granted her research leave; she also received the generous support of Mofid University, including the then-director of the Centre for Human Rights Studies, Dr Hedayat Yousefi. The Institute of Ismaili Studies facilitated and set up the 2020 Zoom interviews, providing technical assistance and general advice. We would like to thank the Communications Department, particularly Salima Bhatia, Susheel Gokarakonda and Rehana Virani, as well as the IT team, particularly Atif Idrees, for technical help with the interviews, as well as Naushin Sharif and Lisa Morgan whose behind-the-scenes support paved the way for the success of these encounters.

We have presented parts of this volume at various fora. While it would be impossible to mention all of these here, they include a workshop organised by Robert Gleave at the University of Exeter as a part of his Law, Authority and Learning in Imami Shiite Islam (LAWALISI) project, where Karen Bauer discussed al-Qurṭubī's interpretation of Q. 4:34; the workshop 'Gender, Authenticity, and Islamic Authority' organised by Sara Omar and Travis Zadeh and Yale University in 2019; and the Freiburg Conversations on Tafsīr and Transregional Studies, 2021, organised by Majid Daneshgar and Johanna Pink. We jointly presented some of the findings from the Prolegomenon at the 2021 virtual meeting of the International Qur'anic Studies Association (IQSA). We would like to thank our colleagues for their helpful interventions on these occasions.

We are grateful for the constructive feedback provided at a crucial juncture by the anonymous peer reviewers. Their comments provoked more than a remedial response and pushed us to be more creative in this volume.

Many people outside of the Institute have also helped with the production of the volume, including Karen Raith at Oxford University Press, Kirsty Adegboro who did our indexing, and the typesetters at RefineCatch.

We reserve our final expression of gratitude for Omar Alí-de-Unzaga, whose vision for Qur'ān and *tafsīr* studies has resulted not only in this project, but has allowed for a wonderful variety of scholarship to emerge from the Institute. We also credit this vision with bringing us together as colleagues, in what, at the time, may have seemed the most unlikely of collaborations.

And, for their endless patience, we dedicate this to Rula al-Jadir and Peter Keevash, and to our children: Dunia, Yousef, Simon and Iris.

Note on translation and conventions

As in the *Anthology of Qur'anic Commentaries, Volume I: On the Nature of the Divine*, in translating the primary texts, we have attempted to remain as faithful as possible to the original Arabic. Thus while the translations will not always read idiomatically in English, the student of Arabic or the interested reader armed with the Arabic text should be able to follow the original fairly closely. In the first volume, the decision was made to omit honorifics from the translations due to the volume's overall length. In this volume we have been able to retain them. While honorifics overtly seem to interrupt the English text, including them is more consonant with the overall flavour of the Arabic originals which were, for their authors, a profound engagement with the divine word. For them, reverence for the Prophet is naturally extended to the Prophet's family, his Companions and major figures in early Islam.

Given the voluminous nature of much of the *tafsīr* material and the obvious restrictions of space, a number of editorial measures were deemed necessary. This is particularly relevant to Ṭabarī's commentary. The chains of transmission (*isnād*s) in Ṭabarī and Ibn Kathīr have been removed from the English translation so that only the crucial transmitters are named in-text. Reports with identical content have often been omitted. Commentators often include material not relevant to the verse at hand, and in these cases an ellipsis [. . .] is used to indicate where the translation has been abridged.

Some of what has been included here may not seem directly relevant to the subject at hand (sc. 'women'). Grammatical discussions, for instance, occupy a substantial space in most of the classical commentaries and we have omitted a certain number of these. However, it would have been unfaithful to the nature of *tafsīr* works to remove all of them. Where the commentaries sideline questions of sex or gender entirely, that is noteworthy in itself, precisely because this shows the nature of the questions that exegetes through time have asked of the Qur'ānic text, and how that may differ from the questions being asked of it by modern readers.

All Qur'ān translations are our own.

Transliteration and dates

The system of transliteration used is essentially that of the *Encyclopaedia of Islam*, with the exception of dj and ḳ, which are represented as j and q respectively. Dates are given in both Hijri (AH) and Common Era (CE) calendars; if they stand alone, they are to be read as Common Era dates. Shamsi dates are indicated by Sh. and the equivalent Common Era date is given.

References

Full references to our sources are given at the first mention and thereafter in short form. By the conclusion of this lengthy project, we often ended up relying on numerous editions of these primary sources, including the online versions at altafsir.com. For that reason, and given the proliferation of editions online and in print in the last decade, we do not give page references to our primary works of *tafsīr* or *ḥadīth*. Instead, references in our primary works of *tafsīr* simply include the *sūra* and verse number; *ḥadīth* references include the author, work, *kitāb*, *bāb* and *ḥadīth* number (the latter of which differ greatly between sources). All encyclopaedia references are given in full in the notes.

Citations from the Qurʾān, whether in transliterated Arabic or in English, are in italics and are identified by [Q.], followed by the *sūra* and verse number. Where the Qurʾān has been paraphrased or is not an exact citation, the relevant text is indicated by [cf. Q.].

Abbreviations

Please note: PA has been used throughout to refer to the Prosopographical appendix to this volume.

EI[1]	*Encyclopaedia of Islam*, 1st edn, Leiden, 1913–38
EI[2]	*Encyclopaedia of Islam*, 2nd edn, Leiden, 1954–2004
EI[3]	*Encyclopaedia of Islam, THREE*
EIr	*Encyclopaedia Iranica*, New York, 1982–
EQ	*Encyclopaedia of the Qurʾān*, Leiden, 2001–2006
ER	*Encyclopaedia of Religion*, 1st edn, New York, 1987
ER[2]	*Encyclopaedia of Religion*, 2nd edn, Detroit, 2005
GAL	*Geschichte der arabischen Literatur*, Leiden, 1898–1949
GAS	*Geschichte der arabischen Schrifttums*, Leiden, 1967–84
GQ	Theodor Nöldeke, *Geschichte des Qorans*, 2nd edn, Leipzig, 1909–38
Lexicon	Edward W. Lane, *An Arabic-English Lexicon*, London, 1863–93
OEMIW	*Oxford Encyclopaedia of the Modern Islamic World*, New York, 1995
TG	Josef van Ess, *Theologie und Gesellschaft im 2. und 3. Jahrhundert Hidschra: Eine Geschichte des religiösen Denkens im frühen Islam*, Berlin, New York, 1991–7

Honorifics:
The Prophet (*ṣlʿm*) = peace and blessings be upon him
The Prophet (*ṣlʿhm*) = peace and blessings be upon him and his family
The Prophet (*ṣlʿ*) = blessings be upon him
The Prophet (*ṣlʿh*) = blessings be upon him and his family
The prophets/imams/etc (*ʿm*) = upon him be peace
Upon her be peace (said of Eve, for instance) (*ʿam*)

Introduction

ISLAMIC TEXTS such as the Qur'ān, Qur'ānic commentaries and *fiqh* manuals played a key role in determining the social and legal status of medieval Muslim women. In the contemporary period, these texts remain authoritative and hence continue to frame debates on women, women's rights and gender equality in Muslim contexts.[1] Such dynamics have shaped Muslims' understanding of their own religion and have contributed to legislation in some Muslim-majority countries. However, the authoritative sources have been, and largely remain, the purview of a scholastic elite, and as such have been inaccessible to many of those who are directly impacted by them in everyday life. Within that scholastic tradition, it is also important to note that the relationship between the Qur'ān and its commentaries only serves to compound the inaccessibility because of the ways in which the scholars have mediated the Qur'ān through these technically complex commentaries. *An Anthology of Qur'anic Commentaries: On Women* is a first

[1] A few of the Western scholarly books on gender that engage medieval sources include: Kecia Ali, *Sexual Ethics and Islam: Feminist Reflections on Qur'ān, Hadith, and Jurisprudence* (London, Oneworld, 2006); eadem, *Marriage and Slavery in Early Islam* (Cambridge, MA, Harvard University Press, 2010); Hina Azam, *Sexual Violation in Islamic Law: Substance, Evidence, and Procedure* (Cambridge, Cambridge University Press, 2015); Asma Barlas, *Believing Women in Islam: Unreading Patriarchal Interpretations of the Qur'an* (Austin, University of Texas Press, 2002); Nimat Hafez Barazangi, *Woman's Identity and the Qur'an: A New Reading* (Tallahassee, University Press of Florida, 2004); Karen Bauer, *Gender Hierarchy in the Qur'ān: Medieval Interpretations, Modern Responses* (Cambridge, Cambridge University Press, 2015); Ayesha S. Chaudhry, *Domestic Violence and the Islamic Tradition: Ethics, Law, and the Muslim Discourse on Gender* (Oxford, Oxford University Press, 2013); Aysha Hidayatullah, *Feminist Edges of the Qur'ān* (Oxford, Oxford University Press, 2014); Manuela Marín and Randi Deguilhem, eds., *Writing the Feminine: Women in Arab Sources* (London, I.B. Tauris, 2002); Ziba Mir-Hosseini, *Islam and Gender: The Religious Debate in Contemporary Iran* (Princeton, NJ, Princeton University Press, 1999); Ziba Mir-Hosseini, Mulki al-Sharmani and Jana Rumminger, eds., *Men in Charge? Rethinking Authority in Muslim Legal Tradition* (London, Oneworld, 2015); Asifa Quraishi and Frank Vogel, eds., *The Islamic Marriage Contract: Case Studies in Islamic Family Law* (Cambridge, MA, Harvard University Press, 2008); Sa'diyya Shaikh, *Sufi Narratives of Intimacy: Ibn 'Arabi, Gender, and Sexuality* (Chapel Hill, University of North Carolina Press, 2012); Barbara Freyer Stowasser, *Women in the Qur'an, Traditions, and Interpretation* (Oxford, Oxford University Press, 1994); Judith Tucker, *Women, Family, and Gender in Islamic Law* (Cambridge, Cambridge University Press, 2008); amina wadud, *Qur'an and Woman: Rereading the Sacred Text from a Woman's Perspective*, 2nd edn (Oxford, Oxford University Press, 1999).

step towards making these authoritative texts on women accessible to a wider audience.[2]

This volume begins with a prolegomenon, 'The Qurʾānic Lexicon on Women', a chronological analysis of the lexicon on women and 'the female' in the Qurʾānic text, showing the emergence of women as pious subjects through time. The subsequent chapters are translations of medieval and modern Qurʾānic commentaries on five verses that lie at the heart of the question of women's status. These verses speak of the creation of the first woman Eve/Ḥawwāʾ (Q. 4:1), Mary, the mother of Jesus (Q. 3:35–6), women's status in marriage (Q. 4:34), the veil (Q. 24:31) and women's testimony in court (Q. 2:282). All of our translations are augmented by clear introductions, thus making these sources accessible to students and non-specialists. We chose these verses because of their resonance and contemporary relevance to women's lived experiences today.

Readers familiar with the *Anthology of Qur'anic Commentaries*, vol. I: *On the Nature of the Divine* will be aware that the volume moved directly from a general introduction to the thematic chapters. But we would have done a great injustice to the intellectual contribution of a volume on women if we had not undertaken a fresh discursive analysis of verses on women in the Qurʾān. This we offer in the Prolegomenon. The Prolegomenon pursues the lexicon on 'women' and 'the female' chronologically through the entire Qurʾān. This lexical-chronological focus differs from existing approaches to the subject; as such, it tells a different type of story about how women are positioned within the overall Qurʾānic kerygma.[3] When the Qurʾān's lexicon on women is analysed according to current theories of Qurʾānic chronology, it shows a development through time. We posit that this development reflects

[2] In her thought-provoking essay entitled 'Who are We Writing for When We Translate Classical Texts?' Marion Katz points out that the people who are most likely to be the audience of classical Islamic texts, namely other scholars, are the ones who are least likely to need translations. Nevertheless, the technical complexity of the texts in this volume makes them difficult to understand without specialist intervention. We hope that our introductions and annotations will serve the purpose of such intervention, and that this work may yet be of some use not only for those teaching and researching women in the Qurʾān and its interpretation but for academics doing comparative work, for academics who are not specialists in *tafsīr*, for scholars of gender who might not otherwise be able to access these texts and for students; because of its subject, this work may also be of interest to non-academics. See Marion Holmes Katz, 'Who are We Writing for When We Translate Classical Texts?' *Islamic Law Blog*, 6 December 2019, https://islamiclaw.blog/2019/12/06/muwaṭṭa'-roundtable-who-are-we-writing-for-when-we-translate-classical-texts/.

[3] For instance, Barlas' *Believing Women in Islam* is a feminist reading of the Qurʾān rather than a lexical analysis of the instances of the term 'believing women' (*muʾmināt*). For a brief summary of the subject of women in the Qurʾān, see Ruth Roded, 'Women and the Qurʾān', *EQ*, V, 523–41.

the emergence of women as pious and social subjects in the Muslim community as the community itself evolves from Mecca to Medina.

While the Prolegomenon gives a glimpse into the place of women in the Qur'ānic worldview, the commentaries translated in the subsequent chapters show how generations of scholars, from the earliest medieval interpreters to modern reformists and conservatives, have interpreted specific threads from this Qur'ānic whole. The main sources for the thematic chapters of this volume are from the genre of Qur'ānic commentaries (*tafsīr*), the one genre that is dedicated to commenting on the entire Qur'ān, which is considered by some to be the authoritative source for formal Muslim discourse on, among other types, those legal, homiletic and narrative passages of the Qur'ān. *Tafsīr* is also a genre that is delimited in key ways: in the medieval period, it was always intended for a scholarly audience and focused on philology, grammar and other technical and scholastic methods of considering Qur'ānic meaning, while modern works of *tafsīr* often incorporate some medieval rulings into modern explanations for a general audience. As a scholarly genre, *tafsīr* was never meant to include every type of meaning that could be assigned to Qur'ānic verses. Our translations of both medieval and modern texts reveal how the modern scholarly debate on women's rights in Islam has been in part shaped by medieval commentaries, and thus by medieval sensibilities. In order to achieve some representation of the range of Muslim thought on these verses, we have gone beyond the genre of Qur'ānic commentary in several instances. Thus we have included some medieval Ismāʿīlī interpretations, which give an idea of the rich diversity of Muslim thought, and we have also included the transcripts of interviews with modern Muslim scholars and exegetes.

Some would argue that it is misleading to centre the debate about women's rights on religious texts. Anthropologist Lila Abu-Lughod has described how Western media, charities and governments often use the trope of the repressed Muslim woman to justify imperialist intervention, whether economic, political or military, in the Muslim-majority world. Abu-Lughod profiles Muslim women who argue that, rather than being oppressed by Islam, they are oppressed by their governments.[4] It is important to note, along with Abu-Lughod, that governments ultimately determine women's rights. It would be naïve to assume that women's social or legal status depends on the interpretations of religious scholars alone; yet it is also problematic to ignore those interpretations, as though religion exists in a sphere separate

[4] Lila Abu-Lughod, *Do Muslim Women Need Saving?* (Cambridge, MA, Harvard University Press, 2013), esp. 211–12.

from state politics, and as though the views of religious leaders are disconnected from believers' conduct in their daily lives, or indeed that the daily lives of religious practitioners have discrete spheres such as 'the religious' and 'the non-religious'.[5]

One of Abu-Lughod's main points is that, far from seeing their religion as oppressive, many Muslim women see it as a source of empowerment.[6] It is self-evident that when people choose to identify as Muslims, they often do so precisely because they feel empowered by this identity; this can involve a deep attachment to the Qur'ān. Furthermore, Muslims may not approach the Qur'ān principally as a legalistic document, to be seen solely in light of the rights it grants or proscriptions it imposes. Many Qur'ānic stories, including that of Eve, Ḥanna (Mary's mother) and Mary, are deeply empowering to women; some would go so far as to revere Mary as enjoying the status of a prophet;[7] the basic aspect of spiritual equality in the text is undeniable. Yet we do not wish to gloss over the difficulties some Muslims face when they wish to reconcile the modern ideal of social egalitarianism with the words of the Qur'ān, with the textual tradition of Qur'ānic commentaries and with that tradition's effect on their lived experience today.[8] Far from skirting vexing Qur'ānic verses or ignoring a history of interpretation that is sometimes at odds with current notions of equal

[5] The scholarly field of the anthropology of ethics and morality makes any such dichotomies between 'the religious' and everything else – be it politics or the social – outright facile and certainly increasingly moot. See Veena Das, 'Ordinary Ethics' in *A Companion to Moral Anthropology*, ed. Didier Fassin (New York, Wiley Blackwell, 2012), 133–49; Michael Lambek, *Ordinary Ethics: Anthropology, Language and Action* (New York, Fordham University Press, 2010); James Laidlaw, *The Subject of Virtue: An Anthropology of Ethics and Freedom* (Cambridge, Cambridge University Press, 2014).

[6] In a related vein, some recent literature is dedicated to Muslim women's religious authority. See especially Masooda Bano and Hilary Kalmbach, eds., *Women, Leadership, and Mosques: Changes in Contemporary Islamic Authority* (Leiden, Brill, 2016); Mirjam Künkler and Devin Stewart, eds., *Women's Religious Authority in Shi'i Islam: Past and Present* (Edinburgh, Edinburgh University Press, 2020).

[7] Maribel Fierro, 'Women as Prophets in Islam' in *Writing the Feminine*, ed. Marín and Deguilhem, 183–98. See also n. 3 in 'Mary' (ch. 2 in this volume).

[8] Progressive Muslims have written extensively about their struggles with the textual tradition. As we note later in the introduction, amina wadud even changed her view from the early view in which she argued that the Qur'ān is gender egalitarian (in *Qur'an and Woman*) to a later one in which she says 'no' to certain aspects of it (in *Inside the Gender Jihad: Women's Reform in Islam* [Oxford, Oneworld, 2006]). Other progressive reflections include Farid Esack, *On Being a Muslim: Finding a Religious Path in the World Today* (London, Oneworld, 2009); Omid Safi, ed., *Progressive Muslims: On Justice, Gender, and Pluralism (Islam in the Twenty-First Century)* (London, Oneworld, 2003); Suha Taji-Farouki, ed., *Modern Muslim Intellectuals and the Qur'an* (Oxford, Oxford University Press in association with the Institute of Ismaili Studies, 2006). See also the website *Critical Muslim*, https://criticalmuslim.com/. Many progressive voices have found a home in the Western academic study of Islam and the Qur'ān.

human rights, our purpose here is to represent this history as faithfully as possible.[9]

Towards a contextualisation of the study of women in the Qur'ān

This book focuses on verses that have to do with women in the Qur'ān, which raises the question of how these verses can be contextualised in the larger picture of sex and gender within the text. Although this is a book primarily on Qur'ānic interpretation, in the following paragraphs we hope to indicate how historical contextualisation might aid the study of women in the Qur'ān.[10]

The concept of biological sex has come under fire from many who point out that there is a third category of intersex (the *khunthā* of Islamic law), that medical issues can exist which call into question a person's biological sex and that, regardless of any biological assignment, people may feel that they are a particular sex or that they do not fall into any binary categorisation. In the Islamic realm, for instance, the *khunthā* may not be an entirely biological category. This is aside from the question of sexuality and sexual preference, which permits an equally varied tapestry. Important contributions exist on sex, sexuality and gender in Islamic contexts,[11] and Islamic masculinities is

[9] We recognise that many Muslim women believe that the sexes should not be treated equally under the law, and they believe that to treat men and women equally is to ignore religious rulings that treat them differently; we represent such views in our translations, particularly in the interviews with Fariba Alasvand. We admit that we cannot escape our own personal perspective, which is that all human beings should have equal rights under the law, other than those people who need extra protection for particular reasons (such as those who may face discrimination). On the issues of agency, postcolonialism and feminist perspectives, see Monica Mookherjee, 'Affective Citizenship: Feminism, Postcolonialism and the Politics of Recognition', *Critical Review of International Social and Political Philosophy* 8.1 (2005), 31–50.

[10] While this is not the place for a full discussion of the history of gender and sex, it is worth noting that Judith Butler famously described sex as a social construct, while Monique Wittig speaks of sex as a category of oppression: 'for there is no sex. There is but sex that is oppressed and sex that oppresses. It is oppression that creates sex and not the contrary.' Monique Wittig, 'The Category of Sex', *Feminist Issues* 2.2 (1982), 63–8.

[11] On sexuality in the Islamic context, see especially Zahra Ayubi, *Gendered Morality: Classical Islamic Ethics of the Self, Family, and Society* (New York, Columbia University Press, 2019); Indira Falk Gesink, 'Intersex Bodies in Premodern Islamic Discourse: Complicating the Binary', *Journal of Middle East Women's Studies* 14.2 (2018), 152–73; Scott Kugle, *Homosexuality in Islam: Critical Reflections on Gay, Lesbian, and Transgender Muslims* (London, Oneworld, 2010); idem, *Living Out Islam: Voices of Gay, Lesbian, and Transgender Muslims* (New York, New York University Press, 2014); Afsaneh Najmabadi, *Women with Mustaches and Men Without Beards: Gender and Sexual Anxieties of Iranian Modernity* (Berkeley, University of California Press, 2005); eadem, *Professing Selves: Transsexuality and Same-Sex Desire in Contemporary Iran* (Durham, NC, Duke University Press, 2014); Kathryn Babayan and Afsaneh

increasingly attended to within this overall gender debate.[12] It may be noted here that the purpose of this volume is not to undertake an in-depth study of sex, gender and biology; it only touches on those issues insofar as the commentaries show how their authors have defined 'woman' and 'man' through time. This reveals how they reify gender norms, espousing a bounded and usually inflexible view of biological sex and sexuality. Gender theorists might assert that the commentators actually create 'sex' through the enforcement of power dynamics. Such views often go well beyond the words of the Qur'ān itself.

The current trend in the field of Qur'ānic studies is to see this text within its late antique context, and we would suggest that this is a fruitful way of understanding the discourse on sex and gender in the Qur'ān. The notions of sex, gender, biology and social roles have been investigated and interrogated in the Bible, in Hellenistic and late antique Judaism, and in late antique Christianity. For instance, it was shown over a decade ago that for the Jewish philosopher Philo of Alexandria (d. *c.* 50), the first Biblical incarnation of Adam was as a genderless spiritual being, described in Genesis 1:26–8 and Genesis 5:1–2, and that embodied gendered creation took place in a separate Biblical account of creation (at Genesis 2:7ff.). And Philo was not an isolated interpreter, but was drawing on an existing tradition: 'for many Hellenistic Jews the oneness of pure spirit is ontologically privileged in the constitution of humanity'.[13]

Feminists have argued that the Qur'ān preserves a genderless space, particularly in its telling of human creation. Recent contributions have also called into question the extent to which female characters in the Qur'ān

Najmabadi, eds., *Islamicate Sexualities: Translations across Temporal Geographies of Desire* (Cambridge, MA, Harvard University Press, 2008); Leslie Pierce, 'Writing Histories of Sexuality in the Middle East', *American Historical Review* 114.5 (2009), 1325–39; Khaled El-Rouayheb, *Before Homosexuality in the Islamic World, 1500–1800* (Chicago, IL, University of Chicago Press, 2005); Everett Rowson, 'The Categorization of Gender and Sexual Irregularity in Medieval Arabic Vice Lists' in *Body Guards: The Cultural Politics of Gender Ambiguity*, ed. Julia Epstein and Kristina Straub (New York, Routledge, 1991), 50–79; idem, 'The Effeminates of Early Medina', *Journal of the American Oriental Society* 111 (1991), 671–93; idem, 'Two Homoerotic Narratives from Mamluk Literature: Al-Safadi's *Law'at al-shaki* and Ibn Daniyal's *al-Mutayyam*' in *Homoeroticism in Classical Arabic Literature*, ed. J.W. Wright Jr. and Everett K. Rowson (New York, Columbia University Press, 1997), 158–91; idem, 'Gender Irregularity as Entertainment: Institutionalized Transvestism at the Caliphal Court in Medieval Baghdad' in *Gender and Difference in the Middle Ages*, ed. Sharon Farmer and Carol Braun Pasternack (Minneapolis, University of Minnesota Press, 2003), 45–72; Elyse Smerdjian, *Off the Straight Path: Illicit Sex, Law, and Community in Ottoman Aleppo* (Albany, State University of New York Press, 2016); Vanja Hamzić, *Sexual and Gender Diversity in the Muslim World: History, Law and Vernacular Knowledge* (London, I.B. Tauris, 2017).

[12] Amanullah De Sondy, *The Crisis of Islamic Masculinities* (London, Bloomsbury Academic, 2013); Lahoucine Ouzagane, ed., *Islamic Masculinities* (London, Zed Books, 2006).

[13] Daniel Boyarin, 'Gender' in *Critical Terms for Religious Studies*, ed. Mark C. Taylor (Chicago, IL, University of Chicago Press, 1998), 120.

adhere to modern ideas of gendered roles.[14] This is not to deny that most Qur'ānic references to women must necessarily be understood as referring to women as a biological sex; rather, it is to say that there is a story beyond biological sex, which might find parallels in the Jewish and Christian traditions and in the late antique milieu. And yet, while verses such as Q. 4:1 indicate a genderless Qur'ānic realm to many readers, it is also worth investigating how notions of gendered biological sex inform Qur'ānic pronouncements.

In order to follow the internal logic by which women and gender are depicted in the Qur'ān, it is necessary to have some understanding of the social structure of early Islamic Arabia and some sense of the Qur'ān's major salvific theme. The *pater familias* had a well-recognised social role across the late antique Mediterranean, and the Qur'ānic treatment of women assumes a hierarchical tribal and familial structure with a male head of household.[15] In the Qur'ānic verses that are chronologically earliest,[16] that is to say the Meccan verses, the social importance of this head of household is apparent in eschatological discussions that presume a male audience, despite clear and simultaneous statements of women's equal creational status with men.

The community's migration from Mecca to Medina is when, according to Muslim historians, they went from a minority fighting against the existing elites, to becoming the elite themselves. Medinan verses clarify social structures for the emergent community. It is thus not surprising that women's worldly situation as a part of a social hierarchy is overwhelmingly addressed in the text's Medinan sections: it is in this period that we find verses such as Q. 4:34, which speaks of the marital hierarchy; but it is also in this period that we find some of the strongest statements of the spiritual equality of men and women, such as Q. 33:35:

> *Indeed, men who submit and women who submit, believing men and believing women, men who are piously obedient and women who are piously obedient, truthful men and truthful women, men who endure and women who endure, humble men and humble women, men who are charitable and women who are charitable, fasting men and fasting women, men and women who safeguard their private parts, those men and women who remember God often, for (all of) them, God has prepared forgiveness and a tremendous reward.*[17]

[14] See for instance Kecia Ali, 'Destabilizing Gender, Reproducing Maternity: Mary in the Qur'ān', *Journal of the International Qur'anic Studies Association* 2 (2017), 89–109.

[15] Robert Hoyland points out that the tribal structure in pre-Islamic Arabia consisted of a progression of groups, from family to tribe, to larger tribal networks; all of these were presumably headed by men. Robert Hoyland, *Arabia and the Arabs: From the Bronze Age to the Coming of Islam* (London, Routledge, 2001), 113–17. See also the Prolegomenon in this volume.

[16] For more on Qur'ānic chronology, see the Prolegomenon below.

[17] All Qur'ān translations in this volume are our own.

Q. 33:35 assures both male and female believers that they can achieve forgiveness and a heavenly reward for the very same righteous actions.[18] Thus women are fully recognised as pious subjects.[19] Evidently the Qurʾān's original audience did not see any contradiction between a worldly hierarchy and spiritual equality; social inequality was not incompatible with loving relations among people.[20] Because for many modern readers the fundamental principle of equality is bound up with the notion of justice, it can be difficult to understand how a social system could be both hierarchical and just, with both elements as part of a coherent and evolving spiritual discourse; yet this is the case in the Qurʾān.

The main purpose of the Qurʾānic narrations is always eschatological, a point that is often lost in discussions of gender. In the Qurʾānic worldview, every worldly act must be undertaken with the aim of reaching the Hereafter, where piety rather than any social standing will determine a person's rank. According to many verses, piety (viz. *taqwā*, *birr*) consists not only in acts of worship to God but also in acts undertaken towards other people, such as charitable giving. Worldly, or social, hierarchies require the fulfilment of social duties as a moral virtue: in the case of marriage, for example, the *pater familias* had a clear moral duty to care for those under his protection. The question remains of how the social world envisioned by the Qurʾān is similar to, or different from, the existing late antique and pre-Islamic social worlds in which it emerged.

Medieval and modern commentators alike have argued that the Qurʾān represented a significant improvement in the rights of women, in that its verses made provision for Muslim women's right to own property, prohibited the burial of live infant girls (which indicates that this may have been a practice) and, perhaps most importantly, addressed women directly, promising them an equal reward for their good deeds. But the assertion that Islam was an unequivocal improvement for women's status is not supported by even a perfunctory survey of the existing research on the Qurʾānic milieu.[21] The

[18] For a summary of medieval commentaries on this verse, see the appendix to this introduction.

[19] This transition from Meccan to Medinan terminology on 'women' and 'the female' are traced in the Prolegomenon.

[20] Hidayatullah, *Feminist Edges of the Qurʾān*, 165.

[21] Leila Ahmed argues that Islam worsened women's lot by suggesting that 'the subordination in the ancient Middle East appears to have become institutionalized with the rise of urban societies and with the rise of the archaic state in particular'. Leila Ahmed, *Women and Gender in Islam* (New Haven, CT, Yale University Press, 1992), 11. She argues that there was a decline in the position of women in the pre-Islamic period coinciding with the fall of goddesses and the rise of gods, and that women in pre-Islamic Arabia had more rights than women under Islam. She identifies the change with Muḥammad becoming firmly established as a statesman and community leader. Ibid., esp. 42–3.

immediate Qur'ānic context of pre-Islamic Arabia and late antique Byzantium seems to have been deeply patriarchal in general; yet that did not prevent women from having rights or even, surprisingly, some freedoms.

The question of women's social status in the late antique Christian and pagan milieu has been the subject of scholarly work for decades, and the most well-known and well-recognised findings show interesting similarities with the Qur'ānic worldview. For instance, women were not prevented from owning property in late antiquity: they were entitled to property and could inherit. There are records of many wealthy women dedicating their property to the Church. The dowry was important, and sometimes a woman's dowry constituted 'her share of the family inheritance'.[22] An engagement was often marked by a gift, and the Roman emperor Constantine (r. 306–37) ruled that if a groom broke the engagement, the gift could be kept by the bride.[23] Men in Roman law were presumed to be the heads of household and women were commonly perceived as weak, 'physically hampered by child-bearing', 'under-educated', dependent and emotionally vulnerable.[24] John Chrysostom (d. 407) wrote that men had 'unrestricted access' to their wives, which in his view ignored the wives' reciprocal prerogative to sexual desire and fulfilment.[25] Women were considered to be at a disadvantage, which generally extended to the intellectual realm as well, even when women themselves chose celibacy or chose philosophical pursuits.[26]

Much less is known of the exact practices in pre-Islamic Arabia. As Robert Hoyland has found, descent was usually patrilineal, but was occasionally reckoned matrilineally.[27] In some instances, women seemed to enjoy sexual freedom, such as the practice of temporary marriage, where a woman could advertise for a mate if she wanted children, and there are records from South Arabia indicating that one woman might have many husbands (polyandry); but this arrangement was not necessarily to the woman's benefit, as it seems that a single woman was often shared among brothers who lived in a household together.[28] Thus it is not necessarily the case that polyandry connotes a

[22] Gillian Clark, *Women in Late Antiquity: Pagan and Christian Lifestyles* (New York, Oxford University Press USA, 1993), 13.

[23] Ibid., 14. Cf. Q. 33:49, in which the believing men are told that if they divorce women before they have touched them, they should provide for them.

[24] Ibid., 56.

[25] Ibid., 91. Cf. Q. 2:223, *Your women are like your sowing fields, so tend to your sowing fields however you desire.*

[26] Ibid., 119–38.

[27] Robert Hoyland, *Arabia and the Arabs*, 129. The whole section on women is useful, viz. 128–34.

[28] Ibid., 131. This may provide context for Qur'ānic passages aimed at organising categories of marriageability and restricting marriage among kin to certain degrees of consanguinity (see Q. 4:23 and 33:50).

woman's free choice of sexual partner. Although women in pre-Islamic Arabia were primarily described as wives and mothers, there are indications that in some pre-Islamic societies they enjoyed financial independence, and that they acted as religious functionaries, queens and entertainers.

The Qur'ānic worldview seems to fit into this pre-Islamic and late antique context. In this context, the idea of sexual and gender egalitarianism – or any social egalitarianism – was either highly uncommon or unknown. Instead of establishing equality in marriage or in society as a whole, the aim of the Qur'ān seems to have been to attach moral probity and the consequent heavenly reward to the enactment of a fair and just social structure. True piety was not through personal or private actions, such as prayer or fasting, alone; rather, those in power were constantly reminded that God had guaranteed rights, dignity and protection to the most vulnerable, and that their own salvation rested on ensuring those rights. The emergence of an explicit recognition of women as pious and social subjects, which is what we show in the Prolegomenon, stands out in this context. Women are seen to have moral agency, which is the type of agency that is valued above all others in the Qur'ān. Hence the Qur'ān recognises the equal intrinsic value of all humans, without challenging the social status position of the *pater familias*.

The genre of Qur'ānic commentary (*tafsīr*)

Most of the works translated in this volume are from the genre of the Qur'ānic commentary called, in Arabic, *tafsīr al-Qur'ān*. The term *tafsīr al-Qur'ān* simply means the explanation, or explication, of the Qur'ān, and in this broad sense this is a widespread activity which takes place in many different genres of text, including poetry, history, law (*fiqh*) and novels; in many types of printed material, including scholarly and popular magazines and journals; and in many types of location, including mosques, classrooms, private homes and, recently, YouTube, blogs, Twitter, TikTok and other online fora. *Tafsīr* in this sense is undertaken by a range of people, and these interpretations are naturally influenced by a range of factors, including the culture and politics of the countries in which they are produced.[29] But the term *tafsīr al-Qur'ān* also refers to a specific genre of text, produced through time by classically trained scholars, and it is such texts that are included in this volume. While

[29] For an excellent introduction to the modern production of *tafsīr*, see Johanna Pink, *Muslim Qur'ānic Interpretation Today: Media, Genealogies and Interpretive Communities* (Sheffield, Equinox, 2019).

exegetical activity can take place anywhere, the genre of *tafsīr* has as its central aim the exposition of the import of Qur'ānic verses and passages.

The genre of *tafsīr* can be considered part of the Muslim 'tradition'. 'Tradition' is a multivalent term; in this context, it usually refers to specific textual genres in which present understanding is always anchored in the received reports. In genres such as law (*fiqh*), history and *tafsīr*, historical precedent is an inevitable part of current interpretations. Modern scholars have described the process of producing and reproducing these textual traditions in various ways. The accretion of historical reports over time, which sometimes involved the erasure of the original report, has been compared to stratigraphy, the geological layering of rock.[30] *Tafsīr* has also been called a 'genealogical' tradition.[31] Johanna Pink describes why the genealogical approach works for *tafsīr*: it is a historical model which does not privilege change over continuity or view 'change as the irreconcilable antagonist of continuity'.[32] Rather, in *tafsīr*, elements of historical continuity are incorporated into an ever-evolving discourse.

Prominent authors in the textual genre of Qur'ānic commentaries are respected, in part, because they seek to represent the interpretations of their forbears with accuracy in textual transmissions leading back to the Prophet and his Companions. One aim of this genre of text is to present an accurate picture of the earliest interpretations of the Qur'ān, which many Muslims consider an exemplary model for today's world. Yet many scholars have observed that the genre's elements of continuity become, inevitably, a part of its change over time.[33] The authors of *tafsīr* consciously draw on prior

[30] Sarah Savant, *The New Muslims of Post-Conquest Iran: Tradition, Memory, and Conversion* (Cambridge, Cambridge University Press, 2013).

[31] Walid Saleh, *The Formation of the Classical Tafsīr Tradition: The Qur'ān Commentary of al-Tha'labī (d. 427/1035)* (Leiden, Brill, 2003), 16; Pink, *Muslim Qur'ānic Interpretation Today*, 8–10.

[32] Pink, *Muslim Qur'ānic Interpretation Today*, 8.

[33] On change, continuity and the nature of Qur'ānic exegesis, see Jane Dammen McAuliffe, 'Qur'ānic Hermeneutics: The Views of al-Ṭabarī and Ibn Kathīr' in *Approaches to the History of the Interpretation of the Qur'ān*, ed. Andrew Rippin (Oxford, Clarendon Press, 1988), 46–62; Norman Calder, '*Tafsīr* from Ṭabarī to Ibn Kathīr: Problems in the Description of a Genre, Illustrated with Reference to the Story of Abraham' in *Approaches to the Qur'ān*, ed. Gerald R. Hawting and Abdul-Kader A. Shareef (London, Routledge, 1993), 101–40; Jane Dammen McAuliffe, Barry D. Walfish and Joseph W. Goering, eds., *With Reverence for the Word: Medieval Scriptural Exegesis in Judaism, Christianity, and Islam* (Oxford, Oxford University Press, 2003); Feras Hamza and Sajjad Rizvi, with Farhana Mayer, eds., *An Anthology of Qur'anic Commentaries*, vol. I: *On the Nature of the Divine* (Oxford, Oxford University Press in association with the Institute of Ismaili Studies, 2008), particularly Hamza's introduction 1–19; Karen Bauer, ed., *Aims, Methods and Contexts of Qur'anic Exegesis (2nd/8th–9th/15th C.)* (Oxford, Oxford University Press in association with the Institute of Ismaili Studies, 2013); eadem, *Gender Hierarchy*; Pink, *Muslim Qur'ānic Interpretation Today*.

generations, keep to a relatively stable format and use common methods, even as they simultaneously incorporate their own views, new methods and the taken-for-granted truths in the sociocultural milieus of their own day and age.[34] In the genre of Qur'ānic commentaries, the authors might claim to be objective reporters of the past, but they are influenced by many factors; premodern *tafsīr* was no less influenced by its geography and politics than modern *tafsīr*.[35] Sometimes 'change' and 'continuity' are one and the same: direct quotes of past interpreters, which seem to indicate an unchanging tradition, can take on new meanings in different contexts.

The notion that the text configures the interpreter, as the interpreter brings their 'pre-judgments' to bear fruitfully on the text, has been well-recognised for decades in the field of religious studies: Gadamer referred to it as the fusion of horizons, where the interpreter seeks to attain the horizon of the text, but the text is flexible enough to accommodate the interpreter's own perspective.[36] Yet it is not entirely uncommon to come across descriptions of *tafsīr* that posit that the commentary genre constitutes an uninterrupted exegetical continuum from the Prophet to the commentator in question. This is perhaps because, as Walid Saleh has argued, scholars often describe the history of *tafsīr* according to their own ideological presuppositions and attachments to particular commentators or modes of interpretation.[37] Here we wish to give a brief synopsis of the genesis and development of *tafsīr* as a genre, in order to situate the reader of this work in the scholarly discipline.[38]

[34] On the contributions of individual authors to the development of this genre, see especially Saleh, *Formation*; Bruce Fudge, *Qur'ānic Hermeneutics: Al-Ṭabrisī and the Craft of Commentary* (London, Routledge, 2011); Tariq Jaffer, *Rāzī: Master of Qur'ānic Interpretation and Theological Reasoning* (New York, Oxford University Press, USA, 2015). A somewhat problematic analysis is presented by Andrew Lane, *A Traditional Muʿtazilite Qur'ān Commentary: The Kashshāf of Jār Allāh al-Zamakhsharī (d. 538/1144)* (Leiden, Brill, 2006); see 'Commentators and their Commentaries', n. 87, in this volume.

[35] For a more detailed analysis of the factors influencing Qur'ānic interpreters, see Bauer, *Gender Hierarchy*, 1–30.

[36] 'A horizon is not a rigid boundary but something that moves with one and invites one to advance further . . . for everything that is given as existent is given in terms of a world and hence brings the world horizon with it.' Hans-Georg Gadamer, *Truth and Method*, 2nd rev. edn, tr. John Weinsheimer and Donald G. Marshall (New York, Continuum, 2004), 245.

[37] Walid Saleh, 'Preliminary Remarks on the Historiography of *Tafsīr* in Arabic: A History of the Book Approach', *Journal of Qur'anic Studies* 12 (2010), 6–40.

[38] For a more detailed account, see Hamza *et al.*, *Anthology*, I, 'Introduction'; also see Michael Pregill, 'Exegesis' in *The Routledge Handbook on Early Islam*, ed. Herbert Berg (Abingdon, Routledge, 2018), 98–125; Walid Saleh, 'The Last of the Nishapuri School of Tafsir: Al-Wahidi and his Significance in the History of Quranic Exegesis', *Journal of the American Oriental Society* 126.2 (2006), 223–43; idem, 'Marginalia and the Periphery: A Tunisian Modern Historian and the History of Qur'anic Exegesis', *Numen* 58.2–3 (2011), 284–313; idem, 'Rereading al-Ṭabarī through al-Māturīdī: New Light on the Third Century Hijrī', *Journal of*

While exegetical activity may have started with Muḥammad, the main authorities for the genre of *tafsīr* are within the generation of the Successors (*tābiʿūn*), with the exception of ʿAbd Allāh b. ʿAbbās (d. 68/687), who is the purported source of many interpretations.[39] However, in this early period, 'one cannot accurately summarise the precise form' of exegetical activity;[40] it was probably not scholarly and may have been more akin to storytelling, or at least bound up with the activities of the famous 'storytellers' (*quṣṣāṣ*). The earliest extant biography of the Prophet, the *Sīra* of Ibn Isḥāq, includes much exegetical activity, such as a *tafsīr* of the entire *sūrat al-Anfāl* (Q. 8). Recent research into this source shows that it was meant to be performed aloud, and that Ibn Isḥāq did perform it.[41] This is one example of how a 'popular' storytelling explanation (*qaṣaṣ*) of the Qurʾān may have developed.

The development of *tafsīr* as a scholarly genre seems to have begun in the second/eighth century and may have been related to the emergence of a class of scholars who desired to differentiate their own approach to the Qurʾān from that of the storytellers and popular tellings of Qurʾānic meaning. Its earliest preserved iteration, namely the *tafsīr* of Muqātil b. Sulaymān al-Balkhī (d. 150/767), retains a sense of the orality of this genre, in that the *tafsīr* is set within the Qurʾānic verses, so that one can read 'with minimal disruption to the flow of the narrative'. In addition to Muqātil's own glosses, his *tafsīr* includes materials attributed to the Jews and Christians, material from the Prophet's biography and pre-Islamic material.[42] These aspects are also all present in the monumental *tafsīr* of Ṭabarī (d. 310/923), but his work additionally contains lengthy grammatical explanations, variant readings and named reports, which Ṭabarī often judges on their relative merits. This work was to become a model and a foil for later works; in their introductions, subsequent authors often describe the ways that they improve on it. Ṭabarī's *Jāmiʿ al-bayān* has several of the stylistic features or hermeneutics that were to become standard: glossing the Qurʾān line by line, including named authorities, and permitting polyvalence, including several, sometimes contradictory, interpretations.[43]

Qur'anic Studies 18.2 (2016), 180–209; Nicolai Sinai, 'The Qur'anic Commentary of Muqātil b. Sulaymān and the Evolution of Early *Tafsīr* Literature' in *Tafsīr and Islamic Intellectual History: Exploring the Boundaries of a Genre*, ed. Andreas Görke and Johanna Pink (Oxford, Oxford University Press in association with the Institute of Ismaili Studies, 2014), 113–43.

39 Hamza *et al.*, *Anthology*, I, 'Introduction', 2.

40 Ibid.

41 This refers to unpublished research being undertaken by Kevin Jaques.

42 Hamza *et al.*, *Anthology*, I, 3.

43 Calder, '*Tafsīr* from Ṭabarī to Ibn Kathīr', 101–38.

As the genre of *tafsīr* developed through time, authors incorporated their own methods, sources and interests. Several recent studies have shown the contribution of individual authors: Thaʿlabī (d. 427/1035), for instance, focused on law and sayings of the Prophet (*ḥadīths*), while Rāzī (d. 606/1209) brought in methods and content from his philosophical (mainly Ashʿarī) epistemology; Qushayrī (d. 465/1072) and Maybudī (*fl.* sixth/twelfth century) both have mystical and Sufi elements in their commentaries.[44] Commentators were also influenced by taken-for-granted truths, by their own common sense and by the exigency to offer coherent and clarificatory glosses to their audience.[45] Medieval exegetes thus trod a line between the timeless and the timely: they always sought to capture the timeless truths of the Qurʾān, but could only do so by recourse to notions that would make sense to their readers. This is not to rule out the possibility that these interpretations contained valuable information about the actual historical meaning of the verse, akin to the way that modern scholars 'find meaning' in the Qurʾān;[46] rather, it is to say that they cannot represent all possible interpretations, and nor were they ever intended to do so.

It is thus all the more important to examine the social history of *tafsīr*, which is a study that remains in its infancy. After the initial early works, this genre may have developed as a regional exercise, centred for centuries around Nishapur, a hub for all kinds of intellectual activities in its heyday. Preliminary research indicates that it was also connected to certain intellectual currents, such as the Shāfiʿī school of law, which was the school of many of the authors of major works.[47] A study of the *tafsīr* works in an Ayyubid library catalogue shows that many of these were penned by Shāfiʿī Nishapuri authors.[48] *Tafsīr* was not a genre that was written for popular consumption: in their introductions to their works, scholars disdained 'ordinary folk'

[44] On Thaʿlabī, see Saleh, *Formation*; on Fakhr al-Dīn al-Rāzī, see Jaffer, *Rāzī*; on Qushayrī, see Martin Nguyen, *Sufi Master and Qur'an Scholar: Abū'l-Qāsim al-Qushayrī and the Laṭāʾif al-Ishārāt* (Oxford, Oxford University Press in association with the Institute of Ismaili Studies, 2012); on Maybudī, see Annabel Keeler, *Sufi Hermeneutics: The Qur'an Commentary of Rashīd al-Dīn Maybudī* (Oxford, Oxford University Press in association with the Institute of Ismaili Studies, 2007).

[45] Bauer, *Gender Hierarchy*, introduction.

[46] Feras Hamza, '*Tafsīr* and Unlocking the Historical Qur'an: Back to Basics?' in *Aims, Methods and Contexts*, ed. Bauer, 19–28.

[47] Saleh posited that there was a Nishapuri school of *tafsīr* (*Formation*); Bauer takes this argument further and argues that *tafsīr* itself was primarily regional and Shāfiʿī (*Gender Hierarchy*, conclusion).

[48] Karen Bauer, '"I Have Seen the People's Antipathy to this Knowledge": The Muslim Exegete and His Audience, 5th/11th–7th/13th Centuries' in *The Islamic Scholarly Tradition: Studies in History, Law, and Thought in Honor of Professor Michael Allan Cook*, ed. Asad Q. Ahmed, Behnam Sadeghi and Michael Bonner (Leiden, Brill, 2011), 293–315.

(*ʿāmma*) and preferred to claim that they were writing for other scholars (*ʿulamāʾ*); indeed, there is little resemblance between the *tafsīr* of the Ḥanbalī Ibn al-Jawzī and his extant book of sermons.[49] Saleh has identified two types of work, the short *madrasa* work and the longer encyclopaedic work; but both of these presumably targeted readerships who were to some extent educated, or 'lettered'. Some authors themselves classified their works as short, medium or long; an author might disdain his own short work, considering only the longest and most complex versions as having been a truly worthy endeavour.[50] This intellectual snobbery relates directly to the cachet which authors in the genre must have gleaned from writing within it: writing a work of *tafsīr* was a way of showing (off) one's scholarly fluency with the accumulated tradition of the past and an acquired mastery of the grammatical difficulties of the Qurʾān's language.

In the modern age of mass literacy, modern works of *tafsīr al-Qurʾān* would serve different purposes: one was to disseminate a single authoritative view of the Qurʾān according to various ideological or scholarly criteria; another was to promote the authoritative status of the author of the work, or to show his (or, occasionally, her) alignment with particular political or social forces. But perhaps the most fundamental difference between medieval and modern works of *tafsīr* is the target audience. Many modern works, such as those of Muḥammad ʿAbduh, Sayyid Quṭb and Muḥammad Husayn Faḍlallāh, began as sermons, directed precisely at the common people with whom medieval exegetes were hardly concerned. Most modern works are written to minimise complex grammatical discussions and prioritise 'common sense' interpretations or straightforward elucidations of 'practical' use. While medieval works were self-consciously scholarly, incorporating conflicting interpretations for an audience who could presumably discern for themselves one truth or many, modern works attempt to convince a common reader of a single authoritative meaning of the Qurʾān. Thus it is probably no accident that in the modern period, the genre tends to be conservative in its approach. As a result, modern scholarly studies of Qurʾānic interpretation do not usually limit themselves to the formal genre known as *tafsīr*.[51]

The modern age of mass literacy has not only affected the writing of modern *tafsīr*, it has also had an effect on the consumption of medieval *tafsīr*.

[49] Saleh, *Formation*; Bauer, 'I Have Seen the People's Antipathy'.

[50] On this, see Karen Bauer, 'Justifying the Genre: A Study of Introductions to Classical Works of *Tafsīr*' in Bauer, *Aims, Methods and Contexts*, 39–66.

[51] See for instance Pink, *Muslim Qurʾānic Interpretation Today*.

What is popular changes through time, and this popularity might stem from sociological and political contexts rather than from scholarly concerns. Saleh points out that, until recently, the most popular book of medieval Qurʾānic commentary in the modern period was that of Bayḍāwī; nowadays, as he argues, it is that of Ibn Kathīr, and he connects this change in popularity to the rise of Salafī movements globally.[52] It is especially important to keep in mind the social history of *tafsīr* when we consider how the authors in this genre treat questions of sex, gender and the rights of women.

Qurʾānic interpretations as a reflection of social power and norms

There is great variety in the commentaries examined in this book; yet within that variety there are also certain constants. No premodern commentator envisioned absolute social equality for men and women in the way that many modern authors might. Some medieval authors asserted that women could be better than men in the spiritual realm,[53] more pious than men and even more intelligent. But, at least within the textual genre of *tafsīr*, they never asserted that women and men could hold the same social status in society. Equally, to our knowledge, no medieval commentator questioned the social hierarchies of their times: none forbade the practice of slavery, for instance. All took for granted the existence of slaves, who had their own place in society and their own set of Islamic laws (the laws on veiling, for instance, differ for slave women and free women).[54] Medieval Qurʾān interpreters did not question the idea of social hierarchies because, for them, social hierarchies were naturally (or divinely) given.[55] These commentaries were produced in cultures where social inequalities were not only taken for granted but were considered – at least by those advocating such hierarchies – to have been positively conceived, a moral good for society as a whole and for the individuals within it. Indeed, such was the importance accorded to social hierarchies that the commentators through time have given precedence to the hierarchical aspects of the Qurʾānic text, despite significant verses that categorically rule out any

52 Saleh, 'Preliminary Remarks on the Historiography of *Tafsīr*'.

53 In particular, see the interpretation of the Fatimid Ismāʿīlī author al-Muʾayyad fī'l-Dīn al-Shīrāzī featured in ch. 1 in this volume.

54 Ali, *Marriage and Slavery in Early Islam*.

55 Aisha Geissinger, *Gender and Muslim Constructions of Exegetical Authority: A Rereading of the Classical Genre of Qurʾān Commentary* (Leiden, Brill, 2015). Bauer, '"The Male is Not Like the Female" (Q. 3:36): The Question of Gender Egalitarianism in the Qurʾān', *Religion Compass* 3.4 (2009), 637–54; Louise Marlow, *Hierarchy and Egalitarianism in Islamic Thought* (Cambridge, Cambridge University Press, 1997); Patricia Crone, *Medieval Islamic Political Thought* (Edinburgh, Edinburgh University Press, 2005).

ontological inferiority of women, let alone justify the misogynistic institutions and attitudes that those interpretations promote.

What evidence is there that the worldly hierarchy took precedence over egalitarianism for medieval interpreters? Those writing in the genre of *tafsīr* often explained that they believed women were inferior to men from the moment of creation (as evidenced in Chapter 1, on Q. 4:1); and they explained hierarchical social institutions by referring to their views of women's innate inferiority (as seen in Chapters 3 and 5, on Q. 4:34 and 2:282). Thus, although some of our authors, such as the Fatimid Ismāʿīlī author al-Muʾayyad fīʾl-Dīn al-Shīrāzī, do mention women's spiritual equality with men, it is uncommon for those sorts of interpretations to appear in the mainstream exegeses of the verses studied in this book. Even when the verse itself seems to indicate such equality, such as Q. 4:1, it was often understood in the medieval period as proof of women's inferiority to men. The influence of social mores is even more apparent in the interpretation of overtly hierarchical verses such as Q. 4:34. Thus, for instance, in his interpretation of Q. 4:34 Zamakhsharī gives a long list of the ways in which men are intrinsically and socially superior to women.[56] Such interpretations refer to common beliefs in the societies in which they were produced, rather than to anything that is actually in the Qurʾān. And yet Zamakhsharī is a respected commentator whose work was widely cited in the medieval period and continues to be cited (and thus to exert influence) today.

The effect of cultural assumptions is apparent in interpretations on women's status: in many of the commentaries in this volume, medieval Muslim authors use the Qurʾān to justify interpretations that privilege men in ways that go well beyond the Qurʾānic text. Qurʾānic commentaries operate at the nexus of culture and religious orthodoxy, precisely because the authors of Qurʾānic commentaries seek to portray themselves as the authentic voices of religious tradition, while being deeply influenced by their own cultural norms.[57]

It is not a coincidence that the scholars producing hierarchical interpretations were exclusively free males, a class of people who were not about to upset the social hierarchies, of which they formed a part, and the commensurate privileges they enjoyed as a result thereof. In short, medieval male scholars had no precedent for interpretations that advocated absolute social equality, nor

[56] See Zamakhsharī's interpretation of Q. 4:34, ch. 3 in this volume, and Rāzī's summary of that interpretation.

[57] Shahab Ahmed would argue that the normative religious texts of Qurʾānic commentaries and *fiqh* are not representative of Islam at all. Shahab Ahmed, *What is Islam? The Importance of Being Islamic* (Princeton, NJ, Princeton University Press, 2016).

would they have had any incentive to offer such interpretations. As free male scholars, they benefitted from the social inequality that they championed.[58]

Many contemporary Muslim scholars are engaged in revisiting, revising and contesting these historical-cultural attitudes. For many Muslims, the idea of social hierarchies no longer seems viable in their cultural contexts, and this is reflected in their interpretations of the Qur'ān. And yet, though notions of equality are widespread, it is still common for modern interpreters to draw on premodern rulings on women's rights and to seek to implement laws on this basis. In this regard, it is crucial to note that 'the status of women' has become a flashpoint for different identities and affiliations, with modern conservative interpreters insisting on maintaining the hegemony of a textual tradition that enshrines laws treating men and women differently, while modern reformists claim legitimacy through a wider vision of justice, rights and ethics, which can sometimes sideline the Qur'ān's hierarchical verses. Each of these views is discussed briefly below.

Modern conservative commentators overwhelmingly believe that the hierarchical verses in the Qur'ān refer to innate differences in the sexes, and that spousal roles, and to some extent other social roles, are biologically determined. These interpretations often rely on fixed ideas of human nature, in which the sexes' abilities to function in the world are determined biologically. While conservatives claim authenticity by virtue of establishing links with tradition, their own interpretations are inextricably linked to the global influence of modern norms: whereas medieval authors justified their commentaries by claiming women's inferiority to men, modern conservatives often find explanations rooted in science, pseudo-science or 'human nature'. As in the medieval period, the scholars putting forth these views often benefit directly from them: they have a vested interest in upholding a tradition of which they claim to be the sole authentic curators.

It is difficult to get away from this hegemonic view within the genre of Qur'ānic commentaries. Outside of the genre of *tafsīr*, modern reformists adopt different methods to deal with this-worldly inequality and social hierarchies implicit in the Qur'ānic text. The most common method is to historicise the text by explaining that the Qur'ānic hierarchies refer to the Qur'ān's original social milieu, but that these can no longer be justified for an entirely different social milieu today, when women and men in many societies enjoy equal access to education and work, and when family sizes are generally smaller than in the medieval period.[59] Another modern strategy is to

[58] This point has also been made by wadud, *Inside the Gender Jihad*, 189.

[59] Prominent modernists who make this argument include Grand Ayatollah Yusuf Saanei and Nasr Hamid Abu Zayd.

overlook or reinterpret these verses, much like the verses on slavery or those that prohibit charging interest on loans are commonly overlooked or 'reinterpreted'. This strategy usually involves prioritising the Qur'ān's egalitarian verses over the Qur'ān's hierarchical verses, but it may also involve a reinterpretation and denial of any hierarchy.[60] A final reformist strategy is to declare that these verses are abrogated, or that there are some verses in the Qur'ān to which believers could turn a blind eye, that is, verses to which they can respond with a hermeneutical 'no'. All of these strategies are apparent in the interviews at the end of Chapter 3, on Q. 4:34.

Muslim reformists may use more than one of the above strategies or may move from one to another. The American amina wadud, for instance, who features in interviews in this volume, denied any hierarchy and affirmed only egalitarianism in her first book, *Qur'an and Woman*, first published in 1992. However, in her 2006 book *Inside the Gender Jihad*, she says that she 'accepts the critiques of moving beyond my apologetics',[61] adding, '[I have] never been locked into a literal meaning of the Qur'anic text when I explore the Qur'anic intent of universal guidance'.[62] She concludes, when reading Q. 4:34, for instance, that 'I simply do not and cannot condone permission for a man to "scourge" or apply *any kind* of strike to a woman . . . This leads me to clarify how I have finally come to say "no" outright to the literal implementation of this passage.'[63]

Feminists and other interpreters who challenge existing norms are routinely dismissed by those who claim that women who are not trained in the traditional texts do not have the authority to interpret the Qur'ān, or that their interpretations are less valid because they pay attention only to part of the text.[64] It is rare to find a modern-day gender-reformist *tafsīr*, or a *tafsīr*

[60] As in the works of Asma Barlas and the early work of amina wadud.

[61] wadud, *Inside the Gender Jihad*, 188.

[62] Ibid., 196.

[63] Ibid., 200.

[64] Regarding modern feminist interpretations, wadud notes that she herself was critiqued by a male progressive Muslim, Ebrahim Moosa, who said that feminists 'make too much of too few verses of the Qur'an'. She replies: 'women's readings of the Qur'an are either expected to be perfect and comprehensive, or they are inadequate. Therefore, rather than finding encouragement from others with prior privilege in engaging in textual analysis, they are castigated for their efforts at contributing, however inconclusively, to new understandings of the Qur'an. Those understandings reveal possible roads toward finding new conceptions of what it means to be human in a religion that has had a history of this very same kind of castigation from the male elites, who were so entrenched in their own struggles for understanding the Divine–human relation that they took for granted their androcentric bias as in fact a reflection of the totality of the divine intent' (wadud, *Inside the Gender Jihad*, 189).

written by anyone who is not overtly a heterosexual male.[65] It is in order to engage the voices of people generally absent from the genre of *tafsīr*, namely reformists and women themselves, that this volume includes the transcripts of interviews with modern Muslim Qur'ān scholars, in which these scholars offer their own interpretations of the select verses. Some of these interviews were conducted by Karen Bauer and Feras Hamza in 2020, and others were conducted in 2011 by Bauer in Qumm, Iran.[66] It should be noted that such interviews represent a snapshot in the interpretations of a particular time and place; in the decade since Bauer undertook her interviews, the interviewees' situations and views may have changed.[67] Yet these transcripts nevertheless give a sense of the changing face of contemporary interpretations.

Those interviews by Bauer and Hamza not only discuss the interpretations of specific verses but also at times delve into the wider principles and methods of Qur'ānic interpretation. They are thus intended as a window into the hermeneutics that underpin the entire venture of modern Qur'ānic interpretation. While a discussion of hermeneutics may seem arcane, at stake here is not only the nature of religious authority among an educated elite. The translations in this volume, and our introductions, are academic and scholarly in nature. But for many women and men, this is not an academic debate. The interpretation of these verses is of immediate social and legal concern: they impact directly on whether a woman can testify in court in certain situations, how women might dress, spousal expectations within marriage and even how women may feel about their own status as believers. This book shows how such verses have been interpreted and reinterpreted through time by scholars who have sought to reconcile the Qur'ānic words with their own social context and their notion of what is true, right and natural.

[65] Though this is not unheard of: see the *tafsīr* of Nusrat Amīn and that of 'Ā'isha 'Abd al-Raḥmān, Bint al-Shāṭi'. On Nusrat Amin, see especially Mirjam Künkler and Roja Fazaeli, 'The Life of Two *Mujtahidas*: Female Religious Authority in Twentieth Century Iran' in *Women, Leadership, and Mosques: Changes in Contemporary Islamic Authority*, ed. Masooda Bano and Hilary Kalmbach (Leiden, Brill, 2016), 127–60; Maryam Rutner, 'Religious Authority, Gendered Recognition, and Instrumentalization of Nusrat Amin in Life and After Death', *Journal of Middle East Women's Studies* 11.1 (2015), 21–41. On Bint al-Shāṭi', see Roxanne Marcotte, 'The Qur'ān in Egypt, 1: Bint al-Shāti' on Women's Emancipation' in *Coming to Terms with the Qur'ān: A Volume in Honor of Professor Issa Boullata, McGill University*, ed. Khaleel Mohammad and Andrew Rippin (New Jersey, Islamic Publications International, 2008), 179–208; Shuruq Naguib, 'Bint al-Shāṭi''s Approach to *tafsīr*: An Egyptian Exegete's Journey from Hermeneutics to Humanity', *Journal of Qur'anic Studies* 17.1 (2015), 45–84.

[66] Some of these interviews have been analysed in Bauer, *Gender Hierarchy*, but here they are presented in full.

[67] Two of the interviewees, Grand Ayatollah Saanei and Nasser Ghorbannia, have since passed away, while Fariba Alasvand has published much more on the subject.

Scholarly objectivity in this work

The contemporary relevance of the subject matter of this book not only raises the question addressed above, of the scholarly objectivity of the authors of works of *tafsīr*, it also raises the question of our own scholarly objectivity as editors of this work. Speaking about her work on modern *tafsīr*, Pink reflects, 'Through my interactions with contemporary Muslim exegetes, I came to realise that I cannot write on contemporary discourse without becoming part of it.'[68] We, too, consider ourselves to have become a part of the discourse presented in this volume. The bulk of this volume is made up of translations, which may be perceived as 'objective' in the sense that such translations record historical debates. But any act of compilation and translation is also, in a sense, an act of authorship. To compile, introduce, annotate and translate medieval and modern commentaries is not only to produce a historical record; it is also to shape that record. And by making these texts available to people who would not otherwise be able to read them, the act of translation may also inform common perceptions about the nature of the historical tradition and therefore the nature of 'Islam' itself.[69] Yet it is the interviews, representing reformist and feminist viewpoints, which are most likely to cause some to question our motivations, and ultimately (perhaps) the scholarliness of this work.

The point that we would like to make here is that the inclusion of women and reformists, who are otherwise marginalised from the *tafsīr* tradition, addresses a basic intellectual responsibility. To omit any mention of these varied perspectives would be to impose an entirely artificial limit on the modern debates over the Qur'ān's meaning by circumscribing these debates within the genre of *tafsīr*. But, as mentioned above, most Qur'ānic interpretation today does not take place in the genre of *tafsīr*. In fact, new works of *tafsīr* are comparatively rare, whereas other fora for interpretation have proliferated. It would thus be a disservice to modern Qur'ānic interpretation to treat the written genre of *tafsīr* as the sole repository, or even the dominant repository, of modern Muslim thought about the Qur'ān.

Equally, it is important to question the ways in which 'objective' discourses about the Qur'ān have been assumed to reside in a particular textual genre whose authors consciously marginalise and disparage other perspectives. Scholars of objectivity have shown how scientific research that adheres to

[68] Pink, *Muslim Qur'ānic Interpretation Today*, 10.

[69] It is extremely common for 'Islam' to be equated with specific historical textual traditions; on this see Ahmed, *What is Islam?*

current models for 'objective' and sound research can incorporate bias; some recent work argues that the very process of determining scientific objectivity is flawed.[70] These biases include androcentricity: many scientific and medical studies, for instance, extrapolate for all humans based on studies of young adult males. Some of these same issues affect the humanities, and particularly a field like Islamic studies, which is dominated by a vast, male-authored textual corpus. In a recent study, Zahra Ayubi has shown that the very notion of morality and goodness is gendered in the medieval Muslim context.[71]

In light of the historical and current bias in all fields of research, scholars of objectivity have reconceptualised what it means to be 'objective'. Sandra Harding, for instance, calls for a shift towards 'fairness and responsibility' rather than adherence to a supposedly disinterested scholarly study.[72] Ahmed El Shamsy highlights how recent contributions have classified the quest for objectivity in terms of 'intellectual virtue' characterised by a commitment to the pursuit of truth.[73] He defines objectivity as 'a moral commitment to pursuing a reality that is not reducible to our preconceived notions and agendas'.[74] Definitions that hinge on the morality and virtue inherent in the pursuit of 'truth' or 'reality' imply that the virtue lies in a scholar's willingness to allow the research to overturn their own desired research outcome or to pursue avenues that might undermine their own personal or scholarly agenda. The pursuit of objective or fair research thus requires a continuous process of self-reflection and self-reflexivity. It is only when scholars recognise their proclivity to bias that they can incorporate methods to ensure that their work is responsible and open to outcomes beyond those biases. An element of self-reflexivity not only informs our decision to include interviews in this volume but also informs the content of those interviews, which include reflections on hermeneutics and bias in Qur'ānic interpretation.

[70] See Sandra Harding, *Objectivity and Diversity: Another Logic of Scientific Research* (Chicago, IL, University of Chicago Press, 2015); Stuart Ritchie, *Science Fictions: How Fraud, Bias, Negligence, and Hype Undermine the Search for Truth* (New York, Metropolitan Books, 2020).

[71] Ayubi, *Gendered Morality*.

[72] See Harding, *Objectivity and Diversity*.

[73] Ahmed El Shamsy, 'How Not to Reform the Study of Islamic Law: A Response to Ayesha Chaudhry', *Islamic Law Blog*, 14 December 2020, https://islamiclaw.blog/2020/12/14/how-not-to-reform-the-study-of-islamic-law-a-response-to-ayesha-chaudhry/. On objectivity as an intellectual virtue, see Moira Howes, 'Objectivity, Intellectual Virtue, and Community' in *Objectivity in Science: New Perspectives from Science and Technology Studies*, ed. Flavia Padovani, Alan Richardson and Jonathan Y. Tsou (New York, Springer, 2015), 173–88.

[74] El Shamsy, 'How Not to Reform the Study of Islamic Law'.

The structure of this work

This work begins with introductory material, including the Prolegomenon on the Qur'ān, and a section on the commentators and their works. Each of the remaining five chapters consists mainly of the translations of eighteen commentaries from the Sunni and Shīʿī traditions, within each of which there will be various degrees of mystical, rationalist and plainly traditionalist interpretations. These works are organised chronologically, starting with the interpretation of Muqātil b. Sulaymān. Each chapter begins with a chapter introduction which situates the verse in its Qur'ānic context, and each individual translation includes its own introduction and annotation to help guide the reader. Most chapters end with interview transcripts.

The selection of verses

The verses selected for this volume are in some sense representative of the ways in which women appear in the Qur'ān. Two verses focus on female characters, and three on women's rights and relationships with others in society. This choice was influenced in part by the depth and breadth of the commentaries, and in part by current interest in these topics. The figures of Mary and Eve (Ḥawwā') have engendered much academic attention, and numerous scholarly articles have been written about them. Q. 4:34, which is the subject of the chapter on marriage, is one of the most controversial verses in the Qur'ān today, and it has been the principal theme of more than one scholarly book. Rulings on the veil have attracted much popular commentary, and to some extent scholarly interest as well. Women's testimony in court is an issue that is directly relevant to many women's lives in Muslim-majority countries. All of these verses have a rich history of interpretation, and some of them have crucial real-world implications for Muslims. These real-world implications have constituted a fundamental part of the selection of these particular verses. The interpretations of these verses can determine whether women have equal rights within the home and in the larger society, how they comport themselves and how they dress. Thus, for modern Muslims, it is of crucial importance to understand how today's interpretations have been arrived at. The medieval exegetical tradition has cast a long shadow over modern understandings of such verses and has had, thereby, a direct impact on women's lives today.

It is important to note that this volume does not include some verses which will always retain an importance for the topic of women in the Qur'ān.

Gender egalitarian verses include Q. 33:35, which was quoted above (*men who submit and women who submit*), Q. 9:71 (*Believing men and believing women, however, are allied to one another: they bid what is right and they forbid what is wrong. They maintain the prayer and they give charity. They obey God and His Messenger: those are the ones to whom God will grant mercy. Verily God is mighty and wise.*); or Q. 66:10–12, which speak of Mary and Pharaoh's wife as exemplary figures. For many modern readers, these verses are examples in which the Qur'ān refers to women's ontological equality with men, and their equal potential for salvation or damnation based on pious acts, rather than accidents of birth or gender. However, for reasons explained earlier, medieval commentators did not tend to comment on these verses' egalitarian implications. Furthermore, such verses seemed to have a less varied and rich history of interpretation than those included in this volume; as an example, we have included a summary of medieval interpretations of Q. 33:35 as an appendix to this introduction. Why did such egalitarian verses not attract much attention? The answer is partly cultural, in that (as mentioned above) elite male interpreters had no particular reason to highlight gender egalitarianism; but there is also a practical element: commentaries on verses that are found in the first part of the Qur'ān tend to be longer and more detailed than commentaries on verses in *sūra*s that come later in the standard version of the scriptural text. Thus, with the exception of the veil verse, the verses we have chosen for this volume are from early *sūra*s (to wit: *sūra*s 2, 3 and 4); and we chose the veil verse as it is the first instance in which the interpreters comment on the veil.[75]

• Prolegomenon: The Qur'ānic lexicon on women

The way that women appear in the Qur'ān's chronological development has important consequences. First, the chronological analysis presented here seems to confirm some theories about the development of the early Islamic community, from a minority opposition to nascent state, in which those with power were instructed on the appropriate limits of that power. Thus the earliest verses on women are presented within an eschatological drama, while the later ones also address the social context of women in the Muslim community. This pattern underpins the main finding of our analysis, which is that women seem to have become an ever-more prominent and important aspect of the Qur'ānic narration through time. In early Meccan verses, 'the female' features mainly in a symbolic way: such verses, for instance, address

[75] The veil is also addressed in Q. 33:59.

pagan hypocrisy by mocking the pagans for worshipping female deities while burying their own infant daughters alive. In later Meccan verses, a period in which stories of Biblical women feature heavily, the believing women in the Qurʾān are also assured that their own pious actions would lead to a heavenly reward. Medinan verses treat women as fully fledged pious and social subjects, who bear clear responsibility for their own pious behaviour. Incidentally, the analysis here calls into question overly simplistic notions of a complete break from tribal and familial ties which have characterised some scholarship on the Qurʾān and early Islam.

- **Q. 4:1, The creation of the first woman**

Q. 4:1 states that God created human beings from a single soul, from which had been created its mate, and from that was spread forth many men and women. This verse has been understood by modern commentators to be a statement about the absolute equality of all human beings. Some even say that this verse indicates that all of humankind was descended from a single cosmic soul. Though there is no mention of the exact manner of Eve's creation in the Qurʾān, most medieval interpretations of this verse assume that the *single soul* refers to Adam, while the *mate* is Eve, and they say that *from it* means that Eve was created from Adam's rib. There are two minority interpretations of this verse. One Shīʿī interpretation attributed to Muḥammad al-Bāqir (d. *c.* 117/735)[76] states that *from it* means that the creation was of the same substance as Adam, the leftover clay after his creation. The second minority interpretation, credited to Abū Muslim al-Iṣfahānī (d. 322/934),[77] states that *from it* means that the creation was of the same type. All of these interpretations (rib, same substance, or same type) are plausible given the ambiguous language of the verse itself. Medieval interpreters assumed that Eve was created from Adam and that she was therefore a secondary creation; they thus related this creation to their claims about women's inherent inferiority in the world. The views put forth in the interviews sharply contrast with these views.

- **Q. 3:35–6, Mary**

Mary is the only woman mentioned by name in the Qurʾān, and as such the text accords her a special status. These verses describe her pre-birth consecration by Anne (Ḥanna), and Ḥanna's surprise at the moment of her birth. According to some of the interpreters, when Ḥanna consecrated Mary to the

[76] On whom, see the PA.
[77] On whom, see the PA.

temple, the people present drew lots for guardianship over her; she was taken under the protection of Zachariah, as later detailed in Q. 3:37. Q. 3:36 also includes the line *the male is not as the female*. Several interpreters explain this line by saying that Ḥanna had planned to consecrate the child in her womb for service in the temple, a service normally only performed by boys; hence her shock and disappointment when she gave birth to a girl. Some interpreters say that the statement indicates that this particular female (Mary) was better than a male.

- **Q. 4:34, Marital relations**

Today, Q. 4:34 is regarded as one of the most controversial verses in the Qurʾān. That is because, on the face of it, this verse sets up a marital hierarchy allowing husbands to discipline their wives and, as a last resort, to strike them. The verse has been the subject of numerous articles and it features prominently in at least two recent scholarly books.[78] While this verse can seem as though it is granting husbands permission to beat their wives, it could instead be seen as a limitation on a man's otherwise unchecked licence over his wife. The medieval interpreters saw this verse as a delineation, and to some extent a delimitation, of men's rights over women. Although the medieval commentators put limitations on husbands, they never questioned a husband's right to rule the family and to discipline his wife. They promoted an unashamedly patriarchal worldview, and many backed it up by saying that men were innately superior to women. The interpretations of this verse have changed in the modern period. Even conservatives, who believe that men should be the head of the family, do not say that women are deficient or inferior compared to men, as the medieval interpreters did. They also limit the extent of the striking which they would permit to the husband in a way that it was not limited in the medieval period. Some scholars have seen the beating as a last resort in the case where the wife committed adultery.[79] Modernists and reformists interpret this verse in a variety of ways. In the interviews included at the end of this chapter, interpreters say, variously, that the verse should be understood as historically situated with no application to today's context, and that it is ultimately to be treated as abrogated; that practical, lived understandings of Islam can abrogate verses such as this one or that Muslims today can say 'no' to a literal application of the verse. The

[78] The books are Bauer, *Gender Hierarchy*, and Chaudhry, *Domestic Violence*.

[79] R.B. Serjeant, for instance, makes this argument about the Prophet's Farewell Pilgrimage Oration. See R.B. Sergeant, 'Early Arabic Prose' in *Arabic Literature to the End of the Umayyad Period (The Cambridge History of Arabic Literature)*, ed. A.F.L. Beeston, T.M. Johnstone, R.B. Serjeant and G.R. Smith (Cambridge, Cambridge University Press, 1983), 121–2.

interpretations of this verse thus raise larger hermeneutical questions about the limits of Qur'ānic reinterpretation.

- **Q. 24:31, The veil**

This chapter is, unsurprisingly, heavily legal in nature, with long discussions of the exact nature of the veil. What is remarkable about these discussions is that the extent of prescribed veiling does not ever cover the face or hands; the face and hands were deemed necessary for women to function in the world, to give testimony at court, and so forth. Medieval scholars also say that the necessity of veiling is restricted to free women, and that slave women must not do it, which indicates that veiling was a type of social and class distinction. The interpreters distinguished in this verse between a manifest and a hidden ornament. Manifest ornament, minimally, could be attributed to a woman's physical features, but also extended in some cases to accessories such as kohl, rings, bangles and so forth. In the interviews, scholars amina wadud and Sa'diyya Shaikh address the question of modesty in the modern world. Both emphasise the importance of context in determining modesty. While wadud focuses on the political implications of the veil and a woman's right to cover, Shaikh argues that modesty may be equally effected without covering up in an age, *pace* the current global health pandemic, when not being covered is the norm.

- **Q. 2:282, Women's testimony**

Q. 2:282 specifies that, in the case of debts, two male witnesses should be called to witness the transaction, and if there are not two men, then a man and two women, so that *where one of the two errs, then one of the two shall remind the other.* This verse thus seems to say that women might run the risk of forgetfulness. Many medieval interpreters also cited a *ḥadīth* on the authority of the Prophet, which says that women were deficient in 'rationality and religion' (*nāqiṣāt al-ʿaql wa'l-dīn*), which confirmed the commentators' views that the Qur'ānic rulings on women referred to an innate deficiency in women. For most, the main interest in the verse was not its gendered elements, but its grammatical features. Based partly on this verse, medieval *fiqh* disallowed women's testimony in a number of cases, such as in murder or adultery. According to some schools of law, women could not even testify in cases of marriage or divorce. Modern responses to this verse are varied, and often represent the political and social circumstances in which they find themselves. Conservative interpreters often justify the ruling in the verse by claiming that there are significant mental differences between the sexes, and that, for instance, women are more emotional, which vindicates the social expectations of their roles as wives and mothers, whereas men are innately more rational. Modern reformists and progressives would argue that this verse made sense in the patriarchal society of pre-Islamic Arabia, but that it can no longer be considered relevant in today's societies, where women are well-educated and hold roles both inside the home and outside in the public domain.

The selection of commentators

The commentaries chosen for this volume include both Sunnī and Shīʿī works and works from the Ismāʿīlī tradition. This selection covers most of the significant interpretations from within the genre of *tafsīr*, but it cannot cover all of the interpretations that have occurred outside of it. Six of the commentators included in this volume do not feature in *An Anthology of Qur'anic Commentaries*, vol. I: *On the Nature of the Divine*, while some from that volume have been omitted from this one. These choices generally reflect our wish to include interesting or unusual interpretations by particular authors and to continually expand the range of commentaries accessible to readers in future volumes in this series. In the modern period, as mentioned above, we have included a selection of interview transcriptions. These include interviews conducted by Bauer and Hamza of two leading feminist interpreters, amina wadud and Sa'diyya Shaikh, and interviews conducted by Bauer in Iran of four leading thinkers: Dr Fariba Alasvand, a professor at the women's Hawzeh in Qumm; Grand Ayatollah Yusuf Saanei, a prominent reformist cleric in Qumm; Mehdi Mehrizi, a scholar of *ḥadīth* in Qumm; and Nasser Ghorbannia, a former professor of law at Mofid University, Qumm. The views of these scholars give some sense of the varied, vibrant and rich current interpretations of the verses in question.

Using this work

This work is intended for anyone interested in the topic of gender in the Qur'ān and in the Islamic interpretive tradition; but it may find its primary use in university classrooms. Because of the culturally sensitive nature of the subject matter, we would highly recommend that the interpretations are always read along with the mini-introductions and the chapter introductions that accompany them. The interpretations in this book can be very difficult to digest for modern readers. They are often quite technically complex; the aspects that are comprehensible are often anchored in such powerful patriarchal worldviews that they would easily sound alien to the modern ear. Our introductions are intended to put these interpretations into their historical intellectual context and, consequently, to make them more comprehensible, even if they may seem unpalatable. Wherever possible, we recommend reading the interpretations in chronological order. That being said, specific interpretations can be excerpted, with their mini-introductions, for ease of use or discussion in classroom settings.

Appendix: A brief synopsis of interpretations of Q. 33:35

> *Indeed, men who submit and women who submit, believing men and believing women, men who are piously obedient and women who are piously obedient, truthful men and truthful women, men who endure and women who endure, humble men and humble women, men who are charitable and women who are charitable, fasting men and fasting women, men and women who safeguard their private parts, those men and women who remember God often, for (all of) them, God has prepared forgiveness and a tremendous reward.*

Q. 33:35 is one of the main Qurʾānic proof-texts cited today for the spiritual equality of men and women. For modern Muslim readers, this verse is a powerful statement in that it shows that God has an abiding interest in women's spirituality as much as men's; however, a survey of the medieval commentators shows that they do not delve into the gender implications of this verse. At most, medieval exegetes refer to an occasion of revelation in which Umm Salama and/or other women ask the Prophet why God addresses men and not women; God answers with this verse, which addresses both women and men as pious subjects. In these occasions of revelation, the questioner recognises that the potential for spiritual transformation or salvation has only been applied directly to men in the community and, in some versions, she worries that this is because something is wrong with women. God is shown to be responsive to these concerns, reassuring women through this verse that the Qurʾān's salvific message applies to them as much as it applies to men. But such occasions of revelation are not mentioned by all commentators; some do not include them and simply explain the verse linguistically, giving the meaning of words such as *believing men* or *men and women who safeguard their private parts*.[80] Even the commentators who include the occasions of revelation usually do not comment on them.[81] It is difficult to avoid the conclusion that, while medieval commentators may have recognised that women here are granted equal potential along with men, for most of them it was not an issue worth discussing – or at least not in this instance. The following are excerpts from some commentators who include an occasion of revelation for this verse, along with a brief introduction to each interpretation.

[80] The following authors make no mention of the women's questions or concerns, and rather focus on the lexical issues in the verse: Qummī, Rāzī, Ṭabrisī, Burūsawī and Kāshānī.

[81] In addition to the commentators cited below, see Ibn Kathīr as a good example of this.

Muqātil

In Muqātil's interpretation, Umm Salama expresses her worry that God has abandoned women, or that there is no good in them. God then immediately answers her pious anxiety by revealing this verse. After his *tafsīr* of Q. 33:35, Muqātil mentions two other verses that were revealed in response to Umm Salama's concerns.

Umm Salama says, 'Why is it that our Lord always mentions men and never mentions women at all in His book? It makes us fear that they are no good, and that God has no need of them, and that He has abandoned them.' So God revealed this verse.

[. . .]

And God, mighty and majestic, also revealed with regard to Umm Salama, may God be pleased with her, at the end of [*sūrat*] *Āl 'Imrān*: *Verily, I do not neglect the work of any worker among you, male or female* [Q. 3:195], and in the *ḥā mīm* [*sūrat*] *al-Mu'min*:[82] *any believer, male or female, who does righteous work* [Q. 40:40; cf. 16:97].[83]

Hūd

Hud records a simple version of Umm Salama's question.

It is mentioned on the authority of Mujāhid that Umm Salama said, 'O Messenger of God, what is it with women, that they are not mentioned along with men when it comes to righteous works?' So God revealed *Indeed, men who submit and women who submit.*[84]

Ṭabarī[85]

Ṭabarī records several instances of questions from Umm Salama or other women to the Prophet. In several of these, women express their anxiety about being beneath

[82] The *sūra* is conventionally known as *Ghāfir*.

[83] Muqātil b. Sulaymān al-Balkhī (d. 150/767), *Tafsīr Muqātil b. Sulaymān*, ed. 'Abd Allāh Maḥmūd Shiḥāta, 5 vols. ([Cairo], al-Hay'a al-Miṣriyya al-'Āmma li'l-Kitāb, 1979–89; repr. Dār Iḥyā' al-Turāth al-'Arabī, 2002), s.v. Q. 33:35.

[84] Hūd b. Muḥakkam al-Hawwārī (fl. fourth/tenth century), *Tafsīr kitāb Allāh al-'azīz*, ed. Belḥāj b. Sa'īd Sharīfī, 4 vols. (Beirut, Dār al-Gharb al-Islāmī, 1990), s.v. Q. 33:35.

[85] The reader will note that Ibn Kathīr cites the Umm Salama tradition via Ṭabarī (not translated here).

God's notice or beneath mention. It is worth noting that Ṭabarī prefaces his exegesis of the verse with a paraphrase of the verse, almost suggesting that more attention be paid to the subject matter.

On the authority of Qatāda,[86] a group of women came into the presence of the wives of the Prophet and they said, 'God mentions you in the Qur'ān, while we receive no mention. Is there nothing worth mentioning about us?'

Mujāhid said, 'Umm Salama said, "So, men are mentioned and we are not", so it was revealed.'

Yaḥyā b. Abd al-Raḥmān b. Ḥāṭib reported that Umm Salama said, 'I said, "O Messenger of God, why is it that men are mentioned in everything, and we are not?"'

Ibn 'Abbās said, 'The wives of the Prophet say, "Why does He always mention believing men (*al-mu'minūn*) and not believing women (*al-mu'mināt*)?"'

Mujāhid said, 'Umm Salama said, "How is it that women are not mentioned like men are in matters to do with righteousness (*fī'l-ṣalāḥ*)?"'

'Abd al-Raḥmān Ibn Shayba, said, 'I heard Umm Salama, the wife of the Prophet (*ṣl'm*), saying, "I asked the Prophet (*ṣl'm*), 'O Messenger of God, what is it about us, that we are we not mentioned in the Qur'ān as much as men are?'" Then she said, "Nothing startled me (*r-w-'*) so much as when one day at noon, while I was doing my hair, I heard him calling from the pulpit; so I did my hair up quickly and went out to another of the wives' chambers (*ḥujurihinna*) and I put my ear next to the palm branches [used as a door between the chamber and the main mosque], and he was saying on the pulpit, 'O People, verily God does say in His book, *Indeed, men who submit and women who submit* [. . .]'."'[87]

Qushayrī

Qushayrī's *tafsīr* of this verse focuses on the pious path, which, while giving spiritual guidance to seekers of any gender, nevertheless sidelines any specifically gendered aspect of this verse.

[86] Bishr ← Yazīd ← Sa'īd ← Qatāda.

[87] Abū Ja'far Muḥammad b. Jarīr al-Ṭabarī (d. 310/923), *Jāmi' al-bayān fī ta'wīl āy al-Qur'ān*, ed. Muḥammad Shākir and Aḥmad Shākir, 30 vols. (Cairo, al-Hay'a al-Miṣriyya al-'Āmma li'l-Kitāb, 1954–69), s.v. Q. 33:35.

As regards His words, majestic be His praise, *Indeed, men who submit and women who submit.* Islam means submission, sincerity of devotion (*ikhlāṣ*) and to make all effort to endure affliction (*mukābāda*). *Believing men and believing women*: Belief (*īmān*) is affirmation and the sum total of all acts of obedience; they also say it is affirmation and verification. It is also said that it refers to when truth (*ḥaqīqa*) breezes through the heart. It can also signify that the heart first acquires life through the intellect (*ḥayāt al-qalb awwalan bi'l-ʿaql*) and according to some through knowledge, for others through understanding from God, for others through the affirmation of oneness, for others through gnosis (*maʿrifa*) and for others belief is that their hearts acquire life through God. *Men who are piously obedient and women who are piously obedient*: pious obedience is sustained devotion (*ʿibāda*). *Truthful men and truthful women* with regard to their covenants (*ʿuhūd*), their commitments (*ʿuqūd*) and observing the bounds imposed on them (*ḥudūd*). *Men who endure and women who endure* maintain praiseworthy traits against blameworthy attributes when unexpected events occur. *Humble men and humble women*: humbleness is to render your inner constitution (*sarīra*) pliant upon the manifestations of the truth. *Men who are charitable and women who are charitable* with their property and their selves so that no quarrel remains between them and those whom they may have degraded or spoken about. *Fasting men and fasting women*: those who abstain from what is impermissible according to the law and the spiritual path (*ṭarīqa*). *Men and women who safeguard their private parts*, outwardly (*ẓāhir*) from what is illicit and, through allusion (*fī'l-ishāra*), from all sins. *Those men and women who remember God often* by their tongues and their hearts and throughout their states, without fail, and without opening themselves up to forgetfulness. *For (all of) them, God has prepared forgiveness and a tremendous reward.* For all of those, they shall have the most beautiful of rewards, the most bountiful recompense.[88]

Zamakhsharī

Zamakhsharī includes two reports about the occasion of revelation. In both instances, the verse is revealed in response to women's anxieties about their spiritual worth.

It is reported that the wives of the Prophet (*ṣlʿm*) said, 'O Messenger of God, God, exalted be He, speaks well of men in the Qurʾān. Is there nothing good

[88] Abū'l-Qāsim al-Qushayrī (d. 465/1073), *Laṭāʾif al-ishārāt*, ed. Ibrāhīm Basyūnī, 6 vols. (Cairo, Dār al-Kātib al-ʿArabī, 1968–71), s.v. Q. 33:35.

about us worth mentioning? We fear lest no act of devotion (*ṭāʿa*) will be accepted from us.' And it is said that the questioner was Umm Salama.

It is reported that when that which was revealed with regard to the wives of the Prophet (*ṣlʿm*) was sent down, other believing women said, 'Has nothing been revealed about us?' So it was revealed.[89]

Qurṭubī

Qurṭubī reports that this *ḥadīth* is found in Tirmidhī.

Tirmidhī reported on the authority of the Ansari woman Umm ʿĀmāra that she approached the Prophet (*ṣlʿm*) and said, 'I see that everything is only for men, and I do not see anything mentioned about women' [. . .] this is a fair (*ḥasan*) but isolated (*gharīb*) *ḥadīth*.[90]

Muḥsin al-Fayḍ al-Kāshānī

In his commentary on Q. 33:35, Muḥsin al-Fayḍ glosses the different types of piety in the verse, drawing on two well-known Shīʿī works, the *Majmaʿ al-bayān* of Ṭabrisī and the *Kitāb al-Kāfī* of Kulaynī.[91] Like other commentators, he pays scant attention to the gender egalitarian implications of this verse; as will be clear from the commentaries included in this volume, he had much more to say about verses that, in his view, were non-egalitarian.

Indeed, men who submit and women who submit: those who accept Islam and those who yield (*munqādūn*) to God's judgment. *Believing men and believing women*: those who affirm what must necessarily be affirmed. In the *Majmaʿ*, on the authority of the Prophet (*ṣlʿh*): 'a [true] Muslim (*s-l-m*) is one from whose words and actions all Muslims are safe (*s-l-m*); the believer (*muʾmin*) is the person from whose wrongful conduct his neighbour is secure

[89] Jār Allāh Maḥmūd b. ʿUmar al-Zamakhsharī (d. 538/1144), *al-Kashshāf ʿan ḥaqāʾiq al-tanzīl wa ʿuyūn al-aqāwīl fī wujūh al-taʾwīl*, 4 vols (Beirut, Dār al-Maʿrifa, 1987), s.v. Q. 33:35.

[90] Muḥammad b. Aḥmad al-Qurṭubī (d. 671/1273), *al-Jāmiʿ li-aḥkām al-Qurʾān*, 20 vols. (Beirut, Dār Iḥyāʾ al-Turāth al-ʿArabī, 1965–7), s.v. Q. 33:35.

[91] Al-Faḍl b. al-Ḥasan al-Ṭabrisī (al-Ṭabarsī) (d. 548/1154), *Majmaʿ al-bayān fī tafsīr al-Qurʾān*, ed. Hāshim al-Rasūlī and Faḍl Allāh al-Ṭabāṭabāʾī al-Yazdī, 10 pts. in 5 vols. (Mashhad, al-Maʿārif al-Islāmiyya, 1976); Muḥammad b. Yaʿqūb al-Kulaynī (d. 329/941), *al-Uṣūl min al-kāfī*, ed. ʿAlī Akbar al-Ghaffārī, 8 vols. (Tehran, Dār al-Kutub al-Islāmiyya, 1955–61).

(*a-m-n*): so none of you is a true believer in me who goes to bed with a full belly while his neighbour starves'. And in the *Kāfī* on the authority of al-Ṣādiq (*'m*), belief (*īmān*) is what is held as reverence by the hearts and *islām* is in marriages, inheritance and preserving life. Belief subsumes Islam, but Islam may not subsume faith. [. . .][92]

In the *Majma'*, on the authority of Muqātil b. Ḥayyān, upon returning from Abyssinia (*ḥabasha*) Asmā' b. 'Umays with her husband Ja'far b. Abī Ṭālib went to see the wives of the Messenger of God (*ṣl'hm*) and asked them, 'Has anything come down about us in the Qur'ān?' They said, 'No'. So she went off to the Messenger of God (*ṣl'hm*) and said, 'O Messenger of God, women are disappointed and at a loss', so he replied, 'Why is that?' She said, 'Because they never receive good mention as men do.' So God, exalted be He, sent down this verse.[93]

[92] In the omitted section, Muḥsin al-Fayḍ, like other interpreters (both Sunnī and Shī'ī), provides a brief description of the types of piety and demeanours indicated in the verse; like others, he makes no particular reference to gender.

[93] Muḥsin al-Fayḍ Muḥammad al-Kāshānī (d. 1091/1680), *Kitāb al-Ṣāfī fī tafsīr al-Qur'ān*, ed. al-Sayyid Muḥsin al-Husaynī al-Amīnī, 7 vols. (Tehran, Dār al-Kutub al-'Ilmiyya, 1998), s.v. Q. 33:35.

Prolegomenon: The Qur'ānic lexicon on women

This prolegomenon is a necessary preamble to reading the commentarial selections on the verses in this anthology on women. Whereas the remainder of this volume focuses on commentaries, which incorporate the bias of their authors as described in the volume introduction, this part offers a glimpse into what the Qur'ān itself says about women, without recourse to the commentarial tradition. This glimpse is enough to highlight aspects of the Qur'ān that were completely missed by the commentators. By taking a historical approach to the text, this Prolegomenon documents a shift in the Qur'ānic lexicon on women, which shows how women gradually assume a place as pious subjects in the Qur'ānic kerygma.[1] Our argument regarding this shift can be summarised thus:

In the early Meccan period, women are most prominently represented by the term 'female' (*unthā*), a term that has symbolic force in anti-pagan rhetoric. Verses emphasising God's creation of the female along with the male, and therefore the creational equality of male and female life, emerge in the earliest period partially as a polemical response to the pagan attitude towards female life, where the pagans bury infant girls and are outraged at the birth of daughters, but give female names to the angels and attribute daughters to God. Since these responses begin in the first revelations of the Qur'ān chronologically, it seems that some of the earliest preaching mocked the pagan practice of worshipping female deities while maltreating their own women and girls. Women also appear in eschatological verses: verses warn the believing man (*mar'*) that his female companion (*ṣāḥiba*), children and close relatives will not avail him on the Day of Judgment. Another theme is the

[1] The term 'kerygma' (Greek, 'proclamation'), which appears in the New Testament and is used extensively in Biblical studies, has recently been adopted by many in the field of Qur'ānic studies to refer to the Qur'ān's oral character. A key argument of stylometric dating of Qur'ānic verses is that certain terms tend to be used within specific time periods. See Behnam Sadeghi, 'The Chronology of the Qur'ān: A Stylometric Research Program', *Arabica* 58 (2011), 210–99. For our chronological arrangement, we have compared the chronology developed by Theodor Nöldeke (d. 1930), which relies in part on some of the early Muslim chronologies and in part on a chronology developed by Gustav Weil, with the mean verse length (MVL) analysis put forth by Nicolai Sinai in his 2017 book *The Qur'an: A Historical-Critical Introduction* (Edinburgh, Edinburgh University Press). Sinai's point of departure is the convergence of MVL with several lexical, literary and thematic features of the text, which was also documented in the aforementioned study by Sadeghi.

houris (*ḥūr ʿīn*), the female beings who form a part of the lush, idyllic portrayals of the Hereafter. Such verses, addressed specifically to men, may indicate that the primary addressees of the earliest pronouncements were male heads of household, who were presumed to have some responsibility for, and leverage over, their kin. Historians of early Islam recognise that the tribal arrangement in pre-Islamic Arabia entailed a male head of household, who was one tier in a hierarchical social structure that also included male elites who saw to the welfare of the whole lineage.[2] The male head of household mirrors the well-recognised figure of the *pater familias* from classical and late antiquity.

In the later Meccan period, women assume a more prominent place in the Qurʾānic kerygma, mainly through stories of women who become exemplary for all believers. Anti-pagan rhetoric escalates in later Meccan verses, with the early Meccan threads brought together and embellished to denounce pagan hypocrisy towards women. The term 'female' is still used in anti-pagan polemic in this period, but it now also appears in verses that reassure believing women that their pious dispositions and behaviours will earn them a place in the afterlife. Thus women are specifically assured of their moral agency. Heavenly companions are no longer described as *ḥūr ʿīn*; rather, believing spouses (*azwāj*) will accompany men to the afterlife.[3]

The lexical and conceptual shift in Medina is dramatic. The term 'female' (*unthā*) is now used largely in legislative passages, and there is a much greater incidence of 'women' (*nisāʾ*) and 'believing women' (*muʾmināt*); indeed, their counterpart, 'female hypocrites' (*munāfiqāt*), appear exclusively in Medinan verses. Moreover, the latter two expressions ('believing women' and 'female hypocrites') are used particularly to emphasise women's moral agency.

In sum, creational equality between the sexes underpins the Qurʾān's kerygma, even as women's status in the community of believers changes over time. In sociological terms, the lexical shifts documented below may indicate a transition from a milieu in which women were considered under the aegis

[2] Robert Hoyland compares this tribal structure to a set of 'Chinese boxes or Russian dolls', in which 'the smaller units, such as households, are segments of more inclusive units, such as lineages, and lineages in turn segments of larger groups, and so on'. Hoyland, *Arabia and the Arabs*, 114.

[3] The shift in descriptions of paradisiacal companions from houris in the early Meccan period to spouses (*azwāj*) in the later Meccan, and purified spouses (*azwāj muṭahhara*) in the Medinan period has been noted by Jane Smith and Yvonne Haddad, Neal Robinson, and Christian Lange. Jane Smith and Yvonne Haddad, 'Women in the Afterlife: The Islamic View as Seen from the Qurʾān and Tradition', *Journal of the American Academy of Religion* 43.1 (1975), 39–50; Neal Robinson, *Discovering the Qur'an: A Contemporary Approach to a Veiled Text*, 2nd edn (Washington, DC, Georgetown University Press, 2003), 87–9; Christian Lange, *Paradise and Hell in Islamic Traditions* (Cambridge, Cambridge University Press, 2016), 51–3.

of the male head of household, to one in which, while still under the latter's protection, they become overtly recognised as pious and social subjects. It must not be supposed, however, that the move from Mecca to Medina was one of an inegalitarian society to an egalitarian one; that would be misreading the entire worldly hierarchy constructed by the Qur'ān. Not only do Medinan rulings differ for women and men, but (as explained in the Introduction) men are given rights over women. Nevertheless, there is a distinct change from largely symbolic references to 'the female' in the pagan milieu of Mecca, to the believing women of Medina, who are addressed in their own right, who have social status, and who are portrayed as making their own moral choices independently. In this way, an individual's piety provides an opportunity for the subverting of the overtly unjust worldly hierarchies in which they find themselves. Social hierarchies in the world, unjust as they may seem, do not foreclose an ultimately just Hereafter.

Early Meccan verses on women

By most accounts, the earliest verse to mention 'the female' is Q. 92:3: [3] *By the One who created the male and the female* [4] *dissimilar indeed are your efforts*. This verse begins with an oath and emphasises God's creative power, which is indicated in part to say that a creation of God's cannot therefore be an object of veneration, a theme that is elaborated below. The mention here of God's creation of both male and female presages later passages which more clearly indicate the sexes' equal ontological worth.

While God in the early Meccan verses is characterised as consciously creating male and female, early verses characterise the pagans by their burial of the infant girl:

> [81:1–9] *Should the sun be darkened,* [2] *should the stars tumble down,* [3] *should the mountains begin to move,* [4] *should the pregnant camels be abandoned,* [5] *should the wild beasts throng,* [6] *should the seas be set alight,*[4] [7] *should the souls be paired up,* [8] *should the infant girl, buried alive (maw'ūda), be asked:* [9] *for what fault was she killed?*

These verses portray end times as completely reversing the current order, and in this formulation the unjustly buried infant girl becomes a symbol of the unjustness of the then-current Meccan social practices. While we cannot know the actual pagan practices, and we admit that the Qur'ān is potentially

[4] Cf. Q. 40:72.

our only source for such practices, it is also worth stating the obvious: this is a text that is intended to convince people of its own worldview, and therefore it will naturally wish to amplify pagan hypocrisy. The very fact that God is outraged at this treatment of infant girls (and, in later passages, adult women) may indicate that such treatment was not entirely accepted among the general populace; the Qur'ānic audience may have been outraged as well.

In this regard, it is significant that the infant girl is the one who is symbolically chosen in the Qur'ān both here in Q. 81:8 and in Q. 16:59 (discussed under 'later Meccan verses on women'). Infanticide and abortion are condemned in Biblical passages and in later Jewish and Christian tradition, but without specifying the sex of the infants: Job 3:16 mentions infants who never saw the light of day;[5] similarly, the *Didascalia Apostolorum* (a late antique church order) says, 'you shall not kill (*tqṭwl*) a child through destruction, nor after he is born shall you kill him (*tqṭlywhy*)'.[6] The significance of the female infant becomes more obvious when we consider how the Qur'ān portrays the pagan concept of God's daughters.

The early Meccan *sūrat al-Najm* (Q. 53) gives more detail about pagan practices.[7] Here is the only mention of al-Lāt, Manāt and al-ʿUzzā, well-recognised pre-Islamic goddesses[8] whom the Qur'ānic pagans (*mushrikūn*) considered to be daughters of God. The Qur'ān emphasises that these names are but a human fabrication:[9]

> [53:19–23] *You see these, al-Lāt and al-ʿUzzā?* [20] *And that other, Manāt, the third one?* [21] *So what is it to be, the male for you, and the female* (al-unthā) *for Him?* [22] *That would indeed be a fraudulent division!* [23] *These are nothing but names*

5 Noted by Nicolai Sinai, 'The Eschatological Kerygma of the Early Qur'an' in *Apocalypticism and Eschatology in Late Antiquity: Encounters in the Abrahamic Religions, 6th–8th Centuries*, ed. Hagit Amirav, Emmanouela Grypeou and Guy Stroumsa (Leuven, Peeters, 2017), 266, who also cites Syriac parallels.

6 Holger Zellentin, *The Qur'ān's Legal Culture: The Didascalia Apostolorum as a Point of Departure* (Tübingen, Mohr Siebeck, 2013), 73.

7 On *sūrat al-Najm*, see Angelika Neuwirth, *Der Koran*, vol. I: *Poetische Prophetie. Frühmekkanische Suren* (Berlin, Verlag der Weltreligionen, 2011), and Nicolai Sinai, 'An Interpretation of *Sūrat al-Najm* (Q. 53)', *Journal of Qur'anic Studies* 13.2 (2011), 1–28. In Nöldeke's chronology, this is the next *sūra* to speak of pagan practices; Sinai also puts it after *sūrat al-Takwīr* (Q. 81).

8 On the goddesses al-Lāt, Manāt and al-ʿUzzā, see Hoyland, *Arabia and the Arabs*, 63 *et passim*; Suleiman Dost, 'An Arabian Qur'ān' (Unpublished PhD dissertation, University of Chicago, 2017), 27–44. Al-Lāt is the most well-attested of the three; on her, see Susanne Krone, *Die Altarabische Gottheit al-Lat* (Berlin, Peter Lang, 1992).

9 On the daughters of God, see Gerald Hawting, *The Idea of Idolatry and the Emergence of Islam: From Polemic to History* (Cambridge, Cambridge University Press, 1999), 130–49; Patricia Crone, 'The Religion of the Qur'ānic Pagans: God and the Lesser Deities' in *The Qur'ānic Pagans and Related Matters: Collected Studies in Three Volumes, Volume 1*, idem, ed. Hanna Siurua (Leiden, Brill, 2016), 52–5.

that you and your fathers have concocted, in which God has invested no authority: they follow only conjectures and the fanciful notions of their souls.

These verses seem, at first glance, to be anti-female with the rhetorical question and answer *so what is it to be, the male for you, and the female for Him? That would indeed be a fraudulent division!* Patricia Crone argues that the Qur'ān 'treats the ideas of many gods, female angels, and daughters of God as practically identical concepts' and that the 'Messenger finds the idea of female angels utterly outrageous', the presumption being that female angels are particularly outrageous due to their gender.[10] The above verses on daughters of God express outrage. But taken in context, the gender of these figures plays an important part in the evolving anti-pagan polemic against them insofar as it shows up pagan inconsistency: while they themselves reject female offspring, the pagans have no compunction in taking God's daughters to be female. The outrage in this verse should be considered as a direct challenge to the very same pagans who have been accused of burying their infant girls.

Pagan hypocrisy towards women is one of three objections to the daughters of God in the Qur'ān. The second, as noted by Crone, concerns the idea that God should have any progeny at all, whether male or female, the abhorrence of which is reiterated throughout the text. This is epitomised in *sūrat al-Ikhlāṣ* (Q. 112),[11] which begins *Say: He is God, One*, while in the later Meccan verses of Q. 19:88–91, the objection to the idea of God's progeny is stronger: $_{[19:88-91]}$ *They say that the Raḥmān has taken a child (walad).* $_{[89]}$ *What a repugnant thing you have trumped up!* $_{[90]}$ *The heavens would almost rupture at the thought of it and the earth would split open, and the mountains would collapse, demolished,* $_{[91]}$ *that they should claim that the Raḥmān has a child.* Given the context of *sūrat Maryam* (Q. 19), the objection in these verses is probably to God having a son (Jesus); however, it should be noted that the word that we have translated as 'child', *walad*, could mean progeny of either sex. In short, the polemic against God having progeny persists throughout the Qur'ān, but the main target of this polemic may have shifted through time from the pagan worship of God's daughters to the Christian doctrine of Jesus as the son of God.

The third objection is the disavowal of worshipping created things, which is also a repeated theme in the Qur'ānic polemic against all forms of

[10] Crone, 'The Religion of the Qur'ānic Pagans', 57.

[11] On this verse and its interpretations, see Hamza *et al.*, *Anthology*, I, 491–575. Nöldeke tentatively dates this *sūra* as early Meccan; Sinai questions whether it can be dated at all. Sinai, *A Historical-Critical Introduction*, 131.

association (*shirk*) that includes idols, graven images and so forth (Q. 29:17; 39:17; 41:37; 109 *et passim*).[12] In our view, it is this objection that sheds light on the repeated assertions that God created the male *and the female* (Q. 49:13; 53:45; 75:39), and it is within this context of Qurʾānic assertions about the nature of the female that we should read the verses on the daughters of God, or the verses that claim pagans give female names to the angels: [53:27–8] *Indeed those who will not believe in the Hereafter will always name the angels with female names* (*tasmiyat al-unthā*) [28] *They do not have any knowledge about that. They follow nothing but conjectures, and indeed conjecture is no substitute for the truth.* These verses refer to the conjectures (*ẓann*) of the pagans. According to the Qurʾān, they give the angels female names because of their conjectures, rather than true knowledge. What is, from the Qurʾānic perspective, the true state of affairs is formulated a few verses later, when the text again refers to the intentional creation of both males and females: [53:45–6] *It is He who created the pair* (*zawjayn*), *the male and the female* (*unthā*), [46] *from a drop of fluid emitted.* The link between these seemingly disparate verses is their common use of the term *unthā* (female). This word, which occurs thirty times in the Qurʾān, and six times in early Meccan *sūras*, is mentioned three times in *sūrat al-Najm*.[13] In the instance cited above, the female is created along with the male in pairs (*zawj*). Both male and female are created by God, and in an entirely physical way, *from a drop of fluid.* Because of the nature of this creation, they cannot be His sons or daughters, and as created beings they cannot be the object of legitimate worship.

Other early Meccan verses echo these themes. *Sūrat al-Ṭūr* (Q. 52) refers to the controversy over God having daughters, asking rhetorically why it should be that God should have daughters while the pagans have sons: [52:39] *Or is it that He should have daughters* (*banāt*) *while you should have sons* (*banūn*)? The term *daughters* is relatively infrequent, occurring only eighteen times in the Qurʾān.[14] Three of the four early Meccan instances of this word refer to the daughters attributed to God (the fourth refers to Lot's daughters). In *sūrat al-Qiyāma* (Q. 75) the trajectory of human creation becomes clearer: God fashioned a primordial human, creating from it the two sexes:

[12] On the religion of the Qurʾānic pagans, see Hawting, *The Idea of Idolatry*, and Crone, 'The Religion of the Qurʾānic Pagans'.

[13] 'Female' (*unthā*) occurs in the following verses: early Meccan (six instances): Q. 37:150, 53:21, 53:27, 53:45, 75:39, 92:3; later Meccan (ten instances): Q. 13:8, 16:58, 16:97, 17:40, 35:11, 40:40, 41:47, 42:49, 42:50, 43:19; Medinan (fourteen instances): Q. 2:178 (twice), 3:36 (twice), 3:195, 4:11, 4:117, 4:124, 4:176, 6:143 (twice), 6:144 (twice), 49:13.

[14] Daughter(s) (*ibna, banāt*) occurs in the following verses: early Meccan (four instances): Q. 15:71, 37:149, 37:153, 52:39; later Meccan (six instances): Q. 6:100, 11:78, 11:79, 16:57, 28:27, 43:16; Medinan (eight instances): Q. 4:23 (thrice), 33:50 (thrice), 33:59, 66:12.

[75:36–9] *Does a person* (*insān*) *suppose that he would be left without purpose?* [37] *Was he not initially a drop of discharged fluid* [38] *then a clot? He then made him a creation well-proportioned* [39] *and from that*[15] *He proceeded with the pair, the male and the female* (*al-unthā*). These verses emphasise God's power and imply that male and female are equal in creation, while rejecting the idea that either males or females could be sons or daughters of God.

In the early Meccan period, female believers (*al-mu'mināt*) are mentioned only once, where they are the subject of repeated attempts by the pagans to lure, entice, or torment them (*f-t-n*), at Q. 85:10: *Indeed those who torment the believing men and the believing women, and do not turn back* [*to God*], *they shall have the punishment of Gehenna: they shall have the chastisement of the Fire.*[16]

While the above paragraphs address the nature of God and the creation of male and female in the early Meccan period, eschatology is another powerful and pervasive undercurrent that runs throughout the Qur'ān.[17] There are many gender-neutral early Meccan warnings to believers. Such verses emphasise that every individual believer is responsible for his or her own salvation, using words like 'soul/self/person' (*nafs*), 'person' (*insān*) or other gender-neutral plurals. Thus Q. 82:5 speaks about the Day of Judgment: *truly then shall a soul know what it has accomplished and what it has left behind* or, later in the same *sūra*, Q. 82:13–14: *Verily the godly* (*abrār*) *shall be in bliss* [14] *and verily, the ungodly shall be in a blaze* (*jaḥīm*).[18] Among many other examples of this type of gender-neutral eschatological rhetoric is Q. 89:23–30:

> [89:23–30] *When on that day Gehenna is brought forth, then on that day shall every person* (*al-insān*) *remember; but what is there now to remember?* [24] *Saying, 'If only I had offered up (something) in my lifetime!'* [25] *On that day, none shall be chastised in the way this person is chastised* [26] *and none shall be bound in the way he is bound* [27] *O soul, you who have become reassured* (*yā ayyuhā'l-nafs al-muṭma'inna*) [28] *return now to your Lord gratified and gratifying.* [29] *Enter now among My servants.* [30] *Enter now My Garden.*

[15] Here the term is *minhu*; the masculine pronoun must refer back to *person* (*insān*) in v. 36.

[16] It should be noted here that this verse and the following verse fit the profile of verses that are considered to be Medinan additions to the Meccan passages, in that they are longer and more complex than the surrounding verses, they both are introduced by the phrase *inna alladhīna*, and they do not seem to fit the rhyme pattern of the rest of the *sūra*. Neuwirth noted this in *Poetische Prophetie*. Indeed, in his chronology, Sinai puts verses 7–11 of this *sūra* as a later addition (see *A Historical-Critical Introduction*, 114–17, Figure 10).

[17] Building on the work of scholars such as Tor Andrae, Sinai calls eschatology the 'first major subject of the Qur'anic proclamations, a sort of stem cell for the genesis of the Qur'an as whole'. Sinai, 'The Eschatological Kerygma of the Early Qur'an', 219.

[18] Also see in this regard, for instance, *sūrat al-Layl* (Q. 92).

While such verses focus on the individual bearing his or her own burden, other early Meccan eschatological verses are addressed to men specifically. In contrast to the gender-neutral verses cited above, these male-orientated verses include vivid imagery of female companionship and other ties of kinship. They have one of two orientations: severing ties of kinship and female companionship on Judgment Day or maintaining/creating these ties in the afterlife. In this context, the 'female companion' (*ṣāḥiba*) emerges as a significant source of comfort in the world. *Ṣāḥiba* occurs only four times in the Qur'ān, all in early Meccan verses. Two occurrences, at Q. 72:3 and 6:101, indicate that such companionship is entirely human, for they say that God does not have a female companion (*ṣāḥiba*) or a son (*walad*). The other two occurrences speak of severing the tie of female companionship; the first example chronologically is at Q. 80:33–7, which reads:[19] [33] *Should the deafening Cry come,* [34] *the day when a man* (*mar'*) *will flee from his brother,* [35] *from his mother, from his father,* [36] *from his female companion* (*ṣāḥiba*) *and from his sons.* [37] *For on that day each of them will be caught up in his own affair.* The second instance is in *sūrat al-Maʿārij* (Q. 70):

> [70:8–13] *On the day when the heaven shall be as molten copper* [9] *and the mountains shall be as tufts of wool* [10] *and no beloved* (*ḥamīm*) *can petition another* [11] *even as they shall be made to see each other; when a criminal* (*mujrim*), *against the chastisement of that day, would ransom his children,* [12] *his female companion* (*ṣāḥiba*), *his brother,* [13] *and the very clan who are his refuge.*

The breach with all of these close degrees of kin, including the 'female companion' (*ṣāḥiba*), emphasises the tension between a believer's worldly and spiritual commitments; such verses warn him first and foremost that his closest attachments in this world will not avail him in the next. Moreover, the passage from *sūrat al-Maʿārij* informs the wrongdoer that on Judgment Day he would ransom those beloved to him in order to save himself. In her discussion of the impact of the earliest Qur'ānic preaching on pagan society, Angelika Neuwirth cites both of these passages, saying that 'an inverted world emerges where the head of the household, instead of sheltering his

[19] For Biblical and Syriac parallels to Q. 80:33–7, see Emran Iqbal El-Badawi, *The Qur'ān and the Aramaic Gospel Traditions* (Abingdon, Routledge, 2014), 170–72, and Sinai, 'The Eschatological Kerygma of the Early Qur'an', 260, who notes the parallel with Mark 13:12–17 and Matthew 24:19, and Syriac parallels in Paul Bedjan, ed., *Homiliae selectae Mar Jacobi Sarugensis*, 5 vols. (Leipzig, Harrassowitz, 1905–10), no. 67, lines 135–40, 243–4; Sinai cites also Edmund Beck, ed. and tr., *Des heiligen Ephraem des Syrers Sermones I–IV*, 8 vols. (Leuven, Peeters, 1970–73), II, no. 2, lines 169–84.

relatives, will be willing to ransom them to save his soul'.[20] For Neuwirth, such images indicate that the new Islamic polity meant to undermine tribal hegemony.[21]

There can be no doubt that the imagery of kinship and companionship effects a rhetorical subversion of tribal kinship structures. But, *pace* Neuwirth, it is worth nuancing the immediate social implications of this. For it is actually the presumption that certain social structures continue that makes this rhetorical point possible: this is precisely why verses that emphasise kinship are addressed to the male. The *pater familias* had enduring responsibility for his family and kin, including wives, children, brothers, parents and others. This point becomes clearer when other kinship verses are taken into consideration.

While the above verses emphasise the severing of worldly ties, particularly for those who have not behaved righteously, others promise that the righteous believers will maintain some of their earthly attachments in the afterlife, as well as having a heavenly pairing with the houris (*ḥūr ʿīn*). The promise of this idealised female comfort and companionship is evidence that these verses are also addressed to men. But gender-neutral eschatological verses imply that women have moral agency as individuals; these male-orientated verses, with their focus on kinship and female companionship, are further evidence for men's place as the fulcrum of the kinship network. Thus Q. 52:17–21:

> [52:17–21] *The God-wary, they shall be amid gardens and bliss,* [18] *rejoicing*[22] *in what their Lord has given them, and for that He has protected them from the chastisement of the Blaze.* [19] *Feast and drink with blessings in return for what you used to do;* [20] *there they are in rows, reclining on couches, paired up with houris (ḥūr ʿīn).* [21] *And those who believe and their offspring follow them in belief, We will unite them with their offspring and We will not diminish them anything of their work; every man (marʾ) shall be held ransom against what he has done.*

At the centre of this formulation of the Garden are adult males who have wives and children in this world. In the Hereafter, the addressees (the

[20] Although Neuwirth cites these *sūras* as an example of the dissolution of tribal structures, there is much evidence from the Qur'ān and from prosopographical and other historical sources to indicate that tribal structures were maintained within the Islamic polity. Angelika Neuwirth, 'From Tribal Genealogy to Divine Covenant: Qur'ānic Re-figurations of Pagan Arab Ideals Based on Biblical Models' in eadem, *Scripture, Poetry and the Making of a Community: Reading the Qur'an as a Literary Text* (Oxford, Oxford University Press in association with the Institute of Ismaili Studies, 2014), 57.

[21] Ibid., 54.

[22] *Fākihīn*, cf. *fructus*, which originally meant 'to enjoy' because of the association of enjoying the harvest (Lat. *frui*, 'to enjoy').

muttaqūn) are reclining on couches with their female companions and those of their offspring who *follow them* (*ittabaʿt-hum*) *in belief* (*bi-īmān*). This might indicate that these heads of household were considered to hold moral sway over those under their protection, which might also, in this context, be considered a kind of social progress: the family would align itself with the new community under the leadership of Muḥammad.

Another early Meccan pericope refers to Abū Lahab and his wife, 'the firewood carrier', implying that they sinned together (Q. 111:2–5). *Sūrat al-Masad* (Q. 111) emphasises Abū Lahab's wealth and status in the world: that he is addressed by name implies that he was well known; but in the Hereafter *his wealth did not avail him, nor what he had earned* (Q. 111:2; cf. 92:11 *et passim*). His wife, who once must have been in a position to command others, ends up carrying the firewood for the blaze that burns him. That she is now engaged in heavy manual labour, led by the rope round her neck, suggests a debasement akin to a slave or an animal; the implication is that because she colluded with him in his bad deeds in the world, she is now forced to stoke the fire that burns him. Whole-household morality also seems to be implied by later Meccan verses that mention the spouses and children of the believers ascending to the Garden along with them (Q. 43:68–70; 25:74–5; 13:22–3), which shall be treated in more detail below.

Whole-household or whole-tribe conversion stories are portrayed in the records of conversion from the *Sīra* of Ibn Isḥāq. Some accounts in this source describe how the conversion of a tribal leader led to the conversion of his tribe. In one case, his wife and father immediately follow the lead of the tribal head.[23] One list of early converts in the *Sīra* includes mostly male converts; where women are listed, their husband or father is listed first.[24] The people on the list were all converted by Abū Bakr, which in turn indicates his own social standing in the new community; or, given that Ibn Isḥāq is a problematic source for early Islamic history,[25] such a list of his converts may indeed be an attempt to retroject Abū Bakr's importance in this early period.

[23] This, for instance, is the pattern in the conversion of al-Ṭufayl b. ʿAmr al-Dawsī, on which see Karen Bauer, 'The Emotions of Conversion and Kinship in the Qur'ān and the *Sīra* of Ibn Isḥāq', *Cultural History* 8.2 (2019), 137–63.

[24] See 'The mention of those Companions who submitted at the invitation of Abū Bakr, may God be pleased with him', in ʿAbd al-Mālik Ibn Hishām, *al-Sīra al-nabawiyya li-Ibn Hishām*, 4 vols. (Beirut, Mu'assasat Ḥusām Rammāl, [n.d.]), I, 191–5.

[25] On Ibn Isḥāq's *Sīra*, see Harald Motzki, ed., *The Biography of Muḥammad: The Issue of the Sources* (Leiden, Brill, 2000), and Sean Anthony, *Muhammad and the Empires of Faith: The Making of the Prophet of Islam* (Berkeley, University of California Press, 2020). Unpublished research by Kevin Jaques indicates that Ibn Isḥāq varied the characters in his accounts according to his audience.

By any reckoning, it is likely that conversion patterns were more complex than this idealised portrayal.[26] Regardless of how conversion actually happened, the presence of the *pater familias* as such a crucial part of the idealisation is significant in and of itself, precisely because it shows the presumption that this is how conversion *should* have occurred.[27]

The paradisiacal female companions (*ḥūr ʿīn*) referenced at Q. 52:20 have generated much discussion in medieval and modern times. *Ḥūr* is a term that occurs only four times in the Qurʾān, all in early Meccan verses (Q. 45:54; 52:20; 55:72; 56:22). Three of these are qualified with *ʿīn*,[28] while these beings are also named as a *newly constituted creation* (*innā anshaʾnāhunna inshāʾan*) (Q. 56:35) in one. The houris form part of vivid descriptions of the Garden in which worldly things such as the sensual pleasures of food and drink, lush natural surroundings and other comforts are mentioned as a way of dismissing this world as illusory, transient and finite (Q. 28:60–61; 31:33; 35:5; 40:39 and *passim*), in contrast to the everlastingly lush Hereafter. Likewise, companionship in the Hereafter is unlike that in this world, which is inevitably blemished by things like self-interest, vain talk, jealousy and rancour (e.g. Q. 15:47). The early Meccan verses exalt the pairing with the houris as one of sensuality, mutual compatibility and amorous affection:[29]

[26] For a more nuanced understanding of the meaning of conversion, of its gradualness and of conversion in kinship and family groups, see Anna Chrysostomides, 'Ties that Bind: The Role of Family Dynamics in the Islamization of the Central Islamic Lands, 700–900 CE' (Unpublished PhD dissertation, University of Oxford, 2017); for a stark warning that we must reject the simplistic accounts presented in early Islamic histories and embrace a more nuanced and ambiguous account, see Harry Munt, 'What Did Conversion to Islam Mean in Seventh-Century Arabia?' in *Islamisation: Comparative Perspectives from History*, ed. Andrew Peacock (Edinburgh, Edinburgh University Press, 2017), 93.

[27] A contrary argument is posed by Montgomery Watt, who uses the list of converts in Ibn Isḥāq presented here to argue that most early converts were young men who were otherwise powerless in the tribal context. W. Montgomery Watt, *Muhammad at Mecca* (Oxford, Clarendon Press, 1960), 87ff.

[28] On the *ḥūr ʿīn* see Stefan Wild, 'Lost in Philology? The Virgins of Paradise and the Luxenberg Hypothesis' in *The Qurʾān in Context: Historical and Literary Investigations into the Qurʾānic Milieu*, ed. Angelika Neuwirth, Nicolai Sinai and Michael Marx (Leiden, Brill, 2010), 625–47. Based on premodern Arabic lexicography and exegesis, he defines the term *ḥūr* as 'having eyes in which the contrast between black and white is very intense' and *ʿīn* as 'wide-eyed' (ibid., 627).

[29] For an argument of the Qurʾānic Hereafter as a 'subdued affair', see Lange, *Paradise and Hell*, 45. Cf. Wild, who describes it as a 'cosmos of sensual delight' in which 'sensual gratification without sexuality seems unthinkable'. Wild, 'Lost in Philology?' 630. Recent reinterpretations are offered by Celine Ibrahim, *Women and Gender in the Qurʾān* (Oxford, Oxford University Press, 2020), 41ff., and Mahdi Tourage, 'Affective Entanglements with the Sexual Imagery of Paradise in the Qur'an', *Body and Religion* 3.1 (2019), 52–70.

> [78:31–3] *Indeed a triumph awaits the God-wary:* [32] *Gardens and vineyards,* [33] *shapely bosomed [females], who are well-matched (kawāʿib atrāb).*
>
> [56:17–38] *Constantly attended to by immortal youths (wildān),* [18] *serving them from goblets and ewers, drinks from a flowing source,* [19] *experiencing neither headache nor dullness,* [20] *and such fruits as they prefer,* [21] *and such meat of fowls as they desire,* [22] *and ḥūr ʿīn* [23] *guarded like pearls,* [24] *a reward for what they used to do.* [25] *In it they shall hear neither idle nor sinful talk,* [26] *only mutual greetings of peace.* [27] *And the Companions of the Right – what about the Companions of the Right?* [28] *Amid thornless lote trees,* [29] *clustered acacia,* [30] *bountiful shade,* [31] *water served* [32] *alongside abundant fruits,* [33] *neither inaccessible nor forbidden,* [34] *and elevated beds.* [35] *Indeed, We have created a newly constituted creation (inshāʾ)* [36] *and made them virgins (abkār),* [37] *loving, well-matched (ʿurub atrāb),* [38] *for the People of the Right.*

The adjectival forms used to describe these figures, such as *kawāʿib*, *ḥūr ʿīn*, *abkār*, *ʿurub* and *atrāb*, are allusive and obscure, consonant with the overall poetic flavour of the early Meccan passages in which they sit. Some of these terms allude to the female form: *kawāʿib* seems to indicate a cleavage of perfect proportions,[30] while *'virgins'* (*abkār*) also appears in Q. 66:5, where the women who have not yet been married (*abkār*) are contrasted with the women who have been married (*thayyibāt*). The notion that these heavenly companions had not been previously married is consistent with the references to them as having *restrained glances* (*qāṣirāt al-ṭarf*) (Q. 37:48; 38:52; 55:56, 72) *not deflowered by human or jinn* (Q. 55:56 and 74). Such verses emphasise their modesty and seclusion, and imply that they are reserved exclusively for the believer. Finally, the houris are described as a *newly constituted creation* (*inshāʾ*) (Q. 56:35).[31]

Other descriptions refer to the houris' compatibility with the believer. *ʿUrub* means loving or amorous.[32] *Atrāb* appears thrice in the Qurʾān (Q. 38:52; 56:37; 78:33), all of which have to do with these companions.[33] According to the oft-cited medieval lexicographer al-Rāghib al-Iṣfahānī

[30] *Kawāʿib*: In Abū Bakr Muḥammad b. al-Ḥasan Ibn Durayd (d. 321/933), *Jamharat al-lugha*, ed. Ramzi Mounir Baalbaki (Beirut, Dār al-ʿIlm li'l-Malāyīn, 1987), s.v. *k-ʿ-b et passim*, the root appears throughout in poetry as a flattering means of describing a shapely bosom, with cleavage of perfect proportions.

[31] For another reading of Q. 56:60–62, see Ibrahim, *Women and Gender*, 42.

[32] Al-Rāghib al-Iṣfahānī, *Mufradāt alfāẓ al-Qurʾān*, ed. Safwan Adnan Dawudi (Damascus, Dār al-Qalam, 2002), 557, s.v. *ʿ-r-b*.

[33] Aside from the use of the root *t-r-b* as 'soil' and as 'coetaneous', another meaning is found in Q. 86:7.

(*fl.* fifth/eleventh century), the *atrāb* 'are coetaneous (*lidāt*), produced together with you, in the same way that the ribs in your ribcage are equal and alike'.[34] Muqātil b. Sulaymān says that the *atrāb* are either virgins or individuals of like age, the idealised thirty-three years-old.[35]

These oblique references could suggest the audience's familiarity with what is being described. Christian images of the Hereafter do not include the kind of sensual and sexual imagery that we see in the Qur'ān.[36] However, an antecedent has been noted in the Zoroastrian *daēnā*, in which a fifteen-year-old maiden greets the believer after his death, and she is rendered more and more beautiful according to his good deeds.[37]

While the fluidity in language seems to indicate that the original audience may have known more about the houris than we can from the Qur'ān alone, it has also allowed the later exegetical tradition much leeway in describing the nature of these idealised females.[38] Contrary to medieval and modern impressions of the heavenly virgins who are the reward for fighters of jihad, the houris are there for all males who are wary of God (*muttaqūn*); they are a reward for those who fulfil the obligations connected with *taqwā* in early Meccan *sūra*s such as giving *zakāt*, praying, believing, sharing their food and wealth with the needy, and so forth.[39] It is also noteworthy that one of the earliest exegetes, Muqātil b. Sulaymān, reconciled the *ḥūr* with this-worldly spouses by saying that the *ḥūr* were purified human spouses, made virginal again through a recreation (cf. 53:47; 56:61–2), and were the perfect

[34] Al-Rāghib al-Iṣfahānī, *Mufradāt*, 712–13. Neal Robinson connects *atrāb* to *turāb*, or soil, and says that its literal meaning is 'of the same soil'. Robinson, *Discovering the Qur'an*, 178. For the meaning of *atrāb*, we have chosen 'well-matched' as it encompasses the twin ideas of being equal in age and in composition.

[35] Muqātil, *Tafsīr Muqātil*, s.v. Q. 78:31. Muqātil also says that the restrained glances in Q. 38:52 means that they restrict their gaze from anyone other than their husbands, because they are enamoured with them (*'āshiq*) (at Q. 38:52).

[36] Wild, 'Lost in Philology?' 643.

[37] Shaul Shaked, 'Eschatology I. In Zoroastrianism and Zoroastrian Influence', *EIr*, VIII, Fasc. 6, 565–9 (available online at http://www.iranicaonline.org/articles/eschatology-I). On the direct link between the *daēnā* and the *ḥūr*, see also Alessandro Bausani, *La Persia Religiosa: Da Zaratustra a Bahâ'u'llâh* (Milan, Il Saggiatore, 1959); Louis Gray, 'Zoroastrian Elements in Muhammedan Eschatology', *Le Muséon*, new series, 3 (1902), 153–84; W. Sundermann, 'Die Jungfrau der guten Taten' in *Recurrent Patterns in Iranian Religions: From Mazdaism to Sufism*, ed. Philippe Gignoux (Paris, Association pour l'Avancement des Études Iraniennes, 1992), 159–73. See also Mircea Eliade, *A History of Religious Ideas*, vol I: *From the Stone Age to the Eleusinian Mysteries* (London, Collins, 1979), 329.

[38] *Pace* Wild, it is perhaps noteworthy that the idea of a number of companions for each man (say, seven or seventy) is a part of the later interpretative tradition.

[39] Jihad becomes an obligation in Medinan *sūras*.

age of thirty-three (the age of everyone in the Hereafter).[40] In this instance, one might say he resolves the tension between the worldly spouses who are more explicitly the subjects of the later Meccan and Medinan Qur'ānic verses and the specially created houri (*ḥūr ʿīn*) of the early Meccan verses.

Many of the above-mentioned themes are brought together in *sūrat al-Ṣāffāt* (Q. 37), which can be classified as early Meccan according to Nicolai Sinai's chronology.[41] This *sūra* thus becomes, in a sense, a summary of the early Meccan verses on women. First, the *sūra* mentions the possibility of wives being dragged into the Fire along with their unjust husbands. The guardians of Hell are instructed: [37:22–3] *Gather those who were unjust together with their mates, and what they used to worship* [23] *besides God, then guide them on the path to the Fire.* The text then mentions the presence of those who have restrained glances, using the feminine adjectival plural:

> [37:40–49] *Except for God's saved servants.* [41] *For them there will be a known reward* [42] *of fruits, and they will be held in honour.* [43] *In the Gardens of bliss,* [44] *upon couches facing one another,* [45] *served with a wine-cup from a fountain,* [46] *pure and delicious to the drinker,* [47] *causing neither headache nor stupefaction.* [48] *And next to them will be those*[f] *with restrained glances,* [49] *resembling hidden white pearls.*

Here the believers are in a place of comfort, facing one another, with their female companions at their side. Towards the end of *sūrat al-Ṣāffāt*, the unacceptability of attributing female progeny to God is once again stressed:

> [37:149–53] *Seek their opinion:*[42] *are daughters consigned to your Lord, and to you sons?* [150] *Or is it that you were witnessing Us creating female angels?* [151] *Truly their mendacity is such that it makes them say* [152] *God has begotten, and truly they speak lies!* [153] *Has He preferred to elect daughters over sons?*[43]

Again, it seems that here the Qur'ānic retort against associationism (*shirk*) is put in the form of rejecting the worship of females in order to show up the Meccans. This passage takes for granted that the audience understands the

[40] With regard to the *inshā'* (*newly constituted creation*) at Q. 56:35, Muqātil says: 'meaning, what is mentioned of the *ḥūr ʿīn* earlier [verse 22], so He starts with this description, that is to say, He has produced the old grey-haired women (*al-ʿujuz al-shumṭ*) of this world by recreating them in the Hereafter after the first creation in this world, *and made them virgins* (*abkār*), meaning young women (*shawābb*), every one of them of a single age, of thirty-three years'. Muqātil, *Tafsīr Muqātil*, IV, 219.

[41] Nöldeke puts it as middle Meccan; so among the early *sūra*s, it would come after the others cited above.

[42] The reader should not miss the irony of the usage of the term *istiftā'* instead of the more neutral root *s-'-l*; the term *istiftā'* is normally used to ask a serious opinion.

[43] Cf. Q. 3:42; 39:4.

hypocrisy of the pagans who attribute daughters to God while themselves preferring their sons and mocks the idea that God would create female angels. The question *Has He preferred to elect daughters over sons?* which overtly seems to express a preference for sons, is in fact a rhetorical riposte to the *mushrikūn*.

In sum, verses from the early Meccan period indicate a threefold objection to the pagan practice of attributing daughters to God and giving the angels female names: God has no progeny; He created both female and male, and it is not acceptable to worship something created; it is absurd of the pagans to attribute daughters to God while killing their own daughters. In the theology expressed in early Meccan verses, women are considered God's creation along with men, while at the same time the elevated status of men in society is affirmed through verses that are addressed specifically to them, emphasising the physical delights of the Garden, including fruit, drinks, springs, gardens, fine clothes and the companionship of the houris. There are hints that this paradisiacal vision may have been orientated towards the figure of the *pater familias*, with the presumption that he had some sway over those under his aegis: early Meccan eschatological verses mentioning kinship ties are addressed to men, and one verse says that his sons may 'follow him' in belief, while verses emphasising individual moral responsibility tend to be gender neutral. In this period, although women have equal creational status with men, no verses have addressed them overtly, whether to emphasise their worldly moral responsibility or to promise them a reward in the afterlife. This may be another indication of the primacy of the male addressee in the initial Qur'ānic revelations.

Later Meccan verses on women

The major difference between the early Meccan and the later Meccan period is that later Meccan *sūra*s include extensive narratives of individual women who must have been familiar to the audience from Biblical or parabiblical accounts. These women are vividly portrayed as characters who follow their own narrative arc. The presence of these exemplary women, while not the focus of this piece, is evidence for the emergence of women as subjects in the nascent Muslim community.

Lexical developments in later Meccan verses, documented here, provide evidence for this shift in women's status. Perhaps the most significant lexical development involves the evolution of the uses of the term 'female' described below, from mainly symbolic references to clear statements of the importance of the female and the possibility of a godly reward for her pious actions. It is also notable that the early Meccan lexicon included certain terms for females, such as 'houri' (*ḥūr*), 'female companion' (*ṣāḥiba*) or 'buried infant girl' (*maw'ūda*), which no longer appear in later periods. In contrast, the term 'women' (*nisā'*) appears for the first time in later Meccan verses and becomes more prevalent in Medinan *sūras*.

As we have seen, in the early Meccan period, the term *unthā* ('female') was used to refer to female angels (Q. 37:150; 53:27), to say that God created the male and the female (Q. 53:45; 75:39; 92:3) and to question the pagans about their hypocrisy of keeping males for themselves and attributing females to God (Q. 53:21). Now, in the later Meccan period, *unthā* is used to demonstrate God's omnipotence and the value of infant girls by saying that God knows what every female carries in her womb (Q. 13:8; 35:11; 41:47), and that it is His choice for some to have males and for others to have females, or a combination of the two (Q. 42:49, 50). As described below, all of this is an implicit answer to the pagans, whose negative reaction to the birth of a girl is emphasised at Q. 16:58. In a rebuke carried over from earlier Meccan *sūras*, two verses ask rhetorically whether God would have adopted female angels (Q. 17:40; 43:19).

Finally, in what may be the most important development of the term, in Q. 16:97 and 40:40 where women are assured that their good deeds will lead to a heavenly reward, it is *unthā* that is used, overtly according women spiritual and human value. It is possible to say that a term that had been used mainly in anti-pagan polemic is now extended to embrace the 'female' of the community of believers:[44]

> [16:97] *Any believer, male or female (unthā), who does righteous work, verily We shall grant him*[45] *a goodly life, and verily We shall repay them their wages equal to the best of their works.*[46]

> [40:40] *Whoever commits an evil work is not requited except with the like of it, while any believer, male or female (unthā), who does righteous work, those, they shall enter the Garden, and be provided for in it without any reckoning.*

Whereas the early Meccan emphasis on the equal ontological worth of the female and the male was mentioned partly as a corrective to the social attitudes of the Meccans and partly to emphasise that humans should not worship a creation of God's (themes that continue throughout the Qur'ān),[47]

[44] These instances also presage the Medinan verses Q. 3:195 and 4:124, which use 'female' in verses about the reward in the Hereafter.

[45] Here the Qur'ān uses the male pronoun but clearly means both men and women.

[46] It could be noted that Q. 16:92 uses a woman as an exemplar of unrighteousness.

[47] Other later Meccan verses include Q. 6:100 and 7:190.

these later Meccan verses stand as a clear recognition of women as members of the community of believers and inhabitants of the afterlife. They also reflect the themes brought forth in the later Meccan stories of Biblical women, in which prominent Biblical women are foregrounded for their moral choices.

The later Meccan period marks a change in the description of the companions in the afterlife from the houris to the 'spouses' (*azwāj*) of the believers. This shift in language may mark a shift in the very nature of the companions being described, from the mysterious houris to real-life spouses.[48] But there may be a connection between the *ḥūr* and the *azwāj*, because both are described as 'reclining' (*muttakiʾūn*) along with the righteous believer. 'Reclining' occurs eight times in the context of Paradise; in early Meccan verses such as Q. 52:20 and 55:76, the believers are reclining with the houris (*ḥūr ʿīn*), while in the later Meccan verse Q. 38:51, they are reclining with those of 'restrained glances' (*qāṣirāt al-ṭarf*), who are coetaneous (*atrāb*). Finally, in Q. 36:56, they are reclining with their mate/pair (*azwāj*). The suggestion is either that the spouses are one and the same as the *ḥūr*, or that the believer is reclining with both spouses and *ḥūr*. Later Meccan verses such as Q. 13:22–3 or 36:55–6, while not explicitly addressed to the *pater familias* as in the early Meccan case, emphasise the importance of kinship ties among offspring and forebears:[49]

> [13:22–3] *Those who are forbearing, desirous of the face of their Lord, who perform the prayer, and expend of that We have provided them, secretly and in public, and who avert evil with good – theirs shall be the Ultimate Abode,* [23] *Gardens of Eden which they shall enter; and those who were righteous from among their fathers, and their spouses (azwājihim), and their offspring, shall enter them, and the angels shall enter unto them from every gate.*
>
> [36:55–6] *Surely the dwellers of the Garden shall on that day be occupied quite joyously;* [56] *they and their spouses (azwāj) shall be in the shade, reclining on raised couches.*
>
> [40:8] *Our Lord, do admit them into Gardens of Eden, as You have promised them, together with the righteous from among their fathers, spouses (azwāj) and seed, for You are surely the one who is Mighty and Wise.*

Although these verses are overtly gender neutral, given the earlier context they may be considered further evidence for the continued importance of a specific family structure revolving around a male head of household, who

48 On this, see Robinson, *Discovering the Qur'an*, 89, and Lange, *Paradise and Hell*, 56.
49 See also Q. 25:74–5.

was presumed to have some influence over those in his protection. In these formulations, like in earlier instances, a single believer is the centrepoint of the family structure, the hub of the wheel. Like the early Meccan Q. 52:17–21 discussed above, these later Meccan instances tell us that it is only the righteous among the spouses and offspring who will ascend along with the *pater familias*.

Some might adduce Q. 43:70 as a counter example, in which the righteousness of the spouses is not mentioned (*Enter the Garden, you and your spouses, you shall be made joyful!*); but this verse is clearly a shortened version of the others. It may be concluded that, although the social status of the *pater familias* entailed a moral responsibility for his household, this does not contradict assertions elsewhere that ultimately everyone is responsible for their own moral choices, and the reward is only attained by the righteous, be they male or female.

The developments described above come as a part of an increasingly sophisticated argument against pagan hypocrisy, in which the pagans' treatment of their women is directly juxtaposed with their exaltation of females to the position of deities. For instance, in *sūrat al-Zukhruf* (Q. 43), the pagan meets the birth of his daughter with despair,[50] despite this (female) being the *very thing that he strikes as a likeness for the All-merciful*:

> [43:15–19] *They have apportioned to Him from among His servants a portion. Assuredly man is an outright ingrate.* [16] *Would He take from among what He has created daughters and single sons out for you?* [17] *When one of them is given the news of the very thing that he strikes as a likeness for the All-merciful (al-Raḥmān),*[51] *his face immediately darkens, barely able to contain himself (kaẓīm).* [18] *'What, one brought up surrounded by ornaments and incoherent in disputes?'* [19] *They make the angels, who are servants of the All-merciful, females (ināth). What, did they witness their creation? This witnessing of theirs will be written down, and they shall be questioned about it.*

In the following verses from *sūrat al-Naḥl* (Q. 16), pagan hypocrisy is summarised, bringing together in direct contrast practices that had heretofore been mentioned separately: burying alive the infant girls, being barely able to contain their outrage at the birth of a girl, and concurrently attributing daughters to God:

> [16:57–9] *They ascribe to God, glory be to Him, daughters, but as for them, whatever they like.* [58] *When one is given the news of a female, his face immediately darkens*

[50] This pagan view is again chastised in Q. 17:40: *Did your Lord prefer you with sons, and [Himself] adopt females from among the angels? Indeed you say a monstrous word!*

[51] That is to say, the birth of a girl.

and he is barely able to contain himself (kaẓīm); [59] *he hides shamefully from his people, because of the evil news that he has been given. Should he hold onto it*[52] *in disgrace, or should he shove it into the earth? How evil are the choices they make!*

Here the unbeliever is faced with a choice when given the news of the birth of a daughter: live in disgrace with this daughter or *shove it into the earth*, burying the infant girl alive. These pagan attitudes and choices, whether by worshipping females or burying them, are morally scandalous; the following later Meccan verses make explicit the value that God places on those very same infant girls:

[42:49–50] *To God belongs the kingdom of the heavens and the earth. He creates whatever He wishes: He gifts females to whomever He wishes, and gifts the males to whomever He wishes,* [50] *or He pairs them males and females, and He makes whomever He will infertile. Indeed He is knowing and powerful.*

Thus, while the pagans devalue women's humanity, God values them along with the males. Many other verses make it clear that God is the creator of humans and knows what is in the wombs, which could be seen as an extension of this theme, as well as emphasising God's power and knowledge. Verses such as Q. 13:8; 16:78; 22:5; 31:34; 35:11 and 41:47 all mention God's knowledge of what is in the wombs. Other verses refer to His purposeful creation of that infant:

[39:6] *He created you from a single soul, then made from it its mate, and He has sent down for you eight pairs of the cattle. He creates you in the bellies of your mothers, creation after creation, in a threefold darkness. This is God, your Lord!*

[16:78] *God has brought you forth from the bellies of your mothers, knowing nothing. He appointed for you hearing, eyesight, and hearts, that you might perchance give thanks.*

God in these verses is involved in every aspect of human formation. In our reading, it is not an accident that many of the verses cited above use the term 'females' as a clear rebuke against those who devalue them. The anti-female practices attributed to the pagans extend to their treatment of grown women: one verse claims that they do not give their wives the meat of freshly slaughtered cattle:

[6:139] *And they say, 'That which is in the bellies of these cattle is exclusively for our males, and forbidden to our spouses.' But if it be still-born, they all share in it. Truly, He will requite them for their allegations. Indeed He is wise and knowing.*

52 Meaning the infant daughter.

The value accorded to some women in the society is indicated in later Meccan verses that emphasise the necessity of being good to parents. Some of these verses are general enjoinders to be good to both parents (see, for instance, Q. 6:151; 17:23; 29:8; or 46:15–17). It is also noteworthy that some verses in the later Meccan period mention the attachment of the prophets to their parents (Q. 14:41; 71:28). One verse from *sūrat Luqmān* (Q. 31) speaks specifically of being good to mothers:

> [31:14] *And We have entrusted every person (al-insān) with [duty towards] his*[53] *parents, his mother bears him, ever weakening, his weaning being in two years. Be thankful to Me, and to your parents. The ultimate destination will be to Me.*

This is an indication of the social value accorded to mothers and of the moral good in treating them well, as well as being a recognition of the travail entailed in pregnancy and birth. This verse presents a direct link between parental mercy and God's mercy.

In sum, there are significant lexical and conceptual developments in later Meccan verses on women and the female (broadly construed). Most obviously, the connection between verses valuing female life in the Qurʾānic worldview and those representing the pagans as denigrating female life, which was implicit in the early Meccan period, is made explicit in the later Meccan period. It is now clear that the treatment of women forms a key line in the Qurʾānic argument against the pagans. Later Meccan verses acknowledge women's value in society, their moral responsibility and their place in the afterlife explicitly, while the male head of household is still recognised as the primary addressee of the text, which hints at his social importance and his potential moral influence over his household.

Medinan verses on women

The Medinan period represents a synthesis of existing Qurʾānic motifs in the context of establishing a new social order: according to traditional accounts, the move to Medina marks the point at which the Muslim community gathers momentum and gradually consolidates its emergent polity to conquer Medina and Mecca – and eventually all of Arabia itself during the lifetime of the Prophet. This new social order revolves around the Prophet Muḥammad as the social and spiritual leader of the community; but it does

[53] The Arabic here uses the masculine pronoun with the understanding that it refers to both men and women.

not entail the wholesale elimination of existing social structures. Rather, the Qur'ān, during this Medinan period, introduces a moral framework to order behaviour within existing social hierarchies such as male and female, free and enslaved.

The community's move from Mecca to Medina is reflected in a significant shift in terminology. For example, in Medinan verses, the term 'believing woman' (*mu'mina*, pl. *mu'mināt*) becomes a predominant form of address to the women of the Medinan community. Likewise, the term 'woman/women' (*n-s-'*), which never appeared in the early Meccan period and only eight times in the late Meccan period, occurs fifty times in the Medinan verses, while 'female hypocrites' (*munāfiqāt*) appears exclusively in Medinan verses. All of this is an indication of the social and religious importance of women in the Medinan milieu, whether as believers or as unbelievers.

The lexical shift in addressing women reflects a shift in the Qur'ān's kerygmatic imperative. The Qur'ānic proclamations are now directed towards those who have already embraced membership of this new religious community and those who may, for expediency, pretend to have membership in it. Thus the kerygmatic turn is also a paradigmatic one, as the content changes from apocalyptic revelations in Mecca to the social life of the nascent community in Medina. Women's increased presence in the Medinan lexicon may, in turn, indicate their enhanced status as pious and social subjects in that community. However, despite any enhanced status that female believers might have enjoyed, the underlying patriarchal structure of society could not have conceivably undergone radical change: male heads of household remain the addressees of many Medinan verses on women. Figure 1 shows how the transition from early to late Mecca and then to Medina is marked by a change in some of the root words associated with each period.

Overall, Medinan *sūra*s are much longer than the Meccan ones, and therefore if the terminology was used with the same frequency in each period, one might expect a mean number of occurrences in the later Meccan verses, with fewer occurrences in the early Meccan period and more occurrences in the later Meccan period; but such is not the case.

While the most obvious changes occur in the frequency of the terms 'believing woman' (*mu'mina*), 'women' (*nisā'*), 'female hypocrites' (*munāfiqāt*) and houris (*ḥūr*), which are each strongly associated with particular periods, on closer analysis there are more subtle, but perhaps no less significant, indications of how the Qur'ānic kerygma changes over time. For instance, it is not surprising that the terms *unthā* and *imra'a* occur most frequently in later Meccan verses, when the Qur'ānic polemic against the pagan mistreatment of women reaches its climax. Specific terms are associated with particular

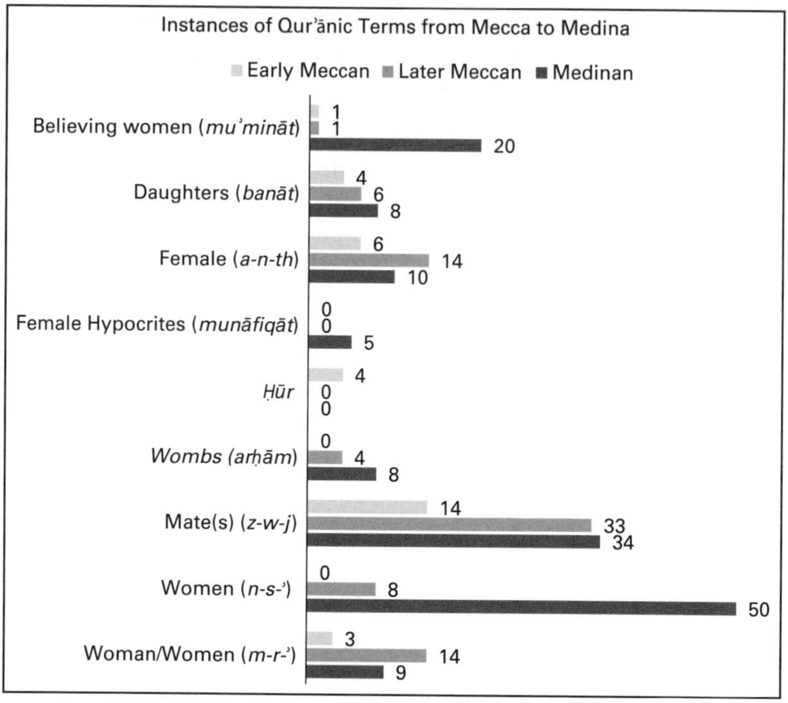

Figure 1. The lexical shift from Mecca to Medina.

sūras: of the fifty Medinan instances of the root *n-s-'* for women, twenty of them occur in *sūra* 4, thus aptly named *sūrat al-Nisā'*.

As noted above, key terms are also used in different ways over time. The use of terms relating to women and the female in Medinan *sūras* shows an increased emphasis on legislation, as anti-pagan rhetoric is eclipsed by verses moderating the morals and behaviour of the Muslim community. One example is the term 'daughters' (*banāt*). In the early Meccan *sūras*, *banāt* is used three times to refer to the daughters of God (Q. 37:149, 153; 52:39) and once to refer to Lot's daughters (Q. 15:71). In the later Meccan period, three verses are dedicated to the daughters of God (Q. 6:100; 16:57; 43:16), while three refer to the daughters of prophets (Q. 11:78, 79; 28:27). In Medinan verses, legislation for the community eclipses the former themes. Six instances refer to the permissible degrees of kinship for marriage (three in Q. 4:23 and three in Q. 33:50); one admonishes the Prophet to tell his wives and daughters to draw their cloaks over themselves, so that they might be recognised in public (Q. 33:59). Only one verse refers to a 'daughter' (Mary, 'daughter of 'Imrān' at Q. 66:12), while none at all speak of the daughters of God. Meanwhile, 'the female' is also used in legislative verses eight times, in reference to female believers and to dietary laws (twice in Q. 2:178, once each in Q. 4:11 and 176, twice in Q. 6:43 and twice in Q. 6:144); twice to indicate that males and females are accorded an equal reward by God (Q. 3:195; 4:124); once in the Mary story, when her mother Ḥanna exclaims that she has borne a female child (Q. 3:36); once to refer to God's creation of males and females (Q. 49:13); and only once to refer to the pagans' invoking of females alongside God (Q. 4:117). This all shows that the anti-pagan rhetoric on women assumes a place in the background, brought back into play through the cyclical recitation of Meccan passages, while the community's own women assume much greater prominence in new Medinan verses.

The number of verses on the equal moral responsibility of all believers now eclipses the anti-pagan verses. The most often-cited verse in this regard is Q. 33:35 (on which, see the appendix to the Introduction). But there are many more such Medinan examples.[54] The following is a representative excerpt in which we have highlighted in bold the instances of the terms 'hypocrite women' and 'believing women' to illustrate the above-mentioned points:

> [9:67–72] *Hypocrite men and* ***hypocrite women*** *are two of a kind: they bid what is wrong and forbid what is right, and are tight-fisted too. They forget all about God, and so He forgets all about them. Truly, the hypocrites are transgressors.* [68] *God promises the hypocrite men and* ***hypocrite women****, together with those who disbelieve, the fire of Hell: in it they shall remain forever, for it is their just deserts. God has cursed them, and for them there will be an abiding chastisement.* [69] *Like those who came before you, who were more powerful than you, and had greater wealth and more children, and enjoyed their share – so too have you enjoyed your share, just like those who came before you enjoyed their share, plunging right in, just like they did: but those, their deeds are worth nothing in either this world or in the Hereafter, and those truly are the losers.* [70] *Has the news not reached them about those who came before them – the people of Noah, 'Ad, and Thamud, and the people of Abraham, the inhabitants of Midian, and those upended towns? Their messengers came to them with clear signs. God did not intend to wrong them, but it was them wronging their own souls.* [71] *Believing men and* ***believing women****, however, are allied to one another: they bid what is right and they forbid what is wrong. They maintain the prayer and they give charity. They obey God and His Messenger: those are the ones to whom God will grant mercy. Verily God is mighty and wise.* [72] *God has promised believing men and* ***believing women*** *gardens with streams beneath them and goodly dwellings in gardens of Eden, abiding therein forever. Still, God's blessing is the greatest (of all things), and that itself is the greatest triumph.*

[54] For instance: Q. 3:61, 195; 4:97–9, 124; 47:19; 48:5–6; 49:11, 13; 57:12–13, 18.

What is striking about the above passage is not just that the tone has changed substantially from the early Meccan anti-pagan rhetoric. It is the way that the language from later Meccan stories is now addressed directly to the hypocrites in Medina. In the beginning of this passage, the audience is told that the hypocrites have forgotten about God, who has thus forgotten about them; this directly parallels the language of the Adam and Eve story in *sūrat Ṭā Hā* (Q. 20). In Q. 20:115, the reader is told that Adam forgot; but the crux of his story is that, unlike the unbelievers, he eventually realises his wrongdoing, repents and remembers. This contrast is made apparent in Q. 20:126, when the unbeliever is warned about the Judgment when God will tell him '*Our signs came to you, and you forgot all about* (*nasayta*) *them; likewise, now you are forgotten about*'. In the Adam and Eve story, Adam and Eve admit that they have wronged themselves (Q. 7:23); likewise, the Queen of Sheba (Q. 27:44) and Moses (Q. 28:16). In all of those instances, the protagonists realise their wrongdoing and repent, submitting to God or asking for His mercy. Here, this language is used to remind the Medinan audience that God does not commit injustice; rather, it is people who commit injustice against themselves and their own souls when they do not repent of their wrongdoing. In the Adam and Eve story, the audience is told that satans are the allies (*awliyā'*) of those who do not believe (Q. 7:27); here, the believers are allies of one another (Q. 9:71).[55] This use of Meccan terminology in a Medinan *sūra* cannot be considered accidental; rather, it is specifically intended to create resonance and contrast.[56] Thus, while the 'hypocrites' are a distinctly Medinan audience, their past parallels and ultimate fate are well known.

Contrary to what one might expect, eschatology is not absent in Medinan verses. Indeed, the reminder of God's reward and punishment is a constant refrain throughout the 'legislative' verses. These and other Medinan verses repeatedly emphasise that both men and women will receive a reward or punishment in the afterlife commensurate with their moral character and their deeds. However, the Hereafter is not described with the same vivid detail as it had been in earlier periods. The lush splendour of early Meccan descriptions and the exaltation of sensual pleasure and sexual companionship are replaced with the somewhat cursory 'gardens with rivers running beneath them'. Some scholars argue that these terse and comparatively less vivid Qur'ānic descriptions of the Gardens are being brought in line with

[55] See also Q. 8:72–3 as an example of believers being allied to one another and unbelievers being allied to one another.

[56] On the use of emotive terms to create resonance, see Karen Bauer, 'Emotion in the Qur'an: An Overview', *Journal of Qur'anic Studies* 19.2 (2017), 1–30.

Biblical traditions, reflecting a change in the audience from pagans to monotheists.[57] However, it is equally plausible that these terser references reflect an audience that is now familiar with the images of the Hereafter already, without the need for any further embellishment in these instances.

Companionship still forms an important part of the Hereafter, but the references to companions in the Garden are now to 'purified spouses' (*azwāj muṭahhara*) in verses Q. 2:25; 3:15; and 4:57. This raises a lingering ambiguity about whether these purified spouses are distinct from the Meccan houris. The purified spouses, unlike the companions described in the early Meccan Qurʾānic verses, are not overtly gendered or sexualised. It might be surmised that these terms are either shorthand for the *ḥūr* of the early Meccan period, or that the earthly spouses become *ḥūr* in the afterlife, or that they are two distinct inhabitants of the Hereafter. Regardless, the blurring of these references indicates a deliberate textual move to embrace an expanded audience, one that speaks to women and men as individuals and as couples. Removed from the obvious context of earlier descriptions, the grammatical construction of 'purified spouses' does not seem to preclude a gender-neutral address.

The centrality of companionship in the world and Hereafter is emphasised in Medinan verses such as Q. 2:102, which speaks of the gravity of rupturing the spousal bond; but despite such allusions in a society for which spousal union was important, other Medinan verses make it clear that, in those instances where a choice is required, the believer must choose God.[58] But it is incorrect to suppose that anti-kin rhetoric entailed a rupture of kinship ties: believers were still admonished to be good to their kin and other needy individuals in society.[59] Such verses reflect a sustained tension throughout the Qurʾānic text between this-worldly and other-worldly commitments, a tension which is especially acute for the *pater familias*, who has obligations to look after the wider social group. In the context of conquest and expanding empire, we can assume that not all of those in his care were even Muslim.

In sum, while one might imagine that in the Medinan period, with the emphasis on jihad and Muslim community building, the rupture with kin would be complete and references to the heavenly maidens would predominate (perhaps as a reward for the fighting members of this conquest society),

[57] Lange, *Paradise and Hell*, 56ff.

[58] See for example Q. 3:14; 4:135; 9:24; 22:1–2; 64:14.

[59] See e.g. Q. 2:83, 180, 215, *et passim*. Also see Bauer, 'The Emotions of Conversion and Kinship', 137–63.

neither is the case. The Hereafter is instead rather less embellished and the heavenly companions, as already mentioned, are referred to as 'purified spouses'. Breaking the spousal bond is equated with grave sin, and several verses mention the continuing importance of being good to kin and vulnerable members of society, treating them with common decency and maintaining existing financial commitments. This-worldly morality thus becomes an expression of piety, insofar as being good in this world is considered a moral imperative.

Conclusion

This Prolegomenon has shown that a chronological analysis of 'women' and 'the female' in the Qur'ān enables an understanding of the subject as one that develops through time, a subset of the development of the Qur'ānic narration as a whole. We began by locating 'the female' in the Qur'ān's anti-pagan polemic and within its eschatological rhetoric. For the pagans, females never attain full personhood: females are idealised as daughters of God, while the *maw'ūda* is an infant girl buried alive. In the Qur'ān, meanwhile, males and females are an equal creation. At the same time, females are idealised in the form of the paradisiacal houris, who are in a sense symbolic of the Qur'ānic view of the ultimately perfect life that awaits believers in the Hereafter. The early Meccan verses are thus sparse in detail about real women and their lives; but there is a symmetry between the *maw'ūda* and the houris, who represent two trajectories: the continual threat to the unbelievers, whose fate in the afterlife will be akin to what they mete out to the *maw'ūda* in this world, and the continual promise to the believers, whose selflessness and self-restraint in this world will earn them a sensory and spiritual bliss in Paradise.

In later Meccan verses, women themselves emerge as pious subjects who have the possibility of attaining the Garden through their own moral agency. Here, women are at the receiving end of the promise and threat that was directed primarily towards men in the earliest Qur'ānic preaching. This development is reflected both in the use of the term 'female' and in the stories of Biblical women such as Mary and the Queen of Sheba, who show moral agency.[60]

In Medinan verses, the worlds represented by Meccan verses are brought together in a new vision that is at once social and moral. Here the nascent

[60] Their stories will be detailed in our forthcoming book on women in the Qur'ān.

Muslim community becomes realised as a political reality, with specific rulings directing believers to treat one another with the moral rectitude that will ensure an ordered life in the world while simultaneously paving the way for the Hereafter. Women achieve a social reality that stands as an answer to their symbolic representation in early Meccan verses. This social reality is imbued with the flavour of the tribal structures in which it stands: the *pater familias* is still presumed to have control of the family, and male elites remain as important figures who look after the well-being of the poor and disenfranchised. At the same time, repeated promises to women show that they are fully responsible moral agents. Spiritual emancipation of women did not translate into social emancipation, as we might expect it in a modern sense, but it certainly highlighted the ultimate spiritual and, in some sense, ontological equality between the sexes in spite of the lingering social hierarchy reserved for men.

The development of the story of women thus parallels the development of the community of Muslims, from a small group of believers in early Mecca to a fully fledged political and social entity with its own rules in Medina, where all subjects are given the choice of pursuing a pious path through their obedience to worldly rulings. We note here that taking a historical-critical approach to a subject that has often been studied in a piecemeal fashion yields tangible results. This analysis is hardly the last word on women in the Qurʾān; but it indicates that 'women' should be considered as an important aspect of the Qurʾānic narration as a whole, rather than as a subject that stands apart from the rest of the text. This has implications for the field of Qurʾānic studies, which has often sidelined the subject of women, and for the field of gender studies, which sometimes examines 'women' in isolation from the Qurʾān's overall kerygma. Perhaps most importantly for this volume, the analysis here shows that the subject of women in the Qurʾān is both more and less than the exegetes make it out to be. More, in the sense that none of the exegetes considered 'women' as a topic to be studied, and as such they could not come to this type of holistic view. Less, in the sense that in the Qurʾān, women are not considered inferior to men, even as they have fewer rights, whereas the commentarial tradition can sometimes extend this legal disadvantage into an ontological inferiority.

The commentators and their commentaries[1]

Muqātil b. Sulaymān al-Balkhī (d. 150/767)

A *MAWLĀ* of the Asad,[2] a traditionist and exegete, Abū'l-Ḥasan Muqātil b. Sulaymān b. Bashīr al-Azdī al-Khurāsānī al-Balkhī (d. 150/767) was born in Balkh (in modern-day Afghanistan) and lived in Marw and Iraq.[3] His scholarly activities took him as far afield as Beirut and Mecca. Muqātil's case is important for the field of Qur'ānic *tafsīr*, as his *tafsīr* is most likely the earliest extant commentary.[4] Given the general sensitivity surrounding the issue of early Islamic texts, scholars tend to be sceptical about the authenticity of early commentaries on the Qur'ān, but they are less so with Muqātil's *tafsīr*.[5] The case for its authenticity is based on the consistently uniform nature of the author's approach in his commentary, and the conformity of these

[1] Substantial parts of this section have been reproduced in toto from Hamza *et al.*, *Anthology*, I; in some cases, the duplicate entries have been lightly edited and updated. We would like to acknowledge that Sajjad Rizvi contributed to many of these entries in volume I. For the entries that we have added in this volume, we have adopted a different approach, in which we translate portions of the commentators' introductions to their own works.

[2] *Mawlā* is a multivocal term in Arabic. In this context, it denotes a retainer or a tribal client, someone who attaches himself to a tribe so that he may be recognised within Arab hierarchies and genealogical arrangements. See Patricia Crone, 'Mawlā', *EI*², VI, 875.

[3] The commentary that we have used in this volume, as noted in the Introduction, is *Tafsīr Muqātil*, edited by ʿAbd Allāh Maḥmūd Shiḥāta. For all of the major *tafsīr* works, we have in fact used other editions and we have also referred to *altafsir.com*. On Muqātil, see the brief but useful entry on him by M. Plessner and A. Rippin, 'Muḳātil b. Sulaymān', *EI*², VII, 508–9; Josef van Ess, *Theologie und Gesellschaft im 2. Und 3. Jahrhundret Hidschra: Eine Geschichte des religiösen Denkens im frühen Islam*, [hereafter *TG*], 4 vols. (Berlin, New York, de Gruyter, 1991–7), I, 212–13, 227; al-Khāṭib Aḥmad b. ʿAlī al-Baghdādī (d. 463/1071), *Ta'rīkh Baghdād*, 14 vols. (Cairo, Maktabat al-Khānjī, 1931), XIII, 402; Paul Nwyia, *Exégèse coranique et langage mystique: Nouvel essai sur le lexique technique des mystiques musulmans* (Beirut, Dar el-Machreq, 1970), 25–34. On the 'confusion' between him and Muqātil b. Ḥayyān (d. 135/753), also an exegete and traditionist from Balkh, see *TG*, II, 510–17; Patricia Crone, 'A Note on Muqātil b. Ḥayyān and Muqātil b. Sulaymān', *Der Islam* 74 (1997), 238–50.

[4] Muqātil's *tafsīr* is edited and appended with a useful introduction to the exegete and his work by ʿAbd Allāh Maḥmūd Shiḥāta; cf. Nwyia, *Exégèse coranique*, 38–108; on the *tafsīr* and its transmission, see *TG*, II, 516–28; also relevant are Kees Versteegh, *Arabic Grammar and Qur'ānic Exegesis in Early Islam* (Leiden, Brill, 1993); Ramzi Baalbaki, *Grammarians and Grammatical Theory in the Medieval Arabic Tradition* (Ashgate, Variorum, 2004).

[5] Even Andrew Rippin, who is generally sceptical of the authenticity of early *tafsīr* texts, accepts the ascription of this text to Muqātil as 'fairly safe'. Andrew Rippin, 'Al-Zuhrī, *naskh al-Qur'ān* and the Problem of Early *Tafsīr* Texts', *Bulletin of the School of Oriental and African Studies* 47 (1984), 23.

characteristics to what we know about Muqātil as an exegete and theologian from later sources that make reference to him. First, for his comments on any Qur'ānic reference to pre-Islamic Judaeo-Christian figures or events, he makes fairly abundant use of Biblical narratives and material that was later deemed *isrā'īliyyāt*.[6] Second, he does not hesitate to interpret anthropomorphic verses about God literally, so that for him God has a hand, an eye and sits on a throne, etcetera.[7] Also included in this *tafsīr* are occasional comments from the transmitter Hudhayl b. Ḥabīb that he did not hear a particular phrase from Muqātil, which lends an air of veracity to the rest of the commentary.[8] Finally, Muqātil undoubtedly believed that all Muslims would attain salvation in the Hereafter, and that even if a Muslim sinner were to end up in Hell, he would eventually exit from Hell on the basis of the belief in the oneness of God, that is, the affirmation of *lā ilāha illā 'llāh* (there is no god except God), a theological conviction that pervades his commentary on eschatological verses in general. These three factors would make him a Murji'ī traditionist.[9] Some studies have suggested, unconvincingly, that he

[6] As noted by Muḥammad Hādī Maʿrifat, *al-Tafsīr wa'l-Mufassirūn fī thawbihi'l-qashīb*, 2 vols. (Mashhad, al-Jāmiʿa al-Raḍawiyya li'l-ʿUlūm al-Islāmiyya, 1997–8), II, 189, 192. For the use of Biblical material in Qur'ānic exegesis, see Ramzī Naʿnaʿa, *al-Isrā'īliyyāt wa āthāruhā fī kutub al-tafsīr* (Damascus, Dār al-Qalam; Beirut, Dār al-Ḍiyā', 1970). Recent contributions by Michael Pregill and Roberto Tottoli question the application of the term '*isrā'īliyyāt*' to early works, showing that the term only emerged in the tenth century as a polemical designation for particular types of transmitted material. See Michael Pregill, 'Isrā'īliyyāt, Myth, and Pseudepigraphy: Wahb b. Munabbih and the Early Islamic Versions of the Fall of Adam and Eve', *Jerusalem Studies in Arabic and Islam* 34 (2008), 215–83; idem, 'Isrā'īliyyāt', *EBR* XIII, 522–8; Roberto Tottoli, 'New Material on the Use and Meaning of the Term *Isrā'īliyyāt*', *Jerusalem Studies in Arabic and Islam* 50 (2021), 1–43. See also Georges Vadja, 'Isrā'īliyyāt', *EI*^{2}, IV, 211–12. More broadly, for the use of *isrā'īliyyāt* to construct the Muslim identity see Uri Rubin, *Between Bible and Qur'ān: The Children of Israel and the Islamic Self-Image* (Princeton, NJ, Darwin Press, 1999); perhaps the earliest overview of this is in M.J. Kister, '*Ḥaddithū ʿan Banī Isrā'īla wa-lā ḥaraja*', *Israel Oriental Studies* 2 (1972), 215–39.

[7] *TG*, II, 528–32 and IV, 373ff.; Nwyia, *Exégèse coranique*, 28. For an argument to the contrary, see Mun'im Sirry, 'Muqātil b. Sulaymān and Anthropomorphism', *Studia Islamica* 107.1 (2012), 38–64.

[8] As noted by Kees Versteegh, 'Grammar and Exegesis: The Origins of Kufan Grammar and the *Tafsīr Muqātil*', *Der Islam* 67.2 (1990), 208; by Nwyia, *Exégèse coranique*, 31; and by Sinai, 'The Qur'anic Commentary of Muqātil b. Sulaymān', 114. Sinai accepts the attribution to Muqātil and suggests a date of sometime before 152/770 (ibid., 117).

[9] The Murji'a (upholders of the doctrine of *irjā'*) were an important early Muslim movement of the turn of the second/eighth century, whose ideology was adopted by the Ḥanafī school at a formative stage, but was later subsumed by the general Sunnī community. The principal ideology of this movement was that all Muslims should suspend judgment (*irjā'*) on the rights and wrongs of the leaders of the community at the time of the schisms – namely, on ʿUthmān b. ʿAffān (*r.* 24–36/644–56) and ʿAlī b. Abī Ṭālib (*r.* 36–41/656–61), both of whom were assassinated. The reason for this ideological plea on the part of the Murji'a was because the stance one adopted towards these early leaders determined one's religio-political affiliation, and in turn fuelled internal schism. In the volatile context of early Islam, the Murji'a thought that if they could put an end to the polemical discussions about the first civil war, then they could also put

was a Zaydī theologian;[10] it has even been suggested that Muqātil was politically a Zaydī,[11] but this seems most improbable and there is certainly no historical evidence to support either claim for his Zaydism. There is plenty of evidence, however, that proves he was a Murjiʾī, at least in terms of theology.[12] Consistent with his traditionalism, he also seems to have held determinist views.[13]

The exegetical corpus ascribed to him is rarely, if at all, acknowledged in the works of later Sunnī traditionists (*aṣḥāb al-ḥadīth*); often exegetical reports are reproduced without explicit mention of his name as transmitter or narrator. It seems likely that this was on account of his disregard for *isnād*s, his perceived exaggerated dependence on the Biblical *isrāʾīliyyāt* material, and his proclivity to interpret Qurʾānic anthropomorphic verses in a quite literal manner.[14] Despite these 'blemishes', and even though he is not

an end to the schism engendered by it. On the Murjiʾa, see Wilferd Madelung, 'Murdjiʾa', *EI*², VII, 605–7, and idem, 'The Early Murjiʾa in Khurāsān and Transoxania and the Spread of Ḥanafism', *Der Islam* 59 (1982), 32–9; *TG*, I, 138–9, 152–221 and II, 164–86, 493–544, 659–63; Khalīl ʿAthāmina, 'The Early Murjiʾa: Some Notes', *Journal of Semitic Studies* 35 (1990), 109–30; Saleh Said Agha, 'A Viewpoint of the Murjiʾa in the Umayyad Period: Evolution Through Application', *Journal of Islamic Studies* 8.1 (1997), 1–42; Patricia Crone and Fritz W. Zimmermann, *The Epistle of Sālim ibn Dakhwān* (Oxford, Oxford University Press, 2001), 219–43. The grandson of ʿAlī b. Abī Ṭālib from his slave-girl wife, al-Ḥasan b. Muḥammad b. al-Ḥanafiyya (d. *c.* 101/719), is supposed to have composed the famous treatise expounding this doctrine of *irjāʾ*. For the text of this work, see Josef van Ess, 'Das *Kitāb al-irǧāʾ* des Ḥasan b. Muḥammad b. al-Ḥanafiyya', *Arabica* 21 (1974), 20–52; *TG*, I, 174–9 and V, 6–12 gives the text itself in German; Michael Cook, *Early Muslim Dogma: A Source-Critical Study* (Cambridge, Cambridge University Press, 1981), 27–43.

10 See M.M. al-Sawwāf, 'Muqātil b. Sulaymān: An Early Zaydī Theologian, with Special Reference to his *Tafsīr al-khams miʾat āya*' (Unpublished PhD dissertation, University of Oxford, 1969); Muḥammad b. Isḥāq Ibn al-Nadīm (d. 385/995), *Kitāb al-Fihrist*, ed. Ibrāhīm Ramaḍān (Beirut, Dār al-Maʿrifa, 1994), 222. For more references, see Hamza *et al.*, *Anthology*, I, 53, n. 7.

11 For example, Nwyia, *Exégèse coranique*, 26.

12 See Claude Gilliot, 'Muqātil, grande exégète, traditionist et théologian maudit', *Journal Asiatique* (Paris) 279 (1991), 39–92. Being from Balkh, Muqātil's background predisposed him to Murjiʾism; see *TG*, II, 531–2; also Feras Hamza, 'To Hell and Back: A Study of the Concepts of Hell and Intercession in Early Islam' (Unpublished PhD dissertation, University of Oxford), 2002, esp. ch. 3, 79–89, for specific examples of Muqātil's Murjiʾī theology of the afterlife.

13 A work entitled *Kitāb al-Radd ʿalāʾl-Qadariyya* is attributed to him.

14 *TG*, II, 529; Aḥmad b. Muḥammad Ibn Khallikān (d. 681/1282), *Wafayāt al-aʿyān*, ed. Iḥsān ʿAbbās, 8 vols. (Beirut, Dār al-Thaqāfa, 1968–72), IV, 343; Baghdādī, *Taʾrīkh*, XIII, 162–4; Abūʾl-Ḥusayn b. ʿUthmān al-Khayyāṭ (d. *c.* 300/912), *Kitāb al-Intiṣār waʾl-radd ʿalā Ibn al-Rawandī al-mulḥid*, ed. and tr. Albert N. Nader, *Le Livre du triomphe et de la réfutation d'Ibn al-Rawandī l'hérétique* (Beirut, Imprimerie Catholique, 1957), 54; Muḥammad Ibn Ḥibbān al-Bustī (d. 354/965), *Kitāb al-Majrūḥīn min al-muḥaddithīn waʾl-ḍuʿafāʾ waʾl-matrukīn*, ed. Maḥmūd Ibrāhīm Zāyid, 3 vols. (Aleppo, Dār al-Waʿy, 1975–6), III, 14; Muḥammad b. Aḥmad al-Dhahabī (d. 748/1348), *Mīzān al-iʿtidāl fī naqd al-rijāl*, ed. ʿAlī Muḥammad Bajawī, 4 vols. (Cairo, ʿĪsā al-Bābī al-Ḥalabī, 1963), no. 8741; Abū ʿAbd Allāh Muḥammad b. Ismāʿīl al-Bukhārī (d. 256/870), *al-Taʾrīkh al-kabīr*, 4 vols. (Hyderabad, Majlis Dāʾirat al-Maʿārif al-ʿUthmāniyya, 1963–78), IV, 4.

explicitly cited by later commentators such as Ṭabarī, it is clear that his work was always a source for Qurʾānic exegetical material.[15]

Muqātil's *tafsīr* is important for modern scholarship because of what it potentially reveals about the nature of the development of the genre itself. There have been two main attempts in Western scholarship to classify this *tafsīr*, with implications for the genre as a whole. For John Wansbrough, Muqātil's *tafsīr* constitutes the earliest phase of exegesis and is thus 'haggadic' (narrative).[16] However, while one cannot ignore that narrative is a driving force in Muqātil's commentary, this designation runs the risk of missing Muqātil's overall method. Sinai points out that although this *tafsīr* includes some long narrative passages, 'structural primacy still rests with the Qur'anic text'.[17] One thing is clear: Muqātil was first and foremost a storyteller; but his method of narrating the Qurʾān as a story incorporated many elements, such as law, narratives and basic lexicography. Narrow categorisations, such as Wansbrough's, may not be adequate to capture this basic point.

Muqātil is the author of two other works on the Qurʾān. One is the *Kitāb Tafsīr al-khams miʾat āya min al-Qurʾān al-karīm*,[18] which organises verses under legal topics and gives basic interpretations of them. The other, called *al-Ashbāh (or al-Wujūh) waʾl-naẓāʾir fīʾl-Qurʾān al-karīm*,[19] examines Qurʾānic expressions by providing several meanings for certain words, with a comment on each meaning and an analogue (*naẓīr*, pl. *naẓāʾir*) where the word is used in the same sense. Other Qurʾānic works attributed to him are not extant.[20] But a third work *Kitāb Mutashābih al-Qurʾān*, in which he deals with the allegorical interpretation of the 'ambiguous' verses in the Qurʾān, is extant in the Sunnī work of Abūʾl-Ḥusayn Muḥammad b. Aḥmad al-Malaṭī (d. 377/986) entitled *Kitāb al-Tanbīh waʾl-radd ʿalā ahl al-ahwāʾ waʾl-bidaʿ* (*The Book of Warning and Refutation of the People of Heresy and Innovation*)

[15] On Ṭabarī's use of Muqātil's Biblical material, see Āmāl ʿAbd al-Raḥmān Rabīʿ, *al-Isrāʾīliyyāt fī tafsīr al-Ṭabarī: Dirāsa fīʾl-lugha waʾl-maṣādir al-ʿibriyya* (Cairo, Dār al-Thaqāfa al-ʿArabiyya, 2000).

[16] John Wansbrough, *Quranic Studies* (London, Oxford University Press, 1977).

[17] Sinai, 'The Qur'anic Commentary of Muqātil b. Sulaymān', 118.

[18] Muqātil b. Sulaymān, *Tafsīr al-khams miʾat āya min al-Qurʾān*, ed. Isaiah Goldfeld (Shafā ʿAmr, Israel, Dār al-Mashriq, 1980).

[19] This work was also edited by ʿAbd Allāh Maḥmūd Shiḥāta. See Muqātil b. Sulaymān, *al-Ashbāh waʾl-naẓāʾir fīʾl-Qurʾān al-karīm*, ed. ʿAbd Allāh Maḥmūd Shiḥāta (Cairo, al-Hayʾa al-Miṣriyya al-ʿĀmma liʾl-Kitāb, 1975); Cf. Nabia Abbott, *Studies in Arabic Literary Papyri*, 3 vols. (Chicago, IL, Chicago University Press, 1957–72), II, 92–106; Nwyia, *Exégèse coranique*, 109–16.

[20] For a list of his works, see Ibn al-Nadīm, *al-Fihrist*, ed. Ibrāhīm Ramaḍān, 222.

which attacks groups of heretics, an interesting fact given his condemnation among Sunnī traditionists.[21]

Hūd b. Muḥakkam al-Hawwārī (*fl.* fourth/tenth century)

Little is known about this Ibāḍī thinker and commentator; even the Ibāḍī sources do not tell us very much.[22] This is partly due to the neglect of the study of the Khārijīs from whom the modern-day Ibāḍiyya are historically descended, albeit they represent a far more moderate form of that Khārijism. Hūd was of the Berber Hawwāra tribe of Ifrīqiyā, who supported the Ibāḍī imams of Tripolitania in North Africa, based in Tāhart,[23] in their struggle against the Fatimids.[24] His father, Muḥakkam (d. *c.* 258/872), was a judge appointed by the Ibāḍī Rustamid Aflaḥ b. ʿAbd al-Wahhāb b. Rustam (d. 258/872) in the Awrās mountains in what is now eastern Algeria.[25] It may

[21] Muḥammad b. Aḥmad al-Malaṭī (d. 377/987), *al-Tanbīh wa'l-radd ʿalā ahl al-ahwā' wa'l-bidaʿ*, ed. Sven Dedering (Istanbul, Maṭbaʿat al-Dawla, 1936); ed. Muḥammad Zāhid al-Kawtharī (Baghdad, Maktabat al-Muthannā, 1968). The use of Muqātil in Malaṭī was noted by Wansbrough, *Quranic Studies*, 165, 211–12.

[22] The commentary we have used in this volume, as noted in the introduction, is *Tafsīr kitāb Allāh al-ʿazīz*, edited by Belḥāj b. Saʿīd Sharīfī. On Hūd, see Abū'l-ʿAbbās Aḥmad b. Saʿīd al-Shammākhī (d. 928/1522), *Kitāb al-Siyar*, 2 vols. (Muscat, Wizārat al-Turāth al-Qawmī, 1987), II, 59; Claude Gilliot, 'Le commentaire coranique de Hūd b. Muḥakkam/Muḥkim', *Arabica* 44 (1997), esp. 179–80; Josef van Ess, 'Untersuchungen zu einigen ibāḍitischen Handschriften', *Zeitschrift der Deutsche Morgenländische Gesellschaft* 126.1 (1976), 42–3; *TG*, II, 656 and IV, 271, where he inconsistently renders his name; see the comments by Belḥāj, the editor of Hūd's *Tafsīr kitāb Allāh al-ʿazīz*, I, 8–13; Muḥammad b. Mūsā Bābāʿammī *et al.*, *Muʿjam aʿlām al-Ibāḍiyya min al-qarn al-awwal al-hijrī ilā'l-ʿaṣr al-ḥāḍir*, 2 vols. (Beirut, Dār al-Gharb al-Islāmī, 2000–2006), II, 443. On this commentary see Sulaiman al-Shuaily, 'Ibāḍī Tafsīr: A Comparison Between the Tafsīrs of Hūd al-Huwwārī and Saʿīd al-Kindī' (Unpublished PhD dissertation, University of Edinburgh, 2001).

[23] Mohamed Talbi, 'Tāhart', *EI*^{2}, X, 99–101. Tāhart was conquered by the Ismāʿīlīs in 909: see Jamil M. Abun-Nasr, *A History of the Maghrib in the Islamic Period* (Cambridge, Cambridge University Press, 1987), 48.

[24] Tadeusz Lewicki, 'Hawwāra', *EI*^{2}, III, 307. More generally on Ibāḍism, see Valerie J. Hoffman, *The Essentials of Ibāḍī Islam* (Syracuse, NY, Syracuse University Press, 2012); on the Ibāḍiyya in North Africa, see Tadeusz Lewicki, 'al-Ibāḍiyya', *EI*^{2}, III, 653–5; ʿAbd al-Raḥmān al-ʿAllāma al-Maghribī Ibn Khaldūn (d. 784/1382), *Kitāb al-ʿIbar*, ed. Yūsuf Asʿad Dāghir, 7 vols. (Beirut, Dār al-Kitāb al-Lubnānī, 1956–61), VI, 282–91; Abū ʿUbayd al-Bakrī (d. 487/1094), *al-Masālik wa'l-mamālik: Kitāb al-Mughrib fī dhikr bilād Ifrīqiyā wa'l-Maghrib*, ed. William MacGuckin de Slane (Algiers, Imprimerie de Gouvernement, 1857), 50, 72, 144.

[25] Cf. Belḥāj's note in Hūd, *Tafsīr kitāb Allāh al-ʿazīz*, 12; Ibn al-Ṣaghīr (*fl.* late third/ninth century), *Akhbār al-a'imma al-Rustamiyyīn*, ed. Muḥammad Nāṣir and Ibrāhīm Baḥāz (Beirut, Dār al-Gharb al-Islāmī, 1986), 49–50; Bābāʿammī *et al.*, *Muʿjam*, II, 355; Abun-Nasr, *A History of the Maghrib*, 47; Elizabeth Savage, *A Gateway to Hell, a Gateway to Paradise: The North African Response to the Arab Conquests* (Princeton, NJ, Darwin Press, 1997), 4–7.

be that, like his father, Hūd too was a judge in the same region. At some stage he seems to have moved to study in Qayrawān, where Ibāḍī scholars lived and studied alongside Mālikīs,[26] and where he first became acquainted with the *tafsīr* of the Basran Yaḥyā b. Sallām (d. 200/815).[27] His famous Ibāḍī contemporaries – Ibn Sallām al-Lawātī (d. *post* 273/886), also a Berber, and his tribesman Ibn al-Ṣaghīr al-Hawwārī[28] – make no mention of him.[29] But later authors mention his fame and knowledge, and especially the importance of his *tafsīr*.[30]

Hūd's commentary is not historical or legendary, as van Ess suggests (based on a manuscript he consulted in Mzab),[31] but rather one primarily based on narrations and theological discussions.[32] It draws upon the (Murji'ī) *tafsīr* of Yaḥyā b. Sallām, of which it is a sort of abridgement.[33] The latter had lived and taught in Qayrawān for a while before moving to Egypt, where he died. He transmitted the commentaries of al-Ḥasan al-Baṣrī, al-Suddī and al-Kalbī.[34] His commentary was well known in Qayrawān and was transmitted by his son Muḥammad (d. 262/875)[35] and, more importantly, by Abū Dāwūd Aḥmad b. Mūsā al-Azdī al-ʿAṭṭār (d. 274/887),[36] whose recension was more widely known. On Ibn Sallām's authority, Hūd quotes a recension of the commentary by al-Ḥasan al-Baṣrī.[37] If one compares the contents

[26] Again, see Belḥāj in Hūd, *Tafsīr kitāb Allāh al-ʿazīz*, 15; Yaḥyā Ibn Sallām al-Ibāḍī (*fl.* third/ninth century), *Kitāb fīhi bad' al-Islām wa sharā'iʿ al-dīn*, ed. Werner Schwartz and Sālim b. Yaʿqūb (Beirut, Dār Iqra', 1985; repr. Wiesbaden, Franz Steiner, 1986), 158–9.

[27] Abū Zakariyyā Yaḥyā b. Sallām b. Abī Thaʿlaba al-Taymī al-Baṣrī (d. 200/815) was a Basran traditionist and commentator who moved to Qayrawān in Ifrīqiyā to teach *ḥadīth* and Qur'ānic commentary. He died in Cairo. See the PA for details.

[28] Ibn al-Ṣaghīr was a third-/ninth-century jurist who served the Rustamids at Tāhart and was a close associate of the imam Muḥammad b. Aflaḥ; see Bābāʿammī *et al.*, *Muʿjam*, II, 236–7.

[29] Belḥāj in Hūd, *Tafsīr kitāb Allāh al-ʿazīz*, 18.

[30] Shammākhī, *Siyar*, 381; Aḥmad b. Saʿīd al-Darjīnī (*fl.* seventh/thirteenth century), *Kitāb Ṭabaqāt al-mashāyikh bi'l-Maghrib*, ed. Ibrāhīm Ṭallay, 2 vols. (Qusanṭīna, Maṭbaʿat al-Baʿth, 1974), II, 395–9. The first mentions of Hūd's *tafsīr* are in Yaḥyā b. Abī Bakr Abū Zakariyyā al-Warjalānī (*fl.* late fifth/eleventh century), *Kitāb Siyar al-a'imma wa akhbārihim*, ed. Ismāʿīl al-ʿArabī (Algiers, al-Maktaba al-Waṭaniyya, 1979), 359, and in Darjīnī, *Ṭabaqāt*, II, 345.

[31] Shammākhī, *Siyar*, 381.

[32] van Ess, 'Untersuchungen', 43.

[33] On this connection, see Gilliot, 'Hūd', 181, nn. 14–17 for references; Belḥāj in Hūd, *Tafsīr kitāb Allāh al-ʿazīz*, 26–32.

[34] Belḥaj in Hūd, *Tafsīr kitāb Allāh al-ʿazīz*, 29–30. For details on these individuals, see the PA.

[35] Muḥammad b. Aḥmad Abū'l-ʿArab al-Tamīmī al-Qayrawānī (d. 333/945), *Ṭabaqāt ʿulamā' Ifrīqiyā wa Tūnis*, ed. ʿAlī al-Shābbī and Naʿīm Ḥasan al-Yāfī (Tunis, al-Dār al-Tūnisiyya li'l-Nashr, 1968), 38–9.

[36] Ibid., 203; Abū Zayd ʿAbd al-Raḥmān al-Dabbāgh (d. 696/1296), *Maʿālim al-īmān fī maʿrifat ahl al-Qayrawān*, 3 vols. (vol. I, ed. Ibrāhīm Shabbūḥ; II, ed. Muḥammad Abū'l-Nūr; III, ed. Muḥammad Māḍūr) (Cairo, Maktabat al-Khānjī, 1968), II, 288.

[37] On al-Ḥasan al-Baṣrī, his commentary and its transmission, see the PA, and *TG*, II, 45, 81–3.

of the work of Ibn Sallām and Hūd, as Belḥāj b. Saʿīd Sharīfī has, one notices a great deal of convergence. However, because Ibn Sallām seems to have been an adherent of Murjiʾism,[38] whose doctrine of faith conflicted with that of Khārijism in general and with Ibāḍism in particular, Hūd adds the necessary Ibāḍī material to express the 'correct' teaching on such issues. For example, he makes it quite clear that one could not be a 'true' believer merely on account of faith (*īmān*) – that which was the classical Murjiʾī position – but required works (*ʿamal*) in addition to attain salvation in the Hereafter.

The edition used here is based on a single manuscript that is incomplete at the beginning. As a consequence, the introduction in which Hūd may have outlined his methodology and theological affiliation is not available to us. The content of the commentary centres on the narrations, most of which go back to al-Ḥasan al-Baṣrī, and deals with both the meaning and sense of the verses, as well as the context of their revelation. Hūd rarely offers his personal opinion; this gives his work a simplicity of style and a succinctness of expression similar to that of other early *ḥadīth*-based commentaries.

ʿAlī b. Ibrāhīm al-Qummī (*fl.* fourth/tenth century)

Abū'l-Ḥasan ʿAlī b. Ibrāhīm b. Hāshim al-Qummī[39] was a contemporary of the eleventh Shīʿī Ithnāʿasharī (Twelver) imam al-Ḥasan al-ʿAskarī (d. 260/874),[40] and his *tafsīr* is possibly the earliest Shīʿī commentary extant,

[38] Belḥāj in Hūd, *Tafsīr kitāb Allāh al-ʿazīz*, 34–5; *TG*, IV, 271.

[39] See the pioneering work on early Twelver Imāmī *tafsīr* by Meier M. Bar-Asher, *Scripture and Exegesis in Early Imāmī Shiism* (Leiden, Brill, 1999), esp. 33–56 for Qummī; Ibn al-Nadīm, *Kitāb al-Fihrist*, ed. Gustav Flügel, 2 vols. (Leipzig, Vogel, 1871–2), 37; idem, *The Fihrist of al-Nadim: A Tenth-Century Survey of Muslim Culture*, tr. Bayard Dodge, 2 vols. (New York, Columbia University Press, 1970), 81; Shaykh al-Ṭāʾifa Abū Jaʿfar Muḥammad b. al-Ḥasan al-Ṭūsī (d. 460/1067), *Fihrist*, ed. Muḥammad Ṣādiq Āl Baḥr al-ʿUlūm (Najaf, al-Maṭbaʿa al-Ḥaydariyya, 1960), 62; Muḥammad b. ʿAlī al-Dāwūdī (d. 945/1538–9), *Ṭabaqāt al-mufassirīn*, ed. ʿAlī Muḥammad ʿUmar, 2 vols. (Cairo, Maktabat Wahba, 1972), I, 385–6; Muḥammad Hādī Maʿrifat, *al-Tafsīr wa'l-mufassirūn fī thawbihi'l-qashīb*, 2 vols. (Mashhad, al-Jāmiʿa al-Raḍawiyya li'l-ʿUlūm al-Islāmiyya, 1997–8), II, 325–7; Carl Brockelmann, *Geschichte der arabischen Literatur* (Leiden, Brill, 1898–1949), [hereafter *GAL*], I, 205; Etan Kohlberg, *A Medieval Muslim Scholar at Work: Ibn Ṭāwūs and His Library* (Leiden, Brill, 1992), 347; see also Maḥmūd Haydūs, *Ḥawl Tafsīr al-Qummī: Dirāsa taḥqīqiyya* (Qumm, Dār al-Kitāb, 2001). On early Shīʿī hermeneutics, see Robert Gleave, 'Early Shiʿi Hermeneutics: Some Exegetical Techniques Attributed to the Shiʿi Imams' in *Aims, Methods and Contexts*, ed. Bauer, 141–72.

[40] The eleventh imam of the Twelver Shīʿa, al-Ḥasan b. ʿAlī was known as al-ʿAskarī because he lived most of his life in the garrison town of ʿAskar Sāmarrāʾ. For more details see the PA, al-ʿAskarī.

at least the earliest full commentary.[41] He was regarded as a 'trustworthy' transmitter (*thiqa*) and of sound convictions (*ṣaḥīḥ al-madhhab*) by the scholars of the Imāmī community.[42] He was a teacher of Muḥammad b. Yaʿqūb al-Kulaynī (d. 329/941),[43] author of *al-Kāfī fī ʿilm al-dīn*, one of the 'Four Books' (*al-kutub al-arbaʿa*) of the Imāmī school comprising the body of canonical narrations, and arguably also the teacher of Ibn Bābawayh al-Qummī, better known as al-Shaykh al-Ṣadūq (d. 381/991), author of *Man lā yaḥḍuruhu'l-faqīh*, another one of the 'Four Books' mentioned.[44]

The commentary in the printed edition[45] used here seems to be one recension by later scholars of a possibly larger 'proto-commentary' by

[41] In this volume, we mainly use ʿAlī b. Ibrāhīm al-Qummī (*fl.* fourth/tenth century), *Tafsīr al-Qummī*, ed. Sayyid Ṭayyib al-Mūsawī al-Jazāʾirī, 2 vols. (Najaf, Maktabat al-Hudā, 1967; repr., Beirut, Muʾassasat al-Aʿlamī li'l-Maṭbūʿāt, 1991); however, we also made recourse to other editions.

[42] Aḥmad b. ʿAlī al-Asadī al-Kūfī al-Najāshī (d. 450/1058), *Rijāl*, ed. Muḥammad Jawād al-Nāʾinī, 2 vols. (Beirut, Dār al-Aḍwāʾ, 1988), 260; al-Ḥasan b. ʿAlī Ibn Dāwūd al-Ḥillī (d. 740–41/1339–40), *Kitāb al-Rijāl*, ed. Muḥammad Ṣādiq Baḥr al-ʿUlūm (Najaf, al-Maṭbaʿa al-Ḥaydariyya, 1972), 135. 'Sound convictions' means that he was not an extremist (*ghālī*) with respect to the status of the imams, a point of controversy in the early Twelver Imāmī community. See Hossein Modarressi, *Crisis and Consolidation in the Formative Period of Shīʿite Islam: Abū Jaʿfar ibn Qiba al-Rāzī and His Contribution to Imāmite Shīʿite Thought* (Princeton, NJ, Darwin Press, 1993), 20–30; M.G.S. Hodgson, 'Ghulāt', *EI²*, II, 1093–5; Wadad al-Qadi, 'The Development of the Term *Ghulāt* in Muslim Literature with Special Reference to the Kaysāniyya' in *Akten des VII. Kongresses für Arabistik und Islamwissenschaft, Göttingen, 15. bis 22. August 1974*, ed. Albert Dietrich (Göttingen, Vandenhoeck and Ruprecht, 1976), 302–9. On the debate about the nature of pre-Buyid Shīʿism and its attitude towards Sunnī approaches to the Qurʾān, see Etan Kohlberg and Muḥammad Amir-Moezzi, eds., *Revelation and Falsification: The Kitāb al-Qirāʾāt of Aḥmad b. Muḥammad al-Sayyārī* (Leiden, Brill, 2009).

[43] Najāshī, *Rijāl*, 378; ʿAbd Allāh b. Muḥammad al-Māmaqānī (d. 1351/1933), *Tanqīḥ al-maqāl fī aḥwāl al-rijāl*, 3 vols. (Najaf, al-Maṭbaʿa al-Murtaḍawiyya, 1930), II, 260 (no. 8102); *GAL*, I, 199; *GAS*, I, 45; Wilferd Madelung, 'al-Kulaynī', *EI²*, V, 362–3. Qummī figures in the two main groups of narrators who constitute the first of the chains of narrations of Kulaynī, *al-Kāfī*; ʿAbd al-Rasūl Ghaffār, *al-Kulaynī wa'l-Kāfī* (Qumm, Muʾassasat al-Nashr al-Islāmī, 1995), 482–3. Cf. Muhammad Marcinkowski, 'A Glance on the First of the Four Canonical *Ḥadīth* Collections of the Twelver-Shīʿites: *Al-Kāfī* by al-Kulaynī (d. 328 or 329 AH/940 or 941 C.E.)', *Hamdard Islamicus* (Karachi) 24.2 (2001), 13–30. Andrew Newman, *The Formative Period of Twelver Shīʿism: Ḥadīth as Discourse Between Qum and Baghdad* (Richmond, Surrey, Curzon Press, 2000), 94–112; Saiyad Nizamuddin Ahmad, 'Twelver Šīʿī *Hadīṯ*: From Tradition to Contemporary Evaluations', *Oriente Moderno* 82 (2002), 125–45.

[44] On the authors of these works, see Syed Waheed Akhtar, *The Early Shīʿite Imāmiyyah Thinkers* (New Delhi, Ashish Publishing House, 1988); Ahmad, 'Twelver Šīʿī *Hadīṭ*'. For a different *fiqh*-led approach, see Robert Gleave, 'Between *Ḥadīth* and *Fiqh*: The "Canonical" Imāmī Collections of *Akhbār*', *Islamic Law and Society* 8.3 (2001), 350–82.

[45] There are two lithographs of Qummī's *Tafsīr* printed in Iran, one from 1313/1895 and another from 1315/1897. The latter, though incomplete, has the *tafsīr* attributed to the eleventh imam al-Ḥasan al-ʿAskarī appended to it: see Muḥammad Ḥusayn al-Jalālī, ed. *al-Tafsīr al-mansūb ilā'l-Imām Abī Muḥammad al-Ḥasan b. ʿAlī al-ʿAskarī* (Qumm, Muʾassasat al-Imām al-Mahdī, 1409/1988).

Qummī himself. This, as Bar-Asher has noted, is because the recension contains material transmitted from Qummī's father via Ibn Abī ʿUmayr (d. 217/831)[46] going back to the sixth Shīʿī imam Jaʿfar al-Ṣādiq (d. 148/765),[47] as well as material transmitted via Abū'l-Jārūd Ziyād b. al-Mundhir b. Ziyād al-Hamadānī al-Khārifī (d. *c.* 146/763) going back to the fifth imam Muḥammad al-Bāqir (d. *c.* 117/735).[48] The presence of Abū'l-Jārūd's material in Qummī's corpus is significant, not least because Abū'l-Jārūd later became the founder of a Zaydī sect, which itself had implications for the relationship between the Twelver Shīʿī community and that of the Zaydīs.[49] But the material from Abū'l-Jārūd appears both as a *riwāyat Abī'l-Jārūd ʿan al-Bāqir* – suggesting an entire, independent, commentary from which material was incorporated into the extant recension of Qummī's *tafsīr* – and as an *isnād* for those reports transmitted via Abū'l-Jārūd that must have belonged to Qummī's proto-commentary.[50] As for those parts that belong to Qummī's original *tafsīr*, they are transmitted on the authority of his student Abū'l-Faḍl al-ʿAbbās b. Muḥammad b. al-Qāsim b. Ḥamza b. Mūsā b. Jaʿfar al-Ṣādiq. Al-Ṭihrānī suggests that, in fact, the work that we have was put together by Abū'l-ʿAbbās in Zaydī Ṭabaristān, hence the inclusion of so much Jārūdī material that was not in Qummī's original work.[51]

It would appear that the present edition was censored and a considerable amount of early material, available in manuscripts of the text, criticising the Companions of the Prophet and the Sunnīs, was omitted.[52] The commentary represents what might be deemed as the earliest phases of 'traditionalist'

[46] See the PA for further details on Ibn Abī ʿUmayr, an important Shīʿī Baghdadi traditionist who knew the seventh, eighth and ninth Twelver imams.

[47] See the PA, Jaʿfar al-Ṣādiq.

[48] See the PA, Muḥammad al-Bāqir.

[49] See the PA, Abū'l-Jārūd.

[50] In other words, there was a proto-commentary by Qummī himself that included reports transmitted via Abū'l-Jārūd, and there was an independent commentary by Abū'l-Jārūd from al-Bāqir; the present recension of Qummī's *tafsīr* is a combination of (parts of) the proto-commentary and the other independent commentary. There are over two hundred citations of Abū'l-Jārūd's *riwāya* in the extant commentary by Qummī: on this material, see Bar-Asher, *Scripture and Exegesis*, 48–56. On the *tafsīr ʿan al-Bāqir*, see Kohlberg, *A Medieval Muslim Scholar*, 319. For a Zaydī recension, see Muḥammad b. Manṣūr al-Murādī (d. *c.* 290/903), *Kitāb Amālī Aḥmad b. ʿĪsā*, MS H.135, Ambrosiana Library, Milan.

[51] Āghā Buzurg Muḥammad Muḥsin al-Ṭihrānī, *al-Dharīʿa ilā taṣānīf al-shīʿa*, 25 vols. (Najaf, Maṭbaʿat al-Gharā', 1936–78), IV, 308; Bar-Asher, *Scripture and Exegesis*, 55.

[52] Mohammad Ali Amir-Moezzi and Sabine Schmidtke, 'Twelver-Shīʿite Resources in Europe. The Shīʿite Collection at the Oriental Department of the University of Cologne, The *Fonds* Henry Corbin and the *Fonds* Shaykhī at the École Pratique des Hautes Études (EPHE), Paris. With a Catalogue of the *Fonds* Shaykhī', *Journal Asiatique* 285.1 (1997), 121; Bar-Asher, *Scripture and Exegesis*, 39–45.

Twelver Shīʿī exegesis, laying the foundations for what later becomes known as Akhbārī *tafsīr*. As such, it narrates reports from the imams that gloss and explain what the verses of the Qurʾān mean and, more importantly, what they signify for the Shīʿa; indeed, the work is heavily cited by later Akhbārīs.[53] But unlike the near-contemporaneous *tafsīr* of ʿAyyāshī, here the author evaluates and weighs up narrations, and includes material which is not only of Shīʿī provenance. Qummī often just quotes a verse and follows the quotation with an explanation of what it means without directly citing his authority. Of course, it is to be understood that he is not expressing his own opinion but an opinion transmitted from the imams as authenticated by the chains of narrations for the *tafsīr* as a whole (deriving as it does ultimately from al-Bāqir and al-Ṣādiq) and by the mention of the imams themselves within many of the parallel exegetical narratives. In Twelver Imāmī sources, Qummī's *tafsīr* is highly respected as a classical text, and because of the proximity in time of the author to the imams, some have even regarded it as the *tafsīr* of the imams themselves and hence considered all of its narrations as 'sound' (*ṣaḥīḥ*)[54] – that, however, is a controversial position. For while the *Tafsīr ʿAlī b. Ibrāhīm*, as it is commonly known, may have been widely used and respected, it did suffer from the detractions of its critics within the larger Shīʿī tradition.[55]

Abū Jaʿfar b. Jarīr al-Ṭabarī (d. 310/923)

Abū Jaʿfar Muḥammad b. Jarīr b. Yazīd al-Ṭabarī is probably the most famous classical Sunnī commentator on the Qurʾān,[56] and has been the subject of a

[53] For a traditional analysis of genres of commentary, see Muḥammad Ḥusayn Dhahabī, *al-Tafsīr wa'l-mufassirūn*, 3 vols. (repr. Cairo, Dār al-Kutub al-Ḥadītha, 1976–89) (orig. pub. 1381/1961–2), I, 13–23, 204–5, 288–89; Maʿrifat, *Tafsīr*, I, 13–112; Andrew Rippin, 'Tafsīr', *EI*², X, 83–8; Calder, 'Tafsīr from Ṭabarī to Ibn Kathīr', 101–40. On Imāmī *tafsīr*, see Mahmoud Ayoub, 'The Speaking Qurʾān and the Silent Qurʾān: A Study of the Principles and Development of Imāmī Shīʿī Tafsīr' in *Approaches to the History of the Interpretation of the Qurʾān*, ed. Andrew Rippin (Berlin, de Gruyter, 1988; repr. Piscataway, NJ, Gorgias Press, 2012). As many of these scholars note, '*maʾthūr*' and '*raʾy*' are to some extent polemical designations.

[54] See the comment by the Safavid scholar Muḥammad Bāqir al-Astarābādī Mīr Dāmād (d. 1040/1630), *al-Rawāshiḥ al-samāwiyya fī sharḥ al-aḥādīth al-Imāmiyya* (Tehran, [lithograph], 1894), 87.

[55] Modarressi (*Tradition and Survival*) has questioned the attribution of the authorship to Qummī in his bibliographical survey of early Shīʿī literature. Hossein Modarressi, *Tradition and Survival: A Bibliographical Survey of Early Shīʿite Literature* (Oxford, Oneworld, 2003).

[56] The work we use in this volume, as noted in the introduction, is Ṭabarī, *Jāmiʿ al-bayān*, ed. Shākir and Shākir; however, like almost all of the major works translated in our chapters, we have also relied on several other editions and on the online version on altafsir.com.

number of academic discussions in western Islamicist[57] and traditional Muslim[58] scholarship in the field of *tafsīr.* Born in Āmul in Northern Iran in 224/839 into a landowning family, he moved to Rayy, near modern-day Tehran, in order to pursue his studies. His most important teacher in this city was Abū ʿAbd Allāh Muḥammad b. Ḥumayd al-Rāzī (d. 248/862), who remained an important source of authority for him as a traditionist and as an authorised transmitter of the narratives from the 'military campaigns' (*maghāzī*) of the Prophet.[59] Ṭabarī continued on to Baghdad, Basra and Kufa to study narrations and to sit at the feet of the major traditionists of his time. He had initially moved to Baghdad to study with the famous traditionist Aḥmad b. Ḥanbal (d. 241/855),[60] but the latter died before Ṭabarī arrived in the capital. Al-Ṭabarī profited most from two traditionists: Muḥammad b. Bashshār, known as Bundār (d. 252/866),[61] in Basra and Abū Kurayb

[57] Clifford Edmund Bosworth, 'al-Ṭabarī', *EI*², X, 11–15; John Cooper, 'Translator's Introduction' in John Cooper, Wilferd Madelung and Alan Jones, eds., *The Commentary on the Qur'ān by Abū Jaʿfar Muḥammad b. Jarīr al-Ṭabarī*, 1 vol. (Oxford, Oxford University Press, 1987), ix–xxxvi; Franz Rosenthal, 'General Introduction' in *The History of al-Ṭabarī*, gen. ed. Ehsan Yarshater, 39 vols. (Albany, NY, State University of New York Press, 1989–98), I (1989), 5–134; Claude Gilliot, *Exégèse, langue, et théologie en Islam: L'exégèse coranique de Tabarī (m. 311/923)* (Paris, Vrin, 1990).

[58] Dhahabī, *Mufassirūn*, I, 205–24; Dāwūdī, *Ṭabaqāt*, II, 106–15; Maʿrifat, *Tafsīr*, II, 312–19; ISESCO, *al-Imām al-Ṭabarī fī dhikrā murūr aḥad ʿasharat qarnan ʿalā wafātih, 310H–1410H*, 2 vols. (Rabat, al-Munaẓẓama al-Islāmiyya li'l-Tarbiyya wa'l-ʿUlūm wa'l-Thaqāfa [ISESCO]; Damascus, Maṭbaʿat al-Kātib al-ʿArabī, 1992); Muḥammad Qāsimzādah, ed. *Yādnāma-yi Ṭabarī: Shaykh al-muʾarrikhīn Abū Jaʿfar Muḥammad b. Jarīr Ṭabarī 225–310 hijrī qamarī* (Tehran, Sāzmān-i Chāp wa Intishārāt-i Wizārat-i Farhang wa Irshād-i Islāmī, Markaz-i Taḥqīqāt-i ʿIlmī-yi Kishwar-i Wizārat-i Farhang va Āmūzish-i ʿĀlī, 1369 Sh./1991); Muḥammad Muṣṭafā al-Zuḥaylī, *al-Imām al-Ṭabarī: Shaykh al-mufassirīn wa ʿumdat al-muʾarrikhīn wa muqaddam al-fuqahāʾ al-muḥaddithīn* (Damascus, Dār al-Qalam, 1990).

[59] The term *maghāzī*, as the title suggests, dealt mainly with the 'military campaigns' of the Prophet, in particular those fought against the Meccans after the emigration to Medina. The earliest such *maghāzī* work is that of al-Wāqidī (d. 208/823). However, some scholars have argued that *maghāzī* was the earliest name for the genre dealing with the biography of the Prophet, and that it becomes known as *sīra*, as in the case of *Sīrat Ibn Isḥāq*, only later. The opposite case has also been made, namely, that *sīra* was the earlier name of the genre. On the relationship between these distinct bodies of material, see Robinson, *Islamic Historiography*, 24–30, and the references provided therein.

[60] Aḥmad b. Ḥanbal b. Hilāl al-Shaybānī al-Marwazī (d. 241/855) was a prominent pietist and traditionist in Baghdad, who opposed the Muʿtazilī consensus especially on the doctrine of the createdness of the Qur'ān (*khalq al-Qur'ān*) and was consequently persecuted during the famous *miḥna* (inquisition) instigated by the ʿAbbāsid caliph al-Ma'mūn shortly before his death in 218/833, and which lasted about twenty years. Ibn Ḥanbal is the progenitor and eponym of the Ḥanbalī *madhdhab*, one of the four Sunnī schools of law. See the PA, Ibn Ḥanbal, for more details.

[61] Baghdādī, *Taʾrīkh*, II, 101–5; Shihāb al-Dīn Aḥmad, Ibn Ḥajar al-ʿAsqalānī (d. 852/1449), *Tahdhīb al-tahdhīb*, 6 vols. (repr. Beirut, Dār Iḥyāʾ al-Turāth al-ʿArabī, 1993), V, 47–9 (no. 6678).

Muḥammad b. al-ʿAlāʾ (d. 248/862)[62] in Kufa.[63] Ṭabarī soon established himself in the caliphal capital as an expert on *ḥadīth* and commentary, as well as on history. He attracted many students and became tutor to one of the sons of the vizier ʿUbayd Allāh b. Yaḥyā b. Khāqān, himself a former student of Ibn Ḥanbal. Ṭabarī even became known as a jurist, and established a short-lived independent school known as the Jarīriyya, although he had originally been a Shāfiʿī. Ṭabarī was accused of Muʿtazilī and Shīʿī sympathies by the Ḥanbalīs, but there is little evidence to support these accusations and Ṭabarī was, in fact, careful to distance himself from Shīʿism.[64] He was known for his precocity; as an old man in his seventies, he recalled that at the age of seven he knew the Qurʾān by heart, at eight he was leading the prayer, and at nine he was studying the narrations from the Prophet.[65]

Ṭabarī's *tafsīr* is one of the oldest Qurʾānic commentaries available to us – a fact that, in itself, makes it invaluable. It circulated in complete form sometime between 283/896 and 290/903. However, given Ṭabarī's method of working, it is likely that he may have used some of the material in lectures prior to completing the commentary; sections of it were almost undoubtedly in circulation well before these dates. Ṭabarī was acknowledged as one of the foremost scholars of his day; his *tafsīr* was instantly recognised by his contemporaries as an important work, and it remains so today. The *tafsīr* also provides an interesting comparison with his other major work, the world history entitled *Taʾrīkh al-rusul waʾl-mulūk*.[66] The two works share much common material, such as the chains of narrations (*isnāds*), the use of authorities (*marājiʿ*) and the consideration of the historical contexts for the revelation of Qurʾānic verses (*asbāb al-nuzūl*). The Qurʾān commentary itself is notable for Ṭabarī's attempt to create a comprehensive collection of traditions in circulation up to his time: it is this aspect of his *tafsīr* (and of his work in general) which is perhaps the most valuable, as his writings comprise the most complete and singular collection of citations from early authorities and works now largely lost to us. The commentary contains a vast body of

[62] Ibn Ḥajar, *Tahdhīb al-tahdhīb*, V, 246–7 (no. 7226).

[63] For more on Ṭabarī's teachers, see Gilliot, *Exégèse, langue, et théologie*, 19–37.

[64] The Ḥanbalīs' antipathy for Ṭabarī appears to have stemmed from his decision not to accept Ibn Ḥanbal's authority as a jurist, although he recognised him as a great *ḥadīth* scholar. This is by no means an opinion in which he was alone. Rosenthal discusses Ṭabarī's relationship with the Hanbalīs in 'General Introduction', 69–78. Cf. *TG*, III, 449–51.

[65] See Rosenthal, 'General introduction', 15, citing Yāqūt b. ʿAbd Allāh al-Ḥamawī (d. 626/1229). *Muʿjam al-udabāʾ*, ed. Aḥmad Farīd Rifāʿī, 20 vols. (Cairo, Dār al-Maʾmūn, 1936–8), XVIII, 49.

[66] Abū Jaʿfar Muḥammad b. Jarīr al-Tabarī (d. 310/923), *Taʾrīkh al-rusul waʾl-mulūk*, ed. Michael Jan de Goeje *et al.* (Leiden, Brill, 1879–1901). The English translation is published as *The History of al-Ṭabarī*, as above.

exegetical material which he gathered during his travels, material through which he establishes a type of 'orthodox' Sunnī interpretation by favouring certain interpreters, chains of transmission and methods, such as grammatical analysis, variant readings and the use of poetic exemplars. There are three layers to his commentary. The first layer considers the relevant narrations on the verse and assesses their appropriateness and soundness; in this section, it is clear that he regards *tafsīr* and *ta'wīl* as synonyms – later tradition would assign the latter for allegorical or allusive commentary associated with esoteric exegesis.[67] The second layer contains philological and periphrastic material, where he especially relies on the Basran grammarian Abū ʿUbayda Maʿmar b. Muthannā (d. 209–10/824–5)[68] and the Kufan grammarian al-Farrā' (d. 207/822).[69] The third layer deals with the variant readings and, given his renown in this discipline, provides us with a major source on these variants at the time of the canonisation of the Qur'ānic readings into the official seven, a process that sought to delimit the minor variants within the text of the scripture.[70] Thus, while this commentary has been called 'encyclopaedic', and indeed it includes many different, sometimes conflicting reports, it also represents Ṭabarī's own effort to create or solidify a genre in a specific form, using particular transmitters and methods, while excluding others.

One other distinguishing aspect of Ṭabarī's approach is his use of *ijtihād* (independent reasoning).[71] He often provides his own views on the content of the various reports, stating which interpretation he considers to be most correct or most sound, often on the basis of a grammatical or philological argument as well as points of theology and dogma. Such instances are frequently prefaced with the phrase 'Abū Jaʿfar says' (*qāla Abū Jaʿfar*), to highlight the fact that it is

67 See Rippin, 'Tafsīr', *EI*², X, 83–8, and Ismail Poonawala, 'Ta'wīl', *EI*², X, 390–92.

68 See the PA, Abū ʿUbayda.

69 See the PA, al-Farrā'.

70 On the canonisation of the seven readings, see Shady Nasser, *The Second Canonisation of the Qur'ān (324/936): Ibn Mujāhid and the Founding of the Seven Readings* (Leiden, Brill, 2020); also see idem, 'Revisiting Ibn Mujāhid's Position on the Seven Canonical Readings: Ibn ʿĀmir's Problematic Reading of *kun fa-yakūna*', *Journal of Qur'anic Studies* 17.1 (2015), 85–113; and idem, *The Transmission of the Variant Readings of the Qur'ān: The Problem of Tawātur and the Emergence of Shawādhdh* (Leiden, Brill, 2012). See also Aḥmad b. Mūsā Ibn Mujāhid (d. 324/936), *Kitāb al-Sabʿa fī'l-qirā'āt*, ed. Shawqī Ḍayf (Cairo, Dār al-Maʿārif, 1972); Christopher Melchert, 'Ibn Mujāhid and the Establishment of Seven Qur'anic Readings', *Studia Islamica* 91 (2000), 5–22; Rudi Paret, 'Kirā'a', *EI*², V, 127–9; A.T. Welch, R. Paret and J.D. Pearson, 'al-Kur'ān', *EI*², V, 406–9; ʿAbd al-Ḥalīm b. Muḥammad al-Hādī Qāba, *al-Qirā'āt al-Qur'āniyya: Tārīkhuhā thubūtuhā ḥujiyyatuhā wa-aḥkāmuhā* (Beirut, Dār al-Gharb al-Islāmī, 1999). See also Aḥmad Mukhtār ʿUmar and ʿAbd al-ʿĀl Sālim Mukarram, eds., *Muʿjam al-qirā'āt al-Qur'āniyya: Maʿa muqaddima fī'l-qirā'āt wa ashhar al-qurrā'*, 8 vols. (Kuwait, Dhāt al-Salāsil; vols. III, V, VI, VIII, Kuwait, Maṭbūʿāt Jāmiʿat al-Kuwayt, 1982–).

71 See Joseph Schacht, 'Idjtihād', *EI*², III, 1026–7; Aron Zysow, 'Ejtehād', *EIr*, VIII, 281–6.

his opinion, even though he tends to support his opinions by appealing to the authority of the *ijmāʿ* (consensus) of previous scholars.

Qāḍī al-Nuʿmān (d. 363/974)

Abū Ḥanīfa al-Nuʿmān b. Muḥammad al-Tamīmī, known as Qāḍī al-Nuʿmān, was raised as an Ismāʿīlī in Qayrawān, North Africa, following the conversion of his father. He served under successive Fatimid caliphs until, in 337/948, the imam-caliph al-Manṣūr (r. 334/946–342/953) appointed him to the prestigious position of chief justice (*qāḍī al-quḍāt*). The imam-caliph al-Muʿizz (d. 365/975) authorised him to hold 'wisdom sessions' (*majālis al-ḥikma*) for the Fatimid initiates on Fridays. When Qāḍī al-Nuʿmān died, al-Muʿizz himself led the funeral prayers.[72]

In this anthology, we have drawn on two of Qāḍī al-Nuʿmān's works: the *Daʿāʾim al-Islām* (Chapters 4 and 5), and the *Asās al-taʾwīl* (Chapters 1 and 2).[73] In his introduction to the *Asās al-taʾwīl*, he explains what he has done in previous works and why that leaves room for this current venture; thus this is a good source for assessing his aims in both works. According to him, his work the *Daʿāʾim al-Islām* dealt with, *inter alia*, the outer aspects (*ẓāhir*) of the sharia, the bounds (*ḥudūd*) of faith (*īmān*), and the difference between faith and submission (*islām*), the duty of devotional loyalty (*wilāya*) and the justification and proof for a hierarchy of leadership, alongside the customary topics of the licit and illicit (*ḥalāl wa ḥarām*) and judgments and rulings. His reason for writing it was so that 'those who are receptive to that might come to know the outer aspects of their religion and that they might have conviction regarding it, and apply it, not to contravene and abandon any of it, since that is the first limit of instruction (*taʿlīm*) and the minimal degree of knowledge and comprehension'.[74] Thus he reaffirms his commitment to adhere to the outward revealed law, regarding this as the starting point and basis for any kind of other, deeper knowledge. This is perhaps an answer to the charge of antinomianism.

72 Farhad Daftary, 'al-Qāḍī al-Nuʿmān' in *Biographical Encyclopaedia of Islamic Philosophy*, ed. Oliver Leaman (London, Bloomsbury, 2006), 165–7.

73 Abū Ḥanīfa al-Tamīmī al-Nuʿmān b. Muḥammad, known as al-Qāḍī al-Nuʿmān (d. 363/974), *Asās al-taʾwīl*, ed. Arif Tamer (Beirut, Dār al-Thaqāfa, 1960); idem, *Daʿāʾim al-Islām*, 3 vols. (Beirut, Dār al-Aḍwāʾ, 1995); tr. Asaf A.A. Fyzee and rev. and annot. by Ismail K. Poonawala, *The Pillars of Islam*, 2 vols. (New Delhi, Oxford University Press, 2002–4). Note that all translations from this work in this volume are our own.

74 Qādī al-Nuʿmān, *Asās al-taʾwīl*, 23.

Qāḍī al-Nuʿmān then mentions that after writing the *Daʿāʾim*, he wrote another book, the *Ḥudūd al-maʿrifa*, in which he focuses on establishing the proofs for the legitimacy of esoteric interpretation (*taʾwīl*) against those who refute it. In that work, he says he has included symbolic (*ramz*) and allusive references through esoteric interpretation, from which those with 'intellect' (*dhawū al-ʿuqūl*) would profit.[75] He then explains that just as the *Maʿrifa* filled a gap left by his first book, the *Daʿāʾim*, the *Asās al-taʾwīl* fits into the gap left by both of those previous efforts; not as a contradiction to either of them but as a complement to both.

In justifying the *Asās al-taʾwīl*, he begins with a trope for introductions, which is to say that he had a duty to write it; but in this case, perhaps, there is some truth to the trope, in that there are not other works like this: 'Once we had achieved our goal from that [*Maʿrifa*], there was a duty upon us towards those seekers (*rāghibūn*). To give them what they deserve, we thought it necessary to furnish them with a book that contains one of the limits (*ḥadd*) in esoteric interpretation beyond the limit of symbol (*ramz*).'[76] The symbolic interpretation was the focus of the *Maʿrifa*; this work, then, goes beyond those symbolic interpretations and ventures further into esoteric territory. Finally, he clarifies that the main purpose of this work is to provide an esoteric complement to the first book on exoteric interpretation:

> In this book, we have expounded upon its bases (*uṣūl*) and the first of its limits (*ḥudūd*) and we have called it the *Asās al-taʾwīl* (*Basis of Interpretation*), and by it we intended to clarify what we had already established in the book *Daʿāʾim al-Islam*, so that this (*Asās*) becomes the basis of the esoteric (*bāṭin*) in the same way in which that one had become the basis of the exoteric (*ẓāhir*), seeking God's help in this, for there is no might nor power except that of God Almighty.[77]

Through these introductory materials, Qāḍī al-Nuʿmān emphasises that the esoteric commentary does not stand on its own, apart from the exoteric; rather, they are supposed to be considered as two parts of a whole, providing the Qurʾānic proof-texts for the reality of the esoteric and the exoteric through the dual aspect of all created beings. This dual aspect is then picked up in his interpretation of Q. 4:1, presented in Chapter 1 of this anthology.

[75] Ibid., 26.

[76] Ibid., 26–7. After justifying the current work, the *Asās*, he explains in more depth what he has done in the *Maʿrifa*, saying that there he 'expends many words to establish the science of interpretation (*taʾwīl*) and the esoteric (*bāṭin*), and to refute those who deny that aspect of the book, the sunna, and the sayings of the Imāms and the [Ismāʿīlī] community (*umma*)' (ibid., 28). Thus, in his formulation, the *Maʿrifa* is a type of general defence of esoteric interpretation, with examples, whereas this one bears a more direct relationship to the *Daʿāʾim*.

[77] Ibid., 27.

Abū'l-Qāsim al-Qushayrī (d. 465/1073)

Abū'l-Qāsim ʿAbd al-Karīm b. Hawāzin al-Qushayrī (d. 465/1073) was an accomplished Sufi scholar of the city of Nishapur, whence the honorary additional agnomen al-Nīsābūrī. The most definitive study of his Qur'ānic commentary, the *Laṭā'if al-ishārāt* (*The Subtleties of the Signs*), to date is that by Martin Nguyen.[78] While recognising his celebrity in that most famous town of Khurasan, Nguyen notes that part of Qushayrī's fame could be accounted for by his talents in other major disciplines of medieval Islamic scholarship: *ḥadīth* scholarship, (Shāfiʿī) jurisprudence and (Ashʿarī) theology. These disciplinary preludes have left their mark on his major Qur'ānic commentary, the *Laṭā'if*, constituting thus a consolidation point in the historical development of the tradition of mystical exegesis.[79] Qushayrī also became celebrated for his famous *al-Risāla al-Qushayriyya* (*Qushayrī's Epistle*),[80] a Sufi reference work consisting of a brief preamble on the principles of *tawḥīd* according to Sufis, followed by four discrete sections dealing with: Sufi technical terminology (e.g. *maqām*, *ḥāl*, *waqt*, *fanā'*, *dhawq*, *nafs*, *rūḥ* and so on); an exposition of the 'waystations' (*maqāmāt*); an exploration of 'spiritual states and charismata' (*aḥwāl wa-karāmāt*); and terminating with brief biographies of the most notable Sufi masters (*aʿlām al-taṣawwuf*). Judging by the endurance of this epistle's attributive title to the author's tribal patronymic, the work must have become a handy reference work for students after his death. Nguyen considers his major exegetical work, the *Laṭā'if*, as being more complex than just a mystical commentary of the Qur'ān, since it incorporates and vindicates the use of traditional scholastic methods (sc. typically *ḥadīth*).[81] Qushayrī's relatively brief introduction to the commentary, partially translated by Nguyen,[82] already suggests that the author is as interested in the application of traditional exegetical methods, such as 'abrogation' (*nāsikh wa'l-mansūkh*), 'narrative passages' (*qaṣaṣ*), 'occasions of revelation' (*asbāb*

[78] Nguyen, *Sufi Master*; also H. Halm, 'al-Ḳushayrī', *EI*², V, 526–7. The version of the work that we most frequently use in this volume is Abū'l-Qāsim al-Qushayrī (d. 465/1073), *Laṭā'if al-ishārāt*, ed. Ibrāhīm Basyūnī, 6 vols. (Cairo, Dār al-Kātib al-ʿArabī, 1968–71).

[79] Nguyen, *Sufi Master*, 2ff. for all of the secondary literature on this commentator and his works.

[80] Abū'l-Qāsim al-Qushayrī, *al-Risāla al-Qushayriyya fī ʿilm al-taṣawwuf*, ed. Maʿrūf Zurayq (Beirut, Dār al-Jīl, 1990).

[81] Nguyen, *Sufi Master*, 121ff.; Keeler, in her study *Sufi Hermeneutics*, notes that the proximity in time between the works of both Qushayrī and Maybudī and the similarity of their hermeneutical premises in these works (sc. spiritual guidance and spiritual edification, 81ff.) would strongly suggest a Khurāsānī school of Sufism by the fifth/eleventh century (see her comment on p. 100, n. 65).

[82] Nguyen, *Sufi Master*, 121ff.

al-nuzūl), 'clear and ambiguous verses' (*muḥkam wa mutashābih*), as he is in recognising that the honour of accessing the most subtle allusions (*ishārāt*), symbols (*rumūz*) and secrets (*asrār*) of the Qur'ān falls upon the 'elect [friends of God]' (*aṣfiyā'*) and into the hearts of [God's] friends (*awliyā'*) through gnosis (*ma'rifa*). In effect, Qushayrī wants to establish a hermeneutical synonymy between the *'ilm* of the *'ulamā'* and the *ma'rifa* of the *awliyā'*, without privileging one over the other, as both are accessible to 'seekers of His path' (*man arāda ṭarīqahu*). This moderating approach to what had historically been distinct intellectual and individualised pursuits (*'ilm* vs *ma'rifa*) can only suggest that the role of the *'ālim* (scholar) in Qushayrī's time was, at least according to Qushayrī, to be a holistic and all-encompassing one: scholasticism and mysticism, one the natural complement of the other.

Mu'ayyad fī'l-Dīn al-Shīrāzī (d. 470/1078)

Mu'ayyad fī'l-Dīn Abū Naṣr Hibat Allāh al-Shīrāzī was born in Shīrāz and became the leading *dā'ī* ('agent of the *da'wa*, the religious, education and political system)[83] under the caliph Mustanṣir (r. 427/1036–487/1094). Mu'ayyad began his spiritual and political journey as a *dā'ī* in Fars; he then undertook a journey from Iran across Iraq and into Syria and eventually Egypt, the seat of the Fatimid caliph, which was fraught with mixed fortunes. The turning point for his career came at the end of 450/1058, when Mustanṣir appointed him as *dā'ī l-du'āt*. This was both a political and a spiritual rank, one rank below the *bāb al-abwāb* ('gate of gates'). It was soon thereafter that Mu'ayyad began to hold weekly lessons on a Thursday for the initiates, called the 'wisdom sessions' (*majālis al-ḥikma*). These have been collected in the work now known as *al-Majālis al-Mu'ayyadiyya*.[84] Despite his elevated appointment, his fortunes again changed in 453/1061 when he was exiled to Jerusalem for a year; after this, he was pardoned by Mustanṣir and then became responsible for the *da'wa* in Yemen and India. His intellectual influence then extended to the Yemeni Sulayhids, hence the Ṭayyibī *da'wa* there. His funeral prayers were led by Mustanṣir.

[83] Since I. Poonawala's entry on al-Mu'ayyad in *EI*², there is now significantly more biographical data available to us in the *EI*³ entry by Tahera Qutbuddin. The biographical data here is a summary of some of her findings. See Tahera Qutbuddin, 'al-Mu'ayyad al-Shīrāzī', *EI*³.

[84] The edition that we use for the translations in this volume is al-Mu'ayyad fī'l-Dīn al-Shīrāzī (d. 470/1078), *al-Majālis al-Mu'ayyadiyya*, ed. Ḥātim Ḥamīd al-Dīn (Mumbai, 1975; 2nd edn. Mumbai, Leaders Press, 2002).

As Tahera Qutbuddin notes, the *Majālis al-Mu'ayyadiyya* presents 'Fatimid doctrine with symbolic *ta'wīl* of Qur'ān verses, Prophetic *ḥadīth*, and precepts of sharīʿa'.[85] In his first two sermons (*majālis*), Mu'ayyad describes his method of interpretations and defends and explains the use of the intellect; but, in itself, the *Majālis* is a demonstration of Mu'ayyad's ability to create a dialogic interplay between fundamental religious concepts and the Fatimid view of those concepts with the Qur'ānic text. This is not a work of *tafsīr* or *ta'wīl* in the traditional sense of a line-by-line interpretation; and yet it draws extensively on Qur'ānic verses to make a point and to teach a lesson. For example, in the tenth *majlis*, some of the didactic elements of these sessions are clear where, in expounding on the statement of faith, 'there is no God but God' (*lā ilāha illā 'llāh*), he says:

> You will have heard the statement of the Messenger of God (*ṣlʿhm*) regarding the words *lā ilāha illā 'llāh* to the effect that if this had been placed on one side of the scale, and if the heavens and the earth and all that is between them were placed on the other side, it would outweigh them. We already know that this is contradicted by the overt (*ẓāhir*) function of eyewitnessing, but is affirmed by the inward (*bāṭin*) function of the intellect (*ʿaql*) and discernment (*baṣīra*) since this phrase is one that comprehends and encompasses the entirety of God's creation from the world of the intellect and the soul to the world of the celestial spheres, the world of nature and the world of humanity, despite its small size and the paucity of its letters. We compare this to the drop of semen, which likewise, despite its scantness and its paucity, encompasses the structures of the outward (*ẓāhir*) and inner (*bāṭin*) shapes of all human forms in terms of hearing, vision, smell, taste, limbs, nerves, organs, until it divides into the simple soul (*al-nafs al-basīṭa*) and the noble intellect which is able to encompass all worlds and what is in them in the same way that the line of a circle encompasses the point at its centre.[86]

Jār Allāh al-Zamakhsharī (d. 538/1144)

Abū'l-Qāsim Jār Allāh Maḥmūd b. ʿUmar al-Zamakhsharī's *tafsīr*, *al-Kashshāf ʿan ḥaqā'iq al-tanzīl wa ʿuyūn al-aqāwīl* (*The Unveiling of the Realities of Revelation and Essences of Divine Sayings*), is a major Muʿtazilī Qur'ān commentary.[87] Popular in both Zaydī and Twelver Imāmī circles, it

[85] Qutbuddin, 'al-Mu'ayyad'.
[86] Al-Mu'ayyad, *al-Majālis*, 40 (*Majlis* 10).
[87] The version we use most frequently for this volume is Zamakhsharī, *al-Kashshāf* (Beirut, 1987). We have also had recourse to other editions. For the view that Zamakhsharī's commentary is not Muʿtazilite, see Lane, *A Traditional Muʿtazilite Qur'ān Commentary*. A refutation of this

was later condensed and 'corrected' – on the basis of Ashʿarī theology – by ʿAbd Allāh b. ʿUmar al-Bayḍāwī (d. 685/1286) in his *Anwār al-tanzīl*.[88]

Zamakhsharī's commentary has, arguably, had an importance second only to Ṭabarī's.[89] Born in Khwārazm,[90] Zamakhsharī trained and taught in Persian Transoxiana, and travelled widely in search of grammatical learning and Qur'ānic commentary. As a theologian, he was influenced by both of the two major schools of Muʿtazilī *kalām* prevalent at this time – the Bahshamiyya associated with Abū Hāshim al-Jubbā'ī (d. 321/933)[91] and that of Abū'l-Ḥusayn al-Baṣrī (d. 436/1044),[92] a dissident student of ʿAbd al-Jabbār (d. 415/1025).[93] Indeed, in many ways, he is one of the last major Sunnī–Muʿtazilī thinkers.

thesis is given by Suleiman Mourad, 'Review of Andrew Lane, *A Tradtitional Muʿtazilite Qur'ān Commentary: The Kashshāf of Jār Allāh al-Zamakhsharī (d. 538/1144)*', *Journal of Semitic Studies* 52.2 (2007), 409–11; for a more detailed refutation of this view and an argument in favour of seeing *al-Kashshāf* as squarely Muʿtazilite, see Kifayat Ullah, *al-Kashshāf: Al-Zamakhsharī's Muʿtazilite Exegesis of the Qur'ān* (Berlin, de Gruyter, 2017); On Zamakhsharī and this work, see also Dhahabī, *Mufassirūn*, I, 429–82; Maʿrifat, *Tafsīr*, II, 480–501; C.H.M. Versteegh, 'Al-Zamakhsharī', *EI*², XI, 432–4; Ibn Khallikān, *Wafayāt*, V, 168–74. On the Muʿtazila and *tafsīr*, see Alena Kulinich, 'Beyond Thoelogy: Muʿtazilite Scholars and Their Authority in al-Rummānī's Tafsīr', *Bulletin of the School of Oriental and African Studies* 78.1 (2015), 135–48; eadem, 'Rethinking Muʿtazilite *Tafsīr*: From Essence to History', *Religion and Culture, Seoul National University* 29 (2015), 227–62; Suleiman Mourad, 'The Survival of the Muʿtazila Tradition of Qur'anic Exegesis in Shīʿī and Sunnī *Tafāsīr*', *Journal of Qur'anic Studies* 12 (2010), 83–100; idem, 'The Revealed Text and the Intended Subtext: Notes on the Hermeneutics of the Qur'ān in Muʿtazilah Discourse as Reflected in the *Tahdhīb* of al-Ḥākim al-Jishumī (d. 494/1101)' in *Islamic Philosophy, Science, Culture, and Religion: Studies in Honor of Dimitri Gutas* (Leiden, Brill, 2012, 367–95); idem, 'The Muʿtazila and their *Tafsīr* Tradition: A Comparative Study of Five Exegetical Glosses on Qur'an 3:178' in *Tafsīr: Interpreting the Qur'an. Critical Concepts in Islamic Studies*, ed. Mustafa Shah (Abingdon, Routledge, 2012), III, 267–83; idem, 'Towards a Reconstruction of the Muʿtazilī Tradition of Qur'anic Exegesis: Reading the Introduction to the *Tahdhīb* of al-Ḥākim al-Jishumī (d. 494/1101) and its Application' in *Aims, Methods and Contexts*, ed. Bauer, 101–40. See also Sabine Schmidtke, 'Muʿtazila', *EQ*, III, 466–71.

88 On the *Anwār al-tanzīl*, see Walid Saleh, 'The Qur'ān Commentary of al-Bayḍāwī: A History of *Anwār al-Tanzīl*', *Journal of Qur'anic Studies* 23.1 (2021), 71–102.

89 Marshall Hodgson, *The Venture of Islam: Conscience and History in a World Civilization*, 3 vols. (Chicago, IL, University of Chicago Press, 1974), II, 308. Saleh, *Formation*, has an altogether different view, see his comments on the neglected but very important *tafsīr* by al-Tha'labī (d. 427/1035) of Nishapur.

90 Khwārazm was an ancient and medieval Central Asian state, nowadays in northwestern Uzbekistan. One of the oldest centres of civilisation in Central Asia, it was conquered by the Arabs in the first/seventh century. In the following centuries, Khwārazm became increasingly prosperous and powerful, and by Zamakasharī's time, its capital city was a significant centre of trade and Arabic learning. The region continued to flourish until the late fourteenth century AD when Timur destroyed the complex irrigation system that brought Khwārazm much of its prosperity. See C.E. Bosworth, 'Khwārazm', *EI*², IV, 1060–65.

91 See the PA, al-Jubbāʾī.

92 See the PA, Abū'l-Ḥusayn al-Baṣrī.

93 See the PA, ʿAbd al-Jabbār.

A significant grammarian, his commentary is quoted by later commentators, more for its discussions of syntax, morphology and philology rather than for its (Muʿtazilī) theology. For example, the later commentator Rāzī quoted Zamakhsharī's *Kashshāf* (sometimes without citing him, see one example in Chapter 4 of this volume); but when Rāzī needed to quote Muʿtazilī views, rather than citing the *Kashshāf*, he cited works of al-Jubbāʾī, Abū'l-Qāsim al-Kaʿbī al-Balkhī[94] and the *Kitāb Tanzīh al-Qurʾān ʿan al-maṭāʿin* of al-Qāḍī ʿAbd al-Jabbār.[95] As a grammatical authority and author of *al-Mufaṣṣal fī'l-naḥw*, a work that arranges its discussions around the parts of speech, Zamakhsharī's views and interpretations on the readings of the verses and their grammatical and philological exegesis were considered reliable and were quoted by a range of commentators of different theological persuasions who came after him. Nevertheless, his Muʿtazilī theological affiliation is quite clear in his interpretation of key verses dealing with anthropomorphism (such as Q. 2:255 and Q. 24:35).[96] There he expresses the five principles (*al-uṣūl al-khamsa*) of Muʿtazilī theology: the utter transcendent uniqueness of the One God (*tawḥīd*); His absolute and rational divine justice (*ʿadl*); the rationality of His promise and threat about an individual's fate in the afterlife (*al-waʿd wa'l-waʿīd*); the status of the grave (Muslim) sinner within the community and in the afterlife (*al-manzila bayn al-manzilatayn*); and the incumbency of active moral agency through commanding good and forbidding evil (*al-amr bi'l-maʿrūf wa'l-nahy ʿan al-munkar*).[97]

Al-Faḍl b. al-Ḥasan al-Ṭabrisī (or Ṭabarsī) (d. 548/1154)

Abū ʿAlī al-Faḍl b. al-Ḥasan al-Ṭabrisī[98] was an important Twelver Imāmī traditionist and scholar, whose theology represents the Twelver Imāmī modification of Muʿtazilī *kalām* initiated by al-Shaykh al-Mufīd (d. 413/1020)

[94] See the PA, al-Kaʿbī.

[95] ʿAbd al-Jabbār b. Aḥmad, al-Qāḍī al-Asadābādī (d. 415/1025), *Kitāb Tanzīh al-Qurʾān ʿan al-maṭāʿin* (Beirut, Dār al-Maʿrifa, 1966); on the work itself; see Maʿrifat, *Tafsīr*, II, 514.

[96] For his interpretation of these verses, see Hamza *et al.*, *Anthology*, I.

[97] Cf. Daniel Gimaret, 'Muʿtazila', *EI*², VII, 783–93; see also the definitive study of the concept of *al-amr bi'l-maʿrūf wa'l-nahy ʿan al-munkar* by Michael Cook, *Commanding Right and Forbidding Wrong in Islamic Thought* (Cambridge, Cambridge University Press, 2000).

[98] For a more complete biography of Ṭabrisī, and an analysis of him as an exegete, see Fudge, *Qurʾānic Hermeneutics*, esp. 28–56. See also Etan Kohlberg, 'al-Ṭabrisī', *EI*², X, 40–41; Muḥsin al-Amīn al-ʿĀmilī, *Aʿyān al-shīʿa*, ed. Ḥasan al-Amīn, 11 vols. (Beirut, Dār al-Taʿāruf, 1986), XLII, 276–82; Dhahabī, *Mufassirūn*, II, 99–144; *GAL*, I, 513–14; Maʿrifat, *Tafsīr*, II, 282–9; Musa A.O. Abdul, *The Qurʾan: Shaykh Tabarsi's Commentary* (Lahore, Sh. Muhammad Ashraf, 1977).

and al-Sharīf al-Murtaḍā (d. 436/1044).[99] His Qurʾān commentary is entitled *Majmaʿ al-bayān fī tafsīr al-Qurʾān* (also called *Majmaʿ al-bayān li-ʿulūm al-Qurʾān*).[100] Ṭabrisī was a student of ʿAbd al-Jabbār b. ʿAbd Allāh al-Muqriʾ al-Rāzī (alive in 503/1109–10), who had himself been a student of the leader of the Twelver Imāmī community in Baghdad, al-Shaykh Abū Jaʿfar al-Ṭūsī (d. 460/1067). The latter was not only the dominant traditionist of his time, collating two of the Four Books of narrations of the classical Imāmī community, but also a commentator whose *al-Tibyān fī tafsīr al-Qurʾān* prefigures the style,[101] structure and theological bent of Ṭabrisī's *Majmaʿ*. Having studied with two important Sunnī commentators – Maḥmūd b. al-Ḥusayn al-Kirmānī (d. *c.* 500/1106–7) and Abū'l-Fatḥ ʿUbayd Allāh al-Qushayrī (d. 521/1127), the son of the famous Sufi commentator and Ashʿarī theologian ʿAbd al-Karīm – Ṭabrisī was familiar with the various methods and traditions of commentary current in Sunnī scholarship. Being Muʿtazilī in his theology, like the Baghdadi Twelver Imāmī scholars before him, his commentary is influenced by that of Zamakhsharī – indeed, he wrote an abridgement of Zamakhsharī's *al-Kashshāf* entitled *al-Kāfī al-shāfī min kitāb al-Kashshāf*. Ṭabrisī also authored another commentary called *Jawāmiʿ al-jāmiʿ*, which is extant.[102] Thus it seems that, in the style of the earlier great Khurāsānī exegete al-Wāḥidī, Ṭabrisī ended up writing three commentaries: a short, a medium and a long.[103]

Majmaʿ al-bayān fī tafsīr al-Qurʾān, Ṭabrisī's principal Qurʾān commentary, is probably the most widely used and admired Twelver Imāmī *tafsīr*. It includes narrations from both Sunnī and Shīʿī narrators, theological discussions, philological observations and periphrastic remarks.[104] The structure of the commentary is fairly consistent and comprises a comprehensive explanation of all aspects of the verse, from the formal consideration of the reading, syntax and philology of the language accompanied with proofs for his positions, to the discussions of the meaning and the citations of narrations that reveal his acute appreciation of the theological significance of the verse. After quoting the verse, Ṭabrisī discusses the readings and provides proofs (*ḥujja*) for them; he analyses the classical language and gives copious examples from

[99] See the PA, al-Ṭūsī.

[100] In this book we have consulted, among other editions, Ṭabrisī, *Majmaʿ al-bayān*, ed. Rasūlī and Yazdī. On the title of the work and the name of the exegete, see Fudge, *Qurʾānic Hermeneutics*, 30–39.

[101] See the PA, al-Ṭūsī.

[102] Al-Faḍl b. al-Ḥasan al-Ṭabrisī (d. 548/1154), *Jawāmiʿ al-jāmiʿ fī tafsīr al-Qurʾān al-majīd*, 2 vols. (Beirut, Dār al-Aḍwāʾ, 1985).

[103] On Wāḥidī, see Saleh, 'The Last of the Nishapuri School of Tafsir'.

[104] Fudge includes excerpts from Ṭabrisī's introduction, see *Qurʾānic Hermeneutics*, esp. 38–44.

classical and pre-Islamic poetry; he discusses the morphology, syntax and philology of the verse again, sometimes providing proofs for his interpretation; he sometimes considers the 'occasion for revelation' (*sabab al-nuzūl*); and finally, he discusses the meaning of the verse, whereins lie the bulk of his theological arguments. All these elements can be reduced to three aspects, which are universally found throughout his commentary – namely, discussion of the meaning *qua* classical language (*lugha*), *qua* syntactical arrangement (*iʿrāb*), and *qua* theological significance (*maʿnā*). Given this framework, one can understand why it was such a successful and influential commentary both in Sunnī and Shīʿī circles and was the basis for the teaching of Qur'ān exegesis.

Fakhr al-Dīn al-Rāzī (d. 606/1209)

Abū ʿAbd Allāh Muḥammad b. ʿUmar b. al-Ḥusayn Fakhr al-Dīn al-Rāzī was one of the most influential and perhaps the most significant Sunnī theologians of the medieval period.[105] He was sometimes known as Ibn al-Khaṭīb because his father, Ḍiyā' al-Dīn Abū'l-Qāsim, had been a preacher (*khaṭīb*) in his hometown.[106] A critically minded Ashʿarī and a philosopher, he studied first in Baghdad and later in Marāgha with the Ashʿarī theologian Abū'l-Qāsim al-Anṣārī, a student of the Imam al-Ḥaramayn Abū'l-Maʿālī

[105] On Rāzī and his Qur'ān commentary, see Jaffer, *Razi*; Georges Anawati, 'Fakhr al-Dīn al-Rāzī', *EI²*, II, 751–5; idem, 'Fakhr al-Dīn al-Rāzī: Tamhīd li-dirāsāt ḥayātih wa mu'allafātih' in *Ilā Ṭāhā Ḥusayn fī ʿīd mīlādihi al-khamsīn/Mélanges Taha Husain*, ed. ʿAbd al-Raḥmān al-Badawī (Cairo, al-Hay'a al-Miṣriyya al-ʿĀmma, 1962), 193–234; Khalīl b. Aybak al-Ṣafadī (d. 764/1362), *al-Wāfī bi'l-wafayāt*, vols. II–VI, ed. Sven Dedering (Wiesbaden, Franz Steiner, 1949–72), vol. VII, ed. Iḥsān ʿAbbās (Wiesbaden, Franz Steiner, 1969), IV, 248–58; Ibn Khallikān, *Wafayāt*, I, 600–602; Aḥmad b. al-Qāsim Ibn Abī Uṣaybiʿa (d. 668/1270), *ʿUyūn al-anbā' fī ṭabaqāt al-aṭibbā'*, ed. ʿĀmir al-Najjār, 6 vols. (Cairo, al-Hay'a al-Miṣriyya al-ʿĀmma li'l-Kitāb, 2001), II, 23–30; ʿAlī b. Yūsuf al-Qifṭī (d. 646/1248), *Ta'rīkh al-ḥukamā'*, ed. Julius Lippert (Leipzig, Dieterich'sche Verlagsbuchhandlung, 1903), 190–92; Tony Street, 'Concerning the Life and Works of Fakhr al-Dīn al-Rāzī' in *Islam: Essays on Scripture, Thought and Society. A Festschrift in Honour of Antony H. Johns*, ed. Peter G. Riddell and Tony Street (Leiden, Brill, 1997), 135–46. Other than Jaffer's study, the following works address Rāzī's thought and his *tafsīr*: Yasin Ceylan, *Theology and Tafsīr in the Major Works of Fakhr al-Dīn al-Rāzī* (Kuala Lumpur, International Institute of Islamic Thought and Civilisation, 1996); Roger Arnaldez, 'L'oeuvre de Fakhr al-Dîn al-Râzî commentateur du Coran et philosophe', *Cahiers de civilization médiévale, Xme–XIIme siècles* 3 (1960), 307–23; idem, 'Trouvailles philosophiques dans le commentaire coranique de Fakhr al-Dīn al-Rāzī', *Études Orientales* 4 (1989), 17–26; idem, *Fakhr al-Dîn al-Râzī: Commentateur du Coran et philosophe* (Paris, Vrin, 2002).

[106] In this work we have used, among other editions: Fakhr al-Dīn Muḥammad b. ʿUmar al-Rāzī (d. 606/1209), *Mafātīḥ al-ghayb aw al-Tafsīr al-kabīr*, 32 pts. in 16 vols. (Beirut, Dār al-Kutub al-ʿIlmiyya, 2000).

al-Juwaynī (d. 478/1085),[107] and with the philosopher Majd al-Dīn al-Jīlī, who was also the teacher of luminaries of the period including the martyred philosopher Shihāb al-Dīn Suhrawardī (exec. 586/1191).[108] Rāzī spent most of his life in the Islamic east, teaching and disputing with anthropomorphists and Muʿtazilī theologians in Transoxiana,[109] and finally settling in Herat with a large circle of students. In the latter period of his life he became known as the 'elder of Islam' (*Shaykh al-Islām*). During his fatal illness in 606/1209, he wrote a creedal work outlining Sunnī beliefs and seemed to abjure the time that he had spent in the vain pursuit of philosophy and philosophical theology. His tomb in Herat became, and remains, a place of veneration.

A committed and philosophically minded theologian, he wrote major critical commentaries on the work of Ibn Sīnā (d. 428/1037), including *Lubāb al-Ishārāt* and a gloss on the *ʿUyūn al-ḥikma*, a work which was gaining currency among rational theologians. In these works he displayed his philosophical acumen and criticised some of the central doctrines of the Muslim Neoplatonic philosophers, including that of the eternity of the universe.[110] In his *kalām* compendia, such as *al-Mabāḥith al-mashriqiyya* and *al-Maṭālib al-ʿāliya*,[111] he continued the project of providing a defensible and viable philosophical theology that was associated with the Ashʿarī school and critical of the excesses of the Avicennan philosophers.[112]

[107] For a study of his thought focusing on his theological work *Lumaʿ al-adilla*, see Mohammad Moslem Adel Saflo, *Al-Juwaynī's Thought and Methodology, with a Translation and Commentary of Lumaʿ al-Adilla* (Berlin, Klaus Swartz, 2000); cf. Imām al-Ḥaramayn Abū'l-Maʿālī al-Juwaynī (d. 478/1085), *Kitāb al-Irshād*; English tr. by Paul Walker, *A Guide to Conclusive Proofs for the Principles of Beliefs* (Reading, Garnet Press, 2000); for a study of his dogmatic theology, see Helmut Klopfer, *Das Dogma des Imâm al-Ḥaramain al-Djuwainî und sein Werk al-ʿAqîdat an-Niẓâmîyya* (Cairo, Salaheddine Boustany; Wiesbaden, Otto Harrassowitz, 1958).

[108] See Hossein Ziai, 'al-Suhrawardī, Shihāb al-Dīn Yaḥyā', *EI*^{2}, IX, 782–4.

[109] For these disputations and their text, see Fathalla Kholeif, *A Study on Fakhr al-Dīn al-Rāzī and His Controversies in Transoxiana* (Beirut, Dar el-Machreq, 1966); Paul Kraus, 'The Controversies of Fakhr al-Dīn al-Rāzī', *Islamic Culture* 12 (1938), 131–53; M. Ṣaghīr Ḥasan Maʿṣūmī, 'Imām Fakhr al-Dīn al-Rāzī and His Critics', *Islamic Studies* (Islamabad) 6 (1967), 355–74; Jane Dammen McAuliffe, 'Fakhr al-Dīn al-Rāzī on God as al-Khāliq' in *God and Creation: An Ecumenical Symposium*, ed. David B. Burrell and Bernard McGinn (Notre Dame, IN, University of Notre Dame Press, 1990), 276–96.

[110] Cf. Muammer İskenderoğlu, *Fakhr al-Dīn al-Rāzī and Thomas Aquinas on the Question of the Eternity of the World* (Leiden, Brill, 2002).

[111] Fakhr al-Dīn al-Rāzī (d. 606/1209), *al-Mabāḥith al-mashriqiyya fī ʿilm al-ilāhiyyāt wa'l-ṭabīʿiyyāt*, ed. Muḥammad al-Baghdādī, 2 vols. (Beirut, Dār al-Kitāb al-ʿArabī, 1990); idem, *al-Maṭālib al-ʿāliya min al-ʿilm al-ilāhi*, ed. Aḥmad Ḥijāzī al-Saqqā, 9 vols. (Beirut, Dār al-Kitāb al-ʿArabī, 1987).

[112] In addition to Rāzī's significance for the study of Muslim theological philosophy, his contribution to the field of ethics, a field itself largely unchartered by modern scholarship, has not been fully appreciated. A principal study in this respect is Ayman Shihadeh, *The Teleological Ethics of Fakhr al-Dīn al-Rāzī* (Leiden, Brill, 2006).

His commentary, *Mafātīḥ al-ghayb* (*Keys to the Unseen*), also known as *al-Tafsīr al-kabīr* (*The Great Commentary*), is a vast compendium of philological, traditionalist, theological and philosophical comments on, and interpretations of, the verses of the Qur'ān.[113] Despite the problems associated with such hermeneutical categories, we can say that his commentary is a substantial expression of the method of *tafsīr bi'l-ra'y* in which the Qur'ān is interpreted through a consideration of theological and philosophical issues (*masā'il*) raised by the verse in question and which are considered carefully in the manner of a *kalām* (dialectic theology) text. The commentary on each verse is divided into various issues and sub-issues, arguments, sub-arguments and counter-arguments, where various lemmas of discursive reasoning are considered, evaluated, rejected or proposed.[114] Thus argument and opinion predominate over the consideration of proof-texts quoted on the authority of the Prophet and his Companions. Often subtle and intricate, it is a scholar's and a theologian's commentary, and possibly the largest commentary of the classical and medieval period. As such, it is a difficult text that presupposes a detailed understanding of theological argumentation and concepts.

Abū ʿAbd Allāh Muḥammad b. Aḥmad al-Qurṭubī (d. 671/1273)

Abū ʿAbd Allāh Muḥammad b. Aḥmad b. Abū Bakr b. Farḥ[115] al-Qurṭubī was a Cordoban Mālikī jurist and the author of many well-known works, of which the best known is his *al-Jāmiʿ li-aḥkām al-Qur'ān wa'l-mubayyin li-mā taḍammanahu min al-sunna wa aḥkām al-furqān* (*The Compendium of Qur'ānic Rulings and the Exposition of What it Contains of Sunna and the Judgments of the Discriminator*).[116] Qurṭubī was born in Montoro or Cordoba.[117] Delfina Serrano Ruano infers 'modest social origins' from 'the fact that both he and his father had to perform manual labour to make a living'; nevertheless, as she shows, he was able to study *ḥadīth* and Qur'ānic

[113] See Dāwūdī, *Ṭabaqāt*, II, 213–17; Dhahabī, *Mufassirūn*, I, 290–96; Maʿrifat, *Tafsīr*, II, 406–29.

[114] For Rāzī's 'toolkit', see Tariq Jaffer, 'Fakhr al-Dīn al-Rāzī's System of Inquiry' in *Aims, Methods and Contexts*, ed. Bauer, 241–61.

[115] For Arnaldez (Roger Arnaldez, 'al-Ḳurṭubī', *EI*²), he is Ibn Abū Bakr Ibn Faraj, while for other authors, including Dhahabī, *al-Tafsīr wa aḥkām*, he is Ibn Abū Bakr b. Farḥ. Dhahabī has a glowing account of the man and his work in *al-Tafsīr wa'l-mufassirūn*, II, 401–7.

[116] One of the editions that we have used in this volume is Muḥammad b. Aḥmad al-Anṣārī al-Qurṭubī (d. 671/1273), *al-Jāmiʿ li-aḥkām al-Qur'ān*, 20 vols. (Beirut, Dār Iḥyā' al-Turāth al-ʿArabī, 1965–7).

[117] To date, the definitive biography of al-Qurṭubī is that of Delfina Serrano Ruano, *EQ*; in what follows, we have drawn on her article.

readings in Cordoba. After Cordoba was conquered by the Christians, the resulting treaty involved the expulsion of the Muslim population, and Qurṭubī left permanently.[118] He went to Alexandria, where he studied *ḥadīth* and *fiqh* with another Qurṭubī, Abū'l-ʿAbbās Aḥmad b. Umar (d. 657/1259). He also studied with Abū Muḥammad ʿAbd al-Muʿṭī al-Iskandarānī (d. 638/1240) the latter's commentary on Qushayrī's *Risāla*. Qurṭubī finally settled in Munyat (today El Minya, Egypt), where he died in 671/1273.

Al-Jāmiʿ li-aḥkām al-Qurʾān has a legal focus, but is by no means confined solely to legislative types of interpretation. The work is perhaps best introduced by its author. Qurṭubī describes his aims thus:

> Since the Book of God suffices to comprehend the sciences of law which alone are able to treat the Sunna and the obligatory acts, brought down from the trustee of the heavens (*amīn al-samāʾ*) (sc. Gabriel) to the trustee of the earth (*amīn al-arḍ*) (sc. Muḥammad), I decided to dedicate my entire life and all of my energies to it, composing this commentary. And, in this commentary, I set out to include a summary of excerpts from other works of *tafsīr*, lexicography, syntax (*iʿrāb*) and variant readings; to refute the deviants and those who interpret in error; to clarify the traditions regarding Qurʾānic legislation and the occasions of revelation, synthesising the context and the rulings in them; and to resolve the disputed ones by referring to the opinions of the pious predecessors and those who came after them. My one rule in this book was to attribute opinions to those who held them, and the *ḥadīth*s to their compilers, for they say that the reason that knowledge is blessed is in the ascription of opinions to their authors. Often, one finds that *ḥadīth* is used in books of jurisprudence and *tafsīr* without attribution, so the only person who would be able to determine the truth of those opinions would be someone who has been able to consult the *ḥadīth* books; anyone without experience in that area would end up perplexed, unable to identify what is sound (*ṣaḥīḥ*) and what is not.[119] But that branch of knowledge is so voluminous that it cannot be used for proofs or inference until it has been correctly attributed [to its author] by the notable imams and the most celebrated of the trustworthy Muslim scholars who have verified it; and we indicate such passages in this book. [. . .] And I leave out many of the stories told by the commentators (*mufassirūn*) and the reports of the historians (*muʾarrikhūn*), except what is essential and what is indispensable for clarification, choosing instead to concentrate on clarifying the legislative verses, by introducing issues (*masāʾil*) that would help explain the meanings of

118 Manuela Marín, 'Des emigrations forcées: Les *ʿulamāʾ* d'al-Andalus face a la conquête chrétienne' in *L'Occident musulman et l'Occident chrétien au Moyen Âge*, ed. Mohammed Hammam (Rabat, La Faculté des Lettres et des Sciences Humaines, Université Mohammed V, 1995), 43–59.

119 Literally: to identify the sound and the diseased.

those verses and that would guide the seeker (*ṭālib*) to what these [verses] entail. Every verse, regardless of whether it includes one or more rulings (*ḥukm*), will contain issues (*masāʾil*) through which I clarify that which it includes of occasions of revelation, exegesis (*tafsīr*), isolated *ḥadīths* (*gharīb*) and the ruling; but if it does not include a ruling (*ḥukm*), I simply mention its exegesis or interpretation (*tafsīr wa-taʾwīl*). [. . .] I have given it the title: *al-Jāmiʿ li-aḥkām al-Qurʾān waʾl-mubayyin li-mā taḍammanahu min al-sunna wa-aḥkām al-furqān* (*The Compendium of Qurʾānic Rulings and the Exposition of What it Contains of Sunna and the Judgments of the Discriminator*).

ʿAbd al-Razzāq Kāshānī (d. 736/1336)

The commentary that has traditionally been attributed to the Andalusian Sufi Ibn ʿArabī (d. 638/1240)[120] is in fact a series of allegorical and mystical interpretations recorded by ʿAbd al-Razzāq al-Kāshānī,[121] a student of the school of Ibn ʿArabī.[122] There is no extant *tafsīr* of Ibn ʿArabī, despite the publication of an anthology taken from his works.[123] The actual title of Kāshānī's commentary, as attested in its manuscript traditions, is *al-Taʾwīlāt*.

Kamāl al-Dīn Abūʾl-Faḍl ʿAbd al-Razzāq b. Jamāl al-Dīn Abīʾl-Ghanāʾim Aḥmad (or Isḥāq) al-Kāshānī (d. 730–36/1329–36)[124] was a major Sufi

[120] Ahmet Ates, 'Ibn ʿArabī', *EI*², III, 707–11; William Chittick, 'Ebn ʿArabī', *EIr*, VII, 664–70; Ṣafadī, *al-Wāfī*, IV, 173–8; Claude Addas, *Quest for the Red Sulphur: The Life of Ibn ʿArabī*, tr. Peter Kingsley (Cambridge, Islamic Texts Society, 1993); orig. pub. as *Ibn ʿArabī, ou, La quête du soufre rouge* (Paris, Gallimard, 1989).

[121] ʿAbd al-Razzāq Kāshānī (d. 736/1336), *Taʾwīlāt al-Qurʾān* (or *Tafsīr al-Qurʾān al-karīm*) popularly but erroneously known as *Tafsīr Ibn ʿArabī*, 2 vols. (Beirut, Dar al-Yaqẓa al-ʿArabiyya, 1968). On this commentator see Pierre Lory, "Abd al-Razzāq al-Kāshānī', *EI*³; Duncan MacDonald, "Abd al-Razzāq al-Kāshānī', *EI*², I, 88–90; ʿAbd al-Razzāq b. Aḥmad Ibn al-Fuwaṭī (d. 723/1323), *Talkhīṣ majmaʿ al-ādāb fī muʿjam al-alqāb*, ed. Muṣṭafā Jawād, 4 vols. (Damascus, Wizārat al-Thaqāfa waʾl-Irshād al-Qawmī, 1962), IV, 180; *GAL*, II, 201–2, *GAL*-S, II, 280–81; Majīd Hādīzādah, 'Kāshānī-nāmah' in *Majmūʿa-yi rasāʾil wa muṣannafāt taʾlīf ʿAbd al-Razzāq Kāshānī*, ed. Majīd Hādīzāda (Tehran, Mīrāth-i Maktūb, 1380 Sh./2000), 23–126.

[122] Dhahabī, *Mufassirūn*, III, 66–82; Maʿrifat, *Tafsīr*, II, 569–86; *GAL*, I, 571, *GAL*-S, I, 791; Osman Yahya, *Historie et classification de l'œuvre d'Ibn ʿArabī: Étude critique*, 2 vols. (Damascus, Institut Français de Damas, 1964), II, 480, 483; Pierre Lory, *Les commentaires ésoteriques du Coran d'après ʿAbd al-Razzāq al-Qāshānī* (Paris, Les Deux Océans, 1980; 2nd rev. edn, 1990).

[123] For details, see Muḥyī al-Dīn Ibn ʿArabī, *Raḥma min al-Raḥmān fī tafsīr wa ishārāt al-Qurʾān*, compilation of all the exegetical comments in Ibn ʿArabī's *Futūḥāt* by Maḥmūd Maḥmūd al-Ghurāb, 2 vols. (Damascus, Dār al-Fikr/Maṭbaʿat al-Nuḍr, 1410/1989); cf. Muḥammad ʿAlī Ayāzī, *al-Mufassirūn: Ḥāyatuhum wa manhajuhum* (Tehran, Wizārat-i Farhang wa Irshād-i Islāmī, 1373 Sh./1994), 464–9. More generally on Ibn ʿArabī's use of *taʾwīl*, see Naṣr Ḥāmid Abū Zayd, *Falsafat al-taʾwīl: Dirāsa fī taʾwīl al-Qurʾān ʿinda Muḥyī al-Dīn Ibn ʿArabī* (Beirut, Dār al-Tanwīr, 1983).

[124] Hādīzāda, 'Kāshānī-nāmah', 28.

figure – likely to have been Twelver Imāmī in affiliation[125] – of the Ilkhanid period in Iran. Although very little is known about his education and early life, at some stage he turned to the Sufi path with two masters: Aṣīl al-Dīn ʿAbd Allāh ʿAlawī (d. 685/1285),[126] who was also a Twelver Imāmī traditionist in Shīrāz; and a Sunnī Sufi of the Suhrawardī tradition, Nūr al-Dīn ʿAbd al-Ṣamad Natanzī (d. 699/1299).[127] Kāshānī mentions the two men in his correspondence with a famous contemporary, ʿAlāʾ al-Dawla Simnānī (d. 736/1336).[128] Other Sufis with whom he associated include Ṣadr al-Dīn b. Fakhr al-Dīn Rūzbihān-i Thānī (d. 685/1286), a respected preacher and grandson of the famous Sufi master of Shīrāz, Rūzbihān Baqlī (d. 606/1209),[129] and Nūr al-Dīn Isfarāyīnī (d. 717/1317), the master of Simnānī.[130] Through his later travels, he met Muʾayyid al-Dīn Jandī (d. *c.* 700/1300), who was himself a student of Ṣadr al-Dīn Qūnawī (d. 673/1274),[131] Ibn ʿArabī's son-in-law. Kāshānī's own commentary on the seminal *Fuṣūṣ al-Ḥikam* (*Bezels of Wisdom*) of Ibn ʿArabī owes much to the previous commentaries of Jandī and Qūnawī. The significance of his Shīʿī Twelver Imāmī affiliation seems to lie in his influence on the Shīʿī tradition of the school of Ibn ʿArabī, a school that came to prominence under Sayyid Ḥaydar Āmulī (d. *post* 787/1385); certainly, Kāshānī is much cited in Āmulī's *Jāmiʿ al-asrār* (*Compendium of Mysteries*).[132]

125 Āghā Buzurg Muḥammad Muḥsin Ṭihrānī, *Ṭabaqāt aʿlām al-shīʿa*, ed. ʿAlī-Naqī Munzawī, 5 vols. (Beirut, Dār al-Kitāb al-ʿArabī, 1971), 112–13; ʿĀmilī, *Aʿyān*, VII, 470; Ḥajjī Khalīfa (Kâtip Çelebi) (d. 1067/1657), *Kashf al-ẓunūn*, 2 vols. (Istanbul, Maṭābiʿ Wikālat al-Maʿārif al-Jalīla, 1941–7), I, 336.

126 Hādīzāda, 'Kāshānī-nāma', 74–6.

127 ʿAbd al-Sattār Jāmī (d. 898/1492), *Nafaḥāt al-uns min ḥaḍarāt al-quds*, ed. Maḥmūd ʿĀbidī (Tehran, Intishārāt-i Iṭṭilāʿāt, 1991), 480; Hādīzāda, 'Kāshānī-nāma', 70–71.

128 Hādīzāda, 'Kāshānī-nāma', 28–9; for a discussion of the correspondence, see Hermann Landolt, 'Der Briefwechsel zwischen Kāšānī und Simnānī über Waḥdat al-Wuǧūd', *Der Islam* 50 (1973), 29–81. On Simnānī, see Jamal J. Elias, *The Throne Carrier of God: The Life and Thought of ʿAlāʾ ad-Dawla as-Simnānī* (Albany, State University of New York Press, 1995); *GAL*, II, 263, *GAL*-S, II, 281; Fritz Meier, "Alāʾ al-Dawla al-Simnānī', *EI*², I, 346–7; Josef van Ess, "Alāʾ al-Dawla Semnānī', *EIr*, I, 774–7; Jāmī, *Nafaḥāt*, 439ff.; Ṣafadī, *al-Wāfī*, VII, 356–7.

129 Hādīzāda, 'Kāshānī-nāma', 73–4; Carl Ernst, *Rūzbihān Baqlī: Mysticism and the Rhetoric of Sainthood in Persian Sufism* (Richmond, Surrey, Curzon Press, 1996), 8–9, especially in the context of the 'existence' of a Rūzbihāniyya Sufi order.

130 Hādīzāda, 'Kāshānī-nāma', 72–3. On Isfarāyīnī and his correspondence with Simnānī, see Nūr al-Dīn ʿAbd al-Raḥmān b. Muḥammad al-Isfarāyīnī (d. 418/1027), *Kāshif al-asrār*, ed. and tr. Hermann Landolt, *Nûruddîn Abdurrahmân-i Isfarâyinî: Le Révélateur des Mystères [Kâshif al-asrâr]* (Paris, Verdier, 1986).

131 William C. Chittick, 'Ṣadr al-Dīn al-Qūnawī', *EI*², VIII, 753–5; *GAL*-S, I, 807–8.

132 See Sayyid Ḥaydar Āmulī (d. *post* 787/1385), *Jāmiʿ al-asrār wa manbaʿ al-anwār* in *La Philosophie Shîʿite*, Bibliothèque Iranienne XVI, ed. Henry Corbin and Osman Yahia (Tehran, Institut Franco-Iranien de Recherche, 1969), 659 *inter alia*; cf. Henri Corbin, *En Islam iranien: Aspects spirituals et philosophiques*. I: *Le shīʿisme duodécimain*; II: *Suhrawardī et les Platoniciens de Perse*; III: *Les fidèles d'amour, shīʿisme st soufisme*; IV: *L'école d'Ispahan, l'école shaykhie, le douziéme imam* (Paris, Gallimard, 1971–2), 149–213.

The commentary with which we are concerned is an allegorical elucidation and interpretation of the divine word, as its alternative name *al-Taʾwīlāt li'l-Qurʾān al-Majīd*[133] suggests. It belongs to the genre known as *al-tafsīr al-ishārī*, or allusive commentary.[134] In particular, Kāshānī's *tafsīr* is largely based on *taṭbīq* – that is, the regular 'application' of macrocosmic references in the Qurʾān to the human microcosm.[135] It is an esoteric and mystical reading that is intended to guide the initiate along the path of spiritual realisation, through subtle, pedagogic allusions to the truth and the inner self. This process of hermeneutics, or *taʾwīl*,[136] is a systematic attempt at locating the experience of the text in the spiritual self and interiorising the word and recognising the signs of God through His explicit revelation (the Qurʾān) and an implicit revelation (the lives of the pious saints and the cosmos).

Much Sufi teaching about the relationship between the word and the world, the inscribed text and the 'cosmic text', is predicated upon the metaphysical notion of the three realities: God, the macrocosmic world and the microcosmic man.[137] The 'text' is a means of expressing each of these realities, realisation being a hermeneutic of that text. Thus Sufi *tafsīr* is not just an explanation, periphrasis or interpretation of the Qurʾān on the linguistic, philosophical, dogmatic and textual levels, it also expresses an understanding of reality both within and without the self. As such, it differs from works that are self-consciously either *bi'l-maʾthūr* or *bi'l-raʾy* in that it rarely contains transmitted narrations or considerations of different opinions. This is reflected in Kāshānī's introduction to his work, in which he emphasises the seeker's direct connection to God and immediate experience of the Qurʾān:

> He has refreshed the sources of the sensory faculties of comprehension of His friends (*awliyāʾ*) so that the beholding may be certain. He has made their inmost hearts sensitive to the [divine] subtleties by the irradiation of rays of love within them. He has made their spirits yearn to witness the beauty of His countenance by means of their annihilation (*fanāʾ*). He then cast upon them [His] speech, wherein they then found spiritual comfort by morning and by

[133] Hādīzāda, 'Kāshānī-nāma', 170–88; Āmulī, *Jāmiʿ*, 498.

[134] More generally on this genre and Sufi *tafsīr*, see Annabel Keeler and Sajjad Rizvi, eds., *The Spirit and the Letter: Approaches to the Esoteric Interpretation of the Qur'an* (Oxford, Oxford University Press in association with the Institute of Ismaili Studies, 2016); Keeler, *Sufi Hermeneutics*.

[135] See Lory, *Les commentaires ésoterique*, 29.

[136] Poonawala, 'Taʾwīl', *EI*², X, 390–92.

[137] For a discussion of Sufism and the three realities, see Sachiko Murata, *The Tao of Islam: A Sourcebook on Gender Relationships in Islamic Thought* (Albany, State University of New York Press, 1992).

> evening. Through that [speech] He brought them closer and closer to Him, such that they became in near communion with Him. Thereat he purified their souls with its [i.e. the Qur'ān's] outward aspect (*ẓāhir*) so that it became like gushing water, and He replenished their hearts with its inward aspect (*bāṭin*) so that it was like a surging sea. But when they wanted to dive [into it] to extract the pearls of its mysteries, the waters rose high above them and they were drowned by its torrent.[138]

Unlike other exegetes who emphasise their reliance on tradition and their 'traditional' lexical methods, Kāshānī here emphasises an emotional connection with God, with love at its centre. Kāshānī thus intentionally goes well beyond the literal (*ẓāhir*) interpretation of the Qur'ān, and his commentary could be seen instead as an explanation and expression of a 'coherent spiritual worldview' in which the text of the Qur'ān is used to encourage a spiritual awakening to the cosmic truths, the nature of spirit, soul and ultimate reality.[139] Thus this commentary provides a type of didactic method for the Sufi path.

Ibn Kathīr (d. 773/1371)

Abū'l-Fidā' 'Imād al-Dīn Ismā'īl b. 'Umar, Ibn Kathīr, was a well-known Syrian Shāfi'ī[140] Ash'arī traditionalist and prolific writer on a range of prominent Islamic disciplines, including biographical dictionaries, *ḥadīth* works and Islamic law. His most famous literary work is perhaps his universal history, the *al-Bidāya wa'l-nihāya fī'l-ta'rīkh*,[141] very much modelled on Ṭabarī's *Ta'rīkh al-rusul wa'l-mulūk*. The historiographically significant sections are the ones on the Mamlūk era (his own) and those that draw on the *Ta'rīkh Dimashq* of Abū Shāma (d. 665/1267), the latter itself being a summary of Ibn 'Asākir's original *Ta'rīkh madīnat Dimashq*.[142] According to Younus Mirza, Ibn Kathīr's most important work remains his Qur'ān

[138] Reproduced from Hamza, 'Unlocking the Historical Qur'an', 29.

[139] Ibid., 26–7.

[140] On Abū 'Abd Allāh Muḥammad b. Idrīs al-Shāfi'ī, see Kecia Ali, *Imām Shāfi'ī: Scholar and Saint* (London, Oneworld Academic, 2011); Joseph E. Lowry, *Early Islamic Legal Theory: The Risāla of Muḥammad Ibn Idrīs al-Shāfi'ī* (Leiden, Brill, 2007); Muḥammad b. Idrīs al-Shāfi'ī (d. 204/820), *The Epistle on Legal Theory*, ed. and tr. Joseph Lowry (New York, New York University Press, 2013).

[141] Abū'l-Fidā' Ismā'īl b. 'Umar 'Imād al-Dīn Ibn Kathīr, *al-Bidāya wa'l-nihāya*, ed. Aḥmad 'Abd al-Wahhāb Futayḥ, 15 vols. (Cairo, Dār al-Ḥadīth, 1992).

[142] 'Alī b. al-Ḥasan b. Hibat Allāh Ibn 'Asākir (d. 571/1176), *Tā'rīkh madīnat Dimashq*, ed. Muḥibb al-Dīn 'Umar al-'Amrāwī, 80 vols. (Beirut, Dār al-Fikr, 1998).

commentary.[143] Saleh argues that Ibn Kathīr's *tafsīr* is important principally because of its substantive relationship to *al-Muqaddima fī uṣūl al-tafsīr*, the treatise on exegesis by Ibn Taymiyya (d. 728/1328), and ultimately Ibn Taymiyya's Ḥanbalī legacy as it was revived by Muḥammad b. ʿAbd al-Wahhāb and Wahhābī ideology some four centuries later: in the introduction to his Qurʾān commentary, Ibn Kathīr includes the entire final two chapters of Ibn Taymiyya's exegetical treatise.[144] In this respect, the curricular pedigree of contemporary Salafism (sc. dependence on 'predecessors', *al-salaf*) can undoubtedly be traced back to Ibn Kathīr as much as to Ibn Taymiyya's work itself. However, Mirza argues that the conflation of Ibn Kathīr with Ibn Taymiyya is a modern one, and stems from a modernist agenda. Though Mirza does not deny that Ibn Taymiyya influenced Ibn Kathīr, he shows that Ibn Kathīr's main impetus for writing his exegesis was to respond to other Shāfiʿī–Ashʿarī scholars who incorporated *kalām* and undertook *ta'wīl* of the Qurʾān; in this regard, Ibn Kathīr's exegesis could be seen as a response to his Shāfiʿī–Ashʿarī colleague Fakhr al-Dīn al-Rāzī.[145]

In his introduction to his work, translated partially below, Ibn Kathīr describes a simplified schema of authoritative exegesis based on a systematic and deliberately delimited generational approach. For him, the best methods of exegesis, beyond intra-Qurʾānic hermeneutics, begin with the Prophet and continue through the first group of Companions (*ṣaḥāba*) and, to a more limited extent, their followers (*tābiʿūn*). The major enhancement offered within this scheme, according to Ibn Kathīr, is the verification of *ḥadīth* materials, sourced in the main from Ṭabarī, but not overtly verified by him. In practice, this approach means that the substance of Ibn Kathīr's *tafsīr* bears a distinct relationship to the *Jāmiʿ al-bayān* of Ṭabarī. At the same time, as Ibn Kathīr states in his introduction, he seeks to define a method of undertaking exegesis and to impose a systematic approach; indeed, this seems to have been a reaction against the major developments that had occurred in the genre in between the time of these two exegetes. By seeking

[143] Younus Mirza, 'Ibn Kathīr', *EI*[3]. For our translations we have drawn on the following edition, in addition to others: Abū'l-Fidāʾ Ismāʿīl ʿImād al-Dīn Ibn Kathīr (d. 774/1373), *Tafsīr al-Qurʾān al-ʿAẓīm*, ed. Khalid Muḥammad Muḥarram (Beirut, al-Maktaba al-ʿAṣriyya, 2006).

[144] Walid Saleh, 'Ibn Taymiyya and the Rise of Radical Hermeneutics: An Analysis of *An Introduction to the Foundations of Qurānic Exegesis*' in *Ibn Taymiyya and His Times*, ed. Yossef Rapoport and Shahab Ahmed (Karachi, Oxford University Press Pakistan, 2010), 124. The relationship between Ibn Kathīr's *Tafsīr* and Ibn Taymiyya's *Muqaddima* was perhaps first noted in Western scholarship by Jane Dammen McAuliffe, 'Qurʾānic Hermeneutics', 46–62, esp. 56ff.

[145] Younus Mirza, 'Was Ibn Kathīr the "Spokesperson" for Ibn Taymiyya? Jonah as a Prophet of Obedience', *Journal of Qur'anic Studies* 16.1 (2014), 1–19; see also idem, 'Ishmael as Abraham's Sacrifice: Ibn Taymiyya and Ibn Kathīr on the Intended Victim', *Islam and Muslim-Christian Relations* 24.3 (2013), 277–98.

a return to some of Ṭabarī's methods and sources, while concurrently refining them in the approach, for instance, to *ḥadīth*s, where Ibn Kathīr cites from the sound (*ṣaḥīḥ*) works, Ibn Kathīr circumscribes the genre.[146] This is apparent when one compares both commentators' introductions to their *tafsīr* works. In the following excerpt from his introduction, Ibn Kathīr describes his own methods:

> If someone were to ask 'what is the soundest method of exegesis (*tafsīr*)?', the answer would be: the soundest method in that regard would be to explain (*tafsīr*) the Qur'ān through the Qur'ān. Thus what may be given in summary form in one place will have been explained in detail in another. If, however, you could not get far by this [method], then you should refer to the Sunna, for it elucidates and clarifies the Qur'ān. Nay, the imam Abū ʿAbd Allāh Muḥammad b. Idrīs al-Shāfiʿī,[147] may God have mercy on him, said: 'Whatever the Messenger of God (*ṣlʿm*) gave as a ruling (*ḥukm*), he did so on the basis of what he had understood from the Qur'ān' [. . .].[148] That is why the Messenger of God (*ṣlʿm*) said, 'Verily, I have been given the Qur'ān and the like of it at the same time', meaning the Sunna. For even the Sunna would be sent down to him by revelation (*waḥy*), just as the Qur'ān came down, except that this [Sunna] is never recited (*tilāwa*) in the way that the Qur'ān is. The imam al-Shāfiʿī, may God have mercy on him, and other imams adduce substantial evidence for this, but this is not the place for that.
>
> The goal is to seek the explanation (*tafsīr*) of the Qur'ān from within it and if you do not find that there, then from the Sunna. It is in this vein that the Messenger of God (*ṣlʿm*) asked Muʿādh [b. Jabal], before sending him to Yemen: 'By what will you pass judgment?', to which he replied, 'By the Book of God', and to which he was then asked, 'And what if you find nothing [there]?', to which he responded, 'By the Sunna of the Messenger of God.' When he was then asked, 'And if you [still] find nothing?', he replied, 'I will make every effort using reason (*ra'y*)', whereupon the Messenger of God (*ṣlʿm*) put his hand firmly upon his [Muʿādh's] chest and said, 'Praise be to God who has made the messenger [Muʿādh] of God's Messenger succeed in attaining what pleases the Messenger of God.' This *ḥadīth* has been [transmitted] via a solid chain of transmission (*isnād jayyid*) in the *Musnad* and *Sunan* collections as we have established [elsewhere] in that instance. The imam Abū Jaʿfar Muḥammad b. Jarīr al-Ṭabarī narrates on the authority of ʿAbd Allāh,[149] meaning Ibn Masʿūd,

[146] Calder, '*Tafsīr* from Ṭabarī to Ibn Kathīr', comments on the way in which Ibn Kathīr circumscribes the genre.

[147] On whom, see the PA.

[148] Ibn Kathīr goes on to elaborate on this first generation of companions and includes the 'ocean of knowledge (*al-ḥibr al-baḥr*)' and the interpreter *par excellence* (*tarjumān*) of the Qur'ān, Ibn ʿAbbās, citing several traditions that confirm the conferral of this honour.

[149] On whom, see the PA, al-Shāfiʿī.

that the latter said, 'By Him besides whom there is no other god, not a single verse of God's Book has been revealed without my knowing regarding to whom it was sent or at which point it was sent. And if I should know of anyone more knowledgeable than me of God's Book and whose location might be reached on camel-back, I would go to him myself.' He [Ibn Masʿūd] also said, 'When one of us had learnt [only] ten verses, he would go no further until he knew their meaning (*maʿnā*) and how to apply them.'[150]

Muḥsin al-Fayḍ al-Kāshānī (d. 1091/1680)

Muḥammad b. Murtaḍā Muḥsin al-Kāshānī, known as al-Fayḍ,[151] whom Majlisī designates as Fayḍ al-Kāshānī, was one of the most important Safavid Qurʾān commentators, who undertook an Akhbārī interpretation of the Qurʾān in his work *al-Ṣāfī fī tafsīr al-Qurʾān*.[152] He grew up in the city of Qumm and moved to Kāshān, acquiring his attributive, and then to Shīrāz upon hearing of the arrival there of the famous scholar al-Sayyid Mājid al-Baḥrānī. At Shīrāz, he came into contact with the most famous scholar of the time, Mullā Ṣadrā, with whom he would come to have an intellectual and a personal relationship: Fayḍ later married Ṣadrā's daughter and they had several children together.[153] Perhaps consequent to this close relationship with Mullā Ṣadrā, Fayḍ al-Kāshānī's literary and intellectual output tended to draw on Sufism and mystical philosophy, and included works of poetry and philosophy as well as his famous Qurʾān commentary. Having spent most of his life in Shīrāz, he returned to Kāshān, where he became the leading authority at the time. His work *al-Ṣāfī* is known as an Akhbārī work, Akhbārī being the Shīʿī doctrine that relies on traditional transmitted sources from the imams,

[150] Ibn Kathīr goes on to elaborate on this first generation of companions and includes the 'ocean of knowledge (*al-ḥibr al-baḥr*)' and the interpreter *par excellence* (*tarjumān*) of the Qurʾān, Ibn ʿAbbās, citing several traditions that confirm the conferral of this honour on him. Ibn Kathīr, *Tafsīr*.

[151] Sometimes he appears under the title Muḥsin al-Kāshānī and sometimes under Fayḍ al-Kāshānī, while it is also worth searching under Muḥammad Muḥsin; Kāshānī is also sometimes shortened to al-Kāshī. Given the several permutations of his name, we have chosen the form Muḥsin al-Fayḍ al-Kāshānī.

[152] Most of the biographical details on Muḥsin al-Fayḍ have been taken from the extensive introduction to the *tafsīr* written by its editor, al-Sayyid Muḥsin al-Husaynī al-Amīnī. See Muḥsin al-Fayḍ al-Kāshānī, *al-Ṣāfī*, I, 11–24.

[153] On whom see Sajjad H. Rizvi, *Mullā Ṣadrā Shīrāzī: His Life and Works and the Sources for Safavid Philosophy* (Oxford, Oxford University Press for the University of Manchester, 2007); idem, *Mulla Sadra and Metaphysics: Modulation of Being* (Abingdon, Routledge, 2009); also see Jari Kaukua, 'Illumination', *EI*[3].

in contrast with the Uṣūlī practice of relying on the sources of interpretation to reformulate law. We note that it is, however, important to exercise caution in using the terms Uṣūlī and Akhbārī, which are polemical terms in some ways akin to the terms *tafsīr bi'l-ra'y* (exegesis according to opinion) and *tafsīr bi'l-ma'thūr* (exegesis according to received interpretation), which many modern scholars have questioned in practice.[154] There is even some controversy about Muḥsin al-Fayḍ's allegiances in this regard, especially when one consults Baḥrānī's biography of him; however, others disputed that there was any question over his alliances.

Muḥsin al-Fayḍ opens his commentary with a passage asserting the primacy of the Prophet's family as sources of knowledge and understanding of the Qur'ān, and lists the types of knowledge contained within the Book. This list is reminiscent of many other authors, including Sunnī authors; but his view is that the truth of these matters cannot be discerned without recourse to the true sources of knowledge, the imams:

> This, my brothers, is in response to what you have requested of me, with regard to the exegesis of the Qur'ān and what has reached us from our infallible (*ma'ṣūm*) imams [. . .] Now, even though the majority of the commentators have plenty to say about the meaning of the Qur'ān, not one of them provides any authority for it (*sulṭān*), and that is because the Qur'ān contains what is abrogating and abrogated (*nāsikh wa'l-mansūkh*), what is unequivocal and equivocal (*muḥkam wa-mutashābih*), what is specific and general (*khāṣṣ wa-'āmm*), what is clarifying and ambiguous (*mubayyan wa-mubham*), what is discrete and contiguous (*maqṭū' wa-mawṣūl*), what are prescriptions and rulings (*farā'iḍ wa-aḥkām*), what is recommended practice and proper etiquette (*sunan wa-ādāb*), what is permitted and forbidden (*ḥalāl wa-ḥarām*), what is resolved upon and where there is licence (*'azīm wa-rukhṣa*), what is exoteric and esoteric (*ẓāhir wa-bāṭin*), what is a limit and a lookout point (*ḥadd wa-maṭla'*), and only the one in whose house this has been sent down would know how to discern these things. Whatever does not issue from that house has no support, and that is what is narrated on the authority of the Prophet (*ṣl'm*), 'Whoever interprets the Qur'ān using his opinion (*ra'y*) and hits upon the truth, verily he has erred (*akhṭa'*).'[155]

There then follows an extensive polemic against the unreliability of Sunnī sources for Qur'ānic exegesis, which serves as an anticipated counterpart for

[154] On the Akhbārīs, see Robert Gleave, *Scripturalist Islam: The History and Doctrines of the Akhbārī Shī'ī School* (Leiden, Brill, 2007); idem, 'Akhbāriyya and Uṣūliyya', *EI*^{3}, where he identifies these as 'polemical internal labels'.

[155] Muḥsin al-Fayḍ, *al-Ṣāfī*, I, 45.

Muḥsin al-Fayḍ's restriction of the Qur'ān's interpretive prerogative to the family of the Prophet and the Ḥuṣaynid lineage. As he himself states, despite the proliferation by his time of commentaries, including Shīʿī ones, not one had done justice to the exegetical content of the Akhbārī tradition, either because these materials have not been verified (via *isnāds*), or they have nor been 'properly connected' (*rabṭ*) to the relevant verses of the Qur'ān in organisational terms. His goal is explicitly to produce such a remedial exegetical work, and he proceeds to elaborate on twelve methodological premises that underpin his commentary, including[156] refutations of several hermeneutical positions with regard to the Qur'ān's status, the relationship of the Prophet's family to the Qur'ān, the occasions for the Qur'ānic revelation, and, *inter alia*, the fourfold theory of hermeneutical levels (*ẓāhir, bāṭin, ḥadd, maṭlaʿ*).[157] His commentary proper is prefaced by a brief exegetical analysis of the standard apotropaic formula used to commence recitation, 'I seek refuge with God from the accursed Satan' (*aʿūdhu bi'llāhi min al-shayṭān al-rajīm*), before proceeding into *sūrat al-Fātiḥa*.

Ismāʿīl Ḥaqqī Burūsawī (or Bursawī) (d. 1137/1725)

Shaykh Abū'l-Fidā' Ismāʿīl b. Muṣṭafā Burūsawī Uskudarī, one of the foremost Ottoman mystics, poets and erudites, was born in Aydos (Aitos, present-day Bulgaria) near Edirne in 1063/1652.[158] After completing his foundational studies in Edirne, he moved to the capital Istanbul in 1084/1673, where Shaykh ʿUthmān Faḍlī initiated him into the Jilvatiyya Sufi order.[159] There he developed an interest in Persian literature that would mark his later literary output, most noticeably in his commentary on the *Mathnawī* of Rūmī entitled *Rūḥ al-Mathnawī*. In 1086/1675, Shaykh ʿUthmān sent him to Skopje (in what was then Bosnia, now Macedonia) to set up a Jilvatī *tekke*.

[156] Ibid., 50.

[157] On this fourfold approach (*historia, allegoria, tropologia* and *anagogia*), see most recently Keeler's note in *Sufi Hermeneutics*, pp. 71ff., esp. n. 13; readers wishing to revisit this fourfold approach, as it derived from Judaeo-Christian exegesis, might see Gerhard Böwering, 'The Scriptural "Senses" in Medieval Ṣūfī Qur'an Exegesis' in *With Reverence for the Word*, ed. Jane Dammen McAuliffe *et al.* (Oxford, Oxford University Press, 2003), 346–365, as well as Claude Gilliot, 'Exegesis of the Qur'ān: Classical and Medieval', *EQ*, II, 100–124, and much earlier, Wansbrough's *Quranic Studies*, esp. 242–6.

[158] For introductions to his biography, see Tahsin Yazici, 'Esmāʿīl Ḥaqqī Borsavī', *EIr*, VIII, 627; G. Kut, 'Ismāʿīl Ḥaḳḳī', *EI*², IV, 191–2; Theodor Menzel, 'Ismail Hakki', *IA*, V, 1114–15; *GAL*, II, 440; *GAL*-S II, 652–3; Mehmet Ali Ayni, *Ismaïl Hakki, philosophe mystique, 1653–1725* (Paris, Paul Geuthner, 1933).

[159] Cf. Abdulbaki Gölpinarli, 'Djilwatiyya', *EI*², II, 542–3.

Encouraged by his shaykh, he began composing sermons and stayed on preaching for six years. He then moved to Bursa where he remained until his death in 1137/1725. A prolific preacher and writer (he composed over one hundred works in Turkish and Arabic), he was a true Ottoman man of letters, versed in a variety of disciplines. Apart from other commentaries on the verses of the classics of Persian Sufism, he wrote a history of his Sufi order, works of homiletics, collections of sermons and a major work on Sufi metaphysics entitled *Kanz-i makhfī* (*The Hidden Treasure*). Many of his works are available in autograph copies in his famous *tekke* in Bursa.

His commentary on the *Mathnawī* aside, his most lasting contribution to scholarship was his major Sufi commentary on the Qur'ān in Arabic, *Rūḥ al-bayān*.[160] He claims in his poem (composed in *saj*ʿ) that his commentary was inspired and sustained by the teaching of his shaykh:

> The great scholar, the authority of his time and foremost of his age, the proof of God to His creation through his knowledge and his mystical intuition, the dawning light of (divine) providence and support, the heir of the mysteries of realised virtues, the contemplator of the (divine) mystery and the renewer of the second millennium, treasury of lordly inspiration, the shaykh of noble lineage named Ibn ʿAffān [ʿUthmān] of Constantinople.[161]

A sustained and original contemplation of the divine discourse, his exegesis is marked by the influence of the school of Ibn ʿArabī (d. 638/1240) and includes copious poetic *shawāhid* from the classics of Persian Sufism. His Sufi affiliations are indicated not only by these verses but also by his recourse to some of the major Sufi commentaries and works available to him, such as the *Rawḥ al-arwāḥ* of Aḥmad Samʿānī (d. 534/1140), the *al-Maqṣad al-asnā fī maʿānī asmā' Allāh al-ḥusnā* of al-Ghazālī (d. 505/1111) on the divine names, and the famous and as yet still unpublished *al-Ta'wīlāt al-Najmiyya*, a major compendium of commentary from the tradition of the Kubrawiyya Sufi order.[162] His

160 In this volume, we mostly rely on the following edition, though we have also had recourse to other editions: Ismāʿīl Ḥaqqī al-Burūsawī (d. 1137/1725), *Rūḥ al-bayān fī tafsīr al-Qur'ān*, ed. ʿAbd al-Laṭīf Ḥasan ʿAbd al-Raḥmān, 10 vols. (Beirut, Dār al-Kutub al-ʿIlmiyya, 2003).

161 Ibid., I, 2.

162 This cycle of commentaries is attributed to Najm al-Dīn Kubrā (d. 618/1221), Najm al-Dīn Dāyā Rāzī (d. 654/1256) and ʿAlā' al-Dawla Simnānī (d. 736/1326). See Fritz Meier, 'Stambuler Handschriften dreier persischer Mystiker: ʿAin al-quḍāt al-Hamadānī, Nağm ad-dīn al-Kubrā, Nağm ad-dīn ad-Dāja', *Der Islam* 24 (1937), 1–39; Süleyman Ateş, 'Üç müfessir bir tefsir', *Ankara Üniversitesi İlahiyat Fakültesi Dergisi* 18 (1970), 85–104; Elias, *The Throne Carrier of God*, 203–12; Henry Corbin, *The Man of Light in Iranian Sufism*, tr. Nancy Pearson (Boulder, CO, Shambala, 1978) (orig. pub. as *L'Homme de lumière dans le soufisme iranien*, Paris, Librairie de Médicis, 1971), 61–131; William Shpall, 'A Note on Najm al-Dīn al-Rāzī and the *Baḥr al-ḥaqā'iq*', *Folia Orientalia* 22 (1981–4), 69–80.

Ottoman context is illustrated through his use of texts commonly used in his time, such as the *ḥadīth* compendium of al-Sakhāwī (d. 902/1497) known as *al-Maqāṣid al-ḥasana*,[163] and the Qurʾānic commentary of the Ottoman jurist Muḥyī al-Dīn Shaykhzāda (d. 951/1544), which is a *marginalia* on the famous Ashʿarī commentary *Anwār al-tanzīl* of al-Bayḍāwī.[164]

As the name indicates, his approach is to elicit the spirit, the essential message of the Qurʾān and its reality. He describes his method as the drawing out of meaning and sense from words, particles and letters, and an attempt to enunciate the (mystical) wisdom and subtle allusions (*maʿārif wa laṭāʾif*) that he had learnt from his experience.[165] The ground of his interpretations and hermeneutics of the text is his own mystical experience as a major Jilvatī shaykh. The work has been edited in ten volumes and is mainly composed in Arabic, with copious quotations of Persian poetry and prose and some sentences in Ottoman Turkish.

Muḥammad ʿAbduh (d. 1323/1905) and Muḥammad Rashīd Riḍā (d. 1354/1935)

The co-authors of the work *Tafsīr al-manār*, Muḥammad ʿAbduh (d. 1323/1905)[166] and his student, Muḥammad Rashīd Riḍā (d. 1354/1935),[167]

163 Muḥammad b. ʿAbd al-Raḥmān al-Sakhāwī (d. 902/1497), *al-Maqāṣid al-ḥasana fī bayān kathīr min al-aḥādīth al-mushtahira ʿalāʾl-alsina*, ed. ʿAbd Allāh Muḥammad al-Ṣiddīq (Beirut, Dār al-Kutub al-ʿIlmiyya, 1979).

164 Muḥyī al-Dīn Muḥammad b. Muṣṭafā Shaykhzāda (d. *c.* 951/1544), *Ḥāshiyat Muḥyī al-Dīn Shaykhzāda ʿalā tafsīr al-qāḍī al-Bayḍāwī*, ed. Muḥammad ʿAbd al-Qādir Shāhīn, 8 vols. (Beirut, Dār al-Kutub al-ʿIlmiyya, 1999).

165 Burūsawī, *Rūḥ al-bayān*, I, 2. The remainder of the *dībāja* is taken up with an explanation of 'seeking refuge in God' (*istiʿādha*) and the *basmala*.

166 The edition we draw upon in this volume, in addition to others, is Muḥammad ʿAbduh (d. 1905) and Muḥammad Rashīd Riḍā (d. 1935), *Tafsīr al-Qurʾān al-ḥakīm al-mashhūr bi-tafsīr al-manār*, ed. Ibrāhīm Shams al-Dīn, 12 vols. (Beirut, Dār al-Kutub al-ʿIlmiyya, 1999). On ʿAbduh, see Johanna Pink, "Abduh, Muḥammad', *EQ*; Muḥammad Rashīd Riḍā, *Taʾrīkh al-Ustādh al-Imām al-Shaykh Muḥammad ʿAbduh*, 3 vols. (Cairo, Maṭbaʿat al-Manār, 1906–31). See also Kenneth Cragg, 'Abduh, Muḥammad', *OEMIW*, 11–12; Joseph Schacht, 'Muḥammad ʿAbduh', *EI*², VII, 418–20.

167 On Riḍā, see Johanna Pink, 'Riḍā, Rashīd', *EQ*, see also Ḥabīb al-Sāmarrāʾī, 'Rashīd Riḍā al-mufassir' (Unpublished PhD dissertation, al-Azhar University, Cairo, 1978); Aḥmad Fahd Barakāt al-Shawābika, *Muḥammad Rashīd Riḍā wa dawruhu fīʾl-ḥayāt al-fikriyya waʾl-siyāsiyya* (Amman, Dār ʿAmmār, 1989); Emad Eldin Shahin, 'Rashīd Riḍā, Muḥammad', *OEMIW*, III, 410–12; W. Ende, 'Rashīd Riḍā', *EI*², VIII, 446–8; Khayr al-Dīn al-Ziriklī, *al-Aʿlām: Qāmūs tarājim li-ashhar al-rijāl waʾl-nisāʾ min al-ʿArab waʾl-mustaʿribīn waʾl-mustashriqīn*, 4th edn, 10 vols. (Beirut, Dār al-ʿIlm liʾl-Malāyīn, 1979), VI, 361–2; ʿUmar Riḍā Kaḥḥāla, *Muʿjam al-muʾallifīn: Tarājim muṣannifī al-kutub al-ʿArabiyya*, 15 vols. (Damascus, al-Maktaba al-ʿArabiyya fī Dimashq, 1376–81/1957–61), IX, 310–12.

were associated with an organisation and an intellectual movement called *al-Manār* (the guiding light), which is also the name they gave to their Qurʾānic commentary.[168] The *Manār* movement emphasised the need to reject differences among Sunnī Muslims based on legal doctrinal affiliation (*madhhab*), to narrow differences between Sunnīs and Shīʿīs, and to reconcile differences among the followers of the three Abrahamic faiths (Judaism, Christianity and Islam). Most importantly, it attempted to provide a programme of reform and renewal coupled with a modernising, scientific and rationalising reading of the divine word.[169]

Muḥammad ʿAbduh was born into a peasant family in Lower Egypt in 1849. He trained at the local Qurʾān school and became associated with the popular Sufism of the Shādhiliyya order prevalent in the region. Moving to study at the premier traditionalist centre in Cairo, al-Azhar, he gained a solid grounding in traditional Sunnī theology, logic and exegesis. In Cairo, he came into contact with the famous Islamic modernist and reformer Sayyid Jamāl al-Dīn Afghānī (Asadābādī)[170] and espoused a programme of theological renewal, fresh revival of legal and ethical norms, and a rejection of unquestioning imitation of established conventions (*taqlīd*). Due to his association with political radicalism, he was exiled between 1882 and 1888, which gave him an opportunity to travel around the Muslim world and even to Paris. This allowed him time to attempt a new diagnosis of what he considered to be a malaise affecting the Muslim consciousness while living under colonial states. During this period, he wrote some important works on his philosophy and the technical tools of thought that he considered to be important for a revival of Islamic thought.[171]

[168] Cf. Fazlur Rahman, *Islam and Modernity: Transformation of an Intellectual Tradition* (Chicago, IL, University of Chicago Press, 1982), esp. ch. 2; Albert Hourani, *Arabic Thought in the Liberal Age, 1798–1939* (Cambridge, Cambridge University Press, 1983); David Commins, *Islamic Reform: Politics and Social Change in Late Ottoman Syria* (New York, Oxford University Press, 1990).

[169] On the commentary, see Marco Brandl, 'Reading the Qurʾān in the Light of al-Manār' (Unpublished PhD dissertation, Oxford University, 2019); Hourani, *Arabic Thought*, 222–44; Jacques Jomier, *Le commentaire coranique du Manâr; tendances modernes de l'éxegèse coranique en Égypte* (Paris, G.-P. Maisonneuve, 1954); Maʿrifat, *Tafsīr*, II, 454–65.

[170] Nikki Keddie, *An Islamic Response to Imperialism: Political and Religious Writings of Sayyid Jamāl ad-Dīn 'al-Afghānī'* (Berkeley, University of California Press, 1968); eadem, *Sayyid Jamāl ad-Dīn 'al-Afghānī': A Political Biography* (Berkeley, University of California Press, 1972); eadem, 'Afghānī, Jamāl al-Dīn al-', *OEMIW*, I, 23–7; Aṣghar Mahdawī and Iraj Afshar, eds., *Majmūʿa-yi asnād wa madārik-i chap-nashūda dar bāra-yi Sayyid Jamāl al-Dīn mashhūr bi-Afghānī/Documents inédits concernant Seyyed Jamāl al-Dīn Afghānī* (Tehran, Dānishgāh-i Tehran; Institut Français de Recherches en Iran, 1342 Sh./1963).

[171] For example, his translation of Afghānī's *Risāla fi'l-radd ʿalā'l-dahriyyīn* came out in 1886, and his philological commentaries on the *Nahj al-Balāgha* in 1885 and the *Maqāmāt* of al-Hamadhānī in 1889.

Muḥammad ʿAbduh's most important theological work was his *Risālat al-tawḥīd* (*Epistle on the Divine Unity*), of which there were two editions: an earlier so-called Neo-Muʿtazilī[172] edition and a later reformist and revivalist Salafī one.[173] As for the *Manār* commentary, he initiated it with his associate Riḍā, who joined him in Cairo in 1897, with the purpose of bringing the rationalised word of God to believers, thereby creating an impetus to action and reform. The journal *al-Manār*, their main political and social mouthpiece, began publication in 1898.[174] Because of ʿAbduh's intellectual leanings toward the opinions of the Muʿtazila, he was considered an heir to this medieval rationalist school. Since most Muslim theologians have had reservations about the views of the Muʿtazila and the language which they use when discussing God, some more traditionally minded scholars have regarded this Muʿtazilī influence as an intellectual flaw in ʿAbduh's philosophy.[175]

Muḥammad Rashīd Riḍā was born in Qalamūn, near Tripoli in Syria, in 1865 to a family that claimed descent from the Prophet Muḥammad. Like ʿAbduh he had an early affiliation with a Sufi order, in his case the Naqshbandiyya, but later in life he became hostile to and critical of Sufism. He moved to Cairo to head the programme of reform with ʿAbduh,[176] and later travelled extensively in search of support for his attempt to weld Islam and modernity: he emphasised the need to apply fresh reasoning (*ijtihād*) in Islamic law and in the arena of socio-political life. After the dissolution of the Ottoman caliphate, he wrote a seminal work on leadership in Muslim society, *al-Khilāfa aw al-imāma al-ʿuẓmā*. In this treatise he proposed the conditions for the rightful leadership of the Muslim community, exhibiting biases in favour of the Saudi Wahhābīs and against the Shīʿa; this was a

[172] On this concept and construct in this context, see Thomas Hildebrandt, 'Waren Ǧamāl al-Dīn al-Afġānī und Muḥammad ʿAbduh Neo-Muʿtaziliten?' *Die Welt des Islams* 42 (2002), 207–62; Robert Caspar, 'Un aspect de la pensée musulmane moderne: Le renouveau du moʿtazilisme', *Mélanges de l'Institut Dominicain d'études orientales du Caire* 4 (1957), 141–202; Detlev Khalid, 'Some Aspects of Neo-Muʿtazilism', *Islamic Studies* (Islamabad) 8 (1969), 319–47.

[173] See Isḥāq Musa'ad and Kenneth Cragg, tr., *The Theology of Unity: The First Translation of a Work by the Father of 20th Century Muslim Thought* [translation of Muḥammad ʿAbduh's *Risālat al-Tawḥīd*] (London, Allen and Unwin, 1966).

[174] Cf. Malcolm Kerr, *Islamic Reform: The Political and Legal Theories of Muḥammad ʿAbduh and Rashīd Riḍā* (Berkeley, University of California Press, 1966).

[175] There is some modern controversy over his Muʿtazilī affiliation, on which see Pink, ''Abduh, Muḥammad'; Hildebrandt, 'Waren Ǧamāl al-Dīn al-Afġānī und Muḥammad ʿAbduh Neo-Muʿtaziliten?' For general information about the Muʿtazila and the question of Muʿtazilī affiliation and interpretation in the modern period, see Richard C. Martin *et al.*, *Defenders of Reason in Islam: Muʿtazilism from Medieval School to Modern Symbol* (Oxford, Oneworld, 1997).

[176] On his relations with the movement, see Assad Nimer Busool, 'Shaykh Muḥammad Rashīd Riḍā's Relations with Jamāl al-Dīn Afghānī and Muḥammad ʿAbduh', *Muslim World* 66 (1976), 272–86.

reversal of his earlier conciliatory stance during the period of his association with ʿAbduh.[177] A respected exegete and jurist, his works remain popular.[178]

ʿAbduh, as the teacher, contributed to the making of the *Manār* commentary by giving lectures in Qurʾānic exegesis (*tafsīr*) from Q. 1 to Q. 4:125, which were published in the journal *al-Manār*. Riḍā, as his student, organised these lectures, abridging parts of them, expanding upon other parts, and adding considerably to the content in certain places. In fact, the commentary *al-Manār* was only started by Riḍā after ʿAbduh's death, and includes much that is exclusively Riḍā's; he continued from Q. 4:125 to Q. 12:107 apparently without any input from ʿAbduh.[179] Thus some modern scholars would question the attribution of ʿAbduh as an author at all. However, Riḍā does present ʿAbduh's views, clearly marking them with phrases such as 'the teacher-imam said'. *Al-Manār* is an incomplete commentary on the Qurʾān, covering only two-fifths of the text (the first twelve parts out of the total thirty) and ending with Q. 12:107. The book appeared in print twenty-six years after ʿAbduh's death and was published posthumously by the press that carried the same name: *al-Manār*. This commentary remains one of the most widely read in the Arab Muslim world.

Al-Manār has a clear agenda of social reform, which manifests in direct calls for social changes, in support of scientific advancement and against the entrenched authority of the scholars (*ʿulamāʾ*); but this reforming agenda has a significant theological dimension. This theological aspect is apparent in the way that the authors address the relationship between divine revelation and rationality, science and the natural world. From the *Manār* perspective, both the divine text and the reality in which humans live (manifested through natural phenomena, science and rational endeavour) are authoritative and harmonious with one another. Although some people may believe that text and reality contradict each other, such apparent contradictions can occur only due to errors in the interpretation of the text, reality, or both. According to Riḍā/ʿAbduh, when the text is silent regarding what can be known about reality (through science or intellectual endeavour), humans should assume that such 'knowledge' is approved by the text; when the text

[177] Henri Laoust, *Le califat dans la doctrine de Rašīd Riḍā*: Traduction annotée d'*al-Ḫilafa au al-Imama al-ʿuẓmā* (Le Califat ou l'Imāma suprême) (Beirut, Institut Français de Damas, 1938); Hamid Enayat, *Modern Islamic Political Thought* (Austin, University of Texas Press, 1982).

[178] His collected *responsa* have been published; see Muḥammad Rashīd Riḍā (d. 1935), *Fatāwā*, ed. Ṣalāḥ al-Dīn al-Munajjid and Yūsuf Khūrī, 6 vols. (Beirut, Dār al-Kitāb al-Jadīd, 1970).

[179] Pink, in both 'ʿAbduh, Muḥammad' and 'Riḍā, Rashīd' describes the extent of ʿAbduh's involvement in the final published *Manār*.

speaks about what cannot be established through science or the human intellect, the text must be accepted.[180] Once again, only when text and reality seem to be in contradiction with one another should the reader suspend judgment about the text's message. It thus becomes apparent in the *Manār* that a human being's highest goal is to fulfil God's will by leading an active and engaged life, learning about the workings of the world, and interpreting His word in the light of such knowledge and experience. This human capacity represents a divine trust, which, coupled with the freedom that allows choice of belief and action in this life, constitute the foundation for human responsibility.

Overall, two concepts are central in the *Manār* commentary: the concept of divinely designed cosmological norms (*sunan kawniyya*) and the concept of divinely designed social norms (*sunan ijtimāʿiyya*). Divinely designed cosmological norms are the laws by which God has organised the universe (including all physical laws discernable by human beings). Divinely designed cosmological norms create order and consistency in nature and the created world. Human beings must recognise that these cosmological norms have come from God and assume no contradiction between them and God's guidance through His prophets (sc. revelation). Divinely designed social norms refer to observed patterns of relationship and behaviour between human beings (e.g. social, cultural and political), and are a direct result of human beings' application of the freedom of choice with which God has endowed them. From the *Manār* perspective, this human freedom (regarded as consistent with both human autonomy and human responsibility) should be neither exaggerated so as to eclipse its divine origin (atheism or agnosticism) nor denied (determinism). Just as humans are permitted to enjoy their freedom, they must use it to choose what will ultimately be most beneficial for their souls in this life and the next.

Sayyid Muḥammad Ḥusayn Faḍl Allāh (d. 2010)

A Lebanese Shīʿī jurist trained in the seminary of Najaf, Sayyid Muḥammad Ḥusayn Faḍl Allāh was born in 1935 in Najaf, the son of a seminarian from

[180] ʿAbduh speaks extensively about the relationship between reason and revelation in his *Risālat al-tawḥīd*, for a brief summary of which see Pink, "Abduh, Muḥammad'; the discussion of evolution in ch. 1 of this volume is an example of how he reconciles science and reason with revelation. Notable in this regard is Riḍā's engagement with tradition, which in some sense seems to be an attempt to reconcile ʿAbduh's more radical views with the socially accepted consensus among the *ʿulamā*ʾ.

the southern Lebanese town of ʿAynātā, near Bint Jubayl.[181] He studied with the foremost Shīʿī *ʿulamāʾ*, including the traditionalist Sayyid Abūʾl-Qāsim al-Khūʾī (d. 1992)[182] and the reforming political thinker and philosopher, Sayyid Muḥammad Bāqir al-Ṣadr (exec. 1980).[183] Al-Ṣadr's ideas on social and intellectual reform, as well as on a programme for the political reorientation of Muslim society, were widely influential.[184] Once back in Lebanon, Faḍl Allāh established himself as a leader-figure in the impoverished Shīʿī southern suburbs of Beirut. After the Iranian revolution and with the rise of Ḥizbullāh,[185] he became a major Shīʿī figure, especially after Ayatollah Khomeini recognised him as a *marjaʿ al-taqlīd* (source of imitation) in 1986.[186]

[181] On him, see, most recently, Bianca Speidel, *Islam as Power: Shiʿi Revivalism in the Oeuvre of Muḥammad Ḥusayn Faḍlallāh* (Abingdon, Routledge, 2021). Also see Olivier Carré, 'Faḍlallāh, Muḥammad Ḥusayn', *OEMIW*, I, 453–6; Lara Deeb, 'Sayyid Muhammad Husayn Fadlallah and Lebanese Shiʿi Youth', *Journal of Shiʿa Islamic Studies* 3.1 (2010), 405–26; Chibli Mallat, *The Renewal of Islamic Law: Muhammad Baqer as-Sadr, Najaf and the Shiʿi International* (Cambridge, Cambridge University Press, 1993); and also his website http://www.bayynat.org. For a view of Faḍl Allāh as an Islamic feminist, see Sophie Chamas, 'Sayyid Muhammad Hussein Fadlallah: Muslim Cleric and Islamic Feminist', *Journal of Alternative Perspectives in Social Sciences* 1.2 (2009), 246–57.

[182] For brief details on him, see Joyce N. Wiley, 'Khoʾi, Aboʾl-Qasim', *OEMIW*, II, 423; see Abdulaziz Sachedina, tr., *The Prolegomena to the Qurʾān* (New York, Oxford University Press, 1998), 3–9.

[183] Mallat, *The Renewal of Islamic Law*; Muḥammad al-Ḥusaynī, *al-Imām al-shahīd al-sayyid Muḥammad Bāqir al-Ṣadr: Dirāsa fī sīratihi wa manhajihi* (Beirut, Dār al-Furāt, 1989); Muḥammad Riḍā al-Nuʿmānī, *al-Shahīd al-Ṣadr: Sanawāt al-miḥna wa-ayyām al-ḥiṣār* (Beirut, Dār al-Hādī, 1997); ʿĀdil Raʾūf, *Muḥammad Bāqir al-Ṣadr bayna diktātūriyyatayn* (Damascus, Markaz al-ʿIrāqī liʾl-Iʿlām waʾl-Dirāsāt, 2001); Talib M. Aziz, 'The Islamic Political Theory of Muhammad Baqir al-Sadr of Iraq' (Unpublished PhD dissertation, University of Utah, 1991); John Walbridge, 'Muhammad Baqir al-Sadr: The Search for New Foundations' in *The Most Learned of the Shiʿa: The Institution of the Marjaʿ Taqlid*, ed. Linda S. Walbridge (New York, Oxford University Press, 2001), 131–9.

[184] Ibrahim M. Abu-Rabiʿ, *Intellectual Origins of Islamic Resurgence in the Modern Arab World* (Albany, State University of New York Press, 1996), 220–47.

[185] On this group, see Eitan Azani, *Hezbollah: The Story of the Party of God, from Revolution to Institutionalization* (New York, Palgrave MacMillan, 2009); Matthew Levitt, *Hezbollah: The Global Footprint of Lebanon's Party of God* (Washington, DC, Georgetown University Press, 2015); Angus Norton, *Hezbollah: A Short History* (Princeton, NJ, Princeton University Press, 2014); Amal Saad-Ghorayeb, *Hizbu'llah: Politics and Religion* (London, Pluto Press, 2002).

[186] On this concept, see Norman Calder, 'Marjaʿ al-taqlīd', *OEMIW*, III, 45–8; Jean Calmard, 'Mard̲j̲aʿ-i tak̲līd', *EI*², VI, 548–56 (which provides a useful list of references); Ahmed Kazemi Mousavi, *Religious Authority in Shiʿite Islam: From the Office of Mufti to the Institution of Marjaʿ* (Kuala Lumpur, International Institute of Islamic Thought and Civilization, 1996); Linda S. Walbridge, ed., *The Most Learned of the Shiʿa: The Institution of the Marjaʿ Taqlīd* (Oxford, Oxford University Press, 2001). Specifically on the *marjaʿiyya* of Faḍl Allāh, see Jaʿfar al-Baḥrānī, *Marjaʿiyyat al-marḥala wa ghubār al-taghyīr liʾl-Sayyid Muḥammad Faḍl Allāh* (Beirut, Dār al-Amīr, 1998); Sayyid Ḥusayn al-Shāmī, *al-Marjaʿiyya al-dīniyya min al-dhāt ilāʾl-muʾassasa* (London, Dar al-Islam Foundation, 1999); Talib M. Azīz, 'Fadlallah and the Remaking of the *Marjaʿiya*' in *The Most Learned of the Shiʿa*, ed. Linda S. Walbridge (New York, Oxford University Press, 2001), 205–15.

Consonant with much reformist Islamist thinking, his writing appeals to a broad cross-section of people. He had written apologetic works on jihad,[187] addressed specific issues of Muslim youth and women, and responded to the needs of Muslims living in the West through a new genre of writing known as *fiqh al-mughtaribīn* (law for those living in the West).[188] His writings on women changed somewhat through time, from his early work in *Min waḥy al-Qurʾān*, translated in this volume, to his book on women and their rights. However, his advocacy for women's rights remained somewhat limited and he never echoed the calls of Muḥammad Jawād Maghniyya for women to be recognised as leaders in Islam, or for them to have equal testimony to men's.

His commentary originated in study circles (*ḥalaqāt*) that he gave in Beirut in the 1970s.[189] These were refined and first printed in 1979. He subsequently supplemented and edited the work. The latest edition came out in 1998 in twenty-four volumes. The style is markedly different from that of medieval works of *tafsīr*, which reflects his desire to appeal to a wider audience (much like the authors of *al-Manār*). He includes lengthy excurses on issues of social importance, such as the status of women (see, for example, his introduction to *sūrat al-Nisāʾ*, in Chapter 1 of this volume).

The commentary is marked by a desire to investigate the existential import of the divine word and communicate its meaning to Muslims living in modern-day Lebanon. Given the communal violence and warfare of recent history, his discourse is noticeably ecumenical in comparison with other Muslim positions,[190] engaging as it does in a meaningful and substantial dialogue with Christians, the other major faith community in Lebanon. This dialogue emerges explicitly in his commentary, especially that on *sūrat Maryam*.[191] It is this engagement, along with his apparent liberalism in trad-

[187] See Muhammad Husayn Faḍl Allāh, *Kitāb al-Jihād* (Beirut, Dār al-Malāk, 1996).

[188] See Muhammad Husayn Faḍl Allāh, *Fiqh al-ḥayāt* (Beirut, Muʾassasat al-ʿĀrif, 1997); idem, *Dunyā al-marʾa* (Beirut, Dār al-Malāk, 1997); idem, *Dunyā al-shabāb* (Beirut, Muʾassasat al-ʿĀrif, 1997); idem, *al-Hijra waʾl-ightirāb* (Beirut, Muʾassasat al-ʿĀrif, 1999).

[189] The edition we have used in this book, in addition to others, is Muḥammad Husayn Faḍl Allāh (d. 2010), *Min waḥy al-Qurʾān*, 24 vols. (Beirut, Dār al-Malāk, 1979; repr. 1998); on Faḍl Allāh's *tafsīr*, see Maʿrifat, *Tafsīr*, II, 474–5.

[190] Muhammad Husayn Faḍl Allāh, *Aḥādīth fī qaḍāyā al-ikhtilāf waʾl-waḥda* (Beirut, Dār al-Malāk, 2000).

[191] Muhammad Husayn Faḍl Allāh, *al-ʿAlāqāt al-Islāmiyya al-Masīḥiyya: Dirāsa marjaʿiyya fīʾl-taʾrīkh waʾl-ḥāḍir waʾl-mustaqbal* (Beirut, Markaz al-Dirāsāt al-Istrātījiyya waʾl-Buḥūth waʾl-Tawthīq, 1994).

itional legal matters that explains his position as one of the foremost Arab Shīʿī leaders of the twentieth and twenty-first century.

Interviewees' biographies

Fariba Alasvand

Fariba Alasvand is a faculty member at the theoretical studies academic department in the seminary (*ḥawza*) in Qumm, specialising in women and family issues in Islam. She received her PhD from al-Zahra seminary in Qumm and has published numerous books and articles, including *A Review of the Convention on the Elimination of all Forms of Discrimination Against Women* (Management of the Hawza ʿIlmiyya of Qumm, 2004), *Women in the Sīra of the Prophet* (Akharin Payam, 2006) and *A Continuous White Line* (Qabasat Isfahan, 2017). Her most recent work is *Law and Fatwa* (2019), and her current research focuses on the nature of gender justice and theories of justice in context. Interview date: 8 June 2011.

Nasser Ghorbannia (d. 2016)

Nasser Ghorbannia was a professor in the Faculty of Law of Mofid University, Qumm, Iran, who specialised in international law and Islamic law. He is the author of *Women's Rights in Islam*. Interview date: 29 May 2011.

Mehdi Mehrizi

Mehdi Mehrizi is an associate professor in the Department of Qur'ān and *ḥadīth* in the Faculty of Law, Theology and Political Science, at Islamic Azad University in Tehran, specialising in *ḥadīth*. He is also the director of the Library of Fiqh, Fiqh Principles, and Law in Qom. He is known for his reformist views and is the author of several books and numerous articles. Interview date: 9 June 2011.

Yusuf Saanei (d. 2020)

Yusuf Saanei was a *Marjaʿ al-Taqlīd* (Grand Ayatollah), who was chairman of the Guardian Council of Iran from 1980 to 1983. He was a prominent opposition leader and reformist, well known for his view that men and women are equal in Islam, that women can lead men in prayer, and that a woman could become a *marjaʿ*. He was also known for his reformist stance on other issues, such as declaring suicide bombing and nuclear weapons illegal according to Islamic legal principles. Interview date: 13 June 2011.

Sa'diyya Shaikh

Sa'diyya Shaikh is an Associate Professor in the Department for the Study of Religions at the University of Cape Town, South Africa. Her research is situated at the intersection of Islamic Studies and Gender Studies. She has a special interest in Sufism and its implications for Islamic feminism and feminist theory. Her book *Sufi Narratives of*

Intimacy: Ibn ʿArabī, Gender and Sexuality is published by the University of North Carolina Press (2012). Interview date: 22 October 2020.

amina wadud

amina wadud is Visiting Professor at the National Islamic University Sunan Kalijaga, Yogjakarta, Indonesia and Visiting Researcher at the Starr King School for the Ministry. Her publications include *Qur'an and Woman* (Oxford, repr. 1999) and *Inside the Gender Jihad* (Oneworld, 2006). Once described as the 'rock star of Islamic feminism', she is best known for her progressive views on gender and sexuality in Islam, for which she has claimed the title the Lady Imam. Interview date: 15 October 2020.

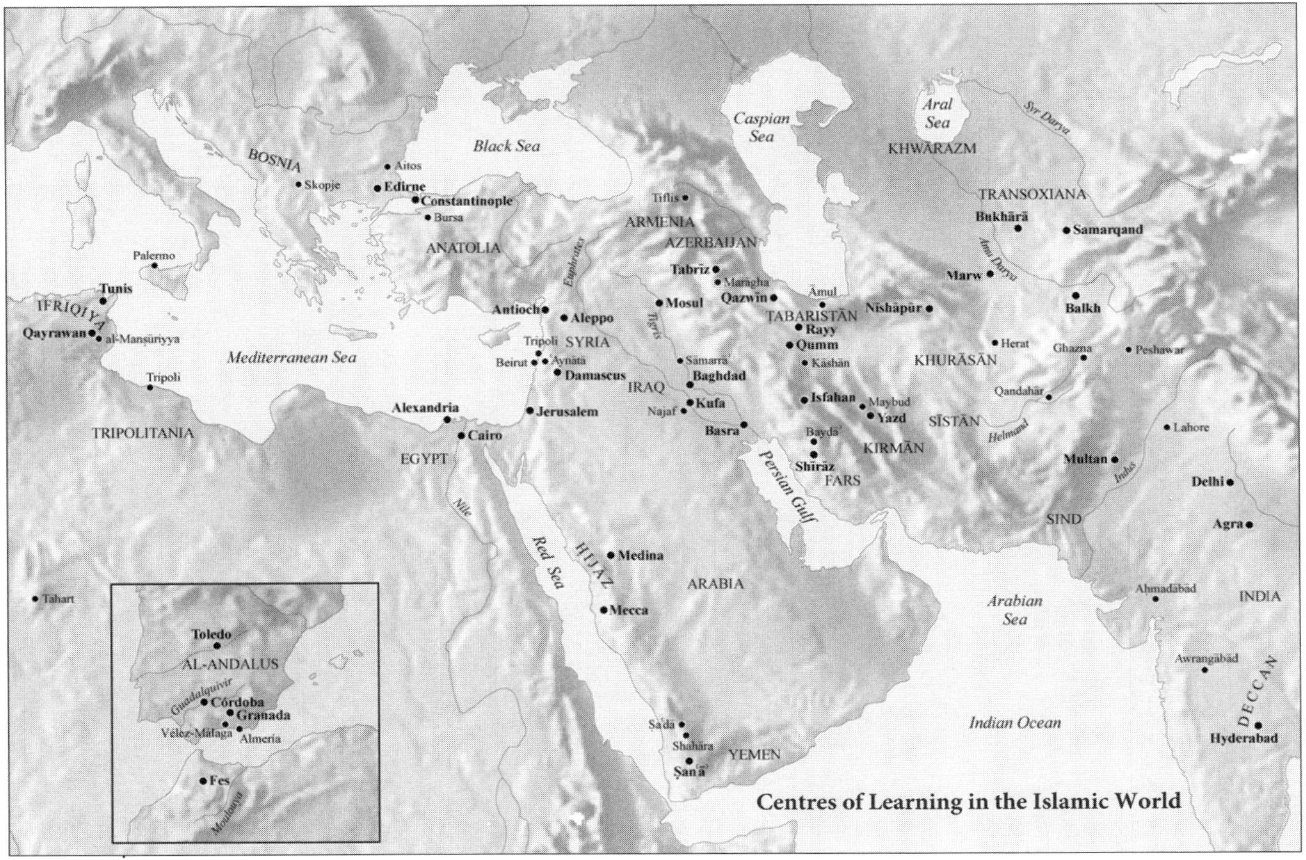

Centres of Learning in the Islamic World

يَـٰٓأَيُّهَا ٱلنَّاسُ ٱتَّقُواْ رَبَّكُمُ ٱلَّذِى خَلَقَكُم مِّن نَّفْسٍ وَٰحِدَةٍ وَخَلَقَ مِنْهَا
زَوْجَهَا وَبَثَّ مِنْهُمَا رِجَالًا كَثِيرًا وَنِسَآءً وَٱتَّقُواْ ٱللَّهَ ٱلَّذِى تَسَآءَلُونَ بِهِۦ
وَٱلْأَرْحَامَ إِنَّ ٱللَّهَ كَانَ عَلَيْكُمْ رَقِيبًا

1 Human creation
(Q. 4:1)

O people! Be wary of your Lord, who created you from a single soul, and from it created its mate, and spread forth from the two many men and women; and be wary of God by whom you petition one another, and the wombs; indeed God is Watcher over you.

Yā ayyuhā'l-nās ittaqū rabbakum alladhī khalaqakum min nafsin wāḥidatin wa-khalaqa minhā zawjahā wa-baththa minhumā rijālan kathīran wa-nisā'an wa'ttaqū Allāha alladhī tasā'alūna bihi wa'l-arḥāma inna Allāha kāna ʿalaykum raqīban

THIS VERSE refers to the foundational moment of the creation of human beings and to the resulting ties that an individual has to God, kin and all of humanity. It begins with humans being enjoined to *taqwā*, or wariness of God. This is a way of encouraging humility before the Divine, of whose power the listener is immediately reminded by the mention of human creation. In Q. 4:1, the nature of this creation is described as being *from a single soul*, from which was created *its mate*, and then from the two of them were spread forth *many men and women*. There are two main views of this initial human creation. The first is that the *single soul* is Adam and *its mate* is Eve; the second, based partly on Q. 75:36–9,[1] is that there was a primordial creation, and from that both men and women were created. Adam and his mate (Eve) are well-recognised Qur'ānic figures, and the first view is ubiquitous in the commentarial tradition.[2] After referring to the original creation and the spreading forth of *many men and women*, the verse goes on to remind people again to be wary (*w-q-y*) of God and with regard to the

[1] Q. 75:36–9 reads: [36] *Does a person (insān) suppose that he would be left without purpose?* [37] *Was he not initially a drop of discharged fluid* [38] *then a clot? He then made him a creation well-proportioned* [39] *and from that (minhu) He proceeded with the pair, the male and the female (al-unthā).*

[2] For an overview of Islamic interpretations of Eve (Ḥawwā'), see Roberto Tottoli, 'Eve', *EI*[3]; see also Cornelia Schöck, 'Adam and Eve', *EQ*, I, 23–6. There are direct linguistic connections between the Qur'ān and the Bible. In Arabic, Ādam can mean 'having a dark complexion' or it can be related to 'the surface of the earth' (*adīm*). Linguistically, it derives from the Hebrew word for 'the surface of the earth'. Ḥawwā' (Eve) is the same as the word for having a ruddy complexion; it is related to the word for 'life' (*ḥayy*) and is derived from the Hebrew term for 'living thing'. For the Biblical story, see Genesis 1:27 and 2:18–25.

womb-ties.[3] It ends with the reminder of God's watchfulness. This verse can be better understood in light of other Qur'ānic instances using the same vocabulary, which are briefly touched on in the following paragraphs.

With its focus on human creation and use of the dual form, it is reasonable to link Q. 4:1 to the Adam and Eve story. The Qur'ān tells the story of Adam and Eve in the Garden in *sūrat al-Aʿrāf* (Q. 7), and deems them the 'two parents' of humankind in Q. 7:27. Thus most of the commentators say the *single soul* is Adam, and its mate (*zawj*), Eve. Adam's creation is described in many verses and in some detail, but the creation of the *zawj* is left vague: Q. 4:1 is traditionally understood to refer to that creation, and is linked linguistically to other verses mentioning the creation of humankind *from a single soul*. In Q. 4:1, the primordial couple are characterised by their procreation of generations thereafter (*and spread forth from the two many men and women*); in other verses, references to the primordial *single soul* and *its mate* are generalised to apply to the prototypical couple. Thus Q. 7:189 refers to the creation of the *single soul* and, from it, *its mate*, while Q. 7:190 is then generalised to refer to any couple. Q. 30:21 never refers to the primordial couple at all, but rather only to the creation of all humans and pairs (*azwāj*), in the context of showing God's power as Creator.[4] Q. 7:190 and Q. 30:21 say mates were created to be a source of solace (*sakan*, *sakīna*, *sukūn*) for one another. Q. 7:189 says that the mate or pair was created so *he might find solace by her side* (*li-yaskuna ilayhā*), while Q. 30:21 says that the mates were created so that you (pl.) might *find solace by their side* (*li-taskunū ilayhā*). In Q. 75:36–9 the creation is from a drop of fluid and a clot – the verses then describe God making a creation, from which is taken male and female: [Q. 75:38–9] *He then made him a creation well-proportioned* [39] *and from that* (*minhu*) *He proceeded with the pair, the male and the female* (*al-unthā*). All of these verses indicate that there is some ambiguity about the nature of the original creation: the Qur'ān does not give details of the exact nature of this creation, and probably does not mean to give such details. Rather, such verses are best understood in the context of explaining God's creative power, which is a central theme in the Qur'ān; creation is considered as His mercy to humankind.

[3] For a brief overview of 'womb' in the Qur'ān, see Marcia Hermansen, 'Womb', *EQ*, V, 522–3.

[4] Q. 30:21 reads: *Of His signs is that He created for you mates from among yourselves* (*min anfusikum*), *that you might find solace by their side, and He ordained love and mercy between you. Indeed, in that are signs for people who are inclined to reflect.*

While the *mate* in Q. 4:1 may be Eve, the nature of the creation *from* the single soul is not specified in the text.[5] Linguistically, *from it* (*minhā*) could mean that the mate was created of the same type as the first creation, and *from it* could also mean that the mate was created from the physical substance/body of the first creation. The Qurʾānic evidence points to *from it* indicating that the second was like the first, or of the same type (cf. Q. 9:128; 16:74; 30:21). But as with many Qurʾānic stories, there is an assumption that the audience had prior knowledge of the events: the ambiguity about the mate and its creation was presumably not ambiguous at all in the Qurʾān's original milieu.

Because the story about the creation of the first woman is never told in detail in the Qurʾān, most of the commentators go well beyond what is written in the text.[6] As described below, the most popular interpretation by far was that the *mate* was Eve, created from Adam's rib, and interpreters through time have used this to say that women are creationally inferior to men. Abū Muslim al-Iṣfaḥānī (d. 322/934) is credited with the interpretation that Eve was created of the same type as Adam, and this is the view preferred by Rāzī. For the Ismāʿīlī Muʾayyad fīʾl-Dīn al-Shīrāzī, the verse has an esoteric meaning in which the single soul is the Prophet Muḥammad, who is paired with ʿAlī, his legatee (*waṣī*). In the modern period, it has been interpreted to mean that creation is from a single universal soul.

With regard to the second part of the verse, all of the commentators agree that the significance of the phrase *and the wombs* is that humans should take care to maintain their connections to their blood relatives and not to sever those connections (cf. Q. 47:22). But the grammatical construction has generated some controversy. The most common reading puts *wombs* in the accusative, meaning that *the wombs*, along with *God*, are the object of *be wary*; the believer should be wary of God and of severing the womb-ties. An alternative reading has *wombs* in the genitive, which would mean: 'be wary of God, by whom you petition one another, and the wombs, by whom you petition one another'. Most of the commentators dispute this last reading, as they deem it to be unacceptable to swear by the wombs (despite

[5] Among those who have argued for equality are amina wadud, *Qur'an and Woman*, and Rifaat Hassan, 'Equal before Allah?' *Harvard Divinity Bulletin* (The Divinity School, Harvard University) 17.2 (January–May 1987), 2–14.

[6] Catherine Bronson, 'Eve in the Formative Period of Islamic Exegesis: Intertextual Boundaries and Hermeneutic Demarcations' in *Tafsīr and Islamic Intellectual History: Exploring the Boundaries of a Genre*, ed. Andreas Görke and Johanna Pink (Oxford, Oxford University Press in association with the Institute of Ismaili Studies, 2014), 27–61; Bauer, *Gender Hierarchy*, ch. 1 and 2; Stowasser, *Women in the Qur'an, Traditions, and Interpretation*, 25–38.

many examples in the Qur'ān of other oaths, as demonstrated by Qurṭubī, for one).[7]

In the Qur'ān, the expression *the wombs* (*al-arḥām*) refers to the ties of blood kinship, as opposed to spiritual or metaphorical brotherhood or parenthood, which are referred to using other terms. Thus the second part of the verse ties in with the first: while the first explains that all humans were created from an original pairing, the second reminds humans that their wariness of God entails respecting the ties of blood kinship in the world. The final line of the verse reminds humans that God *is Watcher over* them, which encourages them to obey His bounds as they are outlined in the previous clauses. While the second part of the verse may not be obviously connected with the question of women's status, it is understood by the commentators to relate to the broader responsibilities of believers towards kin, which is then also applied to non-kin dependents (including women) in Q. 4:2.

Gendered dynamics in commentaries on Q. 4:1: A brief summary

Creation myths are often a locus for the understanding of gender relations. Sa'diyya Shaikh points out that creation myths present 'constructions of religious anthropology and gendered personhood' that are mapped onto social relations between the sexes.[8] Such a dynamic is immediately discernible in the interpretations presented in this chapter. These interpretations demonstrate the move from bare-bones textual foundations to a fully fledged defence of patriarchal social structures. The exegetes saw themselves as a part of an existing tradition, so, for instance, the early commentator Ṭabarī cites Jewish sources on the creation of Eve from Adam's rib.[9] While he does

[7] The persistence of this 'unorthodoxy' should resonate with readers familiar with the vernacular of contemporary Arabic in all of its dialects; note how common it is to swear by 'one's life' (*wa-ḥayātī*), 'your life' (*wa-ḥayātak*), 'the children's lives' (*wa-ḥayāt al-awlād*), 'the mercy due to one's deceased parents' (*wa-raḥmat wālidayk*), and how it is just as common for oaths such as the latter to provoke indignation. Students of classical or modern standard Arabic should guard against the morphological syncretism of the contemporary vernacular in the transliterations given for the examples in this note; but they should also note that this morphological phenomenon in the spoken tongue is likely as old as Arabic itself. For an accessible and comprehensive overview of the Arabic language, see Kees Versteegh, *The Arabic Language* (Edinburgh, Edinburgh University Press, 1997).

[8] Shaikh, *Sufi Narratives*, 141.

[9] While early non-Muslim Western scholarship on Islam tended to deem the Biblical content in the Qur'ān to be 'borrowings', the early Muslim authorities themselves saw the Islamic revelation as the apotheosis of an earlier scriptural tradition and therefore, for them, it was natural to draw on reliable sources from that tradition. On the idea of borrowings and for an example of an early Muslim authority who was renowned for his research into Jewish sources, see Pregill, 'Isrā'īliyyāt, Myth, and Pseudepigraphy', 215–83.

not attach any particular meaning to that creation, over time the exegetes came to suggest that the nature of the first woman's creation was derivative from man and for him (that is, from the rib and for him to find solace), and that this indicates women's creational inferiority to men.[10] In the earliest *tafsīr* works, several *ḥadīth*s were used to bolster the view of women's inferiority, by, for instance, saying that women were created 'crooked'. Later commentators elaborated on women's deficiencies in other ways: Muḥsin al-Fayḍ al-Kāshānī, for instance, said that Eve was created from a rib on the left side, and because the left is the side of material embodiment whereas the right is the side of spiritual enlightenment, women are inherently embodied while men are spiritual in nature.

Only one medieval exegete in this survey affirms that women can be spiritually better than men, and that is the aforementioned Mu'ayyad fī'l-Dīn al-Shīrāzī. Interestingly, his interpretation is not in a book of *tafsīr*, but rather in a book of sermons. This indicates that there were other views of women's nature, but that these views did not necessarily appear in the relatively conservative genre of *tafsīr*. Sa'diyya Shaikh has demonstrated that the Sufi Ibn 'Arabī, who did not write a book of *tafsīr*, in some respects overturns the gendered norms pervasive in works within that genre. For him, women are unable to reach man's level in intellect or religion because of having been incubated in man during creation.[11] However, he also argues that the Prophet loved women because he could witness the 'Real' in them,[12] and that 'There is nothing in the created universe greater in power than women.'[13] Ibn 'Arabī's understanding of gender and of women's place in the cosmos is a nuanced illustration of the complexity of discussions that occurred outside of the genre of *tafsīr* in the medieval period. Nevertheless, one should not equate such interpretations with modern feminism or ideas about women's emancipation.

Modernity has affected both conservative and reformist interpretations of Q. 4:1. While many conservatives adhere to the interpretation of Eve as created from Adam's rib, for them it does not necessarily follow that women are inferior to men. This marks a complete change from the premodern interpretations in the genre of *tafsīr*: whether one is conservative or reformist, the doctrine has transformed from near-consensus on women's creational inferiority to near-consensus on their creational equality with men.

[10] Denise Spellberg, 'Writing the Unwritten Life of the Islamic Eve: Menstruation and the Demonization of Motherhood', *International Journal of Middle East Studies* 28 (1996), 305–24.

[11] Shaikh, *Sufi Narratives*, 153. Also see the interview with her at the end of this chapter.

[12] Ibid., 177.

[13] Ibid., 182.

Contemporary authors who write works of *tafsīr* often do so to show their familiarity with tradition, and thus reformist views are not always apparent within the genre.[14] Some elements of modern reform appear in the interviews included at the end of this chapter. Two of these interviews are of Western feminist scholars, amina wadud and Sa'diyya Shaikh, while three are of scholars from Iran: Fariba Alasvand, Nasser Ghorbannia and Mehdi Mehrizi. What comes to the fore in all of these interviews is that women are no longer seen as inferior to men, by either conservative or reformist commentators. Alasvand, for instance, celebrates women's bodies, saying that breastfeeding can be considered as equal to fighting jihad. Some scholars find inspiration in medieval sources; as described above, Sa'diyya Shaikh delves into the thought of Ibn ʿArabī, which provides an alternate view to the *tafsīr* tradition. But other modern interpreters reject medieval sources. Nasser Ghorbannia, for instance, describes how one can reject *ḥadīth*s if they are not rationally plausible.[15] Rather than rely only on tradition, in his view (and that of other Shīʿī thinkers), one is obliged to use one's rational ability in order to interpret the Qurʾān.

The final part of the verse, describing the womb-tie, is understood by the commentators to refer to the importance of maintaining kinship ties, the severing of which is equated with disobedience to God. According to both medieval and modern interpretations, believers should be good and loving to their relatives, even when their relatives do not reciprocate; such emotional discipline becomes a pious disposition, and fostering kinship ties is thus a form of piety. The implicit notion of self-sacrifice for the sake of marriage and wider kinship ties is widespread, even today. Thus while this part of the verse is not overtly connected to the issue of women's status, the interpretations here are nevertheless important for understanding women's (and men's) place in kinship-based social systems, and how such social systems interact with modern notions of self, individuality, personal freedom and independence.

The question of evolution

One important question to emerge in modern interpretations of this verse is whether Adam was indeed the father of mankind or whether it is possible to

[14] Bauer, *Gender Hierarchy*; Pink, *Muslim Qurʾānic Interpretation Today.*

[15] Modern Shīʿī conservatives and Sunnīs are more likely to find ways around the *ḥadīth*s, such as, for instance, saying that the *ḥadīth*s are a 'joke' or that they were specific to a particular time and place. On the notion that such *ḥadīth*s could have been said in a joking way, see Karen Bauer, '"Traditional" Interpretations of Q. 4:34', *Comparative Islamic Studies* 2.2 (2006), 129–42.

accommodate modern theories of the development of the species, such as evolution. In the commentaries surveyed here, this issue was first brought up by the Egyptian reformist Muḥammad ʿAbduh (d. 1905). ʿAbduh was an advocate for women's rights, albeit perhaps not entirely equal rights between men and women,[16] who argued that women's downtrodden status in his society was largely due to misinterpretations of Islam. However, he did not use Q. 4:1 as an opportunity to discuss women's rights, but rather as an opportunity to defend the theory of evolution as being compatible with Islamic texts and teachings. There can be no doubt that his opinion was controversial and was not universally accepted, even among his followers. Rashīd Riḍā wrote most of the commentary *al-Manār*, which records ʿAbduh's views; in the commentary of Q. 4:1, Riḍā seems to modify this interpretation of ʿAbduh's, and to voice his own disagreement with ʿAbduh's view. Many modern Sunnī interpreters refute ʿAbduh's acceptance of evolution.[17]

Even among reformists today, some of whose views are presented in the interviews at the end of this chapter, the theory of evolution is not always considered to be fact; the term 'theory' is taken *prima facie* to mean that it is unproven as opposed to a well-substantiated and valid scientific consensus. Nevertheless, the idea of the development of the species was accepted in some form by many Iranian reformists, while conservatives (much like Christian conservatives in the West), for the most part, rejected the idea of evolution or human development.

Key terms

Nafs: soul, self or person. This term is grammatically feminine (so any adjective qualifying it must be feminine).

Raḥim/arḥām: literally, womb/wombs. This term also refers to blood kinship, and its multivalence is very much akin to that of 'blood' in English.[18] We have usually translated this term as womb or womb-tie.

Sakan: solace, tranquillity or peace of mind. This is the purpose behind the creation of human pairings (*azwāj*).

16 Anke von Kügelgen, "Abduh, Muḥammad', *EI*[3]. This article notes that ʿAbduh was against polygamy, though he did not agree with putting women in public office.

17 On ʿAbduh's views of evolution, see Marwa Elshakry, *Reading Darwin in Arabic, 1860–1950* (Chicago, IL, University of Chicago Press, 2013); Bauer, *Gender Hierarchy*, 139–52.

18 The term is usually translated as 'kin' or 'kinship'.

Taqwā: a key concept in the Qur'ān, meaning guarding one's soul (*nafs*) against sin (sc. most frequently, *ithm*, *dhanb*, *khaṭī'a*), or misdeeds (*sayyi'āt*) in general, and, hence, the possibility of God's punishment, which is what is entailed in this moral danger that is to be guarded against.[19] Some contemporary translations occasionally render *taqwā* using terms such as 'piety' and 'God-consciousness',[20] while it is more commonly translated as 'fear'.[21] Terms such as 'God-consciousness' capture one of the psychological aspects of *taqwā* but without any reflection of the lexical sense of the root (*w-q-y*). The tendency to default to a translation of *taqwā* as 'fear' in modern Qur'ān translations is largely because of the Muslim exegetical tradition, which, as we shall see, invariably glosses *taqwā* as 'fear'.[22] However, what medieval Muslim scholars took to be an implicit and fundamental valence of this term elides for the modern reader in English the significant nuances of, to borrow one scholar's phrase, the term's 'semantic field', and thus blurs the term *taqwā* with other Qur'ānic words that also connote 'fear'.[23] More significantly, what may be understood as 'righteous/pious fear', arising out of an awe-inspired reverence before an all-encompassing divine power, is considered to be a crucial pious disposition, and one to be cultivated,

[19] Rāghib, *Mufradāt*, s.v. *w-q-y*.

[20] 'God-consciousness' is, for instance, an interpretation taken by John Esposito, *The Oxford Dictionary of Islam* (Oxford, Oxford University Press, 2003).

[21] It is also a question of idiomatic convenience, since 'fear' in English offers adverbial, nominal and verbal forms without constructions begging for an explicit direct object or the clutter of prepositions. Contrast this with 'be wary of' and 'guard against', which, although more precise in terms of the Arabic, are unwieldy in the context of our prose here. Invariably, however, we find ourselves needing to draw on all of the above translations, simply because, in a given Arabic construction or passage, one of the English terms will be more faithful to a given author's usage of *taqwā*. We indicate the Arabic in parentheses in the first instance where we have chosen one of these renderings.

[22] Cf. Rāzī, *Mafātīḥ al-ghayb*. In his commentary on Q. 2:2 *hudā li'l-muttaqīn*, he discusses the richness of the use of the term *taqwā* in the Qur'ān, but recognises that its primary significance is *khashya* (fear). Significantly, for us, he cites Q. 4:1 as an example of that sense, as well as other instances, such as Q. 22:1.

[23] The roots *kh-w-f* (*khawf*) and *kh-sh-y* (*khashya*) are common enough, but even the less frequently occurring *w-j-s* (Q. 11:70; 20:67; 51:28) and *w-j-l* (Q. 8:2; 15:52–3; 22:35; 23:60) overlap, with associated meanings of apprehension, fright or alarm. Fear in the sense of 'apprehension' is one valence within the semantic range of *taqwā*, which is broader, and may, among its other valences, be contrasted with the tendency to conceit, insolence and vainglory, the central theme of the brief *sūrat al-Ḥadīd* (Q. 57) (note vv. 20 and 23 and the concluding command to *taqwā* in v. 28). For an overview of the 'moral' revolution, in the sense of re-evaluation, that is semantically expressed in binaries of opposition and by juxtaposition (as in Q. 49:13: *The noblest of you in the eyes of God is verily the most God-wary* [*inna akramakum 'inda Allāhi atqākum*]), see Toshihiko Izutsu's classic 1959 work (revised by the author in 1966 and republished in what is now a standard edition with a foreword by Charles J. Adams), *Ethico-Religious Concepts in the Qur'ān* (Montreal, McGill-Queen's University Press, 2002), esp. 52ff., 70ff.

according to the Qur'ān.[24] This is one aspect of a complex constellation of devotional pious dispositions that acknowledge God as Watcher (*raqīb*), being in awe of His omnipotence (*qadīr*) and omniscience (*ʿalīm*) while also being grateful for His graces (*dhū faḍlin ʿaẓīm*).[25]

Zawj: one of a pair, mate, spouse, or wife. The correct interpretation of this term depends on context. We sometimes defer to the nominal form of 'pair' to represent the idea of pairing inherent in the term *zawj*.

Muqātil

Although Muqātil was not considered to be a reliable transmitter by later commentators such as Ṭabarī, his interpretation is nevertheless important in that it is the oldest known complete work of *tafsīr*, and thus preserves some early opinions about the meaning of the Qur'ān; and it is clear that later interpreters use his work, though they may not admit to doing so. In the case of this verse, the opinions preserved are widespread. Muqātil begins by saying that the verse is meant to instil fear. He explains *ittaqū rabbakum* by using two synonyms that unambiguously indicate that God used the term *ittaqū* to instil fear in the believer (*khawf*, *khashya*).

Like all subsequent medieval exegetes writing in the genre of *tafsīr*, Muqātil goes on to explain that the *single soul* is Adam and *its mate* is Eve. He explains that the name Eve (Ḥawwā') originates in the word for life (*ḥayy*), because Eve was created from a living being. For him, this means that she was created from Adam's self (or soul) and his rib. Despite his emphasis on the creation of Eve from Adam, Muqātil does not draw inferences from this about the nature of women.[26]

Muqātil interprets *petition one another* as asking one another for what is due; *and the wombs* means guarding against severing the womb-ties (by which he means cutting off relations with kin).

Oh People! Be wary of your Lord. He put fear into them (*yukhāwwifuhum*), saying fear your Lord with reverence (*ikhshū rabbakum*) *who created you from a single soul*, meaning Adam, *and from it created its mate*, meaning from Adam's self, from his rib, Eve (Ḥawwā'). She alone is called Ḥawwā'

[24] Note how in return for practising *taqwā* (*w-q-y*), God 'guards (*w-q-y*)' the righteous from hellfire (Q. 2:20; 3:16, 191; 52:18, 27; 76:11). For a summary overview of how Muslim devotions are anchored in *taqwā*, see the brief essay by William C. Chittick, 'Worship' in *The Cambridge Companion to Classical Islamic Theology*, ed. Tim Winter (Cambridge, Cambridge University Press, 2008), 218–36.

[25] For one argument on the term *taqwā* in the Qur'ān, see Erik S. Ohlander, 'Fear of God (*taqwā*) in the Qur'ān: Some Notes on Semantic Shift and Thematic Context', *Journal of Semitic Studies* 50.1 (2005), 137–52. On the importance of emotional disposition as a form of piety, including fear, see Bauer, 'Emotion in the Qur'ān', 1–30.

[26] See also Bauer, *Gender Hierarchy*, 111–12.

because she was created from the living (*ḥayy*) Adam. He said, glory to Him, *and spread forth from the two many men and women*. It is said that many men and women were created from Adam and Eve; they are a thousand communities (*alf umma*).[27]

And be wary of God by whom you petition one another. He is saying you petition each other in the name of God to claim your rights and needs from one another. *And the wombs*: be wary of (*ittaqū*) severing the womb-ties; rather maintain them.

Indeed God is Watcher: He is watching over (*ḥafīẓ*) your deeds.

Hūd

Hūd takes the same basic interpretation as the others in this chapter, which is to say that Eve is created from Adam's rib, but adds some details: that Eve was created from the last rib on the left side while Adam was sleeping. Hūd's interpretation is notable because it includes three *ḥadīths* that are attributed to early authorities within the *tafsīr* tradition: Mujāhid b. Jabr (d. 104/722), who was a disciple of Ibn ʿAbbās; Ḥasan al-Baṣrī (d. 110/728), an Iraqi commentator; and Abū Hurayra (d. *c.* 59/678–9), a Companion of the Prophet. The latter two transmit from the Prophet himself, and versions of all of these *ḥadīths* are found in many subsequent interpretations. Yet Hūd was not used as a source by later authors; so instead of thinking of him as a progenitor of later tradition, it is possible to think of these *ḥadīths* as being among the most widespread interpretations of the day. Though they are brief, these *ḥadīths* deserve further explanation.

Mujāhid is cited as the source for Adam's first words to Eve: 'Woman, my wife', which Mujāhid quotes in Aramaic transliterated into Arabic as *athā, athatī*; he then quotes the words in languages he claims are Hebrew and Syriac. This version of Mujāhid's *ḥadīth* differs slightly from that in Ṭabarī's *tafsīr*. Ṭabarī's version has Adam saying 'woman' in Aramaic (*nabaṭiyya*), using the same word as Hūd (*athā*); but in it he mentions nothing about 'my wife' and includes neither the Syriac nor the Hebrew cited by Hūd.[28] *Athā*, the word given by both sources for 'woman', seems to be a non-standard spoken form, or it could be that the Hebrew and the Aramaic have been reversed at some point in the transmission process. This makes it probable that neither Hūd nor Ṭabarī actually spoke these languages; instead, they were simply transmitting verbatim material.[29]

[27] Muqātil, *Tafsīr Muqātil*, s.v. Q. 4:1.

[28] See Ṭabarī, below; see also the *tafsīr* attributed to Mujāhid, reconstructed from Ṭabarī: Mujāhid b. Jabr al-Makkī (d. 104/722), *Tafsīr Mujāhid*, ed. ʿAbd al-Raḥmān al-Ṭāhir al-Sūratī, 2 vols. (Beirut, al-Manshūrāt al-ʿIlmiyya, [n.d.]), I, 143.

[29] The standard written form of Aramaic is '*ntt*', which is spoken as *atthā*. Karen Bauer would like to thank Jack Tannous for his help – many years ago now – with the Aramaic here, and with the Syriac and Hebrew in Hūd's exegesis. Rosenthal has commented that the 'local origin of the Arabic tradition is, of course, uncertain'. Rosenthal, *The History of al-Ṭabarī*, I, 274, n. 671. Also see Karen Bauer, 'Room for Interpretation: Qur'anic Exegesis and Gender' (Unpublished PhD dissertation, Princeton University, 2008), 33–4, and eadem, *Gender Hierarchy*, 112–15.

Both other *ḥadīths*, ultimately attributed to the Prophet Muḥammad, say that woman was created from a rib, so one should not try to straighten her, or she will be broken. The addressee of Abū Hurayra's *ḥadīth* is further told that if he leaves her as she is, then he can enjoy her even though she is crooked. The meaning here is obvious: woman is innately defective and crooked. While it is unpalatable to modern sensibilities, interpretations like this one seem to represent a widespread opinion of medieval scholars about women and their abilities.

O people! Be wary of your Lord, who created you from a single soul, meaning Adam, *and from it created its mate*, that is to say, Eve, from the smallest rib (*quṣayrā*)[30] on his left side, while he was sleeping.

Mujāhid [b. Jabr] said, 'So he woke up and said "*Athā, athatī*", meaning "woman, my wife". *Athā* in Syriac is *ishā, ishatī*.[31] That means "woman, my wife", except that it is with a "t" in Hebrew, and with an "sh" in Syriac. *Ithā* means "come here!"'

Al-Ḥasan [al-Baṣrī] said, 'The Messenger of God (*ṣlʿm*) said, "Woman was indeed created from a rib, and if you desire to make her straight you will break her. If you are considerate of that then you will manage to live with her (*taʿish bihā*)."'[32]

Abū Hurayra said, 'The Messenger of God (*ṣlʿm*) said, "Woman was indeed created from a rib; she never settles on one disposition (*khilqa*), for she is like a rib. If you try to straighten her, you will break her, whereas if you leave her as she is, you can enjoy her despite her crookedness".'

His words *and spread forth from the two many men and women*: that is to say, He created from the two many men and women.[33]

And be wary of God by whom you petition one another, and the wombs. In the interpretation of those who read it in the accusative, be wary of severing the womb-ties, and for those who read it in the genitive, then it is as if one were saying, 'I implore you by God and by the womb kinship (*raḥim*).' His words *indeed God is Watcher over you*: that is to say, keeper of your deeds.

[30] The editor of Hūd's *tafsīr*, Belhāj b. Saʿīd Sharīfi, notes that this term is a diminutive, and notes that it might be one of the floating ribs, located between the side and the stomach (Sharīfi, in Hūd, *Tafsīr kitāb Allāh al-ʿazīz*, I, 345).

[31] Actually *ishā, ishatī* is Hebrew for 'woman, my wife'.

[32] Versions of the 'crooked rib' *ḥadīth* are found in Abū ʿAbd Allāh Muḥammad b. Ismāʿīl Bukhārī (d. 256/870), *Ṣaḥīḥ*, *Kitāb aḥadīth al-anbiyāʾ* (60), *Bāb khalq Ādam ṣalāwāt Allāh ʿalayhi wa-dhurrīyatihi* (1), *ḥadīth* no. 6/3331; idem, *al-Adab al-mufrad*, *Kitāb al-ḍayf waʾl-nafaqa* (32), *Bab man qaddama ilā ḍayfihi ṭaʿāman fa-qāma yuṣallī* (317), *ḥadīth* no. 2/747; Muslim b. al-Ḥajjāj (d. 261/875), *Jāmiʿ al-ṣaḥīḥ* (or *Ṣaḥīḥ Muslim*), *Kitāb al-riḍāʿ* (17), *Bāb al-waṣiyya biʾl-nisāʾ* (18), *ḥadīth* nos. 77–80/715, 1467 and 1468. Some of these variants include instructions to men to 'treat women well' (*istawṣū biʾl-nisāʾ khayr*), which are omitted from the commentaries. For editions of these works, see the bibliography; however, it should be noted that we have used various editions.

[33] Hūd, *Tafsīr kitāb Allāh al-ʿazīz*, s.v. Q. 4:1.

Qummī

Qummī's interpretation simply states that Eve was created from Adam's lowest rib; however, this interpretation is important in light of the fact that some later Shīʿī interpretations say that Eve was created from the mud left over from Adam's creation. Qummī draws an equivalence between the piety associated with God-wariness and with preserving the ties to the womb-kin, showing how highly he valued blood kinship.

Be wary of your Lord, who created you from a single soul, meaning Adam (*ʿm*), *and from it created its mate*, meaning Eve. God fashioned (*b-r-ʾ*) her from the lowest of his [Adam's] ribs.[34] *And be wary of God by whom you petition one another, and the wombs.* You will be asked on the Day of Resurrection about wariness (*taqwā*) of God; were you wary of (*taqwā*) Him? And about the womb-ties; did you connect them (*waṣaltumūhā*)?

Indeed God is Watcher over you, that is to say, He has charge [over you] (*kafīl*); and according to one narration of Abū'l-Jārūd,[35] the Watcher and the Keeper.

Ṭabarī

Ṭabarī is famous for including parallel accounts in his commentary, which are often substantially different. However, in the case of Q. 4:1, the parallel accounts are remarkably similar: in all of them, Adam is the single soul, the mate is Eve, and she was created from his rib. The near-agreement of all interpretations is an indication of how widely accepted this version of events was among Sunnī *ʿulamā*ʾ.

Two accounts provide slightly different details about the words that Adam first spoke to Eve and the language he used. In one, he asks her what she is and why she was created; in another, he exclaims, 'My flesh! My blood! My wife!' in a manner somewhat reminiscent of the Biblical account of the story.[36] This account is given on the authority of the 'Jews and other learned people'. In this version, Eve is created from a rib on Adam's left side; but, contrary to this interpretation, the Aramaic Targum of

[34] Qummī, *Tafsīr al-Qummī*, s.v. Q. 4:1.

[35] An early Kūfan scholar and supporter of Zayd b. ʿAlī's failed revolt in 122/740. He was an important early source for narrations on the imams, particularly Muḥammad al-Bāqir and Jaʿfar al-Ṣādiq (d. *c.* 150/767, or shortly thereafter). See the PA. Madelung believes that Abū'l-Jārūd did not recognise the imamates of al-Bāqir and al-Ṣādiq, even though he was associated with both, or at least al-Ṣādiq, and is a source for both a commentary attributed to al-Bāqir and for early Zaydī views. See Wilferd Madelung, 'Abu'l-Jārūd Hamdānī', *EIr*, I, 327.

[36] Genesis 2:23: 'Then the man said: "This at last is bone of my bones and flesh of my flesh; this one shall be called Woman (Heb. *ishshah*), for out of Man (Heb. *ish*) this one was taken."'

pseudo-Jonathan actually says that the rib is Adam's thirteenth rib on his *right* side.[37] Other Jewish accounts offer diverse views, including that the original creation was a being made of both male and female sides, and that this being was later separated into each sex.[38] The idea of a left-side creation might have been of local origin.

Ṭabarī introduces the subject of creation with an excursus on the brotherhood of man. He argues that humans have a duty to care for one another, the strong for the weak, and not oppress one another. Oppression, he reminds the listener, will bring about God's punishment. This is a powerful warning, and is often given in an abbreviated form in the interpretation of verses to do with women and their status; it relates to a larger social obligation by which anyone who is strong and powerful in society has a duty of care to the weaker members.[39]

Ṭabarī explains the final part of the verse by giving the two different interpretations: one, that humans must be wary of God and be wary of severing the womb-ties, and the other, that humans petition in the name of God and the womb-ties. He agrees with the former, and cites a *ḥadīth* on the authority of the Prophet which says to fear God and connect the womb-ties, 'for that helps you subsist in this world and it is better for you in the next'.

He, majestic be His praise, means by His words, *O people! Be wary of your Lord who created you from a single soul*, O you people, be careful of (*ḥ-dh-r*) your Lord lest you contravene him in what he has commanded for you and what he has forbidden from you, lest a punishment befall you, the like of which is unprecedented.

Then He described himself, majestic be His praise. He alone has undertaken the creation of all of mankind from a single individual, and He informed His servants how it was in the beginning of His creation, and that was from the single soul. He thereby alerted them that all of them are the sons of a single man and a single mother, and that they are one from another, and their duties towards one another are obligatory in the same way that the duty of a brother towards his brother is, for they share a lineage going back to a single father and a single mother. That which binds them to look after each

[37] 'The Lord God cast a deep sleep upon Adam, and he slept. And he took one of his ribs – it was the thirteenth rib of the right side – and he closed its place with flesh. And the lord God built the rib he had taken from Adam into a woman and brought her to Adam. And Adam said, "This time, but never again, will woman be created from man as this one had been created from me – bone of my bones and flesh of my flesh. It is fitting to call this one woman, for she has been taken from man."' Pseudo-Jonathan, *Targum Pseudo-Jonathan, Genesis*, tr. Michael Maher (Collegeville, MN, Liturgical Press, 1992), v. 1B, 24. The Palestinian Targum Neofiti in the same series has no mention of which rib was taken.

[38] This is the interpretation of Rabbi Samuel b. Naḥman, in *Midrash Rabbah, Genesis, Volume I*, tr. H. Freedman (London, Soncinco Press, 1961), 54.

[39] On the circle of justice, see Linda T. Darling, *A History of Social Justice and Political Power in the Middle East: The Circle of Justice from Mesopotamia to Globalization* (London, Routledge, 2013).

other's rights, despite the great distance from their joining each other in lineage to the common father, is like the lineage which binds them to their own immediate father, inclining one towards the other thereby, so that they may seek justice for one another, and not injustice, and so the strong among them should make the effort to give the weak one his rights out of common decency (*bi'l-maʿrūf*) according to what God has made incumbent upon him with regard to the weak one.

So He said, *who created you from a single soul*, meaning Adam. This is also as it is in al-Suddī,[40] who said, as for *created you from a single soul*, it was from Adam.[41]

The equivalent of His words *from a single soul* [in which the word 'single' is grammatically feminine] and the thing intended is a man, is the saying of the poet:[42]

> *Abūka khalīfatun waladat-hu ukhrā, wa anta khalīfatun dhāka'l-kamālu*
>
> Your father is a caliph begat by another, and you are a successor of that perfection

He said 'begat by another', meaning a man, but he made the word 'another' feminine because the word 'caliph' is feminine. And God, exalted be His mention, said *from a single soul* (*min nafsin wāḥidatin*) [using the feminine ending for 'single'] due to 'soul' being grammatically feminine, though the meaning is 'from a single man'. If one were to say 'from a single soul' (*min nafsin wāḥidin*) so that the lexical expression was in the masculine form, the meaning would still be correct.

Reports on the interpretation of His words, majestic be His praise, *and from it created its mate, and spread forth from the two many men and women*.

He means by His words, majestic be His praise, *created from it its mate* that from the single soul was created its mate. He means by *zawj*, the second one and, according to what the interpreters have said, its wife, Eve.

[40] Muḥammad b. al-Ḥusayn ← Aḥmad b. Mufaḍḍal ← Asbāṭ ← al-Suddī.

[41] Ṭabarī cites two more reports to the same effect: Bishr b. Muʿādh ← Yazīd b. Zarīʿ ← Saʿīd ← Qatāda said 'meaning Adam'; Sufyān b. Wakīʿ ← his father ← Sufyān ← a man ← Mujāhid said 'Adam.'

[42] Here, Ṭabarī explains why the word 'single' is grammatically feminine (*wāḥida*), although it refers to a man (Adam). 'Single' is an adjective modifying the word 'soul'; the adjective must agree with the gender of its noun. Likewise, he says, a poet has composed a verse in which a feminine pronoun is used to refer to a man.

An account of those who have said this:

Concerning His words *and from it created its mate*, Mujāhid[43] said, 'Eve, from the smallest rib of Adam while he was sleeping, and he woke and said, "Athā", which in Aramaic (*nabaṭiyya*) is "woman".'[44]

Concerning *from it created its mate*, Qatāda[45] said, 'It means Eve, created from Adam, from one of his ribs.'

Al-Suddī[46] said, Adam was made to live in Paradise, and he was walking in it alone: he had no mate in whom to find solace. So he slept deeply, and when he woke there was a woman sitting by his head, whom God had created from his rib. So he asked her, 'What are you?' She said, 'Woman.' He said, 'Why were you created?' She said, 'So that you may find solace in me (*li-taskuna ilayya*).'

Ibn Isḥāq[47] said, He cast a slumber unto Adam, according to what has reached us on the authority of the People of the Book, from among the Jews and other learned people on the authority of 'Abd Allāh b. 'Abbās and others, then He took one of his ribs from the left side and healed the place with flesh while Adam was sleeping, and he did not awaken from his sleep until God had created that mate Eve from his rib. He shaped her as a woman so that Adam could find solace in her. When the slumber was lifted from him, and he awoke from his sleep, and he saw her in the Garden, he said, according to what they claim, and God knows best, 'My flesh! My blood! My wife!' And he found solace in her.

Al-Suddī[48] said, [regarding] *from it created its mate*, 'Eve was made from Adam.'

As for His words *and spread forth from the two many men and women*, this means that from the two of them, meaning from Adam and Eve, peace be upon them, spread out *many men and women*. He had seen them (*qad ra'āhum*), as He says, *like moths scattered* [Q. 101:4]. It is said from this that God spread forth humankind and He made them disperse (*baththa Allāh al-khalq wa-abaththahum*).

The interpreters have said as we have concerning that. An account of those who have said this:

Al-Suddī[49] said: He spread forth humankind.

43 Muḥammad b. 'Amr ← Abū 'Āṣim ← 'Īsā ← Ibn Abī Najīḥ ← Mujāhid.

44 He now gives another *isnād* for the same interpretation: al-Muthannā ← Abū Ḥudhayfa ← Shibl ← Ibn Abī Najīḥ ← Mujāhid said 'likewise'.

45 Bishr b. Mu'ādh ← Yazīd ← Sa'īd ← Qatāda.

46 Mūsā b. Hārūn ← 'Āmr b. Ḥammād ← Asbāṭ ← al-Suddī.

47 Ibn Ḥumayd ← Salama ← Ibn Isḥāq.

48 Muḥammad b. al-Ḥusayn ← Aḥmad b. Mufaḍḍal ← Asbāṭ ← al-Suddī.

49 Muḥammad b. al-Ḥusayn ← Ahmad b. Mufaḍḍal ← Asbāṭ ← al-Suddī.

Reports on the interpretation of His words, exalted be He, *and be wary of God by whom you petition one another, and the wombs.*

The readers differed over the reading of this. The majority of the readers of Medina and Basra read *tassā'alūna* with an intensification (*tashdīd*), meaning *tatasā'alūna*, where one of the two *tā'* [letters] is elided in the *sīn*, turning it into a doubled *sīn*. Some of the Kufan readers read it *tasā'alūna* with a lightening (*takhfīf*), like *tafā'alūna*. Both readings are recognised, both are lexically idiomatic (*faṣīḥ*), I mean with the lightening and the intensification in His words *tasā'alūna bihi*. And the reader would be correct with either of these readings, because, read in either of the two ways, the meaning is unchanged.

As for its interpretation: *be wary of God*, O People, whom, if you petition one another, you petition in His name, where the petitioner asks the petitioned, 'I ask you by God', or 'I implore you by God', or 'I beseech you by God', and the like of that. Exalted be His mention, it is as though He were saying, 'O People, just as you magnify your Lord by your tongues – given that you find it grievous when somebody violates a covenant that they have given you – so also magnify [Him] by being obedient to Him in what He has commanded you to and by shunning what He has forbidden you. So take precautions (*iḥdharū*) against His punishment lest you contravene Him in His commands or His prohibitions.' It is thus in al-Ḍaḥḥāk,[50] who, regarding His words *and be wary of God by whom you petition one another*, said, 'He said, be wary of (*ittaqū*) God through whom you seek contracts and covenants.'[51]

As for His words *the wombs*, the commentators have differed in their interpretations of that. Some of them say that it means: be wary of God (*ittaqū 'llāh*), who, when you ask one another, the one petitioning says, 'I ask you by Him and by the womb-ties (*al-arḥām*).'

An account of those who have said this:

Regarding *be wary of God, by whom you petition one another, and the wombs,* Ibrāhīm[52] said, 'Be wary of God through whom you seek mutual affection (*ta'āṭafūna bihi*) *and the wombs*: He means man petitions by God and by the womb (*al-raḥim*)'.[53]

[50] Al-Muthannā ← Isḥāq ← Abū Zuhayr ← Juwaybir ← al-Ḍaḥḥāk.

[51] Similar reports are given with chains of transmission going back to al-Rabī' b. Anas twice, and Ibn 'Abbās, who glosses *tasā'alūna* as *ta'āṭafūna*, which means seeking mutual affection.

[52] Ḥakkām ← 'Amr ← Manṣūr ← Ibrāhīm.

[53] There follow six further reports on the authority of Yaqūb b. Ibrāhīm ← Hushaym ← Mughīra ← Ibrāhīm; Muḥammad b. Bashshār ← 'Abd al-Raḥmān ← Sufyān ← Manṣūr ← Ibrāhīm; Abu Kurayb ← Hushaym ← Mughīra ← Ibrāhīm; Ibn Bashshār ← 'Abd al-Raḥmān ← Sufyān ← Ibn Abī Najīḥ ← Mujāhid; al-Ḥimmānī ← Sharīk ← Manṣūr or Mughīra ← Ibrāhīm; al-Muthannā ← Suwayd ← Ibn al-Mubārak ← Ma'mar ← al-Ḥasan.

Abū Jaʿfar [al-Ṭabarī] said, according to this interpretation, some of those who read His words *wa'l-arḥāmi* in the genitive case (*khafḍ*) do so coordinating *al-arḥām* with His words *bihi*, as though He meant to say, 'be wary of God and the womb-kin by whom you petition one another', so an overt noun has been coordinated with a genitive pronoun. That is not idiomatically very sound, according to the Arabs, because one does not coordinate an overt noun with something that is pronominal, especially in the genitive, unless it is for poetic licence (*ḍarūrat al-shiʿr*), and that is because of the constraints of poetic form (*ḍīq al-shiʿr*). As for speech, there is no need for the speaker to choose something abhorrent in phrasing and not amenable to syntactical analysis. An example from poetry of coordinating an overt noun with a pronominal in the genitive are the following words of the poet:

Nuʿalliqu fī mithli'l-sawārī suyūfanā
wa-mā baynahā wa'l-kaʿbi ghawṭun nafā'ifu

We hang our swords in the like of masts
Between the swords and the heels an open expanse

The poet coordinated the *kaʿb* (the heel), which is an overt noun, with the suffixed letters in *baynahā*, which is standing in place [of the noun 'swords'].

Others say, rather, the interpretation of *and be wary of God by whom you petition one another* is guard against (*ittaqū*) severing the womb-ties.

An account of those who say this:

Al-Suddī[54] says, regarding His words *be wary of God by whom you petition one another, and the wombs*, that He means be wary of God and be wary of the womb-ties and do not sever them.

Qatāda[55] says, *and be wary of God by whom you petition one another, and the wombs; indeed God is Watcher over you*: it was mentioned to us that the Prophet of God (*ṣlʿm*) used to say, 'Be wary of God and connect the womb-ties, for that helps you subsist in the world and it is better for you in the next'.[56]

[54] Muḥammad b. al-Ḥusayn ← Aḥmad b. al-Mufaḍḍal ← al-Asbāṭ ← al-Suddī.

[55] Bishr b. Muʿādh ← Yazīd ← Saʿīd ← Qatāda.

[56] See Bukhārī, *Ṣaḥīḥ*, *Kitāb al-Adab* (78), *Bāb man busiṭa lahu fī'l-rizq bi-ṣilat al-raḥim* (12), *ḥadīth* no. 17/5986; *Bāb man waṣala waṣalahu Allāh* (13), *ḥadīth* no. 18/5987; a version of this can be found in a collection known as *al-ḥadīth al-qudsī* (*mā jā'a fī khiṭāb rabb al-ʿizza li'l-raḥim*), attributed there to Tirmidhī, in whose own collection see similar reports, viz. *al-Jāmiʿ al-ṣaḥīḥ*, *Kitāb al-Birr wa'l-ṣila* (27), *Bāb mā jā'a fī qaṭīʿat al-raḥim* (9), *ḥadīth* no. 13/1907, *Bāb mā jā'a fī ṣilat al-raḥim* (10), *ḥadīth* nos. 14/1908 and 15/1909, *Bāb mā jā'a fī raḥmat al-muslimīn* (16), *ḥadīth* no. 30/1924; another version of a *ḥadīth* commanding to 'connect the womb-tie' is found in Ibn Māja, *Sunan*, *Kitāb al-Aṭʿima* (29), *Bāb iṭʿām al-ṭaʿām* (1), *ḥadīth* no. 1/3251 (For an edition of this work, see the bibliography). There follow a number of transmissions which say either that the verse means to connect the womb-ties, or that it means to be wary of severing the

Abū Ja'far [al-Ṭabarī] says: In this interpretation, according to those who read it in the accusative (*naṣb*), it means, 'Be wary of God, by whom you petition one another, and be wary of severing the womb-ties', as a coordination of *al-arḥām*, when it is grammatically in the accusative case, with the name of God. He says: I only permit the reading of the accusative in this case, with the meaning 'Be wary (*ittaqū*) lest you should sever the womb-ties', on the basis of what we have already clarified to the effect that the Arabs do not coordinate the named noun with a pronominal in the case of genitive constructions, except for poetic licence.

Reports on the interpretation of His words, exalted be He, *Indeed God is Watcher over you*.

Abū Ja'far [al-Ṭabarī] said, He, exalted be His mention, meant by that: indeed God does not cease to be a Watcher over you, and He means with His words *over you*: over the people to whom He has said, *O people! Be wary of your Lord*. He only said *over you* to mean those who are addressed in the verse, and those sons of Adam who had gone before, because when the second person addressee and the third person who is absent come together in a predicate, the Arabs give the priority to the second person. So they say, when they address a single man or a group who has done something alongside others who are absent, 'You [second person address] did that; you fashioned that.'

He means with His words *Watcher* a keeper (*ḥafīẓ*) who is all-enumerating (*muḥṣī*) of your deeds against you, scrutinising whether you are looking after the sanctity of your womb-ties or how much you are severing them. On the authority of Mujāhid,[57] *Indeed God is Watcher over you* is 'Keeper'. Ibn Wahb said, 'I heard Ibn Abī Zayd[58] [saying] about His words *Indeed God is Watcher over you*, "Over your deeds; He knows them and He comprehends them."' It is in this sense that the words of Abū Du'ād al-Iyādī said:

womb-ties. The chains of transmission are: 'Alī b. Dāwūd ← 'Abd Allāh b. Ṣāliḥ ← Mu'āwiya b. Ṣāliḥ ← 'Alī b. Abī Ṭalḥa ← Ibn 'Abbās; Abū Kurayb ← Hushaym ← Manṣūr ← al-Ḥasan; Sufyān ← Khuṣayf ← 'Ikrima; al-Ḥasan b. Yaḥyā ← 'Abd al-Razzāq ← Ma'mar ← al-Ḥasan; al-Ḥasan b. Yaḥyā ← 'Abd al-Razzāq ← Ma'mar ← Qatāda; Muthannā ← Abu Ḥudhayfa ← Shibl ← Ibn Abī Najīḥ ← Mujāhid; Muthannā ← Isḥāq ← Ibn Abī Ja'far ← his father ← al-Rabī'; al-Muthannā ← Isḥāq ← 'Abd al-Raḥmān ← Ibn Abī Ḥammād; Abū Ja'far al-Khazzāz ← Juwaybir ← al-Ḍaḥḥāk ← Ibn 'Abbās; al-Ḥusayn ← Ḥajjāj ← Ibn Jurayj ← Ibn 'Abbās; al-Ḥusayn ← Ḥajjāj ← Ibn Abī Ja'far ← his father ← al-Rabī'; Yūnus ← Ibn Wahb ← Ibn Zayd. The latter cites *sūrat al-Ra'd*, Q. 13:24, as being related to this verse.

57 Al-Muthannā ← Abū Ḥudhayfā ← Shibl ← Ibn Abī Najīḥ ← Mujāhid.

58 Yūnus ← Ibn Wahb ← Ibn Zayd.

Ka-maqāʿid al-ruqabāʾ
liʾl-ḍurabāʾi aydīhim nawāhidu

Like the minders who sit [in wait],
whose hands are raised [ready to strike] at those casting lots.[59]

Qāḍī al-Nuʿmān

This interpretation represents a distinctly Ismāʿīlī view of Eve's creation. For Qāḍī al-Nuʿmān, Eve was not created from a rib. Rather, she was created as Adam's disciple and as his spiritual legatee. This creation was necessitated by the actions of Iblīs described in Q. 2:34. Q. 2:30–34 describes how God told the angels that He would create Adam, and then commanded them to prostrate to Adam. They all did so except Iblīs, who refused, considering himself above such a thing (*istakbara*), in Q. 2:34. The following verse describes how Adam and his mate dwelt in Paradise. Qāḍī al-Nuʿmān connects Q. 2:34 and Q. 2:35, saying that Eve was created for Adam because Iblīs had been Adam's disciple, only he was banished from that discipleship because he did not show deference to Adam. Thus, according to Qāḍī al-Nuʿmān, God cut him off and banished him, which caused him to despair, and hence he was called Iblīs, the despairing one. Contrary to the discipleship of Iblīs, the discipleship of Eve was perfect and she became Adam's mate and his physical wife as well as the recipient of his spiritual knowledge.[60]

And so [the angels] prostrated themselves, as He, exalted be He, says of them: *Except Iblīs who refused and considered himself above it, and he was among the ingrates* (*al-kāfirūn*) [Q. 2:34]. He was only called 'Iblīs' after this, which is to say when he became despondent (*ablasa*). The grammarians (*aṣḥāb al-lugha*) said that 'Iblīs' is according to the pattern *afʿīl* from *ablasa*, and one says *ablasa al-rajul* when a man despairs (*āyasa*), and it was like that when Iblīs despaired (*āyasa*) of the divine ranking (*ḥadd*), regarding which he had become despondent (*ablasa*). It is also said: *ablasa al-rajul* to mean that he can no longer speak for lack of proof (*ḥujja*), and one can say *ablasa* to mean *ḥazana* (grieve), and *ballasa* to mean *khashaʿa* (humbled).

All of these states came together in Iblīs, for God has said – and He is the most truthful of speakers – *the day when the hour comes, the criminals shall despair* (*yublisu*) [Q. 30:12], and He, mighty and majestic, said, *'What*

59 Ṭabarī, *Jāmiʿ al-bayān*, s.v. Q. 4:1.

60 For more on this interpretation as a part of the Ismāʿīlī cosmology, and relating this interpretation to that of al-Muʾayyad (below), see Karen Bauer, 'Spiritual Hierarchy and Gender Hierarchy in Fāṭimid Ismāʿīlī Interpretations of the Qurʾān', *Journal of Qurʾanic Studies* 14.2 (2012), 29–46.

prevents you from prostrating yourself at My command?' He [Iblīs] *said, 'I surpass him! For you created me from fire, and created him from clay'* [Q. 7:12], meaning 'You have brought me into existence (*ansha'a*) through knowledge, as a spiritual being (*nash'a rūḥaniyya*), and knowledge is my lustrous discipleship (*ta'yīdī al-bāriq*) which no physical being can support; while You have brought him into existence through knowledge that is dense, viscous, speech-bound (*manṭiqī*), natural, corporeal knowledge. So how shall I prostrate myself to someone whom I surpass?' He thus disclosed what he had kept secret, in open declaration (*jāhara*) of his disobedience, whereupon God became wrathful with him (*ghaḍaba 'alayhi*) and cursed him, that is to say, banished (*ṭarada*) him with His words, mighty and majestic, *He said, 'Out from here! Damned shall you be indeed, and verily shall a curse be upon you to the Day of Reckoning'* [Q. 15:34–5]. So He banished him from the ranks of discipleship (*ḥudūd al-ta'yīd*), severing him from these, and banishing him from them. And *la'na* (curse) etymologically means *ṭard* (banishment).

Then God, mighty and majestic, created Eve from Adam, and that is known from His words, exalted be He, *and He created from it its mate*, such was the creation of discipleship, as opposed to a corporeal creation. That is to say, God, exalted be He, commanded Adam, so he undertook her discipleship, her instruction (*ta'līm*) and her spiritual discernment (*tabṣīr*). And He attached her to him, making her his wife and his proof (*ḥujja*). God, glory be to Him, compensated him (*'awwaḍahu*) with her, in exchange for Iblīs.

It is not as the common people (*'āmma*) claim, that God, exalted be He, cast upon Adam a slumber and he slept, and then He drew out one of his ribs and created Eve from it. They have only heard a snippet (*ṭaraf*) of the true interpretation, they are not able to grasp or to know it. All that they are able to hear is that God substituted one of Adam's ribs, using it to fashion Eve, but it is not like that at all. Rather, it is that God, exalted be He, compensated Adam with Eve in exchange for Iblīs, who had stood to be (*mu'ahhal*) Adam's proof (*ḥujja*), as we have said. He made him one of the twelve representatives (*nuqabā'*)[61] because in outward creation (*khalq al-ẓāhir*) they represent the ribs of the human body, since every human has twelve ribs on each side. The right side represents esoteric knowledge (*al-'ilm al-bāṭin*), while the left side

[61] Note that in the Fatimid Ismā'īlī cosmology, each age has a *nāṭiq*, a speaking prophet, and each *nāṭiq* has representatives, *nuqabā'*, who act on his behalf. Twelve are hidden, twelve are manifest, acting openly in the world. The term *ḥadd*/*ḥudūd* refers to any spiritual rankings.

represents exoteric knowledge (*al-ʿilm al-ẓāhir*). The representatives (*nuqabāʾ*) of esoteric knowledge are twelve, and likewise those who represent exoteric knowledge. Then God, glorious and exalted be He, made Adam and his wife live in the Garden, which esoterically (*bāṭin*) constitutes the ranks (*ḥudūd*) of discipleship for the messengers and those below them, all the way down to the representatives (*nuqabāʾ*).

Nothing of what we say here or elsewhere esoterically (*bāṭin*) is a disavowal (*nafī*) on our part of the exoteric (*ẓāhir*); nay, for the two are paired (*muzdawaj*) because God, glory be to Him, and exalted be He, says, *and we have created everything in pairs (zawjayn), so that you might heed* [Q. 51:49].[62]

Qushayrī

Unlike Ṭabarī, Qushayrī does not, in this instance, include several possible interpretations, nor does he name authorities. This is because his ultimate aim is different. For him, the most important aspect of this verse is not the immediate physical creation of the first humans; rather, the importance lies in its broader implications for the nature of humanity as derived from a single original person, by an all-powerful creator. A portion of this interpretation is in rhymed prose, and a portion in verse; it is clearly meant to inspire the believer in a very different manner than the more strictly scholarly work of an exegete such as Ṭabarī. It may be that this text was used to school mystical disciples.[63] Thus Qushayrī's interpretation is not focused on gender and never mentions the actual method of creation of Adam or Eve. He speaks instead of the need to prioritise remembering God over the material world and the self. The people who have forgotten themselves in their remembrance of God are the ones who are rewarded: 'Whoever guards against himself stops at God.' Though all of this may make it seem as though Qushayrī wishes to forsake all things of the world, the last part of the verse shows that this is not so: paraphrasing an oft-cited tradition about 'the womb-tie' (also referenced by Ṭabarī, above), he warns of severing it, 'for whoever severs the womb-tie becomes severed, and whoever connects it is connected', meaning that one should look after one's kin, for severing that connection indicates a severance from God.

His words, majestic be His mention, *O people! Be wary of your Lord, who created you from a single soul, and from it created its mate, and spread forth*

[62] Qāḍī al-Nuʿmān, *Asās al-taʾwīl*, 57–9. Note, however, that this edition has many mistakes including mistakes in the Qurʾānic citations in this passage.

[63] On Qushayrī and his work of *tafsīr*, in addition to the other sources cited in the Commentators section, see Nguyen, *Sufi Master*.

from the two many men and women; and be wary of God by whom you petition one another, and the wombs; indeed God is Watcher over you.

People is a collective noun (*ism jins*), and its etymology (*al-ishtiqāq*) is uncertain. It is said that 'people' (*ins*) are thus named for their perceptibility,[64] on the basis of this allusion:

> O you who have become manifest from the concealment of nonexistence, by virtue of My making you morally responsible,
>
> By My honouring I singled out whomever I wished among you,
>
> I deprived whomever I wished among you of My guidance and knowledge of Me.
>
> I carried you to wherever I wished, or rather I made you reach whatever I wished by the virtue of my disposal.

It is said that you were called an *insān* (human) because of your *nisyān* (forgetfulness), and if you were to forget Me, there is nothing viler, and if you forget to mention Me, then nobody is lower than you.

It is said that whoever forgets the Truth, there is no end to his trials, and whoever forgets the creation, his elevated status is never ending.

It is said, and He says to the sinners (*mudhnibūn*), 'O you who have forgotten my covenant, and rejected My love, and transgressed My bounds, the time has come for you to return to My door, in order to deserve My gentleness and My positive response.' He says to the knowers, 'You who have forgotten your lot for Our sake, you who have not cast your glance and speech from anything other than Us, verily your due from Us is tremendous, and it is incumbent upon Us to give you victory, and your worth has become immense.'

It is said, 'O you who have the intimacy of the breeze of My nearness, and who sought refreshment by witnessing My countenance, and who are strengthened by the magnificence of My stature, you are the most magnificent of my servants to Me'.

His words *Be wary of your Lord* [indicate that] wariness of God (*taqwā*) is the sum of the acts of obedience, the first of which is abandoning polytheism (*shirk*), the last of which is guarding against any other (*ittiqā'*), and the first of the others for you is yourself. Whoever guards against himself (*ittaqā nafsahu*) stops (*w–q-f*) at God, above station and above the witnessing of

[64] The consonantal verbal root *a-n-s* in the Qur'ān is used to indicate that something is perceptible. Moses 'perceives' (*ānasa*) on the side of the 'Mount' (*ṭūr*) in Q. 28:29 (and in Q. 20:10; 27:7); see also other similar sense usage in Q. 4:6, where orphans are to be given their property once they are 'perceived' to have come of age.

[spiritual] states, and he stops there for God's sake, not for the sake of witnessing [his] share of this world or the next.[65]

His words *who created you from a single soul* refer to Adam (*ʿm*), and since our being is created from him and he is created by the Hand, so therefore are we, since the distinction of Adam (*ʿm*) over all of the other males and females of creation became manifest; likewise we were also described. He said, exalted be He, *They are the best of creation* [Q. 98:7].

The lexeme *soul* indicates generality, and generality necessarily implies comprehensiveness.

His words *and from it created its mate*: the Truth (al-Ḥaqq) – glory be to Him – has judged that creatures [should] cohabit so that succession endures, and in order to refer like to like, He has associated shape with shape.

By His words *and spread forth from the two many men and women*, He has made himself known, to those of intellect (*ʿuqalāʾ*), on the basis of the perfection of His power, by the rational demonstration of His lordship and the proofs of His wisdom that He has shown, such that He created this creation in its entirety from the offspring of a single individual, despite the differences in their guises, the variation of their forms and the divergence of their character traits (*akhlāq*); for indeed no two among them resemble one another, for each of them has a form (*ṣūra*), a physical constitution (*khalq*), aspiration (*himma*) and a spiritual state (*ḥāl*). So glory be to Him, whose powers are without limit and whose knowledge has no end.

And be wary of God: the repetition of the command to be wary of God indicates the confirmation of His ruling. *By whom you petition one another, and the wombs*: that is to say, be wary of severing the womb-tie, for whoever severs the womb-tie becomes severed [from God], and whoever connects them is connected [to God].

Indeed God is Watcher over you having oversight and witness, reckoning your breaths against you, and He sees your senses, and He is master of all of your thoughts, and He is the source of your movements and your stillness; and the one who knows that He is Watcher over him should be all the more ashamed before Him.[66]

[65] Qushayrī means here that the final stage of the spiritual path is when the believer no longer pays attention to his reward in this world or the next, and thereby he attains God's true favour. He explains that the first object of polytheism is actually the love of self, and that it is therefore the self that must be guarded against in the first instance. By inference, the obliteration of self in God leads to true spiritual enlightenment.

[66] Qushayrī, *Laṭāʾif al-ishārāt*, s.v. Q. 4:1.

Mu'ayyad fī'l-Dīn al-Shīrāzī

This interpretation, which is not from a work of *tafsīr* but rather from a sermon delivered to a group of Ismāʿīlī devotees, is considerably different in tone and content from the other interpretations of this verse. Muʾayyad himself makes a distinction when he mentions the view of the 'exegetes' (*mufassirūn*). Contrary to these exoteric interpretations, Muʾayyad speaks of its inward meaning, which is hidden from the non-initiates.

According to Muʾayyad, the inner meaning of the verse is that each prophet is an Adam in his own age. Adam in this sense is the spiritual progenitor of the community, just as Adam in the physical sense is the progenitor of humankind. Instead of a community based on the tie of sperm, this spiritual community is based on the tie of spiritual kinship. In this instance, he does not deny the existence of Adam or Eve, but says that, behind their outward manifestations, there is an inward truth: a spiritual kinship that exists amongst his own audience.

The proof for this spiritual kinship is a *ḥadīth* on the authority of the Prophet that has him saying, 'You and I, O ʿAlī, are the two fathers of the believers'.[67] According to Muʾayyad, this indicates a true spiritual lineage between Muḥammad and ʿAlī, through which Muḥammad passed down knowledge to ʿAlī, his legatee or intermediary (*waṣī*), knowledge which binds the community together in a spiritual kinship in the domain of the word of God. The role of the intermediary is to disseminate the truth which he has been given: the inward truths of the Godly word. For Muʾayyad, this puts ʿAlī in the position of a female, in the sense that ʿAlī is pregnant with the knowledge passed down from Muḥammad and is thus the repository for his wisdom.

The gendering of the spiritual hierarchy, in which the passive recipient is female while the teacher is male, is then used to interpret the rest of the verse and Q. 4:34 (the subject of Chapter 3 of this volume). In this interpretation, 'women' are the students, the beneficiaries of knowledge. 'Men' are the teachers and they bestow knowledge. For Muʾayyad, this hierarchy is more true and consistent than the actual worldly gender hierarchy. He represents the worldly gender hierarchy through a *ḥadīth* that has Muḥammad saying that if any human had been ordered to prostrate themselves to any other human, it would be the wives to their husbands. Muʾayyad explains this *ḥadīth* by saying that, although women must be subservient to their husbands in the world, they are sometimes spiritually better than their husbands. However, teachers are always spiritually more advanced than their students. Therefore, according to Muʾayyad, the spiritual hierarchy is more consistent than the worldly gender hierarchy, and the inner meaning of 'men' in the Qurʾān is 'teachers' and 'women', students. Thus, although the outward interpretation of the *ḥadīth* must be obeyed, the inner interpretation is truer.[68]

For the final part of the verse, Muʿayyad focuses on the issue of spiritual kinship. Though he says that it is important to preserve the ties of blood kinship, for him the connection of spiritual kinship is even stronger than worldly kinship, and severing it is a deviation from God's path.

[67] This *ḥadīth* was not found in any of the more prominent *ḥadīth* collections.

[68] On this interpretation, see Bauer, 'Spiritual Hierarchy'.

O Believers! God has appointed rightly guided imams for you as a support and to distinguish you from those who take *as helpers those who lead astray* [Q. 18:51]. Praise God, exalted be He, that He has included you in the true guidance of the imams from the family of your Prophet (*ṣlʿ*) as an excellence and a beneficence, *and remember God's favour on you when you were enemies and He united your hearts, so you became, by His grace, brothers* [Q. 3:103] [. . .][69]

You have received, in the context of revelation, which is always reached by the judgment of the intellect, [the knowledge] that each prophet in his age is the Adam of his cycle (*dawr*), because his existence is a proof of spiritual (*dīn*) lineage, just as the existence of Adam (*ʿm*) is proof of corporeal lineage. The attestation of this is found in the words of the Prophet (*ṣlʿh*) to ʿAlī (*ʿm*), 'You and I, ʿAlī, are the fathers of the believers', indicating the progenitive nature of spirituality (*dīn*) and its modality, and that it is in the domain of the divine word (*kalima ilāhiyya*), which is a surplus of the power of the Messenger, just as there exists physical progeny in the domain of sperm, which is a surplus of the power of manhood. If the sperm is the connection between father and son on account of kinship, then it is more deserving and befitting that the word of God, exalted be He, as a surplus of the power of prophethood, should be the connection between the Prophet (*ṣlʿ*) and the community. The words of the Prophet (*ṣlʿ*), when he said, 'You and I, ʿAlī, are the fathers of the believers', taken as they are, are far removed from metaphor or mutual praise,[70] as alleged by those for whom *all tidings are obscure* [Q. 28:66], the unjust, whose sight (*baṣāʾir*) has been cloaked because they have abandoned the proofs of their religion (*dīn*).

God, exalted be He, said, *Oh People! Be wary of your Lord, who created you from a single soul, and from it created its mate, and spread forth from the two many men and women; and be wary of God by whom you petition one another, and the wombs; indeed God is Watcher over you.* The exegetes say that the *single soul* from which people were created is Adam (*ʿm*) and *its mate* created from it is Eve, *and spread forth from the two many men and women* is creation. We say that one of the wisdoms contained in this verse is that it points out the standing of the Prophet, the legatee (*al-waṣī*) and the imams, upon them be the most excellent peace.

The verse opens with the command of being wary (*taqiyya*),[71] for wariness is a mark of the people of faith, and it is the garment of the [Ismāʿīlī]

[69] We have omitted the rest of the lengthy introduction, which is an explanation of the duality of human nature, warning the believers to take care of their spirits, which is the part of them closest to the angels, and not just their bodies, which is the part of them closest to the earth.

[70] Meaning that, in saying this, the Prophet would be treating ʿAlī with kindliness.

[71] This term has the same root as the word used in the verse, *ittaqū*, meaning 'be wary of God'. *Taqiyya* means fear, caution and piety, and can also refer to the Shīʿī practice of religious dissimulation when under threat.

community (*ahl al-daʿwa*),[72] and by this name they alone are specified; nobody else goes by it other than them. Jaʿfar b. Muḥammad al-Ṣādiq (*ʿm*) said, 'Being wary (*taqiyya*) is my religion and the religion of my fathers, and those who do not practice guarding have no religion.'

Regarding God's words *created you from a single soul*, the single soul from which we were created as a spiritual creation is the Prophet (*ṣlʿh*, the pure ones). For it is from him that the souls who were formed in the form of the abode of the Hereafter have issued, and it is from the surplus of what was revealed to him that they have risen and issued forth. The *mate* created from him, as a rib from one of his ribs, as the being of Eve was created from one of the ribs of Adam (*ʿm*), is the legatee [ʿAlī] (the prayers of God be upon him), who was one of the proofs, and became a mate to the Prophet, pregnant with his knowledge, treasure-keeper of his secret, repository for his knowledge and his wisdom.

Regarding *and spread forth from the two many men and women*, the *men* are the providers of knowledge (*al-ʿulamāʾ al-mufīdūn*), and the *women* are the seekers of knowledge and beneficiaries (*al-mutaʿallimūn al-mustafīdūn*). God, exalted be He, has said, *Men are maintainers of women, by that which God has distinguished the one over the other* [Q. 4:34],[73] meaning that the possessors of knowledge (*ʿulamāʾ*) are in charge (*qawwāmūn*) of the seekers of knowledge (*al-mutaʿallimūn*). God has made their superiority over them manifest, and He has made the seekers of knowledge cleave to them the way a woman cleaves to her husband. The Messenger of God (*ṣlʿ*) said, 'If it were permissible for anyone to prostrate themselves to anyone other than God, I would have ordered that woman prostrate herself before her husband'.[74] In its outward meaning (*ẓāhir*), this is an obligatory ruling, despite the defects in it in certain respects: how many women are better than their husbands, more wary of God and are stronger preservers of God's bounds? If the words are interpreted for their wisdom, they are secure from defect and weakness,

[72] Literally, 'the people of the mission/call', those initiated into the Ismāʿīlī mission. The *ahl al-daʿwa* is the historical self-designation that has been used by the Ismāʿīlī community to distinguish themselves from the non-Ismāʿīlī Muslims, at least since the stabilisation of the Fatimid dynasty in North Africa in the fourth/tenth century. See Farhad Daftary, *The Ismailis: Their Histories and Doctrines* (Cambridge, Cambridge University Press, 1990), esp. 228–32. For an important overview of the polyvalence of this term across Muslim historical, political and theological contexts, see M. Canard, 'Daʿwa', *EI*^{2}, II, 168–70.

[73] Q. 4:34 is the subject of ch. 3 in this volume.

[74] Versions of this *ḥadīth* are found in Abū Dāwūd, *Sunan*, *Kitāb al-Nikāḥ* (12), *Bāb fī ḥaqq al-zawj ʿalā al-imraʾa* (41), *ḥadīth* no. 95/2140; Ibn Māja, *Sunan*, *Kitāb al-Nikāḥ* (9), *Bāb fī ḥaqq al-zawj ʿalā al-imraʾa* (4), *ḥadīth* no. 9/1853; Tirmidhī, *Jāmiʿ*, *Kitāb al-Riḍāʿ* (12), *Bāb mā jāʾa fī ḥaqq al-zawj ʿalā al-marʾa* (10), *ḥadīth* no. 14/1159. For editions of all of these works, see the bibliography.

since the possessor of knowledge is superior to the seeker of knowledge in all aspects and the Prophet (*ṣl*ʿ) said, 'The possessors of knowledge are almost lords (*arbāb*)'.

Then God, glory be to Him, says, as He continues the verse, *be wary of God by whom you petition one another, and the wombs*. He returns to the mention of the command of wariness (*taqiyya*) as a manifestation of the specific meanings with which the verse is concerned, as previously mentioned.

He follows it with His words, magnified be His majesty, *and the wombs*, meaning preserve the overt kinship (*arḥām*), meaning maintain the ties of these rankings (*marātib*), one to the other. Do not be from among those who *sever that which God commands them to connect* [Q. 13:25]. In the act of bringing these together, and the connection of one to the other, is the connecting of the spiritual kinship of religion (*ṣilat al-raḥim al-dīnī*); and in the act of severing one from the other is the deviation (*zaygh*) from God's even path. It is narrated on the authority of the Prophet of God (*ṣl*ʿ) that he said, 'The womb-severer (*qāṭiʿ al-raḥim*) is cursed'.[75] So the ruling regarding the overt action of severing womb-ties is established, but regarding its inner (*bāṭin*) aspect, it is even more established, binding and certain. For indeed he (*ṣl*ʿ) – even though he was naturally inclined towards human kinship (*raḥim al-nās*), lest it be severed – knowing as he did how many a kinship tie was more worthy of being severed than being maintained, was always more inclined towards preserving spiritual kinship (*raḥim al-dīn*), because of having been sent to build a path to the Hereafter. As for whatever concerns this world, people are already fairly solicitous about it, without any need for individuals to instruct them and make them understand it.

God has made you the kinds of people who preserve the spiritual kinship in their religion, and He has gathered you in the band of the one who, when his mercy is sought, he is merciful.[76] Praise be to God who has reinforced the Messenger with the glorious Qur'ān and the 'seven oft-repeated ones' (*al-sabʿ al-mathānī*),[77] rendering what He has revealed by the witnessing of the

[75] This exact *ḥadīth* is not found in the major Sunnī collections, but several *ḥadīths* mention the importance of maintaining womb-ties; see note 56, above.

[76] Reference to the Prophet.

[77] The meaning of these seven '*mathānī*' (lit. pl. doubled) is the subject of much debate within Muslim tradition. In this phrasing, 'oft-repeated', it appears uniquely in Q. 15:87, but see also Q. 39:23 where *mathānī* is qualified by *kitāb mutashābih*. In both cases, the reference is elusive, even as it indicates certain parts of verses of the scripture. Good starting points for further reading on the issue are Welch *et al.*, 'al-Ḳur'ān', *EI*², V, 406–9 Uri Rubin, 'Oft-repeated', *EQ*, II, 575–6; W.M. Watt and R. Bell, *Introduction to the Qur'an* (Edinburgh, Edinburgh University Press, 1970), 134ff. On the figurative nature of 'seven' in this context, see Uri Rubin, 'Exegesis and *Ḥadīth*: The Case of the Seven *Mathānī*' in *Approaches to the Qur'ān*, ed. G.R. Hawting and Abdel-Kader A. Shareef (London, Routledge 1993), 141–56. It is noteworthy that a

intellect a means of constructing [spiritual] edifices, and the rending of the earth with His noble words to reveal spiritual flowers. And God bless the most excellent of what has issued out of the celestial spheres and in whose service the angels are in attendance, Muḥammad the chosen one (*muṣṭafā*), the perceptive intellect of the natural world; and his legatee (*waṣī*), from whose tongue effuses fulfilling bliss, that scorches with the heat of Hell where the sword and its blade touch, ʿAlī b. Abī Ṭālib, bearer of the title *the great tidings* [Q. 78:2]; and the imams from among his seed, the family of mercy and the guides of the community and the effacers of darkness by the light of their wisdom, and grant them much peace. *For God suffices for us and excellent is He as a guardian* [Q. 3:173].[78]

Zamakhsharī

Zamakhsharī, who was a grammarian, combines his analysis of grammar with an analysis of content, so that through the grammar he explains the meaning of the verse and the *sūra* as a whole. Grammatically, he describes how the phrase *from it created its mate* is adjoined to the previous phrase, *created you from a single soul*. He also focuses on the question of why the command to *be wary of your Lord* is not followed by a direct instruction of what the wariness would require of the believer. He explains that, in this instance, the command to be wary of God is followed by a demonstration of God's great power over humanity, in that He created all of humanity from a single person. He argues that, if properly understood, the believer will feel obliged to preserve the rights of their fellow human beings. Thus, like Ṭabarī, Zamakhsharī ultimately interprets this verse as referring to the necessity for people to take care of one another and not to forget their duties towards others less fortunate.

Zamakhsharī's interpretation of the final part of the verse refers to the womb hanging from the throne. This is a reference to the womb that hangs from God's throne, which becomes happy when it encounters someone who has preserved the tie to their womb-kin but conceals itself when it encounters someone who has severed it. This is one example of the way that kinship was evoked in order to encourage morality and decent treatment of relatives and family.

commentator as late as the Ottoman Baghdadi Abū'l-Thanā' Maḥmūd b. ʿAbd Allāh al-Alūsī (1270/1854) titled his exhaustive Qur'ānic commentary *Rūḥ al-maʿānī fī tafsīr al-Qur'ān al-ʿaẓīm wa'l-sabʿ al-mathānī*, ed. ʿAlī ʿAbd al-Bārī ʿAṭiyya, 16 vols. (Beirut, Dār al-Kutub al-ʿIlmiyya, 2005), glossing *sūrat al-Fātiḥa*'s seven verses (counting the *basmala* as v. 1); this reading is given early on in his extensive commentary on the *Fātiḥa* and, obviously again, at Q. 15:87, where he considers other sections or *sūra*s of the Qur'ān as signifying the seven 'oft-repeated' *mathānī*. The mysterious phrase occupies a good deal of Shahrastānī's unique commentary on the *Fātiḥa*, where the emphasis is on the function of the 'doublings'. See Toby Mayer, tr., *Keys to the Arcana: Shahrastānī's Esoteric Commentary on the Qur'an* (Oxford, Oxford University Press in association with the Institute of Ismaili Studies, 2009), esp. 35–46.

[78] Mu'ayyad, *Majālis*, I, 382–6 (s.v. *majlis* 79).

O people! O children of Adam (*banī Ādam*). *Created you from a single soul*: He has made you branch off from a single source, and that is the soul (*nafs*) of Adam, your father. And if you were to say, 'What about the coordination (*'aṭf*) of His words *and from it created its mate*?' I would say that there are two aspects to this.

The first of them is that the coordination is to something elided, as if He had said 'from a single soul, He brought it into being or He began it, and He created from it its mate'. 'He' has been omitted precisely because the meaning already indicates it, and its meaning is: He dispersed you from a single soul. This is its characteristic, that He brought the soul into being from the soil, and created its mate Eve from one of its ribs, *and spread forth from the two* the two sexes (*jins*) of humankind, these two being males and females. He described it [the soul] by explaining and detailing how they were created from it.

And the second [aspect] is that the coordination is with *who created you*. The address in *O people* is to those to whom the Messenger of God (*ṣl'm*) was sent. And the sense is: He created you from the soul of Adam because they are of the very same species (*jins*) branching out from him. He created from the soul your mother, Eve, and He *spread forth from the two many men and women* other than you, innumerable nations.

If you were to say, 'For the arrangement of the words to be sound and succinct, immediately after the command to wariness (*taqwā*) should come its cause, or its motive. So how is it that His creating of them from a single soul, in the detail that He has mentioned, necessitates an enjoinder to God-wariness (*taqwā*)?'

I would respond, because that is something that indicates the immensity of His power, and whoever has power over that kind of thing is all-powerful over everything. Among the things that He has power over is the punishment of disobedient ones, so considering this should cause one to be wary (*taqwā*) of the One who has power over him and to fear (*kh-sh-y*) His punishment. Because that is an indication of the boundless graces to them, it is their duty to be wary of (*taqwā*) Him when they deny and are remiss in their gratitude for these.

Or it may be that by *be wary* He means a specific form of being wary [of Him] (*taqwā*), and that is that they should be wary of Him (*taqwā*) with regard to preserving those rights due between them, not cutting the ties which they are obliged to maintain. And so it would be saying: 'Be wary of (*taqwā*) your Lord who joined you together, making you as branches from a single root, concerning that which is obligatory for some of you to undertake towards others; so preserve that, and do not be neglectful of it.' And this meaning corresponds to the signification of the *sūra*.

It is also read as *khāliq minhā zawjahā wa bāththa minhumā* ('the creator of its mate and the disperser from the two'), using the lexical form of the active participle, and this is a predicate of an elided subject, implying that He is the Creator;[79] and *tasā'alūna bihi* [is to be read as] *tatasā'alūna bihi*, where the *tā'* has been elided in the *sīn*. Some also read *tas'alūna*, which drops the second *tā'*, meaning, you ask one another (*yas'al*) in the name of God and the womb-ties, saying: 'Do this or that for the sake of God and the womb-ties' as a type of affectionate solicitation (*isti'ṭāf*); or 'I implore you by God and by the womb-ties' (*unāshiduka Allāh wa'l-raḥim*); or as in when you ask others on the basis of God and the womb-ties. They say that [the form] *tafā'alūn* stands in for [the form] *taf'alūn* in the case of a plural, as when you may say *ra'aytu al-hilāl wa-tarā'aynāhu*. This is supported by those who read it *taslūna bihi* with or without the *hamza*.

Al-arḥām has been read with all three case endings (*ḥarakāt*).

For the accusative, this can be on the basis of [one of] two aspects, either on the basis of *wa'ttaqū Allāha wa'l-arḥāma* or on the basis of a coordination (*'aṭf*) with a genitive construction, as when you might say *marartu bi-Zaydin wa-'Amra*; this is supported by the reading of Ibn Mas'ūd: *tasā'alūna bihi wa bi'l-arḥāmi*, where the genitive is on account of the coordination of an overt noun with an implicit one [sc. pronoun]. However, this [reading] is not flawless since the suffixed pronoun is attached as a name, and the genitive noun and the genitive preposition are as one. And so, in expressions like *marartu bihi wa-Zayd* and *hādhā ghulāmuhu wa-Zayd*, these are very closely attached; and when attachment is that close, due to repetition, it resembles a coordinated supplement to the word in question, which is not possible, and so it becomes necessary to repeat the preposition [*bi*], as when you would say *marartu bihi wa bi-Zaydin* and *hādhā ghulāmuhu wa ghulām Zaydin*. Do you not see the soundness of your expression when you say *ra'aytuka wa-Zaydan* or *marartu bi-Zaydin wa-'Amrin* in cases where the attachment is not strong [precisely] because it is not repeated? A pretext might be sought against this reading on the basis that there is, implicit, a repetition of the genitive preposition, analogous to *fa-mā bika wa'l-ayyāmi min 'ajabi*.

As for the nominative [reading], that may be on the basis of *it* being a subject whose predicate has been omitted, as though it were being said: 'And the womb-ties, also', meaning 'and the womb-ties are among the things to be guarded' or 'the womb-ties are among the things invoked when people petition one another'. The meaning is that they used to affirm that they had a Creator and used to petition one another by the mention of God and the

[79] Zamakhsharī, *al-Kashshāf*, I, p. 492–3.

womb-tie. So it was said to them, 'Be wary of God who created you and be wary of the One by whom you implore one another, and be wary of the womb-ties and do not sever them' or 'Be wary of God by whose remembrance and the remembrance of womb-ties you solicit one another affectionately'. He, mighty and majestic, by juxtaposing womb-ties with His name, has in effect declared that to keep them connected is paramount, similar to where He says *And your Lord decreed that you should not worship any but Him; and to parents, decency* [Q. 17:23].

[It is reported] on the authority of al-Ḥasan [al-Baṣrī], 'If one were to ask you in God's name, then grant him, and if he were to ask you for the sake of the womb-tie, then grant him [that], for the womb is suspended from the throne (*'arsh*).'[80] The meaning of that is what has been reported on the authority of Ibn 'Abbās, may God be pleased with both of them, 'The womb hangs from the throne. When it is approached by the one who had connected [his womb-ties], it become cheerful and talks to him, but when it is approached by the one who had severed [his womb-ties], it conceals itself from him.'

Ibn 'Uyayna was asked about his words (*ṣl'm*), 'Seek out the goodly for your seed'[81] – meaning, for your children, that is to say that a man should have his child borne lawfully – have you not heard His words, exalted be He, *and be wary of God by whom you petition one another, and the wombs*? The first thing he should do to connect (*ṣila*) is to choose for him a lawful place and not to sever his ties or his kinship, for the fornicator (*'āhir*) has nothing but hard stone.[82] He should then choose propriety (*ṣiḥḥa*) over allegation

[80] A *ḥadīth* about the womb hanging from the throne is found in Muslim, *Ṣaḥīḥ*, *Kitāb al-Birr wa'l-ṣila wa'l-ādāb* (45), *Bāb ṣilat al-raḥim wa-taḥrīm qaṭī'atihā* (6), *ḥadīth* no. 19/2555.

[81] Found in Ibn Māja, *Sunan*, *Kitāb al-Nikāḥ* (9), *Bāb al-akfā'* (46), *ḥadīth* no. 124/1968.

[82] The maxim, found in *ḥadīth*, is 'the bed is for the child, while the hard stone is for the fornicator' (*al-walad li'l-firāsh wa-li'l-'āhiri al-ḥajar*). See for instance Bukhārī, *Ṣaḥīḥ*, *Kitāb al-Ḥudūd* (86), *Bāb li'l-'āhir al-ḥajar* (23), *ḥadīth* no. 46/6818; ibid., *Kitāb al-Farā'iḍ* (85), *Bāb al-walad li'l-firāsh ḥurra kānat aw ama* (18), *ḥadīth* no. 27/6750; Ibn Māja, *Sunan*, *Kitāb al-Nikāḥ* (9), *Bāb al-walad li'l-firāsh wa-li'l-'āhir al-ḥajar*, *ḥadīth*s 160–63/2004–2007; Nasā'ī, *Sunan*, *Kitāb al-Ṭalāq* (27), *Bāb ilḥāq al-walad bi'l-firāsh idhā lam yanfihi ṣāḥib al-firāsh* (48), *ḥadīth*, no. 94/3842. Note that the root *ḥ-j-r*, of course, connotes 'stones', and one would have expected the connotation to be that of 'stoning' as in Islamic law (and indeed this is the way in which the *ḥadīth*s are often translated). However, since this is a pre-Islamic maxim, this transfer of meaning to a penal sense must have occurred later with the maturation of the jurisprudential institution, during the second/eighth century. On this process, and for a survey of the maxim across early Islamic sources, see Uri Rubin, who concentrates on the *firāsh*, and hence, the paternity issue, for the most part: '*Al-walad li'l-firāsh* and the Islamic Campaign against *Zinā*', *Studia Islamica* 78 (1993), 5–26. While 'stone' is, in effect, still the operative word, it is best understood as meaning that the adulterer or fornicator could have no relationship with the child, and the child belonged to the mother's spouse: 'the child belongs to the [matrimonial] bed, and the adulterer has only the hard stone-floor'. The root *ḥ-j-r* can also produce *ḥajr* or *ḥijr*, both of which mean 'isolation', 'restriction' or 'an impediment imposed', suggesting that the adulterer or fornicator could not expect to claim the child. The claims of paternity usually

(*daʿwa*) and not leave him in an immoral predicament where he then pursues his lusts and desires with no guidance from God.[83]

Ṭabrisī

Ṭabrisī gives two possible explanations for the way that Eve was created: either she was created from a rib, which is the opinion of the majority of the exegetes, or she was created from the clay left over after Adam's creation, an interpretation on the authority of Muḥammad al-Bāqir, the fifth Shīʿī imam. The first *tafsīr* source to record this *ḥadīth* is probably ʿAyyāshī's, whose version is much more elaborate, with the imam saying, 'Could not God have created her from something other than a rib?'[84] The implication here might be that women are equal to men because they are created from the same substance, but it should not imply to today's readers that the authors were therefore feminist or had an idea of equality in mind. Ṭabrisī, here, also includes the *ḥadīth* on the authority of the Prophet that women were created from a crooked rib, and men should not attempt to straighten them out. This has appeared already in this chapter in the interpretation of Hūd, an Ibāḍī. That two exegetes from such different backgrounds included this *ḥadīth* may be an indication of how widespread it was. It is noteworthy that Ṭabrisī includes both Sunnī and Shīʿī *ḥadīth*s in his interpretation of this verse.

For the womb-ties, Ṭabrisī emphasises the connection between individuals' pious connection to God and their connection to blood kin in this world. This interpretation includes a variation of the interpretation cited by Qushayrī that whoever connects the womb-ties connects to God, and whoever severs them is severed from God. Furthermore, he cites an interpretation that discourages anger towards a womb-kin, saying that the person who harbours such anger should contact his kin or run the risk of damnation. The link between worldly kin ties and spiritual salvation is clear, and Ṭabrisī draws a linguistic comparison, saying that the name for 'womb', *raḥim*, is derived from God's name, al-Raḥmān (All-merciful). Thus, for him, the womb-tie is directly linked to God's very essence as *al-raḥmān*.

The content of Ṭabrisī's interpretation of the final part of the verse bears some resemblance to that of Ṭabarī and also has echoes of Zamakhsharī, and although he cites some Shīʿī sources, the interpretation itself does not seem particularly Shīʿī: for instance, nothing is said about Fāṭima or any blood connection to the Prophet's line.

involved slave girls who were by far those most frequently embroiled in such extramarital relations. For the lexical possibilities, see Lane, *Lexicon*, s.v. *ḥ-j-r* (518) and s.v. *ʿ-h-r* (2184). Patricia Crone, *Roman, Provincial and Islamic Law: The Origins of the Islamic Patronate* (Cambridge, Cambridge University Press, 1987), 10ff., saw in this instance a clear Jewish influence, as against Goldziher who assumed it to have been carried over from Roman law. Of relevance, and more recent, is Robert Hoyland, *Arabia and the Arabs*, 129, who discusses the possibility that pre-Islamic women could engage in socially acceptable extramarital sex.

[83] Zamakhsharī, *al-Kashshāf*, s.v. Q. 4:1.

[84] Bauer, 'Room for Interpretation', 38; eadem, *Gender Hierarchy*, 123–5.

Reading (*qirāʾa*)

The Kufans read *tasāʾalūna* with a single consonant, while the others double it. Ḥamza reads *al-arḥāmi* in the genitive, while others read it in the accusative. Among the uncommon (*shādhdh*) readings is *arḥām* in the nominative (*waʾl-arḥāmu*).

Proof (*ḥujja*)

Those who read *tasāʾalūna* with a single consonant mean *tatasāʾalūna*, but one *tāʾ* is omitted from the [verbal paradigm] *tatafāʿalūna* [. . .].[85]

Language (*lugha*)

'Spreading forth' (*al-bathth*) is 'dispersion' (*al-nashr*), that is to say, God spread forth humankind, and in this way are His words *like moths scattered about* (*kaʾl-farāsh al-mabthūth*) [Q. 101:4]. Some say *abaththa*, with the same meaning. One says *bathathtuka sirrī* or *abthathtuka sirrī* as two alternative expressions for the same thing.[86] *Al-raqīb* derives from *al-taraqqub*, which is to [lie in] wait (*intiẓār*), and from this is derived *al-ruqbā*,[87] as each of the two parties awaits the death of the other [. . .].[88]

Meaning (*maʿnā*)

God, glory be to Him, began this *sūra* with the admonition and the command of wariness (*taqwā*), so He said, *O people!* which is an address to all morally obliged human beings (*al-mukallafūn*).[89] The vocative in all of God's preceding scriptures was, 'O you wretched ones!' (*yā ayyuhāʾl-masākīn*). As for the Qurʾān, the appeal in that part which was sent down (*nazala*) in

[85] The rest of this lengthy grammatical explanation can be gleaned from Zamakhsharī, above, for this interpretation is practically a replica of it.

[86] Ṭabrisī goes on to discuss another word later in the verse, which does not appear in the part of the verse analysed here.

[87] In jurisprudential discussions, *al-ruqbā* means usufruct for a fixed period or a deathbed gift (*donatio mortis causa*). See A.A.A. Fyzee, *Outlines of Muhammadan Law* (Oxford, Oxford University Press, 1976).

[88] We are omitting here a prolix discussion of the syntax of particles and how they function. This happens under two sections under *iʿrāb* and *al-nuzūl waʾl-naẓm* (revelation and arrangement); but the commentary verges on issues that are not directly relevant.

[89] *Mukallaf* (*k-l-f, taklīf*) has the etymological sense of being charged with something, or having a burden. Therefore, the translation as 'legal competence', which is satisfactory in jurisprudential discussions, loses the sense of moral responsibility that is the primary issue in the context of discussions on the purpose of creation. One could consider the moral responsibility to be prior to the legal responsibility, which is also contained in the term. See D. Gimaret, 'Taklīf', *EI*², X, 139. Because this term refers to one who is literally 'charged with' some duty, elsewhere we render the term 'of legal age', understood in a religious context as being of the age at which an individual becomes legally obliged (by the sharia) to perform their religious duties, usually upon reaching puberty.

Mecca is *O people!* and that which was sent down in Medina is sometimes *O you Believers!* and sometimes *O people!*

[Regarding] *Be wary of your Lord*, its meaning is to be wary of disobedience to your Lord, or going against your Lord by leaving that which He has commanded and pursuing that which He has forbidden. It is said that its meaning is: Be wary of (*ittaqū*) what is due to Him lest you should forsake it. And it is said: Be wary of His punishment. So it is as though He said it is a duty upon you to fear the punishment of the One who has conferred on you the greatest of graces, which is that He has created you from a single soul and brought you into existence. The one whose estimation appreciates this grace is more likely to be God-wary (*taqwā*). It is said that the intention of it is to explain the perfection of His power, as though He said: Who has power to create you from a single soul has all the more power to punish you, and therefore it is your duty to abandon any contravention of Him and to guard against (*tattaqū*) His punishment.

[Regarding] His words *who created you from a single soul*, the intention of the term *soul* here is Adam, according to all of the exegetes, and He did not say a single soul (*nafs wāḥid*) in the masculine, even though the intention is Adam, because the grammatical form (*ṣīgha*) of the expression 'soul' is feminine. It is like the saying of the poet:

> Your father is a caliph who begat another, and you are a successor of that perfection.

So it was made feminine according to the form. If He had said 'from a single soul' (*min nafsin wāḥidin*) [with the word soul in the masculine form], it would have been permissible.

From it created its mate means Eve (ʿ*am*). The majority of exegetes go so far as to say that she was created from one of Adam's ribs. It is narrated on the authority of the Prophet (ʿ*m*) that he said, 'Woman was created from a rib of Adam's, if you try to straighten her, you will break her, whereas if you leave her as she is, with her crookedness, you can enjoy her.'[90] It is narrated on the authority of Abū Jaʿfar al-Bāqir (ʿ*m*) that God created Eve from the surplus clay (*ṭīna*) from which Adam was created. And in the *Tafsīr* of ʿAlī b. Ibrāhīm [al-Qummī], from his lowest rib.

And spread forth from the two many men, that is to say, He dispersed (*nashara*) and divided (*farraqa*) from those two souls, by way of procreation, men *and women*. Moreover, He has done us a tremendous favour by creating us from a single soul, because it is more likely that we will be more solicitous

[90] For the variants of the 'crooked rib' *ḥadīth* in the major Sunnī collections, see above.

towards each other and that we will have mercy on each other because we all go back to the same origin, and because that is the utmost expression of power, and the clearest indication of wisdom and knowledge.[91]

With regard to the meaning of His words *and be wary of God by whom you petition one another*, there are two opinions. One of these is that it is like when they say, *as'aluka bi'llāh an tafʿal kadhā* (I am asking you by God to do so and so), as well as *unshiduka bi'llāh wa bi'l-raḥim* or *nashadtuka Allāha wa'l-raḥim* (I am imploring by God and by the womb). That is what the Arabs used to say, according to al-Ḥasan [al-Baṣrī] and Ibrāhīm [al-Nakhaʿī]. Accordingly, then, His words *wa'l-arḥām* (*and the wombs*) is a coordinated supplement (*ʿaṭf*) to the [syntactical] position occupied by *bihi* (*by whom*). The meaning, then, is: just as you magnify God in speech, magnify Him also by being obedient to Him.

The other [of the two opinions] is that the meaning of *by whom you petition one another* is 'by whom you demand of one another your due and your needs'. As for *and the wombs* (*wa'l-arḥāma*), that is fear 'the womb [ties]' and do not sever them, according to Ibn ʿAbbās, Qatāda, Mujāhid, al-Ḍaḥḥāk, al-Rabīʿ and as related on the authority of Abū Jaʿfar [al-Bāqir] (*ʿm*) in which case it is in the accusative as a coordination with the name of God, exalted be He, and which also indicates that the connecting of womb-ties (*ṣilat al-raḥim*) is an obligation (*wājib*). This is supported by what he reported on the authority of the Prophet (*ṣlʿm*), who said that God said, 'I am the All-merciful (*raḥmān*). I created the womb (*raḥim*) and gave it a name extracted from My name. And so whoever connects it, I shall connect him [to Me], and whoever severs it, I shall cut him off'.[92] There are many reports similar to this one. The connecting of womb-ties can mean accepting kinship ties (*nasab*), or it may be to expend on the maintenance of a womb-kin (*dhū raḥim*) and similar acts.

Al-Aṣbagh b. Nubāta[93] reported on the authority of the Commander of the Believers [ʿAlī b. Abī Ṭālib] (*ʿm*), 'Verily, some of you may become angered [by something] and will not be appeased until they enter hellfire because of that. So, whichever man among you becomes angry with a womb-kin (*dhū raḥim*), let him contact him (*m-s-s*), for the womb-kin, when it comes into contact (*m-s-s*) with [another] womb-kin, becomes settled. For verily it

[91] Ṭabrisī, *Majmaʿ al-bayān*, s.v. Q. 4:1.

[92] A version is found in Tirmidhī, *Jāmiʿ*, *Kitāb al-Birr wa'l-ṣila ʿan rasūl Allāh* (*ṣlʿm*) (27), *Bāb mā jā'a fī qaṭīʿat al-raḥim* (9), *ḥadīth* no. 13/1907. Also see the version cited by Rāzī, below, which is more widely attested.

[93] A close companion of ʿAlī b. Abī Ṭālib who fought alongside him at the Battle of the Camel and at Ṣiffīn. He died after 100/718. See the PA.

[*al-raḥim*] is attached to the throne and calls out, saying, "O Lord, connect whoever connects me and sever whoever severs me."'

Indeed, God is (*kāna*) *Watcher* (*raqīb*) *over you*, that is to say, 'keeper' (*ḥāfiẓ*), according to Mujāhid, and according to Ibn Zayd *raqīb* means 'knower' (*ʿālim*). The meaning [in both cases] is close enough. The reason He uses the expression *kāna*, which indicates a past tense, is that He means He has been Watcher over those of a bygone age, from the time of Adam and his children to the time of the addressees, knowing all that they have done without that burdening Him in any way.[94]

Rāzī

Rāzī's interpretation of Q. 4:1 is probably the most complex medieval interpretation of the verse, for two reasons. The first is because of his in-depth analysis, in which he takes a holistic view of the verse, the *sūra* and the moral obligations on humans. The second is because he incorporates branches of knowledge that have hitherto been overlooked in the genre of *tafsīr*.[95]

For Rāzī, the theme of the *sūra* is that *people* (by which he presumably means men) must be affectionate towards women and children and work to secure their rights for them. This is a common refrain in the interpretations of Q. 4:1, perhaps because the idea that men are responsible for those who are less able to take care of themselves is so prominent in the Qur'ān, and in particular in *sūrat al-Nisāʾ*.

After his initial introduction, Rāzī goes on to address several issues in Q. 4:1. The first is whether the verse is universal or addressed to a particular group of people. He cites the exegete Ibn ʿAbbās as saying that the verse was only addressed to the Meccans, rather than to all people. Rāzī argues against this view, saying (in agreement with all other exegetes) that it is a general address to all legally obligated people [or legal personages, *mukallafūn*] because *people* is in the plural: the reference is to fearing God as the creator of all humans, not just a portion of them, and the obligation of fearing is not specific to the Meccans but rather applies to all people.

The next issue is that the opening, *O people! Be wary of your Lord*, in this verse is identical to the opening of *sūrat al-Ḥajj* (Q. 22). Rāzī explains this by saying that this *sūra*, *sūrat al-Nisāʾ*, indicates the beginning of human life, with references to human creation, and *sūrat al-Ḥajj* indicates the end of it, with its references to Judgment Day.

The third issue for Rāzī is that humans must fear God because He created us from a single soul. This creation, he reminds us, should be understood as the utmost end of goodness, for which humans should be grateful. Furthermore, in his view, the creation from a single soul entails the obligation to be good to orphans, women and those who are weak, because the deeper lesson of this verse is to increase compassion among

94 Ṭabrisī, *Majmaʿ al-bayān*, s.v. Q. 4:1.

95 For more on the hermeneutics and exegetical methods of Fakhr al-Dīn al-Rāzī's *tafsīr*, see Jaffer, *Razi*.

people. Thus people must abandon pride and arrogance, and embrace humility and compassion. Rāzī points out that the idea of creation from a single person does not come naturally to the mind. Instead, it is an idea that is only known through 'traditional proofs'.

Several pages into his commentary, Rāzī reaches the point from which most commentaries start, which is that the meaning of the *single soul* is Adam and the *mate* is Eve. Here, he cites not only the majority interpretation (creation from a rib) but also a minority interpretation on the authority of Abū Muslim al-Iṣfahānī that says Eve was created of the same type as Adam, which he supports by citing several other verses where references to *min nafs* mean 'of the same type'. Though Rāzī cites the first doctrine from al-Qāḍī 'Abd al-Jabbār, he himself prefers the second. He justifies this preference by asking, if God was capable of creating Eve from anything, why would He have created her from a rib? Such justification is seen only in some earlier Shīʿī commentaries.[96]

The interpretation ends with a discussion about whether Adam was created from nothing or from pre-existing material. For Rāzī, this creation was not something from another but was rather from nothing prior.

Rāzī's interpretation of the final part of the verse is heavily grammatical and scholarly, focusing on variant readings and the interpretations of grammatical authorities. One interpretation that has not previously been cited in this selection is that of al-Qāḍī 'Abd al-Jabbār, who is quoted as saying that being wary of God and being wary of the womb-ties have different significations, for wariness of God entails obedience to Him, whereas wariness of the womb-ties entails 'their being maintained and not severed'. He references a dispute over whether the 'womb' and 'the Merciful' are really derived from the same root, as in the interpretation referenced by Ṭabrisī.

Rāzī also cites two legal positions held by the Ḥanafīs that are based on the preservation of ties with blood kin. The first is that close relatives must not be owned as slaves and the second is that gifts given to them must not be taken back. He finishes by saying that the statement of God as Watcher is to remind people of the promise and the threat that they should turn to God in hope and fear.

Know that this *sūra* subsumes many different kinds of legal obligations, and that is because He ordered people in the beginning of this *sūra* to be favourably inclined (*'aṭf*)[97] towards children, women and orphans, and be tenderly compassionate (*ra'fa*) towards them, and to secure their rights for them and protect their wealth for them; and it is in this sense that the *sūra* concludes, that is, with His words, *They request from you a ruling. Say, 'God will give you a ruling with regard to the person who has no descendants or ascendants* (*kalāla*)' [Q. 4:176]. He mentions in the course of this *sūra* other types of duties, such as the command to purification, prayer and fighting the idolaters (*mushrikūn*), and since these obligations are difficult for the souls (*nufūs*)

[96] See also Bauer, *Gender Hierarchy*, 131–2.

[97] The word can also mean affectionate, sympathetic, caring, considerate.

because they are naturally burdensome, then of course He would open the *sūra* with the reason (*ʿilla*) why these difficult obligations must be borne, and that is [out of] wariness of the Lord (*taqwā al-rabb*) who created us and the God which brought us into being. Because of that, He said *O people! Be wary of your Lord, who created you*. There are several issues (*masāʾil*) in this verse.

The first issue (*al-masʾala al-ūlā*): Al-Wāḥidī relates on the authority of Ibn ʿAbbās, with regard to His saying *O people!*, that it is an address to the Meccans. As for the rationalists (Uṣūlīs) from among the exegetes,[98] they unanimously agree that it is a general address to all who are morally obligated (*mukallaf*), and this is the best interpretation on account of several aspects (*wujūh*). The first of these is that the form of the word *people* is in the plural, and He included the definite article which signifies all-inclusiveness. The second of them is that He explained the causative aspect of the matter by means of being wary of (*ittiqāʾ*) Him as the Creator of them from a single soul, and this cause applies generally to the reality of all who are morally obligated (*mukallafūn*), in that they are all of them created from Adam (*ʿm*). When the cause is a general one, then the ruling is general. The third [aspect] is that the obligation of wariness (*taqwā*) is not specific to the Meccans but rather applies to all peoples, and given that the form of the word *people* applies to a totality, and the command to be wary applies to a totality, and the reason for this obligation, which is that they were created from the single soul, also applies to the totality, to prefer the opinion of specification [of the Meccans] is far away [from the truth]. Ibn ʿAbbās [takes it as] proof that His words *Be wary of God by whom you petition one another, and the wombs* are specific to the Arabs since the appeal to God and the womb-ties is a specific custom of theirs. They say, 'I ask you by God and by the wombs' and 'I implore you by God and by the wombs.' But if that was so, then His words *Be wary of God by whom you petition one another, and the wombs* would be specific to the Arabs. If it were so, then in the beginning of the verse, where He says *O people*, it would be specific to them, because His words in the beginning of the verse, *Be wary of your Lord*, and His words after that, *Be wary of God by whom you petition one another, and the wombs*, are both references applied to a single addressee. It is possible that the answer to that is that it is established in the principles of jurisprudence (*uṣūl al-fiqh*) that a specification at the end of the verse does not preclude a generalisation at its beginning, so His words

[98] When Rāzī says the Uṣūlīs, he is speaking of those rationalists who do not rely primarily on tradition. Note that at the end of this section he uses an argument from those who use *uṣūl al-fiqh*. Note too that this discussion is picked up by Riḍā/ʿAbduh below.

O people are general concerning everyone, and His words *fear God by whom you petition one another, and the wombs* are specific to the Arabs.

The second issue (*al-mas'ala al-thāniya*): He made this the starting point (*maṭla'*) of two *sūra*s in the Qur'ān, the first of them being this *sūra*, that is, the fourth *sūra* in the first half of the Qur'ān; the second being *al-Ḥajj*, which is also the fourth *sūra* [but] in the second part of the Qur'ān. Thus He explained the order to wariness (*taqwā*) in this *sūra* with that which would indicate the knowledge of the Beginning, when He created humankind from a single soul, and this indicates the perfection of the power of the Creator, the perfection of His knowledge, the perfection of His wisdom and His majesty. And He explained the enjoinder to wariness of God (*taqwā*) in *sūrat al-Ḥajj* with that which would indicate the perfection of knowledge of the Return, and that is His words *the earthquake of the Hour [of reckoning] is a mighty thing* [Q. 22:1]. So He made the heart of these two *sūra*s a proof of knowledge of the Beginning and knowledge of the Return; then He put the *sūra* indicating the Beginning before the *sūra* indicating the Return. Under this [subject] there are many secrets to be explored.

The third issue (*al-mas'ala al-thālitha*): Know that He ordered us to wariness (*taqwā*), and [since] He mentioned subsequently our creation from a single soul, this gives the sense that the command of wariness is causatively explained by the fact that God created us from a single soul, [therefore] it is necessary to clarify the correspondence between this ruling and that description. So we say: Our doctrine is that He created us from a single soul, which comprises two restrictions. The first of them is that He created us, and the second is the modality (*kayfiyya*) of that creation, which is that He created us from only a single soul. For each of these two restrictions [there] is a transmission concerning the necessity of wariness.

As for the first restriction, it is that He created us and there is no doubt that this signification is a cause (*'illa*) [of wariness], because we are obliged to yield to the obligations imposed by God, and to submit to His commands and His prohibitions. And this can be explained in several aspects (*wujūh*).

The first [aspect] is that He, since He was the creator of us, and the Originator of our essence and our attributes (*dhātinā wa ṣifātinā*), is thus the master of us, and we are His slaves. Lordship requires that His commands for His servants are carried through, and servitude entails yielding to the Lord, Originator and Creator.

The second [aspect] is that the bringing into existence is the utmost in graciousness and the utmost in munificence. You were nothing, and He made you come into existence; dead, and He made you come alive; incapable, and He gave you power; ignorant, and He gave you knowledge. As Abraham (*ʿm*) said, [it was He] *who created me and it is He who guides me, who gives me food and drink* [Q. 26:78–9]. Blessings are entirely from God, and it is obligatory on the servant to accept those blessings by demonstrating submission and yielding, and abandoning recalcitrance and stubbornness – this is the intention of His words *How can you reject God, when you were dead and He gave you life, then He makes you die, then He will give you life* [Q. 2:28].

The third [aspect] is that when He established His existence as Originator and Creator, a god and a lord to us, He made it obligatory for us to devote ourselves to His service, and [obligatory] that we have wariness of (*taqwā*) all that He has forbidden and that He has cautioned against. None of these acts ought to require a reward at all, because these acts of obedience, having been required in return for the aforementioned graces, preclude them requiring reward, because to give what is due to whom it is due entails nothing further. That is assuming that the servant had fulfilled those acts of obedience at the outset. How otherwise, for it is impossible. Enacting the obedience can only come about if God has created the capacity for obedience, and has created the motive for obedience, and only when both the capacity and the motivation are actualised does the combination of the two of them require the issuance of an act of obedience from the servant. And since it is so, then that obedience is a blessing bestowed from God upon His servant, and the master, when He singles out His servant for graces, that grace requires no additional graces. This is the indication of how to explain [why] His being our Creator requires our obedience and avoidance of His prohibitions.

As for the second restriction, that specifying him as our creator from a single soul requires from us obedience and taking precautions (*iḥtirāz*) against disobedience, its explication has several aspects (*wujūh*).

The first [aspect] is that the creation of all individual humans from one single human is more indicative of perfect power. For, if the matter were to do with nature (*ṭabīʿa*) or specific properties, then what would be generated from a single human being would be nothing more than things with attributes of similar shape, and similar in natural created form. But when we see in the individuated forms of people the white, black, red, brown, beautiful, ugly, tall, and short, that indicates that [there is] one managing it and creating it [that] is a voluntary agent (*fāʿil mukhtār*), rather than [it being the result of] natural determinism (*ṭabīʿa muʾaththira*) or a necessitating cause (*ʿilla mūjiba*).[99] Since this point of detail indicates that the manager of the world is a voluntary agent who has power over all contingent beings (*mumkināt*) and has knowledge of all knowable things, then it is obligatory to yield to the obligations He has imposed (*taklīf*), and to His commands and prohibitions. So the connection between His words *be wary of your Lord* and His words *who created you from a single soul* is most beautifully arranged.

The second aspect is that when He mentioned the command to wariness (*taqwā*), He subsequently mentioned the command to be virtuous to orphans, women and the weak. Their creation in their entirety from a single soul has an effect on the meaning, and that is because there is inevitably between kin, correspondence and intermingling, which necessitates an increase in affection, which is why people rejoice in the praise of their relatives and their forbears, and they are saddened by their disparagement and [by] accusations against them. The Prophet said, 'Fāṭima is a piece of my flesh, and what hurts her hurts me'.[100] Given that, then the lesson (*fāʾida*) in mentioning this signification is it becomes a cause for greater compassion of created beings for one another.

The third aspect is that people, when they know that they all come from a single soul, abandon pride and arrogance, and they demonstrate humility and good morals.

The fourth aspect is that this is proof of the Return: since He, exalted be He, is able to bring forth from the loins of one person many different people, and to create from a droplet of sperm an individual of wondrous construction and delicate form, how can the revivification of the dead, their awakening and their spreading forth be far removed? Thus the verse is proof of the Return in this respect: *that He may recompense those who do evil for what they have done and recompense those who have done good with the most beautiful reward* [Q. 53:31].

[99] Rāzī here presents the Aʿsharī position on the nature and role of God with regard to creation and God's active role in daily life, as against the natural determinism of the philosophers. On this debate in general, see S. Nomanul Haq and D.E. Pingree, 'Ṭabīʿa', *EI*², X, 25–8; also, Peter Adamson, 'Creation and the God of Abraham', *Journal of Islamic Studies* 23 (2012), 89–91. On the creation debate, especially between Ghazālī and Rāzī, see David B. Burrell, 'Creation' in *The Cambridge Companion to Classical Islamic Theology*, ed. Winter, 141–79; also, Peter Adamson and Robert Wisnovsky, 'Yaḥyā Ibn ʿAdī on a *Kalām* Argument for Creation' in *Oxford Studies in Medieval Philosophy*, ed. Robert Pasnau (Oxford, Oxford University Press, 2013), I, 205–28; Richard M. Frank, *Al-Ghazālī and the Ashʿarite School* (Durham, NC, Duke University Press, 1994), 36–9.

[100] Muslim, *Ṣaḥīḥ*, *Kitāb Faḍāʾil al-ṣaḥāba, raḍiya Allāhu taʿālā ʿanhum* (44), *Bāb faḍāʾil Fāṭima bint al-nabī ʿalayhā al-ṣalāt waʾl-salām* (15), *ḥadīth* no. 138/2449; another version is found in Tirmidhī, *Jāmiʿ*, *Kitāb al-Manāqib ʿan rasūl Allāh* (*ṣlʿm*) (49), *ḥadīth* no. 4243.

The fifth aspect is that al-Aṣamm[101] said the lesson in it is that the mind does not indicate that the creation would have come from a single individual, but rather this is only known through traditional proofs. The Prophet was illiterate, he did not read a book, nor did he study under a teacher, and when he was informed of this meaning, it was a message about the unknown; so it was a miracle, and so the outcome of His words *created you* is proof of the knowledge of unity and His words *from a single soul* is proof of the knowledge of prophecy.
If it is said: How can it be true that the collective, in its multitude, was created from a single soul with the insignificance (*ṣighar*) of that soul? We say: God has clarified the intention of that since the mate of Adam was created from part of him, and he reached the creation of his progeny through their sperm. That is how it all began, so it is permissible to attribute all creation to Adam.

The fourth issue (*mas'ala*): The Muslims unanimously agree that the intention of the *single soul* here is Adam (*'m*) except that the descriptor is feminine due to the form of the word *soul*. Its parallel [occurs] where God says, *You have slain an innocent soul who has slain none* [Q. 18:74].[102] And the poet says:

> Your father is a caliph who begat another, so you are a successor of that perfection.[103]

They say that 'another' is feminine according to the form of the word caliph.

His words *and from it created its mate* comprise several issues (*masā'il*).
The first issue (*mas'ala*): What is meant by the term *mate* (*zawj*) is Eve. With regard to Eve being created from Adam, there are two opinions. The first, held by the majority, is that when God created Adam He cast upon him a sleep, then He created Eve from one of his left ribs, and when he woke he saw her and inclined towards her and found her familiar (*a-l-f*) because she was created from one of his parts. They find proof for this from a saying of the Prophet: 'Woman was indeed created from the most crooked rib, and if you desire to make her straight you will break her, and if you leave her crooked you can enjoy her'.[104]

[101] Abū Bakr 'Abd al-Raḥmān b. Kaysān, 'al-Aṣamm' (d. 200–201/816–17) was an early influential figure among the Basran Mu'tazila. See the PA and the extensive entry in Josef van Ess, 'al-Aṣamm', *EI*², XII, 89–90.

[102] In Arabic: *al-qatalta nafsan zakiyyatan bi-ghayr nafsin?* The word *zakiyya* has a feminine ending to match *nafs* but refers to a boy in the context of this *sūra*.

[103] As in the examples given earlier, the word 'another' (*ukhrā*) is in the feminine to match 'caliph' (*khalīfa*).

[104] Versions of the 'most crooked rib' *ḥadīth* are found in: Bukhārī, *Ṣaḥīḥ*, *Kitāb Aḥādīth al-anbiyā'* (60), *Bāb khalq Ādam ('m) wa-dhuriyatihi* (1), *ḥadīth* no. 6/3331; Muslim, *Ṣaḥīḥ*, *Kitāb al-Riḍā'a* (17), *Bāb al-waṣiyya bi'l-nisā'* (18), *ḥadīths* no. 77–80/715, 1467–1468. Other 'crooked rib' *ḥadīths* are cited above, see note 32 (Hūd).

The second opinion, which is that of Abū Muslim al-Iṣfahānī, is that *from it created its mate* means from its genus (*jins*), and that is similar to His words *and God made mates for you from among yourselves* (*wa-Allāhu jaʿala lakum min anfusikum azwājan*) [Q. 16:72], and like His words *He called forth a Messenger from among themselves* (*idh baʿatha fīhim rasūlan min anfusihim*) [Q. 3:164] and His words *Verily, there has come a messenger from among yourselves* (*la-qad jāʾakum rasūlun min anfusikum*) [Q. 9:128]. Al-Qāḍī [ʿAbd al-Jabbār] says the first doctrine is stronger, so that His words *created you from a single soul* are true; for if Eve was created in the beginning, then people would have been created from two souls, not from a single soul. It is possible to answer him by saying that the [first instance of the] word *from* is for the initial purpose of creation, and since the beginning of creation and bringing into existence eventuated with Adam, it is correct to say that *He created you from a single soul*. Likewise, since it is established that God is capable of creating Adam from dust, it is also established that he is capable of creating Eve from dust, and because the matter is like that, then what is the point in creating her from one of Adam's ribs?[105]

The second issue (*masʾala*): Ibn ʿAbbās said, 'He was only called by the name Adam because the Almighty created him from all the skins of the earth (*min adīm al-arḍ kullihā*), its red and black, its good and bad, and because of this his sons are red and black, good and bad. And woman was only called Eve (Ḥawwāʾ) because she was created from one of Adam's ribs and therefore was created from something alive (*ḥayy*),[106] so that is undoubtedly why she is called Eve.'

The third issue (*masʾala*): A group of natural philosophers (*ṭabāʾiʿiyyūn*) use this verse to argue the following: His words *created you from a single soul* are proof that the creation of all of them was from a single soul and that His words *and from it created its mate* are proof that its mate was created from it.[107] Then He said, describing Adam, *He created him from dust* [Q. 3:59],[108] proving that Adam was created from dust. He then says, when speaking about the reality

[105] For a discussion of early Twelver Imāmī alternative interpretations, see Bauer, *Gender Hierarchy*, 123ff., citing ʿAyyāshī (*fl.* late third/ninth century), on whom, see Hamza *et al.*, *Anthology*, I, 26–7.

[106] The root *ḥ-y-y* is meant to generate Eve's Arabic name, Ḥawwāʾ.

[107] It is worth noting that the term for 'soul', *nafs* (fem.), is, here in the text, in a genitive relationship with *zawj*, as *zawjuhā*, which means 'its mate', but at the same time customarily encountered as 'her husband or spouse'. Rāzī writes *yadullu ʿalā anna zawjahā makhlūqatun minhā*, that is, the spouse or mate of the soul.

[108] Q. 3:59 reads: *The example of Jesus with God is like Adam; He created him from dust, and He said be, and he was.*

of created beings, *from it We created you* [Q. 20:55].[109] All of these verses prove that accidents (*ḥādith*) can only come into being (*ḥ-d-th*) from some pre-existing matter from which that thing then becomes a created thing,[110] and that the creation of something from pure non-existence (*ʿadam maḥḍ*) and sheer non-being (*nafy ṣarf*) is impossible. The theologians (*mutakallimūn*), however, counter by saying that actually to create something from something [else] is simply impossible (*muḥāl*) to conceive of in the intellect (*ʿuqūl*), since if that created thing were to be identical with the thing that had been in existence before, then it could not have become a created thing in the first place, and if it then cannot become a created thing, then that would preclude it from having been created from something else anyway.

And if we were to say that such a created thing would be something other than that thing which existed before, then [we would effectively be saying that] this thing, which has now been created and come into being, could only have come into being and resulted from pure non-existence (*ʿadam maḥḍ*). It is thus established that for something to be created from something other than it cannot be conceived of by the intellect. As for the word *min* (from) in this verse, it signifies the initial purpose, meaning that the inception of these things coming into being from those [other] things is not because of any need (*ḥāja*) or dependency (*iftiqār*), but perfunctorily as an event and nothing else.

The fourth issue: The author of *al-Kashshāf* [al-Zamakhsharī] read it as follows: *wa-khāliqa minhā zawjihā baththa minhumā* using the active participle which is the predicate of an elided subject, the intended meaning of which is *khāliq* (creator).

[Regarding] His words, exalted be He, *and spread forth from the two many men and women*, there are several issues (*masāʾil*).

The first issue: Al-Wāḥidī says *baththa minhumā*, and by this he means separation (*farq*) and dispersion (*nashr*). Ibn al-Muẓaffar said, *al-bathth* is when you separate things (*tafrīq al-ashyāʾ*), as when one says he dispatches the horses in the raid (*bathth al-khayl fī'l-ghāra*), or the hunter dispatches (*bathth*) his dogs. So God creates creation and then disperses them on the earth. One says 'I spread the carpets' (*bathathtu al-busuṭ*), meaning 'I unfurled (*n-sh-r*) them.' God, exalted be He, says *and carpets spread out* (*zarābī mabthūtha*) [Q. 88:16]. Al-Farrāʾ and al-Zajjāj say, 'Some Arabs say *abaththa Allāhu al-khalq*.'

[109] Q. 20:55 reads: *From it [the earth] We created you, and into it We shall return you, and from it We shall bring you out once again.*

[110] *Al-ḥādith lā yaḥduth illā ʿan mādda sābiqa yaṣīr al-shayʾ makhlūqan minhā.*

The second issue: God does not say 'and spread forth from the two the men and the women' (*wa-baththa minhumā al-rijāl wa'l-nisā'*) because that would entail the two of them having been spread forth from themselves. And that is why He refrained from that expression in favour of His words *spread forth from the two many men and women*. If it were said, 'Why did He not say "and spread forth from the two many men and many women"? And why does he single out the qualifier "many" in the case of the men and not the women?' We would say that the reason is, and God knows best, that the conspicuousness of men is more complete, and their multitude is more obvious, so inevitably they are singled out for being qualified as multitudinous. And this is like an alert to the fact that what is most appropriate for the condition of men is prominence, going out and being visible, and what is appropriate for the condition of women is concealment and passivity.

The third issue: Those who say that all human individuals were like atoms and they were concentrated in the loins of Adam (*'m*) have interpreted His words *spread forth from the two many men and women* literally (*'alā ẓāhirihi*). And those who deny that say that what is meant is that He spread forth from the two of them their progeny, and from that progeny another multitude. So the totality is attributed to them metaphorically.

Regarding His words, exalted be He, *be wary of God by whom you petition one another, and the wombs; indeed God is Watcher over you*, there are several issues (*masā'il*).

The first issue: 'Āṣim, Ḥamza and al-Kisā'ī read *tasā'alūna* with a single consonant (*takhfīf*), while the others read it with an intensification (*tashdīd*) [. . .].[111]

The second issue: Ḥamza alone read *arḥāmi* in the genitive. According to al-Qaffāl, God have mercy on him, this reading, which is not the reading of one of the seven readings, has been reported on the authority of Mujāhid and others. As for the rest of the readers, all of them read it with the ending in the accusative (*wa'l-arḥāma*). The author of the *Kashshāf* [al-Zamakhsharī] reads *wa'l-arḥām* with all three vocalisations. As for Ḥamza's reading, most grammarians think that it is corrupt (*fāsida*) [. . .].[112]

111 As in Zamakhsharī and Ṭabrisī, there follows here a discussion of the vocalisation and the verbal forms.

112 There ensues a dense discussion of the rules for coordination (*'aṭf*) in the context of nouns and pronouns which is of little value when translated into English.

Know that these reasons are not strong reasons for refuting reports cited about these lexical expressions and their variations, and that is because Ḥamza is actually one of the seven readers, and overtly it seems that he would not have come up with this reading on his own. Rather, he would have reported it on the authority of the Messenger of God (*ṣlʿm*). That categorically means that this expression is sound. Analogical reasoning weakens in oral lectures (*samāʿ*), especially reasoning such as these which are 'more feeble than the web of a spider' [cf. Q. 29:41]. But, in addition, there are two other aspects of this reading. One of them is there is an implicit repetition of the genitive preposition, as if it were said: *Tasāʾalūna bihi wa biʾl-arḥāmi*. The second [aspect] is that there is an instance of this in poetry, as recited by Sībawayh:

Faʾl-yawma qad bitta tahjūnā tashtumnā
faʾdhhab fa-mā bika waʾl-ayyāmi min ʿajabi.

Today you have taken to lampooning and insulting us
Go, how curious you are and the passage of time[113]

The odd thing about these grammarians is that they are happy to affirm this lexical expression on the basis of these two unknown verses, but they are not happy to affirm a reading on the basis of it being on the authority of Ḥamza and Mujāhid, even though the two of them were among the greatest of the early scholars (*akābir ʿulamāʾ al-salaf*) of the Qurʾānic sciences. Al-Zajjāj uses as proof for the corruptness of this reading, with respect to its meaning, the words of the Prophet, 'Do not swear an oath in the name of your fathers'.[114] And so, if the term *arḥām* had been coordinated with God's name, that would have entailed the permissibility of swearing an oath by your womb-kin. But one can respond to that by saying that this is narrating something that they used to do in pre-Islamic times, when they used to say, 'I ask you by God and by the wombs', and this narration in the past does not preclude it becoming prohibited in the future. Also, the *ḥadīth* only prohibits swearing oaths in the name of fathers, and this is not the case here, for it is first an oath in the name of God, after which comes juxtaposed the mention of the womb, so this does not contradict the purport of the *ḥadīth*. This is the sum of what there is to be said about reading His words *waʾl-arḥāmi* in the genitive.

As for reading it in the accusative, there are two aspects (*wujūh*).

[113] Rāzī also quotes the line of poetry found in Ṭabarī, above.

[114] Versions are found in Abū Dāwūd, *Sunan*, *Kitāb al-Aymān waʾl-nudhūr* (22), *Bāb fī karāhiyyat al-ḥalf biʾl-abāʾ* (5), *ḥadīth* no. 7/3248; Muslim, *Ṣaḥīḥ*, *Kitāb al-Aymān* (27), *Bāb man ḥalafa biʾl-Lāt waʾl-ʿUzzā faʾl-yaqul lā ilāha illā Allāh* (2), *ḥadīth* no. 9/1648; Nasāʾī, *Sunan*, *Kitāb al-Aymān waʾl-nudhūr* (35), *Bāb al-ḥalf biʾl-ṭawāghīt* (10), *ḥadīth* no. 14/3774.

The first is the preference of Abū ʿAlī al-Fārisī and ʿAlī b. ʿĪsā that it is a coordination with the [syntactical] position of the genitive construction, as in the words:

Fa-lasnā bi'l-jibāli wa lā'l-ḥadīda

We are neither mountains nor iron.

The second, which is the opinion of the majority of the commentators, is that the implied meaning is: be wary of the womb-ties lest you sever them. This is the opinion of Mujāhid, Qatāda, al-Suddī, al-Ḍaḥḥāk, Ibn Zayd, al-Farrā' and al-Zajjāj. According to this aspect, *arḥām* in the accusative is a coordination to the word *Allāh*; in other words, be wary of God and be wary of the wombs, that is to say, be wary of the rights of the womb-ties, connect them and do not sever them.

Al-Wāḥidī, may God have mercy on him, says, it may also be accusative by way of inciting (*ighrā'*),[115] as if you were to say of the womb-ties, preserve them, connect them, as when you would say, 'Lion! Lion!' This interpretation proves that severing womb-ties is prohibited and that it is obligatory to preserve them. As for the reading in the nominative (*rafʿ*), the author of *al-Kashshāf* [says]: the nominative reading is on the basis of [*al-arḥām*] being a subject [of a new sentence], the predicate of which has been omitted (*ḥadhf*), as though it were said 'and the womb-tie as well' (*wa'l-arḥāmu kadhālika*), meaning womb-ties are to be guarded (*taqwā*), or womb-ties are among the things by which petitions are made.

The third issue: God, exalted be He, first said *be wary of your Lord* and then said *be wary of God*. Regarding this repetition, there are several aspects.

The first aspect: [This is] a way of emphasising the matter and urging to it, as you might say to a man, 'Hurry, hurry!' which is more effective than saying, 'Hurry!'

The second aspect: He first commanded wariness [of God] because of the context of the bestowing of graces through [the act of] creation and the like. In the second instance, He commanded wariness [of Him] because of the context of the occurrence of petitions in His name as some seek out their needs from others.

The third aspect: He first says *be wary of your Lord* and then says *and be wary of God*, since '*Lord*' (*rabb*) is an expression used to indicate rearing (*tarbiya*) and kindness (*iḥsān*), whereas '*God*' (*Allāh*) is an expression that indicates vanquishing power (*qahr*) and awe (*hayba*). Thus He commands

115 This term means to goad, spur, or incite someone to take heed before a warning (*al-ighrā' wa'l-taḥdhīr*).

them to be wary of [Him] through [positive] incentive (*targhīb*) and then reiterates the command to that by inspiring awe (*tarhīb*), similar to where He says *and they call upon their Lord in fear* (*khawf*) *and in hope* (*ṭamaʿ*) [Q. 32:16], and *they called upon Us yearning and in awe* (*raghban wa-rahaban*) [Q. 21:90]. It is as though it were said, 'He has reared you and been kind to you, so guard against (*ittaqī*) contravening Him, for He is severe in punishment and tremendous in sway.'

The fourth issue: Know that to petition by God and by the wombs is like saying, 'I ask you by God', 'I seek your intercession by God', 'By God, I hold you to do such and such' and other such [expressions] through which a person emphasises his want when asking another, entreating that person when asking for and seeking his due from that person or his help and assistance.

As for Ḥamza's reading, it is obvious enough in terms of the meaning, the implication being: 'Be wary of God by whom you petition one another and the wombs.' For it was the prevailing custom of the Arabs to entreat a person by reference to the womb-ties, saying, 'I ask you in the name of God and the womb' (*as'aluka bi'llāhi wa'l-raḥimi*), sometimes even singling that [latter] out, 'I ask you in the name of the womb-tie [that binds us]' (*as'aluka bi'l-raḥim*).

The polytheists would write to the Messenger of God (*ṣlʿm*), 'We implore you, by God and by the wombs, that you not send to us so-and-so.'

As for the accusative reading [*bi'l-raḥima*], the meaning then refers back to that [direct object sense], the implication being: 'Be wary of God and be wary of the wombs' (*ittaqū Allāha wa'ttaqū al-arḥāma*).

The Qāḍī [ʿAbd al-Jabbār] said, 'This is one example of when different significations are meant by a single lexical expression, since the signification of "being wary of God" is different to the signification of "being wary of the wombs". For wariness of God entails adhering to obedience of Him and avoiding disobedience of Him, while wariness of the wombs entails [womb-ties] being maintained and not severed with reference to pious acts, preferential treatment and kind behaviour.' This [interpretation] may be defended by [saying] that He, exalted be He, spoke with this expression twice, and according to this implied sense, the problem is resolved.

The fifth issue: Some say that the noun *al-raḥim* is derived from *al-raḥma* (mercy), which is grace (*niʿma*). The argument to support this is what has been reported on the authority of the Prophet (*ṣlʿm*), who said, 'God, exalted be He, says: I am the All-merciful (*raḥmān*) and that is the womb (*raḥim*), and I have given it this name from My name'.[116] The point of comparison, then, is that mercy ensues from some for others because of the context of this state. Others have said, 'Nay, each of the two [nouns] has a root of its own', and dispute over such matters is always nigh.

The sixth issue: The verse indicates the permissibility of petitioning in the name of God, exalted be He. Mujāhid related on the authority of 'Umar that he said, 'The Messenger of God (*ṣl'm*) said, "Whoever asks you in the name of God, then grant him [that request]".'[117] And on the authority of al-Barā' b. 'Āzib, it is [reported] that he said, 'The Messenger of God (*ṣl'm*) enjoined us to seven things, among them, the fulfilling of oaths (*ibrār al-qasam*).'

The seventh issue: His words *and the wombs*, exalted be He, indicate the exalting of the rights of womb-ties and a reiteration to emphasise the prohibition against severing these [womb-ties]. He, exalted be He, said *So would you, if you turned away, cause corruption on the earth and sever your womb-kin?* [Q. 47:22] and *they observe toward a believer neither pact nor covenant* [Q. 9:10]. Regarding the former, they say [that it means] 'kinship' (*qarāba*). He also says, *and your Lord decreed that you should not worship any but Him; and to parents, decency* [Q. 17:23] and *worship God and associate nothing with Him, and to parents, decency; and to kin and orphans, and those in need* [Q. 4:36]. On the authority of 'Abd al-Raḥmān b. 'Awf [it is reported] that the Prophet (*ṣl'm*) said, 'God, exalted be He, says: I am the All-merciful (*r-ḥ-m-n*) and this is the womb (*r-ḥ-m*), whose name I have given from My name. Whoever connects it, I shall connect him and whoever severs it, I shall sever him'.[118] On the authority of Ibn Hurayra, may God be pleased with him, [it is said] that the Prophet said, 'There is no act of obedience to God whose reward is given sooner than the preserving of womb-ties, and there is no deed through which God is disobeyed that is quicker in being punished, than an act of injustice (*baghy*) or a false oath (*yamīn fājira*)'.[119]

It is reported that Anas [b. Mālik] said, 'The Messenger of God (*ṣl'm*) said, "Through an act of charity or the connecting of womb-ties, God increases a

[116] Versions of this *ḥadīth* are found in Abū Dāwūd, *Sunan*, *Kitāb al-Zakāt* (9), *Bāb fī ṣilat al-raḥim* (46), *ḥadīth* no. 139/1694; Tirmidhī, *Jāmi'*, *Kitāb al-Birr wa'l-ṣila 'an rasūl Allāh (ṣl'm)* (27), *Bāb mā jā'a fī qaṭī'at al-raḥim* (9), *ḥadīth* no. 13/1907. Note that this version is slightly different from that cited above by Ṭabrisī.

[117] Versions of this *ḥadīth* are found in Abū Dāwūd, *Sunan*, *Kitāb al-Adab* (43), *Bāb fī'l-rajul yasta'īdh min al-rajul* (118), *ḥadīth* no. 336/5108; Nasā'ī, *Sunan*, *Kitāb al-Zakāt* (23), *Bāb man sa'ala bi'llāh 'azza wa-jalla* (72), *ḥadīth* no. 133/2567.

[118] This is the full version of the *ḥadīth* that was referenced by Ṭabarī, and which was referred to more obliquely by Muqātil, Qummī, and others.

[119] This wording was not found in the major Sunnī *ḥadīth* collections.

lifespan and averts an evil death and wards off danger and what is loathsome".' He (*ṣlʿm*) said, 'The most excellent [form of] charity is one given to a hostile (*kāshiḥ*) womb-relation.' They say that *kāshiḥ* means enemy (*ʿaduww*). So it is thus affirmed, on the basis of evidence from the Book and the Sunna, that maintaining the womb-ties is obligatory, and that reward is merited on account of it.

Those who follow Abū Ḥanīfa,[120] may God be pleased with him, use this principle as a basis for deriving two issues (*masʾala*).

The first of them is that if a man comes to own [as a slave] an unmarriageable (*maḥram*) womb-relative,[121] [then the slave] is freed on that basis, just as in the case of a brother or sister, a paternal uncle or a maternal one. He said, if the ownership were to stand, then, by consensus it would be licit to use them as servants, but using people as servants creates a sense of alienation that propagates the severing of womb-ties. That is illicit based on that principle, so it is obligatory that ownership ceases.

The second of them is that a gift to the unmarriageable womb-kin cannot be taken back because that rescinding creates a sense of alienation that propagates the severing of womb-ties; so it must not be permitted.

The discussion of these two issues appears in [Bayhaqī's] *al-Khilāfiyyāt*.[122]

Then He, exalted be He, concludes this verse with what resembles the promise (*waʿd*) and the threat (*waʿīd*), inspiring awe (*targhīb*), inspiring dread (*tarhīb*), saying *indeed, God is Watcher over you*. *Al-Raqīb* is a watcher (*murāqib*) who keeps a record of all of your deeds, so that is how He acquires that attribute, so He should be both feared (*kh-w-f*) and turned to in hope (*r-j-w*). He, exalted be He, has made it clear that *He knows all that is secret and what is even more concealed (than that)* [Q. 20:7]. Since this is the case, a person must be cautious, fearful (*khāʾifa*), with regard to what they do and what they shun doing.[123]

[120] On whom, see the PA.

[121] The term *maḥram* (pl. *maḥārim*) is semantically equivalent to *muḥarram*, but is retained technically to indicate a category, or categories, of individuals 'unmarriageable' to the person in question by virtue of being too closely related, most often on account of (but not limited to) consanguinity, fosterage, affinity by marriage and sisterly conjunction. See Bernard Weiss, 'Prohibited Degrees', *EQ*, IV, 285–6. This is a major sub-theme of ch. 4, on Q. 24:31, in this volume.

[122] This is a work by the famous Shāfiʿī jurist and Ashʿarī theologian, Abū Bakr al-Bayhaqī (d. 458/1066), about the juridical disagreements between Shāfiʿīs and Ḥanafīs up to his day. He also authored the well-known *Kitāb al-Asmāʾ waʾl-ṣifāt*, a discussion on the proper understanding of God's names and attributes; a brief biography of the scholar is given by J. Robson, 'Al-Bayhaḳī', *EI*², I, 1130.

[123] Rāzī, *Mafātīḥ al-ghayb*, s.v. Q. 4:1.

Qurṭubī

Qurṭubī does not explore the first part of this verse in any depth because he says that he has gone into these matters in the interpretation of various verses in *sūrat al-Baqara*. His epitome of those interpretations is that the *single soul* is Adam.

Qurṭubī has a lengthy and intricate explanation of the second part of the verse (*be wary of God, by whom you petition one another, and the wombs*). He first gives the majority reading, which is that people should be wary of God, and they should be wary of severing the womb-ties. However, he then says that he agrees with the reading taken by Mujāhid, Ḥasan al-Baṣrī and Ibrāhīm al-Nakhaʿī, which is that in pre-Islamic times people used to swear by God and by the wombs, pointing out that there are many oaths in the Qur'ān, such as *by the mount* (Q. 52:1), *by the stars* (Q. 53:1) and so forth. Qurṭubī says that 'it is totally possible that *wa'l-arḥāmi* belongs to the same category, so that He is swearing by it as He does by the created things that indicate His oneness and power, emphasising it to the extent that He has juxtaposed it to Himself. But God knows best.' Thus Qurṭubī agrees with the minority reading of this section of the verse.

Qurṭubī goes on to give some of the implications of this part of the verse, including that the Muslim community should agree on the obligation to maintain rather than sever the womb-tie, even when the mother is an unbeliever. In this regard, he cites a *ḥadīth* in which Asmā' bt. Abī Bakr asks the Prophet whether she should preserve the tie to her mother, and he replies that she should. It is significant that in this particular interpretation the *raḥim* is actually the uterine tie, not a wider network of blood kinship as it has seemed to be in the interpretations of other commentators. This is shown by his citation of Ḥanafī law that the uterine kin may inherit if there are no agnatic relatives.

There are six issues.

The first [issue]: His words, *O people! Be wary of your Lord who created you.* The etymology of the word *nās* has been examined in [*sūrat*] *al-Baqara*, as well as the meanings of *be wary* and the creation and the *mate* and the *sending forth*, and there is no point in repeating it all. This verse is an alert to the fact that He is Creator. He said *single* in the feminine because of the word *soul*, and the word *soul* is feminine, even when the thing that it indicates is male, and it is permissible to say *min nafsin wāḥidin* [*from a single soul*, masculine] out of consideration for the import, since what is intended by *soul* is Adam (*ʿm*) which is what Mujāhid and Qatāda have said. And in the reading of Ibn Abī ʿAbla it is 'one' (*wāḥid*), without the feminine ending. [Regarding] *and spread forth*, the meaning of it is that He divided and spread forth in the earth, and it is like *and carpets spread out* [*wa-zarābī mabthūtha*, Q. 88:16], and this has been introduced in [*sūrat*] *al-Baqara*. And *from the two* means from Adam and Ḥawwā'. Mujāhid said, 'Ḥawwā' was created from the smallest [rib] of Adam', and in a *ḥadīth*, 'woman was created from a crooked rib',[124] and this has been gone into in depth in [*sūrat*] *al-Baqara*.[125]

[Regarding] *many men and women*: He has circumscribed their progeny to two types, which means that the 'effeminate' (*khunthā*)[126] is not a type, but it has a truth that would attribute it to both of these types, which is its Adamic nature; so it would have to follow one of them, as already mentioned in [*sūrat*] *al-Baqara*, where we discuss the additional or deficient genital parts.

The second [issue]: His words, exalted be He, *and be wary of God by whom you petition one another, and the wombs; indeed God is Watcher over you*. He reiterates the command to God-wariness as a way of emphasising and alerting the souls of those being commanded. *Alladhī* is in the accusative as a direct object descriptive clause. *Al-arḥām* is a coordination, that is to say, be wary of disobeying God and fear that you should sever the womb-ties. The Medinese read: *tassā'alūna*, eliding the *tā'* in the *sīn*. The Kufans omit one of the *tā*'s because of the two of them coming together, and they make the *sīn* a single consonant because the meaning is known. It is similar to where He says *wa-lā ta'āwanū 'alā al-ithm* (*do not help one another to sin*) [Q. 5:2], and *tanazzalū* [Q. 97:4], and the like of that. Ibrāhīm al-Nakha'ī, Qatāda, al-A'mash and Ḥamza read it as *al-arḥāmi*, in the genitive (*khafḍ*). The grammarians have discussed this at length. The heads of the Basrans say this is a mispronunciation; you cannot recite with it. As for the Kufans, they just say that it is repugnant and add nothing more; they do not give the reason for its repugnancy. Al-Naḥḥās said, 'As far as I know.' Sībawayh said, 'It is not coordinated with the genitive pronoun, because it is of the status of the indefinite (*tanwīn*), and you cannot coordinate with the indefinite.' Another group says that it is coordinated with the relative clause, for they used to petition one another through it [the womb]. A man would say, 'I petition you in the name of God and the womb.' This is how al-Ḥasan, al-Nakha'ī and Mujāhid have interpreted it, and this is the correct opinion on this issue, as we shall see. Some considered this to be a weak interpretation, among them al-Zajjāj, saying it is repugnant to coordinate an overt noun with a pronoun in the genitive unless the genitive preposition is made manifest, as in His words *fa-khasafnā bihi wa bi-dārihi al-arḍ* (*so We made the earth*

[124] See above, note 32.
[125] Qurṭubī, *al-Jāmi' li-aḥkām al-Qur'ān*, V, 1–2 (s.v. Q. 4:1).
[126] This term is discussed in the exegetical literature in ch. 4, 'The Veil', in this volume.

collapse under him and his dwelling) [Q. 28:81]. It is repugnant to say *marartu bihi wa-Zaydin*. Al-Zajjāj reported on the authority of al-Māzinī because the coordination and the thing with which it is coordinated are correlative. Each one of them takes the place of the other, and just as it is not permissible to say *marartu bi-Zaydin wa-ka* [sic.], likewise it is impermissible to say *marartu bika wa-Zayd*. As for Sībawayh, for him this is repugnant and is only permitted in poetry, as it is said:

Fa'l-yawma qarrabta tahjūnā wa tashtimunā
fa'dhhab fa-mā bika wa'l-ayyāmi min ʿajabi.

Today you have almost[127] lampooned and insulted us
Go, how curious are you and the passage of time

Al-ayyām has been coordinated syntactically with the [pronominal suffix] *kāf* of *bika*, but without [repeating] the [preposition] *bā'* for poetic licence.

And, likewise, the words of the other [poet]:

Nuʿalliqu fī mithli'l-sawārī suyūfanā
wa-mā baynahā wa'l-kaʿbi mahwā[128] *nafānif*[129]

We hang our swords in the like of masts
Between the swords and the heels an airy expanse

Thus the syntactical coordination of *al-kaʿb* with the [suffixed] pronoun in *bayna-hā* is based on poetic licence. Abū ʿAlī [al-Fārisī] said, 'But that is a weak analogy.' In an abridged [version of] *al-Tadhkira*[130] it is reported on the authority of al-Fārisī that Abū'l-ʿAbbās al-Mubarrad said, 'If I were to find myself praying behind an imam, reciting in the following way: *mā antum bi-muṣrikhiyyi* [cf. Q. 14:22] or *ittaqū'llāha alladhī tasā'alūna bihi wa'l-arḥāmi* [cf. Q. 4:1],[131] I would grab my sandals and run.' Al-Zajjāj says, 'Ḥamza's reading, aside from its weakness and repugnance in Arabic, is a grave error with regard to fundamental religious principles, because the Prophet (*ṣlʿm*)

[127] In other versions, *qarrabta* is read *qad bitta*, 'you have taken to [. . .]', given the orthographic similarity between the consonants (*r* and *d*) in manuscripts.

[128] In Ṭabarī's version *ghawṭ* is used; there we translated 'open expanse'.

[129] Rendered as *nafā'if* in Ṭabarī's citation.

[130] On Abū ʿAlī al-Fārisī, see the PA. According to Ibn al-Nadim's *Fihrist*, the work, simply known as *al-Tadhkira* (acknowledged by C. Rabin, 'al-Fārisī', *EI*², II, 803), was composed for the purpose of clarifying 'difficult verses' of the Qur'ān. It is possible that this abridged version was composed by the equally famous Ibn Jinnī (d. 392/1002), who had studied with al-Fārisī for forty years, and became a leading grammarian after al-Fārisī and his successor. J. Pederson, 'Ibn Djinnī', *EI*², III, 755.

[131] Both of these final words are inflected with a *fatḥa* in the standard Qur'ān: *bi-muṣrikhiyya* and *wa'l-arḥāma*.

said, "Do not swear by your fathers",[132] and so if it is not permitted to swear by other than God, then how can you swear by the womb-ties?' I believe that Ismāʿīl b. Isḥaq goes so far as to say that swearing by anything other than God is a grave matter, for indeed it is specifically reserved for God, exalted be He. Al-Naḥḥās said, 'The opinion of some of them [is] that *wa'l-arḥāmi* is an incorrect form of oath, in terms of meaning and syntax, because the *ḥadīth* of the Prophet (*ṣlʿm*) indicates an accusative inflection.' It is narrated on the authority of Shuʿba on the authority of ʿAwn b. Abī Juḥayfa on the authority of al-Mundhir b. Jarīr from his father, who said, we were with the Prophet (*ṣlʿm*) when a group from the tribe of Muḍar turned up barefoot and not fully clothed, and I saw the face of the Messenger of God change when he saw the extent of their destitute state. He then proceeded to perform the *ẓuhr* prayer, saying, *O people! Be wary of your Lord* until [where it says] *and the wombs*. Then he said, 'A man can offer charity with a dinar, or a man can offer charity with a dirham, or a man can offer charity with a measure of dates'. This signification is based on the accusative inflection, because he is urging them to connect their womb-ties. There is also a sound report from the Prophet (*ṣlʿm*) that he said, 'Whoever wishes to swear, let them swear by God or be quiet'.[133] So this refutes the opinion of those who say that the meaning is: I ask you in the name of God and in the name of the wombs. Abū Isḥāq has also said that the meaning of *tasā'alūna bihi* is that you seek what is due to you through Him. And, even here, the genitive inflection is meaningless.

I said, this is what I have come across of the opinions of linguists prohibiting the reading *wa'l-arḥāmi* in the genitive. This is the position of Ibn ʿAṭiyya as well. The imam Abū Naṣr ʿAbd al-Raḥīm b. ʿAbd al-Karīm al-Qushayrī[134] refuted it, preferring the reading of the coordination, saying, 'The likes of this speech is rejected by the leading [authorities] of religion because the readings used by the leading readers have been confirmed on the authority of the Prophet (*ṣlʿm*) by multiple chains of transmission, as the people of this craft know.'

When a thing is confirmed on the authority of the Prophet (*ṣlʿm*), then whoever refutes that is in effect refuting the Prophet himself (*ṣlʿm*) and

[132] See above, note 114 (in Rāzī).

[133] Versions are found in Bukhārī, *Ṣaḥīḥ*, *Kitāb al-Shahādāt* (52), *Bāb kayfa yustakhlaf* (26), *ḥadīth* no. 40/2679; Muslim, *Ṣaḥīḥ*, *Kitāb al-Aymān* (27), *Bāb al-nahy ʿan al-ḥalf bi-ghayr Allāh taʿālā* (1), *ḥadīth* no. 4/1646.

[134] This is the son of the famous Sufi ʿAbd al-Karīm al-Qushayrī (d. 465/1072), one of the commentators selected for our volume (on this Qushayrī, see Nguyen, *Sufi Master*). The son, Ibn ʿAbd al-Karīm (d. 514/1120), was a Shāfiʿī jurist and an Ashʿarī theologian. He became embroiled in a dispute with the Ḥanbalīs of Baghdad which caused a public outcry and forced Niẓām al-Mulk to retire him to Nishapur around 469/1077. See Halm 'al-Ḳushayrī', *EI*², V, 526–7, who accounts for both under the same entry.

deeming repugnant his reading. This is a perilous position and is not to be adopted by the leading lexicographers and grammarians,[135] for the Arabic language should be taken from the Prophet (*ṣlʿm*) and no one should doubt his locution (*faṣāḥa*). As for the *ḥadīth*s mentioned, there is a point to be made, since he (*ṣlʿm*) said to Abū'l-ʿUsharā', *wa abīka law ṭaʿanta fī khāṣiratihi* ('By your father, if you were to stab it [just] in its flank').[136] The prohibition came only concerning swearing by other than God. For this is an entreaty of another person for the sake (*ḥaqq*) of womb kinship (*raḥim*), and so there is no prohibition concerning it. Al-Qushayrī said, 'Some say that this is actually an oath sworn in the name of womb kinship (*iqsām bi'l-raḥim*), that is to say, "fear God and the duty towards womb kinship", as when you might say, "By the truth of your father,[137] do such and such". There are also [examples] in the revelation (*tanzīl*): *by the star* (*wa'l-najmi*, Q. 53:1), *by the mount* (*wa'l-ṭūri*, Q. 52:1), *by the fig* (*wa'l-tīni*, Q. 95:1) and *by your life* (*la-ʿamruka*, Q. 15:72), but that is a strained attempt [at an explanation] (*takalluf*).'

I would say that there is nothing strained about it, for it is totally possible that *wa'l-arḥāmi* belongs to the same category, so that He is swearing by it [the womb] as He does by the created things that indicate His oneness and power, emphasising it to the extent that He has juxtaposed it to Himself. But God knows best. It is God's prerogative to swear by whatever He wills and to prohibit or permit whatever He wills, and so it is not at all unlikely that it may be an invocation (*qasam*). The Arabs swear by the womb-ties (*raḥim*) and it may well be that the [prepositional prefix] *bā'* is intended but omitted, as it has been omitted in the [poet's] saying: [. . .].[138]

[135] In all three instances where we give the translation 'leading', the Arabic gives the term *imām* (pl. *a'imma*). It is used here in its broad honorific Sunnī sense *ex officio* – especially as 'leading authority', 'recognised expert' and also, of course, as 'leader of congregational prayers' (*ṣalāt al-jamāʿa*). This functional usage is in contrast with its very strict and restricted Shīʿī sense of the Huṣaynid descendants of the Prophet. In general, academic convention has it that when used in the former sense, it is retained in lower case (*imām*), and when in the latter, then Imam; however, in this volume the term 'imam' is lower case even in the latter sense.

[136] The reference here is to the legal manner of slaughtering an animal (*dhakāt*, or *tadhkiya*) when the ritual method is impeded, such as when an animal is stuck in a deep well or crevasse. Discussions abound in the chapters on sacrifices (*uḍḥiya*) in the *ḥadīth* manuals. There is a constellation of associated terms in this lexicon (*ḳurbān*, *dhabīḥa*, *hady*, *naḥr*, q.v. all in *EI*) surrounding the major event of the pilgrimage (on which see the substantial entry by A.J. Wensinck, J. Jomier and B. Lewis, 'al-Ḥadjdj', *EI*^{2}, III, 32–8). For a useful summary description of the sacrificial method, see Ersilia Francesca, 'Slaughter', *EQ*, V, 55–6.

[137] Literally, 'by what is truly due to your father *qua* father' (*wa-ḥaqqi abīka*).

[138] Qurṭubī proceeds to demonstrate the viability of the point just made, that a genitive inflection can be retained without the appearance of the genitive inflecting preposition, by citing eight different poetic attestations. There then ensues a brief consideration of the other two vocalisations – *bi'l-arḥāmu*, nominative, where the predicate is implicit, and *bi'l-arḥāma*, accusative, as a syntactical coordination with the direct object clause *bihi*. We pick up the translation at the 'third issue'.

The third [issue]: The [Muslim] community (*milla*) are all of the consensus that the maintaining of womb-ties is an obligation (*w-j-b*) and that severing them is illicit (*ḥ-r-m*). It is soundly reported that when Asmāʾ [bt. Abī Bakr] asked the Prophet (*ṣlʿm*), 'Should I connect the bond (*ṣila*) to my mother?' he replied, 'Yes, connect the bond',[139] commanding that she connect the bond to her, even when she was an unbeliever. It is in order to reiterate its significance that merit is assigned to preserving the [kinship] bond with an unbeliever, so much so that Abū Ḥanīfa and his followers are of the opinion that womb-kin (*dhū raḥim*) may inherit from one another if there are no male agnates (*ʿuṣba*) or a designated obligatory share (*farḍ musammā*), and it is incumbent upon those kin who purchase them to free (*ʿitq*) them on account of the sanctity of the womb relationship (*raḥim*). They reinforce this [position] with what Abū Dāwūd has related on the authority of the Prophet (*ṣlʿm*) saying, 'Whoever comes to own a womb-relation who is within the degrees of sanctity (*muḥarram*), then that [latter] is a free person (*ḥurr*)'. That is the opinion of the majority of scholars (*ahl al-ʿilm*). This has [also] been reported on the authority of ʿUmar b. al-Khaṭṭāb, may God be pleased with him, and that of ʿAbd Allāh b. Masʿūd, and no opposing view to theirs is known among the Companions. That is [also] the opinion of al-Ḥasan al-Baṣrī, Jābir b. Zayd, ʿAṭāʾ [b. Abī Rabāḥ], al-Shaʿbī and al-Zuhrī; and towards this view tended also al-Thawrī, Aḥmad [b. Ḥanbal] and Isḥāq.

Regarding this, the scholars of our school have three opinions. First: that this is specific [only] to parents and grandparents. Second: [it is] the two wings, meaning siblings. Third: [something] similar to the opinion of Abū Ḥanīfa. Al-Shāfiʿī said, 'He is only obliged to free his fathers and mothers but not his siblings or anyone else from among his relatives (*qarāba*) and blood line (*luḥma*).' But the sounder opinion is the first, based on the *ḥadīth* that we have mentioned and which has been verified by al-Tirmidhī and al-Nasāʾī. The best transmission is the version reported by al-Nasāʾī through the *ḥadīth* of Ḍamra [b. Rabīʿa][140] on

[139] Versions are found in Bukhārī, *Ṣaḥīḥ*, *Kitāb al-Hiba wa-faḍluhā wa'l-taḥrīḍ ʿalayhā* (51), *Bāb al-hadiyya li'l-mushrikīn* (29), *ḥadīth* no. 52/2620; Muslim, *Ṣaḥīḥ*, *Kitāb al-Zakāt* (12), *Bāb faḍl al-nafaqa wa'l-ṣadaqa ʿalā'l-aqrabīn wa'l-zawj wa'l-awlād wa'l-wālidayn wa-law kānū mushrikīn* (14), *ḥadīth* no. 62/1003.

[140] Ḍamra b. Rabīʿa Abū ʿAbd Allāh al-Qurashī (d. 202/817) was a Damascene-born *ḥadīth* transmitter who became somewhat of an authority in the town of Ramla, Palestine. Although most of the *rijāl* works deem him reliable and trustworthy, he is mostly known because of the traditionists' consensus that this *ḥadīth* of his on the necessary manumission of an unmarriageable womb-kin once that person is 'owned' was deemed unacceptable, especially by Aḥmad b. Ḥanbal. See Ibn Ḥajar al-ʿAsqalānī, *Tahdhīb al-tahdhīb*, II, 576–7 (s.v. Ḍamra); Muḥammad b. Aḥmad al-Dhahabī, *Siyar aʿlām al-nubalāʾ*, ed. Shuʿayb al-Arnaʾūṭ and Ḥusayn al-Asad, 25 vols. (Beirut, Muʾassasat al-Risāla, 1981–8), IX, 325–7; also, Ibn ʿAsākir, *Tāʾrīkh madīnat Dimashq*, s.v. *ḥarf al-ḍad* (*dhikr man ismuhu* Ḍamra).

the authority of Sufyān on the authority of ʿAbd Allāh b. Dīnār on the authority of Ibn ʿUmar, as follows: The Messenger of God (*ṣlʿm*) said, 'Whoever comes into ownership of a womb-relation that is within the prohibited degrees (*maḥram*), then he is to be freed on that basis'. This is a *ḥadīth* that is affirmed on the basis of a transmission from the most just of individuals and which none of the leading authorities (*aʾimma*) have found any fault that would have required eschewing it, except that al-Nasāʾī comments at the end of it, 'This *ḥadīth* is objectionable (*munkar*).' Others have said that it has only been transmitted (*tafarrada*) by Ḍamra, which [in itself] is the definition of 'objectionable' (*munkar*) or 'deviant' (*shādhdh*) in the technical language of the *ḥadīth* scholars.[141] However, Ḍamra is a trustworthy transmitter (*thiqa*), and if a *ḥadīth* is transmitted only by a single transmitter who happens to be trustworthy, that should not harm it. And God knows best.

The fourth [issue]: They disagree in this regard over those who are of milk kinship (*dhawī al-maḥārim min al-riḍāʿa*).[142] Most scholars say that these are not included in the remit of the *ḥadīth*. The Qāḍī Sharīk is of the opinion that they should be freed (*ʿitq*). The Ẓahirīs and some of the speculative theologians (*mutakallimūn*) say that the father is not to be freed by the son if he should come to own him, supporting this argument on the basis of his words (*ʿm*) 'A son shall not avail a father (*wālid*) except if he should come across him enslaved and then purchases him and sets him free'. They argue that if the purchase (*shirāʾ*) is legitimate, that is an affirmation of the right to ownership (*mulk*), and an owner has full right of disposal (*taṣarruf*). But this is ignorance on their part of the principal aims of the Law (*maqāṣid al-sharʿ*),[143] for God, exalted be He, says *and to parents, decency* [Q. 4:36; 17:23], equating, as obligatory, worship of Him with decency to parents. It is not decent that the father should remain in the possession of his [son] and under his mastery (*sulṭān*). Thus he is obliged to free him, either on the basis of his ownership

[141] On the technical classification of a *ḥadīth* as *munkar* and *shādhdh*, see G.H.A. Juynboll, 'Munkar', *EI*², VII, 576; also, *passim*, in idem, *Muslim Tradition: Studies in Chronology, Provenance and Editorship of Early Ḥadīth* (Cambridge, Cambridge University Press, 1983).

[142] Milk kinship is created between children who have suckled from the same woman, even if there is no actual blood kinship between any of the parties involved. Cf. '*raḍāʿ* or *riḍāʿ*', J. Schacht, J. Burton and J. Chelhod, '*Raḍāʿ* or *Riḍāʿ*', *EI*², VIII, 361–2; Soraya Altorki, 'Milk-Kinship in Arab Society: An Unexplored Problem in the Ethnography of Marriage', *Ethnology* 19.2 (1980), 233–44.

[143] Literally, the phrase means 'the aims of the Law', that is, the theory that if the system (jurisprudence) has been implemented correctly, the aims and purposes of the Law will have been fulfilled, a theory which enjoyed some resurgence in the late-twentieth century. See Robert M. Gleave, 'Maḳāsid al-Sharīʿa', *EI*², XII, 570.

[of him], implementing thus the *ḥadīth* that he 'purchases him and sets him free', or on the basis of decency, implementing the [Qur'ānic] verse. The majority take the *ḥadīth* to mean that because the son is the cause of the freeing of his father by having purchased him, the Law ascribes the act of manumission itself to him since it was precipitated by him.

As for the differences of opinion among the scholars regarding who is to be freed through ownership, the justification for the first opinion is what we have mentioned regarding the significations of the Book and the Sunna. And the justification for the second opinion is to attribute to the father the close and sacred kinship as mentioned in the *ḥadīth*, for there is no one closer to a man than his son and so this is also true for the father, and the brother is also of the same degree of proximity since he is an indicator of the [shared] fatherhood, so much so that one says, 'I am the son of his father (*anā ibn abīhi*).' As for the third opinion, this is dependent on the *ḥadīth* of Ḍamra, which we have already mentioned. And God knows best.

The fifth [issue]: His words, exalted be He, *and the wombs*, the womb (*al-raḥim*) is a term that refers to all kin, regardless of their being in degrees of sanctity (*maḥram*) or not. Abū Ḥanīfa takes into consideration the womb-kin who are in degrees of *maḥram* when prohibiting the rescinding of gifts (*hiba*), but he permits the rescinding of what is due to the paternal cousins even though there is enmity (*qaṭīʿa*) as well as kinship at the same time; that is why so many of the rulings concerning inheritance (*irth*), guardianship (*wilāya*) and other matters are dependent on that [womb kinship]. Taking the *maḥram* relationship into account, however, is a [gratuitous] addition to the text of the Book with no supporting justification. But they consider that on the basis of abrogation (*naskhan*), especially since it alludes to a justification on the basis of enmity [between the relatives], and he [Abū Ḥanīfa] permits it with regard to the rights of paternal cousins and paternal and maternal ones too. And God knows best.

The sixth [issue]: His words, exalted be He, *Indeed God is Watcher over you*, mean Keeper (*ḥafīẓ*), according to Ibn ʿAbbās and Mujāhid. Ibn Zayd [says that it means] Knower (*ʿalīm*). Some say: *raqīb* means *ḥāfiẓ*, with the [active] form *fāʿil*. Thus *raqīb* is one of God's attributes, exalted be He; and *al-raqīb* is one who keeps [records of] and lies in wait for [something].[144]

[144] Qurṭubī, *al-Jāmiʿ li-aḥkām al-Qur'ān*, s.v. Q. 4:1.

Kāshānī

Kāshānī's interpretation was at one time attributed to the mystic Ibn ʿArabī,[145] and in this interpretation one can see the mystical elements of his thought, in that this interpretation is not precisely literal. However, it is very much grounded in a gendered vision of the world: for Kāshānī, woman was the cause of man's downfall, the cause of his ultimate embodiment, and the first woman was created from a rib on his left side, which is the side of generation and corruption, which is to say the world of space and time. Because woman was created from this material, she has the animalistic soul, whereas man's soul is pure and spiritual. This interpretation shows how the very idea and essence of womanhood and femininity was contaminated for some premodern thinkers, who viewed women as lesser beings than men in their very essence.

Kāshānī interprets the womb-ties to be the 'spirits of prophets and saints' from whom the believer may be severed by 'not loving them'. Thus kinship for him is not based on blood but rather a kind of spiritual lineage; an absence of love towards those spiritual kin is what severs the kinship ties. According to him, people should not interrogate the nature of God's oneness, they should just become annihilated in it, for it is this annihilation that creates the true links of kinship.

O people! Be wary of your Lord: be wary of falsely claiming (*intiḥāl*) His attribute when you do good works. Rather, adopt that attribute as a shield for you when you do whatever good works you may do, and say that these have issued from the Absolute Powerful *who created you from a single soul*, which is the rational universal soul (*al-nafs al-nāṭiqa al-kulliyya*) that is the heart of the world (*ʿālam*), being the true Adam (*Ādam al-ḥaqīqī*), *and from it created its mate*, that is, the animal soul that originates from it. They say that she was created from his left rib, from the aspect oriented towards the world of generation (*kawn*), which is weaker than the aspect oriented towards the Truth (*al-ḥaqq*). Were it not for its mate, it [the animal soul] would not have been made to fall (*h-b-ṭ*) to this world. As is commonly known, Iblīs enticed (*s-w-l*) her first,[146] and by leading her astray used this as the means (*w-s-l*) to lead astray Adam. And so there is no doubt that corporeal attachment is not forthcoming except by means of this [soul]. *And spread forth from the two many men* [means] possessors of hearts who tend towards their father [sc. Adam], *and women*, possessors of souls and natures who tend towards their mother [sc. Eve].

[145] Indeed, Kāshānī's commentary (*Taʾwīlāt*) continues to be published under the title of *Tafsīr Ibn ʿArabī;* most probably the title has stuck because of the latter's celebrity.

[146] Often in the Qurʾān, it is 'the soul' (*nafs*) that entices the individual in question to lead him or her astray: see Q. 12:18, 83; 20:96; 47:25.

And be wary of God, of His essence (*dhāt*), against that you should affirm (*ithbāt*) your existence (*wujūd*) and make Him a shield for you when your remnants (*baqiyya*)[147] become manifest at the point of [the soul's] annihilation in [His] oneness. For, otherwise, you will become veiled (*ḥ-j-b*) [from Him] when you come to see the annihilation (*fanā'*); *by whom you petition one another*, [since it is] not by yourselves, *and the wombs*. In other words, be wary of [severing] the true womb-kin, that is, those kin relations that possess sublime principles as disengaged realities (*mufāraqāt*), as well as the spirits of prophets and saints, lest you sever them by not loving them. Let these [ties] act as a shield for you to actualise your felicities and perfections. For the severing of womb-kin through the forsaking of love [for them] means in effect to be oriented away from connectedness (*ittiṣāl*) and oneness (*waḥda*) [with Him] and towards disconnectedness (*infiṣāl*) and multitude (*kathra*) instead: this is the truly loathsome [state] and the absolute distancing (*buʿd*) from the noble presence of the Truth, exalted be He. It is for that reason that the Prophet said, 'Connecting womb-kin (*ṣilat al-raḥim*) increases one's lifespan';[148] in other words, it entails an enduring subsistence (*baqā'*). Know, also, that [the maintaining of] womb-kin represents the outward form of true inward connectedness. The outward works like the inward when it comes to the affirmation of Oneness, and thus the one who is unable to look after the outward is more likely to be unable to look after the inward.

Indeed God is Watcher over you, watching over you lest you become veiled from Him when one of your attributes or when some of your remnants manifest themselves, causing you to suffer chastisement.[149]

Ibn Kathīr

Ibn Kathīr's interpretation of this verse is quite short; nevertheless, he includes several *ḥadīth*s that refer to women's inferiority to men. These *ḥadīth*s allude to a range of ideas: that woman was created for man; that, because of Eve's creation from Adam, women are naturally interested in men; since Adam was created from the earth, men are interested in the world – this is used to justify keeping women indoors; that woman was made from a crooked rib which cannot be straightened. Ibn Kathīr gives these *ḥadīth*s without much commentary, but each of them suggests that woman's

[147] These 'remnants' (*baqiyya*) are aspects of the self that remain spiritually untransformed and attached to this world.

[148] Kāshānī is citing a contracted form of the *ḥadīth* encountered above in Rāzī, 'seventh issue': both articulate the idea through the expressions 'connecting [with] kin' (*ṣilat al-raḥim*) and an 'increase in life-span' (*ziyāda fī'l-ʿumr*).

[149] Kāshānī, *Tafsīr*, s.v. Q. 4:1.

creation from man and for him indicates a deeper reality about the nature of all women. Furthermore, the *ḥadīth* about keeping women indoors also provides a justification for the legal rulings that a husband is permitted to control whether his wife exits the house.[150] Ibn Kathīr interprets the final part of the verse in the same vein as Ṭabarī, which is to say as a moral injunction to all human beings to be affectionate towards one another, and to look after the weaker members of society.

Thus God, exalted be He, commands His creation to be wary (*taqwā*) of Him, which entails worshipping Him alone without partner, and alerts them to His power, with which He created them from *a single soul*, namely Adam (*ʿm*). *And from it He created its mate*, Eve (*ʿam*), created from his left back rib, as he slept. And when he awoke and saw her, he took a liking to her, inclining warmly to her company and she to his. Ibn Abī Ḥātim [al-Rāzī][151] said, 'My father narrated to us that Muḥammad b. Muqātil had narrated from Wakīʿ on the authority of Abū Hilāl from Qatāda that Ibn ʿAbbās said, "Woman was created from man, and she was made to covet (*nahma*) man, and man was created from the earth, and he was made to covet the earth, so lock away your women."' According to a sound *ḥadīth*, 'Woman was created from a rib, and indeed the most crooked part of the rib is the highest [part]. If you set about trying to straighten her, you will break her; but if you decide to enjoy her, you will have to enjoy her with that crookedness.'[152] His words *and spread forth from the two many men and women* [mean] that He spread from the two, from Adam and Eve, many men and women, and he scattered them across all quarters of the earth, with their different kinds (*aṣnāf*), attributes, colours and languages. And after that [one day], to Him will be their return (*maʿād*) and gathering (*maḥshar*).

[150] For more on the husband's right to keep the wife indoors, see Ali, *Marriage and Slavery in Early Islam*.

[151] Ibn Abī Ḥātim al-Rāzī (d. 327/938) was a major *ḥadīth* scholar, critic and transmitter and sat squarely in the *ahl al-ḥadīth* generation that flourished after the death of Ibn Ḥanbal (d. 241/855). In addition, he is credited with authoring the first '*ḥadīth*-criticism' work thus-labelled *al-Jarḥ wa'l-Taʿdīl*, setting a bibliographic precedent for an emerging but not-yet formalised field; he also authored a well-known *ʿIlal al-ḥadīth* (see Pavel Pavlovitch, 'Ibn Abī Ḥātim al-Rāzī', *EI*[3]). According to Pavlovitch, Ibn Ḥātim's father was the direct source of almost fifty per cent of his son's transmissions, with many of the rest being from another major scholar of Rayy, Abū Zurʿa al-Rāzī (q.v. Claude Gilliot, *EI*[3]), who died in 264/878; all of this points to Rayy being a major centre for traditionist scholarship, one thousand kilometres away from Baghdad and within barely a century of the latter's founding.

[152] Permutations of this *ḥadīth* appear elsewhere; see the commentary in Hūd, for instance, above. The thrust of all of these variations is one: the 'crookedness' of the rib is intimately tied to the temperament or nature of women, suggesting at once an inferiority of character and counselling that the success of conjugal life will depend on recognising that nature and 'managing it'.

God, exalted be He, then says, *and be wary of God by whom you petition one another, and the wombs*, that is to say, be wary of God by being obedient to Him. Ibrāhīm, Mujāhid and al-Ḥasan [al-Baṣrī] all say that *by whom you petition one another* is like when one says, 'I ask you by God and by the womb [kin]' (*bi'llāhi wa bi'l-raḥim*). Al-Ḍaḥḥāk said, 'Be wary of (*ittaqū*) God by whom you make contracts (*ʿaqd*) and covenants (*ʿahd*), and be wary of severing womb-ties; rather be dutiful regarding these and maintain them'; that is also the opinion of Ibn ʿAbbās, ʿIkrima, Mujāhid, al-Ḥasan [al-Baṣrī], al-Ḍaḥḥāk, al-Rabīʿ and more than one other person. Some of them read *wa'l-arḥāmi*, in the genitive, as a coordination with the pronoun in *bi-hi*, in other words: the way in which you petition in the name of God and in the name of the wombs (*tasā'alūna bi'llāhi wa bi'l-arḥāmi*), this being the opinion of Mujāhid and others.

As for His words, *Indeed God is Watcher over you*. He watches over all of your states (*aḥwāl*) and your deeds (*aʿmāl*); like where He says, *And God is Witness over all things* [Q. 85:9].

In one sound *ḥadīth*, 'Worship God as if you could see Him. For, though you cannot see Him, He can surely see you';[153] these are words of guidance, but also a command to watch out for the One watching. It is thus for this reason that He, exalted be He, mentions that the origin of all human creation (*al-khalq*) is from a single father and from a single mother – namely, that they might be affectionate (*ʿaṭf*) towards one other and to stir in them compassion towards the oppressed (*ḍuʿafā'*) among them. There is confirmation [to this effect] in the *Ṣaḥīḥ* of Muslim, by way of the *ḥadīth* of Jarīr b. ʿAbd Allāh al-Bajalī:[154] the Messenger of God (*ṣlʿm*), when he was approached by that group of men from the [tribe of] Muḍar, who had turned up in tattered garments, so denuded and destitute, he got up to address the people, and this was just after the midday prayer, and said *O people! Be wary of your Lord, who created you from a single soul* until he had concluded the verse [Q. 4:1]. He then said *O you who believe, be wary of God, and let each soul look to what it has put forth for the morrow* [Q. 59:18], enjoining them to charity (*ṣadaqa*) and adding, 'A man can give charity with a single dinar, a single dirham, a cupful of wheat, or [even] a measure of dates'. The full *ḥadīth*

[153] A widely attested report in which the Prophet is asked by the angel Gabriel to define 'faith' (*īmān*), 'submission' (*islām*), 'virtuousness' (*iḥsān*) and 'the Hour' (*al-sāʿa*). Versions of varying lengths, but with substantially identical narrative focus, appear in all the (six) major Sunnī collections. See Bukhārī, *Ṣaḥīḥ*, *Kitāb al-Tafsīr* (65), *Bāb qawlihi inna'llāha ʿindahu ʿilm al-sāʿa* (66), *ḥadīth* no. 299/4777; ibid., *Kitāb al-Īmān* (2), *Bāb su'āl Jibrīl* (2), *ḥadīth* no. 43/50. Also, in Muslim, *Ṣaḥīḥ*, *Kitāb al-Īmān* (2), *Bāb al-īmān* (also, *islām*) *mā huwa wa bayān khiṣālihi* (1), *ḥadīth* nos. 5 and 7; the *ḥadīth* may also be found in Nawawī's select forty (*al-Arbaʿūn*), at no. 2.

[154] A similar report is cited by Qurṭubī, above, in 'second issue'.

is mentioned [in the *Ṣaḥīḥ*], and that is how it was narrated by Aḥmad [Ibn Ḥanbal][155] and the authors of the *Sunan* collections on the authority of Ibn Masʿūd, where they mention 'the sermon concerning the needy'. And regarding this same incident, [in one version] he recites three verses, of which this verse, *O people! Be wary of your Lord*, is one.[156]

Muḥsin al-Fayḍ al-Kāshānī

This interpretation includes one of the most elaborate descriptions of the inferiority of women in this corpus. Many of the themes here have appeared in prior interpretations; but whereas prior interpretations often were given in a piecemeal fashion, here they are carefully constructed into a whole argument. After a preliminary statement that believers must be wary of God, Muḥsin al-Fayḍ begins his analysis of this verse and its implications for women. He starts by giving the most accepted interpretations: that Eve was created from Adam's smallest rib and that she was created from the side of Adam. Next, he says on the authority of Jaʿfar al-Ṣādiq,[157] that man was created from water and clay, so man's interest is in water and clay, and woman was created from man, so her interest is in men, and therefore women should be kept confined. This bears a strong resemblance to the *ḥadīth* that appeared in Ibn Kathīr's interpretation of a Sunnī source. The clear statement here is that because man is woman's essence, her interests cannot go beyond him; this justifies the legislation, noted above, that allows husbands to confine their wives to the home.

The interpretation moves on to give the *ḥadīth* on the authority of Jaʿfar al-Ṣādiq that Eve was not created from a rib but rather from soil. This *ḥadīth* reports Jaʿfar al-Ṣādiq as saying that the theologians put forth the view that Eve was created from a rib, which is a theological issue, in that one part of Adam would then marry another part. This interpretation is thus similar to previous Shīʿī interpretations in that it questions the veracity of the rib *ḥadīth*, even as it addresses a dialectical enemy (the theologians) and explains how this creation led to women's subservience. In this version, Eve was scooped out from the soil between Adam's legs, so that woman would be subservient to man. After she comes to life, Adam begins to like her and has a conversation with God about her. God tells him that Eve has been created so that Adam may satisfy his desires in her and so that she can obey him; Eve then tells Adam that he must come to her to get engaged, for she will not go to him. The entire tale is at once a statement of and justification for women's subservience, based on women's creation from and for man and on the nature of the first couple's engagement to one another. The dialogue shows that Eve is a sentient person who also understands the rules (perhaps even better than Adam does), but who must nevertheless take her place as subservient to him. Muḥsin al-Fayḍ's opinion is that woman was created from the

155 On whom see the PA, Ibn Ḥanbal.
156 Ibn Kathīr, *Tafsīr*, s.v. Q. 4:1.
157 The sixth of the Twelver Shīʿī imams, eponym of the Jaʿfarī/Imāmī school of law.

left rib, which indicates that the bodily, animalistic part is stronger in women than in men. Because woman was extracted from man, the bodily animalistic aspect is deficient in men and overabundant in women. Thus, like others surveyed here, this interpretation explains women's deficiencies in terms of their physical makeup and the purpose of their creation.[158]

The end of this interpretation is remarkable in that Muḥsin al-Fayḍ considers the question of the exact nature of the propagation of the species after Adam and Eve. There are earlier Shīʿī interpretations that examine this issue, though to our knowledge this is the first time that the Shīʿī discussion of the propagation of the species has been translated. First, he gives an argument that sisters and brothers could not marry, though he then says it might have been possible at one time, but it was later prohibited. The next opinion is that certain sons of Adam were married to houris from Paradise, and others were married to jinn. The good parts of humans come from the lineage of the houris, whereas the bad parts come from the lineage of the jinn. There are several versions of this story. Another story is that Cain and Abel were both products of twin pregnancies, and Cain married Abel's twin while Abel married Cain's, and only after this was sibling marriage prohibited. This leads to a refutation of the Zoroastrians, who are said to practise sibling marriage. When one of the imams is asked about that, he replies that the Zoroastrians continue to do this after sibling marriage was prohibited, while the immediate children of Adam only did so before the prohibition.

In a distinctly Shīʿī interpretation, Muḥsin al-Fayḍ interprets Muḥammad's 'womb-tie' as referring to the imams, who are attached to God's throne.

O people! Be wary of your Lord, who created you from a single soul, that is Adam, upon our Prophet and upon him be blessings and peace. *And from it created its mate*, that is Eve. Al-Qummī says: He created her from his lowest rib, *and spread forth from the two many men and women*, many sons and daughters; and the command to wariness (*taqwā*) of God is a consequence of that, because in it there is an indication of [both] the vanquishing power, which is rightly feared (*kh-sh-y*), and the obvious grace that requires obedience to the One giving it. Al-ʿAyyāshī said that the Commander of the Believers [ʿAlī b. Abī Ṭālib] (*ʿm*), said Eve was created from the rib nearest (*quṣayrā*) to the flank of Adam, the *quṣayrā* being the smallest rib, and God put in its place flesh. And in one transmission, Eve was created from the side of Adam while he was sleeping (*r-q-d*). On the authority of Jaʿfar al-Ṣādiq (*ʿm*), God created Adam from water and clay, and so the aspirations of the sons of Adam are towards water and clay; and God created Eve from Adam, and so the aspirations of women are towards men, thus you should keep them protected in the houses. And in the *Faqīh* and the *ʿIlal*,[159] on his

[158] On this interpretation, see Bauer, *Gender Hierarchy*, 126–9.

[159] Two famous works by Ibn Bābawayh, al-Shaykh al-Ṣadūq (d. 381/991), a foremost Twelver Shīʿī scholar (see the PA): his *Man la Yaḥḍuruh al-faqīh* is considered to be one of the 'four books' (*al-kutub al-arbaʿa*) and a jurisprudential manual for Twelver Imāmī *fiqh*.

authority, [Jaʿfar al-Ṣādiq] (*ʿm*) was asked about the creation of Eve, and it was said to him, 'People around us say that God, mighty and majestic, created Eve from the lowest left rib of Adam.' He said, 'Glory be to God, exalted be He above doing such a thing!' Those who say that, say that God, blessed and exalted, did not have the power to create for Adam a mate from something other than his rib, which gives the repugnant theologian (*mutakallim min ahl al-tashnīʿ*) a right to make speculative arguments that part of Adam married another part, since she was from his rib! God will judge between us and them.' Then he [Jaʿfar al-Ṣādiq] continued, 'When God, blessed and exalted, created Adam from clay and commanded the angels, they prostrated before him. Then stillness (*subāt*) was cast on him, and He created Eve for him. He made her from the hollow which is between his thighs, and that is so that woman would be subservient to man. She began to move, and he noticed her movement, and when he noticed, she moved away from his side. And when he looked upon her, he looked at a beautiful creation which resembled him, although she was female. He spoke to her and she spoke to him in his tongue. He said to her, "Who are you?" And she said, "A creation, which God has created as you see", and Adam said to that, "O Lord, who is this beautiful creation whose company and sight give me solace (*uns*)?" God said, "O Adam, this is my servant Eve; would you like her to be with you, to give you solace, to speak with you and to obey your orders?"[160] Adam said, "Yes, O Lord, and for that I owe you thanks and praise without end." God said, "Dedicate her to Me, for she is My servant who is suitable also for you as a mate (*zawja*) to satisfy desires." And God imparted upon him desires (*shahwa*), and He had taught him before then knowledge of all things, and he said, "O Lord, I dedicate her to you." And God was not satisfied with that. He said, "I would be satisfied if you teach her knowledge of my religion." Adam said, "You shall have that from me, O Lord, if that is what you wish from me." God said, "Verily, I do wish this, for I have already given her to you as a mate, so take her under your wing." Adam said to her, "Come to me", and she said, "No, rather you should come to me", and God Most High ordered Adam to go to her, and he did, and if that had not been, women would have gone out to engage themselves, and this is the story of Eve.'

Al-ʿAyyāshī reports on the authority of al-Bāqir (*ʿm*),[161] who was asked, 'From what thing did God create Eve?' And he said, 'What do they say [of] this creation?' I[162] said, 'They say that God created her from one of Adam's

[160] Muḥsin al-Fayḍ al-Kāshānī, *al-Ṣāfī*, II, 176 (s.v. Q. 4:1).
[161] Also known as Abū Jaʿfar, the father of Jaʿfar al-Ṣādiq.
[162] In ʿAyyāshī's *tafsīr*, the speaker is named as the father of ʿAmr b. Miqdām. See ʿAyyāshī, *Tafsīr ʿAyyāshī* (Qumm, Muʾassasat Baʿtha, 2000), I, 363 (s.v. Q. 4:1).

ribs.' And he said, 'They lie. Was God incapable of creating her from something other than a rib?' So I said, 'Would that I could sacrifice myself to you, son of the Messenger of God. From what thing did He create her?' And he said, 'My father told me on the authority of his fathers; he said, the Messenger of God said that God, blessed and exalted, took a handful of clay and mixed it with His right – and they say both of His hands are right – and He created from it Adam, and some clay was left over, and from this he created Eve.'

In the *ʿIlal* [*al-sharāʾiʿ*] it is also reported on [al-Bāqir's] authority, 'God created Adam from clay, and from its leftover and the rest of it He created Eve.' And in another narration, she was created from his belly, and from his left side, and from the leftover clay from his left rib.

And he [al-Ṣadūq] says in *al-Faqīh*, 'The report which narrates that Eve was created from the left rib of Adam is correct, and its meaning is from the bit of soil which was left over from his right rib, and that is why men have one rib fewer than women do.'

I[163] say, what has been cited to the effect that she was created from the left rib is an indication that the animal, corporeal aspect of women is stronger than it is in men, and the spiritual, angelic aspect is the other way around, and that is because the right stands for the world of the spiritual realm and the left stands for the world of the corporeal kingdom; so the clay represents corporeal matter, whereas the right represents spiritual matter, and there can be no [corporeal] kingdom without a [spiritual] realm, and that is the meaning of the statement [reported by al-Bāqir], 'Both of My hands are right hands.' The left rib missing (*manqūṣ*) from Adam was a metonym for the desires that arise when the bodily realm predominates, since it belongs to the world of creation; that is the leftover clay, which was extracted from his interior and became the [physical] matter for the creation of Eve. The imam indicates, in his *ḥadīth*, that the aspect of the spiritual realm and command is stronger in men than the aspect of [corporeal] kingdom and creation, and it is the other way around with women. The exterior is a sign of the interior, and this is the secret of this deficiency in the bodies of men and women; nobody will obtain the secrets of God except the people of the secret. Calling the speech of the infallibles lies can be attributed to the common people understanding it exoterically (*ẓāhir*), without taking into account the fundamental nature of the *ḥadīth*.

In the *ʿIlal*, [Jaʿfar] al-Ṣādiq (*ʿm*) was asked about the beginning of the issue (*nasl*) from the progeny of Adam and was told that there are some people around us who say that God, exalted be He, revealed to Adam that he

[163] This is now Muḥsin al-Fayḍ giving his own opinion.

should marry his daughters to his sons and that this creation is originally all from these brothers and sisters, to which he responded, 'Glory be to God, exalted be He above doing such a thing!' He continued, 'How can one say this, namely, that God, mighty and majestic, made it so that the origin of His most pure beloved creatures, His prophets and messengers, believing men and believing women, Muslim men and Muslim women, was from something illicit (*ḥarām*), and that He does not have the power to create them from what is licit (*ḥalāl*), when He had taken from them a covenant on the basis of what is licit (*ḥalāl*), wholesome and unadulterated purity. By God, it has come to me that a beast's sister disguised herself to her brother, and when he mounted her and spilt himself in her, thereupon the truth about her was revealed to him, and he came to know it was his sister, and he pulled out his member and bit it off with his own teeth and dropped dead.'

There is another report on his authority [Jaʿfar al-Ṣādiq] (*ʿm*), which is similar to it, and emphasises strongly the illicitness of sisters for brothers, and that was the case throughout the four well-known revealed scriptures (*al-kutub al-arbaʿa*),[164] except that a generation of these creatures shunned the knowledge of the families of the prophets, taking it from other than where they were commanded to, and have thus ended up in the error and ignorance that you see. Towards the end of this [other] report: whoever says this and the like of it[165] only desires to give strength to the arguments of Zoroastrians (Majūs). What is wrong with them? May God fight them. He then proceeds to say that seventy pregnancies (*baṭn*) happened with Adam, and in each pregnancy there was a boy (*ghulām*) and a girl (*jāriya*), up until Abel (Hābīl) was killed. When Abel was killed, Adam was so grief-stricken for Abel that this interrupted his being with women, and he was not able to have intercourse with Eve for five hundred years. When the anguish that he had for him was lifted, he lay with Eve, and God granted him a single offspring with no twin. The name Seth (Shīth) meant 'God's gift' (*hibat Allāh*), and he was the first legatee to receive a testament from among the sons of Adam and he was the first legatee (*waṣī*) to receive a testament (*w-ṣ-y*) from among the sons of Adam (*al-Ādamiyyūn*). After Seth, Japheth (Yāfith) was born to him, also without a twin. When both had reached their maturity, and God, mighty and majestic, willed that the offspring reach the number that you see [today] and that the Pen should decree illicit what God has made illicit in terms of sisters for their brothers, He sent down on a Thursday, in

[164] Presumably the scrolls of Abraham (*ṣuḥuf*), the tablets (*alwāḥ*) of Moses, the psalms (*zabūr*) of David and the Evangel/Gospels (*injīl*) of Jesus. (All are derived from Qurʾānic instances.)

[165] Namely, that Adam's sons and daughters intermarried.

the late afternoon (*ʿaṣr*), a houri (*ḥawrāʾ*) from the Garden named Nazla. God then commanded Adam that he marry her to Seth, which he did. Then on the next day, again in the late afternoon, He sent down another houri named Manzila and commanded Adam to marry her to Japheth, which he did. To Seth was born a male child and to Japheth was born a female child. When these two were old enough, God, exalted be He, commanded Adam to marry Japheth's girl to Seth's boy, which he did. From their issue, then, were born the most excellent of prophets and messengers. May refuge be sought with God against it being as they say, regarding brothers and sisters.

In the *Faqīh*, on his [Jaʿfar al-Ṣādiq's] authority (*ʿm*), Seth was born to Adam, and his name was 'God's gift', and he was the first legatee to receive a testament from among the sons of Adam. [Al-Ṣadūq] narrates the *ḥadīth* providing the full narration.

In his *ʿIlal*, al-ʿAyyāshī also reports on his [Jaʿfar al-Ṣādiq's] authority (*ʿm*) that it was said to him, 'People claim that Adam married his daughter to his son', to which he said, 'Yes, people say that. But do you not know that the Messenger of God (*ṣlʿhm*) said, "If I had come to know that Adam married his daughter to his son, I would have married Zaynab to al-Qāsim, for I would not have wanted to reject Adam's way (*dīn*)".'

In *al-Kāfī*, it is reported on the authority of al-Bāqir (*ʿm*) that it was mentioned to him that the Zoroastrians (Majūs) say marriage (*nikāḥ*) [for them] is like the marriage of sons of Adam, and they use that as an argument against us. As for you [the Shīʿa], they cannot use this as an argument against you: for when 'God's gift' came of age, Adam said, 'O Lord, grant "God's gift" marriage', whereupon God sent down a houri who bore him four male children, and then God raised her back [up to Paradise]. And then when the son of 'God's gift' came of age, he said, 'O Lord, grant the sons of "God's gift" marriage', whereupon God, mighty and majestic, revealed to him that he should ask for the hands of four girls from a man of the jinn, who was a Muslim, for the sons of 'God's gift'. He then married them off. And so all issue with beauty and discernment (*ḥilm*) was from the houri, including prophethood, going back to Adam, and whatever was born of foolishness and impetuosity was from the jinn.

It is also reported on his authority (*ʿm*), by al-ʿAyyāshī, that he [Jaʿfar al-Ṣādiq] said that four males were born to Adam. God then sent down to him four houris (*ḥūr ʿīn*), and he married each one of them to one, and they procreated. God then raised them [the houris] back up and gave these four sons four jinn, and progeny issued from these: whoever was discerning issued from Adam, and whoever was beautiful issued from the houris (*ḥūr ʿīn*), and whoever was created hideous or vile was from the jinn. Another report has it that when 'God's gift' was born to Adam and matured, he asked God to grant him a marriage. God thereupon sent down a houri from Paradise and married her to him, and she bore him four male children. There then was born to Adam another son, and when this one matured he was commanded to marry a jinn (*jānn*). Four girls were born to him, and those sons then married these girls. And whoever was beautiful was from the houri, and whoever was discerning was from Adam, and whoever was a simpleton was from the jinn. After they had procreated, the houri was raised back up to the heaven (*samā'*).

In *al-Faqīh*, also on his authority (*'m*), God, mighty and majestic sent down to Adam a houri from Paradise and married her to one of his sons; the other [son] married the daughter of a jinn (*jānn*). Thus whatever beauty or excellence of character there is in people, that is from the houri, and whatever evil character is from the sons of Adam who are from the jinn.

In the *Qurb al-isnād*, it is reported that ['Alī] al-Riḍā (*'m*) said: Eve carried Abel and a sister at the same time in her belly (*baṭn*), and in the second pregnancy (*baṭn*), Cain and his sister at the same time. Abel married Cain's sister and Cain married Abel's sister. After that, the prohibition [against sibling marriage] took force. In the *Majma'*, the following is reported on the authority of al-Bāqir (*'m*): Eve, Adam's wife (*imra'a*), would give birth each time to a boy and a girl. She first bore Cain (Qābīl) – some say Qābīn – and his twin Aqlīmā, daughter of Adam. In the second pregnancy, [she bore] Abel and his twin Lawzā'. When all had reached maturity, God commanded Adam that Cain should marry Abel's sister and Abel, Cain's sister. Abel was content [to do that] but Cain refused, for his sister was the more beautiful of the two, and said, 'This is not by God's command but your opinion (*ra'y*).' God then commanded both to offer a sacrifice (*qurbān*), and they consented to that. The complete *ḥadīth* appears in [*sūrat*] *al-Mā'ida*, in the commentary on *And recite to them the story of Adam's two sons* [Q. 5:27].

In the *Iḥtijāj*, ['Alī b. al-Ḥusayn Zayn al-'Ābidīn] al-Sajjād[166] (*'m*) said, when conversing with a man from the Quraysh, 'When God accepted Adam's repentance, Adam lay with Eve, for he had not gone into her (*ghashiya*) since he and she were created on the earth. He used to venerate the house and the sacred precinct of the house; so if he wanted to go into her (*gh-sh-y*), he would go out of the sanctuary and would take her with him. Once he had traversed the sanctuary, he would go into her outside of it (*fī'l-ḥill*). Then they performed the major ablutions, in reverence of the sanctuary; then they would return to the environs of the house.

[166] The fourth Shī'ī imam, 'Alī b. Ḥusayn, Zayn al-'Ābidīn (d. 95/712).

'There were twenty male and twenty female children of Adam and Eve, and in every pregnancy (*b-ṭ-n*) was a male and a female. In the first pregnancy, Eve delivered Abel and with him a girl who was called Aqlīmā, and in the second pregnancy was Cain and a girl who was called Lawzā'. Lawzā' was the most beautiful of the daughters of Adam, and when they came of age, Adam feared for them lest they fall into temptation. So he called them to him and said to them, "O, Abel, I wanted to marry you to Lawzā'", and "O, Cain, I want to marry you to Aqlīmā". Cain said, "I am not satisfied with that. Are you going to give me in marriage Abel's ugly sister, and give my beautiful sister in marriage to Abel?" He said, "I will have the two of you draw lots, and if, O, Cain, your arrow is drawn in favour of Lawzā', and if your arrow, O, Abel, is drawn in favour of Aqlīmā, I will give each of you in marriage to that one in whose favour the arrow was drawn." So they were both satisfied with that and drew lots, but Cain's arrow was drawn in favour of Aqlīmā, Abel's sister, and Abel's arrow was drawn in favour of Lawzā', Cain's sister. So he married them in accordance with the lot that God had assigned for them. After that, God prohibited sibling marriage.'

So the Qurashī man said to him, 'So did the two give them children?' He said, 'Yes.' The Qurashī said, 'But is this not the practice of the Zoroastrians (Majūs) today?' He replied, 'The Zoroastrians are doing that after the prohibition from God.' Then he (*'m*) continued, saying to him, 'Do not find these matters strange. These are the ordinances of God which they went by. Did God not create the mate of Adam from him, and then make her permissible to him? That was one of their ordinances, and after that, God revealed the prohibition.'

And if it is asked how these reports are to be reconciled with the former reports, we would say that the former reports are the sound and reliable ones (*mu'tamad 'alayhā*); whereas the latter reports are only cited in order to propitiate the common people (*'āmma*)[167] and are not to be relied upon, even as it is permitted to interpret them in order to reconcile them with the former ones.

And be wary of God by whom you petition one another: that is to say, some of you petition others, saying, 'I ask you by God!' And its root is *tatasā'alūn*, but the initial *tā'* is elided with the *sīn*. It is also read with a single consonant and the omission of the *tā'*. *And the wombs* (*arḥām*): so be wary of (*ittaqū*) severing the womb-ties. That is how it is in the *Majma'* on the authority of al-Bāqir (*'m*). They say that it is derived from the saying, 'I ask you by God and the womb-tie that you do such-and-such.' Or, 'I implore you by God and

[167] By this, he means the Sunnīs.

the womb-tie.' So, in other words, just as you extoll God in your speech, so you should extoll Him by being obedient to Him. On this basis is the reading with the genitive inflection (*jarr*).

Al-Qummī says, 'You will be asked on the Day of Resurrection about wariness (*taqwā*) of God; were you wary of (*taqwā*) Him? And about the womb-ties; did you connect them?'[168]

And in *al-Kāfī* and in al-ʿAyyāshī on the authority of al-Ṣādiq (*ʿm*), it is the womb-ties between people (*arḥām al-nās*) that God, mighty and majestic, commands to be connected and causes to be revered. Do you not see that He has placed them together with him, by which I mean, He has juxtaposed them to His name in the command to wariness (*taqwā*)? And in *al-Kāfī*, also on his [al-Ṣādiq's] authority (*ʿm*), it is reported that the Commander of the Believers [ʿAlī] (*ʿm*) said, 'Connect your womb-tie, even if just by a greeting (*taslīm*)', and then he recited this verse [Q. 4:1].

On the authority of al-Riḍā [ʿAlī b. Mūsā] (*ʿm*), 'The womb-tie (*raḥim*) of the family of Muḥammad, who are the imams, peace and blessings be upon them all, verily cling to the throne, saying, "O Lord, connect whoever connects me, and sever whoever severs me"; and [this tie] keeps flowing thereafter in the womb-ties of the believers', and he recited this verse.

In the *ʿUyūn* on his [al-Riḍā's] authority (*ʿm*), 'God has commanded three things, to which are connected three things, and He commanded wariness of God (*taqwā*) and connection of the womb-tie; and whoever does not connect his kin is not God-wary (*taqwā*).

And on his authority, on the authority of his father, on the authority of their fathers, on the authority of ʿAlī, peace be upon all of them, the Messenger of God (*ṣlʿm*) said, 'When I was carried by night to the heavens, I saw a womb attached to the throne, bemoaning to its Lord a womb-relation. So I said to it, "How many fathers are between you and that womb-relation?" And it said, "We meet forty fathers up."'

Indeed God is Watcher over you, preserver.[169]

Burūsawī

Burūsawī begins by stating that people must preserve each other's rights because God created human beings in all of their different types and colours. He clarifies that people should fear nothing but the Creator. For him, as for others, the single soul is

[168] Note that this is a quote from Qummī, above.
[169] Muḥsin al-Fayḍ, *al-Ṣāfī*, s.v. Q. 4:1.

Adam and the mate is Eve. Eve was created from Adam's rib, and he liked her and was inclined towards her because she was made from a part of him. Burūsawī indicates that Eve was created at the beginning of creation, like Adam was. He ends this part of his interpretation not with a disquisition on women, but with a discussion on the importance of family and kinship relationships, including the interpretation about the womb attached to God's throne.

Burūsawī then emphasises the importance of being wary of God by telling a remarkable anecdote, which may strike some as pure fantasy, about a man who was tempted by a beautiful slave girl. Rather than give in to that temptation, the man smeared his whole body with his own excrement. Later that night, the angel Gabriel went to him and passed his hand over him, which resulted in the man smelling of musk from that day forward. Burūsawī then explains this anecdote by saying that true wariness (*taqwā*) is essential to live a good life, for the believer must always know that God is watching him and he cannot take a single action without God's knowledge. He must therefore perform every action knowing that God will see it; and being mindful of his own inner state will lead to a closer connection with God.

O people! is a general address that entails those existing in the time of the address, and those after them, but not those who have become extinct, and the proof of this is that they were not worshipping according to our holy law (*sharʿ*). Had it been general for all of the children of Adam, then they would have been obligated to worship according to our holy law, which is impossible.

Be wary of your Lord by preserving the duties owed to one another and the connections that must be maintained and cared for, neither forsaking these nor severing what you have been commanded to maintain.

Who created you. He determined your creation, state after state, according to the variation in your forms and colours. *From a single soul.* From a single source, which is the soul of Adam, your father, and he made the gift of creation come after the wariness, so that you are only wary of the Creator. He clarifies that there was one single father. For in the severing caused by the multitudes [of generations over time] is an enjoinder to be compassionate towards one another.

And from it created from that soul, meaning from part of it, *its mate*, your mother Eve, with an extension from one of his [Adam's] left ribs. It is said that God, when He created Adam (*ʿm*) and made him live in the Garden, cast sleep upon him, and while he was between sleeping and waking, He created Eve from his shortest rib; and when he woke up, he found her with him, and he inclined towards her and found her familiar because she was created from one of his parts. Eve was mentioned later, although she was the first among creations, because *and* does not indicate ordering.

And spread forth [means] divided and propagated *from the two*, that is, from that soul and its mate, all people, by way of procreation and progeniture, *many men* (it is masculine in order to encompass a great number) *and women* (in other words, many sons and daughters); it suffices to describe *men* with the adjective *many*, rather than describing women with it, since wisdom (*ḥikma*) rules that there are more of them. The command to be wary of God is made to be consequent upon this story because the purpose of it is to prepare the way for the command to be wary of God with regard to what has to do with the rights of his household and the children of his genus, as proven by the verses that come afterwards. It is as though He had said: Be wary of your Lord who has connected you, making you as trees from a single root, in the obligations you have towards one another, such as the duty to maintain the connections between you; so preserve them and do not be negligent of them.[170]

And be wary of God, that is, when it comes to religion and kinship ties (*nasab*). Do not sever those branches that shoot off from the same root (*jurthūma*). *By whom you petition one another*, among yourselves, when one says to another, 'I ask you by God'; *and the wombs*, that is, when one of you asks the other invoking God and the womb-tie, saying, 'I implore you by God and by the wombs, do such and such', as an emotional entreaty (*istiʿṭāf*). It was the custom of the Arabs that when one of them would entreat another, he would include the womb-tie in the petition and the imploration by God in the entreaty. His words *wa'l-arḥāma* are in the accusative case as a coordination with the [syntactical] locus of the genitive construction, as when you say *marartu bi-Zaydin wa ʿAmra* (I passed by Zayd and ʿAmr), or [as a coordination] with *Allāha*, with the intended meaning 'be wary of God and be wary of the womb-ties', connect them and do not sever them. In juxtaposing the wombs to His name, glory be to Him, He is alerting [us] to the fact that the connection of these ties is of the same status as wariness of Him. It is reported on [the Prophet's] authority (*ṣlʿm*), 'The womb is attached to the Throne (*ʿarsh*) and says, "Whoever connects me, God connects him and whoever severs me, God severs him" '. He (*ṣlʿm*) also said, 'There is no good deed that is rewarded faster than connecting with a womb-relation, and there is no evil deed that is punished faster than illicit sexual acts (*baghy*)'. Therefore, the servant ought to be mindful of these duties, since all [human beings] are siblings (*akhkh*) from a single father and mother – namely, Adam and Eve – and especially believers, since they [also] share the kinship of faith and religion, and likewise through their kinship [of their origins] in clay (*ṭīn*).

Indeed, God is Watcher (*raqīb*) *over you*: *al-raqīb* is *al-murāqib*, one who keeps track of all of your deeds; that is to say, He is keeper and knower of all

[170] Burūsawī, *Rūḥ al-bayān*, II, 159 (s.v. Q. 4:1).

that issues from you of deeds and speech, and of all that is hidden in you of intentions (*niyya*), wishing to recompense you on account of all of that. God thus clarifies how [it is that] *He knows all that is secret and what is even more concealed* [Q. 20:7]. And if this is the case, then a person should be cautious and fearful of what they do and do not do.

Know that wariness (*taqwā*) is the mainstay and the cause of greater ennoblement in this world and the next. There is a story (*ḥikāya*) about a man in Basra who was known as 'the musky one' (*al-miskī*) because a scent of musk always issued from him. He was asked about that, and he related, 'I was the most handsome of people but was [extremely] shy (*ḥayā'*), and so they said to my father, "Why don't you take him to sit in the marketplace? He would then open up to people." He [my father] thus sat me in a draper's shop. An old woman once passed and asked for a piece of cloth. I brought out for her what she wanted. She then said to me, "Can you come with me so that I can pay you for it?" I set off with her until she made me enter a great palace with a magnificent dome. There, inside, was a slave girl on a bed with gold-embroidered cushions. She pulled me close to her chest, and I said, "Goodness, God!" She said, "All is fine!" I said, "My shoes are too tight." I managed to get to the privy, where I defecated and smeared my face and body with it. They thought that I was insane, and so I managed to get away. That same night I came across a man who asked me, "Where do you stand in relation to Joseph, son of Jacob?"[171] and then asked, "Do you know who I am?" I said, "No." He said, "I am [the angel] Gabriel" and then passed his hand over my face and body. From that day on, the smell of musk issues from me, from the scent of Gabriel (*'m*)'. And that is the result of the blessings [that come] from wariness of God (*taqwā*).

Wariness (*taqwā*), as defined in the Law (*shar'*), is preventing a soul from all that can harm it in the Hereafter, and that is according to [several] levels (*marātib*). The first: to protect oneself from the eternal punishment by ridding oneself of all associations with God (*shirk*), and this is the sense of God's words *And He made them commit themselves to the word of wariness (taqwā)* [Q. 48:26]. The second: to shun all sin, which is the commonly acknowledged sense of the word *taqwā* and the one intended in His words, exalted be He, *And if the people of the towns had believed and been God-wary* (*taqwā*) [Q. 7:96] *We would have remitted* [*their sins*] [Q. 5:65].[172] The third: to rise above all that can distract one [from God], which is the veritable piety demanded by His words, exalted be He, *Fear God* (*ittaqū*) *as He should be*

[171] Cf. Q. 12:23ff., the story of Joseph's restraint during the attempts of the wife of the master of the house to seduce him.

[172] The commentary merges the two separate Qur'ānic citations.

feared [Q. 3:102]. It is in this vein that it was narrated about Dhū'l-Nūn al-Miṣrī that when he was approached by one minister (*wazīr*) who was ambitious but manifestly fearful (*kh-sh-y*) of the sultan, he said to him, 'If I were as fearful (*kh-sh-y*) of God as you are of the sultan, I would surely be from among the truthful ones (*ṣiddīqūn*).'

[. . .].[173]

The [spiritual] traveller (*sālik*) thus ought to be wary of his (*taqwā*) Lord and watch out for (*murāqaba*) God in all of his states, as He, exalted be He, says *Indeed God is Watcher over you* [Q. 4:1]. Watchfulness of oneself (*murāqaba*) is a servant's awareness of God's watchfulness, glory be to Him, over him. Thus his maintaining of this awareness is watchfulness (*murāqaba*) of his Lord. This is the root of all good [that can come to a servant] and he can only reach this rank after having reckoned with himself (*muḥāsaba*). And so when he reckons with himself for what has passed and set right his state (*ḥāl*) in the moment (*waqt*),[174] he has adhered to the path of truth and acted virtuously in his relationship with God in terms of looking after his heart, preserving for the sake of God every breath and watching out for (*r-q-b*) God, glory be to Him, in all of his states generally, knowing that there is a Watcher over him. The one who keeps his heart close will always be aware of his states (*aḥwāl*), will see his deeds and will hear his words. But the one who is oblivious to all of that, he has already become separated from the beginnings of connectedness (*waṣla*), and hence all the more so from the realities of proximity (*qurba*).[175]

Sulaymān b. 'Alī said to Ḥumayd al-Ṭawīl, 'Admonish me!' to which he responded, 'If you have been disobedient to God in private while knowing that He sees you, then you have committed a grievous thing, and if [you did it] thinking that He does not see you, then you are an unbeliever, because He says *Indeed God is Watcher over you*.'

A righteous man (*ṣāliḥ*) who had disciples used to single one of them out for sessions more than any of the others. They asked him about that. He said, 'I shall explain.' He gave each student a bird and told each one to slaughter it without anyone seeing him, and gave that student one too. They went off [to do that] and then came back, each one of them having slaughtered his bird,

173 Omitted here is a line of Persian poetry.

174 Technical Sufi terms, on which see 'Abd al-Razzāq Kāshānī (comp.), *A Glossary of Sufi Technical Terms*, ed. and tr. Nabil Safwat (London, Octagon Press, 1991), 101; also William C. Chittick, *The Sufi Path of Knowledge: Ibn al-'Arabī's Metaphysics of Imagination* (Albany, State University of New York Press, 1989).

175 The servant who 'keeps his heart close' to spiritual truth is spiritually awake and will immediately recognise the cause of his spiritual state (*ḥāl*) at any given moment, as well as the consequences of his words and deeds. In effect, he is able to reckon with himself (*muḥāsaba*) before the Day of Reckoning (*yawm al-ḥisāb*) after death.

except this one [student] who came back with the bird alive. He asked him, 'Why did you not slaughter it?' to which he responded, 'You commanded me to slaughter it without anyone seeing me, but I could not find a single place where no one would see.' He said to them [all], 'That is why I always go to see him specifically.'

[. . .][176]

Manār

The *Tafsīr al-manār* is the first modernist *tafsīr* of Q. 4:1, and it differs from other works of *tafsīr* in this chapter. This work was based on interpretations by Muḥammad ʿAbduh, recorded and edited by Rashīd Riḍā, who can be considered as the main author of the text.[177] Though some parts of this commentary are similar to other commentaries (the emphasis on being wary of God and on morality, for instance), other parts are unheard of elsewhere, and two issues stand out: ʿAbduh says that the *single soul* is not Adam, and he says that humans developed by evolution. This is one example of how current worldwide debates influenced the intellectual life in the Middle East at the turn of the twentieth century. A few points from ʿAbduh's unusual interpretation are described below.

After an opening in which he argues that the order to be wary of God is because of the relatedness of all humans, ʿAbduh describes why the *single soul* cannot be Adam. He bases this argument on the indefiniteness of the line: *and spread forth from the two many men and women*. He argues that if this verse referred to all people, it would read 'and spread forth from the two all men and women'. He then points out that every culture has a different idea of human origins and argues that the very idea of Adam came from the Hebrew scriptures, which may have been corrupted. While Ṭabarī had cited the Jewish lore on creation as worth considering (if not necessarily as being authoritative), ʿAbduh sees it as a source that has been corrupted from the message originally brought by Moses. As such, for him it is a 'history of the Jews' rather than a history of humankind, a story that is Jewish in origin rather than divine. In this view, Moses remains a prophet with a divine message, but because that message may have been corrupted, it cannot be trusted more than other sources, such as Chinese lore or, more particularly, archaeological evidence. ʿAbduh then lets himself out of providing a definitive answer to the issue by saying that he only argues about matters beyond thinking and feeling by using the Qur'ān. He claims neither to add to the scripture nor to take away from it; therefore, for him the matter of this *soul* is ambiguous. Riḍā

[176] Omitted here is a line of Persian poetry.

[177] Johanna Pink describes Riḍā as 'the main author of an extensive, incomplete Qur'ānic commentary best known as *Tafsīr al-manār*, which took its name from the journal *al-Manār*, edited by Rashīd Riḍā, in which it was originally published. Originally, the *tafsīr* was based on the exegetical lectures of Muḥammad ʿAbduh, but it was continued and further developed by Rashīd Riḍā to include a wide range of additional material and address specific contemporaneous issues.' Pink, 'Riḍā, Rashīd', *EQ*.

seems to wish to make ʿAbduh's views more palatable, by saying that ʿAbduh does not prevent others from holding the view that Adam is the father of humankind. Riḍa says that some of ʿAbduh's students have become confused by ʿAbduh's focus on archaeological ruins and on the idea that humankind may have a number of different origins. Riḍā asserts that it is possible to believe in this view and still be a Muslim, because the Qurʾān comes from God, who, in His wisdom, sent a text that does not contradict Jewish interpretation or the interpretation of the archaeologists. Furthermore, he asserts that the Qurʾān does not deny the belief in Adam as the father of humankind; it merely leaves the matter ambiguous.

Riḍā is ultimately concerned with the idea that the soul is eternal, while the body fades and dies. He has a doctrine on electricity, which was in his day taken up by the Sufis. According to Riḍā, the creation of the *mate*, Eve, was for the first soul, Adam. He seems to differentiate his own opinion from that of ʿAbduh, who adheres to the view of Abū Muslim al-Iṣfahānī, as explained by Rāzī (on which see above). Thus the interpretation of this verse is a fascinating glimpse into the views of a modernist thinker (ʿAbduh) and into the slightly more conservative views of his disciple (Riḍā). Neither of them is particularly interested in issues of gender, and this is perhaps telling of the most prominent issues of the day, which seem to have been evolution and natural selection, which ultimately leads to an ontological inquiry into the very nature of human existence. Their views on evolution did not gain a foothold in subsequent mainstream Sunnī interpretations of the Qurʾān, though it was addressed by many subsequent Shīʿī thinkers.

Riḍā has a long passage on the womb-ties, a large part of which is a quote from Ibn Taymiyya on the question of intercession and whether one is allowed to petition in the name of the womb-tie. Only a small part of this discussion is directly related to questions of gender. For Ibn Taymiyya and for Riḍā/ʿAbduh alike, the womb-ties are as important as the tie to God, and thus it is important not to neglect these ties.

The teacher-imam [Muḥammad ʿAbduh] says: God, glory be to Him, opens His chapter with a reminder to people, who are addressed, that they issue from a single soul. Such a prelude constitutes a magnificent opening to what the *sūra* contains in the way of rulings on kinship, relations by marriage and whatever is connected to these such as rulings regarding marriage and inheritance. In this way He explains how kinship as a whole is universal, and then mentions womb-ties (*arḥām*) before proceeding to detail rulings that concern these.

It [Q. 4] is called 'the *sūra* of women' because it opens with the mention of women and some of the rulings associated with them. As for His words *O people*, this is a general address, not specific to one group as opposed to another. There is thus no evidence for saying that it was specific to the Meccans, as does the commentator Jalāl [al-Dīn al-Suyūṭī] especially given the fact that the entire *sūra* is Medinan, except for one verse, about which there is some doubt concerning whether it be Meccan or Medinan. The expression *al-nās* (people) is a collective noun for human beings (*bashar*), originally *unās*, but the *hamza* having been elided upon the addition of the definite article (*al-*). I believe that [Fakhr al-Dīn] al-Rāzī attributes the opinion that the address is intended for the Meccans to Ibn ʿAbbās, may God be pleased with him, but he [Rāzī] also adds conversely that the rationalist (*uṣūliyyūn*) exegetes all agree that the address is a general one to all individuals under moral obligation (*mukallafūn*),[178] which is the sounder [of the two opinions]. Three factors lend this [latter opinion] support: the definite article (*lām*) in *al-nās* functioning as all-encompassing (*li'l-istighrāq*) and since they are all created beings and have all been commanded to God-wariness (*taqwā*). I remember that one of the first expressions (*ʿibāra*) I ever heard and understood when I was young was from my father, may God have mercy on him, when he said that God, exalted be He, addressed the people of Mecca with the phrase *O people* and the people of Medina with *O you who believe*, but only once addressed unbelievers with an epithet signifying disbelief, in *sūrat al-Taḥrīm* [Q. 66:7] where He says *O you who have disbelieved, make no excuses this day*, as a way of indicating the manner in which they will be addressed in the Hereafter.

My opinion is that the phrase *O people* occurs frequently in the Meccan *sūra*s, such as [*sūra*s] *al-Aʿrāf*, *Yūnus*, *al-Ḥajj*, *al-Naml* and *al-Malāʾika*;[179] but it also occurs in [*sūra*s] *al-Baqara*, *al-Nisāʾ* and *al-Ḥujurāt* [Q. 49] from among the Medinan *sūra*s, where the Meccan form of address predominates, even as this also subsumes other people. Its occurrence in the Medinan *sūra*s is intended as an address from the outset to all those under religious obligation. I do not believe that Ibn ʿAbbās was of the opinion that the opening words of [*sūrat*] *al-Nisāʾ* were intended as an address to the people of Mecca; he in all likelihood said something akin to what I have just narrated from my father, but the way that transmitters handled it was that they interpreted every instance of this phrase to be such an address. Even Jalāl [al-Dīn] al-Suyūṭī made this mistake, despite the fact that he establishes the *sūra* to be Medinan in his *Itqān*.

[Regarding] His words *be wary of your Lord*: many examples of such [commands] have already been encountered, the last of which comes at the end of the preceding *sūra*. Now, the [harmonious] correspondence (*munāsaba*) between the command to be wary of the Lord of all people, the One who nourishes them with His grace, and the description in His statement *who created you from a single soul* should be clear: creation is the effect of a power, and whoever is described as having this tremendous power ought

[178] Cf. the interpretation of Rāzī given above.
[179] Respectively: Q. 7; 10; 22; 27; and 35 (more conventionally known as *Fāṭir*).

justly to be feared (*taqwā*) and any disobedience of him ought to be avoided. At least that is what some of them have said. The teacher-imam [Muḥammad ʿAbduh], however, says: It is superior to say that this constitutes a prelude for what will follow regarding the rulings on orphans, and the like. And so it is as though He were saying: ʻO People, fear (*khawf*) God, and be wary of overstepping the bounds He has placed for you concerning your actions, and know that you are all kin (*aqribāʾ*) of one another, sharing a single lineage (*nasab*), and that you shall return to a single origin (*aṣl*). Thus it is incumbent upon you to show affection (*ʿaṭf*) to a weak person, such as the orphan who has lost a father, and to preserve his rights (*ḥuqūq*).ʼ

I [Rashīd Riḍā] say: The lexical choice to use the word *rabb* (Lord) here is intended to induce a sentiment of affection. In other words, raise and nurture (*rabbū*) the orphans and connect (*ṣilū*) your womb-ties (*raḥim*), as your Creator raised and nurtured you (*rabbākum*) through His graces (*niʿam*), encompassing you with His munificence (*jūd*) and generosity (*karam*).

The teacher-imam [Muḥammad ʿAbduh] [says]: What is meant by the *single soul* (*al-nafs al-wāḥida*) is not Adam, neither in the text nor in any apparent meaning. Among the exegetes, there are those who say that every vocative (*nidāʾ*) of this type is intended for the Meccans or the Quraysh, and if that is true here then the people of Quraysh ought to understand from it that the *single soul* means the [tribe of] Quraysh or ʿAdnān.[180] But if the address were intended for the Arabs generally, it is possible that they would understand from it that what is meant by the *single soul* is Yaʿrub or Qaḥṭān.[181] If we were to say that the address was to all of those called to Islam – in other words, to all communities (*umam*) – then undoubtedly each community (*umma*) will understand it according to their convictions, and those who believe that all humans are from the line (*sulāla*) of Adam would then understand that what is meant by *single soul* (*al-nafs al-wāḥida*) is Adam. Those who believe that there is a [separate] father for every kind of human being will interpret that ʻsoulʼ (*nafs*) according to what they believe. The larger categories [of races] are the White Caucasian (*qawqāsī*), the Yellow Mongolian (*maghūlī*) and the Black Zanj (*zanjī*), *inter alia*. Indeed, some of these branches may constitute origins in their own right, such as the Red Ethiopians (*ḥabashī*) and the American Indians (*hindī*) and the Malay (*malaqī*).[182]

180 The legendary ancestor of the northern Arabs, as opposed to Qaḥṭān, that of the southern Arabs: see Eva Orthmann, ʻʻAdnānʼ, *EI*³.

181 On the previous points about Arab lineage and Qaḥṭān, see Hoyland, *Arabia and the Arabs*, 231 n. 2, *et passim*.

182 ʿAbduh and Riḍā, *Tafsīr al-manār*, IV, 263.

['Abduh] said: And the textual justification (*qarīna*) that what is meant by the *single soul* (*al-nafs al-wāḥida*) here is not Adam is His words *and spread forth from the two many men and women*, using the indefinite. It would have been more apposite in this respect to have said, 'and spread forth from the two *all* men and women'. How could this [address] indicate a widely acknowledged [single] soul when the address (*khiṭāb*) is general to all nations (*shu'ūb*), and when this knowledge is not acknowledged by all of them? For there are people who may not know of any Adam or Eve, and who will not have heard of either of the two. So, this well-known lineage among the progeny of Noah, for instance, is taken from the Hebrews (*'ibrāniyyūn*), for they are the ones who have connected the history of humankind with Adam, circumscribing it within a more recent historical epoch. The Chinese attribute human lineage to a different father, ascribing his history to a more distant epoch than the one defined by the Hebrews. Science and archaeological research into humans have disproven the Hebrews' version of history, while we Muslims are not obliged to believe in the historical account given by the Jews (*yahūd*); even if they ascribe it to Moses (*'m*), we do not trust that it is from the [original] Torah and that this has survived in the form that Moses [originally] brought it.[183]

He ['Abduh] said: We do not enter into arguments about matters that are beyond rational and sensory perceptions, except on the basis of the revelation with which our Prophet (*ṣl'm*) came, and we do not go beyond this revelation, either by adding or subtracting [anything], as we have already said on several occasions. Here, God, exalted be He, has made the matter of the soul, from which people were created, ambiguous; and He put it in the indefinite, so we leave it ambiguous. And so even if the findings of European researchers (*bāḥithūn ifranj*) are confirmed, namely, that for each human race there is a [separate] father, that still has no bearing on our Book as it does on their Book, the Torah, in which there is a clear text about that [descent]: this is what has driven their researchers to discredit the notion that that [history] comes from God, exalted be He, and is a result of revelations from Him.[184] Instances of other verses where He addresses people with the words *O sons of Adam* do not contradict this, nor do they amount to a categorical textual-proof that all human beings are his progeny, since it suffices for the address to make sense to them if the ones meant here are those progeny of Adam to whom this [address] was directed during the

[183] He indicates here that the Torah has been corrupted.

[184] A good example of 'Abduh's hermeneutical outlook, he is able here to allow for the findings of modern science and, at the same time, to make a supersessionist argument for the Qur'ān.

period of revelation. In addition, in the exegesis (*tafsīr*) of the story of Adam in the earliest sections of [*sūrat*] *al-Baqara* we have already seen how there had been on earth before him a kind (*nawʿ*) of this [human] species (*jins*) who had spread corruption and bloodshed.[185]

For more clarity, I [Riḍā] say: If the vast majority of the exegetes have interpreted the single soul here as being Adam, then they have not taken that from the text of the verse, nor from its obvious sense (*ẓāhir*), but rather from some taken-for-granted notion of theirs that Adam is the father of [all] humankind (*abū'l-bashar*). They have differed concerning phrases, such as where He says, *It is He who created you from a single soul, and made from it its mate, that he might find solace by her side* [Q. 7:189]. Al-Rāzī mentioned three interpretations in his explanation of it. The first interpretation, which he presented on the authority of al-Qaffāl: that God, exalted be He, mentioned this story by way of allegory. What is meant by that is that He created each one of you from *a single soul* and made its *mate* from its type (*jinsihā*), a human, equal to it in its humanity (*insāniyya*). The second interpretation: that the address was to the Quraysh who lived in the time of the Prophet (*fī ʿahd al-nabī*) (*ṣlʿm*), and these were the family of Quṣayy, and that what is meant by the *single soul* is Quṣayy. The third interpretation: that the *single soul* is Adam. He [ʿAbduh] has responded by calling those descriptions that he has come across of Adam and his mate idolatrous (*shirk*), when they are a type of dramatic metaphor. And it has already been mentioned in [*sūrat*] *al-Baqara* how the story of Adam itself is a kind of allegory, just like the allegory which al-Qaffāl uses in understanding the verse in *sūrat al-Aʿrāf*.[186]

It has been transmitted on the authority of the Imāmīs and the Sufis that before the Adam well-known to the People of the Book and to us, there were many Adams. It is said in the *Rūḥ al-maʿānī* [of Alūsī]:[187] The Imāmī author of the *Jāmiʿ al-akhbār* has mentioned, in the fifteenth chapter, a long report in which he transmits that God, exalted be He, created before our father Adam, thirty Adams, and between each Adam and the next Adam was one thousand years; and that the world was in ruins after them for fifty thousand years, then it flourished for another fifty thousand years, and then our father Adam (*ʿm*) was created. Ibn Bābawayh narrated in the *Kitāb al-tawḥīd* on the

[185] See Q. 2:30 where God informs the angels that He intends to appoint a vicegerent (*khalīfa*) on earth, at which point they express their concern that the current inhabitants have not exactly proven to be of the civilised kind.

[186] ʿAbduh clarifies that he interprets this story as a parable in his interpretation of Q. 2:35. The reference to *sūrat al-Aʿrāf* may be a reference to Q. 7:173: *lest you say our forefathers were idolaters*.

[187] On Alūsī, see Hamza *et al.*, *Anthology*, I, 47–8.

authority of [Jaʿfar] al-Ṣādiq in a similarly long *ḥadīth*: you might think that God did not create any humans other than you, but by God He has created a thousand thousand Adams, and you are the last of those Adams. According to al-Maytham in his *al-Sharḥ al-kabīr* of the *Nahj* [*al-balāgha*], it was transmitted on the authority of Muḥammad b. ʿAlī al-Bāqir that he said, 'Before the Adam that is our father, there passed a thousand thousand Adams or more.' The Shaykh al-Akbar [Ibn ʿArabī], in his *Futūḥāt*, [said that] an apparent reading would entail that forty thousand years before Adam was a different Adam. And in the *Kitāb al-Khaṣāʾiṣ* of Ibn Bābawayh – as it is in the margin – would give you to understand that there are multiple Adams even now, when he narrated on the authority of al-Ṣādiq that he said: Indeed, God, exalted be He, possesses twelve thousand worlds, and every single world is bigger than the seven heavens and seven earths, and none of these worlds are able to perceive that God, mighty and majestic, possesses a world other than theirs. Here ends what is relevant for our purposes.

However, on this matter, there are other transmissions in the *Futūḥāt* and elsewhere. It has been transmitted on the authority of Zayn al-ʿArab that the opinion of whoever says there were multiple Adams is disbelief (*kufr*). But this is just an example of his audacity and the audacity of those like him, who pounce at the chance to declare other Muslims as infidels (*takfīr*) on the most baseless of suspicions.

The teacher-imam has two opinions on this point. The first of them is that the plain sense (*ẓāhir*) of this verse precludes that what is meant by the *single soul* could be Adam, regardless of whether he is the father of all humans or not, due to what he has mentioned regarding the contradictions of it in scientific and historical study, and from the [grammatical] indefiniteness of [*many men and women*] spread forth *from it* and *its mate*, even though it is possible to respond to the latter by saying that the indefinite is for those who were born from the two of them directly, as though He had said, 'Spread forth from the two of them many men and women, and spread forth from those, everyone else.' Nevertheless, against the former position, things remain inconclusive.

The second of the two [opinions] is that in the Qurʾān there is no fundamentally conclusive text that all humans (*bashar*) are from the seed (*dhurriya*) of Adam, with what is meant by 'human' here being this animal being possessing the faculty of speech (*ḥayawān nāṭiq*), whose skin shows,[188] who is *erectus*, and who is referred to by the epithet 'human being' (*insān*). Accordingly, what some of the researchers (*bāḥithūn*) and those who share their opinions say, such as that humans have a number of fathers to

[188] *Al-bādī al-bashara*, meaning, not covered in fur.

whom the lines of all of the races of man return, makes no appearance in the Qur'ān.

Thus what the opinion of the teacher-imam counters is the ambiguities that exist in this vein; but this does not prevent those who are convinced that Adam is the father of all humans from [holding] such beliefs. This is because he does not say that the Qur'ān denies such a belief; he only says that it does not establish it as an absolute certainty with no room for interpretation. We are making this explicit in this instance because some people understood from his lessons that the Qur'ān denies this belief, that is to say, the belief that Adam is the father of all humans, but he never stated anything of the sort, either openly or by intimation. All that he was clarifying was that if one were to affirm what researchers say about the study of human remains and their fortunes, and of animals – which is that humans have a number of origins, and the being of Adam is not the father of all of them, in all of the earth, new and old – none of that would negate what the Qur'ān says or contradict it. Nay, it is possible for someone to affirm [those scientific findings] and remain a Muslim and a believer in the Qur'ān; he could even say that if the Qur'ān was from Muḥammad (*ṣlʿm*) then it could not be devoid of a conclusive text supporting the common beliefs of the People of the Book concerning that. But, being from God, it contains what the Jews in former times were not able to refute by claiming that it contravenes their book, and what the researchers in latter times were unable to oppose when it contravenes what has been established [scientifically] according to them.

O, whatever would they say, those people who think that the matter is conclusive on the basis of the text of the Qur'ān, about the person who is certain of the proofs that present themselves to him, that human beings have a number of origins? If he wishes to be a Muslim and he is unable to abandon his certitude about the matter, would they say that his faith is not sound or his Islam is not accepted, even as he may be certain that the Qur'ān is the word of God and that it does not have a text in it that contradicts his certainty?

Thus what appears at first sight from the lexical expression *soul*, regardless of the reports and handed-down traditions, is that it is this quiddity (*māhiya*) or reality (*ḥaqīqa*) through which the human constitutes this being (*kā'in*), one distinguished from other beings (*kā'ināt*); that is to say, He *created you from a single soul*, from a single genus (*jins*) and a single reality (*ḥaqīqa*), and there is no difference in whether this reality began with Adam, according to the People of the Book and the majority of Muslim scholars, or that it began with ones other than him and they perished, as some of the Shīʿa and Sufis say, or even that it began with a number of origins from which a number of races spread, according to some of the researchers, or whether these [multiple] origins, or [this single] origin, were the ones raised above certain [species of] animals, or that he was created independently, as debated by people in our times. God, exalted be He, says in [*sūrat*] *al-Mu'minūn* [Q. 23], verse 12, *We have created humans from an extract of clay* (*wa la-qad khalaqnā al-insāna min sulālatin min ṭīn*), and either in the exegesis of this or in the exegesis of [*sūrat*] *al-Ḥijr* [Q. 15], we shall explain the import of all of the revealed verses concerning the modality (*kayfiyya*) of the creation of human beings.

In any case, and regardless of any opinion or statement, it remains sound to say that all people are from a single soul; it is the humanity through which they are humans, and this is what those who call for the best in people, the righteousness in them, and a defence against harming them, agree upon as being the comprehensive reality for them. You can see them, despite their differences concerning the origin of humans, saying about all types and races of people that they are our brothers in humanity, and they consider humanity the fulcrum of unity and the motive for finding familiarity and mutual affection among humankind, whether they believe that their father is Adam (*'m*) or an ape or something else. This meaning is the one intended by reminding humans that they are from a single soul, because it is a prelude to the words about the rights of orphans and uterine kinship; and these are not stand-alone speeches intended to explain the creation and cosmology in detail, because this is not the aim of religion. And this explanation serves to dissolve the semantic problems in a much clearer way than that of those who have tried to resolve it.

As for the reality of the soul (*nafs*) through which a human being has life, and through which the unity of its species, despite the multitude of races, is confirmed, the Muslim [thinkers] have differed on that, as those before and after[189] them have differed on it. Some of them say that it is one of the accidents of the body (*badan*): it has no independence in itself, but rather it is life itself. The majority say, rather it is the substance. Some of them say it is material, and some of them that it is devoid of matter. Some say it is a part of the body and others say it is a body deposited in a human being. They [also] differ concerning the spirit (*rūḥ*): some say that it is the soul (*nafs*) and some say otherwise; some of them argue for abstention and the impermissibility of

[189] Riḍā's footnote: I mean by 'those after them', those to whom the intellectual life came after them, like the Europeans [*al-ifranj*]. The Muslims had had no partner in this [intellectual] life and they became without a presence in it, since you hear from not one of them an opinion or a school of thought in any of the scientific and philosophical issues, as it was before them. Perhaps one day they will make their return.

speaking about the reality of the spirit (*rūḥ*). All of these doctrines have been transmitted on the authority of the Muslim scholars from the People of the Book, from philosophy and from Sufism, and none of them declared one another an infidel (*yukaffir*) on account of his opinion regarding this. One of the strangest is the doctrine that the spirit is an accident of the corporeal entity (*jism*), which is life. This opinion is transmitted on the authority of the Qāḍī Abū Bakr al-Bāqillānī and his followers from among the Ashʿarī theologians. Despite all of that, he is counted among the imams of the Ashʿarī Sunnīs. It is narrated on the authority of the imam Mālik that the spirit has form, like the body (*jasad*).

Abū ʿAbd Allāh Ibn al-Qayyim [al-Jawziyya] said, concerning the definition of the spirit and explanation of its reality, according to the school of the Sunnīs (*ahl al-Sunna*): It is a body (*jism*), different in quiddity (*māhiya*) from this sensory (*maḥsūs*) body; and it is celestial (*ʿulwī*), luminous (*nūrānī*), subtle (*laṭīf*), living and moving (*mutaḥarrik*), flowing through the substance (*jawhar*) of the organs (*aʿḍāʾ*), running through them like the water flows through a watering place, the stream of oil in the olive or the fire in the coal; so as long as these organs are receptive to the effects that emanate onto (*fayḍ*) them from this subtle body entwined in these limbs, they will benefit from the effects emanating onto them as a result of the senses and voluntary movement. But if these organs are corrupted when they have been overpowered by dense (*ghalīẓa*) parts and are no longer receptive to those effects, that is when the spirit departs from the body and becomes separated into the world of spirits. That ends [ʿAbduh's words].

And I [Riḍā] say that the strongest of the philosophical theories proving the existence (*ithbāt*) of the spirit (*rūḥ*) or the soul (*nafs*) – and these two terms are used to designate a single meaning – is that the mind (*ʿaql*), retention (*ḥifẓ*) and memory (*dh-k-r*; vocalised with a *ḍamma* [*dhukr*]) are not attributes of this body or parts of its quiddity, even though they have been established beyond doubt. So these must have an existential source other than this crude body (*jasad kathīf*). Even in the brain, which is the outer manifestation of these things, fine details eventually unravel until they dissipate and disappear, but as it renews itself time after time, the perceptibles (*mudrakāt*) remain preserved in the soul, which makes them flow back into the new brain after the disappearance of what was before, and so human beings remember them when they need them.

The ancients have said about the existential source, which must be subtle (*laṭīf*), and ethereal due to its subtlety, that it is the soul (*nafs*) and the spirit (*rūḥ*), and these two are near in meaning; they both indicate the most subtle of the existents known by everyone. The terms *al-rūḥ* and *al-rawḥ*, which mean 'breath', have a single origin, whose matter is air (*rīḥ*), since the letter *yā'* in *al-rīḥ* is a *wāw* that has been turned into a *yā'* because of the preceding *kasra* inflection. This subtle meaning, which is the source of perception and life, has been called by two of the most subtle names of existents known to them [namely, *nafs* and *rūḥ*].

If those who had penned those two names [*rūḥ* and *nafs*] had known what the people of our day know, concerning the entities which are more subtle than the air and the soul, like hydrogen and electricity, then they would have given these two names, or a name derived from these two, to the source of life and understanding and the cause of the two of them. Have you not seen that the driver of the electric vehicles like the tram and others refers to the flow of electricity, by which this tram runs, with the term 'breath' (*nafas*)? The naming does not indicate the reality of what is named; it only indicates that those authors imagine the source of life to be something utterly subtle and elusive, despite the power of its effect and the tremendousness of its vestiges.

It was only philosophers, as was their habit, who enquired into the reality of this matter, and they are still enquiring. God Exalted says, *they ask you about the spirit; say the spirit is a matter that belongs to my Lord and you have only been given a little knowledge* [Q. 17:85]. That is to say that the little that you know does not enable you to understand the reality of the soul. Many scholars have said that the verse indicates that there is no point in aspiring to know the reality of the spirit, but I say that it does not indicate that; rather, it indicates that if people are given more knowledge than those questioners were given, then it is possible for them to know it.

I have not found a better way of clarifying or approximating the meaning of the spirit (*rūḥ*) and the soul (*nafs*) in the human being than the analogy of electricity. The materialist, who says that there is no spirit other than an accident (*'araḍ*) which is called life, compares the body to an electric battery, claiming that by virtue of its specific state and by virtue of the materials that are deposited in it, [it] generates electricity, and if something of that were to be missing, it is lost. Likewise, life is generated in the body by virtue of the compounding of an admixture in a specific constitution (*mizāj*), and with its disappearance, it disappears. The one who believes in the [existential] independence of the spirit (*rūḥ*) says that the body resembles an electric vehicle, and is like machines that run with electricity, [whereby energy is] directed to it from the power station where it is generated. If the machine is configured in a [specific] way, in terms of its parts and its instruments, then it is ready to receive the electricity that is directed to it and fulfil its function; but if some of its major parts are missing or if its configuration malfunctions, then it loses power and no longer functions.

Although [people] used to think that electricity was an accident of matter, with no existence in and of itself, more recently they became more inclined to believe that it is the origin of all existing things, that is, it exists in and of itself, and that all other forms of matter exist by virtue of it.[190] This comes close to the doctrine of the spiritualists (*rūḥiyyūn*), [which holds] that the soul is an established reality of humans and the body is animated by it, so it is a preserver of its existence and the regulator of its vital signs. So if it were to leave him, he would be dissolved and return to his elements. One only says that when one looks at the apparent causes and the visible phenomena, for all matters return to God. This new school of thought in electricity is close to the school of thought of those Sufis who believe in the unity of existence (*waḥdat al-wujūd*), and perhaps that is one way of bridging that gap. We shall return to this point of research and expand on the opinions regarding this, according to the philosophers and the naturalists of our age, in a more suitable place for it than this place, if it be in the will of God most High.

As for His words *and from it created its mate*, the meaning of this, according to the way that we have affirmed it, becomes apparent by making the *nafs* a collective noun, and making the pronoun refer back to it, with the meaning 'one of the two', by coordinating it to a corresponding elision, as the majority has stated. That is to say that reality was one first, then He created for it its mate of its type. Its meaning, according to the majority, is that God, exalted be He, created for that soul, which is Adam, a mate from it, and that is Eve; they said that He created her from his left rib while he was sleeping. That is what is made explicit in the second chapter of Genesis (*safar al-takwīn*) and mentioned in some *ḥadīths*. Were it otherwise, it would not occur to the reader of the Qur'ān. There is another opinion, preferred by Abū Muslim, as [Fakhr al-Dīn] al-Rāzī has said, and that is that the meaning of *from it created its mate* is that He created him from its type, so he is like her, as in His words, exalted be He, *Of His signs is that He created for you mates from among yourselves (min anfusikum), that you might find solace by their side, and He ordained love and mercy between you* [Q. 30:21], and His words *and God made mates for you from among yourselves, and made for you, from your mates, children and grandchildren* [Q. 16:72], and His words *He is creator of the heavens and the earth, and He made mates for you from among yourselves (min anfusikum), and mates from the livestock, whereby He multiplies you; there is nothing like Him, and He is the Hearing and the Seeing* [Q. 42:11], and,

190 On the history of the science of electricity and the developments which the authors of *al-Manār* would have very likely had access to, see Paola Bertucci and Giuliano Pancaldi, eds., *Electric Bodies: Episodes in the History of Medical Electricity* (Bologna, Bologna University, 2001).

in a similar vein, His words, mighty and majestic, *Verily, there has come a messenger from among yourselves* (*min anfusikum*) [Q. 9:128], and His words *Truly God conferred a great favour upon the Believers when He called forth a Messenger from among themselves* (*idh baʿatha fīhim rasūlan min anfusihim*) [Q. 3:164]. The like of these latter two are found in [*sūrat*] *al-Baqara* [Q. 2] and [*sūrat*] *al-Jumuʿa* [Q. 62]. There is no difference between the expression of the verse which we are interpreting and the expression of these verses; the meaning in all of them is one. As for he for whom it is established that Eve was created from Adam's rib, he is not obliged to connect that with this verse or to make that an explanation of it, departing from the style of those other verses like it.

The *single soul* has another aspect, which is that it is feminine, and that is why in the verse of [*sūrat*] *al-Aʿrāf* [Q. 7], He has made it feminine where it appears, and made its mate, which was created from it, masculine. So He says: *To find solace by her side* [Q. 7:189]. And, according to this opinion, it is clear that the opening of this *sūra* [Q. 4:1] accords with that, and an aspect of it is that it is usually named 'women'. According to this, it becomes clearer why this *sūra* opens with it and why it is called [*sūrat*] *al-Nisāʾ*. The proponents of this opinion say that it follows from what is established up to our day on the authority of the *ʿulamāʾ* concerning virgin reproduction, which is when the female of some species of animal of this world gives birth to a number of offspring without impregnation by the male. But it is necessary that there had previously been impregnation of some of their lineage. The creation of its mate from it in this way could be from it itself, or it could be of its type. There is another aspect, related to this, which is that the single soul included the male and female organs, like the tapeworm,[191] and it became more sophisticated and its individual parts became two mates. Some modern researchers say this, and the place for verifying it is in the interpretation of another verse.

Al-Zamakhsharī mentioned two aspects concerning the coordination of *and from it created its mate* with what comes before. The first of them is that it is coordinated to the elision, as though He had said, 'from a single soul He created it and began it, and He created from it its mate'; but it has been elided because the meaning is already indicated. It means that He made you lines from a single soul, and this is its attribute, and so forth. The second of them is that it is coordinated with *who created you*, meaning He created you from the soul of Adam because it is of the same type, branching from him, and He

[191] The tapeworm has both male and female sexual organs and can reproduce asexually or through contact with another tapeworm.

created from it your mother Eve, *and spread forth from the two many men and women* other than you, communities too many to enumerate. I say that is sufficient to say many women as well.

The teacher-imam said He used men and women in the indefinite form (*nakkara*) and emphasised this [with] His word *many* as a way of indicating the multitude of types; and that what is intended with the dual form in His words *from the two* is not Adam and Ḥawwāʾ, but rather any mates, and that applies to what we have said regarding the preceding phrase. Mentioning the creation of the pair after mentioning the creation of people does not necessitate its coming later than that in time, and the coordination with the word *and* (*wāw*) does not signify sequence, nor does it preclude the speech being well-ordered and harmonious, as the art of rhetoric demands; it is a form of providing details (*tafsīl*) after a general statement (*ijmāl*). When He says that He has created you from a single soul, this is a general statement, the details (*tafsīl*) of which are then given through the explanation that this creation is from the very same soul which also becomes its mate, and that all progeny is from both of these two mates. Therefore all of the descendants of humans were born of two mates, a male and a female. Thus ends [the words of ʿAbduh].

But one can counter his opinion that the *wāw* ('and') does not imply sequence with reference to verse 6 of [*sūrat*] *al-Zumar, He created you from a single soul, then* [*thumma*] *made from it its mate* [Q. 39:6]. This has been attended to and is mentioned in its appropriate place. The opinion of Abū Muslim and the opinion of the majority that men and women were spread forth from two spouses together can be countered by saying that it precludes them from having been created from a single soul and contradicts that, and it is not a refutation of taking the *single soul* to be an expression of the genus (*jins*) and the all-encompassing reality; so their being from a single genus does not preclude this genus having been created as a pair, a male and a female, and having from it spread forth *many men and women* or, rather, all men and women, as is apparent. Al-Rāzī transmitted on the authority of al-Qāḍī [ʿAbd al-Jabbār] that this objection applies to the opinion preferred by Abū Muslim – namely, that the mate is created of the same genus as that soul, as an independent creation – not the opinion of the majority, which holds that the mate was created from the very same soul when Eve was created from Adam's rib.

On the face of it, however, it applies to both of these opinions, because the reality and the matter itself is that people are created from the two mates, male and female, and those two are two souls, whether created independently or created one from the other as the Exalted One says: *O people, We have created you male and female, and We made you peoples and tribes so that you might know one another* [Q. 49:13]. But it is easier to interpret it according to the majority's opinion, who say that since they were from two souls, one created from the other, in this way they come *from a single soul*. However, to interpret the other way is not difficult, for al-Rāzī has said about it: it is possible to answer by saying that the word *from* indicates the initial purpose, and since the beginning of creation and bringing into existence started with Adam (*ʿm*), it becomes correct to say, 'He created you from a single soul', and also, since it has been established that God is capable of creating Adam from dust, He is also capable of creating Eve from dust, and if it were so, then what is the point in creating her from one of Adam's ribs? That ends [Rāzī's speech]. These are his words, which indicate his preference for what Abū Muslim has preferred, and likewise the teacher-imam.

And be wary of God by whom you petition one another. ʿĀṣim, Ḥamza and al-Kisāʾī read *tasāʾalūna* with a single *sīn*, and its original form is *tatasāʾalūna*, and one of the two *tā*'s has been omitted in order to lighten it. The rest of them read it with the intensification, assimilating the *tāʾ* into the *sīn* due to their proximity to one another in pronunciation (*makhraj*). Each of these two ways is idiomatically correct and well-known among the Arabs in the form of *tatafāʿalūna*. The meaning is: be wary of God, by whom some of you petition others, in that he says, 'I ask you, by God, that you fulfil this need!' hoping thereby to have a positive answer to his request. The meaning of his petitioning by God is that he petitions by his faith in Him and by his magnification of Him. The *bi-* is in it as a causative, that is to say, 'I petition you because of that, that you do such-and-such.'

As for His words *and the wombs*, the majority read it with the accusative inflection. Most of the exegetes (*mufassirūn*) say that it is correlated with the name of the Generous One, that is to say, 'and be wary of (*ittaqū*) the womb-ties, lest you sever them' or 'be wary of losing the rights of the womb-kin, connect them, and do not sever them'. Some of them make it a coordination with the [syntactical] locus of the genitive prefix in *bihi*, and the teacher-imam chose it. Al-Wāḥidī permitted its accusative inflection on the basis of incitement (*ighrāʾ*), like the saying related on the authority of ʿUmar, may God be pleased with him, *yā Sāriya, al-jabala!* (Sāriya, the mountain!), meaning, 'Go to the mountain and take refuge in it.' So the meaning is: and connect the womb-kin and discharge their rights.

The reading of Ḥamza alone is with the genitive, and it is said that it is based on the implied repetition of the genitive, that is to say, *wa'taqqū Allāha alladhī tasāʾalūna bihi wa'l-arḥāmi*. The coordination of an overt noun with a pronoun in the genitive, without the repetition of the genitive preposition, which is the more frequent case, has been heard of. In that vein, Sībawayh has cited the words of the poet:

Nuʿalliqu fī mithli al-sawārī suyūfanā
wa-mā baynahā wa'l-kaʿbi ghawṭun nafa'nif

We hang our swords in the like of masts
Between the swords and the heels an open expanse[192]

Fa'l-yawma qad bitta tahjūna tashtumnā
fa'dhhab fa-mā bika wa'l-ayyām min ʿājab.

Today you have taken to[193] lampooning and insulting us
Go, how curious are you and the passage of time[194]

The Basran grammarians object to this reading of Ḥamza's. Because it is not attested among the Arabs, they do not consider it idiomatic (*faṣīḥ*), nor do they make it a grammatical rule (*qāʿida*); rather, they deem it deviant, and this is their convention. There are expressions (*lughāt*) for which not many poetic citations (*shawāhid*) are transmitted, while still being idiomatic, but these grammarians are obsessed with their grammatical rules, and the teacher-imam has pointed out their error in applying these to the Book of God, exalted be He, in that it is not up to them to make their grammatical rules an argument against any Arabic [expression]. He says here, either the *arḥām* is in the accusative inflection, on the basis that it is coordinated with the Majestic name, or it is in the genitive inflection as a coordination with the pronoun in '*bihi*', and that is permissible with the text of this verse, according to this reading, and it is transmitted according to numerous sources (*mutawātir*), despite what they say. Al-Rāzī said: It never ceases to amaze how these grammarians are happy to affirm this expression on the basis of two unknown poetic verses, but they are not happy to affirm it on the basis of Ḥamza and Mujāhid, although the two of them are among the greatest of the early generations of scholars of the Qur'ānic sciences.

With all of this, those who deny Ḥamza's reading are ignorant of the readings and their associated reports, in their fanaticism for the Basran school of grammarians, while the Kufans consider such a coordination to be based on analogical reasoning; however, this position of theirs has been given weight by some of the leading Basrans. And one or two scholars write at length in defence of this position.

[192] This is the same version of the poetic exemplar as that found in Ṭabarī, except rather than *nafā'if* it has *nafa'nif*. It is thus close to the exemplar found in Rāzī.

[193] In some printed versions of this text, this is *qarrabta*; however, we have emended it to match Ṭabarī's version.

[194] This is the poetic exemplar found in Rāzī.

Some of them object to Ḥamza's reading with respect to the meaning, saying that to mention this [genitive] where the command to wariness (*taqwā*) is mentioned, and instilling hope (*targhīb*) in it, impairs (*mukhill*) the rhetoric because it does not belong (*ajnabī*) in this place; and in addition there is an affirmation that in pre-Islamic times they petitioned one another by the wombs, as one petitions by God, Exalted be He, and [petitioning by the wombs] is [now] among those things forbidden by Islam, with the proof of the *ḥadīth* in the two Sound books, 'Whoever swears, let him swear by God or let him be silent.'[195]

I [Riḍā] answer the first by saying that the mention of petitioning by the wombs is not alien (*ajnabī*) to the command to wariness (*taqwā*) here, because this command is a preface to preserving the rights of kith and kin (*qarāba*) and the womb-ties and adherence to the legislation which the *sūra* brought in that regard. Moreover, some of the exegetes have given authority to the majority reading on the basis of Ḥamza's reading, by justifying the accusative inflection on *al-arḥām* on the basis of it being a coordination with the place of the pronoun in His words *tasā'alūna bihi*, as above.

I answer to the second that swearing by things other than God is not absolutely forbidden, and it is only prohibited to swear when you believe that there is an obligation to fulfil it, not when it is intended purely as an emphatic, as is the way of the Arabs when they use the oath form (*bi-ṣighat al-qasam*), like the emphasis with *an*. And I mean that this answer is on the premise that petitioning by the wombs is an oath on them; and it is a mistake, for indeed to petition by God is not to swear by God, and petitioning by the wombs is not swearing by them. The Shaykh al-Islam Ibn Taymiyya has clarified this distinction by the same premise that he used to investigate the issue of petitions and the means [of petitioning], and he said, and he excelled as is his custom, may God reward him handsomely for his religious duty and for himself in return for what he has stated:[196]

[195] It should be noted that oaths made with reference to God, as in 'by God' (*ta'llāhi*), are relatively rare (the ubiquitous literary and oral *wa'llāhi*, never), when compared with invocations by reference to creation. In fact, one only encounters *ta'llāhi* nine times in the entire Qur'ān, four of them in [*sūrat*] *Yūsuf* (Q. 12). The rarer 'by your Lord' (*fa-wa-rabbika*) appears only three times. However, oaths invoked by creation ('by the sun', 'by the moon', 'by the stars', and so on) are remarkable for their frequency, often as opening lines for the early Meccan *sūras*: see Q. 68; 75; 77; 79; 85; 86; 89; 90; 91; 92; 93; 95; 100; 103. On oaths see Devin Stewart, 'Introductory Oaths and the Question of Composite Sūras' in *Structural Dividers in the Qur'ān*, ed. Marianna Klar (Abingdon, Routledge, 2021), 267–337; idem, 'Divine Epithets and the Dibacchius: Clausulae and Qur'anic Rhythm', *Journal of Qur'anic Studies* 15.2 (2013), 22–64.

As regards petitioning in the name of mortals (*makhlūq*), where the [particle] *bā'* is used as a causative (*sabab*) it cannot be the *bā'* of oaths, and there is a [big] difference between the two.[197] The Prophet (*ṣlʿm*) commanded that oaths should be fulfilled (*ibrār al-qasm*),[198] and it is established on his authority in the two *Ṣaḥīḥ*s[199] that he said, 'Indeed there are among God's servants those for whom, when they swear by God, He will fulfil it for them'.[200] He said that when Anas b. al-Naḍr asked, 'Are you really going to have the teeth of al-Rubayyiʿ broken? Never! By Him who sent you with the truth, she will not have her teeth broken!' The Prophet replied, 'But Anas! The Book of God prescribes retaliation (*qiṣāṣ*)!' However, the people were satisfied and pardoned,[201] whereupon he said (*ṣlʿm*), 'Indeed, there are among God's servants some who, when they swear by God, He fulfils it for them.' And he said, 'Many a person dishevelled and dusty, repulsed from doorways, if he were to swear by God, He would fulfil it [for him]'.[202] Muslim and others narrated it, and he said, 'Shall I tell you of the people of the Garden? Every enfeebled weakling, if he swears by God, He will fulfil it. Shall I tell you about the people of the Fire? [They are] every evil (*ʿutull*),[203] crude (*jawāẓ*) and arrogant (*mustakbir*) one.'[204] This is in the *Ṣaḥīḥ*s, and likewise the *ḥadīth* about Anas b. al-Naḍr, and the others from Muslim's *ḥadīth*s transmitted from a single authority (*mufrad*).

[196] He is now quoting Ibn Taymiyya.

[197] Strictly speaking, the argument being made here is a formal linguistic one, as, substantively, the prefixed particle *bi-* in oaths, as in *bi'llāhi*, is both causative and asseverative.

[198] That is to say, the person who is the object of the oath, and from whom the oath requires an action, should, as far as possible, fulfil the requirement of that oath sworn by another, otherwise, the swearer will be *ḥānith* (a perjurer), having violated his own oath, and will be required to do penance (*kaffāra*).

[199] The *Ṣaḥīḥ* of Bukhārī and the *Ṣaḥīḥ* of Muslim b. al-Ḥajjāj.

[200] This is found in several places in the *Ṣaḥīḥ* of Bukhārī. One instance which tells the full story is *Kitāb al-Jihād* (56), *Bāb qawl Allāh taʿālā min al-mu'minīn rijālun ṣadaqū* [. . .] (12), *ḥadīth* nos. 22 and 23. In this version, by way of background, the narration tells us that on the day of the battle of Uḥud, when other Muslim fighters had turned away from the battleground, Anas b. al-Naḍr (paternal uncle of the famous Companion Anas b. Mālik), stayed on, fought and was killed; but having sworn an oath ('By the Lord of Anas b. al-Naḍr'), he died as a martyr. The story cited in the text above, by Riḍā from Ibn Taymiyya, takes place before Uḥud and centres on Naḍr's sister Rubayyiʿ, who managed to break the front teeth of a slave girl (*jāriya*). The slave girl's guardians demand retaliation and are offered indemnity (*arsh*) instead, but they refuse and take the matter before the Prophet, who reinforces their right to retaliation. However, Anas b. al-Naḍr then intervenes with his oath, 'By Him who has sent you with the truth, my sister's tooth shall not be broken.' Despite having their retaliatory right upheld by the Prophet, the slave girl's guardians relent and accept some form of compensation, giving up the claim to retaliation. It is at that point, seeing how Anas' resolve was vindicated and not his own, that the Prophet remarks, 'There are among God's servants those whom, when they swear an oath in God's name, He fulfills it for them'.

[201] That is, the guardians of the slave girl whose teeth were broken gave up the right to retaliation, as detailed in the previous note.

[202] Nawawī, *Riyāḍ al-ṣāliḥīn, Kitāb al-Muqaddimāt, Bāb faḍl ḍuʿafā' al-muslimīn wa'l-fuqarā' al-khāmilīn* (32), *ḥadīth* no. 257.

[203] Cf. Q. 68:13.

> Swearing an oath by Him on somebody else is when an oath-maker swears on someone else to do something; but if the latter causes the oath-maker to perjure himself (*ḥanatha*) by not fulfilling the oath sworn, then the expiation (*kaffāra*) [for that perjury] falls upon the person swearing the oath (*al-ḥālif*), not on the one sworn on, according to the majority of the jurists. Thus if he were to swear on his servant, his son or his friend, that they do something and then they do not, then the expiation falls on the oath-breaking person who had sworn the oath (*al-ḥālif al-ḥānith*). As for his words, 'I petition you (*sa'altuka*) by God to do such and such', this is a request rather than an oath. In the *ḥadīth*, 'Whoever petitions you by God, grant it to him', there is no expiation for that when the petition is not granted. All believing and unbelieving people petition God, and God responds [even] to the deniers (*kuffār*): when they petition God for sustenance (*rizq*), He provides for them, and He gives them to drink, and when hardship touches them at sea, whomever they petition is a lost cause, except for Him; but when He delivers them to land, they turn away [cf. Q. 17:67], *for indeed humans are ever-ungrateful* [Q. 17:67].[205]
> As for those who swear by God and keep their oaths, they are the favoured ones, for the petition is like the speech of the petitioner to God: 'I petition You, all praise to You; You are God, the Munificent (*al-mannān*), the Creator of the heavens and the earth, O Possessor of majesty and honour' and 'I petition You because You are *God, One* [Q. 112:1], *the Eternal, who does not beget nor is begotten, and to whom none is equal* [Q. 112:2–4]. I petition You, by every name that is Yours, by which You call Yourself or have revealed in Your book, or by which You have taught anyone of your creation, or which You have preferred for Yourself (*ista'tharta bihi*) in what [to us] is the unknown (*'ilm al-ghayb*).' This petition to God, exalted be He, is by His names and His attributes, and that is not an oath on Him, and indeed His acts are entailed by His names and His attributes, so His forgiveness and His mercy are entailed by His names 'the Forgiving' and 'the Merciful', and His pardon is entailed by His name 'the Pardoner'.

Then he [Ibn Taymiyya] said,

> So when the petitioner asks by (*bi-*) something, and the '*bi-*' is causative, he asks for a purpose, which entails the existence of the thing being asked for (*mas'ūl*); and when he says, 'I petition You, all praise to You, You are the God, the Munificent (*al-mannān*), the Creator of the heavens and the earth', the fact that His being is Praised and Munificent, Creator of the heavens and the earth, requires that He be munificent to His servant, the petitioner; and since His existence is praiseworthy, He is required to do what is praiseworthy, and the

[204] Bukhārī, *Ṣaḥīḥ*, *Kitāb al-Adab* (78), *Bāb al-kibr* (61), *ḥadīth* no. 101/6071.

[205] The paraphrase of Q. 17:67 is only in voice: Riḍā uses the third-person plural, whereas the Qur'ān has the second-person plural address.

praising of Him is the reason for the granting of his supplication. So that is why the praying person is commanded to say, 'May God hear the one who praises Him', which is to say that God answers the supplication of whomever praises Him, and the 'hearing' here means answering and accepting.

Then he [Ibn Taymiyya] said,

When the petitioner says to someone else, 'I ask you by God!' then he only petitions him by virtue of his faith in God, and that is a reason for the person whom he has asked granting it; for indeed He, glory be to Him, loves being good to creation, especially when it is a request to avert oppression, for indeed He commands justice and He forbids oppression; and His command is the greatest reason in enjoining action, and if ever there was a cause whose effect was necessary, then it is the command of God, exalted be He. A *ḥadīth* has come about this, which Aḥmad [b. Ḥanbal] narrated in his *Musnad*, and Ibn Māja [reported] on the authority of ʿAṭiyya al-ʿAwfī, on the authority of Abū Saʿīd al-Khudrī on the authority of the Prophet (*ṣlʿm*), that he taught the person who was going to prayer to say in his supplication, 'I petition You by the right that petitioners have over You, and by the right of this walk of mine, for indeed as I walk out [to prayer], it is not out of insolence (*ashir*, cf. Q. 54:25–6) or in reckless ingratitude (*baṭar*) or for the look of it (*riyāʾ*) or for repute (*sumʿa*);[206] rather, I have stepped out [to prayer] in order to guard against Your anger (*ittiqāʾ sakhaṭika*) and to seek to please You (*ibtighāʾa marḍātika*).'[207]

Since this is sound, the right of the petitioner over Him is that He answer them, and the right of the worshipper over Him is that He reward them, and these are rights that He has made obligatory upon Himself towards them. So when He is petitioned in the name of the faith and good deeds (*ʿamal*) which He has made as a cause for answering the supplication, as in His words, exalted be He, *and He answers those who believe and do good deeds, and He gives them increase from His bounty* [Q. 42:26], then He is petitioned by virtue of His promise, because His promise necessarily entails the fulfilment of what He has promised. An example is where the believers say, *Our Lord, we have heard the caller calling, saying: 'Believe in your Lord!' and we believe in our Lord, so forgive us our sins and expunge our evil deeds, and receive us [in death] with the pious ones* [Q. 3:193] and His words, exalted be He, *Indeed a group of My worshippers said, 'Our Lord, we believe so forgive us, have mercy on us, for You are the best of the merciful ones!' But you mocked them, until they made you forget My remembrance while you were laughing at them* [Q. 23:109–10]. This is similar to the Prophet's

[206] Cf. Q. 8:47 *And be not like those who went forth from their homes recklessly ungrateful and just to be seen by people* (*baṭaran wa-riʾāʾa al-nās*).

[207] Cf. Aḥmad b. Ḥanbal, *Musnad*, III, 21, and with slightly different wording, Ibn Māja, *Sunan*, *Kitāb al-Masājid waʾl-jamāʿāt* (4), *Bāb al-mashī ilā al-ṣalāt* (14), *ḥadīth* no. 44/778.

appeal (*ṣlʿm*) on the day of Badr, when he said, 'God! Fulfil for me what you have promised me!' Likewise in the Torah is that God, exalted be He, became angry at the children of Israel and Moses began to petition his Lord, mentioning what He had promised Abraham, for indeed he petitioned Him in the name of His former promise to Abraham. Among the examples of petitioning by good deeds is the petition of the three who took refuge in the cave, for each one of them petitioned in the name of a great deed (*ʿamal ʿaẓīm*) which he had completed with sincere devotion to God, because that deed was something which God loves and is pleased with, in a way which necessarily entails His positive response to the person petitioning. One petitioned in the name of his dutifulness (*birr*) to his parents, and one petitioned in the name of his complete restraint (*ʿiffa*), and the third petitioned in the name of his trustworthiness and his goodness. It is in this vein that Ibn Masʿūd used to say at dawn, 'Dear God! You have commanded me and I have obeyed You. You have called me and I have answered You. Now it is dawn (*saḥar*), so forgive me.' And of the same ilk is the *ḥadīth* on the authority of Ibn ʿUmar, that he used to say at Ṣafā, 'Dear God! You have spoken, and Your words are the truth: *Call Me, I will answer you* [Q. 40:60] and *You do not renege on promises* [Q. 3:194 and *passim*].' Then he mentioned the well-known supplication on the authority of Ibn ʿUmar, which he used to repeat at Ṣafā.

So it has become clear that when one says, 'I petition you by such and such', it is of two types, where the [prefixed] *bāʾ* (*bi-*) functions either for oaths or as a causative; it can thus either function as swearing by God or it can function as a petition sought through Him. As regards the first [type], to swear an oath by created beings cannot be invoked over a created being, so how much more so in the case of the Creator? As for the second [type], it is to petition by some exalted thing, like petitioning by the status due to prophets. Regarding this [latter] there is dispute (*nizāʿ*). It has already been mentioned that Abū Ḥanīfa and his companions considered this impermissible. We say: When someone petitions God, exalted be He, saying, 'I petition you by the right of such-and-such an angel, or a prophet, or a righteous individual, or another, or by the rank (*jāh*) of so-and-so, or by the sanctity (*ḥurma*) of so-and-so', all of that implies that these properly enjoy such a rank before God, and this is sound. For, indeed, these [individuals] have a rank, status and sanctity before God, so that it necessarily entails that God raises their degrees (*daraja*), magnifies their worth (*qadr*) and accepts their intercession when they intercede, even though He, glory be to Him, said, *who can intercede with Him except by His permission?* [Q. 2:255];[208] and it also necessarily entails that whoever follows them and emulates them in the manner recommended for that person (*sunna lahu*) will be among the fortunate (*saʿīd*); and whoever obeys their command which they have communicated on behalf of God will also be among the fortunate. But when a person petitions God by them, it is

[208] See Hamza *et al.*, *Anthology*, I, ch. 2, 127–297, for a discussion of the Throne verse.

> not merely because of their worth and rank that their supplication will receive a response such that he may petition by that [alone]. Rather, it is that their rank is beneficial to him if he follows their way and obeys them in what they have commanded be done on God's authority or when he follows the example that they have established for believers. It benefits him when they pray for him and they intercede on his behalf. But if there does not issue from them for him a supplication or an intercession, or if no reason on his part necessitates a positive response, then there shall be no intercessor for him, nor will his petition in the name of their rank be beneficial for him before God. Rather, he will have petitioned with a matter that is foreign (*ajnabī*) to him and is not a cause of benefit to him. If the man said to a person of great authority: 'I petition you by the obedience to your authority shown by so-and-so, and by your love for him because of his obedience to you, and by his rank with you which is entailed by his obedience to you', then he has petitioned him by a foreign (*ajnabī*) matter, which is neither here nor there for him. So likewise, God's beneficence towards these brought close [to Him], and His love for them and His magnification of their worth alongside their acts of worship of Him, and their acts of obedience to him; there is nothing in that that would necessitate a response to the call of whoever petitions in their name. A response is only obligatory to his call because of a causative factor inherent in him for his obedience to them or because of a reason from them for their intercession on his behalf; but when either of these is missing, then there is no reason.

The end [of the quote].

Then he [Ibn Taymiyya] said in another place:

> It has been clarified that oaths to God, glory be to Him, in the name of anything other than Him, are not permitted, and anyway it is impermissible to swear an oath by invoking a created thing (*makhlūq*). As for reaching Him by the intercession of those who have been given permission (*idhn*) to intercede, that is permissible. For the blind man had requested from the Prophet (*ṣlʿm*) that he supplicate for him, just as his Companions requested that he pray for rain (*al-istisqā'*). And his words 'I turn to You, by Your Prophet Muḥammad, the prophet of mercy' mean by his [the Prophet's] supplication and his intercession for me. That is why this *ḥadīth* ends with 'Dear God! Accept his intercession for me!'[209] and everyone agrees on the permissibility of that which is in the *ḥadīth*; but that is not what concerns us. God, exalted be He, said, *be wary of God by whom you petition one another, and the wombs*, and according to the reading of the majority it is in the accusative inflection, and they may only petition by God alone, and not by the wombs; and their petition of one another by God,

[209] Tirmidhī, *Jāmiʿ*, *Kitāb al-Daʿawāt* (48), *Bāb* 118, *ḥadīth* no. 3578. This fragment is the end of the 'blind man' *ḥadīth* on the previous line. In it, a blind man asks Muḥammad to intercede for him, and he agrees (but cf. Q. 80:2).

exalted be He, is an oath of some of them to others in the name of God, and their making a covenant with one another in the name of God. As for the reading with the genitive inflection (*wa'l-arḥāmi*), a group of the pious predecessors said: It was their way of speaking to say, 'I petition you by God and by the wombs', and this [Qur'ānic verse] was a way of alerting [them] to their manner of petitioning. It is not an indication of its permissibility, and if it had been an indication of its permissibility, then the meaning of his speech 'I petition you by the wombs' would not be an oath by the wombs, for the oath here is not allowed (*lā yasūgh*), but it is occasioned by the wombs, that is to say because the womb-ties are necessary for those who have them towards each other as a right, like the three petitions to God, exalted be He, by their great deeds, and like our petition supplicating the Prophet (*ṣlʿm*), asking for his intercession. An example of this is what the Commander of the Believers, ʿAlī b. Abī Ṭālib, narrated concerning his paternal nephew ʿAbd Allāh b. Jaʿfar: Whenever he used to petition in the name of his father Jaʿfar, ʿAlī would grant that [wish] to him. This is not an instance of making an oath, for indeed it would be greater to make an oath on something other than Jaʿfar; rather, it is an instance of the rights of the womb-kin, because what is due to God is only obligatory because of Jaʿfar and Jaʿfar's right over ʿAlī.[210]

End.

In sum [says Riḍā], the meaning of the verse is that God, exalted be He, says: O People! Be wary of your Lord who created you and who nurtured you through His graces, and be wary of Him in yourselves, and do not overstep His bounds of what He has legislated (*sh-r-ʿ*) regarding the rights and comportment (*adab*) which He granted you in order to put your affairs in order, for indeed He created you from a single soul, so you are of a single species, whose best interests are served by the cooperation of its individuals and their unity and their preserving of each other's rights. Being wary of Him, mighty and majestic, is giving thanks for His lordship, and in that is an exaltation of your human unity and an ascending therein towards perfection. So be wary of God in that which he commands and forbids regarding the rights of the womb-kin, which are singled out from the rights owed to humans in general, by connecting the wombs which He commands you to connect and by guarding against severing that which He has forbidden the severing of. Be wary of him in that, for in wariness of Him is much good for you, and that which causes you to remember Him is your petitioning one another in His generous name, and by His rights over His servants, and His authority (*s-l-ṭ*) that looms high above your hearts, and by the rights of the womb-ties, and what this petition entails in terms of seeking affection and familiarity. So do

[210] Here ends the lengthy quotation from Ibn Taymiyya.

not neglect these two ties between you: the tie of belief in God and magnification of His name, and the tie of the womb. For, if you are negligent in that, you will corrupt your true natures, your homes, families, communities and tribes.

Indeed God is Watcher over you: that is to say, He observes your deeds and how they issue forth from you and their effect on your state. None of that is hidden from Him. For He has prescribed the rulings for you that are best for your affairs, and through them He helps you to attain happiness in this world and the next. *Al-raqīb* is an adjectival form with the same sense of *al-rāqib*, which means someone looking out over him from on high, and from this is derived the *marqab* to denote a place from which a person looks out onto that which is below him. It is used with the sense of preservation, because that is one of its concomitants, and that is how Mujāhid interpreted it. The teacher-imam said: Indeed, God, exalted be He, reminds us here of His watching over us in order to alert us to sincere devotion, meaning that when a person remembers that God is observing him and watching over his deeds, it is more likely that he will be wary of Him and adhere to His bounds.

Faḍl Allāh

In contrast to ʿAbduh and Riḍā, and to almost all prior commentators,[211] Faḍl Allāh focuses heavily on gender in his interpretation. Indeed, he includes a lengthy introduction to *sūrat al-Nisāʾ*, which outlines his vision of the differences and similarities between the sexes. In this vision, women and men are entirely equal as human beings, but they have different, complementary, areas of strength corresponding to their natural roles in the world. The natural distribution of roles is also, he says, the basis for unequal inheritance: because men have more responsibilities, so too should they have a larger inheritance. In his view, treating the sexes equally is a 'failed experiment', and Islam offers a balanced approach. This interpretation uses a mixture of modern and premodern language and concepts to explain why it is appropriate today to follow rulings laid down in the premodern period. While this interpretation is not entirely modern, Faḍl Allāh has an entirely modern focus on gender as a category that needs to be addressed. Yet he uses modern concepts, like independence, to justify premodern laws that allow the husband to control his wife. He says, for instance, that a woman is entirely autonomous 'except in what she cedes' for the sake of marriage.[212]

Though he ultimately promotes an interpretation that follows premodern legal norms, Fadl Allāh overtly critiques the premodern approach to women, which he

[211] With the possible exception of Kāshānī (translated above).

[212] This wording also raises the question of what exactly the woman is ceding, and why, and how that ceding, which Faḍl Allāh describes as voluntary, differs from the expectations of women in medieval *fiqh*. The answer to this question is not in this part of his *tafsīr*.

admits emphasised the negative aspects of being a woman. He says that women's intellect, and humanity, was 'subject to question'. The result, he says, was that many women lived as dependants who were not viewed as having intrinsic human value.

And yet, for Faḍl Allāh, modernity has scarcely been better for women: he goes on to critique the modern 'experiment' of establishing equality between the sexes. In his view, this 'experiment' was a reaction against the imbalanced premodern view of women, but, for him, it is equally unbalanced, because it does away with any reference to the specific nature of each of the sexes, in their strengths and weaknesses. Complementary roles are necessitated, Faḍl Allāh says, because of the innate differences between men and women. According to this view, women have an excess of sentiment and emotionality which may overwhelm their rational sense. These emotions are necessary for women's role in the home and should be considered a strength rather than a weakness; but they mean that women are not naturally inclined to fulfil all roles outside of the home.

The idea of complementarity – which Faḍl Allāh does not name overtly but which informs his interpretation – and women's overabundance of emotion appear, in one form or another, in almost all conservative interpretations of women's roles. In turn, Faḍl Allāh was not the originator of these ideas, which had been in existence since at least the late 1800s and appeared in the genre of *tafsīr* from at least the time of Sayyid Quṭb (d. 1966). The common theme in these modern works, which – as Faḍl Allāh quite rightly points out – distinguishes them from the widespread medieval view, is that modern thinkers tend to emphasise women's human worth, whereas many medieval authors disparage women. At the same time, and in common with the widespread medieval view, modern conservative authors like Faḍl Allāh insist on a particular weakness in women's rationality, which in the medieval period was described as an inherent deficiency and in the modern period is attributed to an overabundance of emotion. Such interpretations are heavily influenced by, and react to, the idea and ideals of feminism, but are perhaps even more influenced by the idea of equality under the law that exists in most European contexts. This is perhaps why Faḍl Allāh chose the legal example of women's testimony to illustrate the correctness of his view.

For all that, his *sūra* introduction outlines a grand theory of the sexes, Faḍl Allāh's interpretation of Q. 4.1 is not particularly focused on gender. Although he argues strongly that the verse speaks of Adam and Eve, he also says that it does not refer to creation from a rib. He cites the *ḥadīth* that says Eve's creation was from the same soil as Adam's creation. He uses this *ḥadīth* and a number of Qur'ānic verses to argue that the mate (Eve) was created of the same type or kind as Adam. Finally, he argues against the interpretation of 'Abduh and the theory of evolution and natural selection. He argues that there was originally no prohibition against brother–sister marriage, which the Zoroastrians still practised at the beginning of Islam, and that the theory of evolution is nothing but a 'speculative proposition' which does not preclude the opposite supposition. Thus, while being aware of science and some scientific advances, it is obvious that Faḍl Allāh has little understanding of the scientific consensus on evolution. In this sense, his interpretation bears a resemblance to modern conservative Christian responses to the fossil evidence.

Introduction to *sūrat al-Nisā*ʾ

The reason for its name

This *sūra* was given the name 'women' because it encompasses many concepts and legal rulings connected to women which clarify the Islamic view of woman, insofar as she is considered one of the two elements from which issued the human life force and insofar as she is the equal of man in those matters connected with the human aspect of her character and her independent responsibility, given that she is an independent legal entity over whom nobody has guardianship with regard to her religious duties and in her capacity for responsibility. So nobody has the right to force her to do what she does not want to do, and there is no way to diminish her legal personhood with regard to the wealth that she possesses. This *sūra* also clarifies the parameters of the marital relationship, its value and its details on the basis of the dignity of woman and man, and [it clarifies] that the health and vitality of the relationship is in their best interests, on the premise of the nature specific to each exemplified by specific physical characteristics and what that anticipates of an active role, in harmony with these characteristics, without detracting from the overall personhood which brings both together as humans.

Perhaps the discussion of inheritance in this *sūra*, in the detailed way in which each kinship or marital relationship has a specific entitlement in the bequest, is connected with women on the basis that it exemplifies an affirmation of her independent personhood which is not neglected by Islam in the way that it was neglected by the laws of the Jāhiliyya which considered her as a commodity to be inherited and passed on to the man along with other types of property, instead of considering her as a person who inherits on the basis of her rights and her distinct role, in the way that people are distinguished in roles.

As for the story that the share of the man is larger than the share of the woman, there is a detailed discussion of that. We shall come to know that it is not based on any diminution of a woman's dignity, but it is all about the distribution of responsibilities, the larger share of which Islam has placed on the man, which then presupposes from the perspective of justice that the greater lot in inheritance should be his.

The Qurʾān discusses women in more than one *sūra*

The discussion about women is not limited to this *sūra*, for we have already met with it in *sūrat al-Baqara* (Q. 2), and we will meet it anew in *sūrat al-Māʾida* (Q. 5), *sūrat al-Nūr* (Q. 24), *sūrat al-Aḥzāb* (Q. 33), *sūrat al-Mujādila*

(Q. 58), *sūrat al-Mumtaḥana* (Q. 60), *sūrat al-Taḥrīm* (Q. 66) and *sūrat al-Ṭalāq* (Q. 65).[213] This *sūra* [*al-Nisāʾ*] treats many of the issues that are connected with the legal and human personhood of a woman. It also discusses the mutual marital rights and obligations between a man and a woman, from which it is manifestly clear that Islam regards a woman as an autonomous human being in opinion, action and faith, and that nobody has power (*sulṭa*) over her except in that which she cedes to him.

The Islamic concept of woman: In regard and in legislation

In light of all of that, it is possible to highlight the intellectual premises and principles which underpin Islamic legislation specific to humans in general and women in particular. There are general rulings premised on the human dimension of the individual and the application in the framework of general responsibility for the man and the woman, like those specific to cases of *kufr* (disbelief) or *īmān* (faith), morals, financial transactions, social relations, and the aspects of upbringing and custodianship. Thus the dynamics (*ḥaraka*) of responsibility extends throughout a woman's personhood and her life – in both positive and negative aspects – just as it is does in a man's life, likewise in both aspects, such that a person would not be able to notice any difference in its nature, even if there may be a difference in detail and terminology. And it is in this framework that the Noble Qurʾān speaks about the reward awaiting believing men and believing women equally in the Hereafter and about the punishment that awaits the disbelieving men and the disbelieving women, the fornicating men and the fornicating women, the thieving men and the thieving women in this world and the Hereafter, without any distinction between men and women, in the specificities of punishment and reward, all of which means that they share in general responsibility, which is itself premised on them sharing in the human species.

Islam thus sets off from a point of specificity concerning masculinity and femininity, hence the particular rulings that deal with the distribution of responsibilities in all of life's details in accordance with the role which God has prepared for each of them, be it in instances within marital life or outside it, within the framework of rule, judiciary and witnessing,[214] and other such matters which we shall attend to in the explanation (*tafsīr*) of the coming verses. And so we will know, through that, how Islam has delineated roles and how it has distributed responsibilities.

[213] It is noteworthy that he only speaks here about *sūras* associated with rulings on women and does not mention *sūrat Maryam* (Q. 19).

[214] That is to say, the public sphere.

This balanced legislative perspective on life constitutes the grounds for governing Islamic rulings, general and specific. And Islam, in all of its credal, moral and legal manifestations, reflects the true nature of human beings and does not seek to venture away from this position which makes humankind always adhere to human reality as it is and as it should be. And this entails that the rulings are accommodating, enlightening and within the reach of practical application. They are not rulings that put pressure on human life, turning it thereby into an unbearably heavy burden, diverting him from the true and realistic path that is necessary for him. Therefore Islam does not posit absolute equality between man and woman in the details of responsibility, but considers them equal in the general human context and differentiates between them in its specificities. In this way it desired for humankind to benefit from the commonalities between man and woman in terms of its development, culture and reality, just as it benefits from the differences between them.

Perhaps the failed experiment, both past and present, of what humanity has granted to women, both conceptually and legislatively, is clear proof of the soundness of Islam's realistic perspective, for both of the experiments prove from two different contexts that the single perspective from a narrow angle does not solve the problem, but rather creates new problems. Historically, the focus was on factors that distinguish men from women, with undue emphasis on the mention of the negative aspects of being a woman, in an unrealistic way, whereas those aspects that are common to both of them, in the context of them both being human, were frequently avoided. There was even some discussion among some philosophers over whether a woman possessed a spirit (*rūḥ*) or not?! [sic] Her intellect was subject to question, and even her humanity, deeply valuable as it is, was subject to neglect.[215] Consequently, she was never considered from the perspective of having a complete essence, combining mind and spirit within a human framework, but rather they solely considered her as a female, simply as an instrument of pleasure. Given that this side of her personhood is associated with shame, given the differing values according to which people live, the stance taken towards her has always been a negative one, exemplified by grief, pain and a feeling of deficiency. The Qur'ān speaks about that; in His words [Q. 16:58–9]: [58] *When one is given the news of a female, his face immediately darkens, and he is barely able to contain himself* (*kaẓīm*); [59] *he hides shamefully from his people, because of the evil news that he has been given. Should he hold onto it in disgrace, or should he shove it into the earth? How evil are the choices they make!*

[215] Note that here and in the preceding lines Faḍl Allāh is critiquing the medieval commentators and thus distinguishing a modern line of interpretation in which women and men have equal value and worth in the world, as well as in the afterlife.

And in this atmosphere women lived on the margins of life, as do large numbers of neglected women, as though they have no intrinsic value but are dependents of a man like any household commodity without feeling or spirit (*rūḥ*). That is how she lost the opportunity to develop her potential and to orient it towards what is beneficial to social life and humankind.

As for the modern experience, it has tried to dilute man and woman completely through the concept of equality, whose concern is circumscribed by a broad human framework that subsumes man and woman, without attending to the specific distinguishing aspects of each of them, which has made it a very unbalanced experience, far from the principle of equilibrium. The contemporary perspective has emerged from the concept of equality between woman and man, in light of the idea of freedoms. They say that woman is enslaved, subjugated and oppressed in the home and at work, and in social relationships, and therefore it is necessary for her to seize her freedom as part and parcel of the movement towards emancipation in human life, so that her potential can burst forth in the construction of human life. Clearly, this perspective is a type of reaction to the harsh reality endured by the woman. But like any reaction, it suffers a lack of balance and composure. Thus woman was granted the freedom in every field and equality was solicited for her in everything, and it was from this point on that things began to set off in the wrong direction, helping to void everything specific to man and woman. Thus each of them was prevented from being able to become a specific type of human, so that humanity could be complementary in its human types in what is common and what is different. As a consequence, women are trying to become masculine (*istirjāl*) and men are trying to become feminine (*taʾannuth*) or transgender (*takhannuth*). So the woman ends up being estranged from herself and the man from himself as well.

It is almost impossible to deny that there have been women geniuses who were able to establish themselves in many fields of knowledge and enterprise, and that women have the capacity to excel in many contexts. But that does not prevent the persistence of a state of emptiness inside the woman and inside the man, and the problem remains in the field of freedom and equality. We still hear the voices that issue from time to time from many groups of women, in more than one country, for a return to the warmth of the domestic family atmosphere which women have lost as a result of the convulsion that was this equality, which indicates that this recent evolution has not solved a problem for women without creating another one. As for Islam, it wants woman to be a female human being, as it wants man to be a male human being, on the basis of the realistic perspective that combines specificity and generality.

How can we understand the legal position on women's testimony?

In this context, the issue arises that Islam regards woman with contempt, suggesting a measure of deficiency in her personhood, which is also noticed where legislation affirms a deficiency of balance in thought (*fikr*), as opposed to her emotional plenitude (*imtilāʾ ʿāṭifī*), which is in law exemplified in the consideration of the testimony of two women in the place of the testimony of a single man.

But that, in our understanding, does not mean an essential deficiency at the intellectual level; rather, all that it implies is judicial precaution against what emotion might lead to in terms of [women] being carried away by tragic emotional circumstances, a matter that leads to upsetting her impartial stance which, in itself, reflects negatively on the veracity of her testimony. And this is what the Noble Qurʾān indicated in the verse that deals with women's testimony; He says: [. . .] *And if there are not two men, then a man and two women who satisfy you as witnesses, where one of the two errs, then one of the two shall remind the other* [. . .] [Q. 2:282].

We remark that He does not justify (*yuʿallal*) this subject on the basis of woman's intrinsic deficiency in terms of her capacity for rational thought (*nāḥiyat al-tafkīr*); rather, He justifies it on the basis of the possibility of her falling under the influence of emotion (*ʿāṭifa*) that has been expressed as 'error' (*ḍalāl*), which is to be far from the straight path. And this remark is confirmed in that the Qurʾān considers the woman as the one who reminds and guides, indicating that when a woman errs in certain situations, there is another woman who intervenes to guide her to the right way.

Weakness is not a woman's inevitable destiny

It is apparent to us, as we discuss this emotional side of woman, that emotions are not necessarily a woman's destiny, nor is she inevitably taxed with them; rather, they are one of the weak points prominent in her personhood, exactly like all of the other weak points that exist in a man and a woman, as we notice in those verses confirming human weakness and its precipitous nature[216] in all matters, and their tendency to deviate in the face of all of that. This is why the Qurʾān has directed various calls to create a state of emotional balance inside the self (*nafs*), as a condition that aids the realisation of justice, as in His words: *Indeed, God commands you to deliver the trusts to their [rightful] owners and, when you judge between people, to judge with fairness* [Q. 4:58], *Do not go near an orphan's property, except with the best possible*

[216] Cf. Q. 20:114; 75:16; 21:37; 17:11, all of which mention a human proclivity to haste (*ʿajal*).

intention, until he comes of age, and observe fully the measure and the balance with justice. We task no soul except according to its capacity. And when you speak, be fair, even if it were your kinfolk [Q. 6:152], *O you who believe, be maintainers of justice and witnesses for the sake of God, even if it should be against yourselves or parents and near kin, and whether it be someone rich or poor, for God has a greater right over them. So do not follow your desires, lest you should be unfair* [Q. 4:135], *and ill-feeling for a people should never lead you to be unjust. Be just. That is nearer to God-wariness. Be wary of God, for indeed God is well-aware of what you do* [Q. 5:8]. These calls are directed equally to men and women, so that both of them may work on anchoring their personhood on a balanced emotional basis, for the purpose of affirming justice in rule, testimony and any given situation, via self-reckoning and being mindful (*murāqaba*) and making a sincere effort (*mujāhada*).

The preceding implicitly means that a woman can overcome the emotional weak points in her personhood and transform them into points of strength so that she might attain a level, in this respect, higher than that of a man and commensurate with the effort expended in the power of endurance and striving on her part, whereas a man might not work on concentrating his potential and capacity, and developing them and strengthening them, which might make him more susceptible to recurring states of weakness, while the woman might work on harnessing and directing her energies to attain power.

The Qurʾān gives the example of a strong woman

The Noble Qurʾān has spoken to us about the typical strong woman who was able to be steadfast in the face of her social milieu without weakness, in its discussion of Mary, the daughter of ʿImrān, who at the beginning surrendered to her feminine weak point, as expressed by God in His words – through her – *she said, 'I wish I had died before this and I were a thing forgotten'* [Q. 19:23]. Soon enough she regained control of herself, and of her situation, after God opened for her the doors of hope and reassurance (*ṭumaʾnīna*), exemplified by the blessed event of the birth, and He called her to seek protection in Him, and to stand firm against the attacks of her community accusing her of evil, and to abstain from speech as an affirmation of her exalted rejection of the lowliness of the accusation, trusting absolutely that she possessed strength of innocence, against the accusation levelled at her. She faced her people, who had come to curse her and malign her and make the most heinous accusations against her, with complete strength and exaltedness, without uttering a single word. Then she indicated the newly born infant so that he might respond to their doubts and their accusations, without concern for their bemusement, fortified by the strength of her faith.

Then there is another Qur'ānic discussion, about the wife of Pharaoh who embodied, in her personhood, strength of will that defies the temptations of the power of wealth and social status and dominion. And so she faced the difficult reality enveloped in the thorny atmosphere of disbelief, surrounded by pain, through God's help first and foremost, and on His special promise exemplified by the effusion of His greatest approval – that is to say, Paradise – imbibing from all of that strength, help and steadfastness.

And God gives the example to those who believe the wife of Pharaoh, who said, *'Lord, build me a house by Your side in the Garden, and deliver me from Pharaoh and his deeds, and save me from this oppressive folk'* [Q. 66:11].

And we note that God desired to give the wife of Pharaoh as an example to believers, whether they were men or women, which suggests that the strong righteous woman can fulfil the role of exemplar for both men and women. This is one of the greatest proof-texts of Islam's respect for woman and its honouring of her, to the extent that it summons believing men to follow her example in this living embodiment of faith that eschews all forms of pleasure and temptation in the context of power, and the symbols and acts epitomised by those who hold it.

Therefore, the Qur'ānic revelation reaffirms to woman her power to overcome the tendency of female human weakness by self-discipline, consciousness and practice on the levels on which she is equal to man or superior to him. This thereby invalidates the conception that some men have that they are of greater worth than a woman, whoever she may be, and who regard her with disdain on the basis of superiority of species. Indeed, the Qur'ān suggests the error of this view because some women are greater than some men on account of an intellect enriched by experience and a will firm in trying moments.

Why this emphasis on weakness in legislation?

Here the question arises: If this human weakness were a general human phenomenon, and if overcoming it is within the reach of all, then why the emphasis on a woman's weakness in the sphere of judicial precaution, to the exclusion of men? Is that not discriminatory in terms of equality? And what is to prevent a woman from becoming a judge or an independent witness if she were strong-willed and open-minded?

To which we respond: Islam does not distinguish between a man and a woman when it deals with their common points of weakness. It requires from each of them the fulfilment of conditions of justness and faith in order to safeguard them from deviance. However, a woman's emotional side is stronger than that of a man, because of what the feminine, motherly nature entails in terms of emotional tendencies that nourish the marital relationship and the relationship between motherliness and children. And since this side is part of the essential makeup of a woman, it is precautionary on the part of the judiciary to invite women to distance themselves from this difficult experience which makes her and society fall into many negative situations so that she might fall under the influence of emotion, far from the course of justice, without detracting from her human dignity, because dignity is not about granting a human being any role that he wants for himself, but about granting him the role that is appropriate to his capabilities and best interests in life.

And in the final instance, there may be some generalisation in this discussion, and it may require some finer detail, but we do not want to delve into this subject from all of its aspects and particularities. All that we want is to give some indication of the general idea in order to pursue the details and particularities in the explanation of the verses, with remarks on the various aspects across the horizons of the Noble Qur'ān.

The *sūra* addresses several topics united by a single goal, which is to organise human consciousness along the path of God-wariness; to keep it from deviating from the way of faith; to anchor it in the authentic bases of the sources of law and creed; to guard it against submission to [base] desires; to organise the family within permitted and forbidden [degrees of] human relationships, and property within the bounds of licit and illicit, and the system of inheritance as a practical means of distributing wealth so that it is not hoarded in the hands of a single individual; [to] lay down the foundations on which the Islamic community rests; to direct believers to assume their responsibilities in the call to God and to confront God's enemies; and to stand up to all intellectual and practical challenges raised by the powers contrary to Islam and the Muslims in the form of lies, calumnies and doubts, so that Islam might live on in the secure bounds maintained by the believers with all of their strength and resources in life. This is what we hope that God grants us success in detailing when we give our exegesis of the clear verses that comprise the sum of this *sūra*.

Q. 4:1[217]

The variation in the Qur'ānic call between *O people!* and *O you who believe*

The *sūra* begins *O people!* (*yā ayyuhā'l-nāsu*) in a divine call for a delving into the various ways of fearing Him, and that is based on Him creating them from

[217] There is a short lexical commentary on the meaning of the words *zawj* (mate, one of a pair, like sandals or slippers), *baththa* (scatter), *arḥām* (wombs) and *raqīb* (preserver, someone who cranes his neck to watch over).

a single soul. This confirms the oneness of their species and their source, and consequently, of the oneness of their shared path towards Him, Exalted be He, that which obliges them to delve into the path of fear of Him, given the profound need of the created being for its Creator in all aspects of life, spiritual and otherwise. Closer inspection of this aspect leads to opening new horizons of the specificities of unity in this human variety, and the splendid magnificence of this harmony between oneness and plurality, in what it suggests in the unity of feeling the vitality of human relationships which the Qurʾān always wants to anchor in spiritual bases that are always connected to God, given that He is the power that brings them together despite their variation.

It is possible that this signification is what has necessitated the variation in the calls, so that there is the call which starts with the words *O people* and the call which starts with the words *O you who believe* when the Qurʾān desires to call humankind to be wary of God. For there is a method that moves the human soul along the feelings of faith and wariness of God in its human aspect. The counterpart to that with regard to the believers is that there is another method with which it addresses the believers in order to stir up their faith, transforming it into an active, vital power that is not frozen in sentiment or absent in abstractions, in order to confirm the coupling of faith and feeling, because of the connection between faith and intellect and feelings and work, on that dynamic path.[218] And in this atmosphere a Muslim preacher, in his operating method, through which he seeks to stir up others via the call, is able to distinguish between that which concerns the human side, with which He speaks to all people, and the faith side, with which He speaks to the believers, and so He does not mix the two when it is required to distinguish [between] them, because that has a major relevance for the realism, flexibility and effectiveness of the method. Perhaps it is expedient in this context not to feel inhibited when there is a need to go beyond the aspect of faith in his address, emphasising instead the human aspect depending on the different scenarios and individuals, because that does not mean neglecting it but enriching it with a new, positive element.

The sense of *taqwā* (wariness of God) in Islamic education

O people! Be wary of your Lord: wariness is that to which God calls His servants in the majority of verses, in that it is practised as an educational method through human action under God's watch and with a profound sense of His presence. There is a big difference between when you say to a person 'do this' and when you call him to do something under the aegis of

[218] See Hamza *et al.*, *Anthology*, I, for the movement of life-force.

being God-wary. The latter method connects the action with God in terms of its motivations and its steps, and in its results. The first method, however, constitutes only an affirmation of the nature of the work which does not actualise for a human being the depth and love for that action, which is actualised by the spiritual effect of being God-wary in life. This is what Islam aims at when it plans to construct a Muslim personhood by means of its laws, the objective of which is to make human commitment to God's rulings an everyday dynamic that renews in that person an abiding sense of God's presence and of responsibility to obey His commands and His prohibitions; otherwise, there is disequilibrium between the nature of faith and the nature of works in that person, when on the contrary, each of the two supports the other.

This is the method we must concentrate on when educating believers, especially those of them who work, in order to remove them from the spiritual desiccation which a believer might suffer as a result of focusing on the work aspect to the detriment of the spirituality of fear of God. That might have another educational value, which is to preserve the vitality of the words of the Qur'ān, animating them in people's lives, transforming them into an active energy that supplies a human being with renewal and dynamism, distancing them from narrow understandings which might be stored up in regressive practices, which believers might practise in certain instances and stages of regression, just as happened with the word *taqwā*, which acquired a traditional meaning, making it one of those words that are restricted to the sphere of acts of worship and individual morality, with little relevance to the life of the common people. And within this framework of education, the words remain as a sign of an Islamic personhood and as one of its symbols, the dynamic of cause and effect in the human being's internal and external reality.

And *taqwā*, in our understanding, is Islam in its vital dynamic sense. Someone could say that it is practically the epitome of the word 'Islam' because it comprehends the intellectual aspect which represents the internal depth and the practical aspect which represents its external dynamic, such that you could set off in your thought, work, emotion, relationships and dealings with others, through God's pleasure in what He has commanded and forbidden as a process of commitment and discipline, 'for God does not miss you where He has commanded you and does not find you where He has prohibited you'. If you have control over your will in those instances that involve the foundational dynamic in life, while being in God's hands, then your commitment shall not fall in the face of the pressure of your desires and your greedy ambitions.

The choice of the word *Lord* (*rabb*) rather than the word 'God' suggests that the first word has the meaning of nurturing (*rabb*), which makes *taqwā* one of the ways in which we are educated and where humans encounter God from a place of practical development of the personhood, and what that entails in concentrating on the quality of the relationship between the human being and his Lord, which is not just a link ending with the final action of creation, but a relationship linked with human existence in spiritual, physical, intellectual and practical growth. Once a human being is in harmony with that, through what God deposited in him in terms of intellect and what He transmitted to him in terms of revelation, then the education proceeds on its natural way. If he were to be recalcitrant in pursuit of his desires, abandoning the call of the intellect (*ʿaql*), then the divine calls, in the context of the promise and the threat (*al-targhīb wa'l-tarhīb*), ambush him, bringing him closer to Heaven and distancing him from the Fire, and tests by way of trial and shock, which wait for him in all places, in order to make him return to his intellect (*ʿaql*) and His Lord.

What is the meaning of the *single soul*?

Who created you from a single soul [refers to] the attribute which the Qurʾān stirs in the mind of the human being, so that he might then conceive of Him from a place of confident connection to Him, in the process of existence, which makes him live the feeling of God in each beat of his heart, in every fold of emotion that he feels, in every movement of his body and in every manifestation of life, so that he is filled up with the sensation of God, as his sensation of life is magnified, finding God in all of that, because it came into being by Him and from Him, and it continues on the basis of Him and it endures through His power.

But what was this *single soul*? Perhaps, as it appears from some of the exegetes (*mufassirūn*), it is an indication of a single reality exemplified in the male and the female, because God – when He created it – originated it on the basis of a pairing (*zawjiyya*), since there are not, according to what the verse indicates, any words about Adam as an individual. But, even though that [understanding] might not be remote from the context (*jaww*) of the verse, it is distanced from its apparent lexical form, for indeed it is apparent that the talk (*ḥadīth*) is not about the nature of human existence, but rather about its beginning and the path of its continuation. So there was a first creation, whom God created in the beginning as a body, and He deposited into him a spirit of His Spirit. Given this context (*jaww*), pairing becomes an essential nature of that creation. So, inevitably, the indication here must be to Adam and Eve, on the basis that the two of them are the direct creation of

God, which was the first foundation from which issued forth the multiplicity (*takāthur*); and that is revealed by the passage *and from it created its mate, and spread forth from the two many men and women*. For, had the matter been [about existence and not Adam and Eve] as that group [of *mufassirūn*] said, there would not have been a place for this passage which speaks about the process of the multiplying on the basis of singularity.

[Regarding] *and from it created its mate*, how do we picture this process of creation? In some of the narrated reports, it has come to us that Eve was created from one of Adam's ribs, and some of them go so far as to count the number of ribs on a man and a woman, on the basis that what is meant by the word *mate* is Eve. Others go so far as to say that the word 'mate' (*zawj*) cannot be meant that way, because both men and women are called 'mate'. So one can say: Such-and-such a man is the mate of such-and-such a woman, just as it is said, such-and-such a woman is the mate of such-and-such a man. According to this, what is meant by the *single soul* is not Adam, and *its mate* is not Eve.

However, we manifestly infer from this verse that, considering it appears in the sequence of creation, this creation is not from one of Adam's ribs, for indeed the verse does not indicate that. Rather, it is possible that the matter can be turned towards the part left over from the clay out of which Adam was created. That has been put forth in a *ḥadīth* on the authority of the imam Muḥammad al-Bāqir (*ʿm*) which is narrated in the *tafsīr al-Mīzān* [Ṭabāṭabāʾī][219] on the authority of the *Nahj al-bayān* of Shaybānī,[220] on the authority of ʿAmr b. Abī al-Miqdām, on the authority of his father, who said,

> I asked Abū Jaʿfar (*ṣlʿhm*), from what thing did God create Eve?' And he replied, 'What do they say about it?' I said, 'They say that God created her from one of Adam's ribs.' He responded, 'They lie; was God incapable of creating her from something other than his rib?' So I said, 'I implore you, from what thing did He create her?' He replied, 'My father informed me, on the authority of his fathers, [that] the Messenger of God (*ṣlʿm*) said, "God, blessed and exalted took a handful of clay, and He mixed it with His right hand, though both of His hands are right hands, and He created from it Adam, and a portion of clay was left over, and He created from it Eve".'

[219] ʿAllāma Muḥammad Ḥusayn Ṭabāṭabāʾī (d. 1360/1981), *al-Mīzān fī tafsīr al-Qurʾān*, 20 vols. (Beirut, Muʾassasat al-Aʿlamī li'l-Maṭbūʿāt, 1973–4).

[220] Muḥammad b. al-Ḥasan al-Shaybānī (d. seventh/thirteenth century), *Nahj al-bayān ʿan kashf maʿānī al-Qurʾān*, ed. Ḥusayn Dargāhī, 5 vols. (Qumm, Nashr al-Hādī, 1998). Not to be confused with the more famous Muḥammad b. al-Ḥasan al-Shaybānī, the jurist and student of Abū Ḥanīfa.

That which confirms this is that God speaks, in other verses, about the subject via the plural, which indicates that the intention behind the creation of the mate is of his kind and [his] original element (*ʿunṣur*), as [seen] in His words, *Of His signs is that He created for you mates from among yourselves (min anfusikum), that you might find solace by their side* [Q. 30:21], and in His words, *And God made mates for you from among yourselves* [Q. 16:72]. And, indeed, it is well known from the very nature of the expression that what is meant by it is that God created for every person a mate of the very same type, not from one of the limbs of his body. And God knows best.

This is on the one hand; and on the other hand we have supposed from the address *a single soul* that the Qurʾān rejects all manner of discrimination, be it on the basis of race (*ʿunṣurī*), ethnicity, colour, language or geography. And indeed these varied elements hold no depth in terms of the humanity of the human being as it is constituted in the single soul, but, rather, are matters accidental to the dynamic of his existence by way of the variety which exemplifies the power of God to vary a single thing, by numerous colours and specificities, without losing, within that diversity, its original nature. In this way, there is no scope for people to see distinctions in these specificities, or glories, and markers of superiority, for they are not specificities at a deep level of existence, but rather they are specificities of shape and extent.

Shaykh Muḥammad ʿAbduh on the subject of the *single soul*

It was published in the *Tafsīr al-manār*,[221] according to what the author of the *Tafsīr al-kāshif*[222] has transmitted on the authority of his teacher Shaykh Muḥammad ʿAbduh, that God, Exalted be He, had made the matter of the soul from which humans were created ambiguous, because He made it an indefinite noun, giving it indefinite form, so we should leave it ambiguous. And that which is suggested in other verses, by His addressing the people as *O children of Adam*, does not contradict this?? [sic] That is an opinion that does not dispel the ambiguity and cannot be considered as a categorical proof-text of the fact that all humans are the children of Adam, for it suffices for the address to be sound for those to whom it was directed during the time of revelation, to be among the children of Adam. Indeed, it has come before in the explanation of the story of Adam, in the beginning of *sūrat al-Baqara*, that on the earth before him there was a species of this genus and that they fell into corruption and shed blood.

[221] By Muḥammad ʿAbduh (see above).

[222] Muḥammad Jawād Maghniyya (d. 1979), *Tafsīr al-kāshif*, 7 vols. (Beirut, Dār al-ʿIlm li'l-Malāyīn, repr. 1990). Maghniyya's interpretation is dealt with briefly in Bauer, *Gender Hierarchy*, 148.

But we mention, according to this opinion, that the Qur'ānic saying *Children of Adam* is not specific to the time of the revelation, but is inclusive of all humans, as in the following speech of His: *When your Lord brought forth from the children of Adam, from their loins their seed* [Q. 7:172], and *Certainly We have honoured the children of Adam and carried them on land and sea, and provided them with all the good things, and preferred them greatly over many that we have created* [Q. 17:70], and, *O children of Adam! Let not Satan tempt you* [Q. 7:27], for indeed these addresses, or speeches, are not directed towards the people in the time of the Call, but are directed towards all people. That suggests that these people who live on this earth are the 'children of Adam', and not the children of some other person.

That does not contradict the text of some narrations indicating the presence of creations resembling these humans before the existence of Adam, because it is manifest – assuming the soundness of the narration – that this species became extinct and it no longer had a role on the earth, which is why God created a new human being which He began with Adam, His vicegerent on the earth.

We have said in the explanation of [*sūrat*] *al-Baqara* that the talk of the angels about the earthly creation, which caused corruption in the earth and shed blood, did not indicate the presence of any previous human experience, so there is another possibility in the *tafsīr*.

How did human propagation begin?

And spread forth from the two many men and women. Perhaps it can be inferred from this verse the idea that, indeed, the sources of the generation of the human species are Adam and Eve, and there is no other non-human element, as some of the narrations attempt to suggest when they say that the beginning of the production of offspring in the second generation was from a houri or a female jinn, one of the two of which would marry some of the sons of Adam, and the other would marry some of the others. It can be deduced from the verse that if this had been true, then He would have said, 'Sent forth from the two of them and from others'. But this inference is imprecise, because this passage speaks about the start of the production of offspring from the two of them, considering the two as the first source, without getting into what happened after them in the specific details of the mating. In this respect, it does not appear to either refute or confirm [those reports].

If it is possible to raise this subject from another angle, instead of making inferences from the verse, perhaps some might wonder whether the beginning of the human production of offspring in the second generation was human in all of its elements and whether this involved a brother marrying his sister. This is a matter rejected by the revealed laws, but perhaps some would go so far as to consider the subject impossible, even in the case of animals.

The answer to that: The matter of the legality, or otherwise, of any marital relationship is subject to the process of legislation insofar as it is either permitted or forbidden, regardless of any innate or essential factors. In light of this, a psychological state of antipathy depends on elements of upbringing, in the consensus that people come to over negative values that find support in legislation.

If we study the method of the revealed laws, we see there are matters that are prohibited in previous laws which subsequent laws came to permit. This is also suggested to us by what God transmitted to us on the authority of Jesus, peace be upon him, concerning His word which the Qurʾān transmitted: *and as one confirming the truth of that which is before me, of the Torah, and to make lawful for you some of the things that were forbidden you. I have brought you a sign from your Lord, so fear God and obey me* [Q. 3:50]. And perhaps matters were the opposite of that, so that prohibition came after permission. And perhaps the basis of this discrepancy is that rules issue forth from what is in the best interests and [to guard against] corrupting behaviours that are delimited by space and time, and the relevant circumstances surrounding an issue are variable depending on various influential factors. It is from this that the principle of abrogation in law emerges, whether in the case of a single system of law or in the framework of several laws.

Given this context, there is nothing to prevent God, glory be to Him, from having permitted the first generation of the children of Adam to marry each other for the purpose of launching the process of the production of offspring in its natural parameters, but not as an act of corruption. The familial system that imposes certain psychological barriers in the matter of the intermarriage of brothers and sisters had not yet, at that time, emerged in the dynamic of life generally, because the society which considers such a system to be part of its dynamic had not yet been born. After that, the prohibition came, because the best interests that called for the permissibility had come to an end at that time. Then, the issue began to involve (*taḥarraka*) conditions of persisting corruption that required legislation against the ruling that deemed it permissible. Therefore the social system which the law connects to the organisation of the family can be considered the foundation for the rule of prohibition which is intended to create a psychological barrier that might prevent a brother from marrying his sister, and that creates an emotional state that is antithetical to any sexual relations between the two, which enables them to live under a single roof in a natural way, without fear of negative eventualities in this framework. The matter did not stop there, but extended to laws that involve a system of forbidding marriage to prohibited kin. Supposing this understanding to be the natural explanation of the subject, there is no problem which requires us to look for a solution.

This interpretation has been confirmed by the *ḥadīth*s that have come to us on the authority of the imams of the *ahl al-bayt*, according to what Ṭabāṭabā'ī in the *Mīzān* said on the authority of the imam ʿAlī b. al-Ḥusayn, [in which] Zayn Abīdīn (*ʿm*) in a conversation with a Qurashī, is describing the marriage of Abel (Hābīl) to Lawzā',[223] the sister of Cain (Qābīl), and the marriage of Cain to Aqlīmā, the sister of Abel:

> The Qurashī said to him: 'And they gave birth to them?' He said, 'Yes.' And the Qurashī said to him: 'This is what the Zoroastrians (Majūs) do today.' So he said, 'The Zoroastrians did that after God's prohibition', and he said to him, 'Do not find this repugnant; they were just God's laws at the time. Did not God create the spouse of Adam from him, and then make her permissible to him? That was one of their laws. After that, God sent down the prohibition.'

Discussing Darwin's theory of human origins[224]

Another point might be raised in this vein, which is that humans were not created as perfect, upright humans but rather were first created as animals, then passed through stages of evolution, until they assumed the human form and characteristics, on the basis of the principle of evolution which Darwin affirmed in his theory 'On the Origin of the Species', in which he attempted to confirm that the theory goes beyond the question of humankind.

But we reject that because of the Islamic viewpoint exemplified in the Noble Qur'ān, drawing support from the indicatory proofs in the appearance of this verse and others that discuss the beginning of creation, and in the way that God has told us about the creation of Adam, who is the first father of the human species, in perfected form, in terms of creation, intellect, perception and complete responsibility for his actions. This suggests that his humanity was an intrinsic part of the dynamics of his existence from the beginning. That is why this theory [of Darwin's] contradicts the religious texts of the Qur'ān, and what is in the noble Sunna, and what they comprise regarding the discussion of the beginning of creation. This is from the Islamic perspective.

[223] See above, the interpretation of Muḥsin al-Fayḍ which includes this report.
[224] See Elshakry, *Reading Darwin in Arabic*, esp. ch. 5, 'Darwin and the Mufti', 161–218.

And as for the perspective of objective science, our exegesis here is not the natural place to discuss it, but there is one aspect that we must raise here, which is that this theory centres on limited experience which cannot embrace all human types, but rather is restricted to specific types such that it would not be sound to make a general inference and then apply it. We add to that, that this experience is not bounded by a single interpretation, but can encompass several observations or interpretations which are beyond the theoretical scope.

Perhaps some researchers have discussed the existence of historically prior types that reveal that humankind predates the time frame which Darwin's types constitute, which means that his inferences do not submit to precise calculation. Whatever the circumstances, there will be one basic truth in all of this, which is that the results coming out of this theory cannot be considered scientific fact but rather are speculative propositions that are subject to conjecture and surmise, because they do not preclude the possibility of the opposite, given the nature of the experience, or given the missing links in the dynamics of the experience. Therefore, it does not represent a scientific basis in the face of the divine revelation that constitutes religious truth.

The relationship with the womb-kin (*al-arḥām*) in Islam

And be wary of God by whom you petition one another, and the wombs; indeed God is Watcher over you. This passage comes as an enjoinder to wariness (*taqwā*), emphasising the line that God wishes his servants to tread and the method (*nahj*) to pursue. It is possible that the suffixing of the reference to majesty in His words *alladhī tasāʾalūna bihi* is an intimation of the strong bond that ties God to man, given the way that others beseech Him and request things in His name. This is the case when they make demands for things they need and for issues they seek to resolve, all of which implies an extended presence in a human being's consciousness. This creates, thus, a profound sensation, and it entails keeping an eye on oneself and self-reckoning, for such leads to a disciplined way of embarking on things that one wills, while treading a path that pleases Him. So if making requests in His name stands as a magnification, then obedience to Him and wariness (*taqwā*) of Him constitute an even more powerful manifestation of that grandeur.

As for the word *wa'l-arḥāma*, this has been read with the genitive inflection (*kasra*), as coordinated with the suffix pronoun in the word *bihi*, and this is in accordance with what is customary among people when they say to one another *unshiduka bi'llāhi wa'l-raḥimi* (I implore you by God and the wombs), where the request is contingent upon the womb, just as it would be in the case of God; this is on the basis of the two being the closest things to humans, for God, glory be to Him, is the Creator and the womb is closeness in terms of lineage.

However, al-Ṭabarī, in his *tafsīr* says,

> That is not idiomatically very sound, according to the Arabs, because one does not coordinate an overt noun with something that is pronominal, especially in the genitive, unless it is for poetic licence (*ḍarūrat al-shiʿr*); and that is because of the constraints of poetic form (*ḍīq al-shiʿr*). As for speech, there is no need for the speaker to choose something abhorrent in phrasing and not amenable to syntactical analysis. An example from poetry of coordinating an overt noun with a pronominal in the genitive is the following words of the poet:
>
> *Nuʿalliqu fī mithla al-sawārī suyūfanā*
> *wa-mā baynahā wa'l-kaʿbi ghawṭun nafāʾif*
>
> We hang our swords in the like of masts
> Between the swords and the heels an open expanse
>
> The poet coordinated the *kaʿb* (the heel), which is an overt noun, with the suffixed letters in *baynahā*, which is standing in place [of the noun 'swords'].[225]

The author of *al-Mīzān* [Ṭabāṭabāʾī] says in this respect:

> However, the narrative thread in the Qurʾān's style in its clarificatory statements does not conform to this. For, if His words *wa'l-arḥāma* were to be taken as an independent copula for *alladhī*, then the implication is that the words would read *wa'ttaqū Allāha alladhī tasāʾalūna bi'l-arḥām* without a pronoun, which is impossible. However, if in sum it and what preceded it constitute a singular copula for *alladhī*, that ends up equating God, majestic be His name, and wombs with regard to their greatness and majesty, which contradicts the style and form of the Qurʾān.

In light of all of that, we find ourselves choosing to read *wa'l-arḥām* in the accusative because it is the most likely and the nearest to being correct, which accords with what has been related by al-Ḍaḥḥāk, that Ibn ʿAbbās used to read it as *wa'l-arḥāma*. On the basis of this opinion: be wary of God when it comes to the wombs, and connect them. On the authority of al-Rabīʿ, with regard to *be wary of God by whom you petition one another, and the wombs*, he said: 'Fear God with regard to the wombs, and hence connect them.' In a *ḥadīth*, it has been reported on the authority of Jamīl b. Darrāj from Abū ʿAbd Allāh [Jaʿfar al-Ṣādiq] (ʿ*m*), that he said, 'I asked him about the words of God, mighty and majestic, *Be wary of God by whom you petition*

[225] See Ṭabarī above.

one another, and the wombs; indeed God is Watcher over you, to which he responded, "That refers to the womb-ties between people, which God, blessed and exalted, has commanded be connected and held in high esteem. Do you not see how He has placed it alongside Himself?"'

The secret of the emphasis on connecting the womb-kin

A person may wonder about the secret regarding this emphasis on the womb-kin and what the Qur'ān suggests in the way of caring for them – connecting them and not severing them – considering that to be an Islamic value. Some might add, in this regard, that this tendency with regard to human relationships might open up the potential for generating and activating a clan mentality in the family, given what the womb-kin represents as a legal specificity that rises to the level of being a major Islamic value, and that this might lead to more close-mindedness within the framework of the family.

However, the issue – as we understand it from the perspective of the wisdom behind the Law (*tashrīʿ*) – does not move towards that sense, but is far, far removed from that. For the issue has to do with the Islamic idea to deepen and extend human relations, and to work towards circumscribing negative reactions that can arise in the self as a result of the continuous interaction that is imposed by kinship ties. That, in turn, could lead to a severe breach and a deepening enmity, particularly when deviant situations occur within the framework of the extended family (*aqribāʾ*). And we witness this frequently in intractable family problems among extended kin to such a level that spite and rancour arise and persist for a long time. So Islam wanted this relationship to have a spiritual basis, in addition to its natural emotional basis that is a result of intrinsic factors to do with emotions, such that both are harmonised with a view to controlling negative situations and preventing the deterioration of human relationships. For, ultimately, a person who is unable to absorb the negative impact of his own traits and his emotional dealings with people to whom he is tied through kinship will be unable to do the same in his dealings with others, with whom he is not connected in any way at the same level.

Perhaps this Islamic method of taking into consideration human relationships is a phenomenon of the [process of the] formulation of Islamic law in all occurrences (*mawārid*) pertaining to the framework of continuous contact on the basis of womb-kin, vicinity or faith as a dynamic of a single creed. We note that the *ḥadīth*s that are reported in these contexts emphasise maintaining connections even in cases where the severing comes from others, being virtuous even in situations where you have been ill-treated, and pardoning, forgiving and being pliant even in instances of aggression.

There could be those who say: These principles constitute the general Islamic ethic and are not specific to these kinds of relationships. We would respond by emphasising the origin of this principle, but with the following remark, which is to say that to highlight these principles when discussing such instances gives it more categoricalness and more emphasis, which in itself suggests that the matter assumes a significance that other matters do not. It has been related by al-Sukūnī with regard to the womb-kin ties (*ṣilat al-raḥim*), on the authority of the imam Jaʿfar al-Ṣādiq (*ʿm*), that he said: 'The Messenger of God (*ṣlʿm*) said, "Do not sever your womb-kin even if he severs you".' And in the book *al-Kāfī* on the authority of ʿAnbasa al-ʿĀbid, he said, 'A man came to Abū ʿAbd Allāh [Jaʿfar al-Ṣādiq] (*ʿm*), and complained about his relatives. And so he said to him, "Restrain your rage (*kaẓm, ghayẓ*) and make sure that you do." To which he responded, "But they do this and that!" So he said, "Do you want to be like them, so that God ends up looking at none of you?"'[226] Also in the *ḥadīth*, it is reported on the authority of Abū Ḥamza al-Thumālī that he said, 'The Commander of the Believers ʿAlī b. Abī Ṭālib (*ʿm*) said in a sermon: "I seek refuge with God from those sins that hasten annihilation." ʿAbd Allāh b. al-Kawwāʾ al-Yashkurī then went up to him and said, "O Commander of the Believers! Are there sins that really hasten annihilation?" He replied, "Of course! Beware the severing of womb-kin: it may be that a household come together and bond even as they are wicked, but God, mighty and majestic, provides for them, and it may be that a household all go their separate ways, each severing the other, so God deprives them even as they are God-wary."'

Thus we find that the matter at hand is not about fostering the asphyxiating atmosphere of family clannishness, but about reaching those horizons where the fundamentality of human relationships is affirmed and one works towards [ensuring] its ethical depth and extent within the personhood of a Muslim individual, so that it does not buckle under the negative conditions that happen from time to time in the way that negativity gives rise to paralysis. As for the boundaries of these relationships, and the scope of movement within them as these impact the individual plane, these are taken care of by the legislations of Islam, where these relationships have a place within the framework of the various branches of jurisprudence,[227] inasmuch as that is harmonised with the other planes in which public relationships operate.

[226] This refers to God looking at His servants who have made it to the Hereafter, cf. Q. 3:77: *those, God shall not speak to them nor look at them on the Day of Resurrection, nor purify them, and they shall have a painful punishment.*

[227] Here he has given some general principles, but is suggesting that one must turn to jurisprudence for a detailed understanding.

We also see this in the plane of faith which puts in place for the Muslim individual the delimiting bounds for his relationships with believers and non-believers with regard to things that he has reservations about and with regard to things which he embraces. It is this that exemplifies the rules governing the dynamics of an individual's relationship to his womb-kin.

A methodological point for extracting Qurʾānic concepts

Perhaps in order to be faithful to the enquiry being made here we might call attention to an important point concerning the way to infer Islamic concepts from the legal sources such as the Book and the Sunna. For it may not be sufficient to extract concepts from Islamic sources by taking their delimitations from a single *ḥadīth* or a single verse; rather, it is imperative that we enter into a comparative exercise between *ḥadīth*s and verses where each of these deals with one aspect of the picture in order for that picture to become more complete by balancing both of its sides. Many have fallen into error by being oblivious to this aspect and by trying to define general concepts in Islam, as in the case of certain studies that talk about Islam as rejecting this world, on the basis of ascetic (*zuhd*) *ḥadīth*s disregarding *ḥadīth*s and verses that speak positively about how human beings are encouraged to set off and embrace the good things of this life and its delights. Or [they fall into] the opposite, which entails being removed from the real picture where asceticism has its place within the psychological framework, which by force of will is able to avoid falling prey to the intense pressures that are produced by the faculty of desire, and gives an equilibrium for the way in which life is embraced without life losing its sensory meaning at the cost of Islamic principles, nor does it impel one to be carried away with desire and swept away by its current. In a word, the method adopted by [Qurʾānic] verses and *ḥadīth*s centres around a governing principle in which an idea in its essence appears in a specific text, but then the bounds and the context for that are put in place by another text, that which forever necessitates balancing between the texts.

Indeed God is Watcher over you: that is to say, preserving your deeds, watching over them and capturing them, which obliges you to embrace this feeling in order to remain restrained within God's delimitations and not to deviate from that in moments of obliviousness.

Interviews

Fariba Alasvand

Dr Alasvand, a professor at the women's Hawzeh in Qumm, is conservative and therefore, in some respects, one might expect her to have similar opinions to those found in the works of *tafsīr* cited above. In this context, what stands out about her interpretation of Q. 4:1 is the ultimately positive message it gives to women. Whereas menstruation and pregnancy were once considered a divinely ordained punishment for women, Dr Alasvand argues that these are simply natural aspects of womanhood and that men are told to look after women when they are in these vulnerable states. She states that a breastfeeding mother is a fighter (*mujāhida*) on God's path. This is a powerful message to send to women: their own natural bodily abilities, such as breastfeeding, are a means of undertaking jihad. Her approach overall could be considered body-positive for women, in that she looks at things that are physically difficult for many women (periods, pregnancy and childbirth, and breastfeeding) and characterises them in a positive way.

Another striking aspect of Dr Alasvand's interpretation is that she argues against *ḥadīth*s that claim that Eve was created from Adam's rib, and argues strongly that this verse and others indicate that women and men are both of the same type. Thus, like Faḍl Allāh and other modern interpreters, she argues against the idea that women are the 'second sex'.

Fariba Alasvand: With regard to your questions about the *tafsīr* of the first verse of *sūrat al-Nisā'*, the most widespread interpretation (*tafsīr*) of this verse, the one given by the majority of Shīʿī commentators, especially recently, is that *it* (*-hā*) [indicates] the type of person, the type of human. This verse indicates that men and women are of a single type. The proof for this, which is present in other verses, is: *Of His signs is that He created for you mates from among yourselves* (*min anfusikum*) [Q. 30:21].
Karen Bauer: [Like] *a messenger from among yourselves* (*rasūlun min anfusikum*) [Q. 9:128]?[228]
Fariba Alasvand: Yes, well done. Of course, the interpretations before said that *min anfusikum* meant 'from the rib'. But with *from among yourselves*, the intention is from your selves, your type. ʿAllāma Ṭabāṭabā'ī has gathered together the evidence on this and has said that *from* (*min*) in this verse is the 'from' of type. *Min* in Arabic is a preposition (*ḥarf jarr*), and it has different types, and this type is the *min* of type. For instance, you can say, 'This bracelet is of (*min*) silver' and it describes its type. The wife is of the same type as the husband; Eve is of Adam.

[228] This is another place in which the term 'from yourselves' is used, so it is a linguistic parallel with the creation in Q. 4:1. This is referenced in earlier interpretations, such as that of Fakhr al-Dīn al-Rāzī above.

Karen Bauer: I understand; they are of the same type. Do you wish to say anything else about this?
Fariba Alasvand: Yes, I just wish to make one point. Many of the *ḥadīth*s have said that the creation was from a rib. I would like to say that its meaning is not that Eve is the second sex. The idea that Eve was created from Adam's rib does not come from this verse. It is present in other sources. It is present in the Torah that God said to Eve: I have created you in this way: you menstruate, you get pregnant, you work, because you have sinned and deceived Adam. Meaning that pregnancy –
Karen Bauer: Is a punishment.
Fariba Alasvand: Yes, these biological issues are called, in the Torah, punishments for Eve. But in the Qurʾān it says that because of these issues, the difficulties that women face, it is necessary for men to find out about women's state, and that they must work well with them. The Islamic religious idea with regard to the menstrual period is that this is a natural issue, but that during this period, women are in a time of hardship (*mashaqqa*) and in a time of illness. Also, in Islamic narrations, we know that when a woman's child is born, and she feeds her baby, she is like a fighter (*mujāhida*) in the path of God. With regard to the Islamic idea of these times that are specific to women, there are many beautiful narrations. In using the narrations, we know that even if woman was created from the rib of Adam, she is not the second sex created for the sake of men. Rather, this verse is an indication of the same type – but there are some narrations, like the one of imam al-Bāqir, which say that just as God was capable of making Adam as an independent being, He was also capable of creating Eve as an independent being. He says that she was not created from the rib of Adam, but as a new creation. If you would like a better explanation, you can ask.
Karen Bauer: I think that's clear to me. The verse does not explain that Eve is from the rib of Adam. She and Adam are of the same substance. They are both from a single soul. But, if she had been from his rib, she would not have been a secondary human, a person under him. Even if she had been from his rib, she would have been equal to him. I hope I've understood.
Fariba Alasvand: Yes, that's right.
Karen Bauer: I now have a new question, on the matter of the creation of humans, and the relationship between that physical creation and the theory of evolution.
Fariba Alasvand: With regard to your new question, there are different opinions held by different *ʿulamāʾ*. For instance, Ayatollah Mishkini says that it is possible to bring together what is said in Darwin's theory and what is present in the Glorious Qurʾān. But, of course, I believe that the theory of

Darwin is a hypothesis (*farḍiyya*) and not all of the scientists believe in it. I mean that this theory has remained a hypothesis, not a physiological truth. It is only a hypothesis; it has not been proven. There is not one single actual proof [that] confirm[s] this hypothesis. Correct? I mean that this belief needs more proof in order to confirm that any single living being is the result of this process. There is not actually proof for the theory of evolution that one being developed from another. The things that were made from one cell are still one cell; and those things that were complicated are still complicated.
Karen Bauer: What about the fossil record that shows changes?
Fariba Alasvand: Probably these were just different beings. There are different species of monkeys and apes, and these were present at all times. There are a lot of similarities between them, and between them and humans. Even in some works of *tafsīr* the idea is present that God Almighty created different beings before humans. So some of the *mufassirūn* explain the words of the angels, when they asked God why He put him on earth, saying *will you set in it someone who will cause corruption in it and shed blood?* [Q. 2:30], by saying there was a physical being that the angels were referring to before this one, which had a physical body. And they knew about this creation; and because of this, the exegetes say that it is possible that there was something resembling humans before humans. But the Qurʾān informs us that God, exalted be He, created this being without anything before it that led to this creation. It is even present in *Nahj al-Balāgha*, which is very beautiful, where there is a very deep interpretation. Imam ʿAlī b. Abī Ṭālib (*ʿm*) said that God created everything, and for everything in this universe there is a particular essence. Angels have a particular essence, and individual beings are not able to go against their particular boundaries. Every type of animal has its own role to play. We have never heard from anyone that a bee is able to do something outside of its boundaries. A bee cannot change its essential existence. In all times and places, bees make honey, they build their houses using their special engineering and they do not go against their nature. The only being that is able to tolerate changes in its life, and in its nature, is the human being. Humans can change their houses, their work and everything. This is, therefore, a special type of creation. Ibn Abī Ṭālib said that for everything there is a special way, and people, who are able to develop in different ways in their life, have their own special place. Of course it is possible to practise cloning. But everything has its special place and is able to change within a particular space and time, rather than from one thing to another. The theory of Darwin contradicts the reality of the created world that was made by God, exalted be He. We say that this theory cannot refute the works of God, exalted be He.

Of course Darwin himself was a religious man; he was a member of the Church, and even he did not deny the existence of God.

Mehdi Mehrizi

Dr Mehrizi is a reformist interpreter, but his interpretation of Q. 4:1 is similar to that of Fariba Alasvand, in that he reads *from it* as 'of the same type'. This is based on a linguistic analysis of other verses with similar phrasing, in which *from it* could not possibly mean 'from the rib'. He then cites an interpretation that he heard from Professor Hossein Modarressi, which says that this verse means that the ideal marriage in Islam is between one man and one woman, because God spread forth all of humanity *from the two*. Finally, Mehrizi says that the theory of evolution may or may not be supported by this verse; religion does not enter into science.

Mehdi Mehrizi: *Be wary of your Lord, who created you from a single soul, and from it created its mate.* The [phrase] *from it created its mate* occurs six times in the Qur'ān: three times in the singular and three times in the plural. Take *khalaqa laka min anfusikum azwājan*, for instance. Nobody says that every single wife was taken from her husband. What is the meaning of *khalaqa laka min anfusikum azwājan*? This and the verse in the singular indicate the truth of reality (*ḥaqīqat al-wāqiʿa*). The single shared essence.
Karen Bauer: Meaning, from the same type.
Mehdi Mehrizi: From the same type, yes; men and women are of the same type.
Karen Bauer: What about *and spread forth from the two*?
Mehdi Mehrizi: Yes, *many men and women* [completes the verse]. The influence of men is the same as the influence of women. *Khalaqa minhā* is commonly interpreted to mean 'created from the man'. But how can we have the feminine pronoun in this case? The word *zawja* is never used in the Qur'ān; only the masculine form, *zawj*, which is used for men and women. Therefore *khalaqa minhā* must mean 'from the same soul'. I spoke with your Professor [Hossein Modarressi] about this verse, and he said something that I found convincing. He said that this verse means that in the Muslim family, there is only one wife, which is indicated by *from it created its mate* and *spread forth from the two many men and women*; not from a man and many women, but from a single man and woman.
Karen Bauer: Ah!
Mehdi Mehrizi: This is the first basis of the family in Islam, one single man and one single woman.
Karen Bauer: I have a second question about this. Many of the modern exegetes say that this single soul is a spiritual soul, not a specific individual

like Adam. But at the same time, what about the physical creation of men and women? My question is about Darwin and evolution, if you would like to speak about this.

Mehdi Mehrizi: Some of the exegetes address this. Ayatollah Mishkini has a book in Farsi concerning the theory of evolution in the Qur'ān. He says that the likes of this verse do not contradict it, nor do they support it. It is not possible to extract from the verse – I believe, as does Mishkini – that it is possible to say that this verse is governed by science. And religion does not enter into this matter.

Nasser Ghorbannia

In this interview, Dr Bauer questioned Dr Ghorbannia on how modern scholars could easily dismiss *ḥadīth*s attributing a deficiency to women. Dr Ghorbannia, a staunch reformist, told her that he could dismiss any *ḥadīth* not in accordance with the principles of Islamic law or with rational understanding of the nature of the sexes. He explained that people are obliged to use their intellect in order to understand the veracity of *ḥadīth*s. This is a radical interpretation which allows for the individual intellect to supersede the transmitted sources.

Nasser Ghorbannia: I do not interpret this verse according to the Christian interpretation. Some of the narrations (of *ḥadīth*) mention that Eve is taken from the same soil as Adam. But the correct interpretation is that Adam and Eve were created from the same soul, and there is no difference between them. They were created from the same spirit and the same soul. *Khalaqa minhā zawjahā*: 'from it' (*minhā*) means from that very same soul, not from Adam. Rather, from that soul, from that spirit.

Karen Bauer: Some *ḥadīth*s say that she was created from the rib.

Nasser Ghorbannia: It is not correct in my opinion, and distinguished Islamic scholars say that this is not correct.

Karen Bauer: But how do you know the *ḥadīth* is not correct? What is the proof that the *ḥadīth* is not correct?

Nasser Ghorbannia: Because this is not reconcilable with the basis of Islamic law and the basis of the Holy Qur'ān. From the other verses of the Holy Qur'ān we infer that men and women are the same. That's the first point. And you know that Islamic traditions have reached us from fourteen hundred years ago. Today, it is possible for us to hear of something happening in the United States, but we don't know if it is correct or incorrect. How can we be absolutely sure that these traditions that we received from fourteen hundred years ago are exactly correct? The Holy Qur'ān said to us that men and women are equal. When traditions are not compatible with the Holy Qurʾān, we do not accept them. This is reason.

Karen Bauer: So you can use your reason, your rationality (*ʿaql*), to deduce this?

Nasser Ghorbannia: Yes, yes, rationality, of course. In our traditions, our imams say to us, and the Prophet told us, that God the creator has sent two messengers to us. One is external, that is the Prophet, and the other messenger is internal, that is rationality and reason. Reason is our prophet.

Karen Bauer: Is this a *ḥadīth*?

Nasser Ghorbannia: Yes, from Jaʿfar al-Ṣādiq (*ʿm*). We have two kinds of prophets, external and internal. The external kind are prophets such as our Prophet and the Christian and Jewish prophets. And the other prophet is internal, by which we mean reason. So we are obliged to interpret the Holy Qurʾān by our reason and by our intellect.

Karen Bauer: Obliged?

Nasser Ghorbannia: Yes, yes, obliged.

Sa'diyya Shaikh

Sa'diyya Shaikh focuses her discussion of Q. 4:1 on the Sufi Ibn ʿArabī, whose interpretation of this verse, and of women's value, is unlike any within the *tafsīr* tradition represented by the interpretations in the previous pages. The Sufi tradition, barely represented in the genre of *tafsīr*, is a ripe ground for exploring the alternative views of the stories common in those very works. In many cases, such as that of Ibn ʿArabī, the exoteric story still has a meaning: he affirms, for instance, that Eve came from Adam's rib. However, that very story is given a different valence in interpretations that recognise deeper wisdom (*ḥikma*), so that, while being true to the story in its outward reading, it is then given the opposite meaning. In this case, Eve eventually becomes a 'superlative being' for Ibn ʿArabī, someone who embodies the divine feminine. It is difficult to gauge the popularity of the Sufi interpretations versus those present in the *tafsīr* tradition. The authors of *tafsīr* were not writing for a popular audience, and indeed their obscure grammatical discussions are hardly digestible. While in some senses such works preserved widespread understandings of the Qurʾānic verses, in other senses they promoted specific types of understanding, which are undermined by the Sufi approach taken by scholars such as Ibn ʿArabī.*

Karen Bauer: We would like to ask you about Q. 4:1. Many premodern commentators relate this verse to Adam and Eve, and especially to the creation of Eve. In your book *Sufi Narratives of Intimacy*, you devote a chapter to Ibn ʿArabī's interpretation of the Adam and Eve myth, culminating in the observation that, for Ibn ʿArabī,

* This interview has been edited for clarity.

> Each modality of being [active and passive] is embedded within the other . . . This idea reiterates the original position that the original Adam was both male and female and that the subsequent gender-specific differentiation made both Adam and Eve into parts of the original whole. Despite this separation, each contained both the modalities of the whole within them – that is, each retained activity and receptivity corresponding to their original source, the original Adam. This view also mirrors the reality of the Godhead.[229]

In your view, is Q. 4:1 related to Ibn ʿArabī's interpretation of Adam and Eve, or does it have other significations that we might not have even picked up on?
Sa'diyya Shaikh: Yes, I think it is very much related to that particular verse, primarily because of the way in which Ibn ʿArabī's interlocutors and peers were talking about gender through the Adam and Eve narrative, and through the creation narratives. [Ibn ʿArabī] weaves together this Qurʾānic verse with other Qurʾānic verses when he speaks about the nature of Adam and Eve. And so there are a number of moves that he makes, in terms of his interpretive style, which are incredibly subversive. In my book, I try to bring together an analysis of these various interpretive moves that he makes when reading the Adam and Eve narratives. Ibn ʿArabī really has three different things that he does with the texts.

Adam and Eve come to symbolise, like they do for other exegetes, a way to think about the relationship between men and women. As you have probably covered in your *tafsīrs*, Adam and Eve come to symbolise the ways in which one thinks about creation, and the ways in which one thinks about the relationships between men and women.

First, one has to contextualise Ibn ʿArabī's interpretation. He is in conversation with a set of thinkers and other exegetes in relation to widely distributed stories about Eve being related to the crooked rib and deficiency, none of which are in the Qurʾān; but as we know, related Biblical stories become integrated as part of the Qurʾānic exegetical literature. Ibn ʿArabī is speaking to an audience for whom the Adam and Eve story becomes a way to speak about Eve being created from the rib of Adam, and since the rib is crooked, and crookedness is indicative of lack, of deficit, of deficiency, or whatever crookedness might imply in the broad sense, it becomes a kind of ontological narrative about deficit, about women's deficit. What Ibn ʿArabī does quite superbly is to be faithful to the tradition and to the *ḥadīth*, as well, while completely morphing, transforming and changing the signification of the rib, and of Eve being derived from Adam.

[229] Shaikh, *Sufi Narratives*, 199.

Looking at the Qur'ānic text itself, there is a verse that states Allāh *created you from a single soul, and from it created its mate*; here, there's no kind of primacy of male or female implicit in the Qur'ānic verse. It's an extremely open and, in fact, very beautiful verse that speaks about ontological pairing and about multiplicity from oneness. Islamic feminists and other people who are thinking about creation can find in this incredibly beautiful and evocative verse not just the notion of oneness – or the shared ontological origin – of men and women but of all human lives. But what many of the medieval exegetes did is they layered and replotted that narrative of that verse in ways that spoke to female deficiency – they argued that the first soul was male, that Ḥawwā' was derived from Adam – and, to be clear, through this reading these medieval exegetes were not doing anything that was outside of the cultural mores. They inherited an entire set of stories, and it's a way of reading these narratives through the close engagement with [the] Biblical narrative, with *ḥadīth* narratives, and so on.

Ibn ʿArabī doesn't say that those rib narratives are not accurate, or that Eve did not come from Adam. He goes along with the story. But what the rib signifies for him instead is the generous capacity for bending and for inclination. And then he presents these beautiful narratives of how Eve is derived from Adam, who experiences emptiness and this yearning for Eve since she is the part that has been removed from him. And because she's taken from Adam, she yearns for him who is her source and her ontological home. In this interpretation, Ibn ʿArabī reconfigures what is previously read as deficit, deficiency, crookedness and derivativeness to create instead a narrative of connection, interiority and oneness. Now, nonetheless, to be clear, even in that narrative, Adam is still the home and Eve is that which is taken from the home. So there's a way in which there's a more benevolent but still androcentric reading of the idea of primary and derivative forms of origin. He holds the narrative of Adam being source and Eve having been taken from [Adam], but he instead completely erased the idea of female deficiency and instead weaves a gendered cosmogony of love, inclination and oneness.

Then he says a very beautiful thing: he says that she bends, and he says, that just as ribs are bent, so Eve bends towards Adam in inclination, and then he says that Adam also bends towards Eve. So, in this way, the notion of ribs being bent becomes re-signified as mutual affection, love, inclination, the desire to come together. So what I think he does superbly is to take a set of narratives that become stories about women's lack, and reframes them in extremely compelling and evocative ways. At the same time, to be clear, in this reading he continues to reinforce the imaginary about Eve being derived.

He just reconfigures what that derivation looks like into a different form of relationality and mutuality.

Karen Bauer: I really enjoyed the way that you have just been talking about the ontological pairing, connection, interiority and oneness. And we know that Ibn ʿArabī was still a medieval thinker and then he didn't, as you said so eloquently and clearly, actually go against some of the legalistic implications for men and women, but he just gave those things a nuance that they didn't have in other texts at all. And I'm wondering if you could just expand on that and expand on whether, in the modern context, you see possibilities of interpreting in that sense, in the senses of ontological pairing, connection, interiority and oneness? Feras, maybe you have something to add there?

Feras Hamza: I think your question is there. I think if Sa'diyya would like to answer about how that can be carried over into modern thinking about the subject.

Sa'diyya Shaikh: So I would love to answer that question. But, actually, I've so far only reflected on one aspect of how Ibn ʿArabī presents the Adam and Eve narrative. He does multiple readings, and so perhaps we can return to what implications that might have once we look at some of his other narratives of Adam and Eve. This is so central in how we think about gender relationships in the Qurʾān, or at least it's been so central in how the exegetes, the *mufassirūn*, give possible different readings of the Qurʾān; it gets invoked in all kinds of ways. In his *Fuṣūṣ* [*al-ḥikām*] and in his *Futūḥāt* [*al-Makiyya*], he addresses this issue in a variety of ways and presents innovative understandings

On the one hand, Ibn ʿArabī is speaking to a dominant and established gendered imaginary, and he pushes away from that to recast a very different form of gendered relationality. He takes the idea of men and women in the form of the archetype of Adam and Eve as being deeply connected, and we've established that.

Then, elsewhere, he tells us there is not just one narrative of creation but four different narratives of creation in the Qurʾān. The creation of Adam is one model of creation, and then the creation of Eve from Adam is the second model of creation, and then the creation of Jesus from Maryam is the third model of creation. And then, the fourth model of creation is that of the rest of humanity, and here he refers to that verse [Q. 4:1] and says, 'from those two, all of humanity'. The rest of us were created from men and women together. So, to summarise, a woman (Eve) comes from a man (Adam) without the mediation of another woman – Eve comes directly from Adam, that's one model of creation. Then you have Jesus, who comes from Maryam, and this is a man coming from a woman without the intermediary of a man.

So those are two different and almost opposite models of creation. He points us to these varied creation models in the Qur'ān, but then reassures us that for the majority, the rest of us, we are from men and women together. Through expanding our view of the Qur'ānic stories of creation, he holds up very different models for thinking about gender, thereby, in my view, pushing us to rethink this idea of Eve simply being created from Adam and all of the patriarchal gendered implications of that singular narrative.

In my book, I've additionally outlined how Ibn ʿArabī uses evocative and poetic images of pregnancy, labour and birthing to describe the original birth of existence from the Divine One. In this metaphor, Ibn ʿArabī describes God, prior to creation, as existing in a state of solitude and oneness. Then he describes a reality within the Divine One, where non-existing latent entities are unable to manifest their potential, experience distress and exert internal pressure within the One, in the same way that a pregnant woman experiences the distress of labour before birthing a child. Then, within the selfsame Divine, through the Breath of the Merciful, these entities are released into existence. So it is this idea of God giving birth to creation, which is a very feminine image: labour, pregnancy and giving birth are Ibn ʿArabī's way of presenting God's creation of all of humanity and of the world.

So there are these very beautiful interpretive moves in which he takes normal gender ideas and introduces unusual readings. Another way he gestures to feminine aspects of the divine is through his commentary on the famous *ḥadīth* of the Prophet [that] says: Three things of the world were made beloved to me – perfume, women and prayer, and the most beloved is prayer. Ibn ʿArabī says that among the three things, perfume, women and prayer, the word 'perfume' in Arabic is grammatically masculine, and so the Prophet, who was an expert in Arabic, should have used a masculine plural, but he instead deliberately used the feminine plural. That wasn't because he was making a mistake. It was because he sought to signify a certain reality of the pre-eminence of the feminine, and then he again brings in the Adam and Eve analogy there. He says Adam is like perfume standing between the *dhāt* or essence, which is the divine feminine whom he comes from, and the female Eve who comes from him. So he, like perfume, stands between these two feminine realities. In Arabic, the word for divine power – *qudra* – is grammatically feminine, as are many other Divine attributes, all signifying the feminine dimensions of God. So the idea that he conveys is that male principle comes from the feminine and gives birth to the feminine.

In my book, I outlined these different modes of reading [that] Ibn ʿArabī provides to give pre-eminence to the feminine. On the one hand, he's working with dominant narratives. He doesn't unsay them. He doesn't say no directly to many of the prevailing narratives. He says: Yes, but the 'rib' means something else. And he doesn't say that Eve doesn't come from Adam, so she comes from Adam, but actually he calls her *naqāwa* (the choicest part),[230] and then she becomes the distilled epitome of creation.

He uses wonderful macrocosmic and microcosmic analogies. In the same way that the *rūḥ* (spirit) is the animating spiritual spark breathed into and giving life to the human being on the microcosmic level, humanity is seen as that *rūḥ* (spirit) breathed into the cosmos or the macrocosm. In Ibn ʿArabī's cosmology, the macrocosm only becomes inspirited when the human being is blown into it. Humanity is seen as a spirit that's blown into the cosmos; in that sense, he uses these subtle metaphors when describing Eve as the epitome, who is symbolised by this microcosmic human. And so he works through, in my view, some very beautiful iterations and different ways of telling the creation story, where he parallels the dominant male narrative where Adam is at the centre, with other narratives, where Eve emerges as this kind of superlative being, and there are yet other narratives where *insāniyya* – humanity and the essence of humanity – is open equally to men and women alike. So, in my book, I describe his approach to these different gender narratives with the image of a whirling dervish who spins the varying stories and thereby renders them fluid. As such, he does not allow us to settle with any particular fixed, reified categories of what men and women, maleness and femaleness, receptivity and activity, might look like or how it might become embodied in a particular kind of person.

I suppose that is the other important thing to recognise about *tafsīr*: [it shows how much a person] reads from [his or her own] state. You can read like Ibn ʿArabī or you can read like an ISIS person. The Qurʾān is open to that full range of readings, contingent on your state, and the Qurʾān tells you, of course, that those of you who have more beautiful or better readings, for them is the reward.[231] And so the idea is that of course there can be uglier readings, and there can be lesser readings. There can be ugly readings and then there can be exquisite readings, all of which are determined by the inner state of the reader.

Just to double back for a second. I wanted to make this point about Ibn ʿArabī, and I have a story that illustrates it rather well. I was at a conference, and I gave a paper on Ibn ʿArabī, and somebody said to me, 'Oh, that's a

[230] See, e.g., ibid., 153, 158, *et passim*.

[231] Cf. Q. 2:121, *those to whom We have given the Book follow its recitation in the way it truly ought to be followed: they believe in it. As for those who deny it, those are the losers*; Q. 7:204, *When the Qurʾān is recited, then listen and pay attention to it; you might receive mercy.*

powerful queer reading of Ibn ʿArabī; and a great use of queer theory.' And I thought at that point, 'Oh, actually, I have never properly read queer theory. All I was doing was reading Ibn ʿArabī.' And I think that the incredible fluidity of Ibn ʿArabī's ideas are profoundly valuable in reading around sexual diversity, in reading around human diversity, in reading about the vast panoramic way in which humans can and must be human. That's what I find so completely exciting about reading with this particular Sufi.

Feras Hamza: One of the things that I think has been inspiring for us is to just realise how much queerness there is in some of the Qurʾānic narrative and the way that it actually subverts aspects of [expected gender norms in] the way it tells stories.

Sometimes there is a germ of queerness in the Qurʾān itself that people don't pick up on. I think Ibn ʿArabī is probably one of those who was able to do that. I guess you've anticipated my much more modern question. Not that I'm fascinated by modern issues, but just to be fair to our audience, and probably students who might be very curious to think, well, since this is what you're suggesting about Ibn ʿArabī's decentring of gender and making it into much more of a fluid process of combinations and permutations, as particularly comes out of your fourth move where the rest of us are just the combination of everything, you know, beyond the pairings that were in the moves 1, 2 and 3. So that would allow room for a lot of the issues to do with gender now, particularly thinking about the LGBTQ+ issues. If a student were to ask you about that, would you say that there is space in Ibn ʿArabī's thinking for that kind of diversity, precisely because he sees things as so fluid?

Sa'diyya Shaikh: Absolutely. I agree completely. I think that, really, it's Ibn ʿArabī's mode of engaging the tradition and engaging the texts. [He has] this capacity to see multiplicity and not reify the divine or the human in any one mode of being. To think about complexity, about how human beings embody the variety of divine attributes in all kinds of ways, opens up a genuine and innate fluidity. Fluidity is his mode of engagement, and fluidity is what queer theory is asking us to be thinking with. So, in some sense, thinking with Ibn ʿArabī is thinking with fluidity. And so I think that it's an incredibly rich space.

One of the critiques that I received from my book – and completely legitimately so – was that I focused a lot on heterosexuality, and really did not expand the ideas around fluidity to think through questions of sexual diversity. And I think that's an area that's ripe for development. In fact, it's something that I'm hoping to work on. One of the reasons, of course, is that I was working so strongly with the Adam and Eve narrative – I was trying to unsay some of the ways in which the dominant heterosexual norms were being fixed by other ways of reading – that I actually didn't pay enough attention at the time, and it was an absence and a lack in terms of my own outlook.

Ibn ʿArabī's sexuality is really interesting. He has some of the most sublime understandings of a heterosexual union, stating that the most profound sages and those people who are deeply accomplished spiritually appreciate that sexual union is the way in which human beings in this life experience an annihilation of ego, using the word *fanāʾ*. He says that, in this life, the most complete *fanāʾ* – and as we know in Sufi terms, or for those of you who don't know, *fanāʾ* is when you lose yourself to the Divine in an experience where your ego dissolves. That experience of annihilation of the ego, of the self, is normally seen as part of a spiritual path where a person might undergo that state of ego-dissolution so that they are witnessing God in an unmediated way, without the obstruction of the ego, and where the spirit is in communion with the Divine. It's a sign of spiritual accomplishment – or, I suppose, perhaps not an accomplishment, but a grace, an enormous divine grace. And people yearn for the experience of *fanāʾ*, and so he actually says that orgasm is the one time that human beings experience *fanāʾ* in this life, because your ego – the egos of the two human beings – dissolve so that you experience the sense of oneness, providing a taste of what is to come in the next life. So, sex is really cool because it actually gives you a taste of what you will experience in the next life if you're a good soul, which of course is a beautiful way of sacralising sexuality.

So he says that some people say sex is animalistic (*ḥayawānī*) not understanding that, actually, *ḥayawān* comes from the word *ḥayy*, which is life, and, he asks us, 'What is more noble than life?' He reconfigures ways in which embodiment is rendered as the lesser principle in binary philosophical schemes and instead reframes embodiment as a deeply alive, vibrant, spiritually important way of being in the world.

We think about embodiment or the 'bodily turn', in contemporary theoretical paradigms, as a way of redressing an entire history of hierarchical binaries that devalued the body. In reality, an affirmative approach to embodiment has [already] characterised some significant parts of the Muslim tradition, in the works of Ibn ʿArabī and other Muslim thinkers, where embodiment was holistically and integrally seen as deeply inspirited. And also, when focusing on some of Ibn ʿArabī's discussions – and a lot of it is about men and women and this correspondence of Adam and Eve, so it is quite a heterosexual unit – every now and then you find these little things that he says that disrupts heterosexism, that he doesn't elaborate on, [yet] I think [they] are ripe for exploration.

For example, he says you only encounter the kind of annihilation through sexual intimacy, [through] a deep ontological oneness with somebody who is like you:[232] your partner, your *zawj* (spouse), or your slave girl (*jāriya*), or your slave boy (*ghulām*). So here he mentions a wife, or a man's slave girl, *jāriya*, or a *ghulām*, which is a slave boy. And I am in no way giving a nod of approval to slavery, but at the same time, one cannot be anachronistic. In those spaces, and in those times, 'those that your right hand possessed' were people that you had sexual relationships with. Unless you're suddenly going to think that Ibn ʿArabī is speaking to women in this instance and saying they could have sex with their slave men, and we all know that in Islamic law, despite some early contestations, women were not having sex with their male slaves. This reference to different kinds of sexual partners appears to be addressed to men, and in this context, he's actually saying that correspondence, that notion of totally becoming one, can also happen during sex with a *ghulām*, meaning with a male slave.

Now, on the one hand, from our current location, one has profound reservations about premodern normative categories of who sexual relationships happen with, and not just deep reservations, but from our perspective, a profound moral rejection of certain ways of thinking around slaves' sexual availability, and we have a deep sense of repulsion when thinking about sex with younger people. All of that aside, I'm simply saying that what he does in that moment, within the sexual norms of that society, is [to] speak about forms of sexuality that are not only heterosexual. And I think it's open to be thought about in both critical and constructive ways.

And the way I read in Ibn ʿArabī [reflects] my mode of reading, [which] is never just to valorise any one thinker. As much as I adore Ibn ʿArabī, I think he is like every other human being, and like you and me, subject to our time, our context, our space, our assumptions. At moments we might each meet rich moments of transcendence, but we are still very much embodied, we are very much historical, we are very much contextual. For example, in one hundred years, people are likely going to look back and say, look at those moronic meat eaters, you know; look at those people who have absolutely no justice towards the earth, and the planet they were living on, and many of us simply don't see that as an ethical impulse at this point. This is not me making excuses for slavery or anything else. [I am] simply [saying], we need to understand social context and human beings as being the products of history and the social context, even as some of them in specific moments are able to transcend them and speak to us in very different ways.

[232] Shaikh, *Sufi Narratives*, 185–7.

Karen Bauer: Sa'diyya, sometimes those readings can be anachronistic as you hinted, and I really appreciate your historical accuracy, and your willingness to be with the text for what it was actually saying. Did you want to say anything else about that for today's world, about today's interpretations of that verse? Do you want to say anything else about either the ontological pairing or connection and interiority, or even about the way that it's being read these days as an anti-hierarchical verse, or as a verse that justifies social egalitarianism?

Sa'diyya Shaikh: So I think this verse is exquisite. It's one of those verses in the Qur'ān that is so appealing because it speaks about intimacy, and our ontological intimacy with one another, and that in fact we are – we come from – one, we are of one, we are to recognise the oneness that we have with one another. So the idea of this kind of ontological intimacy – this notion that we come from one, that we are to therefore petition through this oneness – is about a certain mode of engaging the full recognition of the humanity of others. And I think that's incredibly important in a time where it's not just men and women [who] are not recognising one another. We are living in a context where human beings are just so deeply divided on every axis – whether you are talking about race, whether you are talking about sexuality, gender, you're talking about a world that is still very much defined by all kinds of broader global politics that are deeply othering of human beings. So I think that, indeed, this verse is a very compelling one and [it] urges us to recognise the full humanity of every human life.

amina wadud

amina wadud centres her interpretation of Q. 4:1 on her 'tawhidic paradigm', by which she means that all humans are created equal, and are considered to be absolutely equal. For her, this is a theology of social justice, in which no human can raise him or herself up above another in any kind of hierarchical sense. She also incorporates LGBTQI individuals into her interpretation, saying that every human being has elements of the masculine and the feminine in themselves, so the pairing referred to in the Qur'ān may be understood as not only between a man and a woman but between individuals.

Karen Bauer: In your book *Qur'ān and Woman*, you began with this verse and a discussion of the single soul and its mate (*zawj*: one of a pair, or mate) as an example of gender egalitarianism, with each *zawj* as inherently equal. Is this the kind of verse that would act as a proof-text for your position on religious authority: the equal ability of women and men to act as interpreters of the Qur'ān, prayer leaders, or other positions of religious authority?

amina wadud: Thank you very much for the question, and I had to think about how to respond to this, because the answer is that this is not a text that, necessarily, I would use. Instead, it is a theology that I surmise from the Qur'ān under what I would call the tawhidic paradigm. It relates to this, in that the beginning of understanding is to understand the distinctive nature of the divine reality, Allāh. And that reality according to the Qur'ān, which says *there is nothing like him* (*laysa ka-mithlihi shay'*) [Q. 42:11], is not like things, *shay'*. But *wa-min kulli shay'in, khalaqnā zawjayn* [Q. 51:49], from all things (*shay'*), we created the pair, meaning that duality is a feature of the created world. The conclusion I draw from that is that the nature of Allāh transcends, even though we all have an intimate relationship with Him, but transcends gender. Allāh is neither male nor female, and the reason that that understanding began to have an impact on my relationship to questions of authority and to the issue, for instance, of the issue of women as prayer leaders, is because I also encoded that theology into a rubric of social justice, that says that if you believe in the one God, and that God is *akbar*, or the greatest, then no human being can be above another human being, especially for reasons as arbitrary as gender, or race, or class, or even religion. Rather, human beings act in a relationship of horizontal reciprocity, with Allāh keeping them from what, [in the case of] Shaytan, [He] calls *istikbār* [arrogance],[233] of being superior to another. It allows, therefore, for an exchange, especially in terms of the duties, that is the embodiment of acts, in the context of doing good, it allows an exchange of those positions, so there is no natural hegemony or authority.

Once I understood this for myself, where I could in fact do performances with confidence that I was not in fact defying my 'role' as a woman, then it was also possible for me to accept to perform as the imam of *ṣalāt* (prayer). Before that time, I may have had an inclination, but I didn't understand what it meant in terms of a grounding theologically. Once I had grounded theologically, then it means this: no person's opinion is better than another person's opinion, except in terms of the evidence that they bring forth to their truth-plane. So this is what we understood as a part of the Islamic intellectual tradition all along. There is no fixed answer, and just because you have a beard doesn't mean your answer has to be better, so you're naturally an authority, so everyone should obey you. But, rather, what is the evidentiary basis that you bring? And if your evidentiary base is insufficient, especially juxtaposed to someone else, then that means that that person has

[233] In the Qur'ān, it is Satan who refuses and holds himself above Adam (*abā wa'stakbara*) (Q. 2:34).

authority. And that person could be the trash collector on your street; you know, a blue-collar worker. So to deconstruct the notion of authority for me was only possible when you move toward what I call a democratisation of authority, and again that was brought out of the lived realities, and that is that people are not given the opportunity to speak with regard to laws that are encoded in different countries, supposedly in the name of Islam, but actually in the name of an interpretation of Islam, and those interpretations are predominantly hegemonic and patriarchal.

Karen Bauer: I am interested in the tawhidic paradigm, in terms of no human being being above another human being. In the Qurʾān, from what I understand, and you can please correct me if I am wrong, there is a notion of *faḍl*, which is that *We have distinguished some of you over others* [Q. 4:32], and even some prophets over other prophets [Q. 2:253]. I am wondering how that relates to your tawhidic paradigm. Maybe Feras wants to give some other examples.

Feras Hamza: No, I think I would just value amina's thoughts on this. Because I can see how you can understand these tensions as productive tensions, which is a really valuable thought, but there is a sense in which you talk about contingency, but you talk about agency as well. It is contingent that we are born male and female, that is one of those contingencies of life, but then it sounds like you are being much more agentic towards this assumption of a role. You are saying that we are born male and female and it shouldn't really matter, but then you somehow make it matter, by your subversion of the idea that males should be the authoritative voices, subverting the idea by saying that women should also have a voice. You act as a woman in a social-historical place; after all, your very work, all of it, has meaning precisely because you have gone through this process. You understand these texts, you've been able to bring new light to understand them. So the tension between contingency and agency is very interesting for me here. But I'll let you perhaps respond to Karen's question about the *tafāḍul* (distinction) in creation, that is almost a part of the fabric, I mean that is the point, the point is that we kind of have to endure a kind of creational distinction (*tafāḍul*) until we get to the goal, which is the next life, the *ḥayawān* [cf. Q. 29:64]; the true life.

amina wadud: Yes, I do have a small caveat before I get to the main point, which is that not everyone born in a male or female body ends their life as a male or a female according to their birth. I am a cis-gender female, I was born in a female body, and I am okay with that, but I have many friends, and people whom I work with and people whom I've tried to work for, who are not – they are trans, and it is important for me to just say that.

With regard to *faḍl*, I have spent some time on this as well, because *faḍl* in the way it is used in the Qur'ān is something that is granted from a transcendent location into a concrete, or earthly, or into the known, seen world, and as such *faḍl* cannot be encapsulated into a whole class of people – gender, race, etcetera. And so when the Qur'ān even says *with what God has distinguished the one over the other* (*bi-mā faḍḍala baʿḍahum ʿalā baʿḍin*), the *baʿḍ* – some of them – already lets you know that it is a kind of ambiguous category, and the ambiguity of the category is not something that someone can take on with regard to themselves as an individual, or with regard to a particular classification, like men are superior. It is itself ambiguous enough that when you take it on in that way, you defy the actual or the literal articulation of the Qur'ān. So I like that point about it, but what you find is that over time you have no way to earn, or even to determine what is *tafāḍul*.[234] And so because you cannot, and everywhere that the Qur'ān uses it, it is used as a thing that comes from Allāh to humankind or to the creation, it means that in the process of ethical human development the characteristic of humility defies our taking it on or presuming it belongs to us. And once you take it on, you are on that slippery slope, because remember, once again, Iblīs was created at a certain stage, and yet determined that he was better, and as a consequence the whole movement of oppression or *ẓulm* came into the earth. So I don't think that *faḍl* can be made into something so specific that any specific group of persons can take it on and say, 'That means us'.

Karen Bauer: You've said – and you alluded to this a moment ago –that male and female are 'complementary and contingent equals',[235] and I was wondering what that means, and what are the implications for people who are LGBTQI, non-binary, or cis-gender and heterosexual the way we are?

amina wadud: I have come to abhor the term 'complementary'. Is that going to help? Let's just start from there? The only reason why, is because when we started working on Musawah,[236] which is a term that means reciprocal equality, the best answer we got from well-meaning benevolent patriarchal people was, 'yes, women are complementary'. If a man is wearing an Armani suit, and he is wearing a handkerchief and a tie that complements his suit, he is by no means fully dressed, with just a handkerchief and a tie. And because of that, I don't feel that the term 'complementary' is adequate to express and also to dismantle the persistence of hegemony and arrive at equality and

234 Cf. the discussion of *faḍl* in Chapter 3 (p. 317), in which we argue that God grants *faḍl* in the next life on the basis of people's deeds.

235 wadud, *Inside the Gender Jihad*, 30.

236 Musawah is an organisation that works for equality in Muslim family laws. See https://www.musawah.org/

reciprocity in the way in which I now conceive of it. So when I used it earlier it is because fundamentally I believe that the creation is full of relationships, and relationships between people is the most important relationship that we have on this earth. Even someone [who] is an introvert relies on some kind of relationship; it just may be on terms that are very different from someone who is, say, a very social extrovert. But since relationships are important, then the fundamental relationship, that is the relationship of one human being to one other human being, is constantly being in practice with regard to how we resolve our desires for another, and their ability to fulfil our desires. It starts off as a child, and with the parents, and how much can the parents fulfil everything that this child desires, but also in the ways in which we are also in intimate relationships with *mawaddatan wa-raḥma*, or love and mercy [cf. Q. 30:21], with a partner; it comes into marriage partnerships – how do those work? When we cast marriage partnerships as if they are closed categories – one man and one woman, well, let's be honest, in terms of the Qurʾān, one man and at least the possibility of more than one woman – when we cast them as only that, we forget to require of them some working at how that relationship will go. So when we start to address the lived realities of non-binary people or gender non-conforming people in the full spectrum of LGBTQI, it teaches us something about the nature of human relations that we had neglected because of the presumption that there is an organic and natural relationship between male and female. It isn't natural, it isn't organic. It is work. So for me, when the Prophet, upon him be peace, says that marriage is half of faith, I say, that is half of what you have to work on in order to complete your faith. I don't take it for granted that just because there is a relationship between a man and a woman all the terms of that relationship work, necessarily, or in some set and rigid formula. And, again, this is because of working with gender non-binary people.

It even causes me to return to the use of the word *zawj* in the passage we were talking about before. *Created you from a single soul, and from it created its mate* (*zawj*). I decided to do an investigation of the word *zawj* across the Qurʾān, because I wanted to see whether or not its usage fell always into some type of formulaic, one on top, one on the bottom, one in charge kind of thing, and actually there are several constructs of the pair, because they are the mirror images, they are the opposites, and they are the complements. All of these fit into the notion of 'pair'. And yet the features of interrelationship mean we go through all three. Sometimes we're opposites, sometimes we're complements, and sometimes we're mirrors. I think to return to the idea of humanity as a dynamic, and that each of us have this living potential, means that our nature has to be re-encoded into something other than just a separate identity, and for that I return to the words 'masculine' and 'feminine', as opposed to 'male' and 'female', because each of us is made up of masculine, that is, active and outward-pointing characteristics, and feminine, that is receptive and yielding. We have these in our one composite, and accepting and understanding how these work in tandem within ourselves is another aspect of how I use the word tawhid today, because the tawhidic paradigm also talks about the perfection, the *insān al-kāmil*,[237] the perfection of the relationship between our own parts, so that they work in tandem with each other.

What complicates it for me, and it is a beautiful type of complication, is that when we have a relationship with another person – that is a single body, obviously there are some conjoined twins, but usually a single body – they also combine the masculine and feminine within themselves, and our masculine and feminine [aspects] are always in conversations and complementations with the masculine and feminine in the other body. And I have found that sometimes people have overt kinds of attraction, say in the normative heterosexual context, and yet there are parts of them that are in discord with the other person. It is almost as if the masculine doesn't get along with the masculine of this person, but because she is a female, we forget she has [a masculine part], or the feminine doesn't get along with the feminine part, but because he's male, we forget he has [a feminine part], and as such we don't understand. There is constant give and take, and constant assertion and reception, and we ourselves are a composite of these two aspects or elements.

[237] This is the topic of copious discussion in Sufi work. For an overview, see R. Arnaldez, 'al-Insān al-Kāmil', *EI*^{2}, III, 1239–41; Addas, *Quest for the Red Sulphur*, esp. 276–85; Chittick, *The Sufi Path of Knowledge*, *passim*.

إِذْ قَالَتِ ٱمْرَأَتُ عِمْرَٰنَ رَبِّ إِنِّى نَذَرْتُ لَكَ مَا فِى بَطْنِى مُحَرَّرًا فَتَقَبَّلْ مِنِّىٓ
إِنَّكَ أَنتَ ٱلسَّمِيعُ ٱلْعَلِيمُ ۝ فَلَمَّا وَضَعَتْهَا قَالَتْ رَبِّ إِنِّى وَضَعْتُهَآ أُنثَىٰ
وَٱللَّهُ أَعْلَمُ بِمَا وَضَعَتْ وَلَيْسَ ٱلذَّكَرُ كَٱلْأُنثَىٰ وَإِنِّى سَمَّيْتُهَا مَرْيَمَ وَإِنِّىٓ أُعِيذُهَا
بِكَ وَذُرِّيَّتَهَا مِنَ ٱلشَّيْطَٰنِ ٱلرَّجِيمِ

2 Mary
(Q. 3:35–6)

When the wife of ʿImrān said, 'My Lord, I vow[1] *to You what is in my belly, in consecration. Accept it from me; indeed, You are the Hearer and the Knower.'*

And when she bore her, she said, 'My Lord, I have borne her, a female child,' – and God knew better what she had borne – 'and the male is not as the female. I have named her Mary; I have entrusted the protection of her and her offspring to You against [the evil of] the accursed Satan.'

Idh qālat imraʾat ʿImrān rabbi innī nadhartu laka mā fī baṭnī muḥarraran fa-taqabbal minnī innaka antaʾl-samīʿ al-ʿalīm

Fa-lammā waḍaʿathā qālat rabbī innī waḍaʿtuhā unthā waʾllāhu aʿlamu bi-mā waḍaʿat wa-laysaʾl-dhakaru kaʾl-unthā wa-innī sammaytuhā Maryama wa-innī uʿīdhuhā bika wa-dhurriyatahā min al-shayṭān al-rajīm.

The Qurʾān, as is sufficiently recognised, generally adopts a fairly sparse approach to proper names, the stark exceptions being the names of prophets. However, one name in particular stands out, even among the exceptions, since it also happens to belong to a woman: Mary, mother of Jesus. Indeed, Mary is the only woman named by the Qurʾān. She appears throughout the text in some seventy places, most prominently in the *sūra* that bears her name, *Maryam* (Q. 19). Exemplary women are to be found in various passages across the chapters of the scripture: notably, the wife of Pharaoh in Q. 66:11 (and even here the *sūra* concludes with the mention of Mary, daughter of ʿImrān, Q. 66:12) and *a woman who rules over Sheba* (Q. 27:22–3). Other examples include the wives of the Prophet *in toto*, particularly in Q. 33:32, who are exemplary but under substantial scrutiny as the Qurʾānic narration unfolds. In sum, Mary is singular in receiving mention by name and also in being almost ubiquitously

[1] We are using 'vow' in the archaic sense, with a direct object, which in this context (and as is frequently the case with archaic English) fits the Arabic perfectly, at least in terms of the commentators' periphrastic and paraphrastic exegetical grammatical discussions.

mentioned whenever Jesus is mentioned (sc. ʿĪsā ibn Maryam), whose miracles alone stand out as nothing short of divine[2] (and whose reception in the Christian tradition coalesces into divinity in itself). But, equally, her own status in the Qurʾān suggests a spiritual ranking that displaces the social hierarchy of men over women, and it has given rise to debates on whether she is a prophet.[3] Being assigned an entire *sūra* in the Qurʾān by name, as mostly only male prophets are, invites a closer look at her role and function in the spiritual exemplification pursued by the major religious characters of the sacred text.[4]

[2] See, for instance, the long passage in Q. 5:110, describing the miracles given by God to Jesus, who is almost always referred to as 'Jesus, son of Mary'.

[3] She is known in the Qurʾān as a 'truthful woman' (*ṣiddīqa*); Q. 5:75: *The Messiah, son of Mary, was but a messenger; other messengers before him passed away. His mother was a truthful woman*. The epithet 'truthful' is used of three major prophets in the Qurʾān: Abraham (Q. 19:41), Idrīs (or Enoch, Q. 19:56) and Joseph (Q. 12:46). Moreover, and as the medieval commentators noted, Mary is mentioned in *sūrat al-Anbiyāʾ* (Q. 21), the chapter that enumerates the most prominent prophets in the following sequence: Moses, Aaron, Abraham, Lot, Isaac, Jacob, Noah, David, Solomon, Job, Ishmael, Enoch, Jonah, Zachariah, John, Mary 'and her son' (Q. 21:91). Indeed, on the whole, they made a point of insisting that she was not a prophet, despite this honourable mention (see Qurṭubī, *al-Jāmiʿ li-aḥkām al-Qurʾān*, s.v. Q. 21:91). But a few commentators did believe that she was a prophet. See discussion of this in Jane Smith and Yvonne Haddad, 'The Virgin Mary in Islamic Tradition and Commentary', *Muslim World* 79.3–4 (1989), 161–87, esp. 177ff.; Fierro, 'Women as Prophets in Islam'; Stowasser, *Women in the Qur'an, Traditions, and Interpretation*, 77.

[4] For fuller discussions of Mary in the Qurʾān and Islamic literature, see, in addition to the sources cited above, Muhammad Abdel Haleem, '*Sūrat Maryam* (Q. 19): Comforting Muḥammad', *Journal of Qur'anic Studies* 22.2 (2020), 60–85; Leyla Ozgur Alhassen, 'A Structural Analysis of *Sūrat Maryam*, Verses 1–58', *Journal of Qur'anic Studies* 18.1 (2016), 92–116; Kecia Ali, 'Destabilizing Gender'; Helen Blatherwick, 'Textual Silences and Literary Choices in al-Kisāʾī's Account of the Annunciation and the Birth of Jesus', *Arabica* 66.1–2 (2019), 1–42; Aisha Geissinger, 'Mary in the Qurʾān: Rereading Subversive Births' in *Sacred Tropes: Tanakh, New Testament, and Qur'an as Literature and Culture*, ed. Roberta Sterman Sabbath (Leiden, Brill, 2009), 379–92; Angelika Neuwirth, 'Imagining Mary, Disputing Jesus: Reading *Sūrat Maryam* (Q. 19) and Related Meccan Texts in the Context of the Qurʾānic Communication Process' in *Scripture, Poetry, and the Making of a Community: Reading the Qur'an as a Literary Text* (Oxford, Oxford University Press in association with the Institute of Ismaili Studies, 2014), 328–58: eadem, 'Mary and Jesus: Counterbalancing the Biblical Patriarchs. A Re-reading of *Sūrat Maryam* (Q. 19) in *Sūrat Āl ʿImrān* (Q. 3)' in *Scripture, Poetry, and the Making of a Community*, 359–84; Stowasser, *Women in the Qur'an, Traditions and Interpretations* (ch. 7: 'The Chapter of Mary'), 67–82; Shawkat Toorawa, '*Sūrat Maryam* (Q. 19): Lexicon, Lexical Echoes, English Translation', *Journal of Qur'anic Studies* 13.1 (2011), 25–78. Zeki Saritoprak, 'Mary in Islam', *Oxford Bibliographies* (2015), provides the following additional references to the topic: Tim Winter, 'Mary in Islam' in *Mary: The Complete Resource*, ed. Sara Jane Boss (Oxford, Oxford University Press, 2007), 479–502; Riyad Abu Wandi and Yusuf Qazma Khuri, *ʿĪsā wa Maryam fī'l-Qurʾān wa'l-tafāsīr* (Amman, Dar al-Shurūq, 1996), which surveys Qurʾānic verses relating to Jesus and Mary across classical and modern exegetical work; John Kaltner, 'Mary' in *Ishmael Instructs Isaac: An Introduction to the Qur'an for Bible Readers* (Collegeville, MN, Liturgical Press, 1999), 207–39, provides a comparative look at the accounts of Mary in the Qurʾān and in the Gospels.

We have chosen the preamble to her exemplary life as touched upon in the Qur'ān, namely, the moment of her birth to the wife of ʿImrān, Ḥanna (Anne), in Q. 3:35–6. *Sūrat Āl ʿImrān* (Q. 3) begins with mention of 'Divine oneness' at v. 2,[5] while v. 3 describes the revelation of the Qur'ān, the Torah and the Gospels; indeed, the relationship between these prior scriptures and the Qur'ān, and the relationship among their respective communities of believers are, in our view, the major themes in this *sūra*.[6] Thus it is not surprising that Mary, a revered figure in both Christianity and Islam, is first situated within *sūrat Āl ʿImrān* in terms of her sacred lineage and only subsequently in terms of her own spiritual journey. Verses 33–4 mention Adam, Noah, the descendants of Abraham and the descendants of ʿImrān as *elected* [. . .] *above all worlds, offspring each of the other*. These verses establish a physical lineage for prophecy, a part of which is then elaborated in vv. 35–6. Verse 35 describes the moment that the wife of ʿImrān vows her unborn child to God and humbly asks Him to accept this consecration. In v. 36, she seems to express surprise at having had a female child, tells God that she has named her Mary (Maryam), and entrusts Mary and her offspring to God; meanwhile, the reader is assured that God knew what she had borne. The following verses describe how Mary is 'received' (*taqabbalahā*) by God, 'tended to' (*anbatahā*) by Him and then entrusted to the care of Zachariah. Their interaction is described, and Mary is said to be *chosen above the world's women* in v. 42. This is followed by the visitation of the angels in v. 45 and a description of Jesus at v. 46ff. The reader is assured that this is the true version of the story in v. 60, and the People of the Book are enjoined to hear and recognise this truth in v. 64ff.[7]

From among all of the passages that pertain to Mary in the Qur'ān, we have chosen Q. 3:35–6 for three main reasons. The first is pragmatic, since the exegetical tradition recorded in formal commentaries (*tafsīr*) tends to be

[5] Neuwirth, 'Mary and Jesus', 361. Zahniser identifies God's oneness as the *sūra*'s main theme, but we would bear in mind that it is a theme precisely because it answers potential competition from Christian conceptions. A.H. Matthias Zahniser, 'The Word of God and the Apostleship of ʿĪsā: A Narrative Analysis of Āl ʿImrān (3): 33–62', *Journal of Semitic Studies* 37.1 (Spring 1991), 77–112.

[6] One of the main questions for modern scholars of this *sūra* is the extent to which the Qur'ān accepts previous scriptures. Zahniser ('The Word of God', 85), for instance, argues that the themes of the last two sections of the *sūra* are 'the rejection of the People of the Scriptures and the exhortation to those who believe to turn away from them'. However, cf. Neuwirth, who argues that part of the purpose of this *sūra* is to 'achieve a rapprochement with the Christians', whom she identifies as the Āl ʿImrān of the *sūra*. Neuwirth, 'Mary and Jesus', 359.

[7] Both Zahniser and Neuwirth have published on the structure of *sūrat Āl ʿImrān*. Zahniser divides it into an introduction at vv. 1–32, a narrative section on the family of ʿImrān at vv. 33–62, 'a section in which the phrase "people of the book" is prominent' at vv. 63–99, and, finally, a section on the believers themselves at vv. 100–199. Zahniser, 'The Word of God', 84.

denser in the first parts of the revelation as it is organised, that is from *sūrat al-Baqara* (Q. 2) to about *sūrat al-Kahf* (Q. 18), whereafter, for the most part, the commentators begin to refer the reader to discussions already made and concluded in the earlier parts of their commentaries. In this sense, the final organisation of the order of the Qurʾānic verses into its current form is the order which determines the priorities of exegesis for the authors of our commentaries, with not much regard for the order in which those verses or passages were originally recited by Muḥammad. And this is to be expected, since the Qurʾānic verses were believed to have been finally organised by divine decree, mediated by Gabriel in specific instructions to the Prophet about where verses would finally sit. So, for the authors of *tafsīr*, there are theological premises to be inferred and discovered from the final order of Qurʾānic verses and accordingly they concentrate their exegetical expertise on the larger and longer chapters of the Qurʾān, Q. 1 to Q. 18; hence we focus on the verses which introduce Mary's story in *sūrat Āl ʿImrān* (Q. 3).

A second reason for including these verses is that Ḥanna, Mary's mother, prefigures Mary to some degree, and not just as her progenitor. The entire exchange between a female voice and the Divine in Q. 3:35 breaks with the traditionally male-dominated narrative exchange in which God speaks to His prophets and they speak to Him. Mary enjoys an equally significant moment of narrative focus at the point of her conception of Jesus after the anxiety-ridden visit to her of the angel in Q. 19:16ff.

Finally, it is in this passage that the somewhat apostrophic remark *and the male is not as the female* appears. At first glance, the statement might seem not atypical of a narrative that is largely addressed, at least historically, to a male recipient (the Prophet) and overtly to a largely male audience. Significant exceptions should not be overlooked, particularly when the wives of the Prophet are addressed directly (Q. 33:30–32), or when women are addressed in the third person as believing women (*muʾmināt*) (Q. 33:35 *et passim*). Nevertheless, the statement *and the male is not as the female* is ambiguous and may be read as assuming the superiority of one over the other, though it is not clear which of the two is superior. The commentators are aware of this, as we shall see, especially given that the remark comes immediately after Mary's mother's anticipation of a gift from God.

The gendered norms that inform the exegetes' understanding of the Qurʾānic story of Mary's birth emerge at two points in particular. The first is when Ḥanna vows her child to God, and the second is when she says, '*My Lord, I have borne her, a female child*' and '*the male is not as the female*'. Regarding the first, the exegetes explain that when Ḥanna vowed her offspring to God, she was expecting a male child because the people of that time did not accept that females could be consecrated for service in the temple. The most common reason the exegetes give for not accepting females is the impurity that results from vaginal bleeding, whether during menstruation or postpartum. But some also base their explanations on nature or on social expectations: men are stronger for such service, women are a source of shame because of the social consequences of any bodily 'exposure' (*ʿawra*),[8] and service in the temple entailed mingling with men, which was more likely to lead to censure or libel for a woman than for a man.

The idea that only male children could be consecrated for temple service is directly related to the exegetes' explanations of Ḥanna's statements that *'I have borne her, a female child'* and *'the male is not as the female'*. The exegetes tell us that Ḥanna could not have been informing God; as a righteous woman, she would have known that God was aware of her child's sex. Instead, they explain that because of her vow, Ḥanna was expecting a male child: she could not help but exclaim in surprise when she gave birth to a female instead, for she believed that this female would not be able to serve in the temple and thus her vow would be broken. For the exegetes, this exclamation is emotionally laden. They variously describe it as an expression of distress, sadness, grief, embarrassment or shame. Drawing on a *ḥadīth*, Shīʿī sources say that she had expected to bear a messenger (*rasūl*), which explains her dismay, because women cannot be messengers.

There is merit to the commentators' view that female children could not be consecrated for service in the temple. In Jewish law, vaginal bleeding was considered an impurity that might pollute anyone who, for instance, touched the bleeding woman or sat in the seat where she had sat; women were not allowed in the temple while menstruating.[9] Thus one should not discount the possibility that the Islamic exegetical tradition contains factual information that is helpful for explaining the Qurʾān.[10]

Yet we cannot help but note that the commentators also seem to be influenced, at least to some extent, by their own expectations and gendered presuppositions. Many of the emotions that they attribute to Ḥanna imply a deficiency in Ḥanna's piety, in that her feelings of dismay, disappointment, shame or sadness imply a lack of trust in God's plan. Only three commentators (Rāzī, Qurṭubī and Faḍl Allāh) assert that Ḥanna's vow is in itself proof of her advanced spiritual status, for, to paraphrase Qurṭubī, having children

[8] On this term, see below, 'Key terms'.

[9] For a simple overview of impurity laws in Judaism, see Tirzah Meacham, 'Female Purity (*Niddah*)', *Jewish Women: A Comprehensive Historical Encyclopedia*, Jewish Women's Archive, accessed 23 August 2020, https://jwa.org/encyclopedia/article/female-purity-niddah.

[10] On this see Hamza, 'Unlocking the Historical Qurʾān'.

entails intimacy, and despite her desperate longing for a child, Ḥanna decided to give up her share in that intimacy, dedicating it instead to God. Rāzī, meanwhile, draws a comparison between Ḥanna and Abraham, in that she is inspired by God to give up her child for His sake. For Rāzī, Ḥanna's words are an apology to God for being unable to fulfil her vow. For Qurṭubī, these words are a magnification of Him, for she trusts in His plan for her.

In our view, given the context, Ḥanna's exclamation *'My Lord, I have borne her, a female child'* could certainly indicate surprise or shock; but there is no Qurʾānic evidence that she was dismayed at, or ashamed of, having a daughter rather than a son, or that she doubts that God will accept her vow.[11] Indeed, she simply says to God that she has commended Mary and her offspring to His care, to which God has an entirely favourable response: *so Thereupon her Lord (r-b-b) received her most graciously* (*fa-taqabbalahā rabbuhā bi-qabūlin ḥasanin*) (Q. 3:37). The positivity of God's acceptance might be intended as a subtle rebuke against the Jewish practice of not allowing females to be consecrated in the temple.[12]

Key terms

The verses under consideration here do not contain any terms that are particularly ambiguous; but the following terms, which appear in the exegeses of the verses, merit further explanation.

ʿAwra: exposure, something which is to be concealed or protected. In effect, this potential for exposure and the consequences of such exposure means that in post-Qurʾānic writings this term denotes 'shame' or something 'shameful'. For a more detailed explanation of the term, see Chapter 4, 'Key terms': *ʿawra*.

[11] For Neuwirth, this is a strikingly woman-centred telling of the story, with language related to Ḥanna's physical state (e.g. *I have borne*), and naming her daughter and giving her to the temple herself, with 'the role of the father being sidelined in the story'. In her view, Ḥanna is 'determined to fulfil her vow' despite not having had a son. Neuwirth, 'Mary and Jesus', 373.

[12] The question of whether a menstruating woman could enter or have access to a mosque does not seem to have been of major concern to formal legal discourse in Muslim jurisprudence. There are, of course, conflicting opinions on whether the relevant reports from the Prophet provide a categorical ruling on this, with some schools of law prohibiting it while others permit it if there is a necessity. The historical and contemporary attitudes towards such questions are more likely to reflect interpretations of social power structures and gender relations in a given community. A fascinating study of this issue and the history of women's 'access' to the mosque is Marion Holmes Katz's *Women in the Mosque: A History of Legal Thought and Social Practice* (New York, Columbia University Press, 2014); on this point specifically, also eadem, *Prayer in Islamic Thought and Practice* (Cambridge, Cambridge University Press, 2013), esp. 177ff.

Adhan: hurt or impurity. While in Q. 2:222 the term *adhan* must mean 'hurt', for the exegetes it probably means 'impurity'. This is a secondary meaning of the term, but it alone explains why females were not allowed to serve in the temples in accordance with Jewish law. Many Muslim exegetes and jurists also connected vaginal blood with impurity, and forbade menstruating or postpartum women from praying or handling the Qur'ān.[13]

Muqātil

In Muqātil's commentary, key is the importance of fleshing out the narrative for the purpose of storytelling (*qaṣaṣ*), with background context drawn from his familiarity with Biblical materials (*isrā'īliyyāt*). Background contextual details, which often provide the later commentaries with their own narrative material, are very important to Muqātil's storytelling style of exegesis. He is also keen to demonstrate his knowledge of the religious structure of the Judaic context, making references to where the scribes sat to study the Torah, distinguishing between the *qurrā'* and the *aḥbār*, and relating the latter to the kingly line of the prophet David. The ensuing dispute over guardianship of Mary also takes the form of a narrative reconstructed and recounted between the reciters and Zachariah. Muqātil further demonstrates his narrational expertise by linking the above passage to subsequent verses that conclude the dispute over her guardianship, namely verses 37 and 44. Even when he refers to these other verses, they serve the priority of narrating the overall event coherently. For example, he breaks up the single verse 44 into three separate units in order to gloss its separate parts in various ways, thereby narratively connecting it to the rest of Mary's story.

It is significant that, within the story as told by Muqātil, both Ḥanna and 'Imrān are concerned that only male children could be offered in consecration to God, for girls at that time were considered *'awra*, or something shameful, to be hidden away. In the Qur'ānic telling, God accepts Ḥanna's consecration of the female child. Muqātil implies that this is a way of showing up the former practices.

When the wife of 'Imrān, son of Māthān, *said*, her name being Ḥanna daughter of Fāqūz, the mother of Mary, when she was with child: If God, mighty and majestic, should save me and I should give birth to what is in my belly, I shall assuredly make it consecrated (*muḥarraran*). The children of Māthān were of the progeny of the kings of the Children of Israel from the line of David (*'m*); one who is *muḥarrar* is one who neither labours for the things of this world nor marries, but labours for the Hereafter, cleaving to the prayer niche (*miḥrāb*) and worshipping God, mighty and majestic, in it.

[13] On the development of Islamic purity laws see Marion Katz, *Body of Text: The Emergence of the Sunni Law of Ritual Purity* (Albany, State University of New York Press, 2002).

In that epoch, only male children would be consecrated [for such service]. Her husband therefore said: Have you considered that what is in your belly might be a female child, and if the female child is a [potential] source of shame (*ʿawra*), what will you do? Ḥanna then replied, *'My Lord, I vow to You what is in my belly, in consecration. Accept it from me; indeed, You are the Hearer and the Knower'* of their petition (*duʿā'*), knowing of their vow (*nadhr*), that is, through His acceptance of, and responding to, their supplications.

And when she bore her, she said, 'My Lord, I have borne her, a female child,' – and God knew better what she had borne – 'and the male is not as the female', for the female is *ʿawra*; and here, there is an anteposition (*taqdīm*).[14] God, exalted be He, says to His Prophet (*ṣlʿm*) *and God knew better what she had borne*. Ḥanna then says, *'I have named her Mary'*, and such was [already] her name according to God, mighty and majestic. *'I have entrusted the protection of her and her offspring*, meaning Jesus, *to You against* [*the evil of*] *the accursed Satan'*, meaning the accursed one. God granted her that, and so no satan (*shayṭān*) came near her or her offspring. But Ḥanna feared that a female child would not be accepted as a consecration. So she wrapped her in cloths and placed her in the Holy House (*bayt al-maqdis*), by the prayer niche (*miḥrāb*) where the [scriptural] reciters (*qurrā'*) sat in study. The people then competed for her by drawing lots (*tasāhum*) since she was the daughter of their religious head (*imām*) and master (*sayyid*), and they were the scholars (*aḥbār*) from the progeny of Aaron, to see who among them would take her [into his guardianship]. Zachariah, who was the head of the religious scholars (*aḥbār*) said, 'I shall take her, since I am the most worthy among you for that, for her sister, the mother of John (Yaḥyā), is with me [as my wife].' The reciters (*qurrā'*) said, 'What if there be among the people one closer to her than you? For, if she were to be left to the one most worthy of her from among the people, she would be left to her mother – but she has already been consecrated. So, shall we draw lots for her and the one whose lot emerges, whoever that might be, shall be the most worthy of her?' Thus they drew lots, and God, mighty and majestic, said to Muḥammad (*ṣlʿm*) *and you were not present among them* [Q. 3:44], that is, with them, to witness them, *when they were casting their quills* [Q. 3:44], when they cast lots (*iqtirāʿ*) three times with their quills (*aqlām*), which they used for the writing down of the revelation (*waḥy*), to see which one of them would take charge (*kafala*) of her,

[14] The anteposition (*taqdīm*) is that the words *and God knew better what she had borne* intervene as a parenthetical statement between the two parts of Ḥanna's words, where one would expect the statement *and the male is not as the female* to have come immediately after *I have borne her, a female child*.

that is, which one would keep her to himself. Zachariah cast lots with them and won her. God, mighty and majestic, then said to Muḥammad (*ṣlʿm*), *and you were not present among them when they were casting their quills* [Q. 3:44], about Mary; and that is where He says, *and He made Zachariah her guardian* [Q. 3:37].[15]

Hūd

The commentary by this early Ibāḍī exegete is, as mostly is the case, not entirely distinguishable from other early commentaries where the main focus is on establishing the fuller details of the stories alluded to in the Qurʾān. That, in itself, is an important indication of the emerging traditionalist tendency in the maturing Ibāḍī community of the third/ninth century. Hūd's interpretation is very similar to that of Muqātil, including reference to the *ʿawra* of women and ʿImrān's shame and shock at his wife's consecrating a child whose sex was unknown, for fear that it might be a girl, and that the scholars in the temple drew lots for Mary with their quills. But, unlike Muqātil, Hūd names authorities for most of these interpretations. This does not indicate that Hūd relied on Muqātil, but rather that both relied on widely circulated stories; thus, in Hūd's interpretation, authorities recognised by the wider mainstream pre-classical Sunnī community appear frequently (Mujāhid and Ḥasan al-Baṣrī; though the latter is important in his own right as the teacher of the community's founder, Jābir b. Zayd). However, frequently also, an ambiguous 'some say' (*qāl baʿḍuhum*) is used, and even though this is common to the entire *tafsīr* tradition, its juxtaposition with recognised and named authorities in the case of an Ibāḍī commentary suggests a certain degree of dissimulation on the part of the exegetical tradition, as well as a positioning of itself as being as authoritative as the mainstream tradition.

Hūd differs from Muqātil in the reason he gives for the female not being consecrated to the temple: impurity (*adhan*), as discussed in the chapter introduction. Hūd also includes two further details that are not in Muqātil's commentary: that Mary grew without any breastfeeding from her mother or a wet nurse; and that children are jabbed in their side by a satan as they are born, which makes them cry out, but that Jesus was protected from that jab because he was Mary's son.

When the wife of ʿImrān said, 'My Lord, I vow to You what is in my belly, in consecration. Accept it from me; indeed, You are the Hearer and the Knower.' Mujāhid says, 'Consecrated' (*muḥarraran*) for the house of prayer (*masjid*), abiding [in service] in it. Al-Ḥasan says: This was given to her as inspiration (*ilhām*) until she came to know that it was pleasing to God, and so she made the vow and petitioned God to accept that from her. Some of them have said that the wife of ʿImrān had consecrated what was in her belly [in dedication] to

[15] Muqātil, *Tafsīr Muqātil*, s.v. Q. 3:35–6.

God. They used to consecrate male children, and the one consecrated would, upon being consecrated, abide in the house of prayer (*masjid*), not leaving it, remaining in it and sweeping its floor. It was not possible to do that with women because of the impurity that comes to her, by which is meant, menses (*ḥayḍ*).

His words *and when she bore her, she said, 'My Lord, I have borne her, a female child,' – and God knew better what she had borne* are also read in another way: 'and God knows better what I have borne'. In the case of those who read it with the *sukūn* (*waḍaʿat*), these would be God's [direct] words, whereas in the case of those who read it with *rafʿ*, they would be her [own direct] words. He said *and the male is not as the female*: Al-Kalbī related that the wife of ʿImrān had entered old age and was without child. She then conceived and dedicated what was in her belly as a consecration for the Holy House [in Jerusalem]. In that epoch, the only ones consecrated were male children, and so she made the consecration before knowing what it would be. Her husband therefore asked her: 'How dare you? What have you done? What if it is a female? You know fully well the shameful nature (*ʿawra*) of a woman. So what will you do?' She thus remained distressed at what her husband said to her until she gave birth and said, *'My Lord, I have borne her, a female child,' – and God knew better what she had borne – 'and the male is not as the female'.* She then wrapped her in a cloth and had her sent to the mosque, the mosque of the Holy House, leaving her in it, whereupon the rabbis (*aḥbār*), the descendants of Aaron, competed for [guardianship of] her.

Mujāhid said that when she entered into their presence, Zachariah, who at the time was the chief scholar (*ra's al-aḥbār*), said to them, 'I am the most worthy among you of [guardianship of] her. Her sister lives with me. So, leave her to me.' The scholars, however, said, 'If she were to be left to [the care of] the most worthy of her, she should surely be left to her mother who bore her. But, let us draw lots for her and she will belong [in guardianship] to the one whose lot (*sahm*) emerges.' They thus cast their lots for her with their quills, with which they used to write down the revelation. However, it was Zachariah who won the lot; so he kept her for himself and secured for her wet nurses. When she had grown to be a young woman, he built for her a niche in the mosque, placing the door for it in the middle [of the mosque] where no one could climb up to her except with a ladder, for he did not trust anyone regarding her, except himself.

Al-Ḥasan [al-Baṣrī] said that no wet nurses were [ever] brought for her and she never put her mouth on a breast. God made her grow without suckling. Al-Kalbī said that Zachariah's wife was also barren and in old age, with Zachariah also a very old man. It was then that Zachariah aspired to have a child. As for His words *and I have named her Mary; I have entrusted the protection of her and her offspring to You against [the evil of] the accursed Satan*, lest he lead her and them astray.

They mention that the Messenger of God (*ṣl'm*) said, 'Every son of Adam is jabbed in his side by Satan when his mother gives birth to him, except for Jesus son of Mary, whom he [Satan] went to jab but ended up jabbing the [protective] screen (*ḥijāb*)'.[16] Some say, 'You know the cry that the child makes when its mother gives birth to it? It is from that [jab].' They mention that one of them said, 'Every son of Adam has been jabbed in his side by Satan except for Jesus and his mother: a screen was struck between him and them both, so the jab hit the screen, and nothing penetrated it to them.'[17]

Qummī

Qummī's hermeneutical priority – namely, to uncover the truth of the imamate through his exegesis of the Qur'ān – can be anticipated in his brief gloss to the preceding verse [Q. 3:34] that speaks about God's choosing of the family of Abraham and the family of 'Imrān above all creatures. There, he cites a report from the imam al-Bāqir (*al-'ālim*) that the original revelation had included *Āl Muḥammad* ('the family of Muḥammad) after the words *Āl 'Imrān* ('the family of 'Imrān) in verse 34, but that 'they had dropped this out of the Book' (*asqaṭū Āl Muḥammad min al-kitāb*). In other words, for Qummī, the Book in its current form is incomplete, and even when the explicit mention of the rightful place of the imams and their authority is not to be found, their followers should trust in the veracity of their authority and their claims. Drawing analogously from the exegetical report that then follows concerning verses 35–6, Qummī subtly demonstrates that the followers of the imams should trust in the words of their imams, even when overtly the truth of those words may not be immediately perceptible to them, exactly as 'Imrān and his wife should have trusted in God's promise to them of a male child, a messenger (*rasūl*) who would be blessed and work miracles on the earth, when this did not transpire immediately in Mary, but in her son Jesus. According to Qummī, although 'Imrān had been promised a messenger (*rasūl*), a female could not be a messenger; for him, this explains Ḥanna's surprise and exclamation to God: *'My Lord, I have borne her, a female child'*.

The recognition of the potential incompleteness of the book in pre-Būyid exegetical traditions can also be seen in the works of the later classical Twelver Imāmī commentaries. As we shall see in Ṭabrisī's commentary on these passages, he readily acknowledges that Q. 3:34 included the mention of the family of the Prophet (*Āl Muḥammad*) when read by the 'people of that house' (*Āl al-bayt*).

[16] A version is found in Bukhārī, *Ṣaḥīḥ*, *Kitāb Bidā' al-khalq* (59), *Bāb ṣifāt Iblīs wa-junūdihi* (11), *ḥadīth* no. 95/3286.

[17] Hūd, *Tafsīr kitāb Allāh al-'azīz*, s.v. Q. 3:35–6.

When the wife of ʿImrān said, 'My Lord, I vow to You what is in my belly, in consecration. Accept it from me; indeed, You are the Hearer and the Knower.' For God, blessed and exalted, revealed to (*w-ḥ-y*) ʿImrān, 'I shall endow you with a male child, who will cure the blind and the leper, and give life to the dead by God's permission' [cf. Q. 3:49]. ʿImrān gave his wife this good news and [soon] afterwards she was with child, and said, *'My Lord, I vow to You what is in my belly, in consecration'* for the prayer niche (*miḥrāb*). It was their custom that when they made a vow, they would dedicate the child to the prayer niche.

And when she bore her, she said, 'My Lord, I have borne her, a female child,' – and God knew better what she had borne – 'and the male is not as the female', and You had promised me a male child. *'I have named her Mary; I have entrusted the protection of her and her offspring to You against* [*the evil of*] *the accursed Satan.'* God then endowed Mary with Jesus (*ʿm*). He [Qummī] said: My father [Ibrāhīm b. Hāshim al-Qummī] narrated to me on the authority of al-Ḥasan b. Maḥbūb ← ʿAlī b. Riyāb ← Abū Baṣīr ← Abū ʿAbd Allāh [Jaʿfar al-Ṣādiq] (*ʿm*), who said: If we should tell you something about a man from among us, but then [you see that] it is not in him, it will be in his son, or [even] his son's son. So do not deny it. God revealed to ʿImrān: 'I shall endow you with a male child who will be blessed and who will cure the blind and the leper and will give life to the dead by My permission, and I shall make him a messenger to the Children of Israel' [cf. Q. 3:49]. He [ʿImrān] then related this to his wife Ḥanna, mother of Mary, and when she was pregnant with her, in her mind she was bearing a male child, but *when she bore her, she said, 'My Lord, I have borne her, a female child'* [. . .][18] *'and the male is not as the female'*, since a female could not become a messenger (*rasūl*). God says, *and God knew better what she had borne*: when God then endowed Mary with Jesus (*ʿm*), that was the good news that God had given to ʿImrān and had promised him. So, if we were to tell you something about a man from among us, but it then turns out to be in his son or his son's son, then do not deny it.[19]

Ṭabarī

Ṭabarī's work is distinctive within the early commentarial tradition. Across the religio-political divisions (proto-Sunnī, proto-Shīʿī and the Ibāḍī), *tafsīr* works tended to focus

[18] The intervening *and God knew better what she had borne* [of Q. 3:36] is repositioned by the imam Jaʿfar al-Ṣādiq's report by Qummī in order to allow for the exegetical narrative to be woven around the direct speech of the verse and to make the point about God's knowledge of the Unseen and the trust in the truth of the imams.

[19] Qummī, *Tafsīr al-Qummī*, s.v. Q. 3:35–6.

heavily on narrative exegesis or be strictly devoted to legal and jurisprudential exposition, sometimes to vindicate intra-confessional boundaries, but at other times simply to cement that particular genre and assume a place within its emerging scholastic parameters. Ṭabarī's commentary, in its meticulous handling of *isnād*s and its attention to variant transmissions from the same early authority, is sometimes more akin to the great *ḥadīth* collections (the *Ṣaḥīḥ* works) that themselves contained sections or chapters on Qur'ānic exegesis (see e.g. the two *Ṣaḥīḥ*s of Bukhārī and Muslim, as well as the *Muṣannaf*s of ʿAbd al-Razzāq or Ibn Abī Shayba). Ṭabarī's *tafsīr* differs from these *ḥadīth* collections by virtue of the sources he draws upon and because there is an organising principle behind his exegesis. It is obvious that his commentary on Qur'ānic verses is not simply an unreflective listing of all materials available to him, because he often includes his own views and also because of the way in which he sometimes breaks off from one authority, turns his attention to new exegetical content, only to come back to that former authority and present their view on this new content. It is for this reason that we have chosen to capture the nuances of his chains of transmission, where he is meticulous about the method of transmission between certain chains (*samiʿa* vs. *ḥaddatha*).[20] Ṭabarī opens his commentary on this section with an impressively accurate Biblical genealogy of the family of ʿImrān, Mary's father, traced back through recognisable Biblical cognates like Manasseh, Hezekiah, Jothath, Jehoshaphat, Rehoboam, Solomon and David through to Jesse (Īshā). However, aspects of the story as he tells it differ significantly from the Biblical version, as, for instance, in his view that ʿImrān dies before Mary's birth.

In terms of its content, this commentary elaborates on earlier views, indicating some shared sources, and it prefigures many of the views that are put forth in later commentaries. For Ṭabarī, Ḥanna's piety is shown in her vow to God. Various sources say that this vow was made for her child not to labour in the world, or to be dedicated to the study of the scripture. He summarises the views of early authorities by saying that the correct interpretation of the words *My Lord, I have borne her, a female child* is that Ḥanna said this as an apology to God for not bearing a male child, which she had been expecting; only male children could be vowed to the temple, because men were viewed as having more strength for such service and because women were considered unsuited to enter the temple due to vaginal bleeding (both postpartum and while menstruating).

He, majestic be His praise, means by His words *When the wife of ʿImrān said, 'My Lord, I vow to You what is in my belly, in consecration. Accept it from me*: *idh* (*when*) is semantically connected to *samīʿ* (*the Hearer*).[21] As for the wife of ʿImrān, this is the mother of Mary daughter of ʿImrān, mother of Jesus son

[20] The sources of Ṭabarī's commentary have been studied in great detail in an unpublished PhD dissertation by Fareed Y.Y.M. al-Muftāḥ, 'The Sources of al-Ṭabarī's *Tafsīr*' (Unpublished PhD dissertation, Edinburgh University, 1998). See also Cooper, *The Commentary on the Qur'ān*, esp. the translator's introduction.

[21] This 'Hearer' is of the previous verse, Q. 3:34, *Offspring each of the other, and God is the Hearer and the Knower*. That is to say, 'and God was hearing, when the wife of ʿImrān said. . .'.

of Mary, God's blessings upon him, whose name, according to what has been mentioned to us, was Ḥanna, daughter of Fāqūdh son of Qatīl. The like of this has been narrated to us by Ibn Isḥāq[22] concerning his [Jesus'] lineage (*nasab*). In reports [transmitted] other than from Ibn Ḥumayd, [she was] the daughter of Fāqūd, with a [final] *dāl*, the son of Qatīl. As for her husband, he was ʿImrān son of Yāshham son of Āmūn son of Manshā son of Ḥizqiyā son of Aḥrīq son of Yūwaym son of ʿAzāryā son of Amṣiyā son of Yāwish son of Aḥrihū son of Yāzim son of Yahfāshāṭ son of Ashābrābān son of Raḥbaʿam son of Solomon son of David son of Īshā.[23] Something similar has been narrated to us regarding his genealogy (*nasab*) by Ibn Ḥumayd on the authority of Salama from Ibn Isḥāq.

His words *'My Lord, I vow to You what is in my belly, in consecration'* mean: I have made a vow to You, my Lord, that what is in my belly shall be dedicated in consecration for worship of You, meaning, I have reserved it to serve You and to serve your sanctum (*qudus*)[24] in the temple (*kanīsa*),[25] as one liberated (*ʿatīq*) from service of anything else and designated specifically for You.

Muḥarraran is in the accusative (*naṣb*) as a circumstantial qualifier (*ḥāl*) of *mā*, functioning semantically as *alladhī*. *Accept it from me*: that is, accept from me what I have vowed for You, O Lord. *Indeed, You are the Hearer and*

[22] Reported through Salama from (Muḥammad) Ibn Ḥumayd.

[23] The Biblical genealogy above bears a reasonably close correspondence to that of Matthew 1:1–16; but also see Exodus 6:18–20. Approximately: ʿImrān [= Joachim/Amram]; Yāshham [=?]; Āmūn = Amon; Manshā = Mannaseh; Ḥizqiyā = Hezekiah; Aḥrīq [= Ahaz ?]; Yūwaym [= Jothath ?]; ʿAzāryā [=?]; Amṣiyā = Amos; Yāwish [= Jotham ?]; Aḥrihū [= Jehu ?]; Yāzim [= Joram ?]; Yahfāshāṭ = Jehoshaphat; Ashābrābān = Asa; Raḥbaʿam = Rehoboam; Sulaymān = Solomon; Dāwūd = David; Īshā = Jesse. Our thanks to Stephan Burge and Emran El-Badawi for their advice on this list. The better known of these correspondences may be found in Ṭabarī's chronicle of the Children of Israel in his monumental *Ta'rīkh al-rusul wa'l-mulūk* (*The History of al-Ṭabarī*, vol. III: *The Children of Israel*, tr. William Brinner [New York, State University of New York Press, 1991]). See also the other New Testament genealogy in Luke 3:23–38, *New Revised Standard Version*; on Biblical genealogies, see Burton H. Throckmorton Jr., *Gospel Parallels: A Comparison of the Synoptic Gospels, New Revised Standard Version* (Nashville, Thomas Nelson, 1992 [orig. published 1949]).

[24] Also, *al-quds*, 'the holy', sc. Jerusalem. An introductory but fairly comprehensive account of the history of the presence of this city in Muslim history, art and architecture, and of its variant names, remains that of S.D. Goitein, and O. Grabar, 'al-Ḳuds', in *EI*², V, 302–44.

[25] The commentators persistently refer to the place of worship for which the child was consecrated as *kanīsa* (commonly understood as 'church', but which has historically also meant 'Jewish temple'), which also allows for a paronomastic reference to 'sweeping' (*kanasa*), which was the main task of those male children dedicated to it. Note that the words *ekklēsia*, synagogue, *knesset*, *kanīsa* (Ar.) and, indeed, *katholikos* as *jāmiʿ* all signify a place of gathering or assembly. The Arabic term *kanīsa*, however, does not appear in the Qur'ān. The commentators also use *bayt al-maqdis*, a clear cognate of the Hebrew name for the temple, and *masjid* (mosque or house of prayer/prostration), which demonstrates that they understood the sacred geography and the rites associated with it.

the Knower: You are indeed, O Lord, the One who hears what I say and to whom I supplicate, the One who knows the intentions in me and what I desire. Neither the secret (*sirr*) nor the proclaimed aspects of my affair are hidden from You.

The reason for the vow made by Ḥanna daughter of Fāqūdh, the wife of ʿImrān, mentioned by God in this verse, according to what has reached us, is what has been narrated by:

Salama reported that Ibn Isḥāq[26] said: Zachariah and ʿImrān married sisters. The mother of John (Yaḥyā) lived with Zachariah and the mother of Mary was with ʿImrān. ʿImrān died while Mary's mother was pregnant with Mary, still a child (*janīn*) in her belly. According to what they claimed, she had been unable to conceive until she had reached old age. They were a family of some stature before God. One day, when she was beneath the shade of a tree, she saw a bird feeding its chick and her soul was stirred out of desire for a child. She supplicated to God to endow her with a child. She then conceived Mary, but ʿImrān died. When she discovered that she had a child in her belly, she dedicated it as a vow (*nadhīra*) to God: such a vow means that you make it for the [sole] purpose of the worship of God, confining it to the temple (*kanīsa*), and not to be profited from it through any of the affairs of this world.[27]

Saʿīd reported from Qatāda,[28] concerning His words *When the wife of ʿImrān said, 'My Lord, I vow to You what is in my belly, in consecration'* [to the end of] the verse: the wife of ʿImrān had vowed what was in her belly to God. It was their custom to vow male children, and when the child was consecrated in this way it was appointed to a temple (*kanīsa*), which it would not leave, maintaining it and sweeping it clean (*kanasa*).

[26] Ibn Ḥumayd ← Salama ← Muḥammad b. Isḥāq.

[27] An identical report follows, but with the *isnād* as Ibn Ḥumayd ← Salama ← Ibn Isḥāq ← Muḥammad b. Jaʿfar b. al-Zubayr. Two further reports make the same point, except for the difference in the use of the term designated for the Holy House, or the place of worship. ʿAbd al-Raḥmān b. al-Aswad al-Ṭafāwī ← Muḥammad b. Rabīʿa ← al-Naḍr b. ʿArabī ← Mujāhid: a servant of the church (*bīʿa*); Abū Kurayb ← Jābir b. Nūḥ ← al-Naḍr b. ʿArabī ← Mujāhid: a servant of the temple (*kanīsa*). The commentators would have wondered about the appropriate appellation of the places of worship at the time of Jesus' birth, most likely with Q. 22:40 in mind: *And were it not that God repels people, some by the means of others, monasteries* (or *cloisters*), *churches, prayer-places and places of prostration in which God's name is much mentioned would have been destroyed* (*wa-lawlā dafʿu Allāhi al-nāsa baʿḍahum bi-baʿḍin la-huddimat ṣawāmiʿu wa-biyaʿun wa-ṣalāwātun wa-masājidu yudhkaru fīhā ismu Allāh kathīran*). Three further reports are cited on the authority of al-Shaʿbī and three more on the authority of Mujāhid to the same effect, except that in one report Mujāhid glosses the verse by interpreting *muḥarrar* as signifying one who is 'pure' or 'saved' (*khāliṣ*), unblemished by any affair of this world. In the case of these two authorities, *kanīsa* appears. Two other reports are cited on the authority of Saʿīd b. Jubayr (who uses *bīʿa* and *kanīsa* in the same gloss).

[28] Bishr ← Yazīd ← Saʿīd ← Qatāda.

Maʿmar b. Rashīd reported that Qatāda[29] said, concerning His words *I vow to You what is in my belly, in consecration*, 'She vowed her child to the temple (*kanīsa*).'

Asbāṭ reported that al-Suddī[30] said, [regarding] *When the wife of ʿImrān said, 'My Lord, I vow to You what is in my belly, in consecration. Accept it from me; indeed You are the Hearer and the Knower*, 'The wife of ʿImrān became pregnant and, supposing that what was in her belly was a male child, she dedicated it as a consecration to God, not to labour in this world.'

Al-Rabīʿ[31] said [. . .].

ʿUbayd said, 'I heard al-Ḍaḥḥāk[32] say, regarding His words *I vow to You what is in my belly, in consecration*, "She dedicated her child to God and to be among those who study (*d-r-s*) the scripture (*al-kitāb*) and learn it (*ʿ-l-m*)."'

It is reported on the authority of ʿIkrima[33] that the wife of ʿImrān was a barren (*ʿaqīm*) old woman (*ʿajūz*), whose name was Ḥanna, and she could not give birth [*sic.*]. She used to be envious of women with children and one day said, 'O Lord, upon me shall be the vow in gratitude that if You provide me with a child, I shall give it in charity (*ṣ-d-q*) to the Holy House (*bayt al-maqdis*) to be one of its custodians (*sadana*) and servants (*khādim*).' And he [ʿIkrima] also said, regarding His words *I vow to You what is in my belly, in consecration* (*muḥarraran*): verily she was the consecrated one, daughter of the consecrated ones,[34] as one consecrated to the service of the temple (*kanīsa*).

ʿAbbād b. Manṣūr reported that al-Ḥasan [al-Baṣrī][35] said, regarding His words *when the wife of ʿImrān said* [and] the verse in its entirety, 'She vowed what was in her belly and then relinquished her [in consecration].'[36]

[29] Al-Ḥasan b. Yaḥyā ← ʿAbd al-Razzāq ← Maʿmar [b. Rāshid] ← Qatāda.

[30] Mūsā ← ʿAmr ← Asbāṭ ← al-Suddī.

[31] Al-Muthannā ← Isḥāq ← Ibn Abī Jaʿfar ← his father ← al-Rabīʿ. The report is identical to the first report from Qatāda, above.

[32] Al-Ḥusayn b. al-Faraj heard Abū Muʿādh ← ʿUbayd who heard al-Ḍaḥḥāk.

[33] Al-Qāsim ← al-Ḥusayn ← al-Ḥajjāj ← Ibn Jurayj ← al-Qāsim b. Abī Bazza who reported it to him [Ibn Jurayj] on the authority of ʿIkrima and Abū Bakr ← ʿIkrima.

[34] The first part of the statement by ʿIkrima is an exclamatory eulogising of Mary.

[35] Muḥammad b. Sinān ← Abū Bakr al-Ḥanafī ← ʿAbbād b. Manṣūr ← al-Ḥasan.

[36] Ḥasan is using the polyvalence of the language to indicate Ḥanna's piety but also the irony of the 'double loss' after the gift: *nadharat mā fī baṭnihā thumma sayyabathā*. The verb *s-y-b* (in form II) also means to 'relinquish, set free, abandon'. Cf. also the Qur'ān's use of this root to refer to the she-camel set free to roam (*sāʾiba*) in Q. 5:103.

Reports on the interpretation of His words, exalted be He, *and when she bore her, she said, 'My Lord, I have borne her, a female child,' – and God knew better what she had borne – 'and the male is not as the female. I have named her Mary; I have entrusted the protection of her and her offspring to You against [the evil of] the accursed Satan.'*

By His words, majestic be His praise, *and when she bore her*, He means: when Ḥanna gave birth to the consecrated child (*al-nadhīra*), which is why the feminine [suffixed pronoun] is used (*waḍaʿat-hā*). For, if the [pronominal suffix] *hā* had referred to the *mā* of His words *innī nadhartu laka mā fī baṭnī muḥarraran*,[37] the words would have said *fa lammā waḍaʿat-hu qālat rabbī innī waḍaʿtuhu unthā* (and when she bore it, she said, 'My Lord, I have borne it, a female'). The meaning of His words *waḍaʿtu-hā* is *waladtu-hā* (I have given birth to her). One says of a woman: *waḍaʿat, taḍaʿu waḍʿan*.

She said, 'My Lord, I have borne her, a female child', that is to say, the consecrated one that I have given birth to is a female. *And God knew better what she had borne*. The readers differed over the reading of that. The majority of the readers read it as *waḍaʿat*, as a notification from God, mighty and majestic, Himself that He had full knowledge of what she had borne, regardless of her statement *'My Lord, I have borne her, a female child.'* Some of the earlier authorities read it as *wa'llāhu aʿlamu bi-mā waḍaʿtu* ('And God knew better what I had borne'), as a statement on the part of Mary's mother as the speaker: God knows better what I have given birth to.

The more correct of the two readings is that which has been transmitted via clear proof (*ḥujja*) and in which that [proof] is exhaustively demonstrated, such that its soundness cannot be thwarted. That is the reading of those who read it: *wa'llāhu aʿlamu bi-mā waḍaʿat* (And God knows better what she had borne). No reading that deviates (*shādhdh*) from this can be used in objection to it.

Thus the interpretation of the words is: God knows better than all of His creation what she bore. He, majestic be His praise, then reverts to speaking through her words when she apologises to her Lord for what she had vowed during her pregnancy and consecrated for the service of her Lord: *and the male is not as the female*. For the male has more of the strength needed for service and is more able to maintain it, while the female is not suited in certain circumstances to enter the sanctuary (*quds*) in order to undertake the service of the place of worship because she is affected by menses (*ḥayḍ*) and postpartum bleeding (*nifās*). *I have named her Mary*.

[37] These are the words of verse 35.

As in [the following reports]:

Ibn Isḥāq reported that Muḥammad b. Jaʿfar b. al-Zubayr[38] said, regarding *and when she bore her, she said, 'My Lord, I have borne her, a female child,' – and God knew better what she had borne – 'and the male is not as the female*, 'That is, given that I have vowed it as consecrated to Him [but it is a female].'

Salama reported that Ibn Isḥāq[39] told him, regarding *and the male is not as the female*, 'Because the male has more strength for that than the female.'

Saʿīd reported, on the authority of Qatāda,[40] regarding *and the male is not as the female*: women could not be used for that purpose, that is, to be consecrated for the church so that she is appointed to maintain it, sweep it clean and remain in it, on account of what afflicts her of menses and impurity. That is why she said *and the male is not as the female*.

Maʿmar [b. Rashīd] reported on the authority of Qatāda,[41] regarding *she said, 'My Lord, I have borne her, a female child'*: except that they used to consecrate (*ḥ-r-r*) boys (*ghilmān*). *'And the male is not as the female. I have named her Mary.'*

It is reported that al-Rabīʿ[42] said, 'The wife of ʿImrān had consecrated what was in her belly to God, and she was hoping that He would endow her with a boy, since a woman would not be able to undertake that [task], meaning, to maintain the place of worship, abiding in it and keeping it swept clean, because of the impurity (*adhan*) that befalls her.'

Asbāṭ reported that al-Suddī[43] said, 'The wife of ʿImrān believed that she was carrying a male child (*ghulām*) in her belly, and so she dedicated it (*w-h-b*) to God. But when she bore it, it was a female child (*jāriya*), and so she spoke the words to God in apology: *"My Lord, I have borne her, a female child* [. . .] *and the male is not as the female."* She meant that only boys could be consecrated [for that duty]. God says, *and God knew better what she had borne*; and she said, *I have named her Mary.*'

Qāsim b. Abī Bazza reported that ʿIkrima[44] told him, regarding *and when she bore her, she said, 'My Lord, I have borne her, a female child* [. . .] *and the male is not as the female'* means: menstruation (*maḥīḍ*) and that a woman ought not to be with men; this was her mother speaking these words.

[38] Ibn Ḥumayd ← Salama ← Ibn Isḥāq ← Muḥammad b. Jaʿfar b. al-Zubayr.
[39] Ibn Ḥumayd ← Salama ← Ibn Isḥāq.
[40] Bishr ← Yazīd ← Saʿīd ← Qatāda.
[41] Al-Ḥasan b. Yaḥyā ← ʿAbd al-Razzāq ← Maʿmar [b. Rāshid] ← Qatāda.
[42] Al-Muthannā ← Isḥāq ← Ibn Abī Jaʿfar ← his father ← al-Rabīʿ.
[43] Mūsā ← ʿAmr ← Asbāṭ ← al-Suddī.
[44] Al-Qāsim ← al-Ḥusayn ← al-Ḥajjāj ← Ibn Jurayj ← Qāsim b. Abī Bazza that he was informed by ʿIkrima and on the authority of Abū Bakr from ʿIkrima.

Reports on the interpretation of His words, majestic be His praise, *'I have entrusted the protection of her and her offspring to You against [the evil of] the accursed Satan.'*

By her words *'I have entrusted the protection of her and her offspring to You'*, she meant: I am making You her refuge (*maʿādh*),[45] and her offspring's refuge, from the accursed Satan. The original sense of *maʿādh* is a place to which one returns (*mawʾil*) or a place of shelter (*maljaʾ*) or a place of protection (*maʿqil*).[46] God, exalted be He, accepted her petition and granted her and her offspring protection from the accursed Satan and gave him no way over them.

Yazīd b. ʿAbd Allāh b. Qusayṭ reported that Abū Hurayra[47] said, 'The Messenger of God (*ṣlʿm*) said, "From every soul born, Satan manages to jab them (*ṭaʿna*), and that is when the child gives its first cry, except in the case of Mary daughter of ʿImrān, for when she was about to give birth to her, she said, *'I have entrusted the protection of her and her offspring to You against [the evil of] the accursed Satan'*, whereupon a [protective] veil (*ḥijāb*) was struck around her, and he jabbed [only] it".'[48]

Abū Hurayra[49] said that he heard the Prophet (*ṣlʿm*) say: 'From the Children of Adam there is no soul that is born who is not touched (*m-s-s*) by Satan at birth so that it gives off its first cry when he touches him, except for Mary and her son.'[50]

45 The verb *ʿ-w-dh* appears in various verbal forms in some seventeen instances in the Qurʾān. Most famously, the verb introduces the apotropaic incantations in *sūrat al-Falaq* (Q. 113) and *sūrat al-Nās* (Q. 114) that are considered an essential part of the daily litany of Muslim devotional practice, and are known for that reason as the *muʿawidhatān*. As very short *sūras* they are easily memorised by children learning the Qurʾān and are easily recited by parents over their children for protection against harm or evil. The Qurʾān notes, interestingly, a pre-Islamic practice of seeking this prophylactic through the *jinn* in the *sūra* of the same name (Q. 72). In the case of Mary, one should note her own use of the expression (in Q. 19:18) to protect herself from the approach of the man she does not recognise at first but who then identifies himself as a messenger (sc. Gabriel) from God sent to grant her a child: *She said, 'Truly I seek refuge from you with Him the All-merciful, unless you yourself be God-wary'*. See Kathleen Malone O'Connor, 'Popular and Talismanic Uses of the Qurʾān', *EQ*, IV, 163–82.

46 The verb *ʿ-q-l* also refers to tying up camels with rope (*ʿiqāl*) at their tethering post.

47 Abū Kurayb ← ʿAbda b. Sulaymān ← Muḥammad b. Isḥāq ← Yazīd b. ʿAbd Allāh b. Qusayṭ ← Abū Hurayra.

48 Three further identical reports are provided, also on the authority of Abū Hurayra, but with the additional comment in the third report by Abū Hurayra encouraging people to use the same formula themselves.

49 Ibn Ḥumayd ← Hārūn b. al-Mughīra ← ʿAmr ← Shuʿayb b. Khālid ← Zubayr ← Saʿīd b. al-Musayyab who heard Abū Hurayra say, from the Prophet.

50 Three further reports are provided on the authority of Abū Hurayra to the same effect. Versions of these reports are found in Bukhārī, *Ṣaḥīḥ*, *Kitāb Aḥādīth al-anbiyāʾ* (60), *Bāb qawl Allāh taʿālā waʾdhkur fīʾl-kitāb Maryam idh intabadhat min ahlihā makānan sharqiyyan* [Q. 19:16] (44), *ḥadīth* no. 102/3431; ibid., *Kitāb al-Tafsīr* (65), *Bāb uʿīdhuhā bika wa-dhuriyatahā minaʾl-shayṭān al-rajīm* (2), *ḥadīth* no. 71/4548; Muslim, *Ṣaḥīḥ*, *Kitāb al-Faḍāʾil* (43), *Bāb faḍāʾil ʿĪsā ʿalayhi al-salām* (40), *ḥadīth* no. 193/2366.

Abū Hurayra[51] said, 'The Messenger of God (*ṣlʿm*) said, "No child is born except that Satan has pressed him (*ʿ-ṣ-r*) once or twice, except for Jesus son of Mary, and Mary." The Messenger then recited *'I have entrusted the protection of her and her offspring to You against* [*the evil of*] *the accursed Satan'* [Q. 3:36].

ʿIkrima reported that Ibn ʿAbbās[52] said, 'No child is born but that it gives off its first cry, except Jesus son of Mary, over whom Satan was not given any sway and whom he could not [even] nudge.'

Mundhir b. Nuʿmān al-Afṭas heard Wahb b. Munabbih[53] saying, 'When Jesus was born, the satans came to Iblīs and said, "The idols have all lowered their heads!" He [Iblīs] said, "This must be because of something that has happened", and said, "Stay where you are." He flew off until he had reached the far ends of the earth but could not find anything. He went across the seas but still could not find anything. He flew off further and found Jesus who had been born in a donkey barn with angels encircling him. He returned to them and said, "A prophet was born yesterday; but never has woman been with a child or borne it and I have not been in her presence, except for this one. Despair henceforth that idols should be worshipped. But keep coming at the children of Adam when they are unaware or making haste."'

Qatāda[54] [said], regarding His words *'I have entrusted the protection of her and her offspring to You against* [*the evil of*] *the accursed Satan'*, 'And it was mentioned to us that the Prophet (*ṣlʿm*) used to say [. . .].[55] It was also mentioned to us that the two of them did not commit sin (*dhanb*) as the rest of the Children of Adam do. It was also mentioned to us that Jesus used to walk on water as he would on land because of the certitude (*yaqīn*) and sincere devotion (*ikhlāṣ*) that God, exalted be He, had given him.'[56]

[51] Al-Muthannā ← al-Ḥimmānī ← Qays ← al-Aʿmash ← Abū Ṣāliḥ ← Abū Hurayra ← the Messenger of God.

[52] Ibn Ḥumayd ← Hārūn b. al-Mughīra ← ʿAmr b. Abī Qays ← al-Sammāk ← ʿIkrima ← Ibn ʿAbbās.

[53] Al-Ḥasan b. Yaḥyā ← ʿAbd al-Razzāq ← Mundhir b. Nuʿmān al-Afṭas heard Wahb b. Munabbih.

[54] Bishr ← Yazīd ← Saʿīd ← Qatāda.

[55] The *ḥadīth* of Satan jabbing (*ṭ-ʿ-n*) an impenetrable veil protecting Mary and her child (see Abū Hurayra's first *ḥadīth*, above) is repeated here.

[56] Ṭabarī, *Jāmiʿ al-bayān*, s.v. Q. 3:35–6. Ṭabarī concludes his commentary on these passages with one report on the authority of al-Rabīʿ b. Anas (d. 139/756), a transmitter used often by Ṭabarī (on which, see al-Muftāḥ, 'The Sources of al-Ṭabarī's *Tafsīr*'), in which the Prophet states that Jesus describes how God has granted him and his mother protection from the accursed Satan; and with three reports on the authority of Abū Hurayra, all of which reiterate that Satan had no way of getting to Jesus and that the first cry of a newborn indicates the moment when a child is touched by Satan upon its birth.

Qāḍī al-Nuʿmān

This interpretation represents another way of showing the existential truth of the Ismāʿīlī spiritual hierarchy. In it, Qāḍī al-Nuʿmān brings to light the functions of the various roles of the spiritual hierarchy, as well as the discipleships it entails and the relationships between those key components (*imām*, *ḥujja*, *naqīb*, *dāʿī*, etcetera) within it. He highlights the rupture in the lineage from the Āl ʿImrān to the lineage of Zachariah, which is mapped onto the Fatimid Ismāʿīlī hierarchies: for him, this shift in lineage involves a case of discipleship gone wrong, which is reminiscent of the interpretation of Eve as Adam's proof (*ḥujja*) detailed in Chapter 1 of this volume; both cases become an opportunity for the consummation of a more perfect discipleship. The rupture in spiritual lineage is simultaneously an allusion to the rupture within the Ismāʿīlī *daʿwa* and the wider Imāmī Shīʿism of the time. In this interpretation, 'Mary' is actually an allusion to Zachariah, who, as *ḥujja*, takes the female role in relation to the imam of the age. Though the spiritual hierarchies are thus overtly genderless, with the positions able to be occupied by a male or a female, in this case the Qur'ānic mention of the female does not impede the male nature of the spiritual hierarchy: the feminine here is mapped onto men.

Zachariah (*ʿm*) was the imam during the last days of the cycle (*dawr*) of Moses (*ʿm*), but realised that he would not reach the cycle of Jesus (*ʿm*). ʿImrān had been the master of the age (*ṣāḥib al-zamān*) prior to him [Zachariah] but was unable to establish an imam from his mission (*daʿwa*) and so he established Zachariah, who was not part of his mission, instead; and he placed alongside him a man from his [ʿImrān's] mission expecting him be able to carry out the imamate after him [ʿImrān]. However, [ʿImrān] did not find in him the capacity for the Imamate, which is why he joined him to Zachariah, who is the one whom God, glory be to Him, alludes to (*kannā ʿan*) by [the name] 'Maryam', because thereafter he became a proof (*ḥujja*).[57] And His words, exalted be He, *When the wife of ʿImrān said, 'My Lord, I vow to You what is in my belly, in consecration. Accept it from me; indeed, You are the Hearer and the Knower'*, meaning that the proof (*ḥujja*) of ʿImrān [Zachariah] knew that he would depart from this world before the imam [Jesus] and so he begged God that someone would take his place from among his own mission (*daʿwatihi*), and for him to be an imam after ʿImrān. So when he put him in to the test (*imtiḥān*), it became clear to him that, unless he had been a proof (*ḥujja*), this person would not be capable of establishing the Imamate, because he did not have the necessary ability to clarify through

[57] For a further explanation of this, see Qāḍī al-Nuʿmān, *Asās al-taʾwīl*, 297.

speech or to bear burdens (*iḥtimāl*), which is referred to in His words *And when she bore her, she said, 'My Lord, I have borne her, a female child,' – and God knew better what she had borne.* That is to say, He knew it before he said it. *'And the male is not as the female.* That is to say, not everyone who is fit for the imamate is fit to be a proof (*ḥujja*). *I have named her Mary; I have entrusted the protection of her and her offspring to You against [the evil of] the accursed Satan.'* That is to say, I have fulfilled my vow in him and I have delegated my affair to You, and so preserve him from the furtive machinations of the opponent. *Thereupon her Lord (r-b-b) received her most graciously* that is to say he nurtured (*r-b-b*) that man, his proof (*ḥujja*), after ʿImrān, who is Zachariah (*ʿm*) *graciously*, with the reception of that knowledge and wisdom. *And He tended to her most graciously* that is to say, He raised her (*rabbāhā*) graciously. *And Zachariah was charged with her*, so He put her in his path, and within his embrace, and his supervision (*naẓar*). *And every time Zachariah entered the sanctuary (miḥrāb) to see her, he would find her with provisions and [once] he asked 'O Mary, how is it that you have this?' She said, 'It is from God'* [Q 3:37]. He is saying that each time he spoke to him and touched upon the subject of the path of the Imamate, he would discover that he had knowledge that was more subtle than that with which he had intended to benefit him.[58]

Qushayrī

Qushayrī's brief consideration of these verses is anchored in the overriding importance of spiritual truths as they are obscured by one's spiritual bondage to the material world. The episode with the wife of ʿImrān offers the exegete an opportunity to raise the literal language to a higher metaphor of truth, where true emancipation is emancipation from attachments to this world and its condition. Ultimate spiritual worth overrides social hierarchies taken for granted in this world. For Qushayrī, the wife of ʿImrān does not immediately recognise this, concerned as she was about the social superiority of the male: for the exegete, once elected by God for a purpose, the female (here, Mary) could be the source of as many miraculous affairs as is usually reserved for male prophets and saints. The closing comments of the commentary are phrased in a somewhat apocalyptic tone, portending the coming of Christianity, the end of the pagan Roman empire and the rise of the multiple divisions of the Church: 'an entire world (*ʿālam*) met its salvation on account of her words and an entire world met its destruction on account of her, and discord befell another world because of the two of them'.

[58] Qāḍī al-Nuʿmān, *Asās al-ta'wīl*, 291–2.

One who is emancipated (*muḥarrar*) is one not in bondage (*riqq*) to any creature,[59] whom the Truth, glory be to Him, has emancipated – in His predetermined judgment – from the bondage of being preoccupied [with things of this world] in all aspects and in all states (*aḥwāl*). When the mother of Mary made that vow and bore her, a female child, she was ashamed (*khajal*). Seeing her, she said, *'My Lord, I have borne her, a female child'*, and she is not fit to be consecrated (*muḥarrar*). He, exalted be He, said, *And God knew better what she had borne.* And, by my life, although the male is not as the female manifestly, if the Truth (al-Ḥaqq) accepts her, glory be to Him and exalted be He, every marvellous thing can issue from her.

And when she said *'I vow to You what is in my belly, in consecration'* and said *'Accept it from me'*, He responded [and accepted], and the vestiges of this acceptance were manifested upon her and her son, and an entire world (*ʿālam*) met its salvation on account of her words and an entire world met its destruction on account of her, and discord befell another world because of the two of them.

She said, *'I have named her Mary; I have entrusted protection of her and her offspring to You against* [*the evil of*] *the accursed Satan'*: she sought refuge with God by the easiest means, that Satan should not have a way over anything of what she said, given the way in which he aspires completely to that which governs the hearts.[60]

Zamakhsharī

What is immediately obvious from Zamakhsharī's commentary is his preference for justifying exegetical interpretations by using a dialectical method of hypothetical question and response. Both, of course, are his own creation, but they serve to lend a rationalistic underpinning for what is usually straightforward traditional commentary. He uses this method in several instances, once to establish that the "Imrān' intended here is the one related to Zachariah by marriage and is no connection to the father of another famous Maryam, who was the sister of Moses and Aaron; a second time to establish a grammatical soundness of the suffixed pronoun in *waḍaʿat-hā*; and again, in three further instances, in order to explain what might seem to be redundancies (Ḥanna's announcement of something already known to God; the purport of *the male*

[59] Cf. Qushayrī's *Risāla* where Abū ʿAlī al-Daqqāq narrates a story about Abū Bakr al-Qaḥṭī and his profligate son. When the pious Qaḥṭī was found to be curiously unperturbed by his son's lifestyle, he said, 'We are those who have been emancipated from the bondage to things since pre-eternity' (*innā qad ḥurrirnā ʿan riqq al-ashyāʾ fīʾl-azal*). Qushayrī, *al-Risāla al-Qushayriyya fī ʿilm al-taṣawwuf*, 59.

[60] Qushayrī, *Laṭāʾif al-ishārāt*, s.v. Q. 3:35–6.

is not as the female; and Ḥanna naming the child Mary). Zamakhsharī focuses on Ḥanna's emotions of grief and distress at the birth of a female, implicitly showing her up by saying that God would show her that *this* female is better than a male would have been. Zamakhsharī concludes with a caution to his readers that popular conceptions of Satanic whisperings, prods or touches based on received *ḥadīth* materials are not intended to be taken literally: they are just metaphorical imaginings intended to communicate spiritual truths.

And *when* (*idh*) is in the accusative [syntactically] on account of that;[61] but it is also said that this is because of an implicit mention (*udhkur*). *The wife of ʿImrān* is the wife of ʿImrān son of Matthan, mother of the virgin (*batūl*) Mary and grandmother of Jesus (*ʿm*), and her name was Ḥanna daughter of Fāqūdh. As for His saying *when the wife of ʿImrān said* in the wake of saying *and the family of ʿImrān* [Q. 3:33], this gives weight to the fact that ʿImrān is ʿImrān son of Matthan, the grandfather of Jesus. The alternative opinion is given weight by the fact that Moses is frequently juxtaposed with Abraham in the Qurʾān (*al-dhikr*).[62] If you were to say: ʿImrān son of Yaṣhar had a daughter named Mary, older than Moses and Aaron, and ʿImrān son of Matthan had the virgin Mary, how would you know that this ʿImrān is the father of the virgin Mary and not ʿImrān father of Mary, sister of Moses and Aaron? I would say: That Zachariah was charged with [her] guardianship suffices as proof that ʿImrān is father of the virgin [cf. Q. 3:37]. For Zachariah son of Ādhan and ʿImrān son of Matthan lived in the same era, and Zachariah had married his [the latter's] daughter Īshāʿ [Elizabeth], Mary's sister. Thus John (Yaḥyā) and Jesus were maternal cousins.[63]

It is reported that she [Ḥanna] was sterile and could not conceive, until she reached old age. One time when she was beneath the shade of a tree, she caught sight of a bird feeding its chick, whereupon her soul was moved and she desired a child. She said, 'My Lord, I pledge to You a vow in gratitude that if You should provide me with a child I would give it in charity to the Holy House so that he might be one of its guardians and servants.' She conceived Mary while ʿImrān died during her pregnancy. *In consecration*: liberated for the service of the Holy House with no power for me over him, neither to use

[61] 'That' being the preceding verse's words *wa'llāhu samīʿun ʿalīm*, which Zamakhsharī glosses as God being Hearer and Knower of the wife of ʿImrān and her intention 'when (*idh*) [she said] . . .'.

[62] Here, we have translated *al-dhikr* (the remembrance) as straightforward 'Qurʾān' in order not to obfuscate the reference. This is a term frequently used within the Qurʾān to allude to one of its defining aspects: the fact that it is memorised, oft-mentioned and is sent as a remembrance by God.

[63] See Luke 1:36 where Elizabeth is described as Mary's cousin. Luke 1:41–56 describes Mary and Elizabeth's encounter with one another.

him or to occupy him with anything. This kind of vow was permitted by their Law. It is reported that they used to make these vows and when the boy reached puberty he was given the choice of continuing or leaving. On the authority of al-Shaʿbī, *muḥarrar* means singularly devoted to worship. Consecration was only for boys, but she [Ḥanna] made the assumption on the basis of the implied [expectation of a male child] or because she asked that she be provided with a male child. *And when she bore her*: the [suffixed] pronoun [in *waḍaʿat-hā*] refers to '*what is in my belly*' and it is feminine, either because of the import, since what was in her belly was a female child according to God's knowledge; or, on the basis of interpreting [the implied] 'pregnancy' (*al-ḥublā*) or 'soul' (*al-nafs*) or 'living thing' (*al-nasma*).[64]

If you were to say: How is it possible to say that *unthā* (*a female*) is accusative as a circumstantial qualifier of the [suffixed] pronoun in *waḍaʿat-hā* when it is like you saying *waḍaʿat al-unthā unthā* (she bore the female a female)? I would say that the original [construction] would have been *waḍaʿtu-hu unthā*, 'I have borne it – a female child', but that 'it' has been rendered feminine because the circumstantial qualifier is feminine, since the circumstantial qualification and what is qualified by that are one and the same, exactly as the noun [in] *mā kānat ummuki* (*nor was your mother* [Q. 19:28]) is feminine, since the predicate is feminine. Analogous to this are His words, exalted be He, *fa-in kānatā ithnatayn* (*and if they be two sisters*) [Q. 4:176]. If it is based on the interpretation of an [implicit] *ḥublā* or *nasma*, that is already manifest, as if it were said, 'I have borne the fruit or the living thing, a female child.'

If you were then to say, why did she say *I have borne her, a female child*, and what did she intend by these words? I would say that she said it in distress after seeing the disappointment of what she had hoped for and the contrary of what she had expected. She became sad before her Lord since she had been hoping and expecting to give birth to a male child, which is why she vowed it in consecration for guardianship [of the Holy House]. It is because she spoke in the way that she did, out of grief and sadness, that God, exalted be He, said *and God knew better what she had borne*, as a way of exalting what she had borne and as a way of keeping her unaware of the value of what He had bestowed on her through it; that means 'and God knew better about the thing that she had borne and the great affairs that will ensue from that as a consequence'. *And God knew better what she had borne* is God's address to her: that is to say, you are unaware of the [great] worth of this gifted child

[64] All of these Arabic terms are feminine.

and what God knows of her tremendous affairs and her exalted worth. It [*w-ḍ-ʿ*] is also read as *waḍaʿtu* with the same [ultimate] significance.

Perhaps God, exalted be He, retained a secret and a wisdom in that [statement] – that this female will be better than a male – as a way of consoling her. If you were to say, what is the significance of His words *and the male is not as the female*, I would say that this is an explanation of His statement *and God knew better what she had borne*, as a way of exalting the child born and holding it in high regard, the meaning being 'the male child that she had sought is not as the female child that she has been gifted'. The definite article (*al-*) in the case of both [nouns] is to express familiarity (*ʿahd*). If you were then to say, why are the words *and I have named her Mary* coordinated to those [preceding] words? I would respond that this is a coordination to *I have borne her, a female child*, and that what is between these two [statements] are two parenthetical statements, similar to where He says *and that is indeed a tremendous oath, if you but knew* [Q. 56:76]. If [still] you were to say, why did Ḥanna mention her naming [of the child] to her Lord?, I would say it is because, in their language, 'Maryam' means 'worshipping woman' (*ʿābida*), and she sought thereby proximity [with God] and to ask Him to grant her immunity from sin (*ʿiṣma*) so that her [Mary's] acts would correspond to her name and that her [mother's] expectation of her should be vindicated in her. Do you not see how she followed that [statement] with her request for protection, for her and for her child, from Satan and his leading astray, and that there is the *ḥadīth* reported: 'No child is born but that it is touched by Satan at birth and gives off its first cry because of Satan's touching it, except for Mary and her son'? God knows best about the soundness of this [report], but if it is sound then it means: Satan covets to lead astray every newborn child except for Mary and her son, for they were both preserved from sin (*maʿṣūm*) – likewise is every person who enjoys their attributes, as where He, exalted be He, says [that Satan says] *and I shall pervert them all, except Your servants among them who are saved* [Q. 15:39–40].[65] The first cry of the newborn from the touch of Satan is an imagining (*takhyīl*) and a conceptualisation (*taṣwīr*) of his desire for that child, as though by touching it and striking it with his hand he were saying, 'This is one that I shall lead astray.' A similar image is conjured by the words of Ibn al-Rūmī:

> If it were not for this world announcing to it its adversities
> What would the child cry about when it is born?

[65] Translations predominantly have 'devoted' instead of *saved*, but the standard Qur'ānic vocalisation is *mukhlaṣīn* not *mukhliṣīn*, and while, ultimately, the same type of servant is meant, 'saved' or 'purified' is deemed a more accurate rendering of that vocalisation.

As for the truth of [Satan's] touch (*mass*) or prod (*nakhs*), it is not as the traditionists (*ahl al-ḥashw*) mistakenly imagine (*wahm*).[66] If Iblīs had been given complete sway to prod all people, then this world would have been filled with cries and wails because of the tribulations we suffer as a result of his prods.[67]

Ṭabrisī

Readers familiar with Ṭabrisī's *Majma*ʿ will expect his customary structuring of the major exegetical sections into technical preambles in the form of section headings that deal with specific aspects of the Qurʾānic passages in question. The common ones tend to be *qirāʾa*, *lugha*, *iʿrāb* and *maʿnā*, as these categories can be attended to in most Qurʾānic instances, given the rich body of variant readings in the early and classical periods (and the recognition of their validity), as well as the lexical peculiarities of the text and its basis for Arabic grammar. The use of the section entitled 'Proof' (*ḥujja*) is reserved for bolstering a specific aspect of a passage, which may be a fairly technical point of grammar, as in this case, or it may be a broader theological dimension which Ṭabrisī wants to highlight (regarding, for example, the imamate). It is worth noting that using introductory subdivisions as preludes to a narrative exegesis is something that is picked up in the modern Shīʿī period by the last of our commentators here, Faḍl Allāh. Note also that, despite being a major Shīʿī commentary cited by generations of Qurʾānic commentators thereafter (here, see Muḥsin al-Fayḍ al-Kāshānī), the *Majma*ʿ *al-bayān* is a classical Shīʿī commentary that is very different from the early Shīʿī commentaries of the immediate pre-Būyid period, where the intra-Muslim confessional tensions are more prominent. In Ṭabrisī, by contrast, mainstream sources are acknowledged and cited, and the specifically Imāmī sources of transmission are complementary, not exclusive of the mainstream tradition. A good example of this is his citation from Thaʿlabī on the authority of Abū Hurayra of a Prophetic tradition that identifies the four exemplary women of this world: Mary, Pharaoh's believing wife Āsiya, the Prophet's first wife Khadīja and his daughter Fāṭima. The last of these exemplary women is, of course, the unique source of the Prophetic progeny, the imams.

Reading (*qirāʾa*)

Ibn ʿĀmir and Abū Bakr, on the authority of ʿĀṣim and Yaʿqūb, read *bi-mā waḍaʿtu* (what I have borne), with a *ḍamma* inflection on the *tāʾ*, and this [reading] has also been reported on the authority of ʿAlī [b. Abī Ṭālib] (*ʿm*).

[66] The derogatory epithet, usually in the form *ḥashwiyya* is used by many in the early community, mainly (but not exclusively) the rationalist currents such as the Muʿtazila or the philosophers, to refer to the proto-Sunnī traditionists who gave overarching preponderance to *ḥadīth* reports, even when they were forged or suspect. See Jon Hoover, 'Ḥashwiyya', *EI*^{3}.

[67] Zamakhsharī, *al-Kashshāf*, s.v. Q. 3:35–6.

The rest read it as *waḍaʿat* (what she bore) as [third-person] narrative (*ḥikāya*).

Proof (*ḥujja*)

Those who read it with a *ḍamma* inflection on the *tāʾ* (*waḍaʿtu*) take it to be the speech of Mary's mother. Those who read it with the *sukūn* on the *tāʾ* (*waḍaʿat*) take it to be God's words, exalted be He. The opinion of those who place *sukūn* on the *tāʾ* is strengthened by His words *and God knew better what she had borne*. For, if it had been Mary speaking, she would have said, 'and You knew best what I had borne', since she is addressing God.

Language (*lugha*)

The linguistic meaning of *muḥarrar* can support two senses. One is of a person who has been emancipated (*muʿtaq*), in the sense of 'liberty' (*ḥurriya*); one says *ḥarrartuhu taḥrīran* to mean *aʿtaqtuhu*, that is, I made him *ḥurr*. The other is that of expurgating a text (*kitāb*); one says *ḥarrartu al-kitāb taḥrīran*, in other words, I purged it of corruption and emended it. *Al-taqabbul* is to take something approvingly (*riḍā*), as when receiving a gift. The origin of *al-taqabbul* is *al-muqābala* (countering). The origin of *al-waḍʿ* is to 'put down' (*al-ḥaṭṭ*): *waḍaʿat al-marʾa al-walad* means 'she gave birth to the child'; *al-mawḍiʿ* is the place where something is deposited; *al-ḍiʿa* is 'debasement' (*khasāsa*), because it debases (*taḍaʿu*) the worth (*qadr*) of that person; *al-īḍāʿ* in the context of walking is to have a gentle pace because one lowers (*ḥaṭṭ*) the intensity of the pace. *Al-shayṭān, al-rajīm*: both [terms] have been explained (*tafsīr*) at the beginning of this book.

Syntax (*iʿrāb*)

Regarding the [syntactical] locus of *idh qālat* (*when she said*), there are several opinions. One is that it is accusative by an [implied] 'mention' (*udhkur*), and this is on the authority of al-Akhfash and al-Mubarrad. A second [opinion], on the authority of al-Zajjāj, has it that this [phrase] is [syntactically] dependent on 'He has chosen the family of ʿImrān above [. . .]' (*iṣṭafā āl ʿImrān*).[68] A third, on the authority of ʿAlī b. ʿĪsā,[69] is that this [phrase] is [syntactically] dependent on *the Hearer and the Knower* (*samīʿun ʿalīm*) governed by the meaning of these two attributes, the implication being: And God apprehended (*mudrik*) her words and her intention 'when she said'. A fourth, on the authority of Abū ʿUbayda, is that *idh* is otiose

[68] This is a paraphrase of Q. 3:33.

[69] ʿAlī b. ʿĪsā al-Rummānī (d. 384/994), the famous philologist (see the PA).

(*zā'ida*) and has no syntactical function; but this is an error on the part of the Basrans.

As for *muḥarraran*, it is in the accusative as a circumstantial qualifier (*ḥāl*) of *mā*, the implication being: 'I have vowed to You that which is in my belly, as a thing consecrated', and this [accusative] is governed by [the verb] *nadhartu* ('I vow'). As for His words *unthā*, that is in the accusative because it is a circumstantial qualifier.

Meaning (*maʿnā*)

Since He, glory be to Him, mentioned that He had chosen the family of ʿImrān above [all others], He follows this with the mention of Mary the daughter of ʿImrān, saying, *when the wife of ʿImrān said*, which we have already discussed. Her name was Ḥanna, the grandmother of Jesus. The two were sisters, one of whom was with ʿImrān son of al-Hasham, a descendant of Solomon son of David. On the authority of Ibn ʿAbbās and Muqātil [b. Sulaymān], some say that he was ʿImrān son of Matthan (Māthān) and not ʿImrān the father of Moses, since they are separated by eighteen hundred years. The children of Matthan were the chiefs of the Children of Israel. The other [sister] was with Zachariah; her name was Ashyāʿ and her father's name was Qāqūd b. Qabīl. Thus John (Yaḥyā) and Mary were maternal cousins.[70] On the authority of Mujāhid, *'My Lord, I vow to You what is in my belly'* [means]: I have made it incumbent that I make what is in my belly consecrated, a servant of the church (*bīʿa*) who will serve our places of worship. On the authority of al-Shaʿbī, 'consecrated (*muḥarraran*) for worship (*ʿibāda*)' means sincerely devoted to it (*mukhliṣan*). On the authority of Muḥammad b. Jaʿfar b. al-Zubayr, it is said that [*muḥarraran*] means emancipated (*ʿatīqan*), singularly devoted to the obedience of You, and I shall not use him for my own benefit nor dispose of him for any [worldly] need. One who was consecrated (*muḥarrar*) upon dedication would be assigned to the church for its upkeep, sweeping it clean and serving in it. He would not leave it until he reached puberty, whereupon he would be given the free choice of either remaining in it or departing for elsewhere.

They say that Ḥanna was unable to conceive and supplicated until finally she despaired. One day, beneath a tree, she noticed a bird feeding its chick. Her soul was moved out of desire for a child. She supplicated to God that He provide her with a child, and so she became pregnant with Mary.

[70] See above, note 63. In the Bible, however, the mothers, rather than the children, are cousins.

It is reported on the authority of Abū ʿAbd Allāh [Jaʿfar al-Ṣādiq] that he said: God, exalted be He, revealed (*w-ḥ-y*) to ʿImrān, 'I shall gift you a male child who shall be blessed (*mubārak*), and who shall cure the blind (*akmah*) and the leper (*abraṣ*), and who shall give life to the dead by My permission. I shall appoint him a messenger to the Children of Israel.' He [ʿImrān] told his wife Ḥanna, the mother of Mary, about this. And so when she became pregnant with her, she said, *My Lord, I vow to you what is in my belly, in consecration.*

Accept it from me, that is, my vow, accepting it approvingly. *You are the Hearer*, of what I say, *the Knower*, of my intentions, which is why I can rightly be trusted.

And when she bore her: they say that ʿImrān died while she was still pregnant, and she gave birth some time later, that is, she bore Mary. She had been hoping for a male child, but when she bore a female, she was embarrassed (*khajal*) and ashamed (*ḥayāʾ*); *she said*, with her head bowed, *'My Lord, I have borne her, a female child'*: there are two opinions regarding this. One of them is that what was meant by this was an apology for having vowed unjustly, as it was a female child. The other is that what was meant was to place the mention of her as a female before the petition she would make for her, given [a female's] lesser capacity for effort (*saʿy*)[71] and the deficiency of intellect (*ʿaql anqaṣ*). Thus He mentions this before, so that she might be justified in going on to make the petition with the words *I have entrusted the protection of her and her offspring to You.*

And God knew better what she had borne: He is informing [us], exalted be He, that He knows best about what she would bear, since He is the One who created her and gave her form. According to the other reading: And You, O Lord, know better than I do what I have borne. *And the male is not as the female*, since she is not fit for what the male is suited for. They were only permitted to consecrate males and not females, since the female is not fit for consecration in the way a male is, in terms of serving the Holy House (*bayt al-maqdis*), given what befalls her of menstruation, postpartum bleeding and the need to guard herself against displaying herself indecently (*tabarruj*) before people.

Qatāda said: The custom was only to consecrate male children. She meant that the male was generally superior (*afḍal*) to the female and more suited to [such] things. The [suffixed] *hāʾ* in His words *waḍaʿtu-hā* stands for what is

[71] Although suggesting an inherent physical weakness when compared to that of men, the term *saʿy* can also allude to the necessary fulfilment of religious observance (cf. Q. 17:19, *et passim* s.v. *'s-ʿ-y'* in the Qurʾān).

in His words *what is in my belly*, and that is permissible because *mā* falls on a feminine, standing for something known and indicated by the words *wa innī sammaytu-hā*, that is, 'I have made her name to be Maryam', which in their language means a woman who 'worships' or 'serves', according to what has been said. Mary was the most excellent (*afḍal*) of the women of her time and the most noble (*ajall*).

Al-Thaʿlabī related (*r-w-y*) through an *isnād* on the authority of Abū Hurayra that the Messenger of God (*ṣlʿm*) said, 'It suffices you to know about four only from among all the women of the world: Mary daughter of ʿImrān, Āsiya daughter of Muzāḥim and the wife of Pharaoh, Khadīja bt. Khuwaylid and Fāṭima daughter of Muḥammad'.

I have entrusted the protection of her and her offspring to You against [*the evil of*] *the accursed Satan*: she feared for her against the afflictions that in the main befall women and that is why she said that. Others say that she sought protection for her against the jab of Satan in the side, the one that makes newborns give their first cry. God thus made her and her son, Jesus, immune (*wiqāya*) to him by means of a [protective] veil (*ḥijāb*). Abū Hurayra related that the Prophet (*ṣlʿm*) said, 'No newborn escapes the touch of Satan when it is born and gives off its cry because of that touch of Satan, except for Mary and son'. It is reported on the authority of al-Ḥasan that she sought protection against Satan's leading her astray (*ighwā'*).[72]

Rāzī

Rāzī's enquiry into this passage commences with a survey of the opinions of grammatical authorities, simultaneously demonstrating his breadth of traditional knowledge and allowing him to explore the theological implications of the differences of opinion. Enduring philosophical questions, such as God's (pre-)eternal knowledge and the implications of this knowledge for events as they are narrated temporally in the Qur'ān,[73] are brought into play: how could the Qur'ān narrate that God made the family of ʿImrān one of His elect *when the wife of ʿImrān* uttered the words of Q. 3:35? Or, was it that the *when* (*idh*) here is not really a 'when', but simply a way of indicating an example of why that family had been predesignated as one of the chosen families, precisely because, as history would unfold, the wife of ʿImrān would speak the words of the vow as she ultimately does? Many of these theological questions are bound up in real terms with the grammatical explanations of particles of speech, which some

[72] Ṭabrisī, *Majmaʿ al-bayān*, s.v. Q. 3:35–6.

[73] See Michael E. Marmura, 'Some Aspects of Avicenna's Theory of God's Knowledge of Particulars', *Journal of the American Oriental Society* 82.3 (1962), 299–312.

authorities are wont to overlook even as others insist on their semantic, and hence theological, function. Typical of Rāzī's methodical and systematic approach to passages of the Qur'ān, he divides his exegesis into a series of 'issues', 'opinions' and 'enquiries'.

Rāzī makes several points that differ from those of other commentators. First, he explains that Ḥanna dedicated the child in her womb to God because she was inspired to do so by God, in much the same way that Abraham was inspired by God to sacrifice his son or that Moses' mother was inspired to put her son in a casket in the river. These are parallel examples of the sorts of painful trials to which God put these exemplary parents, making them give up their own children for His sake. Second, Rāzī gives a slightly different explanation for why Ḥanna would say *I have borne her, a female child*. For others, she says these words out of a sense of shame or grief; for Rāzī, she says these words by way of an apology to God that her vow cannot be fulfilled. Unaware of God's great plans for Mary, Ḥanna apologises in distress.

Finally, unlike other commentators, Rāzī gives two opinions on the statement that *the male is not as the female*. The first is a litany of reasons why men were preferred over women for serving in the temple, including that menstruation makes it inappropriate for females to serve there, that men are stronger than women and more fit, that men are able to mingle freely with people whereas women are not, and that men are less likely to be the subject of libel on account of mixing with people. The last two reasons seem to be purely influenced by Rāzī's own social milieu, but they may reflect longstanding notions of honour and shame that find echoes in the Qur'ān, such as in prescriptions for women's modesty, in prescriptions that the wives of the Prophet should stay indoors; and in prescriptions for the *li'ān* procedure, which is intended to set limits on false accusations against a woman's chastity. The second opinion is that the statement 'is actually to give preference to this female child over males', because Ḥanna had desired a male child but God instead gifted her a female. For Rāzī, this indicates Ḥanna's elevated spiritual knowledge, in that she recognises that God's will for her is superior to her own will for herself.

There are several issues (*masā'il*) regarding this:

The first issue: There are several opinions regarding the syntactical function (*iʿrāb*) of *when* (*idh*).

The first [opinion]: Abū 'Ubayda said that it is semantically redundant (*zā'ida*), the meaning being *The wife of 'Imrān said* [. . .]; it has no syntactical function. Al-Zajjāj said, 'Abū 'Ubayda has hardly achieved anything by this, since it is impermissible to annul a single particle from God's Book, exalted be He, and one cannot omit a single particle from God's Book, exalted be He, unless there is extenuating need (*ḍarūra*).'

The second [opinion]: Al-Akhfash and al-Mubarrad said that the implied meaning is 'Mention when the wife of 'Imrān said [. . .]'; and there are many such instances in God's Book, exalted be He.

The third [opinion]: Al-Zajjāj said that the implied meaning is that 'God has chosen the family of 'Imrān above [the beings of] all the worlds, when (*idh*) the wife of ʿImrān said . . .'. However, Ibn al-Anbārī challenged this, saying that God has conjoined [the mention of] the election over others of the family of ʿImrān with the choosing over others of Adam and Noah [Q. 3:33], and since His choosing of Adam and Noah came before ʿImrān's wife's words, it would be impossible to say that that the choosing [of ʿImrān's family] hinged on (*q-y-d*) the moment when the wife of ʿImrān spoke these words. However, it is possible to respond to this by [saying] that the effect (*athar*) of the election of some over others only appears when they were in existence and their acts of obedience became manifest. It is [totally] possible to say that God elected Adam over others in Adam's own time, and Noah when it was the latter's time, and the family of ʿImrān when his wife spoke those words.

The fourth [opinion]: Some say that this depends on what comes before, the implication being that God heard all and knew all[74] when the wife of ʿImrān said these words. But if it were said that God was Hearer and Knower before the wife said those words, and so what is the meaning of the dependency (*q-y-d*), we would say that His hearing, exalted be He, of that speech is tied (*q-y-d*) to the [coming into] existence of that speech, and His knowledge, exalted be He, of the fact that she will mention this, is [also] tied to [the very act of] her mention of that. Change in knowledge or hearing only occurs in relative (*nisab*) and interrelated things (*mutaʿalliqāt*).

The second issue: Zachariah was the son of Ādhin and ʿImrān [was] the son of Māthān, who lived during the same epoch. ʿImrān's wife was Ḥanna daughter of Fāqūdh. Zachariah had married his [ʿImrān's] daughter Elizabeth (Īshāʿ), Mary's sister. John (Yaḥyā) and Jesus (ʿĪsā), peace be upon both, were maternal cousins. As regards the modality (*kayfiyya*) of this vow, there are several reports. The first report is that ʿIkrima said that she [Ḥanna] was barren, unable to give birth. She was jealous of other women's male children. She thus said, 'O Lord, I vow to you that if you provide for me a child, I shall give him in charity to the Holy House [in Jerusalem] to be one of its custodians (*sadana*).' The second report is that Muḥammad b. Isḥāq said that Mary's mother could not conceive children until she became very old. One day, she was beneath the shade of a tree and saw a bird feeding its chick, and her soul stirred in desire of a child. She supplicated her Lord to bestow on her a child, whereupon she became pregnant with Mary. But ʿImrān died, and when she learned of this she consecrated him to God, that is as a servant

[74] The commentator is using the exact Arabic wording of Q. 3:34 *wa'llāhu samīʿun ʿalīm* (*God is Hearer and Knower*), but in order to facilitate the Arabic of the exegetical comment in our narrative, we have modified the English equivalent.

(*khādim*) of the house of prayer (*masjid*). Al-Ḥasan al-Baṣrī said that she did that by inspiration (*ilhām*) from God, and she would not have done it were it not for that, just as when Abraham saw in a dream that he was sacrificing his child and knew that it was a command from God, even if it were not by revelation (*waḥy*), and just as God inspired (*ilhām*) Moses' mother to cast him into the waters, even when it was not by revelation.

The third issue: A consecrated one (*muḥarrar*) is one who is made entirely free (*ḥurran*). One says *ḥarrartu al-ʿabd* to mean I have rid him of bondage (*riqq*) and *ḥarrartu al-kitāb* to mean I emended it [the book] and rid it of all manner of mistakes; *rajul ḥurr* is a man who is purely his own person and on whom no one has any claim; *al-ṭīn al-ḥurr* is [clay] that is free of any sand, pebbles, sludge or blemishes. As for the exegesis (*tafsīr*), they say that it [the child] was vowed purely to worship, according to al-Shaʿbī. It is also said that it was a servant of the church (*bīʿa*) or emancipated from the affairs of this world and vowed to obedience of God. They also say that it would be a servant for those who teach the scripture (*kitāb*) and instruct in churches (*biyaʿ*). The meaning is that she vowed to consecrate that child as an endowment (*waqf*) for the sake of obedience to God. Al-Aṣamm[75] said that the Children of Israel did not take booty (*ghanīma*) or captives (*saby*): their [equivalent of] manumission (*taḥrīr*) was to vow their children in the way we have mentioned. The reason for that was that, according to their religious practice (*dīn*), when a child became capable of service, it was incumbent on it to serve his parents. It was through such vows that they could avoid that type of benefit and appoint them as consecrated in dedication to the service of the house of prayer (*masjid*) and to obedience of God, exalted be He. They also say that the dedicated child (*muḥarrar*) would be placed in the temple (*kanīsa*), serving in it until it reached maturity (*ḥilm*), whereupon it would be given the choice of remaining [in service] or leaving. If it chose not to stay but to leave, it left; but if it chose to stay then there would be no more choice [to leave] thereafter. Every prophet had at least one child from among their progeny consecrated in dedication to the Holy House (*bayt al-maqdis*).

The fourth issue: This consecration (*taḥrīr*) was only permitted in the case of boys (*ghilmān*). As for girls (*jāriya*), they were not [deemed] fit for that on account of being affected by menstruation (*ḥayḍ*) and other impurity (*adhan*). Ḥanna made her vow an absolute one, either because for her it was premised on the implication [that God would thus accept it] or because through this [absolute] vow she sought a means to request a male child.

[75] On whom see ch. 1, note 101, in this volume.

The fifth issue: As regards the accusative form of *muḥarraran* (*in consecration*), there are two justifications. One is that it is in the accusative as a circumstantial qualifier (*ḥāl*) of *mā* (*what* [*is in my belly*]), with the implied sense being: 'I vow to You that which is consecrated in my belly.' The second, which is Ibn Qutayba's opinion, is, 'I vow to You that I shall make what is in my belly consecrated (*muḥarraran*).'

God then says, narrating through her, *Accept it from me; indeed You are the Hearer and the Knower.* 'Acceptance' (*taqabbul*) is to receive something approvingly (*riḍā*). Al-Wāḥidī said that it is derived from *al-muqābala* (countering), since it is received in recompense (*bi'l-jazā'*). And these are the words of one who is only seeking God's satisfaction (*riḍā*), exalted be He, through that action and to be sincerely devoted (*ikhlāṣ*) in worship. He then said, *You are the Hearer and the Knower*, meaning: 'You are the Hearer of my humble request, my supplication and call, and the Knower of the contents of my conscience (*ḍamīr*), my heart and my intention (*niyya*).'

Know that this type of vow was part of the Law (*shar*ʿ) of the Children of Israel, but it is not part of ours, and there is nothing to prevent differences in religious laws regarding such rulings.

God, exalted be He, says *And when she bore her*: know that this [suffixed] pronoun (*waḍaʿat-hā*) either refers to the female child in her belly, with Him knowing that it was a female child, or that it refers to the [feminine] 'soul' (*nafs*) or 'living thing' (*nasama*). Or, one could say that it refers to the 'thing vowed' (*mandhūra*).

God, exalted be He, then says, *she said, 'My Lord, I have borne her, a female child'*: know that the instructive thing (*fā'ida*) about this statement is that the vow had already been made by her to consecrate what was in her belly. She had been given to think that this was a male child, but she does not use that as a condition in her statement, even as their custom was that the child consecrated and made available for the service of the house of prayer (*masjid*) and to obedience of God should be a male child and not a female one. Therefore she said *'My Lord, I have borne her, a female child'*, fearing that her vow would not take on the form expected and apologising for uttering the aforementioned vow. She said that not as a way of apprising God, exalted be He above any need of an apprising, but rather she said that as a way of apologising.

God, exalted be He, then says *and God knew better what she had borne* (*waḍaʿat*): Abū Bakr on the authority of ʿĀṣim and Ibn ʿĀmir read [it] as *waḍaʿtu* ('I have borne'), the implication being that this is a narration of her own speech. The point about saying this is that when she said *'I have borne her, a female child'*, she feared lest she should be seen to be informing God, exalted be He, of that. She thus removed any [such] suspicion by saying *and God knows better what I have borne*. It has already been established that she only said that as an apology and not as a way of apprising [anyone]. The rest [of the readers] read [the verb] in the apocopated form (*jazm*) on the basis that this is God's [direct] speech. On the basis of this reading then, the meaning would be that He, exalted be He, said *and God knew better what she had borne* as an exaltation of her child and as a way of demonstrating her ignorance of the destiny (*qadar*) of that child: meaning, 'And God knew better about the thing that she had borne and the tremendous affair consequent on it and that He will make it and its child[76] a sign (*āya*) for all worlds.' She, in the meantime, was ignorant of this, anticipating nothing of it, which is why she was becoming distressed.

According to the reading of Ibn ʿAbbās, 'And God knew better what you had borne (*waḍaʿti*)' is a [direct] address to her from God, that is to say, 'You are not aware of the destiny of this gifted thing, while God is Knower of the marvels and signs that will come of it.'

God then says, narrating through her, *and the male is not as the female*. There are two opinions regarding this [statement]. The first: that what is meant by this is her preference of the male over the female child. The reason for that preference has several justifications. One of them is that their Law stipulated that only male children and not female ones could be consecrated.[77] The second is that it is appropriate for the male to abide in service of the place of worship, but it is not appropriate for the female because of menses (*ḥayḍ*) and all of the other eventualities that affect women. The third is that the male is fit for this service on account of his strength and tough nature, unlike the female who is weak and incapable of performing this service. The fourth is that the male is not liable to any censure when in service and when mingling with people, but this is not the case with the female. The fifth is that in the case of the male, he is not as likely to be libelled when mixing with people as is a female. All of these aspects entail the preference of the male over the female in this sense.

The second opinion is that what is meant by these words is actually to give preference to this female child over males, as if she had said, 'A male child is what I had desired, but this female child is gifted (*mawhūba*) by God, exalted be He, and the male child desired by me is not like a female child gifted by God.' This statement indicates that that woman was immersed in spiritual

[76] The author means Mary and her child to come, Jesus.

[77] We have emended the Arabic, which says *lā yajūz taḥrīr al-dhukūr dūn al-ināth*, since it translates as the opposite of the point being made. It is likely that *illā* is missing before *al-dhukūr*.

knowledge (*maʿrifa*) of God's majesty, knowing fully that what the Lord does with His servant is [always] better than what the servant desires for himself.

He then, exalted be He, narrates through her a second time, and this is when she says, *I have named her Mary.* This contains several possible enquiries.

The first enquiry is that, manifestly, these words prove what we have mentioned, that ʿImrān had died when Ḥanna was pregnant with Mary, which is why the mother took up the responsibility of naming her when custom had it that this was the responsibility of the father.

The second enquiry is that 'Maryam' in their language meant 'worshipping woman' (*ʿābida*), and so by this naming she sought from God, exalted be He, that He might make her immune (*ʿiṣma*) to the banes (*āffa*) of religion and of this world (*dunyā*), which is confirmed by her subsequent statement, *'I have entrusted the protection of her and her offspring to You against [the evil of] the accursed Satan.'*

The third enquiry is that His words *I have named her Mary* mean, 'I have named her by this appellation (*lafẓ*)', that is to say 'I have made this appellation to be her name', which indicates that a name, the thing named and naming are three different things.

God, exalted be He, then narrates through her a third statement, which is her saying, *'I have entrusted the protection of her and her offspring to You against [the evil of] the accursed Satan.'* This is because, after what she had desired in the way of [the child becoming] a man who would serve the mosque had eluded her, she humbly asked God, exalted be He, to protect it [her child] from the accursed Satan and to make her one of the righteous and obedient. The explanation (*tafsīr*) of *the accursed Satan* (*al-shayṭān al-rajīm*) has already been given at the beginning of this work (*kitāb*).[78]

Qurṭubī

What is immediately clear from Qurṭubī's commentary is the extent to which he has command of the traditional materials – grammatical, theological, legal and narrative. His is the only other major commentary in our anthology that adopts Rāzī's systematic division of key questions and themes into 'issues', which frequently outnumber the subdivisions of the *Mafātīḥ* itself. Qurṭubī, a Mālikī, has an opportunity to take issue with Shāfiʿī scholars on a legal question involving the requirement of an expiation for a woman who breaks her fast to have intercourse with her husband at his

[78] Rāzī, *Mafātīḥ al-ghayb*, s.v. Q. 3:35–6.

request. In this instance, a wife has two competing religious–legal obligations: to maintain her fast, and to obey her husband. In such cases, jurists were divided on the question of whether she was morally responsible for breaking the fast, or whether her husband bore that responsibility. Such discussions are possible because the text in question *and the male is not as the female* is taken as having significance beyond its immediate narrative context – the Levite tradition of service in the Temple – and entailing (or reaffirming) a social and legal distinction between men and women, particularly in cases such as marriage, where a husband has legal rights over his wife.

For Qurṭubī, one has children to foster a sense of intimacy and *sukūn*, which we have translated here as 'solace', but which also has the sense of dwelling and stillness after motion, thus connoting homeliness and comfort. Qurṭubī notes that by devoting her only child to the service of God, Ḥanna relinquished her own share of this intimacy and *sakan* in favour of Him, which shows her pious emancipation from worldly ties. As for her words *'My Lord, I have borne her, a female child'*, Qurṭubī says that this is a way of testifying to the reality of her situation, of proffering an apology for bearing a girl, and of also 'magnifying and exalting God', presumably by accepting His will for her.

There are eight issues regarding this [passage].

The first [issue]: [Regarding] His words, exalted be He, *When* (*idh*) *the wife of ʿImrān said.* Abū ʿUbayda said that *idh* is otiose (*zāʾida*). Muḥammad b. Yazīd said that 'mention when' (*udhkur idh*) is implied. Al-Zajjāj said that the meaning is: 'He chose the family of ʿImrān [to be above others], when the wife of ʿImrān said [. . .]'. She was Ḥanna daughter of Fāqūdh son of Qunbul, the mother of Mary and the grandmother of Jesus (*ʿm*); it is not an Arabic name and 'Ḥanna' is not known in Arabic as a woman's name. There is, in Arabic, Abū Ḥanna al-Badrī, but regarding this [name] they say that it should be Abū Ḥabba, whose name was ʿĀmir, which is more correct. There is a Monastery of Ḥanna (Dayr Ḥanna) in Syria and another monastery also so-called. Abū Nuwās recited:[79]

O Monastery of Ḥanna by Dhāt al-Ukayrāḥ
Whoever chooses to sober up from your intoxication [let them], but I won't

Ḥabba is used frequently [as a name] by the Arabs. Among these are Abū Ḥabba al-Anṣārī, and Abū'l-Sanābil b. Baʿkak who is mentioned in the *ḥadīth* reported by Subayʿa as 'Ḥabba'. 'Khanna', however, is not known, except for one daughter of the Qāḍī Yaḥyā b. Aktham. She is the mother of Muḥammad b. Naṣr. 'Janna' is likewise unknown, except for Abū Janna, the maternal

[79] Noted by Philip F. Kennedy in *Abu Nuwas: A Genius of Poetry* (Oxford, Oneworld, 2005), 135.

uncle of the poet Dhū'l-Rumma. All of this [can be gleaned] from Ibn Mākūlā's book.[80]

The second [issue]: His words, exalted be He, *'My Lord, I vow to You what is in my belly, in consecration'*. The meaning of *vow* (*nadhr*) has been discussed earlier and that it is not incumbent upon a servant unless he makes it incumbent upon himself. It is also said that when she became pregnant, she said, 'If God delivers me and I bear what is in my belly, I shall dedicate it in consecration.' The meaning of *to You* (*laka*) is 'to worship of You' (*li-ʿibādatik*). *Muḥarraran* is in the accusative as a circumstantial qualifier, but is also said to be an adjectival qualification (*naʿt*) of an elided object; that is to say, 'I vow to You what is in my belly: a boy consecrated (*ghulāmān muḥarraran*).' The former [grammatically] is more correct in terms of exegesis (*tafsīr*) and the narrative thread (*siyāq*), as well as the syntax (*iʿrāb*). Syntactically, to make the adjective stand for the thing described (*manʿūt*) is not permitted in certain instances, and in some it is permitted figuratively (*majāz*).

As for the exegesis (*tafsīr*), it is said that the reason why the wife of ʿImrān said that, is that she was ageing but still without child. They were a family of some stature before God. One day, when she was under a tree, she caught sight of a bird feeding its chick, and her soul was moved by this. She then supplicated to God that He grant her a child and vowed [to Him] that if she were to bear one, she would dedicate it in consecration – that is, emancipated and devoted singularly to God, exalted be He – as a servant of the church, confined therein and pledged to worship Him, exalted be He; this was permitted according to their Law (*sharīʿa*). Their children were obliged to obey them [in such cases]. When she bore Mary, she said, *'My Lord, I have borne her, a female child'*, meaning that a female is not fit to be a servant in the temple (*kanīsa*). It is said, because of the menses and the impurity that afflict her. It is also said, because it is not appropriate for her to mingle with men.

She had been hoping for a male child, which is why she made the consecration (*ḥarrarat*).

The third [issue]: Ibn al-ʿArabī said, 'There is no disagreement over the fact that the pregnancy of the wife of ʿImrān was no reason for [making] a vow of consecration, since she was a free woman. If his wife had been a slave girl (*ama*), then there would be no disagreement that a person ought not to vow

[80] Abū'l-Qāsim ʿAlī b. Hibat Allāh, Ibn Mākūlā, (d. between 476 and 488/1083 and 1095) was the famous literary figure of the Ibn Mākūlā family. The reference is to his magnum opus *Kitāb al-Ikmāl*, a treatise on proper names. J.-C. Vadet, 'Ibn Mākūlā', *EI*^{2}, III, 860–61.

away his child. For, whatever his situation may be, if the one vowing were a slave, then no statement of his to that effect would be affirmed, and if he be a free person, then it is not right for that [child] to be his possession, and the same is true of a woman. And so, in what aspect could there be a vow regarding that [child]? The significance of this, and God knows best, is that a person usually desires a child for intimate companionship (*uns*), help and solace. So this woman requested a child in order to have intimate companionship and solace (*sukūn*), but when God, exalted be He, granted her the favour of [blessing her with] a child, she vowed that her share (*ḥaẓẓ*) of intimacy with it should be forsaken and that it would be confined to service of God, exalted be He: that is the vow of the [spiritually] emancipated (*aḥrār*) from among the pious (*abrār*). She wanted it to be emancipated (*ḥ-r-r*) in two respects: emancipated from [the material desires of] this world and from its labours. A Sufi once said to his mother, 'O mother, vow me away to God that I might devote myself to the worship of Him and acquire knowledge.' She said, 'Let it be so.' So he set off, until he eventually gained insight and returned and knocked on her door. She asked, 'Who is it?' He replied to her, 'Your son, so and so.' She said, 'We have given you away to God and shall not go back on this.'

The fourth [issue]: His saying, exalted be He, *muḥarraran* (consecrated) derives from *ḥurriya* (freedom), which is the opposite of *ʿubūdiyya* (servitude); related to this is the *taḥrīr* (emending) of a book, which is to purge it of inconsistencies and corruptions. Khuṣayf reported on the authority of ʿIkrima and Mujāhid that one who is *muḥarrar* is devoted purely to God, mighty and majestic, and is not blemished by anything of this world's affairs. This is well-known in language, when one refers to anything that has been 'saved' (*kh-l-ṣ*) as 'free' (*ḥurr*), with *muḥarrar* having the same meaning. Dhū'l-Rumma recited:

Wa'l-qurṭu fī ḥurrat al-dhifrā muʿallaquhu
Tabāʿada al-ḥablu minhu fa-huwa yaḍṭaribu

The earring suspended upon the free (*ḥurr*) expanse of her nape
And the necklace far away from it as it joggles

Clay (*ṭīn*) that is *ḥurr* is one with no sand in it. A woman who ends up spending the night as one who is *ḥurra* is one whose husband has not managed to attain her on the first night. If he is able to overcome her, then she has, in the space of one night, become white-haired (*shaybā'*).[81]

[81] Lane (*Lexicon*) cites the grammarians as drawing this distinction between the *ḥurr*, the woman who has been married but not deflowered, and the *shaybā'*, a virgin bride 'on the night of her devirgination'. He notes that some relate this root, *sh-w-b*, to the root *sh-y-b* (to become white-haired), as though she has suffered such an affliction on that night that her hair turns white.

The fifth [issue]: [Regarding] His words, exalted be He, *when she bore her, she said, 'My Lord, I have borne her, a female child'*, Ibn ʿAbbās said, 'She said that because only male children were accepted in vows, but God accepted Mary.' *'Female'* (*unthā*) is a circumstantial qualifier, but if you wish, it could also be a substitution (*badal*). It is said that she raised her until she was old enough, then sent her off [to the temple], as reported by Ashhab on the authority of Mālik.[82] It is also said that she wrapped her in a piece of cloth of hers and sent her off to the house of prayer (*masjid*). She thus fulfilled her vow and dissociated from her. It is very possible that there was no partition (*ḥijāb*), as it was in the first years of Islam. For, in [the *Ṣaḥīḥ*s of] both Bukhārī and Muslim it is [reported] that a black woman used to sweep the mosque (*masjid*) during the time of the Messenger of God (*ṣlʿm*), but eventually died, as the *ḥadīth* says.[83]

The sixth [issue]: His words, exalted be He, *and God knew better what she had borne* (*waḍaʿat*) is, according to those who read it as *waḍaʿtu*, part of her speech and so the speech is continuous; this is the reading of Abū Bakr and Ibn ʿĀmir. The import in that is submission (*taslīm*) to God, humbling [oneself] (*khuḍūʿ*) and exalting Him above that anything should be hidden from Him. She was not saying it as a way of informing [God], since God's knowledge of all things is already affirmed in the soul of the believer. She said that as a way of magnifying (*taʿẓīm*) and exalting (*tanzīh*) God, exalted be He. According to the reading of the majority (*jumhūr*), these are part of God's words, which have been positioned ahead: it is implied that these should have come earlier, following on from *I have entrusted the protection of her and her offspring to You [against the evil of] the accursed Satan*, and God knew best what she had borne, as reported by al-Mahdawī. Makkī said, 'It is God's way of alerting to the path of steadfastness (*tathbīt*).' He thus says, 'And God knew better what the mother of Mary bore, whether she said [these words] or not.' This is further strengthened by the fact that if it were the words of Mary's mother, then it would have been more appropriate to say, 'And You know better what I have borne (*wa-anta aʿlam bi-mā waḍaʿtu*)',

[82] Mālik b. Anas, the eponym of the Mālikī school of law.

[83] The woman seems to have been known by the name Miḥjana, or the epithet Umm Miḥjan; see Bukhārī, *Saḥīḥ*, *Kitāb al-Ṣalāt*, *Bāb kans al-masjid wa-iltiqāṭ al-khiraq wa'l-qadhā wa'l-ʿīdān*, *ḥadīth* no. 106. Also cf. Q. 33:53. The implication here is that women frequented sacred places, without a partition between them and the men. The Prophet did not know about her death and she was buried with funeral prayers attended by some of his Companions. However, upon learning of her death, he requested that they point out her grave and he then performed the funeral prayer for her.

since she had made the call to Him at the beginning of the speech when she said, *'My Lord, I have borne her, a female child'*. There is also [another reading] reported on the authority of Ibn ʿAbbās: 'what you have borne' (*bi-mā waḍaʿti*), that is, this would have been said to her.

The seventh [issue]: His words, exalted be He, *and the male is not as the female*, have been used by some Shāfiʿī scholars, like Ibn al-ʿArabī, as proof that obeying her husband by having intercourse with him during the fasting day in Ramadan is not the same for her as it is for him in terms of the obligatory expiation (*kaffāra*) [that would be] incumbent on her.[84] But this is remiss on his part, for this [Qur'ānic] statement entails information about the Law (*sharʿ*) of those before us, which they do not themselves follow [anyway]. With these words this righteous woman only meant to testify to the reality of her situation, and as a continuation of her speech. For she had consecrated her child to serve in the house of prayer (*masjid*), but when she saw that it was a female, whose presence [there] was inappropriate and who was shameful (*ʿawra*), she sought to apologise to God for finding her to be the opposite of what she had intended her to be. 'Mary' is indeclinable because it is a feminine definite noun and is also non-Arabic (*aʿjamī*), as opined by al-Naḥḥās. But God knows best.

The eighth [issue]: [Regarding] His words *I have named her Mary*: this [name] means 'servant of the Lord' in their language. *And I have entrusted the protection of her* means Mary, *and her offspring*, means Jesus. This indicates that 'offspring' (*dhurriyya*) can apply specifically to [immediate] children. In the *Ṣaḥīḥ* of Muslim, Abū Hurayra said that the Messenger of God (*ṣlʿm*), said: 'No child is born but that Satan prods it so that it gives off its first cry, except for the son of Mary and his mother'. Abū Hurayra then added, 'Recite, if you wish, *I have entrusted the protection of her and her offspring to You against [the evil of] the accursed Satan*.' Our scholars say that this *ḥadīth* means that God, exalted be He, responded to the supplication of Mary's mother, for Satan prods (*nakhs*) all of the children of Adam, even the prophets and the saints (*awliyā'*), except for Mary and her son. Qatāda said: 'Every newborn is prodded in his side by Satan, except for Jesus and his mother, between whom

[84] This means that if she breaks the Ramadan fast by obeying her husband's request to have sexual intercourse, then she is not obliged to perform the same type of expiation incumbent on him (because she was not wrong for obeying him, but he was wrong for asking her to break the fast). For Qurṭubī, this is an incorrect interpretation of the phrase, which may imply that he disagrees with the interpretation as a whole, for, according to most jurists, women are not obliged to obey their husbands if the husband asks them to do something that constitutes disobedience to God.

was struck a veil so the jab (*ṭaʿna*) hit the veil and did not penetrate to affect them in any way.' Our scholars say that if this were not the case, there would be nothing special about them both. However, this does not mean that whoever is prodded by Satan is necessarily led astray and perverted. That is a false supposition, for how many a time has Satan placed himself in the path of the prophets and the saints intending all manner of acts to corrupt them and lead them astray, but God made them immune (*ʿiṣma*) to Satan's desires? As He, exalted be He, says, *Verily, My servants over them you shall have no warrant* [Q. 15:42]. And this, despite the fact that every son of Adam has been assigned his counterpart from among the satans, as the Messenger of God (*ṣlʿm*), said. As for Mary and her son, even though they were made immune from his prodding, they were not made immune from his subsequent attempts to latch on to them and to couple himself to them.[85]

Kāshānī

We introduce Kāshānī's commentary a verse earlier, at Q. 3:34, where he presents an ontological mapping of the eternal spirit onto individuals and material bodies generated in time. For Kāshānī, it is essential to understand that the world of the spirit has its own generative process that establishes a spiritual kinship of descent and progeny, mirroring those of the physical world. The best of physical constitutions, or admixtures (*mizāj*), is born at the moment when the purest of spirits and the closest to God come into life or become engendered. The constitution of the Prophet, for example, was, already in pre-eternity, the purest and the closest to God as a spirit, which is precisely what allowed it to become Prophet when engendered in this world. It makes sense to Kāshānī to posit that the messianic figure of the Mahdī, central to Imāmī Shīʿism, but also significant to millenarian and apocalyptic Sunnī *ḥadīth*, will be, insofar as he will be a restorer of God's justice on earth, from the physical progeny of the Prophet Muḥammad. Indeed, Kāshānī takes his ontological scheme a step further to offer that even after engenderment, that physical individual's soul – how it is configured and nourished spiritually – will have a direct effect on the soul of its child. Hence, ʿImrān's spiritual purity and the configuration of his soul led directly to the spiritually superior and blessed figures of Mary and her son Jesus. It is noteworthy here that Kāshānī practically redacts the role of Mary's mother, the wife of ʿImrān, in this process. Though he mentions that her intention had an effect on her child, and that the child is the reflection of the parents' intentions, in the final instance he focuses on male lineage and attributes Mary's truthfulness to her father, rather than to her mother.

Offspring each of the other: meaning in terms of religion and in truth, since generation by birth is of two types, formal and spiritual. Every prophet is a

[85] Qurṭubī, *al-Jāmiʿ li-aḥkām al-Qurʾān*, s.v. Q. 3:35–6.

successor to another prophet, in terms of the affirmation of Oneness (*tawḥīd*), spiritual knowledge (*maʿrifa*) and what concerns the esoteric (*bāṭin*) principles of religion (*uṣūl al-dīn*), and is thus his son, just like those who are sons of [Sufi] shaykhs in our times. As they say, you have three fathers, a father that has given birth to you (*w-l-d*), a father that has raised you (*r-b-b*) and a father that has given you knowledge (*ʿ-l-m*). So just as the existence of the body in the formal birth is generated within the womb of the mother from the seminal infusion of the father, so the existence of the heart in the true birth becomes manifest within the womb of the preparedness of the soul [generated] by the [spiritual] infusion of the shaykh or teacher; it is to this [latter] birth that Jesus (*ʿm*) alluded in his saying: 'He who has not been born again shall not enter the kingdom of heaven (*malakūt al-samāwāt*).'[86]

Know, then, that spiritual birth mostly ensues from the formal one by procreation, which is why, outwardly, prophets were also the progeny and the fruit of a single tree: ʿImrān son of Yaṣhur, father of Moses and Aaron, was a descendant of Levi son of Jacob son of Isaac son of Abraham; and ʿImrān son of Māthān, father of Mary mother of Jesus, was a descendant of Judah son of Jacob. It is also well known that Muḥammad (*ṣlʿm*) was a descendant of Ishmael son of Abraham, and that Abraham was [a descendant] of Noah (*ʿm*). The reason for [all of that] is that the purity or impurity of the spirit corresponds to the constitution (*mizāj*) in terms of uprightness (*iʿtidāl*) or lack of it at the moment of engenderment (*takawwun*). For every one, there is a constitution that corresponds to it and is specific to it, since the [divine] effusion (*fayḍ*) arrives in proportion to that correspondence, and the varying quality of spirits from pre-eternity (*azal*) is in proportion to their kinds and levels in terms of proximity [to] or distance [from the Divine]. Hence, constitutions vary accordingly in sempiternity (*abad*) so that they become connected to these [spirits]. Bodies (*abdān*) that are generated from one another are similar in constitution, for the most part, except perhaps in the case of accidental affairs where there is coincidence. Likewise, then, the spirits that are attached to these [constitutions] are close in terms of rank [to one another], corresponding in attribute, all of which reinforces [the fact] that the Mahdī[87] (*ʿm*) shall be from the progeny of Muḥammad (*ṣlʿm*).

86 John 3:3, 'Jesus answered him, "Very truly, I tell you, no one can see the kingdom of God without being born anew."'

87 For a survey of the concept of *al-mahdī* – lit. 'the guided one', who will return at the end of time as a restorer of justice – from early Umayyad times into its later theological inflections in chiliastic Sunnī *ḥadīth* and Shīʿī imamology, see W. Madelung, 'al-Mahdī', *EI*², V, 1231–8, and the references therein.

And God was the Hearer, when the wife of 'Imrān said *'My Lord, I vow* [. . .]' to where she says *the Knower*, of her intention as she bore witness with the words *indeed, You are the Hearer and the Knower*. Know that the intentions (*niyya*) and configurations (*hay'a*) of the soul (*nafs*) have an effect (*mu'ath-thira*) on the soul of the child, just as [different] nourishments (*ghidhā'*) have [different] effects on its body. Thus, the one whose nourishment is licit and wholesome, whose configurations of the soul are luminous, and whose intentions are sincere and directed towards the Truth (al-Ḥaqq), his child will be a believer, a truthful one, a saint or a prophet. The one whose nourishment is illicit, whose configurations of the soul are dark and vile, whose intentions are corrupt and despicable, his child will be corrupt or a vile disbeliever, since the semen from which the child issues is generated by that nourishment, nurtured in that soul and thus corresponds to it. That is why the Messenger of God said, 'A child is the innermost secret (*sirr*) of its father', and so the truthfulness of Mary and the prophethood of Jesus were the blessing (*baraka*) of the truthfulness (*ṣidq*) of her father.[88]

Ibn Kathīr

Writing in a period well after the crystallisation of the major classical works of Sunnī *ḥadīth* compilations (the two *Ṣaḥīḥ*s of Bukhārī and Muslim, as well as the major *Sunan* works of Ibn Māja and Abū Dāwūd, *inter alia*), Ibn Kathīr had a range of reference works to draw on. His mastery of the *ḥadīth* traditions as they coincide with or vary from a range of works from the *Ṣaḥīḥ*s to the *Sunan*s can be seen below in his attempts to reconcile two seemingly contradictory traditions from the Prophet about the timing of the naming of a newborn child. One tradition has the Prophet naming his son on the night of his birth, while another suggests that the naming of a child is one of the rites completed, alongside the sacrifice (*'aqīqa*, etcetera), on the seventh day after birth. Ibn Kathīr posits that one way to reconcile the two is to understand that on the seventh day, the name is announced publicly (allowing the actual naming to take place on the night of the birth). Overtly, this discussion has nothing to do with the Qur'ānic passage, but this is exactly where *tafsīr* comes into its own: exegetical deftness involves weaving into the commentary strings from the separate body of *ḥadīth* works where the Qur'ānic narrative allows for it. The line *I have named her Mary* allows for that. This example epitomises one of the defining aspects of the *tafsīr* genre and the process by which it solidified as a repository of so many other fields of scholasticism: an instance of interpolation becomes, in effect, an example of interpellation. Note how Ibn Kathīr is also very familiar with, and accurately cites from, Ṭabarī's commentary, another example of the discursive dynamics of the field of Muslim *tafsīr*.

[88] Kashānī, *Tafsīr*, s.v. Q. 3:35–6.

Modern scholars of gender will note that it is Ibn Kathīr's very deftness with the tradition, and his act of interpolation, that enables him to sideline the main gendered story here. He barely comments on Mary or her mother, only asserting that Mary's mother vowed her for service in the place of worship and maintaining that *the male is not as the female* refers to the female's lack of strength for such service.

This wife of ʿImrān is the mother of Mary (*ʿām*), and she is Ḥanna daughter of Fāqūdh, according to Muḥammad b. Isḥāq. She could not conceive. One day, she saw a bird feeding its chick and so she yearned for a child. She supplicated to God, exalted be He, that He grant her a child, and God responded to her petition. Her husband lay with her and she conceived. When the pregnancy reached its full term, she made a vow to consecrate the child, that is, [to make it] devoted solely to worship and to service of the Holy House (*bayt al-maqdis*). She said, *'My Lord, I vow to You what is in my belly, in consecration. Accept it from me; indeed, You are the Hearer and the Knower'*, that is, the Hearer of my supplication, the Knower of my intention. But she did not know whether what was in her belly was a male or a female. *And when she bore her, she said, 'My Lord, I have borne her, a female child – and God knew better what she had borne* (*w-ḍ-ʿ*): this [*w-ḍ-ʿ*] was also read as *waḍaʿtu* ('I had borne'), as the first person ending (*tāʾ al-mutakallim*) and as the completion of her previous statement. It is also read as *waḍaʿat* (*taskīn al-tāʾ*), as being part of God's speech, mighty and majestic be He. *And the male is not as the female*, that is, in terms of strength (*quwwa*) or stamina (*jalad*) for worship and service of the al-Aqṣā mosque.[89]

I have named her Mary: herein is an indication that one is permitted to name [the child] on the day of its birth, as is manifest from the narrative [here], since this is the Law of those before us and has been narrated as something affirmed. With that is affirmed the *sunna* on the authority of the Messenger of God (*ṣlʿm*), when he said, 'This night a child was born to me and I have named him with the name of my father Ibrāhīm (Abraham)' – cited by both of them.[90]

[89] That is to say, the Temple Mount (al-Ḥaram al-Sharīf), the site of the original Jewish temple in Jerusalem, where the al-Aqṣā mosque now stands. It seems that Ibn Kathīr is using the name of the mosque to stand for the earlier Jewish temple, for it was, in a sense, built on the ruins of the temple (though not in the more immediate sense in which the Umayyad Mosque in Damascus, Ibn Kathīr's home, was built in the Christian Basilica of John the Baptist, which had originally been a Roman Temple of Jupiter).

[90] The text has the terse *akhrajāhu* (lit. extracted/selected) in dual form, meaning the two great collections of systematically verified *ḥadīth*s: the *Ṣaḥīḥ* of Bukhārī and that of Muslim b. al-Ḥajjāj. For a full and succinct recent account of this process of canonisation of *ḥadīth* material in compilations, see Stijn Aerts, 'Canon and Canonisation of Ḥadīth', *EI*^{3}. For a standard introduction into the field, see Juynboll, *Muslim Tradition*; more formatively, see Ignaz Goldziher's classic late nineteenth-century study, *Muslim Studies*, II, ed. S.M. Stern, tr. C.R. Barber and S. Stern, with an introduction by Hamid Dabashi (London, Aldine Transaction,

It is also affirmed in both [works][91] that Anas b. Mālik took his brother, who had just been born to his mother, to the Messenger of God (*ṣlʿm*), and he performed the *taḥnīk*[92] for him and named him ʿAbd Allāh. In the *Ṣaḥīḥ* of Bukhārī [it is reported] that a man said, 'O Messenger of God, this night a child was born to me. What should I name it?' To which he replied, 'The name of your child will be ʿAbd al-Raḥmān'. It is also established in the *Ṣaḥīḥ* that when Abū Asyad came to him [the Prophet] with his son in order that he perform the *taḥnīk* for him, he [the Prophet] forgot [about it] and his father [Abū Asyad] asked for the child to be returned home, and then the Messenger of God remembered in a gathering (*majlis*), and [eventually] named him al-Mundhir. As for the *ḥadīth* of Qatāda from al-Ḥasan al-Baṣrī on the authority of Samura b. Jundub: the Messenger of God said, 'Every boy is held in ransom against the [performing of the ceremonial] *ʿaqīqa* for him. On his seventh day, a sacrifice is offered for him, he is named and his head is shaved'. This has been related by Aḥmad [b. Ḥanbal] and the authors of the *Sunan*,[93] and it has been verified (*taṣḥīḥ*) by al-Tirmidhī with this wording. It has also been reported, 'And he [the child] is also blood-smeared (*yudammā*)', which is more sure and preserves the original better, but God knows best. Likewise, the following was reported by al-Zubayr b. Bikār in the *Kitāb al-Nasab*: the Messenger of God (*ṣlʿm*) performed the *ʿaqīqa* for his son Ibrāhīm on the seventh day after his birth and named him Ibrāhīm; but the chain of transmission (*isnād*) for this does not hold and is in conflict with what is in the *Ṣaḥīḥ*. If it were sound, it would have to be interpreted as his [the Prophet's] having announced his name on that [seventh] day.[94] And God knows best.

He then says, narrating the words of Mary's mother, that she says *I have entrusted the protection of her and her offspring to You against* [*the evil of the*]

2006); for a non-Orientalist assessment of these early works (including J. Schacht's work), M.M. Azami's *Studies in Early Hadith Literature* (Indianapolis, IN, American Trust Publications, 1978) is worth consulting. Situating the politics of *ḥadīth* within modernist Muslim concerns, see Jonathan A.C. Brown's *Hadith: Muhammad's Legacy in the Medieval and Modern World* (Oxford, Oneworld, 2009). Still useful as an accessible survey is John Burton's *An Introduction to the Hadith* (Edinburgh, Edinburgh University Press, 1994).

[91] Referring to the *Ṣaḥīḥ*s, see preceding footnote.

[92] This is the ceremonial practice of softening a date skin or a pressed fruit to rub on the lips or palate of a newborn infant, still performed across Muslim communities globally. See, for example, Nathal M. Dessing, *Rituals of Birth, Circumcision, Marriage, and Death among Muslims in the Netherlands* (Leuven, Peeters, 2001), 24ff. More generally, as part of a newborn's welcoming into the practising community, see Françoise Aubaile-Sallenave, "Aqīqa', *EI*[3].

[93] In the main, the *Sunan* works are those of Ibn Māja, Abū Dāwūd and al-Tirmidhī (but al-Nasāʾī and al-Dārimī also produced their own collections).

[94] The attempt to reconcile this report with the one cited by Ibn Kathīr a few lines earlier is because the earlier report, that of the *Ṣaḥīḥ*, mentions that the Prophet gave his son the name on the night of his birth, not seven days later.

accursed Satan, that is to say, I commend her protection to God, mighty and majestic, against the evil of Satan; and she commended [to Him] also the protection of her offspring, who is Jesus (*ʿm*). God responded to her request, as mentioned by ʿAbd al-Razzāq [al-Ṣanʿānī]: we were informed (*anbaʾanā*) by Maʿmar [b. Rāshid] on the authority of al-Zuhrī [reporting] on the authority of Ibn al-Musayyab from Abū Hurayra who said that the Messenger of God (*ṣlʿm*) said, 'No child is born but that Satan touches him upon birth so that it gives off its first cry from his touching of him, except for Mary and her son'. Abū Hurayra then said, 'Recite if you wish *I have entrusted the protection of her and her offspring to You against* [*the evil of*] *the accursed Satan*.' Both [*Ṣaḥīḥ* authors] cite this *ḥadīth* from ʿAbd al-Razzāq. A similar version is reported by Ibn Jarīr [al-Ṭabarī] on the authority of Aḥmad b. al-Faraj ← Baqiyya [b. al-Walīd] ← al-Zubaydī ← al-Zuhrī ← Abū Salama ← Abū Hurayra ← the Prophet (*ṣlʿm*).[95] It is also reported by way of the *ḥadīth* of Qays ← al-Aʿmash ← Abū Ṣāliḥ ← Abū Hurayra who said that the Messenger of God (*ṣlʿm*) said, 'No child is born except that Satan has pressed him (*ʿ-ṣ-r*) once or twice, except for Jesus son of Mary and Mary'. The Messenger then recited *I entrust the protection of her and her offspring to You against the accursed Satan* [Q. 3:36].[96] And [it is also reported] by way of the *ḥadīth* of al-ʿAlāʾ from his father on the authority of Abū Hurayra; and Muslim has also reported it on the authority of Abū Ṭāhir ← Ibn Wahb ← ʿAmr b. al-Ḥārith ← Abū Yūnus ← Abū Hurayra. Ibn Wahb has also reported it on the authority of Ibn Abī Dhuʾab from ʿAjlān, *mawlā* of al-Mushmaʿill, on the authority of Abū Hurayra. Muḥammad b. Isḥāq reports it on the authority of Yazīd b. ʿAbd Allāh b. Qusayṭ from Abū Hurayra on the authority of the Prophet (*ṣlʿm*), as the original *ḥadīth*. In this version, it has also been reported by al-Layth b. Saʿd ← Jaʿfar b. Rabīʿa ← ʿAbd al-Raḥmān b. Hurmuz al-Aʿraj (the Lame) who said that Abū Hurayra said: The Messenger of God (*ṣlʿm*) said, 'Every son of Adam is jabbed by Satan in his side when his mother gives birth to him, except Jesus son of Mary, whom he set off to jab but ended up jabbing the veil'.[97]

Muḥsin al-Fayḍ al-Kāshānī

Fayḍ al-Kāshānī's commentary on these passages very typically draws on the major Imāmī works of Kulaynī, Qummī, ʿAyyāshī and Ṭabrisī, citing narrative materials

[95] This is the third of Abū Hurayra's three reports that conclude the commentary on these Qurʾānic verses in Ṭabarī. Ibn Kathīr accurately cites the chain of transmission.

[96] This report is also cited in Ṭabarī's commentary, above.

[97] Ibn Kathīr, *Tafsīr*, s.v. Q. 3:35–6.

attributed to a chain of imams from ʿAlī b. Abī Ṭālib through Muḥammad al-Bāqir and Jaʿfar al-Ṣādiq to Mūsā al-Kāẓim. The event captured in these Qurʾānic passages, where the wife of ʿImrān anticipates God's promised gift in her immediate progeny, a male child that she will bear, but which comes at one remove as the male child (Jesus) of the female just given to her, becomes a perfect allegory for the gift to mankind of the imams. Thus, as the imams themselves teach, the truth of their authority and divine election must be learnt from them and is to be taken on trust without question, even when it may not reveal itself in that specific epoch or lifetime. This has a significance for the continuing line of the imams during their time, but also for the final return of the twelfth imam at the end of time.

When she said is meant as 'mention when said'. Or, He was *Hearer* of the words of the wife of ʿImrān, *Knower* of her intention when she, *the wife of ʿImrān*, said [. . .]. This was the wife of ʿImrān son of Matthan, the mother of the virgin (*batūl*) Mary, and the grandmother of Jesus. She was the daughter of [one] Fāqūdh, and her name is generally acknowledged as being Ḥanna, as will be reported on the authority of [Jaʿfar] al-Ṣādiq (*ʿm*).

In *al-Kāfī*, on the authority of [Mūsā] al-Kāẓim (*ʿm*), [it is reported] that he said to a Christian (Naṣrānī), 'As for the mother of Mary, her name was Marthār', for which the Arabic [equivalent] is Wahība.

My Lord, I vow to You what is in my belly, in consecration: meaning 'emancipated' (*muʿtaq*) for the service of the Holy House (*bayt al-maqdis*), occupying himself with nothing else. *Accept it from me*, that which I have vowed, *for You are indeed the Hearer* of my words, *the Knower* of my intentions.

And when she bore her, she said, 'My Lord, I have borne her, a female child – and God knew better what she had borne: a parenthetical (*iʿtirāḍ*) statement, being God's words; *and the male is not as the female*: completing the words of the wife of ʿImrān. One reading has it as 'what I have borne' (*bi-mā waḍaʿtu*), as being her words to console herself, that is to say, perhaps God had some secret [wisdom] in all of this, or that a female would be a better thing [ultimately]. And he [Ṭabrisī] reported this [reading] in *al-Majmaʿ* on the authority of ʿAlī [b. Abī Ṭālib] (*ʿm*).[98]

In *al-Kāfī* and in Qummī, on the authority of al-Ṣādiq (*ʿm*), [it is reported] that he said, God revealed to ʿImrān [the following], 'I shall grant you a male child, perfect in stature (*sawiyyan*)[99] and blessed, and he will cure the blind and the leper, and give life to the dead by God's permission. I shall make him a messenger to the Children of Israel.' ʿImrān related this to his wife, Ḥanna,

[98] See Ṭabrisī's commentary above, *s.v.* Reading (*qirāʾa*).

[99] The use of *sawiyyan* here echoes the description of the angel who appeared in the guise of *a man, perfect in stature* (*basharan sawiyyan*) in Q. 19:17.

Mary's mother. When she became pregnant with her, she construed that she was carrying a male child. And when she bore her, she said *My Lord, I have borne her, a female child* and *the male is not as the female*: a girl cannot be a messenger (*rasūl*). God says *and God knew better what she had borne*. When God granted to Mary Jesus (*ʿm*) it was he whom ʿImrān had been given the good news of and whom [God had] promised. Thus, if we [the imams] should say something about a man among us and it should come to pass in his son or his son's son, then do not deny it.

In al-ʿAyyāshī, something similar to this [is reported] on the authority of al-Bāqir (*ʿm*).

On the authority of al-Ṣādiq, God's blessings be upon him (*ṣalāwāt Allāh ʿalayhi*), [it is reported] that one who is *muḥarrar* is assigned to the church, never leaving it. When she bore her, she said, *My Lord, I have borne her, a female child* and *the male is not as the female*: the female menstruates and has to leave the house of prayer (*masjid*), whereas the *muḥarrar* never has to leave the house of prayer. [It is reported] on the authority of one of the two [Imams], peace be upon both: she vowed that what was in her belly would be dedicated to serving worshippers in the temple (*kanīsa*), but the male is not as the female with respect to [such] service. He [the imam] said: She cleaved to it, serving them but struggling with them until she reached puberty, at which point Zachariah commanded that a partition (*ḥijāb*) should be set up for her [to screen her] from the worshippers.

I have named her Mary: she said that as a way of seeking proximity to God and as a petition [to Him] that He protect her [from sin] and make her righteous such that her actions correspond to her name, for 'Mary' in their language means 'worshipping woman' (*ʿābida*). *I have entrusted the protection of her and her offspring to You*, meaning, I seek refuge for her through Your preservation, *against* [*the evil of the*] *accursed Satan* (*al-rajīm*), the outcast one (*maṭrūd*): *al-rajm* is 'to stone'.

In the *Majmaʿ*, on the authority of the Prophet (*ṣlʿm*), 'No child is born but that Satan touches it upon birth so that it gives off its first cry from that touch of his, except for Mary and her son'. They say that this means that Satan covets to lead astray every newborn in such a way that it is affected by that coveting of it by him, except for Mary and her son, whom God made immune by the blessings of this petition for protection (*istiʿādha*).[100]

[100] Muḥsin al-Fayḍ al-Kāshānī, *al-Ṣāfī*, s.v. Q. 3:35–6.

Burūsawī

This major Ottoman-period commentary is interesting for what it shows us about the longevity of the scholastic genre of *tafsīr* itself. Based entirely on the commentary below, if one did not know that it was the work of an Ottoman scholar, Burūsawī, writing *c.* 1700, one would not have guessed that it post-dated the classical commentaries of Ṭabarī, Fakhr al-Dīn al-Rāzī or Qurṭubī by about 500 to 700 years. That is an immense period of time for the continued stability of a genre in terms of formal structure, hermeneutical method, named sources and even the content of the interpretations themselves.[101] Indeed, although not explicitly cited, the *tafsīr* materials of at least Zamakhsharī and Ṭabarī can be gleaned from Burūsawī's exegesis of these passages. The fact that these materials were still relevant and still available to the late seventeenth-/early eighteenth-century Ottoman exegete is significant for the study of the *tafsīr* tradition as a major sub-discipline of Islamic studies. A little over 200 years later, this continuity had become only just discernible (see *Manār* and Faḍl Allāh for these vestiges). By the early twentieth century, stylistic continuity was the exception and not the norm; but, in terms of content, the medieval tradition still exerts an influence in a genre where one of the authors' main objectives is to reconcile that tradition with current norms.

Idh is in the accusative because of *udhkur. The wife of ʿImrān said*: This is the wife of ʿImrān son of Matthan, the mother of the virgin Mary, grandmother of Jesus (*ʿm*), and she was Ḥanna daughter of Fāqūdh. If you were to say, 'But ʿImrān son of Yaṣhar had a daughter whose name was Mary, who was older than Moses and Aaron, and ʿImrān son of Matthan had Mary the virgin, how do you know that this ʿImrān is the father of Mary the virgin, and not ʿImrān father of Maryam sister of Moses and Aaron?' I would respond: It is sufficient to note Zachariah's guardianship as proof that this is ʿImrān the father of the virgin, because Zachariah son of Adhan and ʿImrān son of Matthan both lived in the same epoch and Zachariah had married his daughter Īshāʿ, Mary's sister, so that John (Yaḥyā) and Jesus, peace be upon them both were maternal cousins.

It is reported that she was barren, unable to conceive until she reached old age. One day, when she was under the shade of a tree, she caught sight of a bird feeding its chick and her soul was moved with desire for a child. So, she said, 'O God, I pledge to You a vow in gratitude if You should provide me with a child. I shall give him in charity to the Holy House so that he becomes a guardian and a servant of it.' She became pregnant with Mary but ʿImrān died while she was still carrying her. That is where He says, *My Lord, I vow to You*: a vow (*nadhr*) is what a person makes incumbent upon himself; *what is*

[101] This content, however, is often modified slightly while maintaining a similar form to earlier works.

in my belly: *what* (*mā*) is used to express 'child' because of the mysteriousness of this affair and that it eludes [even] the degrees of those of intellect; *in consecration* (*muḥarrar*): that is, 'emancipated' (*muʿtaq*) for the service of the Holy House, with me having no power over him, neither using him for any other service nor occupying him with any other affair; or, [it means] devoted to God and to worship of Him, neither labouring in the tasks of this world nor marrying, so that he is freed up for the work of the Hereafter. This kind of vow was permitted in their Law, for, according to their religion, when the child reached an age where he could be used for service, he was obliged to serve his parents. It was by way of such vows that they used to forfeit that kind of benefit, making them consecrated (*muḥarrarūn*) to the service of the house of prayer (*masjid*). Among the progeny (*nasl*) of every prophet there was one [child] consecrated to the Holy House, and only male children (*ghulām*) were so consecrated, for the girl (*jāriya*) was not appropriate because of what afflicts her of menses, and other [forms of] impurity (*adhan*), which requires that she leave [the place of worship]. Ḥanna, however, unreservedly vowed what was in her belly, either because she premised it on the fact that it would be a male or because she made the vow [precisely] as a means to request a male child.

Accept it from me: that is, what I have vowed; *al-taqabbul* (acceptance) is to take something approvingly. In reality, this was a petition for the child, for one cannot imagine acceptance before the thing to be accepted has materialised; nay, it was [even] a petition for a male child, given that females were not accepted. *Indeed, You are the Hearer*, of all things that can be heard (*masmūʿāt*), among which is my humbling [before You] and my supplication, *the Knower*, of all that can be known, among which is that which is in my conscience and nothing else.

When she bore her, that is, when she bore the living soul (*nasma*) and it was a female, *she*, Ḥanna, *said*, hoping for a male child, *My Lord, I have* [*indeed*] – the emphasis [*innī*] is a response to her false conviction – *borne her* (*waḍaʿtuhā*), *a female child* (*unthā*), in distress over the disappointment that she perceived for her hopes, contrary to what she had been expecting. The suffixed pronoun [*-hā*] refers to the living soul, and *unthā* is a circumstantial qualifier of it.

And God knew better what she had borne: an exaltation on His part of what she had borne. For, when she became distressed and sorrowful that she had borne a female child, God, exalted be He, said that she was ignorant of the great worth of this gift, and God was the One with knowledge of the thing that she had borne and the marvels and great affair attached to that. For He, exalted be He, shall make that [birth] and the child [in turn] a sign (*āya*) to all worlds, even as she was ignorant of that, knowing nothing of it, which is why she was distressed and sad.

And the male is not as the female: also words spoken by God, clarifying the exaltedness of what she had borne and extolling its status. The definite article (*al-lām*) in both of these [nouns] is for familiarity, that is to say, the male that she was desiring and in whom she was imagining perfectedness, and for whom the most that he could aspire to would have been to be a guardian, is not as the female whom she had been gifted. For her sphere of knowledge and her wish could not encompass the magnificent things that would come of this [female child], who would be superior to what she had requested, but she did not know any of that. Both of these sentences belong to God's speech, as parentheticals between Mary's mother's words *I have borne her, a female child* and her words *I have named her Mary*; and the purpose of these two [parentheticals] is to give solace to Ḥanna's soul and to extol what she had borne.

I have named her Mary: words of Ḥanna, coordinated (*ʿaṭf*) with her words *I have borne her, a female child*. In other words, I have made her name to be Mary. Her purpose in announcing that to the Knower of the Unseen was to seek proximity to Him, exalted be He, and to seek protection (*ʿiṣma*) for her. In their language, Mary means 'worshipping woman' (*ʿābida*) or 'servant of the Lord'. And it was also in order to make it clear that she would not be reneging on her intention, even if what she had borne was a female, and that if she were not suitable by nature for guardianship of the Holy House, then she should be of the worshipping women in it. Manifestly, these words indicate that ʿImrān had died before Ḥanna gave birth to Mary, otherwise the mother would not have taken it upon herself to name the newborn child, for it was customary for the fathers to have the responsibility of the naming.

I have entrusted the protection of her [. . .] *to You*: I seek refuge for her by Your preservation; *and of her offspring*, a coordination with the pronoun in the accusative, that is to say, her children; *against the* [*evil of the*] *accursed Satan*, that is, the one who is outcast. The original meaning of *al-rajm* is 'to stone'. [It is reported] on the authority of the Prophet (*ṣlʿm*), 'No child is born but that Satan touches it upon its birth so that it gives off its first cry from that touch of his, except for Mary and her son'. The meaning of that is: Satan covets to lead astray every newborn so that it becomes affected by him, except for Mary and her son, whom God, exalted be He, made immune (*ʿiṣma*) by the blessings of this petition for protection.[102]

[102] Burūsawī, *Rūḥ al-bayān*, s.v. Q. 3:35–6.

Manār

The *Manār* commentary begins by demonstrating the authors' familiarity with the historical exegetical tradition, which is always a significant window into the discursive nature of Muslim tradition. Beyond repeating some of the major points encountered in the other commentaries above, relating to Mary and her mother, what is ultimately important to note is how telling this commentary here is about the historico-political context in which the authors of the *Manār* lived. From their perspective, as Muslim intellectuals grappling with an increasingly fragmented Muslim caliphate and the continued presence of colonial powers, an opportunity to point to what they perceived as the causes of the apparent atrophy of Muslim societies, playing second fiddle to European cultural and economic hegemony, was not to be wasted. We find a two-pronged oblique attack: one internal to the community and one external. According to ʿAbduh and Riḍā, the lack of accuracy concerning the genealogy of Mary in the Judaeo-Christian scriptural texts and, by internalised analogy, Sufism's own purported ability to trace its genealogy to founding figures of Islam, serves to highlight two major concerns or perceived causes of this religio-cultural atrophy: internal division and external empire. For ʿAbduh and Riḍā, as for previous exegetes, Ḥanna's statement *My Lord, I have borne her, a female child* is a cry of anguish and despair. But, in their view, God rejects this and consequently rejects 'what her statements might insinuate about the vileness of a female child and its lower rank when compared with that of males'. This is an implicit critique of their own society and people's preference for male children.

Indeed, You are the Hearer and the Knower. That is to say that He, glory be to Him, was Hearer of the words of ʿImrān's wife, Knower of her intention (*niyya*) while she was communing with Him and vowing to Him what she bore in her belly in consecration: That is, emancipated from the bonds of others so that it would be dedicated to the worship of Him, glory be to Him, and serve His house; or be singularly devoted to this worship and service, engaging in nothing else. Her praise of Him, exalted be He, during this communion is because He answers prayers and knows [fully] what is in the souls of men and women when they supplicate. The teacher-imam [ʿAbduh] says: The mention of ʿImrān appears twice in these verses. Some say that they both refer to the one person, the father of Mary, inferring the proof of this from the fact they both appear in the same narrative thread. Most of them, however, say that the first one is the father of Moses (*ʿm*) and that the second is the father of Mary, upon her be [God's] satisfaction (*riḍwān*). But between the two there are almost eighteen hundred years. The details mentioned regarding this are drawn from what is acknowledged by the Jews. He [ʿAbduh] adds: The Christians (*masīḥiyyūn*) do not acknowledge that the father of Mary was called ʿImrān, but this is of no consequence, for it is not necessary that they would know every truth about that, and they have no [genealogical] chain of transmission (*sanad*) with which to support [the lineage of] Jesus, and that can be used as a proof argument (*ḥujja*). This is the same for the 'way' (*ṭarīq*) in the case of the Sufis (*mutaṣawwifa*), who claim that they are connected to ʿAlī [b. Abī Ṭālib] or [Abū Bakr] the Righteous one (*al-Ṣiḍḍīq*): they have no supporting chain of transmission to use as a proof argument either. I believe that the genealogy of Jesus [as given] in the Gospels (*injīl*) of Mathew and Luke differ. Had it been written down on the basis of [factual] knowledge, there would not have been this difference.

And when she bore her, she said, 'My Lord, I have borne her, a female child': they say that this is an informing report (*khabar*) but one not intended to inform (*ikhbār*); rather, it is an [expression of] anguish and sadness, and an apology – it is in effect a created statement (*inshāʾ*).[103] That is to say, she vowed to consecrate what was in her belly for the service of God's house and for that [child] to be exclusively devoted to worship Him therein. However, a female is not customarily suited for that, especially given the days of her menstruation. God, exalted be He, says *and God knew better what she had borne*: that is, the status of the female child to which she gave birth and that she would be better than many males. There is thus [on God's part] a rejection of what her statements might insinuate about the vileness of a female child and its lower rank when compared with that of males. He demonstrates this with His words *and the male* that she had asked for and desired *is not as the female* that she bore; nay, this female child is better than the male she had been hoping for. Ibn ʿĀmir and Abū Bakr both on the authority of ʿĀṣim and Yaʿqūb, read it as 'I have borne' (*waḍaʿtu*), as though it were her words. In this case, the meaning would be that the male is not like the female in terms of what each of the two is useful for.

I have named her Mary; I have entrusted the protection of her and her offspring to You against [the evil of] the accursed Satan: *al-ʿawdh* is to seek refuge (*iltijāʾ*) with another and to become attached to that [person]. Thus the meaning of *aʿūdhu biʾllāhi min al-shayṭān* is, 'I seek refuge and with Him and His protection against him [Satan]'; *aʿādhahu bihi minhu* means that 'he becomes a refuge for one from another, barring the latter and protecting the

[103] A *khabar* can be verified or disproved, while an *inshāʾ* is not subject to the same process of validation, being simply a 'creative' utterance. The two terms are considered to counter one another in Arabic rhetoric: see Adrian Gully, *Grammar and Semantics in Medieval Arabic: The Study of Ibn Hisham's 'Mughni l-Labib'* (Surrey, Curzon Press, 1995). There are implications for jurisprudence, for which see Sherman A. Jackson, *Islamic Law and the State: The Constitutional Jurisprudence of 'Shihāb al-Dīn al-Qarafī'* (Leiden, Brill, 1996), esp. 172ff.; also Michael G. Carter, 'Grammar and Law', *EI*[3].

former from him'. 'Seeking refuge with God' is realised through supplication (*du'ā'*) and hope (*rajā'*). *Al-rajīm* is one banished from all good. According to the *ḥadīth* of Abū Hurayra – as in the [*Ṣaḥīḥ*s of the] two venerable ones (*al-shaykhāyn*),[104] as well as by others, with the lexical version here being that of Muslim – 'Every son of Adam is touched by Satan on the day his mother gives birth to him, except for Mary and her son.' Al-Bayḍāwī explained 'touch' (*mass*) here as the desire to lead [the child] astray (*ighwā'*). The teacher-imam said: If the *ḥadīth* is indeed a sound one, then it is meant figuratively (*tamthīl*) and not literally (*ḥaqīqa*). Perhaps that is how al-Bayḍāwī meant it.[105]

Faḍl Allāh

For Faḍl Allāh, spirituality for spiritual growth is a practical philosophy anchored in a pious consciousness that is dynamic, forward-looking and trusting in God. The turbulent social and political decades of the second half of the twentieth century, especially in Lebanon, constitute the backdrop against which his spiritual and religious concerns are foregrounded. His hermeneutical method is to extract the spiritual principles and truths that form the Qur'ānic text's dynamic undercurrent: this is very clear from his constant use of the concept of *ḥaraka*, both in the movement of the narrative of the scripture and when he is fleshing out the ideal outlook for the believer in contemporary times. His interest in the story of Mary's mother is very much tied up with his concerns about contemporary family life in Muslim communities that were undergoing rapid modernisation, and which, in his mind, were somewhat unravelling under the pressure of secularising global currents and unable to adjust to a modernity shorn of pious sensibilities. Mary's mother is not only concerned for her immediate child but also for the future of her progeny in generations to come. Such selfless mindfulness of the present and the future, premised on a solid and unwavering trust in God, is what Faḍl Allāh enjoins his audience, fathers and mothers, to emulate, if only to alleviate their anxieties about the modern day and its precariousness. Mary's mother thus becomes exemplary for the modern Muslim man or woman.

Muḥarraran: 'emancipated' (*muṭlaqan*), such that he does not submit to any human authority (*sulṭa bashariyya*), either to the authority of his parents or to that of others, and is a trusted servant.

[104] Meaning Bukhārī and Muslim.

[105] 'Abduh and Riḍā, *Tafsīr al-manār*, s.v. Q. 3:35–6. The commentary proceeds to compare the figurative nature of this *ḥadīth* with the famous one describing the parting of the Prophet's chest by two angels while still a child in order to remove a 'black clot' from his heart and thus render the Prophet immune to Satan's wiles.

Mary: in their language, 'the worshipping woman' or 'servant woman', according to what they say. That is why she took to naming her thus at the moment of birth; it is as though she prepared her for worship by that naming.

The spiritual outlook of ʿImrān's wife

The story here condenses events, for there are no individual character features given for this woman, *the wife of ʿImrān*. Who was she? What was her name? And what were her personal attributes? [That is] because none of that matters for what the story aims to recount of the spirituality in which the family of ʿImrān chose to live their life, of their tremendous devotion to God, as well as the distinctive type of thinking that marked their consciousness (*waʿy*). This woman had lost her husband after conceiving from him. He may have been a righteous human being who spent his life in service of the House of God (*bayt Allāh*). She thus began to ponder the future of this child and did not think of herself in an egoistic manner, as many do when they consider whom from their children they might benefit, either materially (*māddiyyan*) or notionally (*maʿnawiyyan*), in terms of the wealth that might be acquired or the social status that might be attained. Rather, she thought of him becoming a servant of God. That is what the word *muḥarrar* signifies, so that he does not submit to any human authority (*sulṭa bashariyya*), neither to the authority of his parents nor to that of others. He thus would not work for anyone nor enter into the service of anyone. Rather, he would labour for God and serve His house, becoming thus 'emancipated' in the eyes of others in terms of the authority that he has over himself before them and as a slave (*ʿabd*) before God, on the basis of being a trusted servant (*khādim*) of His.

She thus vowed him to God – and such vows were permitted by their Law – seeking thereby to be close to God, since she had nothing other than that to offer to Him. It is a kind of sacrifice of a living and moving thing which the mother is offering to Her Creator – that he [the child] might remain obedient to Him and in His service. She supplicated sincerely (*ibtihāl*) to Him to accept it from her. For He is the Hearer who hears the supplications of His devoted servants, the Knower who knows the sincerity of their spiritual devotion (*ikhlāṣ rūḥī*) in worshipping Him.

This righteous woman remained in this spiritual state throughout the term of her pregnancy. Then came the promised day that she had been waiting for, when her dream might be realised, but the surprise when it came was [totally] unexpected. The newborn was a female, and a female was not suited to service in the Holy House, as that was the affair of males. She therefore sounded that desperate call of one apologetic and disappointed to announce that the dream had not come true, even if there was no need for her to make that announcement, for *and God knew better what she had borne*: it was He who created it and formed it. *And the male is not as the female*: if the newborn had been a male, the affair would have ended with him becoming a humble servant of the Holy House. But this female that she had borne, she would be eligible for God's ennobling, however that might become manifest, and, through that, His power to produce Jesus from her without a father.

This woman began to think again, as the verse suggests, as she had no desire to drift away from God insofar as her spiritual aspirations. And so if it was not ordained for her to give birth to a male who would become a servant of the Holy House, but instead bear a female, she would return to gentle communion with God concerning her new wishes. She had named her *Mary*, which in their language meant 'worshipping woman', as they say, so that she might become a worshipper of God, obedient to Him with regard to His commands and prohibitions. She then asked God to protect her and her offspring from the accursed Satan, sheltering them from his whisperings, hinderings, plotting, trickery and scheming, that they might be able to journey along the path of obedience without any deviation or slipping.

We are able to discover in this human being a woman who subsists in the most wonderful of relationships with God, with the purest of sentiments (*mashāʿir*) and the greatest emotions of the mind. For she is thinking of the future of her offspring with regard to God, in order to bring them close to Him and to distance them from Satan.

[. . .][106]

What can we infer (*istīḥāʾ*) from these verses?

We can infer from these verses regarding the outlook of ʿImrān's wife and the thread of the story with God's kindnesses towards our lady Mary [the following]:

1. His words, exalted be He, *and the male is not as the female* are not there in order to bestow superiority on the male over the female with respect to human spiritual (*dīniyya*) worth, acting as proof of that concept. Rather,

[106] The commentary moves to the subsequent lines before returning to the lines in question; we pick up the commentary at the point where *the male is not as the female* is discussed, about a page later, under the next major sub-heading.

manifestly it appears to be specific to that instance involving service in the Holy House, which was earmarked for males and not females, given the natural division of labour between males and females, meaning the division of roles on the premise that every person is given the facility to [accomplish] that for which they were created.[107]

2. This righteous mother was fully aware of the role of a woman in life and her need to be a human being full of faith and liberated from both the whisperings of the accursed Satan and his tethers, a woman who is openly dedicated to obedience and to the worship of God so that she may take part in those tasks delegated to her with intellectual, spiritual and practical trustworthiness, making her as trustworthy over her home, her husband, her children and her community as the man is in those tasks delegated to him. This is what made her turn to God so that He might protect her from the accursed Satan. And she did not restrict her [good] wishes to her [Mary] alone, but aspired that He might protect her offspring, too, from Satan, across generations and across time, and that she might live out in those immense dreams of hers that outstretching of faith into the future, her offspring a righteous offspring. For she did not desire to contribute, even if indirectly, in any way to the production of corrupted generations that reject God and His messengers, following other than the path of piety and uprightness of believers, the path of correctness.

That is what we ought to infer for our future aspirations for our children, whom we hope turn out to be righteous Muslims; and that in a way is tied up with our anxieties and practical concerns, making us humble ourselves before God in petition of that and moving us to realise it in a practical way. For that mental and spiritual concern for the righteous well-being of our children in the future becomes itself a lived reality in the way that we raise them, [pushing us] to seek sound methods and to pursue this situation with careful scrutiny and consciousness, monitoring the negative and positive influences of the environment to which they belong, the schools where they study, the company they keep and the classes that they are taught, and so on.

[107] The famous *ḥadīth* that ends with the Prophetic maxim 'and every person is eased onto that for which he has been created' (*wa-kullun muyassarun li-mā khuliqa lahu*) punctuates several reports and seems to have been first attested in the context of predestinarian discussions in early Islam. For the importance of these discussions and of the authenticity of early epistles regarding such questions of theology, the classic work remains that of Cook, *Early Muslim Dogma*. For the *ḥadīth* in question, one version can be found in Bukhārī, *Ṣaḥīḥ*, *Kitāb al-Tawḥīd* (97), *Bāb qawl Allāh taʿālā la-qad yassarnā al-Qurʾān liʾl-dhikr* (54), *ḥadīth* no. 176/7551; Muslim, *Ṣaḥīḥ*, *Kitāb al-Qadar* (46), *Bāb kayfiyyat khalq al-ādamī fī baṭn ummihi wa-kitābat rizqihi wa-ajalihi wa-ʿamalihi wa-shaqāwatihi wa-saʿādatihi* (1), *ḥadīth* no. 15/2649.

A lack of concern, conversely, turns into a [daily] reality of negligence that leaves their affairs without any proper and thorough planning.

3. God, indeed, received her [Mary] in a beautiful way, responded to the supplications of her righteous mother and protected her from the accursed Satan in a real and practical way, setting up for her a wholesome and pure environment that would ensure her growth naturally without negative or deviant influences: by means of Zachariah's guardianship of her, he who was from among the righteous prophets. He [Zachariah] embraced her and committed himself to raising her, orienting her and training her spiritually and practically so that she might become an extraordinary human being in the future by the extraordinary spiritual energy that stirred within her and that secured for her God's love and satisfaction, because of her devotional practices, which in turn made her a receptacle for God's guardianship, providing her with solicitude to an extraordinary extent. These divine kindnesses that surrounded Mary, as a result of the granting [by God] of her righteous mother's petition and sincere plea, can happen to any human being who opens their heart to God in sincere prayer that He look after their children and protect them from the accursed Satan and set up for them – out of the hidden mysteries of His knowledge – good opportunities to attain the highest degrees of faith and piety. For God has taken it upon Himself to heed the call of His faithful servants in what constitutes their welfare. This matter should compel us to seek refuge with Him concerning our current labours and our future concerns for our lives and the lives of our children. And this, so that hope might remain alive in us through trust in God, ridding our hearts of the fear of what the future holds in the way of phantoms, and relying on the safety provided in Him, for He is the One who answers the calls of the supplicant and gives security to the fearful.[108]

[108] Faḍl Allāh, *Min waḥy al-Qur'ān*, s.v. Q. 3:35–6.

ٱلرِّجَالُ قَوَّٰمُونَ عَلَى ٱلنِّسَآءِ بِمَا فَضَّلَ ٱللَّهُ بَعْضَهُمْ عَلَىٰ بَعْضٍ وَبِمَآ أَنفَقُوا۟
مِنْ أَمْوَٰلِهِمْ فَٱلصَّٰلِحَٰتُ قَٰنِتَٰتٌ حَٰفِظَٰتٌ لِّلْغَيْبِ بِمَا حَفِظَ ٱللَّهُ وَٱلَّٰتِى تَخَافُونَ
نُشُوزَهُنَّ فَعِظُوهُنَّ وَٱهْجُرُوهُنَّ فِى ٱلْمَضَاجِعِ وَٱضْرِبُوهُنَّ فَإِنْ أَطَعْنَكُمْ
فَلَا تَبْغُوا۟ عَلَيْهِنَّ سَبِيلًا إِنَّ ٱللَّهَ كَانَ عَلِيًّا كَبِيرًا

3 Marital roles
(Q. 4:34)

Men are maintainers of women, by that which God has distinguished the one over the other, and by that which they expend of their property. So, righteous women are devoutly obedient women, those who safeguard during absence what for God is to be safeguarded; and if you fear the women's defiance, then admonish them, and forsake them in the beds, and strike them; but if they obey you, seek not a way against them. Indeed God is high, mighty.

Al-rijālu qawwāmūna ʿalāʾl-nisāʾi bi-mā faḍḍala Allāhu baʿḍahum ʿalā baʿḍin wa-bimā anfaqū min amwālihim faʾl-ṣāliḥātu qānitātun ḥāfiẓātun liʾl-ghaybi bi-mā ḥafiẓa Allāhu waʾllātī takhāfūna nushūza-hunna fa-ʿiẓūhunna waʾhjurūhunna fīʾl-maḍājiʿ, waʾḍribuhunna fa-in aṭaʿnakum fa-lā tabghū ʿalayhinna sabīlan inna Allāha kāna ʿaliyyan kabīran

Because of the prerogative that Q. 4:34 grants to men over women, it may be considered one of the most controversial verses in the Qurʾān today. Based on its social context, we read this verse as a restriction of husbands' rights.[1] Yet, as many scholars have shown, commentaries on this verse from within the *tafsīr* tradition are pervaded by patriarchal views of marital relations. Moreover, scholars such as amina wadud and Hadia Mubarak have pointed to a modern tendency to elide the *tafsīr* tradition and the Qurʾān itself, so that the Qurʾān is always read through the lens of *tafsīr*, and the biases of the authors of *tafsīr* are read into the Qurʾān.[2] Sa'diyya Shaikh describes how such interpretations 'foster a mode of gender relations that practically disempowers Muslim women'.[3]

In what follows, the authors' presumption of male superiority will become obvious; so too will the authors' presumption of a patriarchal society in

[1] This view that Q. 4:34 is a restriction has been taken by many feminist interpreters, perhaps most prominently by Barlas, *Believing Women in Islam*.

[2] wadud, *Qur'an and Woman*, especially 1–11; Hadia Mubarak, 'Breaking the Interpretive Monopoly: A Re-examination of Verse 4:34', *Hawwa* 2.3 (2004), 261–89.

[3] Sa'diyya Shaikh, 'Exegetical Violence: *Nushūz* in Qurʾānic Gender Ideology', *Journal for Islamic Studies* 17 (1997), 49–73.

which men are empowered over women. In these texts, women's own voices and experiences are absent, even as the authors themselves justify such patriarchy as natural and right and seek to encourage husbands to act justly towards their wives and not to oppress them. Against the background of the textual tradition, contemporary reformists and feminists have offered their own responses to this verse; a selection of these responses is represented in the interviews at the end of the chapter.[4] Many modern Muslim interpreters are concerned with ethical considerations and what is best to do in today's context of universal human rights. Their renewed engagement with difficult Qurʾānic passages takes several forms: semantic reconsideration, where the canonical lexicon is etymologically re-examined; cultural contextualisation, in which the overt meaning of the passage is accepted but its application today is rejected; rejection of such passages or judging them to be abrogated; reinterpretation of such passages through daily practice and lived realities, rather than solely through the textual tradition or traditionalist male communal authorities.[5] However, reformist interpretations of the Qurʾān are routinely dismissed or ignored as having less religious validity or scholarly merit than traditional interpretations, particularly when those reformists are women.[6] Furthermore, as Kecia Ali has documented, women's scholarship is often marginalised, especially in the academic fields of Qurʾānic studies and the study of early Islam.[7] The interviews at the end of this chapter are one attempt to give a platform to voices that might otherwise be excluded from discussions of the Qurʾān or the textual tradition of *tafsīr*, which, in part through a methodological conservatism, also tends to preserve an ideological conservatism on the issue of gender equality.

[4] Aysha Hidayatullah has documented what she calls 'first wave' and 'second wave' Muslim feminist responses to difficult Qurʾānic verses like Q. 4:34. As mentioned earlier in this volume, the first wave denied any problem with the Qurʾān, while the second wave argues that such verses pose a problem for notions of justice that are based on worldly egalitarianism. See Hidayatullah, *Feminist Edges of the Qurʾān*.

[5] For re-engagement with the text, see, for instance, Mir-Hosseini, al-Sharmani and Rumminger, *Men in Charge?*; Chaudhry, *Domestic Violence and the Islamic Tradition*; Murad H. Elsaidi, 'Human Rights and Islamic Law: A Legal Analysis Challenging the Husband's Authority to Punish "Rebellious" Wives', *Muslim World Journal of Human Rights* 7.2 (2011), 1–25. For an interpretation based on lived realities, see Sa'diyya Shaikh, 'A *Tafsir* of Praxis: Gender, Marital Violence, and Resistance in a South African Muslim Community' in *Violence against Women in Contemporary World Religions: Roots and Cures*, ed. Daniel C. Maguire and Sa'diyya Shaikh (Cleveland, OH, Pilgrim Press, 2007), 66–89.

[6] On this, see, for instance, wadud, *Inside the Gender Jihad*, 189.

[7] On this, see particularly Kecia Ali, 'The Omnipresent Male Scholar', *Critical Muslim* 8 (September 2013), 61–73; eadem, 'The Politics of Citation', *Gender Avenger* blog, 31 May 2019, accessed 21 September 2020, https://www.genderavenger.com/blog/politics-of-citation; eadem, 'No Manthology is an Island', *Journal of Feminist Studies in Religion* blog, 4 June 2019, accessed 21 September 2020, https://www.fsrinc.org/no-manthology-is-an-island/.

The following paragraphs offer a brief summary of the different parts of Q. 4:34 and a brief overview of the interpretations taken in the commentaries and interviews that comprise this chapter; this is followed by a 'Key terms' section that describes specific words in further detail.

Q. 4:34 begins by stating that men are *maintainers* (*qawwāmūn*) of women. This multivalent term indicates both support/maintenance and a prerogative over them (see 'Key terms': *qawwāmūn*). The reason for this position with regard to women is that God has given men a *faḍl* over them ('Key terms': *faḍl*), which linguistically echoes Q. 4:32. *By that which they expend of their property* refers here to maintenance: the word for 'spending' is from the root *n-f-q*, which also describes maintenance. Thus, in the Qur'ān, men's position over women is related to their financial duties towards them, and presumably to their relative position in society, which is taken for granted in the Qur'ānic discourse (on which, see the Prolegomenon).

Men's privileged status is confirmed by many *ḥadīths*; the most widely cited is the verse's occasion of revelation, which the commentators often cite when initially describing men's position as *maintainers*. Even the earliest commentator, Muqātil b. Sulaymān, recounts a story of a woman, Ḥabība bt. Zayd, whose husband slaps her. Her father becomes angry and goes with her to the Prophet; the Prophet orders retaliation (*qiṣāṣ*) against the husband, which could mean a financial penalty or an in-kind return of the offence. However, as they are leaving, Muḥammad calls them, saying, 'I wanted one thing and God wanted another, and that which God wants is [always] better'. Thus, according to this version of the story, although the Prophet wanted to limit husbands' rights to hit their wives, God established this verse as a confirmation of that right. Some modern interpreters believe that this *ḥadīth* is fabricated because the Prophet would not have wanted something that God did not want. Furthermore, unlike the general Qur'ānic context, this *ḥadīth* establishes the striking as a right rather than as a limitation, and it bears a close relationship to *fiqh* rulings which grant husbands almost unlimited power to hit their wives without legal consequence.

After the initial statement of the relationship between men and women, Q. 4:34 goes on to describe *righteous women* (*ṣāliḥāt*) as being *devoutly obedient women* (*qānitāt*) (cf. Q. 33:35) who *safeguard during absence what for God is to be safeguarded*, meaning – according to the commentators – that a wife should safeguard her chastity and her husband's property in his absence. Many commentators say that God safeguards the women who safeguard Him, meaning that when they are devoutly obedient, He protects them.

The last part of the verse is in command form, and tells husbands that if they fear that their wives will defy them ('Key terms': *nushūz*), they may chastise them in three steps: admonishment, forsaking in the bed, and striking. It concludes by telling the husbands that if their wives obey, they should not seek a way against them, and reminds the husbands of God's might and exaltedness. This establishes a Qur'ānic limit on the husbands' rights, in that they are not allowed to chastise their wives without reason, and reminds them of God's power over them, a nuance which is not lost on the commentators.

As shall be documented below, the commentators have a specific idea of fairness and justice within the marital hierarchy.[8] This takes different forms, including limiting the extent of the wife's obedience and encouraging men not to take full advantage of their rights over their wives. Ṭabarī cites the early authority Ibn ʿAbbās as saying that a wife owes her husband obedience only in certain matters, not in all matters, and, in a separate chain of narration, that when a wife is righteous, her husband should be righteous to her. Other commentators make it clear that a wife's main duty is to agree to sexual relations with her husband. According to legal rulings, and by extension *tafsīr*, a man establishes himself as the 'owner' of the right to sexual relations with his wife when he pays the bridal payment to her.[9] For them, a wife's main form of disobedience is her refusal to engage in sexual relations with her husband.

Though medieval commentators never question a man's right to be in charge of his wife, and only in rare instances do they question his right to chastise her physically, they frequently warn husbands against overstepping the bounds, saying that God will punish them for any abuses of authority. In the words of Rāzī: 'When the women are too weak to defend themselves against your injustice, and when they are incapable of demanding justice from you, then know that God, glory be to Him, is high, vanquishing, mighty, powerful, and will take vengeance on you for them, and He will give them the full share of the rights that you owe them.' Rāzī is under no illusion

[8] On medieval interpretations of Q. 4:34 and a more detailed analysis of the exegetes' notions of fairness and justice, see Bauer, *Gender Hierarchy*, 161–218 (ch. 5: 'Who Does the Housework? The Ethics and Etiquette of Marriage').

[9] In the words of Kecia Ali, '[The jurists'] central notion about marriage was that the marriage contract granted a husband, in exchange for payment of dower, a form of authority or domination (*milk*) over his wife's sexual (and usually reproductive) capacity. The same term, *milk*, was used – though with a somewhat different semantic range – for ownership of a slave. It was the exclusive *milk* over a particular woman – as a slave or as a wife – that rendered sexual access licit.' Ali, *Marriage and Slavery in Early Islam*, 6.

that God will intervene to protect women in this world; rather, he refers to God punishing unjust husbands and vindicating victimised wives in the Hereafter. While most commentators are not as outspoken as Rāzī, they nevertheless recognise that legal permission does not equal moral good; they can recognise a space in which it is morally better for the husband not to exercise his full rights.

Even those commentators who did not limit a wife's obedience still limited a husband's response: all recognised that there were three steps to be taken in sequence and if the wife obeyed at any step, then they could go no further. To qualify the striking, they referenced the Prophet's Farewell Pilgrimage Oration, which has him say that any strike should be non-severe, or non-injurious (*ghayr mubarriḥ*). A few commentators question the husband's moral prerogative to strike his wife, even as they recognise his legal prerogative to do so. Following Shāfiʿī, Rāzī recommends not hitting. For some commentators, the social status of the wife makes a difference to her husband's rights: Qurṭubī recommends that husbands should not strike their wives if the wives are nobly born, for such treatment befits slave women more than free women;[10] Rashīd Riḍā cites a *ḥadīth* that asks, 'Is not one of you ashamed to strike his wife as he strikes a slave, striking her at the beginning of the day and then making love with her at its end?' These interpretations and *ḥadīth*s recognise the degradation involved in a physical chastisement, even when it does not cause injury.

Commenting on the final part of the verse, *God is high, mighty*, many pre-modern commentators say that husbands have no right to task their wives with loving them, often explaining that 'her heart is not in her hands', meaning she can only be chastised for her outward behaviour, not her inner state.[11] This highlights the difference between their conceptions of marriage

[10] Manuela Marín, 'Disciplining Wives: A Historical Reading of Qur'ân 4:34', *Studia Islamica* 97 (2003), 5–40.

[11] There is an interesting jurisprudential undertone to this point, namely that a person is judged according to their intentions and actions, not their emotions, and this seems to be the view of the exegetes: Qushayrī, below, goes so far as to say that God controls a person's feelings and that a wife cannot be held responsible for her feelings. However, the notion that a person is only judged on actions and intentions deserves some qualification. According to the Qur'ān, God knows a person's innermost feelings (*sirr*: Q. 6:3; 9:78; 20:7 *et passim*), the implication being that the pious person must eventually come to control his or her impulses so that their emotions are aligned with what satisfies God and not with what satisfies their desires. And yet there is a recognition, both in the Qur'ān and by the exegetes, that these desires persist and must constantly be guarded against. A repeated Qur'ānic example is that people must control their love of worldly things and, for instance, give alms (*zakāt*); on following one's desires, see also Q. 7:176 *et passim*. Thus, for the exegetes, the wife demonstrates her obedience to God by controlling her actions and obeying the ordinances that, in their view, He has imposed: which is to say, agreeing to sexual relations with her husband. It may be noted here, however, that nowhere does the Qur'ān itself specify this as a wife's duty.

as a hierarchical social institution, in which husbands have the right to enforce particular behaviours and in which marriage brings families together (see Q. 4:35, in which the families negotiate with each other when the marital dispute from Q. 4:34 persists), and modern conceptions of a love-based match between two people who come together as equal individuals. This also indicates that the medieval commentators' view of marriage is akin to the just rule of a state. If the subject/woman is in an outward state of obedience, the ruler/husband has no right to ask for more.

Contemporary conservative commentators seek to justify the marital hierarchy by referring to the innate differences between the sexes. For them, as for medieval commentators, the marital hierarchy is not based on a particular social circumstance, but rather on the innate qualities of the sexes. Modern conservative commentators often omit the warnings, ubiquitous in medieval commentaries, of God's punishment of husbands who overstep; an example below is the interpretation of Faḍl Allāh. By omitting such warnings, conservatives overlook the potential for abuse within the marital hierarchy, even as they argue that the husband's power over his wife is limited in key ways. Thus, unlike medieval commentators, their modern conservative counterparts do not admit the possibility of structural violence in a hierarchical marriage, but they often say, for instance, that the husband's beating should be 'light' or a 'slap', language that seeks to mitigate the violence inherent in such acts.

In sharp contrast to the conservative views represented in the written commentarial tradition, reformist interpreters, such as those who are interviewed at the end of this chapter, reconceptualise the nature of marriage so that it is not inherently hierarchical. Reformists recognise that the marital roles are flexible, not based on the inherent nature of the sexes. For many reformists, husbands and wives should be free to choose for themselves who works and the division of household labour. Some interpreters even say that this verse has been abrogated because it was only specific to a certain time and place.

This is a verse which tests the limits of what it means to be commonly decent to one's spouse, and is thus an occasion for observing the ways in which interpreters negotiate the boundaries of acceptability. The above paragraphs have given a basic summary of the commentaries presented below; but any close reading will reveal differences in tone and substance among both medieval and modern commentators. Some stress the limits on men's authority, some stress women's deficiencies or 'natural' differences between the sexes. The interpretations of Q. 4:34 provide a test-case on the ways that current social concerns and norms affect interpretation.

Key terms

Faḍl: distinction, surplus, preference over another, superiority or merit; used throughout the Qur'ān to denote God's creational prerogative as a result of which, for example, some people are distinguished over others by having been granted more wealth (Q. 4:32); certain messengers (Q. 2:253) and prophets (Q. 17:55) have been given a distinction over others; certain creation (humankind) is superior to other creation (Q. 17:70); and even some food is distinguished from other food in flavour (Q. 13:4). *Faḍl* is a theme throughout *sūrat al-Nisā'*, with the root appearing some fourteen times in the *sūra*, out of 104 occurrences in the Qur'ān as a whole (i.e. thirteen per cent of all occurrences). In Q. 4:32, the implication seems to be that the divine prerogative of creating distinctions among people is purposeful: in that instance, people are admonished not to *covet that by which God has distinguished some of you over others; men have been given a share of what they earn, and women have been given a share of what they earn*. The distinction mentioned here may relate to rulings on inheritance that appear several verses earlier, and thus it may refer to men's worldly prerogative; as explained above, the exegetes relate the advantage here to men's prerogative over women in Q. 4:34.[12] And yet, according to Q. 17:21, God's *faḍl* in the Hereafter is contrasted with that in this world: in the Hereafter, the distinction (*tafḍīl*) among people will be greater (than the distinctions in this world); in that sense, spiritual *faḍl* may be considered to supersede the *faḍl* in this world. *Faḍl* in *sūrat al-Nisā'* appears first in Q. 4:32, and while the *faḍl* in that verse and in Q. 4:34 may be construed as material bounty, at the end of *sūrat al-Nisā'* this theme comes to its natural conclusion: in Q. 4:173, we are told that God will grant His *faḍl* to those who believe and do righteous deeds, and indeed Q. 4:175 is a clear indication of His *faḍl* as a spiritual reward: *As for those who believe and hold fast to Him, He will admit them to His mercy and faḍl, and He will guide them along a straight path to Him*. The spiritual *faḍl* that God grants on the basis of a person's deeds in Q. 4:173 and Q. 4:175 is thus qualitatively different from the *faḍl* that He grants to men over women in Q. 4:34. Ultimately, the *faḍl* that God grants to some in this world entails prerogatives in this world, while the *faḍl* that He grants by virtue of human

[12] Though, note that at the end of Q. 4:32, both women and men are then enjoined to seek of God's *faḍl*; here, at least, God's *faḍl* in this world (the prerogative He grants to some of His creation) and His *faḍl* in the next (the bounty He grants in the Hereafter) may be elided into one.

behaviour is related to a person's piety, and is associated with closeness to Him and a prerogative in the Hereafter.

Maʿrūf: something that adheres to custom, is correct and right in a moral sense, or is well-known, which we have translated in this work in various ways, usually 'common decency' and 'what is expected'. This term often comes up in reference to how men should treat women and also in reference to women's obedience. When the commentators say that women should obey *bi'l-maʿrūf*, they mean that they should obey in those matters in which it is correct and right that they obey, those matters that are expected of them or those matters that are customary.[13]

Mubarriḥ: something that is severe, violent, injurious or harmful. In its verbal form, this can also mean annoying or hurting someone. In his Farewell Pilgrimage Oration, the Prophet is attributed with saying that if a husband strikes his wife, it should be non-*mubarriḥ*: not severe, injurious, violent, or harmful.

Nushūz: in its Qurʾānic usage, denotes something that 'rises up'. The word appears four times in the Qurʾān: Q. 58:11, *If it is said, rise, then rise!* (*wa-idhā qīla'nshuzū, fa'nshuzū*); Q. 2:259, *look at the bones, how we raise them* (*nunshizuhā*) *and clothe them with flesh*; Q. 4:34, *if you fear the women's defiance*; and Q. 4:128, *if a woman should fear nushūz or desertion from her husband, there is no sin on the two of them if they reach a reconcilement; for reconcilement is better*. Q. 58:11 admonishes the believers to have appropriate comportment: in gatherings, people must rise if asked; while Q. 2:259 refers to a repeated Qurʾānic theme of God raising the dead. In the specific context of nuptial relationships (Q. 4:34 and 128), it connotes 'rising up as an act of [moral] rebellion', 'a turning against', so to speak, the expected mutual commitments of the nuptial bond. Nevertheless, *nushūz* is contextualised differently in these verses. In Q. 4:34, a woman's *nushūz* is to be remedied by verbal admonishment, forsaking in the beds and, in the final instance, by striking; none of these measures, however, may be taken when women return to obedience (*but if they obey you, seek not a way against them*). Thus *nushūz* for women entails some perceived measure of disobedience, and we gloss it as 'defiance'. In contrast, Q. 4:128 suggests that the husband's *nushūz* or *iʿrāḍ* ('rejection', 'shunning', 'objecting to') is most likely to constitute not disobedience *per se*, but a disappointment of the wife's expectations of his nuptial

[13] For a more detailed discussion of *maʿrūf*, see Michael Cook, *Commanding Right and Forbidding Wrong*.

commitment, however that materialises for her.[14] So, whereas a wife's obedience is necessary to remedy the *nushūz*, for the husband, 'making peace' (*ṣulḥ*) suffices as redress, though this is a voluntary act, even as it is a moral good.[15] The husband's *nushūz*, therefore, may be glossed as 'turning against', as opposed to 'defiance'.

Qunūt: in the Qur'ān *qunūt* is pious obedience, as opposed to *ṭāʿa*, which may be pious or worldly obedience. Note that the exegetes gloss women's *qunūt* as *ṭāʿa* to their husbands and to God, which shows how they perceive obedience to the husband as an aspect of women's piety.

Qawwāmūn (*ʿalā*): the intensive nominal form suggests a repeated action derived from the verbal substantive *al-qiyām ʿalā*,[16] to attend to; to be attendant to something, meaning to be looking after it, a figurative implication of the act of repeatedly getting up for the sake of something.[17] *Qawwāmūn* is a form that occurs three times in the Qur'ān, all of which are temporally and physically proximate: all are from the Medinan period and they appear in neighbouring *sūras*: *sūrat al-Nisā'* (Q. 4) and *sūrat al-Mā'ida* (Q. 5). Each of the uses of the term is modified by a different preposition, which may or may not indicate a different significance. In Q. 4:34, the term has a dual sense in which men 'stand over' women (*qawwāmūn* **ʿalā**) and they are *maintainers of women*, the latter being proximate to the meaning in Q. 4:135 and Q. 5:8, in which the term means standing up for something. In Q. 4:135, believers stand up for justice (*qawwāmūn* ***bi'****l-qisṭ*) and are God's witnesses (*shuhadā'* ***li'****llāhi*); in Q. 5:8, these prepositions are reversed, so that they stand up for God (*qawwāmūn* ***li'****llāhi*) and bear witness to justice (*shuhadā'* ***bi'****l-qisṭ*). Thus the term, to a large extent, connotes a positive value (cf. also Q. 13:33), in which God is *qā'im ʿalā* humankind. In the context of

[14] Even though the Qur'ānic passage in question states *nushūzan aw* ('or') *iʿrāḍan*, there is a strong sense in which the two are not alternative scenarios, but that the latter is in effect a gloss on the first; that is to say, a woman might fear that her husband is no longer taking an interest in her or upholding his side of the marital commitment. For a summary capturing this, see Rāzī, *Mafātīḥ al-ghayb*, s.v. Q. 4:128. But also see Muqātil, *Tafsīr Muqātil*, s.v. Q. 4:35, in which he defines the husband's *nushūz* as [his refusal to pay] maintenance or his taking another wife (*iḍrār*); see also his *tafsīr* of Q. 4:128 in which he glosses the husband's *nushūz* with reference to a story in which the husband takes a younger wife and gives her more maintenance than the first wife.

[15] Cf. Q. 2:228, where, in the case of divorce, a husband has the prerogative to take his wife back if there is a willingness on his part to make peace (*in aradū iṣlāḥan*); thus the reconcilement is at the husband's hand. Q. 2:228 goes on to say that men have *a degree over* women, which is a further indication of that prerogative.

[16] Cf. Hamza *et al.*, *Anthology*, I, 129, where the editors discuss the related term *qayyūm* in the context of God's attributes, as in Q. 2:255.

[17] See Rāghib, *Mufradāt*, 690, s.v. *q-w-m*.

Q. 4:34 it appears in the masculine plural (*qawwāmūn*) and is glossed immediately by a relative clause that contains the noun *faḍl* (see above). Therefore, the expression has, for the exegetical tradition, become an undemanding and straightforward assertion that men have been granted privileges over women, partially as a result of their duties towards them, translating, in turn, into a kind of natural patriarchy.

Taʾdīb: to discipline, both physically and morally, as might naturally be found in the context of children, but which, in the premodern world, would have extended to the entire household – women, dependants and slaves included. Not a Qurʾānic term, but the gloss of choice for the exegetes when explaining the husband's moral duties within a conjugal relationship.

Muqātil

Muqātil's *tafsīr* is the first wholly extant *tafsīr*, and it is apparent that by this time, there was already a well-established occasion of revelation for this verse and an established narrative about the verse's basic meaning and the rights that it grants to men in marriage. In this interpretation, *qawwāmūn* means *musallaṭūn*, meaning that men have been granted power over women; Muqātil asserts that they have been given the power to discipline and guide them, establishing thus a husband's patriarchy over his wife (or wives). One of the reasons that Muqātil gives for the husband's rights is the latter's financial means. However, the husbands' powers are not unrestricted, and Muqātil reminds husbands of the limits of their rights over their wives. First, he states that the husbands' *fear* of their wives' *defiance* (*nushūz*) means that they know of their wives' *nushūz* – it is not enough to suspect it: this establishes the first limit. The second limit is set when Muqātil reminds husbands that if their wives were to return to obedience, they could not then strike them. Finally, he says that the striking should not be severe or injurious.

Men are maintainers of women was sent down concerning Saʿd b. al-Rabīʿ b. ʿAmr, who was a tribal chief (*naqīb*),[18] and his wife Ḥabība bt. Zayd b. Abī Zuhayr. Both were of the Anṣār from the Ḥārith clan of the tribe of Khazraj. The report is that he slapped his wife, whereupon she went to her family. Her father then set off with her to the Prophet (*ṣlʿm*) and protested, 'I married my

[18] This is a title that indicates a position of some authority within the tribal structure. On *niqāba* and the various functions of the *naqīb* in early Islamic history, see Teresa Bernheimer, *The ʿAlids: The First Family of Islam, 750–1200* (Edinburgh, Edinburgh University Press, 2013), esp. ch. 4. See also C.E. Bosworth and J. Burton Page, 'Naḳīb', *EI*^{2}, VII, 926. For its later developments and institutionalisation under the ʿAbbāsids, see A. Havemann, 'Naḳīb al-As͟hrāf', *EI*^{2}, VII, 927.

darling to him and gave her to his bed, and he slapped her!' So the Prophet (*ṣl'm*) said, 'Let her retaliate (*q-ṣ-ṣ*) against her husband'. She went to her husband in order to retaliate, but then the Prophet (*ṣl'm*) said, 'Come back! Gabriel (*'m*) has just come to me, saying that God has sent down *men are maintainers* (*qawwāmūn*) *of women*'.[19] That is to say, they are empowered (*musallaṭūn*) over women *by that which God has distinguished the one over the other*, which is that a man has a distinction (*faḍl*) over his wife in [terms of] rights; *and by that which they expend of their property*, meaning they have been distinguished (*fuḍḍilū*) on account of the bridal payment (*mahr*) that he delivers to her,[20] so husbands have been empowered (*musallaṭūn*) to discipline and guide them.[21] So there can be no retaliation between a man and his wife, except in cases of [loss of] life or serious wounding.[22] 'At that, the Prophet (*ṣl'm*) said: "We wanted one thing and God wanted another, and that which God wants is [always] better".'

He then describes such women, saying: *So, righteous women*, in terms of religion, *are devoutly obedient women*, meaning obedient to God and to their husbands. *Those who safeguard during absence*, in their husband's absence, they safeguard their chastity[23] and their husband's property. *What for God is to be safeguarded*, meaning in return for God's safeguarding of the women.

And if you fear the women's defiance means you come to know of your wives' disobedience, meaning [as in the case of] Sa'd.[24] So God means that if you were to know of their disobedience towards their husbands *then admonish them* by [reminding them of] God, and if they do not accept the admonishment, *forsake them in the beds*. He [God] is saying: Do not have sexual relations (*jimā'*) with her at all, and if they return to obedience

[19] The report pauses here and Muqātil comments, 'that is to say . . .'

[20] We have translated both *mahr* and *ṣadāq* as 'bridal payment' rather than 'dowry'. 'Dowry' traditionally means the money that a bride brings to the marriage, whereas they mean here the money that the husband brings to it.

[21] Literally, the phrase *al-akhdh 'alā aydīhinna* means 'taking them by the hand'; the meaning is made clear by the context in which it is used in Ṭabarī's *tafsīr* (see below).

[22] The report now resumes.

[23] *Furūj* means 'the openings' (sc. vaginas).

[24] Muqātil intends to weave the report about Sa'd into his exegesis of the verses above, hence the return to referencing Sa'd. There is a manuscript variant that has *sh-h-d*, as opposed to *s-'-d*, hence giving *shahdan* instead of *Sa'dan*. However, in addition to the fact that this is an unusual conjugation of the verb for 'witnessing' (*shāhidan, shuhūdan* or *shahādatan* would have been the standard forms), a few lines further below in Muqātil's commentary, in his gloss to the nuptial rupture (*shiqāqa baynihimā*) in Q. 4:35, again Muqātil refers this to Sa'd and his wife. We thus believe *s-'-d* to be the correct reading of the consonantal skeleton. The alternation between 'your wives' and 'towards their husbands', that is, the shift in address, is because the dispute between Sa'd and his wife had become public, which made it clearer (at least from the husband's perspective) that the wife, in this case, Sa'd's, had indeed been disobedient.

towards their husbands with the admonishment and the forsaking [then that is the end of it]. If not, *strike them* with a non-severe (*ghayr mubarriḥ*) strike, meaning one that does not leave any mark.

But if they obey you, seek not a way against them, meaning any pretext [to strike them]. He means to say: Do not task her with love for you when that is beyond her capacity.[25]

Indeed God is high, meaning He is raised above His creation, *mighty*.[26]

Hūd

Like Muqātil, Hūd says that *qawwāmūn* means that men are in authority of disciplining women and guiding them. Hūd uses some of the same language as Muqātil (*musallaṭūn* and *al-akhdh ʿalā aydīhinna*), even though there is no evidence of any transmission between them. This indicates that they are probably drawing on a common source, which could be Ḥasan al-Baṣrī. These terms are a classic expression of men's patriarchal role: husbands are supposed to guide their wives to do right (literally, 'take their hand') and discipline them when they go wrong, just as a parent does for a child. The exegetes present this disciplining not as harsh cruelty but as a necessary step in the guidance of women.

Hūd says that the reason for this is that God made men superior to women in terms of the amount of inheritance they receive and the value of their testimony, both of which are legal instances where two women equal one man. According to Hūd, *by that which they expend* refers to the bridal payment. But it is clear that Hūd does not refer solely to a financial advantage that God has given to men over women, because he then quotes a *ḥadīth* which says that a woman without a husband is a poor thing, even if she is property, because *men are maintainers of women*. Thus for Hūd and others who quote this *ḥadīth*, men's *qiwāma* refers to them managing women's affairs.

Hūd cites the same *asbāb al-nuzūl* as Muqātil, but with some details missing; that might be because his primary interest in the *asbāb* seems to be legal. He quotes Ḥasan al-Baṣrī to say that there is no legal basis for retaliation between a man and his wife, other than in the case of her death or serious wounding; he clarifies that the strike is meant to correct the wife rather than to injure her.

Hūd defines *nushūz* as a wife's disobedience in specifically refusing to allow her husband to sleep with her. The three punishments should be undertaken in order, and if she relents, then he cannot seek a pretext to strike her. According to Hūd, the striking should not leave a mark. This seems to conflict with the rather wider leeway that Ḥasan al-Baṣrī has granted to husbands. We can assume that Ḥasan's

[25] In this, Muqātil and other exegetes echo God's approach towards human beings in that God does not task humans with things that are beyond their capacity. See e.g. Q. 2:286, in which *God does not task any soul beyond its capacity, et passim*. Hūd attributes this interpretation to Kalbī. See below.

[26] Muqātil, *Tafsīr Muqātil*, s.v. Q. 4:34.

interpretation represents the legal limit, whereas Hūd's represents the 'correct' or moral interpretation of the verse. Finally, Hūd cites Kalbī as saying that husbands should not try to make their wives love them and clarifying that all of the punishments are to take place only around the matter of his need of her. This again represents a limit on husbands' behaviour, by limiting the place and scope of the chastisement.

Men are maintainers of women, that is to say, they have been empowered to discipline women (*musallaṭūn ʿalā adab al-nisāʾ*) and to guide them (*wa'l-akhdh ʿalā aydīhinna*) *by that which God has distinguished the one over the other.* He made the testimony of two women equal to the testimony of a single man, and men have been given more in inheritance. *And by that which they expend of their property*, meaning the bridal payment (*ṣadāq*).

It is mentioned that the Messenger of God (*ṣlʿm*) said, 'The woman who does not have a husband is impoverished (*miskīna*)'. It was asked, 'Even if she is wealthy?' He replied, 'Yes, even if she is wealthy, *men are maintainers of women*'.[27]

Some have mentioned that a person said, 'It was mentioned to us that a man slapped his wife in the time of the Prophet (*ṣlʿm*), so the woman came to the Prophet of God (*ṣlʿm*). The Prophet of God (*ṣlʿm*) wanted her to retaliate against him, and so God sent down *men are maintainers of women*.' It is mentioned on the authority of al-Ḥasan [al-Baṣrī] that a man slapped his wife, and the matter was raised with the Prophet, who said, 'What you have done is evil'.[28] So God sent down *Men are maintainers of women*. So there can be no retaliation between a man and his wife in matters, other than a wound by which the skin of her head or face is split open (*mūḍiḥa*).'[29] That is to say, he saw that [striking] as a corrective measure.

His words *so, righteous women* meaning the women who are good to their husbands *are devoutly obedient women* that is to say, obedient to their husbands, in the interpretation (*tafsīr*) of al-Ḥasan [al-Baṣrī]. Others have said obedient to God and to their husbands. *Those who safeguard during absence* their chastity, in the absence of their husbands. *What for God is to be*

[27] This *ḥadīth* is not found in the major Sunnī collections.

[28] The editor of the edition of Hūd's *tafsīr* footnotes this, saying: 'I cannot find among my books of *tafsīr* and *ḥadīth* any which present the occasion of revelation for this verse, including the expression: "What you have done is evil". The nearest is that which is reported by Jalāl al-Dīn al-Suyūṭī in his *al-Durr al-manthūr fī'l-tafsīr bi'l-ma'thūr*, in a *ḥadīth* verified by Ibn Mardawayh on the authority of ʿAlī. He says, "He has no right".' Bālḥājj b. Saʿīd Sharīfī, in Hūd, *Tafsīr kitāb Allāh al-ʿazīz*, I, 377; Jalāl al-Dīn al-Suyūṭī (d. 911/1505), *al-Durr al-manthūr fī'l-tafsīr bi'l-ma'thūr*, 6 vols. (Beirut, Dār al-Maʿrifa, [197–?]), II, 151.

[29] According to Lane (*Lexicon*), *mūḍiḥa* is a wound where the skin is broken and the bone shows; he notes that this is the only type of wound for which retaliation is allowed.

safeguarded, that is to say, in return for God's safeguarding of the women, according to the interpretation of al-Ḥasan.[30] Other interpreters have said: In the absence of their husbands, they safeguard those rights of his which God has laid down.

His words *And if you fear the women's defiance*, their disobedience, meaning she rises up (*nashaza*) against her husband and does not allow him to sleep with her (*yaghshāhā*).[31] *Then admonish them, and forsake them in the beds, and strike them*. Some say that he should begin by admonishing her with words, and if she persists then he should forsake her, and if she persists then he may strike her non-severely, that is to say, without leaving a mark. Some of them say, 'Then they raise the issue with the authorities.'

[Regarding] His words *but if they obey you, seek not a way against them*: if she gives him leave to sleep with her (*yaghshāhā*), then he should not seek a pretext [to strike her]. Al-Ḥasan says God's words *forsake them in the beds* mean that he should not come near her. Al-Kalbī says *but if they obey you, seek not a way against them* means do not task them with love. The admonishment towards them is only in the bed, and the cursing[32] is in the bed, and the hitting is in the bed. It is not for love, but his need of her.

Indeed God is high, mighty.[33]

Qummī

Qummī's interpretation is unusual in that it does not mention men having any specific superiority over women. Instead, he focuses solely on men's maintenance of their wives. Otherwise, this brief interpretation incorporates several elements that have already been seen in the interpretations of Muqātil and Hūd. The *nushūz* is restricted to the bed and is defined as the wife rising from the marital bed, which is to say refusing to have sexual relations with her husband. For Qummī, like other commentators, if the wife agrees and lies with her husband, then the husband should 'seek not a way against her', which is to say that he should not punish her if she complies. Like both Muqātil and Hūd, Qummī says that the husband should not task his wife with love. Finally, he states that the punishments must all take place in bed, which, as in previous sources, is a limit on the husband's authority to chastise his wife.

[30] This is, again, a direct word-for-word parallel of the interpretation of Muqātil, but there it is not attributed to al-Ḥasan al-Baṣrī.

[31] Literally, 'to cover her', cf. Q. 7:189.

[32] This is an alternative interpretation of 'forsake them in the beds'.

[33] Hūd, *Tafsīr kitāb Allāh al-ʿazīz*, s.v. Q. 4:34.

Men are maintainers of women, by that which God has distinguished the one over the other, and by that which they expend of their property, meaning God made it incumbent upon men to maintain women, and then God praised women, saying *so, righteous women are devoutly obedient women, those who safeguard during absence what for God is to be safeguarded*, meaning she safeguards herself when her husband is absent from her; and in a narration of Abū'l-Jārūd on the authority of Abū Jaʿfar [al-Bāqir] (*ʿm*) concerning His words *devoutly obedient women* (*qānitāt*),[34] he says 'obedient' (*muṭīʿāt*).

[Regarding] His words *and if you fear the women's defiance, then admonish them, and forsake them in the beds, and strike them; but if they obey you, seek not a way against them*. That is, when the wife rises up from her husband's bed, he says to her, 'Be wary of God (*ittaqī 'llāha*) and return to your bed!' and that is the admonishment. If she obeys him that is the end of it; if not, he insults her, and that is the forsaking. If she returns to her bed then that is the end of it; if not, he may strike her non-severely, and if she obeys him and lies with him in the bed then God says *but if they obey you, seek not a way against them*. [Al-Qummī] says do not task them with love, and He made the admonishment, the insulting and the striking in the bed.[35]

Indeed God is high, mighty.[36]

Ṭabarī

In the first part of the verse, Ṭabarī seems to circumscribe the limits of wifely obedience. Women are supposed to obey their husbands, but only in those matters in which God has ordered them to obey. The focus is on the legal aspects of the verse: first, the husband's financial duties, and second, the occasion of the verse's revelation, which justifies the legal extent to which a man can strike his wife without being liable for retaliation. Ṭabarī's interpretation veers off the beaten path when he describes the second punishment of the recalcitrant wife, and, as has been well-documented elsewhere, he proposes an interpretation that is so unusual that many later commentators censure him.[37] Ṭabarī does not believe that the husband should forsake his wife in the bed because the wife's main duty is to have sexual relations with her husband when he wishes, and so she would welcome him forsaking the bed. Instead, he finds an unusual

[34] See 'Key terms' above. In the Qur'ān, *q-n-t* refers to pious obedience, whereas *ṭ-w-ʿ* can be used to refer to any type of obedience; so here pious obedience is being glossed as a more general type of spousal obedience.

[35] Meaning, the only reason that a husband can undertake these measures is because of his wife's refusal of sex.

[36] Qummī, *Tafsīr al-Qummī*, s.v. Q. 4:34.

[37] Shaikh, 'Exegetical Violence', 65; Marín, 'Disciplining Wives', 24–5; Bauer, 'Room for Interpretation', 78–9; Bauer, *Gender Hierarchy*, 1–3, 210–11.

interpretation of the root *h-j-r*, which involves tying up a camel with a rope, and argues that the husband must tie the wife up with a rope and strike her until she complies. His interpretation was roundly rejected by subsequent commentators, who asserted that he had gone beyond the limits.

Amazingly, otherwise, Ṭabarī comes across as moderate in his interpretation. He limits a wife's obedience, for instance, saying that it means she should be good to his family. The striking should be *ghayr mubarriḥ*, 'without leaving a mark'. He goes on to clarify that the husband should undertake these steps in order and should not seek to harm his wife, nor expect love from her, 'for that is not in their hands. So do not strike them or harm them because of it.' He concludes by reminding men that God is exalted over everything. Thus if a husband seeks to harm and hurt his wife, God will avenge him on her behalf. In this interpretation, God is the wife's ultimate protector. There is an implicit comparison to a just ruler, who likewise should not abuse his power; and just as implicit is the recognition that such abuses are possible or even likely in these hierarchical relationships.

Reports on the interpretation of His words, *majestic be His praise, Men are maintainers of women, by that which God has distinguished the one over the other, and by that which they expend of their property.*

Abū Jaʿfar [al-Ṭabarī] said, 'He, majestic be His praise, means by His words *Men are maintainers of women* that men have a prerogative over their wives (*ahl qiyām ʿalā nisāʾihim*), in terms of disciplining them and guiding them in what is incumbent upon them towards God and towards themselves.'

By that which God has distinguished the one over the other means by that which God distinguished men (*faḍḍala*) over their wives, because they deliver their bridal payment to them, they maintain them with their property, and they provide for them sufficiently. That is the distinction (*tafḍīl*) which God, blessed and exalted, has given men over women, and that is why they have acquired the prerogative of maintaining them (*qawwām*), executors of the command over them, in that part of women's affairs which God has appointed to men.[38] The interpreters (*ahl al-taʾwīl*) have said something similar to what we have said in that respect.

An account of those who have said this:

ʿAlī b. Abī Ṭalḥa reported that Ibn ʿAbbās[39] said, '*Men are maintainers of women* means commanders (*umarāʾ*); she must obey him in those matters in which God has ordered her to obey. Obedience to him is that she is good to his family and she safeguards his property. His distinction over her is by virtue of his maintenance payments (*nafaqa*) and his efforts (*saʿy*).'

[38] Here Ibn ʿAbbās circumscribes the limits of a wife's obedience; she does not have to obey in every matter.

[39] Al-Muthannā ← ʿAbd Allāh b. Ṣāliḥ ← Muʿāwiya b. Ṣāliḥ ← ʿAlī b. Abī Ṭalḥa ← Ibn ʿAbbās.

Juwaybir reported that al-Ḍaḥḥāk[40] said, concerning His words *Men are maintainers of women*, 'The man undertakes to command the woman to obey God, and if she refuses, then he has the right to strike her non-severely; he has a distinction (*faḍl*) over her by virtue of his maintenance payments and his efforts.'

Al-Suddī[41] said about *men are maintainers of women*, 'They guide them and discipline them.' Ibn al-Mubārak reported from Sufyān[42] that he said, '*by that which God has distinguished the one over the other* is by virtue of God's distinction (*tafḍīl*) of men over women'.

It has been reported that this verse was sent down regarding a man who slapped his wife, and that dispute was brought before the Prophet (*ṣlʿm*), who judged in her favour with retaliation.

An account of those who have said this:

Qatāda reported from al-Ḥasan [al-Baṣrī][43] that he said that a man slapped his wife. She went to the Prophet (*ṣlʿm*), who wanted to give her retaliation against him, so God sent down *Men are maintainers of women, by that which God has distinguished the one over the other, and by that which they expend of their property*, so the Prophet (*ṣlʿm*) called to him and recited it to him and said, 'I wanted one thing and God wanted another'.

Saʿīd [b. Jubayr] reported from Qatāda[44] about His words *Men are maintainers of women, by that which God has distinguished the one over the other, and by that which they expend of their property*, that he [Qatāda] mentioned to us that a man slapped his wife, so she went to the Prophet (*ṣlʿm*), and then he said the like of what was said above.

Maʿmar related on the authority of Qatāda[45] about His words *men are maintainers of women* that he [Qatāda] said a man struck (*ṣakka*) his wife and she went to the Prophet (*ṣlʿm*) who wanted to keep her from him, so God sent down *men are maintainers of women*.

Al-Ḥasan [al-Baṣrī][46] said that a man from among the Anṣār slapped his wife, so she went and sought retaliation. The Prophet (*ṣlʿm*) decreed that there was retaliation between the two of them, and so His words *do not be hasty with the Qurʾān before its revelation to you is concluded* [Q. 20:114] were

[40] Al-Muthannā ← Isḥāq ← Abū Zuhayr ← Juwaybir ← al-Ḍaḥḥāk.
[41] Muḥammad b. al-Ḥusayn ← Aḥmad b. al-Mufaḍḍal ← Asbāṭ ← al-Suddī.
[42] Al-Muthannā ← Ḥibbān b. Mūsā ← Ibn al-Mubārak ← Sufyān.
[43] Muḥammad b. Bashshār ← ʿAbd al-Aʿlā ← Saʿīd ← Qatāda ← al-Ḥasan.
[44] Bishr b. Muʿādh ← Yazīd ← Saʿīd ← Qatāda.
[45] Al-Ḥasan b. Yaḥyā ← ʿAbd al-Razzāq ← Maʿmar ← Qatāda.
[46] Ibn Wakīʿ ← his father ← Jarīr b. Ḥāzim ← al-Ḥasan.

sent down, and then *men are maintainers of women, by that which God has distinguished the one over the other* was sent down.

Ḥajjāj said, on the authority of Ibn Jurayj[47] that he [Ibn Jurayj] said: A man slapped his wife and the Prophet (*ṣl'm*) wanted retaliation, and while they were in that state the verse was revealed.

Asbāṭ said on the authority of al-Suddī,[48] as for *men are maintainers of women*, there were words between a man from the Anṣār and his wife, and so he slapped her. Her family set off to mention that to the Prophet (*ṣl'm*), so he informed them: *Men are maintainers of women* – to the end of the verse.

Al-Zuhrī used to say, 'There is no retaliation between a man and his wife except in cases of [loss of] life.'[49]

Ma'mar said, 'I heard al-Zuhrī[50] saying, "Even if a man splits his wife's head open (*shajja*), or wounds her, there is not any retaliation (*qawad*) against him, although he owes bloodwit (*'aql*), except if he assaults her and kills her, in which case he is killed for her."'

As for His words *and by that which they expend of their property*, it means with the bridal payment that they deliver to them and expend upon them in maintenance, as in [the following reports]:[51]

'Alī b. Abū Ṭalḥa reported that Ibn 'Abbās[52] said, 'His distinction (*faḍl*) over her is based on his maintenance and his efforts.'

Juwaybir reported from al-Ḍaḥḥāk, likewise.[53]

Ibn Mubārak reported, 'I heard Sufyān saying[54] '*By that which they expend of their property* is because of the bridal payment (*mahr*) that they deliver.'

Abū Ja'far [al-Ṭabarī] said: Therefore, the interpretation of the words is as follows: men are maintainers of their wives because of God's distinction (*tafḍīl*) of men over women and because they maintain them from their property. And the 'which' (*bi-mā*) in His words *by that which God has distinguished the one over the other* and in His words *by that which they expend* functions for the verbal noun (*maṣdar*).

[47] Al-Qāsim ← al-Ḥusayn ← Ḥajjāj ← Ibn Jurayj.

[48] Muḥammad b. al-Ḥusayn ← Aḥmad b. Mufaḍḍal ← Asbāṭ ← al-Suddī.

[49] Here, Zuhrī gives a legal opinion, which is that the husband does not owe any compensatory payment or in-kind retaliation for any injury he may inflict on his wife, other than when she dies as a result of the beating.

[50] Al-Ḥasan b. Yaḥyā ← Abd al-Razzāq ← Ma'mar ← al-Zuhrī.

[51] The following reports clarify that the early commentators considered a husband's payment of maintenance to be integral to his prerogative over his wife.

[52] Al-Muthannā ← Abū Ṣāliḥ ← Mu'āwiya b. Ṣāliḥ ← 'Alī b. Abī Ṭalḥa ← Ibn 'Abbās.

[53] Al-Muthannā ← Isḥāq ← Abū Zuhayr ← Juwaybir ← al-Ḍaḥḥāk.

[54] Al-Muthannā ← Ḥibbān b. Mūsā ← Ibn Mubārak ← Sufyān.

Reports on the interpretation of His words, exalted be He, *so, righteous women are devoutly obedient women, those who safeguard during absence what for God is to be safeguarded.*

Abū Jaʿfar [al-Ṭabarī] said: He means with His words, majestic be His praise, *righteous women* those who are upright in terms of their religion and those who do what is good, as when ʿAbd Allāh b. Mubārak said, 'I heard Sufyān[55] saying: "Righteous women do good."'

Are devoutly obedient women means obedient to God and to their husbands, as in the following reports:

Ibn Abī Najīḥ reported that Mujāhid[56] said His word *devoutly obedient women* is 'obedient' (*muṭīʿāt*).

[From another source] Ibn Abī Najīḥ reported that Mujāhid[57] said *devoutly obedient women* is 'obedient' (*muṭīʿāt*).

Ibn Abī Ṭalḥa reported that Ibn ʿAbbās[58] said *devoutly obedient women* is 'obedient' (*muṭīʿāt*).

[Hereafter are four further reports glossing *devoutly obedient women* as either 'obedient' or as 'obedient to their husbands'.]

Therefore we have clarified the meaning of 'devout obedience' (*qunūt*) in the above, and it is 'obedience' (*ṭāʿa*), and we have indicated the correctness of that with evidential examples (*shawāhid*) that are too many to enumerate.

As for His words *those who safeguard during absence*, He means safeguarding themselves when their husbands are absent from them, in respect of their own chastity and their husbands' property and the duties prescribed for them of what is due to God in that respect and otherwise, as in the following reports:

Qatāda[59] said, [regarding] *those who safeguard during absence*: 'Safeguarding what God has entrusted to them with that which is due to Him, and safeguarding their husbands in their absence.'

Al-Suddī[60] said, '*Those who safeguard during absence*: she safeguards for her husband his property and her chastity, until he returns, as God has commanded her.'

Ḥajjāj related that Ibn Jurayj[61] said, 'I asked ʿAṭāʾ, "What is the meaning of His words *those who safeguard during absence*?" He replied, "Safeguarding for the husband."'

55 Al-Muthannā ← Hibbān b. Mūsā ← ʿAbd Allāh b. Mubārak ← Sufyān.
56 Muḥammad b. ʿAmr ← Abū ʿĀṣim ← ʿĪsā ← Ibn Abī Najīḥ ← Mujāhid.
57 Al-Muthannā ← Abū Ḥudhayfa ← Shibl ← Ibn Abī Najīḥ ← Mujāhid.
58 ʿAlī ← Dāwūd ← Abū Ṣāliḥ ← Muʿāwiya b. Ṣāliḥ ← ʿAlī b. Abī Ṭalḥa ← Ibn ʿAbbās.
59 Bishr b. Muʿādh ← Yazīd ← Saʿīd ← Qatāda.
60 Muḥammad b. al-Ḥusayn ← Aḥmad b. al-Mufaḍḍal ← Asbāṭ ← al-Suddī.
61 Al-Qāsim ← al-Ḥusayn ← Ḥajjāj ← Ibn Jurayj.

Ḥajjāj [also] related that Ibn Jurayj[62] said, 'I asked 'Aṭā' about *those who safeguard during absence*, and he said "safeguarding for the husbands".'

Sufyān[63] said, '*Those who safeguard during absence* safeguarding their affairs for their husband when he is absent'.

Abū Hurayra[64] reported that the Messenger of God (*ṣl'm*) said, 'The best of women is she who, when you look at her, makes you happy, when you order her, obeys you, and when you are absent from her safeguards for you your property and her self'.[65] He said, 'Then the Messenger of God (*ṣl'm*) recited *men are maintainers of women*, to the end of the verse.'

Abū Ja'far [al-Ṭabarī] said: This report on the authority of the Messenger of God (*ṣl'm*) indicates the soundness of what we have said about the interpretation of that, and its meaning is: righteous women are righteous in terms of their religion, obedient to their husbands, safeguarding for them their own persons and the husbands' property.

As for His words *what for God is to be safeguarded*, the readers have differed about its reading. In the reading according to the majority of the Muslim garrison cities, *bimā ḥafiẓa Allāhu* puts the name of God in the nominative so that the meaning is: in return for God's safeguarding of the women, having made them to be so, as in the following reports:

Ibn Jurayj[66] said, 'I asked 'Aṭā' about His words *what for God is to be safeguarded*, and he said, "They have been safeguarded by God."'

Ibn Mubārak[67] said, 'I heard Sufyān saying about His words *what for God is to be safeguarded*, "In return for God's safeguarding her, in having made her so".'

Abū Ja'far Yazīd b. al-Qa'qā' al-Madanī read it thus: *by that which safeguards God (Allāha)*[68] meaning with their safeguarding of God through obedience to Him, and fulfilling the duty towards Him which He commanded them to safeguard in the absence of their husbands, as when one says to

[62] Zakariyyā b. Yaḥyā b. Abī Zā'ida ← Ḥajjāj ← Ibn Jurayj.

[63] Al-Muthannā ← Ḥibbān b. Mūsā ← Ibn Mubārak ← Sufyān.

[64] Al-Muthannā ← Abū Ṣāliḥ ← Abū Ma'shar ← Sa'īd b. Abī Sa'īd al-Miqbarī ← Abū Hurayra.

[65] Versions of this *ḥadīth* appear in Abū Dāwūd, *Sunan*, *Kitāb al-Zakāt* (9), *Bāb fī ḥuqūq al-māl* (33), *ḥadīth* no. 109/1664; Nasā'ī, *Sunan*, *Kitāb al-Nikāḥ* (26), *Bāb ayyu'l-nisā' khayr* (14), *ḥadīth* no. 36/3231.

[66] Zakariyyā b. Yaḥyā b. Abī Zā'ida ← Ḥajjāj ← Ibn Jurayj.

[67] Al-Muthannā ← Ḥibbān b. Mūsā ← Ibn Mubārak ← Sufyān.

[68] The word 'God' is in the accusative case in this reading, which means that God is the object of the verb 'safeguard'. In other words, it means safeguarding what is owed to God, since God Himself does not need safeguarding. Ṭabarī disagrees with this reading.

another, 'You have not safeguarded God in such and such', with the meaning, you neither paid attention to Him nor did you regard Him.[69]

Abū Jaʿfar [al-Ṭabarī] said that the correct reading is the reading that Muslims have provided, such that the one whom this [reading] has reached has no excuse [to deviate] and such that it affirms the proof [of its correctness] to him, and thus precludes what is known to be the reading solely of Abū Jaʿfar [Yazīd b. al-Qaʿqāʿ al-Madanī] and by which he has deviated from them; rather, that [correct] reading is the one that makes the name of God, Blessed and Exalted, nominative – *bi-mā ḥafiẓa Allāhu* (*what for God is to be safeguarded*) – since that is correct in Arabic and accords with the Arabic language (*kalām al-ʿArab*), and since it is hideous to make it accusative (*Allāha*) because that is alien to the speech of the Arabs (*manṭiq al-ʿArab*). For the Arabs do not omit the subject of the verb along with the verbal conjugations, because if the subject is omitted, there would be no identifiable subject of the verb. And in this phrase there is something omitted, but there is no need to mention it, because it is indicated by the overt sense of the speech. And the meaning of *so, righteous women are devoutly obedient women, those who safeguard during absence what for God is to be safeguarded* is: so treat them well and act righteously towards them (*fa-aḥsinū ilayhinna wa-aṣliḥū*).[70] The like of that has been mentioned in the reading of Ibn Masʿūd.

Ṭalḥa b. Muṣarrif[71] reported that in the reading of ʿAbd Allāh [Ibn Masʿūd] it is: 'so, righteous women are devoutly obedient women during absence (*qānitāt li'l-ghayb*) because of what God has made [to be] safeguarded, so be righteous to them (*aṣliḥū ilayhinna*), *and if you fear the women's defiance* [. . .]'.[72]

[69] Some versions of the text have *lāḥaẓtahu*, which is 'to pay regard to Him', while in some it is *rāqabtahu*, which is 'to watch/pay attention to Him'.

[70] Note that in this interpretation, *what for God is to be safeguarded* seems to be the righteous women themselves; when women are righteous, they have been safeguarded by God, and their husbands should behave righteously towards them.

[71] Al-Muthannā ← Isḥāq ← ʿAbd al-Raḥmān b. Abī Ḥammād ← ʿĪsā al-Aʿmā ← Ṭalḥa b. Muṣarrif.

[72] Note that this is a variant reading, meaning that it preserves an alternative wording to the currently accepted wording of the verse. This variant, which includes the phrase 'be righteous to them', is one of two attributed to Ibn Masʿūd. Zamakhsharī (at note 144) attributes to Ibn Masʿūd the phrase 'be righteous to them' and also credits him with a variant plural form of the terms *ṣāliḥāt*, *qānitāt* and *ḥāfiẓāt*: *ṣawāliḥ*, *qawānit*, *ḥawāfiẓ*. Ṭabrisī (at note 149) does not mention Ibn Masʿūd, and attributes *ṣawāliḥ*, *qawānit* to Ṭalḥa b. Muṣarrif, who is, according to Ṭabarī, the transmitter of Ibn Masʿūd's reading. Rāzī (at note 157), citing Zamakhsharī, attributes *ṣawāliḥ qawānit ḥawāfiẓ* to Ibn Masʿūd and omits the original variant attributed to him here in Ṭabarī ('be righteous to them'). Neither of these readings are in Ibn Mujāhid's *Kitāb al-Sabʿa fī'l-qirāʾāt*.

Aḥmad b. Mufaḍḍal said that Asbāṭ reported on the authority of al-Suddī[73] *so, righteous women are devoutly obedient women, those who safeguard during absence what for God is to be safeguarded* [means] so be good to them (*fa-aḥsinū ilayhinna*).

ʿAlī b. Abī Ṭalḥa reported that Ibn ʿAbbās[74] said, regarding His words *so, righteous women are devoutly obedient women*, 'So be righteous to them (*fa-aṣliḥū ilayhinna*).'

ʿAlī b. Abī Ṭalḥa reported that Ibn ʿAbbās[75] said, 'His words *so, righteous women are devoutly obedient women* mean that if they are like this, then you should be righteous to them (*fa-aṣliḥu ilayhinna*).'

Reports on the interpretation of His words *if you fear the women's defiance, then admonish them*.[76]

The interpreters differ with regard to the meaning of His words *if you fear the women's defiance* (*nushūz*). Some of them say that its meaning is: those women of whose *nushūz* you know (*taʿlam*). The justification for turning *fear* (*khawf*) in this instance into knowledge (*ʿilm*) is that it is analogous to turning suspicion into knowledge, because the two meanings approximate each other, given that suspicion is a kind of doubt and that fear is always associated with hope, and they are both together performed by a man in his heart. As the poet said,

> Do not bury me in the waterless desert, for indeed I fear
> that if I were to die, I should not taste it

It ['for indeed I fear'] means 'for indeed I know'. And as another said,

> Words have come to me from Nuṣayb that he has said,
> I did not fear from you, O Sallām, to be denigrating me.

With [I did not fear] meaning I did not suspect.

A group of interpreters said the meaning of *fear* in this instance is the fear which is the opposite of hope (*rajāʾ*). They say the meaning of that is: when you see from her what you have feared – that she is committing *nushūz*

[73] Muḥammad b. al-Ḥusayn ← Aḥmad b. al-Mufaḍḍal ← Asbāṭ ← al-Suddī.

[74] ʿAlī b. Dāwūd ← ʿAbd Allāh ← Muʿāwiya b. Ṣāliḥ ← ʿAlī b. Abī Ṭalḥa ← Ibn ʿAbbās.

[75] ʿAlī b. Dāwūd ← ʿAbd Allāh b. Ṣāliḥ ← Muʿāwiya ← ʿAlī b. Abī Ṭalḥa ← Ibn ʿAbbās.

[76] The following reports discuss whether the husband must know of his wife's disobedience in order to undertake her chastisement or whether he can chastise her upon suspicion of her disobedience. These reports may be a holdover from an older understanding of *nushūz* as a specific act, because if it were simply that the wife refused sexual relations with her husband, he would surely know this.

against you by looking at that which she should not look at, and coming and going – and you fall into doubt regarding her, then admonish her and forsake her. And among those who say that is Muḥammad b. Kaʿb.

As for His saying *nushūzahunna*, it means their rising up (*istiʿlāʾ*) against their husbands, raising themselves (*irtifāʿ*) from the bed in their disobedience, disagreeing with their husbands about that in which it is obligatory for them to obey them, their hatred and shunning (*iʿrāḍ* [cf. Q. 4:128]) of them. The root meaning of *nushūz* is 'to become raised' (*irtifāʿ*), and from that [root] it is said of the place of high ground that it is *nashz* and *nashāz*.

He [al-Ṭabarī] says: *Then admonish them* means remind them of God, and make them fear His punishment in pursuing what God has forbidden her in terms of disobeying her husband in those matters in which it is obligatory for her to obey him. Regarding that, the interpreters have said the like of what we have said.

An account of those who have said that *nushūz* is hatred and disobedience to the husband:

Asbāṭ reported that al-Suddī[77] said, '*if you fear the women's defiance* [means] their hatred'.

Yūnus told me that Ibn Wahb reported that Ibn Zayd said, regarding His words *if you fear the women's defiance*, 'those whose disobedience you fear'. He said that *nushūz* is disobeying him and disagreeing with him.

ʿAlī b. Abī Ṭalḥa reported that Ibn ʿAbbās[78] said [regarding] His words *if you fear the women's defiance*, 'That woman commits *nushūz*, takes her husband's rights lightly and does not obey his order.'

Ibn Jurayj reported that ʿAṭāʾ[79] said, '*Nushūz* is when she loves to be apart from him, and the man's *nushūz* is also like that.'

An account of those who say what we have said concerning His words *admonish them*:[80]

ʿAlī b. Abī Ṭalḥa reported that Ibn ʿAbbās[81] said that *admonish them* means admonish them with the Book of God, and he said, God orders him,

[77] Muḥammad b. al-Ḥusayn ← Aḥmad b. Mufaḍḍal ← Asbāṭ ← al-Suddī.

[78] Al-Muthannā ← ʿAbd Allāh b. Ṣāliḥ ← Muʿāwiya ← ʿAlī b. Abī Ṭalḥa ← Ibn ʿAbbās.

[79] Al-Muthannā ← Isḥāq ← Rawḥ [b. Zinbaʿ al-Judhāmī] ← Ibn Jurayj ← ʿAṭāʾ.

[80] All of the following reports assume that when a wife fulfils her marital duty of agreeing to sexual relations with her husband, it is a form of obedience to God. For the interpreters, the worldly hierarchy has been established by God and therefore obedience to it becomes a pious act; this is all the more so when the wife does not love the husband but she obeys in any case (on which see below).

[81] Al-Muthannā ← ʿAbd Allāh b. Ṣāliḥ ← Muʿāwiya ← ʿAlī b. Abī Ṭalḥa ← Ibn ʿAbbās.

when she commits *nushūz*, to admonish her and remind her of God, and of the greatness of his rights over her.

Ibn Abī Najīḥ reported that Mujāhid[82] said [regarding] *if you fear the women's defiance*, 'When a woman rises up (*nashazat*) from the bed of her husband, he should say to her, "Be wary of God (*ittaqī 'llāha*), and return to your bed!" And if she obeys him, then there is no way for him [to take action] against her.'

Al-Ḥasan [al-Baṣrī][83] said, 'When the woman defies (*nashazat*) her husband, he admonishes her with his tongue, ordering her to be wary of God (*ittaqī 'llāha*) and to obey him.'

Muḥammad b. Kaʿb al-Quraẓī[84] said, 'When a man notices that she regards him lightly, he says to her verbally, "I have seen you do such and such, so stop it!" And if she conducts herself so as to please him, then there is no way for him against her; and if she refuses, then he forsakes her bed.'

Ibn Abī Najīḥ reported that Mujāhid[85] said, about His words *admonish them*, 'When the woman rises up (*nashazat*) from the bed of her husband, then he says to her: "Be wary of God (*ittaqī 'llāha*), and return!"'

ʿAṭā'[86] said, regarding *admonish them*, 'Verbally'.

Ibn Jurayj[87] said, regarding *admonish them*, 'with his tongue'.[88]

Reports on the interpretation of His words, exalted be He, *forsake them in the beds*.

Abū Jaʿfar [al-Ṭabarī] said that the interpreters have differed concerning the interpretation of that. Some of them say that the meaning of it is that you admonish them for their *nushūz* against you, O husbands, and if they refuse to reconsider their duty in that respect, and their obligations towards you, then forsake them by renouncing sexual relations when you lie with them.

An account of those who have said this:

ʿAlī b. Abī Ṭalḥa reported that Ibn ʿAbbās[89] said, 'His words *admonish them, and forsake them in the beds* mean admonish them, and if they obey you then that is the end of it, and if not then forsake them.'

[82] Al-Muthannā ← Abū Ḥudhayfa ← Shibl ← Ibn Abī Najīḥ ← Mujāhid.
[83] Al-Muthannā ← ʿAmr b. ʿAwn ← Hushaym ← Yūnus ← al-Ḥasan.
[84] Ibn Wakīʿ ← his father ← Mūsā b. ʿUbayda ← Muḥammad b. Kaʿb al-Quraẓī.
[85] Al-Muthannā ← Ḥibbān b. Mūsā ← Ibn al-Mubārak ← Shibl ← Ibn Abī Najīḥ ← Mujāhid.
[86] Ibn Wakīʿ ← his father ← Isrā'īl ← Jābir ← ʿAṭā'.
[87] Al-Qāsim ← al-Ḥusayn ← Ḥajjāj ← Ibn Jurayj.
[88] There is another report like this on a different chain of transmission.
[89] Al-Muthannā ← ʿAbd Allāh b. Ṣāliḥ ← Muʿāwiya b. Ṣāliḥ ← ʿAlī b. Abī Ṭalḥa ← Ibn ʿAbbās.

Ibn ʿAbbās[90] said, [regarding] *forsake them in the beds*, ʻBy *forsake*, He means that the man and his wife are on one single bed and he does not have sexual relations with her.ʼ

ʿAṭāʾ b. al-Sāʾib reported that Saʿīd b. Jubayr[91] said, ʻthe "forsaking" is forsaking sexual relationsʼ.

Asbāṭ reported that al-Suddī[92] said, ʻAs for *if you fear the women's defiance*, indeed it is her husband's obligation to admonish her, and if she does not acquiesce then let him forsake her in the bed.ʼ

It is said, he lies down next to her and turns his back on her, and he mounts and does not speak to her. In my text (*kitāb*) it is like this: ʻHe mounts her and does not speak to her.ʼ

Juwaybir reported that al-Ḍaḥḥāk[93] said, with regard to His words *forsake them in the beds*, ʻHe lies with her and forsakes speaking with her and turns his back to her.ʼ

Saʿīd b. Jubayr reported that Ibn ʿAbbās[94] said, [regarding] *forsake them in the beds*, ʻHe should not have sexual relations with herʼ.

Others say, rather, the meaning of that is: Forsake them and forsake speaking to them while they have left the beds until they return to your beds.[95]

An account of those who have said this:

Abū'l-Ḍuḥā reported that Ibn ʿAbbās[96] said, concerning His words *forsake them in the beds*, ʻIt is not leaving off of speaking; rather, the forsaking has to do with the bed.ʼ

ʿAṭāʾ b. al-Sāʾib reported that Saʿīd b. Jubayr[97] used to say, concerning *forsake them in the beds*, ʻUntil they come to your bedsʼ.

ʿAṭāʾ reported that Saʿīd b. Jubayr said, concerning *forsake them in the beds*, ʻIn sexual relationsʼ.

ʿAlī b. Abī Ṭalḥa reported that Ibn ʿAbbās said, concerning *forsake them in the beds*, ʻHe admonishes her, and if she accepts that is the end of it, but if not he forsakes her in the bed and does not speak to her other than to leave the marriage, which is hard on her.ʼ

[90] Muḥammad b. Saʿd ← his father ← his uncle ← his father ← his father ← Ibn ʿAbbās.

[91] Ibn Ḥumayd ← Jarīr ← ʿAṭāʾ b. al-Sāʾib ← Saʿīd b. Jubayr.

[92] Muḥammad b. al-Ḥusayn ← Aḥmad b. Mufaḍḍal ← Asbāṭ ← al-Suddī.

[93] Al-Muthannā ← ʿAmr b. ʿAwn ← Hushaym ← Juwaybir ← al-Ḍaḥḥāk.

[94] Al-Muthannā ← Ḥibbān b. Mūsā ← Ibn Mubārak ← Sharīk ← ʿAṭāʾ b. al-Sāʾib ← Saʿīd b. Jubayr ← Ibn ʿAbbās.

[95] The debate here is between those who believe that the husband forsakes speaking to his wife but continues to engage in sexual relations with her, and those who believe that the forsaking entails the forsaking of sexual relations.

[96] Abū Kurayb and Abū Sāʾib ← Ibn Idrīs ← al-Ḥasan b. ʿUbayd Allāh ← Abū'l-Ḍuḥā ← Ibn ʿAbbās.

[97] Ibn Ḥumayd ← Yaḥyā b. Wāḍiḥ ← Abū Ḥamza ← ʿAṭāʾ b. al-Sāʾib ← Saʿīd b. Jubayr.

'Ikrima said, regarding *forsake them in the beds*, 'Speaking and talking'. [There follow nine further reports to similar effect.]

Others say that the meaning of His words *forsake them in the beds* is to say harsh words to them while they are abandoning your beds.

An account of those who have said this:

Abū Ṣāliḥ reported that Ibn 'Abbās[98] said, concerning His words *forsake them in the beds*, 'He speaks in harsh language to her with his tongue, and he is coarse with her in speech, but he does not refrain from having sexual relations with her.'

And the like of this was reported on the authority of 'Ikrima.[99] He said, 'The forsaking is in utterance, he is coarse to her. It is not in terms of sexual relations.'

Mughīra reported that Abū'l-Ḍuḥā[100] said, concerning His words *forsake them in the beds*, 'He forsakes her in speech, and does not forsake lying with her in bed until she returns to what he wants.'

Al-Ḥasan [al-Baṣrī][101] said, 'He should not forsake her except in the sleeping places, in the beds; he does not have the right to forsake her in words or in anything except the mattress.'

Ya'lā reported that Sufyān[102] said, with regard to His words *forsake them in the beds*, 'When [commencing] sexual relations with her, he says to her, "Come and do it!" – words in which there is coarseness. If she does that, then he cannot task her with loving him, for indeed her heart is not in her hands.'

Abū Ja'far [al-Ṭabarī] said that the term *forsake* (*h-j-r*) has only three possible meanings in the speech of the Arabs. The first of them is that a man forsakes the words of another man and his conversation, and that is that he rejects him and leaves him. From this usage, it is said, 'A man forsook his wife' (*hajara fulān ahlahu, yahjuruhā hajran wa hijrānan*). The second meaning is a plethora of words with frequent repetition, like the speech of someone being derisory. From this usage, it is said: *Hajara* so-and-so in his words, when he raves and speaks at length without ceasing so that becomes his manner and custom (*hijjīrāhu wa ihjīrahu*). An example of this is the words of Dhū'l-Rumma:[103]

[98] Ḥasan b. Yaḥyā ← 'Abd al-Razzāq ← al-Thawrī ← a man ← Abū Ṣāliḥ ← Ibn 'Abbās.

[99] Al-Thawrī ← Khaṣīf ← 'Ikrima.

[100] Ya'qūb b. Ibrāhīm ← Hushaym ← Mughīra ← Abū'l-Ḍuḥā.

[101] Al-Muthannā ← Ḥibbān b. Mūsā ← Ibn Mubārak ← 'Abd al-Wārith b. Sa'īd ← a man ← al-Ḥasan [al-Baṣrī].

[102] Al-Muthannā ← Isḥāq ← Ya'lā ← Sufyān.

[103] A poet of the Umayyad era; see Nefeli Papoutsakis, 'Dhū l-Rumma', *EI*^{3}.

He threw and he missed, for fate always vanquishes
They diverged so that war and woe become his custom

The third meaning is to *hajr* a camel, when its owner ties it with the *hijār*, which is a rope tied on its flank and the joint of its forelegs; and from this usage, Imrū' al-Qays said:

They espied their ruin in the dunes of the open desert,
And they well-nigh hastened to the [animal] ropes (*hijār*).

As for the opinion that it is coarseness and noxiousness, that is only in the form *ihjār*. It is said from that usage: so and so *ahjara* in his speech, when he says the *hujr*, which is abominable speech (*yuhjiru ihjāran wa'hujran*).

Since there is no justification for the *hajr* except one of those three meanings, and the woman whose *nushūz* you fear is only ordered by her husband in the admonishment to return to obeying him in those matters which are her obligation towards him – accepting him when he calls her to his bed – it cannot be that the wife would be ordered to obey God and her husband in that matter, and then her husband would be ordered to forsake her in the very matter about which he had admonished her. Since that is the case, it invalidates the opinion of the person who says that the *hajr* is that the husband forsakes sexual relations with his wife. It may be, since this meaning is incorrect, that the meaning is forsaking words with them because of their forsaking you in the beds, but that is also incomprehensible, because God, may His mention be glorified, has informed by the tongue of His Prophet (*ṣl'm*) that it is not permissible for a Muslim to forsake his brother more than thrice.[104] Even if it were permissible, the forsaking in words would have no comprehensible meaning, because if she was departing from him, and in defiance of him, then it would be to her delight if he did not speak to her or see her and if she did not see him. How could the man have been ordered – in a situation where his wife hates him, and her leaving him – to abstain from that which, by abstaining from it, makes her happy – such as abstaining from sexual relations with her and abstaining from speaking and conversing with her – while being commanded to strike her in order to deter her from disobeying him when he calls her to the bed and other matters in which it is necessary for her to obey him?

Since those two aspects are proven false, the meaning might be: forsake them in your speech to them, which means, if you were to speak to them, reply, but harshly. If that was its meaning, then there would be no purpose in

[104] Versions of this *ḥadīth* are found in Nawawī, *Riyāḍ al-ṣāliḥīn*, *Kitāb al-Umūr al-manhī 'anhā* (17), *Bāb taḥrīm al-hijrān bayn al-muslimīn* (280), *ḥadīth* nos. 85/1595 and 87/1597.

using the *hajr* to allude to the pronouns standing in for the women themselves, I mean with the pronominal suffix (*-hunna*) in His words *forsake them* (*wa'hjurū-hunna*), because if He had meant that by it, then the verb would not be transitive, because one can only say '*hajara* so-and-so (*fulān*) with words'; you cannot say 'someone *hajara fulānun fulānan*'.

Since all of these possible meanings that we have mentioned contain the above-mentioned defects, the closest interpretation to the truth with regard to His words *forsake them* is that its meaning is oriented towards tying with the *hijār* in the way that we have mentioned from the sayings of the Arabs regarding the camel, when the owner ties it with a rope as we have described (*hajarahu fa-huwa yahjuruhu hajran*). Since that is the meaning, the interpretation of the words is: those whose *nushūz* you fear, admonish them for their *nushūz* against you, and if they heed the admonishment, then there is no way for you against them, and if they refuse to return from their *nushūz*, then tie them fast with ropes in the bed, meaning in the rooms and sleeping chambers in which they lie down, and in which their husbands lie with them.

An account of those who have said this:

Ḥakīm b. Muʿāwiya reported that his father[105] said that he went to the Prophet (*ṣlʿm*) and said, 'What are the rights of our wives over us?' He said, 'He feeds her, he clothes her, and he does not strike her face, and he does not disfigure her[106] or forsake (*hajr*) her, except in the sleeping chambers.'[107]

[On another chain of transmission] Ḥakīm b. Muʿāwiya reported that his father[108] reported that the Prophet (*ṣlʿm*) said the like of it.

Bahz b. Ḥakīm reported that his grandfather[109] said, 'I said, "O Messenger of God, what can we take from our women, and what do we leave to them?" He said, "Your sowing fields, so tend your sowing fields as you will [cf. Q. 2:223],[110] except that you must not strike her face, nor disfigure her, nor

[105] ʿAbbās b. Abī Ṭālib ← Yaḥyā b. Abī Bukayr ← Shibl ← Abū Quzaʿa ← ʿAmr b. Dinār ← Ḥakīm b. Muʿāwiya ← his father.

[106] This is the meaning if the verb is in form 2, as it is in some editions; if it is in form 1, then the meaning is 'revile'.

[107] Versions of this *ḥadīth* are found in Abū Dāwūd, *Sunan*, *Kitāb al-Nikāḥ* (12), *Bāb fī ḥaqq al-mar'a ʿalā zawjihā* (42), *ḥadīth* no. 97/2142; Ibn Ḥajar al-ʿAsqalānī, *Bulūgh al-marām*, *Kitāb al-Nikāḥ* (8), *ḥadīth* nos. 63/1018; 205/1141 and 206/1142; Ibn Māja, *Sunan*, *Kitāb al-Nikāḥ* (9), *Bāb ḥaqq al-mar'a ʿalā'l-zawj* (3), *ḥadīth* no. 6/1850; Nawawī, *Riyāḍ al-ṣāliḥīn*, *Kitāb al-Muqaddimāt*, *Bāb al-waṣiyya bi'l-nisā'* (34), *ḥadīth* no. 277.

[108] Al-Ḥasan b. ʿArafa ← Yazīd ← Shuʿba b. al-Ḥajjāj ← Abū Quzaʿa ← Ḥakīm b. Muʿāwiya ← his father.

[109] Al-Muthannā ← Ḥibbān b. Mūsā ← Ibn Mubārak ← Bahz b. Ḥakīm ← his grandfather.

[110] This report uses the same vocabulary as the Qur'ānic verse, but it is in the singular rather than the plural.

forsake (*hajr*) her, except in the sleeping rooms; and feed them from what you eat, and clothe them as you are clothed [cf. Q. 5:89]. How can you do otherwise when you have been intimate with each other [cf. Q. 4:21]?"'

A number of interpreters have said the like of what we have said regarding this interpretation.

An account of those who have said this:

Al-Ḥasan [al-Baṣrī][111] said, 'When a woman rises up (*nashazat*) against her husband, let him admonish her with his tongue, and if she accepts then that is the end of it, and if not, he strikes her non-severely, and if she returns, then that is the end of it, and if not, then it is permissible for him to take what he wants from her (*ya'khudh minhā*) or to release her [by divorcing her].'

Abū'l-Ḍuḥā reported that Ibn 'Abbās[112] said, regarding His words *forsake them in the beds, and strike them*, 'He does that to her and strikes her until she obeys him in the bed, and if she obeys him in the bed and lies with him then he does not have a way against her.'

Yaḥyā b. Bishr reported that he heard 'Ikrima[113] say about His words *forsake them in the beds and strike them*, 'A non-severe strike', he said, 'The Messenger of God (*ṣl'm*) said, "strike them when they disobey you in what is expected of them (*ma'rūf*), non-severely".'

Abū Ja'far [al-Ṭabarī] said, none of the interpreters whom we have mentioned requires that the *hajr* has a meaning other than 'striking', and they do not require *hajr* if it takes any form from among the many forms in which a woman can look as though she has been struck, as indicated by the report that 'Ikrima narrates on the authority of the Prophet (*ṣl'm*), who commanded that the women be struck when they disobey their husbands in what is expected of them (*ma'rūf*), without any [mention of] the command from him to the husbands to forsake (*hajr*) them, according to the reasoning we have described.

If someone were to suspect that our interpretation of the report on the authority of the Prophet (*ṣl'm*) as narrated by 'Ikrima is wrong, but that it is correct that the Prophet (*ṣl'm*) did not implement the command for a husband to forsake (*hajr*) his wife when she disobeys him in what is expected of her (*ma'rūf*) and instead commanded him to strike her before the forsaking (*hajr*), and that this is proof of the soundness of our opinion that the meaning of *hajr* is as we have explained it, that would entail that God's

111 Al-Muthannā ← 'Amr b. 'Awn ← Hushaym ← al-Ḥasan.
112 Ibn Ḥumayd ← Jarīr ← Ḥasan b. 'Ubayd Allāh ← Abū'l-Ḍuḥā ← Ibn 'Abbās.
113 Al-Muthannā ← Ḥibbān ← Ibn Mubārak ← Yaḥyā b. Bishr ← 'Ikrima.

command to the husband to admonish her when she defies him is meaningless, since there is no mention of admonishment in ʿIkrima's report from the Prophet. In fact, the matter is the opposite of what the suspecter thinks, and that is because his words (*ṣlʿm*) 'when they disobey you in what is expected of them [. . .]' are a clear proof that he [the Prophet] did not permit a man to strike his wife except after he had admonished her about her defiance (*nushūz*), namely that she should not be disobedient to him, and after there had issued from him to her a command containing an admonishment of what is expected of her, as commanded by God, exalted be His mention.

Reports on the interpretation of His words, exalted be He, *strike them*. Abū Jaʿfar [al-Ṭabarī] said He means by that, majestic be His praise, admonish them, oh men, for their *nushūz*, and if they refuse to return (*iyāb*) to what is obligatory upon them towards you, then secure them with ropes in their sleeping chambers and strike them in order to make them return from their disobedience to the duties that are incumbent upon them in terms of obeying God in those rights of yours that are necessary for them to fulfil.

The commentators have said that the attribute of the striking which God has permitted to the husband of the wife who rises up is that it must be non-severe (*ghayr mubarriḥ*).

An account of those who have said this:[114]

ʿAṭāʾ reported that Saʿīd b. Jubayr[115] said [concerning] *strike them*, a non-severe (*ghayr mubarriḥ*) strike.

[Ṭabarī includes nine further reports specifying only that the strike be *ghayr mubarriḥ*. We have translated reports below that define the term *ghayr mubarriḥ*.]

ʿAlī b. Abī Ṭalḥa reported that Ibn ʿAbbās[116] said, [concerning] *forsake them in the beds, and strike them*, 'You forsake her in the bed, and if she accepts then that is the end of it, and if not then God has permitted you to strike her non-severely. Do not break her bones, and if she accepts you then that is the end of it, and if not then it is permissible for you to take ransom (*fidya*) from her.'

Saʿīd reported that Qatāda[117] said, [concerning] *and forsake them in the beds, and strike them*, 'You forsake them in the beds, and if they refuse you

[114] The following reports seek to mitigate the extent of the beating that the husband can inflict on the wife.

[115] Ibn Ḥumayd ← Ḥakkām ← ʿAmr ← ʿAṭāʾ ← Saʿīd b. Jubayr.

[116] Al-Muthannā ← Abū Ṣāliḥ ← Muʿāwiya ← ʿAlī b. Abī Ṭalḥa ← Ibn ʿAbbās.

[117] Bishr b. Maʿādh ← Yazīd b. Zurayʿ ← Saʿīd ← Qatāda.

then strike them non-severely. That is to say, without blemishing (*ghayr shāʿin*).'

Ibn Jurayj reported that ʿAṭā'[118] said, 'I asked Ibn ʿAbbās, "What is a non-severe (*ghayr mubarriḥ*) strike?"' He said, "He strikes her with a tooth-stick [*siwāk*][119] or something resembling it."'

[And on another chain of transmission] Ibn Jurayj reported that ʿAṭā'[120] said, 'I asked Ibn ʿAbbās, "What is a non-severe strike?" He replied, "With a tooth-stick or the like."'

[On a third chain of transmission] Ibn Jurayj reported that ʿAṭā'[121] said, 'The Messenger of God (*ṣlʿm*) said in his oration, "a non-severe strike (*ḍarb ghayr mubarriḥ*)" [meaning] a tooth-stick or the like.'

Al-Ḥusayn reported that Ḥajjāj[122] said, 'The Messenger of God (*ṣlʿm*) said, "Do not forsake women, except in the beds, and strike them non-severely", not leaving a trace (*ghayr mu'aththir*).'

Asbāṭ reported that al-Suddī[123] said [concerning] *strike them*, 'If she accepts at the forsaking then that is the end of it, and if not, then strike her non-severely.'

Mūsā b. ʿUbayda reported that Muḥammad b. Kaʿb[124] said, 'You leave her bed if you do not see that she inclines (*n-z-ʿ*), and if she still does not incline then strike non-severely.'

Al-Ḥasan[125] said, 'A non-severe strike, not leaving a trace.'

Reports on the interpretation of His words, exalted be He, *but if they obey you, seek not a way against them*.

Abū Jaʿfar [al-Ṭabarī] said, He means by that, majestic be His praise, if they obey you, oh people, [meaning] your women from whom you fear *nushūz*, when you admonish them, then do not forsake them in the beds. And if they do not obey you, then *forsake them in the beds, and strike them*; and if they return to obeying you at that and return to the duties upon them, then do

118 Al-Muthannā ← Isḥāq ← Ibn ʿUyayna ← Ibn Jurayj ← ʿAṭā'.

119 A *siwāk* should be considered as a small stick used for brushing the teeth. Cf. Chaudhry, *Domestic Violence and the Islamic Tradition*, 83, n. 93. Here, Chaudhry argues from her own experience of 'markets in the Middle East and South Asia' that a *siwāk* should be considered a switch or branch. However, we are not sure that there is lexicographic support for this interpretation in the medieval period.

120 Ibrāhīm b. Saʿīd al-Jawharī ← Ibn ʿUyayna ← Ibn Jurayj ← ʿAṭā'.

121 Al-Muthannā ← Ḥibbān b. Mūsā ← Ibn Mubārak ← Ibn ʿUyayna ← Ibn Jurayj ← ʿAṭā'.

122 Al-Qāsim ← al-Ḥusayn ← Ḥajjāj ← the Messenger of God.

123 Muḥammad b. Ḥusayn ← Aḥmad b. Mufaḍḍal ← Asbāṭ ← al-Suddī.

124 Ibn Wakīʿ ← his father ← Mūsā b. ʿUbayda ← Muḥammad b. Kaʿb.

125 Al-Muthannā ← Ḥibbān ← Ibn Mubārak ← ʿAbd al-Wārith b. Saʿīd ← someone ← al-Ḥasan.

not seek a way of harming them; [do not do] what is loathsome to them (*makrūhihinna*); and do not seek out a way to that which is illicit to you of their bodies and their property through pretexts (*ʿilal*) – and that is that one of you might say to one of them while she is being obedient to him, 'You do not love me and you hate me', and strike her for that or harm her. So God, exalted be He, says to men, *but if they obey you* – which is to say, despite their hatred of you – do not commit an outrage against them, nor should you task them with love for you, for that is not in their hands. So do not strike them or harm them because of it.[126]

The meaning of His words *seek not* is do not ask for or request. When someone says, 'I sought the lost object (*ḍālla*)', it means that he sought something out. The poet has said, describing death:

> It sought you, yet you did not seek it until you found it, as though
> you had made a tryst with it the eve before

Meaning, it requested you but you did not request it.

The commentators (*ahl al-taʾwīl*) have said the like of what we have said about this.

An account of those who have said this:

ʿAlī b. Abī Ṭalḥa reported that Ibn ʿAbbās[127] said, concerning His words *but if they obey you, seek not a way against them*, 'If she obeys you, then do not transgress against her through these pretexts (*ʿilal*).'

Abū'l-Ḍuḥā reported that Ibn ʿAbbās[128] said, 'When she obeys him and lies with him, then he does not have a way against her.'

Ḥasan b. Yaḥyā told us that ʿAbd al-Razzāq reported that Ibn Jurayj said regarding His words *seek not a way against her*, 'A pretext (*ʿilal*)'.

ʿAbd al-Razzāq reported that al-Thawrī said, concerning *but if they obey you*, 'She comes to the bed although she hates him.'

Sufyān[129] said, 'If she does that, then he should not task her with loving him, because her heart is not in her hands.'

Ibn Abī Najīḥ reported that Mujāhid[130] said, 'If she obeys him, then she lies with him, for God says *but if they obey you seek not a way against them*.'

Qatāda[131] used to say about *but if they obey you, seek not a way against them*, 'If she obeys you then do not seek a pretext against her.'

[126] Here Ṭabarī emphasises the importance of the wife obeying the duties imposed on her, despite anything she might be feeling.

[127] Al-Muthannā ← ʿAbd Allāh b. Ṣāliḥ ← Muʿāwiya b. Sāliḥ ← ʿAlī b. Abī Ṭalḥa ← Ibn ʿAbbās.

[128] Ibn Ḥumayd ← Jarīr ← al-Ḥasan b. ʿUbayd Allāh ← Abū'l-Ḍuḥā ← Ibn ʿAbbās.

[129] Al-Muthannā ← Isḥāq ← Yaʿlā ← Sufyān.

[130] Al-Muthannā ← Abū Ḥudhayfa ← Shibl ← Ibn Abī Najīḥ ← Mujāhid.

[131] Bishr b. Muʿādh ← Yazīd ← Saʿīd ← Qatāda.

The [final] word regarding the interpretation of His words, exalted be He, *indeed God is high, mighty*.

Abū Jaʿfar [al-Ṭabarī] says, 'Indeed God is the one who is exalted over everything. So, O people, do not seek a way against your wives, when they obey you in those rights which God has made incumbent upon them, because your hand is over their hands, for God is higher than you and higher than everything, and He is higher over you than you are over them. He is greater than you and greater than everything, and you are in His hands and in His fist. So be wary of God, lest you should be unjust towards them and seek a way against them while they are being obedient to you, for your Lord, who is higher than you and than everything, and greater than you and greater than everything, will make them triumph over you.[132]

Qushayrī

This brief interpretation begins with the reason for the verse, which is that men are stronger in their hearts and their spiritual practices (*qulūb wa-himam*). 'Hearts' means their spirits and their minds, according to the medieval Muslim understanding of the term. There is a strong focus here on the gentler side of the verse, on being kind and on what husbands should and should not do. First, husbands should 'develop their instruction gradually and gently'. As in other interpretations, if a wife obeys then the husband is not authorised to chastise her further. For Qushayrī, 'the etiquette of good companionship is implicit in this verse'. If the wife is a poor companion to her husband, that authorises his actions, but if she is not, then the husband must act well towards her, not rejecting her or holding a grudge against her. Men cannot expect love from their wives, for God alone controls love in the heart.

God has distinguished men with strength and has made the burden upon them greater, for the burden is commensurate with strength. It is about the heart and its aspiration (*himam*), not individuated beings and corpora.[133]

If you fear the women's defiance, develop their instruction gradually and gently, and if the matter is resolved through the admonishment then do not use the stick to strike. The etiquette of good companionship is implicit in this verse.

[132] Ṭabarī, *Jāmiʿ al-bayān*, s.v. Q. 4:34. Here, Ṭabarī includes a harsh warning to husbands that they must not abuse their wives, which is an implicit recognition of the possibility of such abuse and the wife's lack of worldly recourse for it.

[133] The Arabic term here is *juthath* (sing. *juththa*) which signifies a corpse. The contrast here is between the living heart and the dead body, meaning that someone can be alive in a bodily sense but can remain spiritually dead. For Qushayrī, the person who is truly alive is he whose heart aspires to the spiritual realm.

Then He said, *but if they obey you, seek not a way against them*, meaning, if she stops at once her poor companionship and returns to obedience, then do not take vengeance on her for what has passed, and do not decline to accept her excuses, or reject her.

It is said, *but if they obey you, seek not a way against them* by exceeding the bounds of what she deserves in your resentment.[134]

[. . .][135] They say that she owes you bodily obedience, and as for affection and inclination towards you in the heart, that is up to God; so do not task her with that aspect of her which God has not made yours, for indeed the hearts are in God's control, and He makes them love whatever He wishes and makes them loathe whatever He wishes.

They say [concerning] *but if they obey you, seek not a way against them*, do not forget her past loyalty on account of a moment's uncharacteristic dryness, for perhaps matters will go back to being beautiful again.[136]

Zamakhsharī

Zamakhsharī's interpretation is along similar lines to its predecessors, but many of its aspects give the impression of his misogyny, even within the context of a patriarchal society. He first emphasises that men do not deserve their position because of the use of brute force or power, but rather because of their innate superiority to women. His interpretation is noteworthy for its long list enumerating the aspects of this superiority. He also focuses quite heavily on the *asbāb al-nuzūl* with Ḥabība bt. Zayd, and he makes an addition to this *ḥadīth*, which was not in previous versions of it: in his version, Ḥabība rises up against her husband Saʿd. As mentioned above, this *ḥadīth* justifies laws on the amount of force that husbands are allowed to use against their wives. In Zamakhsharī's view, there is no retaliation against a husband for an injury he causes his wife, 'even if he were to split open her head'. Zamakhsharī also includes a *ḥadīth* that talks about women's merits in terms of how pleasing she is to her husband (rather than, for instance, her innate piety): 'The best of women is she who, when you look at her makes you happy, when you order her, obeys you, and when you are absent from her safeguards for you your property and her self'. When describing the phrase *strike them*, he cites two more *ḥadīth*s, one which says, 'Hang your whip where your household (*ahl*) can see it', and one on the authority of Asmāʾ bt. Abī Bakr, who said that her husband would strike his wives so much that he would break the rod on them.

[134] That is to say, what (in his view) she might 'deserve' by way of discipline or punishment. Here, Qushayrī is warning husbands that they should not act on their impulses but should control themselves when disciplining their wives.

[135] The omitted content moves to the interpretation of Q. 4:35.

[136] Qushayrī, *Laṭāʾif al-ishārāt*, s.v. Q. 4:34. Here, Qushayrī encourages husbands not to be too harsh with their wives.

All of this represents a development in ways of interpreting the verse, in that he is incorporating more *ḥadīths*; but it also represents the development of a sustained argument for the husband's ultimate authority over his wife. In his interpretation of the final phrase of the verse, *but if they obey you, seek not a way against them. Indeed God is high, mighty,* Zamakhsharī, like others, reminds men that they should not hold grudges or transgress, for God has more power over them than they have over their wives. On the whole, this interpretation, with its focus on the reasons why men deserve their status over their wives, could mark a change in the nature of the genre itself: as the discipline of *tafsīr* grew more sophisticated, the interpretations contained more detailed explanations; equally, it could signal that Zamakhsharī held a particularly dim view of women.

Men are maintainers of women: they undertake to command and forbid them, as rulers govern their subjects. They are called *quwwām* for that reason.

The pronoun in *the one* refers to both men and women. That is to say, men are only in control (*musayṭirūn*) of women because of the distinction (*tafḍīl*) that God has given *the one*, and they are the men, *over the other*, and they are the women. In this is a proof that guardianship is only earned by distinction (*tafḍīl*), not domination (*taghallub*), haughtiness (*istiṭāla*) or force (*qahr*).

Concerning men's distinction, they have mentioned intellect (*ʿaql*), determination (*ḥazm*), resolve (*ʿazm*), and strength (*quwwa*), writing in the majority of cases, horsemanship, marksmanship, and that among them are prophets and scholars, they have the greater and lesser imamate,[137] they wage jihad, they call the prayer and give the Friday sermon, they are able to undertake ritual seclusion (*iʿtikāf*), they say the magnifications during Eid al-Aḍḥā (*takbīrāt al-tashrīq*), according to Abū Ḥanīfa they are able to testify in *ḥudūd*-crimes and those involving retaliation (*qiṣāṣ*),[138] [they have] more shares and agnatic priority in inheritance,[139] [greater] bloodwit, the *qasāma*-oath,[140] authority in marriage, divorce, and the return of the wife after a revocable divorce, [greater] number of spouses, lineage is through the male line, and they have beards and turbans.

And by that which they expend: because of what men spend from their property in marrying women, in the bridal payment and maintenance. It was narrated that Ḥabība bt. Zayd b. Abī Zuhayr, the wife of Saʿd b. Rabīʿ, a

137 Meaning: they rule the state and lead the prayers.

138 Other schools differ as to what testimony is permitted to women. On women's testimony, see ch. 5 in this volume.

139 Meaning that, in inheritance, related men who do not have an obligatory assigned portion can come to inherit in cases where the only obligatory inheritors are women.

140 Pronouncing an oath fifty times, which establishes guilt or innocence in cases of murder.

tribal chief (*naqīb*) of the Anṣār, rose up against him (*nashazat ʿalayhi*), so he slapped her. So her father went with her to the Messenger of God (*ṣlʿm*) and said, 'I gave my darling to his bed and he slapped her!' The Messenger ordered her to retaliate against him, and then God sent down [this verse]. The Messenger (*ṣlʿm*) said, 'We wanted one thing and God wanted another, and that which God wants is better', and he lifted the order of retaliation.

The [jurists] differ concerning that. It is said: There is no retaliation between a man and his wife, except in cases of death, even if he were to split open her head, though that necessitates the blood money. It is also said that there is no retaliation except in cases of wounding and murder; as for a slap and the like, then no.

So, righteous women are devoutly obedient women: they are obedient and they undertake (*qāʾimāt*) what is obligatory upon them towards their husbands.

Those who safeguard during absence: 'being absent' (*ghayb*) is the opposite of 'being witness to' (*shahāda*), that is to say, women are safeguarders of what is due to the absent one. When their husbands are not in a position to witness them, they safeguard what ought to be safeguarded during an absence, such as their chastity, homes and property.

On the authority of the Prophet (*ṣlʿm*), 'The best of women is she who, when you look at her makes you happy, when you order her, obeys you, and when you are absent from her safeguards for you your property and her self',[141] and he recited this verse. It is said that *absence* means their secrets.

What for God is to be safeguarded: what God has safeguarded for them when He entrusted them to the care of their husbands in His book, and which the Messenger (*ṣlʿm*) ordered, saying, 'Behave well towards women';[142] or that with which God safeguards them, protects them from and grants them success to preserve in the absence; or by that which He safeguards for them when He promises them the great reward for safeguarding the absent one, or the severe punishment He threatens them with upon betrayal.

The '*mā*' is a particle relating to the verb. And it has been recited '*bi-mā ḥafiẓa Allāha*' in the accusative, on the basis of the *mā* being a connective.[143] In other words, so that the wives safeguard in the absence in the way that safeguards what is due to God, and what is entrusted by God, which is chastity, self-fortification, compassion (*shafaqa*) towards the husbands and being well-disposed to them.

[141] This *ḥadīth* first appears in the interpretation of Ṭabarī; see above, note 65.

[142] This is a reference to the Farewell Pilgrimage Oration.

[143] This is the reading that Ṭabarī and others attribute to Abū Jaʿfar Yazīd b. al-Qaʿqāʿ al-Madanī.

The reading of Ibn Masʿūd is: 'Righteous women are devoutly obedient women, safeguarders of the absence (*ṣawāliḥ qawānit ḥawāfiẓ li'l-ghayb*) that which for God is to be safeguarded, so be righteous to them (*aṣliḥū ilayhinna*).'[144]

Her *nushūz* or *nushūṣ* is that she is disobedient to her husband and she no longer feels comfortable in his presence. Its original sense is agitation.

In the beds: in the sleeping places. That is to say, do not enter into the women under the covers; or it may denote a euphemism for sexual relations (*jimāʿ*). It is said that he turns his back to her in the bed, and it is said that *in the beds* is in their sleeping chambers, where they spend the night. In other words, do not spend the night with them. It is [also] read as *fī'l-maḍjaʿ* and *fī'l-muḍṭajaʿ*. That is, in order to ascertain their state and to verify the matter of their *nushūz*, He orders admonishing them first, then forsaking them in the beds, and then the striking if the admonishment and the forsaking has had no effect on them.

It is said that its meaning is to force them to have sexual relations with you, and tie them up, from tying the camel, which is secured with ropes. This is the interpretation of the obtuse (*min tafsīr al-thuqalāʾ*).[145]

They have said that the strike must be non-severe, not wounding her or breaking her bones, and avoiding the face. On the authority of the Prophet (*ṣlʿm*), 'Hang your whip where your household (*ahl*) can see it'. And, on the authority of Asmāʾ bt. Abī Bakr al-Ṣiddīq, may God be pleased with both of them, 'I was the fourth of the four wives of al-Zubayr b. al-ʿAwwām, and when he became angry with one of us, he would strike us with the wooden pole from the clothes rack until it broke on us.' And some couplets are recited on the authority of al-Zubayr, including, 'If her children were not around her, I would strike her.'

Seek not a way against them: Do not expose them to harm, reprimands and accusations; forgive them and treat it as though it had never been, after their return to obedience and compliance and leaving off of their *nushūz*.[146]

[144] Note that these variant terms for 'righteous women', 'obedient' and 'safeguarding', are not attributed to Ibn Masʿūd by Ṭabarī (at note 72), and Ṭabrisī (at note 149) attributes them to Ṭalḥa b. Musarrif. We have not italicised the reading as it is non-standard.

[145] The *thuqalāʾ min al-nās* are the people who are disliked. Many other commentators disagreed with Ṭabarī's view as well. See Bauer, 'Room for Interpretation', 165–79; Chaudhry, *Domestic Violence and the Islamic Tradition*, 78–80; Bauer, *Gender Hierarchy*, 1–3, 208–11.

[146] Here and in the following paragraph Zamakhsharī emphasises the importance of forgiveness by reminding men of God's forgiving nature; he encourages husbands to be just rulers over their wives, in emulation of God's example towards humanity.

Indeed God is high, mighty: Be wary of Him, and know that His power over you is greater than your power over those who are under your hand. It is narrated that Abū Masʿūd the Anṣārī raised his whip in order to strike a young male slave of his, and the Messenger of God (*ṣlʿm*) caught sight of him and called out to him: 'Oh Abū Masʿūd, God has more power over you than you have over him', so he threw away the whip and freed that slave. Or it may mean that God is exalted and mighty, and if you disobey Him, despite the exaltedness of His affairs and the greatness of His rule, then you repent, He will relent; so all the more should you be willing to forgive those who transgress against you if they relent.[147]

Ṭabrisī

Ṭabrisī divides his commentary into different sections, including sections on the vowelling of the verse ('the reading'), 'the language', meaning the form of the words and grammar; the occasion of revelation (*asbāb al-nuzūl*); and the 'meaning'. These specialised subheadings indicate that the genre is becoming ever more sophisticated and complex. Ṭabrisī cites Muqātil b. Sulaymān as the source of the *asbāb al-nuzūl* of Ḥabība bt. Zayd, but the version that he cites is slightly different from the one that we have of Muqātil's; instead, it resembles more the version found in Zamakhsharī, because it has Ḥabība defying her husband before he slaps her. Ṭabrisī connects men's preference over women with their ability to manage their affairs, discipline them and have control over them. Thus, as has now become typical for the genre, wives are put in the position of children with regard to their husbands, who are described as being superior in several innate and learned characteristics; here, these include their 'knowledge (*ʿilm*), intellect (*ʿaql*), soundness of opinion'. Like other commentators, Ṭabrisī warns husbands against seeking an excuse for striking their wives when the wives are obedient. Seeking a pretext against them is not permissible, nor is expecting love from them. He ends by saying that God is on the women's side, and He will 'secure victory on their behalf when they are incapable of it'. This is a clear warning to men who seek to abuse their privilege. It should be noted that, although Ṭabrisī is a Shīʿī, his interpretation draws on, and resembles, many Sunnī commentaries.

Reading (*qirāʾa*)

Abū Jaʿfar [Yazīd b. al-Qaʿqāʿ al-Madanī] alone reads *by that which God has distinguished* with 'God' in the accusative.[148] The rest read it in the

[147] Zamakhsharī, *al-Kashshāf*, s.v. Q. 4:34.
[148] See Ṭabarī's interpretation, above.

nominative. There is a deviant reading, 'so, righteous ones are devoutly obedient ones' (*ṣawāliḥ qawānit*), which is the reading of Ṭalḥa b. Muṣarrif.[149]
[. . .]

Language (*lugha*)

One can say 'a man is *qayyim*, *qayyām*, or *qawwām*'; *qawwām* is an emphatic construction indicating augmentation (*takthīr*). The origin of *qunūt* is 'continuous obedience', and from that is the *qunūt* supplication in the *witr* prayer,[150] from the long period of standing in it.

The origin of *nushūz* is rising up against the spouse and standing in opposition to him, and it is derived from the saying so-and-so is on an elevation, that is to say, it is raised. One says of a woman: *nashazat, tanshuzu* and *tanshizu*.

The *hajr* is forsaking out of hatred: one says, 'I have forsaken a man' when I have stayed away from conversing with him out of hatred; the *hājira* is noon, because it is the time in which he abandons work; and the man ties the camel when he fastens it with the *hijār* (rope). The origin of *al-ḍujūʿ* is *istilqāʾ* (to lie down). One can say: *Ḍajaʿ ḍujūʿan wa iḍṭjāʿan* when he lies down for sleep. Anything that you tip, you can say that you have *aḍjaʿtuhu*. *Bughya* is a request or a desire, and one says, 'I sought an object' when one asks for it, and the poet says, describing death:

> It sought you, yet you did not seek it until you found it, as though
> you had made a tryst with it the eve before

Syntax (*iʿrāb*)

The *bāʾ* where He says *bi-mā faḍḍala Allāhu wa bi-mā anfaqū* is syntactically attached to His statement *qawwāmūn*; and the *mā* in both instances is relating to the verbal action (*maṣdariyya*) and requires no referent for what is conjoined to it because it is a particle. And as for His words *bi-mā ḥafiẓa Allāhu*, the *mā* also relates to the verbal action so that the implied sense is that God preserves the women. For those who read *bi-mā ḥafiẓa Allāha* in the accusative, the *mā* is a suffixed noun (*ism mawṣūl*), with the implied

[149] On these readings, see the text at notes 72, 144.

[150] Typically, the *qunūt* is a formulaic supplication performed just after rising up from the genuflexion (*rukūʿ*) during the *witr* (single) unit of prayer, usually after the late-evening or late-night prayer, constituting the joined third (like the *maghrib* prayer) or separated third of a unit of three (two completed with the *taslīm*, followed immediately by a third single unit). There is some disagreement and historical variation regarding this and the *witr*; see A.J. Wensinck, 'Ḳunūt', *EI*², V, 395.

sense being with that which preserves God, that is to say, preserves the command of God.

Occasions of revelation (*asbāb al-nuzūl*)

Muqātil said that this verse was revealed with regard to Saʿd b. al-Rabīʿ b. ʿAmr, who was a tribal chief (*naqīb*), and his wife, Ḥabība bt. Zayd b. Abī Zuhayr, both of whom were among the Anṣār. She rose up against him and so he slapped her, and her father went with her to the Prophet (*ṣlʿm*) and said, 'I gave my darling to his bed, and he slapped her!' So the Prophet (*ṣlʿm*) replied, 'Let her retaliate against her husband', and so she went out with her father to retaliate against him, and then the Prophet (*ṣlʿm*) said, 'Come back! Gabriel has just come to me, saying that God has sent down this verse'. The Prophet (*ṣlʿm*) then said, 'I wanted one thing and God wanted another, and that which God wants is better', and he lifted the order of retaliation. Kalbī says that it was revealed concerning Saʿd b. Rabīʿ and his wife Khawla bt. Muḥammad b. Maslama, and he mentioned a story the like of this. And Abū Rawq said that it was sent down concerning Jamīla bt. ʿAbd Allāh b. Ubayy and her husband Thābit b. Qays b. Shammās, and he mentioned something close to it.

Meaning (*maʿnā*)

When He, exalted be He, clarified the distinction (*faḍl*) of men over women,[151] He mentioned subsequently their distinction (*faḍl*) in undertaking the affairs of women, and He said, *Men are maintainers of women*, meaning responsible for (*qayyimūn*) women, empowered over them (*musallaṭūn ʿalayhinna*) in management (*tadbīr*), discipline (*taʾdīb*), spiritual instruction (*riyāḍa*) and education (*taʿlīm*).

By that which God has distinguished the one over the other: this is a clarification of the reason for giving men authority (*tawliya*) over women. That is to say, God only tasked them with authority in their affairs because they have superiority (*ziyādat al-faḍl*) over the women, in terms of knowledge (*ʿilm*), intellect (*ʿaql*), soundness of opinion (*ḥusn al-raʾy*), as well as resolve (*ʿazm*).

And by that which they expend of their property on the women, the bridal payment and the maintenance; all of that is a clarification of the proof of their responsibility for them, and giving men authority over their affairs.

[151] This may refer to Q. 4:32.

So, righteous women are devoutly obedient women, that is to say, obedient to God and to their husbands, according to Qatāda, al-Thawrī and ʿAṭāʾ, and it is also understood as safeguarding (*ḥafiẓāt*). It is substituted in His words, *O Mary, be devoutly obedient* (*uqnūti*) *to your Lord* [Q. 3:43], meaning, persist in obedience to Him.

Those who safeguard during absence, meaning, themselves and their chastity while their husbands are absent, on the authority of Qatāda, ʿAṭāʾ and al-Thawrī. It is also said: Safeguarding the property of their husbands when the husbands are absent and looking after their rights and that which is inviolable. The best interpretation is that they bear responsibility for both matters, because there is no incompatibility between these two things.

What for God is to be safeguarded, that is to say, that which God has preserved for them, in their bridal payments and the obligation (*ilzām*) of their husbands to pay their maintenance, according to al-Zajjāj, and it is said: What God has preserved for them, and His protection from sin (*ʿiṣma*). Had God not preserved them and protected them from sin, they would not preserve their husbands in their absence.

And if you fear the women's defiance (*nushūz*) means that the women from whom you fear *nushūz*, in its manifest causes and its indications. And the *nushūz* of a woman is her disobedience to her husband and her raising herself up against him, and going against him. Al-Farrāʾ said that its meaning is that you know of their *nushūz*. He said that the 'fearing' means 'knowing', because fearing *nushūz* is having knowledge of its occurrence.

Admonish them and forsake them in the beds means to admonish them first with words and friendly advice, and if the admonition has no effect, and if the words of advice leave no impression, then forsake them in the beds. On the authority of Saʿīd b. Jubayr, who said, 'It means sexual relations, and He only mentions beds because they are singled out for sexual relations'. It is said that its meaning is forsake them on the mattresses and in the sleeping places, and that is because her love or hatred of the husband will thereby become clear.[152] If she has any inclination towards him, then she would not endure the separation from him in the beds, and if she were not that way, then she would endure it. That is on the authority of al-Ḥasan and Qatāda and ʿAṭāʾ. And what has been reported on the authority of Abū Jaʿfar goes back to this meaning. He said, 'He turns his back on her.' In the *tafsīr* of al-Kalbī on the authority of Ibn ʿAbbās, 'Admonish them with the Book of God first, and that

[152] Here, in contradiction with earlier sources, the wife's hatred can constitute, in itself, *nushūz*; although, below, Ṭabrisī cites the view that the husband must not task his wife with love, and that if she is outwardly obedient to him he must not seek a pretext against her.

is to say to them, "Be wary of God (*ittaqī 'llāha*) and return to obeying me!"' and if she returns, then that is the end of it. If not, he should speak coarsely to her, and if she returns then that is the end of it. If not, he should strike her non-severely. It is said, with regard to the meaning of *ghayr mubarriḥ* (non-severely), that it should not cut her flesh or break her bones. It is narrated on the authority of Abū Jaʿfar that the striking is with a tooth-stick.

But if they obey you: if they return to obeying you and carrying out your orders, *seek not a way against them*, that is to say, do not seek from them a pretext [for beating] under false pretences. It is said, on the authority of Abū Muslim and Abū ʿAlī al-Jubbāʾī, [do not seek] a way to the striking and the forsaking, which is [only] permitted to you in the case of *nushūz*. And it is said on the authority of Sufyān b. ʿUyayna that its meaning is that you must not task her with love. And so it could be that the meaning is that if things are outwardly put straight for you, then do not seek a pretext against them on the basis of what they may inwardly hide.

God is high, mighty: He is ever-above tasking [anyone] with anything other than what is right (*al-ḥaqq*) in accordance with [their] capacity. Highness and mightiness are among the attributes of God, and the benefit in mentioning them here is the clarification of His being on the women's side and of His power to secure victory on their behalf when they are incapable of it. It is said that what is meant by it is that He, exalted be He, despite His highness and mightiness, does not task you with more than you have the capacity to bear, and likewise you should not task women with that which they do not have the capacity to bear.[153]

Rāzī

It is notable that Rāzī's commentary on Q. 4:34 includes none of the philosophical musings that dominate his commentary on other verses. Rāzī begins by making direct reference to Q. 4:32, *Do not covet that by which God has distinguished some of you over others*. He explains that men have been made maintainers of women because they have been given more inheritance, as indicated by that verse and others. For him, this is why men have to pay for women's maintenance and their bridal payment, so that the excess from one side becomes equal with the other. But his interpretation is not that men's station is merited solely because of their financial maintenance of their wives: husbands deserve to be in charge of their wives, he argues, because of both essential characteristics and legal rulings. The essential characteristics comprise knowledge and ability; he includes a near-verbatim quote (without attribution) of Zamakhsharī's

[153] Ṭabrisī, *Majmaʿ al-bayān*, s.v. Q. 4:34.

explanation of the many ways that men are superior to women. Such superiority justifies men's rights over women; nevertheless, Rāzī has a distinct emphasis on fairness in marriage: he says, for instance, that the wives must preserve their husbands' rights, just as the husbands are ordered to preserve their wives' rights and *retain them in common decency* (Q. 2:229).

Rāzī defines the fear of *nushūz* as a suspicion rather than an actual proof of the act. He says that the suspicion could arise from speech or act: for instance, if the wife used to 'respond to him when he called to her' or 'yield to him in conversation', but then she changed, or if she used to hurry to bed happily and then she changed. Thus, although Rāzī also includes the interpretation that the wife does not have to love the husband, it is clear that she must have the right attitude.

Rāzī is the first commentator in this study to include the opinion of Shāfiʿī, which is that it is permissible for husbands to strike their wives, but it is better not to.[154] He then cites a different occasion for the revelation of the verse, which is that the women of the Quraysh were controlled by their husbands, but the women of Medina controlled their households; this caused the Qurashī husbands to complain when they moved to Medina. After the revelation of this verse, the women became agitated and complained to the Prophet, who disparaged the husbands who beat them. Shāfiʿī uses this to say that the best husbands do not strike; and then he outlines the rules for striking, which is that if it must be done it should be no more than twenty or forty strikes. He also cites those who say that the striking should be with a scarf or a handkerchief rather than a stick and emphasises that the lighter option is the better one. This is in direct contradiction to previous harsh interpretations such as that of Zamakhsharī.

Rāzī concludes by saying that the phrase *God is high, mighty* is a direct threat to the husbands to ensure that they are not unjust to their wives. In line with previous commentators, he says that God will vanquish the unjustly punished wife.

Know that He said *do not covet that by which God has distinguished some of you over others* [Q. 4:32]. We have mentioned that the occasion of revelation for this verse was when women were speaking about the distinction (*tafḍīl*) that God gave to men over women in inheritance, and God, exalted be He, mentioned in this verse that He only distinguished men over women in inheritance because men are *maintainers of women*. So, indeed, even if they enjoy each other equally, God has ordered men to pay women the bridal payment, and men to bestow maintenance on women liberally. The surplus from one of the two sides has become equivalent with a surplus from the other side, and it is as though there is no actual distinction (*faḍl*) at all. This is a clarification of the modality of the arrangement of verses (*naẓm*).[155]

There are several issues (*masāʾil*) in this verse:

[154] See Kecia Ali, '"The Best of You Will Not Strike": Al-Shāfiʿī on Qurʾan, Sunnah, and Wife-Beating', *Journal of Comparative Islamic Studies* 2.2 (2006), 143–55.

[155] Rāzī, here, affirms a type of equality in the distribution of wealth, saying that men are granted more in inheritance because of their financial duties towards their wives.

The first issue (*mas'ala*): *Qawwām* is a noun used for someone who goes out of his way to be in charge of a matter (*qiyām bi'l-amr*). One says, so-and-so is the *qayyim* of a woman, or is her *qawām*, to mean the one who manages her affairs and takes it upon himself to preserve her. Ibn ʿAbbās said, 'This verse was sent down with regard to the daughter of Muḥammad b. Salama and her husband Saʿd b. al-Rabīʿ, who was a tribal chief (*naqīb*) of the Anṣār. He gave her a proper slap, and so she rose up from his bed (*nashaza*) and went to the Messenger (*ṣlʿm*), and made this complaint, that he had slapped her and that the mark of the slap was still on her face. So the Messenger said, 'Retaliate against him'. Then he said to her, 'Wait (*uṣburī*), let me see'. Then this verse was sent down, *Men are maintainers of women*; that is to say empowered (*musallaṭūn*) over their discipline and guidance (*al-akhdh fawq aydīhinna*). It is as though He made him a commander (*amīr*) over her and the executor of rulings that concern her. When this verse was revealed, the Prophet (*ṣlʿm*) said, 'We wanted one thing and God wanted another, and that which God wants is better', and the order of retaliation was lifted. So, having established for men authority (*sulṭan*) over women, and the power to carry that [authority] through (*nafādh al-amr*), He proceeds to clarify that this is justified on the basis of two things (*amrayn*):

The first is His words: *by that which God has distinguished the one over the other.* Know that men's distinction (*faḍl*) over women is obtained in more than one aspect (*wujūh*); some of them are essential attributes (*ṣifāt ḥaqīqiyya*) and some of them are legal rulings. As for the essential attributes, know that the existence of essential distinctions (*faḍā'il ḥaqīqiyya*) returns to two matters: knowledge and capability (*qudra*). There is no doubt that men's intellect (*ʿaql*) and knowledge are greater, and there is also no doubt that they have a more complete ability to undertake toilsome labour. These two matters result in men's distinction over women in intellect (*ʿaql*), determination (*ḥazm*), and strength (*quwwa*), writing in the majority of cases, horsemanship, marksmanship, and that among them are prophets and scholars, they have the greater and lesser imamate, they wage jihad, they call the prayer and give the Friday sermon, they are able to undertake ritual seclusion (*iʿtikāf*), they are able to testify in *ḥudūd*-crimes and those involving retaliation (*qiṣāṣ*) by consensus, and in marriage according to Shāfiʿī, may God be pleased with him, [they have] more shares and agnatic priority in inheritance, they bear the bloodwit in murder and manslaughter, the *qasāma*-oath, authority in marriage, divorce and the return of the wife after a revocable divorce, [greater] number of spouses, lineage is through the male line, and all of that indicates the distinction of men over women.[156]

[156] This is almost an exact replica of the interpretation of Zamakhsharī. See above, p. 349.

The second reason (*sabab*) this distinction obtains is His words *and by that which they expend of their property*, meaning, the man is distinguished over the woman because he gives her the bridal payment and he pays maintenance to her.

Moreover, God divided women into two groups. He described the righteous women among them as being *devoutly obedient women, those who safeguard during absence what for God is to be safeguarded*. This comprises several issues (*masāʾil*):

The first issue (*masʾala*): The author of the *Kashshāf* [al-Zamakhsharī] said that the reading of Ibn Masʿūd is, 'So righteous ones are obedient ones, safeguarding' (*faʾl-ṣawāliḥ qawānit, ḥawāfiẓ liʾl-ghayb*).[157]

The second issue (*masʾala*): His words *devoutly obedient women, those who safeguard*, there are two aspects (*wujūh*) to this. The first is *obedient*, that is to say obedient to God, and *safeguard during absence*, that is to say, fulfilling their duties towards (*qāʾimāt al-ḥuqūq*) their husbands. The performance of the rights of God precede, and then He causes that to be succeeded by the rights of the husband. The second aspect is the status of the woman is either to be determined when the husband is present or when he is absent. As for her status while her husband is present, God describes it as that of devout obedience (*qānita*). The origin of the term *qunūt* is 'persistent obedience', and the meaning is that the wives fulfil their duties towards their husbands, and the obvious interpretation is that this is an informative statement, except that the intention of it is a command to obedience.

Know that a woman cannot be good unless she is obedient to her husband, because God, exalted be He, said *so, righteous women are devoutly obedient women*, and the definite article in the plural indicates the total inclusion of a group. This entails that for a woman to be good, she must be devoutly obedient to God (*qānita*) and to her husband (*muṭīʿa*). Al-Wāḥidī, may God have mercy on him, said, 'The import of the word *qunūt* is obedience, which is general obedience to God and to husbands.'

As for the state of the woman in the absence of her husband, God, exalted be He, has described her with His words: *those who safeguard during absence*. Know that absence is the opposite of presence and the meaning is that the

[157] As noted above, this reading attributed to Ibn Masʿūd differs entirely from the reading that Ṭabarī attributes to him, and it also differs from the reading attributed to him by Zamakhsharī, in that this version includes the variant plurals (*ṣawāliḥ qawānit*, *ḥawāfiẓ*) and omits the phrase 'so be good to them'. See the text at notes 72, 144 and 149.

wives are preservers of the requirements in cases of absence, and that has several aspects (*wujūh*). The first of them is that she preserves herself from adultery, lest some disrepute attach itself to her husband on account of her adultery, and so that he does not become associated with a child made from sperm that is not his. The second of them is the safeguarding of his property from perishing. The third of them is the safeguarding of the house from what is inappropriate. On the authority of the Prophet (*ṣlʿm*), 'The best of women is she who, when you look at her, makes you happy, when you order her, obeys you, and when you are absent from her safeguards for you your property and her self',[158] and he recited this verse.

The third issue (*mas'ala*): *Mā* (that which) in His words *by that which God has preserved*: it has two aspects (*wajh*).

The first [aspect] is that it means 'that which' (*alladhī*), in which case the referent of *alladhī* has been omitted, and the implied sense is 'by that which God preserves *for them*'. The meaning is that it is their responsibility to preserve the rights of the husband in return for their rights over their husbands that God has preserved when He ordered the husbands to be just to the women, to *retain them in common decency* [Q. 2:229] and to give them their marriage portion. And thus His words are equivalent to saying 'this for that'.

The second aspect (*wajh*) is that the *mā* relates to the verb, the implication being 'in return for God's safeguarding' (*bi-ḥifẓ Allāh*),' and given this implication, there are two aspects. The first is that the women safeguard for the absent by that which God has safeguarded for them; that is to say, the safeguarding will not be possible for them except through success granted by God. This would be an example of associating the verbal infinitive with the subject. The second is that the meaning is that the woman is only able to safeguard during absence because of their safeguarding of God, that is, because of the women's safeguarding of God's ordinances and His orders. If the woman does not attempt to undertake the duties of God and strive in safeguarding His orders, then she will not be obedient to her husband. This is an example of attaching the verbal infinitive to the object.

Know that God, exalted be He, when He mentioned the righteous women, mentioned after that those who are not righteous, and said, *if you fear the women's defiance*. Know that '*fear*' is an expression for the state reached in

[158] This *ḥadīth* is first cited by Ṭabarī, see above, note 65.

the heart upon a suspicion of an occurrence of a deplorable matter in the future. Al-Shāfiʿī, may God be pleased with him, said, [regarding] *if you fear the women's defiance* (*nushūz*), the *nushūz* could be in speech and it could be in act. The speech, for example, is that she used to respond to him when he called to her, and she would yield to him in conversation if he spoke to her, and then she changed.[159] The action, for example, is if she would stand up when he entered the room, or she hastened to his command and hurried to his bed happily when he sought her out, and then she stopped doing all of that. These are the signs indicating her *nushūz* and her disobedience, such that he suspects her *nushūz*. These states are the preamble that necessitate 'fear' of the *nushūz*. As for *nushūz* [itself], it is her disobedience of the husband and rising up against him in opposition. Its origin is from the saying that something *nashaza* if it rose up, and from that one says that the earth is *nushz or nushr* when it is raised up.

Then the Exalted said, *then admonish them, and forsake them in the beds, and strike them*. In this are several issues (*masā'il*):

The first issue (*mas'ala*): Al-Shāfiʿī said, may God be pleased with him, 'As for the admonishment, it is that he says to her, "Be wary of God (*ittaqī 'llāha*), for I have a right over you, and back away from what you are doing, and know that obedience to me is a duty upon you"', and the like. And he should not strike her at this moment, because it is possible that will suffice.

If she persists in the *nushūz*, then at that point he should forsake her in the bed, including refraining from speaking to her. Al-Shāfiʿī said, may God be pleased with him, 'In his forsaking, he does not exceed three words'; and also, 'When he forsakes her in the bed, if she loves her husband, this will be difficult for her and she will abandon her *nushūz*.' And if she hates him, then that forsaking will suit her, and that is a proof of the perfectness of her *nushūz*. Among them are those who interpret that to be forsaking sexual relations with her face-to-face (*mubāshara*), because adding the term 'forsaking' to the term 'beds' suggests that.

If, after the forsaking, she continues with the *nushūz*, then he may strike her. Al-Shāfiʿī said, may God be pleased with him, 'The striking is permitted, but not doing it is better.' It is narrated on the authority of ʿUmar b. al-Khaṭṭāb, may God be pleased with him, that he said: We the people of the

[159] Here Rāzī expands the scope of a wife's *nushūz* to include her general attitude towards her husband in speech and actions. He indicates that a wife should yield to her husband in conversation and should rise when he enters a room; both of these actions are indications of his social standing being higher than hers within the household.

Quraysh, our men controlled (*mulk*) our women. Then we went to Medina and we found that their women controlled their men. So our women mixed with their women and became emboldened against their husbands, which is to say they rose up (*nashazna*) and were insolent (*ijtara'*). So I went to the Prophet (*ṣlʿm*), and I said to him, 'The wives have become emboldened against their husbands', so he granted permission to strike them. Then a group of women, all of them complaining about their husbands, went round the chambers of the Prophet's wives. So he said (*ṣlʿm*), 'Muḥammad's[160] household were visited at night by a group of seventy women, all of whom were complaining about their husbands, and you will not find those men to be the best among you'.[161] And its meaning is that those who strike their wives were not better than those who did not strike.

Al-Shāfiʿī, may God be pleased with him, said: This *ḥadīth* indicates that it is a priority to eschew striking.[162] But if you were to strike her, then that striking must be such that it could never result in her perishing (*halāk*), it should be dispersed around her body; he should not keep doing it in the same place, he should avoid the face because all of the beauty is gathered there, and the strikes should be fewer than forty.[163] Among our companions are those who say he should not reach twenty [strikes], because that is the full legal limit (*ḥadd*) in the case of [striking] a slave. And among them are those who say the striking should be with a folded handkerchief or with his hand, and he should not strike her with a whip or with a stick. And in sum, according to the best interpretation, the lighter option should be considered in this situation.

I say, [al-Shāfiʿī] indicates that God ordered husbands to begin with the admonishment, then ascend from it to the forsaking in the beds, then ascend from that to the striking. And that [gradation] is as good as saying explicitly

160 Note that the Prophet seems to be speaking in the third person here.

161 Versions are found in Abū Dāwūd, *Sunan*, *Kitāb al-Nikāḥ* (12), *Bāb fī ḍarb al-nisāʾ* (43), *ḥadīth* no. 101/2146; Ibn Māja, *Sunan*, *Kitāb al-Nikāḥ* (9), *Bāb ḍarb al-nisāʾ* (51), *ḥadīth* no. 141/1985; Nawawī, *Riyāḍ al-ṣāliḥīn*, *Kitāb al-Muqaddimāt*, *Bāb al-waṣiyya bi'l-nisāʾ* (34), *ḥadīth* no. 279. Note also the *ḥadīth* in which the Prophet is reported to have said, 'The best of you is the best to his wife, and I am the best to my wives', versions of which are found in Ibn Māja, *Sunan*, *Kitāb al-Nikāḥ* (9), *Bāb ḥusn maʿāsharat al-nisāʾ* (50), *ḥadīth* nos. 133/1977 and 134/1978; Tirmidhī, *Jāmiʿ*, *Kitāb al-Manāqib* (49), *ḥadīth* no. 4269 and *Kitāb al-Riḍāʿ* (12), *Bāb mā jāʾa fī ḥaqq al-marʾa ʿalā zawjihā* (11), *ḥadīth* no. 17/1162.

162 Here, Rāzī cites Shāfiʿī and the example of the Prophet to discourage husbands from beating their wives. However, he recognises that in the law they have the right to strike them, and in light of that he also recommends limiting the beating if they do strike them. The exegetes often recommend behaviour which falls well short of these legal limits; this is one way of recognising that what may be allowed legally may not be the best action morally.

163 The standard *taʿzīr* punishment must be fewer than forty blows, as recommended here.

that whenever you can reach the goal with the lightest option, that should suffice, and that it is an obligation to be content with it. You should not embark on the harsher route. And God knows best.

The second issue (*mas'ala*): Our companions differ [on this]. Some of them say the ruling of this verse has legislative force on the basis of the sequencing. Although the outward sense of the lexical expression suggests amalgamation (*jamʿ*), the force of the verse indicates a sequencing. The Commander of the Believers, ʿAlī b. Abī Ṭālib, may God be pleased with him, said: 'He should admonish her with his tongue, and if she stops then there is no way for him against her, and if she refuses then he forsakes her bed, and if she still refuses, he strikes her, and if she does not learn the lesson from the striking, they call for two arbiters.' Others said, 'This sequencing is observed upon fearing the *nushūz*, and as for when the *nushūz* is verified, there is no harm in doing them all at once.' One of our companions says that our school states that upon fearing the *nushūz*, he admonishes her, but can he forsake her? He has the option, upon commencement of the *nushūz*, to admonish her, or forsake her, or strike her.

Then He says, exalted be He, *but if they obey you*, that is to say, if they return from their *nushūz* and become obedient at this disciplining, *seek not a way against them*, that is to say, do not seek a path to striking them or forsaking them by way of damage and harm.[164]

Indeed God is high, mighty. His highness is not the height of direction, and His mightiness is not the mightiness of the body; rather, He is high and mighty because of the perfect nature of His power and because His will is always executed through all contingent beings. These two attributes have been mentioned in this place in an excess of goodness, and His clarification is of several aspects (*wujūh*):

The first is that the intention of it is to threaten the husbands not to be unjust towards women, meaning that when the women are too weak to defend themselves against your injustice, and when they are incapable of demanding justice from you, then know that God, glory be to Him, is high, vanquishing, mighty, powerful, and will take vengeance on you for them, and He will give them the full share of the rights that you owe them. So do not become deluded on account of your power over them[165] or your being greater than them by a degree [cf. Q. 2:228].

[164] Here, again, Rāzī encourages men to be moderate towards their wives.
[165] Literally: your hand being higher than theirs.

The second is that if they have obeyed you, do not to seek a way against them on account of your hand being higher than theirs. For God is higher than you and mightier than everything, and He is exalted above tasking [people] except rightfully.

The third is that He, exalted be He, despite his greatness and mightiness, only ever tasks you with that which you are capable of, so likewise do not task them with loving you, for they may not be capable of doing so.

The fourth is that, although He is high and mighty, he does not punish the sinner if he repents. Rather, He forgives him. So, if a woman turns away from her *nushūz*, then all the more should you accept her repentance and abandon her punishment.

The fifth is that God, despite His highness and mightiness, is content with what is outwardly manifest from the servant, and He does not invade the innermost secrets. So all the more should you be content with the outward state of your wives; do not fall into the trap of inspecting what she loves and hates in her heart and her inner self (*ḍamīr*).[166]

Qurṭubī

One might assume that Qurṭubī, writing a work of legal interpretation, would focus on the laws in this verse. However, the majority of this interpretation is very much grounded within the *tafsīr* tradition rather than the legal tradition. Methodologically, this interpretation is notable for its inclusion of numerous *ḥadīths*, only some of which have been mentioned in prior interpretations of this verse. In terms of content, Qurṭubī suggests that striking depends on a wife's social status. He says that husbands should not strike nobly born women – for them, verbal chastisement is enough; but slaves and lower-class women may be struck with a stick.[167]

For the first part of the verse, Qurṭubī focuses on the necessity of men's maintenance in exchange for women's obedience; it later becomes clear that this is connected to men's legal status as *qawwām* over women. He first situates the verse in a discussion of inheritance among several women, which led to the revelation of Q. 4:32 (*Do not covet that by which God has distinguished some of you over others*). Like Rāzī, Qurṭubī says that men's duty to maintain women in Q. 4:34 makes up for their surplus in inheritance in Q. 4:32. He then defines *qawwāmūn* as 'absolute power of oversight' and 'earnestly protecting' something. This, he says, explains why men undertake the management of women, keeping them in the house, preventing them from coming out, 'and [why] it is her duty to obey and accept his command in everything that is not

166 Rāzī, *Mafātīḥ al-ghayb*, s.v. Q. 4:34.
167 This interpretation has been analysed by Manuela Marín, 'Disciplining Wives', 5–40.

disobedience to God'. Thus, for Qurṭubī, women's obedience is not limited to sex, as it seemed to be for Ṭabarī and other early commentators. Qurṭubī then explains that when a husband does not pay maintenance he is no longer *qawwām*, and 'she is entitled to dissolve the contract' of marriage. This is in accordance with Mālikī *fiqh*, which holds that men's position depends on them upholding their financial responsibilities.

In terms of a wife's obedience, Qurṭubī says that the wife owes her husband good and beautiful companionship, and she should recognise 'the degree that he has above her' (cf. Q. 2:228). To explain this degree, Qurṭubī cites a *ḥadīth* that says that if the Prophet had ordered anyone to prostrate themselves before anyone else, he would have made a wife prostrate herself before her husband. This is the very same *ḥadīth* that was used by the Ismāʿīlī Mu'ayyad to undermine the idea of a marital hierarchy, because some women are better than their husbands. But here it is taken quite literally to be a reference to men's superiority to women, and it is backed up by other *ḥadīth*s that talk about the importance of a husband being pleased with his wife: she should not refuse his advances even if she is on the back of a camel, and if she spends the night away from her husband, the angels curse her until morning. In these instances, then, 'good companionship' is not restricted as it was in Ṭabarī.

Qurṭubī also refers to the controversy created by Ṭabarī's interpretation of 'tie them fast with ropes in the bed', and he cites the Mālikī Ibn ʿArabī's refutation of this interpretation, in which it is clear that Ṭabarī's view goes beyond the bounds of propriety. Qurṭubī's own view is that the husband should turn his back on his recalcitrant wife, because if the wife loves him, this will be hard on her and 'she will return to righteousness'; but if she accepts it, then it is proof of her *nushūz*. Any strike must be an 'educating strike', of which 'the intention of it is correction, nothing more'. He ends by asking the husbands to be gentle with their wives and to remember that God's power over them is greater than their own power over their wives. However, he also says that women's disobedience is equivalent to a grave sin. Even given this, men should only strike women who are of a social class where it is acceptable to treat them in this manner.

His words [Q. 4:34] consist of eleven issues (*mas'ala*).

The first issue: His words, exalted be He, *Men are maintainers of women* are a subject and a predicate (*ibtidā' wa-khabar*); that is to say, men undertake (*yaqūmūn*) to *expend* on women and to defend them, and also, if they are able, to be judges (*ḥukkām*) and rulers (*umarā'*), and to go on military raids (*ghazw*), and women cannot do that. It is said *qawwām* and *qayyim*. The verse was revealed with regard to Saʿd b. al-Rabīʿ, whose wife Ḥabība bt. Zayd b. Khārija b. Abī Zuhayr turned on him (*nashazat ʿalayhi*), and so he slapped her. Then her father said, 'O Messenger of God, I gave my darling to his bed, and he slapped her!' And he (*ṣlʿm*) said, 'Let her retaliate against her husband'. So she went out with her father in order to take vengeance on him, when Muḥammad said (*ṣlʿm*), 'Come back! This is Gabriel, who has come to me'. Then God revealed this verse, and Muḥammad (*ṣlʿm*) said, 'We wanted one thing and God wanted something else'; and in another narration, 'I wanted one thing, but that which God wants is better'. So it contradicted the first ruling [ordering the retaliation]. It has been said, with regard to this rejected ruling that was revealed, *do not be hasty with the Qur'ān before its revelation to you is concluded* [Q. 20:114].

Al-Ḥasan [al-Baṣrī][168] said, 'A woman came to the Prophet (*ṣlʿm*), and she said, "Indeed my husband slapped my face." So he (*ṣlʿm*) said, "There is retaliation between the two of you". Then God revealed: *Do not be hasty with the Qur'ān before its revelation to you is concluded*, and the Prophet held back (*amsaka*) until He revealed: *Men are maintainers of women*.' Abū Rawq said, 'It was revealed concerning Jamīla bt. Ubayy and her husband, Thābit b. Qays b. Shammās.' Kalbī said, 'It was revealed concerning ʿUmayra bt. Muḥammad b. Maslama and her husband, Saʿd b. al-Rabīʿ. It is said he provoked her, which is the saying of Umm Salama, mentioned before.'

An aspect of the arrangement [of the Qur'ānic verses] is that the women were speaking about men's distinction over women in inheritance, and so *do not covet* [Q. 4:32] was revealed.[169] Then God, exalted be He, clarified the distinction (*faḍl*) of men over women in inheritance, which is why the bridal money (*mahr*) and maintenance are incumbent upon them, such that the benefit of the distinction given to them returns to the women.

It is said: Indeed, men have a distinction (*tafḍīl*) over women in their surplus of intellect (*ʿaql*) and management (*tadbīr*), and the prerogative (*ḥaqq al-qiyām*) over the women was granted to them on account of that. It is said that men have an excess of strength in the self and natural characteristics that women do not have, because heat and dryness predominate in the nature of men; so in him is strength and power, while moisture and coldness predominate in the nature of women, which comprises gentleness and weakness.[170] So He gave men the right of *qiyām* over women because of that and in His words: *by that which they expend of their property*.

The second issue: This verse indicates that men can discipline their wives. But when the women preserve the rights of their husbands, men ought not to make companionship with them unpleasant.

[168] Ismāʿīl b. Isḥāq ← al-Ḥajjāj b. al-Minhāl and ʿĀrim b. al-Faḍl – and the wording is that of al-Ḥajjāj – ← Jarīr b. Ḥāzim ← al-Ḥasan al-Baṣrī.

[169] The full verse reads: *Do not covet that by which God has distinguished some of you over others; men have been given a share of what they earn, and women have been given a share of what they earn* (Q. 4:32).

[170] Here, Qurṭubī cites ancient Greek medical ideas of the humours in order to explain the differences between the sexes.

Qawwām is an intensive form based on the form *fa''āl*, which is for emphasis, and it is from undertaking to maintain (*qiyām 'alā*) something, maintaining absolute power of oversight (*istibdād bi'l-naẓar fīhi*) and earnestly protecting it. So the *qiyām* of men over women is of this sort, and it is that he undertakes her management and discipline (*tadbīr wa-ta'dīb*), keeps her in her house, prevents her from coming out, and it is her duty to obey and accept his command in everything that is not disobedience to God. This is justified by men's distinction (*faḍīla*), the maintenance, the intellect, and the strength in undertaking the jihad, the inheritance, commanding right and forbidding wrong. Some of them have the view that it is due to the beard, but this is nothing, for there could be a beard without anything else that we have mentioned. We have refuted this in our interpretation of [*sūrat*] *al-Baqara*.

The third issue: The *'ulamā'* have understood from His words *by that which they expend of their property*, that when he is unable to maintain her, then he is not *qawwām* over her, and thus, since he is not *qawwām* over her, she is entitled to dissolve the contract [of marriage], due to the cessation of the goal for which the marriage was contracted. There is a clear indication in this respect that the marriage can be dissolved in times of hardship when he is unable to provide maintenance and clothing, and this is according to the school of Mālik and al-Shāfi'ī. However, Abū Ḥanīfa says that it is not dissolved, due to His words *and if any man shall be in difficulty, then let him have respite until things ease* [Q. 2:280]. And the opinion concerning this has been introduced in that *sūra*.

The fourth issue: *So, righteous women are devoutly obedient women, those who safeguard during absence* is all a predicate, and what is intended by it is to command obedience to the husband, and to maintain (*qiyām*) what is due to him (*ḥaqq*) in terms of his property and herself while he is absent. In the *Musnad* of Abū Dāwūd al-Ṭayālisī, it is reported on the authority of Abū Hurayra that the Messenger of God (*ṣl'm*) said, 'The best of women is she who, when you look at her, makes you happy, when you order her, obeys you, and when you are absent from her safeguards for you your property and her self',[171] and he recited this verse, *Men are maintainers of women* – to the end of the verse. He said (*ṣl'm*), to 'Umar, 'There is no greater treasure to a man than a good woman, who when he looks at her makes him happy, and when

[171] See note 65 above.

he orders her obeys him, and when he is absent from her, safeguards him', as verified by Abū Dāwūd.

Ibn Masʿūd's *muṣḥaf* reads *fa'l-ṣawāliḥ qawānit ḥawāfiẓ* ('So, righteous ones are obedient ones, guarding ones'). This is a specifically feminine construction. Ibn Jinnī said that this broken form of the plural is closer in lexical expression to its signification because that implies a multitude, which is what is meant here.

The *mā* in His words *bi-mā hafiẓa Allāhu* relates to the verbal noun (*maṣdariyya*); that is to say, in return for God's safeguarding of the women. It is also correct for it to have the sense of *alladhi*, so that the referent of *hifẓ* is a pronoun in the accusative. And in the reading of Abū Jaʿfar [Yazīd b. al-Qaʿqāʿ al-Madanī], *bi-mā hafiẓa Allāha* [with Allāh] in the accusative. Al-Naḥḥās said the nominative is the clearer [of the two inflections]; that is to say that they are preservers of the absence of their husbands in return for God's safeguarding and help and fulfilment. And it is also said that they preserve God in terms of their bridal payments and living together well. It is said: The women safeguarding God by that which God has made them preserve for Him of the fulfilment of trusts owed to their husbands. The signification of the reading in the accusative is 'by their safeguarding of God', that is to say, their safeguarding of His commands and his religion. And with regard to the implied sense, it is also said, 'by that which they preserve of God', and the verb was made singular as in the following: *fa-inna'l-ḥawādith awdā bihā*. It is also said that the meaning is 'by safeguarding God', as in *ḥafiẓtu'llāha*.

The fifth issue: His words *if you fear the women's defiance*. '*Allātī*' is the plural of *allatī*, and it has been discussed before. Ibn ʿAbbās said, '*You fear*; meaning, you know and you arc surc.' And it is said, 'He is awaiting it (*ʿalā bābihi*)'. *Nushūz* is disobedience, and it is taken from *al-nashz* – what is raised from the ground. One says, 'a man *yanshuz wa yanshiz*', when he was seated and then he rose up standing. And it is used in His words, *If it is said, rise, then rise!* [Q. 58:11]; that is to say, rise up and go out to war or obey one of God's commands.

So the meaning is that you fear the women's disobedience and their deeming themselves above that which God has made obligatory upon them with regard to obedience to the husband. Abū Manṣūr al-Lughawī said that *nushūz* is the antipathy of each of the spouses for his companion. It is said: *Nashazat, tanshiz,* and she is a *nāshiz* without the feminine ending. *Nashaṣat, tanshuṣ* signifies a woman with whom cohabiting is intolerable. Ibn Fāris said: The woman *nashazat*, making life difficult for her husband, and he *nashaza* against her when he strikes her and is rough with her. Ibn Durayd says, the woman *nashazat*, and *nashasat* and *nashaṣat*, with a single meaning.

The sixth issue: His words *admonish them*. That is to say, with God's book, remind them of what God has made obligatory for them with regard to good companionship and living together beautifully with the husband, and recognising the degree he has above her [cf. Q. 2:228]. It is said: Indeed, the Prophet (*ṣl'm*) said, 'If I had ordered anyone to prostrate themselves before anyone else, I would have ordered the woman to prostrate herself to her husband'.[172] And he said, 'She must not refuse his advances even when she is on the back of a camel'.[173] And he said, 'When a woman spends the night away from the bed of her husband, the angels curse her until morning',[174] while another narration has 'until she returns and places her hand into his hand'. There are other similar transmissions.

The seventh issue: His words *and forsake them in the beds* (*wa'hjurūhunna fi'l-maḍājiʿ*). Ibn Masʿūd and Nakhaʿī and others read: *fi'l-maḍjaʿ* in the singular, as though it were a collective noun standing in for the plural. The *hijr* in the *maḍājiʿ* is that he lies in bed with her (*yuḍājiʿuhā*) and then he turns his back on her and does not have sexual relations with her (*lā yujāmiʿuhā*), and this interpretation is on the authority of Ibn ʿAbbās and others. Mujāhid says, 'Avoid the women's beds', and there is an implied omission. This is supported by *ihjurūhunna* from *hijrān*, which is distance. It is said, *hajarahu*, which is to say, causing a separation from something, and keeping far away from it, and it is not possible to be far from her other than by leaving the bedside. Those who give it this meaning include Ibrāhīm al-Nakhaʿī, al-Shaʿbī, Qatāda and al-Ḥasan al-Baṣrī, while this is narrated by Ibn Wahb and Ibn al-Qāsim on the authority of Mālik, and Ibn al-ʿArabī preferred it. They understood the matter on the basis of the fuller sense of the term. And this saying is like when you say, 'He left him for the sake of God.' And that saying is from Mālik.

[172] Versions of this *ḥadīth* are found in Abū Dāwūd, *Sunan*, *Kitāb al-Nikāḥ* (12), *Bāb fī ḥaqq al-zawj ʿalā'l-mar'a* (41), *ḥadīth* no. 95/2140; Tirmidhī, *Jāmiʿ*, *Kitāb al-Riḍāʿ* (12), *Bāb mā jā' fī ḥaqq al-zawj ʿalā'l-mar'a* (10), *ḥadīth* no. 14/1159; Tirmidhī's narration is cited by Nawawī, *Riyāḍ al-ṣāliḥīn*, *Kitāb al-Muqaddimāt*, *Bāb ḥaqq al-zawj ʿalā'l-mar'a* (35), *ḥadīth* no. 285.

[173] Ibn Māja, *Sunan*, *Kitāb al-Nikāḥ* (9), *ḥadīth* no. 9/1853.

[174] Versions of this *ḥadīth* are found in Muslim, *Ṣaḥīḥ*, *Kitāb al-Nikāḥ* (16), *Bāb taḥrīm imtināʿihā min firāsh zawjihā* (20), *ḥadīth* nos. 140/1436, 141, 143; Abū Dāwūd, *Sunan*, *Kitāb al-Nikāḥ* (12), *Bāb fī ḥaqq al-zawj ʿalā'l-mar'a* (41), *ḥadīth* no. 96/2141; Nawawī, *Riyāḍ al-ṣāliḥīn*, *Kitāb al-Muqaddimāt*, *Bāb ḥaqq al-zawj ʿalā'l-mar'a* (35), *ḥadīth* no. 281.

I said: This opinion is sound. When the husband turns away from her bed, if she loves him then that is unbearable for her and so she will return to righteousness, and if she hates him, then her *nushūz* becomes manifest, and it becomes clear that the *nushūz* is on her part.

It is said that *ihjurūhunna* is from *hujr*, which is vile speech; that is to say, speak rudely to her while lying with her for sexual relations and otherwise, and Sufyān said that was its meaning. It is narrated on the authority of Ibn ʿAbbās.

It is said, 'Affix them with ropes in their rooms, from the saying "tie" (*hajr*) the camel, hold it fast with a *hijār*, which is a rope with which the camel is tied.' This is the preference of Ṭabarī, and he criticised all other opinions. His opinions on this topic need further consideration. The judge Abū Bakr [Ibn] al-ʿArabī refuted him in his *Aḥkām*, and he says: What a lapse from one so learned in the Qurʾān and the Sunna! And that which brought him to this interpretation is a *ḥadīth* conveyed by only one narrator (*ḥadīth gharīb*), and it was narrated on the authority of Ibn Wahb on the authority of Mālik, from Asmāʾ bt. Abī Bakr al-Ṣiddīq, who was the wife of al-Zubayr b. al-ʿAwwām, and she would always go out until he was taken to task for it. So he reprimanded her (*ʿataba ʿalayhā*) and her co-wife (*wa ʿalā al-ḍurra*), tying the hair of one of them to the other and striking them both severely. The co-wife was more circumspect (*aḥsan ittiqāʾan*), while Asmāʾ was not mindful at all (*lā tattaqī*), and so he struck her more. She complained to her father, Abū Bakr, and he told her, 'My little girl, be patient, for al-Zubayr is a good man, and perhaps he will be your husband in heaven, and it has reached me that a man, if he deflowers a girl, will marry her in heaven'. [Al-Ṭabarī] considered the tying and the securing as a possibility in the lexical expression together with the actions of al-Zubayr, so that is how he got to that interpretation.

This *hajr* is limited to a month, according to the *ʿulamāʾ*, as the Prophet (*ṣlʿm*) did when he confided in Ḥafṣa, she divulged it to ʿĀʾisha, and they both made a cause against him [cf. Q. 66:3]. There is no sense going as far as four months, which God has set down as the period of [waiting] as an exemption for the forswearer.[175]

The eighth issue: His words, exalted be He, *and strike them*. God ordered that he begin first with the admonition of the women, then he forsakes her, and if this does not have a salutary effect on her, then he strikes her, and

[175] Cf. Q. 2:226. For a brief description of the *īlāʾ*, see 'Īlāʾ', *EI*[2]. For a discussion of taking oaths on the Qurʾān, see G.R. Hawting, 'Oaths', *EQ*, III, 561–6. As Hawting says, this is likely to come up in *fiqh* in the books of *nikāḥ* and *ṭalāq*.

indeed it is this which restores (*yuṣāliḥ*) her to him by fulfilling his rights. The striking in this verse is a disciplining strike (*ḍarb al-adab*) – not a severe one (*ghayr al-mubarriḥ*) – where no bones are broken and no permanent marks are left on the limbs, as is the case with a fist-strike (*lakaza*) or the like. The intention of it is correction, nothing more. Undoubtedly, if it leads to death then you need an indemnity (*ḍamān*).[176] This is like the doctrine with regard to the teacher striking his pupil, when [he is] being instructed in the Qur'ān and manners (*adab*). In the *Ṣaḥīḥ* of Muslim:

> Be wary of God with regard to women, for you have taken them as a trust from God, and sexual relations with them have been made lawful to you by the word of God. You have the right over them that they should not allow anyone whom you dislike to tread on your bedding,[177] and if they do that, then strike them with a non-severe strike.[178]

The *ḥadīth* is published among the long *ḥadīths* of Jābir [b. ʿAbd Allāh] about the Ḥajj, that is to say, do not let any of your relatives or non-related women whom you dislike come into your houses.

And an interpretation like this is borne out by what al-Tirmidhī narrated, and declared sound on the authority of ʿAmr b. al-Aḥwaṣ, which is that he saw the Farewell Pilgrimage Oration (*ḥajjat al-wadāʿ*) by the Messenger of God, and he thanked God and lauded Him and reminded them of God, and orated:

> Treat women well, for they are your captives, and you have no power over them other than that except if they come with clear indecency (*fāḥisha mubayyana*), and if they do that, then forsake them in the beds and strike them non-severely, but if they obey you, then do not seek a way against them. Indeed, you have rights over your wives, and they have rights over you. As for your rights over your wives, they should not allow anyone whom you do not like to tread on your bedding, nor should they allow anyone whom you dislike into your houses (*buyūt*). Their rights over you are that you should be good to them with regard to their clothing and food.[179]

[176] An indemnity: the restoration of like-for-like.

[177] *Furūsh* is literally bedding or carpets, and it implies an intimacy in which the stranger is allowed into the inner sanctum of the house.

[178] Found in Muslim, *Ṣaḥīḥ*, *Kitāb al-Ḥajj* (15), *Bāb ḥajjat al-nabī* (*ṣlʿm*) (19), *ḥadīth* no. 159/1218.

[179] Versions of this *ḥadīth* are found in Tirmidhī, *Jāmiʿ*, *Kitāb al-Riḍāʿ* (12), *Bāb mā jāʾa fī ḥaqq al-marʾa ʿalā zawjihā* (11), *ḥadīth* no. 18/1163 and *Kitāb Tafsīr al-Qurʾān* (47), *ḥadīth* no. 3367; Ibn Māja, *Sunan*, *Kitāb al-Nikāh* (9), *Bāb ḥaqq al-marʾa ʿalāʾl-zawj* (3), *ḥadīth* no. 7/1851; Nawawī, *Riyāḍ al-ṣāliḥīn*, *Kitāb al-Muqaddimāt*, *Bāb al-waṣiyya biʾl-nisāʾ* (34), *ḥadīth* no. 276. Truncated versions are found in Ibn Ḥajar al-ʿAsqalānī, *Bulūgh al-marām*, *Kitāb al-Nikāḥ* (8), *ḥadīths* no. 1141 and 1142.

He [al-Tirmidhī] said: This is a well-attested (*ḥasan*), sound *ḥadīth*. As for his words 'clear indecency' (*fāḥisha mubayyana*), he meant to say that the women should not let anyone whom their spouses hate enter, and they should not make them angry. The intention is not unlawful sexual intercourse (*zinā*). If it were that, it would be prohibited, and it would be necessary to apply the *ḥadd* penalty.

He said (*ṣlʿm*), 'Strike the women if they disobey you in what is expected of them (*maʿrūf*), a non-severe strike'. 'Aṭā' said, 'I said to Ibn 'Abbās, "What is a non-severe strike?" He said, "With a toothbrush or the like".' It is narrated on the authority of 'Umar, may God be pleased with him, that he struck his wife and he was reproached for it, and so he said, 'I heard the Messenger of God (*ṣlʿm*) say, "A man is not asked why he strikes his wife (*ahl*)".'[180]

The ninth issue: His words *but if they obey you*. That is to say, they desist from their *nushūz*, *seek not a way against them*: do not commit anything against them either in word or deed. This is a prohibition against oppressing them even as the superiority (*faḍl*) over them and the capacity to discipline them have been affirmed. It is said, its meaning is do not task them with love for you, for this is not their choice.

The tenth issue: His words *indeed God is high, mighty*, which are an indication to the husband that he should *lower your wing* (*ikhfiḍ janāḥaka*),[181] and show a gentle side (*līn al-jānib*). That is to say, to the extent that you have power over them, you should remember the power of God [over you], for His hand has power over every hand. Let no man be high-handed towards his wife, for God is watching, and due to that, here is a beautiful description [of God's] exaltedness and might.[182]

The eleventh issue: Since that is established, know that God did not order anything in His book about the striking unequivocally, except here and with regard to the greater *ḥudūd* punishments. So the women's disobedience to their husbands is made equal to the grave sin[183] and their husbands, not the

[180] Versions of this *ḥadīth* are found in Ibn Māja, *Sunan*, *Kitāb al-Nikāḥ* (9), *ḥadīth* no. 142/1986 and in Abū Dāwūd, *Sunan*, *Kitāb al-Nikāḥ* (12), *Bāb fī ḍarb al-nisā'* (43), *ḥadīth* no. 102/2147.

[181] Cf. Q. 15:88; 17:24; 26:215.

[182] Here, Qurṭubī marks a difference between God and men, who should not be characterised in that way.

[183] For an extensive but accessible overview of the lexicon and theology of sin in the Qur'ān, including *kabā'ir*, see Muhammad Qasim Zaman, 'Sin, Major and Minor', *EQ*, V, 19–28.

imams, have been given authority over that; and He gave that authority to them rather than to the judges, without witnesses or documents, as a way of entrusting wives to their husbands.

Al-Muhallab said, 'Striking women is only permissible in the case of their holding themselves back from their husbands sexually.' They differ with regard to the necessity of the right to strike when it has to do with housework (*khidma*), for analogical reasoning (*qiyās*) would suggest that if he is allowed to strike her with regard to matters of sex (*mubāḍaʿa*) then it would be permissible with regard to housework (*khidma*), which is a duty towards him out of common decency (*maʿrūf*).[184]

Ibn Khwayzmandād said: *Nushūz* entails forfeiture of the maintenance payment and all of the marital rights, and it is possible, along with that, for the husband to strike her a disciplinary, non-severe strike and to undertake the admonishment and forsaking until she reverts from her *nushūz*; and when she returns, then her rights are restored. Likewise is everything that requires discipline, and it remains for the husband to discipline her.

There is a difference in the case of disciplining the high-ranking women and the low-ranking women. Discipline of the high-ranking women is with reprimand (*ʿadhl*), and the discipline of the low-ranking women is with the whip (*sawṭ*). The Prophet (*ṣlʿm*) said, 'Sensible is the one[185] who hangs his whip and disciplines his household (*ahl*)'. And he said, 'Indeed Abū Jahm never put his stick down'. Bashshār said: The free person is reproached (*yulḥā*), but for the slave, the stick. *Yulḥā* means to reproach. Ibn Durayd said, 'Censure for the free is ever a deterrence, while there is no deterring the slave except by the stick' (*wa'l-lawm li'l-ḥurr muqīm rādiʿ, wa'l-ʿabd lā yardaʿahu illā'l-ʿaṣā*).[186]

Ibn al-Mundhir said, 'The learned people agree on the necessity of paying maintenance when they have both reached pubescence (*bālighūn*), other than the *nāshiz* who withholds herself from him.' Abū 'Umar[187] said, 'Whoever's wife commits *nushūz* after he has entered her, she forfeits her maintenance unless she is pregnant.' But Ibn al-Qāsim opposed the majority of the jurists with regard to maintenance for the *nāshiza*, and he made it

[184] There is a legal dispute about the housework, with some schools holding that it is a wife's obligation and other schools holding that it is not a wife's obligation. See Ali, *Marriage and Slavery*, 75–6; Bauer, *Gender Hierarchy*, 161ff.; eadem, 'Room for Interpretation'.

[185] Literally, 'God has mercy upon', but this has the vernacular equivalent of saying 'the sensible one'.

[186] Cf. Abū Dāwūd, *Sunan*, *Kitāb al-Ṭahāra*, *ḥadīth* no. 142: 'Do not beat your wife as you beat your slave girl'.

[187] See the PA, this volume, s.v. Ḥafṣ b. Sulaymān.

obligatory. And when the *nāshiz* returns to her husband, then her maintenance is obligatory from that moment forward.

The maintenance of the wife is not annulled for anything except *nushūz*, not from sickness, menstruation, postpartum bleeding (*nifās*), fasting, Ḥajj, or the husband's absence; nor is it permitted for him to withhold the *nafaqa* from her against a claim of something other than what we have mentioned.[188] And God knows best.[189]

Ibn Kathīr

Ibn Kathīr's interpretation is notable for the number of sound *ḥadīth*s it includes in order to justify the opinions that are, by now, familiar to the reader. For him, *qawwāmūn* means that men are managers of women, that they are their heads, they judge them and they punish them, because men are inherently better than women and women are unsuited to positions of leadership. He supports his view with reference to the *ḥadīth* that says, 'A people who entrust their affairs to a woman will never succeed', which was widely cited against women in positions of judging or other leadership roles.[190] Ibn Kathīr also quotes Ṭabarī by saying that women must obey in those matters in which God has commanded their obedience, which means being good to her husband's family and safeguarding his property. This is a somewhat more restricted view of women's obedience than that put forth by other commentators, such as Qurṭubī.

'Righteous women' are also defined through *ḥadīth* citation. Ibn Kathīr cites the 'best of women' *ḥadīth* and another *ḥadīth* that says that 'when a woman prays her five and fasts her month[191] and preserves her chastity and obeys her husband, it will be said to her "enter Paradise by any door you wish"', though he admits it is a single transmission.

Ibn Kathīr defines *nushūz* as a woman's defiance of, rejection of, and hatefulness to her husband; he equates a wife's obedience to her husband with her obedience to God. To bolster these opinions, he cites a *ḥadīth* stating that a woman will be cursed by the angels until morning if her husband calls her to bed and she refuses, or if she spends a night away from his bed. For him, the striking should be non-injurious, as in the Farewell Pilgrimage Oration, which means that he should not leave a mark or, according to the jurists, that he should not break their bones. He cites the *ḥadīth* against striking which says 'Do not strike God's female servants' and one that has the Prophet Muḥammad saying 'Those men are not the best of you' about men who struck

[188] See Ali, *Marriage and Slavery*, 65–96 (ch. 3: 'Maintaining Relations', esp. 89ff., on the husband's failure to maintain his wife).

[189] Qurṭubī, *al-Jāmiʿ li-aḥkām al-Qurʾān*, s.v. Q. 4:34.

[190] See Karen Bauer, 'Debates on Women's Status as Judges and Witnesses in Post-formative Islamic Law', *Journal of the American Oriental Society* 130.1 (2010), 21.

[191] Meaning her five daily prayers and the month of Ramadan.

their wives. These *ḥadīths* were cited by Fakhr al-Dīn al-Rāzī, another Shāfiʿī. So, in this instance, it seems as though al-Shāfiʿī's opinion had some influence on Shāfiʿī Qur'ān commentators. However, Ibn Kathīr also cites the *ḥadīth* where ʿUmar reports that the Prophet said: 'Do not ask a man why he struck his wife'.

Men are maintainers of women is that the man is *qayyim* over the woman; that is to say, her head and her elder (*kabīruhā*), the ruler over her and the person who disciplines her if she becomes crooked.

By that which God distinguished the one over the other, because men are superior to women (*afḍal*) and men are better than women (*khayr*), and due to this, men have been singled out for prophethood, and, likewise, supreme sovereignty (*al-mulk al-aʿẓam*), due to his words (*ṣlʿm*), 'A people who entrust their affairs to a woman will never succeed',[192] which al-Bukhārī narrated from among the sayings of ʿAbd al-Raḥman b. Abī Bukra on the authority of his father. Likewise, [men hold] the position of judgeship and other matters.

By that which they expend of their property [entails] paying the bridal payment and maintenance, and the things that God has tasked him with and made necessary for him towards her in His book and in the *sunna* of the Prophet (*ṣlʿm*). So man is inherently superior to woman (*al-rajul afḍal min al-mar'a fī nafsihi*), and he has a distinction over her and the right of munificence towards her (*faḍl ʿalayhā wa'l-ifḍāl*), which is in accordance with his being *qayyim* over her, as God has said, *Men have a degree over them* [Q. 2:228]. ʿAlī b. Abī Ṭalḥa reported that Ibn ʿAbbās said, '*Men are maintainers of women* means commanders (*umarā'*); she must obey him in those matters in which God has ordered her to obey. Obedience to him is that she is good to his family and she preserves his property'.[193] The like of this was reported by Muqātil, al-Suddī and al-Ḍaḥḥāk.

Al-Ḥasan al-Baṣrī said that a woman came to the Prophet (*ṣlʿm*) complaining that her husband had slapped her, and the Messenger of God (*ṣlʿm*) said, 'Retaliation', so God sent down *men are maintainers of women*, and she returned without retaliation. Ibn Jurayj and Ibn Abī Ḥātim narrated it, from several paths on his authority. Likewise, this narration (*khabar*) has been transmitted by Qatada and Ibn Jurayj and al-Suddī. Ibn Jarīr [al-Ṭabarī] has made all of that available. Ibn Mardawayh provides an *isnād* through another means. He said [. . .] on the authority of Mūsā b. Ismāʿīl[194] b. Mūsā

[192] Versions of this *ḥadīth* are found in Bukhārī, *Ṣaḥīḥ*, *Kitāb al-Fitan* (92), *Bāb al-fitna allatī tamūju ka-mawj al-baḥr*, *ḥadīth* no. 50/7099; also, Tirmidhī, *Jāmiʿ*, *Kitab al-fitan* (33), *ḥadīth* no. 105/2262; Ibn Ḥajar al-ʿAsqalānī, *Bulūgh al-marām*, *Kitāb al-Qaḍā'* (14), *ḥadīth* no. 13/1409.

[193] This is a verbatim quote from Ṭabarī, see above.

[194] Ismāʿīl was the elder son of Mūsā al-Kāẓim, the seventh Shīʿī imam.

[al-Kāẓim] b. Jaʿfar [al-Ṣādiq] b. Muḥammad [al-Bāqir] said that his father [Ismāʿīl b. Mūsā] told him, on the authority of his grandfather [Mūsā al-Kāẓim], on the authority of Jaʿfar b. Muḥammad [Jaʿfar al-Ṣādiq], on the authority of his father [Muḥammad b. ʿAlī al-Bāqir], on the authority of ʿAlī [b. al-Ḥusayn, Zayn al-ʿĀbidīn],[195] that he said: A man from the Anṣār came to the Messenger of God with a wife of his, and she said, 'O Messenger of God!' Her husband so-and-so, son of so-and-so, the Anṣārī, had struck her and left a mark on her face. So, the Messenger of God (*ṣlʿm*) said, 'He cannot do that!' Then God sent down *men are maintainers of women* – that is, in terms of discipline – and so the Messenger of God said, 'I wanted one thing and God wanted something else'. Likewise, Qatāda, Ibn Jurayj and al-Suddī transmitted this report, skipping one link in the chain of transmission (*arsala*), and Ibn Jarīr [al-Ṭabarī] made all of that available.

Al-Shaʿbī said, concerning this verse *men are maintainers of women, by that which God has distinguished the one over the other, and by that which they expend of their property*, that it is the bridal payment which he gives to her. Have you not seen that if he slanders her (*qadhafahā*), then he can perform the *liʿān* procedure,[196] but if she slanders him then she is whipped?

Regarding His words, exalted be He, *so, righteous women* from among the women *are devoutly obedient women*. Ibn ʿAbbās and more than one commentator said, 'Obedient to their husbands'.

Those who safeguard during absence. Al-Suddī and others have said that she preserves her chastity and his property in her husband's absence.

His words *what for God is to be safeguarded*, that is to say, the safeguarding is from his safeguarding God. Ibn Jarīr [al-Ṭabarī] reported that Abū Hurayra[197] said that the Messenger of God (*ṣlʿm*) said, 'The best of women is she who, when you look at her, makes you happy, when you order her, obeys you, and when you are absent from her safeguards for you your property and her self';[198] then the Messenger of God (*ṣlʿm*) recited this verse, *men are*

[195] Note that this *ḥadīth* is cited on the authority of the Shīʿī imams. Aḥmad b. ʿAlī al-Nasāʾī ← Muḥammad b. Hibat Allāh al-Hāshimī ← Muḥammad b. Muḥammad al-Ashʿath ← Mūsā b. Ismāʿīl b. Mūsā [al-Kāẓim] b. Jaʿfar [al-Ṣādiq] b. Muḥammad [al-Bāqir] ← his father [Ismāʿīl b. Mūsā] ← his grandfather [Mūsā al-Kāẓim] ← Jaʿfar b. Muḥammad [Jaʿfar al-Ṣādiq] ← his father [Muḥammad b. ʿAlī al-Bāqir] ← ʿAlī [b. al-Ḥusayn, Zayn al-ʿĀbidīn].

[196] This is a procedure in which a husband may accuse his wife of adultery without witnesses by swearing four times to it and invoking God's curse upon him if he is lying, and a wife may protest her innocence, invoking God's curse upon her if she is lying. For a brief summary, see Devin J. Stewart, 'Curse', *EQ*, I, 492.

[197] Ibn Jarīr ← al-Muthannā ← Abū Ṣāliḥ ← Abū Maʿshar ← Saʿīd b. Abī Saʿīd al-Miqbarī ← Abū Hurayra ← the Messenger of God.

[198] See above, note 65.

maintainers of women – to its end. Ibn Abī Ḥātim [al-Rāzī][199] [also] narrated something like this.

Imam Aḥmad [Ibn Ḥanbal] reported that ʿAbd al-Raḥmān b. ʿAwf[200] narrated that the Messenger of God (*ṣlʿm*) said: 'When a woman prays her five, and fasts her month, and preserves her chastity, and obeys her husband, it will be said to her, "Enter Paradise by any door you wish."' This was a unique transmission (*tafarrud bihi*) on the authority of Aḥmad by way of ʿAbd Allāh b. Qāriẓ on the authority of ʿAbd al-Raḥmān b. ʿAwf.

His words *if you fear the women's defiance* [are regarding] the women whom you fear are committing *nushūz* against their husbands. And *nushūz* is rising up, so the *nāshiz* woman is the one who raises herself up against her husband, abandoning his order, rejecting him and being hateful to him. When the signs of *nushūz* become apparent to him, then he should admonish her and make her fear the punishment of God with regard to her disobedience to him; for, indeed God has made [fulfilment of] her husband's rights and obedience to him a duty upon her, and He has forbidden her from disobeying him when He made him surpass and exceed her (*al-faḍl wa'l-ifḍāl*). The Messenger of God (*ṣlʿm*) said, 'If I were to order anyone to prostrate themselves before anyone else, I would have ordered the woman to prostrate herself to her husband because of the greatness of his rights over her'.[201] Al-Bukhārī narrated it on the authority of Abū Hurayra, may God be pleased with him.

The Messenger of God (*ṣlʿm*) said, 'When a man calls his wife to his bed and she refuses, the angels curse her until morning' as reported by Muslim, and in another wording: 'If a woman spends the night away from the bed of her husband the angels curse her until morning'.[202] Because of this, the Exalted said: *If you fear the women's defiance, then admonish them.*

About His words, *and forsake them in the beds*, ʿAlī b. Abī Ṭalḥa said, on the authority of Ibn ʿAbbās, that the forsaking is that he does not have sexual relations with her or lie with her, and he turns his back to her. Such has been said by more than one, and others add – among them al-Suddī, al-Ḍaḥḥāk, ʿIkrima and Ibn ʿAbbās in one narration – that he does not speak to her along with all of that, or converse with her. ʿAlī b. Abī Ṭalḥa says also, on the authority of Ibn ʿAbbās, 'He admonishes her, and if she accepts that, it is the

[199] Ibn Abī Ḥātim ← Yūnus b. Ḥabīb ← Abū Dāwūd al-Ṭayālisī ← Muḥammad b. ʿAbd al-Raḥmān b. Abī Dhuʾab ← Saʿīd al-Miqbarī.

[200] Imam Aḥmad ← Yaḥyā b. Isḥāq ← Ibn Lahīʿa ← ʿAbd Allāh b. Abī Jaʿfar ← Ibn Qāriẓ ← ʿAbd al-Raḥmān b. ʿAwf.

[201] See above, note 172.

[202] See above, note 174.

end of the matter, and if not, then he should forsake her in the bed and should only speak to her to repudiate the marriage, and that is hard on her.'

Mujāhid, Shaʿbī, Ibrāhīm, Muḥammad b. Kaʿb, Miqsam and Qatāda said that the forsaking is that he does not lie with her. Abū Dāwūd[203] reported that the Prophet said, 'If you fear their *nushūz*, then forsake them in the beds'. Ḥammād said it means [forsake] the marriage. In the *Sunan* [of Abū Dāwūd] and the *Musnad* [of Aḥmad b. Ḥanbal], it is reported that Muʿāwiya b. Ḥayda al-Qushayrī said, 'O Messenger of God, what is the right of one of our wives over us?' He replied, 'That you feed her when you eat, you clothe her as you clothe yourself and you do not strike her face or disfigure her (*tuqabbiḥ*), and that you do not forsake her, except within the sleeping chamber (*bayt*)'.[204]

[Regarding] His words *and strike them*: if they are not deterred by the admonishment or by the forsaking, then you may strike them non-severely, as it has been established in the *Ṣaḥīḥ* of Muslim on the authority of Jābir who reported that the Prophet said in the Farewell Pilgrimage Oration, 'Be wary of your Lord with regard to women, for they are with you as captives, and you have the right over them that they not let anyone tread on your bedding whom you dislike, and if they do that, then strike them non-severely (*ghayr mubarriḥ*). Their rights are to their sustenance and clothing, out of common decency (*bi'l-maʿrūf*)'.[205] Such was said by Ibn ʿAbbās and more than one other.

[Regarding] striking non-severely (*ghayr mubarriḥ*), al-Ḥasan al-Baṣrī said that it means without leaving a mark (*ghayr mu'aththir*). The jurists have said that he should not break her limbs or leave any mark on her. ʿAlī b. Abī Ṭalḥa said on the authority of Ibn ʿAbbās, he forsakes her in the bed, and if she accepts then that is the end of the matter, and if not then God has permitted you to strike a non-severe strike without breaking her bones, and if she accepts then that is the end of the matter, and if not then God has made it lawful for you to take the redemption (*fidya*)[206] from her.

Iyās b. ʿAbd Allāh b. Abī Dhubāb[207] reported that the Prophet said, 'Do not strike God's female servants'. ʿUmar, may God be pleased with him, went to

[203] Abū Dāwūd ← Mūsā b. Ismaʿīl ← Ḥammād b. Salama ← ʿAlī b. Zayd ← Abū Murra al-Ruqāshī ← his uncle ← the Prophet.

[204] See above, note 107.

[205] Note that this version of the *ḥadīth* differs from that in Muslim's *Ṣaḥīḥ* (cited above by Qurṭubī); it seems to be a mix of Muslim's version with Tirmidhī's.

[206] Cf. Q. 2:229.

[207] Sufyān b. ʿUyayna ← al-Zuhrī ← ʿAbd Allāh b. ʿAbd Allāh b. ʿUmar ← Iyās b. ʿAbd Allāh b. Abī Dhubāb ← the Prophet.

the Messenger of God and said, 'The women are emboldened against their husbands!' and so the Messenger of God gave permission to strike them. Then many women surrounded the family of Muḥammad, complaining about their husbands, and so the Messenger of God said, 'Many women complaining about their husbands have surrounded the family of the Messenger of God, and those men are not the best of you'. This was narrated by Abū Dāwūd and al-Nasā'ī and Ibn Māja. Imam Aḥmad [Ibn Ḥanbal][208] reported that Ash'ath b. Qays said, 'I stayed with 'Umar, may God be pleased with him, as a guest, and he grabbed his wife and he struck her, and said, "O Ash'ath, preserve on my authority three things which I have preserved on the authority of the Messenger of God. Do not ask a man about why he strikes his wife, do not sleep except after the *witr* prayer", and he forgot the third.' Such was narrated by Abū Dāwūd and al-Nasā'ī and Ibn Māja from a *ḥadīth* of 'Abd al-Raḥmān b. Mahdī on the authority of Abū 'Awāna on the authority of Dāwūd.

[Regarding] His words *but if they obey you, seek not a way against them*, if the woman obeys her husband in all that he wants from her, within the bounds that God has permitted to him from her, then there is no path for him against her after that, and he does not have the right to strike her or to forsake her.

His words *indeed God is High, Mighty*, are a threat to men if they wrong women without reason, for God is the exalted and mighty guardian of the women, and He will take vengeance on anyone who oppresses them and wrongs them.[209]

Muḥsin al-Fayḍ al-Kāshānī

Although Muḥsin al-Fayḍ al-Kāshānī takes a typical view of the verse, in that he defines *qawwāmūn* as 'managers' – like the ruler who governs his subjects – because of men's innate superiority of mind, strength and management, he also introduces one distinctly Shī'ī *ḥadīth*. It confirms men's superiority over women by saying that men are superior to women in the same manner that water is superior to the earth, because water brings the earth to life. He also mentions that women's menstruation impedes their worship because of their 'impurity'. Thus, although menstruating women avoid prayers because they are ordered to do so, the avoidance is nevertheless considered to

[208] Imam Aḥmad ← Sulaymān b. Dāwūd, meaning Abū Dāwūd Ṭayālisī ← Abū 'Awāna ← Dāwūd al-Awdī ← 'Abd al-Raḥmān al-Sulamī ← al-Ash'ath b. Qays.

[209] Ibn Kathīr, *Tafsīr*, s.v. Q. 4:34.

be a defect in their religiosity. Muḥsin al-Fayḍ cites a familiar *ḥadīth*, but on a different chain of transmitters: 'the best of women' *ḥadīth* here has a slightly different wording and is cited on the authority of the Shīʿī imam Jaʿfar al-Ṣādiq. He defines *nushūz* as rising up and disobedience; he says that the admonishment is verbal, that *forsake them in the beds* means the husband should turn his back to his wife, and if that does not work, he should strike her without breaking her bones or cutting her flesh. He cites Imam al-Bāqir to say that this striking should be with a tooth-stick, and he finally reminds men that God's power over them 'is greater than your power over those who are under your hand'.

Men are maintainers of women: they manage them (*yaqūmūn ʿalayhinna*) with the management (*qiyām*) of the ruler governing his subjects, *by that which God has distinguished the one over the other*, because of the distinction (*tafḍīl*) of men over women in terms of their completeness of intellect (*ʿaql*) and good management, and his excess of strength for good deeds and acts of obedience.

And by that which they expend of their property in marrying them, for instance the bridal payment and the maintenance. In the *ʿIlal*, on the authority of the Prophet (*ṣlʿhm*) he was asked, 'What is the distinction (*faḍl*) of men over women?' And he said, 'It is like the distinction of the water over the earth, for it is because of water that the earth comes to life and it is through men that women came to life, and if it had not been for men, the women would not have been created'.[210] Then he recited this verse and said, 'Have you not seen how women menstruate and it is not possible for them to perform worship because of their impurity, while men are not struck by such menstrual discharge'.

Righteous women are devoutly obedient women. Qummī, on the authority of [Imam] al-Bāqir (*ʿm*) says that they are obedient.

Those who safeguard during absence their selves and the property of their husbands. In the *Kāfī* on the authority of [Jaʿfar] al-Ṣādiq (*ʿm*) on the authority of his fathers, peace be upon them, the Prophet (*ṣlʿhm*) says, 'There is no greater benefit to a Muslim man after Islam than a Muslim wife, a woman who makes him happy when he looks at her, and obeys him when he orders her, and safeguards for him herself and his property when he is absent from her'.

And if you fear the women's defiance. Their *nushūz* is raising themselves above obeying you, and their disobedience to you.

Then admonish them verbally.

[210] This is a reference to Eve.

And forsake them in the beds if the admonishment does not have a salutary effect. In the *Majmaʿ* [Imam] al-Bāqir (*ʿm*) says that he should turn his back to her.

And strike them, if the forsaking has no benefit, with a strike that is not strong (*ghayr shadīd*), not cutting her flesh or breaking her bones. In the *Majmaʿ* [Imam] al-Bāqir (*ʿm*) says that he should strike with a tooth-stick.

But if they obey you, seek not a way against them through reprimand and harm.

For God is high, mighty. Beware of him, for his power over you is greater than your power over those who are under your hand.[211]

Burūsawī

Burūsawī dispenses with the interpretation of the words of the verse in a rather cursory manner; the real interest here is in the numerous *ḥadīth*s purported to have been said by the Prophet Muḥammad to his wife ʿĀʾisha, which come after the verse's interpretation. As for the verse itself, for Burūsawī, *qawwāmūn* means the managers of women's affairs, a privilege men have been given for a number of reasons – for instance, that men are more determined and wise than women; that they are skilled in a number of worldly things that women are not, such as archery, penmanship, and so forth; and because they spend of their property on maintenance and the bridal payment. *Fear* for him means to know or to suspect in one's heart that *nushūz* might be occurring. The admonition is supposed to soften the wives, forsaking them in the beds means not having sexual relations with them, and the striking should be done non-severely; these three measures are to be conducted in stages, by degrees. If the wives obey, their husbands are not allowed to seek to harm them; and, in a refrain that has now become familiar, he states that God has greater authority over the husbands than husbands have over their wives.

After his *tafsīr* of the verse, Burūsawī gives his readers some advice. First, women about whom questions arise must be divorced unless their husbands are really in love with them. There follow the *ḥadīth*s referenced above, apparently addressed by the Prophet to ʿĀʾisha. These include admonishments that whenever a woman says anything bad about her husband, her tongue will be lengthened and tied around her neck on Judgment Day; that the woman who visits tombs is cursed until she returns; that the Prophet is the opponent of every woman whose husband has divorced her; that women who lighten their husbands' obligation to pay the bridal payment will be rewarded; that wives must perform supplications for their husbands before they supplicate for themselves, and so forth. All of these *ḥadīth*s serve to emphasise women's secondary importance to her husband, and that her husband's good favour will stand her in good stead with God; we did not find these *ḥadīth*s in the sound collections.

[211] Muḥsin al-Fayḍ al-Kāshānī, *al-Ṣāfī*, s.v. Q. 4:34.

Burūsawī goes on to say that men are often perfect, but that the only perfect women were Mary and Āsiya, the wife of the Pharaoh, the women who are referenced in Q. 66:11–12. Notably, his short list of perfect women does not include Fāṭima or any of the wives of the Prophet, but he does mention that ʿĀʾisha is superior to other women. He finishes by saying that women do not have a full share in the religion, because of the Qurʾānic verse on inheritance that says *for the male, like the share of two females* (Q. 4:11). In his argument, women have only one-third of religion and men have two-thirds. Needless to say, this interpretation rests heavily on cultural assumptions about women's abilities and their overall nature. It is likely that these ideas about women were widespread in Burūsawī's time.

Men are maintainers of women: they manage the affairs (*qāʾimūn biʾl-amr*) in promoting that which is beneficial and forbidding that which is disgraceful. It is the management by which a leader governs his people. They are empowered (*musallaṭūn*) to discipline women, and the proof of that is in matters both earned and innate.

So He said, *by that which God has distinguished the one over the other*: the explicit pronoun is for both parties in the majority of cases; that is to say, because of His making men superior to women in determination (*ḥazm*), resolve (*ʿazm*), strength, noble chivalry (*futuwwa*), provisions, marksmanship, heroism (*ḥamāsa*), generosity, they are up to the task of penning the sermon, possessing the craft of penmanship as well as other indications that require [that they enjoy] extra [merit], alongside the noble character traits that make for a comprehensive felicity.

And by that which they expend of their property: because they spend of their property when they marry them, in matters such as the bridal payment and maintenance, and this is a clear indication of the necessity of the husband's duty of maintenance payments for the wives.

It is narrated about Saʿd b. al-Rabīʿ, who was one of the tribal chiefs (*naqīb*) of the Anṣār, may God be pleased with them, that his wife Ḥabība bt. Zayd b. Abī Zuhayr committed *nushūz* against him, so he slapped her. Then her father went with her to the Messenger of God (*ṣlʿm*), and the two of them complained, so he said (*ṣlʿm*), 'Let her retaliate against him'; so this verse was sent down, and then he (*ṣlʿm*) said, 'I wanted one thing and God wanted another, and that which God wants is better', and he lifted the order of retaliation. So there is no retaliation for a slap or the like; the ruling [of retaliation] is for the loss of life, and what is less than that is treated in the books of positive law (*furūʿ*). *So, righteous women* among women *are devoutly obedient women*: obedient to God, exalted be He, undertaking the duties towards their husbands (*qāʾimāt bi-ḥuqūq al-azwāj*). *Those who safeguard during absence*: the duties during absence; that is, what is necessary for the wives to safeguard, of their chastity, property and houses, during the absence of their husbands.

The Prophet (*ṣl'm*) said, 'The best of women is one who when you look at her, makes you happy, when you order her, obeys you, and when you are absent from her, safeguards her[212] property (*māluhā*) and her self for you', and then he recited this verse. The reason why 'property' (*māl*) is suffixed with her (*-hā*) is to indicate that, in terms of the right of disposal, his property is her property. *What for God is to be safeguarded*: the [particle] *mā* may denote an infinitive, that is to say, by God's safeguarding, exalted be He, of the women, that is, in commanding them to safeguard during the absence, and urging them to that with the promise [of reward] and the threat [of punishment] or by granting them success to [achieve] it. Or it [the *mā* of *bi-mā*] may be a relative particle, in other words, 'with what' (*bi'lladhī*) God has safeguarded for the women from the men of bridal payment, expenditure, constantly safeguarding the women and warding off [any harm] from them.

And if you fear the women's defiance: addresses husbands and guides them with regard to the manner in which to manage (*qiyām*) women. Fear is a state that ensues in the heart upon the occurrence of reprehensible things, and upon the suspicion or knowledge of such occurrences. It may be that one of the two of these is meant, which is to say you suspect their disobedience and their raising themselves above obedience to you. *Then admonish them*: advise them, instilling hope or fear (*tarhīb wa targhīb*). The imam Abū Manṣūr said that the admonition is speech that softens hard hearts, and instils an aversion to repulsive natural characteristics, by reminding of the [negative] consequences. *And forsake them*, after that, if the admonishment and advice has had no effect. The forsaking is abandoning out of hatred (*qalā*) [of the behaviour]. *In the beds*, that is to say, in the sleeping places. So do not let them enter under the covers, or have sexual relations with them face to face (*mubāshara*). It is the plural of *maḍja'* and it is the place where one lies on one's side to sleep. *And strike them*. If what you have done, in terms of admonishing and forsaking, has no salutary effect, [then strike them] non-severely, not blemishing or fracturing or breaking the skin. The three matters are sequential, and he ought to follow the sequence therein.

But if they obey you: if they are obedient to you overtly, since that constitutes the full force of a deterrent, *then seek not a way against them* by rebuking

[212] In the standard version of this *ḥadīth*, it is 'his' or 'your' property; yet, having adopted this alternative possessive pronoun reading, Burūsawī makes a point of it by saying that it proves that women have the right to spend their husbands' wealth.

them or harming them; that is to say, refrain from assaulting them and consider what had issued from them as though it had never been – for, truly, the one who repents from sin is as one who had never sinned.

Indeed God is high, that is to say, God is higher above you in power than you are over them. *Mighty*: He is a mightier judge over you than you can ever be over them. In sum, be wary and forgive them if they relent, for you disobey Him despite the exaltedness of His status and the mightiness of His dominion (*sulṭān*), but when you repent, He still turns towards you [in forgiveness], and so all the more should you be forgiving of whoever commits a wrong against you if that person relents.

The author of *al-Shirʿa*[213] and the commentary therein stated the following: if he were to witness or come to know of something sinful (*fujūr*) on his wife's part – that is to say, an immoral act (*fisq*), mendacity (*kadhib*) or an inclination to what is not right (*bāṭil*) – then he should divorce her, unless he cannot bear to be without her, in which case he should hold on to her.

It is narrated that a man came to the Messenger of God (*ṣlʿm*) and said, 'O Messenger of God, I have a wife who does not reject the hand of the man who touches her.' He said, 'Divorce her'. The man replied, 'I love her!' So the Prophet said, 'Then, hold on to her',[214] fearing for him that if he divorced her, he would follow her and become corrupt along with her, and taking into consideration that it is more important for the marriage to continue since it wards off corruption from him, despite the constraint on his heart. Thus men have to bear loathsome things, but a man should never turn into a cuckold (*dayyūth*). As a knower (*ʿārif*) once said:

[. . .][215]

Some scholars (*ʿulamāʾ*) used to say that to bear a single harm from a woman is in reality to bear from her the equivalent of twenty acts of harm, such as when a boy avoids being slapped, a pot avoids being broken, a calf avoids being struck, a cat avoids being shooed away, a cat is prevented from eating the remains from the small table for serving food (*khuwān*) and the fallen-off scraps, a robe is prevented from being scorched, and a guest is prevented from departing.

213 We have been unable to find details on this work.

214 Versions of this *ḥadīth* are found in Abū Dāwūd, *Sunan*, *Kitāb al-Nikāḥ* (12), *Bāb nahī ʿan tazwīj man lam yalid minaʾl-nisāʾ* (4), *ḥadīth* no. 4/2049; Ibn Ḥajar al-ʿAsqalānī, *Bulūgh al-marām*, *Kitāb al-Nikāḥ* (8), *ḥadīth* no. 156/1099; Nasāʾī, *Sunan*, *Kitāb al-Ṭalāq* (27), *Bāb mā jāʾa fīʾl-khulʿ* (34), *ḥadīth* nos. 76/3464 and 77/3465 and *Kitāb al-Nikāḥ* (26), *Bāb tazwīj al-zāniya* (12), *ḥadīth* no. 34/3229.

215 One Persian line.

The Messenger of God (*ṣlʿm*) said, 'You are all shepherds and you are all responsible for your flock'.[216] And he also said, 'Whenever a woman dies and her husband is pleased with her, she enters heaven'.[217] And he also said, 'Whenever a woman wrongs her husband in this world, his mate from among the virgins of Paradise (*ḥūr ʿīn*) says, "Do not wrong him, or you will battle it out with God, and he is a temporary visitor to you and is about to leave you for us!"'[218]

The Prophet (*ṣlʿm*) said in a speech to ʿĀʾisha, may God be pleased with her: Whenever a woman harms her husband with her tongue, then, indeed, on the Day of Judgment God makes her tongue seventy measures (*dhirāʿ*) [long], and then it is tied around her neck, O ʿĀʾisha! And whichever woman prays to her Lord and supplicates for herself subsequently supplicates for her husband; her face is struck during her prayer until she supplicates for her husband and subsequently supplicates for herself. O ʿĀʾisha! Any woman who mourns for her dead for more than three days, God invalidates her deeds. O ʿĀʾisha! Any woman who wails over her dead, indeed God makes her tongue seventy measures long and she is pulled to the Fire with whoever follows her. O ʿĀʾisha! Whenever a woman is afflicted by a calamity and slaps her face and rends her garments, indeed she is with the wife of Lot and Noah in the Fire [cf. Q. 66:10], and she will despair of any good to come and the intercession of any intercessor on the Day of Resurrection. O ʿĀʾisha! Whenever a woman visits tombs, indeed God curses her, and she is cursed by everything dry and moist until she returns. The moment she returns to her house it will be in God's anger and abhorrence until the next day, and if she were to die at that moment, she would be among the inhabitants of the Fire. O ʿĀʾisha! Strive! And do not refrain from striving, for verily you are the companions of Joseph and the young women of David, and the ones who got Adam expelled from heaven, and the disobedient wives of Noah and Lot. O ʿĀʾisha! Gabriel kept entrusting me with women, until I thought that he was going to prohibit divorcing them. O ʿĀʾisha! I am the opponent of every woman whose husband has divorced her.

[216] Found in Bukhārī, *al-Adab al-mufrad*, *Kitāb al-Malaka* (9), *Bāb al-ʿabd rāʿin* (104), *ḥadīth* no. 51/206 and *Kitāb al-Riʿāya* (10), *Bāb al-rajul rāʿin fī ahlihi* (108), *ḥadīth* no. 1/212 and *Kitāb al-Riʿāya* (10), *Bāb al-marʾa rāʿiya*, *ḥadīth* no. 3/214. For full references, see the bibliography.

[217] Tirmidhī, *Jāmiʿ*, *Kitāb al-Riḍāʿ* (12), *Bāb mā jāʾa fī ḥaqq al-zawj ʿalāʾl-marʾa* (10), *ḥadīth* no. 16/1161; Ibn Māja, *Sunan*, *Kitāb al-Nikāḥ* (9), *Bāb ḥaqq al-zawj ʿalāʾl-marʾa* (4), *ḥadīth* no. 10/1854; Nawawī, *Riyāḍ al-ṣāliḥīn*, *Kitāb al-Muqaddimāt*, *Bāb ḥaqq al-zawj ʿalāʾl-marʾa* (35), *ḥadīth* no. 286.

[218] Versions of this *ḥadīth* are found in Tirmidhī, *Jāmiʿ*, *Kitāb al-Riḍāʿ* (12), *ḥadīth* no. 29/1174; Nawawī, *Riyāḍ al-ṣāliḥīn*, *Kitāb al-Muqaddimāt*, *Bāb ḥaqq al-zawj ʿalāʾl-marʾa* (35), *ḥadīth* no. 287.

Then he said: O ʿĀʾisha! The woman who conceives from her husband, whenever she bears a child, is like the reward of the person who fasts by day and stays up at night, and the raider in the path of God. O ʿĀʾisha! When she gets the birth pangs, with every contraction she has the equivalent of a freeing of a soul, and with each suckling the setting free of a slave. O ʿĀʾisha! When a woman lightens her bridal payment, she gets for it the equivalent of a blessed pilgrimage and an accepted lesser pilgrimage; God forgives her all of her sins, the past and the present, those hidden and those manifest, the wilful ones and the accidental ones, the first and the last. O ʿĀʾisha, the woman who is patient, enduring the harms [which] her husband [inflicts on her], she is like the one who is splattered with her own blood when fighting in the path of God, and she is among the women who are devoutly obedient, those who remember [God] often, and who submit and are believing and repentant women.[219]

It is such in the *Rawḍat al-ʿulamāʾ*, and there is more, but I have shortened and omitted some of it.

The allusion of the verse is that God, exalted be He, made men *qawwāmūn* over women, because women's coming into being was subsequent to men's coming into being, and men are the roots, while women are the branches. Just as the tree is derived from the fruit from which they were created, so too women were created from men's rib; likewise, before she was created, Eve was a rib of Adam's (*ʿm*) and he was her basis. So men stand over women, in terms of correcting their religious and worldly affairs. God, exalted be He, said, *Guard yourselves and your households from a fire* [Q. 66:6].

He has singled out men because they are perfectly prepared (*istiʿdādiyyat al-kamāliyya*) for the caliphate and prophecy; for men's existence is the original, and women's existence is dependent on their existence for generation and reproduction. [The Prophet] (*ṣlʿm*) said, 'Many a man has reached perfection, but among women only Āsiya, the daughter of Muzāḥim and wife of Pharaoh, and Mary, the daughter of ʿImrān [cf. Q. 66:11–12], have reached it. ʿĀʾisha's superiority over other women is like the superiority of *tharīd*[220] over all other food'.[221] Despite this, women were still not perfect enough to make them suitable for the caliphate or prophecy. Their perfection is only in relation to other women, not to men, because women are, in

[219] For one occurrence of the *q-n-t* as it relates to women (*qānitāt*), see Q. 4:34. In the Arabic, the participial female plural constructions strongly echo Q. 33:35.

[220] Crumbled bread moistened with broth.

[221] The second half of this *ḥadīth*, on ʿĀʾisha's superiority, is found in several of the sound books (e.g. Bukhārī, *Ṣaḥīḥ*, *Kitāb al-Aṭʿima* (70), *ḥadīth* no. 47/5419).

relation to men, deficient in intellect (*ʿaql*) and religion,[222] so much so that he [the Prophet] said, concerning ʿĀʾisha, may God be pleased with her, despite her superiority over other women, 'Take two thirds of your religion from this little fair one (*ḥumayrāʾ*)'.[223] So this is, in relation to men, a deficiency, because he did not say to take all of your religion [from her]; but in relation to other women it is a perfection because it is on the basis of His words *for the male, like the share of two females* [Q. 4:11]. So the share of women in religion is one-third and perfection is two-thirds, by analogy with the male's share being double that of the female.[224]

Manār

Though Rashīd Riḍā dedicated much of his life to publicising his teacher ʿAbduh's views,[225] they did sometimes disagree.[226] This verse is one instance where their disagreements are substantial, at least when it comes to undertaking disciplinary measures against women. While ʿAbduh takes a typical view, allowing that husbands can strike wives if this will work to cure the wives' misbehaviour, Riḍā does not believe that it can be justified at all: he is entirely against husbands striking wives.

Despite his modernist stance on the 'striking' aspect of Q. 4:34, Riḍā does not believe that women and men are equal: he says that men have the duty to protect and to maintain women financially because God made men stronger and more powerful than women. It is important to note here that Riḍā does not use the typical explanation that men are also more intelligent or rational than women. He goes on to say that men's acquired qualities support their innate, natural ability to maintain women, because men pay women their bridal payment as a form of remuneration for acquiescing to men's governing them. Thus Riḍā says that women voluntarily cede their complete equality with men in return for financial remuneration. This is because, according to him, women innately like to be under men's headship and control. Drawing an analogy with the body, Riḍā claims that one cannot say that the head is greater or better than other parts of the body. Instead, each part fulfils an important function. According to him, men are natural breadwinners, while women's natural

[222] This is a reference to a *ḥadīth*, a version of which is found in Nawawī, *Riyāḍ al-ṣāliḥīn*, *Kitāb al-Istighfār* (19), *ḥadīth* no. 11/1879.

[223] *Ḥumayrāʾ*: see Lane, *Lexicon*, s.v. *ḥ-m-r*, where he mentions that this epithet *aḥmar/ ḥamrāʾ* was applied to white-skinned men/women, as saying *abyaḍ* might have other connotations. He also says the diminutive was applied to ʿĀʾisha.

[224] Burūsawī, *Rūḥ al-bayān*, s.v. Q. 4:34.

[225] However, there have been questions about whether Riḍā was really very close to ʿAbduh at all or whether, on the contrary, he sought to use the connection for his own self-publicity. Riḍā, for instance, was not invited to ʿAbduh's funeral.

[226] On the difference between Riḍā and ʿAbduh on polygamy, see Johanna Pink, 'Modern and Contemporary Interpretation of the Qurʾān' in *The Wiley Blackwell Companion to the Qurʾān*, 2nd edn, ed. Andrew Rippin and Jawid Mojaddedi (Oxford, Wiley, 2017), 483–4.

function is being pregnant, breastfeeding, and raising children. This is an early argument for the complementarity of the sexes, of the type that has become extremely widespread in conservative interpretations today.

Riḍā quotes ʿAbduh as saying that women in marriage have their own right of disposal and that they have the agency to accept or reject the conditions of marriage. For him, the husband's right of oversight includes the right to keep their wives in the house and not let them out, even for a visit to their kin, and to control when and how much maintenance to give them. ʿAbduh also said that *the one over the other* meant men over women, because men and women come together to become a full person, with the man being the head and the woman being the body. Thus it is possible to say that, in this case, ʿAbduh upholds some crucial aspects of premodern interpretations which grant men great leeway over their wives and which consider men to be innately superior to women and in this regard he and Riḍā disagree.

As mentioned above, however, the biggest difference between Riḍā and ʿAbduh is in their response to the phrase *strike them*. ʿAbduh defends the practice of physical chastisement of wives by describing those who are opposed to it as followers of European customs. He says that the Europeans believe themselves to be better than the Muslims on account of their treatment of women, but critiques the 'European' view by asking how they manage to control their wives' disobedience if they do not resort to striking them. He also critiques their perception of the striking itself: 'They probably imagine a weak, delicate woman, well-behaved and refined, and an uncouth, crude man oppressing her, his whip feeding off her tender flesh and quenching its thirst off of her innocent blood.' The striking, according to ʿAbduh, is obviously not for such circumstances; it is only permitted when the husband knows that this will cure the wife's disobedience.

Riḍā responds to all of this by saying that certain *ḥadīth*s exist that show that striking women is 'repugnant'. One of these, on the authority of the Prophet, asks whether a man would strike his wife like he would strike a slave and then go to her in the evening to have sexual relations. Riḍā builds on this point and finally argues that striking women is never permitted. In his view, if a wife is incapable of behaving herself 'by virtue of her bad upbringing', then the husband should take pity on her and leave her. He should not force her or himself to endure a marriage that is not working.

Since God, exalted be He, forbade both men and women from coveting 'the distinction (*faḍḍala*) that He gave to one over the other' [cf. Q. 4:32], and directed them to depend on what they had earned in the matter of livelihood, and ordered them to grant inheritors their share, and since one of the reasons for this clarification is the mention of the distinction (*tafḍīl*) given to men over women in inheritance and jihad, one might ask about the reason for this singling out, and the answer to this question is, in His words, exalted be He: *men are maintainers of women, by that which God has distinguished the one over the other, and by that which they expend of their property*. That is to say, it is their task, as is known and customary, to provide protection, care, guardianship and sufficiency. The corollary of this would be for God to impose jihad on men and not women, for it entails protection of them, and that their share in inheritance should be more than the women's share, because the requirement of maintenance falls on men and not women. The reason for this is that God distinguished men over women (*faḍḍala*) when He created them originally, and He gave men what He did not give women of might and power, so the variance in terms of legal obligations and rulings is the result of variance in their innate nature and predisposition.

There is also another reason which has to do with acquisition, and which supports the reason of innate nature, and that is what men expend of their property on women, for the bridal payment is a form of compensation for women and remuneration for their being, after marriage, under the headship of men; for the Law (*sharīʿa*) has honoured woman by requiring for her some remuneration as entailed by innate nature and the arrangement of living together, which is that the husband is her maintainer (*qayyim*). As such, this has become a matter relegated to customary practice (*umūr ʿurfiyya*) which people settle on via contracts, for their best interests. It is as though the woman has voluntarily ceded complete equality and has permitted man to have one degree over her – that being the degree of maintenance (*qiyāma*) and headship – and she is content with financial remuneration in place of it. So God then says in Q. 2:228: *Women have rights like their obligations, according to common decency* (*maʿrūf*), *but men have a degree over them.* So, the verse made this degree obligatory on them, as entailed by innate nature, which is why to honour a woman is to give her compensation and remuneration in place of this degree, making this a customary matter so that she may be of good heart, calm [lit. a cool breast] and comforted [lit. cool eyes]. It cannot be said that innate nature does not compel a woman to accept a contract that places her under the headship of a man without compensation, for we see in some nations women pay dowries (*mahr*) to men so that they might be under the men's headship. Is this not motivated by innate nature, which only some would disobey? We have already explained the wisdom behind the recent practice of referring to bridal payment (*muhūr*) by the term 'wages' (*ujūr*), similar to what has just been mentioned here: this is [a matter that is] absolutely clear, even if some of the exegetes (*mufassirūn*), as you may know, have not come to this conclusion. For some of them take the expenditure of one's property here to also include the bridal payment and the maintenance required for a woman after marriage.

The teacher-imam [ʿAbduh] says: *Qiyām* here means headship (*riyāsa*), under which the one who is subject to the headship (*marʾūs*) has some right of disposal and choice, and it does not mean that this person under that headship ends up under duress, or stripped of agency and incapable of doing anything except that which his master (*ra'īs*) commands. When a person is *qayyim* over another,[227] this is a reference to that person's right-guidance (*irshād*) and supervision [of the other] when the latter is executing what the former is guiding him to. That is to say, [it involves] supervising that person's actions and keeping them disciplined (*tarbiya*): among such [actions] is preserving [the integrity of] the home and not leaving it, not even, for example, to visit one's kin, except on those times and occasions when the man permits it and is content for it [to take place]. I also believe that this extends to the matter of maintenance, where the man commands, such that he should estimate an overall amount, be it a daily, monthly or annual allowance. She should then expend what he has allowed for, but in a manner that she considers will be satisfactory to him and that is commensurate with his comfortable or restricted means.

He said: The intention of distinguishing (*tafḍīl*) one over the other is the distinguishing of men over women. For, if He had said, 'by that which men are distinguished (*faḍḍala*) over women', or if He had said 'the distinction (*tafḍīl*) of men over women', it would have been more succinct and clearer according to our view of the intention. But the wisdom behind this expression is the very same wisdom in His words *do not covet that by which God has distinguished some of you over others* [Q. 4:32], the point of which is to say that woman is to man and man is to woman the same way that organs are to the body of a single person: the man is the head and the woman is the body.

I [Riḍā] say: This means that a man should not transgress on the basis of his superior [*faḍl*] strength over a woman, and the woman should not deem his superiority burdensome or consider it diminishing of her worth. For there is no shame if a person's head is superior to his hand, or his heart is more noble than his belly, for instance; for the deeming superior [*tafḍīl*] of certain organs of the body over others by making some of them more major than others is simply for the good of the entire body, with no harm in that to any given organ. In fact, the well-being of all of the organs is realised and established thereby. Likewise, wisdom has it that man is superior to woman in terms of power and ability to earn a living and provide protection, which allows her to perform her natural functions (*waẓīfa fiṭriyya*), that is, becoming pregnant, giving birth and bringing up the children, with peace of

[227] This 'other' is to be understood as the woman throughout. We have retained the generic third person masculine because that is what the Arabic text is using to make an overtly universal argument, which very soon becomes clearly about the extent of the wife's compliance with her husband's demands and expectations.

mind, provided for with the means of livelihood she requires. And in the very same expression lies another wisdom, which is that this preference is only of one sex over the other, and not every individual man over every individual woman, for how many a woman is superior to her husband in knowledge, work, and even in physical strength and capacity to earn a living?

And the teacher [ʿAbduh] did not point this meaning out, despite its being manifest from the expression, and despite the confirmation of reality, even as some might claim its weakness. In these two meanings allowed for by the expression it is obvious that it is consummately succinct, reaching a degree of inimitability, because it allows for all of these interpretations. We have said in the interpretation of the verse *do not covet that by which God has distinguished some of you over others* [Q. 4:32] that the expression encompasses what each sex has in the way of superiority (*faḍḍala bihi*) over the other, and what individuals have over individuals of their own sex and over individuals of the other sex. But none of these conceptualisations are forthcoming here, even though the lexical expression (*ʿibāra*) is one and the same, because the context there is different from the context here, even as we have pointed out there the weakness of the conceptualisation of the superiority of women over men by way of what is specific to them of pregnancy and childbirth, since men do not covet that. We now return to the words of the teacher.

He [ʿAbduh] said: His superiority has two facets, the natural and the acquired. The natural is that the temperament (*mizāj*) of men is stronger, more perfect, more complete, and more beautiful, and you might find it strange that I say that the man is more beautiful than the woman; but this is the beauty that follows from the completeness of the physical form and its perfection. And what is man in his living body except one among many species of animal, with one and the same physical form? We can see that the male of all of the animals is more perfect and more beautiful than the female, as you can see in roosters and hens, in rams and ewes, as well as in lions and lionesses. One of the aspects of the perfection of the male creation and its beauty is the hair of the beard and the moustaches, and because of that a bald man is always considered to be deficient in physical form: he wishes that there were a treatment to make his hair grow, even if he were a person who would regularly shave his beard. Consequent upon the strength of temperament and perfect physical nature are the strength of the intellect and the ability to examine matters, their principles and goals, in a sound way. There is a saying among physicians and learned people: 'A sound mind is in a sound body'. The result of that, furthermore, is perfectedness for work relating to earning livelihood, for men have a greater capacity for earning livelihood, for inventions and for handling matters; which is to say that because of this they are responsible for maintaining women, protecting them and undertaking the general management in the marital society which unites the house. It is necessary for every society to have a leader to whom they can refer in order that the general welfare [of all] is one. [Thus] ends [the teacher's words], with more clarification and elaboration.

I [Riḍā] say: This leadership puts the contract of marriage in the hands of men, for it is they who ratify it with the agreement of women, and they dissolve it with divorce. The first thing that the majority of well-known *mufassirūn* mention about this superiority is prophecy, the greater and lesser imamate, undertaking religious rites like calling and holding the prayer, and giving the sermon at Friday congregational prayers and others. There is no doubt that these prerogatives follow from the perfect preparedness of men and the absence of distractions for them from these works, given what there is in prophethood of special election and singling out. But these are not the reasons for the *qiyām* of men over women's affairs; the reason is that indicated by the causative [prefixed particle] *bi-*, because prophecy (*nubuwwa*) is a specific singling out [of a man] and cannot form the basis for such a ruling, just as it does not follow from this that every man is better than every woman just because prophets have all been men. As for the imamate and the sermon and their substance, as has been recognised, these belong to men because that is what the law (*shar*ʿ) has laid down; it does not necessarily entail that men should be distinguished in every ruling. And even if the sharia had allowed women to deliver the sermon on Fridays or at the Hajj, or to perform the call to prayer and to lead it, that would still not preclude men becoming *qawwāmūn* over women given [men's] innate nature (*fiṭra*). Nevertheless, the majority of the commentators fail to refer to the ways of innate nature when trying to justify the wisdom behind the rulings of this innate-nature religion (*dīn al-fiṭra*), seeking instead such [justifications] from other rulings.

God, exalted be He, said, *so, righteous women are devoutly obedient women who safeguard during absence what for God is to be safeguarded*. This is a detailing of the situation of women in domestic life where a woman is under the leadership of the man. He mentions that herein are two groups, the righteous women and the women who are not righteous, and that among the attributes of 'righteous' women is devout obedience (*qunūt*), which is acquiescence (*sukūn*) and obedience to God, exalted be He, and likewise to their husbands with common decency (*ma*ʿ*rūf*), safeguarding [the sanctity of their] absence.

Al-Thawrī and Qatāda said: *Safeguarding during absence* [means] that they safeguard in the absence of their husbands that which it is necessary to safeguard in terms of their person and property. Ibn Jarīr and al-Bayhaqī narrate a *ḥadīth* on the authority of Abū Hurayra, that the Prophet (*ṣlʿm*) said, 'The best of women is she who, when she looks at you, makes you happy, when you command her, she obeys you, and who during your absence from her safeguards your property and her self',[228] and he recited the verse. The teacher-imam said that *ghayb* ('absent', 'unseen') here denotes anything that one may be loath to reveal; that is to say, they safeguard all that is private (*khāṣṣ*) in conjugal affairs and personal to that couple, so that none of these women should come to know about anything private to the husband.

I further believe that these words of His extend to include the necessity of concealing all that may take place between the women and their husbands in privy, especially allusions to sexual relations (*ḥadīth al-rafath*), and thus how much more so regarding [his] honour. In my view this is one of the most rhetorically exquisite of Qurʾānic allusions (*kināyāt*) to moral purity (*nazāha*). Pure virgins would read this and comprehend the hidden things it is alluding to, while being at a safe distance from any feelings of shame with which the verse's furthest edges might touch their tender nature, for their hearts shall be safe from any such effects that might bring blushes to their cheeks. And all the more so when safeguarding what is absent is connected to *what God has safeguarded*. So, this rapid transition from the subtle mention of what is 'absent' to the overt mention of God dispels the self from brooding about things that are behind closed doors, things that are hidden and secret, making it instead preoccupied with mindfulness of Him, mighty and majestic.

And they interpret *what for God is to be safeguarded* as meaning with what He safeguards for the women in terms of the bridal payment and the obligation to maintain them, intending that the women safeguard the rights of men in their absence in return for the bridal payment and the obligation of maintenance, both themselves having been safeguarded for women by God's ruling, exalted be He. Between you and me, I can already see you agreeing with me that this interpretation is weak, and [it is] farcical that the honouring of such righteous women by the testimony of God Himself for their safeguarding of [the sanctity of] that absence, from an illicit touch, a forbidden look or an eavesdropping, should be contingent on a few pennies (*darāhim*) they are paid or on a couple of spoonfuls they sit around waiting for. Perhaps after rejecting this opinion you will find more palatable what I find palatable, which is that the *bi-* (what) of the saying *what for God is to be*

228 Note that this version of the *ḥadīth* differs from the version given in other commentaries.

safeguarded is the exact match of the *bi-* in 'there is no might or power except with God' (*lā ḥawla wa-lā quwwata illā bi'llāhi*) [cf. Q. 18:39], and that the meaning is that they [are able to] safeguard during absence by God's safeguarding [of them], that is, by that safeguarding [ability] which God grants them in return for their being righteous women. For the righteous woman, as a result of her mindfulness (*murāqaba*) of God, exalted be He, and her fear of Him, becomes safeguarded from [committing] any treachery, and strong enough to preserve trust. Or, it is that [the meaning is] the women safeguard it because God has commanded that it be preserved. They thus obey Him and disobey all desires (*hawā*). One hopes that the full import of this verse might reach the women of our times, those who delight in exposing marital secrets and who do not safeguard [the sanctity of] absence with regard to such!

The teacher-imam says: This type of women, men have no right (*sulṭān*) to discipline them; their power (*sulṭān*) is over that second type [of women], which He has identified and regarding whose ruling He makes clear: *if you fear the women's defiance, then admonish them, and forsake them in the beds, and strike them. Nushūz* in its origin means rising up, and the woman who does not fulfil the rights of her husband has raised herself up against him and has attempted to be above her chief, but she has also raised herself up above her own nature (*ṭabīʿa*) and that which the natural order (*niẓām al-fiṭra*) necessitates. She becomes like something that juts out (*nāshiz*) from the earth and which is no longer even. Some of them have explained 'fear of *nushūz*' as merely anticipating it, while others as actually having knowledge of it. But one could ask: Why has the lexical expression 'fear' been replaced with the lexical expression 'knowledge', or why did He not say, 'those who commit *nushūz*'? There is no doubt that the Qurʾānic expression has a subtle wisdom, and it is that God, exalted be He, when He wished that the companionship between the two spouses be a companionship of love, affection, satisfaction and union (*maḥabba wa-mawadda wa-tarāḍin wa-iltiʾām*) [cf. Q. 30:21], did not want to attribute *nushūz* to women in a way that suggests that it would naturally issue from them; He chose instead to express that in a way that indicates that it would not naturally issue from them, because it breaks the norms which govern the natural system and by which living together becomes goodly. In this expression is a subtle indication of the standing of woman and what is the priority with regard to her affairs, and of what is necessary for the man in terms of managing her and being as nice as possible (*ḥusn al-talaṭuf*) when dealing with her, when he perceives from her something that he fears would lead to her defiance and her neglecting to undertake marital duties.

Thus, first, he should begin with such admonishment as he sees necessary and that will have an effect on her. The admonishment differs according to each woman's disposition (*ḥāl*). Some women are affected when made to fear God, mighty and majestic be He, and His punishment for such *nushūz*. Other women are affected by threats (*tahdīd*) and warnings of negative consequences in this world, like enemies rejoicing in her misfortune, or her being prevented from [having] some of the things she may desire, such as nice clothes and jewellery. An intelligent man will know well enough which admonishment should affect the heart of his wife.

As for being forsaken, this should be a sufficiently disciplinary measure for any woman who loves her husband, because his forsaking her will be hard on her. Some of the commentators, among them Ibn Jarīr al-Ṭabarī, go so far as to say that the woman who raises herself up will not be affected by the forsaking of her husband, meaning his avoidance of her, and they say that the meaning of *ihjurūhunna* (forsake them) is to secure them with the ropes used for tying a camel. What they have said is worthless, and they have no idea about women's character traits and their natures, for indeed there are women who love their husbands, even as recklessness and frivolity make the *nushūz* against him an attractive option. Some of them raise themselves up as a test for their husbands, in order for it to become clear to her or to other people the extent of his passion for her and his desire for her to be pleased. And I say that there are some women who commit *nushūz* to force her husband to satisfy her with what she demands of jewellery and accessories. And for some of them, their parents are the ones who tempt her to *nushūz* for their own personal goals.

The teacher-imam did not speak about the 'forsaking in the beds' because it is self-evident, and how often have the commentators (*mufassirūn*) tried to explain self-evident matters which the uneducated masses understand effortlessly? For, if you were to say to the common man that so-and-so forsook his wife in bed, or in the sleeping place, or in the resting place, or the place of sleep, then he would understand the intention of your words. But some of the commentators (*mufassirūn*) have foregrounded what is meant by the allusion, to the detriment of the moral purity that is intended in the Book. Some have said that the meaning is forsake their sleeping-quarters, which is where they spend the night; and some have said that the forsaking of them is on account of *the beds* – that is to say, on account of their disobedience to you in them. This is subsumed by the meaning of *nushūz*, so what is the point of making it the aim of the punishment? Some of those who explain the forsaking as securing with ropes say: You tie them up in order to force them to do that which they are refusing to do, and al-Zamakhsharī called this the explanation of the obtuse (*tafsīr al-thuqalāʾ*).

The correct meaning is that which springs to mind, O reader, and that which springs to the mind of all who know these words of the language. You may say the expression indicates the prohibition of the meaning which some of them have given it. For He says *and forsake them in the beds*, and this is not realised by forsaking the bed itself, which is the mattress, nor is it realised by forsaking the room in which the lying down occurs. It is only realised by forsaking in the bed itself. To propose forsaking the bed or the room is a greater punishment; God, exalted be He, did not permit it, and it might be the cause of a greater estrangement. Forsaking in the bed itself is a meaning which is not realised by forsaking the bed or the room in which it is found, because coming together in the bed is that which awakens the marital feelings, and it makes each of the spouses feel inner tranquillity towards the other, and the disturbances caused by earlier events cease. If the man forsakes the woman and avoids her in this place, it is very likely that those feelings and the inner tranquillity will prompt her to ask him about the reason, and [will] bring her back down from the high ground of rebellion to the even plain of harmony. And I can almost see the reader being completely convinced that this is the intended meaning, even if, like me, reader, you had never seen this interpretation by anyone, living or dead.

As for the striking, the condition has been imposed on it that it be non-severe (*ghayr mubarriḥ*). Ibn Jarīr [al-Ṭabarī] has narrated that on a chain of transmission going back to the Prophet (*ṣlʿm*). *Tabrīḥ* is severe damage, and it is narrated on the authority of Ibn ʿAbbās in his *tafsīr* that the striking be with a tooth-stick and the like – that is to say, like a strike with the hand or a small cane. And it was narrated on the authority of Muqātil about the occasion of revelation of the verse that it was about Saʿd b. al-Rabīʿ b. ʿAmr, one of the tribal chiefs (*naqīb*), and about his wife Ḥabība bt. Zayd b. Abī Zuhayr, and the matter was that she had risen up against him, and he slapped her and so her father went with her to the Prophet and said, 'I gave my darling to his bed, and he slapped her!' The Prophet replied, 'Let her retaliate against her husband'. So she departed with her father in order to retaliate against him, and the Prophet said, 'Come back! This is Gabriel, who has just come to me, and God has sent down this verse', and he recited it, and he said, 'I wanted one thing and God wanted another, and that which God wanted is better'. Kalbī said it was revealed about Saʿd b. Rabīʿ and his wife Khawla bt. Muḥammad b. Salama, and he mentioned the story, and it is said that it was revealed with regard to other men.

Some among us who follow European manners (*muqallidāt al-ifranj*) find the legality of striking a 'defiant' woman (*nāshiz*) too much, yet they do not find it too much when she rises up and raises herself against him, and even though he is the master of the house, she renders him subject (*mar'ūs*), nay, despicable (*muḥtaqar*). Furthermore, she persists in her 'defiance' (*nushūz*), so that she will not yield to his admonishment or his advice, nor is she bothered by his turning away from her or his forsaking of her. I do not know how they might deal with such rebellious women, or how they think the women's husbands should manage them. They probably imagine a weak, delicate woman, well-behaved and refined, and an uncouth, crude man oppressing her, his whip feeding off her tender flesh and quenching its thirst off of her innocent blood. They probably also claim that God has permitted him such violence, and that even when he is committing such a crime and a transgression against her, he remains blameless, as happens in the case of many of those heartless and uncouth individuals with ossified character traits.

Heaven forbid that God should permit the likes of this oppression or that He should be pleased by it. Indeed, it is only men who are thugs and brutes who oppress women out of pure animosity (*'udwān*). Many *ḥadīth*s have been reported that enjoin the likes of these men to look after women, and the [following] verse, in what it provides of arbitration, allows for what is due to them. Indeed, there are women who are husband-hating, who rebel against them, who rebuff their husbands, who despise their husbands, who are ungrateful for the maintenance that they provide. They rebel against them out of obduracy and obstinacy, and [for] making them bear what they have no capacity to bear. And what possible corrupting force might befall the earth if a God-wary, meritorious man is permitted to mitigate the obduracy of one of these women and overturn her self-conceited rebellion by striking her across the hand with a tooth-stick or a smack to the back of the neck? If it is too burdensome to the men's nature to permit such a thing, then let them know that their nature has become so frail that they have become stunted and that many of their European exemplars actually strike these educated and refined women of theirs – flimsily dressed women who are deviant and a cause of deviance. Their sages and scholars have done this, their kings and princes. It is a necessity that cannot even be eschewed by those who go to extremes to honour women who are learned, so why would you deem it odious to permit it out of necessity in a religion that was sent universally for the civilised and uncivilised alike, for all races of humankind.

The teacher-imam [says]: The legality of striking women is not repugnant to the intellect or innate nature, such that it would need interpretation. For it is something that is needed in situations where the social environment becomes corrupted and corrupt character traits predominate. Indeed, it becomes permissible if a man considers that a woman's return from *nushūz* depends on it. So if the social environment becomes sound again, and women are able to become mindful of advice and heed the admonition, or be deterred by the forsaking (*hajr*), then it would be obligatory to do without the striking. For each condition there is a ruling to suit it in the sharia, and we are ordered in every condition to treat women with gentleness and to avoid oppressing them, and to *retain them out of common decency, or to release them kindly* [Q. 2:229]; and there are many *ḥadīth*s on the care of women.

I [Riḍā] say: Among these *ḥadīth*s are those which make the striking repugnant and which make people averse to it. Among them is the *ḥadīth* of ʿAbd Allāh b. Zamʿa in the two *Saḥiḥ*s. He said that the Messenger of God said, 'Will one of you strike his wife as he would strike a slave and then make love to her at the end of the day?'[229] And in a narration on the authority of ʿĀʾisha, according to ʿAbd al-Razzāq [al-Ṣanʿānī], 'Is not one of you ashamed to strike his wife as he strikes a slave, striking her at the beginning of the day and then making love to her at the end of it?' He [the Prophet] is here reminding the man that if he knew in himself that he would need that sexual relationship and that private union with his wife – which is the most powerful and complete union between any two human beings, with each of them being bonded to the other in complete unity, so that each one of the two will feel that their connection to the other is stronger than the connection of some of their limbs to their other [limbs] – if, again, he could not do without this union and connection that innate nature demands, how could it be seemly for him to make his wife, who is like his own self, into something contemptuous, akin to the contemptibility of his slave, by striking her with his hand or whip? Verily, the nature of the noble and humble man would keep him away from such crudeness, and it would prevent him from seeking the maximal form of union with one whom he has reduced to the status of a slave girl. So the *ḥadīth* is the most powerful condemnation of the striking of women. And I recall that I was guided to this exalted meaning before I had discovered its noble wording. Whenever I heard of a man striking his wife, I would say 'Good God! How could a person lead a marital life with a woman

[229] Versions of this *ḥadīth* are found in Bukhārī, *Ṣaḥīḥ*, *Kitāb al-Adab* (78), *Bāb qawl Allāh taʿālā* [Q. 49:11] (43), *ḥadīth* no. 72/6042 and *Kitāb al-Tafsīr* (65), *Bāb sūrat al-Shams* (91), *ḥadīth* no. 463/4942; Muslim, *Ṣaḥīḥ*, *Kitāb al-Janna wa-ṣifat naʿīmihā wa-ahlihā* (53), *Bāb al-nār yadkhuluhā al-jabbārūn waʾl-janna yadkhuluhā al-ḍuʿafāʾ* (13), *ḥadīth* no. 60/2855; Nawawī, *Riyāḍ al-ṣāliḥīn*, *Kitāb al-Muqaddimāt*, *Bāb al-waṣiyya biʾl-nisāʾ* (34), *ḥadīth* no. 274; Tirmidhī, *Jāmiʿ*, *Kitāb Tafsīr al-Qurʾān* (47), *ḥadīth* no. 3666. An attenuated version, reading, 'None of you should whip his wife as a slave is whipped', is found in Ibn Ḥajar al-ʿAsqalānī, *Bulūgh al-marām*, *Kitāb al-Nikāḥ* (8), *ḥadīth* no. 113/1064.

whom he beats?' Sometimes he assaults her with beating as though he is a wolf and she is a sheep, and sometimes he humbles himself to her like a slave begging for the utmost limit of intimacy!

However, we do not deny that people vary [in character], and that among them are those who are not suited to this sort of life. If his wife is not capable, by virtue of her bad upbringing, to honour him to the extent that he deserves, and she does not back down from her *nushūz* via the admonishment and the forsaking, then he should separate himself from her with decency, and let her go kindly, unless he hopes to reconcile with her through the mediation recommended in the [subsequent] verse. But he should never strike. The best of men do not strike women, and it is only out of necessity that this has been permitted to them. Al-Bayhaqī narrated from among the *ḥadīth*s of Umm Kulthūm, the daughter of [Abū Bakr] al-Ṣiddīq, may God be pleased with both of them, that she said that men had been forbidden from striking women, but when they started to complain about them to the Messenger of God (*ṣlʿm*), he permitted it but said, 'The best of you will never strike'. If ever there was a licence (*rukhṣa*) that sounded like a prohibition, it would be this one! In sum, to strike is a bitter medicine, for which the virtuous free man has no need, even though it can never be eliminated from all houses in every situation, and even as it is a common form of discipline for men and women alike.

Nevertheless, the majority of jurists have identified *nushūz* that has legal consequences, and which renders striking permissible, if needed in order to counteract that [defiance], with just a few forms of behaviour like disobeying the man in bed, and leaving the house without a [good] reason (*ʿudhr*). Some of them consider that her refraining from adorning herself when he demands constitutes *nushūz*. They say that he may also strike her if she abandons her religious obligations, like the major ablution and prayer. The apparent meaning is that *nushūz* is more general and encompasses any disobedience which is caused by rising up and refusal, and that is the sense of this phrase: *but if they obey you, seek not a way against them*. The teacher-imam said: That is to say, *if they obey you* in any one of these disciplinary measures, then do not seek to transgress by overstepping these bounds to other measures, and begin with what God has begun, which is the admonishment, and if that has no effect then he forsakes her, and if that has no effect, then he strikes her, and if that also has no effect, then they resort to the mediation. One understands from this that there is no way against the obedient women, even with admonishment and advice, much less forsaking and striking.

I say: Many commentators (*mufassirūn*) have explicitly required this sequence in disciplining, even if the syntactical coordination with the letter *wāw* ('and') does not actually imply such a sequence. Some of them say that this is indicated by the narrative and common-sense arguments, for if it had been the opposite, then the strongest measure would suffice, and [one would] have no need of the weakest, and this would be meaningless. Some of them say that the sequencing can be derived from the inclusion of the *wāw* ('and') in sections [of the Qur'ānic verse] that vary in intensity, and are sequenced in a matter that is [itself] graduated, and so the text itself is the proper indicator of sequence. The meaning of *seek not a way against them* is: do not look for a way to end up harming them in word or deed, with 'seek' (*baghy*) meaning 'look for [a way to]' (*ṭalab*). But it can also mean exceeding the bounds by aggressing. In other words, do not seek any injustice towards them by any means. So, whenever things are overtly correct, do not seek the secrets folded within.

Indeed God is high, mighty. Indeed, his power (*sulṭān*) over you is greater than your power over your wives. If you transgress against them, He will punish you, while if you disregard their lapses, out of generosity and swallowing your pride, He will disregard yours.

The teacher-imam said: He concluded with this after forbidding injustice, as the man is only unjust to the woman because he feels himself to be superior to her, and [because of] his being [physically] larger and more capable than her. So He, exalted be He, reminds them of His mightiness and His greatness and His power over the man in order that he might be admonished and become humbled (*yakhshaʿ*), and be wary of God with regard to her.[230] Know that men who try to oppress women in order to be masters in their houses will beget only those who will be slaves to others. In other words, their children will grow up under such injustice and will end up being like degraded slaves before those by whose side they will need to live.[231]

Faḍl Allāh

Faḍl Allāh's lengthy interpretation contains few original points; he is broadly conservative on women's issues, and he supports the interpretation which places the husband in charge of the marriage and gives him the right to admonish the wife, abandon her in the bed, and strike her. In terms of content, there are two main departures from prior interpretations, both of which mark this out as a modern work of *tafsīr*. The first

[230] 'Be wary of God with regard to her' is a reference to the Prophet's Farewell Pilgrimage Oration in which he admonishes men to 'be wary of God with regard to women'.

[231] ʿAbduḥ and Riḍā, *Tafsīr al-manār*, s.v. Q. 4:34.

is that Faḍl Allāh makes an effort to respond to the issue of equality between the sexes, and the second is that, unlike medieval commentators, he does not address the issue of men who abuse their rights over their wives.

Faḍl Allāh is distinctly modern in his emphasis on certain types of equality between the spouses, which is a clear response to feminist discourses. He addresses specifically the 'nature of *qiwāma*' in Islam, saying that it does not mean mastery or control. This interpretation thus seems to contradict medieval interpretations directly, and, underscoring this, Faḍl Allāh addresses 'the personhood of the woman' throughout his interpretation. Like some medieval commentators, such as Ṭabarī, he claims that the nature of the marital contract is limited, and, as in medieval commentaries, he asserts that a wife's main obligation is to give her husband sexual access, therefore she should not leave the house without her husband's permission. This, according to Faḍl Allāh, is because men have more need of sex than women do, and so having constant sexual access to their wives prevents them from falling into immoral situations. Thus Faḍl Allāh's vision of the ideal roles of husband and wife rely on a particular conception of masculinity and male sexuality in which men are presumed to have uncontrollable sexual urges. Like some other modern Shīʿī interpreters, Faḍl Allāh says that the wife has no obligations other than sexual availability to her husband, and he states that she can demand a wage for doing the housework. In his view, marriage is not a matter of commercial transaction but of emotional commitment in which wives' good companionship to their husbands is the equivalent of their jihad. Whereas medieval commentators all mentioned husbands' obligations to their wives, this interpretation is excessively focused on women's responsibilities towards their husbands; Faḍl Allāh barely mentions the husbands' obligation to the wives. For him, marital roles are based on innate characteristics and are connected to other rulings in *fiqh*, such as that on women's testimony.

While he maintains medieval rulings, Faḍl Allāh couches these in modern language. Thus he describes the husband's chastisement of his wife in terms of the emotions that each is supposed to feel: 'it is an even-tempered striking for discipline that gives her a taste of humiliation'. The idea of humiliating the wife is not present in any medieval commentary, and it is something that Riḍā argues against explicitly. Unlike medieval commentators, Faḍl Allāh does not say that a husband must be careful and not oppress his wife because God is watching over him. Instead, he focuses on securing the wife's obedience. This interpretation shows that a person who is otherwise considered to be a modernist or reformist might have deeply conservative, even radically conservative, views when it comes to women's rights.[232]

The lexical meaning

Qawwāmūn: Managers of the affairs of others in terms of the administrative matters and guardianship which are needed in marital life. One says: A man is *qayyim*, or *qayyām* or *qawwām*. And this is an emphatic construction denoting frequency (*takthīr*).

[232] While in later writings he changed his views on certain matters such as women leaving the house without permission, he maintained his view on women's testimony.

Qānitāt: The root sense of *qunūt* is continuous obedience, from which is derived the word '*qunūt*' in the *witr* prayer, due to the length of the standing (*qiyām*) in it. The intention of the word is that the wives are obedient to their husbands with a continual obedience. They are obedient in their responsibilities towards the males in those matters that God has ordered them to be obedient.[233]

Ḥāfiẓāt li'l-ghayb: The wives preserve for their husbands in the husbands' absence – as made obligatory by marriage – themselves, their property, their secrets and their honour, and other matters from among those matters which God wishes for them to preserve and safeguard.

Nushūzahunna: This refers to the wives' disobedience and arrogance, and their raising themselves above their husbands. Al-Rāghib [al-Iṣfahānī][234] said: The *nushūz* of the woman is her hatred of her husband, her raising herself over obedience to him, and raising her eye from him to another. *Nashaz* is rising up from the ground, and the canine tooth (*nāb*) is *nāshiz*.

Wa'hjurūhunna: Abandoning out of hatred.[235] One says: '*Hajartu al-rajul*' to mean, I have stopped talking to him out of hatred. The *hājira* is noon because it is the time in which they abandon their work [in the heat of the sun].

Maḍāji': The root sense of *ḍujū'an* is to lie down to sleep (*istilqā'*). One says *ḍaja'a*, *ḍujū'an* or *iḍṭijā'an* to mean lying down to sleep.

The occasion (*munāsaba*) of revelation

In the *Asbāb al-nuzūl* of al-Wāḥidī, he cites Muqātil: This verse was revealed about Sa'd b. al-Rabī', who was one of the tribal chiefs (*naqīb*), and his wife, Ḥabība bt. Zayd b. Abī Hurayra, and they were both Anṣār, and she rose up (*nashazat*) against him, so he slapped her. Her father went with her to the Prophet (*ṣl'm*) and said: 'I gave my darling to his bed and he slapped her!' So the Prophet (*ṣl'm*) said, 'Let her seek retaliation from her husband'. So she left with her father, intending to seek retaliation against him, and the Prophet said, 'Come back! This is Gabriel (*'m*) who has come to me, and God, exalted be He, has sent down this verse'. The Messenger of God said, 'I wanted one thing and God wanted another, and that which God wanted was better', and he waived the order of retaliation.

233 This refers to Ṭabarī's interpretation.
234 In his work, the *Mufradāt*.
235 Cf. Q. 93:3.

Al-Kalbī said that this verse was sent down with regard to Saʿd b. Rabīʿ and his wife Khwala bt. Muḥammad b. Maslama, and he mentioned a similar version of the story.

On the basis of this narration, we note that the verse does not negate the ruling on retaliation because it deals with the matter of the role of the husband in marital life in his status as manager (*qaymūma*) of the woman, or in his managing her (*qiyāma ʿalayhā*) with the meaning of being (*kawnihi*) the one responsible for her in the sphere of marriage, keeping in mind what God made for him in terms of particular rights, although that does not cancel her rights to retaliation as a person who is an injured party, in a situation in which the man has no right.

Do you not see that if there was a man who had taken her money from her, she would have the right to retaliate and seek recompense against him for his money whether he is willing or not? And the explanation of that is that there is no contradiction between *qiwāma* and her established right to recompense from an act of aggression.[236]

Likewise, if a man attacks (*hajama*) his wife by striking her, would it be prohibited for her to defend herself, even if that meant striking him back? We do not see that there is any relationship, near or far, between the two verses. Perhaps these numerous narrations in the names of people regarding whom it was sent down are a proof that this is not the case of a *ḥadīth* to do with the historical occasion of revelation of the verse in any trustworthy way, but rather is a personal effort on the part of those concerned to discuss the occasion of revelation, but in a way that cannot be verified.

And in the *Tafsīr al-mīzān* [by Ṭabāṭabāʾī] – on the very same subject – in the outward sense of the narrations, there is another problem, and that is they outwardly suggest that the Prophet's saying '*qiṣāṣ*' is a clarification of what the ruling would be when an enquirer seeks a legal opinion (*istiftāʾ*) and not a judgment in the absence of the two sides of the case, which would require the sending down of the verse to demonstrate the error of the Prophet in his judgment and his legislation, which contradicts his infallibility (*ʿiṣma*). Nor is it a case of abrogation (*naskh*), for that is when a ruling is annulled before it has been implemented. When God, glory be to Him, gets involved (*taṣarruf*) in some of the Prophet's rulings, whether by lifting them or laying them down, that is only in his rulings and his opinions within the remit of his authority (*wilāya*), not with regard to the rulings that he has legislated for his community, for that would be an invalid demonstration of error.

[236] That is to say, the *qiwāma* status does not override an infringement of her actual rights. This verse should not be used as an excuse for domestic violence.

But one can respond to the author of the *Mīzān* by saying that the Prophet ruled for *qiṣāṣ* – assuming the soundness of the narration – based on the verse of retaliation, which entails the retaliation of the injured party against the aggressor in a like manner. God, however, sent down the verse of *qiwāma* that abrogates the ruling of a woman's retaliation against her husband when he has aggressed (*ʿudwān*) against her. So, it is not a case of abrogation before enactment, given that the ruling is universal and operative in its wording (*ṣīgha*) in the way that it comprehends men and women alike.

Men are maintainers of women

In these two verses [Q. 4:34–5] are some prominent features of the Qurʾānic planning for the legislation concerning the family and the relationship of the man and woman as spouses. The first verse confirms the principle (*mabdaʾ*) of the prerogative (*qiwāma*) of men over women, and so they have the right of authority (*qaymūma*) within marital life, in relation to what is required of administrative affairs and guardianship. And that is on the basis of two points, one of which the verse leaves implicit and the other of which it makes explicit. The first is the distinction (*tafḍīl*) of men over women on the basis of some individual characteristics hidden in their makeup. The second is the payment men make of their property for the marital home and for women. On the face of it, both points together are the basis of the ruling, not each one on its own.

On this basis, it is possible for us to make an observation that, according to some of the exegetes, the matter of *qiwāma* is comprehensive of marital life and other matters, using the idea of distinction as an independent justification. This is in light of the man's administration (*idāra*) of rulership (*ḥukm*) and judgeship (*qaḍāʾ*) and other matters that represent his dominance in public life. These things are exclusively his, and not the woman's, and are considered one manifestation of his authority (*qiwāma*). But we do not understand that from this verse, whose overall feel suggests that it is talking about the marital home. That is because this derivative of substantive law cannot be considered a derivative of rulings for a comprehensive issue. Rather, it constitutes, in accordance with manifest customary practice, a subsidiary derivation that indicates the comprehensive scope for that ruling. Were it otherwise, it would have been more apposite to talk about judgeship, rulership and jihad first, rather than about how to impose order in the home.

That is on the one hand. On the other, the verse is talking about the authority (*qiwāma*) with regard to the role that a man undertakes vis-à-vis a woman, so that the case, in all of its practical details, is about a man and a woman [as a married couple]. But that is not within the remit of authority (*qiwāma*) when the latter has to do with rulership and judgeship, for the sway in both of these instances is one that is held over all people subsumed by that rulership or judgeship, and it sits outside the context which this verse seems to inhabit, according to its lexical form. However, a person might [easily] project on rulership in conjugal life some features from rulership elsewhere, given the greater importance of public matters over private matters.

We might register another remark about some of the words that discuss the nature of the legal ruling. In some instances where the wife assumes the burden of maintenance of the marital home, should she then have the right to authority (*qiwāma*) on the basis that expenditure is a Qurʾānic justification for that [*qiwāma*]? In sum, this is to remark that the ruling is based on both points together, not on either one of them independently. This is on the one hand. On the other, the act of expenditure (*infāq*) that the Qurʾān talks about is an act of expenditure that is premised on responsibility in the way that Islam obliges the husband to pay the wife maintenance and bridal payment, not the expenditure premised on charitable donation. It is as though the verse wants to consider this a requirement of the husband and his fulfilment of it a premise for the ruling, which is why many *ḥadīth*s, which jurisprudents base themselves on when giving legal opinions, say that if the husband ceases to fulfil the maintenance it becomes possible for the Islamic official, after giving him the option of divorce or continued maintenance, to grant her a divorce without his [the husband's] consent, because authority (*qiwāma*) is invalidated once one of the two matters on which *qiwāma* depends is invalidated. And God knows best.

Now, what is the nature of authority (*qiwāma*) in marital life, and what are its limits in detail? What is the meaning of *al-tafḍīl*? And why is the maintenance the responsibility of the husband, not the wife, in the plan laid out by Islam for marital life?

What is the nature of *qiwāma* in Islam?

As for the answer to the first question, some people might imagine that it involves mastery (*siyāda*) and control (*sayṭara*), such that a woman's word does not count against her husband's word, and she has no standing before him – whether in her private affairs or public ones – and she has no choice in the management of her life and property, and in this way she becomes a discarded mass, devoid of any independent and particular human traits. She is a dependent, not an independent, human being.

But this is so far from the Islamic approach with regard to family law. For marriage does not annihilate the woman as a person in all matters not covered by the marital contract, given that a woman is committed to other things in life; rather, all that it binds her to, from a legal perspective, is what she binds herself to. Indeed, the marital contract, by its very nature, is conceptually circumscribed to particular requirements it imposes, which each of the two of them is required to fulfil on the basis of the contract. It is this conceptualisation that obliges the wife to respond to her husband's sexual need every time he desires her. It is not for her to deprive him of that or to set up physical or psychological barriers which prevent him from fulfilling his need unless there are exceptional circumstances in which there is a legal or health impediment that would be outside the scope of her natural will. So it is not for her, then, to leave his house without his permission under normal circumstances, if that is contrary to his right in this context. And the husband has to fulfil the desire of his wife in that which coincides with the understanding of living together companionably (*muʿāshara bi'l-maʿrūf*) and protecting her from deviance.

Perhaps the focus on the sexual aspect of the marital relationship and the strong emphasis on adherence to it, based as it is on the consideration that the sexual need and the implications it brings of reassurance, love and spiritual solace, is a fundamental aspect of this contract, since it is intended to be a way of regulating instinctual needs within an ambience of spiritual and psychological tranquillity. As for this insistence on fulfilling the desire of the husband in a perfunctory (*ḥāsim*) and mechanistic (*daqīq*) manner, perhaps that arises from the fact that it is man's nature to be more quickly aroused in this respect than a woman, who needs – in most cases – more complicated preparation for that, which requires the husband to hold himself back, lest he stray from the straight line in a way that would destroy the relationship and cause it to swerve into a bottomless abyss. Nevertheless, based on personal jurisprudential *ijtihād*,[237] he has to reciprocate in situations when he fears that she might deviate and there is a possibility of her falling into illicitness (*ḥarām*).

The husband is obliged to provide to his wife maintenance in accordance with his means and common decency (*bi'l-maʿrūf*), in the way that her material needs require, according to her circumstances. And the husband has the right to end the marital relationship with divorce, in principle, while maintaining the decency which Islam made in its planning to build the

[237] Meaning, development of the law; we understand this to mean that Faḍl Allāh is, here, referring to his own jurisprudential opinions.

Islamic personhood so that such decency would prevent him from engaging in improvised behaviours without justification. And this is what the marital contract requires in the way of commitment from both sides, whereby each one of them is free in all individual matters that have to do with other tasks, whether affairs of domestic tasks or social and financial status, when that does not conflict with their private marital commitments. It is not for the man to impose on his wife the role of managing the marital home, except on the basis of her commitment to that, within an agreement that they have come to, even in the case of the custody of the children and looking after them. For it is not the responsibility of the wife, from the perspective of religious law, but rather the responsibility of the husband, and she has the right to demand the wage for it, given that Islam respects her labour in the framework of its human and material worth. And it is not for a woman to impose on her husband maintenance above and beyond her needs, or to respond to some of her personal or social needs that are outside of the commitments of her marital contract.

And so we find that Islam granted each one of them considerable room to manoeuvre with freedom in that which confirms the humanity of their will and their worth, within the scope of the relationship. It has not left the matter to personal mood or fleeting desire, whereby each of them acts in a way that they should not towards the other. Rather, it reveals to both of them that a materialistic foundation is not one on which marriage ought to be based. Marriage is not a fixed material corporation that submits to precise accounting in the context of profit and loss. Instead, it is a spiritual, dynamic relationship premised on humanity that deems the personality of each of them to be a spiritual extension of the personality of the other. It wills both of them to set off on the basis of love expressed through the healthy intimate affection (*ʿāṭifa*) that each of them feels towards the other, and on the basis of the compassion which expresses each of their consciousness of the circumstances of the other in terms of feelings, thoughts, connectedness and conduct, proceeding [ultimately] from the divine will. And this is what the noble verse articulates: *Of His signs is that He created for you mates from among yourselves (min anfusikum), that you might find solace by their side, and He ordained love and mercy between you. Indeed, in that are signs for people who are inclined to reflect* (Q. 30:21), and also His words *they are like a garment unto you and you a garment unto them* (Q. 2:187).

The noble *ḥadīth* considers that a woman's beautiful companionship (*muʿāshara*) towards her husband is a jihad, just as it appears in his words (God be pleased with him and his family), 'a woman's jihad is living with her husband beautifully (*ḥusn al-tabaʿʿul*)' and in other religious texts which seek to make the point that devotion to this relationship and patience with its negative moments are a stance that brings the human closer to God, exactly as in acts of worship, jihad and the like.

And in light of all of that, the marital relationship in the consciousness of each of them moves with a spirit of giving, sacrifice and love, far from the static materialistic calculations. So we find the woman exhausting herself in the service of her husband and children in everything that she is able to expend or exert of herself, her property and her life. Likewise, we find the man continuously goes about (*ḥ-r-k*) dedicating his whole life to his wife and children, to the extent of depriving himself of many of his desires for the sake of their well-being. That is the case when the marital relationship proceeds along a sound and balanced line. And Islam proceeds on that basis, so that the two spouses feel that their life together is not ruled by the law (*qānūn*) and his and her commitments to that, but rather alongside that [law] stands a human state in which the person feels the spirit of giving for the sake of others in his desire to attain God's satisfaction and as a confirmation of the spiritual side of his humanity in all of that.

And with this, we come to know that authority (*qiwāma*) implies the right (*ḥaqq*) of bearing the responsibility for the marital house, on the basis of the sharia commitments imposed by the marital contract, or what is required by the legal state (*ḥāla qānūniyya*) in terms of the property the man possesses within the marital home and in his capacity to implement the sharia in certain specific aspects connected with attaining his rights – as we shall see – in that divorce is in his hand. In everything else, other than that, he has no right to be in charge (*qiwāma*) [of her].

We thus find that the matter is not about annihilating a woman as a person but rather confirming her personhood by holding her to the commitment that she herself has made, even as Islam has given her the right to impose whatever conditions she wishes in the marital contract, as long as it does not overtly contradict Islam.

The limits of men's distinction (*tafḍīl*) over women

As for the subject of distinction (*tafḍīl*) in this noble passage *by that which God has distinguished the one over the other*, many have mentioned that it is an indication of the distinction (*tafḍīl*) of men over women in perceptive (*idrāk*) and intellectual (*ta'aqqul*) capacity, which suggests that a woman's intellect (*'aql*) is inferior to a man's intellect, and they confirm this idea with the sayings that have been preserved about women that discuss women's intellectual deficiency. And some add to that by talking about the physical aspect which makes the man able to undertake much hard labour requiring exertion that a woman is unable to undertake.

However, are we really able to pass judgment on this subject in the manner that they do? And is this among the subjects pertaining to the unseen, which does not submit to experience and observation, so that we end up relegating the matter to the realm of the unseen and assigning it an obscure and foggy ruling? In response: we have reservations about that, because we have no way of confirming it, but we may attempt to understand via the equality between men and women in the sharia – in most aspects – that the degree of awareness and intellect from which proceeds the specification of responsibility in work and movement is one and the same for both parties. For, just as one witnesses in everyday life, there is proof that many women in life circumstances, both public and private, equivalent to those of men, have been able to prove their ability in focus, awareness and subtle perception in all matters presented to them, both theoretical (*fikriyya*) and practical (*ʿamaliyya*).

As for the *ḥadīth*s about the deficiency of women's intellects, in some of them, proof has been sought from the Noble Qurʾān, in that the testimony of two women takes the place of the testimony of a single man, which means that the matter is not evaluated in a positive way, but in a negative way. But how are we to comprehend that? In response: the matter may have more to do with the intensity of a woman's potential for an emotional reaction, which God has deposited in her, and its influence on her as a female and as a mother. So that has a great effect [in that it results] in her overreaction when tragic events strike or in emotional cases, which leads her to deviate from equilibrium and the ability to consider matters calmly, especially when these are connected to the problems that take place within marital life. And this is exemplified in the noble verse which speaks about the invalidity of a single female witness in contrast to the acceptability of a single male witness in His words *if one of them errs the other reminds her* (Q. 2:282), which suggests the possibility of deviation.[238] So, as a safeguard for justice, it prescribes including another woman with her who may remind her and guide her to the straight path. This means that the matter entails the potential, rather than the inevitability, of an overreaction to a situation, precisely because one of the two women is presumed to be able to remain composed and to rectify the matter in case of an error.

In the beginning of the *sūra* we have already alluded to the fact that this emotional female weakness may become balanced by means of a protracted process of instruction (*tarbiyya*). But divine legislation (*tashrīʿ*) is mindful of

[238] Cf. ch. 5, this volume.

all humans, and it legislates on the basis of the general nature of things. In light of this, it is possible that authority (*qiwāma*) is precisely due to the weakness of the man's emotional side, since he is less likely than a woman to overreact in emergency situations. It could also be that the matter is connected to the physiological situations which the woman as a mother encounters, such as pregnancy, breastfeeding, child rearing and the like, all of which leave her little room to devote herself to, and concentrate on, the administrative matters of marital life. Therefore, the preference is premised on essential characteristics that give the man the power to face a situation far more calmly than a woman when it comes to cases of divorce and specific personal needs.[239] There may also be hidden things of which we have no knowledge, which only God knows about, concerning the makeup of the man and the woman.

As for the reason for the man's specialisation in the responsibility of maintenance, perhaps it is connected with what Islam laid down for him in terms of the organisation of the family, in consideration of the fundamental role of motherhood in the woman's life, which would deprive her of the opportunity to realise self-sufficiency for the family, because Islam sees that the family has much to gain from the woman's care for the house, more than it gains from her distance from it for work. Rather, the work of women, on the basis of what we have seen from experience and our contemporary reality, brings about many negative spiritual and material results for the family, especially for the children who have lost the mother's care, which is picked up by servants and nurseries. And it is this that leads to the working mother's exhaustion, which is a combination of the toil of work and the toil of the home in the majority of instances. We are not here to affirm the unlawfulness of women's work, or attack it in principle, but we confirm the Islamic truth that does not consider that it is better, in the case of conflicts with the spiritual and material growth and development of family life.

The Qur'ān draws the outlines of a noble portrait for believing women

So, righteous women are devoutly obedient women, those who safeguard during absence what for God is to be safeguarded. This is one of those radiant

[239] By which he means sex.

portraits of mindful (*wāʿiyāt*) believing women who comprehend their divinely legislated responsibilities towards their husbands in what God prescribes for them through the marital contract of strictures (*quyūd*) and commitments (*iltizāmāt*). They thus humbly submit (*khushūʿ*) to God when they face any situation in which there are tempting factors and the lures of the soul that commands itself to wrongdoing [cf. Q. 12:53]. They instead adopt a stance of pure and powerful faith that rejects all such [temptation], certain that the worth of a believer's faith is to adhere to her compact and her covenant, doing it no harm either big or small. With that [commitment], they guard their husbands during their absences as a result of what marriage imposes on them of trust (*amāna*) over the self, property, secrets and honour (*ʿirḍ*) among other things that God has [made to be] guarded in His laws (*tashrīʿ*) and has willed for wives to guard in their practical lives.

Marital commitment transforms marital life into something entrusted to both spouses for safekeeping, in all that it entails of commitments and responsibilities. Both of them thereby lose their individual freedom. In the case of the wife, she is not free to give herself to whomever she wishes, nor is she free to dispose of her husband's property as she wishes without his approval, nor to divulge to others secrets of marital life or personal secrets about her husband, for all of that is entrusted to her for safekeeping by God; yet, that is not a stricture imposed through servitude, as some people are wont to consider it, depicting the institution of marriage as the climax of tragedy for a woman, mourning the freedom that she loses as a result thereof. The secret of what we have said is that marital strictures affirm the element of freedom and do not annul it, since these [strictures] issue from the voluntary will of a woman who is free, which itself is a prerequisite for the soundness of the [marriage] contract; they do not issue from the will of another seeking to dominate her life. The concept of freedom [here] is encountered in the idea that a human being's decision is a consequence of that person's free will, for it is up to him to make a decision or not to make it. But once he has willed [it] and has committed to that decision, that commitment becomes a confirmation of the meaning of freedom, one natural result of which is that decision.

How does the Qurʾān treat the problem of *nushūz*?

And if you fear the women's defiance. There is another type of woman that differs greatly from this type, and that is the type that rebels (*tamarrud*) against her husband's divinely legislated rights (*ḥuqūq sharʿiyya*), which are incumbent on her on the basis of her commitment in the marriage contract.

That is the meaning of *nushūz* in the sense of 'rising up' (*irtifāʿ*). Here, the word is used to express metonymically how a woman rises up in disobedience to her husband. Once the signs of that appear in the wife and the husband recognises, after having studied the situation with a fair mind, that it has not arisen out of circumstances to do with the sharia or health, then he is obliged to deal with the situation realistically without overreaction or obduracy, providing an Islamic solution to this problem and establishing order in the marital home on the basis of what was agreed upon in the contract.

In this vein, some people might enquire about cases where psychologically the wife is not in a comfortable enough state to take part in sexual activity. How can sharia legislation then pressure her, in such a situation, and oblige her to respond to her husband's desires, which might then contribute to the destruction of her personality and to giving her complexes at a fundamental level towards that relationship in the future? The response is that Islam does not consider this matter romantically (*shāʿiriyya*) in the way presupposed by the question. Rather, it considers marriage a contractual relationship founded on the true welfare of both spouses, where both commit to relinquish some of their freedom in favour of the mutual duties imposed by the contract on each towards the other. That is the difference between solitary life and communal life: for to be part of a small or large group means to behave as one part of a totality, not as an independent individual. You relinquish some of your freedom for the benefit of that role. In light of that, God willed that marriage protect the couple from sexual deviance and from searching for illicit means. He has required the wife to be responsive to her husband's lawful desires, deeming that a means of [gaining] proximity to God and bestowing upon that responsiveness a spiritual significance that provides her a spiritual state as a replacement for her individual state, in order to guard her husband from seeking out his desires outside of the confines of the marital home, which in the end would result in the destruction of the marriage. Through this, He willed for her to overcome her mood in favour of his desire. For, in losing some of this mood, she gains a firm foothold in confirming the concept of love and mercy [cf. Q. 30:21] in their marital life.

As for the reason for emphasising this aspect in the case of a man, we alluded to it before this discussion, namely that the libido (*ʿunṣur al-ithāra*),[240] which leads to the awakening of sexual desire, is greater in the case of the

[240] Literally, 'the urge element'.

man than the woman. That is why, we note, it is the man who drives a woman to deviance through his various methods, whereas we find that a woman's deviance mostly comes about as a result of a state of material, not sexual, [need]. With the man, it is the converse, since [the need for] sex in his case is an almost daily state, depending on the extent of his libido.

The way in which the question considers this problem does not treat the topic in a realistic way, since it demands the husband to suppress his desire out of respect for hers. We might raise another question: what does a husband do if his wife is experiencing a state of complex sexual frigidity? And what does he do if she is living in protracted psychological crises? Do we demand of him that he freeze his desire so that the matter then turns into a psychological problem? Or do we demand that he seek [to sate] it out outside of the confines of the home, when either way the solution will not be to the benefit of the woman in either the near or the distant future?

We do not deny that there are certain negative aspects to the Islamic solution, but the extent of the positives is higher and greater. We have mentioned more than once that Islam seeks to balance negatives and positives in the way that it anchors legal cases within the parameters of the unlawful and the lawful. In every permissive legislation there are inevitably negatives associated with doing the action, just as in every prohibitive legislation inevitably there are positives when [the action is] avoided. No legislation anywhere in the world, whether religious or otherwise, is one hundred percent positive or negative. By its very nature, it requires the laying out of limits for human beings and then delimiting their freedom on the basis of that, which generates many problems and negatives.

In this vein, we would like to raise a salient point, which is that Islam does not want a man, the husband, to live in a sexual relationship that is barren and cold. Rather, it wants him, in a virtuous and decent way, to set up the conditions that would arouse the woman's desire, by adorning himself for her just as he likes her to adorn herself for him,[241] and respecting her need for sexual satisfaction when he engages in the relationship, not concluding the act until he senses that she has attained what she wants from him. In light of this, the man can, under such conditions, overcome negative psychological states by careful emotive methods, just as the woman is able to achieve the same via self-suggestive methods (*al-asālīb al-īḥāʾiyya al-dhātiyya*), or by means of certain spiritual moods that impel her to attend to her husband's desire, for spiritual reasons, by striving to dissuade him in a way that does

[241] This refers to a *ḥadīth* on the authority of Ibn ʿAbbās found in Ṭabarī's *tafsīr* of Q. 2:228.

not choke him emotionally or cause him to overreact when she is not able to do that at any given point.

From the command given to the husband to live together companionably (*muʿāshara bi'l-maʿrūf*),[242] we might glean certain indications that he should suppress his desire in situations where there is a lot of pressure from the requirement to fulfil that desire, and that this may seem to be at odds with the concept of *maʿrūf*, which Islam wants for him. But all of this belongs within the framework of ethical (*akhlāqī*) self-constitution, which constructs the Muslim personality on spiritual foundations that carry [specific] values (*qiyam*) and ideas (*afkār*), the best method for [evincing] the best kind of human being, and has nothing to do with that requirement, which itself is based on a realistic consideration of the welfare (*maṣāliḥ*) and corruption (*mafāsid*), when one examines the human condition according to its material reality, treating it thereby in a realistic way and arriving at a spiritual cure.

The Qurʾān delimits the methods for dealing with a woman's rebelliousness (*nushūz*)

The first: admonition (*mawʿiẓa*)

Then admonish them: This is the first approach that Islam desires that spouses adopt to deal with cases of rebellion on the part of the wife against conjugal duties, which is the method of admonition. This is done by pursuing thoughtful and spiritual approaches that might caution her against the implications of her act on both this-worldly and other-worldly levels. The husband should make her fear (*khawf*) God's punishment for her disobeying Him concerning those of the husband's rights to which He has obligated her, and the fact that that could lead to the destruction of marital life, reflecting negatively on her future and the future of the children, where there are children. In order to achieve this goal, it is imperative to follow those approaches that will lead to the desired goal, which is her return to the straight way and eschewing deviance.

The approaches vary in accordance with the mental capacity (*dhihniyya*) of the wife intellectually, spiritually and emotionally. All of that must be studied, noting the weak points and strong points of her individual and religious personality, whereafter the situation may be confronted with wisdom

[242] Cf. Q. 4:19.

and flexibility and a time frame for the stages necessary to secure her consent and commitment. But since certain cases require more time, one should not be content with just one or two impromptu words in passing, as some people are wont to do when treating such cases, using hackneyed phrases in a very dry way, bereft of spirit and life, and meaningless for both the speaker and the listener.

The second: forsaking in bed

And forsake them in the beds: This is the second approach that Islam wants the husband to pursue when the first approach, admonition, fails. [It is] a psychological technique of disciplining (*ta'dīb nafsī*), which is to forsake (*hajr*) her in bed by refusing all relations with her (*muqāṭaʿa*), according to some commentators; or to turn his back on her when they sleep in the same place; or to suggest to her, in one way or another, that he does not desire her or care about her. Perhaps this approach, negative as it is, has the greatest effect on the nature of a woman, because her husband's interest in her is considered to be a very important factor in her self-esteem, as affirmed by psychoanalysts in the field.

The third: striking

This is the third approach, which is the approach of striking; but this does not constitute unreasonable striking, which a person commits in an emotional outburst due to a sharp temper, psychological problems, or the need to let off steam. Rather, it is an even-tempered striking for discipline (*ta'dīb*) that gives her a taste of humiliation. The reported *ḥadīth*s show that it is a non-severe strike that does not make the flesh bleed or break the bones, which suggests that it is more of a psychological approach than a physical one. Some have reservations about Islam on account of this approach, since it violates respect for a woman, her dignity and consideration of her as a human being. But in our view, the matter must be tackled from another side: are disciplinary penal methods, such as imprisonment, physical striking and the like, in conflict with basic human dignity, such that the call to remove the punishment becomes the basis of legislation, regardless of the difference between a man and a woman? But this is not something that can be accepted by any nation or people who seek to safeguard their way of life by safeguarding order, and the penal system is part of that general legal framework, considering it as a deterrent factor for criminals and deviants who stray far into criminality and deviance.

In light of this, we must pursue the thought: the marital relationship is one of those human relationships, while it endures, that submits to a fixed arrangement that preserves its equilibrium. But if rebellion occurs against the commitments therein, then what is the solution? Is it left to chance, or is a way of treatment sought?

The former is out of the question because that would mean throwing the relationship to the wind, so the latter is imperative. If the peaceful ways such as admonition and forsaking have been exhausted, that is evidence that the woman does not submit to regular humane methods based on respect, because a woman who does not listen, or respond to psychological pressures, or is not ready to discuss the pros and cons of the matter through calm dialogue is a woman who does not wish to enter into normal relations with others, so how is a man to deal with her? Does he divorce her? Or does he submit her to the relevant courts? Or does he resolve the problem in his own private way?

Divorce is not a solution. It is actually a method of running away from the problem by destroying the very structure within which it arises, whereas Islam attempts to make divorce the last resort, considering that it is the most loathsome of things that have been made lawful by God. As for legal recourse, that is not practical in the likes of these daily incidents which lead to the exposure of many personal and practical secrets. At the same time, many of these instances cannot be proven through legal means, for private activities – especially the sexual aspects of a relationship – are never consummated in front of people. So how can you deal with it and prove anything reasonably in such instances, given what that entails of repeated court appearances, and given the recurrence of these incidents? The subject can only be considered one of those privileges granted to the husband, given his authority (*qiwāma*) over the wife within the framework of marital life. This is exactly like the disciplinary methods that law leaves to the discretion of a manager in everyday emergencies, where employees are constantly straying. But that [privilege] must proceed from a commitment of faith, which will prevent him from pursuing striking outside of the limits permitted by God. For, once he has transgressed God's limits, the wife has the right to raise the matter with a sharia judge in order to make him return to the correct path, because when the matter takes on a different course, it requires the authorities to intervene in order to repulse the aggression and save the victim of that aggression.

We do not deny that in matters such as these, the implementation [of these steps] submits to certain types of personal exploitation on the part of the husband. But the fault in that is not the fault of the legislation; rather, it is a problem of the society, which never proceeds to implement the comprehensive framework in a balanced, enforced way. Perhaps one of the most salient pieces of evidence for this are acts of individual and communal injustice, which do not proceed from the sharia, that allow for exploitation, because of certain loopholes present in it. But this arises out of private and public circumstances that encourage all that is imposed by the struggle between the strong and the weak in life.

But if they obey you, seek not a way against them. These procedures are not imposed as a way of letting off steam, or as an encouragement of acts of injustice, or to impose personal mastery (*sulṭa*); rather, they were imposed in order to confront a problem that required a solution that would help the marital home to stay together and to subsist, and to impel the wife to undertake her responsibilities towards her husband as a fulfilment of God's law. So if the goal is realised at any of the particular stages on the course towards a solution, then it is incumbent on the husband to refrain from any other negative behaviour, because God has not granted him any mastery over her, small or great, outside of the parameters of the prescribed divinely legislated rights.[243]

[243] Faḍl Allāh, *Min waḥy al-Qur'ān*, s.v. Q. 4:34.

Interviews

Grand Ayatollah Saanei

Grand Ayatollah Saanei's style is a didactic question-and-answer format; he is a strong orator and an imposing individual. He begins by addressing the 'problem' with the Qur'ānic verse, which is that it would not be just for men to be in charge of women. He answers this by arguing first that the verse is only connected with marriage, and not other matters, and then by saying that it is not a command, but a verse that instead informs the listener or reader about reality. The words at the beginning of the verse are not in the form of an order; they are descriptive. For Grand Ayatollah Saanei, this description follows the characteristics of other informative sentences that have been put in the place of laws; but it is not legally binding. According to him, this sentence expresses a preference but is not an obligatory command, so the spouses can arrange the household however they want. If they agree that they should bear joint responsibility for it, they can do so. He then moves on to the second part of the verse, which includes the command to *strike them*. His argument is that this is a type of joke and is not a serious matter. It would not be striking with a stick, but rather the type of thing that is 'appropriate between a man and his wife', such as 'striking' with a toothbrush. When I asked him in the interview whether this was the best way to bring women round, he insisted that it was a joke rather than anything serious. For him, there is an issue if any striking is severe, or intended to cause harm; but that is not the case here. In this case, for him, it is a type of tap to get the wife's attention. Such an action is not obligatory.

Ayatollah Saanei: *Men are maintainers of women, by that which God has distinguished the one over the other, and by that which they expend of their property.*

The problem with this verse is that it has empowered men over women (*musallaṭūn ʿalā al-mar'a*). The meaning of *qawwām* is that they are their guardians, and they are their commanders. And this command is contrary to justice. How is it possible for men to be commanders over women?

The answer is that *qawwāmūn* means 'those who undertake such affairs'; it is about management (*tadbīr*). But in this verse, the 'management' has to do solely with marriage, and not with other matters. It does not mean that women cannot have a place in parliament, or that they cannot make mutual decisions. It does not give [men] the right to leadership (*riyāsa*) and power (*salṭana*) and guardianship (*wilāya*) and other matters. The verse is, firstly, connected with marriage. This is the first point.

The second point is that the verse is not an indication of a ruling that is incumbent and necessary for obedience to God (*laysa madlūl al-āya ḥukm al-wujūb wa'l-ilzām al-ilāhī*). We cannot derive from this verse that God has made man *qayyām* over his wife, as He made the Prophet *qayyām* over the people. Rather, the indication of the verse is that it is an informative statement (*jumlatun khabariyya*), telling about reality (*ikhbār li'l-wāqiʿiyya*) – the visible reality, as it is in many societies today and in the past. In the small kingdom, that is, the house, it is necessary to have a director (*mudīr*) and a manager (*mudabbir*). And, so, people have given the role of manager and director to the husband. This is information (*ikhbār*) about the real situation, just as when God, exalted be He, informs us that the sun is hot, and that the sun and the moon are *for reckoning* (*ḥusbān*) [Q. 6:96]. Is the fact that the sun and the moon rise and set a law, or is it a clarification for the purpose of knowledge (*bayān ʿilmī*)?

Karen Bauer: A clarification for the purpose of information.

Ayatollah Saanei: Yes, and there are some clarifications (*bayān*) that are informative. In the story of Joseph, he said that twelve stars bowed down to him. Is the story of Joseph historical and informative, or is it legal (*qānūniyya*)?

Karen Bauer: Historical.

Ayatollah Saanei: The story of Abraham. Is it historical or legal? It's historical! *We will tell you the best of stories* [Q. 12:3]. Or it may be an indication of a present reality. *When one is given the news of a female, his face immediately darkens, barely able to contain himself* (*kaẓīm*) [Q. 16:58]. Is this a statement of information, or a law?

Karen Bauer: Information (*ikhbār*).

Ayatollah Saanei: Information! Yes. It is not in the form of an order! The *dustūr*, or order, has a specific mode of expression in Arabic. Rise and pray (*aqīmū al-ṣalāt*)! It is an order. A command. The means of expression is specific. This verse does not have the form of an order. Men are *qawwāmūn* over women. It means that men take care of women, they manage women. *By that which God has distinguished the one over the other*, not 'distinguished men over women', but 'the one over the other'. There is a superiority of men and a superiority of women. *And by that which they expend*. The maintenance is the man's responsibility. If one household wants to give the administration (*mudīra*) to the wife, that does not contradict the divine law. This verse is not a clarification of the law, but is, rather, an informative verse. If a man wants to make his wife the director of the house, it doesn't contradict the revelation, and it doesn't constitute disobedience to God, because this verse is not a legal verse, but an *ikhbār wāqiʿiyya*. The information has been renewed (*qad yatajaddad*). So the verse is information, the phrase is an informative phrase (*jumla khabariyya*).

The third point is regarding putting an informative sentence in the place of a law. Sometimes these informative sentences stand in the place of a law or an order. If the father wants the son to wash his hands, he says: Wash your hands! And this is an order. But he may say: My son, he washes his hands. It is informing about it, but it is in the place of an order. But the informative sentences in place of a law, according to me and to some of the other *ʿulamāʾ*, do not assume the place of a necessary duty or an absolute requirement. It is what is preferred. If the man is the *mudabbir*, it is better than if the woman is the *mudabbira*. In my opinion, and in the opinion of some of the other *ʿulamāʾ*, when an informative sentence comes in the place of the law, we cannot derive from that an obligatory command. If it says 'he washes his hands', it means 'wash your hands', but it is not an obligatory ruling (*luzūm*). It is, instead, preferred (*maṭlūb*), not a necessity or a law. The law must have clear orders, not roundabout ones.

Karen Bauer: But what about the next part of the verse, *if you fear the women's defiance*?

Ayatollah Saanei: Strike them! In this verse, there is not an obligatory ruling (*laysa dustūr ilzāmiyya*). Not in this verse. It is instead a type of joke (*mizāḥ*) and a way of making the wife return to the husband. The first thing to do is admonish them. There is no violence in an admonishment. It is simply a time in which the husband appeals to the wife's emotions and arouses her desire. The second step is to abandon them in the beds. This is turning their backs on them. The third is to strike them. But the striking is a type of joke. It is not striking them with a sword, but rather striking them in a way that is appropriate between a man and his wife in specific circumstances. And this is clarified in [Imam] al-Bāqir (*ʿm*). Al-Bāqir said that the striking is with a toothbrush. Have you seen the *siwāk* (traditional toothbrush)? A strike with that is nothing but a game (*laʿib*), a joke (*mizāḥ*). The striking is not a violent striking, but a joking type of striking in order to bring the woman round. It is not a striking of power and might. This opinion is given on the authority of al-Bāqir (*ʿm*) in the *tafsīr Majmaʿ al-bayān*.

Karen Bauer: And now – in the present time, now, in our days – ?

Ayatollah Saanei: Our days!

Karen Bauer: Is this the best way? Striking? Should people still follow this verse?

Ayatollah Saanei: If a man follows this verse, there is no harm in it. If he goes against it, there is no harm in that (*lā baʾsa ʿalayhi*).

Karen Bauer: Hmmm.

Ayatollah Saanei: The problem is violent striking. But this striking is not severe! It is to bring about love (*jalb al-maḥabba*). The admonishment is

done from love (*jalb al-maḥabba*), the abandoning in the beds is done from love (*jalb al-maḥabba*) and the striking is with a toothbrush. These English![244]
Hedayat Yousefi:[245] Some of the *'ulamā'* have said that *nushūz* is only to do with sexual matters. Is that correct?
Ayatollah Saanei: The *nushūz* is only in matters between a husband and wife, and it is not about any other matters. *Righteous women are devoutly obedient* – in other words, obedient to the husband in marital matters,[246] not obedient in all matters. If a man is responsible for paying the maintenance and takes care of her, then our rationality tells us that she should be obedient to him in marital matters and not go against him. Because the husband pays the maintenance. He bears the responsibility for maintaining her. He bears the responsibility of management. Therefore, in this case, should the wife be obedient in marital matters or should she be recalcitrant? [Silence] Obedient! *Righteous women are devoutly obedient women* indicates the thing that the mind also agrees with, which is that the wife should be obedient in sexual matters. And after that, *those who safeguard during absence*, in other words, safeguarding themselves for them. And then *if you fear the women's defiance* – in other words, *nushūz* in sexual matters.
Karen Bauer: What about when he doesn't pay the maintenance (*nafaqa*)?
Ayatollah Saanei: Well then it is her right to leave the marriage. If he doesn't maintain her, she can leave. She can go to the court and leave the marriage.
Karen Bauer: And in our day, many women work –
Ayatollah Saanei: That is what I explained before! It is not a legal order (*ḥukm qānūn*)!
Karen Bauer: Okay.
Ayatollah Saanei: It's a statement about reality! If the woman wants to be the director, the *mudabbira*, then there's no harm in it. If she wants to be *muqayamma* and to pay maintenance for the man – then there's no harm in it! It is not an obligatory ruling! It is not obligatory! It is a statement of reality.

[244] Here he means to say that Karen Bauer was looking at things with the presuppositions of her cultural background, rather than giving the Qur'ānic text the benefit of the doubt and understanding his view: that the intention is not to harm, but to bring about a loving atmosphere.

[245] Various people accompanied Karen Bauer on her interviews in Iran, and these other interlocutors often gave more depth and richness to the interviews; sometimes they even added their own views. Dr Hedayat Yousefi was, at the time, the acting director of the Centre for the Study of Human Rights at Mofid University, the centre which had sponsored Karen Bauer's visit to Iran to conduct the interviews. In this instance, he knew that this was a question that she had asked other clerics, and asked it because he could see that she had forgotten to ask it.

[246] This is a euphemism for sexual relations.

Fariba Alasvand

Fariba Alasvand discussed many things in our interview, including the importance of taking into account all of the Qur'ānic verses on women. For her, it is important to understand the legal culture of the Qur'ān as a whole in order to understand the particular verses in question. She explained that the legal culture of the Qur'ān promotes a generosity among the spouses, which means that the husband should not oppress his wife, even if he might have the ability to do so. He should not prevent her from leaving the house for things like work or to take a walk. Crucially, spouses should make decisions in consultation with each other. However, in the event that the spouses disagree, the husband's word carries the day. Equally, wives may work to support the household, but they are never *qawwāmāt* over their husbands. Thus, for Alasvand, the spouses have roles that are determined by their sex, which is an indicator of certain aspects of their innate nature. Unlike some other commentators, Alasvand admitted that some people today might use these concepts for harmful ends. But she insists that this is not the fault of the system, but rather of the people who abuse it. When I asked whether striking would be the best way to make a woman understand and be willing to have sex with her husband, Alasvand responded that the time for an emotional appeal is during the admonishment, where the husband uses soft and gentle words to try to convince the wife. The striking must not be painful and must not leave a mark, otherwise the husband is liable to pay for it.

In communication via email in 2021, a decade after this interview took place, Dr. Alasvand shared some of her recent research on the terminology of the family, such as *qawwāmiyya*. In this research she describes how the medieval interpreters – particularly Sunnī interpreters – were influenced by their own cultural presuppositions in their understanding of the term, which, in her view, led to errors in their understanding. She describes a change in the culture of interpretation in the modern period, to a more holistic view of the term. Her work represents an important trend among the *ʿulamāʾ*; although she critiques feminist interpretations, she concurrently makes room for new understandings of key Qur'ānic terminology.

Karen Bauer: I would like to ask about [Q. 2:228], *Women have rights like their obligations, according to common decency (maʿrūf), but men have a degree over them.* Maybe there is a connection between this and *men are qawwamun over women* [Q. 4:34].

Fariba Alasvand: In order to understand what the Qur'ān has said, it is necessary to gather together all of the verses, and to see what the Qur'ān says with regards to all of them. For instance, in the time of Imam al-Ṣādiq, there was a heretic[247] who was named Ibn Abī'l-ʿAwjāʾ.[248] He looked into many

[247] She used the term *zindīq* in Arabic, while also saying 'materialist' in English. *Zindīq* would normally, however, be understood as 'heretic' while 'materialist' would be *dahrī*.

[248] On Ibn Abī'l-ʿAwjāʾ and whether he was a historical figure, see Ghasem Bostani, 'Ibn Abī Al-Awja: His Historical Existence and the Evaluations of the Claims about Him', *Quranic Sciences and Tradition* 50.1 (2017), 9–31, doi: 10.22059/jqst.2017.224588.668787.

questions in the Qur'ān, and he had a specific view of the words of the Qur'ān. You know that there is no contradiction in the Qur'ān, but he would read one verse and then read a second verse as though it contradicted the first verse. And the imam said that there is in the Qur'ān the general and specific, the *muṭlaq* and the *muqayyad*. Understanding and knowing the Qur'ān requires knowing and understanding all of it. In order to take a theory or a specific view, we must look at the situation in general. I have written in my book, in the first chapter, entitled 'the place of human beings.' This chapter consists of philosophical research connected with moral philosophy. And in this chapter are two sections, one about philosophy and one about the Qur'ān. And in another chapter I have undertaken research on laws. Legal verses have a particular context. In my philosophical chapter, I wrote about Ibn Sina, and others. I wrote about the gauge (*mi'yār*) of human beings in the Qur'ān. I have written about the human being as a human being: the essential humanity of people. The research is on this gauge (*mi'yār*).

With regards to the Qur'ān, we must consider (*'aql*) basic matters. We must consider the source of all life, God, blessed and exalted, and we must consider the goals of life, the purpose. We must consider the context of the Qur'ān, and of the sending of the Prophet – the basic fundamentals of life. Humans are the one being that is able to consider these matters, and to know about these issues: a human being is called 'human' if he is capable of thinking of moral matters, of good and bad. We call this 'practical reasoning' (*al-'aql al-'amalī*). We know the difference between theoretical reasoning (*al-'aql al-naẓarī*) and practical reasoning: theoretical reasoning (*'aql*) understands what is present and what is not present, and practical reasoning (*'aql*) is understands what is a good action and what is a detestable action. The one who is able to think in this way, and to tell the difference between good and bad, this is a person (*insān*) in the Noble Qur'ān. And also, the human being is the one being that is able to look and to understand the reality of things as they are in particular times and places. In the mystical (*'irfān*) Islam we call this 'witnessing' (*shuhūd*): direct understanding of the higher reality (*al-dark al-mubāshir bi'l-nisba ilā al-ḥaqā'iq al-'ulyā*).

Karen Bauer: And all of these types of *'aql*, put together, comprise the intellect (*'aql*) . . . And this intellect (*'aql*) is humanity?

Fariba Alasvand: Yes, all of this, these are the gauge that need to be present in order to call a person a person. The human being is a being that is rational, a being that is moral. And in this regard, in the Qur'ān, the human being is the one who is able to obtain happiness. Happiness is possible through a good life in this world, and in reaching the Garden, the Hereafter. I believe that the Qur'ān speaks of the equality of men and women from these bases. It says that *Any believer, male or female* (*unthā*), *who does righteous work, verily We shall grant him a goodly life, and verily We shall repay them their wages equal to the best of their works* [Q. 16:97].

So what is the meaning of the 'degree' [that men have over women] in this regard? Of course with regard to these fixed (*muḥkama*) philosophical issues in the Qur'ān, we may reach the following result: this degree is not a degree of humanity;[249] the degree is of course a degree of difference. The ground in which this verse is based is that of rights: *Women have rights like their obligations, according to common decency* (*ma'rūf*), *but men have a degree over them* (Q. 2:228). This verse suggests (*yutraḥ*) a society in which they did not believe in any rights for women. The Qur'ān emphasised (*akkada*) that women have rights like their obligations. Meaning that they do not simply have duties; rather, they also have rights. But *men have a degree over them* (*li'l-rijāl 'alayhinna daraja*) means that men have a particular right with regards to women. And in the Shī'ī narrations, this verse is interpreted – for instance, in the narrations of Imam al-Riḍā, he says that men have the right of inheritance, or the right of *qawwāmiyya*. Only the right of inheritance or *qawwāmiyya*. To interpret this verse with regards to the *qawwāmiyya* indicates the chain of organization of the hierarchy within the house (*silsilat al-marātib li'l-riyāsa fī'l-bayt*). Meaning in Islamic thought, in the society of the family, there is a hierarchical chain: the people sharing in the house need a director. For sure, they need some administration. The presence of the administration is necesitated by differences (*li-farḍ al-ikhtilāfāt*), because the original principle of the Muslim house is consultation (*tashāwur*). Even in the Noble Qur'ān, the concept of consultation is mentioned even in the situation of deciding when the woman should stop nursing the child [Q. 2:233]. The issue of consultation is an important issue in Islam. I believe that the rights and duties in Islam have their own culture. The legal culture is more important than the letter of the law.

Karen Bauer: This is an important point.

Fariba Alasvand: For instance, God, exalted be He, gave the headship (*riyāsa*) of the household to the man. But the culture of that control is very specific. The head of the people is their servant (*ra'īs al-qawm khādimuhum*). The headship is not dictatorial (*istibdād*). Instead, the head of the people is their servant (*ra'īs al-qawm khādimuhum*). So much so, that it is necessary for the head to engage in consultation (*yajib 'alā al-ra'īs al-tashāwur*) [Cf.

[249] Alasvand is here emphasising that women and men are ontologically equal.

Q. 42:38]. Even if the head is a prophet, he consults with regard to the command [Cf. Q. 3:159]. Many Shīʿī narrations deal with the issue of consultation and assure us (*akkadū ʿalā*) that whoever is dictatorial in their opinions is an oppressor (*ẓālim*), meaning that whoever is selfish is also oppressive. This issue is called the culture of rights: people have their rights, but Islam gives to those rights a particular culture. It is necessary for the husband to engage in consultation with his wife. Freedom and happiness are present in the house through the use of both of their minds.

Karen Bauer: I have a question. If there is a discussion between the two of them, and there is a difference in their two opinions, what happens?

Fariba Alasvand: In some issues, the *qawwāmiyya* refers to this. If there is a difference between them, and the difference is not resolved by consultation, then the opinion of the husband holds, in certain specific instances.

Karen Bauer: For instance?

Fariba Alasvand: For instance, in the choice of house, in all of the issues of marital life; not in any one particular issue. For instance, differences in opinion between the children and the parents.

Karen Bauer: But the wife is not a child! The husband and wife are both – they both have rationality, they both have the same human value, and so why does the decision go to the husband and why isn't it resolved through consultation and discussion between the two of them?

Fariba Alasvand: First, there is consultation and agreement. In Muslim houses, for instance in Iran, the majority of the decisions are based on consultation and agreement. In most situations, the opinion is that of the wife, and the husband agrees with her! But in certain specific situations, the final decision is given to one person. The meaning of this is not that the others do not have rational sense (*ʿaql*); but in any administration, we may discuss, and we may consult, and not reach a conclusion. Of course, one person has to be in charge of that administration. It is necessary. There is a new idea about the house, connected with someone called Anthony Giddens.[250] He believes in a democratic family. But there is an obscure point about his view. I would like to ask of Anthony Giddens: if there are differences between the wife and the husband and –

[250] Anthony Giddens is a prominent English sociologist who in his book *The Transformation of Intimacy: Sexuality, Love, and Eroticism in Modern Societies* (Palo Alto, CA, Stanford University Press, 1992) put forth a vision of an egalitarian family based in part on women achieving sexual equality and an equal right to sexual pleasure in marriage. By referring to Giddens, Alasvand is showing that she is familiar with academic theories of family relationships; many such works have been translated into Farsi.

Karen Bauer: And they cannot resolve it, then how could they resolve it?
Fariba Alasvand: Yes, but he believes that conversation can resolve it – but the conversation could last until when? This will constantly be happening in the house.
Karen Bauer: Well, my question is this: why does the man have this power [to decide]?
Fariba Alasvand: Yes, well, in Islam, the man has a duty to pay maintenance, and *men are maintainers of women* (*al-rijālu qawwāmūna ʿalā al-nisāʾ*) means undertaking the administration of the house. Therefore, the man, who undertakes this responsibility, of course should have an advantage, and that advantage is the administration of the family. And our jurists say that the man who does not give the maintenance to his household, does not have the *qawwāmiyya*.
Karen Bauer: If he does not have work in that time, and she does have work at that time, or, for instance, if, unfortunately, my husband lost his work, then I would be paying for the house. I know that in Islamic law it is not necessary for me to maintain the house, but this is an ideal. However, in our world, sometimes the wife works and maintains the house. I know that this is not her [Islamic] responsibility, but in reality, it happens.
Fariba Alasvand: The financial maintenance of the house leads to the household administration. But Islam ensures (*akkada*) that the gender role of the man is to pay the maintenance (*al-dawr al-jinsī li'l-rajul al-infāq*). The intention of 'gender role' is the role that it is necessary for the man and the woman to adhere to with regard to biology and to law (*ḥuqūq*). For instance, pregnancy is a woman's role, with regard to her natural capacity. And the maintenance is a gender role. Men and women both work in the society, and this is not connected to gender. In the Islamic legal system, women's salary is kept for themselves, while men's salary pays for both men and women, as you have said. And the important point for Islam is the preservation of this system. Meaning that the woman can work if she likes, and she can take her salary for herself, and it is necessary for the husband to pay maintenance to her, for the house and the children. And if there is a difference of opinion under this system, then of course the last word must go to the husband. In the contract [of marriage] it is possible for the woman to include clauses that limit the man's *qawwāmiyya* over her. The wife may impose a condition on her husband that she may choose the house or the city in which they live.
Karen Bauer: Or if he were to marry another person, then she would have the power of divorce, for instance.
Fariba Alasvand: Yes. Well done. The intention of these points is to preserve the unity of the family. But in the West, I believe that the place of the family

is not connected with these issues. The wife is a person, the husband is a person, and they are both thinking and mature. But, of course, if they wish to preserve the family, it is necessary [to dispense with this sort of attitude]. The basis for Western life is individuality, but in Islam it is communality. It is present in the narrations, that the woman is the head of the family: a person came to Imam al-Ḥusayn and asked, 'Why are there beautiful carpets and so forth in your house?' He replied, 'We pay the maintenance and the bridal payment to our wives, and they spend it how they wish.' That means that the woman is free in her husband's house. For you, everything leads to individuality, but for us everything is communal. For instance, even when children have grown up, they must respect their parents, and the parents have a greater right over their children. That does not mean that the children are always children.

Karen Bauer: So – even if the woman is paying maintenance for the house, [the husband] has the right of *qiwāma* over her? Is this due to something in him, with regard to his mind (*ʿaql*)?

Fariba Alasvand: The *qiwāma* means the administration of the house. And the ruling that is necessary, in exchange for the *qiwāma*, is the *tamkīn* of the wife. And *tamkīn* has a specific meaning: the intimate relations between a husband and wife. The man is *qawwām* over the woman, in this regard, and over her leaving the house. Leaving the house does not mean that it is not possible for the woman to leave the house, but rather it means that they must both agree to it. For instance, my husband is a scholar (*muʿammam*). Of course, I work outside of the house, and I leave the house to go walking, and it is not necessary for the woman to get permission for every little thing.

Karen Bauer: Yes, my husband is the same way, he is a professor in a university. But if our husbands were not at that level, if they had limited views, if they had not gone to university, if they were not cultured, if we were in a small village, and he does not know – but it is possible that I have gone to the university –

Fariba Alasvand: Yes, well done (*aḥsantī*). This issue about which you've spoken is that for all rights there is a culture, and [the moral] culture is very important, it is more important than the rights themselves. It is necessary for us to look at Islamic rights in light of Islamic culture. I believe that we cannot reach happiness simply by taking advantage of our rights. For instance, in Islam men have *qawwāmiyya*. You may say that we must take the *qawwāmiyya* from men and give it to women, because it is possible for men to take advantage of this issue. Just as it is possible for the mother, by virtue of her heightened feelings, to take advantage of (*yastabidd*) the children. The powerful may take advantage of the weak. Oppression of the weak may occur on the part of any powerful person.

Karen Bauer: Yes, true.

Fariba Alasvand: And, of course, reaching happiness is not simply taking advantage of all of one's rights, as you have in the West. In some points in the past, women have been oppressed, and now it is possible for men to take advantage of women. Everyone who has power, in terms of their physiology or in terms of their rights, may oppress others. I will give you an example of what I mean by the 'cultural rights'. It is necessary in Islamic law that the man pays the woman's maintenance according to what she has been accustomed to. But in some cases the husband must pay more than what was in her father's house. Of course, I understand that Muslims may derive an incorrect meaning from *qawwāmiyya*. But all of the people may take an incorrect meaning from all laws. We internalise our norms, which has to do not with the laws, but primarily with the upbringing within the home, and secondarily with the official education that one receives in school.

Karen Bauer: And what about *nushūz*? I understand (and if I have not understood correctly, please correct me) that *nushūz* relates specifically to the sexual relations between a wife and husband. If the wife refuses him, then this is *nushūz*. Is this correct?

Fariba Alasvand: Yes, when the wife refuses her husband. But *nushūz* is a ruling (*ḥukm*) with regard to the wife and with regard to the husband. The *nushūz* of the wife is her refusal of the husband in sexual matters, and the *nushūz* of the husband is non-payment of maintenance and not engaging in sexual relations for more than four months. God, exalted be He, has provided a cure for these very particular marital issues. Maybe there is a sexual problem between the husband and wife. But this issue is a private matter, between a wife and a husband: Islam does not permit anyone else to see this kind of behaviour. So it is not possible for any husband to go to the court and say 'my wife has stopped doing this'. In this matter, in Islamic law, the word of the husband is not accepted in a court of law. Why? Because it may be possible for all husbands to claim that their wives have stopped performing their sexual duties. We have a solution to this matter. You may say that it is possible for a husband to divorce his wife. Yes, of course after divorce the problem will be solved, but with regard to the head, not the heart.

We say that in the marital realm, Islam gives a sure-fire technique to solve these problems. What is this solution? The Qur'ān ensures a three-fold organised solution. The first is the admonishment. And admonishment is tender (*layyin*), emotional words, because the sexual relationship, especially for the woman, is an emotional issue. She has the view of the feelings, while the man's view is exclusively to biology. And if the admonishment does not work, then they move on to the second stage. And in the Qur'ān, *tafsīr* and Islamic law, it is not possible for the husband to go to the second stage unless he has failed in the previous stage. So, then, after the admonishment he moves on to the next stage, which is the forsaking in the bed. This means that he turns his face away from her. And if this fails, then he can go on to the third and strongest stage. It is not possible to move on unless he has no other options.

In Islam, in commanding right and forbidding wrong [cf. Q. 3:104, 110 *et passim*], it is necessary [when someone commits a public wrong] first to say something, but if the solution to the problem cannot be found in that way then it can be solved through striking – of course [in public lawbreaking] this matter is in the power of the judge. But in the sexual relationship between the husband and wife, there is no other person present, and it is up to them to solve the problem themselves. If the wife does not undertake her duties, there are of course other options. Maybe the husband will go to another woman, for example. Maybe he will have a sexual relationship with another woman. But we search for the solution to this problem [by keeping it] between the husband and the wife. So after the admonishment and the abandonment, we go to the third option, and that is the striking. But [we must consider] the culture of rights at the time of this verse. The Prophet was always saying to the people, 'Do not strike anyone except the cursed one (*la'īn*), and do not honour anyone except the blessed (*karīm*)'. He always said it. And Imam al-Ṣādiq says to us that the hitting is with the *siwāk*, which is a very soft strike. In Imāmī jurisprudence (*fiqh*), for instance, in the thought of Imam Khomeini, it must not leave any mark or any bruise, and it should cause no pain. If there is pain and it leaves a scar, then you can accept blood money (*diya*) for it.

Karen Bauer: Because you have said before that the sexual relationship for the woman is something special, and something emotional, and she might have feelings about it, is this striking the best way to get to her heart? Is this the best way to – if she is emotional and sensitive in this regard, is this going to change her to become correct? If my husband struck me, even just like this [slaps own hand lightly], it would be a shock to me. It would not make me feel like . . .

Fariba Alasvand: This issue is solved in the Qur'ān at the time of the admonishment. The admonishment is kind words, emotional words; the majority of women will return to the correct path after the admonishment. This is the first stage. But with this issue, there is a rational necessity (*lā buddiyya ʿaqliyya*). These issues are solved through the rational necessity.

All men understand intuitively through experiential knowledge of the law that living well with women requires women's own backing (*mu'āwana*). If the woman does not like to live together, or to share in sexual matters, then the man and the woman do not both taste the sweetness of the sexual relationship. The difference between women and men in this regard leads to many problems. Not all men, Muslim or non-Muslim, are capable of understanding the other person. They cannot walk in the other person's shoes.

Karen Bauer: So if the man was *nāshiz* by not having [intimate] relations with her for four months, then it is not her right to admonish him, or abandon him in the bed, or strike him?

Fariba Alasvand: We must look at the physical differences between the spouses on this issue. Women, from the point of view of the physical body, are not able to work as men work. It is because of this that the law, the court and the judge help women in this issue. They help her to obtain her rights. It is possible for her to take her husband to court and for the judge to force the man in this issue, to return natural order to the house.

Mehdi Mehrizi

Mehdi Mehrizi's interpretation is radical in that he suggests that Q. 4:34 has been abrogated. His proof is a different occasion of revelation than that of Ḥabība bt. Zayd. That occasion must be false, according to Mehrizi, because it states that God wanted one thing and the Prophet wanted something else. Mehrizi questions how the Prophet could possibly want something different from what God wanted. The real occasion, he contends, is one that had been mentioned by Fakhr al-Dīn al-Rāzī, which is that this verse was revealed in a time of war. According to Mehrizi, the men needed to feel masculine at that moment. After this verse was revealed, according to Mehrizi, the Prophet said that women should not be struck except in cases of manifest lewdness, just like men. Mehrizi also questions the wording of the verse. The end of the verse is an order – 'strike them!' – but, he points out, no interpreter ever interpreted it as an order which had to be obeyed. He therefore says that even if there was an order originally, it was subsequently removed. He ends the interview by describing how interpreters are influenced by their own opinions and their milieu.

Karen Bauer: And as for *al-rijālu qawwāmūna ʿalā al-nisāʾ* [Q. 4:34]?

Mehdi Mehrizi: Yes, I say in an article that this verse has been abrogated.

Karen Bauer: Abrogated! Oh! The whole verse?

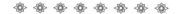

Mehdi Mehrizi: Yes. I have proofs for this matter. I have written on this. I speak about Ayatollah Maʿrifa. He also, after reading my article, said that this verse was abrogated by degrees (*nusikhat tadrījiyyan*). He said that the matter of the striking is like the matter of slavery. Islam wished to abrogate this with the passage of time. I have spoken about this issue in this book. My proof is that this verse was revealed three years after the Hijra of the Prophet to Medina. All of the exegetes say that a woman complained about her husband and went to the Prophet –

Karen Bauer: Yes, Ḥabība bt. Zayd.

Mehdi Mehrizi: And with regard to the striking, the Messenger ordered *qiṣāṣ* (retaliation), but in the end, the Messenger said, 'I wanted one thing and God wanted something different, and what God wants is better'. But how can this be? How could it be like this?

The *muhājirūn* who came to Medina from Mecca were very strict (*mutashaddidūn*) with regard to women's issues. For instance, 'Umar b. al-Khaṭṭāb said to the Prophet: 'Our women have been disobedient'; this matter was difficult for the *muhājirūn*. This verse was revealed before the battle of Uḥud, when there was a crisis, and they said, 'How can we sacrifice (*nuḍaḥḥī*) ourselves for our religion, while we are not able to strike our own women?' This verse was revealed. The morning after this verse was revealed, seventy women went to the house of the Prophet and said, 'Our husbands struck us last night!' So after this verse was revealed, seventy women complained! And after this verse, the Prophet spoke about striking, in another context. He said, 'Do not strike anyone except for the cursed one (*la'īn*), and do not honour anyone except the blessed (*karīm*)' (*lā yaḍribu illā al-la'īn, wa lā yukrima illā al-karīm*). And he said in his Farewell Pilgrimage Oration, which was his last speech ever, 'Do not strike women, except in the case of manifest lewdness (*fāḥisha mubayyana*)'.

Karen Bauer: And [the striking should be] non-severe (*ghayr mubarriḥ*)?

Mehdi Mehrizi: No, no, no! Do not strike women at all, except in the case of manifest lewdness. And this applies to the man as well: the man is struck in cases of manifest lewdness, just as the woman is struck in those cases. And there is another matter regarding this [issue]. It is in the form of a command: strike them! And an order is given in cases of obligation (*wujūb*) or in cases of preponderance *rujḥān* [of evidence]

Hedayat Yousefi: In fiqh, we say that this is either as a command, an order, that you must do, or it is better that you do it. It is *wājib* or it is better (*istaḥabba*).

Mehdi Mehrizi: But no exegetes have said that the striking is either prescribed (*mustaḥabbun*) or necessary (*wājib*). All of them say that the meaning is that it is permitted (*jawāz*). There is a tenet in the principles of Islamic jurisprudence (*uṣūl al-fiqh*) that if there is a prohibition and afterwards a command, then it means that it is permissible. For instance, if you were to go to the doctor and he said, 'Do not eat hummus', but then after you have been cured, and taken medicine, he says, 'Eat hummus', what is the meaning of this order to eat? It means that the prohibition has been removed. So *strike them* removes the prohibition on striking that had existed before, which was the Prophet's prohibition on striking women in the first three years of the Hijra. And because of this, they say that this verse was revealed with regard to a specific matter and in a specific situation. It wished to end the *fitna* (crisis).

Karen Bauer: The *asbāb al-nuzūl* about Habiba bt. Zayd that you mentioned earlier, is this refuted because the Prophet is infallible, and therefore it would not be possible for him to say, 'I wanted one thing and God wanted another'?

Mehdi Mehrizi: The matter was like that for some time, but then the Prophet said: Do not strike those except for the *laʿīn* and do not honour those except for the honourable ones.

Karen Bauer: What about . . . there are other verses – for instance, *Your women are like your sowing fields* [Q. 2:223] . . .?

Mehdi Mehrizi: *Your women are like your sowing fields, so tend to your sowing fields however you desire.*

Karen Bauer: What about that?

Mehdi Mehrizi: I speak about this matter, in that this is a matter which indicates that women should be honoured. This indicates that the woman is a human being which resembles a field. She is a field for birth, for propagation of the people. He means to say that just as much as you respect the ground that gives you fruit, so should you also respect your wife, because she brings you children and she helps you to propagate the species. Just as the ground is respected, so should your wife be respected.

Karen Bauer: And then what about the wife who cannot have babies?

Mehdi Mehrizi: It is speaking generally and typically. It says that woman in general is a source for production, and you should respect them as such. If your earth is not good, you can step on it, but if your ground is fertile, you respect it.

Karen Bauer: So the verse of tillage orders men to respect their wives, because the wives may –

Mehdi Mehrizi: I believe that this verse wishes to clarify the responsibility (*raʿiyya*) of man to woman. A woman is not a toy for the man to play with. Some *ḥadīth*s say that the men in the time before Islam sought to use women in any way they wished. This verse says no, they can't do that. *Your women are like your sowing fields*. They are the source of life, they are the source of birth, they are the source of the propagation of the species. So it is necessary for you to behave towards her as you would your tillage. Not like a toy. There are around three hundred verses about women in the Qur'ān.

Karen Bauer: Oh yes, I know.

Mehdi Mehrizi: There are about eighteen problematic verses. And in one of my articles I've written about these problems. I have divided these verses into three types. The section on exegetes is about the problems in exegesis. The section on exegetes says that all of them interpret according to . . .
Karen Bauer: Their opinion!
Mehdi Mehrizi: Their opinion, and their thoughts, and their place and culture. Culture affects the *tafsīr.* The culture of an Arab exegete, the culture of an Iranian exegete, and so forth.

Sa'diyya Shaikh

Sa'diyya Shaikh speaks here about her work on the '*tafsīr* of praxis'. In an article of that name, she describes the interpretation of the Qur'ān by lay women through their lived realities of domestic abuse; but in this interview she clarifies that all *tafsīr* is a '*tafsīr* of praxis', by which she means that all *tafsīr* is affected by the concerns and preconceptions of its authors, and no author of *tafsīr* can escape their own personal circumstances. Shaikh herself conducted interviews of Muslim women who had suffered spousal abuse, and in response to Q. 4:34, most of Shaikh's interviewees rejected the interpretations of their local religious authorities by rejecting the idea that any form of wife beating could be moral; only one interviewee felt that she should be a better Muslim and more patient with her husband. In our conversation, we questioned what it might mean to have a method based on lived experience rather than traditional interpretations, and whether that decentring of interpretative authority could become a means of social change. In her response, Shaikh admitted that not every woman would take an emancipatory reading of Q. 4:34. It is thus unclear whether highlighting women's experiences would lead to reinterpretation or social change. The interview moved on to a discussion of the hermeneutics of modern reformist Qur'ānic interpretation. On the whole, reformists reject the idea that this verse should be implemented, but they follow different methods for explaining its presence in the Qur'ān. The most common method is historical contextualisation. Some reformists say that this verse is abrogated; Shaikh argues that her interview subjects were abrogating the verse in practice. Feras Hamza raised the question of whether the Qur'ān's 'barbed wire moments' could be considered an impetus for a deeper moral engagement, a type of moral test.[251] In his view, a problem occurs when the Qur'ān's passages that outline boundaries, edges or rules are mistaken for its morally prescriptive content.

[251] With regard to Q. 4:34, Laury Silvers has presented a similar argument: 'I argue that the purpose of the existence of this verse would be to remind human beings of the extraordinary burden of freedom. Specifically, human responsibility is only meaningful if we choose from comprehensive possibilities: ranging, in this case, from gladly accepting the right to beat one's wife to properly refusing to interpret this verse as a permission, let alone a command of God.' Laury Silvers, '"In the Book We Have Left out Nothing": The Ethical Problem of the Existence of Verse 4:34 in the Qur'an', *Comparative Islamic Studies* 2.2 (2008), 171–80.

Karen Bauer: So we'd like to talk about what you have defined as the '*tafsīr* of praxis'. You've coined the term '*tafsīr* of praxis', which refers to a type of Qur'ānic hermeneutics that is not based on the textual tradition but is informed by the 'full, embodied realities of Muslim women'.[252] This is because, as you described, everyone's experience and cultural presuppositions inform their exegesis, so including the voices 'of women who have survived violent marriages allows' you to 'expand the types of experiential perspectives informing understandings of Qur'anic ethics'. Those are your words. You describe your approach as follows:

> My approach explicitly foregrounds how a group of Muslim women think and speak in relation to the text and engage God, ethics, and religion through the realities of their suffering and oppression. What they often emerge with is an understanding of Islam that provides a very different ethical and existential vision than that of traditional male scholars, their husbands, and clerics around them. By suggesting that their experiences constitute a mode of '*tafsir*', I argue for a transformation and redefinition of traditional boundaries of what counts as Qur'anic exegesis. I maintain that this more expansive approach to *tafsir* will allow contemporary Muslims to engage dynamically with Islamic ethics, Qur'anic texts, and their embodied realities.[253]

I would say this was a paradigm-shifting article in the field when you wrote about the *tafsīr* of praxis. So we're interested in exploring these findings and thinking about their wider implications [for the verses in this book]. I'm wondering if you have any further words you would like to say about the *tafsīr* of praxis, and anything else you would like to share about it.

Sa'diyya Shaikh: One of the things that I wanted to do in my work, and I hope that I did so successfully, was to make the point that in fact all *tafsīr* is a *tafsīr* of praxis. The idea is that exegesis itself is fundamentally a lived enterprise and people do not set all of who they are on one side and say, 'We will read the Qur'ān in some kind of abstract, neutral, scholarly way that doesn't bring the fullness of our lived experiences into our reading.' By nature of being human, all *tafsīr* is a *tafsīr* of praxis. In one sense, the conceptualisation of this category was to render visible the fact that *all* readings are premised on and reflect the interpreter's lived experiential reality. One of the things that I did in that article was to illustrate how people like Zamakhsharī and Rāzī also [do this]. When you are reading *tafsīr*, you have to go and read the greats, those influential classical scholars like Ṭabarī, Rāzī and

[252] Shaikh, 'A *Tafsir* of Praxis', 69.
[253] Ibid., 70.

Zamakhsharī. One of the things that I foregrounded – and I think, Karen, that you've done this beautifully in your work as well – is how these different *tafsīr* scholars did very different things. You have, for example, Ṭabarī reading, in a very narrow way, this notion of *qiwāma*, and then you have Zamakhsharī and Rāzī doing very different things.

Yet all of these men brought the normative assumptions of their society into their reading. Zamakhsharī, for example, in interpreting male *qiwāma*, uses a political analogy of his time. He states that a man stands in the same relationship to a woman that a sovereign political ruler stands in relation to his subjects, who are to obey their leader's commands. So he is projecting and interpreting the Qur'ān through his own real experiences of a specific political power dynamic within his society. The earlier Ṭabarī, however, understands *qiwāma* to be primarily about maintenance in marriage and men providing financially for the upkeep of their wives. Tabari does not interpret this specific verse in ways that justify men's overall authority over women and reads it to reflect a specific financial role of husbands. So his approach limits understandings of *qiwāma*, perhaps in ways that find resonance with the views of many contemporary feminists. However, Zamakhsharī and Rāzī project more androcentric social, political and gender norms which informed their lived experiential realities onto the reading of male *qiwāma*. They discuss male *qiwāma* as founded on men's superiority over women, invoking some of the following examples of men's purported superiority: men can ride horses better, they can grow beards, they have better intellects.[254] These scholars project their specific social conditioning and the prevailing gender norms of their societies onto their readings of the Qur'ān.

So when we say 'a *tafsīr* of praxis', [we mean that] in fact all *tafsīr* is a *tafsīr* of praxis. Part of conceptualising that is not only to bring women's experiences in, but to show that any interpreter, as an embodied and socially situated person, invariably brings their specific cultural lenses and lived experiences to their interpretation of the Qur'ān. To deny that is to then render the very particular readings of a small group of people universal, and in fact they are not: they are partial. All of our readings are partial – Ibn 'Arabī's readings are partial, Karen's readings are partial, my readings are partial, Zamakhsharī's readings are partial. The notion of partiality needs to be recognised; so that's one of the central things that this article highlights. And in feminist scholarship, across the board, there is a very important epistemological insight on the fact that all knowledge is imbued by

[254] See the interpretation of Zamakhsharī and that of Rāzī, above.

a particular form of experience, and we need to recognise that particular locations in society, in terms of power, render understandings of knowledge by virtue of those contexts. So I sought to highlight this insight by conceptualising the category '*tafsīr* of praxis'.

The other thing that I intended was to reconceptualise authority, because when we name an interpretive practice as a *tafsīr*, we actually say we are gifting you with the authoritative capacity to interpret the Qur'ān and related ethics for us. So I foregrounded how regular women living their lives, trying to be good Muslims in a relationship with God, for whom their religious life means a lot to them, and their desire to be good Muslims means a lot to them, negotiate what they think being 'good Muslims' means in the context of very fraught and, in some cases, very violent relationships. When they made sense of what it meant to be a good Muslim, as well as what it meant to be living in that abusive relationship and at times resisting, at times being defeated by it, that was connected to a desire of making sense of what it means to be Muslim: they were essentially grappling with how to live Islamic ethics and what the Qur'ān meant to them. They were deeply interrogating their religious worldview, where the Qur'ān is a fundamental part of them. And so they were effectively doing a *tafsīr*, they were doing an interpretation; we just do not recognise it as a *tafsīr* because they are not a part of an elite group, who are generally brown men in the Muslim context. They're not in that elite group of scholarly, educated, brown men. But the reality is that what they are effectively doing is interpretation. And so the *tafsīr* of praxis is done by regular women, not scholars, who probably don't read the Qur'ān in Arabic – many of them don't – but in fact, the Qur'ān was an intimate part of their spiritual landscape. The way they made sense of the world was deeply imbued by the ethos of the Qur'ān.

What I want to then bring to bear in this conversation is that exegesis is not exclusively this narrow reading. It is not: 'Let us read the text and see what this word means, what that word means; how does it connect to other words?' Yes indeed, that is one important mode of reading, but when you engage the Qur'ān as a way that informs your life, even though you may not be reading it in its grammatical form and in this very specific [scholarly] mode of reading, you are still reading the Qur'ān in an existential mode, and I want to recognise that as a mode of interpretation. So that articulation is about expanding the notion of the authority of interpretation, of stretching it, by saying it is not solely the realm and preserve of an elite group of brown men; and contemporary brown elite men also tend to look at previous contexts where elite groups of premodern men determine their interpretation. I'm essentially saying, let us rethink notions of authority. Let us think about what meaning-making is, in terms of the Qur'ān, in this very embodied, lived sense reflected by lay women.

One of the women that I interviewed was a counsellor. She herself was previously in an abusive marriage where she was violently treated by her spouse, and she had left him. She was very strong; she became a counsellor to battered women and was deeply invested in Islam as a source of women's [empowerment]. It is how she survived. Because of God, she says, she survived a violent marriage, and this profound spiritual strength supported her to get through the struggle. She also stated, 'I gave the Qur'ān as a gift to a friend, who is not Muslim, but I struck out verse 4:34. I blacked out *waḍribūhunna* because, if you don't understand the Qur'ān in context, it can be a permission for violence.' I found that to be incredibly powerful. This is a laywoman; this is not someone who spends a huge amount of time studying the Qur'ān as a scholarly text or as an exegetical text. For her, the Qur'ān is a meaning-giving text that guides her life. Hers was a very powerful claim about reading and interpretation: to say that how one chooses to read the text is open to this violent reading, and she rejected that violent reading. I thought that was a very interesting kind of exceptional response, a response worth noting.

Feras Hamza: I am interested in your work on this because it resonated with me in terms of a lot of work being done in anthropology, for instance – the idea of ordinary ethics, everyday ethics. And it is sort of saying that the experience of every person, the average person, is worth something, it is worth bringing it in, to break up the ivory tower in which academics live and in which they have their erudite discussions about what a verse of the Qur'ān is saying, while in the meantime there are all of these real-life problems. But I do want to push you on this, if just for the sake of perhaps you elucidating even more the *tafsīr* of praxis. I mean, this requires some degree of sophistication, does it not, on the part of the subject herself? To make this move, to think that my experience is worth something – who is the person who validates this so that it becomes the authoritative reading or so that it revises male behaviour? I mean, shouldn't males, for example, be promoting this *tafsīr* of praxis by women so that it will raise that profile? In sum, how does this translate into a call for change, a call for reform? You yourself have championed these women by identifying that their experiences are in fact moments of *tafsīr*, and that makes infinite sense. So the question is, how to translate that into a call for action, and how does that change the current situation? So just your thoughts on that, actually, the more practical aspect of it, if you can. Thank you.

Sa'diyya Shaikh: Thank you Feras. The reality is that it doesn't always work that way. People read the Qur'ān, they have a way of understanding the

Qur'ān through a whole plethora of influences, and those include what you've been taught at madrasa, what your mother says, what your father says, what your shaykh says, what your teacher (*ustādh*) says, what your friends are saying. So one of the women did that, while another one was saying, 'I need to be a better Muslim, I need to be more patient; if I was more patient, this violence wouldn't happen.' So she had embodied a whole different type of subjectivity that did not problematise the husband's violence. But I think that you are right; we read from a composite reality involving a whole complexity of things. That's not ultimately reducible to a solitary subject, receiving the Qur'ān. That having been said, I think we need to be thinking at the level of social engagement. We have to be thinking about different modes of ethical engagement. As a mother of a teenage boy and teenage girl, [I am acutely conscious that] we have to be having more robust conversations. How do we have different ways of Islamic education for young people? How do we think about how we model different modes of gender relationships? How do we model our lived ways of being Muslims? I think that is really critical.

I do think that when reading the Qur'ān we need varied forms of literacy, so that it is not simply about reading words and understanding grammar, but about forms of literacy that enable us to cultivate a moral compass in ourselves and enable this also for other lives around us. What kinds of ways of being Muslim do we enable, individually and collectively, in our communities through the refinement of one's moral compass? Because if we work with that, if we are alive to that, then the dignity of every other life becomes an intrinsic part of how we engage the Qur'ān, which means that our modes of reading are contingent on our hearts. And that is not a simple thing; it is not that you sit there in *ḥalaqa* (a session) refining your heart. Really, the workshop of the world is the space for the refinement of the heart, in every relationship, through *ʿibādāt* (worship) and through *muʿāmalāt* (interactions/social acts), through the social aspect and through worship, through a variety of modes of engaging.

The question is, what enables social change? I think that is the broader question, Feras; and what modes of reading enable that? And that is a very complicated thing that we need to attend to in the specificities of our lives embedded within communities and contexts; but we need a different form of engagement. I think we need to stop unthinkingly inscribing forms of authority that no longer resonate with our understandings of justice and human dignity as the starting point. When you read things about female deficiency – or any human being's deficiency [being] fundamentally based on something that they have no control over – that immediately is a red flag.

How do we teach people to recognise that as an ethical, spiritual red flag? That's the challenge. I think that's the broader ethical challenge to many communities. Absolutely.

Feras Hamza: Thank you, over to you, Karen.

Karen Bauer: I really appreciated that answer, Sa'diyya, thinking about new ways and different ways of engaging. I think that one of the things that we found, because we have done a reading of the Qur'ān's verses on women, was just how much those sorts of verses that we read now as giving permission for men to have rights over women were actually, in their own context, about men looking after women and limiting what might have otherwise been an unlimited male prerogative. So if you come from a scenario in which nobody has rights, except for one sort of person in society, and then you imagine reading it through that lens, then you will get a very different reading from the reading [you would get] if you imagine everybody as having equal rights automatically. And I think that somehow connects with what you were saying about Q. 4:34 and the ways in which the *tafsīr* of praxis could potentially become a model for change.

You mentioned earlier that there was a woman who struck it out, and you actually described how, in their practice of it, women had essentially abrogated the verse. I was wondering if you could speak about this concept of abrogation.

Sa'diyya Shaikh: Yes, Karen, I think that many of us already know or have encountered the arguments, which to me are eminently sensible. Any kind of mildly historically perceptive lens will have us understand that the Qur'ān was, of course, speaking to a set of historical assumptions and contextual gender norms. What else would it be speaking to as a force for change? And, in fact, Qur'ānic gender teachings were clearly reformative of a number of dominant patriarchal norms of the seventh century. In our current political context, where gender equality is a powerful discourse, the extent of the gender reforms in Qur'ānic teachings is not always evident. The argument that the gendered ideas, as reflected in Q. 4:34, are descriptive rather than prescriptive is, to me, self-evident. It makes me wonder how one could not know this. How could a reader not know that this kind of verse is descriptive of its context rather than prescriptive of the ways in which people ought to be in this time?[255] So I think this notion of reading the Qur'ān contextually – recognising that there are verses that reflect seventh-century norms, and

[255] Note, however, that much feminist research assumes that the Qur'ān is an entirely gender-egalitarian text.

[that such verses] needed to do so in order for its audience to relate to it, and then also that most often the Qur'ān simultaneously ameliorated and reformed those gender norms to improve conditions for women on the receiving end of patriarchy – to recognise the Qur'ānic dynamics of contextual reform is important.

The other thing that gets entirely silenced – which I think is an important historical retrieval in relation to the Qur'ān – is the perspective of women themselves. For example, the revelation of the Qur'ānic verse in *al-Aḥzāb*, Q. 33:35, that says: *believing men and believing women*, was prompted by the questions of Umm Salama, the wife of the Prophet, who asked the Prophet: 'Does God only speak to men?' For me, she asked the Prophet this question very seriously, since the Qur'ān uses Arabic language which is grammatically gendered, such that the plural that includes women is a masculine plural. For all Muslim women in androcentric worlds, she asks: How do I know that I specifically am being spoken to? Is it that God only speaks to men, or is God speaking to all of us?[256] So she is asking, what we would call in the contemporary context, a profoundly feminist question. She's asking about female subjectivity and clarifying the absolute integrity of female subjectivity as subjects addressed by God. Asma Barlas does a beautiful job of rendering that narrative, and I think that this requires reiteration, that not only did the Prophet (*ṣlʿm*) not immediately respond to the question by trying to pacify her [Umm Salama] by saying, 'well of course God is referring to you, just be quiet', he actually waited for God to intervene. Then you have the revelation of this verse [Q. 33:35], which says 'for believing men and believing women, for men and women who surrender, for men and women who fast, for men and women who are chaste, for men and women who give charity, for men and women who are obedient'. So it is bringing every single moral virtue and articulating it in a gender-inclusive manner. For me, those moments are important in terms of the Qur'ān articulating such a clear vision of moral equality.

The other question that I'd like to come back to is, why is it that things that are descriptive of a patriarchy become foregrounded as the Qur'ānic gender narrative, and those narratives that are very clearly addressing human equality and dignity rendered peripheral? This verse [Q. 33:35], for example, why can't this be the way that we think about Islamic thought? Why can't it be the foundation of how we think about gender relations? The Qur'ān is, in

[256] This relates to the *asbāb al-nuzūl* of Q. 33:35, in which Umm Salama was said to have asked the Prophet why God only addresses men in the Qur'ān. See the appendix to the introduction, in which we have translated several of these narratives.

some sense, you could say, ambivalent; I would say it is holding a contextual descriptive register and a utopian, ontological register of equality, and it's urging us as believers towards that vision. That is my way of reading it. The question is, why are those verses that speak to human equality, that call husbands and wives garments to one another [Q. 2:187], that say that you are *awliyāʾ* of one another [Q. 9:71] – meaning you are friends, supporters, maintainers of one another – not rendered central to defining our humanity? Why are the verses describing seventh-century norms rendered [central]? And that is a question of interpretation: who decides what is the Qurʾānic vision when the Qurʾān holds these different registers? We can't say the Qurʾān is a feminist document; that is simplistic and incomplete. We have to look at the Qurʾān in a holistic way to be thinking about these different registers.

So Umm Salama asks this question, and it is not just the Qurʾānic verse that emerges as important. It is the entire way that [. . .] premodern Muslim women [were] asking a critical question on female subjectivity: Am I, as a woman, being addressed? Is my entire sisterhood being addressed here? And not only does the Prophet not respond in a hurried manner, the Prophet is quiet, and God considers this a question worth responding to. Also, by responding in this very profound manner, it is actually a mode of how we are to engage with the Qurʾān. We are to interrogate things that do not render us visible. It is saying that questioning, interrogating, critically reading is a way that is divinely backed up. Perhaps God is saying, 'Cool, do this. I've got something to say to you, and thanks for asking', and that is something that is worthy of doing.

There are things that we never hear about. Why do we not hear about the *sūra* of the *mujādila*, the woman who contests and wrestles with God? And you know there is a pre-Islamic practice where her husband says, 'Your back is like the back of my mother', and in the norms of that time, that is what renders the marriage invalid, and the couple are not supposed to have sex thereafter, and they're not supposed to be a married couple because he has now, in some sense, annulled the marriage, and that was the normative practice of the time. She goes to the Prophet and says my husband has made a mistake; we want to be together, can you undo it? and he says, 'No, I really can't undo it. This is the norm. You are now no longer sexually involved. He has taken this promise, this oath.' So she says, no, take it to God. I'm sorry, Prophet, I don't like your response. Could you please take it to the source? And then the Prophet does that, and in the meantime she and her sisters prayed, saying please God, bring me some respite, listen to me, dear God. And God does, and he calls [the *sūra*] the *Mujādila* [Q. 58], the woman who argues. So the issue, of course, is women who argue with God, women who contest any taking away of their dignity, is a Qur'ānic model. And it is a Qur'ānic model that God responds. God, thus, is encouraging female subjects or any marginalised subjects to wrestle with anything that denies their dignity and their equality and their full respect. There is a Qur'ānic model for this and [yet] it is rendered invisible. It is completely subdued; nobody talks about it. I think all of that speaks to the question of what modes of reading do we bring? What ways of reading do we bring to the Qur'ān?

And so to answer Feras's earlier question, as well: how do we 'do' change? How we do change is also how we reread the tradition. The tradition itself is so complex and diverse. Early Muslim women were certainly not quiet women who succumbed to male authority and obedience. They were a bunch of robust, questioning, critical women. Umm Salama actually gave counsel to the Prophet in the middle of what was really a rebellion amongst his men who did not want to actually accept the treaty of Ḥudaybiya.[257] These men said: 'We are powerful – we can actually go ahead and take on the enemies.' But Umm Salama said no, no, no. He [the Prophet] wanted peace. He wanted a kind of strategic exit, and she gave him a solution. These [women] were political analysts; these were women who were on the ground, were engaged with politics and their community. The [first] wife of the Prophet was older than him, proposed marriage to him, was essentially his employer. We have models in Islamic history of powerful, strong, Muslim women who were certainly not meek, who refused abuse of any kind. What does it take to retrieve those legacies, those genealogies, those historical memories, and those historical models of women and female subjectivity? That is part of the work of what Islamic feminists have done, and Islamic feminists have started this project in very interesting ways, thankfully (*al-ḥamdu li'llāh*).

Karen Bauer: So this is part of what we were considering, Sa'diyya, when we wrote the volume introduction, but also why we felt pretty passionately that we wanted to include some interviews and have some women speaking. Because the whole *tafsīr* tradition is mediating the Qur'ānic text, which

[257] The location just outside Mecca where, in 6/628, the Prophet and his followers, having been prevented from continuing towards Mecca to perform the pilgrimage (*ḥajj*), negotiated the famous truce (*ṣulḥ*) with the Meccans (apparently through the mediation of 'Uthmān b. 'Affān, the future third caliph) to the effect that 'the believers' would turn back to Medina on the condition that they be allowed to return the following year to perform the rite: see W. Montgomery Watt, 'al-Ḥudaybiya', *EI*², III, 539, and the primary references provided therein.

means a lot to all Muslims, or to most of them, and that is a lot of people, and it is mediating it through such a narrow textual tradition, controlled by such a narrow, small group of people. And as you say, there are the greats, and you have to engage with them to some extent, but it was important for us to show that actually that tradition in no way defines the [whole spectrum of] Muslim engagement with the Qur'ān and certainly doesn't define how modern Muslims engage with it and the way that modern Muslims approach it in terms of gender.

Sa'diyya Shaikh: Now there are two things. One thing that I think it is really important to say is that the *tafsīr* cannon is essentially men's voices, men talking to other men. We really ought to recognise the very selective, partial mode of interpretation that the *tafsīr* canon presents to us. It is small. It is selective. It is elite. The other point – that Shahab Ahmed made absolutely brilliantly in his book[258] – is that when [we] are talking about the modern context, we may say 'go to the *tafsīr* canon', [but] in the premodern context, you never went to a *tafsīr* scholar. Actually, so much of it was mediated through Sufi poetry, through music (*qawali*), through all kinds of popular ways of Qur'ān transmission that really weren't about reading texts. So, this contemporary obsession with [the genre of] *tafsīr* is the product of modernity, literacy and books as becoming the repositories of knowledge and the repositories of religious authority, whereas [throughout] Muslim history, you've had this whole plethora of very different artistic, Sufi mediations, philosophical mediations, that come through poetry and music and art, stories you get told and listen to, about the ethical ways of being a Muslim – and the Qur'ān is so intricately woven through all of these cultural artifacts and mediated through them, not through some *tafsīr* canon with a bunch of dudes telling you what to do, or how to understand God's word.

Karen Bauer: Yes Sa'diyya, I agree. Do you have any more that you would like to say about Q. 4:34? You describe women who were subject to spousal abuse, but who were encouraged to stay in their marriages by their families and by religious authorities; these women themselves interpreted the religious values of patience and female obedience as a reason for them to stay.[259] Yet all but one of these women 'contested their husbands' violence in ethical and religious terms'. They asked their husbands, for instance, how they could beat them and then go to the mosque to pray; one woman said she could not pray behind her husband because she could not respect him. For them, then,

[258] Ahmed, *What is Islam?*
[259] Shaikh, 'A *Tafsir* of Praxis', 77.

'violent male behaviour was viewed as inconsistent with the practice of Islam and the divine imperatives for human beings'. You conclude that 'hence their experiential "*tafsir*" abrogated the literal and patriarchal readings of Q. 4:34'.[260] Do you believe the literal sense of this verse is abrogated, based on women's experiences or modern ways of considering human rights?
Sa'diyya Shaikh: In the article, essentially what I argue is that women were existentially abrogating those verses, at least abrogating the literal meaning of those verses. Effectively, these women who had been beaten by their husbands rejected that abuse on religious grounds. One of them said, 'I won't perform my *ṣalāt* (prayer) with this man, because I know that a man who violates me like that cannot be my leader [in prayer].' The other one said [to her husband], 'You want to ask Allāh for forgiveness, and you haven't even asked my forgiveness. Allāh can never forgive you if you don't ask for my forgiveness.' So there is this very clear assertion that violence against them was unjust, was ungodly, was not something that God would tolerate, and so the abuser's, this violent partner's, religiosity and spirituality were completely compromised by virtue of his violence. So these women's approach is essentially an abrogation of any violent reading of that verse. These are not necessarily highly educated people; they are not highly trained in the Qur'ānic literature in the way that one thinks of the educated *'ulamā'* (scholars), but they were very clear from their living, embodied engagement with the text that violence and abuse by their husbands are ungodly, un-Qur'ānic and un-Islamic. Fundamentally, they were on the receiving end of such injustice, violence and violation, and they completely, in their bones, and in their being [knew] – it wasn't even a question for seven out of the eight women that I was in conversation with; for them, it was an absolute knowledge through their experience – that this abuse by their husbands was ungodly and un-Islamic. They abrogated any violent reading of the Qur'ān.

My position is the same as I have echoed before, which is that Q. 4:34 is descriptive, not prescriptive. And of course, you can go [the Qur'ān translation of] Laleh Bakhtiar, God have mercy on her, who has just passed, that actually says very clearly that there are different ways to interpret the word '*wa'ḍribūhunna*' – that it can also mean 'to depart', etcetera. Other people would say that the context of revelation shows that it was indeed physical chastisement. But the Qur'ān is open to our modes of engagement, and this is true in terms of the broader Qur'ānic message, the prophetic example and much of tradition. So we never read these verses outside of an entire textured

[260] Ibid., 86.

way of thinking about historical context, of ethics, of what gender meant, what gender relationships were normative at the time, how these understandings develop subsequently, what our understanding of human dignity is in this moment. And, of course, the argument is that the Prophet, even in the most dire of breakdowns in terms of his family, in the midst of such incredible disagreements, actually removed himself from the company of his wives; he moved away from them when there was intense marital conflict. So the prophetic *sunna* (example) in cases of intense marital conflict is to withdraw, to move away from your spouse if you are in a state of marital disharmony. It is not to hit them. This is simply not what the Prophet did. He did not hit a spouse that he was angry with. This is quite clear in that regard. So that would be my reading.

I have another idea from Ibn ʿArabī that I would love to share with you, because it shows this mode of *tafsīr* that I think is fantastic.

Karen Bauer: Yes, sure.

Sa'diyya Shaikh: Okay, so there is a wonderful reading of Ibn ʿArabī. There is clearly a Qurʾānic verse that is speaking to ʿĀʾisha and Ḥafṣa, and one does not know the details of the *sabab* (the context of revelation) here, but these were two of the Prophet's wives, and there was [some] way in which they had ganged up against him. The verse says, *if you back each other up against the Prophet, then know that God is his master, and Gabriel, the righteous among the believers, and the angels after that are his supporters* [Q. 66:4]. So here is Ibn ʿArabī's reflection. Ibn ʿArabī is talking about the attribute of God, *al-Qawī*, [the] Strong, and he uses these two women, Ḥafṣa and ʿĀʾisha to exemplify the divine quality of strength. He says that from these two women we, as believers, can learn strength. Here the Prophet needs God, the angels, and all of the believers and Gabriel to support him against these two women, which means that they are really strong. And from there, he says, 'God mentions only the strong ones, who possess power and strength. So the righteous believers act with conviction, and that is the strongest of actions, and if you understand this, you set off on the path.' Now, if you read the very next verse after this, where really God is upbraiding Ḥafṣa and ʿĀʾisha [in Q. 66:5], Ibn ʿArabī takes this very verse, that is a reprimand to these two women, and says that if they didn't want to be his [the Prophet's] wives, fine – he could divorce them and get better wives, if that is what they wanted. If they wanted to give the Prophet a hard time, God was there, the angels were there, the righteous believers were there, and Gabriel was there, and the Prophet has all of this support. And Ibn ʿArabī's reflection is not 'check out these women who are impossible wives to live with'. No. His reflection is that this verse is indicative of the strength of these two women, and righteous believers must acquire the attribute of strength in their actions and in their beliefs. He sees them as models of the embodiment of the attribute of *qawī*, which is really incredible. And he's taking something literally that speaks at one level, and he's completely reconstituting it to mean something else, so that he does a very interesting gender interpretation in this reading. He uses ʿĀʾisha and Ḥafṣa as models that the believers should follow; not that they should be upbraided by the Prophet, but rather that they embody a quality that believers should learn and embody.

I think that's a fascinating example of the extraordinary hermeneutical play in the Islamic tradition that we need to be thinking about. This example is not simply to show you what a cool thinker Ibn ʿArabī is, but actually to demonstrate a model of enormous hermeneutical freedom, and that people read and interpret from their state. So Qurʾānic verses that are reflective of a descriptive reality can, in fact, be read in very different modes, and can be read from a higher [state], and can get to beautiful, internally discerning ways of engaging the human condition; even something that seems, at face value, to be a divine slap on the wrist to Ḥafṣa and ʿĀʾisha becomes something very different. They become a model of strength, of action, of conviction, of resolve of what believers should be. That is Ibn ʿArabī reading from a state, from an exalted state, so that is indeed a model to be followed when reading the Qurʾān.

Feras Hamza: Thank you, Sa'diyya. I might explore something perhaps of the nature of Muslim readers not having an alternative way of dealing with texts, or reading texts, beyond the letter itself. As somebody who knows the tradition scholastically but also in that lived experience way that you talk about, which is also so terribly important – philosophy as a way of life – I am just conscious that actually I don't find any method of reading away from those difficult verses; a satisfactory method. I think that the difficult verses are themselves there for some kind of purpose, for some kind of ethical stimulus, and I think the problem with the Qurʾān, for me, is that its boundaries are mistaken for its content. That is, those barbed wire moments in the Qurʾān that either have to do with the beating verse or the punishment for fornicators, or punishment for thieves. For me, these constitute the ethical challenges: what kind of person will you be, faced with this kind of legal injunction? It is a real challenge to character, and those edges – I call them 'barbed wire' because I think of the modern correlate of the state and all of its various ways of having deterrents as well, and we forget how often these problems we face in our current contemporary paradigms of constitutions and laws all have deterrents, they have terrifying aspects, we do horrible things to other human beings through law, which looks very nice and is all cosmetic and done up; we treat [illegal] aliens and immigrants in such ways, and refugees and so on. So it is not a Qur'ānic problem *per se*, but in the Qur'ān, the issue for me is that these moments that jar, jar for a purpose. The dissonance there is what creates possibilities for moral growth and moral action.

I think that often these boundaries are confused for the contents, and the contents are not laid out explicitly. You are given guidelines, but there is an immense sphere of possibility. So, substantively, the Qur'ānic world should not be defined by these barbed wire moments, or these rough edges, or these difficult verses, and I think they are important, they are not just to be argued away or explained away, or interpreted in ways that make us feel better about the ethical system that we want. Because I think also that one of the Qur'ān's fundamental underlying currents is that the life of this world is a life of trouble; it is not a utopia. It is really a chance for you to be tested, to have your mettle tested, I suppose, so [the world] is not really the point. The point is *al-ḥayawān* [Q. 29:64], the true life, the next life. So I think sometimes these problematic verses are taken as the stipulations of the law as opposed to stimuli for moral engagement.

Sa'diyya Shaikh: Feras, absolutely, I agree with you completely. And in fact, Karen will also be familiar with this work, but Laury Silvers, some years ago, did one of the best readings of Q. 4:34 that I have ever seen. And I am sad, because the details of the argument are not very clear in my head at the moment, but it essentially echoes what you have to say, which is in fact these difficult verses in the Qur'ān are ways in which your moral subjectivity and your ethical responsibility to do the right thing come into being. Effectively, everything that is available is not everything you should do.[261] [. . .] And that is one way to think about it, [but] for those people on the receiving end of bad readings of [Q.] 4:34, many might well say, 'I'd rather it not be there, and I don't need to be on the receiving end of some man distilling his moral agency', and so I think it is worth looking at from a variety of perspectives.

amina wadud

amina wadud identifies several methods by which she rejects the literal implementation of Q. 4:34. One is to contextualise the verse historically; another is to identify its general and particular elements (the *'āmm* and the *khāṣṣ*), a tool of traditional exegesis

[261] Silvers, 'In the Book We Have Left out Nothing'.

that she uses to subvert the interpretations that traditional exegetes took for granted. Ultimately, her 'no' to the literal implementation of this verse is based on her privileging the context over the text, by which she means that a verse must be seen to achieve the overall ethos of the Qur'ān's moral ethics. For her, justice for women can only be determined by women themselves; women are harmed not only by violence itself but by the threat of violence. Much like Sa'diyya Shaikh's view of the *tafsīr* of praxis, her view of context over text grew out of her activist work within Muslim communities. Such work led her, like Sa'diyya Shaikh, to privilege women's experience as an important factor in the interpretation of the Qur'ān – those very experiences that have been marginalised throughout the history of interpretations of this verse.

amina wadud's comment on *yaqīn* in this interview, though made in passing, alludes to an important dynamic shared by what may be termed traditionalist as well as rationalist Muslim Qur'ānic hermeneutics (even as the approaches criss-cross and are varied).[262] The Sufi interpretive tradition also drew on such hermeneutics, but combined them with ritual praxis in order to map out a psycho-spiritual framework or the key concepts of what may be termed a spiritual ontology, verifying such findings whenever possible in the Qur'ānic text, even when the Qur'ānic references themselves were allusive. A good example of such spiritual hermeneutics are Sufi elaborations on the soul (*nafs*), its state (*ḥāl*) and its journey (cf. *ṭarīqa*) in this world and the next. To take one example of how such intra-Qur'ānic textual references provide clues to a broader spiritual psychology, there is the Sufi tripartite categorisation of the soul into *ammāra* (goading [to evil]), *lawwāma* (reproaching), *muṭma'inna* (reassured); all three of these terms appear as single occurrences, without any overt connections or systematic linkage in the Qur'ān. The term *yaqīn* is very much analogous. The word denotes 'knowledge (*'ilm*) about which there is no doubt (*shakk*)'. In the Qur'ān, it appears on four occasions in prefixed constructions: as *'ilm al-yaqīn* (knowledge of certainty) and *'ayn al-yaqīn* (the very) in Q. 102:5–7, and as *ḥaqq al-yaqīn* in Q. 56:95 and in Q. 69:51. In their writings on the psychology of the soul (*nafs*), Sufis ordered these three levels into a hierarchy of consciousness to denote the capacities of the soul's metaphysical knowledge (cf. *gnosis*) on its journey towards perfectedness from this life into the next.[263]

262 Cf. Rippin, 'Tafsīr', *EI*², X, 83–8.

263 See William C. Chittick, 'On Sufi Psychology: A Debate between the Soul and the Spirit' in *Consciousness and Reality: Studies in Memory of Toshihiko Izutsu*, ed. Sayyid Jalāl al-Dīn Āshtiyānī *et al.* (Leiden, Brill, 2000), 341–66; Mohamed A. Mahmoud, *Quest for Divinity: A Critical Examination of the Thought of Mahmud Muhammad Taha* (New York, Syracuse University Press, 2007), esp. 145ff.; see also Qushayrī, *al-Risāla al-Qushayriyya fī 'ilm al-taṣawwuf*, s.v. *muṣṭalaḥāt al-taṣawwuf: 'ilm al-yaqīn* (no. 22), 85; Abū 'Abd al-Raḥmān al-Sulamī (d. 412/1021), *Ḥaqā'iq al-tafsīr*, ed. Sayyid 'Imrān, 2 vols. (Beirut, Dār al-Kutub al-'Ilmiyya, 2001), I, 417–18, s.v. Q. 101:5–7 on the various levels; and on technical usage, see 'Alī b. Muḥammad al-Jurjānī (d. 816/1413 or 838/1434), *Kitāb al-Ta'rīfāt*, ed. Ibrāhīm al-Abyārī (Beirut, Dār al-Kitāb al-'Arabī, 1985), 332, *ḥadīth* no. 1644.

Karen Bauer: amina, on Q. 4:34 you have said:

> There is no getting around this one, even though I have tried through different methods for two decades. I simply do not and cannot condone permission for a man to 'scourge' or apply *any kind* of strike to a woman. [. . .] This leads me to clarify how I have finally come to say 'no' outright to the literal implementation of this passage. This also has implications in implementing the *ḥudūd* (penal code) ordinances. This verse, and the literal implementation of the *ḥudūd*, both imply an ethical standard of human actions that are archaic and barbarian at this time in history. They are unjust in the ways that human beings have come to experience and understand justice, and hence unacceptable to universal notions of human dignity.[264]

We are wondering, what does it mean to say 'no' to the literal interpretation or implementation of a verse? Can anyone say 'no' to parts of the Qur'ān, and in what circumstances might that happen?

amina wadud: I also had to evolve to this location from where I was when I first published, and the evolution was born, one hundred per cent, in the field of the struggles for gender justice and equality, particularly in [my] participating as one of the founding members of 'Sisters in Islam'[265] and as one of the resource people for the Musawah[266] movement, which is a movement for reform in Muslim personal status law. That is because when you have a passage like this one, that literally says, *and strike them* whether or not there are caveats to go with that, it leads to a very slippery slope in the context of another global movement, which is a movement to eradicate all forms of violence against women. Now, trying to wed these two things – that is, my field of interpretation and theology and the sort of activism in terms of policy reform and the like – was actually almost as beautiful to me as coming across the Qur'ān not long after I became Muslim.

When you are interpreting the Qur'ān simply on the basis of linguistics, philosophy and even ethics, in the abstract way in which ethics are often done, it is possible for you to deliberate a long time over the nuances of the language, and that is all you do. When, however, you are faced with the lived reality, there is a consequence in how you relate to texts. When I first began working with activist groups, I would say that I could be identified as [someone who privileged] text over context. By the time that process was over, I had been converted to context over text. And I want to tell you that

[264] wadud, *Inside the Gender Jihad*, 200.
[265] An activist organisation in Malaysia co-founded with Zainah Anwar.
[266] Website: https://www.musawah.org/

this verse is precisely the way to demonstrate that an application of a verse must achieve the overall Qur'ānic ethos or the principles, virtues, or values, like justice. Justice for women can only be determined by women, and all of the research into domestic violence – be it in the context of Muslim families or not – confirms that not only violence but the potential threat of violence is harmful for women. So I had to grapple with how to get from the command form *waḍribūhunna* [strike them] to the lived reality, and I was challenged because I was accused of being so Qur'ān-centric that I could not see beyond it, and everything had to be confirmed in it. I did not feel that way in my gut, but I also was not clear how to get there. So writing that chapter in *Inside the Gender Jihad* is a representation of the evolutionary process, and that evolutionary process actually becomes a methodology.

That methodology hinges upon the awareness that there is both *ʿāmm* and *khāṣṣ* in the Qur'ān. There are general statements and there are specific statements, and specific statements have no implementation component to them. So if the wives of the Prophet are ordered to not marry after he dies, there is no general rule that comes from that. We don't have you burning yourself on the funeral pyre like they did in parts of the Indian tradition in the past. So it's not an *ʿāmm*. But as soon as you realise that the purview of certain verses is not universal, it is easy to go to a particular passage and determine the purview of its application. And given the history of interpretation with regard to this passage, even in the context of the dominant male tradition, where they start to make caveats, such as *bi-miswāk* or *ramziyyan*, with a dental stick, or in a metaphorical way, as soon as they start to give caveats that are also not a part of the literal Qur'ān, it says that human beings intervened with the meaning of the Qur'ān for the purpose of achieving certain social goods, or *maṣlaḥa*, and now we come to the final stage.

The third stage for me was feminist interpretation that brought doubt on whether or not we have fully understood this passage. And if you look at Laleh Bakhtiar's book,[267] she is talking about thirty different interpretations of the term *ḍarb*, so there is this idea that maybe we don't know what it means, in the literal sense of it. But the final stage is to say we use the measurements and evidentiary basis of women's lived realities of domestic violence to determine whether this verse can be used as a rubric of application in the context of community, and the answer is 'no'. It does not remove [the

[267] Laleh Bakhtiar, tr., *The Sublime Quran* (Chicago, IL, Kazi Publications, 2007).

verse] from the Qur'ān; it simply says that all of the understandings of it in the context of seventh-century Arabia is not going to be matched in the context of twenty-first-, twenty-third-, twenty-fifth-century global realities of Islam. So when people talk about the methodology of lived reality, it is not just how you feel, it is also constructing a corollary between evidence in the context of certain practices, and how those practices might be understood if you take them literally, even out of the Qur'ān.

Feras Hamza: To me, amina, it is interesting that you should refer to quite a hermeneutically specific technique, which is to identify the *ʿāmm* versus the *khāṣṣ*. I am interested in how you have been able to mine the traditional toolkit for your purpose, which is a wider purpose that serves justice for women and so on. Are there any more of these tools that are just as useful? They are traditional tools, these categories of how you approach the Qur'ān. It is very interesting; I did not know about the method that you have used, and it struck me because I have worked with medieval texts, and this is a kind of hermeneutic that is identified and used. That is interesting for me, what do you feel about that? You are trying to use the tools of tradition, but to rejuvenate that tradition's reading of the text, of the scripture. Could you expand on that?

amina wadud: Yes, it's rather a fun project actually. Even now when I teach workshops with activists, I start with the *ʿulūm al-Qur'ān* [sciences of the Qur'ān], and the reason that I do is to demystify the Qur'ān, and to stop having it stand outside of it, and have us stand inside of it. The *ʿāmm* and *khāṣṣ*, which as you notice are not the full categories, because there is *khāṣṣ*, *ʿāmm* and universal, and universal wasn't articulated by the classical exegetes, because, actually, the notion of universal is a kind of twentieth-century thing. But the use of the existing disciplines of Qur'ānic studies indicates to me that it is a discipline, and the object of the discipline is the comprehension of the revelation; and if the revelation has as its goal *hudan li'l-muttaqīn* [Q. 2:2] – that is, guidance [to the God-wary] – then the revelation's past is not complete unless and until humans actually use it.

Karen asked a question earlier that I think is appropriate to bring in here, which is, can you say 'no' in other places? People say 'no' to the Qur'ān all the damn time, and we don't make a big deal out of it until there is a power base, and that power base has been encoded in the context of patriarchy that has run through our intellectual tradition as if it is one and the same, even, as Allāh. So it is really important to understand that, for example, when the Qur'ān says that you can't eat the meat of pigs (*laḥm al-khinzīr*) unless you are under duress, there are people who don't eat meat at all, and in not eating meat that is permitted in the Qur'ān they give an ethical Islamic justification for it, and that means that they are saying 'no' to the Qur'ān's permission to eat meat. But you never hear about this when you start talking about the politics of Islam. It is only about these situations with regard to gender, and I would say also with regard to sexuality – all of a sudden it is a done deal, and what makes the deal done, supposedly, is the classical discourse. Well, the classical discourse is: 'you are men and we are men' (*antum rijāl wa-naḥnu rijāl*); the classical discourse is just discourse, and according to people like [Abdolkarim] Soroush, they fulfilled the justice of their time, and we must fulfil the justice of our time. And the justice in the classical period – across traditions, not just in Islam – was that there was a treatment owed to a person relative to their status that differed from the treatment owed to a person in a different status. We have now replaced that with a universal human rights understanding which is about equality and reciprocity. And equality and reciprocity across gender are at loggerheads in the context of Muslim discourse because so much was written in the milieu of well-meaning people who had what Ayesha Chaudhry calls an 'idealised cosmology' which was in fact hegemonic.[268] We live in an idealised cosmology that is egalitarian, and neither of these idealised cosmologies is superior to another, but they have a facility with regard to context. Remember what I said, I have now become context over text? One of the things about our context is that you do not have to agree with Qur'ānic statements about slavery, just because the institution of slavery was not condemned in the Qur'ān, because that was then and this is now. Now we know that every human being deserves *la-qad karramnā banī Ādam* [*And verily We have give to the children of Adam an honoured station* Q. 17:70] – they deserve *karāma* (honour), and slavery is not an institution of *karāma* or dignity. It is a systemic thing, it is a paradigm shift, where the Qur'ān articulated enough on a trajectory that, if we were to follow it, we would get to the place where we are, but we tend to want to recede on certain issues, because of the literal text. And I have finally been freed of the necessity to justify any specific text because of the whole of the text and because of the author of the text, whom we believe to be Allāh.

Feras Hamza: amina, I think you raised a really interesting point here with regards to the text and our relationship with it. In a sense aren't you saying that we work into the Qur'ān from within a cultural perspective? We have a universal ethic now of egalitarianism, so in a sense we have to make that fit

[268] Chaudhry, *Domestic Violence and the Islamic Tradition*, 12–13 *et passim*.

into the Qur'ān – how could the Qur'ān be denying that? It does seem to be working from a cultural context into the Qur'ān; it is not really working from the Qur'ān into our culture, and that might not come very intuitively to a lot of people. It is very sophisticated and astute to imagine that there is some correlation between any ideal cultural value at any point in time and the Qur'ān's eternal truth, and I think – isn't it the case? – that a lot of people assume that the truth comes from the Qur'ān, and then they have to do all kinds of gymnastics to square that with their cultural context, whereas for you it just seems effortless, because you are saying, 'We just happen to have a universal ethic here, which seems reasonable, which is to be equal, to have egalitarianism and so on, and so surely the Qur'ān has it, so let's go back to the Qur'ān and work out how that fits.' Just for the sake of argument, and just for the sake of fleshing out what I think is a really interesting perspective, how do you see that? How do you see the relationship between reading from the text or working into the text?

amina wadud: Yes, I think that once again there is a little bit of politics in this conversation – which is superior, our current milieu or the Qur'ān? – which is not where I am going at all. Where I am going instead is that the purpose of the Qur'ān is human beings and their well-being. Therefore, we are the markers. If the Qur'ān would become obsolete, we would lose so much, and the way to do it is to grapple with those articulations that did not pursue the full trajectory, as encoded in the Qur'ān itself, and to make them stop points or milestones along the way to the completion of what is called in Sufi terms *al-insān al-kāmil*[269] – in other words, the completion of the full breadth of our capacity as human beings having human lives. And because every human being at every point in history had a human life, how we understand that history is again on the path of that trajectory. In other words, because for some people the Prophet is the epitome of the sacred light in everything and because the revelation came to him, there is a tendency to understand the prophetic perfection as if it removed him from the rampant patriarchy of his time and culture, in which he also participated in the most benevolent way. How do you grapple with this unless you understand that we are put in a certain time in the place that is the earth for this human adventure, and we have tools, we have *āyāt* (signs), we have ways to push us towards the achievement of greater and greater ethical completions of our humanity? And the Qur'ān and its *āyāt* are part of the signs. It is part of the way forward.

[269] See ch. 1, n. 237, this volume.

But the Qur'ān itself points us to *āyāt* in the implicit realm, which is everything else around us, which is lived reality. The lived reality must be addressed by the Qur'ān in order for the Qur'ān to be relevant to it. So if you wish to keep the Qur'ān alive, then you must grapple with the places where Qur'ānic articulation is locked into the means of articulation that were available in the seventh century.

For example, everywhere that the Qur'ān talks about the movement between the sun and the earth, it uses words we still use in our language, like sunrise and sunset, but [really] the sun does not move. I mean, it moves, because our whole galaxy is moving, but it is the earth's rotation on its axis that causes the sun to appear to set and rise, and I have done some investigation of this just a little bit further because I was curious: did anybody get this? Because it is pretty clear from the perspective of the God that I know that it is not the sun that is moving, so why is it that that is the language that is used? Well, [that language] was the signifier that identified the perception of the experience vis-à-vis the earth and the sun, and as such the language is not scientifically accurate. Does that mean that Allāh made a mistake? No. Again from the context of seventh-century Arabia certain principles and ideals were established, but the fulfilment of them sometimes took, in fact, the trajectory of the process of living or life of human beings. And that is why slavery was never condemned in the Qur'ān, and yet I don't know anybody who doesn't find it abhorrent.

So we are dealing with [these questions]: what is the nature of living ethics, and what is the relationship of the Qur'ān to that living ethics? For me, the Qur'ān is always a companion. But the only way for the Qur'ān to be a companion to me, and I say this with all sincerity personally, is that I had to grapple with the places that, no matter how much you do with it, [it says what it says]. And I just cannot condone a man beating his wife. So what does that mean? I grappled with this and it was almost one of those dark nights of the soul, until I went through the process of the development of the methodology that I show in that book [*Inside the Gender Jihad*]. So we do have to grapple with specifics, and we have to determine their application in real contexts, and if we do not do that, what we have said is 'humanity does not matter, because the Qur'ān is superior'. I am saying: the Qur'ān is addressed to humanity, because humanity matters.

Karen Bauer: I do have to say that with regard to one of the points that you made very early on, about gender exceptionalism, I do say to my students all the time, if you look at the question of interest, charging interest (*ribā*), or anything like that, you will notice a lot of very conservative people have performed a lot of gymnastics in order to be able to do modern banking.

And if you look at other questions like slavery, as you mentioned, you'll notice that people have no problem reinterpreting it. So it is sometimes hard for people to grasp that gender is actually the exception, rather than the rule, in terms of reinterpretation. And I think that is such a significant point that it bears repeating.

[. . .]

We have reached our final question, and our final question has to do with the nature of the text itself. In your book *Inside the Gender Jihad*, you mention the 'silence' of the text: 'The text is silent. It needs interpretation, and had always historically and currently been subjected to interpretation. We make it speak for us by asking of it. If we are narrow, we will get a narrow response or answer. If we are open, it will open us to even greater possibilities'.[270] We are curious as to what it means to say that the text is 'silent' and that it gains meaning from interpretation. Are there certain people who can make the text speak, and what kind of commitment might it take to make it speak? Does this even relate to what you have said before about the text being a 'window' to look through? Thank you.

amina wadud: Yes, this quotation actually started with Imam ʿAlī may God be pleased with him (*raḍī Allāhu ʿanhu*) – that the text is silent and we make it speak. I think it is interesting because, of course, he was in the oral culture, so the idea of a silent text has different potential meanings than what I understand, and my understanding of it is related to the existence of a physical Qurʾān in the home of many if not all Muslims, and yet it is not a companion text to their daily lives, but rather the interpretation, or what the imam says, or the Mullah says, or the *mawlānā* says, in context is what they think is holy or sacred, and I think that is quite interesting. So the text can remain wrapped in a lovely cloth on the top shelf, but it is still silent.

Now, having said that, I am going to be honest: the fact that I fell in love with the Qurʾān means that I have a privilege. It means that from the beginning it spoke to me, but I don't mean to say that it has to speak to everybody in that way. What I mean to say is that the Qurʾān gives us such a wide repertoire of actual statements, but many of us have not come to align ourselves with the Qurʾān in any way. I ask people in certain settings, 'Tell me about your favourite verse in the Qurʾān. Why is it your favourite?' You know, there is sometimes something in the Qurʾān that speaks to you, and when it does, then own it. And when you own it, that becomes the key to unlocking the

[270] wadud, *Inside the Gender Jihad*, 197.

door which is the Qur'ān, because the Qur'ān is a portal into the ultimate reality. If you don't have the key to unlock it, then you could pass back and forth through the door but you won't notice anything. You want to find a way to be able to have a personal relationship. I really try to encourage people, even just in translation, to become intimate with the Qur'ān and to have the Qur'ān be intimate to them. Without that, then the Qur'ān does not speak to you. So it is silent. Just like in the cartoon with Lionel,[271] the adults are talking 'wah wah wah' – there are lots of words, but they are not transformative. So there is a kind of silence.

But I have become interested in what I call the ambiguities of the Qur'ān, which is where this statement actually came from when I was writing it. That is, if you look at it, the Qur'ān sometimes fills in gaps along the lines of a certain trajectory and it sometimes leaves a gap, which I think is very interesting. I want to give some specific examples of it. There is a short *sūra* at the end, and at the moment I can only think of the verse *you will not encompass all of His knowledge* [Q. 2:255], but there is a short *sūra* at the end, which actually goes through transitions of knowledge, from *ʿilm al-yaqīn* to *ḥaqq al-yaqīn* [cf. Q. 102] etcetera, and I find it fascinating because it is one of the shortest *sūra*s, and if you take an evolution of the potential with regard to language itself, and you watch the places where the Qur'ān fills in the gap and the places where the gap is maintained, you can surmise the filling of the gap in the middle, because the trajectory is clear. Like you can teach children about sequencing when they are little. In the sequence of the Qur'ān, look at the places where the sequences have blank spots, and I think those are fascinating, and that is the silence that I was talking about at that time.

But, also, because the Qur'ān shifts between verbs or active participles or nouns, there is a 'do' version and a 'be' version. As I am working on ambiguity, and embracing ambiguity in the Qur'ān, I think that we need to study the extent to which the Qur'ān gives a verbal base and a verbal noun base for certain things, and which things are only done in noun form and which things are only done in verb form. It is a big project, not one that I have taken on, but I am very interested in it because when you are just reading the Qur'ān it is not sufficient to gather the data. But I am curious about ways in which the Qur'ān manipulates the language itself to make its message, because I have seen the ways in which the Qur'ān says a thing lends itself to deeper and deeper levels of understanding for the purpose of guidance. Somehow, it takes a human being from its current state to its next highest

[271] 'Peanuts', Charles Schultz.

state, so we arrive at our own perfected soul. And so I am very much interested in what goes unsaid in the Qur'ān, what is said only in verbal form, what is said only in noun form, and what we might surmise from the way in which these things build in that sequence with something missing or not, in what ways we fill in that gap based on our understanding of how the sequence should go. This is a really interesting linguistic project, which, unfortunately, I don't think I am going to have the opportunity to be able to pursue. But I am very interested in the fact that the 'literal' thing that people usually say about the Qur'ān is usually about application. They do not say 'literal' in terms of all of this other beautiful stuff in the Qur'ān. So this is not about the *qaṭʿī* (categorical) it is about the breath – the *nafas al-Raḥmān*; it is about the breath that breathes life into this text, and how we engage with that language and how our capacity to engage with it sweeps us up into realms of possibilities. And that to me is exquisitely divine.

Feras Hamza: That is a really lovely reflection on the oral context in which the Qur'ān must have emerged in the seventh century through the mouth of the Prophet, to all of those who knew their words very well, who could speak their words with beautiful rhetoric and poetry, but this Qur'ān comes with a message, and your word 'transformative' is very interesting here because it wasn't just empty words, it was words constructed in a particular way, with a view to effecting a particular impact.

amina wadud: Not just descriptive, but prescriptive.

Feras Hamza: I think it is interesting that a lot of language that you yourself use to talk about your hermeneutics uses these three steps of prefiguring, configuring and refiguring, which is a hermeneutical approach that has been touched on by certain thinkers in the European tradition, though not to do with the Qur'ān – they applied it to other religious texts. But it is interesting that we're yet to do this for the Qur'ān, and it is something that I'm quite interested in – how do we look at language and how does it impact the narration itself. And we both, Karen and I, work on the Qur'ān all the time, and so it is constantly with us, and we certainly do value the thought that you expressed earlier, which is that you get out of it as much as you give to it, and the idea that the piecemeal approach never really works. One has the sense that the Qur'ān is, like you said, a portal, but also when you actually begin to recite or read it, you feel like you are joining a continuing narration, it is not like it ever stops; it is there, but you just are not conscious of it, like a carousel, always going around and you step on and step off. And I am interested in the hermeneutics of that. Maybe you could just add a little bit – any thoughts provoked by my own commentary on your commentary. I just want to explore that with you a little bit more – the world of hermeneutics and how that is enhanced by our own recitation of the Qur'ān, reading Arabic, knowing Arabic; that is also a privileged position. It is not a position that can be extracted by reading an English translation of the Qur'ān. But I have to say that if you know the Qur'ān in Arabic and you can read it in English, you can always make a better translation of the English. There is always a way of enhancing the English. But to go back to the point, what do we do with this question of language? Because the Qur'ān is faceted at a linguistic, composite level as you were saying.

amina wadud: Yes, I think that I have borrowed from some Sufi commentators who expressed the idea that there is a multiplicity of interpretations with every word. Because in my lifetime, as I said, I was really privileged. I fell in love with the Qur'ān in an English translation that I can no longer tolerate, which is really funny. And I turned that love into a life work: I went to graduate school for the study of the Qur'ān. And yet, as I say, I am still doing short blurbs of Qur'ānic commentary for my Patreon [web] page, and usually the ones that I write for the page are just the short *sūra*s that you tend to repeat again and again for your performance of *ṣalāt* (*prayer*), and sometimes I am standing there, praying *ṣalāt* and thinking, 'Oh you know this is just so much fun, I think I will just write about it for the page'. So I do. I give a little bit of *tafsīr* just to remind us to reflect on it. In that respect, Professor Hamza, I think that some people are lucky in that, when they immerse themselves in the study, they don't lose the beauty. Other people are only interested in the politics of how to control other people through the Qur'ān. But when you allow for it, I think the Qur'ān responds to you at every state and every station when you return to it, and that is why the more you put into it the more you get out of it. Unfortunately, when you are just learning – kids may be forced to memorise and get slapped on the hand with a ruler – you kind of don't understand what we're talking about; but, fortunately, as mature adults, our relationship is one of a tremendous amount of love and inspiration from the Qur'ān itself, and that is why it is when people ask, 'How can you believe in the Qur'ān? It's not equal, etcetera', I say, 'You know, there are sixty-seven problematic verses, but I would by no means throw the baby away with the bath [water].' There is so much beauty, and there is so much challenge. I require myself to read the Qur'ān every day during the month of Ramadan. It used to be that I would finish the Qur'ān every Ramadan, but I am getting older and it takes longer; and, unfortunately, no matter what I do I am always interested in the interpretive part, so I can't just read, I am thinking. I am managing about a half, and this time it may have even been a third, so it is getting less and less. And yet, every time I read it, I find something new; and I find that fascinating, because even when I am reciting the [parts] that I have already memorised, new things still come to me. And that is, I think, what the Sufis meant with regard to the spectrum of possible meaning. And that is that the Qur'ān is a portal into the ultimate reality, and if you are privileged to find the keys to unlock and be able to walk through that portal, what a lovely view.

وَقُل لِّلْمُؤْمِنَٰتِ يَغْضُضْنَ مِنْ أَبْصَٰرِهِنَّ وَيَحْفَظْنَ فُرُوجَهُنَّ وَلَا يُبْدِينَ
زِينَتَهُنَّ إِلَّا مَا ظَهَرَ مِنْهَا وَلْيَضْرِبْنَ بِخُمُرِهِنَّ عَلَىٰ جُيُوبِهِنَّ وَلَا يُبْدِينَ زِينَتَهُنَّ
إِلَّا لِبُعُولَتِهِنَّ أَوْ ءَابَآئِهِنَّ أَوْ ءَابَآءِ بُعُولَتِهِنَّ أَوْ أَبْنَآئِهِنَّ أَوْ أَبْنَآءِ بُعُولَتِهِنَّ أَوْ إِخْوَٰنِهِنَّ
أَوْ بَنِىٓ إِخْوَٰنِهِنَّ أَوْ بَنِىٓ أَخَوَٰتِهِنَّ أَوْ نِسَآئِهِنَّ أَوْ مَا مَلَكَتْ أَيْمَٰنُهُنَّ أَوِ
ٱلتَّٰبِعِينَ غَيْرِ أُو۟لِى ٱلْإِرْبَةِ مِنَ ٱلرِّجَالِ أَوِ ٱلطِّفْلِ ٱلَّذِينَ لَمْ يَظْهَرُوا۟ عَلَىٰ عَوْرَٰتِ
ٱلنِّسَآءِ وَلَا يَضْرِبْنَ بِأَرْجُلِهِنَّ لِيُعْلَمَ مَا يُخْفِينَ مِن زِينَتِهِنَّ وَتُوبُوٓا۟ إِلَى ٱللَّهِ جَمِيعًا
أَيُّهَ ٱلْمُؤْمِنُونَ لَعَلَّكُمْ تُفْلِحُونَ

4 The veil
(Q. 24:31)

And tell the believing women to lower their gaze and safeguard their private parts, and let them not reveal their ornament except what is apparent of it, and let them cast their wraps over their cleavage, and let them not reveal their ornament except to their husbands, or their fathers, or their husbands' fathers, or their sons, or their husbands' sons, or their brothers, or their brothers' sons or sisters' sons, or their womenfolk or what their right hands possess, or their male dependants lacking (sexual) desire or children uninitiated to the exposedness of women. And let them not stamp their feet to make known what they hide of their ornament. Turn to God in repentance all together O believers so that you may prosper.

Wa qul li'l-mu'mināt yaghḍuḍna min abṣārihinna wa-yaḥfaẓna furūjahunna wa-lā yubdīna zīnatahunna illā mā ẓahara minhā wa'l-yaḍribna bi-khumūrihinna ʿalā juyūbihinna wa-lā yubdīna zīnatahunna illā li-buʿūlatihinna aw ābā'ihinna aw ābā'i buʿūlatihinna aw abnā'ihinna aw abnā'i buʿūlatihinna aw ikhwānihinna aw banī ikhwānihinna aw banī akhawātihinna aw nisā'ihinna aw mā malakat aymānuhunna aw al-tābiʿīna ghayri ūlī'l-irbati min al rijāl aw al-ṭifl alladhīna lam yaẓharū ʿalā ʿawrāt al-nisā' wa-lā yaḍribna bi-arjulihinna li-yuʿlama mā yukhfīna min zīnatihinna wa-tūbū ilā Allāhi jamīʿan ayyuha'l-mu'minūn laʿallakum tufliḥūn

THE VERSES of Q. 24:31 are one of two loci in the Qur'ān that, over time, have come to be regarded as the proof-texts, however indirectly and allusively, for the general Muslim jurisprudential requirement for a woman to 'veil'. In reality, the relationship between the Qur'ānic discourse on this topic and the body of jurisprudential (*fiqh*) elaborations is complex, as are the cultural politics of veiling. Since at least the so-called 'Islamic awakening' of the 1970s, the veil has come to symbolise a constellation of political and cultural ideals, often in conflict with local and national governments in the Islamic world, but also with cultural values perceived as global exports of a liberal capitalist and secularising Euro-American political economy. It has become symbolic of two tensions simultaneously: that experienced by Muslim women within their Muslim communities on the one hand, and, on the other hand, between traditional conceptions of cultural identity and what are perceived as secularising public sensibilities preferred by national governments hoping for greater alignment with Euro-American modernity.[1]

For women themselves, the liberal ideals of choice and freedom can intersect to produce hybrid subjectivities, where a Muslim woman in a non-Muslim majority country may choose to veil precisely because it is her choice: liberal values are internalised to justify traditionalist conceptions of public identity and, by extension, traditionalist modes of reasoning.[2] Such intersections are frequently overlooked in a Western political discourse that deploys the Islamic veil as a symbol of a cultural intransigence with regard to women's rights and as a throwback to oppressive and illiberal premodern religio-political traditions.[3] The veil thus acts metonymically for 'women' or 'women's rights' in the Islamic world and beyond. Where women are subject to oppressive social structures (which in itself is a global challenge, and not peculiarly Islamic), the institution of the veil is an obvious target. It would be easy to dismiss the discourse on the veil as a distraction from the challenges to women's equality and rights in large parts of Muslim societies where social structures indeed remain largely oppressive of women. But in many

[1] For an important nuancing of the idea of 'the secular' and its relationship to 'the sacred', Talal Asad's *Formations of the Secular: Christianity, Islam and Modernity* (Stanford, CA, Stanford University Press, 2003) is essential reading. In a similar vein, Talal Asad *et al.*, in *Is Critique Secular: Blasphemy, Injury and Free Speech* (New York, Fordham University Press, 2013), rethink and critique conventional dichotomies where, for instance, 'free speech' and 'religious thought' could never inhabit the same epistemological space, let alone be used in the same breath.

[2] A classic example is found in the ethnographic work documented in Irene Zempi, '"It's part of me, I feel naked without it": Choice, Agency and Identity for Muslim Women who Wear the Niqab', *Ethnic and Racial Studies* 39.10 (2016), 1738–54. Against the construction of the *niqāb* (full face veil) through the lens of Islamic terrorism, the interviews with British women who wore the *niqāb* show that they frame it as an expression of personal choice, as well as religious piety, public modesty and belonging to the global *umma*.

[3] For instance, Boris Johnson's comparison of Muslim women in burkas to 'letterboxes' was his way of situating himself on the domestic political front as a defender of 'Britishness' by implying the backwardness and un-Britishness of those who would choose to dress in this manner: 'If you tell me that the burka is oppressive, then I am with you . . . I would go further and say that it is absolutely ridiculous that people should choose to go around looking like letterboxes.' 'Boris Johnson Faces Criticism over Burka "Letter Box" Jibe', BBC News, 6 August 2018, https://www.bbc.co.uk/news/uk-politics-45083275. He subsequently apologised for the remarks.

instances, the veil has become symbolic of those very tensions that animate the larger debates over women's rights and the subtle interplay between modernity, tradition and notions of cultural and religious authenticity.

A cursory look at the anthropology of dress with regard to veiling practices reveals a rich spectrum of expressions of modesty, which suggests that veiling can never be understood as a monolithic phenomenon.[4] The choice to veil or not to veil has the power to challenge norms about how women ought to be in modern societies, particularly in those instances where cultural ideals demand a structuring and a disciplining of the 'woman-subject', leaving no room for alternative expressions of social agency or cultural identity.[5] This is as true in societies where the dominant practice is not to veil, as it is in societies where the dominant practice is veiling.[6] Often, nuanced examinations of the concepts of modesty and privacy are missed entirely.[7] In sum, the multiple social and political intersections within which the veil appears across cultural geographies requires contextualised interpretations of the kind perhaps only offered by focused ethnographic studies.[8] Veiling practices, much like the individuals practising them, can accommodate contradictory aims and motivations. Agency can become ambiguous: women comply with social norms and contest them when they veil or choose not to.[9]

While it may seem that the objectification of the 'veiling Muslim woman' – through the reification of the veil and its reduction into a single phenomenon

[4] See 'Key terms': *khimār.*

[5] Cf. Nadia Fadil and Mayanthi Fernando, 'Rediscovering the "Everyday" Muslim: Notes on an Anthropological Divide', *HAU Journal of Ethnographic Theory* 5.2 (2015), 59–88. The authors challenge the normativity of liberal-secular approaches to 'the everyday' in the field of anthropology, where in fact 'the everyday' can be shown to have been used to disqualify 'pious practice' from ethnographic attention, thus framing it as ontologically aberrant.

[6] Perhaps because this is such a politically laden topic, social or legal pressure on women to veil in conservative social milieux (whether in the Muslim-majority world or outside of it) is the subject of much less academic research than its counterpart, women's choice to veil in liberal, secular societies. For a rich discussion, see Leila Ahmed, *A Quiet Revolution: The Veil's Resurgence, from the Middle East to America* (New Haven, CT, Yale University Press, 2012).

[7] See, for example, Fadwa El Guindi's classic study of the concept of 'modesty' among several other significations of veiling, including that among communities of men, *Veil: Modesty, Privacy and Resistance* (Oxford, Berg, 1999); on the veil of 'masculinity', see 117–28.

[8] For example, Lila Abu-Lughod's *Veiled Sentiments: Honor and Poetry in a Bedouin Society* (Berkeley, University of California Press, 1999).

[9] Arlene E. MacLeod, 'Hegemonic Relations and Gender Resistance: The New Veiling as Accommodating Protest in Cairo', *Signs: Journal of Women in Culture and Society* 17.3 (1992), 533–57: The veil can reflect social class and is a mode of social communication (about marital status, education, origin). It can signal political sentiment, national protest, as well as fashion (cultural identity), and cannot be reduced to a Gramscian 'false consciousness'. Confronted with a criss-cross of power relations (men, class, economics), for some women the veil offers a suitable response to negotiate a maze of obligations and social pressures.

with a single meaning, shorn of any subjectivities – is entirely modern, such objectification has a precursor in this verse's medieval interpretations, in which the woman herself is objectified as a legal category around which parameters needed to be established clearly, as we shall see. The following paragraphs briefly describe the veil's place in the Qur'ān, in the legal literature and in the commentaries in this chapter.

The believers' dress is discussed in three Qur'ānic verses: Q. 7:39, 24:31 and 33:59.[10] Q. 7:31, from the later Meccan period, reads in part, *O children of Adam! Adorn yourselves* (*zīna*) *at every place of worship*, which some early commentators framed as a rebuke of pagan practices. For instance, in Ṭabarī's commentary on this verse, he describes women performing prayer rituals nearly naked, with their breasts exposed and a mere cloth covering their private parts; he glosses *ornament* here as 'clothing', with the meaning that the believers should clothe themselves decently when praying.[11] An instance of clothing specific to women is found in Q. 33:59, which instructs the Prophet to tell his wives and daughters 'and the women of the believers' to *draw their cloaks closely about themselves: that makes it more likely for them to be recognised and not harmed*. In this instance, along with the preceding and following verses, the overt Qur'ānic context seems to distinguish Muslim women from non-Muslims; there is the sense that this status confers on them a special protection. The preceding verse warns: *those who harm the believing men and the believing women without cause certainly bear the guilt of slander and flagrant sin*; while the following verse warns that the hypocrites should cease tormenting the believers

The verse in question in this chapter, which is also from the Medinan period, thus comes amid an intra-Qur'ānic discussion of modesty as a function of believers' status *qua* believers in contexts where they might be harassed or where they might not act with the pious comportment expected of them on account of that status in the social sphere. The first half of *sūrat al-Nūr*, the *sūra* in which this verse is found, further specifies particular aspects of moral comportment with regard to what may be considered 'public' and 'private' spaces and acts, with a particular focus on sexual ethics. *Sūrat al-Nūr*, which means 'the *sūra* of light', begins with something much more stark: the punishment of fornicators. The narrator, understood to be God, here asserts that fornicators should be punished with lashes and fornicators

[10] These verses are all discussed in Omar Anchassi, 'Status Distinctions and Sartorial Difference: Slavery, Sexual Ethics, and the Social Logic of Veiling in Islamic Law', *Islamic Law and Society* (2021), 1–31.

[11] Ṭabarī, *Jāmiʿ al-bayān*, s.v. Q. 7:31; Anchassi notes that this practice was mentioned by several early commentators.

of both sexes belong together (vv. 2–3). This is then mitigated: the fornication must be witnessed by four people, or sworn on a sacred oath, or the accuser will be flogged (vv. 4–11); the audience is chastised for believing unproven allegations, for punishing people without proof, and for spreading indecency (*fāḥisha*) among the believers (vv. 12–19). Thus fornication, an act of moral wrong, is still considered relatively private: it is only subject to punishment within the community when it becomes 'public' by being witnessed by a number of people. Meanwhile, making unjust or unproven accusations and spreading rumours are also crimes, themes that are repeated in vv. 23–5. The *sūra* then outlines physical spaces of privacy: houses and bodies. Houses are private spaces: believers must not enter unoccupied houses, and should knock before entering any houses (vv. 27–9), and they must preserve their own and others' bodily privacy by casting down their looks and guarding their private parts (v. 30); women should *cast their wraps over their cleavage* (v. 31). Believers should marry each other when possible. All of these rulings are punctuated by reminders that God will forgive anyone who repents.

What might initially seem to be a straightforward condemnation of illicit sex is thus nuanced through the idea that those who engage in such behaviour are suited to one another and will face their ultimate reckoning in the Hereafter (v. 26). Meanwhile, believers' licit sexual conduct with one another is connected with a wider notion of modesty that involves maintaining a modicum of bodily privacy, controlling the gaze, not entering others' houses unbidden, and a strict regulation of any interference with others' private affairs. This part of the *sūra* culminates in an assertion of God's nature as light and guidance: *God is the light of the heavens and earth.* [. . .] *God guides to His light whom He will* (v. 35).[12] The description of God as light (*nūr*) gives the *sūra* its name and is instrumentally connected to the instructions on socio-moral comportment in the verses that precede it. The beginning and the end point of such proper comportment is God: He guides the behaviour of the community and suggests that those who follow such guidance should find one another in the world, just as they will find Him in the Hereafter.

It is in this context that Q. 24:31 outlines the actions to be undertaken by believing women: lowering their gazes, casting their wraps over their cleavage and not displaying their ornament, except what is apparent of it. There follows a list of the people before whom a woman may display her ornament, including blood kin and members of the household, or people

[12] On this verse and its interpretations, see Hamza *et al.*, *Anthology*, I, 347–453. Note also that God's light is a precursor to the believers' own light which, they are told elsewhere, will *move swiftly before them* on the Day of Judgment (Q. 57:12).

who will be coming and going in the house, such as slaves, children and 'followers' (see 'Key terms': *tābiʿūn*). Believers are finally instructed to turn all together to God in repentance. Taken at face value, this verse seems to encourage moderate norms of modesty and social decency in public, with a generally more relaxed atmosphere within the house. None of the verses in the Qurʾān mention covering women's hair or faces.

Much has been written on the legal interpretations (*fiqh*) of the veiling verses. As is described below, the authors of *tafsīr* agree that free women's faces and hands should remain uncovered as they go about their daily business. While early jurists agree, post-classical jurists began to insist that women cover their faces.[13] In both *tafsīr* and *fiqh*, enslaved women only needed to cover between the navel and the knees, just the same as men. In the *tafsīr* of this verse the veiling practices of slave women receive almost no attention; rather, they are discussed as members of the household before whom (free) women's veiling is exempt. In *fiqh*, the difference in veiling status for free women and slave women became a matter of significant debate.[14]

For the commentators surveyed in this chapter, the major issue in this verse is identifying what constitutes a woman's ornament (*zīna*), precisely because that ornament should not come within the purview or gaze of certain categories of individuals – in the main, those who are not related to that woman. This is provoked by the Qurʾānic verse's proviso that women

[13] Eli Alshech, 'Out of Sight and Therefore Out of Mind: Early Sunnī Islamic Modesty Regulations and the Creation of Spheres of Privacy', *Journal of Near Eastern Studies* 66.4 (2007), 267–90.

[14] Modern scholars explain the difference between free women's veiling and slave women's veiling in three main ways, all summarised by Anchassi. Eli Alshech argues for a public–private divide and shows how the rulings on veiling changed through time. As the fear of *fitna* increased, slaves and free women were gradually asked to cover more. Ze'ev Maghen argues that with regard to veiling, Islamic law adhered to a 'building strong walls' approach as opposed to a 'building strong men' approach. Omar Anchassi draws on Hina Azam's notions of 'theocentric' versus 'proprietary' systems of sexual ethics. Azam argues that under the theocentric model, sexuality was a moral space judged primarily by God, while under a proprietary model, sexuality is a commodity that can be monetised. Anchassi uses this model to argue that early arguments for slave women to be unveiled is rooted in a proprietary notion of sexual ethics, in which their social status trumped the fear of temptation; through time, as the fear of temptation increased, the model became more theocentric and jurists began to insist that slave women cover. See Alshech, 'Out of Sight'; idem, '"Do Not Enter Houses Other than Your Own": The Evolution of the Notion of a Private Domestic Sphere in Early Sunnī Islamic Thought', *Islamic Law and Society* 11.3 (2004), 291–332; Anchassi, 'Status Distinctions'; Azam, *Sexual Violation in Islamic Law*, or for an accessible summary, eadem, 'Competing Approaches to Rape in Islamic Law' in *Feminism, Law, and Religion*, ed. Marie Fallinger, Elizabeth Schiltz and Susan Stabile (Burlington, VT, Ashgate, 2013), 327–44; Ze'ev Maghen, 'See No Evil: Morality and Methodology in Ibn al-Qaṭṭān al-Fāsī's *Aḥkām al-Naẓar bi-Ḥāssat al-Baṣar*', *Islamic Law and Society* 14.3 (2007), 342–90.

could reveal their ornaments, but only *what is apparent of it* (*illā mā ẓahara minhā*). Here, the commentators expand the exegetical space by reflecting on the nature of the ornament itself: is it the woman's body or parts of it that are considered natural physical adornments, or is it what she adorns herself or those parts with, of jewellery or other accessories? Hence, there are two interrelated questions: what are a woman's ornaments (*zīna*) and who can see them?

All of the commentaries agree that a woman's entire body is a *zīna*, and it is the fact of a woman's *zīna* that becomes the potential for her exposedness (*'awra*). The term *'awra*, discussed further below, is used by the commentators to refer to women's potential to be in a state, however temporary and partial, of nudity, nakedness, or indecent exposure, and thus becomes, for them, equated with shame. Denoting 'woman' as *'awra* facilitates an objectification of women in this male-dominated scholastic field, as the commentators are then able to set the parameters for women's modesty and, ultimately, for their activities in private as well as public life.

For the commentators, only the husband has the right of full access to his wife's entire body, even as some are reluctant to extend that right to him actually gazing at her private parts; but this remains the minority point of view. What vestiges of *zīna* can be exposed to other categories of individuals, beyond the husband, in the way of relatives, kin or otherwise, and non-relatives is the point of contention. It is the outer boundaries of the group of those whose gaze is permitted that is most difficult to define. This group is important precisely because they enjoy regular access to the household; most are exempted: because of their degrees of consanguinity, they are not allowed to be married to the women in question (*maḥram*). But the household was also comprised of others – slaves or dependants (elderly or otherwise) – and these had to be identified in order for them to be licitly in the presence of the women of the household who may not be dressed as they would be in public. It is thus the minimum requirement for the covering of a woman's body, or the maximum of the woman's body that could be exposed to a household member, that becomes a focus of the commentators' exegeses. This leads to discussions about the ornament being of two kinds: 'hidden' and 'manifest'.

The consensus seems to be that a woman's manifest ornament is her hands and face, and the commentators proceed to corroborate this with reports from the Prophet. They all agree that in public women should have their face and hands showing, since they need these to be identified and to be able to pursue various aspects of public life. Many specifically mention that a woman must have her face showing in order to testify in court. It is important to note that because all of the commentators agree that some part of that *zīna* may be exposed to non-relatives (as per the Qur'ānic verse), none of them mandate that a woman cover herself entirely, whether in private or in public. This makes the modern turn to the full *niqāb* in various Muslim contexts all the more unusual and interesting for the study of contemporary identity.

One final point ought to be mentioned with regard to the issue of the veil and the lines drawn for women, and between them and men in public and private life. The commentaries, even when they are sparse, betray a broader geographical, socio-cultural legacy. The generally fastidious method by which the commentaries zero in on aims specific to their exegetical imperatives, be these legalistic, sectarian, moralistic, pietistic or spiritual, can all too easily mask the historical affinities of West-Arabian society, here Mecca and Medina, with its Graeco-Roman, now Byzantine, late antique periphery.[15] Every now and then, a historical report or series of reports marshalled by the exegetes to vindicate and reinforce the legal and moral strictures as they were deposited in the Qur'ān unwittingly provide us with a window, no more than a tantalising one, into a liminal stage in the transition from an ambiguous cultural model,[16]

[15] The Islamo-Arabic conceptual vocabulary as it emerges in the Qur'ān bears a striking resemblance to the lexicon of terms used in late antique Christian writings to discuss women's modesty, dress (including veiling and hair-binding) and the norms governing their appearance in public, and this can be gleaned from contexts as wide apart as North Africa (cf. Tertullian, third century) to the Byzantine East (cf. *Didascalia Apostolorum*, c. 230): on both of these, see the fascinating contribution of Gabriel Radle, 'The Veiling of Women in Byzantium: Liturgy, Hair, and Identity in a Medieval Rite of Passage', *Speculum: A Journal of Medieval Studies* 94.4 (2019), 1070–1115. Although Radle does not make the connections with the Islamo-Arabic milieu or language, the Islamicist should find lots to ponder: compare, for example, the ancient Greek word for veil, κρήδεμνον (lit. battlement), and the Arabic term for a chaste woman, *muḥṣin* (lit. fortified). Parallel cultural dispositions, such as veiling in the case of men as an emotional response or as a pious disposition of humility (cf. Greek αἰδώς), suggested by the Qur'ānic references to the Prophet as *muzzammil* (*sūrat al-Muzzammil*, Q. 73) and *muddaththir* (*surat al-Muddaththir*, Q. 74) have scarcely received attention, *pace* Abu-Lughod's remarks in *Veiled Sentiments*, 117–28 and 148. On the Greek side, see Douglas L. Cairns, 'The Meaning of the Veil in Ancient Greek Culture' in *Women's Dress in the Ancient Greek World*, ed. Lloyd Llewellyn-Jones (London, Duckworth and the Classical Press of Wales, 2002), 73–93.

[16] Ambiguous, simply because we know almost nothing with any level of certainty or detail about pre-Islamic Mecca from the record of its own inhabitants – given that it was not a literary society (though not an unlettered one, given the emergence of the Qur'ān itself) – and this *pace* the immense scholarship devoted to filling in some of the blanks. See Robert Hoyland's *Seeing Islam as Others Saw It: A Survey and Evaluation of Christian, Jewish and Zoroastrian Writings on Early Islam* (Princeton, NJ, Darwin Press, 1997); Patricia Crone, *Meccan Trade and the Rise of Islam* (Princeton, NJ, Princeton University Press, 1987); eadem, *Roman, Provincial and Islamic Law: The Origins of the Islamic Patronate* (Cambridge, Cambridge University Press, 1987); Walter E. Kaegi, *Byzantium and the Early Islamic Conquests* (Cambridge, Cambridge University Press, 1992); also Michael G. Morony, *Iraq After the Muslim Conquest* (Princeton, NJ, Princeton University Press, 1984). We suggest that the pattern on the 'other side' of the cultural zone could not have been very different to that of West Arabia. Epigraphic, sigillographic and numismatic evidence remains silent without the support of documentary texts. As it happens, the earliest document we have is the Qur'ān itself.

what may be termed as 'Graeco-Mediterranean', to an unequivocal Islamo-Arabic one.[17]

Key terms

ʿAwra: in the Qurʾān, this is exposedness, something which should be concealed or protected. But by the time of the commentaries, this potential for exposure and the consequences of such exposure mean that for the commentators it denotes 'shame' or 'shameful parts'.[18] Thus our translations of this term differ between the original Qurʾānic context (exposedness) and the commentaries (shameful parts) as described below.

ʿAwra appears four times in the Qurʾān. In three cases, the term refers to 'exposedness', that is, twice to homes being left exposed and unguarded during expeditions into battle (Q. 33:13)[19] and once to individuals in a household being exposed because of the loose garb worn in the privacy of the home around the resting periods (Q. 24:58). In fact, the reference to the *ʿawrāt* of women in Q. 24:31 merely seems to prefigure that of the general household in Q. 24:58 as a matter of social modesty; however, the subject of this phrase in Q. 24:31 is children who are not yet sexually conscious.

The term comes to denote a 'defect' of some sort, originally in the eye: *al-aʿwar* being a person with only one functioning eye;[20] it can also connote harm or hurt as the cause of the defect. In addition, there is the valence of something that is 'marred' or 'blemished' because of some defect. The social visibility of such defects extended the sense of the term into 'something shameful' to be covered up from public eyes, whence the figurative notion of *ʿār* for a crime or affliction that mars the reputation of a group or community. Anxiety over both of these came to be associated with women in general.[21] This in itself speaks volumes about the objectification of women in a wide range of Muslim societies as things to be hidden or out of sight of the public

[17] That is to say, what ultimately became the Arabic-Islamic tradition could have easily become an alternative Arabised cultural paradigm.

[18] Rāghib, for instance, says, '*ʿawra* is a person's *sawʾa* (unseemliness), but that is a metonym (*kināya*); its original sense is something that is shameful (*ʿār*)'. Rāghib, *Mufradāt*, 595–6, s.v. *ʿ-w-r*.

[19] The verse reads: *They claim, 'Our houses are exposed', but they are not exposed* (*yaqūlūn inna buyūtanā ʿawratun, wa-mā hiya bi-ʿawratin*).

[20] Cf. in this vein the pejorative connotation associated with the apocalyptic figure of the false messiah, often referred to as *al-aʿwar al-dajjāl*, 'the one-eyed impostor'. David B. Cook, 'Dajjāl', *EI*^{3}; Farhang Mehrvash, tr. Farzin Negahban, 'Dajjāl', *EIsl*.

[21] Cf. the Urdu word for 'woman', *aurat*, the final *tāʾ* being an orthographical carry-over from the Arabic feminine suffix.

gaze. In effect, a synecdoche is extended beyond what may be considered the 'parts' of a woman liable to 'exposure', which in the Qur'ān are not always denoted exclusively by this term: the natural state of nakedness and therefore unseemliness of men and women in the story of Adam and Eve is referred to with the term *saw'a*, also a pejorative word connoting something 'evil' (cf. *sū'*; see Q. 7:26–7).[22]

Farj/jayb: *farj* literally means an 'opening' but has, especially in its more frequent plural form *furūj*, been understood as the genitals or *pudenda* (note the Latin etymology of 'something to be ashamed of'). With *jayb* we are on less solid ground, since the *jayb* is usually an opening or aperture in the garment, but, presumably, since such apertures were sewn into the tops of garments, they could, by extension, refer to the neckline and down to the cleavage and bosom. It should be noted that the only other Qur'ānic occurrence for *jayb* is the episode with Moses' 'glowing hand', which he inserts into his bosom through, presumably, the *jayb* of his garment (Q. 27:12 and 28:32, on which compare the Biblical parallel in Exodus 4:6).[23]

Khimār: outer garment, wrap, or veil. In the Qur'ān, the root *kh-m-r* only appears once to denote some kind of wrap that should be used to cover the *jayb* (pl. *juyūb*), the garment aperture (and by extension the bosom or cleavage). Other root occurrences are restricted to the word *khamr*, wine. Undoubtedly, the lexicographers drew the analogy of something that 'veils', 'covers' or 'obscures' the mind, from the intoxicant effect of wine. All other 'veil-type' clothing is extra-Qur'ānic, with no mention of the extensive and rich lexicon for women's veils from different cultural geographies. In the written tradition, there are many different veiling terms in different contexts, including *ḥijāb*, *jilbāb*, *khimār*, *qināʿ* or *miqnaʿa*, *niqāb*, *mindīl*, *shaʿriyya*, *mulā'a* (in Egypt), the Ottoman *yashmaq*, the Arabian Gulf *burquʿ*, or the Moroccan *lithām*, and the 'veiling' garments known as *fūṭa*, *izār*, *milḥafa*, *takhlīla* in Morocco and Algeria.[24]

Maḥram: the basic sense of the root (*ḥ-r-m*) denotes something 'illicit' or 'inviolable', with significant ritual and legal derivates such as *ḥarām*,

[22] Cf. Abu-Lughod, *Veiled Sentiments*, 140–42.

[23] Gabriel Reynolds suggests that this is a 'pointed response' to Moses' leprous hand as described in Exodus 4:6; he points out that the description of the hand as 'white as snow' in that Aramaic *Targum Omqelos* is similar to the Qur'ānic depiction. Gabriel Said Reynolds, *The Qur'an and the Bible: Text and Commentary* (New Haven, CT, Yale University Press, 2018), 489.

[24] These have all been superbly documented by Yedida K. Stillman in *Arab Dress, A Short History: From the Dawn of Islam to Modern Times*, 2nd rev. edn, ed. Norman A. Stillman (Leiden, Brill, 2003), esp. 138–60. Note the non-Muslim veiling practices of Rabati Jewish women.

muḥarram (ritually prohibited or sacrosanct, as in the holy months) and *iḥrām* for both the act of entering into pilgrim sanctity and the cloth used for that purpose. Technically, it has come to denote those individuals in degrees of kinship by blood or breast-suckling that preclude marriage between the individuals involved, typically as enumerated by Q. 24:31. A *maḥram* is also, by extension, a male guardian who may accompany a woman in public when she needs to discharge religious and legal duties or engage in commercial transactions, precisely because there could be no suspicion of sexual activity or involvement between the two. Kinship in itself does not mean unmarriageability, since first cousins on both the paternal and maternal sides could marry the woman in question. Hence, the exegetes' discussion of why uncles are excluded from Q. 24:31, which identifies categories of individuals before whom a woman might adopt looser garments, thus bearing more of her physical parts than she would before a marriageable kin.

Tābiʿūn: literally, 'those who follow'. The category of economic dependency naturally included free married women and their children in a given household. But the term 'follower' is used here precisely in order to capture other kinds of dependants who may be attached to a household customarily over a period of time, but who do not fit into either the category of marriageability or unmarriageability. This category of dependency may have included various household hands performing a range of domestic chores or menial tasks, and who had no social attachment or source of livelihood other than the household to which they were attached.

Zīna: the root *z-y-n* occurs forty-six times in the Qurʾān, to describe beauty, adornment and ornament. In this verse, it is 'ornament', and may simply refer to women's accessories and jewellery, but for the commentators it comes to constitute one side of the social lens through which women were construed, the other being *ʿawra*. Together, the two terms frame the boundaries within which women were socially regulated by a pervasive societal patriarchy and its male-dominated juridical institutions.

Muqātil

As a storyteller and an exegete, Muqātil prefaces his exegesis of the verse by providing us with the occasion on which the verse was revealed, the characters involved and the location. More importantly, reflecting a still early stage in the formation of the ethical and legal boundaries of the Muslim community, the exegetical impulse seems to be to delineate a clear separation between pre-Islamic customs, here of moral laxity, and the moral bounds of Islam that were being established by scriptural revelation. Conversely, more ambiguously and less clearly distinguished is the relationship between the believers following the Prophet and other monotheists such as the People of the Book. It is entirely possible that the boundaries of the early Muslim community were ambiguous enough to include Jews and Christians, perceived as monotheists within the same Abrahamic tradition. This becomes clear when Muqātil mentions the 'believing women' in the presence of whom the (Muslim) women addressed by the Qur'ānic verse are permitted to reveal their ornament.[25] Readers will note how, by the time of the classical tradition, from Ṭabarī onwards, the boundaries harden, such that Muslim women are not permitted to reveal their ornament, or take off their veils, before Jewish or Christian women, and this is gradually reinforced by a tradition reported on the authority of the caliph ʿUmar b. al-Khaṭṭāb (r. 13–23/634–44).

This verse and the following one were revealed in [the case of] Asmāʾ bt. Murshid. She owned a date palm grove, named al-Waʿl, in the lands of Banū Ḥāritha. Women would enter it uncovered with their breasts, legs and hair showing. On one occasion Asmāʾ remarked, 'O how vile this is!' God, exalted be He, then revealed: *And tell the believing women to lower their gaze and safeguard their private parts, and let them not reveal their ornament except what is apparent of it*, meaning the face, the palms of the hands and where the bracelet sits; *and let them cast their wraps over their cleavage*, meaning their breasts (*ṣudūr*), *and let them not reveal their ornament*, by which God means that they should not take off their *jilbāb*,[26] *except to their husbands* (*buʿūl*, sing. *baʿl*), meaning their spouses, *or their fathers, or their husbands' fathers, or their sons, or their husbands' sons, or their brothers, or their brothers' sons*; He then says *or their womenfolk*, meaning all women who belong to the believing women; *or what their right hands possess* of slave girls, *or their male dependants*, meaning a man who follows another man and belongs with him but is not one of his slaves, *lacking (sexual) desire*, meaning those who have no need (*ḥāja*) for women, such as the frail old man, or one who is impotent.[27]

[25] Cf. Fred M. Donner's thesis that the earliest self-conception of the Muslim community was ecumenical enough to include other monotheists and that *muslimūn* is only redefined definitively as denoting the new community, what we refer to as Muslims, around the time of the caliph ʿAbd al-Malik b. Marwān (r. 65–86/685–705): *Muhammad and the Believers: At the Origins of Islam* (Cambridge, MA, Belknap Press of Harvard University Press, 2010), esp. 57–69.

[26] A long robe.

[27] Or suffering from a deformity of the member, or erectile dysfunction or dyspareunia. Muqātil, *Tafsīr Muqātil*, s.v. Q. 24:31.

Hūd

The Basran roots of Ibāḍism are always present in the *tafsīr* of Hūd, who gives priority of report to the leader of the intellectual circles of Basra in his time, al-Ḥasan al-Baṣrī (d. 110/728), a scholar and ascetic to whom both Ibāḍism and Muʿtazilism owe their roots through students of his. The cross-fertilisation of these latter two meant that Ibāḍism always retained some of the rationalist elements of Muʿtazilism, even as the former ultimately settled into a fully traditionalist community. Hūd's exegesis contains interesting early evidence for what might at best only be considered a liminal stage of attitudes towards modesty in public and private spheres, for both men and women, to some sort of veiling and physical manifestation of modesty in the private and social or public sphere. The somewhat hyperbolic description by Anas b. Mālik about the exposed breasts of ʿUmar's slave girls as they were serving the former in the house of the latter suggests clearly, given ʿUmar's well-known stern pious character, that slave women's social status was indicated precisely by their enforced exposure to the male gaze, which in turn suggests that free women were distinguished in public by their covering. As Hūd relates, ʿUmar himself went to hit a slave woman who had covered her head in public, chastising her for dressing above her station. The difference between free women's covering and slave women's covering is mandated in the legal opinions attributed to the early jurists, according to whom Muslim slave women could be perfectly pious while covering nothing other than the area between the navel and the knees.

As for His words *And tell the believing women to lower their gaze and safeguard their private parts*, this means: to lower their gaze from what it is not permissible for them to look at. And this applies to free women and slave girls. As regards His words *and let them not reveal their ornament except what is apparent of it*, some have said that *except for what is apparent of it* refers to 'clothing', which is also what al-Ḥasan [al-Baṣrī] said. It has also been mentioned on the authority of Mujāhid from Ibn ʿAbbās that he said that *what is apparent of it* refers to kohl (*kuḥl*) and rings (*khātam*). They mention also that when ʿĀʾisha was asked about 'apparent ornament' (*zīna ẓāhira*), she said, covering her wrist with her garment as she spoke, that this was bracelets (*qulb*), meaning bangles (*siwār*), and rings without stones (*fatakha*).[28]

The scholars (*ʿulamāʾ*) say that this verse pertains to free women, for in the case of slave girls ʿUmar b. al-Khaṭṭāb once saw a slave girl wearing a veil (*qināʿ*), whereupon he raised his stick over her [to strike her], saying, 'Uncover your head and do not imitate free women.' They mention on the authority of Anas b. Mālik that he said, "Umar's slave girls used to serve us with their heads uncovered, their breasts quivering and their anklets showing.'

[28] Also, sometimes, *fatkha*, denoting a ring worn around a toe.

As for His words *and let them cast their wraps over their cleavage*, this means: she draws her wrap down over her *jayb*, which is the neckline (*naḥr*). *And let them not reveal their ornament*: this is hidden adornment (*zīna bāṭina*). For there are two types of ornament: a manifest ornament, which we have explained, and a hidden ornament, which we will explain in due course, God willing. *Except to their husbands* (*buʿūl*): their spouses (*zawj*), *their husbands' fathers*: the fathers of their spouses, *or their sons, or their husbands' sons, or their brothers, or their brothers' sons or sisters' sons, or their women-folk*, Muslim women, who are able to see those parts of her that are allowed to be seen by unmarriageables (*dhū'l-maḥram*). But neither a Jewish nor a Christian woman is permitted to see that.

Thus these are the three categories of inviolability (*ḥurma*), each one greater than the next. One is the spouse, to whom all of her is permitted, a licence not granted to anyone else. Another is the father and the son, the brother, the paternal uncle, the maternal uncle, the nephew and niece, and those suckling infants who are considered in this case as kin. According to al-Ḥasan, they are only allowed to cast their gaze on these women's hair, breasts, legs and such like. Al-Ḥasan stated: a woman should not take off her veil (*khimār*) before her father or before her son or her brother. Ibn ʿAbbās said that they can look at the parts [of the body] where the earrings are, the necklace, bracelets and anklets. These are the hidden ornaments. A third category of inviolability (*ḥurma*) includes the father-in-law, the stepson and dependants, about whom God has stated *their male dependants lacking (sexual) desire*, that is to say, those without any need for women. These were men who lived in Medina and whose nature had become not to desire women on account of their poverty. Another opinion has it that this refers to imbeciles (*aḥmaq*) whom no woman would desire and of whom no man could find himself jealous. Al-Ḥasan also said that it refers to the man who follows (*t-b-ʿ*) another to serve him food and drink.

As for a woman's male slave (*mamlūk*), there is nothing wrong with her being in his presence wearing a thick, full-length shirt (*darʿ ṣafīq*) without any long outer garment (*jilbāb*).

They mention that ʿUmar b. al-Khaṭṭāb said, 'A woman shall not travel, except in the company of a kinsman who is unmarriageable (*dhū maḥram minhā*).' They also mention that ʿUmar b. al-Khaṭṭāb said, 'A woman shall not be alone with a man who is not an unmarriageable kin of hers, even if it be said that that person were her husband's [protective] male relation (*ḥamw*). For death shall be her protector!'

Another opinion has it that a woman should not take off her wrap (*khimār*) before her male slave, unless he should enter into her presence unexpectedly, in which case that is fine. Some think that *what their right hands possess* refers to slave girls and not male slaves (*ʿabīd*). Ibn Lahīʿa on the authority of Abū'l-Zubayr from Jābir b. Abd Allāh said, 'A woman should not take off her wrap (*khimār*) in the presence of her master's (*sayyid*) slaves.'

As for His words *or children uninitiated to the exposedness of women*, this means those who have not attained puberty (*ḥulm*) or the age of marriage (*nikāḥ*).

As for His words *and let them not stamp their feet to make known what they hide of their ornament*: women would stamp their feet when they passed by a gathering of seated men (*majlis*) so that the clanking of their anklets would be heard. Another opinion has it that they would strike one leg against the other until the ringing of the anklets could be heard. They were then forbidden to do that.

As for His words *Turn to God in repentance*, from all such sins; *all together O believers so that you may prosper* means [so] that you may prosper and enter Paradise.[29]

Qummī

This commentary includes a considerable number of reports (*akhbār*) on the authority of the ʿAlid imams that function as the narrative (*riwāya*) equivalent of the Sunnī *ḥadīth* reports. Certain intermediate names in the transmission are oft-cited trusted authorities – in this case, Abū Baṣīr (d. 150/767) and Abū'l-Jārūd (d. after 150/767).[30] Somewhat indicative of the overall tendency of all of the commentators to want to distinguish various extents of 'ornament' and to elucidate which category of individuals are permitted to see them, Qummī's commentary divides access into three groups: the general public – that is, 'foreigners' to the household who might gaze only on the accessories a woman is wearing; familiars to the household, who are close enough in kinship to be unmarriageable, might be able to see more of a woman's physical ornament (parts of her body, unveiled, such as the head and neckline); and finally the male spouse for whom the entire body is permitted visually.

It was narrated to me from my father on the authority of Muḥammad b. Abī ʿUmayr, on the authority of Abū Baṣīr that Abū ʿAbd Allāh [Jaʿfar al-Ṣādiq] (*ʿm*) said:

[29] Hūd, *Tafsīr kitāb Allāh al-ʿazīz*, s.v. Q. 24:31.

[30] Abū'l-Jārūd was the eponymous founder of Jārūdī Zaydism, and a long-time companion of both the fifth and sixth imams, al-Bāqir and al-Ṣādiq, neither of whose imamates he actually recognised. On this issue and the relationship of the material ascribed to Abū'l-Jārūd in Qummī's *Tafsīr*, see Bar-Asher, *Scripture and Exegesis*, 46–56.

> Every verse in the Qur'ān that mentions private parts (*furūj*) refers to fornication (*zinā*), except this one, which refers to the gaze. Therefore, it is illicit for a believing man to gaze at the private parts of his [Muslim] brother [and] for a woman to gaze at the private parts of her [Muslim] sister.[31]

According to Abū'l-Jarūd's report from Abū Jaʿfar [al-Bāqir] (*ʿm*), concerning His statement *and let them not reveal their ornament except what is apparent of it*, by *of it*:

> It refers to garments (*thawb*), kohl, rings, palm dyes and bracelets. Ornament is of three types: the ornament for people, the ornament for unmarriageable relatives and the ornament for the husband. As for the ornament for people, we have already mentioned it. As for the ornament for unmarriageable relatives, this is the place of the necklace and above, and the bangle and what is further down [the arm], and from the anklet to what is below that. As for the ornament for the husband, it is the entire body.[32]

As for His words *their male dependants lacking (sexual) desire*, this refers to the elderly decrepit male who has no desire for women,[33] and the child who has no consciousness of the shameful parts (*ʿawra*) of women. As for His statement *and let them not stamp their feet to make known what they hide of their ornament*, He means: let them not strike one foot against the other so that the jangly anklets ring out.[34]

Ṭabarī

Ṭabarī's commentary is always to be noted for the extensive support he summons in the way of chains of transmission for various exegetical opinions. Often, a variant chain of transmission (*isnād*) is provided for the very same interpretation that is reported by the very same final transmitter in the chain. The clearest example of this here is the bundle of interpretations attributed to Mujāhid. What may seem like redundancy to the reader is in fact meticulousness on the part of the historian, who is keen to establish various lines of transmission for similarly worded reports and exegeses. The discussion around *zīna* begins with a detailing of the types of clothing and accessories constituting the 'apparent' form of ornament for a woman, but quickly moves to consider the non-adorned physical parts which may legitimately be left uncovered: the most salient of these parts are the face, hands and fingers, regardless of whether these are adorned with dyes or accessories. The reasoning behind this licence

[31] Note that this passage is quoted exactly by Muḥsin al-Fayḍ al-Kāshānī, below.
[32] Note that this passage is quoted verbatim by Muḥsin al-Fayḍ al-Kāshānī, below.
[33] Fayḍ al-Kāshānī cites this phrase, though Qummī adds the word *kabīr*.
[34] Qummī, *Tafsīr al-Qummī*, s.v. Q. 24:31.

is traced to a woman's physical appearance during the performance of the ritual prayer (*ṣalāt*): in effect, her comportment and physical appearance during prayer, being a moment of ritual sanctity, suggests that sets the standard for public appearance outside of prayer. Having been written in a later urban context with a cosmopolitan demographic and extended settled households means that Ṭabarī's commentary, perhaps more so than earlier commentaries, is likely to offer additional scenarios in which visual access to a woman's ornament – be it her dress and accessories or her physical parts – comes into question. Thus, for example, non-Muslim women (in this instance, Christians), slaves and male dependants are included in various ways within which the exegetes circumscribe the framework of licit or illicit for a woman's *zīna*.

Exalted be His mention, He says to His prophet Muḥammad: *And tell*, O Muḥammad, *the believing women*, from your community (*umma*), *to lower their gaze*, from that which God loathes for it to be gazed at and has prohibited you from looking at, *and safeguard their private parts*. He is saying: let them guard their private parts, lest one for whom it is not lawful should see them, by wearing over them what conceals them from their sight.

As for His words *and let them not reveal their ornament*, He is saying: let them not manifest their ornament to people who are not unmarriageable to them (*maḥram*). The ornament is of two types. One is that which is hidden, such as anklets, bracelets, earrings and necklaces; the other, that which is apparent. But there are differences of opinion regarding what is intended by it in this verse.

One opinion has it that it refers to the apparent ornament of clothing (*thiyāb*).

An account of those who said this:

Ibn Masʿūd[35] said, 'Ornament is of two types: the apparent type is clothing and the hidden one is anklets, earrings and bracelets.'

ʿAbd Allāh [b. ʿUmar] said, 'This [ornament] is clothing (*thiyāb*).'[36]

Abū Isḥāq said, 'Do you not see where He says *Adorn yourselves* (*zīna*) *at every place of worship* [Q. 7:31]?'

Ibn Masʿūd[37] said, 'This [ornament] is a robe (*ridāʾ*).'

Others have said that *what is apparent of it* refers to what she has been permitted to reveal, and this is kohl, rings, bracelets and the face (*wajh*).

[35] Ibn Ḥumayd ← Hārūn b. al-Mughīra ← al-Ḥajjāj ← Abū Isḥāq ← Abū'l-Aḥwāṣ ← Ibn Masʿūd.

[36] There are five transmissions to the same effect from Ibn ʿUmar via different chains, with the penultimate one preceded by two identical opinions: one transmitted from Ibrahim al-Nakhaʿī and the other from al-Ḥasan al-Baṣrī.

[37] Al-Qāsim ← al-Ḥusayn ← Ḥajjāj ← Muḥammad b. al-Faḍl ← al-Aʿmash ← Mālik b. al-Ḥārith ← ʿAbd al-Raḥmān b. Zayd ← Ibn Masʿūd.

An account of those who have said this:

Saʿīd b. Jubayr reported that Ibn ʿAbbās[38] said, 'Kohl and rings'. Likewise is the opinion of Saʿīd b. Jubayr, but without a transmission from Ibn ʿAbbās.[39]

Al-Ḍaḥḥāk reported that Ibn ʿAbbās[40] said, '*What is apparent of it* refers to kohl and the cheeks (*khaddān*).'

Saʿīd b. Jubayr[41] said, 'It is the face (*wajh*) and the palms (*kaff*).'

ʿAṭāʾ [b. Abī Rabāḥ][42] said, 'It is the palms (*kaffān*) and the face (*wajh*).'

Qatāda[43] said, 'It is kohl, bracelets and rings.'

Ibn ʿAbbās[44] said, '*What is apparent of it* is the face, the eye kohl, palm dye and rings, all of which are revealed for anyone to see when they enter her house.'

Qatāda[45] said, 'The two manacles (*masakatān*), rings and kohl. And it has reached me that the Prophet said, "It is not lawful for a woman who believes in God and the Last Day to bare her hands up to here",[46] and he clasped his arm about halfway up.'

As regards His words *except what is apparent of it*, al-Miswar b. al-Makhrama[47] said, 'The two *qulb*s, meaning bracelets (*siwār*), the ring and kohl.'

Ibn ʿAbbās[48] said, '*And let them not reveal their ornament except for what is apparent of it* [refers to] rings and bracelets.'

Ibn Jurayj said, as did ʿĀʾisha, 'Bracelets (*qulb*) and rings (*fatkha*).' ʿĀʾisha said, 'The daughter of my maternal half-brother, ʿAbd Allāh b. al-Ṭufayl, entered upon me all adorned, and thereupon the Prophet came in, but stopped [to turn back].' ʿĀʾisha continued, 'But, O Messenger of God, she is my niece and a maid (*jāriya*)', to which he said, 'Once a woman has come of age (*ʿarakat*), she is not permitted to show anything other than her face, and otherwise not more than this much',[49] and he clasped his arm leaving the space of another fist's length between his clasp and the palm of his hand. This is also indicated by what Abū ʿAlī reported. Ibn Jurayj and Mujāhid both said that *except what is apparent of it* refers to kohl, dye and rings.

38 Abū Kurayb ← Marwān ← Muslim al-Malāʾī ← Saʿīd b. Jubayr ← Ibn ʿAbbās.

39 ʿAmr b. ʿAbd al-Ḥamīd ← al-Āmulī ← Marwān ← Muslim al-Malāʾī ← Saʿīd b. Jubayr.

40 Ibn Ḥumayd ← Hārūn ← Abū ʿAbd Allāh Nahshal ← al-Ḍaḥḥāk ← Ibn ʿAbbās.

41 Ibn Bashshār ← Abū ʿĀṣim ← Sufyān ← ʿAbd Allāh b. Muslim b. Hurmuz ← Saʿīd b. Jubayr.

42 ʿAlī b. Sahl ← al-Walīd b. Muslim ← Abū ʿAmr ← ʿAṭāʾ.

43 Ibn Bashshār ← Ibn Abī ʿAdī ← Saʿīd ← Qatāda.

44 ʿAlī ← ʿAbd Allāh ← Muʿāwiya ← ʿAlī ← Ibn ʿAbbās.

45 Al-Ḥasan ← ʿAbd al-Razzāq ← Maʿmar ← Qatāda.

46 This *ḥadīth* does not seem to be in the canonical collections or in the *Muṣannaf* of ʿAbd al-Razzāq.

47 Al-Ḥasan ← ʿAbd al-Razzāq ← Maʿmar ← al-Zuhrī ← someone ← al-Miswar b. Makhrama. Al-Miswar b. Makhrama (d. 64/684) was a long-standing companion of the caliph ʿUmar.

48 Al-Qāsim ← al-Ḥusayn ← Ḥajjāj ← Ibn Jurayj ← Ibn ʿAbbās.

49 This *ḥadīth* does not seem to be in the canonical collections or in the *Muṣannaf*.

According to ʿĀmir,[50] this refers to kohl, dye and garments (*thiyāb*).

According to Ibn Zayd,[51] this refers to adornment such as kohl, dye and rings. This is what he used to say and what people opined.

According to ʿUmar b. Abī Sulma,[52] when al-Awzāʿī was asked about *and let them not reveal their ornament except what is apparent of it*, he said, 'The palms of the hands and the face.'[53]

Others are of the opinion that it means the face and garments.[54]

However, the most likely of these opinions to be correct is the one that takes [*ornament* to] mean the face and the palms of the hands, and if it were so, it could include kohl, rings, bracelets, dyes (*khiḍāb*)[55] and garments. The reason that we believe this to be the most likely interpretation is because all are of the consensus that a person who performs the ritual prayers is required to cover up their shameful parts (*ʿawra*) during prayer, and that a woman is permitted to reveal her face and hands[56] during prayer but required to cover up everything else of her body except for what, according to the report from the Prophet, she was permitted to leave showing, that is, half of her arm. If that then is their consensus, it gives us to know, thereby, that she is permitted to reveal that part of her body that is not considered *ʿawra*, as is the case with men. For what is not considered *ʿawra* is not unlawful to bare. And if it is permitted for her to reveal that, we can know that this is what God has excepted with His words *except for what is apparent of it*, since all of that is apparent in her case.

As for His words *and let them cast their wraps over their cleavage*, this means let them cast their veils over their necklines in order to cover therewith their hair, their neck and their earrings.

It is reported that ʿĀʾisha[57] said, 'When this verse was revealed, women tore off the inner lining of garments (*mirṭ*) and used it to veil themselves.'

[50] Ibn Ḥumayd ← Jarīr ← ʿĀṣim ← ʿĀmir.

[51] Yūnus ← Ibn Wahb ← Ibn Zayd.

[52] Ibn ʿAbd al-Raḥīm al-Barqī ← ʿAmr b. Abī Sulma.

[53] An identical opinion is then reported on the authority of al-Ḍaḥḥāk with the following chain: ʿAmr b. Bunduq ← Marwān ← Juwaybir ← al-Ḍaḥḥāk.

[54] Two reports via different transmission from al-Ḥasan al-Baṣrī are cited by Ṭabarī in support of this interpretation. The first chain is: Ibn ʿAbd al-Aʿlā ← al-Muʿtamir ← Yūnus ← al-Ḥasan [al-Baṣrī]. The second is: Ibn Bashshār ← both Ibn Abī ʿAdī and ʿAbd al-Aʿlā ← Saʿīd [b. Jubayr] ← Qatāda ← al-Ḥasan [al-Baṣrī].

[55] This probably refers to the practice of dyeing the hands or fingertips with *ḥinna*, though it can also refer to dyeing the hair.

[56] This explanation confirms that when the commentators use the term *kaff*, they are referring to the hands in general, as opposed to the back of the hands or palms (cf. Lane, *Lexicon*, suppl. *k-f-f*), signifying the importance of the fingers, as these wrap around to create a handful (*kaff*) and also effect a slap (*kaff*).

[57] Ibn Wakīʿ ← Zayd b. Ḥabbāb ← Ibrāhīm b. Nāfiʿ ← al-Ḥasan b. Muslim b. Yanāq ← Ṣafiyya bt. Shayba ← ʿĀʾisha.

It is also reported from the Prophet's wife ʿĀʾisha[58] that she said, 'May God have mercy on the first women Emigrants when the verse *and let them cast their wraps over their cleavage* was revealed. When God sent down *and let them cast their wraps over their cleavage*, they tore off what they could from their thickest garments (*murūṭ*) and used it to veil themselves.'

With His words *and let them not reveal their ornament except to their husbands*, He is saying let them not reveal their ornament, which is the hidden and not the apparent one – such as the anklets, earrings and gold bracelets and what a woman has been commanded to cover with her veil of what is above the neckline and all that is other than what they have been permitted to uncover and reveal during ritual prayer and in the presence of outsiders, such as the arms and everything above that – except to their husbands. The commentators have said the like of what we have said on this subject.

An account of those who said this:

Ibrāhīm [al-Nakhaʿī][59] said [of] *and let them not reveal their ornament except to their husbands, or their fathers* that this is everything above the arms (*dhirāʿ*). And [via another transmission] that regarding this verse Ibrāhīm[60] said *And let them not reveal their ornament except to their husbands, or their fathers, or their husbands' fathers*: what is above the neckline (*jayb*). Shuʿba said, 'Manṣūr wrote to me about this and I read it back to him.'

Regarding *And let them not reveal their ornament except to their husbands*, Qatāda[61] said, 'She can reveal to such [individuals] the head (*raʾs*).'

Regarding *and let them not reveal their ornament except to their husbands* to where He says *the exposedness of women*, Ibn ʿAbbās[62] said, 'The ornaments that women may reveal to them are earrings, necklace (*qilāda*) and her bracelets; but as for her anklets, her upper arms (*miʿḍad*), her neckline (*naḥr*) and her hair (*shaʿr*), these she can only reveal to her husband (*zawj*).'

[58] Ibn Wahb ← Qurra b. ʿAbd al-Raḥmān ← Ibn Shihāb [al-Zuhrī] ← ʿUrwa ← ʿĀʾisha.

[59] Ibn Bashshār ← ʿAbd al-Raḥmān ← Sufyān ← Manṣūr ← Ṭalḥa b. Muṣarrif ← Ibrāhīm [al-Nakhaʿī].

[60] Ibn al-Muthannā ← Muḥammad b. Jaʿfar ← Shuʿba ← Manṣūr ← someone narrating ← Ṭalḥa ← Ibrāhīm [al-Nakhaʿī].

[61] Yaʿqūb ← Ibn ʿUlayya ← Saʿīd b. Abī ʿArūba ← Qatāda. On Ismāʿīl b. Ibrāhīm b. ʿUlayya (d. 193/808–9), the Basran traditionist, see Michael Cook, 'The Opponents of the Writing of Tradition in Early Islam', *Arabica* 44.4 (1997), 437–530; also Andrew Rippin and Roberto Tottoli, eds., *Books and Written Culture of the Islamic World: Studies Presented to Claude Gilliot on the Occasion of His 75th Birthday* (Leiden, Brill, 2014), esp. 373ff.

[62] ʿAlī ← Abū Ṣāliḥ ← Muʿāwiya ← ʿAlī ← Ibn ʿAbbās.

Regarding His words *and let them not reveal their ornament except to their husbands*, Ibn Masʿūd[63] said that this refers to a neck chain (*ṭawq*) and earrings. God, majestic be His praise, means to say, 'Tell the believing free women (*ḥarāʾir*) not to manifest this hidden (*khafiyya*) ornament, which is not apparent (*ẓāhira*), except to their spouses (*buʿūl*), that is, their husbands (*azwāj*) – the singular of which is *baʿl* – or to their fathers, or to the husbands' sons, or to their brothers, or to their brothers' sons.' By *or their brothers* (*ikhwānihinna*) is [also] meant their sisters (*ikhwātihinna*), or the sons of their brothers, or the sons of their sisters, or their womenfolk, meaning Muslim women (*nisāʾ al-muslimīn*).

Regarding His words *or their womenfolk*, Ibn Jurayj[64] said, 'I heard that this referred to Muslim women, for it is not permissible that a Muslim woman should bare her nakedness to a pagan woman (*mushrika*) unless she be her slave girl (*ama*), which explains why He says *or what their right hands possess*.'

It is reported from ʿUbāda b. Nusayy[65] that it was reprehensible (*k-r-h*) for a Christian woman (*naṣrāniyya*) to greet a Muslim woman with a kiss or to see her shameful parts (*ʿawra*), as one interpretation of *or their womenfolk*.

It is [also] reported from ʿUbāda[66] that he said: 'Umar b. al-Khaṭṭāb sent a letter to Abū ʿUbayda b. al-Jarrāḥ, God's mercy be on both of them, saying, 'It has reached me that [Muslim] women are going into the public baths with women from the People of the Book. Put a stop to that and prevent it from happening.' Abū ʿUbayda then took up the task, imploring God, 'O Lord, whatever woman enters the baths without cause or illness, seeking a glow (*bayāḍ*) for her face, blacken her face *on the day when the faces will glow* [Q. 3:106].'[67]

As for His words *or what their right hands possess*, the interpreters differ regarding the interpretation of this. Some say that this means 'or their slaves' (*mamālīk*), before whom it is acceptable for her to manifest that ornament which she manifests to those others.

An account of those who said this:

Regarding His words *or what their right hands possess* (*mā malakat aymānuhunna*), Makhlad al-Tamīmī[68] said that the reading (*qirāʾa*) is more likely to be 'your right hands' (*aymānukum*).

[63] Al-Qāsim ← al-Ḥusayn ← Ḥajjāj ← Ibn Jurayj ← Ibn Masʿūd.

[64] Al-Qāsim ← al-Ḥusayn ← Ḥajjāj ← Ibn Jurayj.

[65] Al-Ḥusayn ← ʿĪsā b. Yūnus ← Hishām b. al-Ghāzī ← ʿUbāda b. Nusayy.

[66] ʿĪsā b. Yūnus ← Hishām ← ʿUbāda [b. Nusayy].

[67] Cf. Q. 3:106: *on the day when some faces will glow and others will be blackened* (*yawma tabyaḍḍu wujūhun wa-taswaddu wujūh*).

[68] Al-Qāsim ← al-Ḥusayn ← Ḥajjāj ← Ibn Jurayj ← ʿAmr b. Dīnār ← Makhlad al-Tamīmī.

Others say, nay. Rather, the meaning of this is what their right hands possess of pagan slave girls (*imāʾ al-mushrikīn*), as we have already mentioned on the authority of Ibn Jurayj before. Where He says *or their womenfolk*, this meant Muslim women and not pagan women, and so he said that *or what their right hands possess* means slave girls (*imāʾ*) who are pagan (*mushrikāt*).

Reports on the interpretation of His words, exalted be He, *or their male dependants lacking (sexual) desire or children uninitiated to the exposedness of women. And let them not stamp their feet to make known what they hide of their ornament. Turn to God in repentance all together O believers so that you may prosper.*

God, exalted be His mention, means those [men] who depend on you (*t-b-ʿ*) for the daily food they receive in your houses, who have no desire (*irb*) for women or need (*ḥāja*) for them, or want (*yurīd*) them. The commentators have said the like of what we have said on this subject.

An account of those who said this:

Regarding *or their male dependants lacking (sexual) desire*, Ibn ʿAbbās[69] said, 'In those early days (*al-zamān al-awwal*), a man would follow another around without any threat of jealousy (*yughār ʿalayhi*) and the woman would take off her wrap (*khimār*) in his presence. This would [typically] be the fool (*aḥmaq*) who had no need (*ḥāja*) for women.'

Regarding *or their male dependants lacking (sexual) desire*, Ibn ʿAbbās[70] said, 'This is the man who would follow a group of people around, being a simpleton (*mughaffal*), neither caring for nor desiring women. In front of such a person, the ornament that she is permitted to reveal would be her earrings, neck chain and bracelets. But as for her anklets, upper arm ornaments (*miʿḍād*), her neckline or hair, these she can only reveal to her spouse (*zawj*).'

Qatāda,[71] regarding His words *or their* [*male*] *dependants*, said, 'These are those dependants (*t-b-ʿ*) who follow you around (*t-b-ʿ*) to acquire sustenance (*ṭaʿām*).'

Ibn Abī Najīḥ reported that Mujāhid[72] said, regarding [His words] *or their male dependants lacking (sexual) desire*, 'It refers to those who seek

[69] Muḥammad b. Saʿd ← his father ← his [paternal] uncle ← his father ← his father ← Ibn ʿAbbās.

[70] ʿAlī ← Abū Ṣāliḥ ← Muʿāwiya ← ʿAlī ← Ibn ʿAbbās.

[71] Al-Ḥasan ← ʿAbd al-Razzāq ← Maʿmar ← Qatāda.

[72] Ibn Bashshār ← ʿAbd al-Raḥmān ← Ismāʿīl b. ʿUlayya ← Ibn Abī Najīḥ ← Mujāhid.

sustenance (*ṭaʿām*) and not women.' Something similar is reported on the authority of Mujāhid [via another chain of transmission].[73]

[Others report that] Mujāhid[74] said, 'Those whose only concern is their belly and are not to be feared when it comes to women.' Something similar is reported on the authority of Mujāhid.[75]

Regarding His words *lacking (sexual) desire*, Manṣūr reported that Mujāhid[76] said, 'The dimwit (*ablah*).'

Layth reported that Mujāhid[77] said, 'This is the dimwit (*ablah*) who knows nothing about women.'

Regarding His words *or their male dependants lacking (sexual) desire*, Ibn Abī Najīḥ reported that Mujāhid[78] said, 'Those who have no desire for women, like so-and-so (*fulān*).'

Regarding *lacking (sexual) desire*, Ibn ʿAbbās[79] said, 'This is the one before whom women are not ashamed (*ḥayāʾ*).'

Regarding *lacking (sexual) desire*, al-Shaʿbī[80] said, 'This is the man who follows another man and his retinue and whose desire has not led him to become aware of women's shameful parts (*ʿawra*).' Al-Shaʿbī[81] said *lacking (sexual) desire* means the one who has no desire for women.

Saʿīd b. Jubayr[82] said, 'This is the mentally impaired (*maʿtūh*).'

Regarding His words *or their male dependants lacking (sexual) desire*, al-Zuhrī[83] said, 'This is the fool (*aḥmaq*) who has no aspiration (*himma*) or desire (*irb*) for women.' And with the same [transmission], a similar interpretation is transmitted by the father [of Ibn Ṭāwūs],[84] who said that this is the fool who has no aspiration for women.

Ibn ʿAbbās[85] said, 'That this is the one who has no need of women'.

Regarding His words *or their male dependants lacking (sexual) desire*, Ibn Zayd[86] said, 'This is the person who follows a group of people around, as if he

[73] ʿAbd al-Raḥmān ← Sufyān ← Ibn Abī Najīḥ ← Mujāhid.
[74] Muḥammad b. ʿAmr ← Abū ʿĀṣim ← ʿĪsā ← al-Ḥārith ← al-Ḥasan ← Warqāʾ ← Ibn Abī Najīḥ ← Mujāhid.
[75] Al-Qāsim ← al-Ḥusayn ← Ḥajjāj ← Ibn Jurayj ← Mujāhid.
[76] Ismāʿīl b. Mūsā al-Suddī ← Sharīk ← Manṣūr ← Mujāhid.
[77] Abū Kurayb ← Ibn Idrīs ← Layth ← Mujāhid.
[78] Yaʿqūb ← Ibn ʿUlayya ← Ibn Abī Najīḥ ← Mujāhid.
[79] Abū Kurayb ← Ibn ʿAṭiyya ← Isrāʾīl ← Abū Isḥāq ← his narrator ← Ibn ʿAbbās.
[80] Ibn Ḥumayd ← Jarīr ← al-Mughīra ← al-Shaʿbī.
[81] Ibn Bashshār ← Yaḥyā b. Saʿīd ← Shuʿba ← al-Mughīra ← al-Shaʿbī.
[82] ʿAbd al-Raḥmān ← Ḥammād b. Salama ← ʿAṭāʾ b. al-Sāʾib ← Saʿīd b. Jubayr.
[83] Al-Ḥasan ← ʿAbd al-Razzāq ← Maʿmar ← al-Zuhrī.
[84] [Al-Ḥasan ← ʿAbd al-Razzāq ←] Maʿmar ← Ibn Ṭāwūs ← his father.
[85] Al-Qāsim ← al-Ḥusayn ← Ḥajjāj ← Ibn Jurayj ← Ibn ʿAbbās.
[86] Yūnus ← Ibn Wahb ← Ibn Zayd.

were one of them and had grown up among them, except that he does not follow them around out of any desire for their women, nor does he have any desire for women, but simply follows them because they have extended their company (*irfāq*) to him.'

'Ā'isha[87] said, 'There was an effeminate (*mukhannath*)[88] who used to enter upon the wives of the Prophet, since they considered him to be of those with no interest [in women] (*ghayr ūlī'l-irba*). One day, the Prophet came in when he [the effeminate] was with some of his wives and he was describing a woman, saying, "When she comes along, she comes along with four and when she leaves, she leaves with eight", whereupon the Prophet said, '"I do not think this person knows what he is talking about. Do not let him into your presence [again]."[89] He was then barred from them (*ḥajabūhu*).'

'Ikrima[90] said, regarding *or their male dependants lacking (sexual) desire*, 'This is the effeminate one whose penis (*zubb*) does not become erect (*qāma*).'

The readers disagree regarding [the inflection of] His words *ghayr ūlī'l-irba*. Some of the Syrians, the Medinese and the Kufans read it as *ghayra ūlī'l-irba*, with *ghayra* in the accusative (*naṣb*). There are two ways in which *ghayra* in the accusative might function. One of them severs it from *al-tābiʿīn* as *al-tābiʿīn* is a proper noun and not an indefinite. The other considers it as an exceptive clause (*istithnā'*), so that *ghayr* means *illā* (except). So it would be as though He had said, 'except those [lacking sexual desire]'. Others, not from among those I have mentioned, read it *ghayri* [in the genitive], as an adjectival qualifier (*naʿt*) for *al-tābiʿīn*, and it is certainly permissible to describe *al-tābiʿīn* with *ghayr* where *al-tābiʿīn* is a proper noun and not an indefinite, because *al-tābiʿīn* is a proper noun not circumscribed by time. The

[87] Al-Ḥasan ← 'Abd al-Razzāq ← Maʿmar ← al-Zuhrī ← 'Urwa ← 'Ā'isha.

[88] See Rowson, 'The Effeminates', 671–93 (esp. 674 on this incident). More broadly on sexualities, see Stephen O. Murray and Will Roscoe, eds., *Islamic Homosexualities: Culture, History, and Literature* (New York, New York University Press, 1997). Contemporary anthropological studies in landscapes that have historically seen less social and cultural transformation preserve unique windows into the past. The ethnographic work done on this subject by Unni Wikan in Oman is insightful: 'The Omani *Xanith*: A Third Gender Role?' *Man* 13.3 (1978), 473–5; eadem, 'Man Becomes Woman: Transsexualism in Oman as a Key to Gender Roles', *Man* 12.2 (1977), 304–19; eadem, *Behind the Veil in Arabia: Women in Oman* (Chicago, IL, University of Chicago Press, 1982), esp. 168ff.

[89] This *ḥadīth*, as preserved in Ṭabarī, has 'I do not think' (*lā arā*); however, this appears to be a scribal or typographical error. The versions of the *ḥadīth* in the collections of Muslim and Abū Dāwūd have 'I think' (*alā arā*); this is reflected in the translations of the *ḥadīth* elsewhere in this chapter, which preserve the correct version. Versions of this *ḥadīth* are in Muslim, *Ṣaḥīḥ*, *Kitāb al-Salām* (39), *Bāb manʿ al-mukhannath min al-dukhūl 'alā'l-nisā' al-ajānib* (13), *ḥadīth* no. 45/2181, and Abū Dāwūd, *Sunan*, *Kitāb al-Libās* (34), *Bāb fī qawlihi 'ghayr ūlī'l-irbati'* (35), *ḥadīth* no. 88/4107.

[90] Saʿd b. 'Abd Allāh b. al-Ḥakam al-Miṣrī ← Ḥafṣ b. 'Umar al-'Adanī ← al-Ḥakam b. Abān ← 'Ikrima.

interpretation of the words based on this reading would be: 'or those whose character (*ṣifa*) is so'. In my opinion, both [grammatical] readings are close in meaning and of frequent enough occurrence in the major towns (*amṣār*), and so whichever of the two a reader chooses is correct. However, the genitive inflection (*khafḍ*) is the stronger [of the two] in the Arabic language, and this reading is more pleasing to me (*aʿjab ilayya*). *Al-irba* is based on [the paradigm of] *fuʿla* from *al-irb*, similar [in pattern] to *jalsa* from *julūs* [or] *mashya* from *mashī*, and it means 'need' (*ḥāja*). One says *lā irba lī fīka* to mean *lā ḥājata lī fīka* (I have no need of you). Likewise, [one says] *aribtu li-kadhā wa-kadhā* to mean *iḥtajtu ilayhi*, and so I am one who is *ārib lahu araban*. As for *al-urba* with the *ḍamma* on the *alif*, this means *al-ʿuqda*.

As for His words *or children uninitiated to the exposedness of women*, He means children who, on account of their youth, have not been exposed to women's nakedness through sexual intercourse (*jimāʿ*) and thus initiated to it. The commentators have said the like of what we have said on this subject.

An account of those who have said this:

Mujāhid[91] said, 'They have no knowledge of what is involved, on account of their youth and prepubescence (*qabl al-ḥulum*).' Another similar report is given by Mujāhid.[92]

As for His words *and let them not stamp their feet to make known what they hide of their ornament*, He means: 'Let them not wear ornaments around their ankles, so that if they were moving or walking between people, they would know what they were hiding.' The commentators have said the like of what we have said on this subject.

An account of who said this:

The father of al-Muʿtamir[93] related to us from his father the following: 'A Ḥadramī claimed that a woman who had two silver anklets (*burra*) with beads (*jazʿ*) and [who,] when she passed by some people, stamped her feet, and one of the anklets (*khilkhāl*) fell onto the beads making a sound, whereupon God revealed *and let them not stamp their feet to make known what they hide of their ornament*.'

Regarding *and let them not stamp their feet to make known what they hide of their ornament*, Abū Mālik[94] said, 'They used to wear beads (*kharaz*) around their ankles, and when passing through groups of seated men they

[91] Muḥammad ← Abū ʿĀṣim ← ʿĪsā ← al-Ḥārith ← al-Ḥasan ← Warqāʾ narrated to all of us ← Ibn Abī Najīḥ ← Mujāhid.
[92] Al-Qāsim ← al-Ḥusayn ← Ḥajjāj ← Ibn Jurayj ← Mujāhid.
[93] Ibn ʿAbd al-Aʿlā ← al-Muʿtamir ← his father.
[94] Ibn Bashshār ← ʿAbd al-Raḥmān ← Sufyān ← al-Suddī ← Abū Mālik.

would shake their ankles in order to make known what they hide of their ornament.'

Regarding *and let them not stamp their feet*, Ibn ʿAbbās[95] said, 'That is that she should [not] strike one anklet against the other in the presence of men or shake her anklets among men. God forbade that because it is of the work of Satan (*ʿamal al-shayṭān*).'[96]

And regarding *and let them not stamp their feet to make known what they hide of their ornament*, Qatāda[97] said, '[Ornament is] the bells (*ajrās*) on their accessories (*ḥulī*), which they wear around their feet at the place of the anklet (*khilkhāl*). God has prohibited them from stamping their feet so that these bells be heard.'

As regards His words *turn to God in repentance all together O believers*, He means: return, O believers, to obedience of God in what He has commanded you and in what He has forbidden you, such as lowering the gaze, guarding the private parts (*farj*) and refraining from entering the houses of others without asking permission or uttering salutations (*taslīm*), in addition to other things that He has commanded or prohibited, *so that you may prosper*, [meaning,] so that you may flourish and attain your requests from Him, having obeyed His commands and prohibitions.[98]

Qāḍī al-Nuʿmān

This commentary comes from Qāḍī al-Nuʿmān's *Daʿāʾim*, which is the closest that he comes to writing a book of positive law. As such it makes an interesting point of comparison between Fāṭimid approaches and that in other legal schools. Echoing the 'distinction' imperative that we find in the earliest commentary, that is, the need to distinguish between free Muslim women and female slaves, we are here introduced to another necessary distinction where women are encouraged to don accessories in order not to be mistaken for men; this, of course, suggests that there was already a good degree of physical veiling – perhaps by both women and men – in public. This discussion of women-specific ornament is extended, somewhat unexpectedly, into a discussion of the permissibility or otherwise of boys and men to wear gold and silver or 'to accessorise', neither of which is remotely connected to the focus of this verse. Such moments in the commentaries suggest that norms of modesty and

95 ʿAlī ← ʿAbd Allāh ← Muʿāwiya ← ʿAlī ← Ibn ʿAbbās.

96 A similar report identifying the verse's reference to 'anklets' (*khilkāl*) is reported by Qatāda. Another report from Ibn Zayd identifies shaking the 'little ornamental bells' (*ajrās*) on the anklets as the practice that elicited this prohibition.

97 Al-Ḥasan ← ʿAbd al-Razzāq ← Maʿmar ← Qatāda.

98 Ṭabarī, *Jāmiʿ al-bayān*, s.v. Q. 24:31.

gender-specific comportment were moral virtues that the Muslim public needed to be reminded of. However, based on a reported Prophetic precedent, allowances are made for men to wear certain types of accessories, such as rings that marked out their special status within the religious community, a practice that continues to this day, especially among Sayyids and Sufi shaykhs.

It has been reported to us from Jaʿfar b. Muḥammad [al-Ṣādiq] on the authority of his father [al-Bāqir] on the authority of his fathers, on the authority of the Messenger of God (*ṣlʿhm*), that he said: 'When a woman goes to pray, she should be wearing some pieces of jewellery, unless she does not have any.' He forbade women to be without accessories and enjoined them not to resemble men, cursing those of them who did that.

[It is reported] from Abū Jaʿfar Muḥammad b. ʿAlī [al-Bāqir] (*ʿm*), that he said, 'A woman should not go without ornament, even if it is just a necklace around her neck.'

[It is reported] from the Messenger of God (*ṣlʿhm*), that he forbade women to strike the ground with their feet, whereby a woman would make her anklet jingle and thus make known what is hidden of her ornament, meaning whenever she was out of the house but not in the presence of unmarriageable kin. That is because of His words *and tell the believing women to lower their gaze and to safeguard their private parts* to where He says *and let them not stamp their feet to make known what they hide of their ornament.*

And [it is reported] from Abū Jaʿfar Muḥammad b. ʿAlī [al-Bāqir] (*ʿm*) that he was asked about gold ornament for women and that he said, 'That is fine, it is just reprehensible (*makrūh*) for men.'

And [it is reported] from Jaʿfar b. Muḥammad [al-Ṣādiq] (*ʿm*) that he was asked whether boys could wear gold, to which he replied, 'My father used to adorn his children and women with both gold and silver, and it is fine also to adorn swords and [Qurʾān] manuscripts (*muṣḥaf*) with gold or silver.'

And [it is reported] from the Messenger of God (*ṣlʿhm*) that he saw a man with an iron (*ḥadīd*) ring on one of his fingers and thereupon remarked, 'That is the adornment of the people of hellfire: cast it off yourself! I sense the scent and hallmark of the Magians (*Majūsiyya*) in you.' And so he [the man] took it off and wore a gold ring instead. But he [the Prophet] said, 'Your finger remains in hellfire as long as that ring remains on it', to which the man replied, 'O Messenger of God, should I not wear a ring at all then?' 'Better not to, but if you so wish, then wear a silverplate and make sure it is not a heavy one'.[99]

[99] In Bukhārī, *Ṣaḥīḥ*, *Kitāb al-Libās*, *Bāb khawātīm al-dhahab* includes many reports about the Prophet throwing away his gold ring for a silver one, but they do not reflect this wording.

[It is reported] from ʿAlī (ʿm) that he said, 'Do not let your boys wear iron rings.'

[It is also reported] from ʿAlī (ʿm) that he said, 'The Messenger of God's ring (*ṣlʿm*) was made of silver as was the pommel of his sword.'

[It is reported] from the Messenger of God (*ṣlʿhm*) that he forbade men from gold adornments, saying, 'That is forbidden (*ḥarām*) in [the life of] this world'.[100]

[It is reported] from him [ʿAlī] (ʿm) that he [the Prophet] used to wear a ring on his right hand and forbade wearing them on the left.

[It is reported] from him [ʿAlī] (ʿm) that he said, 'For the one who wears a ring (*takhattama*) of agate (*ʿaqīq*), God will seal (*khatama*) for him his end with the best promise (*ḥusnā*).[101] And verily the best of [precious] stones is quartz (*ballūr*).'

[It is reported] from al-Ḥusayn b. ʿAlī (ʿm) that he said: The Messenger of God (*ṣlʿhm*) said to me, My son, sleep on your back, and your stomach will stay flat; drink water in sips and your food will go down gently. Colour the edge of your eyelid with kohl on odd days (*watran*), and your vision will be illuminated. Anoint with oil every now and then (*ghibban*)[102] and you will have emulated the custom (*sunna*) of your Prophet. Wear new sandals, for they [when worn out] are like the jangly anklets [of women], and [new] turbans, for they are the crowns of the Arabs. And when you prepare a stew, make plenty of gravy, so if your neighbour receives no portion of the meat, he will at least have some of its gravy, as the gravy is made of the meat. Wear a ring of ruby (*yāqūt*) or agate (*ʿaqīq*), for it brings good fortune (*maymūn*) and is blessed (*mubārak*): every time a man looks at it, his face will increase in light, and to pray wearing one is worth seventy prayers. Wear the ring on your right hand, for that is my practice and the practice of the messengers, and whoso shuns my practice does not belong with me. Do not wear it on the left hand and do not wear [anything] other than ruby or agate'.

[It is reported] from the Messenger of God (*ṣlʿhm*) that on his ring was inscribed: 'Muḥammad [is] the Messenger of God.'

And [it is reported] from ʿAlī (ʿm) that inscribed on his [ʿAlī's] ring were [the words]: "ʿAlī believes in God.' And from Jaʿfar b. Muḥammad [al-Ṣādiq]

[100] A somewhat similar *ḥadīth* is found in Nasāʾī, *Sunan*, *Kitāb al-Zīna* (48), *Bāb taḥrīm al-dhahab ʿalā al-rijāl* (40), *ḥadīth* no. 109/5148. This *ḥadīth* forbids men from wearing gold and silk, as do many others.

[101] The statement plays on the common root for *kh-t-m*, meaning 'seal', 'ring' and 'to conclude'.

[102] There is a strand of *ḥadīth* that emphasises the importance of not making a routine of grooming oneself in the case of men, lest it become a feminine-like habit (see *ḥadīth al-tarajjul*).

(ʿ*m*), 'O Lord ease [matters] for me. You are my trust, so preserve me from the evil of Your creatures.' And from him (ʿ*m*), [it is reported] that he said, 'Let no one pray wearing a ring on which images (*tamāthīl*) have been etched.'[103]

Qushayrī

Qushayrī's hermeneutics in his *Laṭāʾif* are all present here in condensed form. Even as the legal parameters of the verse are fully operative for him, he is concerned not so much with explicating in detail the verse's enjoinder to women to veil or the various degrees of consanguinity before whom they might be permitted to lower their guard, but with extracting for his reader, in standard Sufi fashion, the spiritual kernel of a verse which, on the face of it, is so obviously legalistic. The reader's attention is immediately turned to the spiritual dimensions that underpin the need to veil and not to reveal ornaments: just as the carnal pleasures of this world are disfigurements in the hellfire to which they lead, so too to delight in one's righteousness (so that it becomes self-righteousness) is to disfigure that righteousness. The shared moral–legal lexicon of Sufism (of *adab*, *walāya*, *sirr*, *khawāṭir*, *ruqiyy*, *ḥāl*, *ghafla*, *tawba*, *tawfīq*, *ʿāmma*, *khāṣṣa*) and the spiritual hierarchies into which it divides creation pervade the verse's commentary. Qushayrī, true to his exegetical style,[104] uses rhyme, parallelisms and aphorisms to convey the spiritual wisdoms embedded in what might otherwise be taken as a passage containing straightforward divine prescriptions. On the legalistic elements of the verse, it is notable that Qushayrī draws a parallel between the modesty required of women and men, holding both fully legally accountable for their actions and allowing to both the possibility of attaining the spiritual state which lies beyond worldly desires.

And tell the believing women to lower their gaze and safeguard their private parts, and let them not reveal their ornament except what is apparent of it, and let them cast their wraps over their cleavage. To require this from women is the same as requiring it from men, since legal obligation (*taklīf*) extends to both sexes (*jins*), and it is thus an obligation for women to shun things that are prohibited (*maḥẓūrāt*). This recommendation (*nadb*) and supererogatory act (*nafl*) in their case is a means to safeguard the heart against any distractions or ignoble passing desires (*khawāṭir*). Once women have risen above (*r-q-y*) this state, their hearts will be blind to all that is other than the Worshipped One. God singles out His mercy for whomever He will.

[103] Qāḍī al-Nuʿmān, *Daʿāʾim al-Islām*, II, 162–5.
[104] See Nguyen, *Sufi Master*, 121–42.

And let them not reveal of their ornament except what is apparent of it, that which God has permitted, glory be to Him, as jurisprudence clarifies as exempt from this prohibition. Beyond that, it is a duty for women to protect themselves against any penalties that may ultimately befall them, taking care not to make that a cause for the hearts of His servants into temptation (*fitna*). Just as God, glory be to Him, preserves His friends (*awliyāʾ*) from what is damaging to their religious practice (*dīn*), He also safeguards them from being the cause of others falling into temptation. It may be that they are not the cause of any benefit to any of [His] creatures, but at least no temptation befalls anyone because of them.

In sum, whatever constitutes a servant's 'ornament' (*zīnat al-ʿabd*) should not be revealed. And so, just as a woman has shameful parts (*ʿawra*), and she is not permitted to reveal her ornament, so too the one who reveals to creation the ornament of those innermost secrets (*sarāʾir*) arising from the purity of his [spiritual] states (*aḥwāl*) and the integrity (*zakāʾ*) of his acts, turns his ornament (*zīna*) into a disfigurement (*shayn*), except in cases where something of it manifests itself to others, but not by the person's doing or intention; that is exempt, for one is not liable for an action over which [one] has no control or charge. And thus, as detailed in the explications of the Law (*sharīʿa*), women who are within degrees of unmarriageability (*dhawāt al-maḥārim*) are exempt from this prohibition.

As for His words, majestic be His mention, *or their male dependants lacking (sexual) desire or children uninitiated to the exposedness of women*: in all of these [cases] the moral stipulations of the Law (*ādāb al-sharʿ*), and whether something is permissible and prohibited, should be taken into consideration.

As for His words, majestic be His mention, *Turn to God in repentance all together O believers so that you may prosper*: turning in repentance (*tawba*) is to turn away from blameworthy acts towards their praiseworthy counterparts. All believers are commanded to turn in repentance. One [kind of] repentance is from a slip (*zalla*), which is the repentance of the common folk (*ʿawāmm*); another is repentance from heedlessness (*ghafla*), which is the repentance of the elite (*khawāṣṣ*) – one repentance is to avoid punishment, the other repentance is to be heedful of the command.

They say that He has commanded all to repentance: the disobedient to turn away from disobedience and towards obedience; the obedient from seeing only an act of obedience to seeing, instead, God-given success (*tawfīq*); and the elite of the elite from seeing only God-given success to witnessing the One who gives success [Himself]. They also say that He has commanded all to repentance, lest the disobedient one feel shame in turning in repentance on his own. They say that giving aid to the powerful while giving it [also] to the weak, out of compassion for them, is a sign of nobleness (*karam*).

With regard to His words *so that you may prosper*, it becomes clear that He has commanded them to repent so that they themselves benefit, and not for His sake – their obedience thereby becoming an act of self-adornment.

They say that those who are most in need of repentance are the ones who believe that they have no need of it.[105]

Zamakhsharī

Zamakhsharī's exegesis begins with an interesting parallel to some of the earliest commentaries, namely the preamble that the mention of safeguarding the *furūj* here is not – as everywhere else in the Qur'ān – intended to be a reference to safeguarding against illicit sexual activity, but rather to the need to exercise modesty by dressing modestly. The reader will encounter here the story relating to the blind man who enters the Prophet's house while some of his wives are present, and they, to their surprise, are then commanded to 'take your cover' (*iḥtajibā*). This *ḥadīth* foregrounds the possibility of female desire, which is why Zamakhsharī relates it to the verse's command to women to lower their gaze. The Prophet's command to his wives – *iḥtajibā*! – is a recognition that his wives might desire their male visitor. The term uses the root *ḥ-j-b*, which throughout the Qur'ān refers to a 'screen', 'barrier' or 'partition', and never a veiling garment, for which the closest Qur'ānic term is *khimār*, and perhaps less so the *jilbāb* of Q. 33:59. Note, for instance, Q. 19:17, where Mary screens herself off from her family just before going into labour. More significant for the *ḥadīth* here, however, is Q. 33:53, where those visiting the Prophet's house are enjoined to speak from behind a partition (*ḥijāb*) when speaking to his wives. So, while the term *iḥtajibā* might be interpreted by a modern audience to mean 'veil yourselves', at the time of the episode above it would have meant 'take your cover', as in retreat behind a screen, since the import of the *ḥadīth* is to shield the Prophet's wives' gaze from the blind man who enters. The Prophet's wives' surprise may indicate a cultural model in which male desire was more readily acknowledged than female desire. Coupled with Zamakhsharī's prelude regarding the need for women to lower their gaze from men, a reciprocal ethic of modesty, implicit in the Qur'ān's own wording to all believers to lower their gaze in Q. 24:30 and repeated here to believing women specifically, is thus recognised. Both men and women are morally obliged to turn their gaze away. Zamakhsharī remarks that the term *juyūb* properly refers to the typical openings of a garment at the top and that broad cuts or loose clothes at the time allowed for more exposure of the area from the breasts to the neck, which suggests that the purpose of the Qur'ānic verse was to enjoin modest dressing in general, even

[105] Qushayrī, *Laṭā'if al-ishārāt*, s.v. Q. 24:31.

as he – like most of the commentators – is naturally concerned to gloss the term with the word 'breasts' (*ṣudūr*), thereby establishing what for them was a minimum for pious decorum.

The indication[106] is that the matter concerning 'the gaze' (*naẓar*) is more expansive (*awsaʿ*).[107] Do you not see how in the case of unmarriageable women, there is nothing wrong with looking at their hair, their chests (*ṣudūr*), their breasts (*thady*), their arms, legs and feet? Likewise in the case of slave girls on display and the non-Muslim woman (*ajnabiyya*) whose face, hands and feet may be looked at, according to one of the two reports? As for the matter of the private parts (*farj*), this is restricted. It should suffice for you to know this difference, given that one is permitted to look [at everything] except for what has been interdicted and that sexual activity has been prohibited except for what has been exempted.[108] It is possible that the intended meaning is: while safeguarding the private parts from illicit sexual activity, to safeguard them also from being revealed. According to Ibn Zayd, every mention in the Qurʾān of the safeguarding of private parts is [safeguarding them] against illicit sex (*zinā*), except for this [verse] here, where the intended meaning is to cover up (*istitār*). He then informs [us] that He is All-aware (*khabīr*) of their acts and states, how their eyes wander, and what they fashion with all of their limbs and senses; so it is their responsibility, once they realise that, to be mindful (*taqwā*) and cautious of Him in every motion and at every rest.

Women have also been commanded to lower their gaze. It is not permissible for a woman to look upon a stranger and catch sight of what is below his belly to his knees. Should she experience desire, she must lower her gaze immediately. Nor, similarly, should she look at another woman, except where likewise [permitted]. Lowering her gaze from the outset is what she ought to do, and is more virtuous. To this relates the *ḥadīth* of Ibn Umm Maktūm from Umm Salama, may God be pleased with her, who said:

[106] The commentary on Q. 24:31 is intimately tied to the commentary on the previous verse enjoining all believers – but understood here as men, because of the contrast with women in Q. 24:31 – to lower their gaze and safeguard their private parts. The question for the exegetes is the relationship between lowering the gaze and the safeguarding of private parts from illicit sexual activity, especially because in Q. 24:30, the partitive particle *min* is used with *abṣār* but not with *furūj*. We begin the selection at this nexus.

[107] That is to say, the scope of proscription and permission is more difficult to define, since the private parts are restricted to specific functions (sexual relations), whereas 'sight' can involve various contexts.

[108] Zamakhsharī is operating with juridical categories to invert the relationship: all looking is generally permitted except for what has been prohibited, and all sexual acts are prohibited except for what has been permitted.

> I was in the Prophet's house (*ṣl'm*), and Maymūna was with him. Ibn Umm Maktūm came – and this was after we had been commanded to screen ourselves (*ḥijāb*) [cf. Q. 33:53] – and entered, whereupon he [the Prophet] said, 'Take your cover (*iḥtajibā*)',[109] to which we said, 'O Messenger of God, is he not blind and unable to see us?' to which he replied, 'And are you two blind, that you do not see him?'[110]

If you were to ask why the lowering of the gaze [in this verse] is mentioned before the guarding of the private parts, I would say that it is because sight is the vehicle for fornication (*zinā*) and the captain of vice (*fujūr*). The temptation that comes through it is more intense and more frequent, such that a person is well-nigh incapable of guarding against it.

Al-zīna (ornament) is any jewellery, kohl or dye that a woman uses to adorn herself with. The 'outward' of that, such as the ring, the (finger) band, kohl or dye, can be shown to the stranger. As for what is hidden of that, such as the bracelet (*siwār*), the jingly anklet (*khilkhāl*), the bangle (*dumluj*) or the necklace (*qilāda*), the tiara (*iklīl*), the scarf (*wishāḥ*) and earrings (*qurṭ*), then she should not make it visible except to those mentioned. The reason for mentioning *ornament* (*zīna*) only and not specifying parts [of the body] is to emphasise to the utmost degree the command of preserving and concealing oneself [from the gaze], for these ornaments are on parts of the body that are forbidden to be seen by other than those [mentioned],[111] such as the arm, the leg, the shoulder, the neck, the head, the breast and the ears. He has thus forbidden that these ornaments themselves be gazed upon so that it may be known that the reason that these should not be looked at is because they are worn on those places [which are forbidden to be seen]. So much so, that to look at these places without these things being worn on them is not a question for discussion when it comes to permissibility.[112] To look at those very parts is absolutely forbidden, is well established as something illicit and bears witness to the fact that women are obliged to take precautions to cover these up and to be certain about when to reveal them. If you were to say: What do

[109] Note the discussion of this *ḥadīth* in the introduction to Zamakhsharī's *tafsīr* of this verse.

[110] This version of the *ḥadīth* is found in Tirmidhī, *Jāmi'*, *Kitāb al-Adab* (43), *ḥadīth* no. 3005; Abū Dāwūd, *Sunan*, *Kitāb al-Libās* (34), *Bāb fī qawlihi 'azza wa-jalla 'Qul lil-mu'mināt* [. . .]' (36), *ḥadīth* no. 93/4112; Nawawī, *Riyāḍ al-ṣāliḥīn*, *Kitāb al-Umūr al-manhī 'anhā* (17), *Bāb taḥrīm al-naẓar ilā al-mar'a al-ajnabiyya*, *ḥadīth* no. 116/1626 (note that Nawawī, however, compiled his collection roughly a century after Zamakhsharī's death).

[111] Meaning the categories of individuals listed in the verse for whom it is lawful to display a certain degree of ornament.

[112] The text tortuously makes the argument that if a woman's accessories are forbidden to be viewed, then the places on which she wears these accessories are *ipso facto* forbidden to be looked at.

you say about hair extensions (*qarāmīl*) – is it licit for those individuals to look at them? I would respond: Yes. You might then say: But is not the place for these the back (*ẓahr*) and it is forbidden to them to look at her back and belly (*baṭn*), and it may be that some of the hair becomes apparent when the extensions fall down to below her navel? I would say: Yes, it is as you have it, but the issue regarding hair extensions is different from all other types of adornment since they always sit on top of clothing, and it is permitted for non-relatives to look at the outer garment that covers the back and the front, and so how much more so for these individuals, unless it is transparent, in which case it is not permitted to look at it and you would not be permitted to look at her hair extensions as these sit on top of it.

If you were to ask: what is meant by the places of ornament (*mawqiʿ al-zīna*)? Is it that entire part of the limb (*ʿuḍw*) or just what is worn on it of ornament? I would say that the sound opinion is that it means that entire part of the body, given how the 'places of hidden ornament' (*mawāqiʿ al-zīna al-khafiyya*) is explained. Likewise is the case with the 'places of manifest ornament' (*mawāqiʿ al-zīna al-ẓāhira*): the face is the place of the kohl on the eyes; dye marks the area around the brows and the sides [of the face]; lotion covers the cheeks; and the hands and feet are the places for rings and bands as well as henna dye. If you were to say: Why is the 'apparent ornament' permitted unexceptionally? I would say that is because to cover these would involve some hardship, for a woman cannot avoid using her hands to go about her work and she needs to uncover her face, especially when she gives testimony, is summoned to court, or at the marriage ceremony. She also needs to make her way through the streets, which means her feet are uncovered, and this is especially the case with poorer women. That is the intended meaning of His words *except for what is apparent of it*, in other words, except for what is customarily and habitually manifested and what has always been manifest. However, exceptional permission has been granted with regard to 'hidden ornament' to those mentioned [in the verse], because they are specifically likely to need to go in to see women and to mix with them, and also because there is minimal expectation of any temptation befalling them with regard to those women, given the repugnance of touching close kin. In addition, a woman needs these men when travelling, and when riding and dismounting and so on.

It used to be the case that the apertures (*juyūb*) [of their garments] were [cut] broad and their necklines, chests and all around would be visible from them. They would also drape their wraps over their backs leaving these exposed. Thus they were commanded to drape their wraps over their front in order to cover those parts. It is possible that what is meant by *juyūb* is the breast (*ṣudūr*), the name for that being an extension of what sits under and at this place; from this [same root] derives the saying about someone that he is *nāṣiḥ al-jayb* [to mean 'trustworthy'] and when you say *ḍarabat bi-khimārihā ʿalā jaybihā* (she pulled her wrap across her bosom), it is like saying *ḍarabtu bi-yadī ʿalāʾl-ḥāʾiṭ* to mean that I placed it [my hand] on it [the wall]. It is reported from ʿĀʾisha, may God be pleased with her, that she said: I have not seen women more excellent than the women of the Anṣār. When this verse was sent down, each one of them went off to grab their embroidered cloths to tear off parts, wrapping themselves with these and looking as though they had ravens atop their heads.[113]

Some have read [it as] *jiyūbihinna* with a *kasra* on the initial *jīm* because of the [subsequent] *yāʾ*, similar to *biyūtan ghayri biyūtikum* (houses other than your houses).[114]

With regard to *their womenfolk* (*nisāʾihinna*), the opinion on the authority of Ibn ʿAbbās, may God be pleased with both of them,[115] is that this refers to believing women (*muʾmināt*), since it is not seemly for a believing woman (*muʾmina*) to go naked before a pagan (*mushrika*) or a woman from the People of the Book (*kitābiyya*). Overtly, *their womenfolk* and *what their right hands possess* would seem to refer to all those women, free and slaves, who are in their service, for women are all equally permitted to look at one another. However, one opinion has it that *what their right hands possess* includes men and women altogether.

It is reported from ʿĀʾisha, may God be pleased with her, that she had permitted her male slave (*ʿabd*) to look at her. She also said to [her slave] Dhakwān, 'Once you have placed me in my grave and come out, you shall be a free man (*ḥurr*).' Something similar was reported on the authority of Saʿīd b. al-Musayyab, but then he qualified this, saying, 'Do not be deluded by this verse of [*sūrat*] *al-Nūr*, for indeed what is meant here is slave girls (*imāʾ*).'[116]

[113] The fact that these extra garments were embroidered or figured (*muraḥḥal*) suggests the zeal to observe the commandment, and the black colour of the garments and the haphazard way in which they presumably wrapped their heads with them is what made the women seem as though they had black birds atop their heads.

[114] The parallel given is from Q. 24:27 where *b-y-t* is also a case of an initial consonant followed by a *yāʾ*.

[115] Meaning Ibn ʿAbbās and his father. The reader should not fail to note how this benediction becomes one example of the construction of ʿAbbāsid historical memory. On this issue in general, see Tayeb El-Hibri, *Reinterpreting Islamic Historiography: Hārūn al-Rashīd and the Narrative of the ʿAbbāsid Caliphate* (Cambridge, Cambridge University Press, 1999).

[116] Saʿīd b. al-Musayyab is frequently cited by the other exegetes as having adopted a strict position on this issue (see, for example, Qurṭubī, 'Fourteenth [issue]', later in this chapter, where he makes his opinion clear that *what your right hands possess* cannot refer to women's male slaves, only her female slaves).

And this is the sound opinion, for a woman's slave (*ʿabd*) is a non-relative, whether he is castrated or virile. Maysūn bt. Baḥdal al-Kilābiyya said that when Muʿāwiya came in to see her with a castrate in his company she quickly veiled her face (*q-n-ʿ*) from him, whereupon he said, 'But he is a castrate!', to which she replied, 'O Muʿāwiya, do you suppose that just because someone mutilated him, will make licit what God has made illicit?'

According to Abū Ḥanīfa it is not permitted to take castrates into service, or retain them, or sell or purchase them. However, there is nothing from any of the predecessors (*salaf*) about retaining them. If you were to say that it has been reported that a castrate was gifted to the Messenger of God (*ṣlʿm*) and he accepted it, I would respond that he would not have accepted something that would have been a source of tribulation for all, unless he were an unclad youth. If this were the case, then perhaps he accepted him in order to set him free later on or for some other reason.

Irba is a need. It is said that this refers to those who follow you around in order to secure for themselves leftovers of your food, and have no need for women, as they are dimwits (*bulah*) who know nothing about them; or these could be old men who are righteous who lower their gaze when in the company of women; or they could be impotent men.

Some have read *ghayra*, in the accusative, as signifying an exceptive [clause] or a circumstantial qualifier; if [read] *ghayri*, in the genitive, then this constitutes a descriptive [clause]. The singular serves the purpose of the plural since it is a collective noun, and what comes afterwards [of the plural verb] clearly shows that the plural is meant;[117] a similar case is that of *and He [then] brings you forth as children.*[118]

Lam yaẓharū (*uninitiated*) is derived either from [the construction] *ẓahara ʿalā al-shayʾ* to mean 'he has come to discover something', that is, they [the children] do not know what shameful parts (*ʿawra*) are and cannot distinguish between those parts and others'; or it is derived from *ẓahara ʿalā fulān* to mean 'he has the strength to [challenge] someone' and *ẓahara ʿalāʾl-Qurʾān* to mean 'he has the capacity to memorise it'. In other words, these [are children who] have not reached the age (*awān*) of sexual capacity. One reading has *ʿawarāt*,[119] which is the tongue of the [tribe of] Hudhayl.

If you were to say: Why did God not mention paternal and maternal uncles?[120] I would say that when al-Shaʿbī was asked about this, he said: Lest

[117] The Arabic has *aw al-ṭifl* (sing. form) *alladhīna lam yaẓharū* (pl. conjugation).

[118] Q. 40:67: *thumma yukhrijukum* (pl. suffix) *ṭiflan* (sing. form).

[119] The standard Qurʾānic vocalisation is *ʿawrāt* for the plural of *ʿawra*.

[120] That is to say, why were uncles not included among those in the verse before whom women could reveal their ornament, such as the fathers and the fathers-in-law.

the paternal uncle describe her to his son and the maternal uncle do the same. The sense then is that all kinship ties subsume the father and the son within unmarriageability (*maḥramiyya*), except for the paternal uncle and the maternal uncle and their sons, for if this father were to see her, he might describe her to his son who is not unmarriageable to her, and his imagining of her through that description verges on his gazing on her, which is another eloquent proof of the obligation for the women to take precautions to cover up.

Women used to strike the ground with their feet so that their anklets would jangle, and people would know that they were wearing anklets. They also say that women used to strike one foot against the other so that people would know that they were wearing anklets on both feet. And since they have been prohibited from making sounds with their accessories after having been prohibited from manifesting them, it will be known from this that the prohibition against revealing the very places of the ornaments is of the highest priority. The weak servant is barely able to be mindful of God's commands and prohibitions in every case, even if he were to discipline and exert himself [to that task]. He will never be without some shortcoming that issues from him, which is why He has enjoined all believers to repentance and seeking forgiveness, giving hope of prosperity to them if they repent and seek forgiveness.

On the authority of Ibn ʿAbbās, may God be pleased with both of them: 'Repent from what you used to do in the *jāhiliyya* and perhaps you might find fortune in this world and in the next'. If you were to say: But has not repentance been made by entering into Islam and does Islam not annul what came before? What, then, is the significance of this repentance? I would say that what He meant by it is what the scholars say: Whoever commits a sin and repents from it is required to renew that repentance every time he remembers that [sin], for he is required to adhere to this remorse with resolve until such time as he meets his Lord.

Some read *ayyuhu'l-mu'minūn* with a *ḍamma* inflected *hā'*: the justification for this is that, whereas it would have been inflected with a *fatḥa* as preceding the *alif* [of the definite article], once the *alif* has been elided because of the coming together of two vowelless consonants, its inflection adopts the inflection of the preceding vowel.[121]

[121] Zamakhsharī, *al-Kashshāf*, s.v. Q. 24:31.

Ṭabrisī

Most of Ṭabrisī's prefatory discussion to the verse focuses on establishing the syntactical status of the phrase *lacking (sexual) desire* (*ghayr ūlī'l-irbati*), and whether the phrase should be read as an exceptive clause to, or an adjectival qualifier of, the preceding term *their male dependants* (*al-tābiʿīn* [. . .] *min al-rijāl*). In other words, if read with an accusative inflection (*ghayra*), the verse would mean 'those male dependants who have no such need', whereas with the oblique inflection (*ghayri*), it would be simply qualifying this group of people as having no need by their having assumed this role of male dependant in the first place: males can only function as dependants when they do not have any such need. Naturally, the commentators realise that there may be males who become dependants but who also have such needs, and in front of whom believing women cannot reveal their ornament, hence the inquiry into the implications of both the accusative and the oblique inflections. Ṭabrisī, as elsewhere and in contradistinction to earlier (pre-Buwayhid) Imāmī commentaries,[122] draws on authorities from the Sunnī and Shīʿī tradition when discussing the opinions regarding 'manifest' and 'hidden' ornament. It is noteworthy that where he does cite Sunnī authorities, he is careful to conclude where he can with a reference to one of the imams to show that the Sunnī tradition accords with the Imāmī one. As a cumulative and discursive tradition, with every commentary additional items are included for consideration. Ṭabrisī, here, considers the question of a woman's ornament, not only from the perspective of keeping it hidden but of accentuating it for the husband, for whom it is a restricted privilege and prerogative. The category of 'father' and 'son' are extended vertically to include 'grandfathers' and 'grandsons' among those in the presence of whom a woman does not need to fully veil. We also see here the inclusion of Zoroastrian women, alongside the Jewish or the Christian, reflecting perhaps the ethnic demographic within which Ṭabrisī was composing his work. The question of whether a woman's male slave is permitted the same licence as her female slave remains contentious. We begin this commentary with Ṭabrisī's interpretation of the preceding verse, Q. 24:30.

Meaning (*al-maʿnā*)

Glory be to Him. God then makes clear what is lawful to see and what is unlawful, and says, *Tell* O Muḥammad *the believers*[123] *to lower their gaze* from that which it is not licit for them to look at, *and safeguard their private parts* [Q. 24:30] from those unlawful to them and from lewdnesses (*fāḥisha*) [. . .] Ibn Zayd stated that every instance in the Qur'ān in which the

[122] On this distinction and turning point for the approach within Imāmī exegesis, see Bar-Asher, *Scripture and Exegesis*, esp. 71–86 (and the references therein), in which the 'anti-Sunnī tendency and hostile attitude to the Companions of the Prophet', a defining characteristic of the earliest Imāmī exegetical compositions, is heavily toned down in the classical Shīʿī works of Ṭūsī and Ṭabrisī.

[123] Understood here as 'believing men'.

'safeguarding of private parts' is mentioned, it is fornication (*zinā*) that is meant, except in this instance. For, here, what is intended is covering up (*satr*) lest anyone should look at them, which is also what has been related on the authority of Abū ʿAbd Allāh [al-Ṣādiq] (ʿ*m*), who said, 'It is unlawful for a man to look upon the private parts of his fellow man or for a woman to look upon the private parts of her fellow woman' [. . .].[124]

And tell the believing women to lower their gaze and safeguard their private parts: He has commanded women just as He commanded men in terms of lowering the gaze and guarding the private parts. *And let them not reveal their ornament*: that is, let them not reveal those places of ornament (*mawāḍiʿ al-zīna*) to anyone other than one unmarriageable (*maḥram*) to them or one in a similar legal relation. He did not intend the actual ornament itself, for that may be lawfully seen, but what is intended are the actual parts where these ornaments are [worn]. They say that there are two kinds of 'ornament' (*zīna*): a manifest one and a hidden one. The manifest one is not to be covered up and it is permitted to look at, because of His words *except what is apparent of it*.

There are three opinions with regard to this matter. One, on the authority of Ibn Masʿūd, is that 'manifest' [ornament] constitutes clothing (*thiyāb*), while the 'hidden' ones are anklets, earrings and bracelets. The second one, on the authority of Ibn ʿAbbās, is that the 'manifest' refers to kohl, rings, the cheeks and the palms when they have been dyed (*khiḍāb*), or, on the authority of Qatāda, kohl, bracelets and rings. The third opinion, on the authority of al-Ḍaḥḥāk and ʿAṭāʾ, has it refer to the face and the palms; or, on the authority of al-Ḥasan [al-Baṣrī], it is the face and the fingertips (*banān*); or, the palms of the hands and the fingers (*aṣābiʿ*) according to the commentary (*tafsīr*) of ʿAlī b. Ibrāhīm [al-Qummī].

And let them cast their wraps (*khumur*) *over their cleavage*: *khumur*, plural of *khimār*, are veils (*maqāniʿ*), coverings for a woman's head that droops over her neckline (*jayb*). They were commanded to throw these veils (*maqāniʿ*) over their bosoms (*ṣudūr*) in order to cover their necklines (*nuḥūr*); it was said that they used to let these veils fall on the backs of their shoulders revealing their bosoms (*ṣudūr*). Necklines (*juyūb*) are used metonymically to refer to bosoms (*ṣudūr*), because it as though the one is draped over the other. They said that the command was issued here for them to cover their hair, earrings and necklines. Ibn ʿAbbās said that she should cover her hair, her

[124] We pick up Ṭabrisī's commentary a few lines down, where Q. 24:31 begins. The nature of the continuous flow of the commentaries means that passages preceding the verse in question are of relevance insofar as they provide a prelude to the sections that follow, as can be seen here.

chest (*ṣadr*), her breastbones (*tarāʾib*) and the sides of her face down the neckline (*sawālif*).

And let them not reveal their ornament – that is to say, the hidden ornament, which must not be uncovered during ritual prayer. On the authority of Ibn ʿAbbās, this is also said to mean that they should not take off their long garments (*jilbāb*) or their wraps (*khimār*), *except to their husbands*, that is, they should reveal to their spouses the parts of their bodies that are their ornament, in order to draw out their inclinations and stir their sexual appetite (*shahwa*). For it is reported that the Prophet (*ṣlʿhm*) said:

> Cursed be from among women the woman who dyes not (*saltāʾ*) and the one who wears no kohl (*marhāʾ*).[125] And cursed be the woman who when her husband calls to intercourse she procrastinates [by saying] 'I will!' (*musawwifa*), and the one who when he calls to her claims she is in menses (*ḥayḍ*) but is not (*mufsila*).

Or their fathers, or their husbands' fathers, or their sons, or their husbands' sons, or their brothers or their brothers' sons or sisters' sons, all of whom are [males] not lawful for her to marry and are unmarriageable to her on account of issue (*sabab*) and kinship (*nasab*). And included in this category are the forefathers of the husband, however high up, and the grandchildren, however far down, to whom it is permitted to reveal the ornament without provoking sexual desire (*shahwa*) and who are permitted to look intentionally if it is not for pleasure (*ladhdha*). *Or their womenfolk*, meaning believing women. But they are not permitted to bare themselves before a Jewish or a Christian or a Zoroastrian (*majūsiyya*) woman, unless the latter be a slave girl (*ama*), which is itself the meaning of His words *or what their right hands possess*, that is to say, slave girls (*imāʾ*).

It is reported on the authority of Ibn Jurayj, Mujāhid, al-Ḥasan and Saʿīd b. al-Musayyab that they said, 'It is not permissible for a slave (*ʿabd*) to gaze upon the hair of his mistress (*mawlātihi*).' It is also said that this refers to both male slaves (*ʿabīd*) and female slaves (*imāʾ*); this has also been reported on the authority of Abū ʿAbd Allāh [Jaʿfar al-Ṣādiq] (*ʿm*). Al-Jubbāʾī is reported to have said that what is meant is a slave (*mamlūk*) who has not attained the age of manhood (*rijāl*).

Or their male dependants lacking (sexual) desire: There are differences of opinion regarding the meaning of this. They say that a 'dependant' (*tābiʿ*) is one who follows (*t-b-ʿ*) you in order to acquire your sustenance, and who has no [sexual] need of women – in other words, the simpleton (*ablah*) – the one who has a master [as guardian] over him, according to Ibn ʿAbbās, Qatāda

[125] This does not seem to be in the canonical collections.

and Sa'īd b. Jubayr, and that is also what has been related on the authority of Abū 'Abd Allāh [al-Ṣādiq].

Others, like 'Ikrima and al-Sha'bī, say that this refers to an impotent one (*'anīn*), who has no need (*irb*) for women precisely on account of his [sexual] incapacity. According to al-Shafi'ī, it refers to one [who is a] partial eunuch (*khaṣiyy*) or a complete eunuch (*majbūb*) who has no desire (*raghba*) for women, but there is no precedence for this opinion. According to Yazīd b. Abī Ḥabīb, the reference is to the decrepit elderly man (*al-shaykh al-himm*)[126] on account of the evanescence of his [sexual] need (*irb*). According to Abū Ḥanīfa and his companions, the reference is to the young slave. *Or children*, that is, a group of children, *uninitiated to the exposedness of women*, by which He means young boys that have not come to know about women's shameful parts (*'awra*) and have not the virility for these, for lack of [sexual] appetite (*shahwa*). They also say that [it is because] they are not capable of copulating with women. However, as soon as they do attain that [sexual] appetite, then the same ruling for men governs them.

And let them not stamp their feet to make known what they hide of their ornament: Qatāda said that women used to stamp their feet in order to let the jangling of their anklets be heard, which is why He then forbade them to do that. According to Ibn 'Abbās, the verse intended to prohibit women from stamping their feet to reveal their anklets or the sound of these as they went about.

Turn to God in repentance all together O believers so that you may prosper, that is, [so] that you may win the reward of Paradise. According to the *ḥadīth*, the Prophet said, 'O people, turn to God in repentance, for I repent to God a hundred times every day'; [this was] cited by Muslim in his *Ṣaḥīḥ*. And by *repentance* (*tawba*) is meant total devotion (*inqiṭā'*) to God, exalted be He.[127]

Rāzī

Rāzī's commentary is always most striking for the systematic way in which he attempts to address issues raised by a particular verse or passage. Indeed, this predilection to break up the commentary into issues (*masā'il*), aspects (*wujūh*) and divisions (*aqsām*), which in turn sometimes subdivide into further inquiries (see the hypothetical scenarios he sets up below to address the verse's injunctions), frequently makes the text difficult to follow; at times, even Razi, as manuscript editors note, loses track of his

[126] In some editions this is '*al-shaykh al-haram*'.
[127] Ṭabrisī, *Majma' al-bayān*, s.v. Q. 24:31.

subdivisions. Most of his commentary, like that of others here in this volume, centres on identifying how much of the body women are permitted to show in the presence of various classes of individuals mentioned in the verse. The recurring question throughout is the definition of *ʿawra* and which parts of the body, in males and females, when exposed constitute *ʿawra*. Once this question has been broached, it is juxtaposed against the question of the degrees of familiarity that justify 'visual' access to various parts of the female body as well as its external ornament (jewellery, etc). The question of course is complicated by whether *zīna* (ornament) refers to what the commentarial tradition regards as the main loci of a woman's physical identity (hands, face and hair) or whether it refers to something more (the arms, legs, cleavage and so on). What is interesting is the extent to which household presence determines much of this privy access, as slave girls (whose standing is determined by their legal status as slaves and not by their religious affiliation) are permitted greater intimacy than free women who may be Jews or Christians. In addition, the presence of males in the household is of concern if they are not usually full-time occupants (uncles, etcetera) or if they are likely to be stirred by sexual desire in the presence of the women of the house. That *ʿawra*, strictly speaking, in the main is considered to be the portion of the body between the navel and the knees is in itself surprising and allows for a degree of variance in opinion regarding the limits of exposure between men and women as well as women and other women depending on the degrees of relationship between them. In his discussion of the first issue, below, Rāzī is citing directly from the commentary of Zamakhsharī, a testament to the latter's established authority as a grammarian and for the affinity between the two commentators in their tendency to a rationalising approach to exegesis, despite their differing schools of law: Zamakhsharī was a Ḥanafī, Rāzī was a Shāfiʿī.

Know that He, glory be to Him, has commanded men to lower their gaze and safeguard their private parts and has commanded women what He has commanded men, but adding in their case that they should not reveal their ornament except to specific categories of people. As for His words *to lower their gaze*, there are several issues.

The first issue: The majority have said that the [particle] *min* here is partitive, with the intended meaning being to lower one's gaze from what is illicit and restricting it to what is licit. For al-Akhfash, this [*min*] may very likely be redundant, by analogy with where He says *mā lakum min ilāhin ghayruhu* [*you have no god other than Him*, Q. 7:59] and *fa-mā minkum min aḥadin ʿanhu ḥājizīn* [*and not one of you could have held Us off from him*, Q. 69:47]; Sībawayh, however, rejects this [opinion]. If one were to ask how it [the *min*] has been inserted regarding the lowering of the gaze and not the safeguarding of the private parts, we would say that this is proof that the matter of looking is broader. Do you not see how when it comes to unmarriageable persons (*maḥārim*), it is acceptable to look at their hair and breasts (*ṣudūr*), likewise slave girls when they are being displayed for sale (*al-mustaʿraḍāt*).[128] As for the matter of the private parts, that is narrower [in scope].[129] It is enough of a difference to note that sight has been permitted except in certain cases, whereas the sexual act has been prohibited except in certain cases. Some have said that *to lower their gaze* means to look less, since sight, when it is not used, is in effect lowered and barred from its function. In accordance with this, the [particle] *min* is neither redundant nor partitive but is a relative [particle] for the verb *al-ghaḍḍ*. One says *ghaḍaḍtu min fulān* to mean 'I detracted from his worth' (*naqaṣtu min qadarihi*).

The second issue: Know that shameful parts (*ʿawrāt*) may be divided into four [types]: shameful parts of a man in the presence of another man; shameful parts of a woman in the presence of another woman; shameful parts of a woman in the presence of a man; and shameful parts of a man in the presence of a woman.

As for a man in the presence of another man, it is permissible for him to look at his entire body except for the shameful parts (*ʿawra*), which is between the navel (*surra*) and the knees, with the navel and the knees themselves not being shameful parts (*ʿawra*). But according to Abū Ḥanīfa, God have mercy on him, the knees constitute shameful parts. Mālik said that the thighs are not shameful parts, even though the proof that they are shameful is what has been reported on the authority of Ḥudhayfa, that the Prophet (*ṣlʿm*) came across him sitting in a mosque with his thigh showing, and so he said (*ṣlʿm*), 'Cover up your thigh, for it is a shameful part (*ʿawra*)'.[130] And he also said to ʿAlī, God be pleased with him, 'Do not reveal your thighs or look upon the thighs of another person, either living or dead'.[131] Moreover, if it happens that looking at another's face or the rest of his body stirs desires or causes fear of falling into temptation (*fitna*), because he is a hairless youth (*amrad*), then it is not permitted to look at him. It is not permissible for a man to lie with (*muḍājaʿa*) another man, even if each of them were on either side of the bed, because of what Abū Saʿīd al-Khudrī reported that the Prophet said, [which is:] 'A man should not lie next to another man in a single garment,

[128] Many published documents of sale of enslaved women show that they were subject to thorough physical inspection. See Yusuf Raghib, *Actes de vente d'esclaves et d'animaux en Égypte médiévale*, 2 vols. (Paris, Institut Français d'Archéologie Orientale, 2002).

[129] Note how this entire preamble is taken almost verbatim from Zamakhsharī's commentary, but without explicit acknowledgement.

[130] Found in Tirmidhī, *Jāmiʿ*, *Kitāb al-Adab* (43), *ḥadīth* no. 2798.

[131] Versions of this *ḥadīth* are found in Ibn Ḥanbal, *Musnad*, *Min musnad ʿAlī b. Abī Ṭālib*, *ḥadīth* no. 2149; Abū Dāwūd, *Sunan*, *Kitāb al-Janāʾiz* (21), *Bāb fī satr al-mayyit ʿinda ghaslihi* (32), *ḥadīth* no. 52/3140; Ibn Māja, *Sunan*, *Kitāb al-Janāʾiz* (6), *Bāb mā jāʾa fīʾl-ṣalāt ʿalāʾl-qabr* (32), *ḥadīth* 95/1527.

nor should a woman lie next to another woman in a single garment'.[132] It is also reprehensible (*k-r-h*) [for a man] to embrace or to kiss the face [of another man], except one's son out of affection (*shafaqa*). A handshake is recommended (*mustaḥabb*), because of what Anas has reported: A man said, 'O Messenger of God, when a man among us comes across one of his brethren or friends, should he bow before him?' to which he said, 'No'. So he asked, 'Should he then embrace him and kiss him?' to which he also said, 'No'. So he said, 'Then should he shake hands with him?' to which he said, 'Yes'.[133]

As for a woman's shameful parts in the presence of another woman, it is like a man's shameful parts in the presence of another man. She is permitted to look at her entire body except for what is between the navel and the knees. But when there is fear of temptation, then it is not permitted, and it is not permitted for them to lie together. Is a woman from among the People of the Book (*dhimiyya*) permitted to look at the body of a Muslim woman? They say that this is permissible, as is the case with a Muslim woman before another Muslim woman. But the sounder opinion is that this is not permissible, for the very fact that she is an outsider (*ajnabiyya*) in religious terms. God, exalted be He, says *or their womenfolk*, and a woman from among the People of the Book is not of our womenfolk.

As for the shameful part of a woman in the presence of a man, the woman is either an [unrelated] outsider (*ajnabiyya*), or an unmarriageable relative (*dhāt raḥim muḥarram*), or a woman taken in temporary relationship for pleasure (*mustamtaʿa*).[134] If she be an outsider, she could be either a free woman or a slave girl (*ama*). If she be a free woman, then her entire body is a shameful part (*ʿawra*) and he is not permitted to look at any part of her, except for the face and palms, for she needs to reveal her face during transactions of sale or purchase and to extend her palms to take and give. By 'palm' (*kaff*), we mean the inside and outside [of her hands] up to the elbows (*kūʿ*). But they also say that the top side of the hand is a shameful part (*ʿawra*).

[132] Versions of this *ḥadīth* are found in Muslim, *Ṣaḥīḥ*, *Kitāb al-Ḥayḍ* (3), *Bāb taḥrīm al-naẓar ilā'l-ʿawrāt* (17), *ḥadīth* no. 90/338; Abū Dāwūd, *Sunan*, *Kitāb al-Ḥammām* (33), *Bāb mā jāʾa fī'l-taʿriya* (3), *ḥadīth* no. 10/4018; Tirmidhī, *Jāmiʿ*, *Kitāb al-Adab* (43), *ḥadīth* no. 3023.

[133] A version is found in Nawawī, *Riyāḍ al-ṣāliḥīn*, *Kitāb al-Salām* (5), *Bāb istijāb al-muṣāfaḥa ʿinda'l-liqāʾ* (143), *ḥadīth* no. 45/888. It should be noted that Nawawī lived after Rāzī.

[134] On temporary marriage (*mutʿa*) see Shahla Haeri, *Law of Desire: Temporary Marriage in Shiʿi Iran* (Syracuse, NY, Syracuse University Press, 1989); Ziba Mir-Hosseini, *Islam and Gender: The Religious Debate in Contemporary Iran* (Princeton, Princeton University Press, 1999), 69–71; Sachiko Murata, *Mutʿa: Temporary Marriage in Islamic Law* (London, Mohammadi Press, 1987); Khaled Sindawi, *Temporary Marriage in Sunni and Shiʿite Islam: A Comparative Study* (Wiesbaden, Harrassowitz Verlag, 2013); for actual disputes see Mir-Hosseini, *Marriage on Trial: Islamic Family Law in Iran and Morocco* (London, I.B. Tauris, 1993), 162–180;. See also Heffening, 'Mutʿa', *EI*², and the references therein.

Know also that we have mentioned that it is not permissible to look at any part of her body, but it is permissible to look at her face and palms. In each of these opinions there is, however, an exception. As for the opinion that it is permissible to look at her face and palms, then know that this can be of three divisions: it is either where there is no motive (*gharaḍ*) or temptation (*fitna*), or where there is [the possibility of] temptation but no motive, or where there is both [the possibility of] temptation and a motive.[135]

As for **the first division**: know that it is not permissible [for a man] to look intentionally at the face of an unrelated woman (*ajnabiyya*) without a [justifying] motive. If his eyes should fall upon her inadvertently, then he should lower his gaze, because of His words *tell the believers to lower their gaze* [Q. 24:30]. They say that it is permissible [to look] if it is not liable to become a source of temptation; this is the opinion of Abū Ḥanīfa, God have mercy on him. But [the man] is not permitted to look at [that woman] again, because of His words *Indeed, the hearing and the sight and the heart – of each of these it will be asked* [Q. 17:36] and because of his [the Prophet's] words (*ṣlʿm*), 'O, ʿAlī, do not follow the [first] look with [another] look, for the first is [lawfully] yours but the second one is not',[136] and that Jābir b. ʿAbd Allāh said, 'I asked the Messenger of God (*ṣlʿm*) about the inadvertent look and he commanded me to turn my eyes away',[137] and [finally] because it is predominantly the case that it is not possible to avoid the first [look], as it tends to occur spontaneously (*ʿafwan*) whether it be intentional or unintentional.

As for **the second division**: this is when it involves a motive but not temptation and may be one of several cases. One case is when [a man] wishes to take a woman in marriage (*nikāḥ*) and thus looks at her face and her palms. Abū Hurayra, may God be pleased with him, related that a man wanted to marry a woman from among the Anṣār [of Medina]. The Messenger of God (*ṣlʿm*) said to him, 'Cast your eye on her, for there is something in the eyes of the Anṣār'.[138] He (*ṣlʿm*) also said, 'If one of you should propose (*khaṭaba*) to a woman, then there is nothing wrong in looking at her if he is looking at her in order to propose [marriage]'.[139] Al-Mughīra b. Shuʿba

[135] Note that these divisions are not in order in his discussion.

[136] Versions of this *ḥadīth* are found in Abū Dāwūd, *Sunan*, *Kitāb al-Nikāḥ* (12), *Bāb mā yu'maru bihi min ghaḍḍ al-baṣar* (44), *ḥadīth* no. 104/2149; Ibn Ḥanbal, *Musnad*, *Min musnad ʿAlī b. Abī Ṭālib*, *ḥadīth* no. 1373; Tirmidhī, *Jāmiʿ*, *Kitāb al-Adab* (43), *ḥadīth* no. 3004.

[137] A version is found in Tirmidhī, *Jāmiʿ*, *Kitāb al-Adab* (43), *ḥadīth* no. 3003.

[138] Versions are found in Muslim, *Ṣaḥīḥ*, *Kitāb al-Nikāḥ* (16), *Bāb nadb al-naẓar ilā wajh al-mar'a* (12), *ḥadīth* no. 87/1424; Nasā'ī, *Sunan*, *Kitāb al-Nikāḥ* (26), *Bāb idhā istashāra rajul rajulan fī'l-mar'a* (23), *ḥadīth* no. 51, 52/3247.

[139] This *ḥadīth* is not found in this exact wording, but cf. Abū Dāwūd, *Sunan*, *Kitāb al-Nikāḥ* (12), *Bāb fī'l-ʿadl*, *ḥadīth* no. 37/2082.

said, 'I proposed to a woman and he (*ṣl'm*) asked me, "Have you looked at her?" to which I said, "No". He said, "Look, for that will make it more likely to last between you".'[140] All of that proves that it is permitted [for a man] to look at [a woman's] face and her palms with desire (*shahwa*) if he intends to marry her, and this is also indicated by His words, exalted be He, *women are not lawful for you beyond that, nor [is it lawful] for you to change them for other wives, even though their beauty impress you* [Q. 33:52], for their beauty could not impress him unless he were to see their faces. A second case is when [a man] wishes to purchase a slave girl (*jāriya*), in which case he is permitted to look at all that, but not her shameful parts (*'awra*). The third case is during a contractual transaction (*mubāya'a*), when he should look at her face thoroughly (*muta'ammil*) so that he might recognise her when he needs her. The fourth case is when he looks at her as she bears witness and looks only at her face, because acknowledgement can only be confirmed thereby.[141]

As for **the third division**: this is when [a man] looks at [a woman] out of desire (*shahwa*), which is forbidden. He (*ṣl'm*) said, 'The eyes [too] fornicate'.[142] Jābir [b. Abd Allāh] said, 'I asked the Messenger of God about the inadvertent look, and he commanded me to turn my eyes away.'[143] They say that in the Torah is written: 'the look seeds in the heart desire', and perchance a look gives birth to enduring grief.

Another point to add is that it is not permissible for an unrelated man (*ajnabī*) to look at the body of an unrelated woman (*ajnabiyya*); but they make exceptions. One of these is that it is permissible for a trustworthy physician (*ṭabīb*) to look at her for the purposes of treatment (*mu'ālaja*). It is also permissible for a circumciser (*khattān*) to look at the private parts (*farj*) of the one to be circumcised (*makhtūn*) as an unavoidable necessity. The second [exception] is that it is possible to look intentionally at the private parts of both parties involved in fornication (*zinā*) in order to bear witness to the act of fornication. Likewise, private parts may be viewed in order to bear witness to a birth and to look at the breasts of the wet nurse (*murḍi'a*) in order to bear witness to

[140] Versions of this *ḥadīth* are found in Ibn Māja, *Sunan*, *Kitāb al-Nikāḥ*, *ḥadīth* no. 1937; Nasā'ī, *Sunan*, *Kitāb al-Nikāḥ* (26), *Bāb ibāḥat al-naẓar qabl al-tazwīj* (17), *ḥadīth* nos. 39/3234, 40/3235.

[141] Note that the commentators assume that a woman cannot wear a face covering to bear legal witness.

[142] Cf. the sermon on the Mount in Matthew 5:27–30, where the heart commits adultery through the eyes; also cf. Abū Dāwūd, *Sunan*, *Kitāb al-Adab*, no. 4904 (*wa'l-'aynu taznī*).

[143] Versions are found in Muslim, *Ṣaḥīḥ*, *Kitāb al-Adab* (38), *Bāb naẓar al-fujā'a* (10), *ḥadīth* no. 59/2159; Tirmidhī, *Jāmi'*, *Kitāb al-Adab* (43), *ḥadīth* no. 3003.

suckling.[144] Abū Saʿīd al-Iṣṭakhrī (d. 328/940)[145] said: It is not permissible for a man to look at these parts intentionally, for the recommended [jurisprudential] practice (*mandūb*) is to conceal (*satr*)[146] an act of fornication (*zinā*); and in the case of parturition (*wilāda*) and wet-nursing (*riḍāʿ*), a woman's testimony is acceptable and so there is no need for a man to look in order to bear witness. The third [exception] is when a woman is drowning or in a fire, in which case [a man] is permitted to look at her body in order to save her. If this unrelated woman (*ajnabiyya*) be a slave girl (*ama*), some say that what counts as shameful parts (*ʿawra*) is what is between the navel and the knees. Others have said that her shameful parts (*ʿawra*) are the parts that are not revealed during her work (*mihna*) and hence her head, arms, legs, neckline and chest do not count as shameful parts. However, the opposite opinion to what has been mentioned exists with reference to her back, her belly and what is above the arms. A man is certainly not permitted to touch [a woman] nor her him, and this is forbidden whether it be for cupping (*ḥijāma*) or applying kohl (*iktiḥāl*) or anything else, for touching is more powerful than looking, judging by the fact that the emission of fluids (*inzāl*) as a result of touching breaks a person's fast, whereas if it is the result of looking, it does not break it. Abū Ḥanīfa, may God have mercy on him, said: It is permissible to touch a slave girl in those places where he is permitted to look. But if the woman is unmarriageable to him, whether in terms of blood (*nasab*), suckling (*riḍāʿ*) or in-lawship (*ṣihriyya*), then what is between her navel and knees constitutes her shameful parts to him, just as in the case of a man. Others, however, have said that her shameful part is what is revealed while she is working (*mihna*), this being the opinion of Abū Ḥanīfa, may God have mercy on him. All of these details shall, God willing, be presented in the exegesis (*tafsīr*) of the verse.

144 In permitting a man to look at birth, Rāzī is going against the majority Shāfiʿī view on the matter, which does not permit men to testify to a live birth. Men's absence from childbirth justifies the opinion that permits women to testify to birth, even without the testimony of a man. He acknowledges his departure from the majority view obliquely by citing Abū Saʿīd al-Iṣṭakhrī in the following line.

145 Abū Saʿīd al-Ḥasan b. Aḥmad b. Yazīd al-Iṣṭakhrī was a well-known Shāfiʿī jurist of Baghdad and *qāḍī* of Sijistān during the reign of the caliph al-Muqtadir (d. 328/940). See Dhahabī, *Siyar*, XV, 250–52.

146 Cf. Ziba Mir-Hosseini, 'Islamic Law and the Question of Gender Equality' in *Routledge Handbook of Islamic Law*, ed. Khaled Abou El Fadl *et al.* (Abingdon, Routledge, 2019), 340–54. The concept of *sitr* is central to both Islamic jurisprudence and private piety. So long as a transgression has not inadvertently or intentionally been brought to public light, a sinning individual is enjoined to keep the transgression 'under wraps', so to speak, exercising the divine 'covering' (*sitr*; God is al-Sattār), all the while engaging in repentance and regret. See Ahmad El Shamsy, 'Shame, Sin, and Virtue: Islamic Notions of Privacy' in *Public and Private in Ancient Mediterranean Law and Religion*, ed. Clifford Ando and Jörg Rüpke (Berlin, de Gruyter, 2015), 237–49. See also Norman Calder, *Islamic Jurisprudence in the Classical Era*, ed. Colin Imber (Cambridge, Cambridge University Press, 2010), esp. 55ff.

If the woman is a wife taken in temporary marriage (*mustamtaʿa ka-zawja*) or a slave girl (*ama*) whom he is permitted to enjoy temporarily, he is permitted to look at her entire body, including her private parts (*farj*), even as it is considered loathsome (*k-r-h*) that he should look at the private part (*farj*) itself – for it is said that this brings about blindness (*ṭams*). Some say that it is never permissible [for him] to look at her private parts, regardless of whether the slave girl (*ama*) be property (*qunna*), a housekeeper (*mudabbira*), the mother of a child (*umm walad*) or held in security (*marhūna*). If she were a Zoroastrian (*majūsiyya*), an apostate (*murtadda*), or an idolatress (*wathaniyya*), or shared between him and another man,[147] or married or manumitted (*mukātaba*), then she is to be considered as one unrelated (*ajnabiyya*).

ʿAmr b. Shuʿayb related on the authority of his father from his father that the Prophet (*ṣlʿm*) said, 'If one of you should give in marriage a slave girl (*jāriya*) to his slave (*ʿabd*) or his hired hand (*ajīr*), let him not look at what is below the navel and above the knees'.[148]

As for the shameful parts in the case of a man before a woman, there is some debate (*naẓar*): if he be unrelated to her, then what is between the navel and the knees is shameful for him to expose, while it has also been said his entire body except for the face and palms, which is the case for her with him. The first [opinion] is sounder and it is the opposite case for the woman in terms of the man, for a woman's body in itself is shameful (*ʿawra*), on the basis of the fact that her prayers are not sound if her body is uncovered; with the body of a man, it is the opposite. It is still not permissible for her to look intentionally if she fears temptation or to look again at his face, according to what has been reported from Umm Salama, that she and Maymūna were with the Prophet (*ṣlʿm*) when the son of Umm Maktūm came in to see her and the Prophet said, 'Take [your] cover (*iḥtajibā*) before him', at which point [Umm Salama relates], 'I said, "O Messenger of God, is he not blind and unable to see us?" to which he (*ṣlʿm*) said, "And are you two blind that you do not see him?"'[149] And if he is her guardian (*maḥram*), what is between his navel and knees is shameful for him to expose to her. If he be her spouse or master (*sayyid*), for whom it is permissible to have sexual relations with her (*waṭʾ*), then she is permitted to look at his entire body, [though] it is deemed loathsome for her to look at his private parts (*farj*), as is the case with him

[147] This must not be a reference to her being sexually shared, but merely shared as a servant, for sexual sharing is not legally permitted.

[148] Abū Dāwūd, *Sunan*, *Kitāb al-Libās* (34), *Bāb fī qawlihi ʿazza wa-jalla wa qul li'l-muʾmināt yaghḍuḍna* (36), *ḥadīth* no. 93/4112.

[149] See above, note 110.

before her. It is also not permitted for a man to be naked (*ʿāriyan*) in the house of a maternal uncle when he has something with which to cover his shameful parts, for it has been reported that the Prophet was asked about this and said, 'It is worthier that he be ashamed (*yastaḥī*) before God[150] [than before his uncle]'. It is reported that the Messenger said, 'Beware of being naked, for in your company are those who never leave you, except when you are relieving yourselves (*ghāʾiṭ*) and when a man is intimate with his wife (*ahl*)'.[151] But God knows best.

The third issue: Al-Shiblī was asked about His words *to lower their gaze*, and he commented, '[Lower] the eyes from illicit things and the eyes of the heart from all that is not God, exalted be He'. His words, exalted be He, *and safeguard their private parts* mean from what is not licit. Abū'l-ʿĀliya is reported to have said, 'Every instance in the Qurʾān where He says *safeguard their private parts* refers to fornication (*zinā*), except for the one in [*sūrat*] *al-Nūr*, where it means that no one's eyes should fall on them.'[152] But this [opinion] is weak because it specifies without any proof (*dalāla*). The apparent reading requires that the meaning be to guard them from all that God has made illicit for them, be it fornication, touching, or looking, and if the intended meaning were to restrict looking, then both touching (*lams*) and the sexual act (*waṭʾ*) would necessarily be included by the import of this verse, since they are more severe than looking (*naẓar*). Thus, if God has designated looking [as forbidden], then it is already implied in the meaning of the address that the sexual act or touching are forbidden. Likewise, where God says *then do not say to them, 'Fie!'* [Q. 17:23], this necessarily means prohibiting what is greater than that, such as cursing or beating [. . .]

As for His words *And tell the believing women to lower their gaze and safeguard their private parts*, interpretations are as we have already mentioned. If one were to ask: why He has placed the lowering of gazes before the safeguarding of private parts? We would say: Because the eyes are a conduit for fornication (*zinā*) and lead the way to sin (*fujūr*); the trial (*balwā*) that a person undergoes because of them is always greater and more severe and it is almost impossible to guard against [looking].

As for His saying *And let them not reveal their ornament except what is apparent of it*, this belongs to those rulings that are specifically for women,

150 Cf. Tirmidhī, *Jāmiʿ*, *Kitāb al-Adab* (43), *ḥadīth* no. 3024.
151 Ibid., *Jāmiʿ*, *Kitāb al-Adab* (43), *ḥadīth* no. 3030.
152 In Ṭabrisī and elsewhere, this *ḥadīth* is attributed to Ibn Zayd and to Jaʿfar al-Ṣādiq.

most of the time; we say 'most of the time' since a man is [also] forbidden from revealing his ornament, whether jewellery or clothes, to women unrelated to him because of the temptations (*fitna*) that might arise thereby. There are several issues here.

The first issue: Opinions differ over what is meant by *their ornament*. Know that 'ornament' (*zīna*) can be used to refer to beautiful features (*maḥāsin al-khalq*) that God has created and to all that human beings adorn themselves with, such as beautiful garments and accessories and other things. Some, however, reject the term *zīna* as referring to physical features (*khalq*), since one almost never refers to physical traits when one says 'of her ornament', but refers to what is added to those physical traits in the way of kohl or colour and the like. It is more accurate, though, to say that physical traits are subsumed by the term *zīna*, and this is indicated in two ways. One is that many women, as far as their physical traits are concerned, go without any of what is considered ornament, and, so, if we were to take the term as signifying physical characteristics we would have fulfilled the general sense of the term but without excluding things other than the physical appearance. The second way [that this is indicated] is that His words *and let them cast their wraps over their cleavage* indicate that what is meant by *ornament* (*zīna*) generally comprehends physical appearance and other than that. It is as though God has forbidden them from revealing the fair traits of their appearance by requiring them to cover these with a wrap (*khimār*). When some say, however, that *ornament* expresses what is other than physical appearance, they have in effect confined it to three matters: the first of them is paints (*aṣbāgh*), such as kohl, face dyes (*khiḍāb*) to brand (*wasma*) her brows, milk lotion (*ghumra*) on her cheeks, and henna (*ḥinā'*) on her palms and feet; the second of them is jewellery, such as rings, bangles, anklets, bracelets, necklaces, tiaras, cinctures and earrings; and the third of them is garments, as in where God says *adorn yourselves* (*zīnatakum*) *at every place of worship* [Q. 7:31], meaning garments (*thiyāb*).

The second issue: Opinions differ over what is meant by His words *except what is apparent of it*. As for those who take *ornament* to refer to physical traits, al-Qaffāl has said that the meaning of the verse would be '[except] what a person habitually leaves apparent, which in the case of women are the face and hands, and in the case of men, the face, hands and legs'. And so the command came to cover up what is not revealed by necessity, and permission [was] granted for them to reveal what is normally revealed and what by necessity is made apparent, since the legal rulings in Islam are meant to be natural (*ḥanīfiyya*),[153] easy (*sahla*) and solicitous (*samḥa*). Since the revealing of the face and hands is necessary (*ḍarūra*), beyond any doubt, they are in agreement that neither of these can be a shameful part (*ʿawra*). As for the feet, their exposure is not considered necessary and indeed they disagree as to whether these can be considered as a shameful part or not. There are two views on this matter: the sounder is that things like the top of the foot is a shameful part (*ʿawra*). As for a woman's voice, there are two views, the sounder one being that it is not shameful (*ʿawra*), for the wives of the Prophet (*ṣlʿm*) used to relate traditions (*akhbār*) to men. As for those who interpret *ornament* to mean something other than physical traits, they say that He, glory be to Him, mentions *ornament* because there can be disagreement over the fact that it is permissible to look at it when it is not part of a woman's limbs. The moment that God prohibited looking at it when it has to do with the bodies of women, that becomes a superlative emphasis of the illicitness of looking at a woman's body parts. On the basis of this statement, it is permissible to look at the ornament on a [woman's] face, such as a tattoo (*washma*) or face paint (*ghumra*), and the ornament on her body, such as colour, rings and likewise her clothes. [Thus] the reason for permitting looking at her is that it would be inhibiting (*ḥaraj*) for her to cover these up, since a woman will invariably use her hands to handle things and will need to reveal her face during witness, in court or at the point of marriage.[154]

The third issue: They agree that His words *and let them not reveal their ornament except what is apparent of it* are specific to free women (*ḥarāʾir*) and not slave girls (*imāʾ*). The meaning therein is clear and that is that a slave girl is chattel (*māl*) and it is imperative to exercise caution when selling or purchasing her, and this can only be [exercised] if one could look at her to inspect her, contrary to the case with free women.

As for His words *and let them cast their wraps over their cleavage*: *khimār* is the singular of *khumur*, which are veils (*maqāniʿ*). The exegetes state that [Jāhilī] women before Islam used to fasten their *khimār*s behind them. And,

[153] Or somehow 'intuitive', as these early scholars understood the term. In the vast majority of instances, *ḥanīfiyya* was associated with a form of monotheistic 'submission' that preceded Judaism and Christianity and was used to qualify the practice of Abraham (see esp. Q. 3:67), bypassing Judaeo-Christian practices and institutions to establish Abraham's monotheism as a historical precursor to what the Prophet Muḥammad preached and re-established, according to the Qur'ān. See W. Montgomery Watt, 'Ḥanīf', *EI*².

[154] Ironically, the Muslim medieval tradition's position on this point has not been factored in by contemporary Muslim women facing resistance to their donning of *niqāb*s and *burka*s by European governments in European public spheres ('The Islamic Veil across Europe', BBC News, 31 May 2018, https://www.bbc.com/news/world-europe-13038095).

so, with their garment cut (*juyūb*) at the front, their necklines and pendants would be revealed. They were thus commanded to cast their veils (*maqāniʿ*) over their cleavages (*juyūb*) in order to cover their necks and necklines and the surrounding hair, ear and neck jewellery, and where the knot was drawn. The expression *ḍ-r-b* (strike) is intended as an emphatic act of drawing and *bi-* is attached [to emphasise juxtaposition]. On the authority of ʿĀʾisha, may God be pleased with her, [it is reported], 'I have not seen women more excellent than the those of the Anṣār: when this verse was sent down, each one of them took to ripping out parts of their garments' inner lining and covered their heads to the back.' Some read *jiyūbihinna* with a *kasra* on the *jīm* because of the subsequent *yāʾ*, and likewise *biyūtan ghayra biyūtikum*.

As for His words *and let them not reveal their ornament*, know that after God speaks about ornament in the abstract sense, He then speaks about subtle [forms of] ornament that He has forbidden women to reveal to non-relatives. And while this subtle ornament must be hidden from all, He excepts twelve figures (*ṣūra*): **the first** is their spouses; **the second**, their fathers and whomever is older from both the males and the females, such as paternal grandparents and maternal grandparents; **the third**, the parents of their spouses; **the fourth and fifth**, their sons and the sons of their spouses, and included in this are the grandchildren even lower down, whether male or female, such as the children of their sons and the children of their daughters; **the sixth**, their brothers, whether from the side of the father or [the side of] the mother, or from both; **the seventh**, their nephews and nieces; **the eighth**, the children of their sisters. All of these are unmarriageable. Herein are several questions:

The first question: Are those matters illicit for unmarriageable individuals licit when it comes to a slave girl (*mamlūka*) or an unbelieving woman (*kāfira*)?

The response: If [the man] owns the woman and she is considered unmarriageable to him, then he is permitted to look at her front and back, [though] not in a desirous manner, but rather out of the prerogative of ownership, which is different between people in such cases.

The second question: What about opinions regarding the paternal uncle and the maternal uncle?

The response: The overt view is that they are like all other unmarriageable individuals and are permitted to look, and this is the opinion of al-Ḥasan al-Baṣrī, who said that [this] is because the verse does not mention suckling relationships (*riḍāʿ*), and these count as kinship (*nasab*). Moreover, God says in *sūrat al-Aḥzāb*: *There is no blame on these women concerning their fathers*

[Q. 33:55] to the end of the verse.[155] And while there is no mention of spouses or their sons there [in Q. 24:31], these are mentioned here [in Q 33:55]. Sometimes He mentions a part to turn attention to the whole. Al-Shaʿbī said, 'God does not mention these two [the uncles, in Q. 24:31] lest they then describe them [the women] to their sons and so on.' This means that all of the relationships of kin share the rights of [access because of] unmarriageability, except the paternal uncle and the maternal uncle and their sons. For, if one of these fathers were to see her, he might then describe her to his son, who is not unmarriageable, and thus end up giving him a picture of her by describing her after seeing her. This is another example of a rhetorically powerful proof of the obligation on women to exercise caution and cover up.
The third question: What is the reason for permitting these [individuals] to look at a woman's ornament?
The response: It is because they are specifically in need of entering into their presence and mingling with them, and because of the unlikelihood of falling into temptation in their case, and on account of the natural tendency (*ṭabʿ*) to be averse to sitting with strangers. A woman also needs their company during travel, and [help] while dismounting and mounting.

The ninth [excepted figure]:[156] His words *or their womenfolk*, regarding which there are two opinions. One says that this means womenfolk who are of the same religion, which is the opinion of most of the first generations [of authorities]: Ibn ʿAbbās said, 'A Muslim woman should not bare herself before women of the People of the Book (*ahl al-dhimma*) and should not reveal to the unbelieving woman, except what she reveals to those unrelated to her, unless the woman be her slave girl (*ama*), because God says *or what their right hands possess*.' ʿUmar [b. al-Khaṭṭāb] once wrote to Abū ʿUbayda commanding him to forbid the women of the People of the Book (*ahl al-kitāb*) from entering the baths (*ḥammām*) with the [Muslim] women believers. The other opinion says that the phrase *their womenfolk* refers to any women, which is the correct stance (*madhhab*); still, the opinion of the pious predecessors (*al-salaf*) is sustained out of respect (*istiḥbāb*) and takes priority.

The tenth [excepted figure]: His words *or what their right hands possess*. On the face of it, the statement refers to slaves (*ʿabīd*) and slave girls (*imāʾ*). There is a difference of opinion here. Some have interpreted the verse on the basis

[155] The reference is to an extended passage in *sūrat al-Aḥzāb* (Q. 33) that prescribes the proper behaviour in the presence of the Prophet's wives and access to them in their household.

[156] Rāzī here resumes the list of twelve categories of those before whom women may reveal their ornament.

of this apparent sense (*ẓāhir*), claiming that there is nothing wrong with these women revealing to their slaves what ornament they reveal to those who are unmarriageable to them, an opinion related on the authority of ʿĀʾisha and Umm Salama, may God be pleased with both of them. They use this verse as proof, even as this is apparent enough, and [use] also what Anas [b. Mālik] reported, namely that he [the Prophet] (*ṣlʿm*) came to Fāṭima with a slave whom he had brought as a gift for her while she was in a garment that [was so short that] if she covered her head with it, it would barely reach her legs, and if she were to cover her legs with it, it would barely reach her head. When the Prophet saw how she was [garbed], he said to her, 'Do not be troubled, for he is [as] your father and your young lad (*ghulām*)'.[157] [It has been reported] on the authority of Mujāhid that the mothers of the believers[158] did not veil themselves before their slaves in manumission so long as they still owed [as little as] a dirham. [It has been reported] on the authority of ʿĀʾisha, may God be pleased with her, that she said to Dhakwān, 'Once you have put me in my grave and come out, then you are a free man (*ḥurr*).' It has [also] been reported on the authority of ʿĀʾisha that a slave would be looking at her while she was brushing her hair. Ibn Masʿūd, Mujāhid, al-Ḥasan [al-Baṣrī], Ibn Sīrīn and Saʿīd b. al-Musayyab, may God be pleased with them, have said, 'A slave should not look at the hair of his mistress', which is also the opinion of Abū Ḥanīfa, may God be pleased with him. They have based their proof for this on several things. The first: his [the Prophet's] words (*ṣlʿm*), 'It is not permissible for a woman who believes in God and the Last Day to travel for more than three days except if she be with an unmarriageable guardian'.[159] A slave (*ʿabd*) is not unmarriageable to her and so cannot accompany her on travel; and since he is not permitted to travel with her he is not permitted to look at her hair, as is the case with a free man who is not related. The second: her ownership of the slave does not make licit what was illicit for him before ownership. The ownership of men by women is not the same as the ownership of women by men, for there is no disagreement among them regarding the fact that, as a result of her ownership of the slave, she is not permitted to enjoy (*tamattuʿ*) him sexually in any way, as a man does his slave girl. The third: even if a slave is not permitted to marry his mistress (*mawlāt*), that prohibition against him is temporary (*ʿāriḍ*), as in the case of one who has four wives but is not permitted to marry others. And

[157] Cf. Abū Dāwūd, *Sunan*, *Kitāb al-Libās*, *Bāb fīʾl-ʿabd yanẓur ilā shaʿr mawlātihi*, *ḥadīth* no. 4106.

[158] This appellation, *ummahāt al-muʾminīn* in Arabic, refers to the wives of the Prophet.

[159] Cf. Abū Dāwūd, *Sunan*, *Kitāb al-Manāsik waʾl-ḥajj* (11), *Bāb fīʾl-marʾa taḥujju bi-ghayr maḥram* (2), *ḥadīth* no. 6/1726; Muslim, *Ṣaḥīḥ*, *Kitāb al-Ḥajj* (15), *Bāb safar al-marʾa maʿ maḥramin ilā ḥajjin wa-ghayrihi* (74), *ḥadīth* nos. 462–75.

since this prohibition (*ḥurma*) is not indefinite, the slave remains of the same status as all other unrelated individuals. If this [interpretation] holds, it becomes apparent that the meaning of His words *or what their right hands possess* refers to slave girls (*imāʾ*). And if one were to say, 'But slave girls are included in His words *their womenfolk*' so what is the use of this repetition, we would say that *their womenfolk* and *what their right hands possess* mean those free women and slave girls who are in their company. The proof-text of that is that He, glory be to Him, first mentions the situation with men – in His words *and let them not reveal their ornament except to their husbands* to the end of what is mentioned – and so it is possible for someone to suppose that men are specifically meant by that, whether they be unmarriageable or not unmarriageable. He then adds to that 'slave girls' with His words *or what their right hands possess*, lest it is thought that this licence is confined to free women, for the apparent meaning of His words *or their womenfolk* requires that they be free women and not slave girls. This is similar to His words *two witnesses of your menfolk* (*min rijālikum*) [Q. 2:282] referring to free men, given the attribution [of these men] to us. Likewise, His words *or their womenfolk* refer to free women; He then adds to these 'the slave girls', permitting to them what He has permitted to free women.

The eleventh [excepted figure]: His words, exalted be He, *or their male dependants lacking (sexual) desire*, regarding which there are several issues.

The first issue: It is said that these are men who follow you around to receive whatever surplus is there of your food and have no need for women, since they are simpletons (*balah*) who have no awareness of women, or righteous elderly men (*shuyūkh ṣulaḥāʾ*) who, in the company of women, lower their gazes. It is common knowledge that castrates (*khaṣiyy*) and impotents (*ʿanīn*) and their like may not have a desire (*irba*) for the sexual act (*jimāʿ*) itself, but may have a strong desire for all other forms of sexual pleasure (*tamattuʿ*), which prevents them from being the intended reference [of the verse]. The intended meaning must be based on those of whom it is known that they have no desire of any form of pleasure, either because of the lack of [sexual] appetite (*shahwa*) or for lack of knowledge (*maʿrifa*), or because of poverty (*faqr*) and disability (*maskana*). It is over these three aspects that scholars have disagreed. Some have said that these [male dependants] are the destitute in dire poverty. Others have said that they are the mentally impaired (*maʿtūh*), the dimwits (*ablah*) or young boys (*ṣabiyy*). Still others have said that [*male dependants*] refer to old men and any man who lacks sexual appetite (*shahwa*). There is nothing to prevent all [of the above] from being included in that [last category]. Hishām b. ʿUrwa related, on the authority of Zaynab bt. Umm Salama from Umm Salama, that the Prophet (*ṣlʿm*) entered into her presence while an effeminate (*mukhannath*) was with her, and [the effeminate] turned to the brother of Umm Salama and said to him, 'If God grants you the conquest of al-Ṭāʾif tomorrow, I shall tell you where to find Ghaylān's daughter, for she comes with four and leaves with eight.' And the Prophet said, 'Let not this one enter into your presence anymore'.[160] The Prophet had permitted the effeminate to enter and be with the women when he presumed that he was one of those 'without desire [for women]', but when he came to know that this [effeminate] knew all about the affairs of the women and what they looked like, he realised that he was [one] of those with desire and thus barred him thereafter. Concerning partial castrates (*khaṣiyy*) and full castrates (*majbūb*), there are three positions (*awjuh*). The first: it is permissible [for women] to reveal the inner ornament in their presence; the second: it is not permitted; the third: it is permitted only for the partial castrate but not the full castrate.

The second issue: *Al-irba* (need, desire) is [based on the pattern] *fuʿla*, derived from *al-irb*, similar to *al-mashya* (a walk) or *al-jalsa* (a sitting), derived as they are [respectively] from *al-mashy* and *al-julūs*; *al-irb* means a need (*ḥāja*) and a craving (*walaʿ*) for something, desiring it strongly (*shahwa*); *al-irba* is the need for women; *al-irba* is also the intellect (*ʿaql*), from which derives *al-arīb* (an expert).

The third issue: Regarding *ghayr*, there are two readings. Ibn ʿĀmir and Abū Bakr on the authority of ʿĀṣim and Abū Jaʿfar read it *ghayra*, as an exceptive or as a circumstantial qualifier (*ḥāl*) meaning 'dependants who are impotent with regard to women'. The other reading is *ghayri*, as an adjectival clause.

The twelfth [excepted figure]: His words *or children uninitiated to the exposedness of women*, regarding which there are several issues.

The first issue: *Al-ṭifl* (the child) is a singular noun, but it stands here for the plural since it has the meaning of a collective noun (*jins*), since what comes after it indicates that it is the plural that is meant, analogous to His words *thumma nukhrijukum ṭiflan* [*then We bring you forth as infants*, Q. 22:5].

[160] Cf. Bukhārī, *Ṣaḥīḥ*, *Kitāb al-Nikāḥ* (67), *Bāb mā yunhā min dukhūl al-mutashabbihīna bi'l-nisāʾi ʿalā'l-marʾa* (113), *ḥadīth* no. 168/5325 and *Kitāb al-Maghāzī*, *Bāb ghazwat al-Ṭāʾif fī Shawwāl sanat thamān* (56), *ḥadīth* no. 354/4324; Mālik, *Muwaṭṭaʾ*, *Kitāb al-Waṣiyya* (37), *ḥadīth* no. 5/1462.

The second issue: To be initiated to something happens in two ways. The first is to have knowledge of it, as in where He says *for if they should come to know of you, they will stone you* [*innahum in yaẓharū ʿalaykum yarjumūnakum*, Q. 18:20], that is, they become aware of you. The second is to overcome something and spring upon it, as in His words *and they prevailed* (*fa aṣbaḥū ẓāhirīn* [Q. 61:14]). According to the first way, the meaning would be, children who have no concept of the nakedness of women and do not know what that is because of their young age, which is the opinion of Ibn Qutayba. According to the second way, it is those who have not reached the age at which they would be able to have sexual relations (*ityān*) with women, which is the opinion of al-Farrāʾ and al-Zajjāj.

The third issue: For a child who is oblivious to the shamefulness (*ʿawra*) of women because of his young age, there is then no shame (*ʿawra*) for a woman in his presence. But if he starts to notice it at a young age, because he is pubescent, then a woman is required to hide from him what is between her navel and knees. As regards the obligation to cover what is other than that, there are two aspects: one is that there is no obligation, because the [heavenly] pen [that records deeds] has not begun to write in his case; the other is that the obligation stands, as in the case of a man, since he [the boy] might have the [sexual] appetite for her and she for him, which is the intended meaning of His words *or children uninitiated to the exposedness of women*. The term *ṭifl* (child) comprehends him up until the time of puberty. As for the elderly man (*shaykh*), if he still has a sexual appetite then he is considered like a young man (*shābb*), but if he has no desire left, there are two opinions: the first, that [exposing] the inner ornament (*zīna bāṭina*) in his presence is permitted, and what is a shameful part (*ʿawra*) in his presence would be what is between the navel and the knees; the second, that in his presence the entire body is considered shameful (*ʿawra*), except for the outer ornament (*zīna ẓāhira*). With this concludes the last of the scenarios that God has made the exception.

Regarding these [individuals], al-Ḥasan was of the opinion that even though all of them are permitted to see the inner ornament (*zīna bāṭina*), they nevertheless fall into three categories.[161] The first of these is the husband, who has the privilege of intimacy (*ḥurma*) that no other has, making for him licit everything about her; the second [right of] intimacy belongs to the son, the father, the brother, the grandfather, the father-in-law and every

[161] In other words, they do not all have equal access to that 'hidden ornament', as Rāzī will conclude below.

unmarriageable relative and those of suckling relationships who are like blood relatives (*nasab*) and for whom it is permissible to look at the hair, the breasts, the legs, the arms and the like; the third [right of intimacy] is for *male dependants lacking (sexual) desire*, likewise for a woman's slave boy (*mamlūk*), and it is acceptable for a young woman (*shābba*) to be in front of them dressed in a shirt (*darʿ*) and in a thick veil (*khimār*) not necessarily with a wrap (*milḥaf*). But it is not permissible for any of these individuals to see [a woman's] hair or skin (*bashar*); it is always best to cover (*satr*). Moreover, it is not licit for a young woman to sit in front of a stranger (*gharīb*) without an outer garment (*jilbāb*).

This, then, captures the details of these various ranks [of intimacy].

As for His words *and let them not stamp their feet to make known what they hide of their ornament*, Ibn ʿAbbās as well as Qatāda related that [when] passing by other people, the women would strike their legs together so that their anklets would clank. And one knows that when a man who is overpowered by his desires hears the sound of the anklets, this will be even more incentive for him to gaze at the women. God, exalted be He, has given the justification for that by saying *to make known what they hide of their ornament*, pointing out thereby that the reason for which this [act] was prohibited was lest their ornament of jewellery be known. There are several lessons (*fāʾida*) in this verse. The first one is: Since the sound that suggests the presence of ornament is prohibited, all the more so is the prohibition of revealing the ornament itself. The second one is: women are prohibited from raising their voices when speaking, lest outsiders (*ajānib*) should overhear, since the sound of their voices is more likely to cause temptation than the sound of their anklets. [This] is why they deem it reprehensible for a woman to make the call to prayer (*adhān*), [for it] requires raising one's voice, and a woman is forbidden from doing that. The third one is: the verse is proof that it is forbidden to look at a woman's face with desire, since that is more likely to stir temptation (*fitna*).

As regards His words *turn to God in repentance all together O believers so that you may* (*laʿallakum*) *prosper*, there are several issues.

The first issue: There are two aspects to *repentance* (*tawba*). One of these is that the obligations which God imposes in every matter cannot always be fulfilled by a servant who is weak, even if he should discipline himself and make every effort; [he] will always be liable to some shortcoming on his part. That is why He has enjoined all believers to turn in repentance and to ask forgiveness, giving them hope of prospering after repentance and forgiveness. The other [aspect of repentance]: Ibn ʿAbbās, may God be pleased with them both, said, 'Repent of what you used to do in the previous age of ignorance (the *jāhiliyya*) so that you may be felicitous in this world and in the next.' If one were to ask, 'If the act of repentance in [embracing] Islam were sound and this [act of] Islam cancels what was before it, what is the meaning of this repentance here?' we would say, as some scholars have said, that the one who has sinned and repented from his sin is required to renew his repentance every time he recalls that [sin], since he is required to continue to be remorseful until he should meet his Lord.

The second issue: One reading has *ayyuhu'l-mu'minūn*, and the reason for this is that – even though it [the *hā'*] carried a *fatḥa* inflection, preceding as it does an *alif*, with the *alif* elided because of the coming of two unvowelled letters – a diphthong emerges. And God knows best.

The third issue: The explanation of *laʿalla* (*so that*) has already been mentioned in *sūrat al-Baqara* where He says: *Worship your Lord who has created you and those that were before you, so that you will guard yourselves* [*against evil*] [Q. 2:21]. And God knows best.[162]

Qurṭubī

Qurṭubī is somewhat prolix in his interpretation, enumerating twenty-three issues within the main body of the verse and two issues in the final phrase. Perhaps his interest stems from the verse's overt legal implications, and the evident disagreements in law that arose from it (see, for instance, the twentieth issue). In line with the jurisprudential focus of his *tafsīr*, legalistic terminology pervades Qurṭubī's commentary (for example, *yajūz*, 'permissible'; *wujūb*, 'obligatory'; *ḥarām*, 'forbidden'; *makrūh*, 'reprehensible/hateful'; *kabīra* 'grave sin'), as he is concerned to corroborate jurisprudential methodologies with reference to Qur'ānic statements and to demonstrate at the same time, thereby, the complementary relationship between the body of *fiqh* and scriptural injunctions. In this vein, it is also noteworthy that he dedicates considerable space to identifying degrees of intimacy permitted, not just at the first degree (woman–father) but also several degrees in generations upwards (woman–grandparents) and downwards (mother–grandchildren). He is equally concerned with establishing legal age, even when that may not be aligned with physical age (the case with 'young boys'). The somewhat ambiguous category of *dependants that are without (sexual) desire* also permits him to investigate various categories of overtly male genders (including that of effeminates) in order to establish the legal limits for intimacy and access to believing women.

His words *and tell the believing women to lower their gaze and safeguard their private parts, and let them not reveal their ornament* up to His words *their ornament* comprise twenty-three issues.

[162] Rāzī, *Mafātīḥ al-ghayb*, s.v. Q. 24:31.

The first [issue]: As for His words, exalted be He, *and tell the believing women* (*mu'mināt*), God, glory be to Him, has specified the address to females here for emphasis (*li'l-ta'kīd*). For His words *tell the believers* (*qul li'l-mu'minīn*) [Q. 24:30] suffice, given that it is a general expression subsuming male and female believers, as in every general address in the Qur'ān. The doubling of the consonant (*taḍ'īf*) occurs in *yaghḍuḍna* but not in *yaghuḍḍū* because the third verbal consonant (*lām al-fi'l*) in the second instance is vowelless, whereas it is vowelled in the first; both, however, are apocopated on the basis of occupying an apodosis.[163] He begins with the mention of 'lowering [the gaze]' before 'private parts' because sight is the messenger of the heart, just as a fever is the messenger of death (*al-ḥummā rā'id al-mawt*). This meaning is understood by one poet:

> Do you not see how the eye leads the heart, so that whatever the eyes become fond of so too does the heart?

And in a report (*khabar*), 'Sight is one of Iblīs' poison arrows. So whoever lowers his gaze, God occasions in his heart a sweetness (*ḥalāwa*).'[164] Mujāhid said, 'When a woman comes forth, Satan sits over her head and beautifies her (*zayyanahā*) for whomever will look, and when she departs, he sits at her buttocks, beautifying her for whomever will look.'

It is reported that Khālid b. 'Imrān said, 'Do not seek to look [again] after looking [the first time], for perhaps a servant [of God] may catch sight of something that will make rot set in his heart as rot sets in a leather skin and renders it useless.' God has therefore commanded believing men and women to lower their gaze from what is unlawful for them, and so it is not lawful for a man to look at a woman, or a woman at a man; for what ties her to him ties him to her, and what she wants from him is what he wants from her. In the *Ṣaḥīḥ* of Muslim, Abū Hurayra is reported to have said, 'I heard the Messenger of God saying, "God has verily prescribed for the son of Adam his lot of fornication (*zinā*) and he will commit that unfailingly, for the eyes fornicate and their act of fornication is to look"'[165] [to the end of that] *ḥadīth*.

[163] On the varied uses of the grammatical concept of apodosis (*jawāb*), see Arik Sadan, 'The Meaning of the Technical Term *Jawāb* in Arabic Grammar', *Jerusalem Studies in Arabic and Islam* 37 (2010), 129–37.

[164] That is to say, God grants a delight that compensates for what would have been experienced by the visual act.

[165] Cf. Abū Dāwūd, *Sunan*, *Kitāb al-Nikāḥ* (12), *Bāb mā yu'maru bihi min ghaḍḍ al-baṣar* (44), *ḥadīth* nos. 107/2152 and 108/2153; Bukhārī, *Ṣaḥīḥ*, *Kitāb al-Qadar* (82), *Bāb 'wa ḥarāmun 'alā qaryatin ahlaknāhā* [. . .]' (9), *ḥadīth* no. 18/6612 and *Kitāb al-Isti'dhān* (79), *Bāb zinā al-jawāriḥ dūna al-faraj* (12), *ḥadīth* no. 17/6243; Muslim, *Ṣaḥīḥ*, *Kitāb al-Qadar* (46), *Bāb quddiru 'alā ibn Ādam ḥaẓẓuhu mina'l-zinā* (5), *ḥadīth* no. 32/2657.

With regard to gazing at women who are not yet menstruating, al-Zuhrī said, 'It is not right for he who desires to look at them to cast his eyes on any part of them, even if they be immature of age.' 'Aṭā' [b. Abī Rabāḥ] was averse to [men] gazing at the slave girls on sale in Mecca, except where the one looking intended to purchase one. In both of the *Ṣaḥīḥ* compilations,[166] when a woman of the Khath'amiyya [tribe] came to ask him [the Prophet] (*ṣl'm*) a question and al-Faḍl [b. 'Abbās][167] set about gazing at her, he turned the latter's face away. He (*ṣl'm*) said, 'Jealousy for [someone] (*ghayra*) is part of faith (*īmān*),[168] whereas [sexual] indiscretion (*midhā'*) is hypocrisy (*nifāq*)'. *Midhā'* is when a man gathers together men and women and leaves them to indiscretion among themselves, and is related to the term *al-madhy*, which is said to denote sending men off to women, as in when they say *madhaytu al-faras*, meaning: 'I sent the horse out to pasture. Every male commits indiscretion and every female hits back (*qadhā*).'[169] Thus it is not lawful for a woman who believes in God and the Last Day to reveal her ornament except to whom it is lawful or to whom she is definitively unmarriageable (*muḥarram*), for he is safe from having his nature (*ṭab'*) stirred by her, given that he has no hope of [ever marrying] her.

The second [issue]: Al-Tirmidhī has reported on the authority of Nabhān, *mawlā* of Umm Salama, that the Prophet said to both her [Umm Salama] and Maymūna when Ibn Umm Maktūm entered upon her, 'Take your cover'. The two women then said, 'He is blind', to which he (*ṣl'm*) said, 'And are you two blind that you do not see him?' Some say that this *ḥadīth* is not sound (*yaṣuḥḥ*) according to the transmitters (*ahl al-naql*), since the one reporting it from Umm Salama is her *mawlā* Nabhān, who is not one of those whose *ḥadīth*s can be used as proof (*ḥujja*). Assuming its soundness, however, and that it is from him (*ṣl'm*), it may be understood as a strict measure (*taghlīẓ*) imposed on his wives on account of their revered status (*ḥurma*),[170] just as He

[166] That is, of Bukhārī and Muslim.

[167] He was the Prophet's cousin and the brother of the famous 'Abd Allāh b. 'Abbās, who was accompanying the Prophet on that day.

[168] This *ḥadīth* does not seem to be in the canonical collections in this wording. On jealousy, see Marion Holmes Katz, 'Beyond *Ḥalāl* and *Ḥarām*: *Ghayra* ('Jealousy') as a Masculine Virtue in the Work of Ibn Qayyim al-Jawziyya', *Cultural History* 8.2 (2019), 202–25.

[169] There is subtle word play here since *al-madhy* is also the term for the pre-ejaculate emitted when the sexual appetite is stirred in both men and women, as opposed to the seminal fluid itself, *al-maniyy*. Moreover, *al-qadhā* is something that falls into the eye and irritates it, suggesting that what would be a sight for sore eyes is an eyesore in spiritual terms.

[170] Also, of course, with the resonances of 'out of bounds' and 'sacrosanct', as wives of the Prophet, they could not be subsequently married to anyone else, including after the Prophet's death (Q. 33:53).

was strict with them in the matter of the screen (*amr al-ḥijāb*),[171] as pointed out by Abū Dāwūd and other leading scholars (*a'imma*).

There then remains the significance of the established sound *ḥadīth*, namely that the Prophet had commanded Fāṭima bt. Qays to spend her waiting period (*ʿidda*) in the house of Umm Sharīk, but then said, 'That woman is frequented by my companions, so spend your waiting period in the house of Ibn Umm Maktūm instead, for he is a blind man and will not see anything of you when you take your clothes off'. We have said that on the basis of this *ḥadīth*, some scholars (*ʿulamā'*) infer that it is permissible for a woman to see of a man what is not permitted for him to see of her, such as the hair and where the earrings hang; however, when it comes to the shameful parts (*ʿawra*), then no. That is why there is a specific statement within the general address: His words *and tell the believing women to lower [of] their gaze*. [The particle] *min* [*of*] here is then a partitive (*tabʿīḍ*), as in the previous verse. Ibn al-ʿArabī says, He commanded her to move from the house of Umm Sharīk to the house of Ibn Umm Maktūm because that is more fitting for her than staying in the house of Umm Sharīk, since Umm Sharīk was liable to frequent visitation and many would end up seeing her [Fāṭima], whereas in the house of Ibn Umm Maktūm, no one would see her. And so her refraining from looking at him would be deemed closer to that [command] and more fitting, which is why she was granted licence for that.

And God knows best.

The third [issue]: Out of caution against temptation (*fitna*), God commanded women not to reveal their ornament to onlookers, except for those exempted by the remainder of the verse. He then made an exception for what is apparent (*ẓāhir*) of ornament. But people differed over the extent of this [exception]. Ibn Masʿūd said, 'The apparent ornament is garments (*thiyāb*)', to which Ibn Jubayr added, 'The face'. Saʿīd b. Jubayr, ʿAṭā' and al-Awzāʿī said, 'The face, the palms of the hands and garments'. Ibn ʿAbbās, Qatāda and al-Miswar b. Makhrama said, 'The apparent of ornament is kohl, bracelets, and dye to halfway up the arm, as well as earrings and large rings.' What is similar to these, it is permissible for a woman to reveal to anyone who enters her presence. In explaining the meaning of 'halfway up the arm' (*niṣf al-dhirāʿ*), al-Ṭabarī mentions on the authority of Qatāda a *ḥadīth* from the Prophet, in which he said, 'It is not lawful for a woman who believes in God and the Last

[171] Again, with reference to Q. 33:53, the term *ḥijāb* here refers to the separation by physical screen required between those who came to speak to the Prophet's wives and the latter in the Prophet's house.

Day once she has begun menstruating to reveal anything other than her face and her hands up to here', clasping his arm halfway up.[172]

Ibn 'Aṭiyya said: It seems to me, on the basis of the lexical expressions of the verse, that a woman is enjoined not to reveal [anything] and to make a concerted effort to conceal all that is ornament. But an exception has been made for what becomes apparent [of ornament] on the basis of the need to move around to accomplish what is unavoidable or to attend to the remedying of some matter and the like. And so *what is apparent* in such a situation, precipitated by necessity, in the case of women is thus exempt.

I say: This is a fair enough opinion. However, since the face and hands are customarily predominantly showing, and so too during acts of worship such as the ritual prayers and the pilgrimage, then it could reasonably be that the exception refers to these two [parts of the body]. This [interpretation] is supported by what has been related by Abū Dāwūd [in a report] on the authority of 'Ā'isha, may God be pleased with her, that she said: On one occasion, Asmā', the daughter of Abū Bakr, may God be pleased with both of them, entered upon the Prophet wearing light garments, and the Messenger of God turned away, saying, 'O Asmā', verily when a woman is of menstruating age, it is not right for anything other than these to be visible of her', and he pointed to the face and hands.[173]

This is the stronger [argument], if one were to be on the side of caution and to guard against corrupting public morality. Thus a woman is not to reveal of her ornament anything except what is apparent of her face and hands. And God is the One who grants success, besides Whom there is no other lord. One of our scholars, Ibn Khwayz-i Mandād, has said, 'If a woman were [so] beautiful that her face and hands were feared for their temptation, then she is obliged to conceal them. If she were anile or haggard, she is permitted to reveal her face and hands.'

The fourth [issue]: *Ornament* divides into two [kinds]: a natural one (*khilqiyya*) and an acquired one (*muktasaba*). The natural one is her face, for that is the source of ornament and the beauty of the created form (*khilqa*) and what gives the animate being its meaning (*ma'nā al-ḥayawāniyya*), because of the benefits that it brings about and the paths to knowledge. As for the acquired ornament, this is the effort she makes to acquire a fairer physical appearance, such as clothes, jewellery, kohl and dyes; it is in this

[172] Cited by Ṭabarī, but not found in the canonical collections.

[173] Abū Dāwūd, *Sunan*, *Kitāb al-Libās* (34), *Bāb fīmā tubdī al-mar'a min zīnatihā* (33), *ḥadīth* no. 85/4104.

sense that God says, *adorn yourselves (zīna) at every place of worship* [Q. 7:31]. The poet also says:

> They adorn themselves as fair as you shall ever see, and when they go without, they are the best of those who go without.

The fifth [issue]: Ornament is either apparent or hidden. That which is apparent is always lawful for all people, unmarriageable (*maḥārim*) and unrelated (*ajānib*). We have already mentioned the [various] opinions of the scholars regarding this. As for what is hidden, it is not lawful for it to be revealed, except before those whom God has named in this verse or who stand in their place.

There is a difference of opinion over bracelets (*siwār*). ʿĀʾisha said, 'They count as apparent ornament since they are around the hands (*yadd*).' But Mujāhid said, 'They count as hidden ornament since they sit before the palms (*kaff*) and actually around the arms.' Ibn al-ʿArabī said, 'As for dye, it is [a] hidden ornament if it is used on the feet (*qadam*).'

The sixth [issue]: *And let them cast their wraps over their cleavage.* [. . .][174] The occasion (*sabab*) for this verse was that whenever women at that time covered their heads with 'veils' (*akhmira*), which were 'covers' (*maqāniʿ*), they would let [these veils] hang down along their backs. Al-Naqqāsh said, 'as the Nabataeans used to do, where the upper chest (*naḥr*), the neck itself (*ʿunuq*) and both ears (*udhunān*) are uncovered'.[175] God therefore commanded that the veiling cloth (*khimār*) should be folded over to cover the exposed neckline (*jayb*) in order to conceal the breast. Al-Bukhārī relates that ʿĀʾisha said, 'May God have mercy on the first women Emigrants (*muhājirāt*). When *and let them cast their wraps over their cleavage* was revealed, they tore off [parts of] their shawls (*izār*/pl. *uzur*)[176] and veiled themselves with them.' On one occasion, there entered upon ʿĀʾisha Ḥafṣa, the daughter of her brother ʿAbd al-Raḥmān, may God be pleased with them all, veiled in a thin cloth through which her neck and what is around it could be seen, whereupon she [ʿĀʾisha] tore it off and said to her, 'You should wear something thick to veil [yourself].'

The seventh [issue]: *Khumur* is the plural of *khimār*, which is what is used to cover the head, and from this derives the expression *ikhtamarat al-marʾa* or

[174] A brief grammatical discussion ensues here regarding the vowelling of the jussive particle *l-* in *waʾl-yaḍribna*, and whether it is to be inflected with a *kasra* or a *sukūn*.

[175] Cf. the French *décolletage*.

[176] Also, a 'loin cloth'.

takhammarat (the woman veiled) or that she is *ḥasanatu'l-khimra* (beautifully veiled); *juyūb* is the plural of *jayb*, which is where the shirt or garment is cut,[177]and it derives [etymologically] from *al-jawb*, which means to cut (*qaṭ'*). The common reading is to have *juyūbihinna* with a *ḍamma* on the *jīm*. However, some Kufans read *jiyūbihinna* with a *kasra* because of the *yā'*, just as they read the same in the case of *biyūt* (houses) and *shiyūkh* (old men). Nevertheless, the first grammarians do not permit such readings and say *bayt, buyūt* and *fils, fulūs*. Al-Zajjāj's opinion was that it was possible to substitute the *ḍamma* with a *kasra*, and that what has been reported on the authority of Ḥamza of the possibility of combining *ḍamma* and *kasra* is simply impossible and can hardly be pronounced, except as a way of actually suggesting that it is not possible.[178] Muqātil said, '*Over their juyūb*' means [over] their breasts (*ṣudūr*), meaning the place of the *juyūb* (cleavage).

The eighth [issue]: There is evidence in this verse that the *jayb* can only be that of the breast area of a garment. Such were the necklines of the garments of our predecessors (*salaf*), may God be pleased with them, like the ones made by women here in al-Andalus and by the men and boys of the Egyptian provinces. Al-Bukhārī, may God have mercy on him, has written on this issue under the 'Chapter on the neckline of a shirt around the breast', narrating the *ḥadīth* of Abū Hurayra, in which he says: 'God's Messenger gave the example of the niggardly and the charitable as that of two men wearing iron gowns (*jubba*) with their hands forced up towards their chests and throats [. . .]' [to the end of] the *ḥadīth*, which has already been mentioned in full.[179] And in this [same chapter], Abū Hurayra said, 'I saw the Messenger of God doing like this with his fingers [when asked] about where his neckline was. And if I had seen that he was trying to make it wider [I would have said so], but it could not be any wider.' This makes it clear that his neckline was around his upper chest, because if it were around his shoulder edges, the hands would not have been forced to the chest and throat. This is a fair inference [from the *ḥadīth*].

177 In other words, the neckline of a dress, robe or shirt.

178 Cf. Q. 89:9 for a related sense of the verbal root *j-w-b*. Ḥamza b. Ḥabīb al-Zayyāt (d. 156/772) was one of the recognised seven readers of the Qur'ān (see the PA).

179 Bukhārī, *Ṣaḥīḥ*, *Kitāb al-Zakāt* (24), *Bāb mathal al-mutaṣaddiq wa'l-bakhīl* (28), *ḥadīth* no. 46/1443. Whereas for the one who expends in charity, the robe sits comfortably and widens almost to cover him completely, for the niggardly one, the robe becomes so tight that his arms become stuck against his throat, as when one tries to put one's arms through a shirt that is far too small in size.

The ninth [issue]: As for His words *except to their husbands (illā li-buʿūlatihinna)*, *baʿl* is the spouse (*zawj*) and the master (*sayyid*) in the language of the Arabs. An example of that is the Prophet's *ḥadīth* from [the archangel] Gabriel: 'When the slave girl shall give birth to her master', which is an allusion to the great number of captured slave girls (*sarārī*) as a result of the great number of conquests (*futūḥāt*), when children will issue forth from slave girls and every mother will be manumitted (*ʿ-t-q*) by her own child, as though he were her master, the one bestowing the favour of manumission on her, since freedom comes to her as a result of him; this was also recognised by Ibn al-ʿArabī. I say that related to this is what he (*ʿm*) said with regard to Mārya: 'Her son made her a freewoman (*aʿtaqahā*)',[180] so that, thereafter, manumission (*ʿitq*) was attributed to him. And that is among the best interpretations of this *ḥadīth*. But God knows best. A matter [to be noted]: the spouse or the master sees his woman's ornament and more, since every part of her body is permissible for him to taste (*ladhdha*) and to look at (*naẓar*). It is for this reason that He begins [in this verse] with husbandship (*buʿūla*), since husbands get to see far more than this. God says [in Q. 23:5–6] *and those who safeguard their private parts except from their wives or what their right hands possess, for then they are not blameworthy.*

The tenth [issue]: People differ over the permissibility of a man to look at his wife's private parts (*farj*). There are two opinions: one of them is that this is permissible, since if it is permitted for him to enjoy it, then to look at it is subsumed by that prerogative. The other is that this is not permissible, based on the statement of ʿĀʾisha, may God be pleased with her, regarding her situation with God's messenger (*ṣlʿm*): 'I never saw his, nor he mine.' But the first [of these two opinions] is the sounder one, while the second can be sustained on the basis of good manners (*adab*), as stated by Ibn al-ʿArabī. Aṣbagh, a scholar of ours, stated that it is permitted for him to lick it with his tongue.[181] Ibn Khwayz-i Mandād said, 'As for the spouse (*zawj*) or master (*sayyid*), he is permitted to look at the entire body and the outside of the private parts (*ẓāhir al-farj*), but not inside (*bāṭin*). Likewise, it is permitted for a woman to look at the shameful part (*ʿawra*) of her husband and for the slave girl at the nakedness of her master.' I say that it has been reported that the Prophet (*ṣlʿm*) said, 'Beholding the private parts (*farj*) begets blindness (*ṭams*)',[182] that

[180] The Prophet's slave-girl Mārya the Copt, the only woman after Khadīja to bear him issue, gave birth to Ibrāhīm, who died in infancy at eighteen months old, according to the historical sources.

[181] Note that this is a rare instance in which the focus shifts from the husband's sexual pleasure to an act that he performs for his wife's sexual pleasure.

[182] This is not found in the canonical collections.

is blindness (*ʿamā*), namely in the beholder. It is also said that their child is born blind, but God knows best.

The eleventh [issue]: After God begins with the mention of spouses, He follows that with the unmarriageable individuals (*dhū'l-maḥram*) and treats them equally in terms of revealing ornament, even though their ranks differ according to what the souls of human beings conceal. There is thus no doubt that it requires more caution for a woman to uncover before spouse's child than before a father or a brother. There are different levels of what can be revealed to them. What is revealed to the father cannot be revealed to the child of the husband. The *qāḍī* Ismāʿīl reported on the authority of al-Ḥasan and al-Ḥusayn, may God be pleased with both of them, that they never saw the mothers of the believers [uncovered]. Ibn ʿAbbās said, however, that it is permitted for them [the children] to see the women. Ismāʿīl said, I reckon that al-Ḥasan and al-Ḥusayn were of that opinion because the sons of the husbands (*abnā' al-buʿūla*) were not mentioned in the verse relating to the wives of the Prophet (*ṣlʿm*) – that is, where He says *there is no blame on these women [the Prophet's wives] concerning their fathers* [Q. 33:55], whereas in *sūrat al-Nūr* [Q. 24:31], He says, *And let them not reveal their ornament except to their husbands* [. . .]. Thus Ibn ʿAbbās based his opinion on this verse, while al-Ḥasan and al-Ḥusayn based their opinion on the other verse.

The twelfth [issue]: Where He says *or their husbands' sons*, He means the male issue of the husbands, which can include the grandchildren, however far down, whether male or female, such as the grandchildren of the sons or the grandchildren of the daughters. Likewise the fathers of the husbands and the grandfathers, however high up on the male side, the fathers of the fathers and the fathers of the mothers, and their children however far down, as well as the children of the daughters however far down, such that the children of the sons and the children of the daughters are of equal status [in this regard]. Likewise their sisters who issue from the fathers or the mothers or from one of the two classes [of relatives]. Also [included] are the children of brothers and the children of sisters, however far down, whether they be males or females, such as the children of the sisters' sons and the children of the sisters' daughters. All of those represent what is forbidden for those [relatives] resulting from marriage, for they are inferred by virtue of having been born [to them] and these are all unmarriageables (*maḥārim*), as already mentioned in [*sūrat*] *al-Nisā'*. The majority are of the opinion that the paternal uncle and the maternal uncle are considered like all unmarriageables for whom it is permitted to look at what these are permitted to look at.

But there is no mention in this verse of the suckling relatives, which, as mentioned already, are considered like a blood relationship. According to al-Shaʿbī and ʿIkrima, however, the paternal uncle and the maternal uncle do not belong with the unmarriageables (*mahārim*). ʿIkrima said that He has not mentioned either of the two in the verse because they are both extensions of their children.

The thirteenth [issue]: His words *or their womenfolk* mean Muslim women, which include slave girls (*imāʾ*) who are believers but exclude women who are polytheists from among the People of the Book (*ahl al-dhimma*) and others. It is therefore not licit for a believing woman to reveal anything of her body to a polytheist woman unless she is her slave girl, which are [indicated by] His words *or what their right hands possess*. Ibn Jurayj, as well as ʿUbāda b. Nusayy and Hishām the reader, deemed it reprehensible (*makrūh*) for a Christian woman to greet a Muslim woman with a kiss or to see her naked, basing themselves on the interpretation of *or their womenfolk*. ʿUbāda b. Nusayy said: ʿUmar, may God be pleased with him, wrote to Abū ʿUbayda b. al-Jarrāḥ: 'It has reached me that the women of the People of the Book are entering the baths alongside Muslim women: put a stop to this and prevent it, for it is not licit for a woman from the People of the Book to see a Muslim woman naked.' Upon receiving this, Abū ʿUbayda got up and beseeched God saying, 'If any woman should enter the baths with no reason other than to seek a glow (*b-y-ḍ*) for [the skin of] her face, may God blacken (*s-w-d*) her face on the day when certain faces shall glow [cf. Q. 3:106].'

Ibn ʿAbbās said, 'It is not licit for a Muslim woman to be seen by a Jewish or Christian woman lest she describe her to her husband.' Regarding this opinion, there is disagreement among the jurisprudents (*fuqahāʾ*): if the unbelieving woman be a Muslim woman's slave girl, then she is permitted to look at her mistress, but anyone else, no, and that is because of the absence of a religious bond (*walāya*) between Muslims and unbelievers, and because of what we have already mentioned. And God knows best.

The fourteenth [issue]: His words *or what their right hands possess*. The apparent meaning (*ẓāhir*) of the verse would include slaves and slave girls who are [either] Muslims or from the People of the Book (*kitābiyyāt*); and this is the opinion of a group of scholars and is the apparent [meaning] according to the position (*madhhab*) of ʿĀʾisha and Umm Salama, may God be pleased with them both. Ibn ʿAbbās said, 'It is acceptable for a slave to look at his mistress's hair.' Ashhab said, Mālik [b. Anas] was asked if a woman could take off her wrap (*khimār*) in front of a castrate (*khaṣiyy*).

He [Mālik] said, 'Yes, as long as he is her property or someone else's, but not if he is a free man. And even if he were a potent scoundrel, with neither looks nor charm, as long as she owns him, he can look at her hair.' Ashhab said that Mālik said, 'It is not befitting for a slave girl (*jāriya*) who tends to a boy or a woman to enter the latrine when a man is there.' God, exalted be He, says *or what their right hands possess.* Ashhab reported from Mālik, 'The young halfwit can look at his mistress's hair, but I do not condone this in the case of the husband's slave boy (*ghulām*).' Saʿīd b. al-Musayyab said, 'Do not be deluded by the verse *or what their right hands possess*, for what is meant by it are the slave girls and not the slave boys.' Al-Shaʿbī found it reprehensible for a slave to look at the hair of his mistress, which is also the opinion of Mujāhid and ʿAṭāʾ [b. Abī Rabāḥ]. Abū Dāwūd reported on the authority of Anas [b. Mālik] that God's Messenger (*ṣlʿm*) came to Fāṭima with a slave whom he wanted to gift to her, and Fāṭima was wearing a garment (*thawb*) which, if she were to cover her head with it would not reach her legs, and which if she were to cover her legs with it would not reach her head. When the Prophet (*ṣlʿm*) saw her reaction, he said, 'There is no shame on you, for he is as your father or slave'.

The fifteenth [issue]: His words *or male dependants lacking (sexual) desire* mean 'other than those who have a [sexual] need (*ḥāja*)'; *al-irba* means *al-ḥāja*. One says *aribtu*, *ārib* or *araban*: *al-irb*, *al-irba*, *al-maʾruba* and *al-arab* mean *al-ḥāja*, the plural of which is *maʾārib*, that is 'needs' (*ḥawāʾij*), like His saying *and in it I have other needs* (*maʾārib*) [Q. 20:18], which has already been discussed. [The poet] Ṭarafa recited: 'When a man utters ignorance, sin and obscenities, the day has come where his needs (*maʾārib*) are forlorn.' People have disagreed over the meaning of His words *or male dependants lacking (sexual) desire*. Some have said that this means the fool (*aḥmaq*) who has no need of women. Others have said [that this means] the dimwit (*ablah*). Another group have said that it refers to the man who follows people around to eat with them and keep their company, being a weakling (*ḍaʿīf*) with no concern or desire for women. Some have said that this is the impotent (*ʿanīn*) man; others the eunuch (*khaṣiyy*) or the effeminate (*mukhannath*). Some have said that it is the elderly man (*shaykh*) or the boy who has no [sexual] awareness [of women]. But all of these disagreements come close in meaning and come together in the sense of an individual who has no comprehension of, or aspiration with which to take notice of, the matter of women. Such was the character of Hīt, the effeminate one who was in the house of the Messenger of God (*ṣlʿm*).[183]

[183] On these characters, see Rowson, 'The Effeminates of Early Medina', 671–93.

When he [the Prophet] (*ṣlʿm*) heard the way he would describe the attractive traits of a woman, Bādiya bt. Ghaylān, he commanded that the women veil themselves in his presence. This *ḥadīth* was verified by Muslim, Abū Dāwūd and Mālik in his *Muwaṭṭaʾ*, and by others such as Hishām b. ʿUrwa from [his father] ʿUrwa on the authority of ʿĀʾisha. Abū ʿUmar reported that ʿAbd al-Malik b. Ḥabīb told him, on the authority of Ḥabīb, Mālik's scribe (*kātib*), that he [Ḥabīb] said, 'I said to Mālik, "Sufyān has added in his *ḥadīth* that the effeminate one was called Hīt, but there is no [mention of] Hīt in your book", to which Mālik replied, "He is right, that is who he is."' The Prophet (*ṣlʿm*) banished him to al-Ḥimā, a place near Dhūʾl-Ḥulayfa, just north of its mosque [. . .].[184]

Al-Wāqidī and al-Kalbī both mention that Hīt the effeminate said to ʿAbd Allāh b. Umayya al-Makhzūmī, the brother of Umm Salama from her father, whose mother was ʿĀtika, the maternal aunt of God's Messenger (*ṣlʿm*), while he [ʿAbd Allāh] was in his sister Umm Salama's house and the Messenger of God (*ṣlʿm*) was listening: 'If God should grant you the conquest of al-Ṭāʾif, then you should aim for Bādiya bt. Ghaylān b. Salama al-Thaqafī: from the front she is well-rounded and from the back twice so, with a mouth like a daisy;[185] when she sits she is solid and upright, and when she speaks it is like song; between her legs a vessel upturned [. . .].'[186] So the Prophet (*ṣlʿm*) said to him, 'Verily, you have ogled her without restraint, O enemy of God'.[187] He then banished him from Medina to al-Ḥimā. He reported that when al-Ṭāʾif was taken, ʿAbd al-Raḥmān b. ʿAwf married her and she bore him Burayha, in the report of al-Kalbī. Hīt remained in that place until the death of the Prophet (*ṣlʿm*). When [the caliph] Abū Bakr took over, his case was brought before him, but he refused to allow him to return. When ʿUmar [b. al-Khaṭṭāb] took over, he was also mentioned to him, but he [also] refused [to allow him back]. People approached [the caliph] ʿUthmān about him, saying that he had grown old [and] weak and become needy, and so he [ʿUthmān] allowed him to come into the city every Friday to beg, but then

184 A substantial discussion ensues on the variations in transmission of the contents of this story that essentially revolves around the presence of an effeminate in the household of the Prophet. The interest that the exegetes had in these variations – in this case, the details concerning this Hīt character – demonstrates the extent to which the generation of late Umayyad and early ʿAbbāsid scholars of *ḥadīth* (Sufyān al-Thawrī, Mālik b. Anas, Hishām b. ʿUrwa and al-Wāqidī) were scrutinised for being the seminal link between the Prophet's age and their own, in which the literary tradition properly begins to crystalise.

185 Or, upper chest (*thaghr*).

186 This already somewhat abstruse description of Bādiya is followed by couplets in which the poet Qays b. al-Khaṭīm describes her delightful and attractive build. On Qays, see Iṣfahānī, *Aghānī*, III, 5ff.

187 On this *ḥadīth* see note 160.

[made him] return to his place. They say that Hīt was a *mawlā* of ʿAbd Allāh b. [Abū] Umayya al-Makhzūmī, who also had a *mawlā* called Ṭuways,[188] and that is why people started to refer to effeminates (*khunnath*). Abū ʿUmar said, 'They say [her name as] Bādiya or Bādina, although the correct version is to say it with the *yā*ʾ, and that is the majority view.' Likewise al-Zubayrī mentions it with *yā*ʾ.

The sixteenth [issue]: He qualifies *dependants* (*tābiʿīn*) with [the preposition] *ghayri* (meaning, other than those)[189] because dependants are not the ones intended *per se* and the lexical expression [*tābiʿīn*] functions like an indefinite noun (*nakira*), except that *ghayr* cannot serve an indefinite noun, and it is therefore possible to take it as an adjectival qualifier of a definite noun (*maʿrifa*); you can also consider it a substitution (*badal*) if you wish. Views on this are similar to those regarding *ghayri'l-maghḍūbi ʿalayhim* (*not of those against whom there is wrath* [Q. 1:7]). ʿĀṣim and Ibn ʿĀmir read *ghayra* accusatively (*naṣb*) so that it is [understood] as an exceptive clause (*istithnā*ʾ), that is to say, 'they [women] may reveal their ornament to dependants except those among them who have [sexual] desire'. It is also possible for it to be [understood] as a circumstantial qualifier (*ḥāl*), with the sense: 'those who are dependent on them [the women] but are [sexually] unable (*ʿājiz*) with regard to the women', which is the opinion of Abū Ḥātim, the one to which the circumstantial qualifier refers to being the male among the dependants.

The seventeenth [issue]: His words, exalted be He, *aw al-ṭifl* (*or children*) is a collective noun (*ism jins*) indicating a plural (*jamʿ*), the proof of which is the [plural] adjectival *alladhīna*. However, the codex (*muṣḥaf*) of Ḥafṣa has *aw al-aṭfāl* in the plural form. They say that a 'child' (*ṭifl*) is one who has not reached puberty (*rāhaqa al-ḥulum*). *Yaẓharū* means 'who have not become aware [of women] via copulation', that is, 'who have not revealed their nakedness in order to copulate, on account of their young age'. They also say that [it means] 'they have not reached [the age] to physically be able to be with women'. One says *ẓahartu ʿalā* to mean *ʿalimtuhu* (I have come to know it)

[188] On Ṭuways as well as Hīt, and their relationship to the clans of Medina, see Iṣfahānī, *Aghānī*, III, 22–5.

[189] In the translation of the Qurʾānic verse, for idiomatic purposes, this exclusionary or negatory sense of *ghayri* is captured in the English 'lacking'. So, *al-tābiʿīna ghayri ūlī'l-irba*, 'dependants lacking [sexual] desire', is literally rendered as 'dependants other than those with [sexual] desire'. It is always challenging to balance the exigencies of idiomatic English for a wide readership against the commentators' interest and facility in submitting the Arabic to linguistic analysis.

and *ẓahartu ʿalā* to mean *qahartuhu* (I have dominated it). The majority agree on the vowelless *wāw* in *ʿawrāt* because of the cumbersomeness of a vowel on the *wāw*. A report on the authority of Ibn ʿAbbās has the *wāw* with a *fatḥa*, on the analogy with *jafna, jafanāt*. Al-Farrā' relates that *ʿawarāt* is the dialect (*lugha*) of Qays, with a *fatḥa* on the *wāw*. Al-Naḥḥās [says]: This is the [correct] analogy (*qiyās*) since it is not a descriptive, as when you say *jafna, jafanāt*. However, the vowelless [version] is best in the case of *ʿawrāt* and the likes of it, because when a *wāw* is vowelled and when what precedes it is also vowelled, it turns into an *alif*, and if that were the case the meaning would be lost.

The eighteenth [issue]: Scholars disagree over the requirement to conceal (*satr*) what is other than the face and hands, there being two views: one of them is that it is not required, since there is no legal obligation (*taklīf*) for that, which is the sound opinion (*ṣaḥīḥ*); the other [opinion] is that it is required because the man may feel desire and so might [the woman]. If the boy has reached puberty (*rāhaqa*), then he is to be treated as a mature adult (*bāligh*) in terms of the requirement for veiling (*satr*). Similar is the case of the old man (*shaykh*) who has lost his [sexual] desire (*shahwa*). But this too is a source of disagreement in two ways, as is the case with the young boy (*ṣabiyy*). The sounder opinion is that the sanctity of concealment (*ḥurma*) holds, like the opinion of Ibn al-ʿArabī.

The nineteenth [issue]: Muslims share the consensus that the two unseemly parts (*saw'atān*) constitute shameful parts (*ʿawra*) in the case of the man and the woman, and the woman is in her entirety a shameful part (*ʿawra*), except for her face and hands, about which there is disagreement. With regard to men, most scholars agree that the shameful part is between his navel and knees, none of which should be seen, as has already been [discussed] sufficiently in [*sūrat*] *al-Aʿrāf* [Q. 7].

The [issue] completing the twenty: The rationalists (*aṣḥāb al-ra'y*) [say]: a woman's exposure (*ʿawra*) in the presence of her slave (*ʿabd*) refers to what is between her navel and her knees. Ibn al-ʿArabī [says]: 'It is as though they considered her a man and him [the slave] a woman.' God, exalted be He, has forbidden it absolutely to look (*naẓar*) at a woman or desire her for [sexual] pleasure (*ladhdha*) but exempted, in terms of the desire for [sexual] pleasure, spouses and what right hands possess, and then exempted the *ornament* [from being prohibited] to twelve individuals, the slave being among these. But why bother with this view? This is corrupted analogical reasoning (*naẓar fāsid*) and an effort to reason (*ijtihād*) which is far from being robust. Some have interpreted (*ta'wīl*) His words *or what their right hands possess* to be referring to slave girls (*imā'*) but not slave boys (*'abīd*); among these are Sa'īd b. al-Musayyab. But how can this be interpreted as male slaves to whom women are attached? This is very far [from the truth]. Ibn al-'Arabī said, 'The implication is "or what their right hands possess of those who do not have [sexual] desire or male dependants who have no [sexual] desire", which is also related by al-Mahdawī.'

The twenty-first [issue]: His words, exalted be He, *and let them not stamp their feet* [to the end of] the verse, mean 'let not a woman stamp her foot when she walks, lest she make a sound with her anklet. For to make audible the sound of the *ornament* is like revealing the *ornament* itself, or worse, whereas the purpose [here] is chasteness (*tasattur*). Al-Ṭabarī records an *isnād* on the authority of al-Mu'tamir [b. Sulaymān] from his father that the latter said, 'Ḥaḍramī claimed that a woman had worn two silver anklets and beads around her ankles, and when passing by some folk struck her leg on the ground so that the anklets hit the beads and clattered, whereupon this verse was sent down.' Hearing this [kind of] *ornament* is more likely to stir desire than [actually] revealing it, as al-Zajjāj stated.

The twenty-second [issue]: If a woman does that with her jewellery out of joy, then it is considered loathsome (*makrūh*), but if she does it for show and to attract men, then that is illicit and reprehensible (*ḥarām madhmūm*). Likewise for the man who strikes his sandal: if he does it out of vanity, then that it is forbidden, for self-conceitedness (*'ujb*) is a grave sin (*kabīra*), and even if he should do it [just] for show, that is still not allowed.

The twenty-third [issue]: [Abū Muḥammad] Makkī [b. Abī Ṭālib],[190] may God have mercy on him, said, 'No verse in God's book contains more pronominalisations (*ḍamā'ir*) than this one, bringing together a total of twenty-five pronominalisations for *the believing women*, oblique ones (*makhfūḍ*) and nominative ones (*marfū'*).

As regards His words *turn to God in repentance all together O believers*, there are two issues.

[190] Abū Muḥammad Makkī b. Abī Ṭālib Ḥammūsh al-Qaysī al-Qayrawānī (d. 437/1046) was a famous North African, later Andalusian (Cordoban), Qur'ānic reader: see Dhahabī, *Siyar*, XVII, 591–2. Attributed to him is a Qur'ānic commentary: *al-Hidāya ilā bulūgh al-nihāya*.

The first one: His words *turn* [. . .] *in repentance* are an imperative (*amr*). There is no disagreement among the community that turning in repentance (*tawba*) is obligatory (*wājib*) and that it is an individual duty (*farḍ muta'ayyan*). This has already been discussed in [*sūrat*] *al-Nisā'* [Q. 4] and elsewhere, and so there is no point in repeating it [here]. The meaning is: 'And turn in repentance to God, for you are never beyond lapse or shortcoming when it comes to fulfilling the rights owed to God, exalted be He.' So, never abandon repentance in any state.

The second one: The majority read *ayyuha*, with a *fatḥa* on the *hā'*, while Ibn 'Āmir read it with a *ḍamma*, the reason being that the *hā'* should constitute part of the same word and so the inflection follows [the declension of] the one called [by the vocative] therein. But Abū 'Alī [al-Fārisī] considered that an extremely weak reasoning, saying that the final part of the noun is [actually] the second *yā'* of *ayy*, so the *ḍamma* inflection ought to fall on the last letter of the noun. If it were permissible to place a *ḍamma* in this case on account of its juxtaposition to the word, it would also be permissible to place a *ḍamma* on the *mīm* of *Allāhumma*, on account of its juxtaposition to the word that is extended in form. The correct view, however, is that if a given recitation has been established on the authority of the Prophet (*ṣl'm*), then there is no option but to assume its soundness linguistically, for the Qur'ān is the ultimate authority (*ḥujja*).[191]

Ibn Kathīr

Ibn Kathīr is keen to demonstrate his command of the *ḥadīth* corpus by including many variants, authorities and collections with detailed chains of transmission (*isnāds*). This lends his commentary on this verse a somewhat repetitive quality. He begins by explaining that, with this verse, God is jealously guarding or protecting Muslim women for their husbands; and his interpretation is pervaded by the concern that men other than their husbands might see something of them. He focuses extensively on the liminal character of the effeminate and whether he might be allowed to see women, as he would have no desire for them; as do prior authors, he concludes that in some cases effeminates too are a danger. Equally, Christian or Jewish women are a danger, as they might describe a Muslim woman to their husbands (Muslim women

[191] Qurṭubī, *al-Jāmi' li-aḥkām al-Qur'ān*, s.v. Q. 24:31. Qurṭubī concludes his commentary on this part of the verse with further grammatical reflection, prompted by a poetic citation from Farrā', on the relationship between a final *yā'* and a subsequent definite article *al-* and the effect that this elision has on the vocalisation or otherwise of the final *yā'*, referring to instances in the Qur'ān such as *ghayra muḥillī'l-ṣaydi* [Q. 5:1], *yā-ayyuha'l-sāḥiru* [Q. 43:49] and *ayyuha'l-thaqalān* [Q. 55:31].

are presumed to have higher moral standards). One of the main themes in this *tafsīr*, as for previous authors, is to stress that God seeks to distinguish Muslim women from non-Muslims, with the initial impetus of the verse having been the Jāhilī women's brazenness, walking about with loose garments and 'their breasts all but hanging out'. The Muslim protagonist of this story, Asmā' bt. Marthad, is disgusted by their conduct, and thus this verse is seen as protecting Muslim women's interests, rather than imposing something unwanted or unnecessary on them.

This is an imperative from God, exalted be He, to believing women, a jealous guarding (*ghayra*)[192] [of them] on the part of God for their husbands, His believing servants, and a way of distinguishing them from the attributes of the women of the *jāhiliyya* and the actions of idolatrous women (*mushrikāt*). The occasion for the revelation of this verse is the one mentioned by Muqātil b. Ḥayyān: It has reached us, but God knows best, that Jābir b. ʿAbd Allāh al-Anṣārī related how when Asmā' bt. Marthad was staying in a place in the lands of the Banū Ḥāritha, women would walk in on her without any covers wrapped around them (*muttazirāt*) and so their anklets, breasts and locks would be revealed. So Asmā' commented, 'How disgusting that is!' and God revealed *and tell the believing women to lower their gaze* [to the end of] the verse. Thus His words *and tell the believing women to lower their gaze* means from what God has forbidden them to look at, other than their husbands. That is why many scholars are of the opinion that a woman should not look at a man who is a non-relative (*ajnabī*) with desire, or even without desire for that matter. Most of them base their argument on the reports in Abū Dāwūd and al-Tirmidhī of a *ḥadīth* of al-Zuhrī on the authority of Nabhān, the *mawlā* of Umm Salama, who narrated to him [al-Zuhrī] that Umm Salama had told him [Nabhān] that she was with the Messenger of God (*ṣlʿm*) with Maymūna, and she [Umm Salama] said, 'While we were with him, Ibn Umm Maktūm walked in on him – and this was after we had been commanded to screen ourselves (*ḥ-j-b*) – and the Messenger of God said, "Take [your] cover (*iḥtajibā*) from him", to which I said, "But, Messenger of God, is he not blind and unable to see us, nor does he know us?" to which the Messenger of God said, "And you two, are you blind? Do you not see him?"'[193]

Al-Tirmidhī there states that this *ḥadīth* is fair (*ḥasan*) and sound (*ṣaḥīḥ*). Other scholars, however, are of the opinion that it is permissible for women to look at male non-relatives, provided that it is not out of desire (*shahwa*), as established in the *Ṣaḥīḥ* where it is mentioned that the Messenger of God

[192] Unlike in English, the term 'jealousy' (*ghayra*) in Arabic also has the sense of caretaking something sacred, so a jealous guarding of it from harm.

[193] The wording here is slightly different than in Tirmidhī's version, on which see above, note 110.

(*ṣlʿm*) was watching the Abyssinians (*ḥabasha*) as they sparred with their spears on the Festive Day (*ʿīd*) in the mosque while ʿĀʾisha, mother of the believers, also watched them from behind him so that he was concealing her from them, until she became bored and left.

As regards His words *and safeguard their private parts*, Saʿīd b. Jubayr said, 'from abominable acts (*fāḥisha*)', while Qatāda and Sufyān [al-Thawrī] said, 'from what is not licit for them', and Muqātil said, 'from fornication (*zinā*)'. Abū'l-ʿĀliya said, 'Every verse revealed in the Qurʾān in which the safeguarding of private parts is mentioned refers to fornication, except for this verse, *and to safeguard their private parts*, meaning that no one should see them.'

His words, exalted be He, *and let them not reveal their ornament except what is apparent of it* mean that the women should not reveal anything of their ornament to non-relatives except what is impossible to conceal, which, as Ibn Masʿūd says, are things like the garments (*ridāʾ*) and robes (*thiyāb*), that is, in the way that was customary for Arab women, draping a head-covering (*miqnaʿa*) over their garments to conceal them and the edges of clothes that are visible: in such instances there is no blame (*ḥaraj*) on a woman since she is unable to cover it [entirely]. Analogous to this, in terms of women's clothing, is what is revealed by a woman's wrapper (*izār*) and cannot be concealed. Those who share Ibn Masʿūd's opinion are al-Ḥasan [al-Baṣrī], Ibn Sīrīn, Abū'l-Jawzāʾ as well as Ibrāhīm al-Nakhaʿī and others. Al-Aʿmash reported from Saʿīd b. Jubayr on the authority of Ibn ʿAbbās that *and let them not reveal their ornament except what is apparent of it* refers to the face, hands and rings; a similar opinion has been reported from Ibn ʿUmar, ʿAṭāʾ [b. Abī Rabāḥ], ʿIkrima, Saʿīd b. Jubayr, Abū'l-Shaʿthāʾ, al-Ḍaḥḥāk, Ibrāhīm al-Nakhaʿī and others. This can possibly be considered as an explication (*tafsīr*) of what is meant by the ornament that women are forbidden from revealing. In addition, Abū Isḥāq al-Subayʿī on the authority of Abū'l-Aḥwaṣ from ʿAbd Allāh [b. Jābir] said, regarding *and let them not reveal their ornament*, that *ornament* means earrings, gold bracelets, anklets and necklaces. And in another report from him, via the same chain (*isnād*), he commented: 'There are two types of ornament, an ornament which is only seen by the husband, such as the ring or the bangle, and another ornament that is seen by a non-relative, that which is apparent (*ẓāhir*) of the clothes (*thiyāb*).'

Al-Zuhrī said that the women should not reveal to any of those enumerated by God [in the verse], for whom she is unmarriageable, anything except bracelets (*aswira*), veils (*akhmira*) and earrings (*aqriṭa*), but without completely uncovering herself. But to all other people, nothing should be revealed of her except the ring.

Mālik reported from al-Zuhrī that *except what is apparent of it* means a ring (*khātam*) or an anklet (*khilkhāl*).

It is possible that Ibn ʿAbbās and his followers wished to explain *what is apparent of it* as the face and hands, which is the accepted (*mashhūr*) opinion among the majority (*al-jumhūr*), and one finds reassurance of it in the *ḥadīth* reported by Abū Dāwūd in his *Sunan*: Yaʿqūb b. Kaʿb al-Anṭākī and Muʾammil b. al-Faḍl al-Ḥarrānī both narrated,

> Al-Walīd b. Saʿīd b. Bishr on the authority of Qatāda from Khālid b. Durayk from ʿĀʾisha, may God be pleased with her, said that Asmāʾ, the daughter of Abū Bakr, walked in on the Prophet (*ṣlʿm*) scantily clad (*thiyāb riqāq*) and he turned [his face] away from her saying, 'O Asmāʾ, when a woman reaches menses (*maḥīḍ*), it is not right that anything should be seen of her except this',[194] and he indicated his face and hands.

But Abū Dāwūd and Abū Ḥātim al-Rāzī think that this [*ḥadīth*] is a *mursal* one,[195] since Khālid b. Durayk never transmitted (*s-m-ʿ*) from ʿĀʾisha, may God be pleased with her, but God knows best.

His words *and let them cast their wraps over their cleavage* refer to drapes (*maqāniʿ*) that can be folded over to cover their breasts to conceal what is underneath in the chest area, so that they are at variance with the dress of women of the *jāhiliyya* who did not used to do that; nay, their women would pass by men with their breasts all but hanging out without any cover, even baring their necks, locks and earrings. God thus commanded the believing women to be modest in dress and behaviour, as He, exalted be, He said, *O Prophet, tell your wives and daughters and the wives of believers to draw their cloaks closely about themselves: that makes it more likely for them to be recognised and not harmed* [Q. 33:59]. And in this noble verse [Q. 24:31], He says, *and let them cast their wraps over their cleavage*: *khumur* is the plural of *khimār* and it is what is used to 'cover' (*yukhmar*) the head, which is what people call *maqāniʿ*. Saʿīd b. Jubayr said that *wa'l-yaḍribna* (let them cast over) means *wa'l-yashdidna* (let them fasten) *their wraps over their cleavage*, meaning over the neck area (*naḥr*) and breast (*ṣadr*) so that nothing of that may be seen.

194 Cf. Abū Dāwūd, *Sunan*, *Kitāb al-Libās* (34), *Bāb mā tubdī minhā al-marʾatu min zīnatihā* (33), *ḥadīth* no. 85/4104.

195 This technical classification of *ḥadīth*s as *mursal* indicates that there is a missing link in the chain, in this case between the Prophet's contemporaries, here his wife ʿĀʾisha, and the generation of Successors (such as Qatāda). Khālid b. Durayk sits alongside Qatāda in generational terms and may not have had direct contact with ʿĀʾisha, as Ibn Kathīr cautions above. See G.H.A. Juynboll, *Muslim Tradition: Studies in Chronology, Provenance and Authorship of Early Hadith* (Cambridge, Cambridge University Press, 1983).

Al-Bukhārī relates that ʿĀʾisha,[196] may God be pleased with her, said, 'May God have mercy on the first of the Emigrant women. When God sent down *and let them cast their wraps over their cleavage*, they shredded lengths of cloth to veil themselves with them.' He [Bukhārī] also said that Abū Nuʿaym narrated from Ibrāhīm b. Nāfiʿ from al-Ḥasan b. Muslim from Ṣafiyya bt. Shayba that ʿĀʾisha, may God be pleased with her, used to say, 'When this verse was revealed *and let them cast their wraps over their cleavage*, the women took their wrappers (*uzur*), tore out the inner linings and veiled themselves with these.' Ibn Abī Ḥātim said: My father narrated to us that Ṣafiyya bt. Shayba[197] said,

> While we were with ʿĀʾisha, the women of the Quraysh were mentioned and their merits spoken of, whereafter ʿĀʾisha, may God be pleased with her, said, 'Verily, the women of the Quraysh are meritorious, but by God I have not seen women more praiseworthy than the women of the Anṣār in the sincerity of their affirmation of the Book of God and their belief in the Revelation. Verily, when *and let them cast their wraps over their cleavage* of *sūrat al-Nūr* was sent down, their men hurried to them to recite to them what God had sent down in it for them. Each man would recite to his wife, daughter or sister and to any kinswoman, and every woman grabbed her embroidered woollens using [pieces of] them to bind around their heads (*iʿtajarat*) as an affirmation and act of faith in what God had sent down of His Book. You would see them behind the Messenger of God (*ṣlʿm*) turbaned, looking like ravens sat atop their heads.'

Abū Dāwūd reported the same, but in another way, on the authority of Ṣafiyya bt. Shayba.

Ibn Jarīr [al-Ṭabarī] said: Yūnus narrated to us that ʿĀʾisha[198] said, 'May God have mercy on the first Emigrant women when God sent down *and let them cast their wraps over their cleavage*; they tore up the shoulder pads of their woollens to veil themselves therewith.'

Abū Dāwūd also reported this by way of a *ḥadīth* from Ibn Wahb.

As for His words, exalted be He, *and let them not reveal their ornament except to their husbands* (*buʿūl*) mean '[to] their spouses (*azwāj*)'. *Or their fathers, or their husbands' fathers, or their sons, or their husbands' sons, or their brothers or their brothers' sons or sisters' sons*: all of these are unmarriageable (*maḥārim*) to the woman and she is permitted to be

[196] Al-Bukhārī ← Aḥmad b. Shabīb ← his father ← Yūnus ← Ibn Abī Shihāb ← ʿUrwa [b. Hishām] ← ʿĀʾisha.

[197] Ibn Abī Ḥātim ← his father ← Aḥmad b. ʿAbd Allāh b. Yūnus ← al-Zanjī b. Khālid ← ʿAbd Allāh b. ʿUthmān b. Khathyam ← Ṣafiyya bt. Shayba.

[198] Yūnus ← Ibn Wahb ← Qurra b. ʿAbd al-Raḥmān ← Ibn Shihāb ← ʿUrwa ← ʿĀʾisha.

before them in full ornament, but without premeditation or ostentation (*tabahruj*).[199]

Ibn al-Mundhir reports, on the authority of al-Shaʿbī and ʿIkrima,[200] the following regarding this verse: *and let them not reveal their ornament except to their husbands, or their fathers, or their husbands' fathers*, reciting it to the end and saying that the paternal uncle and maternal uncle are not mentioned because they are able to describe [the woman in question] to their sons,[201] and so [the woman] should not take off her veil in front of either the paternal or maternal uncle. As for the husband himself, all of that [*ornament*] is only for him and so she can make herself up in whatever way that is not permitted in the presence of anyone other than him.

As for His words *or their womenfolk* means that she may appear in her *ornament* also before other women who are Muslims but not before the women of the People of the Book (*ahl al-dhimma*), lest these describe her to their husbands; and although this is to be guarded against in the case of all women, it is even more strict with the women of the People of the Book, for there is nothing to prevent these women from doing such a thing, whereas the Muslim woman knows that this is illicit (*ḥarām*) and is naturally discouraged (*z-j-r*) from it.

The Messenger of God (*ṣlʿm*) has indeed said, 'Let not a woman see another woman and describe her to her husband as though he were able to see her',[202] as has been verified (*kh-r-j*) in the two *Ṣaḥīḥ*s on the authority of Ibn Masʿūd.

Saʿīd b. Manṣur reports in his *Sunan*: Ismāʿīl b. ʿAyyāsh has narrated (*ḥ-d-th*) on the authority of al-Ḥārith b. Qays[203] that ʿUmar b. al-Khaṭṭāb wrote to Abū ʿUbayda: 'To wit, it has reached me that some of the Muslim women are frequenting the baths with polytheist women, and this is within your power. It is not licit for a woman who believes in God and the Last Day that anyone other than the women of her community (*milla*) should see her naked.'

[199] There is a striking lexical similarity between *tabahruj* and the verb *tabarruj*, which means to make an ostentatious and deliberate display of one's ornament, in effect 'to flaunt oneself'; *tabarruj* is associated with pre-Islamic customs as per the Qurʾānic occurrence in Q. 33:33: *wa-lā tabarrajna tabarruj al-jāhiliyya al-ūlā* (*and do not flaunt yourself as they used to in the age of paganism* [*al-jāhiliyya*]).

[200] Mūsā meaning Abū Hārūn ← Abū Bakr, meaning Ibn Abī Shayba ← ʿAffān ← Ḥammād b. Salama ← Dāwūd ← al-Shaʿbī and ʿIkrima.

[201] Even though these two are not marriageable, their sons as first cousins of the woman in question are eligible to be married to her, thus these two uncles are precluded from being privy to the ornament that may be displayed to unmarriageables.

[202] Cf. Bukhārī, *Ṣaḥīḥ*, *Kitāb al-Nikāḥ* (67), *Bāb lā tubāshiru al-marʾa al-marʾa fa-tanʿatahā li-zawjihā* (118), *ḥadīth* no. 173/5240.

[203] Ismāʿīl b. ʿAyyāsh ← Hishām b. al-Ghāzī ← ʿUbāda b. Nusayy ← his father ← al-Ḥārith b. Qays.

Mujāhid says, with regard to *or their womenfolk*, 'Their Muslim womenfolk and not the polytheist women, for it is not permitted for a Muslim woman to reveal herself bare before a polytheist woman (*mushrika*)'.

'Abd Allāh reports in his commentary on the authority of al-Kalbī from Abū Ṣāliḥ that Ibn 'Abbās said, [concerning] *or their womenfolk*, 'These are Muslim women who should not reveal this [*ornament*] to a Jewish woman or a Christian, meaning the neckline, earrings, necklaces (*wishāḥ*) and what only an unmarriageable is allowed to see.'

Sa'īd reports that Mujāhid[204] said, 'A Muslim woman should not take off her veil (*khimār*) in front of a polytheist woman, for God, exalted be He, says *or their womenfolk*, and such a [polytheist] woman does not belong among her womenfolk.'

On the authority of Makḥūl and 'Ubāda b. Nusayy, it is reported that they both considered it loathsome (*makrūh*) that a Muslim woman should greet a Christian, Jewish or Zoroastrian (*majūs*) woman with a kiss.

As for what has been reported by Ibn Abī Ḥātim that 'Alī b. al-Ḥusayn narrated that Abū 'Umayr narrated that Ḍamra said: 'Ibn 'Aṭā' reported on the authority of his father that he [the latter] said, "When the Companions of the Messenger of God (*ṣl'm*) reached Jerusalem (*bayt al-maqdis*), their women found themselves before Jewish and Christian women."' If this [report] is sound, then it is to be interpreted as a case of necessity (*ḍarūra*) or a humiliating situation (*imtihān*), and no nakedness should be revealed necessarily, but God knows best.

As for His words, exalted be He, *or what their right hands possess*: Ibn Jarīr [al-Ṭabarī] said that this means 'from among the polytheist women', before whom she is permitted to reveal her ornament, even if she be a polytheist, since she would be her slave girl. This is the opinion of Sa'īd b. al-Musayyab.

The majority say, rather, she is permitted to appear before any slave (*raqīq*), whether male or female. They use as proof the *ḥadīth* reported by Abū Dāwūd, where Muḥammad b. 'Īsā narrated that Abū Jamī' Sālim b. Dīnār from Thābit on the authority of Anas [b. Mālik] that the Messenger of God (*ṣl'm*) had brought [his daughter] Fāṭima a slave boy whom he intended to gift to her while – as he related – Fāṭima was wearing a robe which, if she were to use [it] to veil her head, would not reach her legs, and if she were to cover her legs with it, [it] would not reach her head. When the Prophet (*ṣl'm*) saw what had transpired, he said, 'Do not worry! He is both [like] a father to you and a young boy'.

[204] Sa'īd ← Jarīr ← Layth ← Mujāhid.

The *ḥāfiẓ* Ibn ʿAsākir in his *Taʾrīkh*, in the biographical entry (*tarjama*) on Khadīj al-Ḥimṣī, the *mawlā* of Muʿāwiya, mentions that ʿAbd Allāh b. Masʿada al-Fazārī, whose skin was a very dark black colour, had been gifted by the Prophet (*ṣlʿm*) to his daughter Fāṭima, who brought him up and subsequently freed him. Much later on, he rose to prominence [fighting] alongside Muʿāwiya [b. Abī Sufyān] during the battle of Ṣiffīn, becoming one of the severest opponents of ʿAlī b. Abī Ṭālib, may God be pleased with him. The imam Aḥmad [b. Ḥanbal] reported that Sufyān b. ʿUyayna narrated from al-Zuhrī from Nabhān on the authority of Umm Salama who mentioned that the Messenger of God (*ṣlʿm*) said, 'If any woman among you should have a slave to be manumitted but who still had service to complete, let her veil herself from him'; this [*ḥadīth*] has also been reported by Abū Dāwūd from Musaddid on the authority of Sufyān [al-Thawrī].

His words, exalted be He, *or their male dependants lacking (sexual) desire*, mean hired hands (*ujarāʾ*) and dependants (*atbāʿ*) who are not equals but whose minds are distracted and flabby, with no aspiration for women or any desire for them.

Ibn ʿAbbās said, 'This is the fool (*mughaffal*) who has no desire (*shahwa*).'

Mujāhid said, 'This is the simpleton (*ablah*).'

ʿIkrima said, 'This is the effeminate (*mukhannath*) whose penis (*dhakar*) does not become erect'; and more than one early scholar (*salaf*) was of the same opinion.

In the *Ṣaḥīḥ*, in one of the *ḥadīth*s of al-Zuhrī from ʿUrwa, ʿĀʾisha reported,

> An effeminate used to walk in on the family of the Messenger of God (*ṣlʿm*), and they used to consider him among those lacking (sexual) desire (*ghayr ūlīʾl-irba*). On one occasion, the Prophet walked in while he was describing a woman, saying how she had a fourfold waistline from the front and double that from the back, whereupon the Messenger of God (*ṣlʿm*) [said], 'I see that this one knows exactly what goes on in here. Let him not enter into your presence anymore'. He thus banished him to al-Baydāʾ, and he came back [to Medina] only on Fridays to seek food.

The imam Aḥmad [b. Ḥanbal] reported on the authority of Umm Salama[205] that the Messenger of God (*ṣlʿm*) came in while she was [sitting] with an effeminate alongside ʿAbd Allāh b. Abī Umayya – that is, her brother – and the effeminate was saying, 'O ʿAbd Allāh, if God should give you victory over Ṭāʾif tomorrow, then seek out for yourself the daughter of Ghaylān, for she verily sports a fourfold waistline from the front and double that from the

[205] Aḥmad [b. Ḥanbal] ← Abū Muʿāwiya ← Hishām b. ʿUrwa ←his father ← Zaynab the daughter of Abū Salama ← Umm Salama.

back.' He said [continuing his report] that the Messenger of God (*ṣlʿm*) overheard him and then said to Umm Salama, 'Do not let him enter into your presence [anymore]'.[206] Both [Bukhārī and Muslim] have verified this in the two *Ṣaḥīḥ* collections in the *ḥadīth* version of Hishām b. ʿUrwa.

The imam Aḥmad [b. Ḥanbal] said that ʿAbd al-Razzāq [al-Ṣanʿānī] narrated that Maʿmar [b. Rāshid] narrated from al-Zuhrī from ʿUrwa b. al-Zubayr on the authority of ʿĀʾisha, may God be pleased with her:

> An effeminate man used to walk in on the wives of the Prophet (*ṣlʿm*), and they considered him from among those without (sexual) desire [for women]. On one occasion, the Prophet (*ṣlʿm*) walked in while he was with [the Prophet's] wives describing some woman, saying, 'From the front she has a fourfold waistline and from the back twice that.' The Prophet (*ṣlʿm*) then said, 'I see this one knows everything in here. Let him not come in [anymore]'. They banned him thereafter.

Muslim, Abū Dāwūd and al-Nasāʾī also reported this [*ḥadīth*] via ʿAbd al-Razzāq on the authority of Umm Salama.

His words *or children uninitiated to the exposedness of women* mean that on account of their youth, [children] have no comprehension of women's affairs (*aḥwāl*) or [conception] of their nakedness when they hear their soft speech, [or see] their swinging gait, their movements and postures. When a child is too young to understand any of that, then there is no problem in him entering into the presence of women, whereas if he were an adolescent, or near enough, and aware of all of that, and perceives it and discriminates between the hideous woman and the fair one, then he cannot [be permitted to] enter into the presence of women.

It is confirmed in the two *Ṣaḥīḥ* collections on the authority of the Messenger of God (*ṣlʿm*) that he said, 'Beware of entering into the presence of women', to which they said, 'O Messenger of God, what about an in-law?' to which he responded, 'In-law, in death!' (*al-ḥamw al-mawt*).[207]

His words *and let them not stamp their feet* [to the end of] the verse: Women in the time of the *jāhiliyya* used to walk through the streets with anklets around their feet, but whose jangle could not be heard. She would then strike the ground with her foot and the men would hear their ringing. God therefore forbade believing women from doing the same. Similarly, if

[206] See above, note 160.

[207] Versions are found in Bukhārī, *Ṣaḥīḥ*, *Kitāb al-Nikāḥ* (67), *Bāb lā yakhluwanna rajulun biʾmraʾatin illā dhū maḥram* (111), *ḥadīth* no. 165/5232; Muslim, *Ṣaḥīḥ*, *Kitāb al-Salām* (39), *Bāb taḥrīm al-khalwati biʾl-ajnabiyyati waʾl-dukhūli ʿalayhā* (8), *ḥadīth* no. 28/2172; Tirmidhī, *Jāmiʿ*, *Kitāb al-Riḍāʿ* (12), *Bāb mā jaʾa fī karāhiyyat al-dukhūli ʿalāʾl-mughībāt* (16), *ḥadīth* no. 26/1171.

she were to make a motion in order to reveal any part of her concealed ornament, then this would be included in the prohibition here on account of His words, exalted be He, *and let them not stamp their feet* [to the end of] the verse. To that extent, she should refrain from putting on perfumes or scents when leaving home, lest men catch her scent.

Abū ʿĪsā al-Tirmidhī reported, on the authority of the Prophet (*ṣlʿm*),[208] 'Every eye fornicates (*zāniya*), and when a woman perfumes herself and passes by a session (*majlis*), then she is a such-and-such',[209] meaning [that she is] a fornicator (*zāniya*). And in the same section [this has been transmitted] on the authority of Abū Hurayra. This is a fair and sound [*ḥadīth*], reported also by Abū Dāwūd and al-Nasāʾī via the *ḥadīth* of Thābit b. ʿAmāra. Abū Dāwūd reported on the authority of Abū Hurayra,[210] may God be pleased with him, who said that a woman passed him, the scent of whose perfume he smelled as the tail of her garment whirled up dust. He said to her, 'O slave girl of the Almighty, have you just come from the mosque?' to which she said, 'Yes.' He asked her, 'Have you put on perfume?' She said, 'Yes.' He then said, 'I have indeed heard my love Abū'l-Qāsim (*ṣlʿm*) say, "God does not accept the prayers of a woman perfumed in this mosque until she goes back home and performs the major ablution (*ghusl*) as though from major impurity (*janāba*)."'[211] This has been reported by Ibn Māja from Abū Bakr Ibn Abī Shayba on the authority of Sufyān, he being Ibn ʿUyayna.

Al-Tirmidhī also reported via the *ḥadīth* of Mūsā b. ʿUbayda from Ayyūb b. Khālid on the authority of Maymūna bt. Saʿad that the Messenger of God (*ṣlʿm*) said, 'The woman who swaggers with her garment trailing in ornament among other than her family is like the darkness on the Day of Resurrection that has no light'.[212] In the same vein, women are forbidden from walking in the middle of the road because of the exposure of their ornament that this would cause.

Abū Dāwūd said that al-Taghlibī narrated that ʿAbd al-ʿAzīz, meaning Ibn Muḥammad, narrated from Ibn Abī al-Yamān from Shaddād b. Abī ʿAmr b. Ḥamās from his father from Ḥamza b. Abī Usayd al-Anṣārī on the authority of his father that he heard the Prophet (*ṣlʿm*), who was exiting the mosque

[208] Abū ʿĪsā al-Tirmidhī ← Muḥammad b. Bashshār ← Yaḥyā b. Saʿīd al-Qaṭṭān ← Thābit b. ʿAmāra al-Ḥanafī ← Ghunaym b. Qays ← Abū Mūsā [al-Ashʿarī], may God be pleased with him.

[209] A version is found in Tirmidhī, *Jāmiʿ*, *Kitāb al-Adab* (43), *ḥadīth* no. 3015.

[210] Abū Dāwud ← Muḥammad b. Kathīr ← Sufyān ← ʿĀṣim b. ʿUbayd Allāh ← ʿUbayd *mawlā* Abū Ruham ← Abū Hurayra.

[211] Versions found in Abū Dāwūd, *Sunan*, *Kitāb al-Tarajjul* (35), *Bāb mā jāʾa fī'l-marʾa tataṭayyabu li'l-khurūj* (7), *ḥadīth* no. 16/4174; Ibn Māja, *Sunan*, *Kitāb al-Fitan* (36), *Bāb fitnat al-nisāʾ* (19), *ḥadīth* no. 77/4002.

[212] Tirmidhī, *Jāmiʿ*, *Kitāb al-Riḍāʿ* (12), *ḥadīth* no. 22/1167.

while some men and women were intermingling along the road, say to the women, 'Stay back and do not fill up the road, but go along its edges'.[213] And so women would cleave to the walls so closely that sometimes their robes would snag on the walls.

[Regarding] His words *turn to God in repentance all together O believers so that you may prosper*: Adopt these beautiful attributes and splendid character traits that I have commanded you to, and abandon the despicable character traits and attributes of the people of the *jāhiliyya*. For true and total prosperity is to do what God and His Messenger have commanded and to abandon what they both have forbidden. And God, exalted be He, is the One to be sought for assistance.[214]

Muḥsin al-Fayḍ al-Kāshānī

Muḥsin al-Fayḍ, as an Akhbārī, focuses his interpretation on reports of the imams; and rather than simply naming chains of authority, as did previous authors, he names the books in which the reports are found. He names at least five separate Shīʿī *ḥadīth* collections, which is a way of emphasising his own scholarly credentials as well as exemplifying the Akhbārī approach. The reports that he cites often echo themes in Sunnī interpretations, or even their exact wording. Thus Muḥsin al-Fayd quotes an interpretation from Qummī that credits Jaʿfar al-Ṣādiq with a particular report; the same interpretation is also attributed to Ibn Zayd by Ṭabrisī, and, in Sunnī sources, to Abū'l-ʿĀliya. The interpretation in question specifies that all of the verses in the Qur'ān mentioning *private parts* refer to fornication, except for this one; this one mentions covering as a way of preventing fornication. Unlike Ṭabrisī, Muḥsin al-Fayḍ does not include reports on Sunnī sources; thus he does not attribute this report to Ibn Zayd. Traditions that speak of the Prophet's wives remain absent from this account, as does the occasion of revelation mentioned in some Sunnī sources. In addition, the entire question of the effeminate does not arise. Notably, however, one of the reports included here specifies *only* the hands (not the face) as a woman's 'manifest ornament'; others include the face, which is the more accepted opinion.

And tell the believing women to lower their gaze and safeguard their private parts. [According to] al-Qummī on the authority of [Jaʿfar] al-Ṣādiq (*ʿm*):

> Every verse in the Qur'ān that mentions private parts (*furūj*) refers to fornication (*zinā*), except this one, which refers to the gaze. Therefore, it is illicit for a

[213] Abū Dāwūd, *Sunan*, *Kitāb al-Adab* (43), *Bāb fī mashī al-nisā' maʿa al-rijāl fi'l-ṭarīq* (181), *ḥadīth* no. 500/5272.

[214] Ibn Kathīr, *Tafsīr*, s.v. Q. 24:31.

> believing man to gaze at the private parts of his [Muslim] brother [and] for a woman to gaze at the private parts of her [Muslim] sister.[215]

In the *Kāfī*, also on his authority (*ʿm*), there is a *ḥadīth* in which he mentions: Faith has been prescribed for the limbs. And for the eyes, it has been prescribed that they do not gaze at what God has made illicit for them, and that they turn away from what God has forbidden of that which is not licit for them, which is also one part of faith. God, blessed and exalted, says, *and tell the believers*[216] *to lower their gaze and safeguard their private parts* [Q. 24:30], prohibiting them from gazing at their nakedness (*ʿawrāt*) and from a man gazing at the private parts (*farj*) of his brother and he should safeguard his private parts from being gazed at. And He says *and tell the believing women to lower their gaze and safeguard their private parts*, [meaning] that a woman should not gaze at the private parts of her sister and that she should safeguard against her private parts being seen. He [al-Kulaynī][217] said: Everything relating to safeguarding private parts refers to illicit fornication (*zinā*), except for this verse which refers to gazing.

[It is reported] on the authority of al-Bāqir (*ʿm*) that he said, 'A young man from the Anṣār encountered a woman in Medina – women then used to wrap veils (*yataqannaʿna*) around the backs of their heads – and he kept looking at her as she approached, and when she passed him, he kept looking [back] at her as he entered a narrow passageway', which he [al-Bāqir] named as belonging to the Banū-something [tribe], 'and kept looking at her from behind until his face was struck by a pole in the wall or a piece of glass, which tore his face. When the woman was out of sight, he saw that blood was flowing onto his garment and his chest. He then said, "By God, I shall go to the Messenger of God (*ṣlʿh*), and I shall tell him the news [of what happened]."' He [al-Bāqir] said, 'And when he came to him and the Messenger of God (*ṣlʿh*) saw him, he said, "What is this from?" And when he [the young man] informed him, Gabriel came down with this verse: *And let them not reveal their ornament except what is apparent of it*.'

In the *Kāfī*, [it is reported] on the authority of al-Ṣādiq (*ʿm*) concerning His words, exalted be He, *except what is apparent of it*, that he said, 'Apparent ornament is kohl and rings', and in a [different version of the] report, 'Rings and manacles (*maska*)', [otherwise] known as *qulab*, vocalised *qulb* (sing.), which is a bracelet (*siwār*).

[215] This is an exact quote from Qummī, above.

[216] This is *mu'minīn*, which is 'believers', but here it may be understood as 'believing men' since the believing women are specified in the following verse.

[217] Author of the *Kāfī*.

In the *Jawāmiʿ*, on their authority, peace be upon them, [the apparent ornament] is the two hands and the fingers. According to al-Qummī, al-Bāqir (*ʿm*), regarding this verse, said,

> It refers to garments (*thawb*), kohl, rings, palm dyes and bracelets. Ornament is of three types: the ornament for people, the ornament for unmarriageable relatives and the ornament for the husband. As for the ornament for people, we have already mentioned it. As for the ornament for unmarriageable relatives, this is the place of the necklace and above, and the bangle and what is further down [the arm], and from the anklet to what is below that. As for the ornament for the husband, it is the entire body.[218]

In the *Majmaʿ*,[219] on the authority of the Prophet (*ṣlʿh*): 'What is beneath the shirt belongs to the husband, and what is above the shirt belongs to the son and the brother. And for those who are not unmarriageable, there are four types of garment: a shift (*dirʿ*), a wrap (*khimār*), a cloak (*jilbāb*) and a wrap (*izār*)'.

In the *Kāfī* [it is reported] on the authority of al-Ṣādiq (*ʿm*) that he was asked what was licit for a man to see of a woman if he were not an unmarriageable relative, to which he replied, 'The face, the hands and the feet.' [It is reported] on his authority also, 'There is nothing wrong with looking at the heads of the [women of] Tihāma, the nomadic Bedouin (*aʿrāb*), the inhabitants of the flood plains (*sawād*) and the uncouth foreign infidels (*ʿulūj*), because when they are forbidden from [doing] something, they do not desist.' He continues, 'And the woman who is insane or who is demented, there is nothing wrong in looking at her hair or body, if it be unintentional.' And [it is reported] also on his authority (*ʿm*) that he said the Messenger of God (*ṣlʿh*) said, 'It is not forbidden (*ḥurma*) to look at the hair or hands of the women of the People of the Book (*ahl al-dhimma*)'. Also [it is reported] from him (*ʿm*) that he was asked about the case of a man who wanted to marry a woman, but wanted to have good look at her, at her face and from behind; to which he replied that there was nothing wrong with that. In another report [he replied] 'There is nothing wrong with him looking at her face and wrists (*miʿṣam*) if he wishes to marry her'. I say that [it should be read] *miʿṣam*, which is like *minbar* [in grammatical form] and is the place where the bracelet is [worn]. In yet another [version of the] report, 'He is permitted to look at her hair and beautiful features, so long as he is not lustful (*ladhdha*)'. And in another [report], 'He should purchase her at the highest price'.

[218] Note that this is a verbatim quote of what is in the *tafsīr* of Qummī, above.
[219] This refers to the *Majmaʿ al-bayān* of Ṭabrisī.

In the *Khiṣāl*, the Prophet (*ṣl'h*) said to the Commander of the Believers ['Alī b. Abī Ṭālib] (*'m*), 'O 'Alī! The first look is yours, but the second [will be held] against you and is not for you'. In another report, 'Yours to have is the first glance at a woman, but do not prolong it with another look, and beware of temptation (*fitna*)'.

And let them cast their wraps over their cleavage, in order to conceal their necks, *and let them not reveal their ornament*, which He has repeated in order to clarify the ones to whom the revealing is permitted and the ones to whom it is not permitted; *except to their husbands*, for these are the ones for whom the *ornament* is intended, and they are permitted to look at the entire body, as has already been mentioned; *or their fathers, or their husbands' fathers, or their sons, or their husbands' sons, or their brothers or their brothers' sons or sisters' sons* – what these are permitted to see of her has already been mentioned.

In the *Kāfī* [it is reported] on the authority of al-Ṣādiq (*'m*) that he was asked about whether a woman's arms (*dhirā'*) constitute the ornament regarding which God, exalted be He, says *and let them not reveal their ornament except to their husbands*, to which he replied, 'Yes, and also the ornament that is beneath the veil and what is below the bracelets'; *or their womenfolk* means believing women.

In both *al-Kāfī* and *al-Faqīh*, on the authority of al-Ṣādiq (*'m*), [it is reported that] he said, 'A woman should not bare herself to a Jewish or Christian woman, for they may describe her to their husbands.'

Or what their right hands possess means slaves (*'abīd*) and slave girls (*imā'*), as stated in the *Majma'* on the authority of al-Ṣādiq (*'m*). Regarding this verse, [it is reported] in *al-Kāfī* on his authority (*'m*) that he said, 'There is nothing wrong with a slave (*mamlūk*) seeing the hair and legs [of his mistress]'; in another version, 'the hair and legs of his mistress (*mawlāt*); and in yet another, 'There is nothing wrong with his looking at her hair if he is a trusted one (*ma'mūn*).' Also [reported] on his authority (*'m*) is, 'A slave is not permitted to look at any part of his lady's body, except at her hair but without intending it.'

Or their male dependants lacking (sexual) desire: that is, those without need (*ḥāja*) for women; *irba* signifies 'intellect' (*'aql*) and excellence of opinion (*ra'y*). *Ghayr* is also read as *ghayra* in the accusative; *male*, according to al-Qummī, is decrepit old man who has no need of women.[220] In the *Kāfī*, on the authority of al-Bāqir (*'m*), he said, 'He is the fool (*aḥmaq*) who does not lie with women.' In the *Majma'*, also on his authority (*'m*), the *dependant*

220 Cf. Qummī, above.

is the one who follows you around in order to acquire some of your food and has no need for women, such as the imbecile (*ablah*) who is under a person's guardianship.

In the *Kāfī*, it is reported on the authority of [Mūsā] al-Kāẓim (*ʿm*) that he was asked about the man whose eunuch (*khaṣiyy*) enters into the presence of his women to give them ablution bowls and thus sees their hair, to which he [the imam] said, 'No.'

Or children uninitiated to the exposedness of women because of their inability to discriminate and attain knowledge thereof, or because they have not yet reached the stage of desire in attaining that knowledge and being overcome by it.

And let them not stamp their feet to make known what they hide of their ornament so that their anklets rattle and it becomes known that they are wearing anklets, for that creates a proclivity in men [to desire them]; *turn to God in repentance all together O believers*, since it is barely any of you who do not fall short in abstaining from desires; an alternative reading [of *ayyuha*] is *ayyuhu*; *so that you may prosper* with felicity in both abodes.[221]

Burūsawī

This commentary is notable for its hybrid approach to the question at hand. Burūsawī cites all of the Sunnī schools of law on the question of veiling, what is considered *ʿawra*, and other matters. For Ḥanafī *fiqh*, his main source is Abū'l-Layth al-Samarqandī, whom he quotes extensively, which in turn may indicate that he had a copy of the book from which the interpretations are taken. After discussing the legal implications of a passage, Burūsawī includes Sufi interpretations that indicate that this verse has a hidden meaning for the knower/gnostic: he who reveals his works, and his inner ecstatic state, has rendered that state a blight, where it was once considered beautiful. Here, his interpretation strongly resembles that of the much more concise Qushayrī (above). Finally, he quotes extensively from Persian poetry. Thus he combines a number of different sources and approaches to *tafsīr* and the Qurʾānic sciences. Burūsawī also cites extensively from books *verbatim*, indicating the beginning and end of the quoted passage in question; this again marks a change from earlier citation practices within this genre. In terms of content, it is notable that he does not discuss the effeminate, but rather focuses on whether a man who was impotent or castrated, or otherwise physically impaired, could see a woman's ornament (the answer was no). Yet he mentions that if a boy reaches manhood and is physically beautiful to other men, then he must veil just as a woman does, covering everything but the face and hands. It is unclear if he is referring to a socially recognised practice of queer men

[221] Muḥsin al-Fayḍ al-Kāshānī, *al-Ṣāfī*, s.v. Q. 24:31.

veiling. Burūsawī ends his exegesis of the verse with a somewhat lengthy explanation of the reasons why one should turn in repentance to God. Agreeing with earlier interpretations, he says that every believer must repent, even one who is a spiritual initiate. He then connects the state of repentance with the annihilation of the self (*fanāʾ*), saying that the seeker can become veiled in a spiritual station and hence needs to repent from that spiritual stasis in order to ultimately experience God in a direct way. In the act of continual repentance, and asking forgiveness of God, the seeker annihilates the self and is able to experience oneness with the Divine.

And tell the believing women to lower their gaze and not look at what is illicit for them to see of a man, which, according to Abū Ḥanīfa and Aḥmad [b. Ḥanbal], is the shameful parts (*ʿawra*), but which, according to Mālik [b. Anas], is anything other than the face (*wajh*) and the extremities (*aṭrāf*). The sounder position is that of the Shāfiʿī school of law (*madhhab*), which is that she should not look at him and he should not look at her; *and safeguard their private parts* by safeguarding themselves against fornication (*zinā*) and covering up (*tasattur*).

There is no disagreement among the imams concerning the requirement to conceal the *shameful parts* (*ʿawra*) from the eyes of people. But they have differed over what exactly constitutes the *shameful parts* (*ʿawra*).

Abū Ḥanīfa says that a man's shameful part (*ʿawra*) is what is from below his navel to below his knee, the knee being a shameful part (*ʿawra*). The *Niṣāb al-iḥtisāb*[222] has it that a person whose knee is not covered should be reprehended (*n-k-r*) mildly (*bi-rifq*) because the issue over whether it constitutes a shameful part (*ʿawra*) is a widely known debate. As for the one who does not cover up his thighs, then he should be severely reprimanded (*ʿ-n-f*) but not beaten, because there is disagreement over whether these constitute a shameful part (*ʿawra*) among some of the traditionists (*ahl al-ḥadīth*). But he whose unseemly part (*sawʾa*) is not covered up should be punished (*a-d-b*) as the fact that this is a shameful part (*ʿawra*) is not in dispute, given the repugnancy of it being revealed. The end [of the *Niṣāb*]. And akin to the case of the man is that of the slave girl (*ama*), whose belly and back are given priority because these constitute an area that is conducive to desire, the slave girl to be manumitted upon completion of payments (*mukātaba*), the (slave) mother of a child (*umm walad*) and the slave girl to be manumitted upon [the] death of [her] owner (*mudabbara*).[223] The entire [body of the] free woman (*ḥurra*) is

[222] ʿUmar b. Muḥammad al-Sanāmī (d. 734/1334), *Niṣāb al-iḥtisāb* (Mecca, Maktabat al-Ṭālib al-Jāmiʿī, 1986).

[223] See R. Brunschvig, "Abd', *EI*², I, 25–40, for a detailed account of the various technical terms and categories applied to the institution of slavery in the Muslim jurisprudential literature.

considered a shameful part (*ʿawra*), except for her face and hands; according to him [Abū Ḥanīfa], the sound opinion is that her feet are a shameful part (*ʿawra*), except when she is performing the ritual prayer (*ṣalāt*).

Mālik [b. Anas] has it that the shameful part (*ʿawra*) of a man are his private parts (*farj*), front and back, and his thighs, and that this is the same for the slave girl (*ama*), and the slave girl freed upon [her] owner's death (*mudabbara*) and the slave girl freed upon purchase with a term (*muʿtaqa*). The free woman is entirely a shameful part (*ʿawra*) except for her face and hands. According to him, it is also recommended (*mustaḥabb*) that the [slave] mother of a child (*umm walad*) conceal what the free woman is required to conceal of her body; likewise the slave girl under contract of payment (*mukātaba*).

Al-Shāfiʿī and Aḥmad [b. Ḥanbal] both say that the shameful part (*ʿawra*) of a man is what is between the navel and the knees, and that the knees themselves are not a shameful part (*ʿawra*); likewise the slave girl (*ama*), the contractual slave girl (*mukātaba*), the (slave) mother of a child (*umm walad*), the slave girl to be freed upon [her] owner's death (*mudabbara*) and the one partially freed upon purchase (*muʿtaq baʿḍuhā*). The free woman is entirely a shameful part (*ʿawra*) except for [her] face and hands, according to al-Shāfiʿī, and except for [her] face only, according to Aḥmad [b. Ḥanbal], if correctly understood.

As for a man's navel, this is unanimously (*bi'l-ittifāq*) considered not to be a shameful part (*ʿawra*), as stated in the *Fatḥ al-Raḥmān*.[224]

The lowering of the gaze (*ghaḍḍ*) is mentioned before [the safeguarding of private parts] because the gaze (*naẓar*) wants fornication and leads to corruption (*fasād*), all of which mean that God, exalted be He, has juxtaposed the prohibition to gaze at what is illicit, with the mention of the safeguarding of private parts as a warning about the tremendous danger of the gaze (*naẓar*), for it summons one to commit the act. In one *ḥadīth*, 'Sight is one of Iblīs' arrows (*sahm*)', and it is said, 'He who lets his eyes wander, has hastened his death.' [. . .]

And let them not reveal their ornament, let alone the parts where these sit. One can say *badā buduwan* or *buduwwan* to mean 'something has become clearly manifest' (*ẓahara ẓuhūran bayyinan*) and *abdā* for *aẓhara*; *except what is apparent of it* [. . .]: rings, the extremities of garments, kohl or eye ornaments, dyes or palm ornaments, for it is manifestly difficult (*ḥaraj*) to conceal these. Ibn al-Shaykh said, '*Ornament* (*zīna*) is whatever a woman

[224] This is likely to be Mujīr al-Dīn b. Muḥammad al-ʿUlaymī al-Maqdisī (d. 927/1521), *Fatḥ al-Raḥmān fī tafsīr al-Qur'ān*, ed. Nūr al-Dīn Ṭālib, 7 vols. ([Cairo], Dār al-Nawādir, 2009).

adorns herself with in the way of jewellery (*ḥuliyy*), kohl, robes (*thawb*) or [face] paint (*ṣibgh*). As for what is apparent on her – such as the ring (*khātam*) or gold band (*fatkha*), which is a ring without a gem (*faṣṣ*), kohl or paint – there is nothing wrong with revealing these in front of non-relatives, but on condition of certainty that it will not stir up desire (*shahwa*). As for what is hidden on her – such as bracelets and bangles, things which a woman wears around her wrists, or necklaces or earrings – it is not licit for her to reveal these except to the women mentioned later in His words [beginning with] *except to their husbands* [to the end of] the verse.

There is an allusion in the *Taʾwīlāt al-Najmiyya*[225] to the [importance of] keeping secret what God has adorned their innermost mysteries (*sarāʾir*) with in the way of pure states and augmented works, for when these are manifested, the beautiful becomes beastly, except for what has become manifest of these by way of an oncoming of truth (*wārid ḥaqq*) or a kind of charisma (*karāma*) that manifests itself on that person without any action or effort on his part: that is exempt, since one is not accountable for what is not of one's will (*taṣarruf*) or deliberate effort (*takalluf*). The end [of the *Najmiyya*].

In the *Ḥaqāʾiq* of al-Baqlī,[226] the author says that there is therein a proof-text (*istishhād*) [that indicates] that it is not permissible for the [spiritual] knowers (*ʿārif*) to reveal the ornament that is the truths of their gnosis (*maʿrifa*) and what God unveils for them from the world of the angelic realm (*malakūt*) and the lights of the Essence (*anwār al-dhāt*) and Attributes (*ṣifāt*), or [to reveal their] ecstasies (*mawājīd*), except what becomes manifest of these when one is overcome, such as gasps and cries, turning from one colour to another,[227] and what rolls off their tongues involuntarily in the way of ecstatic utterances (*shaṭḥ*) and conforming allusions (*ishārāt*). Such states are the noblest of ornaments for spiritual knowers. They say, 'The most beautiful ornament for a servant is obedience (*ṭāʿa*), which ornament, if he makes it manifest, disappears.' Some have said that the wisdom [hidden] in this verse for the people of spiritual knowledge is that the one who makes manifest anything of his deeds – except that which is apparent of him without any intention on his part – shall forsake thereby the sight of the Truth (*ruʾyat* al-Ḥaqq), the sight of the Truth (al-Ḥaqq) shall be lost to the one upon whom alights the sight of creation (*khalq*). The shaykh al-Saʿdī, sanctified be his secret, said: [. . .]

225 Cf. Hamza *et al.*, *Anthology*, I, 46 (and n. 244 thereat).

226 Rūzbihān b. Abū'l-Naṣr al-Baqlī al-Shīrāzī (d. 606/1209), *ʿArāʾis al-bayān fī ḥaqāʾiq al-Qurʾān* (Beirut, Dār al-Kutub al-ʿIlmiyya, 2008).

227 Literally, the commentator has 'to turn yellow and to turn red'.

And let them cast their wraps over their cleavage: *Cast* (*ḍ-r-b*) has as implicit the sense of 'throw over' (*ilqā'*), which is why its [intransitive] sense is governed by [the preposition] 'over' (*'alā*). *Khumur* is the plural of *khimār*, which is what a woman covers her head with and conceals herself with: otherwise, it cannot be called a *khimār*. In the *Mufradāt* [of al-Rāghib], the root sense of *kh-m-r* is to conceal (*s-t-r*) something. What one uses to cover oneself with is called a *khimār*, but customary usage (*ta'āruf*) has meant that it has come to designate what a woman uses to cover her head. *Juyūb* is the plural of *jayb* and it is what has been cut into (*j-w-b*) of a shirt (*qamīṣ*) in order for the head to go through. The meaning, then, is that [women] should cast their shawls (*maqāni'*) over their *juyūb* in order to conceal thereby their hair, earrings and necklines from non-relatives (*ajānib*). [. . .]

There is, herein, proof that a woman's chest (*ṣadr*) and her neck (*naḥr*) both constitute shameful parts (*'awra*), and thus cannot be seen by a non-relative.

And let them not reveal their ornament, that is to say, [their] hidden ornament, such as bangles, gold bracelets, necklaces, earrings and the like, let alone revealing the areas where these items are worn. He has repeated this [phrase] in order to clarify those to whom it is licit to reveal [the ornament] and those to whom it is not licit to reveal [it].

Abū'l-Layth [al-Samarqandī][228] said that women should not manifest the places where the ornaments are worn, such as the breast (*ṣadr*), the legs (*sāq*), the arms (*sā'id*) or the head (*ra's*), for the breast is the place of the necklace, the leg is the place of the anklet, the arm is the place of the bracelet and the head is the place of the headband (*iklīl*). He also mentions [the term] *al-zāniya* (fornicating woman), by which he meant the place where the ornament sits (*mawḍi' al-zīna*). The end [of the excerpt].

Except to their husbands: The author of the *Mufradāt*[229] says that *al-ba'l* is the male of a pair, the plural being *bu'ūla*, like [the pattern of] *faḥl* and [its plural] *fuḥūla*. The end [of this excerpt]. That is to say, [women should reveal their ornament] only to their husbands, for these are the ones for whom the ornament is intended and they have the right to gaze at the entire bodies of their wives, even that place in question, especially if gazing at it serves to strengthen desire, except that it is considered odious to gaze at the private parts themselves by general agreement (*bi'l-ittifāq*), even at his own, as it is reported that this brings about blindness and effaces the light of the eyes. In

[228] He was a fourth-/tenth-century Ḥanafī theologian and jurist whose works survived in Ottoman Turkish manuscripts: see Joseph Schacht, 'Abū'l-Layth al-Samarḳandī', *EI*².

[229] Al-Rāghib al-Iṣfahānī, *Mufradāt*.

'Ā'isha's words, may God be pleased with her, 'He never saw anything of my private parts, nor me of his.' In the *Niṣāb*, the author says that the above refers to the hidden ornament, which may be revealed to the husband in order to summon him to her and to stir up desire of her; that is why the Messenger of God cursed the woman who does not put on colour (*salqā'*) and the one that does not wear kohl on her eyes [for her husband] (*marhā'*). [. . .]

Or their husbands' sons, or their brothers, or their brothers' sons or sisters' sons.

The justification (*'illa*) for this is the frequency of necessary intermingling between these males and the women, and the diminished risk of [falling into] temptation on the part of both, given the natural repulsion on both sides to sexual contact (*mumāssa*) between kin. They are permitted to look at what is revealed of the women during service (*khidma*).

The author of *Fatḥ al-Raḥmān* says that according to al-Shāfi'ī, it is permissible for all of those mentioned to see the inner ornament (*zīna bāṭina*), except what is between the navel and the knees, which is only licit for the husband.

According to Mālik, they can look at the face and the extremities.

According to Abū Ḥanīfa, they can look at the face, the head, the breast, the legs and the arms, but not the back or the belly or the thighs.

According to Aḥmad [b. Ḥanbal], they can look at what most commonly (*ghāliban*) is manifest, such as the face, the neck, the feet, the hands and the legs.

Abū'l-Layth said that there are four levels [of permissibility] when it comes to looking at women: with respect to the permissibility to look at all of a woman's parts, that is in the case of a husband looking at his wife or slave girl; with respect to the permissibility to look at the face and hands, that is the case of a man looking at a woman to whom he is marriageable, as long as each of them trusts himself or herself [not to fall into temptation], in which case there is nothing wrong with looking when there is a need; with respect to the permissibility to look at the breast, the head, the legs and the arms, that is the case of a man looking at a woman with whom he has womb-ties and to whom he is unmarriageable, such as his mother, his sister, his paternal aunt or maternal aunt, his father's wife or his son's wife or his wife's mother, whether this [womb-tie] be due to suckling (*riḍā'*) or to blood kinship (*nasab*); and with respect to the non-permissibility of looking at any part [of her], that is when he fears falling into sin if he were to look. The end [of the passage].

The lack of any mention of the paternal uncles or the maternal uncles is because it is more prudent that the women be covered up in their presence, lest they describe the women to their sons, since for the sons to imagine the women through such descriptions would be tantamount to them seeing them [in person].

Or their womenfolk who are devoted to them in companionship or service, being free believing women, since unbelieving women (*kawāfir*) are not concerned with the sin of describing their mistress to other men, in which case when such male non-relatives picture her it would in effect be like them looking at her. The act then of describing the places of ornament of believing women to male non-relatives counts as a sin (*ithm*) for believing women. Thus what is meant by *their womenfolk* is the women of their religious community, which is the opinion of the majority of the [pious] predecessors (*salaf*). The imam says that the opinion of the [pious] predecessors is to be considered recommended (*istiḥbāb*), even as the opinion of the school of law (*madhhab*) is that what is meant by *their womenfolk* is all women.

The *faqīr*[230] says the following: Most of the recognised works of commentary (*tafāsīr*) are loaded with the opinions of the [pious] predecessors, and they consider a woman who is a Jew or a Christian or a Zoroastrian or a pagan like the male non-relative in terms of [this] ruling, prohibiting thereby a Muslim woman from revealing her body before such a woman, unless the latter be her slave girl (*ama*), just as they have prohibited her from baring herself (*tajarrud*) before non-relatives. Overtly, the justification seems to be [based on] two things: incongruity in terms of religious faith, given that belief and unbelief separate them, and the lack of any assurance against their being described in the way mentioned. Thus it is necessary for the chaste women (*ʿafāʾif*) to avoid corrupt women (*fawāsiq*) and their company or [to avoid] baring themselves to them. It is for that reason that no marriage relationships (*munākaḥa*) are allowed between the Sunnīs and the Muʿtazila, as [stated] in the *Majmaʿ al-fatāwā*; this is because differences of creed and attribute amount to discrepancy in terms of religious practice (*dīn*) and essence (*dhāt*). May God set right the women of our times, for their character traits (*akhlāq*) resemble the character traits of unbelieving women. How, then, can a [believing] woman given to chastity and piety mix with unbelieving women in public baths (*ḥammāmāt*) and the like? ʿUmar b. al-Khaṭṭāb, may God be pleased with him, wrote to Abū ʿUbayda asking him to forbid the women of the People of the Book (*kitābiyyāt*) to enter the public baths with Muslim women.

Or what their right hands possess: slave girls, for a woman's male slave is like a male non-relative to her, whether he be castrated or potent (*faḥl*); that

[230] Burūsawī, the author himself.

is the opinion of Abū Ḥanīfa, may God have mercy on him, and is what the generality of the scholars follow. Thus she is not permitted to go on the pilgrimage with him or to travel with him, even if it may be permitted for him to see her if he is sure that there is no sexual desire on his part.

Shaykhzāda (Ibn al-Shaykh)[231] says, if one were to ask, 'What is the purpose of specifically mentioning slave girls after His words *or their womenfolk*?' the answer would be: And God knows best, that when He, exalted be He, says *or their womenfolk*, this is meant to indicate that it is not licit for a [Muslim] woman to reveal her ornament to unbelieving women, whether they be free women or slaves owned by others or by her. And so when He says *or what their right hands possess* without restriction, that is, whether these women be believers or idolaters (*mushrikāt*), it can be inferred that it is licit for a slave girl to look at her mistress's ornament, whether this slave girl be a Muslim or an unbeliever, because of the unavoidable necessity of revealing to her unbelieving slave girl the places of her hidden ornament when she is making use of her services. In this way, the [unbelieving] slave girl is distinct from the [unbelieving] free woman.

Or their male dependants lacking (sexual) desire: *irba* means 'need' (*ḥāja*). That is to say, men who are followers of the household and who have no need for women, the likes of decrepit old men and the disfigured (*mamsūkh*), spelled with a *khā'*; those whose potency and genitalia have lost their original health and have acquired a contrary state that prevents them from having any [sexual] need (*ḥāja*) for women, or for women to have any desire for them. Such a *mamsūkh* is called a *mukhannath*, whose genitalia are limp and whose manner of speaking is effeminate by virtue of birth, and as such has no need for women. As regards the full castrate (*majbūb*) and the partial eunuch (*khaṣiyy*), there is a difference of opinion: the full castrate is the one whose penis (*dhakar*) and testicles (*khiṣya*) have both been cut off (*j-b-b*), whereas the partial castrate is the one whose testicles only have been cut off. The opinion of choice here is that the partial castrate, the full castrate, as well as the impotent (*'anīn*), are, like others who are potent, not permitted to look [at women] because they will always feel desire, even if their members (*āla*) are of no help to them [in this regard].

[. . .]

Some have said that His words *and tell the believers to lower their gaze* [Q. 24:30] are unambiguous (*muḥkam*), whereas His words *and male dependants* are general, and what is unambiguous takes priority in terms of

[231] See the PA.

implementation. Thus there is no dispensation (*rukhṣa*) for those mentioned, such as the partial castrate and the like, to look at the beauties of women, even if there is no probability (*iḥtimāl*) of vice (*fitna*).

[According to] the *Kashshāf*:[232] 'It is not licit to retain castrates, employ them, sell them or buy them, for nothing has been transmitted to the effect that the [pious] predecessors used to retain them.' The end [of the citation].

In the *Niṣāb*, I have read in one of the volumes that Muʿāwiya walked in on some women, and with him was a castrated slave. One of the women was repulsed by him, whereupon Muʿāwiya exclaimed, 'But he is like a woman!' to which she replied, 'Are you suggesting that the fact that he has been mutilated makes licit what God had made illicit to the eyes!' and he was taken aback by her perspicacity and insight. The end [of the citation].

In the *Bustān*,[233] it is said that one should not castrate any son of Adam, for there is nothing to be gained from it, as a castrate is not permitted to look at women, just as the potent man is likewise not permitted to look, which is in contrast to the castration of animals. Do you not see that a castrated sheep has tastier meat and more fat, as has been elaborated on by others?

Or children uninitiated to the exposedness of women, due to the fact that they have not attained the ability to discriminate (*tamyīz*), meaning discovering (*iṭṭilāʿ*), or because they have not reached the level of desire in order to be generative, meaning to have mastery or power [over women]. [. . .]

Ṭifl is a collective noun acting as a plural, sufficiently indicated by the description [in the verse], similar to the [use of the] term *ʿaduww* (enemy) where He, exalted, says *for they are enemies* (*ʿaduwwun*) *to me* [Q. 26:77].

In the *Mufradāt*, the author says that a *ṭifl* is a child (*walad*), as long as he remains tender (*nāʿim*); *al-ṭufaylī* is a man well-known for attending any invitation.

In his commentary on the *Fātiḥa*, Master Fanārī says that the definition of a child (*ṭifl*) is [applied to an individual] from the moment that it is born and begins to cry until the completion of six years. The end [of the citation].

ʿAwra is the unseemly part (*saw'a*) of a human being, and functions metonymically; it derives from *ʿār* (shameful), and this is on account of the shame it provokes when this [nakedness] becomes manifest and is censured; that is why a woman is called *ʿawra*. Related to that is the word *ʿawrā'*, meaning a vile word, as stated in the *Mufradāt*.

232 Of Zamakhsharī (see above).

233 This is likely to be ʿImād al-Dīn Abū Hāmid Muḥammad b. Muḥammad al-Iṣfaḥānī (597/1201), *al-Bustān al-jāmiʿ li-jāmiʿ tawārīkh ahl al-zamān*, ed. ʿUmar ʿAbd al-Salām Tadmurī (Beirut, al-Maktaba al-ʿAṣriyya, 2002).

In the *Fatḥ al-qarīb*,[234] it is said: *ʿAwra* is anything that causes one to be ashamed (*istaḥā*) when it is manifested.

According to one *ḥadīth*: A woman is *ʿawra*, and He made her very being *ʿawra*, for once she appears, all become ashamed (*yustaḥyā minhu*) just as one does when one becomes ashamed when the *ʿawra* appears.

The linguists say that *ʿawra* is thus called because of its vileness when it appears and because the eyes are [naturally] turned away from it, and [the term] is derived from *al-ʿawr*, which signifies deficiency (*naqṣ*), shame (*ʿayb*) and vileness (*qubḥ*), and is related to *ʿawr al-ʿayn* (blind in one eye).

The *faqīr* says: One is given to understand from the statement about the child (*ṭifl*) that piety (*taqwā*) consists of preventing young boys (*ṣibyān*) from being in the presence of women when they have reached seven years of age. For the seven-year-old boy, even as he has not yet attained [sexual] desire, has attained the ability to discriminate (*tamyīz*), and even some who have not yet reached puberty can have [sexual] desire and thus no good would come from mixing with women [at that age].

In the *Multaqat* of al-Nāṣirī,[235] if a boy (*ghulām*) reaches manhood but is not comely (*ṣabīḥ*), then the ruling for men applies to him; but if he were comely, then he is treated according to the ruling governing women and is considered shameful (*ʿawra*) from head to toe, meaning that it is illicit to look at him out of desire. As for greeting (*salām*) and looking at him, but not out of desire, there is nothing wrong with that; this is why he is not commanded to the face veil (*niqāb*). The author [of the cited work] mentions a story of a dead scholar who was seen in a dream with a blackened face, and when asked about that, he replied, 'I saw a young boy in such-and-such a place and so I gazed at him and my face was burnt by the Fire.'

The *qāḍī* says: I heard the imam say that two satans (*shayṭān*) accompany every woman, while eighteen satans accompany a young boy.

It is loathsome to sit with youth (*aḥdāth*), boys (*ṣibyān*) and those of little intellect (*sufahāʾ*), because it is not dignified (*mahāba*), as [mentioned] in the *Bustān*.

In the *Anwār al-mashāriq*, the author states that it is forbidden (*ḥ-r-m*) for a man to gaze at the face of a beardless youth (*amrad*) if he be of fair features, whether it be a look of desire or otherwise and whether the one looking feels secure from temptation (*fitna*) or fears [falling into] it. A person who visits

[234] Probably: Muḥammad b. Qāsim al-Ghazī (d. 918/1512), *Fatḥ al-qarīb al-mujīb fī sharḥ alfāẓ al-taqrīb*, which exists in manuscript form but apparently has not been published. A digitised manuscript exists at the internet archive.

[235] The *Multaqat* is a Ḥanafī legal compendium by Nāṣir al-Dīn al-Ḥusaynī al-Samarqandī al-Madanī (d. 556/1161).

the baths should take care to preserve his eyes, hands and everything else from the shameful parts (*ʿawra*) of another, and should preserve his own nakedness from the gaze of others. The one who reveals his nakedness should be reprimanded (*inkār*).

And let them not stamp their feet to make known what they hide, that is, what they hide from sight, *of their ornament*: that is to say, [women] should not strike the ground with their feet to make their anklets jangle and thus make known that they are wearing anklets, for that provokes an inclination (*mayl*) to them on the part of the men and suggests that the women have an inclination for the men. And since it is illicit for the women to make non-relatives hear the sound of their anklets, then raising their voices to make their speech audible to non-relatives is all the more illicit, for the sound of a woman's [voice] is more likely to cause temptation than the sound of her anklet. That is why they consider it loathsome for a woman to make the call to prayer, since this [call] requires that they raise their voices.

The *faqīr* says: With this subtle analogy (*qiyās*), the question of women uttering remembrance aloud (*jahrī*) in some towns may be clarified. In the case of women, congregation (*jamʿiyya*) and voicing aloud (*jahr*) is to be greatly prohibited. They would be committing a great sin (*ithm ʿaẓīm*) by doing that, for if congregating and speaking aloud were to be a recommended (*mustaḥabb*) thing for them, then it would also be recommended in the ritual prayers (*ṣalāt*), the call to prayer (*adhān*) and the pilgrimage invocation (*talbiya*).

The author of the *Niṣāb al-iḥtisāb* says: One of the things that should be reckoned with in the case of women is their donning of anklet bells (*jalājil*) around their legs. Since it is loathsome for a child (*ṣaghīr*) to wear anklet bells around their legs, it is even more loathsome for an adult woman [to wear them], as their condition (*ḥāl*) is [always] premised on their being hidden (*tasattur*).

Turn to God in repentance all together O believers, since none of you will be innocent of remissness with regard to His commands and prohibitions, especially when it comes to refraining from desires (*shahawāt*); and *jamīʿan* (*all together*) is a circumstantial qualifier (*ḥāl*) of the subject of the verb *tūbū* (repent), that is to say, while your state is one of being together; [. . .] and *O believers* is an emphatic (*taʾkīd*) statement to solicit a response, and is a declaration that the attribute of having faith inevitably requires obedience (*imtithāl*) [of the command]. There is in this verse proof that sin (*dhanb*) does not exclude a servant from faith, since He says *O believers* after He has commanded [them] to turn in repentance, which is always attached to sin; *so that you may prosper* [means so] that you may secure felicity in both abodes.

God, exalted be He, has enjoined all believers to repentance and to seek forgiveness, as the weaker servant is never able to avoid a shortfalling on his part, even if he were to make a great effort (*ijtihād*) to be mindful of God's charges (*takālīf*). [. . .]

In the *Ta'wīlāt al-Najmiyya*, it is said that this indicates that repentance from sin is required of the initiate (*mubtadi'*), just as it is required from the one halfway along (*mutawassiṭ*) and from the one who has reached the end (*muntahī*), for the good deeds (*ḥasanāt*) of the pious (*abrār*) are the bad deeds (*sayyi'āt*) of the ones brought near (*muqarrabūn*). The Messenger of God (*ṣl'm*) used to say, 'Turn in repentance to God all together, for I verily repent to Him a hundred times each day'. Thus the repentance of the initiate is from forbidden things (*muḥarramāt*), and the repentance of the one halfway along is from the things additionally made licit (*zawā'id al-muḥallalāt*), and the repentance of the one who has reached the end is to shun all that is other than God entirely and to turn to God entirely.

So that you may prosper: The prosperity of the initiate is to be [turned] away from the Fire to the Garden; and that of the one halfway along is to be [turned] away from the garden of the earth to the highest of 'Illiyūn,[236] the stations (*maqāmāt*) and degrees (*darajāt*) of proximity (*qurb*); and that of the one who has reached the end is to be [turned] from the incarceration of metaphorical existence (*ḥabs al-wujūd al-majāzī*) to true existence (*wujūd ḥaqīqī*) and from the darkness of creation (*ẓulmat al-khalqiyya*) to the light of Lordship (*nūr al-rubūbiyya*). [. . .]

Some of the great masters (*al-kibār*) have said that God, exalted be He, demands repentance from all believers. And whoever believes in God and refrains from associating [others with Him] (*shirk*) has verily repented, and his repentance and return to God are sound, even if a passing inclination (*khāṭir*) should visit him and he were to commit an act of disobedience (*ma'ṣiya*) during that repentance. For when a believer is guilty of an act of disobedience, his chest becomes constricted, his heart anguished, and his spirit remorseful. The secret [workings] of this applies generally (*'umūm*). But the allusion here is specifically (*kuṣūṣ*) that they are [in a state of being] veiled, by virtue of being indefinite (*nakira*) in origin, such that any proximity to Him that they might encounter, or peacefulness in their stations (*maqām*), or in their witnessings (*mushāhada*), or in their spiritual knowledge (*ma'rifa*) is because of their affirmation of [His] Oneness (*tawḥīd*). That is to say: You are [all] behind the veils in this [spiritual] station. Repent from

[236] This is a reference to an afterlife place of reward (Q. 83:18–19), the root of which suggests 'high' or 'height' ('-*l*-*y*).

these [states] to Me, for to admire these [states] is the greatest form of idolatry (*shirk*) with regard to [the cultivation of] spiritual knowledge (*maʿrifa*). For the one who thinks that he has arrived (*w-ṣ-l*) shall harvest no knowledge of His existence (*wujūd*) or of the quintessence (*kunh*) of the majesty (*jalāl*) of His might (*ʿizza*). It is because of this that He has made repentance obligatory on them with every breath, and that is why the beloved (*ḥabīb*) of God [Muḥammad] cast himself headlong into the ocean of annihilation (*baḥr al-fanāʾ*), saying, 'Verily, my heart is all-consumed and I ask forgiveness of God a hundred times a day'. Thus it is understood that after every [moment of] repentance there follows closely another repentance, until you finally repent from all repentance and fall into the ocean of annihilation, overcome by the vision of eternity (*qidam*) and subsistence (*baqāʾ*). Our Lord! Appoint us among those who have been annihilated and granted subsistence.[237]

Faḍl Allāh

Faḍl Allāh frequently uses experiential language in his commentary; for instance, he often mentions the concept of *ḥaraka*, which is motion as a process of 'substantial transformation' (*jawhariyya*, cf. Mullā Ṣadra).[238] His unnecessarily dense language, complicated sentence structure and use of technical terms tend to obscure a relatively straightforward argument, which is that women should veil because they are inherently tempting to men; by removing the temptation as much as is reasonable and possible, people are protected from falling prey to their base instincts and are thus enabled to live a life that is more pure. For Faḍl Allāh, women know of their own power over men. The 'feminine part' of women is what attracts men, and it is why men seek women out; if faced with women showing their adornment in public life, they are unlikely to be able to control their 'instinctual emotions'. Thus women must only show themselves to their husbands. In the main, along with other modern conservative commentators, Faḍl Allāh uses modern language and arguments in order to bolster medieval *fiqh*; thus, for him, along with the medieval consensus, women should not cover their faces. He argues strongly against the *niqāb* (face covering). However, whereas several premodern commentators argued strongly for women to

[237] Burūsawī, *Rūḥ al-bayān*, s.v. Q. 24:31.

[238] On Faḍl Allāh's break with the traditional approach to *marjaʿiyya*, see Morgan Clarke, 'After the Ayatollah: Institutionalisation and Succession in the *marjaʿiyya* of Sayyid Muḥammad Ḥusayn Faḍl Allāh', *Die Welt des Islams* 56.2 (2016), 153–86; also Walbridge, *The Most Learned of the Shiʿa*, esp. ch. 12; Aziz, 'Fadlallah and the Remaking of the *Marjaʿiya*', 205–15. More recently, a consideration of Faḍl Allāh's intellectual formation and commentary on the Qurʾān has been written by Maria Pakkala, '"Take not Jews and Christians as Intimates!" Depictions of Jews and Christians in Modern Shīʿī Qurʾānic Exegesis' (Unpublished PhD dissertation, University of Helsinki, 2019).

wear makeup and other adornment that made them more feminine, and all took it for granted that women would wear kohl around their eyes (listing this as one of the 'visible adornments'), for Faḍl Allāh, women's makeup is artificial adornment and is thus prohibited.

The lexical meanings

Al-ghaḍḍ is to close the folds of [the] eyelid, one over the other. [Ṭabrisī] says in the *Majmaʿ*: The original meaning of *al-ghaḍḍ* is diminution (*nuqṣān*). One says, 'He lowered his voice (*ghaḍḍa min ṣawtihi*) or his eyes.' *Bi-khumurihinna*: *Khumur* is the plural of *khimār*, and [it] is what a woman covers her head with. *Juyūbihinna*: [This is] the plural of *jayb*, which is an opening at the top of the garment, and what is meant by that here are the breasts (*ṣudūr*). *Buʿūlatihinna*: *Buʿūla* is 'husbands' (*azwāj*). *Al-irba* is 'need' (*ḥāja*).

Regarding the rulings governing gazing and concealing

One of the objectives of Islam is to penetrate the inner being of man in order to purify his spirit and nurture him as an individual by setting firm a trajectory of uprightness for his life, such that his adherence to that path becomes a part of his internal constitution and so that acts issue forth from him in a spontaneous manner, and not as a result of sudden instances of [devotional] commitment that at times place pressure on his [spiritual] movement but that at other times recede. That is why God's laws (*tashrīʿ*) submit to a scheme in which rulings vary according to a variety of instances, the object of which is to encompass the human being in all of his dimensions so that the path might become upright and [his] experience might acquire depth, and so that the general idea [for his spiritual development] might be set in motion from a position of strength.

That is why He has set the relationship between a man and woman, and the latter's relationship to him, to be governed by precise laws (*qawāʿid*), which regulate situations in which desire is awakened and the body's basic instinct (*gharīza*) is stirred (*ḥaraka*).[239] This is so that the relationship might remain natural and pristine (*naẓīfa*), subsumed under the broader moral

[239] Faḍl Allāh is able to play on the various nuances of the single word *ḥaraka* to remain within reference to his philosophical/existential concept.

(*akhlāqī*) frame for the purity of the spirit[240] and the body, and so that [it should rest] on the basis of a principle of chasteness (*ʿiffa*) in both of their persons, which takes shape as a result of persistent practice and which animates this thought in [their] essential being (*dhāt*) and effects an immunity (*manāʿa*) along the [path of spiritual] movement.

These verses are there to speak about two important topics in this respect, the topic of gazing and that of the revealing of ornaments, [precisely] because of the effect these have on the awakening of instinctual emotions (*mashāʿir gharīziyya*). A look can reflect instinctual attraction, feeding as it does the imagination, and has an unsettling effect, steering feelings towards deviance (*inḥirāf*). For the very tangible images that a human being may see stoke the fire of instinct and interact with subtle elements in a human's essential make-up, affecting him negatively.

As for the revealing of the ornament, this prompts a psychological state of mind (*jaww nafsī*) in which a woman's seductive self stirs in her an emotional awareness of her physical beauty and of the seductive talents that she possesses, which invite the admiration of men and stir their basic instincts. That means that the feminine aspect is of immense importance to a woman's personality during her life; it secures for her a distinct place in the heart of a man or in his life. That also makes her [constantly] monitor situations in which there is a reaction to her beauty, and this [in turn] becomes for her a series of different ways of moving about to be seductive, ending up with her unrelenting attention to her ornament and to [ways of] animating her instincts. She thereby begins to forsake attending to the other aspects of personhood, which in turn has a negative effect on life in Muslim society and on moral behaviour in general.

Objections and responsa

Some people will be given to think that all of this means that Islam attempts to oppress a woman by extinguishing that primordial feminine dimension [which is] so deeply embedded in her personhood; that it attempts to limit her ability to express that aspect of her personhood when she reveals the ornament bestowed upon her by God as one of His greatest graces to humankind; and that it wills that men and women live in [sexual] repression when

[240] It is clear that Faḍl Allāh intends the soul here, but given modern standard Arabic's loss of the original meaning of *nafs*, only *rūḥ* might invoke that idea in the mind of a modern audience.

faced with instances of beauty in life, which creates in them an intractable [psychological] complex, as is the case frequently with individuals faced with situations of privation and repression.

Such people consider that the prohibition against the revealing of ornament and forbidding [men] from looking at women constitute an unjustified fear of beauty, which is one of the manifestations of God's power in His creation and one of His graces to humankind and in life. These very people might add that the measure of chasteness is a human being's ability not to succumb to deviance when confronted with instances in which [sexual] instinct is stirred by physical beauty, through the power of the moral constitution that one possesses, which allows him to face all of that in a natural way. 'Chasteness' is not to escape from such situations, because escape reflects an essential weakness in the face of the factors leading to deviance; that means that power is only in play when one distances oneself from the problem and not when one confronts it. The moral law in human beings exists so that they can be near a firestorm and not be burned by it, not so that they should run far away from it.

The response to all of that is: Islam does not desire to obliterate a woman's femininity; nay, it seeks to emphasise it as a natural human condition, connected to the extension of a human being's life and as attending to one's instinctive sexual needs, as is the case with food and drink and the like, all of which impose more than one [kind of] need that is stirred in both men and women at the level of spiritual feelings that each of the two experience along the trajectory of their relationship, including the sensual pleasures that each of them enjoy when [sexual] instinct calls. Islam, however, does not want the feminine aspect in a woman as well as the masculine aspect in a man to eclipse the other dimensions of their personhood and render life entirely in the service of that [aspect], with the result that a woman goes around in society seeking only what stirs, or is stirred by, her feminine spirit and a man goes around looking only for what sexually stirs his masculine spirit. But, rather, it wants that aspect specific to each of the two to function within the sphere of a conjugal relationship that is established on the basis of the freedom to choose a partner who is suitable in terms of behaviour (*sulūkiyyan*), appearance (*jamāliyyan*) and mindset (*nafsiyyan*), so that with that [partner] he [or she] is able to relieve the hunger of [sexual] instinct (*gharīza*) and satisfy the maternal or paternal instincts (*naz'a*) [inherent] in a human being, paving the way for an environment (*jaww*) congenial to a spiritual and emotional partnership in more than one way.

Islam posits marriage as the legal basis for sexual relations and as a [sexual] release for that male and female, and there is a need to open up to this important aspect of life; it also considers female society as an arena in which women should be able to be free to reveal their ornament and to satisfy their inclination to manifest their corporeal beauty and to attain, as a result of that, self-fulfilment at this level. But it does not give her the room to set out in public life from her position as a female, nor does it give the man freedom to enjoy a woman's beauty unrestrained, even with respect to just looking, since that disturbs the peace of a balanced psychological state and ultimately only transforms the entire affair to resemble something like sexual chaos.

As for the issue of psychological complexes that arise and the question of wondering about the causes of a fear of beauty, which is a manifestation of divine power and grace, and the matter of considering modesty (*'iffa*) as a stance under some kind of [ethical] trial and not extrinsic to it, it suffices to counter that by alluding to a critical point, which is that a complex in the self almost always arises as a result of engrossed indulgence of illicit things or in things desired but out of reach. That precipitates a violent struggle within [the self] between the divine law or reality and desire or need. The complex emotional state, wavering between instances of pull and attraction, is thus transformed into a psychological complex that asphyxiates the inner comfort of the self.

To wit, prohibition should not become a complex, and that [is possible] when a human being faces the prohibitions of the divine law and subsists in a life of faith, which opens up his heart and mind to God across the horizons of His pleasure on the premise that human beings need to be mindful of Him in the same way that they need Him to exist, with the full sense that His knowledge of what sets him right and what corrupts him is greater than his knowledge of that in himself. The conceptual comparison made by faith between general [public] welfare – which, across many of its horizons, does not drift far from the welfare of the human individual – and private welfare – which, in some respects, may satisfy some desire of his, even as it clashes with many other more important and more pressing needs of his in other respects – is a comparison that will keep him connected to reality and will open his eyes to the negative and positive consequences of choices made in that [reality] until he is able to form his own personal convictions about the meaningfulness of a social sphere open to [the full possibilities of] life in instances of prohibition, so that desisting from that [prohibited thing] leaves but a few subtle vestiges in him that pass in terms of sense and feeling in a very transitory way. As for the issue of beauty and its interaction with human artistic or aesthetic values, it cannot be circumscribed within this specific sphere, where values are mixed up with natural instincts and artistic sentiment with sexual sentiment, a matter that has a negative effect on the social peace at the level of general [social] principles, which means that the guardianship of this public matter falls under the responsibility of divine laws in order to diminish in everyday spaces the factors that lead to deviance and to restrict these spheres of complexity that harm the system of public morality.

According to Islam, art and beauty do not constitute absolute values, but rather represent two instances of wondrous creation that allow human beings to catch sight of God and of life from a spiritual and moral standpoint and keep them away from spheres in which this standpoint is completely displaced, as is the case with all sweet things in life whose sweetness a human being should experience both spiritually and materially, but in a manner that does not lead to his fall. Life cannot be viewed on the basis of absolutes, either when evaluating its concepts or its contents, for life itself does not hold any absolutes, even when it comes to its own existence, but rather is based on a series of limits imposed in more than one arena. That is why one can only confront matters in a relational way that balances between one limit and another as each [of these] impacts the major issues of life positively or negatively. In light of this, art and beauty and other concepts implied in existence must be in the service of the social order in which human beings find themselves, instead of the social order itself being in the service of these [concepts]. For that [latter] would damage the harmony of art and the aesthetics of beauty and would result in a disfigurement of forms and ugliness in reality.

As for the matter of modesty being intrinsic to the [human] experience as opposed to extrinsic, that is correct, but a human being invariably needs edification in order not to fall into the Fire and to forsake the experience [itself]. The restraints of the Law in the sphere of human relationships always have as their objective the protection of the social milieu against any negative consequences that might steer these relationships into a sphere of volatility, and not one of stability, which means that it [the Law] has that much more immunity and capacity to counter severe [social] pressures within which lie in store the winds of insanity at more than one level. That is why these [restraints] are directed at giving more depth to the experiential dimension of the self and [are] not meant as a means to escape it.

Rounding off this exposition, we are thus able to arrive at a definitive conclusion: the rules governing 'looking' [at] and the revealing of a woman's ornament are wholly connected to the overall concept that Islam wishes to animate in the life of a human being for the purpose of [creating] a pristine relationship [with others] and a purified personality, alongside balanced behaviour within the society of men and women. One should not consider these legislations in an abstract manner and divorce them from the things with which they are organically connected, exactly like in any scientific study of an Islamic legal ruling, where one must recognise the sphere to which it is connected and within which it operates, and that for the purpose of understanding its general trajectory and the course along which it moves.

Lowering the gaze

Tell the believing women to lower their gaze: Most of the commentators [say] that the command to lower [the gaze] here means avoiding looking altogether. Some might understand it metonymically as referring to lowering the eyes so that the beholder does not behold the entirety of the thing looked at; that is because some have mentioned that *ghaḍḍ al-baṣar* means to sever it (*kasr*), as opposed to what others have mentioned, namely that it means to close the eyelids, which prevents looking altogether.

The *ḥadīth* that is reported regarding the reason for the revelation [of this verse] somewhat suggests the more common meaning, however. In the *Kāfī*, the following is transmitted via a chain on the authority of Saʿad al-Iskāf from Abū Jaʿfar [al-Ṣādiq] (*ʿm*): A young man from the Anṣār came across a woman in Medina – and women then used to veil themselves behind the ears – and he looked at her as she came towards him. As she passed him, he kept looking as he entered into an alleyway, the name of which he said was the Banū something [street], and when he turned to look at her, his face was struck by a pole or a piece of glass sticking out of the wall and which gashed his face. When the woman had gone, he looked down and saw blood pouring down his chest and robe. He then said, 'By God, I shall go to the Messenger of God (*ṣlʿm*) and tell him [about this].' And so when he came to him, the Messenger of God (*ṣlʿm*) saw him and asked, 'What happened?' And he told him. Gabriel then came down with this verse: *And tell the believers to lower their gaze and safeguard their private parts. That is purer for them. Surely God is aware of what they contrive* [Q. 24:30].

But the thought might occur that in the story it sounds like the young man was staring with eyes wide open in a desirous and lascivious manner, which does not entail that the required thing is to avoid looking [altogether], but rather to lower the gaze and sever it such that it does not constitute a gaping stare that inspects the entire details of the body and the tempting parts of it. The meaning of the verse then stands for desisting from looking in a desirous or covetous way. We are able to confirm this view by probing deeply the sense of the word *min*, overtly a partitive [preposition], which means that what is required is to lower part of the gaze and not all of it. That is because coordinating the plural forms where He says *yaghuḍḍū min abṣārihim* [Q. 24:30] entails necessarily that it [the command] be distributed among [several] individuals, with the meaning thus being: let each man lower of his gaze, and not his entire gaze. Some mention that the import of this partitive is connected to the subject of looking and not with the manner of it. In other words: to lower the gaze away from what is illicit and confining it to what is licit. However, the case is the opposite of what is apparent, since what is immediately understood from the word *baṣar* is the eye and the partitive must thus be connected to it and not to what it is directed at or what it looks at. Al-Akhfash, according to what the author of *al-Kashshāf* has transmitted, permits that it be a redundant [particle], whereas Sībawayh rejects that. Perhaps the latter is correct, since there is no evidence to indicate that it is redundant.

The author of the *Mīzān* commentary [Ṭabāṭabāʾī] mentions that the word *min* indicates an incipient purpose, and is neither redundant nor generic or partitive, responding to every opinion on that matter, so that the meaning is: let them sever [their gazes], starting with their eyes. But this contradicts the apparent sense, since the verse is set up to talk about the manner of looking and not about anything incipient or anything to do with ultimate purpose. In light of that, the apparent sense of the verse is that one should avoid deliberately looking at those things that are illicit for him when he comes across them. This then leads him not to counter those kinds of things that turn up in front of him, and which he encounters by chance, with a full stare, but rather with a diminished look, so that he is turned away from any prolonged inspection of every detail of that [forbidden thing].

Disagreement over the signification of the verse

There is another disagreement over what is signified by the verse, and that has to do with its comprising an apparently unqualified attachment, such that it is illicit to look at the bodies of believing women, without any qualification and including all parts of the body. Because when one omits an attachment it suggests a comprehensive [statement], especially when we note that by its very nature the desired principle does not accord with the passage indicating the nature of legal responsibility (*taklīf*) with regard to the acts of believers. For there is no point in talking about the obligation of lowering [the gaze] without talking about what that [gaze] might be attached to. They might consider that directing the command to lower [the gaze] once to the believing men and once to the believing women makes it clear that believing men should lower their gaze from believing women and that believing women should lower their gaze from believing men. Thus the attachment is mentioned as an equation, so that it has a comprehensive signification for both parties.

But there is yet another point of view, which is that it might well be that the verse appears in order to affirm the principle [of lowering the gaze] as a prelude to talking about the legal rulings, so that talking about the details [of that principle] would occur in other sections of the Book. This may be inferred on the basis of the illicitness of revealing [one's] ornament, for example; or that what is illicit for a woman to reveal is illicit for a man to look at; or that something may become manifest of a woman's 'inviolables', which men are not permitted to violate; or from the details described by the Prophet Muḥammad (*ṣlʿm*) regarding those parts of a woman's body or a man's body that it is illicit to look at. It is perhaps this that some exegetes point to in their opinions that it is obligatory to lower the gaze from what is illicit and to restrict the sight to what is permitted when these [illicit parts] are manifest. This can be inferred from specific proofs and that is why the omission of the attached referent does not imply comprehensiveness, since the equation of [the mention of] believing men and believing women with a view to legal responsibility [for each] does not make it apparent that either of the two sides is the one intended as the object of the gaze categorically. It may be that there are some reports that indicate that the referent of the obligation to lower the gaze is the private parts, as mentioned in the *Kāfī* in those reports on the authority of the imam Jaʿfar al-Ṣādiq (*ʿm*) where he says: He has thus forbidden them to look at their private parts and [forbidden] a man to look at the private parts of his fellow [believer]. This is supported by the fact that the mention of the referent in the second sentence proves that that is what is intended by the first sentence in which the referent is omitted.

The safeguarding of private parts

And safeguard their private parts: The apparent sense of the safeguarding of the private parts is safeguarding them from acts of fornication. However, disparate *ḥadīth*s have been transmitted suggesting that what is meant by this here is the safeguarding of these [private parts] from sight, as is mentioned in the *ḥadīth* on the authority of the imam Jaʿfar al-Ṣādiq (*ʿm*) where he says: Everything in the Qurʾān about the safeguarding of private parts is about fornication, with the exception of this verse where it is [safeguarding them] from sight. This has been reported on the authority of Ibn Zayd as transmitted from the author of *al-Kashshāf* [al-Zamakhsharī], who said: Everything in the Qur'ān about the preservation of private parts is about fornication, except in this case where what is meant is to cover up (*istitār*).

This [sense] appears close enough and is suggested by the overall thrust of this section of the *sūra*, where the discussion revolves around matters of covering up and looking, as in the details of covering up that God desires in the case of women, which makes the question in this case not far off from that. In consequence, this verse – and what follows – comes to constitute a clarification of what one should lower one's gaze from and what one should cover up from sight. This is especially so when we recognise that guarding private parts from sight is an obligation for both men and women, whether the onlooker be a man or a woman, since looking at private parts is forbidden for men and women with their counterparts and others, and God knows best [. . .].[241]

The parts to be covered up

And tell the believing women to lower their gaze so that they do not fill their eyes with what is forbidden to look at and so that they do not do it intentionally; *and safeguard their private parts* from acts of fornication, or from gazing, covering them up from the eyes of male and female onlookers. In this section of the verse, a discussion might arise about its being about the illicitness of women looking at men, by way of correspondence to men looking at women, which has already been discussed. This can well be confirmed by the well-known *ḥadīth* on the authority of the Messenger (*ṣlʿm*) about the story of Ibn Umm Maktūm transmitted through Umm Salama, may God be pleased with her, where she says: I was at the Prophet's house and there was Maymūna with him. Ibn Umm Maktūm then walked in – and this was after we had been commanded to veil – and he entered into our presence, whereupon he [the Prophet] said, 'Take your cover'. We then said, 'But O Messenger of God, is he not blind and unable to see us?' He said, 'And you two, are you blind, that you do not see him?'

We might mention here a couple of *ḥadīth*s in support, as well as some in contradiction. An example is the story of Fāṭima bt. Qays, as reported by Muslim and Abū Dāwūd, where it is said that when her husband divorced her, the Messenger of God (*ṣlʿm*) commanded her to sit out her waiting

241 There is an ensuing brief commentary by Faḍl Allāh that concludes Q. 24:30, which we omit here.

period (*ʿidda*) in the house of Umm Sharīk, the Anṣārī woman, but then said, 'Actually, my companions frequently visit that woman, so wait out your period in the house of Umm Maktūm, for he [Ibn Umm Maktūm] is a blind man and you will be able to take off your clothes [when you want to]'. Some have tried to reconcile both matters, saying: Women looking at men who are non-relatives is not of the same severity as men looking at women who are non-relatives. And so, even as it is not licit for the women to deliberately turn their eyes to look at the men face to face during communal sessions, the women are allowed to look at the men while they pass them in the street, or while the men are engaged in licit activities from a distance. Indeed, there is nothing wrong with women looking at men at home when there is a real need.

However, we note that the narrative thread is the same when it comes to the command directed at believing men and the command directed at believing women, which itself suggests that the ruling appears on this subject to issue a principle rather than details, leaving this last to other passages, or [to issue] from the point of view of the inner significance beneath extended gazing and eyeing that then suggests [sensual] provocation. The command then appears in order to be circumscribed to looking, indicating a natural fleeting situation, not a deliberate provocative one, or as [issuing] from a specific motive, which is the private parts, in one possible interpretation as previously discussed. We would be able to infer this signification from the customary manner of life among Muslims, where men are not veiled from women and women are not forbidden from looking at men in a spontaneous way in public and private life. If that were explicitly forbidden, the matter would have been a pressing one for Muslim society and a matter about which there would be much inquiry with respect to the legal obligations under the Law. But we find that this has not left much of a trace in Islamic jurisprudence, either during the early period of Islam or at any other later time.

The illicitness of women revealing ornament

And let them not reveal their ornament: Some have mentioned that what is meant by *ornament* here is the places where ornaments sit, since the things used for ornament, such as earrings and bracelets, are not in themselves forbidden to be revealed. Therefore, the prohibition against revealing the ornament stands in as [a prohibition against] revealing the places where it sits, for covering up ornaments cannot be separated from covering its locations. The author of *al-Kashshāf*, in applying an analogy to this, says: The reason for mentioning *ornament* [. . .].[242]

Some might indeed mention that what is meant by *ornament* is its overt signification: the jewellery and clothes and the like that one adorns oneself with, in the ways in which women generally adorn their heads, their faces and other parts of their body, and which in our day is generally expressed with the term 'make-up' (*tajmīl*). Therefore, the verse appears as an overt prohibition against the sort of self-exposure (*tabarruj*) by which a woman reveals her entire ornament. It may be that this interpretation (*iḥtimāl*) is the one that emerges by virtue of the word's lexical import (*madlūl lughawī*), signifying what a woman uses to adorn herself with of those external items. This does not contradict the idea that it is permitted to reveal ornament *qua* ornament, because what is intended thereby is ornament as it sits on some part of the body, and not anywhere else. However, there is a *ḥadīth* related on the authority of the imam Jaʿfar al-Ṣādiq (*ʿm*) reported in *al-Kāfī* with a chain of transmission via al-Fuḍayl [b. Yasār], in which the following is said: I asked Abū ʿAbd Allāh [al-Ṣādiq] (*ʿm*), about a woman's arms, and whether they constitute [part of her] ornament, about which God says *And let them not reveal their ornament except to their husbands*. He said, 'Yes, and also all ornament other than the veil (*khimār*) and the bracelets (*siwār*)', which confirms that what is meant by this [verse] is the places where the ornaments sit.

Ornament that is permitted

Except what is apparent of it: Overtly, what is meant by this is the face, the hands and the feet, as related in the report on the authority of the imam Jaʿfar al-Ṣādiq (*ʿm*) where he says: What is a man permitted to see of a woman when he is not unmarriageable to her? He [the imam] said, 'The face, the hands and the feet'. It is apparent from some reports [transmitted] on his authority regarding His words, mighty and majestic, that regarding *except what is apparent of it*, he [the imam] said that the apparent ornament is kohl and rings, and in others [he said] a ring or a band (*fatkha*), which is a *qulab*; this also suggests the meaning already mentioned, namely that what is intended is the ornament itself in that part [of the body] and not only where it sits.

242 At this point, and as indicated in the edition of Faḍl Allāh's text by Faḍl Allāh himself, Zamakhsharī's comments on the same verse in his *al-Kashshāf* is quoted verbatim at length (see *q.v.* Zamakhsharī, above).

Some commentaries hold that what is meant by His words *what is apparent of it* is 'that which is apparent and cannot be concealed' or 'ornament that appears, but unintentionally'. The sentence [in the verse] proves that women ought not reveal such ornament deliberately unless it becomes apparent without any intention on her part, such as when a garment becomes sparse when winds blow and something of the ornament is revealed, for example, or in cases where that [ornament] is itself apparent and cannot be hidden, such as garments that women wear over their clothes, since that cannot be [completely] hidden, but is something that would draw attention being worn as it is by a woman. There is no reprimand on the part of God, exalted be He, for that. That is the meaning of this verse pointed out by [the likes of] ʿAbd Allāh b. Masʿūd, al-Ḥasan al-Baṣrī, Ibn Sīrīn and Ibrāhīm al-Nakhaʿī. Such commentators add that the other commentators say the opposite of that, namely that the meaning of *what is apparent of it* is what a human being makes apparent by habit, subsuming in that [interpretation] a woman's face and hands, including everything on them that is ornament. In other words, it is acceptable, according to them, for a woman to adorn her face with kohl, powder or paint, and her hands with henna, rings, bangles and bracelets, and walk among people with her face and hands revealed. This meaning of the verse has been reported on the authority of ʿAbd Allāh b. ʿAbbās and his students, and is the opinion of a large group of Ḥanafī jurisprudents.

Those [first] commentators would respond to that by saying: As for us, we are barely able to comprehend on what linguistic basis it is possible for the meaning of *what is apparent* to be what a human being makes apparent deliberately. And this is very clear and can hardly be missed by anyone. The overall sense of the verse then is that the Qurʾān prohibits revealing ornament but grants licence (*r-kh-ṣ*) when it becomes apparent unintentionally. To then take liberty with this licence to the point of [making it mean] what is made apparent deliberately is something that contravenes the Qurʾān and contradicts the reports, both of which establish that women at the time of the Prophet did not used to expose themselves before non-relatives with their faces unveiled (*sāfirāt*) and that the command to veil also included [veiling] the face so that the full body veil (*niqāb*) had formed part of women's dress, except in the case of [entering into] pilgrim sanctity (*iḥrām*).

It seems that such exercising of individual reasoning when understanding the Qurʾān and its legal rulings depends on the [social] context and the surrounding environment governing the manner of veiling in which the commentator lived, in a way that made the form familiar to his taste and understanding. And this leads him to understand the Qurʾān on that basis. It may well be that this was the reason behind many of the legal opinions (*fatwa*) by jurisprudents declaring the obligation to cover up the face and hands. But we would like to debate this understanding by focusing on the phrase *except what is apparent of it*, which this kind of commentator understood as signifying occasional and spontaneous display not resulting from any personal choice on the part of that person. And we can then indeed note that this does not lead to the conclusion desired by him, since the appearance of something by itself may issue out of the very nature of that social situation to which people are habituated during their lifetime, such that they practise it in an involuntary way that comes about on account of the habit and custom for that thing to be apparent. The original sense in this regard is for these to appear, as the author of the commentary *al-Kashshāf* has said.

The reports do not establish that the command was to fully veil (*niqāb*) with the face being covered. Indeed, the allusion to casting wraps over cleavage, as comes later in the verse, suggests that there is no requirement to veil the face; if it were so, it would have been more befitting that it should be mentioned, considering that revealing it is one of those matters that is not confined to a specific group of people who lived in the first generations of Islam, whereas the revealing of cleavage was something that was part of all ages.

We are in fact able to infer the permissibility of revealing the face and hands in a categorical way on the basis of the emphatic prohibition of covering them up during the state of pilgrim sanctity (*iḥrām*), for that is the state in which it would be confirmed whether something must be covered up out of obligation. For, to reveal is not something that accords with the naturally pure state in which the pilgrim is required to distance himself from instances of temptation. That in turn leads us to infer that this matter, which in ordinary situations is permitted, becomes obligatory during the state of pilgrim sanctity – so that a woman might suffer the heat of the sun on her face just as a man suffers its heat on his head – as related by the tradition which says, 'A woman's state of pilgrim sanctity is on the basis of her face, while a man enters pilgrim sanctity on the basis of his head'.

Casting wraps over cleavage

And let them cast their wraps over their cleavage: cast their wraps, which are head coverings (*aghṭiyat al-ra's*), over their *juyūb*, the *jayb* being – according to some opinions – the opening of a shirt garment; and what is meant by this is the breast, on the basis of naming something by the place in which it sits. In light of that, it is an obligation for women to conceal their breasts and necklines (*naḥr*) with the cover that [also] conceals their heads. They mention that during the time of the *jāhiliyya*, women's shirt openings were wide enough to reveal their necklines and breasts and the surrounding area. Moreover, they used to let their veils hang behind them and so these would be revealed. They were thus commanded to let them hang at the front in order to cover those [parts].

And let them not reveal their ornament except to their husbands: their male spouses (*azwāj*), for the husband is entitled to see what he wishes of his wife; *or their fathers, or their husbands' fathers*, including the fathers and grandfathers on the father's and mother's side, given the good character of the father in all cases, *or their sons*, including children and their children, *or their husbands' sons*, including their grandchildren, *or their brothers*, from the father and the mother, or from either of the two, *or their brothers' sons or sisters' sons*, being the children and grandchildren. As for the permissibility of revealing the ornament to these, that is due to the relationship that the woman has with them, a relationship of a specific nature, governed by psychological barriers that prevent them from entertaining sexual thoughts or from being attracted by instinct to her, given the legal rulings, social traditions and human values deeply entrenched in the consciousness of people that make them unmarriageable to her; that renders sexual attraction to them a case of [sexual] deviance, which is far removed from what is familiar and from what is the natural state of affairs for human relationships.

However, this matter is also likely to admit many forms of psychological unsettling that may drive a human being to deviant and abnormal behaviour, or to assaulting his daughter, or sister, or sister's daughter or his brother on account of immoral orientations that stir up instinctual desire in the direction of rebelliousness and towards what is illicit, or on account of pornographic films and erotic novels and the like, of which we hear a lot in our contemporary world. Thus there must be continuous monitoring of the movement of relationships and regulation of [sexually] provocative conditions and an effort to find external restraints in addition to internal restraints within the depths of the self. Experiments have proven that reliance on traditional approaches in such matters does not realise any guarantees of immunity. It is thus fairly easy to dissipate spiritual and moral values when faced with a cultural orientation that is in contradiction with these [values] in all manner of deviant ways.

Or their womenfolk: There is disagreement over what is meant by *womenfolk* here. Does it mean Muslim women, since a Muslim woman is not permitted to reveal her ornament to a non-Muslim woman, and so she is required to cover up before her just as she would cover up before non-relative males? Or does it mean all women, so that this juxtaposition becomes notably more consonant with the preceding mode of articulation? What the *ḥadīth*s reported on the authority of the family of the Prophet, peace be upon them, suggest is that it is reprehensible to reveal ornament before non-Muslim women. In the book *al-Faqīh*,[243] the following is mentioned: Ḥafṣ b. al-Bukhturī reported on the authority of Abū ʿAbd Allāh Jaʿfar al-Ṣādiq (*ʿm*) that he said: A woman should not reveal herself in front of a Jewish or Christian woman, for they can then describe her to their husbands. The verification of that [report] may be delegated to the books of jurisprudence.

Or what their right hands possess, of slave girls and female servants. Some say that this includes [male] slaves, and this has been reported on the authority of the imam Jaʿfar al-Ṣādiq (*ʿm*). The issue is a matter of jurisprudential debate among Muslim jurists.

Or their male dependants lacking (sexual) desire: These are individuals who have no desire for women, from among servants and hired hands, who are of an advanced age, or who have some physical weakness that impedes their sexual capacity, or who suffer from a mental disability that places them in a state of stable unawareness. Revealing the ornament to these will not result in any arousal or impinge on a woman's chasteness.

Or children uninitiated to the exposedness of women: These are children who have not reached the age of discrimination and are ignorant of the function of women's private parts when it comes to the [sexual] instinct and are unable to distinguish these from the other parts of the body. They also say that this is a euphemism for prepubescence, and so what is meant by *uninitiated to the exposedness of women* is that they do not have the physical capacity or the familiarity, meaning the capacity to master matters that are unseemly when explicitly said to women, such as coitus and the like.

And let them not stamp their feet to make known what they hide of their ornament, such as anklets, necklaces, earrings and bangles. From this we are able to infer the obligation to shun what arouses men and drives them to entertain thoughts of illicit relationships.

Turn to God in repentance all together O believers so that you may prosper [means] so that you might set aright your corrupted deeds and keep your distance from factors that lead to deviance, and so that you might set off along the path of faith that is driven by Qurʾānic moral basis. For, that sets up for you the means for prosperity in this world and in the Hereafter, as repentance signifies being remorseful of deviant forms of behaviour that have taken place in the past and a resolve to set aright deeds in the future.[244]

243 *Mān lā yaḥḍuruhu al-faqīh* by al-Shaykh al-Ṣadūq.
244 Faḍl Allāh, *Min waḥy al-Qurʾān*, s.v. Q. 24:31.

Interviews

Sa'diyya Shaikh

Sa'diyya Shaikh argues that modesty in the dress and in one's gaze involves not sexualising oneself or another; these injunctions are the same for both men and women, with the additional stipulation on women to cover the bosom. In her view, approaching one another in a non-sexualised way allows for a deeper level of engagement as human beings. Speaking from a South African context, she considers herself to be in modest dress without any head covering. For Shaikh, styles of dress that seem to be the opposite (either face coverings or miniskirts) might inadvertently draw equal levels of attention to the body in ways that are not optimally nourishing for women.

Karen Bauer: If you agree that modesty is a virtue in the Qurʾān, what does that mean today, and how may men and women embrace an ethic of modesty to be implemented in the public sphere, and how indeed does that relate to Q. 24:31 about believing women lowering their gaze and the sort of modesty that was enjoined on them there?

Sa'diyya Shaikh: We all know that the verse before the verse that you describe was speaking about men also lowering their gaze and guarding their private parts. The extra part [in Q. 24:31] is really about not displaying your bosom and *ornament*, for people to cover up the bosom.

I think that the notion of modesty is a really important virtue for both men and women alike. And what I really appreciate about this verse is that the locus for modesty is an internal locus, first of all. The idea of lowering your gaze is about a certain internal way of engaging the other. Lowering the gaze means that you do not boldly stare at people in a sexual way. It has a whole level of signification about not sexualising people through your gaze, and about guarding your chastity and your private parts. It is about essentially rejecting promiscuity as a way of engaging. And in terms of Qurʾānic verses and in terms of social engagements, I think that those points are incredibly important.

We are in an age right now where it seems that in popular culture, the more flesh you show, for both men and women, the more liberated you are. In fact, I think the more hostage you are to a certain kind of body, to a certain kind of embodiment, to a certain way of engaging the other that is premised primarily [on the body], the more restricted is your humanity. No doubt the body is a beautiful thing that should be celebrated, but there are certain ways in which modesty protects that celebration in the context of intimate relationships. The idea of having one's body on display has become a different kind of marker. Now, earlier Western feminist notions of bra burning and particularly strong ways of asserting the female body were forms of resistance to dominant patriarchal modes of women's embodiment. Now, versions of popular culture – and that is not feminist necessarily, because many Western feminists argue against it as well – seem to say that the sexier you are and the more flesh you show, the more liberated you are, when in fact, in my view, it often reflects being hostage to the lower self. It is a hostage to the lower self and it does not allow human beings to be able to engage with the fullness of one another.

Physical modesty, and sexual modesty, is an important Islamic virtue, and it is an important virtue for this time, and how we think about that must be about ways that allow men and women [to interact] with each other, men with each other, women with each other, to engage in ways that allow us to be fully embodied human beings, that allow us to respect each other for those parts of ourselves that truly matter. And within an Islamic framework that is about what kind of human being you are, not necessarily about how a particular body is physically present in the world.

What I think is important to retain is modesty as a virtue, and modesty as a way of engaging. One of the things that I tell my students – which some Muslim students find offensive and some Western feminists find very offensive as well – is that actually a *niqāb* [face covering] and a bikini for me might be seen to signify similar ways of the objectification of women's bodies. Young Muslim women in my class often get very upset with that, and the Western feminists say, 'Well, we can show as much body as we like; it is my body', and they also get very upset with that. And what both end up doing is to illustrate that when you centre the body in this kind of way, when you are wearing a *niqāb* and all I can see of you are your eyes, and I don't see any other part of your body, in this contemporary context that makes you the subject of a gaze, a gaze where you are actually rendered anonymous beyond your eyes, and so your physical objectification happens in a certain way. Specifically, if you are walking down the street in South Africa, if there is a *niqābī* woman walking, and that is becoming increasingly more of a practice here, it attracts a particular kind of gaze, and in my analysis, what is being done is [they are implicitly saying]: My body is so significant that I cover all of it up so that you cannot engage it. That for me is an objectification. If I cannot see your face (that part that engages me as a unique, distinct human being) – and here I am speaking about face covering, I am not speaking about a head covering; I am speaking about *niqāb*, that covers my face and covers the distinctive way in which I recognise another human being – for me, that is one form of objectification. A woman with a bikini, where everything shows, is another form of objectification. 'I am my sexuality. I am my curves, I am my boobs. Look at me.' That is an objectification. Both of those modes of objectification are deeply problematic for me spiritually.

This is probably not going to be popular, and I am certainly not saying that this is the only way to read it, but for me, in both cases, one is making way too much of the body. We are, as human beings – in terms of a Qur'ānic and a particular kind of impetus – multi-layered. The body is beautiful, and it is meant to be celebrated, but it is also meant to be modestly covered.

To be modestly covered and to be modest are defined by context. I always say to my students that I am perfectly in hijab [with no head covering]. So hijab is then what modesty dictates. For me, personally, you will not find me in a miniskirt, because for me hijab means that I dress modestly in a way that allows me the privacy of my body and allows me to guard my private parts or cover them. And I think that enables a different level of engagement with others. Modesty allows someone to relate to another human being not simply as a body.

amina wadud

amina wadud chooses to wear a headscarf in certain formal settings, while eschewing it when she is out and about in her neighbourhood. Wadud says that wearing a headscarf in formal settings is a response to the politics of veiling in the public sphere, in which she chooses to show solidarity with those Muslim women who wear the headscarf. For her, the headscarf is a visual indication of being Muslim. Wadud rejects any type of coercion over veiling, whether that be to uncover or to cover, and prioritises Muslim women's right to choose how to present themselves.

Karen Bauer: In *Inside the Gender Jihad*, you speak about your own journey from your conversion, to wearing hijab for thirty years as a Muslim, and now to wearing it sometimes but not all the time. You've explained this through your phrase, 'If you think that the difference between Heaven and Hell is forty-five inches of material, boy will you be surprised'; and you also contrast the notion of modest dress with *taqwā*, quoting the verse *the best garment is the garment of taqwā* (Q. 7:26); finally, you note that it is impossible to tell from the outside whether a woman's hijab is coerced or donned from choice. Building on your equality paradigm, we would like to explore the implications of shared responsibility for modesty. If you agree that modesty is a virtue in the Qur'ān, what does that mean, and how may men and women embrace an ethic of modesty to be implemented in the public sphere?

amina wadud: I still prioritise modesty and I still feel that modesty has some correlation to items of clothing, and that does not mean that I consider a naked child to be immodest, for example. So the question then is how does it evolve, and how do we consider it in what we call the public sphere.

Unfortunately, we cannot have a conversation about Muslim women's dress today without the politics of Muslim women's dress being on the table, and until both politics have been resolved, then I will always err on the side of a person who covers by choice, and I will be adamant in terms of choosing to wear a veil in public settings. Public settings for me are formal. For me, for example, when I walk in my neighbourhood every day, I am not covering my hair, I am wearing a t-shirt, and I am wearing spandex pants [leggings]. [The veil] is not something I would go to the market with. I have determined, according to my own bodily integrity, that there is only so much I will uncover in front of one person at one time. But that is me personally.

What I want to discuss instead is: what is the cultural milieu of respect for bodily integrity when we have all kinds of complications in society? Muslim women whose choice of how to demonstrate their modesty through the Islamic fashions of head covering and the like are making expressions of their own agency, and I am not in favour of anyone who determines how much of that agency they should express. So I am opposed to any of the bans that are put into place in any country on the planet, no matter what their majority population is. A woman should have full choice. Just as I believe a woman should have full choice not to have to cover. And yet, in the milieu of certain Muslim majority contexts, it is impossible to imagine a woman exercising that choice and still being able to walk down the street. So both circumstances reveal a kind of cultural milieu, and operating within that milieu is not the same thing as choice. Sometimes it is a question of convenience. Unfortunately, we do not have the capacity to remove the politics from the conversation.

As for what I think the Qurʾān intended, I believe that the Qurʾān intended for us to maintain a respectful decorum between women and men, or between persons who might be attracted to each other even if they are not in the same age group, because there are places where a child can be seen as being attractive. There is a new movie out called *Cutie* and people are arguing about whether or not it participates in or challenges certain rubrics of understanding preteen girls in their own identities. But the extent to which there is not the level of consciousness raised in societies enough for girls to be protected in the company of certain men, and therefore I would err on the side of putting a barrier between them and the men by way of dress. So it is hard to express the spectrum of choice and at the same time the immersion into worlds that do not respect bodily integrity [such as in spaces that, for instance, sexualise children].

Because my ancestors were brought to the Americas in chains on slave ships, and my poor mothers were put [naked] on the auction block – my Muslim heritage goes all the way back to my birth family on my mother's side; they came to America already as Muslims – the idea that you do not have the right to choose which parts of you to cover in certain places became my personal motivation that I do not uncover certain parts of me in certain situations, in accordance with my fullest right to choose and to observe the integrity that is necessary. That became a part of my consideration of the Islamic rubrics, and the politics of the discussions as I said, which doesn't allow you to just have a personal opinion.

But I did come away with the understanding that the Qurʾān does encode modesty for both women and men, and the ways in which modesty is expressed in context vary, and the ways in which we negotiate with those variants are also diverse. By the time we put all of this in there, then the trajectory of modesty, which is an expression of *taqwā*, or God-consciousness, is almost lost, and that is really a shame, because I would like people to have the option. But in reality, I know so many Muslim women in so many circumstances who are not able to understand for themselves what would be their expression, if it were not for so many forces on the outside. And because of context over text, I will prioritise the complication of Muslim women being able to assert their full choices over anything that is in the text, especially considering that the text is so ambiguous.

I think the specific words that were used in the Qurʾān were expressions of modesty that were used in the [first-/]seventh-century context, like *jalābībihinna* [*their cloaks*, Q. 33:59] – the *jilbāb* was not a universal form of dress, and yet it is an explicit phrase in the Qurʾān. I used to believe that it means you always have to wear a *jilbāb*, an outer coat, and I did that for a few years, as I also chose to cover my face for a few years. But as I grew in terms of my relationship with society, that is, I became a single parent, and I went to work in an elementary school, I exercised different choices in terms of how I encoded modesty on my body, and I was thankful that I was in a place where I could do that. So again, like other things, my understanding of what the Qurʾān intends with regard to dress has evolved, and it has not left the politics of the veil, unfortunately.

Feras Hamza: amina, can I just pick up on that? Are you saying one of two things, which is that in our particular historical juncture, it just so happens that the veil is politicised, that there is the politics of the veil, and yet at the same time are you also saying that in certain social settings the veil is important because neither the women nor the men involved in the sexualities of that landscape at the time are mature enough to understand these bounds of modesty and encoding modesty on themselves? Are these two things true for you? It is not really about the veil, but it just happens to be about the veil? Can you elaborate there?

amina wadud: Well, I definitely think that the discourses over the veil are not always about the veil but are about something else. However, I want to properly clarify between something that I consider to be choice, when choice might include forms of nakedness, and any comments that I may have made about the veil, because I do not see the veil or nakedness as the two options. What I meant in terms of bodily integrity – and I observe certain places where that is not being observed by other people – has to do with nakedness. I mean, is it possible – I was warned not to put naked pictures of my grandchildren on my Facebook page by a Jewish activist woman who said, 'You just don't know who is perusing Facebook' because of paedophilia. And she was right, and I thought to myself it is a shame that she is right. So it is in terms of nakedness that I am speaking, and because my ancestors weren't just forced out of the veils, the veils of the women coming from Africa, Islam having preceded the slave route by a thousand years in Africa, they were stripped naked. And from it I have a DNA, I have a genetic codification that says nobody gets to see parts of my body except as I will. But I am never going to exercise nakedness. One of my daughters took me to a naked hot springs. I wore a bathing suit the whole time and I thought to myself, 'This is not me. I can't do this. There are too many things to see.' I kept lowering my gaze; I can't even walk because I'm so busy lowering my gaze. 'This is not me – it's just not me!' So some of the comments that I made are about choices about levels of nakedness, and they don't have to do with choosing to veil.

So choosing veiling and different levels of veiling in the modern society is so politicised that, even in places where the cultural milieu is veiling, a woman really does not have full choice. So a woman in a 'Western society' who does choose to veil, including choosing to cover her face, to wear *niqāb*, is not in defiance of the cultural milieu, she is in the midst of the politics of de-veiling. And the politics of de-veiling are about as strong as the politics of veiling in places like the Gulf region where everybody wears it even though nobody wears it when they go anywhere else. And that is real, and because that is real it means I can't have a discussion about the hijab in isolation, as if I can solve this problem by looking at the few passages that are in the Qurʾān with regard to it, because we cannot. There is a heavy political component to it, and resolving that political component, to me, has to come first. Unfortunately, it comes first with the price paid by women themselves in those spaces.

... وَٱسۡتَشۡهِدُواْ شَهِيدَيۡنِ مِن رِّجَالِكُمۡ فَإِن لَّمۡ يَكُونَا رَجُلَيۡنِ فَرَجُلٞ وَٱمۡرَأَتَانِ مِمَّن تَرۡضَوۡنَ مِنَ ٱلشُّهَدَآءِ أَن تَضِلَّ إِحۡدَىٰهُمَا فَتُذَكِّرَ إِحۡدَىٰهُمَا ٱلۡأُخۡرَىٰ...

5 Women's testimony (Q. 2:282)

Call to witness two witnesses from your menfolk, and if there are not two men, then a man and two women who satisfy you as witnesses, where one of the two errs, then one of the two shall remind the other

Wa'stashhidū shahīdayn min rijālikum fa-in lam yakūnā rajulayn fa-rajulun wa'mra'atān mimman tarḍawna mina'l-shuhadā'i an taḍilla iḥdāhumā fa-tudhakkira iḥdāhumā al-ukhrā

The selection chosen here is a short excerpt from the longest verse in the Qur'ān, which has to do with the contracting of debts; this excerpt is significant in that it includes the possibility of women giving testimony. The verse sits in *sūrat al-Baqara*, a Medinan *sūra* that has long legalistic passages which, in our view, seem to be intended to protect those whose rights might not otherwise be secured, including women. In these cases, care for the underprivileged or disadvantaged is one part of a believer's duty to God, which also includes paying *zakāt* for the needy along with praying, fasting and being grateful. Q. 2:282 comes after a long passage on the moral good of charitable giving in Q. 2:261–77, while the verses immediately preceding this one deal with usury and debt. The main subject of Q. 2:282–3 is the necessity of recording debts in writing, with witnesses. This seems to be a continuation of the overall concern in this verse group: to secure financial rights for those who might otherwise be disabused of those rights, by encouraging charitable giving and accurate recording of any debts.

In this context sits the excerpt we have selected, which mentions that the debt must be witnessed by two men or a man and two women *so that if one of the two errs, then one of the two shall remind the other*. This echoes Qur'ānic inheritance rules where males get the share of two females, while the ruling on blood money in Q. 2:178 stipulates *a free man for a free man, a slave for a slave, a female for a female*.[1] For contemporary readers, two women's testimony in the place of one man's seems preposterous; for the Qur'ānic audience it made utter sense. In analogous legal systems such as Jewish law,

[1] Drawing an analogy with women's inheritance, exegetes and jurists often argued that women's bloodwit was worth half of a man's.

women had no right to testify at all, while in ancient Roman law, which influenced Byzantine law, they were considered legally incompetent.[2] Seen in this light, the Qurʾān guarantees women rights as social subjects. Yet (as described below) medieval Muslim jurists interpreted this verse narrowly, granting women limited rights to testify. These interpretations have cast a long shadow in Muslim-majority countries where modern codifications of medieval jurisprudential opinions have had real consequences for women's lives.[3] In many countries, women's testimony is still counted as half of a man's in certain types of cases, and they are not empowered to testify at all in other types of cases.[4]

Such profound modern implications could hardly be predicted from the medieval commentaries surveyed in this chapter. Indeed, for these medieval commentators, gender seems entirely peripheral: a Qurʾānic moment that includes and recognises women becomes for them a grammatical curiosity, an opportunity to ponder a rare use of the particle *an* (that), to explain why God repeated the phrase *one of the two* rather than just saying 'she', or to delve into a number of other obscurities at length. In some instances, these ponderous grammatical discussions are put to the service of the exegetes' misogynistic outlook. Ṭabrisī explains that the phrase *who satisfy you as witnesses* could not refer to the two men; rather, it is the women whose

[2] On Jewish law, see Orit Malka, 'Disqualified Witnesses Between Tannaitic Halakha and Roman Law: The Archaeology of a Legal Institution', *Law and History Review* 37.4 (2019), 903–36. She notes that some of the categories of people whose testimony is not allowed include women, minors, slaves and gentiles. In these cases, their 'social and biological' identities prevent their testimony, whereas in the case of Jewish males, it is their ability to maintain an 'ethics of self-control'. Thus there may be a parallel with the Qurʾānic injunction to only allow those *who satisfy you as witnesses*, which is presumably a reference to moral character. On Roman law, see Suzanne Dixon, 'Infirmitas Sexus: Womanly Weakness in Roman Law', *Legal History Review* 52.4 (1984), 343–71.

[3] Moamen Gouda and Niklas Potrafke argue that women face more discrimination and have fewer rights in countries in which 'Islam' is the source of legislation. Moamen Gouda and Niklas Potrafke, 'Gender Equality in Muslim-Majority Countries', *Economic Systems* 40.4 (2016), 683–98.

[4] 'According to a survey of legal systems of Arab States carried out by Freedom House (2010), women's testimony is only worth half of men's in the following countries: Algeria (in criminal cases), Bahrain (in religious courts), Egypt (in family matters), Iraq (in some cases), Jordan (in religious courts), Kuwait (in family courts), Libya (in some cases), Morocco (in family matters), Palestine (in cases related to marriage, divorce and child custody), Qatar (in family matters), Saudi Arabia, Syria (in religious courts), and the United Arab Emirates (in some civil matters). In Yemen, women are not allowed to testify at all in cases of adultery and retribution. The only Arab countries in which women's testimony is considered to be equal to men's in all circumstances are Oman and Tunisia.' Source: UN Economic and Social Commission for Western Asia, 'Against Wind and Tides: A Review of the Status of Women and Gender Equality in the Arab Region (Beijing +20)' (7 January 2016), p. 56, n. 256, accessed 1 July 2019, https://sustainabledevelopment.un.org/content/documents/2283ESCWA_Women%20and%20Gender%20Equality%20in%20the%20Arab%20Region_Beijing20.pdf.

reliability is in question. Most exegetes mention women's right to testify almost as an afterthought. Women's lesser rights in this regard are usually attributed to their innate lack of capacity, and particularly to their intellectual deficiency. Some support this view with recourse to a *ḥadīth* on the authority of the Prophet that says that women are the 'majority of the inhabitants of Hell'[5] because of their deficiency in intellect and religion (*'aql wa-dīn*). Although many commentators refer in passing to the legal rulings on women's testimony, such rulings seem to concern them but little; the impact of the verse is not their bailiwick.

The scope of women's testimony was a source of vibrant debate from an early period. For instance, 'Abd al-Razzāq al-Ṣan'ānī (d. 211/826), in his *ḥadīth* compilation, *al-Muṣannaf*,[6] records sixteen different reports of early authorities on the question of women's testimony with men in *ḥudūd*-crimes and other matters, and several pages of opinions on women's testimony in childbirth or suckling. These opinions are varied: according to Sha'bī, women's testimony is admissible with that of men's only regarding marriage and divorce. According to Zuhrī, however, the testimony of women is not admissible in cases of *ḥadd*-crimes, divorce or marriage, even alongside that of men. Qatāda takes the opposite view of Sha'bī's. 'Alī b. Abī Ṭālib's opinion is also recorded, to the effect that women's testimony is not admissible in cases of divorce, marriage, *ḥudūd*-crimes or bloodwit (*dimā'*). 'Umar is also recorded as being in agreement with 'Alī on this issue, as reported by Zuhrī via Sa'īd b. al-Musayyab. For Ibn Ḥujayr, the testimony of women is accepted in all matters other than fornication or adultery (*zinā*), because that is not something they should be looking at. And according to 'Aṭā' b. Abī Rabāḥ

[5] Versions of this *ḥadīth*, in full or in part, are found in the following sources: Bukhārī, *Ṣaḥīḥ*, *Kitāb al-Zakāt* (24), *Bāb al-zakāt 'alā'l-aqārib* (44), *ḥadīth* no. 64/1462; ibid., *Kitāb al-Ḥayḍ* (6), *Bāb tark al-ḥā'iḍ al-ṣawm* (6), *ḥadīth* no. 9/304; ibid., *Kitāb al-Īmān* (2), *Bāb kufrān al-'ashīr wa-kufrin dūna kufrin* (21), *ḥadīth* no. 22/29; ibid., *Kitāb al-Riqāq* (81), *Bāb faḍl al-faqr* (16), *ḥadīth* no. 38/6449; *Bāb ṣifat al-janna wa'l-nār* (51), *ḥadīth* nos. 135/6546 and 136/6547; ibid., *Kitāb al-Nikāḥ* (67), *Bāb* 87, *ḥadīth* no. 130/5196 and *Bāb kufrān al-'ashīr* (88), *ḥadīth* no. 131/5197; ibid., *Kitāb Bad' al-khalq* (59), *Bāb mā jā'a fī ṣifat al-janna wa-annahā makhlūqa* (8), *ḥadīth* no. 52/3241; Ibn Māja, *Sunan*, *Kitāb al-Fitan* (36), *Bāb fitnat al-mar'a* (19), *ḥadīth* no. 78/4003; Muslim, *Ṣaḥīḥ*, *Kitāb al-Riqāq* (49), *Bāb akthar ahl al-janna al-fuqarā' wa-akthar ahl al-nār al-nisā' wa-bayān al-fitnati bi'l-nisā'* (1), *ḥadīth* nos. 1/2736 and 2/2737; ibid., *Kitāb al-Kusūf* (10), *Bāb mā 'uriḍa li'l-nabī (ṣl'm) fī ṣalāt al-kusūf min amr al-janna wa'l-nār* (3), *ḥadīth* no. 18/907; Nasā'ī, *Sunan*, *Kitāb al-Kusūf* (16), *Bāb qadr al-qirā'a li-ṣalāt al-kusūf* (17), *ḥadīth* no. 35/1493; Nawawī, *Riyāḍ al-ṣāliḥīn*, *Kitāb al-Istighfār* (19), *Bāb al-amr bi'l-istighfār wa-faḍlihi* (371), *ḥadīth* no. 11/1879; Tirmidhī, *Jāmi'*, *Kitāb al-Īmān* (40), *Bāb mā jā'a fī istikmāl al-īmān wa-ziyādatihi wa-nuqṣānihi* (6), *ḥadīth* no. 8/2613. Saffarīnī (d. 1189/1774) explained this *ḥadīth* by saying that there are more women in this world, and that is why there would be more of them in Hell. Lange, *Paradise and Hell*, 90.

[6] 'Abd al-Razzāq al-Ṣan'ānī, *Muṣannaf*, VIII, 139–40, *Bāb hal tajūz shahādat al-nisā' ma'a al-rijāl fī'l-ḥudūd wa-ghayrih*, *ḥadīth* nos. 15401–17.

the testimony of women alongside that of men is allowed in all cases, even in adultery or fornication (*zinā*) but in this latter as long as there are two women alongside three men. Almost all early authorities cited by ʿAbd al-Razzāq permitted women's testimony without men in matters such as childbirth, and in many cases they permitted a single woman to testify.

These early debates crystallised into post-formative legal school views. Most schools of law interpreted the restrictions in Q. 2:282 as broadly as possible and only allowed for women's testimony in specific cases, such as contracting a debt and other monetary matters, or matters that men did not see, such as childbirth; nevertheless, there were dissenting views within them and between them on marriage, divorce and other matters.[7] A few schools took a broader view. The earliest legal school, the Ḥanafīs, allowed two women's testimony with one man's in all matters except crimes of *ḥudūd* or *qiṣāṣ*. According to the now-defunct Ẓāhirī school, a woman's word was worth half that of a man's in all cases, and women's word was accepted without men's word in all cases: eight women could testify to adultery or fornication. Other than the Ẓāhirīs, no schools accepted women's testimony unless there was also a male witness, except in cases where men were not present (such as at childbirth); but jurists were careful to explain that this was out of necessity, rather than because a woman's word was, in itself, as acceptable as a man's word. Medieval jurists consistently described women as deficient in reason (*nāqiṣāt ʿaql*).[8]

The modern laws on this verse can be attributed more directly to debates in these works of *fiqh*; yet modern scholarly interpretations of this verse are also often intertwined with identity politics and state politics. Modern commentaries on this verse foreground contemporary concerns about women's innate capacities and their participation in the public sphere; such responses tend to fall in one of two broad perspectives – conservative and reformist – which have political as well as social implications. Conservatives seek to preserve key elements of medieval *fiqh*, but with new justifications, thereby supporting state laws that treat women unequally; but they do not use the same justifications as medieval commentators. Reformists tend to engage directly with the Qurʾān and its social context, arguing for

[7] Bauer, 'Debates on Women's Status', 1–21.

[8] Cf. Mohammad Fadel, 'Two Women, One Man: Knowledge, Power, and Gender in Medieval Sunni Legal Thought', *International Journal of Middle East Studies* 29.2 (1997), 185–204, in which he argues for the opposite; this view is refuted in Bauer, 'Debates on Women's Status'. On women's expert testimony, see Ron Shaham, 'Women as Expert Witnesses in Pre-Modern Islamic Courts' in *Law, Custom, and Statute in the Muslim World: Studies in Honor of Aharon Layish*, ed. Ron Shaham (Leiden, Brill, 2007), 41–65.

women's equal participation today and against discriminatory legislation. Conservatives are heavily represented in the written genre of *tafsīr*; an example is the interpretation of Faḍl Allāh below. But these views are also widespread among religious scholars in the public sphere, as represented by the interview with Fariba Alasvand. Dr Alasvand, a hugely popular teacher in the Hawzeh in Qumm, argues that women's testimony should be counted as less than men's because of innate, scientifically proven differences between the sexes. She, and other modern conservatives, rejects any notion of women's inferiority while still upholding laws that treat men and women differently.

Modern reformist views are often absent from the written genre of *tafsīr*; hence we represent them here through the inclusion of interviews of religious scholars. These reformist interpreters generally agreed that the Qurʾānic context gave women rights that they might not otherwise have had, and that the testimony of two women for one man reflected a social milieu in which women were not actively involved in financial matters. To paraphrase the words of Grand Ayatollah Saanei, anyone can see that women are as intelligent as men and that they see and hear the same things, so why would the Qurʾān discriminate against them? For him and other reformists, the answer has to be that these rules applied to a certain time and place. For them, the Qurʾānic rulings establish fairness and justice; but the boundaries of those fair and just rulings are not fixed with the letter of those rulings: what was fair and just in first-/seventh-century Arabia may no longer be fair and just today.

The sociopolitical relevance of this verse in modern times is one reason that its modern interpretations are so varied and the debate so vigorous. That the corresponding vigour in the medieval period was reserved for grammatical issues exposes the ways in which the *tafsīr* tradition is limited by its genre and its authors' own social status and class as elite male scholars. On the whole, they took women's inferiority for granted, and, by doing so, they were able to diminish any Qurʾānic suggestion that secured women a place as social subjects in the public sphere.

Key terms

Ḍalāl: in the Qurʾānic context, this is error or going astray. 'The errant' (*al-ḍāllūn*) is used perhaps most famously in *sūrat al-Fātiḥa* (Q. 1), where those who err are contrasted with those on the 'straight path' (*al-ṣirāṭ al-mustaqīm*). Straying from the path is also used in other instances, and in

Q. 16:125, the audience is told that God knows who has strayed and who has been guided. God offers guidance; but He is not affected by human error: when people err, they only err against themselves, as per Q. 34:50. The sense in which people lead themselves astray in Q. 34:50 hints at another connotation of *ḍalāl*, which is being lost. Those who worship other than God are lost, and their own idols will desert them or be lost to them in their time of need, thus Q. 6:24, which reads: *Look at them now, having told themselves [all those] lies, they can no longer find* (*ḍalla ʿanhum*) *the things they used to fabricate* (also cf. Q. 10:30). Similarly, in Q. 17:67, when people are in difficulty at sea, *those whom you invoke other than Him are nowhere to be found* (*ḍalla*). In Q. 2:282, the commentators usually gloss *ḍall* as 'forget', because the testimony is 'lost' or has 'gone astray' from the woman, meaning that she has forgotten it.

Naṣb: the *fatḥa* vowelling of the inflection, indicating both the accusative case for nouns and the subjunctive mood for verbs.

Rafʿ: the *ḍamma* vowelling of the inflection, and thus the nominative case in nouns, the indicative mood for verbs.

Tashdīd* and *takhfīf: *tashdīd* is the doubling of the medial letter (from the adding of the *shadda* over that letter), and indicates an intensive form; it is usually translated as 'intensification'. *Takhfīf* indicates a single medial letter in a word and is usually translated as 'lightening'.

Muqātil

Muqātil's paraphrastic *tafsīr* of this portion of Q. 2:282 entails a basic gloss of terms. His main concern is that whoever testifies, male or female, should be satisfying, meaning suitable, as witnesses. He glosses the term *errs* as 'forgets', and says that if one woman forgets her testimony, the other should remind her of it. Commentators such as Muqātil parse phrases so finely that it can be difficult to render into English. For instance, the phrase that we have translated as: *where one of the two errs, then one of the two shall remind the other* is parsed piece-by-piece in the following way: *where she errs*, the woman, meaning where she forgets, *one of the two*, the testimony, *then one of the two shall remind*, of the testimony, *the other*. Our translations below render this paraphrastic parsing somewhat more idiomatic and comprehensible.

God, glory be to Him, then says *call to witness*, concerning your rights, *two witnesses from your menfolk, and if there are not two men, then a man and two women who satisfy you as witnesses*. He means: let not a man call to witness concerning his rights, except one who is satisfactory, whether the witness be a man or a woman. Then He says: *Where one of the two errs*, the woman, meaning, lest she forgets the testimony, *then one of the two shall remind the other* of the testimony. He means the woman who has remembered the testimony of the two shall remind the other one.[9]

Hūd

Hūd's interpretation is more detailed than Muqātil's, including different legal opinions on testimony and a *ḥadīth* on the authority of the Prophet about the types of people from whom testimony is not accepted. This is a nascent example of what will become, in later texts, a more fully fledged discussion of the legal opinions on testimony. Hūd gives two variant readings of the term *remind* (*tudhakkir*): one with a single medial letter and one with a double medial letter. The first case would render the word 'remember' and the second 'remind'.

His words *call to witness two witnesses from your menfolk*, that is to say, from your free men; *and if there are not two men*, then let it be *a man and two women who satisfy you as witnesses*. They mention that the Messenger of God (*ṣlʿm*) said, 'Unacceptable is the testimony of someone who is characterised by *ẓinna*, or *ḥinna* or *jinna*'.[10] And the explanation of one characterised by *ẓinna* is one who has been accused (*muttaham*); *al-ḥinna* means enmity (*ʿadāwa*) between two men; and *al-jinna* means insanity (*junūn*). They have mentioned on the authority of Shurayḥ that he said: I do not admit the testimony of one who is a disputant (*khaṣm*), or a partner[11] (*al-sharīk*), or a person whose testimony can save himself from being implicated (*dāfiʿ al-maghram*), or the testimony of the hired hand (*ajīr*) on behalf of the one who has hired him on the estate in question.

His words *where one of the two errs*, that is to say, lest one of the two forgets the testimony, *then one of the two shall remind* [*tudhakkir*] *the other*, that is, she who has remembered the testimony reminds the other. It [*tudhakkir*] may be read lightened (*takhfīf*) or intensified (*tathqīl*),[12] and for those who read it lightened, it has the sense: it was mentioned to her and she remembered (*dhukira lahā fa-dhakarat*). And it may be that a person reminds (*yudhakkir*) his companion, but he does not remember (*lā yadhkur*); but this

[9] Muqātil, *Tafsīr Muqātil*, I, 229, s.v. Q. 2:282.

[10] The Arabic has *lā tajūzu shahādatu dhī'l-ẓinnati wa-dhī'l-ḥinnati wa-dhī'l-jinna*.

[11] In this context, the partnership is commercial, that is, someone with a vested interest.

[12] That is to say, with a single medial consonant or a doubled one, *tathqīl* being a synonym of *tashdīd* (see Versteegh, *Arabic Grammar*, 113ff.)

is a woman who has been reminded (*dhukkirat*), and so in either case she will have been reminded.[13]

Qummī

This is a very brief gloss in which Qummī says that *errs* is 'forgets' and that one woman reminds the other.

It has been related in a report (*khabar*) that *sūrat al-Baqara* contains five hundred rulings and that in this verse there are fifteen rulings [. . .]. *Call to witness two witnesses from your menfolk*: [thus far there are] eight rulings. *If there are not two men, then a man and two women who satisfy you as witnesses, where one of the two errs, then one of the two shall remind the other*, meaning that if one of the two of them forgets then the other will remind her: nine rulings.[14]

Ṭabarī

Ṭabarī's interpretation includes both legal rulings and an unusual variant reading and interpretation of the verse. Much of his interpretation is taken up with the question of the phrase that we have translated as *where one of the two errs, then one of the two shall remind the other*. Ṭabarī discusses variant readings of this phrase, focusing on the term *an* (where) and on the term *remind*, the latter of which can be read with a lightening (*takhfīf*) or with an intensification (*tashdīd*) of the medial letter. With a lightening, it might be taken to mean 'make like a man', which is indeed the reading of Sufyān b. ʿUyayna. In Ibn ʿUyayna's reading, rather than one woman reminding the other, she makes the other like a man. Ṭabarī vehemently disagrees with this reading, because it goes against the majority view and because, in his argument, the woman who forgets is more in need of reminding than she is of being made like a man. Thus the interpretation makes little sense to Ṭabarī, but he is not opposed to the idea that women could be like men in their strength of memory. This is an interesting case in which a debate over semantics and grammar is resolved not only using grammar but also using common sense and Ṭabarī's own notions of right and wrong.

[13] Hūd, *Tafsīr kitāb Allāh al-ʿazīz*, I, 259–60, s.v. Q. 2:282.
[14] Qummī, *Tafsīr al-Qummī*, I, 94–5, s.v. Q. 2:282.

Reports on the interpretation of His words, exalted be He, *call to witness two witnesses from your menfolk.*

By this, He, majestic be His praise, means 'and call to witness, concerning your rights, two witnesses. One says, so-and-so is my witness (*shahīd*) regarding this property, or my testifier (*shāhid*) to it. As for His words *from your menfolk*, He means from your free Muslim men, not your slaves, and not free men who are unbelievers.

As in [the following reports]:[15]

It is reported by Ibn Abī Najīḥ from Mujāhid[16] that he said [regarding] *call to witness two witnesses from your menfolk*: free men.

It is reported by Dāwūd b. Abī Hind from Mujāhid[17] the like of this.

Reports on the interpretation of His words, exalted be He, *and if there are not two men, then a man and two women who satisfy you as witnesses.*

By this, He, majestic be His praise, means that, if there are not two men, then let it be a man and two women who testify. The words *al-rajul* and *imra'atān* are in the nominative case (*raf*ʿ) as a response to [an implied] 'let it be' (*kawn*). And so, if you wish,[18] you may take it as: 'if there are not two men, then let a man and two women testify to that' (*fa'l-yashhad rajulun wa'mra'atān*);[19] you might also wish it thus: 'if there are not two men, then a man and two women who can testify to it (*yashhadūna ʿalayhi*)'. But even if you were to say, 'if there are not two men, then a man and two women', that would still be correct.[20] All of these are possible.

If it had been the case that *fa-rajulun wa'imra'atān* were in the accusative (*naṣb*),[21] that could still be possible, based on the implication (*ta'wīl*) being: if there are not two men, then 'call to witness' a man and two women (*fa'stashhidū rajulan wa'mra'atayn*). As for His words *who satisfy you as witnesses*, He means from the just (pl. *ʿudūl*) whose religious observance (*dīn*) and righteousness (*ṣalāḥ*) satisfy you, as narrated to me by al-Muthannā

[15] The following narrations serve to confirm that the expression *your menfolk* refers to the witness's status as a free Muslim.

[16] Ibn Wakīʿ ← Ubayy ← Sufyān ← Ibn Abī Najīḥ ← Mujāhid.

[17] Yūnus ← ʿAlī b. Saʿīd ← Hushaym ← Dāwūd b. Abī Hind ← Mujāhid.

[18] Ṭabarī here is offering two ways of supplying implicit verbs in order to justify and retain a nominative inflection for the two nouns *rajulun* and *imra'atān*, in addition to the way that the statement is given in the Qur'ānic verse without any verb.

[19] This is an unattributed quotation of the grammarian Farrā''s interpretation of the same verse.

[20] Ṭabarī, and his source, Farrā', are not suggesting that the reader change the words of the Qur'ān. Rather, these suggestions refer to the way that the meaning of the verse might be taught to believers in oral teaching sessions.

[21] That is to say: *fa-rajulan wa'mra'atayn*.

who said that al-Rabīʿ[22] said: His words *call to witness two witnesses from your menfolk*, this is about debts (*dayn*); and *if there are not two men, then a man and two women*, that too concerns debts; and regarding *who satisfy you as witnesses*: those who are just.

Juwaybir reported from al-Ḍaḥḥāk that he said,[23] '*Call to witness two witnesses from your menfolk*: God, mighty and majestic, has commanded that they call to testimony two just ones from their menfolk, and *if there are not two men, then a man and two women who satisfy you as witnesses*.'

Reports on the interpretation of His words, exalted be He, *where one of the two errs, then one of the two shall remind the other.*

The readers differ in how they recite that. The majority of the Ḥijāzīs and the Medinese, and some[24] of the Iraqis read:[25] *an taḍilla iḥdāhumā fa-tudhakkira iḥdāhumā al-ukhrā* with a *fatḥa* on the *alif* of *an*, rendering *taḍilla* and *tudhakkira* as subjunctives (*naṣb*), the meaning being: if there are not two men, then a man and two women, so that one of the two of them might remind the other if she were to forget. That, according to them, is a case of pre-positioning (*muqaddam*), but the import of it is a post-positioning (*taʾkhīr*),[26] because the 'reminding', according to them, is what ought to occupy the position of '[where] she errs', the meaning being that which we have provided according to their interpretation (*qawl*).

They also add: we have rendered *tudhakkira* subjunctive, because when the conditional (*al-jazāʾ*)[27] comes first (*taqaddama*) it becomes syntactically connected (*ittaṣala*) to that which comes before it, its apodosis (*jawāb*) ends up referring back to it, as you would say in speech, 'It truly delights me that (*an*) the beggar should ask and be given',[28] with the meaning, 'It truly delights me that the beggar should be given if he were to ask (*in saʾala*) or when he

[22] Al-Muthannā ← Isḥāq ← Ibn Abī Jaʿfar ← his father ← Rabīʿ.

[23] Al-Muthannā ← Isḥāq ← Abū Zuhayr ← Juwaybir ← al-Ḍaḥḥāk.

[24] Or 'one of the Iraqis reads [. . .]'.

[25] We have kept the following readings in transliteration, as the meaning of each one will be explained just after the reading is given.

[26] The technical terms, formally *taqdīm* and *taʾkhīr*, constitute a literary technique for rhetorical purposes in which the normal word order is reversed (cf. Greek *hysteron proteron*); see Versteegh, *Arabic Grammar*, 121ff.

[27] This is a rare term used to denote, literally, 'the requital' and it is usually found in the following combination *jawāb al-jazāʾ*. See Manuela E.B. Giolfo, '*Fa-*' in *The Subjunctive Mood in Arabic Grammatical Thought*, ed. Arik Sadan (Leiden, Brill, 2012), 127–71; also eadem, '*Yaqūm* vs *Qāma* in the Conditional Context: A Relativistic Interpretation of the Frontier Between the Prefixed and the Suffixed Conjugations of the Arabic Language' in *The Foundations of Arabic Linguistics: Sībawayhi and Early Arabic Grammatical Theory*, ed. Amal E. Marogy (Leiden, Brill, 2012), 135–60.

[28] The Arabic is *innahu la-yuʿjibanī an yasʾala al-sāʾilu fa-yuʿṭā*.

asks (*idhā sa'ala*)', where what delights you is 'the giving', not 'the asking'. But in that statement, 'that he should ask' – coming as it does first – becomes connected to what has preceded it: the words 'it truly delights me' (*la-yuʿjibanī*), which renders a *fatḥa* on the *an* and is [at the same time] rendered subjunctive (*nuṣiba*) by it. Then, after that comes the speaker's words *fa-yuʿṭā* (and that he should be given), which is rendered subjunctive on account of the subjunctive construction of his words *la-yuʿjibanī an yas'al* (it truly delights me that he should ask), in syntactical agreement, even if the import was meant to be that of a conditional (*jazā'*).

Others also read it in that way, except that they would read it with an unvowelled (*taskīn*) *dhāl* in *tudhkira* and without doubling (*takhfīf*) its *kāf*. But even those who read it like that differ amongst themselves concerning the interpretation of this very reading. Some had it mean: one of them renders the other a male by virtue of the two women coming together [in agreement]. In this sense, if her [one woman's] testimony were to concur with that of her female companion and if the latter's testimony were admissible – and given that the testimony of one male is admissible in the case of debts, whereas the sole testimony of either one of the two women is not admissible in the case of debts, unless both of the women concur with each another on a single testimony – only then does their testimony become on a par with the testimony of a single male. Thus, according to the opinion of those who interpret this [verse] with that meaning, it is as though each of the two women renders herself and her companion into one male (*dhakar*). Reference here is made to the sayings of the Arabs *adhkarat bi-fulānin ummuhu*, which is to say she gave birth to a male and, as such, [it is also said] of her *tudhkiru bihi* or *hiya imra'atun mudhkiratun* to mean that she gives birth to male children. This is an opinion reported to have been held by Sufyān b. ʿUyayna.

This was narrated to me by Abū ʿUbayd al-Qāsim b. Sallām,[29] who reported that Sufyān b. ʿUyayna said, 'The interpretation of His words *fa-tudhakkira iḥdāhumā al-ukhrā* is not about making someone remember (*dhikr*), as in when someone has forgotten (*nisyān*) something; rather, it derives from 'male' (*dhakar*), with the meaning that when one woman testifies with another, the testimony of the two of them becomes like the testimony of a male.' Others, however, among these [interpreters] did consider it to be about remembering [something] after having forgotten [it].

[29] A Baghdadi philologist and the author of works on the Qur'ān, died 224/838. See Reinhard Weipert, 'Abū ʿUbayd al-Qāsim b. Sallām', *EI*[3]; see also the PA.

Still, there were others who read it as *in taḍilla iḥdāhumā fa-tudhakkiru iḥdāhumā al-ukhrā* – with a *kasra* on *in* and the indicative (*rafʿ*) mood with a doubling (*tashdīd*)[30] in the case of *tudhakkiru* – as constituting the subject (*ibtidāʾ*)[31] of the predicate clause indicating what the two women would do. That is, if one of the two should forget her testimony, the other shall remind her, by way of 'the remembering woman' (*al-dhākira*) steadying 'the forgetful one' (*al-nāsiya*) and reminding her of that – and they read it as being [syntactically] cut off from what comes before.[32]

The meaning of the words, according to those who read it like that, is thus similar: 'Call to witness two witnesses of your menfolk, and if there are not two men then a man and two women who satisfy you as witnesses, so that if one of the two of them should forget, the other shall remind her.' That reading is one where the predicate (*khabar*) comes at the beginning (*istiʾnāf*) to describe the action of one of them forgetting her testimony and then reminding the forgetful one. This is the reading of al-Aʿmash and those who learned it from him. The reason al-Aʿmash only renders *taḍilla* a subjunctive (*naṣaba*) is because it is apocopated (*jazm*) by the conditional particle (*ḥarf jazāʾ*), namely *in*. So, interpreting the passage on the basis of his reading it as having been *in taḍlil*, one would say: When one of the two *lām* letters is elided with the other, he gave it the lightest of vowellings and made *tudhakiru* an indicative (*rafaʿa*) on account of the *fa-* since it constitutes the response (*jawāb*) to the conditional (*jazāʾ*).

According to us, however, the correct reading here is the reading of those who read *an*, with a *fatḥa* in His words *an taḍilla iḥdāhumā*, and the doubling of the letter *kāf* in His words *fa-tudhakkira iḥdāhumā al-ukhrā*, producing a subjunctive inflection on the *rāʾ*, the meaning thus being: if there are not two men, then let one man and two women testify, so that if one of the two of them should err, the other shall remind her. As for the subjunctive inflection of *tudhakkira*, that is because of the coordination with *taḍilla*; *an* carries a *fatḥa* because it comes to occupy the position of a *kay* ('in order

30 A doubling of the middle consonant; in other words, the second verbal form.

31 Literally, 'as the beginning (*ibtidāʾ*) of the announcement (*khabar*) of what the women would do': Arabic grammatical terms do not have the semantic remove that modern English does with its hybrid inherited grammatical taxonomy. This, which also allows for synonymy (cf. *ibtidāʾ* and *istiʾnāf*), permits the commentators considerable room for rhetorical paronomasia, moulding the lexical forms of the grammatical technical terms into verbs, nouns, participles and so on while speaking about the one grammatical category.

32 In other words, syntactically, the statement *in taḍilla iḥdāhumā fa-tudhakkiru iḥdāhumā al-ukhrā* is a stand-alone sentence and not explicative of the preceding statement about the need for two women if there are not two men; in this reading, it stands as a cautionary parenthetical (but hardly a revision of the position that two women are needed in the place of a single man). On *istiʾnāf* and *inqiṭāʿ*, see Versteegh, *Arabic Grammar*, 117 and 132–4.

that'), which functions as a conditional; the ensuing response is provided for sufficiently by that *fatḥa*, by which I mean the *fatḥa* of the *an*, derived from a *kay*, and the coordination (*nasaq*)[33] of the second one, by which I mean *tudhakkira* with *taḍilla* so that it be known that that which has replaced the operator (*ʿāmil*), which is itself obvious, has already been indicated and its meaning and function, that of the *kay*, have been fulfilled.

The reason we have chosen this reading in particular is because of the conclusivity of the argument given the consensus on this among the earliest readers and the later ones, and also because in the case of al-Aʿmash and those who follow him, they are alone in reading it the way they do. One cannot simply abandon a reading that is copiously attested among Muslims in favour of another one. As for our choice of *fa-tudhakkir* with a doubled *kāf*, it is based on the sense of the fulfilling of the reminder by one of them to the other and making it known to her that this has been completed, so that the woman is reminded. Thus the doubling of the letter (*tashdīd*) is preferable to the single letter (*takhfīf*).

As for what has been related on the authority of Ibn ʿUyayna about the interpretation that we have mentioned, that is a mistaken interpretation, and meaningless, for a number of reasons. The first of these is that it goes against the opinion of the majority of the interpreters (*ahl al-taʾwīl*). The second is that it is commonly assumed that when one of the two women errs in the testimony that she gives, she has in effect departed from it by virtue of having forgotten it, just as when a man errs regarding his debt, and becomes confused about it, he ends up transgressing what is right. And so if one of the two women should end up in such a predicament, how could it be possible for her to make the other a male (*dhakar*) alongside her, given this forgetfulness in her testimony and her erring concerning it? The one of the two women who is erring in her testimony is doubtless more in need of reminding (*tadhkīr*) than of being made like a male (*idhkār*); that is, unless he meant that the remembering woman (*dhākira*), should her companion fail to remember the testimony, actually impels her to remember what she is struggling to remember and had thus forgotten, thereby strengthening her memory so that she makes her ability to remember what she had forgotten equivalent to the ability of a male. It is like when one says of a thing with the ability to function that it is *dhakar* ('male'), and as one says of a sword whose strike is sharp that it is *sayfun dhukrun*, and a manly man *rajulun dhukrun*, meaning consummate in

[33] The usual term for coordination is *ʿaṭf*. However, see Versteegh (*Arabic Grammar*, esp. 7 and 153) on the genealogical trajectory of this apparently Kufan term for 'coordination'.

action, strong in smite and of sound resolve.[34] If this then is what Ibn ʿUyayna had meant, where does that place it among the [various] interpretations? In fact, if his interpretation of it is this, then his interpretation would lean towards our interpretation of it, even though the meaning of his reading would actually contradict that of the reading that we prefer, by changing the correct reading with his chosen reading of a lightened (*takhfīf*) *tudhkira*. Still, we do not know of anyone who reads it like that, or who prefers reading it like he does with that meaning. So, the correct opinion concerning His words, if the matter is generally as we have indicated, is the one that we prefer.

An account of those who have interpreted His words *where one of the two errs, then one of the two shall remind the other* as we have:

Saʿīd reported that Qatāda[35] said, about His words *Call to witness two witnesses from your menfolk, and if there are not two men, then a man and two women who satisfy you as witnesses, where one of the two errs, then one of the two shall remind the other*: God knew that there would be dues (*ḥuqūq*) [from one person to another] and thus He created trust between some of them for the sake of others. Seek then that trust provided by God, for that is greater obedience to your Lord, and is more likely to guarantee your property (*māl*). I swear by my life, if a man were a God-fearing person, the writing down [of the debt] can only increase him in good, and if he were corrupt, then he will be more likely to fulfil [commitments] when he knows that there will be witnesses against him.

Al-Rabīʿ,[36] regarding *where one of the two errs, then one of the two shall remind the other*, said: If one of the two of them forgets, then the other will remind her.[37]

Qāḍī al-Nuʿmān

Qāḍī al-Nuʿmān gives the rulings for women's testimony according to his legal interpretation. According to him, women could testify without men in those matters that

[34] Note the construction of maleness/masculinity, in which 'maleness' indicates functionality and is associated with strength and weaponry.

[35] Bishr ← Yazīd ← Saʿīd ← Qatāda.

[36] Muthannā ← Isḥāq ← Ibn Abī Jaʿfar ← His father ← al-Rabīʿ.

[37] Ṭabarī, *Jāmiʿ al-bayān*, s.v. Q. 2:282. There follow three further reports, on different authorities, to the same effect – see Ṭabarī, *Jāmiʿ al-Bayān*, II, 1620–23, s.v. Q. 2:282 – and in the last of these it is said that both variants of the third person verbal form (i.e. *fa-tudhkira* and *fa-tudhakkira*) are acceptable (alternative) expressions and mean the same thing, but that Ṭabarī's preference is for *tudhakkira*.

men do not see, such as birth, menstruation and so forth. Note that this interpretation, which was widespread in the medieval period, was predicated on the idea that men were never present at childbirth. For Qāḍī al-Nuʿmān, women's testimony is not permitted in divorce or in *ḥudūd*-crimes, except that it seems that it is accepted in the event of a killing, as long as the witness swore a fifty-fold oath.

It is related that ʿAlī [b. Abī Ṭālib] and Abū Jaʿfar and Abū ʿAbd Allāh (*ʿm*), said: In marriage, the testimony of those women and slaves who may testify to property is permitted. The testimony of women is not permitted in divorce, nor in *ḥudūd*-crimes, though it is permitted in property, and in those matters that nobody sees except women, such as looking at other women, testifying to the first cry after birth (*istihlāl*), childbirth, parentage, menstruation and everything that resembles that. In this matter the testimony of the midwife is permitted, if she is satisfactory. The testimony of women in cases of murder is abominable (*laṭkh*), so with it there must be fifty-fold oath (*qasāma*).[38]

Zamakhsharī

Zamakhsharī's primary interest seems not to be the status of women, but rather the grammatical difficulties of this part of the verse, and the variant readings. Zamakhsharī is a Ḥanafī, and, according to the Ḥanafī school, women's testimony is permitted alongside men's in anything that is not *ḥudūd* or *qiṣāṣ*. Zamakhsharī's *tafsīr* is also notable in that he says that God *intends* for one of the women to err, because her error is the cause of the second woman's reminding her. This interpretation raises the question of whether God could intend an error. Indeed, Zamakhsharī admits that the first objection would be: how can her error be the intention of God Almighty? However, for him, it is this very error that is mitigated against by the introduction of the second witness, so while it may be intended, it is also resolved.

Call to witness two witnesses: ask that two witnesses testify on your behalf in cases of debt *from your menfolk*, the male believers. Free status (*ḥurriya*) and legal age (*bulūgh*) in addition to being Muslim are the conditions, according to most of the *ʿulamāʾ*. And according to ʿAlī [b. Abī Ṭālib], may God be pleased with him, the testimony of a slave is not admissible in any situation, but according to Shurayḥ, Ibn Sīrīn, and ʿUthmān al-Battī,[39] it is admissible.

[38] On the *qasāma*, see J. Pedersen and Linant de Bellefonds, 'Ḳasam', *EI²*, IV, 688–90. Qāḍī al-Nuʿmān, *Daʿāʾim al-Islām*, II, 514.

[39] ʿUthmān al-Battī (d. 143/761) is an important figure in the discussion among Islamicists about the authenticity of early Islamic texts. Michael Cook (along with Schacht) regards the famous epistle of Abū Ḥanīfa to Battī as one of the earliest extant texts. See Cook, *Early Muslim Dogma*, esp. 27ff.

In addition, according to Abū Ḥanīfa, the testimony of unbelievers against one another is permitted, despite their different confessional communities (*milal*).

And if there are not, if the two witnesses are not, *two men then a man and two women*, then let a man and two women testify. The testimony of women alongside that of men is acceptable according to Abū Ḥanīfa in matters other than *ḥudūd* crimes and retaliation (*qiṣāṣ*).

Who satisfy you: those whom you know to be just.

Where one of the two errs: when one of the two is unable to provide the testimony because she has forgotten it, [*taḍilla*] being derived from *ḍalla al-ṭarīq* (he has lost his way) when he cannot find it (*lam yahtadi lahu*). And it [the verb] is subjunctive (*intiṣāb*) because it serves as an object (*maf'ūl lahu*); in other words, intending thereby that she errs. If you were to say: How could God, exalted be He, intend for her to err?[40] I would say: Since erring is a cause (*sabab*) for reminding, and the reminding is effected (*musabbab*) by that [erring], and since they consider both cause and effect as having equal status given that they are in apposition and are interconnected, then the intention for the error from which reminding ensues becomes, in effect, an intention for the reminding.

It is as though it were said: 'With the intention being that one reminds the other if she were to err'. Analogous (*naẓīr*) to this is when one says, 'I have prepared the wooden beam so that when (*an*) the wall begins to lean, I might prop it up' (*an yamīla al-ḥā'iṭ fa-ad'amahu*) and 'I prepared the weapons so that when (*an*) the enemy should come, I might ward him off' (*an yajī'a 'adūwwun fa-adfa'ahu*).

Fa-tudhkira has been read as either lightened or as *fa-tudhakkira* (doubled), with both constituting alternative expressions (*lughatān*), and in addition: *fa-tudhākir*. Ḥamza read it as *in tadilla iḥdāhumā*, as a conditional with *fa-tudhakkiru* indicative (*raf'*) and doubled (*tashdīd*), such as where He says: *Wa man 'āda fa-yantaqimu Allāhu minhu* (*and whoever relapses, God shall inflict vengeance on him* [Q. 5:95]). Another reading taking the form of a passive construction with the feminine [third person] is *an tuḍalla iḥdāhumā*. An example of an extravagant explanation in the commentaries (*min bida' al-tafāsīr*) is when they claim that it is *fa-tudhkiru*, that is, the one makes the other a male (*dhakar*), meaning that when the two of them join together they assume the status of a male.[41]

[40] Note that the Arabic relative clause particle *an*, which we render as 'where' for lexical flexibility, may also be rendered as 'that'.

[41] Zamakhsharī, *al-Kashshāf*, I, 403, s.v. Q. 2:282.

Ṭabrisī

Of all of the commentaries surveyed in this chapter, it is perhaps Ṭabrisī's which most exemplifies the lexical and grammatical impetus in *tafsīr*. He expounds at great length on the different readings and gives extensive explanations for the variant readings. Gender is, for him, a secondary concern, but his biases creep into his grammatical explanations, such as when he explains that the two women are the ones who must be satisfying. Ṭabrisī attributes the two-women-one-man rule to women's innate proclivity for forgetfulness: 'This is because forgetfulness overcomes women more than it overcomes men'. This is perhaps the most interesting part of this interpretation for those who study gender, because it shows that by his time the commentators are interested in explaining why a verse has a particular ruling, rather than simply reproducing the ruling itself.

Reading (*qirā'a*)

Ḥamza alone read *in taḍilla*, with a *kasra* on the *hamza*, while the rest [read it] with a *fatḥa* [*an*]. Ibn Kathīr, Abū ʿAmr and Qutayba read *fa-tudhkira* lightened (*takhfīf*) and in the subjunctive (*naṣb*). Ḥamza also read *fa-tudhakkiru* in the intensive form (*tashdīd*) and in the indicative (*rafʿ*). The rest of them read *fa-tudhakkira* in the intensive form (*tashdīd*) and in the subjunctive.

Proof (*ḥujja*)

The justification (*wajh*) for Ḥamza's reading *in taḍilla iḥdāhumā* with the *kasra* on the *hamza* is that he considers *in* to be a conditional particle (*li'l-jazā'*) and the *fa-* where He says *fa-tudhakkiru* introduces the response to the conditional (*jawāb al-jazā'*). The syntactical locus for the conditional (*sharṭ*) and its response (*jazā'*)[42] are both in the indicative mood (*rafʿ*) because they both describe indefinites, in this case the two women, where He says *fa-rajulun wa'mra'atān*. Thus His words *rajulun wa'mra'atān* are the predicate (*khabar*) of an elided subject clause (*mubtada' maḥdhūf*), the implication (*taqdīr*)[43] being: 'then the ones to testify shall be a man and two women'

[42] This is a good example of the fluidity with which the medieval exegetes drew on grammatical terms and the synonymy available to them as a result of the influences of both the Basran and Kufan schools of grammar. On all of these issues, the reader is advised to consult the works of Versteegh in the bibliography and also the two-part study by Mustafa Shah: 'Exploring the Genesis of Early Arabic Linguistic Thought: Qur'anic Readers and Grammarians of the Kūfan Tradition (Part I)', *Journal of Qur'anic Studies* 5.1 (2003), 47–78 and idem, 'Exploring the Genesis of Early Arabic Linguistic Thought: Qur'anic Readers and Grammarians of the Basran Tradition (Part II)', *Journal of Qur'anic Studies* 5.2 (2003), 1–47.

[43] Conceptually, *taqdīr* is a very interesting grammatical term, which literally means 'estimating'. It is often used by exegetes to postulate, as it were, what the underlying structure may be or what the speaker intended to say, had the speaker said it in full, and they do this by supplying elements or paraphrasing the statement in question; cf. Versteegh, *Arabic Grammar*, 99, 150; Gully, *Grammar and Semantics in Medieval Arabic*, 215ff.; K. Versteegh, 'Taqdīr', *EALL*, IV, 442–6.

(*fa-man yashhad rajulun wa'mra'atān*). It could also be that *rajulun* is in the nominative as indicating a new subject (*ibtidā'*) and *imra'atān* [likewise nominative] as indicating a coordination with that [subject], with the predicate of the subject in this case having been elided; here the implied meaning would be: 'then a man and two women shall testify' (*fa-rajulun wa'mra'atān yashhadūn*).

As regards His words *who satisfy you as witnesses*, what is mentioned here refers back to those just described, the one man and two women, and cannot be a reference to the *two witnesses* (*shahīdayn*) mentioned earlier because of the disagreement in syntactical inflection of those described. Do you not see how *shahīdayn* is accusative while *rajulun wa'mra'atān* are inflected in the nominative? Given this, you will then know that the adjectival qualification (*waṣf*), which itself is an adverbial qualifier (*ẓarf*), is one that describes *fa-rajulun wa'mra'atān* and not the earlier-mentioned *shahīdayn*. Thus the conditional and its response are adjectival qualifications of *imra'atān* (two women), since a conditional is a sentence that can be used to describe just as it can be used to connect [clauses], similar to where He says *those whom, if We give them mastery over a land, establish the prayer* [Q. 22:41].[44]

As for the *lām* in His words *an taḍill*, for those who take *an* as introducing a conditional and functioning to apocopate (*jazm*), it is vowelled with a *fatḥa* because of the coming together of two unvowelled consonants (*sākinān*); even if it were inflected with a *kasra* because of the preceding *kasra*, this still would have been acceptable by analogy (*qiyās*).[45] As for His words *fa-tudhakkiru* (will remind), they are [to be taken as] analogous to Sībawayh's statement regarding His words, exalted be He, *wa-man 'āda fa-yantaqimu Allāhu minhu* [Q. 5:95][46] and the other verses that he recited [as proof] along-side this one to the effect that what follows the *fa-* in *fa-tudhakkiru* is an elided subject (*mubtada' maḥdhūf*), which, if you were to supply it, would have been *fa-humā tudhakkiru iḥdāhumā al-ukhrā*. In this way, the 'reminding' (*dhikr*) refers back to the missing subject, that is, the [elided] pronoun in His words *iḥdāhumā*. As for the origin (*aṣl*) of *tudhakkir*, that is *al-dhikr* (to remind), the opposite of *al-nisyān* (to forget): *dhakkartu* is a transitive verb that can take a given direct object (*maf'ūl*), but if you were to

[44] *Alladhīna in makkannāhum fī'l-arḍi aqāmū'l-ṣalāt*: the *in makkannāhum fī'l-arḍi* thus constitutes an adjectival qualification of *alladhīna*.

[45] The two terms *naql* (transmission) and *qiyās* (analogy) constituted methodological principles of linguistic methods for the Basran and the Kufan grammarians, from which could be derived grammatical analyses of the kind presented above.

[46] *And whoever relapses, God shall inflict vengeance on him*. Ṭabrisī is interested in the indicative-mood inflection of the verb *fa-yantaqimu*.

add to it a *hamza* or to double its *ʿayn*, it would take a different direct object,[47] which is similar to the [difference between] *farraḥtuhu* and *afraḥtuhu*. Thus those who read *fa-tudhakkiru* are those who apply a doubling [of the medial consonant], and those who read *fa-tudhkiru* are those who add a *hamza*, and both are palatable (*sāʾigh*).

The second direct object in His words *then one of the two shall remind the other* (*fa-tudhakkiru iḥdāhumā al-ukrā*) has been omitted, the meaning being: then one of the two shall remind the other of the testimony that they have committed to provide.

As for the majority reading, it is *an taḍilla* with a *fatḥa* on the [initial] *alif* [of *an*], so the *an* is connected (*taʿalluq*) to a verb in ellipsis (*muḍmar*), which is indicated by the [context of the] speech. This [elided verb] can be one of three things: the first is that His words *and if there are not two men, then a man and two women* indicates that you may say 'and call to witness a man and two women' (*waʾstashhidū rajulan waʾmraʾatayn*). On that basis, the implication is 'let a man and two women testify', where *an* is connected to this [elided] verb. The second is the opinion of Abūʾl-Ḥasan, namely that the implication is 'let there be (*faʾl-yakun*) a man and two women', according to which, then, the meaning would be 'let the testimony of a man and two women take place (*faʾl-yaḥduth*)', where the first part of the [genitive] annexation (*muḍāf*) has been omitted and its place taken up by the part to which it is annexed (*muḍāf ilayhi*). The third is where the predicate of the subject is suppressed, which in this case is *fa-rajulun waʾmraʾatān*, that is to say, 'then a man and two women should testify' (*fa-rajulun waʾmraʾatayn*). In this way 'should testify' (*yashhadūn*) governs (*ʿāmil fī*) *an*, and the place of the ellipsis, according to those who place a *fatḥa* on the *hamza* in *an taḍilla*, is *qabla an* (before that [she errs]). As for those who place a *kasra* on *in*, that is because the conditional and its response have been concluded. As for the [correct inflection] for *an*, that should be with an initial *a-* (*naṣb*), the implication being: so that if one of the two shall err, then [the other] shall remind (*li-an taḍilla iḥdāhumā fa-tudhakkir*).

If an objection was made that testimony takes place on the basis of recollection (*dhikr*) and memory (*ḥifẓ*), not errancy (*ḍalāl*), which in effect is memory lapse (*nisyān*), the response would be: Sībawayh's opinion is that He

[47] The *ʿayn* here means the second consonant *-k-* of *dh-k-r*, as grammarians used the paradigm of *f-ʿ-l* (*faʿala*) for the primary verbal form. Similarly, by *lām*, they would mean the third consonant of a typical tri-consonantal verbal stem. As for *hamz* or *hamza*, they meant the glottal stop of an initial *alif*; by *taḍʿīf* is meant *tathqīl*, where the consonant is 'doubled', hence the opposite of *takhfīf*. In sum, the discussion is about what we would call the second and fourth verbal forms (*dhakkara* and *adhkara*, respectively). The difference in direct object meant by Ṭabrisī is the difference between a direct object and an indirect object.

has commanded [two women] to come forth as witnesses in order that one might remind the other and the reason why He mentions *an taḍilla* is because that is the cause for the reminder. It is like when one says, 'I have prepared such and such so that if the wall should bend, I would prop it up', by which he does not mean that he is desiring for the wall to bend; rather, he is simply giving the occasion and motive for the propping up. As for reading His words *fa-tudhakkira* or *fa-tudhkira* in the subjunctive, that is because it is coordinated (*ʿaṭf*) with the [other] verb made subjunctive by the *an* [. . .].[48]

Meaning (*maʿnā*)

God, glory be to Him, then gives the command to call to witness, saying, *call to witness two witnesses from your menfolk*, meaning: request witnesses, and have them bear witness over the document (*al-maktūb*), two of your men, which is to say from the people of your religious community. Mujāhid said that these should be from those who are free (*aḥrār*), educated (*ʿālimūn*), of legal age (*bālighūn*) and Muslim, and not slaves (*ʿabīd*) or unbelievers (*kuffār*). Free status is not a necessary condition, according to us, for the admissibility of testimony; only being Muslim and justness (*ʿadāla*) are conditions; this is also the opinion of Shurayḥ, al-Laythī and Abū Thawr. Some say that this is a command for judges (*quḍāt*) when issuing judgments concerning rights: they should seek out two witnesses to advocate for the plaintiff (*muddaʿī*) when the defendant (*muddaʿā ʿalayhi*) denies [the charges]. The *sīn* in these two instances then signifies the [verbal] *sīn* of question and request.[49]

If there are not two men, meaning, if the two witnesses are not male, *then a man and two women*, that is to say, let there be a man and two women, or let a man and two women testify, *who satisfy you as witnesses*: their justness [satisfies you]. This proves that that justness is a prerequisite for testimony and that we are not enacting piety by simply calling to witness those who are satisfactory in an absolute sense, because He says, *who satisfy you*. He did not say 'who are satisfactory', for there is no way for us to know who is satisfactory to God, exalted be He, but rather our piety lies in calling to witness someone who is satisfactory to us on the face of it (*fī'l-ẓāhir*), that is, one

[48] Ṭabrisī provides his commentary by parsing the verse or passage of verses into analytical categories (*qirāʾa*, *ḥujja*, *iʿrāb*, *lugha*, *maʿnā* and occasionally *nuzūl* among other less frequent ones), filling each with those parts of the verse that may be relevant. The remainder of the *ḥujja* section above continues into other parts of this long verse. We provide elliptical brackets and move on to where our section of the verse (the testimony) emerges again for discussion, now under *maʿnā*.

[49] By his comment on the *sīn*, Ṭabrisī means to explain why the tenth verbal paradigm, *istafʿilū*, sc. *istashhidū*, is used instead of the fourth, *ashhidū*, which would have also been a grammatical possibility.

whose religious practice and trustworthiness satisfy us, and whom we know for his discretion (*satr*) and righteousness (*ṣalāḥ*).

Where one of the two errs, that is to say, if one of the two women should forget, *then one of the two shall remind the other*: this is said to derive from 'reminding' (*dhikr*), the opposite of forgetting (*nisyān*), as [reported] on the authority of al-Rabīʿ, al-Suddī, al-Ḍaḥḥāk and the majority of the interpreters. The implication (*taqdīr*) is that one of them reminds the other of the testimony which they have both undertaken to bear. As for those who read *fa-tudhkiru*, as a lightened (*takhfīf*) form, from *al-idhkār*, this also carries the same meaning, that is to say, one says to her, 'Do you remember the day when we witnessed in such-and-such a place, and in the presence of such-and-such a man or woman?' until she remembers the testimony. Such forgetfulness overcomes women more than it overcomes men. Some also say that [the verb] is related to *dhakar* (male), that is, this [coming together of the two women] makes her like a man, [as reported] on the authority of Sufyān b. ʿUyayna; but the former [interpretation] is the stronger one.

And if it were asked: why did He repeat the expression *iḥdāhumā* (*one of the two*)? Why did He not say 'so that she might remind the other'? The response to this has two aspects. One of them is that this was repeated so that the agent of the verb might precede the object. For, if He were to say 'she then reminds the other' (*fa-tudhakkiruhā al-ukhrā*), He would have caused the object of the action to separate the agent of the verb and the verb itself, which is [stylistically] loathsome (*makrūh*).

The second of them is what al-Ḥusayn b. ʿAlī al-Maghribī said, which is that it meant that if one of the two testimonies should be erroneous, which is to say, that it becomes lost through forgetfulness, then one of the two women will remind the other (*fa-tudhakkir iḥdā al-mara'tayn al-ukhrā*), with the effect that the repetition of the word *iḥdāhumā* is not rendered meaningless. This is supported by the fact that the one who forgets a testimony is not called *ḍall*; but you can say *ḍallat al-shahāda* when it is gone amiss, similar to where God says, glory be to Him, *ḍallū ʿannā* (*they have gone amiss from us*) [Q. 40:74], that is to say, they were lost to us.[50]

Rāzī

Building on the points made by Zamakhsharī, Rāzī first explains his view of women's innate inferiority by saying that 'forgetfulness dominates women's natures, due to the

[50] Ṭabrisī, *Majmaʿ al-bayān*, II, 398, s.v. Q. 2:282.

predominance of coldness and moisture in their physical constitution', hence the need for two women. The argument about the humours – coldness and moisture versus warmth and dryness – had existed since the time of the ancient Greeks; it appeared to explain women's role in the *tafsīr* of Abū'l-Layth al-Samarqandī (d. 373/983), over three hundred years before Fakhr al-Dīn al-Rāzī. It seems likely that the Greek notion of the humours was widespread in Islamic lands, and that this was one way of describing the differences in intellect between men and women that most commentators believed to be innate. While it seems to be a far-fetched explanation to modern sensibilities, in those times it would have been considered scientific and true.

Rāzī's interpretation is therefore predicated on the idea of women's inferiority. For him, the phrase *where one of the two errs, then one of the two shall remind the other* serves two purposes: the first is to attain the testimony, which can only happen with two women and one man, and the second is to 'highlight the superiority of a man over a woman'. For him, these goals are only reached through the error of one of the women.

Rāzī mentions the interpretation of Sufyān b. ʿUyayna, but only to refute it. Finally, true to his exegetical parsing method, Rāzī embarks on the commentary to Q. 2:282 by noting that it contains the third of several (financial) legal rulings (*aḥkām sharʿiyya*) mentioned at this point of the *sūra* (sc. Q. 2, *sūrat al-Baqara*), at what he calls 'the verse of mutual loaning' (*āyat al-mudāyana*).[51] Rāzī's use of subdivisions is extensive in his commentary, and ranges from terms like *ḥujja* (proof), *su'āl/jawāb* (question/response) and *lāzim* (concomitant) to *qawl* (opinion), *nawʿ* (type/species), *wajh* (aspect) and *mas'ala* (issue), with this last being by far the most frequent analytic category. We pick up the commentary at the point at which Rāzī is offering the second matter that God is commanding to be considered in this verse (the first being the writing down of the debt).

The second type of matter taken into consideration by God, exalted be He, with regard to the contracting of debts (*mudāyana*) is 'the calling to witness' (*ishhād*), where He says *call to witness two witnesses from your menfolk*. Know also that the purpose of writing down [the debt contract] (*kitāba*) is the calling forth of witnesses (*istishhād*) in order to allow for testimony if the person were to deny knowledge [of the debt] (*juḥūd*) and to be able to secure what is owed. There are several issues regarding this verse.

[51] 'The verse of mutual loaning' is also known as *āyat al-dayn*, although the sixth infinitive is the more accurate, extracted as it is from the opening words of the verse itself (*idhā tadāyantum*). It would be even more precise to think of it as signifying 'the verse of mutual contracts involving debts'. Rāzī offers a distinction between *qarḍ* and *dayn*, where the latter is time-bound and the former is an outright loan. Indeed, Islamic jurisprudence does make a distinction between the two: see Imran A.K. Nyazee, *Outlines of Islamic Jurisprudence* (Islamabad, Center for Excellence in Research, 1998; 6th edn, 2016), esp. ch. 19, 307ff.; also Hiroyuki Yanagihashi, 'Contract Law', *EI*[3]; somewhat outdated but containing a useful overview of obligations and contracts is Joseph Schacht's *An Introduction to Islamic Law* (Oxford, Clarendon Press, 1964), 144–60.

The first issue: *Istashhidū* means *ashhidū*. One says *ashhadtu al-rajul* or *istashhadtuhu* with the same import; and *alshahīdān* are the same as *al-shāhidan*, where the paradigm *faʿīl* has the import of *fāʿil*.

The second issue: The genitive construction (*iḍāfa*) of His words *from your menfolk* (*min rijālikum*) has involves several aspects. The first is that it means from your religious community (*milla*), namely, the Muslims. The second is that some take this to be free men (*aḥrār*), while the third is that *from your menfolk* are those whom you consider fit for testimony on account of [their] justness (*ʿadāla*).

The third issue: There are multiple conditions for testimony, and these are mentioned in works of jurisprudence (*fiqh*). Here, we will mention just one issue, which is that, according to Shurayḥ and Ibn Sīrīn and Aḥmad, the testimony of slaves (*ʿabd*) is admissible, whereas according to al-Shāfiʿī and Abū Ḥanīfa, may God be pleased with the two of them, it is not. Shurayḥ's proof for his argument (*ḥujja*) is that God's words *call to witness two witnesses from your menfolk* are general, extending to slaves and others, and this is also indicated by the import of the text (*naṣṣ*). That is because a person's intellect (*ʿaql*), along with his faith (*dīn*) and justness, would prevent him from mendacity (*kadhib*). Thus, if he were to testify when all of these conditions have been met, the plaintiff's statement would be confirmed, and that in turn becomes a means to reinstate his rights. Moreover, intellect, faith and justice should not vary on account of being free or being a slave (*riqq*). The testimony of slaves must then be admissible. The proof argument of al-Shāfiʿī[52] and Abū Ḥanīfa, may God be pleased with the two of them, is His words, exalted be He, *let not witnesses refuse when they are summoned* [Q. 2:282], which entails that whoever is called to witness be obliged to go to the location where testimony is to be given, and it is illicit for that person not to go to present his testimony. Given that the verse indicates that whoever is called to witness is obliged to present himself, whereas the consensus indicates that slaves are not obliged to present themselves, which then means that it is not obligatory for the slave to come forth as a witness, this deduction (*istidlāl*) presents itself as a fair one (*ḥasan*). As for His words, exalted be He, *call to witness two witnesses from your menfolk*, we have clarified that some of them have said *call to witness two witnesses from your menfolk* whom you consider fit to provide testimony. Given this implication, why would you say that slaves are in such a predicament?

[52] Rāzī was a Shāfiʿī.

He, exalted be He, then says *and if there are not two men, then a man and two women*. Concerning the nominative (*irtifāʿ*) case in *rajulun wa'mra'atān* (a man and two women), four aspects ensue. The first is: let there be one man and two women; the second: let one man and two women testify; the third: the witnesses [required] shall consist in a man and two women; the fourth: a man and two women should testify. All of these assumptions (*taqdīrāt*) are permissible and sound possibilities, as mentioned by ʿAlī b. Īsā [al-Rummānī], may God have mercy on him.

He then said, *who satisfy you as witnesses*, which is like His words regarding divorce (*ṭalāq*): *and call to witness two who are just from among you* [Q. 65:2]. Know then that this verse does not indicate that anyone may be sound for the purpose of testimony. The jurists (*fuqahā'*) say there are ten conditions for accepting testimony, that the witness be free (*ḥurr*), of legal age (*bāligh*), Muslim, just (*ʿadl*), knowledgeable about what he is testifying to, neither drawing to himself any benefit by that testimony, nor doing it in order to ward off any harm from himself, nor know frequent mistake-making (*ghalaṭ*), nor for forsaking virtuousness (*muruwwa*), and without any enmity existing between him and whomever he might be testifying against.

Then He said, *where one of the two errs, then one of the two shall remind the other*. The import here is that forgetfulness dominates women's natures, due to the predominance of coldness (*bard*) and moisture (*ruṭūba*) in their physical constitution (*amzija*). Hence, it is less reasonable to assume that forgetfulness should occur in the case of both women than in one of them alone. Thus two women have been made to stand in place of one man, so when one of the two of them should err, she shall be reminded by the other, which is the intention of this verse. Herein, however, several issues are involved.

The first issue: Ḥamza reads *in taḍalla* and *fa-tudhakkiru*, the meaning of which constitutes a conditional. The syntactical locus for *taḍill* is an apocopation (*jazm*), even as that is not indicated by any [consonantal] doubling (*taḍʿīf*); *fa-tudhakkiru* is thus rendered an indicative, because what comes after the conditional (*jazā'*) constitutes the beginning [of the statement] (*mubtada'*).

As for all of the other readers, they read it as being *an* with a *fatḥa* for two reasons (*wajh*). One is the implication that it signifies *li-an taḍilla* (so that if she were to err), but where the prepositional particle (*khāfiḍ*) has been omitted. The other is that it is the object of occasion (*mafʿūl lahu*), that is to say, intended for when she might err.[53]

[53] Note the relationship between this interpretation and that of Zamakhsharī above.

However, if one were to object: how could it be correct to say this when 'calling to witness' is something done for the purpose of 'reminding', not for 'causing errancy', we would say: There are two objectives here. The first of them is that the testimony take place, which is not attained except when one of the two women reminds the other; and the second is that it is intended to highlight the superiority of a man over a woman, in order to then clarify that when two women take the place of one man, that is justness in such cases, and that can only occur when one of the two women errs. Therefore, if each of these two matters, by which I mean the calling to witness and the clarification of the superiority of a man over a woman, is what is intended – and this can only happen through the error of the one of them and the reminding of the other – then undoubtedly these two matters become required. That is what occurred to me by way of response at the time of penning this section. Grammarians will have other responses, copiously covering this in their books, but I did not find any of them convincing. And God knows best.

The second issue: Regarding 'erring' (*ḍalāl*) where He says, *where one of the two errs*, there are two aspects. One of them is that this connotes 'forgetting' (*nisyān*), as He, exalted be He, has said: *Lost to them now* (*wa-ḍalla ʿanhum*) *are the fallacies they used to invent* (*mā kānū yaftarūn*) [Q. 16:87],[54] that is to say, they have gone from them (*dhahaba ʿanhum*). The second is that this derives from 'losing one's way' (*ḍalla fī'l-ṭarīq*) in the sense of not being able to find it. Both of these aspects are quite similar [in meaning]. Abū ʿAmr's opinion was that *ḍalāl* originally meant 'absence' (*ghaybūba*).

The third issue: Nāfiʿ, Ibn ʿĀmir, as well as ʿĀṣim and al-Kisāʾī read *fa-tudhakkira*, doubled and in the subjunctive, whereas Ḥamza read it *fa-tudhakkiru*, doubled and in the indicative, while Ibn Kathīr and Abū ʿAmr read *fa-tudhkira*, lightened and in the subjunctive. Both are [related] lexical forms: *dhakara* and *adhkara*, just like *nazala* and *anzala*; but the doubled [form] is the one more widely used. God, exalted be He, said, *Remind, then* (*fa-dhakkir*)*; for, if anything, you are meant to be a reminder* [Q. 88:21]. Those who read it lightened allow for the verb to remain transitive by the *alif* of *afʿala* (*hamzat al-ifʿāl*).[55]

[54] It must be said that this is not the optimal choice for an analogous Qurʾānic usage (cf. Q. 25:17 and Q. 32:10 for a more obvious sense of 'lost' regarding *ḍ-l-l*). Rāzī's citation (also in Q. 6:24) suggests more the sense that the false deities or idols referred to in the Qurʾānic context have abandoned those who had trumped them up, even though, of course, the fact that they 'cannot find' these suggests 'lost'. Lane (*Lexicon*, Book I, 1797) discusses *an* or *in taḍilla*.

[55] In other words, the fourth verbal form.

The majority of the exegetes (*al-mufassirūn*) are of the opinion that this act of reminding (*al-tadhkīr wa'l-idhkār*) relates to forgetfulness, with the exception of what has been related on the authority of Sufyān b. ʿUyayna, namely that concerning His words *fa-tudhkiru iḥdāhumā al-ukhrā*, he read it as 'she makes her a male' (*tajʿaluhā dhakaran*), meaning that the sum of the testimony of the two women equals the testimony of one man. This reasoning (*wajh*) has also been recorded on the authority of Abū ʿAmr b. al-ʿAlāʾ, who said: When a woman testifies then the other one comes to testify alongside her, she makes her [equal to] a male (*adhkarat-hā*), because the two of them together take the place of one man. However, this reasoning (*wajh*) is considered invalid (*bāṭil*) by the agreement of the majority of the exegetes. Two aspects (*wajh*) prove its weakness. The first is that whatever status women may attain, if a man is not with the two of them their testimony is not admissible. Hence, the second woman could never make the first like a male. The second aspect is that His words *fa-tudhakkir* are counterpoised (*muqābil*) to His preceding words *an taḍilla iḥdāhumā*, and so, since the 'errancy' (*ḍalāl*) is elucidated by the 'forgetting' (*nisyān*), then likewise the 'reminding' (*idhkār*) will be elucidated by that which has been counterpoised to the 'forgetting'.[56]

Qurṭubī

Qurṭubī's interpretation is heavily focused on law, detailing the rulings from his Mālikī school.[57] In the following passage, he explains the controversy over whether women can testify when there is a second man who could testify, or whether they can only testify if there is not a second man who could testify. Qurṭubī's view is that if two men do not come, then a man and two women may testify: 'In this verse, God, exalted be He, has permitted the testimony of two women with a man even when there are two men available, even has He has not mentioned this in other verses'. He goes on to say that women's testimony, however, is only accepted in monetary matters, and is not accepted in issues of marriage, divorce or other matters. He justifies this by saying that monetary matters cause the most problems, so 'God has allowed for many ways of documenting [these issues].'

Qurṭubī explains that women's testimony is accepted without men's testimony in certain matters, but that this is out of necessity, since men do not see these things.[58]

[56] Rāzī, *Mafātīḥ al-ghayb*, s.v. Q. 2:282.

[57] In his preamble to the commentary on Q. 2:282, Qurṭubī advises that 'fifty-two issues' are raised by this verse.

[58] See Shaham, 'Women as Expert Witnesses' and Bauer, 'Debates on Women's Status'.

Thus, for him, the permission for women's testimony in no way implies that women's abilities are equal to men's, just that it is necessary in some limited circumstances. In those matters where men testify, the women's testimony is never acceptable without the man's. In those matters where only women attend, such as childbirth, the testimony of two women is acceptable. Qurṭubī admits that this matter is open to debate within the Mālikī school.

Finally, Qurṭubī gives a number of variant readings of *then one of the two shall remind the other.* He himself agrees with the reading of Sibawayh and argues against the reading of Ibn ʿUyayna, because, in his view, it does not deal with the issue of forgetting.

The twenty-fourth [issue]: Regarding His words, exalted be He, *Call to witness (istashhidū) two witnesses from your menfolk*, *istishhād* is when a call is made for testimony (*shahāda*). There is disagreement over whether it is obligatory (*farḍ*) or highly recommended (*nadb*), but the sound view is that it is a highly recommended act, as shall be explained, God willing.

The twenty-fifth [issue]: Regarding His words, exalted be He, *two witnesses*, God, glory be to Him, in His wisdom ordered (*rattaba*) testimonies relating to rights, both financial (*māliyya*) and corporeal (*badaniyya*), as well as *ḥudūd*-punishments in such a way that in each of these jurisdictions (*fann*) He has assigned two witnesses, except in fornication (*zinā*), as will become clear in *sūrat al-Nisāʾ* [Q. 4]; *witness* (*shahīd*) is an emphatic construction,[59] and in that form is an indication of someone who testifies frequently, intimating as it were the [person's] justness.[60] And God knows best.

The twenty-sixth [issue]: His words *from your menfolk*: this text [explicitly] disqualifies unbelievers (*kuffār*), those not of legal age (*ṣibyān*) and women (*nisāʾ*), but the expression itself [*menfolk*] can extend to [male] slaves (*ʿabīd*). However, Mujāhid said: What is meant here is free men (*aḥrār*). This was the preferred opinion of the Qāḍī Abū Isḥāq,[61] who has written at great length on this. The scholars differ with regard to the testimony of slaves. Shurayḥ, ʿUthmān al-Battī, Aḥmad [b. Ḥanbal], Isḥāq, and Abū Thawr[62] say that the testimony of a slave is permitted if he is just, giving weight to the lexical

[59] That is, it is an intensive substantive (*faʿīl*) form (cf. *shāhid*, *fāʿil*).

[60] By Qurṭubī's time, the institution of the professional witness (*shāhid ʿadl*) was well established. See R. Peters, <u>*Sh*</u>*āhid*, *EI*[2], IX, 207–8.

[61] Abū Isḥāq al-Isfarāʾīnī (d. 418/1027) was a medieval Sunnī theologian and Shāfiʿī jurisprudent. On him, see Angelika Brodersen, 'Abū Isḥāq Isfarāyīnī', *EI*[3].

[62] Abū Thawr Ibrāhīm b. Khālid al-Kalbī (d. 240/854) was a Baghdadi Shāfiʿī, who met Shāfiʿī. On him, see the PA.

expression of the verse (*lafẓ al-āya*).[63] Mālik [b. Anas], Abū Ḥanīfa and al-Shāfiʿī, as well as the majority of scholars, are of the opinion that a slave's testimony is not admissible, giving weight to the limitations of being a slave (*naqṣ al-riqq*), while al-Shaʿbī and al-Nakhaʿī permitted it in minor matters. However, the correct opinion is that of the majority, since God, exalted be He, says, *O you who believe when you contract debts*, continuing this address all the way to where He says *from your menfolk*, so that the address overtly (*ẓāhir*) is directed at those who contract debts; but slaves do not have that power, at least not without the permission of their masters. If the objection were to be made that the specification [of believers] at the beginning of the verse does not preclude a generalisation [of 'your menfolk'] at the end of it, one would respond that this specification is repeated by His words *let not witnesses refuse when summoned* [Q. 2:282], which will be explained in due course. In addition, His words *from your menfolk* are proof that a blind man can legitimately be considered a witness, but only if he knew something with absolute certainty (*yaqīnan*), as related on the authority of Ibn ʿAbbās, who said, 'The Messenger of God (*ṣlʿm*) was asked about testimony and he said, "Do you see the sun? Testify to what you see like this or stay away"'.[64] This is proof of the precondition that a witness should have seen with his own eyes (*muʿāyana*) that regarding which he is testifying, and not [proof] that he might testify by inference (*istidlāl*), which is liable to error. Yes, [a man] may lie with (*waṭʾ*) his wife if he were to recognise her voice, since embarking on sexual activity (*waṭʾ*) is permitted in this case by the preponderance of assumption (*ẓann*).[65] So if a woman[66] were to come to him in the bridal procession (*zuffat ilayhi*)[67] and it were said to him, 'this is your wife', even if

[63] That is to say, they base their argument on *your menfolk*, which would overtly include Muslim men and the male slaves they owned.

[64] A version of this *ḥadīth* is found in Ibn Ḥajar, *Bulūgh al-marām*, *Kitāb al-Qaḍāʾ* (14), *Bāb al-shahādāt* (1), *ḥadīth* no. 24/1420.

[65] The term *ẓann* represents human surmise or conjecture, but, however strong, still represents a potentially fallible opinion in contrast to *bayyina* (a clear proof): cf. the many uses of *ẓ-n-n* in the Qurʾān, where it can range from 'assume' to 'think' to 'trust' or even 'to be sure' (Q. 9:118; 38:24), yet still without clear or manifest proof. Qurṭubī's text, especially his examples, strongly suggests that he was drawing on Abū Ḥāmid al-Ghazālī's famous jurisprudential work *al-Muṣṭaṣfā*, on which, regarding the issues of uncertainty, see Baber Johansen, 'Dissent and Uncertainty in the Process of Legal Norm Construction in Muslim Sunnī Law' in *Law and Tradition in Classical Islamic Thought: Studies in Honor of Professor Hossein Modarressi*, ed. Michael Cook *et al.* (New York, Palgrave Macmillan, 2013), 127–44; Mohammad Fadel, '*Istaftī qalbaka wa in aftāka al-nāsu wa aftūka*: The Ethical Obligations of the *Muqallid* between Autonomy and Trust' in *Islamic Law in Theory: Studies on Jurisprudence in Honor of Bernard Weiss*, ed. A. Kevin Reinhart and Robert Gleave (Leiden, Brill, 2014), 105–26.

[66] Meaning, his new bride.

[67] This term indicates the festive pageant with which a bride is conducted to her husband's house following their marriage.

he did not know her, it would be permissible for him to have intercourse with her (*waṭʾ*). Likewise, it is permissible for him to accept a gift brought to him on the word of the messenger. But if he were to be told by someone that Zayd had affirmed this, or sold that, or had falsely accused someone, or had usurped something, he would not be permitted to testify against him on the basis of that information, because certainty (*yaqīn*) is the correct path in testimony.[68] In the absence of that [certainty], one is permitted to draw on a preponderance of conjecture (*ghālib al-ẓann*), which is why al-Shāfiʿī as well as Ibn Abī Layla and Abū Yūsuf all said: If he knew that thing before becoming blind, his testimony about it would still be admissible even after becoming blind, so that the blindness that would otherwise have represented an obstacle between him and the accused (*mashhūd ʿalayhi*) becomes like prolonged absence (*ghayba*) or death (*mawt*) in relation to one accused. This is the juridical opinion (*madhhab*) of these [scholars]. There is no justification (*wajh*) for preventing a blind man from testifying about what he had alighted on when he was able to see, and his testimony is valid to the degree that the report is copiously affirmed, just as one may report a ruling transmitted from the Messenger (*ṣlʿm*) by a great number of individuals (*tawātur*). Some scholars admit the testimony of a blind man in what is established on the basis of sound (*ṣawt*), because they believe that an inference made on this basis can rise to the level of certainty (*ḥadd al-yaqīn*) and that resemblance (*ishtibāh*) in sound is equal to resemblances in form (*ṣuwar*) or colour (*alwān*). But this is a weak argument (*ḍaʿīf*), since it would entail admitting as reliable something heard in the case of someone who has full sight. I say that Mālik's stance (*madhhab*) with regard to the testimony of a blind person on the basis of hearing (*ṣawt*) is admissible in cases of divorce and the like if the voice is recognised [by the testifier]. Ibn Qāsim reported: I said to Mālik, 'So a man hears his neighbour through the wall but does not see him and he hears him divorcing his wife and can proceed to testify against him if he recognises the voice (*ṣawt*)?' He said: Mālik said that his testimony is admissible. This is also the opinion of ʿAlī b. Abī Ṭālib, al-Qāsim b. Muḥammad, Shurayḥ al-Kindī, al-Shaʿbī, ʿAṭāʾ b. Abī Rabāḥ, Yaḥyā b. Saʿīd, Rabīʿa, Ibrāhīm al-Nakhaʿī, as well as Mālik and Layth.

The twenty-seventh [issue]: *If there are not two men, then a man and two women*. The meaning is that if the summoner does not come with two men,

[68] In this last example, with the proverbial Zayd, it is because 'testimony' involves the fate of a third party and not the person himself that the issue is so categorically attached to 'certainty'.

then let him come with a man and two women, and this is the opinion of the majority (*jumhūr*); *rajulun* (man) is in the nominative case as a subject (*ibtidāʾ*) and coordinated with it is *imraʾatān* (two women), the predicate having been omitted. That is to say, a man and two women should take the place of the two [male] witnesses. The accusative (*naṣb*) can be used, but not in the Qurʾān, as if it were: *istashhidū rajulan waʾmraʾatayn* (then call to witness a man and two women). Sībawayh related (*ḥakā*) *in khanjaran fa-khanjaran*.[69] Some scholars say, rather, the meaning is 'if there are not two men', that is to say, 'if no two [men] can be found'. Thus the testimony of two women is not permitted unless there are no men. Ibn ʿAṭiyya, however, says, 'But this [argument] is weak, because the wording of the verse does not permit such an interpretation. Rather, what is apparent from its meaning is the opinion held by the majority.' That is to say, if the two called to testify are not two men, that is to say, if the plaintiff is remiss about that, or has done it intentionally for some reason, then let him call a man and two women to testify.

In this verse, God, exalted be He, has permitted the testimony of two women with a man even when there are two men available, even as He has not mentioned this in other verses, and so, for the majority, it is admissible specifically to monetary matters (*amwāl*),[70] on the condition that a man is always with the two women. And this is the case specifically in financial matters, and not in other ones, because God has allowed for many ways of documenting (*tawthīq*) wealth, because of the many ways in which it can be acquired and because of the frequency with which troubles befall people as a result of it. So He made it documentable, sometimes by writing (*kitba*), and sometimes by verbal testimony (*ishhād*), and sometimes by depositing a security (*rahn*) and sometimes by a guarantee (*ḍamān*): and in all of these cases, the testimony of women with a man is allowed for. Let no reasonable person be under the illusion that God's words *when you contract debts* [Q. 2:282] apply to the debt of bridal payment after consummation (*maʿ al-buḍʿ*) or for reconciliation (*ṣulḥ*) after the intentional spilling of blood (*damm al-ʿamd*). In those cases, the testimony does not pertain to debts, but is testimony for the contraction of marriage (*nikāḥ*).

[69] There are varying possibilities here for which of the two terms can be in the accusative or nominative; commonly, the phrase would be *in khanjaran fa-khanjarun*, but this all depends on what one takes to be the ellipsis (for example, the verbs in both cases, such as *kāna*). The force of *Sībawayh ḥakā* ('Sibawayh related') is that he used poetic attestations to support grammatical rules, as did other early grammarians; on Sībawayh, see the detailed study of Amal Marogy, *Kitāb Sībawayhi: Syntax and Pragmatics* (Leiden, Brill, 2010).

[70] The meaning of this term is wider than it seems in English, encompassing anything that has a monetary value: property, monetary matters, chattel and so forth.

Scholars (*ʿulamāʾ*) have permitted women's testimony alone in those cases which none other than women are privy to, out of necessity (*ḍarūra*). Likewise, the testimony of those who have not attained legal age (*ṣibyān*) is permitted in cases of mutual injury out of necessity.[71]

The thirtieth [issue]: If it is affirmed that judgment may be passed on the basis of an oath and a witness, then as the Qāḍī Abū Aḥmad ʿAbd al-Wahhāb said: This is permitted in the case of property (*amwāl*) and matters related to that, except for corporeal rights (*ḥuqūq al-abdān*), given the consensus on this of all those who admit an oath alongside a witness. He says that this is because matters relating to property rights are of a lower degree that corporeal rights, by virtue of the fact that women's testimony is acceptable regarding these [. . .].[72]

Al-Mahdawī says that the testimony of women is not permitted in *ḥudūd*-crimes according to the opinions of the majority of jurists (*ʿāmmat al-fuqahāʾ*), as well as in cases of marriage or divorce, again according to the majority of the scholars (*akthar al-ʿulamāʾ*), which is the opinion of the school (*madhhab*) of Mālik and al-Shāfiʿī and others: women can only testify in matters relating to property (*amwāl*). In all cases in which they cannot testify for someone, they also cannot testify against another witness, whether there be a man with them or not. They cannot reproduce their testimony unless they are with a man, and it must have come from a situation in which she was with a man and a woman [in the first place]. Judgment can be passed on the authority of two women in every matter that is only attended by women, like birth (*wilāda*), the live birth of a child (*istihlāl*) and the like. All of this is according to the school of Mālik and there are minor differences regarding that.

The thirty-first [issue]: God's statement, exalted be He, *who satisfy you as witnesses* (*mimman tarḍawna minaʾl-shuhadāʾ*) occupies the syntactical locus of a subject clause (*rafʿ*) because it functions as an adjectival clause (*ṣifa*) for *a man and two women*. Ibn Bukayr and others say that this is

[71] Issues twenty-eight and twenty-nine comprise a long discussion of whether youths can testify, and the rules on the admissibility of swearing an oath (*yamīn*), where one person swears an oath alongside another who testifies. This latter was a point of major dispute between the majority of the Andalusians, with it being rejected by the Ḥanafīs but permitted by almost all of the Mālikīs and the Shāfiʿīs on the basis of the precedent of the Companions and even the Prophet himself, according to them.

[72] Women's testimony, thus, is permitted in matters perceived to be of a lesser offence. There follows another lengthy discussion about the admissibility of oath and testimony in cases of injury, concerning which there is further dispute.

addressing the arbiters (*ḥukkām*). But Ibn ʿAṭiyya claims that this is not proper (*nabīl*), the address being to all people. The ones caught up in this matter are the arbiters themselves. There are many cases of this in God's Book, where the address is generalised even as it specifically singles out some.

The thirty-second [issue]: Where God, exalted be He, says *who satisfy you as witnesses* (*mimman tarḍawna mina'l-shuhadā'*) this proves that among [those called to be] witnesses there may some who are unsatisfactory. Thus people cannot be assumed to be just unless they have proven to be so; this concept is something over and above (*zā'id*) being a Muslim, as the opinion of the majority stands. Abū Ḥanīfa said that every Muslim who is overtly a Muslim and untainted by some manifest corruption (*fisq*) may be considered a just person, even if his [moral] status (*majhūl al-ḥāl*) is unknown.[73] ʿUthmān al-Battī and Abū Thawr said that these [witnesses] are the just (*ʿudūl*) Muslim individuals, even if they be slaves (*ʿabīd*). I say that they have generalised the [applicability of the] rule, entailing thereby preference for the testimony of the nomad (*badawī*) over that of the townsman (*qarawī*) if he be just and satisfactory: this is the opinion of al-Shāfiʿī and those who agree with him, and he is reckoned among our authorities and co-religionists. Being a nomad is like his being from another city (*balad*), and the generalisations in the Qur'ān that indicate the admissibility of the testimony of just individuals treats the townsman and the nomad as equals. God, exalted be He, says, *who satisfy you as witnesses* (*mimman tarḍawna mina'l-shuhadā'*), and [elsewhere] He says, *and call to witness two who are just from among you* [Q. 65:2], where *from among you* (*minkum*) is an address for [all] Muslims. This categorically entails that the import of 'justness' (*ʿadāla*) be additional to being a Muslim, necessarily, because an adjective (*ṣifa*) is additional to the thing it describes (*mawṣūf*). Likewise, *who satisfy you as witnesses* (*mimman tarḍawna mina'l-shuhadā'*) is also similar, unlike what Abū Ḥanīfa said. And he is not to be classified as *satisfactory* until his status is investigated. It is necessary not to be content with his being outwardly a Muslim. [. . .][74]

The thirty-sixth [issue]: His words, exalted be He, *where one of the two errs*. Abū ʿUbayd said the meaning of *one of the two errs* is 'she forgets'. Erring in

[73] Thus Qurṭubī draws a distinction between legal schools. In his school's view (the Mālikī), one must know of the justness or probity of the individual, whereas the Ḥanafīs assume that, in the absence of overt corruption, any Muslim is just.

[74] Further discussion ensues on the additional requirements of constituting a 'satisfactory witness', that is, being Muslim in itself is not a guarantee of satisfactoriness.

testimony means forgetting one part of it and remembering only another, such that a person becomes confused (*ḥayrān*) in the middle of it, 'errant' (*ḍāll*). One who forgets their testimony entirely cannot be described as having erred in it. Ḥamza read *in*, with a *kasra* in the conditional sense (*jazā'*), where the *fa-* in His words *fa-tudhakkiru* constitutes its response (*jawāb*). Both the conditional clause and its response are in the indicative (*raf'*) [together] constituting an adjectival qualification of *a man and two women*; *tudhakkiru* is in the indicative mood, opening a new sentence (*isti'nāf*), as in the case of His words, *and whoever relapses, God shall inflict vengeance on him* (*fa-yantaqimu*) [Q. 5:95], this being the opinion of Sībawayh.

Those who place a *fatḥa* on the *an* take it to be an direct object of reason (*maf'ūl lahu*), with its operating agent (*'āmil*) omitted; *fa-tudhakkira* is then read in the subjunctive, according to the majority, as a coordination to the [other] verb in the subjunctive because of *an*. Al-Naḥḥās[75] said it is possible to read *taḍalla* and *tiḍalla*. Those who say *taḍalla* do so on the basis of the linguistic variant *ḍalilta taḍalla*, and in accordance with this you can say *tiḍalla* with a *kasra*, in order to indicate that the past tense is vowelled *fa'ilta*. ['Āṣim] al-Juḥdarī and 'Īsā b. 'Umar [al-Thaqafī][76] read *an tuḍalla* (she errs), with the meaning of *tunsā* (she forgets), and this is what was related about those two by Abū 'Amr al-Dānī. Al-Naqqāsh related, on the authority of al-Juḥdarī, [the reading] *tuḍilla* with the meaning *an tuḍilla al-shahāda* (that the woman loses the testimony), as when one says: *Aḍlaltu al-faras wa'l-ba'īr* (I have lost the horse and the camel) when they have disappeared from you and you cannot find them, and they end up dead.

The thirty-seventh [issue]: In His words *fa-tudhkira*, Ibn Kathīr[77] and Abū 'Amr lighten the *dhāl* and *kāf*, and according to this, the meaning would be that she renders her male in testimony, because the testimony of a woman is [only] half a testimony, and when there are two female witnesses, the bringing together of them adds up to the testimony of one male, according to Sufyān b. 'Uyayna and Abū 'Amr b. al-'Alā'. This is remote [from the truth] since, in relation to error, which means forgetfulness, there can only be

[75] The grammarian.

[76] 'Īsā b. 'Umar al-Thaqafī, Abū 'Umar al-Thaqafī al-Naḥwī al-Baṣrī (d. 149/766), a Qur'ān reader. On him, see Theodor Nöldeke and Friedrich Schwally, *et al.*, *The History of the Qur'an*, ed. and tr. Wolfgang H. Behn (Leiden, Brill, 2013), 474ff.; he is also mentioned by Kohlberg and Amir-Moezzi, *Revelation and Falsification*.

[77] He is referring here to the Qur'ān reader.

reminding, which is why the majority of readers read *fa-tudhakkira* as doubled; that is to say, she alerts her when she becomes heedless and forgets.

I say: This refers back to the reading of Abū ʿAmr, to mean if one of the two of them forgets, then the other one reminds her (*fa-tudhkiruhā al-ukhrā*), as in when one says *tadhakkartu* when remembering something, or *adhkartuhu* to remind someone else, as well as *dhakkartuhu*, all with the same meaning, as mentioned in the *Ṣaḥīḥ* works.[78]

Ibn Kathīr

Ibn Kathīr, a Shāfiʿī, starts his interpretation[79] of this part of the verse by stating his school's ruling that women's testimony is only allowed in monetary matters, not in other issues such as marriage and divorce. He justifies the ruling in which two women have been put in place of one man in testimony by citing a well-known *ḥadīth* on the authority of the Prophet. According to this *ḥadīth*, which is found in the *Ṣaḥīḥ* of Muslim, the Prophet tells a group of women that they are the majority of the inhabitants of Hell because they curse a lot, are ungrateful to their husbands, and are deficient in intellect and religion. The ruling that two women can testify in place of one of the male witnesses is explained by women's deficiency in intellect.

This *ḥadīth*, which is considered to be sound (*ṣaḥīḥ*) and on the authority of the Prophet himself, reflects medieval cultural attitudes about women's intellect and abilities, and may, in turn, have influenced modern cultural attitudes: it is still referenced today. Although it does not appear in many works of *tafsīr* on this verse, it is referenced as early as Thaʿlabī (d. 427/1035). Ibn Kathīr's method of bringing in the whole, sound *ḥadīth* in order to comment on the Qurʾān represents a development in the genre of *tafsīr*. In many works up to this point, the *ḥadīth* might simply have been cited in a shortened form.

As for His words *call to witness two witnesses from your menfolk*, this is a command to include testimony (*ishhād*) alongside written documentation as a further means of certification (*tawthiqa*). *And if there are not two men, then a man and two women*, but this is only in the case of financial affairs (*amwāl*) and those things that are acquired through money (*māl*).

The reason why two women take the place of one man is because of women's deficiency in intellect (*ʿaql*), as recorded by Muslim in his *Ṣaḥīḥ*:

[78] Qurṭubī, *al-Jāmiʿ li-aḥkām al-Qurʾān*, III, 389–98 (s.v. Q. 2:282), selections.

[79] At the beginning of his exegesis, he mentions a *ḥadīth* which seems to make the point that men are given to forgetfulness, because it describes Adam forgetting something on his deathbed and being reminded by the angels. This shows the importance of witnesses, because, had the angels not witnessed the incident, then Adam would have thought an injustice had been committed against him. The unstated implication is that since men are forgetful, women must be all the more so.

Abū Hurayra[80] reported that the Prophet said, 'O women! Give alms and ask for God's forgiveness as often as you can, for I have seen you as the majority of the inhabitants of the Fire'. A very discerning woman (*imra'a minhunna jazlatun*) among them said, 'What is it about us, O Messenger of God, that makes us the majority of the inhabitants of Hell?' He said, 'You curse (*laʿn*) a lot and you are ungrateful to your husbands (*kufr al-ʿashīr*), and I have not seen anyone more deficient in intellect (*ʿaql*) or religion (*dīn*) who can nevertheless vanquish even the shrewdest man (*dhū lubb*) than you women'. She said, 'O Messenger of God, what does it mean to have deficiency in intellect and religion?' He replied, 'As for the deficiency in intellect, that is because the testimony of two women is equal to the testimony of one man, and so this is the deficiency in intellect. Also, a woman will spend days without praying and break her fast in Ramadan: there is the deficiency in religion'.

As for His words *who satisfy you as witnesses*, there is proof here that justness is a precondition for being a witness. Herein is a restriction (*muqayyad*) that al-Shāfiʿī[81] applies to every Qur'ānic stipulation for calling witnesses but where there is no reference to any precondition; he adduced this verse, which proves that the witness ought to be just (*ʿadl*) and satisfactory (*marḍī*), to reject [the testimony of] one whose moral probity is not manifest (*mastūr*).[82]

His words *where one of the two errs* mean the two women; if one [of the two] should forget the testimony, *then one of the two shall remind the other*, that is to say that a recollection (*dhikr*) will occur to her on account of the testimony that takes place. In this respect, others have read *fa-tudhakkir* in the intensive form derived from *al-tidhkār* (the reminding). Those who say that the witness of the one woman with the other makes it equivalent to the testimony of a man have gone too far. The sound opinion is the one that was [mentioned] first. And God knows best.[83]

Muḥsin al-Fayḍ al-Kāshānī

Muḥsin al-Fayḍ al-Kāshānī uses this segment of Q. 2:282 as an opportunity to promote the imams. When discussing the qualities needed in a witness, he incidentally slips

[80] Qutayba ← Ismāʿīl b. Jaʿfar ← ʿAmr b. Abī ʿAmr ← al-Miqbarī ← Abū Hurayra ← the Prophet.

[81] Like most authors of works of *tafsīr* from his time and before, Ibn Kathīr followed the Shāfiʿī school of law. On the significance of Shāfiʿī's early contribution to the formation of Islamic jurisprudence, see Joseph E. Lowry, *The Risāla of Muḥammad Ibn Idrīs al-Shāfiʿī*.

[82] We would like to thank Joseph E. Lowry for clarifying the jurisprudential usage and connotation of the status of *mastūr*.

[83] Ibn Kathīr, *Tafsīr*, I, 343, s.v. Q. 2:282.

in a defence of the sort of person whom one should follow. This person will be 'a righteous, chaste, discerning, reckoning person who eschews disobedience (*maʿṣiya*) and desire (*hawā*), partiality (*mayl*) and bias (*taḥāmul*)'. It is this sort of person whose petitions to God will be granted. This commentary thus becomes a full-blown defence of intercession.

Call to witness, regarding debts, *two witnesses from your menfolk*: your free men, but not your slaves. For God has made slaves too occupied with service to their masters (*mawālī*) for them to bear the responsibility of witnessing and testifying. And let these [witnesses] be Muslims among you, for God has made that an honour (*sharaf*) for Muslims who are just by admitting their testimony, making that an honour for them in advance and a reward for them in this world before they reach the Hereafter, as stated in the commentary (*tafsīr*) of the imam on the authority of the Prophet (*ṣlʿhm*). I say that this proviso that only free men can be summoned to witness does not preclude admitting the testimony of slaves when summoned and if they be just individuals; this is corroborated on the authority of the People of the House, peace be upon them.

And if there are not, meaning the two witnesses, *two men, then a man and two women who satisfy you*. He (*ʿm*) means those who satisfy you on account of their religious character (*dīn*), their trustworthiness (*amāna*), righteousness (*ṣalāḥ*), chasteness (*ʿiffa*), and his alertness, whenever he may be testifying, as well as his reckoning (*taḥṣīl*) and discernment (*tamyīz*); not every righteous person (*ṣāliḥ*) is discerning (*mumayyiz*) or reckoning (*muḥaṣṣil*), nor is every reckoning or discerning person a righteous one. For indeed there are, from among the servants of God, those who are qualified on the basis of their righteousness and chasteness, but who, if they were to testify, their testimony would not be accepted, on account of the weakness of their discernment. But if he were a righteous, chaste, discerning, reckoning person who eschews disobedience (*maʿṣiya*) and desire (*hawā*), partiality (*mayl*) and bias (*taḥāmul*), you should cleave to that kind of meritorious man and follow his lead and his guidance, and if the rain should fail, then through him seek rain, and if your crops should cease to grow, then seek that they should shoot forth through him, and if you are deprived of your provision, then seek the copious flow of provisions through him. For he is the kind of person whose requests are never thwarted, nor are his petitions rejected. As for *an taḍilla iḥdāhumā* it is also read [as *in*] with a *kasra* on the *hamza*; *fa-tudhakkira* is also read in the indicative, with a lightening of the consonant, and in the subjunctive mood, derived from *al-idhkār* (reminding). As for *iḥdāhumā al-ukhrā* in the *tafsīr* of the imam [al-Ṣādiq], on the authority of the

Commander of the Believers (*amīr al-muʾminīn*),[84] when one of them errs in the testimony and forgets it, the other reminds her, so the two of them are rectified (*istiqāma*) for the delivery of the testimony. I say: This is based on the saying 'he lost the path' (*ḍalla al-ṭarīq*), meaning that he could not find it, and this is the reasoning for the consideration of number. He [the imam] (*ʿm*) said that God made the testimony of two women equal to the testimony of one man, because of the deficiency of their intellect and in their religion.[85]

Burūsawī

This is a straightforward interpretation of women's testimony. It briefly outlines the rules in the Ḥanafī school, which is that women may testify in everything except in *ḥudūd* and *qiṣāṣ*. The phrase *who satisfy you as witnesses* is taken to mean that the individuals must be distinguished by particular characteristics, by which, according to him, women are rarely distinguished. This explains why women are considered to be weaker in testimony than men.

Call to witness two witnesses, that is to say, ask the two of them to undertake to testify in cases of debt contracted between you. They are called 'witnesses' as a way of referring to someone about to embark on a role as though he had already assumed it. As for *from your menfolk* (*min rijālikum*), it is semantically attached (*mutaʿalliq*) to *call to witness two witnesses* (*istashhidū*), that is to say, from the people of your religious community, meaning those who are free men, who have reached legal age and who are Muslim, for the discourse here is about their mutual transactions (*muʿāmalāt*), and the Law (*al-sharʿ*) never addresses slaves directly.[86] And as for the case in which the debt is contracted between unbelievers, or if the accused were an unbeliever, then it is permitted to call to witness an unbeliever, in our opinion.

And if there are not, that is to say, two [male] witnesses together – it is a negation of a generality, not a generality of a negation[87] – *two men*, either out of exigency or for some other reason, *then a man and two women* let a man and two women testify. The testimony of women alongside men in monetary matters is permitted according to consensus, but not in *ḥudūd*-crimes or

[84] ʿAlī b. Abī Ṭālib.

[85] Muḥsin al-Fayḍ al-Kāshānī, *al-Ṣāfī*, I, 234, s.v. Q. 2:282.

[86] The Qurʾān never addresses slaves using direct speech, only free men or free women.

[87] That is to say, Burūsawī is here concerned with whether the negative applies to the two being men, or whether it applies to the two men being unavailable.

retaliation (*qiṣāṣ*), in which case it must be men. As for *who satisfy you* (*mimman tarḍawna*), it is semantically attached to something omitted, which functions as an adjectival qualification of the man and the two women, that is to say, being satisfactory to you. The specific mention of the qualification in their case, even when this is usually considered in the case of any witness, is because of how rare it is for women to have that quality. As for *as witnesses* (*min al-shuhadā'*), this is semantically attached to something omitted that functions as a circumstantial qualifier (*ḥāl*) for the omitted pronoun (*ḍamīr*) whose referent is the relative clause (*mawṣūl*), that is to say, 'who satisfy you, being individuals from among witnesses, because you know them to be just and you trust them'; including 'women' in the term *witnesses* (*al-shuhadā'*) is by virtue of preponderance (*taghlīb*).[88]

Where one of the two errs, that is to say, one of the two women witnesses, *then one of the two shall remind the other.* This is used as a justification for considering number in the case of women. In reality, the justification is the need for a reminder, but since 'the erring' is the occasion for that ['reminding'], it is understood to be one and the same, as when you might say, 'I prepared the weapon so that when an enemy comes I might ward him off', where 'the preparing' is actually for the purpose of that warding off, not for the coming of the enemy. Nevertheless, the coming has been placed first because it is the occasion for it. It is as though it were said, 'So that one of the two might remind the other if she errs in her testimony by forgetting.'[89]

Manār

Muḥammad ʿAbduh is the first commentator to introduce the idea that the ruling on two women/one man might refer to the social circumstances in which women found themselves. Indeed, his student Rashīd Riḍā mentions that some commentators have used women's deficiencies as a part of this interpretation, which is a reference to the *ḥadīth* cited by Ibn Kathīr that states that women were deficient in reason and religion. ʿAbduh argues against the idea that this verse refers to women's physical makeup, saying:

> The exegetes have discussed this [matter] and have attributed its cause to physical constitution, adding that the constitution of women is blighted by coldness, which [always] entails forgetfulness; but this is not something that has been corroborated.

[88] That is to say, the plural is the masculine plural form because of the preponderance of men as witnesses: grammarians usually cite the example of *O believers* (*yā ayyuhā'lladhīna āmanū*), which will naturally include women.

[89] Burūsawī, *Rūḥ al-bayān*, s.v. Q. 2:282.

> The correct reason is that financial transactions, compensation claims (*muʿāwaḍāt*) and the like are not her concern, and for that reason her memory in such cases tends to be weak.

ʿAbduh argues that women have a better memory than men for matters of the household with which they are concerned. For him, this proves that people have a good memory for those things that concern them, which, he says, 'is not contradicted by the fact that in our times there are some foreign women (*ajānib*) who do work in the fields of finance'. He thus implies that in countries where women are involved in financial transactions, their word could be accepted in those matters. However, he states that he is ruling for the majority in his own culture, and thus he himself accepts two women's and one man's testimony. Indeed, when explaining why the Qur'ān's author calls for two women with one man, Riḍā says that it is because 'of the weakness of women's testimony and people's lack of trust in it'. Thus, even in his own time, it seems that women were not trusted to give a reliable version of events.

It is important to note that ʿAbduh's views on women were informed by the heady milieu around him. There were women in Egypt at the time who were fighting for gender equality and fighting against the traditional patriarchal interpretation of the Qur'ānic verses. Zaynab Fawwāz was one such woman; her writings and work have been largely ignored in modern times.[90]

It might be imagined that ʿAbduh's interpretation gave rise to a whole raft of reformist views on this verse, and indeed reformists often say that this verse was only appropriate because women's lack of education at the time of the Prophet, and that it may be reinterpreted today. But such reformists are not commonly writing works of *tafsīr*. Within this genre, ʿAbduh's interpretation was not taken up. The genre of *tafsīr* on this issue represents the mainstream conservative view that remains today, which is that women's testimony is worth less than men's.

Call to witness two witnesses from your menfolk: that is to say, request that those from among you who were present at that [moment][91] testify to that [debt], or make them give testimony regarding it. A witness (*al-shahīd*) is someone who witnesses something and is present and has observed it closely (*bi-imʿān*), as can be evinced from this intensive form (*ṣīghat al-mubālagha*);[92] 'he called him to witness' (*istashhadahu*) means requested (*sa'ala*) that he testify, that is to say, that he be witness to that matter when needed. *Al-shahīd* is used to designate one who is trustworthy (*amīn*) in testimony, as in [the lexicon] *al-Qāmūs*.[93] It

[90] On Zaynab Fawwāz, see Marilyn Booth, *Classes of Ladies of Cloistered Spaces: Writing Feminist History through Biography in Fin-de-Siècle Egypt* (Edinburgh, Edinburgh University Press, 2015).

[91] The moment when the debt was contracted (sc. *idhā tadāyantum*).

[92] The form being *shahīd* as opposed to *shāhid*.

[93] *Al-Qāmūs al-muḥīṭ* is a famous dictionary compiled by the fourteenth-century lexicographer Fīrūzābādī; on the title of the lexicon, cf. Greek Ωκεανός. The authors here indicate that, because this quality is applied to God and to humans, humans must attempt to embody some element of the God-like quality.

may be that this adjectival noun (*waṣf*) is based on the intensive form (*ṣīghat al-mubālagha*), but in this case the interpretation [of this usage] is based on *shahīd* as a name for God, exalted be He, even though there is no evidence that it is specific [to Him].[94] The context, along with the form, indicates that some attribute of perfectedness is to be taken into consideration in the case of those called to witness, just as it is considered in the case of the scribe (*kātib*) and the legal guardian (*walī*).[95] The explanation that we have just given with regard to the meaning of *shahīd* refutes the opinion of those who say that what is meant by *shahīdayn* is the two who will testify (*shāhidayn*) to that [debt] claim on the basis of some figurative sense of the former.[96]

His words *from your menfolk*, where the address here is to believers, indicates that those who are not from them cannot be called to witness. But even though calling others to witness is not permitted by the Law or in practice, based on the import of this qualification (*ṣifa*),[97] this cannot be counted as a proof-text that the testimony of one such [other], should he testify, will not be sound or that it will not constitute proof of anything: it is just that the scholars (*ʿulamāʾ*) are in agreement (*ittifāq*) over the legal conditions for testimony, among which are being Muslim and being just, because of both this verse and where He says *and call to witness two who are just from among you* [Q. 65:2]. In addition, they take God's words, exalted be He, in the bequest verse (*āyat al-waṣiyya*) – *two who are just from among you, or two others not from among you* [Q. 5:106] – to be specific to that instance. Some, however, have interpreted this differently, as shall be discussed when we reach its place. I myself cannot recall anything on the authority of the teacher-imam [ʿAbduh] regarding this matter; but the great scholar Ibn al-Qayyim has ascertained that an instance of a clear proof (*bayyina*) in the

[94] The author means to indicate that the term can be applied to humans to mean 'witness' (*shāhid*), because it is so used in reference to God (nine times, cf. Q. 58:6) but is not exclusive to Him, and because *shahīd* based on the intensive *faʿīl* form is more commonly used for 'martyr' (which, of course, also meant 'witness' in Greek, μάρτυς: cf. usage from the Old Testament to the New Testament, e.g. Luke 24:48, and its religio-metaphoric sense in both Christian and Muslim tradition); for a fuller discussion of the term in Muslim tradition, see E. Kohlberg, 'Shahīd', *EI*², IX, 204–7.

[95] Both of these roles are referenced in this long verse as they pertain to the documenting of debts.

[96] In other words, there is no need to rely on any figurative sense of *shahīd* to make it mean *shāhid* (witness); the entire point here is simply to inquire into why (the dual form of) *shahīd* and not *shāhid* is used in the verse.

[97] That is, the qualification that the male witnesses be men who belong to the Muslim community (*min rijālikum*), because, as the authors will note, Q. 5:106 allows for 'outsiders', which is to say non-Muslims, but the jurists restrict this exception to testimony for bequests in cases of the death of the bequeather during travel away from home.

Law is more comprehensive than testimony, so everything by which the truth might be ascertained constitutes a clear proof, as in instances of categorical evidence (*qarāʾin qaṭʿiyya*). For it is possible for the testimony of a non-Muslim to be counted as a clear proof in this very self-same sense inferred from the Book, the Sunna and language, if it serves to make things clear for the judge (*ḥākim*).

If there are not, that is to say, from those two whom you have called to act as witnesses, *two men* – the exegetes (*mufassirūn*) here take the person subject [of *yakūnā*] to refer to the two witnesses, on the basis of their being so desired or so required – *then a man and two women* may be called to witness; or let a man and two women be called to testify. Our estimation [of the meaning] here is preferable to the majority's interpretation [of it] as being that of making them testify (*ishhād*). It is just that they follow the terminology (*iṣṭilāḥ*) of the jurisprudents (*fuqahāʾ*) whereas we follow the arrangement (*naẓm*) of the Qurʾān.

As regards *who satisfy you as witnesses*, they say: From among those whose religious conduct and justness satisfy you, being [qualified] witnesses.[98] The reason that He describes a man and two women in this way is on account of the weakness of women's testimony and people's lack of trust in it. That is why the matter in this case is delegated to the satisfaction of those summoning witnesses (*mustashhidūn*). He then explains the justification (*ʿilla*) of making two women take the place of one man with His words, mighty and majestic be He: *where one of the two errs, then one of the two shall remind the other.* He is thus cautioning that if one of the two should err, that is to say, that she should make a mistake because of not being on top of the details (*ḍabṭ*), and on account of her carelessness, then either one of the two women shall remind the other about what the facts were, with the result that the testimony of the one will complete the testimony of the other. It is essentially to say that each of the two is liable to making mistakes (*khaṭaʾ*) or losing her way (*ḍalāl*), that is, becoming lost and unable to be guided to what had happened exactly. It thus became necessary for two [women] to take the place of one man, because when one of the two of them reminds the other, they both end up equivalent [in testimony] to one man. This is why He overtly repeats the expression *one of the two* (*iḥdāhumā*). The meaning here is not 'lest one should forget, then the other one reminds her', as many exegetes have understood it. One of them (and he is al-Ḥusayn b. ʿAlī al-Maghribī) says that its meaning is: 'If either of the two testimonies should

[98] Having qualified by virtue of being 'from among them'.

be lost to (*taḍilla ʿan*) either one of the two women, then the one woman shall remind the other of it.' Thus He has made the first use of the term 'one' (*iḥdā*) to be a reference to the testimony (*al-shāhada*) and the second use of the term to [one of the two] women. Al-Ṭabrisī endorses this interpretation by saying that forgetting one's testimony cannot be referred to with the term *ḍalāl* ('erring'), because *ḍalāl* means 'loss' (*ḍayāʿ*), and yet a woman is not lost [in this instance]. The fact that there is a difference between error (*ḍalāl*) and forgetting (*nisyān*) can be inferred from His words *lost to us* [Q. 7:37], and likewise from *My Lord does not err nor does He forget* [Q. 20:52]. It would seem that the teacher-imam has affirmed this [distinction] where he mentions it. But some have rejected this because of its fragmenting effect (*tafkīk*), and because interpreting 'error' as 'forgetfulness' has been reported on the authority of Saʿīd b. Jubayr, al-Ḍaḥḥāk and others, with Ibn al-Athīr transmitting it literally (*lughatan*). But my opinion is that what I have already mentioned [in this respect] avails of the need for that. Al-Alūsī[99] mentions that the justification for His not saying 'and so she reminds her' (*fa-tudhakkiruhā*) but [saying] *the one of the two shall remind the other* is on account of the fact that in *Ṭirāz al-majālis*[100] he came across an instance where al-Khafājī asks the Chief Justice (*qāḍī al-quḍāt*) Shihāb al-Dīn al-Ghaznawī about the mystery (*sirr*) of the repetition of *iḥdā* (*one of the* [*two*]), referencing what al-Maghribī had once said, as follows:[101]

> O chief of the sublime, most pious masters, you whose morning dew is cast across all mankind,
>
> What is the secret of repeating *iḥdā* (the one) instead of *tudhdhikiruhā* (she would remind her) in the verse about those called to witness in *al-Baqara*
>
> When overtly condensing [the phrase] with a [suffixed] pronoun instead of repeating *iḥdāhumā* would seem more appropriate, if something did need repeating,
>
> And when applying *iḥdā* to the first of the two in the same testimony is not deemed satisfactory in the eyes of the experts?
>
> So, plunge into [the depths of] your intellect and extract if you will the essence of this from your ocean of knowledge, then send back to us some of the gems [of its mystery].

99 On whom, see Hamza *et al.*, *Anthology*, I.

100 Aḥmad b. Muḥammad Shihāb al-Dīn al-Khafājī (d. 1069/1659), *Ṭirāz al-majālis* (Cairo, Būlāq, 1867).

101 The following is a long passage in rhyming verse.

The judge answered:

> O you from whom great and widespread knowledge is benefitted, and whose merits are well known to all beings,
>
> O you who have singlehandedly devoted yourself to scaling heights, your question is certainly a worthy one even as secrets may lie concealed.
>
> The words *taḍillu iḥdāhumā* (one of them errs) can indeed apply to both of them, and so it has no need of being manifest;
>
> And if it had come with a [suffixed] pronoun, that would have entailed designating only one of the two to be considered in the judgment
>
> And as you have alluded, the one to whom you may offer this [as a] solution and who has probed [this question], this is not satisfactory
>
> But this is all that this feeble mind permits, and God alone knows best the true meaning of what He mentions.

Some cite women's essential nature as a justification for the erring or forgetting [in this verse], on the basis of their being deficient in intellect and religion. Others justify it on the basis of the preponderance of moisture in their physical constitution (*amzāj*). The teacher-imam said: The exegetes have discussed this [matter] and have attributed its cause to physical constitution, adding that the constitution of women is blighted by coldness, which [always] entails forgetfulness; but this is not something that has been corroborated. The correct reason is that financial transactions, compensation claims (*muʿāwaḍāt*) and the like are not her concern, and for that reason her memory in such cases tends to be weak, whereas she is not like that in household affairs, which do concern her; in these [matters], her memory is stronger than that of a man, meaning that it is human nature that, whether male or female, the memory is stronger regarding matters that concern them and with which they are predominantly occupied. This, of course, is not contradicted by the fact that in our times there are some foreign women (*ajānib*) who do work in the fields of finance; but they are a minority, and this cannot be used as a justification. Rulings that apply for the generality are only ever based on the majority case and what constitutes sound judgment in that respect.

The teacher-imam said: God, exalted be He, made the testimony of two women a single testimony. So, if one of the two were to omit something of her testimony – that is, if she were to forget it or if she could no longer recall it – then the other would remind her and complete her testimony. And it is the judge's prerogative, nay it is his duty, to question one of the two in the presence of the other and rely on one part of the testimony from one of them and on the remaining part from the other. He [ʿAbduh] said that this is an obligation (*wājib*), even if judges do not actually practice this, out of ignorance on their part. As for men, he [the judge] should not deal with them in the same way. Rather, he needs to discriminate between the two men, such that if one of the two witnesses were to fall short or forget, then the other is not permitted to remind him. Indeed, if he [the witness] were to leave something out, the [entire] testimony would become invalid, as in, for example, if he were to omit something that would otherwise have elucidated the truth. Thus his testimony on its own is insufficient as proof to elucidate that [truth]. Therefore, one cannot rely on it, nor on the testimony of the other man alone, even if that itself did elucidate something [of the truth].[102]

Faḍl Allāh

In his explanation of why two women's testimony should equal that of a man's, and why women should be excluded from certain matters, Faḍl Allāh immediately refers to what he terms 'women's emotional side' (*al-jānib al-ʿāṭifī*).[103] His view hinges on the idea of the complementarity of the sexes. According to this widespread argument, women are by nature full of tender emotions, which helps them to form deep attachments to their children and husbands, thereby making them suited to fulfil their main role in life within the home. For him and others who take this view, men are not as easily swayed. When they are emotional, they tend towards anger rather than affection; this is because of their role as the primary breadwinner outside of the house. By their very natures, the sexes are therefore suited to complementary roles, with the man undertaking more public-facing duties. For Faḍl Allāh, women should not be prevented from working outside of the home: in this interpretation, he says that women can do so with their husbands' permission, while in later writings he may have softened that view to allow them to work in any case; but working outside of the house is not a woman's primary role, as it is for men. He stresses that women's affectionate side does not detract from their personal value; rather, it is that by giving them this trait, God has protected women from inclining with more force towards some other aspect.

Faḍl Allāh includes two section headings in his explanation of this part of the verse: 'Why is the testimony of two women equivalent to that of a single man?', in which he explains that women have a stronger affectionate side than men, and 'Legal stipulations (*tashrīʿ*) and the general typological characteristics', in which he addresses a possible objection to his view. This objection is framed as a question from someone who admits that women are more affectionate than men, but argues that modern educational methods 'diminish this aspect in a woman' and 'invigorate the emotional side of a man to the extent of pervertedness'. Faḍl Allāh answers this contrived

[102] ʿAbduh and Riḍā, *Tafsīr al-manār*, s.v. Q. 2:282.

[103] The term used by Faḍl Allāh to indicate women's emotions is *ʿāṭif* (pl. *ʿawāṭif*), which could also be understood to refer to affection and tender caring, rather than every emotion.

question by explaining that laws are not made based on individuals, but on types. He argues that if individuals pay attention to their typological characteristics, this will have a positive result for them. Finally, Faḍl Allāh admits that there might be negative aspects to this ruling, and that it is not entirely positive.

After laying out the general precepts behind the ruling, Faḍl Allāh explains the grammatical difficulties of the verse and its meaning in a way that is reminiscent of other commentators, except that he relies mainly on Shīʿī sources, including the highly influential Ṭabāṭabāʾī.

Call to witness two witnesses from your menfolk: God ordained that testimony (*shahāda*) be one of the ways of establishing the truth, and this by means of the proof provided by two just witnesses. And they must be mature, of sound mind, rightly guided and observant Muslims, which is deduced from His words *from your menfolk*; in other words, those who follow your religion.

But why is the testimony of two women equivalent to that of a single man?

If there are not two men, then a man and two women, for the two of them stand in place of one man in testimony. As for the reason for that, it is because of what God, glory be to Him, mentioned when He said: *Where one of the two errs, then one of the two shall remind the other.* The basis of this may be the vigour of the emotional aspect (*al-jānib al-ʿāṭifī*) entailed by the maternal nature (*umūma*), which, in order to bear its responsibilities and the heavy and exhausting burdens of these, requires a great deal of emotional capital (*raṣīd*), as is also entailed by feminine nature (*unūtha*), which is suggestive of tender (*ʿāṭifiyya*) and delicate (*murhafa*) feelings (*mashāʿir*), which in turn arouse affection (*ḥanān*), emotion (*ʿāṭifa*) and reassurance (*ṭumaʾnīna*) in a conjugal context (*jaww*). Emotions may overcome a woman and cause her to deviate from the path of justness in testimony, and to stray from right-guidedness (*hudā*), especially in cases involving testimony that are imbued with some tragic element on the part of the defendant or the plaintiff. Thus emotions may steer [her] to take into consideration that [person's] welfare, as a result of tragic personal circumstances that encompass him. Therefore, it is necessary to have another woman to correct her mistakes, and to remind her of her responsibility, allowing the judge thereby the opportunity to enact his prerogative (*ḥurriya*) in order to arrive at the truth. This is not about denigrating women, because for her, personally, emotions are not in tension with [her] personal values, but are themselves noble human values. It is just that

God wishes for her to be restrained by internal as well as external factors to protect her from inclining towards her more dominant aspect as a precaution, so that human beings might attain the justice that God willed for them in all cases and situations, be it on the individual or on the communal level.

Legal stipulations (*tashrīʿ*) and the general typological characteristics

Some people might say: We concede that a woman's emotional capital may be larger than that of a man, but we also know that, in spite of all of that, instructive discipline (*tarbiya muwajjaha*) can diminish this aspect in a woman, steering her towards a balanced approach, just as a deviant (*munḥarifa*) form of discipline, or the lack of a sound disciplining, may invigorate the emotional side of a man to the extent of pervertedness (*inḥirāf*), diminishing his rational side to a great extent. How then are we to confront such an eventuality? Do we reverse the case and say that an emotional man will require another man to remind him if he were to stray? And should the testimony of an emotionally balanced woman alongside the testimony of a man suffice? Or should legal rulings (*tashrīʿ*) remain as they are, giving preponderance to the role of the man over the role of the woman, however weak the man may be and however strong the woman may be?

Our response to that would be to say that the legal stipulations pertaining to men and women, and the manner in which their practical roles in all aspects of life are distributed, do not issue from specific individual traits when considering the reasoning and procedures of the Law. Essential character traits of individuals are not subject to the precepts that generally govern things, precisely because these [traits] can even vary in the same person, depending on the varying circumstances and the positive and negative effects that these might have on the dynamics of that personality in practice. Rather, it is imperative that legal stipulations emanate from the general typological characteristics that represent the essential dimensions of a human being at an ontological level (*takwīnī*): this enables the establishing of general precepts for all cases and all matters.[104]

[104] Faḍl Allāh at this point is touching on the subheading of the sections to introduce his key argument: legal requirements and stipulations are generally made on the basis of general characteristics – that is, the general characteristics of being male and the general characteristics of being female – and not on the basis of individuals, male or female (presumably because these constitute 'exceptional' traits and not 'typical' ones). This argument is commonly applied in contemporary discourse over women's testimony, but it was also occasionally used in the premodern period.

In light of that, it is necessary for us to take into consideration the typological element that constitutes the personality of a man or a woman in terms of their very natures, whether these be positives or negatives in certain cases, but at the same time to draw on [the strengths of] specific individual traits when examining the details of a given issue, as a way of pursuing justice in the sphere of law (*qaḍāʾ*). In addition, an edificatory instruction and its positive aspect, or a deviant form of instruction and its negative aspect, might each generate a second nature that is either active or passive in a human being. Nevertheless, this should not prevent one from being alert to moments of weakness in certain situations, and it means that the cautious approach adopted by justice is in harmony with the typological dimension of a human being's personality.[105]

We must point out in this vein that the nature of divine legislation does not preclude negatives existing alongside positives, because there is no such thing as an act that is entirely good or entirely evil. Rather, there is good that is accompanied by some evil, or evil accompanied by some good, which means that when a legal case considers something to be obligatory or licit, it must submit to a predominance of good over evil; whereas when it is to do with something being illicit, it is subject to the opposite, which is that there is more evil than there is good. Inevitably, then, there will be negatives in all situations, but these will vary; sometimes they are intense and sometimes negligible, sometimes they are augmented, sometimes diminished, depending on the nature of the topic under divine legislation. And God knows best the truths of His rulings.

There are two points to be made with regard to the exegesis [of this passage].

The first: [Regarding] His words, exalted be He, *one of the two shall remind the other.*[106] A noun (*ẓāhir*) here takes the place of a pronoun (*muḍmar*), and some may say that it would have been more appropriate to say 'the other reminds her'. However, the author of *al-Mīzān* [Ṭabāṭabāʾī] responded to that by saying, 'The subtlety here has to do with the varying lexical import in both instances, and so what is meant by the first *iḥdāhumā* is not any specification [of one of the two women], and by the second *iḥdāhumā* it is one of the two after the erring of the other woman: so the

[105] In other words, first nature, that of being a man or a woman, is generally the safer side to err on and is the reason why laws like the one that regulates the nature of testimony are as they are.

[106] This is the same discussion encountered in earlier commentaries (Qurṭubī, for example, or *Manār*, above) about why the Qurʾān does not say *fa-tudhakkiruhā al-ukhrā* instead of *fa-tudhakkira iḥdāhumā al-ukhrā*.

import of the two differs.'[107] This is a good [explanation]. But it could also be [like that] for emphasis (*ta'kīd*), and indeed this may be closer [to being the explanation], because the first instance of the word *iḥdāhumā* already contains the first import which he [Ṭabāṭabā'ī] used to explain [the import of] the second, and so it is possible that one can do without it [being repeated]. There are, however, two other possibilities, as mentioned by the author of the *Majmaʿ* [*al-bayān*].[108] The first is that it was repeated precisely so that the subject of the verb should precede the object, and had He said *fa-tudhakkiruhā al-ukhrā* (then the other shall remind her), then He would have caused the object of the action to separate the subject of the verb and the verb itself, which is [stylistically] loathsome (*makrūh*). The second of them is what al-Ḥusayn b. ʿAlī al-Maghribī said, which is that it means 'if one of the two testimonies were erroneous', which is to say, if it were to be lost through forgetfulness, then one of the two women will remind the other (*fa-tudhakkir iḥdā al-mara'tayn al-ukhrā*), so that the repetition of the word *iḥdāhumā* (the one of them) does not end up being meaningless. This [last] is supported because one who forgets a testimony cannot be called *ḍāll*, but you can say *ḍallat al-shahāda* to mean that it has been lost.[109] But both of these [possibilities] are far from the truth.

The second is that the commentators explain *ḍalāl* (error) – where He says *where one of the two errs* – as *nisyān* (forgetfulness). In the commentary *al-Kashshāf*, [al-Zamakhsharī] has, '[It is] when one of the two is unable to provide the testimony because she has forgotten it'.[110] In the *Majmaʿ al-bayān*, [al-Ṭabrisī] has, 'that is to say, [if] one of the two women should forget'. In light of that, he explains His words *fa-tudhakkira* (*she shall remind*) by saying:

> *Where one of the two errs*, that is to say, if one of the two women should forget, then *one of the two shall remind the other*: this is said to derive from 'reminding' (*dhikr*), the opposite of forgetting (*nisyān*), as [reported] on the authority of al-Rabīʿ, al-Suddī, al-Ḍaḥḥāk and the majority of the interpreters. The implication (*taqdīr*) is that one of them reminds the other of the testimony which they have both undertaken to bear. As for those who read *fa-tudhkiru*, as a lightened (*takhfīf*) form, from *al-idhkār*, this also carries the same meaning, that is to say, one says to her, 'Do you remember the day when we witnessed in such-and-such a place, and in the presence of such-and-such a

[107] Ṭabāṭabā'ī, *al-Mīzān*, II, 440.
[108] Ṭabrisī.
[109] Footnoted in the text: *Majmaʿ al-bayān*, I, 513. See Ṭabrisī, above.
[110] Footnoted in the text: *al-Kashshāf*, I, 403. See Zamakhsharī, above.

> man or woman?' until she remembers the testimony. Such forgetfulness overcomes women more than it overcomes men.[111]

We observe, in addition to that, that they have attempted to explain the term *errs* on the basis of the term *remind*, having established that the word *tadhkīr* (reminding) operates to restore a mental detail to the memory of the one who has forgotten. But the closest [to the truth] is that the words 'she errs' (*taḍilla*) are the ones that could explain the reminding. Since what is required for the soundness of testimony is that the witness not be influenced by any situation that would lead to the testimony contravening reality, be it through forgetfulness or through error arising from matters becoming confused for him, as a result of not seeing something properly, or by unwittingly not comprehending the subject-matter. Therefore, forgetfulness has no specific relevance to the topic, but rather the relevance is specifically that of error (*ḍalāl*), which is to stray far from the truth, as a result of inherent causes.

It could be said that what should be obligatory is the justness of the female witness (*shāhida*). How can the woman be liable to deficiency in perception or poor comprehension and then proceed to give testimony on the basis of that, when justice requires her to examine in detail that to which she is testifying, so that proceeding to give testimony in a state of error then conflicts with justice? The answer to this is: it could be that this occurs without any attention to the basis of the error, as in many cases where things are examined in depth and a person only alights on one aspect of that thing. But that is not incompatible with justice, just as forgetfulness is not incompatible with it, because it is possible that the two states are involuntary.

That is on the one hand. And on the other hand, reminding (*tadhkīr*) may consist in bringing something out of heedlessness (*ghafla*), just as it may consist in bringing something out of forgetfulness (*nisyān*), or from a state of erroneousness (*khaṭa'*) as compounded ignorance (*jahl*). It is in this sense that His words, exalted be He, *give the reminder, perhaps the reminder might be of benefit* [Q. 87:9] are meant, as well as other verses which consider 'reminding' to be the [central] message of the prophets, as individuals who deliver God's messages to people in order to bring them out of their erroneous ways so that they might then take note of the reality of matters and the issue of [their final] destiny (*maṣīr*), since they may very well misconstrue the true nature and details of both of these during their life [on earth].

What is odd about these discussions is that women should be more forgetful than men, even though that has not been established either

[111] Footnoted in the text: *Majma' al-bayān*, I, 513. See Ṭabrisī, above.

scientifically or by experience. Rather, they are on an equal par, for the causes of forgetfulness can inhabit both men and women, affecting them [equally]. And it could occur to men as a result of some internal or external circumstance, the pressure of which leads them to that [forgetfulness] but which might not occur in the case of women. That is why, indeed, the interpretation which is more accurate – and God knows best – could be that what is meant by 'error' is its broader signification, which consists in departing from the truth in testimony, either as a result of error, or obliviousness, or forgetfulness: that way, 'reminding' can come to subsume any state in which it is necessary to alert another to error.

Who satisfy you as witnesses: manifestly, here it is about being satisfied with noting a state of trustworthiness [in them] that ensues from justness, which is rectitude along the legal path, enjoining as that does truthfulness and preventing mendacity.[112]

[112] Faḍl Allāh, *Min waḥy al-Qur'ān*, s.v. Q. 2:282.

Interviews

Fariba Alasvand

Fariba Alasvand begins her interpretation by detailing some of the premodern rulings on testimony, pointing out that they differ according to circumstance. In some matters only women testify, while in others both men and women testify, and in yet others only men testify. Her argument is that testimony is a responsibility rather than a right, and that God 'extricated us from a difficult responsibility, by not forcing us to do that'. According to her, the lessening of responsibility on women also has scientific proof, in that women pay attention to details and are less reliable as witnesses. She goes on to detail other reasons why women's testimony should be less generally acceptable than men's, referring to a book of popular science. Alasvand does not see a conflict between her interpretations and modernity – in fact, she tells me that she likes to read scientific views and show how the Islamic view is aligned with science. Her conservative view represents a majority among scholars.

The idea that a woman would argue against her own equality may understandably be mystifying to modern thinkers: one might expect that because Alasvand is a woman, she would be the most radical proponent of women's rights. That is simply not the case. She is recognised by the establishment as a *mujtahida* – a woman qualified to give juristic interpretations. In order to attain that status, she has had to work within the system. In Karen Bauer's trip to Qumm, Iran, in 2011, she met few women who were reformers, and those who supported reform were not religious leaders. Rather, they followed male reformists like Grand Ayatollah Saanei. Alasvand represents the majority conservative view, and does it in an eloquent, intelligent and sympathetic manner, which makes her a highly influential scholar, particularly among women.

Fariba Alasvand: I have discussed the issue of women's testimony well in my book. The first thing that I have said is that there are different types of testimony in Islam. In some issues, Islam accepts only the testimony of women. In some issues, Islam accepts the testimony of men and women equally. In financial issues, the testimony of women is accepted with men, but two women and one man. The important issue here is that we have a dialogue about it. In all of the countries of the world, testimony is a duty, not a right. It is an obligation.
Karen Bauer: A responsibility?
Fariba Alasvand: Yes, a responsibility. It is a mistake for women to say that they wish to claim their rights and have the equal right to testimony with men. No. God has in this way extricated us [women] from a difficult responsibility, by not forcing us to do that. Even with regard to [giving] testimony, in terms of [matters like] bribes (*rashwa*), it is a very important and critical job, like being a judge. If you testify against me, I might take revenge against you. That is why it is a very hard task. It is not something that you like to do.

It is so critical and important. So, Islam has divided this responsibility among several people, and among women the division is greater, which shows the blessings of God and the favour of God towards us. We have scientific proof that women pay attention to details, so they remember less; there is more possibility for them to forget, because they pay attention only to details. Men have a general view towards everything, and so there is less probability that they [will] forget things.

Fatemeh Muslimi [Karen Bauer's research assistant]: She [Karen] doesn't agree.

Fariba Alasvand: What part does she not agree with? She didn't say.

Fatemeh Muslimi: I know from her look!

Karen Bauer: Yes, we talked about it before. She knows that I think that this is individual. Some individuals have a good memory, some individuals have a bad memory.

Fariba Alasvand: The law is not based on individuals, but rather on types. In order to understand these types, you should read a book by Allan and Barbara Pease, their book is called *Why Men Don't Listen and Women Can't read Maps*.[113] They have done research and they have shown that when you pay attention to more details, you may forget some other points. But if you have a general view, a bird's-eye view, you can remember better. This does not mean that one of them is flawed and the other is without flaws. This means that women and men have different functions, and so this is actually perfection for each of them.[114]

Karen Bauer: So, my question is, is this because – as some other people that we have talked to say – that this is because women's emotions overpower their rationality? Do you agree with this? Or [in your opinion] is it just due to physiological differences in our [women's] power of concentration?

Fariba Alasvand: The Qur'ān speaks about the forgetting, but not about this. Of course, if you take the scientific proof for it, as mentioned by Allan and Barbara Pease, then there is proof for that. Women's emotions do overpower their reason. They show that when women have an emotional response,

[113] Allan and Barbara Pease, *Why Men Don't Listen and Women Can't Read Maps* (London, Orion, 2001). This book purports to explain the differences between men and women using current neuroscientific research (as of 2001); it is remarkable that conservatives now draw on science rather than just traditional sources to bolster their view of the nature of the sexes. On this interview, see Bauer, *Gender Hierarchy*, 73–80.

[114] The arguments that women and men are different but equal, and that the law is based on types not on individuals, is already attested, and appears in this volume in the interpretation of ʿAbduh/Riḍā.

all parts of the brain are affected. When men have an emotional response, only one part of their brain is affected. So, men can control it. But I believe that we should turn to the Qur'ān, which only addresses the issue of forgetfulness. And this is the case when men become angry, all parts of their brain are affected.

Karen Bauer: Well, that's exactly my question, because I have heard now so many times that women are emotional, but men are not emotional; yet when men are angry, they are very emotional!

Fariba Alasvand: The issue of anger is different from being emotional. When they are angry all parts of their brain are affected. They say that 'anger is the key to all evil' (*al-ghaḍab miftāḥ kull al-sharr*). It is not a matter of rights, as you see it. It is a matter of removing responsibility, and you should be happy with that. It is not about determining the person's social status or position towards men, but about removing responsibility. So, you should not mix the philosophical arguments with those related to human rights.

Karen Bauer: Is there anything else that you wanted to add at all?

Fariba Alasvand: There are a lot of conversations about women's rights, and a lot of ideas – Islamic ideas – about women, but we do not have any more time.[115]

Karen Bauer: Yes, it's true. We could talk for many hours, I can see this.

Fariba Alasvand: In our office, we look into women's studies, in the modern view. I mean that we try to relate Islamic ideas and modern ideas about women. For example, we explain the Islamic ideas and the Islamic view in modern terms. For example, we wrote some articles about gender identity, and there are some articles in a book by me and the Director of the Centre, in which we explain gender roles and sexual identity: meaning, we have a critical view about it – we take into consideration all of the scientific points and then we explain the Islamic view. One of the points that is very important, that we could put in bold, is that the physiological aspects of womanhood are an advantage rather than a disadvantage.

Karen Bauer: Hmm, very interesting. A very interesting point of view.

Fariba Alasvand: Being a woman is a reality, and we need to take everything into consideration from this framework. First it is necessary to see yourself as a woman, and from there take everything else into account. For instance, the issue of the menstrual period is very important, and you need to plan for

[115] Note that at this point the interview had been going on for nearly two hours.

it. Now it has been established that for three weeks out of the month, women are under the influence of premenstrual syndrome (PMS).[116]

Karen Bauer: Three weeks!!!

Fariba Alasvand: For three weeks you are involved with that, and for only one week are you relaxed.

Karen Bauer: Do you think so?

Fatemeh Muslimi: Think what?

Karen Bauer: Have you noticed that? I've never noticed that. Maybe for one week I'm involved with it.

Fariba Alasvand: No, only one week can you be completely relaxed. But three weeks out of every month a woman is involved with this. They have counted two thousand signals for that. But this [science] shows that for up to three weeks, women can be involved with PMS. It depends. And in this time, one is not able to be relaxed. This affects all of women's issues. You cannot, for instance, buy shoes when you have your period, because the size of your feet may change; so it affects everything that has to do with women, everything in your life. So, you should consider the reality of the differences between women and men, and then make a programme. You should not think that women and men are equal and not take into consideration our differences.

Yūsuf Saanei

Grand Ayatollah Saanei has a persuasive style of speaking. He begins this interview by showing that he understands the problems that many modern readers have with the verse, because of the innate similarities between men and women: 'Their sight is like a man. Their hearing is like a man. Their perception is the same: this is a certainty. Their understanding is like that of a man, so why are two women put in the place of one man?' His answer is that science has proved that this legal difference between them is not justifiable, and therefore women's testimony should be accepted equally to men's in most cases.[117] He justifies this view by putting the verse into its historical context. He asserts that in the time of the Prophet, and indeed through his own childhood, most women were not well-educated in monetary matters. This verse is about debts, and people who know nothing of a matter are not very good at remembering it; for him, this is the reason that the verse specifies two women should take the place of one man in testimony.

[116] Also known as premenstrual tension (PMT).

[117] The way this is phrased in the interview makes it seem as though he supports full equality between women's and men's testimony. However, his son's book on the subject, which gives more detailed analysis of his views, clarifies that women's testimony is still not accepted in certain matters such as homosexuality. This is detailed in Bauer, *Gender Hierarchy*, 89–94.

Linguistically, he says that the word 'err' means 'forget' and that 'the two women have been put in the place of one man because of the possibility of forgetfulness'. He admits that the grammar of the verse limits the possibility of forgetfulness to women, but he says that this is not because women are naturally more forgetful than men. Rather, it is because at the time of the revelation, and in subsequent eras, mathematics was a somewhat specialised subject. Saanei then says that from this proof we may generalise, so that if men are poor at remembering something then there should be four of them, while two women will suffice to testify to something about which they are knowledgeable.

Perhaps most interestingly, Saanei dismisses the 'deficiency' *ḥadīth* out of hand: 'The *ḥadīth* that says that women are deficient in their minds is false (*bāṭil*).'

Finally, he ends by saying that the testimony of women is not acceptable in certain matters, which is connected to lewdness. That is due to the need to keep certain matters hidden, according to him.

Yusuf Saanei: I will start from the fourth question, which is about the witnessing verse. The problem is this: two women have been put in the place of one man. In the instance when both women and men see and hear something, and men and women both see as well as each other, one man is enough. But if a woman sees and hears the same thing, then two of them are needed in place of one man. Their sight is like a man. Their hearing is like a man. Their perception is the same: this is a certainty. Their understanding is like that of a man, so why are two women put in place of one man? Why does Islam do this to women, putting two of them in the place of one man? I am restating the problem to show that I understand it well. If one understands the problem, it is much easier to answer it.

According to the scientific method, the difference between male and female is not justifiable. And in the place where a man's testimony is enough, a woman's testimony is also enough, without any difference between them. What we can deduce (*mustafād*) from the verse is that there is no difference between the testimony of a woman or that of a man. In some issues, it is necessary to have one witness, whether woman or man. In some matters, it is necessary to have two witnesses, women or men. This is my reading and understanding of the verse.

Karen Bauer: Uh . . .

Yusuf Saanei: Are you saying, from where do you get this understanding?

Karen Bauer: Yes.

Yusuf Saanei: We say that this blessed verse is in the section on debts (*bāb al-dayn*). And it was revealed 1,400 years ago. Or more than 1,400 years. And women at that time were not in the same situation as we see them in today, in that women were in their houses; they did not go outside the house, and they did not study sums. They were not able to do any kinds of maths. I have seen a woman from my neighbourhood; when her father came with the bill, if the sum came to three hundred thousand, she was not able to add it up. She said, 'three hundred tomans!' She didn't know three hundred thousand. That time was different from this time. Even learned men, when they were writing in their books, were ignorant of certain matters. If they wanted to add one thousand and one hundred, they would write a one with three zeroes, and then a one with two zeroes. Meaning that they did not know how to add up the two. And in the time of the revelation, this verse reflects a social situation in which women were poor with regard to their knowledge of monetary matters, and ignorant of sums. This is the first issue.

The second issue is that whoever is ignorant of a matter, their forgetfulness is greater than those who are learned in that matter. Is that true?

Karen Bauer: Yes, that's true.

Yusuf Saanei: In that time, God's Book said: When one of the two errs, then the second woman will remind the first. Her error (*taḍilla*) is forgetfulness. *Where one of the two errs* means 'when one of them forgets'. All of the exegetes say that the word *ḍalla* is related to the reminding, meaning that it is forgetfulness. The proof of the ruling, the philosophy of the ruling, is that one woman comes forward. What is the philosophy of the Qur'ān? What can we extract from the Qur'ān? *An* is a mark of *ta'līl* in Arabic, with the meaning of 'so' (*kay*). The philosophy is that, if (*idhā*) one of them errs, then the other one will remind her. If one of them forgets, then the other will remind her. *An taḍilla* is the proof (*'illa*) of the verse. The two women have been put in the place of one man because of the possibility of forgetfulness. We say: Is this forgetfulness with regard to all people, or only with regard to women? Why has the testimony of two men not been put in the place of the testimony of one man? We must say, with regard to the grammar of the verse, that this is specific to women. This verse has to do with women, and it is specific to women. But we do not say that women are naturally more forgetful than men! We say that in the circumstances of the revelation of the verse, they were indeed very forgetful, because they were ignorant of mathematical matters and sums. They did not know 100 from 1,000 tomans. [This was such in the populace] to the extent that when the caliph went to the treasury, he did not know how to count out 500 dinars: how, if he did not know how to do that, could women be expected to know? Therefore, the testimony of two women was put in the place of the testimony of one man in debts, so that if one of them erred, the other could remind her. This is the philosophy of the verse. And this philosophy is present in the instance (*wurūd*) of the verse. A pillar of the creed (*'aqīda*) is that the rulings (*aḥkām*) and the regulations (*qawānīn*) are pursuant (*tābi'ūn*) to the goals, the philosophy and the proofs [in the verse]. So, the goals (*ahdāf*) may generalise the rule, or they may make the rule more specific (*yuʿammim/yukhaṣṣiṣ al-qānūn*). If a physician says to an ill person, do not eat pomegranates because they are sour (*ḥāmiḍ*), what is understood from this? Should he not eat just pomegranates, or should he avoid all sour things (*ḥāmiḍ*)?

Hedayat Yousefi: All sour things (*ḥāmiḍ*).

Yusuf Saanei: Yes, all sour things (*muṭlaq al-ḥāmiḍ*)! 'Don't eat pomegranates' is a ruling specific to pomegranates. But from this proof (*ʿilla*) we can generalise: do not eat any sour things (*ḥāmiḍ*). And it is permissible to eat all sweet things. The ruling revolves around the proof, and the regulations revolve around the goals (*ahdāf*). Before we write laws, we first write down the goals of that law. Then we can follow the spirit of the law through the letter of the law. The goal (*hadaf*) and the proof (*ʿilla*) are the forgetfulness. Forgetfulness is common among women, and in this case the ignorance is specific to debts. The regulations (*qānūn*) follow the philosophy by saying that when a woman is knowledgeable in a certain area, then the testimony of two of them is enough. And when a man is ignorant in a certain matter, then there must be four men. Shaykh al-Mufīd [Abū ʿAbd Allah Muḥammad b. Nuʿman al-ʿUkbarī al-Baghdādī, d. 412/1022], one of the great Shīʿī *ʿulamāʾ*, said, in the chapter on marriage, that the testimony of two women is enough. In the chapter on marriage. Why is that so? In the Eastern world – in Iran, in Syria, in these areas – the matter of marriage is in the hands of women. Even now it's like that. It's changed a little bit these days. But tell me, are women learned about marriage matters, or are they not learned about these matters? Are men more knowledgeable about these matters? No! They are ignorant, and women are knowledgeable. That's why the Shaykh al-Mufīd said that.

Karen Bauer: And this is not only in . . .

Yusuf Saanei: It's in all matters! All matters! It is clear that if the ignorance of the two witnesses in a certain matter is greater than their knowledge of it, it is necessary from this verse that there be four of them. Men or women. And when their forgetfulness is not great, then two suffice, men or women. This is the *ḥukm* based on the *ʿilla*, and the *ḥukm* follows that *ʿilla*, and it follows the *ahdāf*. And this is the knowledge of justice. And this is the knowledge of truth. And God is great! Mighty!

Karen Bauer: Why, in the Middle Ages, did the *ʿulamāʾ* say that in some matters two women were sufficient, but not four?

Yusuf Saanei: As for what some of the *ʿulamāʾ* have said, what I say is mentioned in the Qurʾān! All that we have said is in the Qurʾān and the Sunna of the Prophet. The things that others have said are false. The *ḥadīth* that says that women are deficient in their minds is false (*bāṭil*) from its source! The idea of the deficiency of women's reason is oppressive to women! How could they be deficient in reason? How could God have given more rational power to men and not given it to women? God, exalted be He, when He created His creation, both men and women, He described it in *sūrat al-Mu'minūn* [Q. 23:12–14]: *Certainly we created a person* (*al-insān*) *from an extract of clay, then We made him a small seed in a firm resting place, then We made the seed a clot, then We made the clot a lump of flesh, then we made the lump of flesh bones, then We clothed the bones with flesh, then We created it as another creation, so blessed be God, the most excellent of the creators* (*tabāraka Allāhu aḥsanu al-khāliqīn*). The man or the woman who glorifies God is the best of creation. The idea of the deficiency of women's reason is oppression of women! How could they be deficient in reason? How could God have given more rationality to men than to women? *We have created you male and female* (*innā khalaqnākum min dhakarin wa-unthā*) [Q. 49:13] – all of us are sons of Adam and Eve.

I have a final point to make. In some matters, women's testimony alone is not at all accepted. Like in the matter of adultery. This matter requires the testimony of four men. Likewise, *ḥudūd* or murder. This is not because of any deficiency, but because of keeping matters hidden (*al-umūr*). This is why the testimony of two men is not acceptable, because the goal is to narrow the incidence, and to cover up lewdness (*li-yastur al-fāḥisha*).
All of these matters are present in this book.

Mehdi Mehrizi

The views of Mehdi Mehrizi are firmly reformist. Like Grand Ayatollah Saanei, Mehrizi says that it is important to look for the cause of the ruling, its *'illa* (proof). For him, as for other reformists, if the situation changes through time, then so does the ruling. In his view, it is important to pay attention to the wording of the verse. The verse does not say 'if' the woman errs, it says 'when' the woman errs. Thus, for him, the ruling is only sound *when* one of the two women errs. When one does not err, then her testimony is as valid as a man's. He also makes the point that women of the Prophet's time assumed that their word would be accepted. The word of Fāṭima, the daughter of the Prophet, was accepted in the incident of Fadak, which involved a parcel of land that she claimed had been left to her by her father. According to a *ḥadīth* in *al-Kāfī*, a Shī'ī *ḥadīth* collection, Abū Bakr accepted her word on the matter. For Mehrizi, this shows that women's word is not always worth half of men's word or less, because both Fāṭima and Abū Bakr believed that her word alone was enough. However, Mehrizi does admit that this interpretation is a matter of difference between the Shī'as and the Sunnīs.

Mehdi Mehrizi: With regard to the witnessing verse, in *sūrat al-Baqara*.
Karen Bauer: Yes.
Mehdi Mehrizi: I do not interpret this verse to mean that the testimony of a woman in court is half of that of a man. Even in *fiqh* they say that there are different stages (*marḥala*): *marḥalat al-taḥammul* and *marḥalat al-adā'*. *Marḥalat al-adā'* is in the court and the *marḥalat al-taḥammul* is expert testimony. God says in this verse, *Call to witness two witnesses from your menfolk, and if there are not two men, then a man and two women who satisfy you as witnesses, where one of the two errs, then one of the two shall remind the other.* This verse says that there is an obligation of witnessing; when a person wants to lend money or contract a debt with another person, it is necessary for them to write it down, or, if they cannot write, to call two men, or a man and two women to witness. This is about the rights concerning debt. I, for instance, give you something, and we can write it out, that on this day, I gave you that, in this way. Or if we don't write it, two people can witness to it, or a man and woman. And then if there is a dispute, it goes to the judge at the court. And it is in that context that we have to seek recourse to the writing or to the witnessing. Does this verse necessitate testimony? No. The jurists say that this verse means that women's testimony is half that of a man. But the verse does not speak about that matter. That is the first point.

The second point is giving the cause (*taʿlīl*) in this verse. *Where one of the two errs, then one of the two shall remind the other* (*an taḍilla iḥdāhumā fa-tudhakkira iḥdāhumā al-ukhrā*). This construction occurs in the Qur'ān several times. For instance, in *sūrat al-Ḥujurāt* [Q. 49], in the verse about a piece of news: *O you who believe, if a morally corrupt person comes to you with a piece of news, seek clarification lest you accuse a people in ignorance and end up regretting what you have done* (*in jā'akum fāsiqun bi-nabā'in fa-tabayyanū an tuṣībū qawman bi-jahālatin, fa-tuṣbiḥū ʿalā mā faʿaltum nādimīn*) [Q. 49:6]. All of the jurists and *uṣulī*s who interpret this verse say that '*an*' is a cause (*ʿilla*): if the *fāsiq* gives evidence, and if they are certain that he is truthful, it is not necessary to do anything to further ascertain his truthfulness (*tabayyun*). Seeking to further ascertain his truthfulness (*tabayyun*) is a means [*ṭarīq*], an incidental (*ʿaraḍī*). It is not a subject or a goal (*mawḍūʿī aw hadafī*) that if the *fāsiq* should say something, then we must do nothing further to ascertain his truthfulness (*tabayyun*). No. It is necessary for us to undertake a preliminary investigation (*faḥṣ*) to see whether he is truthful or lying; then, if he is truthful, it is not necessary to seek to further ascertain his truthfulness [*tabayyun*], through verification (*taḥqīq*). This is the context of this verse. It is giving cause (*taʿlīl*). For instance, if we were to look at a group of Bedouin, we might find a woman who does not concern herself with financial matters. She works, but she doesn't deal with the real financial matters. Financial matters are men's business. When one of them errs, the other will remind her. This [forgetfulness] gives the cause for this justification [*taʿlīl*]. And when the cause goes away, then the effect goes away as well (*idhā intafat al-ʿilla yantafī al-maʿlūl*).

Karen Bauer: I have a question about the *ʿilla* and the *ḥukm*. I don't understand the difference between the *ʿilla* and the *ḥukm*.

Mehdi Mehrizi: In Imāmī *fiqh*, they ask what is the *ʿilla* in its essence, what is it in its *ḥurma*? Alcohol is forbidden (*ḥarām*), for instance. Why? The jurists say that the reason for making alcohol forbidden is drunkenness. Drunkenness is the *ʿilla*. If drunkenness is possible through the use of something other than alcohol, it is forbidden just like alcohol.

Karen Bauer: For instance, drugs.

Mehdi Mehrizi: Yes, like drugs or some other thing, made, for instance, from dates [date wine]. Typically, the jurists (*fuqahā'*) interpret the *ʿilla* in *fiqh* commandments (*aḥkām al-fiqh*) [*wājib*, etc.] as a justification (*ḥikma*). It is possible that the *ḥikma* goes (*tantafī al-ḥikma*) but the *ḥukm* remains (*wa-lākin al-ḥukm mawjūd*). If we know for sure (*qaṭʿan*) that something is the cause (*ʿilla*) of the *ḥukm*, then the *ḥukm* revolves around the axis of the *ʿilla*. When there is an *ʿilla*, then there is a *ḥukm*; and if the *ʿilla* goes, then the *ḥukm* goes. But most of the time, they interpret the causes (*ʿilal*) to be rulings (*ḥikam*).

But if the situation and the time changes, then the *ʿilla* changes and the ruling changes. *Where one of the two errs, then one of the two shall remind the other*, but when one of them does not err – for instance, today, many women work in banks, many women are directors of factories, they have, for instance, a company, they have an interest in banks; a woman in this day and age does not differ from a man with respect to financial matters. And the verse makes things explicit (*tuṣarriḥ*) in this matter. That is the second point.

The third point is that I might ask: how is that possible? For instance, in the *Kitāb al-Kāfī*, there is a *ḥadīth* regarding the incident of Fadak. This was an incident that occurred in which there was a difference between Fāṭima and Abū Bakr. Fāṭima went to Abū Bakr and said, 'Fadak is ours.' She went – not ʿAlī – and said that Fadak is ours, and Abū Bakr judged in favour of Fāṭima. This *ḥadīth* is possible in *al-Kāfī*. How could it possible [if women's word is not accepted]? If Fāṭima did not believe, and Abū Bakr did not believe, that the testimony of women was worth that of half of a man – and this is in a financial matter. The matter of Fadak is a difference in opinion between the Shīʿa and the Sunnīs.

❁ ❁ ❁ ❁ ❁ ❁ ❁ ❁

Nasser Ghorbannia (d. 2016)

Like other reformists, Nasser Ghorbannia seeks to contextualise this verse in its time and place. Like Alasvand, he says that testimony is a duty, rather than a right, and that the Qur'ān was protecting women from the potentially unpleasant consequences of fulfilling that duty. Today, however, people who testify in court are protected and, therefore, the law on testimony can change. Currently, however, he said that the laws had not changed in some Muslim countries; but if a Muslim in England wanted to testify, then she could, because the laws of the land permit women's testimony and grant that it is equal to men's. Like Grand Ayatollah Saanei, he argues that the deficiency *ḥadīth* is unsound.

Ghorbannia did not argue for absolute equality for men and women: when I asked about women leading the prayer, he said that women do not have the right to lead the prayer, but that women do have the right to teach men and to be a judge. In my interpretation, Ghorbannia was treading carefully in this interview and was careful not to go against the ruling conservative majority, which was in government at the time (2011).

Nasser Ghorbannia: The testimony of women is a very important question.
Hamid Shivapour [professor of law, Mofid University]: And challengeable.
Nasser Ghorbannia: Yes, challengeable. In my opinion, this verse is not related to giving testimony. There [was] a difference between men and women in giving testimony, because of the situation of women at that time, because women were concerned only with the family. And at that time, they did not take part in society, in trading, in watching the affairs in society. It was possible for women to forget what they had witnessed. For that reason, the Holy Qur'ān says to people, to guide people: if you are, for example, concluding a contract, invite one man and one man, or one man and two women to testify and be witnesses to that. This is one point. Another point is that, not only according to Islamic law and Islamic jurisprudence but also according to modern law, civil law, common law, testimony is not a right; it is an obligation, it is a duty. The Holy Qur'ān said that women are not obliged [to testify]; they do not have the duty to take part in court and to testify. You know that at that time, and this time also, testimony was acceptable *only* in the court, and not out of court. The Holy Qur'ān has exempted women from taking part in the court and from testifying. Today, for example, in the

statute of the international criminal courts, one point has been emphasised: protection of the people who testify. We think that the Holy Qurʾān has protected women. And I think that to understand this is not difficult.

Karen Bauer: OK, two questions. The first direct question. So now, women can testify? One woman and one man are equal in testimony? Today, in this day and age, this would be the reinterpretation?

Nasser Ghorbannia: Sometimes in testimony, no. But sometimes, the judge and the court can rely on the expert testimony of only one woman. And sometimes only the testimony of women is acceptable, not men.

Karen Bauer: For instance, women can testify [alone] in childbirth, in the birth of a live child, parentage.

Nasser Ghorbannia: Yes, in affairs related to women.

Karen Bauer: Because only women are there, seeing it.

Nasser Ghorbannia: Yes.

Karen Bauer: I'm going to ask you one more question about that. But first, I'm going to ask about when you said 'at that time'. You said that 'at that time' women were not involved in trade. Maybe you meant that women at that time were not *directly* involved. Khadīja was in trade, but the Prophet Muḥammad was her representative; that's how they got to know each other. So is that what you mean, that she wasn't directly involved, so therefore maybe women's testimony – women were protected from testimony. Is that what you meant?

Nasser Ghorbannia: Yes.

Karen Bauer: So, it's not really that women never took part in economic affairs, but that maybe they were not as likely to be directly [involved]?

Nasser Ghorbannia: You understand correctly.

Karen Bauer: Thank you. So then today, in some countries, women do testify in court in the same cases as men. In some countries women's and men's testimony are considered to be equal.

Nasser Ghorbannia: In Islamic countries, or Western countries?

Karen Bauer: Well, in England.

Nasser Ghorbannia: It's popular [meaning: cultural], it's not forbidden.

Karen Bauer: Do you mean, because of the culture there, even if I were a Muslim in England [I could testify equally to men]?

Nasser Ghorbannia: Even a Muslim. When a court in England permits them to give testimony, they can testify. In all cases. This is a good question.

Karen Bauer: What about the *ḥadīth* [about women being] 'deficient in reason and rationality'?

Nasser Ghorbannia: All of your questions are challengeable. But I've tried to answer these questions in my books. Absolutely, I can say that this tradition is not correct. It is not from Imam ʿAlī (ʿ*m*). Ayatollah Motahheri wrote many books on Islamic Law. One of his books is the 'System of the Rights of Women in Islam' (*Niẓām-e ḥuqūq al-zan dar Islam*).[118]

Hamid Shivapour: It is an important book.

Nasser Ghorbannia: Very important. Of course, our great leader Imam Khomeini has said about his books, that all of his books are useful. He has assessed this *ḥadīth*. He tried to interpret this tradition, this *ḥadīth*, and then finally, he asked himself, 'Why do we make ourselves tired? This narration is not correct.' And it's not from Imam ʿAlī (ʿ*m*). But, unfortunately, it's popular.

Fatemeh Muslimi: What about the idea that women are deficient in their faith?

Nasser Ghorbannia: No.

Fatemeh Muslimi [to Karen Bauer]: So the previous interpretation, that we heard yesterday, was that women have fewer prayers than men.

Karen Bauer: Because of the [menstrual] period.

Fatemeh Muslimi: But he [Ghorbannia] says it's completely wrong.

Nasser Ghorbannia: Yes. Absolutely, I reject this *ḥadīth* and say that it's not from Imam ʿAli. Of course, some of our Islamic scholars, such as Professor Javadi-Amoli, have said that the prophet ʿAlī (ʿ*m*) has said this narration only in a specific situation, about one woman, Ayesha. Because Imam ʿAlī was upset about one woman, he has said this. And I believe that this justification is not correct.

Fatemeh Muslimi: Yes.

Nasser Ghorbannia: Because Imam ʿAlī was infallible, and it is not possible that because he was upset by one woman he has made a general ruling about all women.

Karen Bauer: So what about the question of authority? Some people say that women can be teachers for other women, but not teachers for men. But there are more sensitive issues, for instance, like leading the prayer. Some people say that women should not lead the prayers for men.

Nasser Ghorbannia: Worshipping has a specific situation. Women have no right to be the leader of collective prayer. This is correct. It is not very important. Men have the right to be the imam of the prayer. I have the right, but I do not want to be the imam. Because really, actually, it is a responsibility. An imam of the Friday prayer or in the Imāmī Jamāʿāt, accepts the responsibility of other people. It is really not a very important thing.

[118] Published in English as Murtada Mutahhari, *Woman and Her Rights* (CreateSpace Independent Publishing Platform, 2015).

Karen Bauer: Some people want to. There was one woman, an American woman called amina wadud.

Nasser Ghorbannia: Anyway, according to Islamic law, women do not have the right to be the imam in prayer. But women have the right to be a teacher for men or women, yes, there is no difference. But it is important that women observe Islamic morality and Islamic ethos. This is the test. And of course, in my opinion, a woman has a right to be a judge.

Karen Bauer: Ah!

Nasser Ghorbannia: Yes, this is possible. So practically, in Iranian society, women are teachers, are professors, are working in medical clinics and in hospitals, and sometimes they are limousine drivers, and they work hard.

Karen Bauer: [Women have the right to be] a judge in all matters?

Nasser Ghorbannia: Yes, I believe in all matters. In criminal and civil matters, and family matters.

Karen Bauer: I believe that there is some precedent for it. Ardabili said that women may be judges if there was consensus.

Nasser Ghorbannia: I haven't seen it, but in my opinion, yes.

Prosopographical appendix[1]

This is intended as a brief point of reference for some of the major figures mentioned in this volume. To facilitate reference, the entries are given according to the way in which they are cited in the primary text, not necessarily by their first name or surname. Individuals referred to in more than one way are cross-referenced. We begin with a short entry on the wives of the Prophet.

Wives of the Prophet: Several of the Prophet's wives are mentioned in this volume (most prominently, ʿĀʾisha, Ḥafṣa, Umm Salama and Maymūna). For primary source material on them in the earliest Muslim biographical dictionaries, the reader is advised to consult the last volume of Muḥammad Ibn Saʿd's *Kitāb al-Ṭabaqāt al-kabīr* (or the penultimate, if the edition contains a separate final volume for indices), which is reserved for entries on women (*fīʾl-nisāʾ*); thus, in Eduard Sachau's nine-volume edition (Leiden, Brill, 1921), vol. VIII is the reference point. For an analysis of Ibn Saʿd's volume on women, see Amira Abou-Taleb, 'Constructing the Image of the Model Muslim Woman: Gender Discourse in Ibn Saʿd's *Kitāb al-ṭabaqāt al-kubrā*' in *Islamic Interpretive Tradition and Gender Justice: Processes of Canonization, Subversion, and Change*, ed. Nevin Reda and Yasmin Amin (Montreal, McGill-Queen's University Press, 2020), 179–208. An abridged version of vol. VIII has been translated by Aisha Bewley as *The Women of Madina* (London, Taha Publishers, 1997); for a review of this translation see Farhana Mayer's review in *Journal of Qur'anic Studies* 2.1 (2000) 139–41. For a general overview of these early Muslim female figures, some of whom were important sources for *ḥadīth* transmission (viz. ʿĀʾisha, Ḥafṣa and Umm Salama), see Yasmin Amin, 'The Prophet's Wives' in *The Oxford Encyclopedia of Islam and Women*, ed. Natana J. DeLong-Bais (Oxford, Oxford University Press, 2013), 426–9, and Barbara Freyer Stowasser, 'Wives of the Prophet', *EQ*, V, 507–21. Stowasser provides prosopographical details on the thirteen women, with separate sections dedicated to their appearance in the Qurʾān (cf. Q. 33), in classical *ḥadīth* works, and in hagiographies as well as modern studies on them by Muslim and non-Muslim scholars. Another useful overview is found in her *Women in the Qur'an, Traditions, and Interpretation*. Of the Prophet's wives, ʿĀʾisha and Ḥafṣa have attracted the most scholarly attention, perhaps because of the prominent roles each played in Islamic history's formative period, which may have been facilitated by their status as daughters, respectively, of the Prophet's key allies Abū Bakr and ʿUmar. ʿĀʾisha was a source of information about the Prophet himself and hence, ultimately, for aspects of what later crystallised as Muslim jurisprudence (*fiqh*); but she also became politically active at the time of the

[1] With a few exceptions, entries from Hamza *et al.*, *Anthology*, I, have been reproduced verbatim.

assassination of the caliph ʿUthmān b. ʿAffān (36/656) and the ensuing 'Battle of the Camel' (36/656) in which she sided with the prominent Meccans Ṭalḥa and al-Zubayr (both died in the same event) against ʿAlī b. Abī Ṭālib. On ʿĀʾisha, see Muḥammad Ibn Saʿd, *Kitāb al-Ṭabaqāt al-kabīr*, ed. Eduard Sachau, 9 vols. (Leiden, Brill, 1921), VIII, 39–56; Denise A. Spellberg, *Politics, Gender, and the Islamic Past: The Legacy of ʿAʾisha Bint Abi Bakr*, rev. edn (New York, Columbia University Press, 1996); eadem, "ʿĀʾisha bint Abī Bakr', *EQ*, I, 56–60; Aisha/Ash Geissinger, 'The Exegetical Traditions of ʿĀʾisha: Notes on Their Impact and Significance', *Journal of Qurʾanic Studies* 6.1 (2004), 1–20; eadem, "Aʾisha bint Abi Bakr and Her Contributions to the Formation of Islamic Tradition', *Religion Compass* 5.1 (2011), 37–49. Ḥafṣa's prominence is on account of her role in the coming together, ultimately, of a final standardised text of the Qurʾān, since she is reported to have kept her own copy (*ṣaḥīfa*) of how she had heard it from the Prophet himself. On this, see Ruqayya Khan, 'Did a Woman Edit the Qurʾān? Hafṣa [sic] and Her Famed "Codex"', *Journal of the American Academy of Religion* 82.1 (2014), 174–216, and for the rebuttal of this view, see Sean Anthony and Catherine Bronson, 'Did Ḥafṣah Edit the Qurʾān? A Response with Notes on the Codices of the Prophet's Wives', *Journal of the International Qurʾanic Studies Association* 1 (2016), 93–125; on Ḥafṣa more generally see Uri Rubin, 'Ḥafṣa', *EQ*, II, 398. For Umm Salama's role in the transmission of *ḥadīth*, see Yasmin Amin, 'Umm Salama and her Ḥadīth' (Unpublished MA thesis, American University of Cairo, 2011), http://dar.aucegypt.edu/handle/10526/1524; eadem, 'Umm Salama's Contributions: Qur'an, Hadith, and Early Muslim History as Sources for Gender Justice' in *Muslim Women and Gender Justice: Concepts, Sources, and Histories*, ed. Dina el Omari *et al.* (London, Routledge, 2019) 185–203; eadem, 'Umm Salamah: A Female Authority Legitimating the Authorities' in *Female Religious Authority in Shiʿi Islam: Past and Present*, ed. Mirjam Künkler and Devin Stewart (Edinburgh, Edinburgh University Press, 2021), 47–77.

ʿAbd Allāh b. ʿUmar b. al-Khaṭṭāb (d. 73/693). One of the most prominent figures of the first generation of Muslims and those authorities quoted for traditions. He distanced himself from all political allegiances during the first civil war. On account of his piety, he was offered the caliphate three times, but refused on each occasion; *see* L. Veccia Vaglieri, "Abd Allāh b. ʿUmar' *EI*², I, 53–4.

ʿAbd al-Jabbār. *See* al-Qāḍī ʿAbd al-Jabbār.

ʿAbd al-Razzāq al-Ṣanʿānī [Abū Bakr b. Hammām b. Nāfiʿ al-Ḥimyarī] (d. 211/826). An early Yemeni traditionist who compiled a *Muṣannaf* and a *Tafsīr* on the basis of transmissions from Maʿmar b. Rāshid [*q.v.*]. It has been argued that his work is an important source for early *ḥadīth* and law in Mecca; *see GAS*, I, 81, 99; Ibn Saʿd, *Ṭabaqāt*, V, 399; Khalīfa b. Khayyāṭ, *Ṭabaqāt*, ed. Akram Ḍiyāʾ al-ʿUmarī (Baghdad, Maṭbaʿat al-ʿĀnī, 1967), 289; Bukhārī, *Taʾrīkh*, III, ii, 130; Dhahabī, *Tadhkira*, I, 364; Ibn Khallikān, *Wafayāt*, II, 371; Ibn Ḥajar, *Tahdhīb*, VI, 310; Harald Motzki, '*The Muṣannaf* of ʿAbd al-Razzāq al-Ṣanʿānī as a Source of Authentic *aḥādīth* of the First Century AH', *Journal of Near Eastern Studies* 50 (1991), 1–21; idem, *The Origins of Islamic Jurisprudence: Meccan Fiqh Before the Classical Schools* (Leiden, Brill, 2002), esp. 51–74.

Abū ʿAlī al-Fārisī (d. 377/987). One of the outstanding grammarians of the fourth/tenth century. He also famously consorted with the poet al-Mutanabbī at the court of Sayf al-Dawla in Aleppo; *see* Rabin, ʿal-Fārisīʾ, *EI²*, II, 802–3.

Abūʾl-ʿĀliya, Rufayʿ b. Mihrān [al-Riyāḥī] (d. 92/710). A Basran narrator, counted among the renowned first generation of Successors. Although he is said to have been a commentator in his own right, he is more usually recognised as a traditionist and a Qurʾān reader, and figures prominently in chains of transmission such as those in Ṭabarī's *Tafsīr*; *see* Regis Blachère, ʿAbūʾl-ʿĀliyaʾ, *EI²*, I, 104–5; Ibn Saʿd, *Ṭabaqāt*, VII, 81–5; Ibn Ḥajar, *Tahdhīb*, III, 284–6; *GAS*, I, 34; Dhahabī, *Siyar*, IV, 207.

Abū ʿAmr [Zabbān] b. al-ʿAlāʾ (d. 154/771). A Basran reciter and one of the seven established readers; *see* Regis Blachère, ʿAbū ʿAmrʾ, *EI²*, I, 105–6; *GAL*, I, 99, suppl. I, 158. As an authority on grammar, he is frequently cited along with Abū ʿAlī al-Fārisī [*q.v.*] (especially in the commentaries by Ṭabrisī and Razī).

Abū Ḥanīfa, al-Nuʿmān b. Thābit (d. 150/767). The eponymous progenitor of the Sunnī Ḥanafī school of law and an early theologian of Kufa. The school was not at first included among the ʿorthodoxʾ Sunnī schools of law, and this was probably due to the fact that Abū Ḥanīfa's theological views were associated with early Murjiʾism (an early anti-sectarian movement, later subsumed by Sunnism) and that his use of *raʾy* (personal opinion) as well as *qiyās* (legal analogy), although the jurisprudential norm at the time, were frowned upon by the proponents of *ḥadīth*, which at the time of Abū Ḥanīfa had become the only authoritative and legitimate source of law next to the text of the Qurʾān. A number of creeds (cf. *al-Fiqh al-akbar* and *al-Fiqh*) are attributed to him. He spent most of his life in Kufa, but died in Baghdad where a mausoleum was built at the site which is now in the Aʿẓamiyya district of the city (*al-imām al-aʿẓam*, ʿthe greatest imamʾ, being Abū Ḥanīfa's epithet); *see* Joseph Schacht, ʿAbū Ḥanīfaʾ, *EI²*, I, 123–4; Dhahabī, *Siyar*, VI, 390–403.

Abū Hurayra [ʿAbd Allāh b. ʿĀmir al-Dawsī] (d. *c.* 59/678–9). A Companion of the Prophet, who accepted Islam in the eighth year of the Hijra. He transmitted a large corpus of narrations that are found in the major Sunnī collections; *see* James Robson, ʿAbū Hurayraʾ, *EI²*, I, 129; Dhahabī, *Tadhkira*, I, 31–5; Dhahabī, *Siyar*, II, 578; Ibn Ḥajar, *Tahdhīb*, XII, 262–7.

Abūʾl-Ḥusayn al-Baṣrī [Muḥammad b. ʿAlī b. al-Ṭayyib] (d. 436/1044). A dissident from the Basran school of Abū Hāshim and an important influence on Imāmī *kalām*; *see* Aḥmad b. Yaḥyā Ibn al-Murtaḍā, *Ṭabaqāt al-muʿtazila*, ed. Susanna Diwald-Wilzer (Wiesbaden, Franz Steiner, 1961), 118; Wilferd Madelung, ʿAbūʾl-Ḥusayn al-Baṣrīʾ, *EI²*, suppl. Fasc. I, 25–6; Daniel Gimaret, ʿAbūʾl-Ḥosayn Baṣrīʾ, *EIr*, I, 322–4; Ibn Khallikān, *Wafayāt*, IV, 271ff.; Ṣafadī, *Wāfī*, IV, 125; Qifṭī, *Taʾrīkh*, 293ff.; Maḥmūd b. Muḥammad al-Malāḥimī al-Khwārizmī Ibn al-Malāḥimī, *Kitāb al-Muʿtamad fī uṣūl al-dīn*, ed. Martin McDermott and Wilferd Madelung (London, al-Hoda, 1991).

Abū Jaʿfar Muḥammad b. Abūʾl-Ḥasan b. Bābawayh al-Qummī. *See* Ibn Bābawayh.

Abū Jaʿfar Muḥammad b. ʿAlī al-Bāqir. *See* al-Bāqir.

Abū Jaʿfar Yazīd b. Qaʿqāʿ al-Madanī (al-Makhzūmī?) (d. 130/748). One of the ten readers and three Medinan reciters included in the longer list of often recognised recitations established in the fourth/tenth century. His readings are based on his narrations from his masters, ʿAbd Allāh b. ʿAyyāsh b. Abī Rabīʿa, ʿAbd Allāh b. ʿAbbās and Abū Hurayra; *see* Dhahabī, *Ṭabaqāt*, I, 72–6; Alford T. Welch, 'Ḳur'ān', *EI*[2], V, 409; Aḥmad Pākatchī, 'Abū Jaʿfar Yazīd b. Qaʿqāʿ', *EIsl.*, I, 172–5; Ibn Saʿd, *Ṭabaqāt*, II, 654; Ibn al-Nadīm, *Fihrist*, ed. Flügel, 33; Ibn Mujāhid, *Kitāb al-Sabʿa fī'l-qirā'āt*, 56–8; Dhahabī, *Siyar*, V, 287; Ibn Khallikān, *Wafayāt*, VI, 274, who claims that Abū Jaʿfar was a Persian originally called Jundub b. Fayrūz.

Abū'l-Jārūd, Ziyād b. al-Mundhir b. Ziyād al-Hamadānī al-Khārifī (d. *c.* 146/763). An associate of Muḥammad al-Bāqir and a major transmitter of exegetical traditions from al-Bāqir in the *tafsīr* of Qummī. However, there seems to have been some tension between him and al-Bāqir's son Jaʿfar al-Ṣādiq [*q.v.*], which may have been related to his Zaydī leaning, especially since he supported the revolt of Zayd b. ʿAlī in 740; *see* Wilferd Madelung, 'Abū'l-Jārūd', *EIr*, I, 327; ʿĀmilī, *Aʿyān*, XXXII, 338–46; Ibn Ḥajar, *Tahdhīb*, III, 386–7; *TG*, II, 253–60; Ibn al-Nadīm, *Fihrist*, 221; Najāshī, *Rijāl*, 128–9; Abū'l-Fatḥ Muḥammad b. ʿAbd al-Karīm al-Shahrastānī, *al-Milal wa'l-niḥal*, ed. Muḥammad Sayyid al-Kaylānī, 2 vols. (Cairo, Muṣṭafā al-Bābī al-Ḥalabī, 1961), I, 157–9; al-Ḥasan b. Mūsā al-Nawbakhtī, *Firaq al-Shīʿa*, ed. Muḥammad Ṣādiq Āl Baḥr al-ʿUlūm (Najaf, al-Maktaba al-Murtaḍawiyya, 1932), 48; Saʿd b. ʿAbd Allāh al-Ashʿarī al-Qummī, *Kitāb al-Maqālāt wa'l-firaq*, ed. Muḥammad Jawād Mashkūr (Tehran, Markaz Intishārāt ʿIlmī wa Farhangī, 1963), 71–2; *TG*, II, 253–5; also *see* (pseudo-) al-Nashi' al-Akbar, *Masā'il al-imāma*, ed. Josef van Ess, *Frühe muʿtazilitische Häresiograph: Zwei Werke des Naši al-Akbar (gest. 293 H.) herausgegeben und eingeleitet* (Beirut, Franz Steiner, 1971), 42–5; Madelung 1979, 136–7. For extensive citations, *see* Modarressi, *Tradition and Survival*, 121–5.

Abū Kurayb Muʿāwiya b. al-ʿAlā' (d. 247/861 or 248/862). According to Rosenthal he is one of Ṭabarī's most frequently cited sources in the *History* as well as the *Tafsīr*; *see* Ibn Ḥajar, *Tahdhīb*, IX, 385–6.

Abū'l-Layth Naṣr b. Muḥammad al-Samarqandī (d. end of fourth/tenth century, probably 375/985) wrote a work of *tafsīr* but is primarily known for his work as a Ḥanafī theologian and jurist. See Schacht, 'Abū'l-Layth al-Samarḳandī', *EI*[2], for a list of extant works, some published.

Abū Muslim al-Iṣfahānī, Muḥammad b. Baḥr (d. 322/934). A Muʿtazilī commentator of Northern Iran, who was much quoted by later commentators with Muʿtazilī leanings such as al-Sharīf al-Murtaḍā and al-Ṭūsī. His commentary, *Jāmiʿ al-ta'wīl li-muḥkam al-tanzīl* (or *Sharḥ al-tanzīl*) is known for its allegorical method; *see* Wilferd Madelung, 'Abū Moslem', *EIr*, I, 340–41; Ibn al-Nadīm, *Fihrist*, 34, 136; *GAS*, I, 423; Ṣafadī, *Wāfī*, II, 244; Ibn al-Murtaḍā, *Ṭabaqāt*, 91; *GAL*, I, 209–10; Sayyid Muḥammad-Riḍā Ghiyāthī Kirmānī, *Barrasī-ye ārā' wa naẓarāt-i tafsīrī-yi Abū Muslim Muḥammad b. Baḥr al-Iṣfahānī* (Qumm, Intishārāt-i Ḥuḍūr, 1378 Sh./1999).

Abū Saʿīd al-Khudrī, Saʿd b. Mālik b. Sinān (d. 73 or 74/692 or 693). A Companion of the Prophet who was recognised as a legal authority in Medina; *see* Dhahabī, *Siyar*, III, 168–72, no. 28.

Abū Ṣāliḥ Dhakwān al-Sammān (d. 101/719). A narrator from Abū Hurayra and a source for al-Aʿmash; *see* Ibn Ḥajar, *Tahdhīb*, I, 416–17; *GAS*, I, 79, 81, 97; Dhahabī, *Tadhkira*, I, 89–90.

Abū ʿUbayd al-Qāsim b. Sallām (d. 224/838). Born in Herat, he moved to Basra to become one of its most renowned philologists and lexicographers, especially in the Qurʾān and *ḥadīth* sciences. He studied under many Iraqi luminaries such as Aṣmaʿī (d. 213/828) as well as Kisāʾī (d. 189/805) and Farrāʾ (d. 207/822). From Shāfiʿī he acquired expertise in jurisprudence and returned to tutor in Khurāsān before eventually settling in Baghdad and spent his final years in Mecca after his pilgrimage in 219/834. On his works and their relationships to key figures of the third/ninth century, see now Reinhard Weipert, 'Abū ʿUbayd al-Qāsim b. Sallām', *EI*[3], as well as the classic study of his *Kitāb al-Īmān* by Wilferd Madelung, 'Early Sunni Doctrine Concerning Faith as Reflected in the *Kitāb al-Īmān* by Abū ʿUbayd al-Qāsim b. Sallām (d. 224/838)', *Studia Islamica* 32 (1970), 233–54.

Abū ʿUbayda Maʿmar b. al-Muthannā al-Taymī (d. *c.* 209–10/824–5). Of Jewish origin, he was an important figure of the second/eighth century. He studied under the leading philologists of the school of Basra, Abū ʿAmr b. al-ʿAlāʾ and Yūnus b. Ḥabīb. He was remembered above all for his philological work on the Qurʾān (*Majāz al-Qurʾān*, one of the earliest *tafsīr* works consisting of brief notes on selected Qurʾānic words and phrases), and on the *ḥadīth* (*Gharīb al-ḥadīth*). He was accused of having Khārijī leanings; *see GAL*, I, 103; *GAS*, I, 8, 27, 36, 43; H.A.R. Gibb, 'Abū ʿUbayda', *EI*[2], I, 158; Ibn Khallikān, *Wafayāt*, V, 241; Wilferd Madelung, *Religious and Ethnic Movements in Medieval Islam* (London, Routledge, 1992), 47–56; Michael Lecker, 'Biographical Notes on Abū ʿUbayda Maʿmar b. al-Muthannā', *Studia Islamica* 81 (1995), 71–100, especially 89–92 on his expertise in *tafsīr*; *see* Maʿmar b. al-Muthannā al-Taymī Abū ʿUbayda, *Majāz al-Qurān*, ed. Fuat Sezgin, 2 vols. (Cairo, Maktabat al-Khānjī, 1954–62).

ʿĀʾisha, Umm ʿAbd Allāh ʿĀʾisha bint Abī Bakr (d. 58/678). See above, s.v. 'Wives of the Prophet'.

al-Akhfash (al-Akbar), Abūʾl-Khaṭṭāb ʿAbd al-Ḥamīd b. ʿAbd al-Majīd al-Akhfash (d. 177/793), belonged to the Basran school of grammar, and famously known for collecting numerous dialectal terms; among his most distinguished pupils were Sībawayhi [*q.v.*], Abū Zayd al-Anṣārī [*q.v.*], Abū ʿUbayda [*q.v.*] and al-Aṣmaʿī [*q.v.*]; *see* C. Brockelmann and C. Pellat, 'al-Akhfash', *EI*[2], I, 321.

al-Akhfash, Harūn b. Mūsa b. Sharīk al-Naḥawī (d. 271/884–5). One of a number of individuals with this cognomen (Jalāl al-Dīn Ṣuyūṭī, *al-Muzhir fī ʿulūm al-lugha wa-anwāʿihā*, ed. Muḥammad Aḥmad Jād al-Mawlā *et al.*, 2 vols. [Cairo, ʿĪsā al-Bābī al-Ḥalabī, n.d.]), II, 453–4, mentions him at the end of his list of such individuals; on the three famous Akhfashs, *see* C. Brockelmann and C. Pellat, 'al-A<u>kh</u>fa<u>sh</u>', *EI*[2], I, 321; on this Akhfash, *see* Ibn Khallikān, *Wafayāt*, III, 486; Dhahabī, *Siyar*, XIII, 566.

ʿAlī b. Abī Ṭalḥa. There is some confusion over the date of his death, which according to the biographers is either 120/737 or 143/760; Ibn Ḥajar gives the latter, but Rosenthal places it at around 750, in view of the other transmitters in the chain; *see* Rosenthal, *History*, 215, n. 334; Ibn Ḥajar, *Tahdhīb*, VI, 339–41.

ʿAlī b. ʿĪsā al-Rummānī (d. 384/994). By profession a *warrāq*, that is, a copyist of manuscripts (usually *maṣāḥif* and *ḥadīth* compilations), and a seller of books and paper. He also authored a work on Qurʾānic philology and other shorter lexical treatises; his commentary on the Qurʾān is largely lost. Dogmatically, he belonged to the Muʿtazilī Ikhshīdiyya school of Baghdad; *see* J. Flanagan, 'al-Rummānī', *EI*², VIII, 614–15; on copyists and booksellers, *see* M.A.J. Beg, 'Warrāḳ', *EI*², XI, 150.

ʿAlī al-Riḍā, Abūʾl-Ḥasan ʿAlī b. Mūsā b. Jaʿfar al-Ṣādiq (d. 203/818). The eighth imam of the Twelver Shīʿa. As part of his efforts to win support among the Shīʿī community, the ʿAbbāsid caliph al-Maʾmūn summoned him to Marw in the year 201/816, and appointed him as heir to the caliphate, giving him the title of al-Riḍā. Al-Riḍā, however, died just over a year later; Bernard Lewis, "ʿAlī al-Riḍā', *EI*², I, 399–400.

al-Aʿmash Sulaymān b. Mihrān al-Asadī (d. 148/756). A Kufan traditionist and Qurʾān reader; *see* C. Brockelmann and C. Pellat, 'al-Aʿmash', *EI*², I, 431; *GAS*, I, 81, 310–11, 360; Dhahabī, *Tadhkira*, I, 154.

ʿĀmir b. al-Ṭufayl (d. *c*. 8/629). Arab poet said to have plotted to assassinate the Prophet; he remained a pagan to his death; *see* Werner Caskel, "ʿĀmir b. al-Ṭufayl', *EI*², I, 442.

Anas b. Mālik, Abū Ḥamza (d. between 91 and 93/709 and 711). A prolific traditionist and Companion of the Prophet, to whom he was given at an early age as a servant by his mother. He was among those, such as Jābir b. ʿAbd Allāh al-Anṣārī, humiliated by al-Ḥajjāj, having had his neck tied with a seal in the wake of Ibn al-Ashʿath's failed revolt against the Marwānid regime; *see* A.J. Wensinck and J. Robson, 'Anas b. Mālik', *EI*², I, 482.

al-Aṣamm, Abū Bakr ʿAbd al-Raḥmān b. Kaysān (d. 200–201/816–17). A major Basran theologian (*mutakallim*) and exegete. Although known to have authored a considerable number of early treatises on jurisprudence and theology (twenty-six, according to Ibn al-Nadīm), none are extant. It can be safely assumed that al-Aṣamm was a Muʿtazilī of sorts; he was a proponent of free will in this protracted early Islamic theological debate, and affirmed the doctrine of the created (*khalq*) Qurʾān. However, because he did not agree with the fourth of the five Muʿtazilī tenets (*al-uṣūl al-khamsa*), that of the *manzila bayn al-manzilatayn* (the intermediate state between *īmān* and *kufr*, to which belonged the *fāsiq*), he remained outside the fold of what may be considered mainstream Muʿtazilism in Basra: see Gregor M. Schwarb, 'al-Aṣamm', *EI*³; also Michael Cook, *Commanding Right and Forbidding Wrong*, esp. 196ff. on 'Early Muʿtazilite Doctrine'.

al-Aṣbagh b. Nubāta al-Mujāshiʿī (d. after 100/718). A companion and close confidant of ʿAlī b. Abī Ṭālib. He fought alongside him at the Battle of the Camel and Ṣiffin; *see* Najāshī, *Rijāl*, I, 69–71; *TG*, I, 291–2.

ʿĀṣim, Abū Bakr b. Bahdala al-Asadī (d. 127–8/745). The head of the Kufan school of Qurʾānic readers, his reading represents one of the seven established systems for the recitation of the Qurʾān; his pupil was the famous reader Ḥafṣ [*q.v.*], who transmitted ʿĀṣim's reading (known as *Ḥafṣ ʿan ʿĀṣim*); *see* Arthur Jeffery, "ʿĀṣim', *EI*², I, 706–7.

al-ʿAskarī, Abū Muḥammad al-Ḥasan b. ʿAlī (d. 254/868). Known as al-ʿAskarī because he lived most of his life in the garrison town of ʿAskar Sāmarrāʾ. In the Twelver Shīʿī tradition, he is the father of the twelfth and last imam, the Mahdī, who is expected as the redeemer of the last days; *see* Joseph Eliash, 'Ḥasan al-ʿAskarī', *EI*², III, 246–7.

Asmāʾ bt. Abī Bakr (d. 73/693). She was the elder half-sister of ʿĀʾisha and an early convert to Islam in Mecca. After the Hijra, she married al-Zubayr b. al-ʿAwwām and bore him ʿAbd Allāh b. Zubayr, who was a leader in the fight against ʿAbd Allāh b. Marwān in the second *fitna*. H.A.R. Gibb, 'Asmā'', *EI*², I, 158–9.

ʿAṭāʾ b. Abī Rabāḥ Aslam al-Qurashī, Abū Muḥammad (d. 114/732 or 115/732 or 733). A Yemeni by birth and of Nubian parentage, he exercised his personal opinion (*raʾy*) in legal matters, like most of his contemporaries. He is traditionally regarded as a member of the Meccan school of commentary and associated with the students of Ibn ʿAbbās [*q.v.*] as well as being an important transmitter of *ḥadīth* prophetic sayings. He was suspected of Murjiʾī sympathies, for which he was briefly imprisoned. As an authority for Ibn Jurayj [*q.v.*], he is an important source for material in the *Muṣannaf* of ʿAbd al-Razzāq [*q.v.*]; *see* Ibn Saʿd, *Ṭabaqāt*, V, 344–6; Khalīfa b. Khayyāt, *Ṭabaqāt*, 280; Bukhārī, *Taʾrīkh*, III, ii, 463–4; Ibn Khallikān, *Wafayāt*, II, 423–5; Dhahabī, *Mufassirūn*, I, 113–14; Maʿrifat, *Tafsīr*, I, 362–6; *GAS*, I, 31; Ibn Saʿd, *Ṭabaqāt*, V, 467–70; J. Schacht, "Aṭā'', *EI*², I, 730; Dhahabī, *Tadhkira*, I, 98; Ibn Ḥajar, *Tahdhīb*, VII, 199–203; Nöldeke, *GQ*, II, 167; Motzki, *Origins*, 246–62.

ʿAṭiyya b. Saʿd al-ʿAwfī (d. 111/729). A Kufan Shīʿī transmitter of reports from Ibn ʿAbbās and a source for al-Kalbī. He was considered a 'weak' transmitter (*ḍaʿīf*); *see GAS*, I, 30; Ibn Saʿd, *Ṭabaqāt*, VI, 212–13; Ibn Ḥajar, *Tahdhīb*, VII, 224–6; Abū'l-Ḥajjāj Yūsuf al-Mizzī, *Tahdhīb al-kamāl fī asmāʾ al-rijāl*, ed. Bashshār ʿAwwād Maʿrūf, 35 vols. (Beirut, Muʾassasat al-Risāla, 1998), XX, 145–9, no. 3956.

al-ʿAyyāshī, Abū'l-Naḍr Muḥammad b. Masʿūd al-Sulamī (fl. late third/ninth century). A contemporary of Kulaynī and a prominent scholar of the third/ninth century. He had been a Sunnī but converted to Shīʿīsm early in his life and eventually studied in the major centres of Imāmī learning such as Baghdad and Qumm. He was a prolific author who wrote a work of commentary; the extant commentary is incomplete. But ʿAyyāshī's comments on later *sūra*s do appear in the works of other Imāmī commentators. For more details, see Hamza *et al.*, *Anthology*, I, 26–7.

al-Bāqillānī, Qāḍī Abū Bakr (d. 403/1013). Ashʿarī theologian and Mālikī jurisprudent who contributed systematic works on Ashʿarī theology. Five of the fifty-two works known to be extant are worthy of mentioning here: *Iʿjāz al-Qurʾān*, *Kitāb al-Tamhīd*, *al-Manāqib*, *al-Intiṣār*, *al-Inṣāf*. See R.J. McCarthy, 'al-Bāḳillānī', *EI*², I, 959; see also Yusuf Ibish, 'The Life and Works of al-Bāqillānī', *Islamic Studies* 4.3 (1965) 225–36.

al-Bāqir, Abū Jaʿfar Muḥammad b. ʿAlī (d. *c.* 117/735). Shīʿī imam; *see* E. Kohlberg, 'Muḥammad b. ʿAlī al-Bāḳir', *EI*[2], VII, 397–9; for further details, and on his intellectual heritage, *see* Arzina Lalani, *Early Shīʿī Thought: The Teachings of Imam Muḥammad al-Bāqir* (London, I.B. Tauris in association with the Institute of Ismaili Studies, 2000).

al-Bayḍāwī, ʿAbd Allāh b. ʿUmar (d. 685/1286). A Shāfiʿī jurist, and one of the most renowned commentators on the Qur'ān. He was born in a city known as al-Bayḍā' (hence the name al-Bayḍāwī) in Fars and worked as a judge in Shīrāz. In his commentary, *Anwār al-tanzīl*, he followed the method of Zamakhsharī, but omitted the opinions of Muʿtazilī theology, substituting them with traditionalist theology; *see* Ziriklī, *Aʿlām*, IV, 110. Al-Bayḍāwī's commentary, published in Germany in 1846–8, is among the works on which Western scholars have based their studies of the Qur'ān since the late eighteenth century.

al-Bayhaqī, Abū Bakr Aḥmad b. al-Ḥusayn b. ʿAlī (d. 458/1066). Author of the well-known *Kitāb al-Asmā' wa'l-ṣifāt*, a discussion on the proper understanding of God's names and attributes. A brief biography of the scholar is given by J. Robson, 'Al-Bayhaḳī', *EI*[2], I, 1130.

Bishr b. Muʿādh al-ʿAqadī (d. in or *ante* 245/859). *See* Ibn Ḥajar, *Tahdhīb*, I, 458.

al-Ḍaḥḥāk b. Makhlad al-Shaybānī al-Baṣrī, Abū ʿĀṣim al-Nabīl (d. *c.* 212–14/827–9). *See* Ibn Ḥajar, *Tahdhīb*, II, 570–72, no. 3457; Ibn Saʿd, *Ṭabaqāt*, VII, 295; Ibn al-Nadīm, *Fihrist*, 123; C. Pellat, 'Abū ʿĀṣim al-Nabil', *EI*[2], suppl. I, 17–18.

al-Ḍaḥḥāk b. Muzāḥim al-Hilālī (d. 102/720). A famous traditionist who is said to have put together a *tafsīr*, based on what he heard from Saʿīd b. Jubayr [*q.v.*] at a meeting in Rayy; he famously never met Ibn ʿAbbās; Dhahabī, *Siyar*, IV; 598–600, no. 238; Mizzī, *Rijāl*, XIII, 291; Ibn Ḥajar, *Tahdhīb*, II, 572–3, no. 3458. Ṭabarī is said to have used al-Ḍaḥḥāk's (written) commentary as one of his sources; *see* Rosenthal, *History*, 109; *GAS*, I, 29–30.

Fanārī, Shams al-Dīn Muḥammad b. Ḥamza al-Fanārī (d. 834/1431). A renowned Ḥanafī jurist and philosopher, was the first *shaykh al-islām* (a title equivalent to chief *muftī*) of the Ottoman Empire under Murād II in Bursa; *see* J.R. Walsh, 'Fenārīzāde', *EI*[2], II, 879; Aḥmad b. Muṣṭafā Tāshköprülüzāde, *al-Shaqā'iq al-nuʿmāniyya*, tr. Mecdī Efendi as *Ḥaqā'iq ush-sharā'iʿ* (Istanbul, n.p., 1296/1878), 47–53. His commentary on the first chapter of the Qur'ān was well known as part of his larger, incomplete commentary known as *ʿAyn al-aʿyān fī tafsīr al-Qur'ān*; *see* Khalīfa, *Kashf*, 406, 428, 1014.

al-Farrā', Abū Zakariyyā Yaḥyā b. Ziyād al-Kūfī (d. 207/822). An early Kufan grammarian and author of a periphrastic commentary on the Qur'ān, namely *Kitāb Maʿānī'l-Qur'ān*. Cf. R. Blachère, 'al-Farrā'', *EI*[2], II, 806–8; Ibn Khallikān, *Wafayāt*, II, 229; Ibn al-Nadīm, *Fihrist*, 34, 61, 66; Abū'l-Ṭayyib al-Lughawī, *Marātib al-naḥwiyyīn*, ed. Muḥammad Abū'l-Faḍl Ibrāhīm (Cairo, Maktabat Nahḍat Miṣr, 1955), 88ff.; Naphtali Kinberg, *A Lexicon of al-Farrā's Terminology in His Qur'ān Commentary, with Full Definitions, English Summaries, and Extensive Citations* (Leiden, Brill, 1996); *GAS*, I, 36, 48, 371.

al-Fīrūzābādī, Majd al-Dīn Muḥammad b. Yaʿqūb (d. 817/1415) is the author of *al-Qāmūs al-muḥīṭ*, a unilingual dictionary of great importance in the study of classical and middle Arabic, as well as other works, including a commentary on the Qurʾān, a commentary on a famous poem, and books on history and prophetic traditions (*ḥadīth*). He was born in Kārizīn (or Kārazīn) in Fars and studied in Baghdad, Damascus, Jerusalem, Cairo and Mecca, acquiring great erudition in the fields of Arabic language and literature as well as the religious sciences. A *tafsīr*, entitled *Tanwīr al-miqbās min tafsīr Ibn ʿAbbās* has, as shown by Andrew Rippin, '*Tafsīr Ibn ʿAbbās* and Criteria for Dating Early *tafsīr* Texts', *Jerusalem Studies in Arabic and Islam* 18 (1994), been wrongly attributed to him. It is more likely that the work belongs to Muḥammad al-Dīnawarī (d. 308/920); H. Fleisch, 'Fīrūzābādī', *EI*², II, 926.

al-Fuḍayl b. Yasār al-Nahdī (d. ante 148/765). A 'trustworthy' transmitter (*thiqa*) of *ḥadīth* from Basra, he transmitted from both Muḥammad al-Bāqir and Jaʿfar al-Ṣādiq, dying during the latter's lifetime; *see* Abū ʿAlī Muḥammad b. Ismāʿīl al-Ḥāʾirī al-Māzandarānī, *Muntahā al-maqāl fī aḥwāl al-rijāl*, ed. Muʾassasat Āl al-Bayt, 8 vols. (Qumm, Muʾassasat Āl al-Bayt, 1995), V, 213–14, no. 2300.

al-Ghazālī, Abū Ḥāmid Muḥammad b. Muḥammad (d. 505/1111). One of the most significant thinkers in the history of Islam. He wrote many books on theology, philosophy and legal theory; *see* W. Montgomery Watt, 'al-Ghazālī', *EI*², II, 1038–42; various, 'al-Ġazālī', *EIr*, X, 358–77; *GAL*, I, 535–46.

Ḥafṣ b. Sulaymān b. al-Mughīra, Abū ʿUmar al-Asadī al-Fākhirī al-Bazzāz (d. 180/796). Transmitter of the 'reading' of ʿĀṣim, a cloth merchant, his fame rests solely on the knowledge he acquired of the 'reading' of the master of Kufa; *see* Bernard Lewis, ed., 'Ḥafṣ b. Sulaymān', *EI*², III, 63.

al-Ḥajājj b. Muḥammad al-Miṣṣīṣī al-Aʿwar (d. 206/812). Transmitted the Qurʾān interpretations of Ibn Jurayj [*q.v.*]; see Ibn Ḥajar, *Tahdhīb*, II, 205–6; al-Khaṭīb al-Baghdādī, *Taʾrīkh Madīnat al-Salām*, ed. Bashshār ʿAwwād Maʿrūf, 23 vols. (Baghdad, Dār al-Gharb al-Islāmī, 2001), VIII, 236–9; Dhahabī, *Siyar*, IX, 447–50.

Ḥammād [b. ʿĪsā al-Juhanī] (d. 209/825). A Shīʿī traditionist from Kufa, a follower of Jaʿfar al-Ṣādiq, Mūsā al-Kāẓim and ʿAlī al-Riḍā.

Ḥammād b. ʿUthmān b. ʿAmr al-Fazārī (d. 190/805). Kufan traditionist; *see* Najāshī, *Rijāl*, I, 339.

Hammām, Abū ʿUqba Hammām b. Munabbih b. Kāmil al-Ṣanʿānī (d. 130/747). The brother of Wahb b. Munabbih. A small collection (*ṣaḥīfa*) of his narrations is mentioned in some sources; *see GAS*, I, 81, 86; Ibn Ḥajar, *Tahdhīb*, XI, 67.

Ḥamza b. Ḥabīb Abū ʿUmāra al-Taymī al-Zayyāt (d. 156/772). One of the seven established readers of the Qurʾān. He was interested in *ḥadīth* and religious duties (*farāʾiḍ*), but he was most famous for his 'reading'; among his pupils were Sufyān al-Thawrī [*q.v.*] and al-Kisāʾī [*q. v.*], but his readings were passed on by his immediate disciples, Khalaf b. Hishām [*q.v.*] at Baghdad and Khallād b. Khālid. His reading became widespread in the Maghrib, but was eventually replaced by that of Nāfiʿ [*q.v.*], the preferred reading of the Mālikīs, whose school came to dominate that region; *see* C. Pellat, 'Ḥamza b. Ḥabīb', *EI*[2], III, 155; Najāshī, *Rijāl*, I, 111–18.

al-Ḥasan al-Baṣrī, Abū Saʿīd b. Abī'l-Ḥasan b. Yasār (d. 110/728). A famous pietist of the second generation of Muslims. He was renowned as a commentator of the school of Iraq in the traditional accounts and as a proto-Sufi; *see* ʿAlī b. ʿUthmān Hujwīrī, *Kashf al-maḥjūb*, ed. V. Zhukovski (repr. Tehran, Tehran University Press, 1979), 86–7; Aḥmad b. ʿAbd Allāh Abū Nuʿaym al-Iṣfahānī, *Ḥilyat al-awliyāʾ wa-ṭabaqāt al-aṣfiyāʾ*, 10 vols. (Cairo, Maktabat al-Khānjī, 1932–9), II, 131–6; Arthur John Arberry, *Muslim Saints and Mystics: Extracts from Attār's Tadhkīrat al-auliyāʾ* (London, Routledge, 1979), 19–26; Dhahabī, *Mufassirūn*, I, 124–5; Dāwūdī, *Ṭabaqāt*, I, 147, where it is claimed that he was *mawlā* of Zayb b. Thābit, the Companion of the Prophet, who traditionally is regarded as the compiler of the Qurʾān in the reign of ʿUthmān; *see* Maʿrifat, *Tafsīr*, I, 371–85; *GAS*, I, 30; H. Ritter, 'al-Ḥasan', *EI*[2], III, 347–8; Cook, *Early Muslim Dogma*; *TG*, 11, 41ff.

Hushaym b. Bashīr b. Abī Khāzim (d. 183/799). A famous traditionist of his time who settled in Baghdad. He narrated from al-Zuhrī [*q.v.*] and others. Those who narrated from him included Ibn Ḥanbal; *see* Ibn Ḥajar, *Tahdhīb*, XI, 59–64; *GAS*, I, 38; Dhahabī, *Tadhkira*, I, 248–9.

Ibn ʿAbbās, ʿAbd Allāh b. ʿAbbās b. ʿAbd al-Muṭṭalib (d. 68/687). The cousin of the Prophet, traditionally accepted as the founder of the discipline of Qurʾānic exegesis; *see* Dāwūdī, *Ṭabaqāt*, I, 232–3; Maʿrifat, *Tafsīr*, I, 224–31; Dhahabī, *Mufassirūn*, I, 65–83; L. Veccia Vaglieri, "Abd Allāh b. ʿAbbās', *EI*[2], I, 40–41; Ibn Saʿd, *Ṭabaqāt*, II/2, 119–23, V, 74–5, 216–17; Ibn Ḥajar, *Tahdhīb*, V, no. 474; *GAS*, I, 25–8. On his '*tafsīr*', debates on its authenticity and his significance in the traditional accounts, *see* Claude Gilliot, 'Portrait "mythique" d'Ibn ʿAbbās', *Arabica* 32 (1985), 127–84; Isaiah Goldfield, 'The "Tafsīr" of ʿAbdallāh b. ʿAbbās', *Der Islam* 58 (1981), 125–35; Rippin, *Tafsīr Ibn ʿAbbās*, 38–83; cf. Wilferd Madelung, "Abd Allāh b. ʿAbbās and Shīʿite Law' in *Law, Christianity and Modernism in Islamic Society: Proceedings of the Eighteenth Congress of the Union Européene des Arabisants et Islamisants*, ed. U. Vermeulen and J.M.F. van Reeth (Leuven, Peeters, 1998), 13–25; M.A. Abū'l-Naṣr, *ʿAbd Allāh b. ʿAbbās: Ḥibr al-umma wa tarjumān al-Qurʾān* (Beirut, Muʾassasat al-Risāla, 1992).

Ibn Abī Ḥātim al-Rāzī (d. 327/938). A major *ḥadīth* scholar, critic and transmitter of the early fourth/tenth century, who sat squarely in the *ahl al-ḥadīth* generation that flourished after the death of Ibn Ḥanbal (d. 241/855). In addition, he is credited with authoring the first '*ḥadīth*-criticism' work thus-labelled *al-Jarḥ wa'l-taʿdīl*, setting a bibliographic precedent for an emerging but not-yet formalised field; he also authored the well-known *ʿIlal al-ḥadīth* (see Pavel Pavlovitch, 'Ibn Abī Ḥātim al-Rāzī', *EI*[3]).

Ibn Abī ʿUmayr, Abū Aḥmad Muḥammad b. ʿĪsā al-Azdī (d. 217/831). A Baghdadi Shīʿī traditionist, who narrated from Mūsā al-Kāẓim, ʿAlī al-Riḍā and Muḥammad al-Jawād. He was al-Kāẓim's agent in Baghdad. He was appointed as a judge (*qāḍī*) by the Abbasid caliph al-Maʾmūn. He wrote important works on theological issues such as human free will (*qadar*) and the unicity of God (*tawḥīd*), but none of the works are extant; *see TG*, I, 384–6; Najāshī, *Rijāl*, II, 204–8; Abū ʿAmr Muḥammad b. ʿUmar b. ʿAbd al-ʿAzīz Kishshī (Kashshī), *Rijāl al-Kishshī*, ed. Aḥmad al-Ḥusaynī (Karbala, Muʾassasat al-ʿIlmī li'l-Maṭbūʿāt, 1960–2), 363–5; al-Ḥasan b. ʿAlī Ibn Dāwūd al-Ḥillī, *Kitāb al-Rijāl*, ed. Muḥammad Ṣādiq Baḥr al-ʿUlūm (Najaf, al-Maṭbaʿa al-Ḥaydariyya, 1972), 159–60, describes him as 'the most trustworthy of people' (*awthaq al-nās*); ʿAbd Allāh b. Muḥammad Māmaqānī, *Tanqīḥ al-maqāl fī aḥwāl al-rijāl*, 3 vols. (Najaf, al-Maṭbaʿa al-Murtaḍawiyya, 1930), III, 61–4, no. 10272.

Ibn ʿĀmir, Abū ʿUmar ʿAbd Allāh b. ʿĀmir al-Yaḥsūbī (d. 118/736). One of the seven established Qurʾān readers. Of South Arabian origin, he settled in Damascus where he was appointed judge (*qāḍī*) by the caliph al-Walīd b. ʿAbd al-Malik and chief of police by the later caliph Yazīd b. al-Walīd; his reading was adopted by the inhabitants of Damascus; *see* Joseph Schacht, 'Ibn ʿĀmir', *EI*[2], III, 704.

Ibn al-Anbārī, Abū'l-Barakāt ʿAbd al-Raḥmān b. Muḥammad b. ʿUbayd Allāh b. Abī Saʿīd Kamāl al-Dīn (d. 577/1181). Arabic philologist, compiler of a biographical history of philology, a manual of grammar and a collection of the differences between the Basran and Kufan schools of grammar; *see* C. Brockelmann, 'al-Anbārī', *EI*[2], I, 485–6; Ibn Khallikān, *Wafayāt*, III, 139–40; Dhahabī, *Siyar*, XXI, 113–15.

Ibn al-ʿArabī, Abū Bakr Muḥammad b. ʿAbd Allāh al-Maʿāfirī (d. 543/1148). A native of Seville, he spent periods studying in Damascus and Baghdad, including under Abū Ḥamid al-Ghazālī. He also spent periods with traditionists in Cairo, and finally returned to Seville where he worked on his major contributions which included a Qurʾān commentary, *Aḥkām al-Qurʾān*.

Ibn ʿAsākir, Thiqat al-Dīn Abū'l-Qāsim ʿAlī b. Abī Muḥammad al-Ḥasan b. Hibat Allāh b. ʿAbd Allāh b. Ḥusayn al-Dimashqī al-Shāfiʿī al-Ḥafiẓ (d. 571/1176). Sunnī historian of Damascus; *see* N. Elisséeff, 'Ibn ʿAsākir', *EI*[2], III, 713–15; *GAL*, I, 33; Ibn Khallikān, *Wafayāt*, III, 309–11.

Ibn Bābawayh al-Qummī, Abū Jaʿfar Muḥammad b. Abū'l-Ḥasan, known as al-Shaykh al-Ṣadūq (d. 381/991–2). Universally regarded among Twelver Shīʿīs as one of their foremost doctors and traditionists; author of *Man lā yaḥḍuruhu'l-faqīh*, one of the 'four books' (*al-kutub al-arbaʿa*) or established Shīʿī manuals that were composed during the fourth/tenth and fifth/eleventh centuries and are the basis for Twelver jurisprudence; *see* Shaykh al-Ṭāʾifa Abū Jaʿfar Muḥammad b. al-Ḥasan al-Ṭūsī, *Fihrist*, ed. Muḥammad Ṣādiq Āl Baḥr al-ʿUlūm (Najaf, al-Maṭbaʿa al-Ḥaydariyya, 1960), 184; ʿInāyat Allāh ʿAlī al-Quhpāʾī (al-Quhbāʾī), *Majmaʿ al-rijāl*, ed. Ḍiyāʾ al-Dīn al-ʿAllāma al-Iṣfahānī, 7 vols. (Isfahan, Maṭbaʿat Rūshīn, 1964–8), V, 269–73; Māmaqānī, *Tanqīḥ*, III, 154–5; ʿĀmilī, *Aʿyān*, XLVI, 153–6; Ṭihrānī, *Ṭabaqāt*, 187–8; *GAL*, I, 187–8; *GAS*, I, 544–9; Wilferd Madelung, 'Ebn Bābawayh', *EIr*, VIII, 2–4; Asaf Fyzee, 'Ibn Bābawayh', *EI*[2], III, 726–7; cf. Marcinkowski, 'A Glance', 199–222.

Ibn Ḥanbal, Abū ʿAbd Allāh Aḥmad b. Muḥammad b. Hilāl al-Shaybānī al-Marwazī (d. 241/855). A prominent traditionist in Baghdad, who opposed the Muʿtazilī consensus especially on the doctrine of the createdness of the

Qur'ān and was consequently persecuted. He is regarded as the progenitor of one of the Sunnī legal schools; *see* H. Laoust, 'Aḥmad b. Ḥanbal', *EI*², I, 272–7; Dhahabī, *Siyar*, XI, 232–98; Muḥammad Abū Zahra, *Ibn Ḥanbal: ḥayātuhu wa ʿaṣruhu, ārā'uhu wa fiqhuhu* (Cairo, Dār al-Fikr al-ʿArabī, 1947); *GAS*, I, 510; *TG*, III, 456–65, 473–6.

Ibn Ḥumayd, Abū ʿAbd Allāh Muḥammad b. Ḥumayd al-Rāzī (d. 248/862). Ṭabarī studied with him in Rayy (at which time Ibn Ḥumayd was in his seventies) and is one of his most frequently cited sources in Ṭabarī's *tafsīr*. There is no consensus on his reliability, since Ibn Ḥanbal had nothing but praise for him, while others, such as Nasā'ī and Bukhārī did not think much of him at all and he was even accused of random fabrication of chains of transmission (*isnāds*). Despite this, many besides Ṭabarī transmitted from him, including Abū Dāwūd, al-Tirmidhī, al-Qazwīnī, Ibn Abī'l-Dunyā and al-Baghawī; *see* Dhahabī, *Siyar*, XI, 503–6; Ibn Ḥajar, *Tahdhīb*, IX, 127–31; Sezgin, *GAS*, I, 289; Rosenthal, *History*.

Ibn Isḥāq (d. *c.* 150/767). The famous historian to whom a biography (*sīra*) of the Prophet is attributed, though we only have it in a recension by a later scholar, Ibn Hishām (d. 218/833); *see* J.M.B. Jones, 'Ibn Isḥāḳ', *EI*², III, 810–11; Ibn Ḥajar, *Tahdhīb*, IX, 38–46; Sezgin, *GAS*, I, 288–90.

Ibn Jinnī, Abū'l-Fatḥ ʿUthmān (d. 392/1002). A famous grammarian from Aleppo of Byzantine origin, most celebrated in the branch of grammar known as *taṣrīf* (essentially, morphology). He founded the science of Arabic etymology (*al-ishtiqāq al-akbar*) and authored two famous grammatical works, one on the Arabic language and the other on its vowels and consonants; he also wrote a commentary on the *Dīwān* of his famous contemporary, the poet al-Mutanabbī (d. 354/955); *see* Johannes Pedersen, 'Ibn D̲j̲innī', *EI*², III, 754.

Ibn Jurayj, Abū'l-Walīd ʿAbd al-Malik b. ʿAbd al-ʿAzīz b. Jurayj al-Rūmī al-Umawī (d. *c.* 149–51/766–8). An important Meccan traditionist and narrator who reported from the second generation. He brought together *ḥadīth*s from ʿAṭā' b. Abī Rabāḥ [*q.v.*], al-Zuhrī [*q.v.*], Mujāhid [*q.v.*] and ʿIkrima [*q.v.*] and passed them on to the likes of Wakīʿ, Ibn al-Mubārak and Sufyān b. ʿUyayna [*q.v*]. He reportedly had both a written collection of narrations and a *tafsīr*; *see* Ibn Ḥajar, *Tahdhīb*, VI, 402–6; Ibn Saʿd, *Ṭabaqāt*, V, 361–2; Khalīfa b. Khayyāṭ, *Ṭabaqāt*, 283; Bukhārī, *Ta'rīkh*, III, I, 422–3; Ibn Khallikān, *Wafayāt*, II, 348; Dhahabī, *Tadhkira*, 169–71; Dhahabī, *Siyar*, VI, 325–36; *GAS*, I, 91; C. Pellat, 'Ibn D̲j̲urayd̲j̲', *EI*², suppl. 5–6, 386; Motzki, *Origins*, 268–85.

Ibn Kaysān, al-Ḥasan b. Muḥammad b. Aḥmad, Abū Muḥammad al-Ḥarbī (d. 358/968). Qur'ān reader and grammarian. Dhahabī, *Siyar*, XVI, 136.

Ibn Māja, Abū ʿAbd Allāh Muḥammad b. Yazīd al-Qazwīnī (d. 273/887). Famous compiler of *ḥadīth* whose most well-known work is the *Kitāb al-Sunan*, or *Sunan*. He was criticised by some for including many 'weak' reports in his collection; *see* J.W. Fück, 'Ibn Mād̲j̲a, *EI*², III, 856.

Ibn Mardawayh, Aḥmad b. Mūsā b. Mardawayh b. Fūrak b. Mūsā b. Jaʿfar al-Iṣbahānī, Abū Bakr (d. 410/1019). Famous collector of *ḥadīth*; *see* Dhahabī, *Siyar*, XVII, 308–11.

Ibn Masʿūd, ʿAbd Allāh b. Ghāfil Hudhayl al-Hudhalī (d. 32/652–3). A famous Companion of the Prophet and a Qurʾān reader. He was of Bedouin origin and one of the earliest Muslims (in some accounts the third convert), receiving the Qurʾān directly from the Prophet. In 21/642 he settled permanently in Kufa, where his teaching was highly esteemed, and his ʿAlid tendencies, especially with regard to exegesis, were better received; *see* J.-C. Vadet, 'Ibn Masʿūd', *EI*², III, 873–5; Ibn Saʿd, *Ṭabaqāt*, VII, 342; Maʿrifat, *Tafsīr*, I, 217–23; Dhahabī, *Mufassirūn*, I, 838. On what can be reconstructed of Ibn Masʿūd's version of the Qurʾān, *see* Arthur Jeffery, *Materials for the History of the Text of the Qurʾān: The Old Codices* (Leiden, Brill, 1937), 20–113.

Ibn Qaʿqāʿ. *See* Abū Jaʿfar Yazīd b. Qaʿqāʿ al-Madanī (al-Makhzūmī?).

Ibn Qutayba, ʿAbd Allāh b. Muslim b. Qutayba (d. 276/889). One of the great Sunnī polygraphs of the third/ninth century, both a Ḥanbalī theologian and litterateur (*adīb*); *see* Gérard Lecomte, 'Ibn Qutayba', *EI*², III, 844–7.

Ibn Saʿd, Abū ʿAbd Allāh Muḥammad b. Saʿd b. Manīʿ (d. 230/845). The author of the well-known *Kitāb al-Ṭabaqāt al-kabīr*, a major biographical dictionary of the strata of society; *see* Ibn Ḥajar, *Tahdhīb*, IX, 182–3, J.W. Fück, 'Ibn Saʿd', *EI*², III, 922–3; *GAS*, I, 300–301.

Ibn Sallām, Abū Zakariyyā Yaḥyā b. Abī Thaʿlaba (d. 200/815). One of the earliest Ibāḍī Basran authors who made his name in Qayrawan; *see* Belḥāj's remarks in Hūd's *Tafsīr kitāb Allāh al-ʿazīz*, I, 21–2; *TG*, IV, 271; Abūʾl-ʿArab, *Ṭabaqāt*, 37–9; Abū Bakr ʿAbd Allāh Mālikī b. Muḥammad, *Kitāb Riyāḍ al-nufūs fī ṭabaqāt ʿulamāʾ Qayrawān wa Ifrīqiyā*, ed. Ḥusayn Muʾnis (Cairo, Maktabat al-Nahḍa al-Miṣriyya, 1951–60), 122–5; Dāwūdī, *Ṭabaqāt*, II, 371; Dhahabī, *Siyar*, IX, 396; idem, *Mīzān al-iʿtidāl*, IV, 380; Abūʾl-Khayr Shams al-Dīn Muḥammad b. Muḥammad b. Muḥammad b. ʿAlī b. Yūsuf Ibn al-Jazarī, *Ghāyat al-nihāya fī ṭabaqāt al-qurrāʾ*, ed. G. Bergstraesser, 2 vols. (Beirut, Dār al-Kutub al-ʿIlmiyya, 1971), II, 373; Abū Bakr Muḥammad b. Khayr b. ʿUmar b. Khalīfa al-Lamtūnī al-Amawī Ibn Khayr al-Ishbīlī, *Fahrasat mā rawāhu ʿan shuyūkhi-hi min al-dawāwīn al-muṣannafa fī durūb al-ʿilm wa-anwāʿ al-maʿārif*, ed. Francisco Codera and Julián Ribera Tarragó (Baghdad, Maktabat al-Muthannā, 1963), 56–7; Hamadi Sammoud, 'Un exégète oriental en Ifriqiya: Yaḥyâ Ibn Sallâm (742–815)', *Institut des belles-lettres arabes*, 126 (1970), 227–42; Gilliot, 'Hūd', *Arabica* 44 (1997), 181–2. On the Basran Ibāḍiyya, *see TG*, II, 186–233.

Ibn Sīrīn, Abū Bakr Muḥammad (d. 110/728). Traditionist, jurist and also first renowned Muslim interpreter of dreams; *see* T. Fahd, 'Ibn Sīrīn', *EI*², III, 947–8; Ibn Khallikān, *Wafayāt*, IV, 181–3; Dhahabī, *Siyar*, IV, 606–22.

Ibn Taymiyya (d. 728/1328). Famous Ḥanbalī scholar whose works attracted many modern jurists because of his erudition and clarity of prose. His extensive writings (and some dictations) have been collected in the *Responsa* (*al-Fatāwā*, 37 volumes), *Epistles* (*al-Rasāʾil*, 6 volumes), and other similar collections. His writings span all of the religious sciences and Islamic intellectual history; *see* Muḥammad Ḥasan Ismāʿīl, *Kitāb al-Radd ʿalā al-manṭiqiyyūn* (Beirut, Dār al-Kutub al-ʿIlmiyya, 1998).

Ibn ʿUmar. *See* ʿAbd Allāh b. ʿUmar b. al-Khaṭṭāb.

Ibn ʿUyayna, Sufyān (d. 196/811). A Ḥijāzi scholar, mainly a traditionist (*muḥaddith*) and one of the principal transmitters from Ibn Shihāb al-Zuhrī (d. 124/742), among others such as ʿAmr b. Dīnār (d. 126/744) and ʿAbd Allāh b. Dīnār (d. 127/745). To Ibn ʿUyayna was attributed a phenomenal memory and he had apparently memorised close to 7,000 *ḥadīths*; see Susan A. Spectorsky, 'Sufyān b. ʿUyayna', *EI*[2], IX, 772.

Ibn Wahb, Abū Muḥammad ʿAbd Allāh b. Wahb b. Muslim al-Fihrī (d. c. 195–6/810–11). An Egyptian narrator and *mufassir*; *see* J. David-Weill, 'Ibn Wahb', *EI*[2], III, 963; Sulaymān b. Aḥmad al-Ṭabarānī, *al-Muʿjam al-kabīr*, ed. Ḥamdī ʿAbd al-Majīd al-Salafī, 11 vols. (Baghdad, Wizārat al-Awqāf wa'l-Shu'ūn al-Dīniyya, 1984), XI, no. 11830; Yaḥyā Ibn Sallām al-Ibāḍī, *Kitāb al-Taṣārīf* (Tunis, al-Sharika al-Tūnisiyya li'l-Tawzīʿ, 1979), 150.

Ibn Zayd, ʿAbd al-Raḥmān b. Zayd b. Aslam al-ʿUmarī (d. 182/798). Known as an expert in *tafsīr*, he was an important source of narrations for both ʿAbd al-Razzāq and Ibn Wahb; *see GAS*, I, 38; Ibn Ḥajar, *Tahdhīb*, VI, 177–8.

ʿIkrima, Abū ʿAbd Allāh ʿIkrima al-Barbarī (d. 105/723–4). Probably the most famous transmitter of the 'commentary' of Ibn ʿAbbās represented in the traditional accounts. His trustworthiness was disputed in the biographical dictionaries and among commentators; *see* Dhahabī, *Mufassirūn*, I, 107–13; Dhahabī, *Siyar*, V, 12–36; Dāwūdī, *Ṭabaqāt*, I, 380–81; Maʿrifat, *Tafsīr*, I, 348–62; Joseph Schacht, 'ʿIkrima', *EI*[2], III, 1081–2.

Jābir b. ʿAbd Allāh, Abū ʿAbd Allāh, al-Salamī al-Khazrajī al-Anṣārī (d. 78/697). A Companion of the Prophet, accompanying him on numerous expeditions. He is said to have fought alongside ʿAlī at Ṣiffin (37/657). He is noted as the most prolific narrator of traditions from the Prophet, and regarded highly by *ḥadīth* scholars. Many transmitted his traditions which he is supposed to have collected in his compilatory collection (*ṣaḥīfa*). He enjoys special status in Shīʿī tradition, since the *ḥadīths* recorded on his authority in Shīʿī sources bear on the special qualities of ʿAlī and the graces granted him by God. Significantly, he is credited with the *ḥadīth* about the appointment of ʿAlī as legatee (*waṣī*) by the Prophet, among numerous other traditions that bear upon the virtues of the imams after ʿAlī; *see* M.J. Kister, 'Dj̲ābir b. ʿAbd Allāh', *EI*[2], suppl. 3–4, 230–32. Dhahabī, *Tadhkira*, I, 43–4, describes him as the 'jurist of Medina'; *see* Aḥmad b. Yaḥyā Balādhurī, *Ansāb al-ashrāf*, ed. Muḥammad Bāqir al-Maḥmūdī, 3 vols. (Beirut, Dār al-Taʿāruf li'l-Maṭbūʿāt, 1974–7), I, 248 (also ed. Maḥmūd Firdaws al-ʿAẓm [Damascus, Dār al-Yaqaẓa al-ʿArabiyya, 1997]; 6 vols., IV and V ed. Iḥsān ʿAbbās [Wiesbaden, Franz Steiner, 1978–2002]); Khalīfa b. Khayyāṭ, *Ta'rīkh*, 65; Abū Jaʿfar Muḥammad b. Jarīr al-Ṭabarī, *Ta'rīkh* (*Dhayl al-mudhayyal*), tr. Landau-Tasseron (New York, State University of New York Press, 1998), 58–9.

Jābir b. Zayd, Abū'l-Shaʿthā', al-Azdī (d. between 93/711 and 104/722). Given the lack of prosopographical certainty about the eponymous ʿAbd Allāh b. Ibāḍ (d. 89/708) and his religio-political contribution to the foundations of Ibāḍism, Jābir can be considered the major early source for Ibāḍī doctrine as it coalesced in Basra and the fledgling community's leader there before the Ibāḍī imamate was established in exile in Oman; see John C. Wilkinson, *Ibâḍism: Origins and Early Development in Oman* (Oxford, Oxford University Press, 2010), 154 and also 161–210. Jābir, crucially, is acknowledged by Sunnī sources as a student of Ibn ʿAbbās (and at times his links to Ibāḍism are denied for that very reason by these sources), and he was also associated as such with al-Haṣan al-Baṣrī (d. 110/728), the foremost intellectual figure of Basra at the time. Jābir himself had students who would become major sources for Sunnī traditionism, key among them Qatāda b. Diʿāma (d. 117/735) and ʿAmr b. Dīnār (d. 126/744). Ibāḍī sources often cite traditions directly from Jābir b. Zayd, so that he effectively functions as the equivalent of an Ibn ʿAbbās for Sunnī sources or a Jaʿfar al-Ṣādiq for Shīʿī ones, in terms of both frequency of citation and authoritativeness. R. Rubinacci's entry on him in *EI*[2] has now been superseded by that of E. Francesca in *EI*[2], II, 359–60, with a much-expanded bibliography of more recent studies on Ibāḍism in the last two decades, but curiously missing P. Crone and F. W. Zimmermann, *The Epistle of Sālim Ibn Dhakhwān* (see esp. 301ff. and n. 4, on the reason for the divergence regarding his death date).

Jaʿfar al-Ṣādiq, Abū ʿAbd Allāh Jaʿfar b. Muḥammad b. ʿAlī b. al-Ḥusayn b. ʿAlī b. Abī Ṭālib, known as al-Ṣādiq (the truthful one) (d. 148/765). Successor to Muḥammad al-Bāqir [*q.v.*], he was the imam of the Shīʿa of his time, accepted both by Ismāʿīlī and Twelver Shīʿīs, and an authority on *ḥadīth* and jurisprudence (*fiqh*) for Sunnī scholars. He is attributed the authorship of a commentary on the Qurʾān, which has reached us in two recensions, one being the so-called Shīʿī recension and the other the so-called Sufi recension; *see* Marshall G. Hodgson, 'Dja̱ʿfar al-Ṣādiḳ', *EI*[2], II, 374–5.

al-Jubbāʾī, Abū ʿAlī al-Jubbāʾī, Muḥammad b. ʿAbd al-Wahhāb (d. 303/915–16). One of the most celebrated of the Basran Muʿtazila, who differed from the Baghdad Muʿtazila over the question of human free will. Abūʾl-Ḥasan al-Ashʿarī (d. 323/935) studied with him before making his definitive break with the Muʿtazila and dedicating his efforts to refuting Muʿtazilism, especially that of his former master al-Jubbāʾī; *see* Louis Gardet, 'al-Dju̱bbāʾī', *EI*[2], II, 569–70. A *tafsīr*, based upon various statements attributed to him, has been put together by Daniel Gimaret, *Une lecture Muʿtazilite du Coran: Le Tafsīr d'Abū ʿAlī al-Djubbāʾī (m. 303/915) partiellement reconstitute à partir de ses citeurs* (Louvain-Paris, École Pratique des Hautes Études, Peeters, 1996). On his son, Abū Hāshim ʿAbd al-Salām b. Muḥammad al-Jubbāʾī, *see* Ibn al-Murtaḍā, *Ṭabaqāt al-Muʿtazila*, 94–100, 105, 107–10, 114, 130; L. Gardet, 'al-Dju̱bbāʾī', *EI*[2], II, 570; *GAS*, I, 623–4.

Juwaynī, Abūʾl-Maʿālī ʿAbd al-Malik (478/1085). A major Ashʿarī theologian, he wrote an influential manual on the theology of that school entitled *Kitāb al-Irshād ilā qawāṭiʿ al-adilla fī uṣūl al-iʿtiqād*, tr. Paul Walker 2000. He taught in Mecca and Medina, where he got his sobriquet 'imam of the two holy Cities' (*imām al-ḥaramayn*); *see* Louis Gardet, 'al-Dju̱waynī', *EI*[2], II, 605–6.

al-Kaʿbī, Abūʾl-Qāsim ʿAbd Allāh b. Aḥmad b. Maḥmūd al-Balkhī (d. 317/929). A well-known scholar, theologian and head of a branch of the Muʿtazila called al-Kaʿbiyya; *see* Ibn Khallikān, *Wafayāt*, III, 45; Albert Nader, 'al-Balkẖī', *EI*[2], I,

1002; Ibn al-Murtaḍā, *Ṭabaqāt al-Muʿtazila*, 88–9 *inter alia*; *GAS*, I, 622–3; Dhahabī, *Tadhkira*, 803.

al-Kalbī, Abū'l-Naḍr Muḥammad b. al-Sā'ib b. Bishr (d. 146/763). Renowned as a Qur'ān commentator (*mufassir*) and contemporary of another early *mufassir*, Muqātil b. Sulaymān al-Balkhī (d. 150/767). A Shīʿī, he was interested in what may be termed universal history and the history of religions, especially pre-Islamic, Jewish and Christian; but he was also renowned for other branches of knowledge: poetry, literature, philology, genealogy, tradition and ancient legends. His commentary on the Qur'ān, now lost, is supposed to have been the longest ever composed and in it he is said to have espoused pro-ʿAlid interpretations of particular verses. He was known as a transmitter of exegetical sayings going back to Ibn ʿAbbās [*q.v.*]; *see* W. Atallah, 'al-Kalbī', *EI*[2], IV, 495–6; Ibn Saʿd, *Ṭabaqāt*, VI, 358ff.; ʿAbd Allāh b. Muslim b. Qutayba Ibn Qutayba, *Kitāb al-Maʿārif*, ed. Tharwat ʿUkāsha (Cairo, Maṭbaʿat Dār al-Kutub, 1960), 535; Ibn al-Nadīm, *al-Fihrist*, 107ff.; Ibn Khallikān, *Wafayāt*, IV, 309–11; Yūsuf Yaghmūrī, *Nūr al-qabas fī akhbār al-najāt wa'l-udabā' wa'l-shuʿarā'*, ed. R. Sellheim (Wiesbaden, Franz Steiner, 1964), 256–62; Ṣafadī, *Wāfī*, III, 83; Ibn al-Athīr, *Lubāb*, III, 47. On his *tafsīr*, of which scholars have consulted manuscripts from various collections (Chester Beatty MS 4224, Ayasofya MS 118 and Hamidiye MS 40), *see* Dāwūdī, *Ṭabaqāt*, II, 149; Rippin, '*Tafsīr Ibn ʿAbbās*', 50–56; Wansbrough, 130–36, 140–47 inter alia; Marco Schöller, '*Sīra* and *tafsīr*: Muḥammad al-Kalbī on the Jews of Medina' in *The Biography of Muḥammad: The Issue of Sources*, ed. H. Motzki (Leiden, Brill, 2000), 18–48. It has been suggested that the *tafsīr* is identical to *al-Wāḍiḥ fī tafsīr al-Qur'ān* of Abū Muḥammad al-Dīnawarī (d. 307/920); *see* Rippin, 'Al-Zuhrī', 23; *GAS*, I, 34–5. On the use of his narrations in Shīʿī sources, *see* Furāt b. Furāt al-Kūfī, *Tafsīr*, ed. Muḥammad al-Kāẓim, 2 vols. (Beirut, Mu'assasat al-Nuʿmān, 1412/1992), I, 121–2 on Q. 5:11; Abū Jaʿfar Muḥammad b. al-Ḥasan al-Ṭūsī, *al-Tibyān fī tafsīr al-Qur'ān*, ed. Āghā Buzurg al-Ṭihrānī, 10 vols. (Najaf, al-Maṭbaʿa al-ʿIlmiyya, 1957–63), X, 369 and Ṭabrisī, *Majmaʿ al-bayān*, XXX, 137 on Q. 93:7; cf. Kohlberg, *A Medieval Muslim Scholar*, 343, on the use of his *tafsīr* by Ibn Ṭāwūs (d. 673/1275); Uri Rubin, *The Eye of the Beholder: The Life of Muḥammad as Viewed by the Early Muslims* (Princeton, Darwin Press, 1995), 91 and 94. He was accused of being unreliable (*matrūk*) and of being a Shīʿī; *see* Abū ʿAbd Allāh Muḥammad b. Ismāʿīl Bukhārī, *Kitāb al-Ḍuʿafā'*, ed. M. Zāhid (Beirut, Dār al-Maʿrifa, 1986), 105ff.; idem, *Ta'rīkh*, I, 101; Ibn Kathīr, *Tafsīr*, II, 71 on Q. 5:56; Ibn al-Athīr, *Lubāb*, III, 47; Ibn Khallikān, *Wafayāt*, IV, 310; Ṣafadī, *Wāfī*, III, 83; Taqī al-Dīn Aḥmad Ibn Taymiyya, *al-Muqaddima fī uṣūl al-tafsīr*, ed. A. Zamarlī (Beirut, Mu'assasat al-Risāla, 1994), 69ff. where he is criticised alongside other early *mufassirūn* such as Wāqidī, Thaʿlabī and others.

al-Kisā'ī, Abū'l-Ḥasan ʿAlī b. Ḥamza al-Kisā'ī (d. *c.* 189/805). A well-known philologist and Qur'ān reader; had close relations with the ʿAbbāsid court for many years, as tutor of the caliph al-Mahdī's son al-Rashīd and later the latter's sons, al-Amīn and al-Ma'mūn; his is the latest of the seven established Qur'ānic readings; *see* R. Sellheim, 'al-Kisā'ī', *EI*[2], V, 174–5.

Makkī b. Abī Ṭālib Ḥammūsh al-Qaysī (d. 437/1045). Born in Qayrawān, was a well-known scholar of grammar and the Qur'ān in al-Andalus. Works of his on Qur'ānic topics that are extant include *Kitāb al-Kashf*; *Mushkil i'rāb al-Qur'ān*; *Tafsīr al-mushkil min gharīb al-Qur'ān*; see Dāwūdī, *Ṭabaqāt*, II, 331–2; Ibn Khallikān, *Wafayāt*, IV, 361; Muṣṭafā Ibrāhīm Mashannī, *Madrasat al-Tafsīr fī'l-Andalus* (Beirut, Mu'assasat al-Risāla, 1986).

Mālik b. Anas (d. 179/796). The eponym of the Mālikī school of law, who lived in Medina and was also called the Imam of Medina. His *Kitāb al-Muwaṭṭa'* is the earliest work of law that survives. On him see Yasin Dutton, *The Origins of Islamic Law: The Qur'an, the Muwaṭṭa' and the Madinan 'Amal* (Surrey, Curzon, 1999); Paul Gledhill, 'The Development of Systematic Thought in Early Mālikī Jurisprudence' (Unpublished PhD thesis, Oxford University, 2014); Joseph Schacht, 'Mālik b. Anas', *EI*², VI, 263–5.

Ma'mar b. Rāshid (d. 154/770–71). A Basran traditionist, he is usually known as the narrator for the *tafsīr* of Qatāda [*q.v.*] and was the main source for much of 'Abd al-Razzāq's narrations in his *al-Muṣannaf* and his *Tafsīr*. Cf. *GAS*, I, 81, 290–91; Dhahabī, *Tadhkira*, I, 364; Ibn Ḥajar, *Tahdhīb*, X, 243–6.

Mu'āwiya b. 'Ammār b. Khabbāb al-Duhanī (d. 175/791). A 'trustworthy' transmitter (*thiqa*) of *ḥadīth* from Kufa and author of several works, including a book on prayers (*Kitāb al-Ṣalāt*) and one on divorce (*Kitāb al-Ṭalāq*), Najāshī, *Rijāl*, II, 346–8; Kishshī, *Rijāl*, 260; Muḥammad Taqī al-Shushtarī, *Qāmūs al-rijāl*, 14 vols. (Tehran, Markaz Nashr al-Kitāb, 1968), IX, 42.

al-Mubarrad, Abū'l-'Abbās Muḥammad b. Yazīd al-Thumālī (d. *c.* 286/900). A major figure in the Basran school of grammar and a prolific author; *see* R. Sellheim, 'al-Mubarrad', *EI*², VII, 279–82; *GAL*, I, 109; *GAS*, IX, 78–81; Ibn al-Nadīm, *Fihrist*, 59.

Muḥammad b. Abī 'Umayr [Abū Aḥmad Zayd b. 'Īsā al-Azdī]. *See* Ibn Abī 'Umayr.

Muḥammad b. 'Alī, Abū Ja'far al-Bāqir. *See* al-Bāqir, Abū Ja'far Muḥammad b. 'Alī.

Muḥammad b. al-Ḥanafiyya (d. 81/700–701). Son of 'Alī b. Abī Ṭālib from Khawla, a woman of the Banū Ḥanīfa. He was generally a pacifist, not wishing to involve himself with the various disputes between the leading Muslim factions during the first two civil wars. However, an Iraqi enthusiast, al-Mukhtār, stirred up a revolutionary movement in the former's name: Muḥammad tried to avoid any contact with al-Mukhtār but eventually needed his help to escape imprisonment under the contender to the caliphate, 'Abd Allāh b. al-Zubayr. After the failure of al-Mukhtār's revolt and the defeat a few years later of Ibn al-Zubayr, Ibn al-Ḥanafiyya visited the Marwānid caliph in Damascus and recognised his legitimacy, thereafter returning to Medina where he eventually died; *see* Fr. Buhl, 'Muḥammad b. al-Ḥanafiyya', *EI*², VII, 402–3.

Muḥammad b. Ka'b, Abū Ḥamza al-Quraẓī (d. 112/731). A narrator of *ḥadīth* regarded as a reliable authority; *see* Ibn Khallikān, *Wafayāt*, V, 218; Dhahabī, *Siyar*, V, 65–8; *GAS*, I, 32; Khalīfa b. Khayyāṭ, *Ta'rīkh*, 363; Ṭabarī, *Ta'rīkh* (*Dhayl al-mudhayyal*), 2496–7, tr. Landau-Tasseron, 231.

Muḥammad b. Saʿd b. Muḥammad b. al-Ḥasan b. ʿAṭiyya b. Saʿd b. Junāda al-ʿAwfī (d. 276/889). An important direct source of Ṭabarī, represented a complete tradition of narrations that are reflected in a family chain of narrators going back to Ibn ʿAbbās; *see* Khaṭīb, *Ta'rīkh Baghdād*, V, 322; Gilliot, *Éxègese, langue, et théologie*, 25. This *isnād* appears 1,560 times in Ṭabarī's *tafsīr*.

Mujāhid b. Jabr, Abū'l-Ḥajājj al-Makkī (d. 104/722). An important disciple of the *tafsīr* school of Ibn ʿAbbās, he also narrated exegetical material from ʿAlī b. Abī Ṭālib and Ubayy b. Kaʿb [*q.v.*]. He is regarded as one of the initiators of the commentary method according to one's personal opinion (*bi'l-ra'y*); *see* Dhahabī, *Mufassirūn*, I, 107; Maʿrifat, *Tafsīr*, I, 335–42; Ibn Saʿd, *Ṭabaqāt*, V, 446–67; Ibn Ḥajar, *Tahdhīb*, X, 43–4; *GAS*, I, 29; Nöldeke, *GQ*, II, 167; Ibn al-Nadīm, *Fihrist*, 33; Dhahabī, *Tadhkira*, 92–3; Yāqūt, *Muʿjam al-udabā'*, V, 72; Andrew Rippin, 'Mudjāhid', EI^2, VII, 293; F. Leemhuis, 'MS 1075 *tafsīr* of the Cairene Dār al-Kutub and Mujāhid's *tafsīr*' in *Proceedings of the Ninth Congress of the Union Européene des Arabisants et Islamisants*, ed. R. Peters (Leiden, Brill, 1981), 169–81. The *tafsīr* attributed to him has been edited by ʿAbd al-Raḥmān al-Ṭāhir al-Sūratī: Mujāhid, *Tafsīr*.

Muqāṭil b. Ḥayyān b. Du'āl Dūz, Abū Bisṭām al-Nabaṭī (d. 153/770). *Ḥadīth* authority. Dhahabī, *Siyar*, VI, 340; on the possible confusion between him and Muqāṭil b. Sulaymān, *see* Crone, 'A Note', 238–50.

al-Muthannā b. Ibrāhīm al-Āmulī. One of Ṭabarī's teachers whilst he was a student at Rayy. He is an important source for Ṭabarī but very little is known about him.

Nāfiʿ b. ʿAbd al-Raḥmān al-Laythī (d. 169/785). One of the seven established Qur'ān readers who lived and died in Medina. His pupils Warsh (d. 197/812) and Qālūn (d. 220/835) were the main transmitters of his reading; the transmission of the Qur'ān from Warsh on the authority of Nāfiʿ (known as *Warsh ʿan Nāfiʿ*) is still used in the Muslim world today, especially in North-west Africa; *see* Andrew Rippin, 'Nāfiʿ al-Laythī', EI^2, VII, 878; Najāshī, *Rijāl*, I, 107–11.

al-Nakhaʿī, Ibrāhīm b. Yazīd (d. 96/717). A Kufan traditionist and jurist who transmitted a great deal of material from Anas b. Mālik [*q.v.*] and ʿĀ'isha [*q.v.*]. He was a proponent of the use of *ra'y* (personal opinion) if it was based on a sound knowledge of the existing body of tradition. He influenced a number of theological currents which manifested themselves in the later legal schools, primarily the Ḥanafī one; *see* Gerard Lecomte, 'Ibrāhīm al-Nakhaʿī', EI^2, VII, 921–2; Ibn Ḥajar, *Tahdhīb*, I, 177–9; Dhahabī, *Siyar*, IV, 520–29.

al-Nawawī, Muḥyī al-Dīn Yaḥyā b. Sharaf (d. 676/1277). A Shāfiʿī jurist famous for his knowledge of *ḥadīth* and his commentary on Muslim's *Ṣaḥīḥ*; *see* Willi Heffening, 'al-Nawawī', EI^2, VII, 1041–2.

al-Qāḍī ʿAbd al-Jabbār, Abū'l-Ḥasan ʿAbd al-Jabbār b. Aḥmad b. ʿAbd al-Jabbār al-Hamadhānī al-Asadābādī (d. 415/1025). The most significant scholar of the late Muʿtazilī school of Abū Hāshim al-Jubbā'ī. In Muʿtazilī sources, he was known as *qāḍī al-quḍāt* because he had been judge of Rayy under the patronage of the vizier al-Ṣāḥib b. ʿAbbād (d. 385/995). A prolific author and theologian, he penned the monumental *al-Mughnī fī abwāb al-ʿadl waʾl-tawḥīd* and also wrote two short works on the allegorical and allusive commentary on the Qurʾān; *see* Wilferd Madelung, "Abd al-Jabbār', *EIr*, I, 116–18; Wilferd Madelung, 'The Theology of al-Zamakhsharī' in *Actas del XII Congreso de la U.E.A.I. (Malaga, 1984)* (Madrid, Union Européene d'Arabistants et d'Islamisants), 485–95; Samuel M. Stern, "Abd al-Djabbār', *EI*[2], I, 59–60; Ibn al-Murtaḍā, *Ṭabaqāt*, 112–13, 119; Dāwūdī, *Ṭabaqāt*, I, 256–8; Dhahabī 1961–2, I, 391–403; Maʿrifat, *Tafsīr*, II, 514; *GAS*, I, 624–6; Ibn al-Nadīm, *Fihrist*, 374.

al-Qaffāl, Abū Bakr Muḥammad b. ʿAlī (d. 365/976). A native of Shāsh (Tashkent), he was a student of Ṭabarī, a traditionist and an adherent of the Shāfiʿī school, who introduced that rite to Transoxiana in Central Asia; *see GAS*, I, 497–8; al-Ṣafadī, *Wāfī*, IV, 112–14; Dāwūdī, *Ṭabaqāt*, II, 198–200; Ibn Khallikān, *Wafayāt*, IV, 2001; Dhahabī, *Siyar*, XVI, 283–5; Claude Gilliot, 'The Beginnings of Qurʾānic Exegesis' in *The Qurʾan: Formative Interpretation*, ed. Andrew Rippin (Aldershot, Ashgate Variorum, 1999), 137–8. Qaffāl wrote a book on legal theory, a commentary on Shāfiʿī's book on legal theory and a commentary on the Qurʾān; *see* Ismāʿīl, *Kitāb al-Radd*, 129.

Qatāda b. Diʿāma al-Sadūsī (d. 117/735). A Basran, he was blind from birth, but proverbial for his memory and knowledge of genealogies, lexicography, historical traditions, Qurʾānic exegesis and readings. He was a pupil of al-Ḥasan al-Baṣrī [*q.v.*] and Ibn Sīrīn; *see* C. Pellat, 'Ḳatāda b. Diʿāma', *EI*[2], IV, 748; Dhahabī, *Siyar*, V, 269–83, no. 132; idem, *Mufassirūn*, I, 125–7; idem, *Ṭabaqāt*, II, 43–4; Ibn Khallikān, *Wafayāt*, IV, 85–6; Dhahabī, *Tadhkira*, I, 115–17; Ibn Ḥajar, *Tahdhīb*, VIII, 351–6; Ibn Saʿd, *Ṭabaqāt*, VII, 329–31; *GAS*, I, 31; Nöldeke, *GQ*, II, 168.

Rabīʿ b. Anas al-Bakrī (d. 139/756). A Basran narrator of the second generation of Muslims; *see GAS*, I, 34; Ibn Ḥajar, *Tahdhīb*, III, 238–9; Maʿrifat, *Tafsīr*, I, 411.

al-Rāghib, Abūʾl-Qāsim al-Ḥusayn b. Muḥammad, better known as al-Rāghib al-Iṣfahānī (d. *ante* 441/1050). For someone so frequently cited and well-known for opinions on issues ranging from Qurʾānic lexicography to ethics (al-Ghazālī is famously reputed to have carried with him on his travels a copy of Rāghib's principal work on Islamic ethics), it is extremely rare to find an informative biographical entry on al-Rāghib al-Iṣfahānī in the Muslim literary tradition. Al-Dhahabī can only tell us that he was an astute scholar, an impressive inquirer and the author of several compilations. Although the traditional death date ascribed to Rāghib is 503/1108, alternative dates have been adduced: between 440/1048 and 470/1077 (Dhahabī, *Siyar*, XVIII, 120–21); the middle of the fifth/eleventh century (Wilferd Madelung, 'Ar-Rāghib al-Iṣfahānī und die Ethik al-Ghazālīs' in *Islamwissenschaftliche Abhandlungen Fritz Meier zum 60sten Geburtstag*, ed. R. Gramlich [Wiesbaden, Steiner, 1974], 152–63). As E. Rowson has pointed out, Rāghib frequently alludes to contemporaries who can be identified as belonging to the circle of the Buyid vizier Ibn ʿAbbad (d. 385/995), and later his successor, al-Ḍabbī (d. 399/1008). Rāghib is best known for his contribution to the field of Islamic ethics, where his principal works are *al-Dharīʿa ilā makārim al-sharīʿa* and *Tafṣīl al-nashʾatayn wa-taḥṣīl al-saʿādatayn*. He wrote works of philosophy and he is also the author of a *tafsīr*, now mostly lost, and one of the most celebrated dictionaries of Qurʾānic terms, the *Mufrādāt al-Qurʾān*; *see* Everett K. Rowson, 'Al-Rāghib al-Iṣfahānī', *EI*², VIII, 389–90.

al-Rummānī, ʿAlī b. ʿĪsā (d. 384/994). Seminal thinker in linguistics and the literary sciences; *see* J. Flanagan, 'Al-Rummānī', *EI*², VIII, 614–15; *GAL*, I, 20, 113, S I, 175; Ibn Khallikān, *Wafayāt*, III, 299; Dhahabī, *Siyar*, XII, 533.

Saʿīd b. Jubayr b. Hishām al-Asadī al-Wālibī (d. 95/714). A famous scholar, traditionist and Qurʾān reciter (*muqriʾ*), renowned for his knowledge, especially that of the Qurʾān. He was killed by al-Ḥajājj for having taken part in the rebellion of Ibn al-Ashʿath, together with other famous figures, Mujāhid b. Jabr [*q.v.*], Ṭalq b. Ḥabīb and ʿAṭāʾ b. Abī Rabāḥ [*q.v.*]; *see* Dhahabī, *Siyar*, IV, 321–43, no. 116; Dhahabī, *Tadhkira*, I, 76–7; Ibn Ḥajar, *Tahdhīb*, IV, 11–14; *GAS*, I, 28–9; Gérard Lecomte, 'Sufyān al-Thawrī: Quelques remarques sur le personnage et son oeuvre', *Bulletin d'études orientales de l'Institut Français de Damas* 30 (1978), 51–60.

al-Sakhāwī, Shams al-Dīn (d. 902/1497). A famous Egyptian traditionist, prosopographer and historian; *see* Carl F. Petry, 'al-Sakhāwī', *EI*², VIII, 881–2.

al-Shaʿbī, ʿĀmir b. Sharāḥīl (d. 103/721–110/728). Famous early legal expert and transmitter of *ḥadīth*; *see* G.H.A. Juynboll, 'Al-Shaʿbī', *EI*², IX, 162–3; Ibn Khallikān, *Wafayāt*, III, 12–15; Dhahabī, *Siyar*, IV, 294–319.

al-Shāfiʿī, Abū ʿAbd Allāh Muḥammad b. Idrīs (d. 204/820). The eponym of the Shāfiʿī school of law. He was considered the 'renewer' (*mujaddid*) of the second/eighth century. He was probably born in Gaza, but after the death of his father, moved with his mother to Mecca. Having spent time with the tribe of Hudhayl, he acquired great skill as a poet and is said to have been admired in this respect by later literary luminaries such as al-Jāḥiẓ (d. 255/869). He was also an excellent archer, but abandoned these activities for a quest for knowledge. At Mecca he studied with the eponym of another school of law, Mālik b. Anas (d. 179/795), the author of the famous legal manual *al-Muwaṭṭaʾ*. Shāfiʿī spent many years in Iraq where he met with the two progenitors of the other Sunnī schools, Abū Ḥanīfa [*q.v.*] and Aḥmad b. Ḥanbal [*q.v.*], before spending time in Yemen and finally settling in Egypt where he composed his two most famous works, the *Kitāb al-Umm* and *al-Risāla*; *see* E. Chaumont, 'Al-Shāfiʿī', *EI*², IX, 181.

Shaykhzāda, Muḥammad b. Muṣliḥ (Ibn al-Shaykh). (d. 951/1544). *Shaykh al-Islām* (chief *muftī*) of Istanbul and author of a commentary on Bayḍāwī's *Tafsīr ḥāshiyat Muḥyī al-Dīn Shaykhzāda ʿalā tafsīr al-qāḍī al-Bayḍāwī*.

al-Shiblī, Abū Bakr Dulaf b. Jaḥdar (d. 334/945). A celebrated but controversial mystic of Baghdad. A disciple of Junayd, he also associated for a time with al-Ḥallāj. Shiblī left behind no authenticated written works, but two works attributed to him have been published: *Dīwān*, ed. K.M. al-Shaybī (Baghdad, Dār al-Taḍāmun, 1967), and *Ādāb al-mulūk*, ed. B. Radtke (Beirut, Franz Steiner Verlag, 1991). Otherwise, many sayings and a number of poems have been preserved in works of Sufi literature. His ecstatic utterances (*shaṭḥiyyāt*) were included and commented on by Rūzbihān Baqlī in his *Sharḥ-i shaṭḥiyyāt*.

On Shiblī, *see* Farīd al-Dīn ʿAṭṭār, *Tadhkirat al-awliyāʾ*, ed. M. Estiʿlāmī; partial Eng. tr. Arberry as *Muslim Saints and Mystics*; Florian Sobieroj, 'Al-Shiblī', *EI*[2], IX, 432–3; Dhahabī, *Siyar*, XV, 367ff ; Abū Nuʿaym, *Ḥilya*, X, 366–75.

Sībawayh (d. *c.* 180/796). Pioneer Arabic grammarian and author of a single untitled work known as *Kitāb Sībawayhi*, acknowledged as the founding text of Arabic grammatical science. He was a student of al-Akhfash al-Akbar [*q.v.*] and al-Khalīl b. Aḥmad; for extensive references *see* Michael G. Carter, 'Sībawayhi', *EI*[2], IX, 524–30.

al-Suddī, Ismāʿīl b. ʿAbd al-Raḥmān (d. 127/745). A popular Kufan preacher, with regard to whom opinions diverged greatly; some considered him mendacious, undoubtedly on account of his 'preaching' and the 'popular' nature of his Qurʾānic exegesis, associated with the role of the popular storyteller/preacher (*qāṣṣ*); *see* G.H.A. Juynboll, 'Al-Suddī', *EI*[2], IX, 762; Ibn Ḥajar, *Tahdhīb*, I, 313; *GAS*, I, 32–3.

Sufyān al-Thawrī (d. 161/788). One of the key figures in the generation of *tābiʿūn* who, alongside Mujāhid b. Jabr [*q.v.*], Muqātil b. Sulaymān, ʿAbd al-Razzāq al-Ṣanʿānī [*q.v.*] is a major source for early exegesis, and to whom with some confidence we can attribute the emergence of a formal genre of *tafsīr*. Although a *tafsīr* has been published in his name, edited by I.A. ʿArshī (Beirut, 1983), Versteegh has little confidence in the authenticity of this work, and considers it to be a compilation from later sources. C.H.M. Versteegh, 'Grammar and Exegesis: The Origins of Kufan Grammar and the *Tafsīr Muqātil*', *Der Islam* 67.2 (1990), 206–42.

al-Sulamī, Abū ʿAbd al-Raḥmān Muḥammad b. al-Ḥusayn (d. 412/1021). An important Sufi hagiographer and Qurʾān commentator from Nishapur; *see* Gerhard Böwering, 'al-Sulamī', *EI*[2], IX, 811–12; Dhahabī, *Siyar*, XVII, 247–55; *GAS*, I, 671–4; Süleyman Ateş, *Sülemî ve Tasavvufî Tefsirî* (Sönmez, Cağaloğlu, 1969). His significant *tafsīr*, *Ḥaqāʾiq al-tafsīr*, has been uncritically edited and published in two volumes.

al-Suyūṭī, Jalāl al-Dīn (d. 911/1505). A Shāfiʿī jurist, he wrote treatises on law and legal theory. He was the student of Jalāl al-Dīn al-Maḥallī (on whom *see* C. Pellat, 'al-Maḥallī', *EI*[2], V, 1223). Suyūṭī completed the commentary begun by his master Maḥallī and this *tafsīr*, which came to be known as *Tafsīr al-Jalālayn*, 'the Commentary of the two Jalāls', and has enjoyed lasting popularity even to this day (for an English translation see Hamza *et al.*, *Anthology*, I). Since Suyūṭī was responsible for the final form of the commentary and the bulk of its content some scholars have referred to it as his work, Maḥallī having composed the commentary only on the *sūrat al-Fātiḥa* and then from *sūrat al-Kahf* (Q. 18) onwards. Suyūṭī lived most of his life in Cairo and some biographers have attributed 600 books and booklets to him. He is known, *inter alia*, as a linguist, historian, and legal scholar. Jalāl al-Dīn al-Suyūṭī, *Ḥusn al-muḥāḍara fī akhbār Miṣr waʾl-Qāhira*, 2 vols. (Cairo, Būlāq, 1880–81), I, 252; Najm al-Dīn Ghazzī, *al-Kawākib al-sāʾira fī aʿyān al-miʾa al-ʿāshira*, ed. Jibrāʾīl Sulaymān Jabbūr, 3 vols. (Beirut, American University of Beirut Press, 1945), I, 226; Muḥammad b. Aḥmad Ibn Iyās, *Badāʾiʿ al-zuhūr fī waqāʾiʿ al-duhūr*, 3 vols. plus index prepared by Muḥammad ʿAlī Biblāwī and ʿAlī Afandī Ṣubḥī (Cairo, Būlāq, 1893–6), IV, 83. Cf. Eric Geoffroy, 'Al-Suyūṭī', *EI*², IX, 913–16; Elizabeth M. Sartain, *Jalāl al-Dīn al-Suyūṭī: Biography and Background* (Cambridge, Cambridge University Press, 1975); M.A. Sharaf, *Jalāl al-Dīn al-Suyūṭī: Manhajuhu wa ārāʾuhu al-kalāmiyya* (Beirut, Dār al-Nahḍa al-ʿArabiyya, 1981).

Ṭarafa, ʿAmr b. al-ʿAbd b. Sufyān (*fl. c.* 543–69). Pre-Islamic poet and composer of a *muʿallaqa* poem which is among the most famous pre-Islamic poems; *see* J.E. Montgomery, 'Ṭarafa', *EI*², X, 219–20; ʿAzmī Sukar, *Muʿjam al-shuʿarāʾ fī taʾrīkh al-Ṭabarī* (Sidon, al-Maktaba al-ʿAriyya, 1999), 246.

al-Thaʿlabī, Aḥmad b. Muḥammad (d. 427/1035). A prominent commentator of the Qurʾān and collector of stories. He is famous for two works: a massive *tafsīr*, which draws upon the work of Muqāṭil b. Sulaymān (d. 150/767) and al-Kalbī [*q.v.*], and a *Qiṣaṣ al-anbiyāʾ* work on the stories of the lives of pre-Muḥammadan prophets. His major commentary, *al-Kashf waʾl-bayān ʿan tafsīr al-Qurʾān* has been uncritically and incompletely edited in four volumes, although Isaiah Goldfield edited the bibliographical introduction: Thaʿlabī, *Qurʾanic Commentary*; *see* Andrew Rippin, 'al-Thaʿlabī', *EI*², X, 434; Saleh, *Formation*; Dhahabī, *Tafsīr*, I, 227–34; Nöldeke, *GQ*, II, 173–4; *GAL*, I, 350.

al-Ṭūsī, Abū Jaʿfar Muḥammad b. al-Ḥasan (d. 459 or 460/1066–7). Originally from Khorasan, he moved to Buyid-dominated Baghdad, where he studied with two of the main Imāmī authorities of all time, al-Shaykh al-Mufīd (d. 413/1022) and al-Sharīf al-Murtaḍā (d. 436/1044), later becoming the leading Twelver scholar of his time. He wrote two of what were to become the 'four books' (*al-kutub al-arbaʿa*) of Imāmī jurisprudence: *al-Istibṣār*, and *Tahdhīb al-aḥkām* (the latter being a commentary on al-Mufīd's *al-Muqniʿa*). He wrote the first great Imāmī rationalist Qurʾān commentary: Ṭūsī, *Tibyān*; *see* Mohammad A. Amir-Moezzi, 'al-Ṭūsī', *EI*², X, 745–6; Akhtar, *The Early Shīʿite Imāmiyyah Thinkers*, 205–46; ʿAlī Dawānī, ed. *Hazāra-yi Shaykh Ṭūsī*, 2 vols. (Tehran, Dār al-Tablīgh-i Islāmī, 1362 Sh./1983; orig. pub. Tehran, Amīr Kabīr, 1349 Sh./1970); Āghā Buzurg Muḥammad Muḥsin Ṭihrānī, *Zindagī-nāma-yi Shaykh Ṭūsī* (Tehran, Farhangistān-i Adab wa Hunar-i Īrān, 1981). Cf. Muhammad I. Marcinkowski, 'Rapprochement and Fealty during the Būyids and Early Saljūqs: The Life and Times of Muḥammad ibn al-Ḥasan al-Ṭūsī', *Islamic Studies* (Islamabad) 40.2, 273–96.

Ubayy b. Kaʿb, Abūʾl-Mundhir (d. 18 or 30/635 or 651). Traditionally regarded as the founder of the Medinan 'school' of commentary, he had been a Jewish rabbi before his conversion to Islam. He acted as the Prophet's secretary. An early collector of the Qurʾān, known as 'master of the readers' (*sayyid al-qurrāʾ*), he was renowned for his memory and his ability to recite the entire Qurʾān in eight nights. He is said to have collected his own copy of the Qurʾān prior to the collection ordered by the caliph ʿUthmān; *see* Dhahabī, *Mufassirūn*, I, 91–3; Maʿrifat, *Tafsīr*, I, 223–4, 316–17; Andrew Rippin, 'Ubayy b. Kaʿb', *EI*², X, 964–5; Ibn Saʿd, *Ṭabaqāt*, III/3, 59–62; Dhahabī, *Siyar*, I, 389–402; Nöldeke, *GQ*, III, 83–97; cf. Jeffery, *Materials for the History of the Text of the Qurʾān*, 114–81.

Wahb b. Munabbih (d. between 110/728 and 114/732). A South-Arabian storyteller of Persian descent and an important figure in the early Islamic storytelling tradition. He was classed among the experts in the *isrāʾīliyyāt*, and there is some controversy about whether he was one of the *ahl al-Kitāb* before his conversion to Islam. A *ṣaḥīfa* is attributed to Wahb, on which see R.G. Khouri 'Wahb b. Munabbih', *EI*², XI, 34–6.

al-Wāḥidī, Abū'l-Ḥasan al-Naysābūrī (d. 468/1075). Famous exegete, grammarian and scholar of Mutanabbī's poetry. His most famous work is on the occasions of the revelation of the Qurʾānic verses, the *Asbāb al-nuzūl*; *see GAL*, I, 411–12; Ibn Khallikān, *Wafayāt*, III, 303–4; Dhahabī, *Siyar*, XVIII, 339–42.

al-Wāqidī, Muḥammad b. ʿUmar (d. 207/822). A philologist, traditionist, exegete and author of a work on the campaigns of the Prophet: Wāqidī, *Kitāb al-Maghāzī*; *see* S. Leder, 'al-Wāqidī', *EI*², XI, 101–3; Dhahabī, *Siyar*, IX, 469; Ibn Saʿd, *Ṭabaqāt*, V, 314–21, VII, 77; Ibn al-Nadīm, *Fihrist*, 111. He was accused of being Shīʿī and of being an unreliable source. For a modern debate on the latter, see Chase F. Robinson, *Islamic Historiography* (Cambridge, Cambridge University Press, 2003), 29–30.

Yaḥyā b. Sallām. *See* Ibn Sallām.

Yaʿqūb b. Shuʿayb b. Maytham al-Tammār (*fl.* early second/eighth century). Narrated from Jaʿfar al-Ṣādiq, and was the grandson of a close companion of ʿAlī b. Abī Ṭālib who had been executed in Kufa for his Shīʿism; *see* Najāshī, *Rijāl*, II, 427; Ibn Dāwūd, *Kitāb al-Rijāl*, 206.

Yūnus b. ʿAbd al-Aʿlā b. Maysara (d. 264/877). A great Egyptian scholar, a Qurʾān reciter (*muqriʾ*) who followed the reading of Warsh from Nāfiʿ [*q.v.*], and a *ḥāfiẓ* (one who has memorised the entire Qurʾān), who transmitted from the likes of Sufyān b. ʿUyayna, and transmitted to Muslim, Ibn Māja [*q.v.*], al-Nasāʾī and Abū Ḥātim; *see* Ibn Ḥajar, *Tahdhīb*, XI, 440; Dhahabī, *Siyar*, XII, 348–51.

Yūnus b. Ḥabīb al-Naḥwī (d 439/1047). Compiler of books on *tafsīr*, language, parables and anecdotes; *see* Ibn Khallikān, *Wafayāt*, VII, 244–9; Dhahabī, *Siyar*, VIII, 171.

al-Zajjāj, Ibrāhīm b. al-Sarī (d. 311/923). An Arabic grammarian who worked in Baghdad; among his pupils were Abū ʿAlī al-Fārisī [*q.v.*], Ibn Wallād and al-Rummānī [*q.v.*]. He is regarded as the link between the two grammarian schools of Kufa and Basra and the new grammar that was developed in Baghdad in the fourth/tenth century under the influence of Greek logic. His main work dealt with Qurʾānic philology: Ibrāhīm b. al-Sarī al-Zajjāj, *Maʿānī al-Qurʾān wa iʿrābuhu*, ed. ʿAbd al-Jalīl ʿAbduh Shalabī (Beirut, al-Maktaba al-ʿAṣriyya, 1973); *see* C.H.M. Versteegh, 'Al-Zadjdjādj', *EI*², XI, 377–8. *GAS*, I, 49; *GAL*, I, 109–10; Ibn al-Nadīm, *Fihrist*, 60–61; Dhahabī, *Siyar*, XIV, 360.

Zayd b. ʿAlī (d. 122/740). A grandson of al-Ḥusayn b. ʿAlī b. Abī Ṭālib and a noted expert on periphrastic exegesis of the Qurʾān; *see* Wilferd Madelung, 'Zayd b. ʿAlī', *EI*², XI, 473–4; Ibn Saʿd, *Ṭabaqāt*, V, 239–40; Abū'l-Faraj Iṣfahānī, *Maqātil al-Ṭālibiyyīn*, ed. Aḥmad Ṣaqr (Cairo, Dār Iḥyāʾ al-Kutub al-ʿArabiyya, 1949), 127–51; *GAS*, I, 552–60; Balādhurī, *Ansāb*, ed. Maḥmūdī, II, 520–41; Cornelis van Arendonk, *Les debuts de l'imāmat zaidite au Yemen*, tr. Jacques Ryckmans (Leiden, Brill, 1960), 28–31; Jaʿfar Subḥānī, *Manshūr-i ʿaqāʾid-i Imāmiyyah*, ed. and tr. R.S. Kazemi as *Doctrines of Shiʿi Islam: A Compendium of Imami Beliefs and Practices* (London, I.B. Tauris), 2001, 57–220.

Zayn al-ʿĀbidīn, ʿAlī b. al-Ḥusayn b. ʿAlī al-Sajjād (d. 94–5/712–13). The fourth Shīʿī imam, brother of Zaynab bt. ʿAlī. After the massacre at Karbala, Zayn al-ʿAbidīn retired to a quiet life of piety and charity in Medina and was not active in politics. Though respected and revered by both Sunnī and Shīʿī sources, the details of his life and his dealings with the political authorities vary considerably between them. See E. Kohlberg, 'Zayn al-ʿAbidīn', *EI*², XI, 482–3.

al-Zuhrī, Muḥammad b. Muslim b. ʿUbayd Allāh b. Shihāb b. Zuhra (d. 124/742). A prominent (and pre-eminent) traditionist and jurist of the third generation of Muslims in Medina. His main teachers were ʿUrwa b. al-Zubayr (d. 93/712), the nephew of ʿĀʾisha [*q.v.*], and Saʿīd b. al-Musayyab [*q.v.*]. An important source for the legal pronouncements of Ibn Jurayj [*q.v.*], he was also an important source for the *Sīra* of Ibn Isḥāq [*q.v.*]; *see* Michael Lecker, 'al-Zuhrī', *EI*², XI, 565–6; idem, 'Biographical Notes', 21–63; Khalīfa b. Khayyāṭ, *Ṭabaqāt*, 261; Robinson, *Islamic Historiography*, 24ff. Motzki, '*The Muṣannaf* of ʿAbd al-Razzāq', 1–21.

Bibliography

PRIMARY SOURCES

ʿAbd al-Jabbār b. Aḥmad, al-Qāḍī al-Asadābādī (d. 415/1025). *Kitāb Tanzīh al-Qurʾān ʿan al-maṭāʿin*. Beirut, Dār al-Maʿrifa, 1966.

ʿAbduh, Muḥammad (d. 1905) and Muḥammad Rashīd Riḍā (d. 1935). *Tafsīr al-Qurʾān al-ḥakīm al-mashhūr bi-tafsīr al-manār*, ed. Ibrāhīm Shams al-Dīn, 12 vols. Beirut, Dār al-Kutub al-ʿIlmiyya, 1999.

Abūʾl-ʿArab, Muḥammad b. Aḥmad al-Tamīmī al-Qayrawānī (d. 333/945). *Ṭabaqāt ʿulamāʾ Ifrīqiyā wa-Tūnis*, ed. ʿAlī al-Shābbī and Naʿīm Ḥasan al-Yāfī. Tunis, al-Dār al-Tūnisiyya liʾl-Nashr, 1968.

Abū Dāwūd al-Sijistānī (d. 275/889). *Sunan*, ed. Muḥammad Muḥyī al-Dīn ʿAbd al-Ḥamīd, 4 vols. Beirut, Dār al-Fikr, [198–?].

Abū Nuʿaym al-Iṣfahānī, Aḥmad b. ʿAbd Allāh (d. 430/1038). *Ḥilyat al-awliyāʾ wa-ṭabaqāt al-aṣfiyāʾ*, 10 vols. Cairo, Maktabat al-Khānjī, 1932–9.

Abūʾl-Ṭayyib al-Lughawī (d. 351/962). *Marātib al-naḥwiyyīn*, ed. Muḥammad Abūʾl-Faḍl Ibrāhīm. Cairo, Maktabat Nahḍat Miṣr, 1955.

Abū ʿUbayda, Maʿmar b. al-Muthannā al-Taymī (d. *c.* 209–10/824–5). *Majāz al-Qurān*, ed. Fuat Sezgin, 2 vols. Cairo, Maktabat al-Khānjī, 1954–62.

Abū Zakariyyā al-Warjalānī, Yaḥyā b. Abī Bakr (*fl.* late fifth/eleventh century). *Kitāb Siyar al-aʾimma wa akhbārihim*, ed. Ismāʿīl al-ʿArabī. Algiers, al-Maktaba al-Waṭaniyya, 1979.

al-Alūsī, Abūʾl-Thanāʾ Maḥmūd b. ʿAbd Allāh (d. 1270/1854). *Rūḥ al-maʿānī fī tafsīr al-Qurʾān al-ʿaẓīm waʾl-sabʿ al-mathānī*, ed. ʿAlī ʿAbd al-Bārī ʿAṭiyya, 16 vols. Beirut, Dār al-Kutub al-ʿIlmiyya, 2005.

Āmulī, Sayyid Ḥaydar (d. *post* 787/1385). *Jāmiʿ al-asrār wa manbaʿ al-anwār* in *La Philosophie Shîʿite*, Bibliothèque Iranienne XVI, ed. Henry Corbin and Osman Yahia. Tehran, Institut Franco-Iranien de Recherche, 1969.

al-ʿAskarī, al-Ḥasan b. ʿAlī (attrib.) (d. 260/873–4). *Al-Tafsīr al-mansūb ilāʾl-Imām Abī Muḥammad al-Ḥasan b. ʿAlī al-ʿAskarī. See* secondary sources, Jalālī, *Tafsīr al-mansūb.*

ʿAṭṭār, Farīd al-Dīn (d. *c.* 618/1221). *Tadhkīrat al-awliyāʾ*, ed. M. Estiʿlāmī. 6th Repr. Tehran, Intishārāt-i Ḥikmat, 1370 Sh./1991; partial English tr. A.J. Arberry as *Muslim Saints and Mystics: Extracts from Attār's Tadhkīrat al-auliyāʾ*. London, George Allen and Unwin, 1979.

al-ʿAyyāshī, Muḥammad b. Masʿūd (d. 320/932). *Tafsīr ʿAyyāshī*. Qumm, Muʾassasat al-Baʿtha, 2000.

al-Baghdādī, al-Khāṭib Aḥmad b. ʿAlī (d. 463/1071). *Taʾrīkh Baghdād*, 14 vols. Cairo, Maktabat al-Khānjī, 1931; also published as *Taʾrīkh madīnat al-Salām*, ed. Bashshār ʿAwwād Maʿrūf, 23 vols. Baghdad, Dār al-Gharb al-Islāmī, 2001.

Bakhtiar, Laleh, tr. *The Sublime Quran*. Chicago, Kazi Publications, 2007.

al-Bakrī, Abū ʿUbayd (d. 487/1094). *al-Masālik waʾl-mamālik: Kitāb al-Mughrib fī dhikr bilād Ifrīqiyā waʾl-Maghrib*, ed. William MacGuckin de Slane. Algiers, Imprimerie de Gouvernement, 1857.

al-Balādhurī, Aḥmad b. Yaḥyā (d. 279/892). *Ansāb al-ashrāf*, ed. Muḥammad Bāqir al-Maḥmūdī, 3 vols. Beirut, Dār al-Taʿāruf li'l-Maṭbūʿāt, 1974–1977; ed. Maḥmūd Firdaws al-ʿAẓm. Damascus, Dār al-Yaqaẓa al-ʿArabiyya, 1997; 6 vols., IV and V ed. Iḥsān ʿAbbās. Wiesbaden, Franz Steiner, 1978–2002.

al-Baqlī, Rūzbihān b. Abū'l-Naṣr al-Shīrāzī (d. 606/1209). *ʿArā'is al-bayān fī ḥaqā'iq al-Qur'ān*. Beirut, Dār al-Kutub al-ʿIlmiyya, 2008.

al-Bayhaqī, Aḥmad b. al-Ḥusayn (d. 458/1066). *al-Khilāfiyyāt bayn al-imāmayn al-Shāfiʿī wa-Abī Ḥanīfa wa-aṣḥābihi*, ed. Maḥmūd b. ʿAbd al-Fattāḥ al-Naḥḥāl, 8 vols. Cairo, al-Rawḍa li'l-Nashr wa'l-Tawzīʿ, Cairo, 2015.

al-Bukhārī, Abū ʿAbd Allāh Muḥammad b. Ismāʿīl (d. 256/870). *Al-Adab al-mufrad*, ed. Muḥammad Fū'ād b. ʿAbd al-Bāqī. Cairo, al-Maṭbaʿa al-Salafiyya, 1955.

——. *Kitāb al-Ḍuʿafā' al-ṣaghīr*, ed. M. Zāhid, Beirut, Dār al-Maʿrifa, 1986.

——. *Ṣaḥīḥ (Recueil des traditions mahometanes)*, ed. Ludolf Krehl and Theodor Willem Juynboll, 4 vols. Leiden, Brill, 1908.

——. *Al-Ta'rīkh al-kabīr*, 4 vols. Hyderabad, Majlis Dā'irat al-Maʿārif al-ʿUthmāniyya, 1963–78.

al-Burūsawī, Ismāʿīl Ḥaqqī (d. 1137/1725). *Rūḥ al-bayān fī tafsīr al-Qur'ān*, ed. ʿAbd al-Laṭīf Ḥasan ʿAbd al-Raḥmān, 10 vols. Beirut, Dār al-Kutub al-ʿIlmiyya, 2003.

al-Dabbāgh, Abū Zayd ʿAbd al-Raḥmān (d. 696/1296). *Maʿālim al-īmān fī maʿrifat ahl al-Qayrawān*, 3 vols. (vol. I, ed. Ibrāhīm Shabbūḥ; vol. II, ed. Muḥammad Abū'l-Nūr; vol. III, ed. Muḥammad Māḍūr). Cairo, Maktabat al-Khānjī, 1968.

al-Darjīnī, Aḥmad b. Saʿīd (*fl.* seventh/thirteenth century). *Kitāb Ṭabaqāt al-mashāyikh bi'l-Maghrib*, ed. Ibrāhīm Ṭallay, 2 vols. Qusanṭīna, Maṭbaʿat al-Baʿth, 1974.

al-Dāwūdī, Muḥammad b. ʿAlī (d. 945/1538–9). *Ṭabaqāt al-mufassirīn*, ed. ʿAlī Muḥammad ʿUmar, 2 vols. Cairo, Maktabat Wahba, 1972.

al-Dhahabī, Muḥammad b. Aḥmad (d. 748/1348). *Mīzān al-iʿtidāl fī naqd al-rijāl*, ed. ʿAlī Muḥammad Bajawī, 4 vols. Cairo, ʿĪsā al-Bābī al-Ḥalabī, 1963.

——. *Siyar aʿlām al-nubalā'*, ed. Shuʿayb al-Arna'ūṭ and Ḥusayn al-Asad, 25 vols. Beirut, Mu'assasat al-Risāla, 1981–8.

——. *Tadhkirat al-ḥuffāẓ* 4 vols. Hyderabad, Maṭbaʿat Majlis Dā'irat al-Maʿārif al-ʿUthmāniyya, 1968–70.

Faḍl Allāh, Muhammad Husayn (d. 2010). *Aḥādīth fī qaḍāyā al-ikhtilāf wa'l-waḥda*. Beirut, Dār al-Malāk, 2000.

——. *Al-ʿAlāqāt al-Islāmiyya al-Masīḥiyya: Dirāsa marjaʿiyya fī'l-ta'rīkh wa'l-ḥāḍir wa'l-mustaqbal*. Beirut, Markaz al-Dirāsāt al-Istrātījiyya wa'l-Buḥūth wa'l-Tawthīq, 1994.

——. *Dunyā al-mar'a*. Beirut, Dār al-Malāk, 1997.

——. *Dunyā al-shabāb*. Beirut, Mu'assasat al-ʿĀrif, 1997.

——. *Fiqh al-ḥayāt*. Beirut, Mu'assasat al-ʿĀrif, 1997.

——. *Al-Hijra wa'l-ightirāb*. Beirut, Mu'assasat al-ʿĀrif, 1999.

——. *Kitāb al-Jihād*. Beirut, Dār al-Malāk, 1996.

——. *Min waḥy al-Qur'ān*, 24 vols. Beirut, Dār al-Malāk, 1979. Repr. 1998.

Fīrūzābādī, Muḥammad b. Yaʿqūb (d. 817/1415). *Al-Qāmūs al-muḥīṭ*, 4 vols. Beirut, Dār al-Jīl, n.d. Repr. Cairo, Muṣṭafā al-Bābī al-Ḥalabī, 1952.

al-Ghazālī, Abū Ḥāmid (d. 505/1111). *Al-Muṣṭaṣfā min ʿilm al-uṣūl*, ed. Muḥammad Yūsuf Najm, 2 vols. Beirut, Dār Ṣādir, 1995.

Ghazzī, Najm al-Dīn (d. 1061/1651). *Al-Kawākib al-sā'ira fī a'yān al-mi'a al-'āshira*, ed. Jibrā'īl Sulaymān Jabbūr, 3 vols. Beirut, American University of Beirut Press, 1945.

Hūd b. Muḥakkam al-Hawwārī (d. *c.* 290/903) *Tafsīr kitāb Allāh al-'azīz*, ed. Belḥāj b. Sa'īd Sharīfī, 4 vols. Beirut, Dār al-Gharb al-Islāmī, 1990.

Hujwīrī, 'Alī b. 'Uthmān (d. 465–9/1072–7). *Kashf al-Maḥjūb*, ed. V. Zhukovski. Repr. Tehran, Tehran University Press, 1979.

Ibn Abī Uṣaybi'a, Aḥmad b. al-Qāsim (d. 668/1270). *'Uyūn al-anbā' fī ṭabaqāt al-aṭibbā'*, ed. 'Āmir al-Najjār, 6 vols. Cairo, al-Hay'a al-Miṣriyya al-'Āmma li'l-Kitāb, 2001.

Ibn 'Arabī, Muḥyī al-Dīn (d. 638/1240). *Raḥma min al-Raḥmān fī tafsīr wa ishārāt al-Qur'ān*, compilation of all the exegetical comments in Ibn 'Arabī's *Futūḥāt* by Maḥmūd Maḥmūd al-Ghurāb, 2 vols. Damascus, Dār al-Fikr/Maṭba'at al-Nuḍr, 1410/1989.

Ibn 'Asākir, 'Alī b. al-Ḥasan b. Hibat Allāh (d. 571/1176). *Tā'rīkh madīnat Dimashq*, ed. Muḥibb al-Dīn 'Umar al-'Amrāwī, 80 vols. Beirut, Dār al-Fikr, 1998.

Ibn al-Athīr, Majd al-Dīn al-Mubārak b. Muḥammad (d. 606/1210). *Al-Lubāb fī tahdhīb al-ansāb*, ed. H. Qudsī. Cairo, 1938.

Ibn Dāwūd al-Ḥillī, al-Ḥasan b. 'Alī (d. 740–41/1339–40). *Kitāb al-Rijāl*, ed. Muḥammad Ṣādiq Baḥr al-'Ulūm. Najaf, al-Maṭba'a al-Ḥaydariyya, 1972.

Ibn Durayd, Abū Bakr Muḥammad b. al-Ḥasan (d. 321/933). *Jamharat al-lugha*, ed. Ramzi Mounir Baalbaki. Beirut, Dār al-'Ilm li'l-Malāyīn, 1987.

Ibn al-Fuwaṭī, 'Abd al-Razzāq b. Aḥmad (d. 723/1323). *Talkhīṣ majma' al-ādāb fī mu'jam al-alqāb*, ed. Muṣṭafā Jawād, 4 vols. Damascus, Wizārat al-Thaqāfa wa'l-Irshād al-Qawmī, 1962.

Ibn Ḥajar al-'Asqalānī, Shihāb al-Dīn Aḥmad (d. 852/1449). *Bulūgh al-marām*, ed. Raḍwān Muḥammad Raḍwān. [Cairo], Dār al-Kitāb al-'Arabī bi-Miṣr, [1954].

——. *Tahdhīb al-tahdhīb*, 6 vols. Repr. Beirut, Dār Iḥyā' al-Turāth al-'Arabī, 1993.

Ibn Ḥanbal, Aḥmad (d. 241/855). *Musnad*, ed. Muḥammad Naṣr al-Dīn al-Albānī, 6 vols. Beirut, al-Maktab al-Islāmī and Dār Ṣādir, n.d.

Ibn Ḥibbān al-Bustī, Muḥammad (d. 354/965). *Kitāb al-Majrūḥīn min al-muḥaddithīn wa'l-ḍu'afā' wa'l-matrukīn*, ed. Maḥmūd Ibrāhīm Zāyid, 3 vols. Aleppo, Dār al-Wa'y, 1975–6.

Ibn Hishām, 'Abd al-Mālik (d. 218/833). *Al-Sīra al-nabawiyya li'Ibn Hishām*, 4 vols. Beirut, Mu'assasat Ḥusām Rammāl, [n.d.]; ed. Ferdinand Wüstenfeld, *Dad Lebens Muhammed's nach Ibn Ishâq bearbeitet von Abd el-Malik Ibn Hichâm*, 2 vols. Göttingen, Dietrichs, 1858–60; tr. Alfred Guillaume, *The Life of Muhammad: A Translation of Ibn Isḥāq's Sīrat Rasūl Allāh*. London, Oxford University Press, 1955. Repr. Karachi, Oxford University Press, 1982.

Ibn Iyās, Muḥammad b. Aḥmad (d. *c.* 930/1524). *Badā'i' al-zuhūr fī waqā'i' al-duhūr*, 3 vols. plus index prepared by Muḥammad 'Alī Biblāwī and 'Alī Afandī Ṣubḥī. Cairo, Būlāq, 1893–6.

Ibn al-Jazarī, Abū'l-Khayr Shams al-Dīn Muḥammad b. Muḥammad b. Muḥammad b. 'Alī b. Yūsuf (d. 833/1429). *Ghāyat al-nihāya fī ṭabaqāt al-qurrā'*, ed. G. Bergstraesser, 2 vols. Beirut, Dār al-Kutub al-'Ilmiyya, 1971.

Ibn Kathīr, Abū'l-Fidā' Ismā'īl 'Imād al-Dīn (d. 774/1373). *Al-Bidāya wa'l-nihāya*, ed. Aḥmad 'Abd al-Wahhāb Futayḥ, 15 vols. Cairo, Dār al-Ḥadīth, 1992.

——. *Tafsīr al-Qur'ān al-'aẓīm*, ed. Khalid Muḥammad Muḥarram, 4 vols. Beirut, al-Maktaba al-'Aṣriyya, 2006.

Ibn Khaldūn, ʿAbd al-Raḥmān al-ʿAllāma al-Maghribī (d. 784/1382). *Kitāb al-ʿIbar*, ed. Yūsuf Asʿad Dāghir, 7 vols. Beirut, Dār al-Kitāb al-Lubnānī, 1956–61.
Ibn Khallikān, Aḥmad b. Muḥammad (d. 681/1282). *Wafayāt al-aʿyān*, ed. Iḥsān ʿAbbās, 8 vols. Beirut, Dār al-Thaqāfa, 1968–72.
Ibn Khayr al-Ishbīlī, Abū Bakr Muḥammad b. Khayr b. ʿUmar b. Khalīfa al-Lamtūnī al-Amawī (d. 575/1179). *Fahrasat mā rawāhu ʿan shuyūkhi-hi min al-dawāwīn al-muṣannafa fī durūb al-ʿilm wa-anwāʿ al-maʿārif*, ed. Francisco Codera and Julián Ribera Tarragó. Baghdad, Maktabat al-Muthannā, 1963.
Ibn Māja, Muḥammad b. Yazīd al-Qazwīnī (d. 273/887). *Sunan*, ed. Ṣidqī Jamīl al-ʿAṭṭār, 2 vols. Beirut, Dār al-Fikr, 1995.
Ibn al-Malāḥimī, Maḥmūd b. Muḥammad al-Malāḥimī al-Khwārizmī (d. 536/1141). *Kitāb al-Muʿtamad fī uṣūl al-dīn*, ed. Martin McDermott and Wilferd Madelung. London, al-Hoda, 1991.
Ibn Mujāhid, Aḥmad b. Mūsā (d. 324/936). *Kitāb al-Sabʿa fīʾl-qirāʾāt*, ed. Shawqī Ḍayf. Cairo, Dār al-Maʿārif, 1972.
Ibn al-Murtaḍā, Aḥmad b. Yaḥyā (d. 840/1437). *Ṭabaqāt al-muʿtazila*, ed. Susanna Diwald-Wilzer. Wiesbaden, Franz Steiner, 1961.
Ibn al-Nadīm, Muḥammad b. Isḥāq (d. 385/995). *Kitāb al-Fihrist*, ed. Gustav Flügel, 2 vols. Leipzig, Vogel, 1871–2; ed. Ibrāhīm Ramaḍān. Beirut, Dār al-Maʿrifa, 1994. Trans. Bayard Dodge, *The Fihrist of al-Nadīm: A Tenth-Century Survey of Muslim Culture*, 2 vols. New York, Columbia University Press, 1970.
Ibn Qutayba, ʿAbd Allāh b. Muslim b. Qutayba (d. 276/889). *Kitāb al-Maʿārif*, ed. Tharwat ʿUkāsha. Cairo, Maṭbaʿat Dār al-Kutub, 1960.
Ibn Saʿd, Muḥammad (d. 230/845). *Kitāb al-Ṭabaqāt al-kabīr*, ed. Eduard Sachau, 9 vols. Leiden, Brill, 1921; vol. VIII (abridged), tr. Aisha Bewley as *The Women of Madina*. London, Taha Publishers, 1997.
Ibn al-Ṣaghīr (*fl.* late third/ninth century). *Akhbār al-aʾimma al-Rustamiyyīn*, ed. Muḥammad Nāṣir and Ibrāhīm Baḥāz. Beirut, Dār al-Gharb al-Islāmī, 1986.
Ibn Sallām al-Ibāḍī, Yaḥyā (*fl.* third/ninth century). *Kitāb fīhi badʾ al-islām wa sharāʾiʿ al-dīn*, ed. Werner Schwartz and Sālim b. Yaʿqūb. Beirut, Dār Iqraʾ, 1985. Repr. Wiesbaden, Franz Steiner, 1986.
——. *Kitāb al-Taṣārīf*. Tunis, al-Sharika al-Tūnisiyya liʾl-Tawzīʿ, 1979.
Ibn Taymiyya, Taqī al-Dīn Aḥmad (d. 728/1328). *Al-Muqaddima fī uṣūl al-tafsīr*, ed. A. Zamarlī. Beirut, Muʾassasat al-Risāla, 1994.
Iṣfahānī, Abūʾl-Faraj (d. 356/967). *Kitāb al-Aghānī*, ed. Iḥsān ʿAbbās, 25 vols. Beirut, Dār Ṣādir, 2004.
——. *Maqātil al-Ṭālibiyyīn*, ed. Aḥmad Ṣaqr. Cairo, Dār Iḥyāʾ al-Kutub al-ʿArabiyya, 1949.
al-Iṣfahānī, ʿImād al-Dīn Abū Hāmid Muḥammad b. Muḥammad (d. 597/1201). *Al-Bustān al-jāmiʿ li-jāmiʿ tawārīkh ahl al-zamān*, ed. ʿUmar ʿAbd al-Salām Tadmurī. Beirut, al-Maktaba al-ʿAṣriyya, 2002.
al-Isfarāyīnī, Nūr al-Dīn ʿAbd al-Raḥmān b. Muḥammad (d. 418/1027). *Kāshif al-asrār*, ed. and tr. Hermann Landolt, *Nûruddîn Abdurrahmân-i Isfarâyînî: Le Révélateur des Mystères [Kâshif al-asrâr]*. Paris, Verdier, 1986.
Jāmī, ʿAbd al-Sattār (d. 898/1492). *Nafaḥāt al-uns min ḥaḍarāt al-quds*, ed. Maḥmūd ʿĀbidī. Tehran, Intishārāt-i Iṭṭilāʿāt, 1991.
al-Jurjānī, ʿAlī b. Muḥammad (d. 816/1413 or 838/1434). *Kitāb al-Taʿrīfāt*, ed. Ibrāhīm al-Abyārī. Beirut, Dār al-Kitāb al-ʿArabī, 1985.

al-Juwaynī, Imām al-Ḥaramayn Abū'l-Ma'ālī (d. 478/1085). *Kitāb al-Irshād*. Translated into English by Paul Walker as *A Guide to Conclusive Proofs for the Principles of Beliefs*. Great Books of Islamic Civilisation. Reading, Garnet Press, 2000.

Kāshānī, 'Abd al-Razzāq (d. 730–36/1329–35). *A Glossary of Sufi Technical Terms*, ed. and tr. Nabil Safwat. London, Octagon Press, 1991.

——. *Tafsīr al-Qur'ān al-karīm* (or *Ta'wīlāt al-Qur'ān*, popularly but erroneously known as *Tafsīr Ibn 'Arabī*), 2 vols. Beirut, Dār al-Yaqẓa al-'Arabiyya, 1968. Repr. Beirut, Dār Ṣādir, 2002.

al-Kāshānī, Muḥsin al-Fayḍ Muḥammad (d. 1091/1680). *Kitāb al-Ṣāfī fī tafsīr al-Qur'ān*, ed. al-Sayyid Muḥsin al-Husaynī al-Amīnī, 7 vols. Tehran, Dār al-Kutub al-'Ilmiyya, 1998; *Tafsīr al-Ṣāfī* ed. Ḥusayn al-A'lamī, 5 vols. Beirut, 1982. Repr. Tehran, Maktabat al-Ṣadr, 1994.

al-Khafājī, Aḥmad b. Muḥammad Shihāb al-Dīn (d. 1069/1659). *Ṭirāz al-majālis*. Cairo, Būlāq, 1867.

Khalīfa, Ḥajjī (Kâtip Çelebi) (d. 1067/1657). *Kashf al-ẓunūn*, 2 vols. Istanbul, Maṭābi' Wikālat al-Ma'ārif al-Jalīla, 1941–7.

Khalīfa b. Khayyāṭ (d. 240/854–5). *Ṭabaqāt*, ed. Akram Ḍiyā' al-'Umarī. Baghdad, Maṭba'at al-'Ānī, 1967.

al-Khayyāṭ, Abū'l-Ḥusayn b. 'Uthmān (d. *c.* 300/912). *Kitāb Intiṣār wa'l-radd 'alā Ibn al-Rawandī al-mulḥid*, ed. and tr. Albert N. Nader, *Le Livre du triomphe et de la réfutation d'Ibn al-Rawandī l'hérétique*. Beirut, Imprimerie Catholique, 1957.

al-Khū'ī, Abū'l-Qāsim b. 'Alī Akbar al-Mūsawī (d. 1413/1992). *Al-Bayān fī tafsīr al-Qur'ān*. Beirut, Manshūrāt Mu'assasat al-A'lamī, 1974; tr. with introduction by 'Abd al-'Azīz A. Sachedina, *The Prolegomena to the Qur'ān*. New York, Oxford University Press, 1998.

al-Kishshī (al-Kashshī) (*fl.* fourth/tenth century). Abū 'Amr Muḥammad b. 'Umar b. 'Abd al-'Azīz. *Rijāl al-Kishshī*, ed. Aḥmad al-Ḥusaynī. Karbala, Mu'assasat al-'Ilmī li'l-Maṭbū'āt, 1960–62.

al-Kūfī, Furāt b. Furāt (*fl.* late third/ninth century). *Tafsīr*, ed. Muḥammad al-Kāẓim, 2 vols. Beirut, Mu'assasat al-Nu'mān, 1412/1992.

al-Kulaynī, Muḥammad b. Ya'qūb (d. 329/941). *Al-Uṣūl min al-kāfī*, ed. 'Alī Akbar al-Ghaffārī, 8 vols. Tehran, Dār al-Kutub al-Islāmiyya, 1955–61.

Maghniyya, Muḥammad Jawad (d. 1979). *Tafsīr al-kāshif*, 7 vols. Repr. Beirut, Dār al-'Ilm li'l-Malāyīn, 1990.

al-Majlisī, Muḥammad Bāqir (d. 1110/1699). *Biḥār al-anwār*, 104 vols. Beirut, Mu'assasat al-Wafā', 1983.

al-Malaṭī, Muḥammad b. Aḥmad (d. 377/987). *Al-Tanbīh wa'l-radd 'alā ahl al-ahwā' wa'l-bida'*, ed. Sven Dedering. Istanbul, Maṭba'at al-Dawla, 1936; ed. Muḥammad Zāhid al-Kawtharī. Baghdad, Maktabat al-Muthannā, 1968.

Mālik b. Anas (d. 179/795). *Muwaṭṭa'*, ed. Muḥammad Fū'ād 'Abd al-Bāqī, 2 vols. Cairo, 1951. Repr. Cairo, Dār Iḥyā' al-Kutub al-'Arabiyya, [1986?].

al-Mālikī, Abū Bakr 'Abd Allāh b. Muḥammad (d. *c.* 460/1068). *Kitāb Riyāḍ al-nufūs fī ṭabaqāt 'ulamā' al-Qayrawān wa-Ifrīqiyā*, ed. Ḥusayn Mu'nis. Cairo, Maktabat al-Nahḍa al-Miṣriyya, 1951–60.

al-Māmaqānī, 'Abd Allāh b. Muḥammad (d. 1351/1933). *Tanqīḥ al-maqāl fī aḥwāl al-rijāl*, 3 vols. Najaf, al-Maṭba'a al-Murtaḍawiyya, 1930.

al-Māzandarānī, Abū 'Alī Muḥammad b. Ismā'īl al-Ḥā'irī (d. 1086/1676). *Muntahā al-maqāl fī aḥwāl al-rijāl*, ed. Mu'assasat Āl al-Bayt, 8 vols. Qumm, Mu'assasat Āl al-Bayt, 1995.

Midrash Rabbah, Genesis, Volume I, tr. H. Freedman. London, Soncino Press, 1961.

Mīr Dāmād, Muḥammad Bāqir al-Astarābādī (d. 1040/1630). *Al-Rawāshiḥ al-samāwiyya fī sharḥ al-aḥādīth al-Imāmiyya*. Tehran, [lithograph], 1894.

al-Mizzī, Abū'l-Ḥajjāj Yūsuf (d. 742/1341). *Tahdhīb al-kamāl fī asmā' al-rijāl*, ed. Bashshār 'Awwād Ma'rūf, 35 vols. Beirut, Mu'assasat al-Risāla, 1998.

Mujāhid b. Jabr al-Makkī (d. 104/722). *Tafsīr Mujāhid*, ed. 'Abd al-Raḥmān al-Ṭāhir al-Sūratī, 2 vols. Beirut, al-Manshūrāt al-'Ilmiyya, [n.d.].

Mujīr al-Dīn b. Muḥammad al-'Ulaymī al-Maqdisī (d. 927/1521). *Fatḥ al-Raḥmān fī tafsīr al-Qur'ān*, ed. Nūr al-Dīn Ṭālib, 7 vols. [Cairo], Dār al-Nawādir, 2009.

Muqātil b. Sulaymān al-Balkhī (d. 150/767). *Al-Ashbāh wa'l-naẓā'ir fī'l-Qur'ān al-karīm*, ed. 'Abd Allāh Maḥmūd Shiḥāta. Cairo, al-Hay'a al-Miṣriyya al-'Āmma li'l-Kitāb, 1975.

——. *Tafsīr al-khams mi'at āya min al-Qur'ān*, ed. Isaiah Goldfeld. Shafā 'Amr, Israel, Dār al-Mashriq, 1980.

——. *Tafsīr Muqātil b. Sulaymān*, ed. 'Abd Allāh Maḥmūd Shiḥāta, 5 vols. [Cairo], al-Hay'a al-Miṣriyya al-'Āmma li'l-Kitāb, 1979–89. Repr. Beirut, Dār Iḥyā' al-Turāth al-'Arabī, 2002.

al-Murādī, Muḥammad b. Mansūr (d. *c.* 290/903). *Kitāb Amālī Aḥmad b. 'Īsā*. MS H.135, Ambrosiana Library, Milan.

Muslim b. al-Ḥajjāj al-Qushayrī (d. 261/875). *Jāmi' al-ṣaḥīḥ* (or *Ṣaḥīḥ Muslim*), ed. Maḥmūd Fū'ād 'Abd al-Bāqī, 5 vols. Cairo, Dār Iḥyā' al-Kutub al-'Arabiyya, 1955–6.

al-Najāshī, Aḥmad b. 'Alī al-Asadī al-Kūfī (d. *c.* 279/906). *Rijāl*, ed. Muḥammad Jawād al-Nā'inī, 2 vols. Beirut, Dār al-Aḍwā', 1988.

Nasā'ī, Aḥmad b. Shu'ayb (d. 303/915). *Sunan*, 8 vols. Cairo, Muṣṭafā al-Bābī al-Ḥalabī, 1964–6.

al-Nashi' al-Akbar (d. 293/906). *Masā'il al-imāma*, ed. Josef van Ess, *Frühe mu'tazilitische Häresiograph: Zwei Werke des Naši al-Akbar (gest. 293 H.) herausgegeben und eingeleitet*. Beirut, Franz Steiner, 1971.

Nawawī, Abū Zakariyyā Yaḥyā b. Sharaf al-Dimashqī (d. 676/1277). *Riyāḍ al-ṣāliḥīn*. Beirut, Dār al-Fikr, 2001.

al-Nawbakhtī, al-Ḥasan b. Mūsā (*fl.* fourth/tenth century). *Firaq al-Shī'a*, ed. Muḥammad Ṣādiq Āl Baḥr al-'Ulūm. Najaf, al-Maktaba al-Murtaḍawiyya, 1932.

al-Nu'mān b. Muḥammad, Abū Ḥanīfa al-Tamīmī, known as al-Qāḍī al-Nu'mān (d. 363/974). *Asās al-ta'wīl*, ed. Arif Tamer. Beirut, Dār al-Thaqāfa, 1960.

——. *Da'ā'im al-Islām*, 3 vols. Beirut, Dār al-Aḍwā', 1995; tr. Asaf A.A. Fyzee and rev. and annotated by Ismail K. Poonawala, *The Pillars of Islam*, 2 vols. New Delhi, Oxford University Press, 2002–4.

Pseudo-Jonathan. *Targum Pseudo-Jonathan, Genesis*, tr. Michael Maher. Collegeville, MN, Liturgical Press, 1992.

al-Qifṭī, 'Alī b. Yūsuf (d. 646/1248). *Ta'rīkh al-ḥukamā'*, ed. Julius Lippert. Leipzig, Dieterich'sche Verlagsbuchhandlung, 1903.

al-Quhpā'ī (al-Quhbā'ī), 'Ināyat Allāh 'Alī (*fl.* eleventh/seventeenth century). *Majma' al-rijāl*, ed. Ḍiyā' al-Dīn al-'Allāma al-Iṣfahānī, 7 vols. Isfahan, Maṭba'at Rūshīn, 1964–8.

al-Qummī, 'Alī b. Ibrāhīm (*fl.* fourth/tenth century). *Tafsīr al-Qummī*, ed. Sayyid Ṭayyib al-Mūsawī al-Jazā'irī, 2 vols. Najaf, Maktabat al-Hudā, 1967. Repr. Beirut, Mu'assasat al-A'lamī li'l-Maṭbū'āt, 1991.

al-Qummī, Saʿd b. ʿAbd Allāh al-Ashʿarī (third/ninth century). *Kitāb al-Maqālāt wa'l-firaq*, ed. Muḥammad Jawād Mashkūr. Tehran, Markaz Intishārāt ʿIlmī wa Farhangī, 1963.

al-Qurṭubī, Muḥammad b. Aḥmad al-Anṣārī (d. 671/1273). *Al-Jāmiʿ li-aḥkām al-Qur'ān*, 20 vols. Beirut, Dār Iḥyā' al-Turāth al-ʿArabī, 1965–7.

al-Qushayrī, Abū'l-Qāsim ʿAbd al-Karīm b. Hawāzin (d. 465/1073). *Al-Risāla al-Qushayriyya fī ʿilm al-taṣawwuf*, ed. Maʿrūf Zurayq. Beirut, Dār al-Jīl, 1990.

——. *Tafsīr al-Qushayrī, al-musammā: Laṭā'if al-ishārāt*, ed. ʿAbd al-Laṭīf Ḥasan b. ʿAbd al-Raḥmān, 3 vols. Beirut, Dār al-Kutub al-ʿIlmiyya, 1971. Repr. 2000; *Laṭā'if al-ishārāt*, ed. Ibrāhīm Basyūnī, 6 vols. Cairo, Dār al-Kātib al-ʿArabī, 1968–71.

al-Rāghib al-Iṣfahānī (*fl.* fifth/eleventh century). *Mufradāt alfāẓ al-Qur'ān*, ed. Ṣafwān ʿAdnan Dawūdī. Damascus, Dār al-Qalam, 2002.

al-Rāzī, Fakhr al-Dīn Muḥammad b. ʿUmar (d. 606/1209). *Al-Mabāḥith al-mashriqiyya fī ʿilm al-ilāhiyyāt wa'l-ṭabīʿiyyāt*, ed. Muḥammad al-Baghdādī, 2 vols. Beirut, Dār al-Kitāb al-ʿArabī, 1990.

——. *Mafātīḥ al-ghayb aw al-Tafsīr al-kabīr*, 32 pts. in 16 vols. plus indices (*fahāris*). Beirut, Dār al-Kutub al-ʿIlmiyya, 2000.

——. *al-Maṭālib al-ʿāliya min al-ʿilm al-ilāhi*, ed. Aḥmad Ḥijāzī al-Saqqā, 9 vols. Beirut, Dār al-Kitāb al-ʿArabī, 1987.

Riḍā, Muḥammad Rashīd (d. 1935). *Fatāwā*, ed. Ṣalāḥ al-Dīn al-Munajjid and Yūsuf Khūrī, 6 vols. Beirut, Dār al-Kitāb al-Jadīd, 1970.

al-Ṣafadī, Khalīl b. Aybak (d. 764/1362). *Al-Wāfī bi'l-wafayāt*, vols. II–VI, ed. Sven Dedering. Wiesbaden, Franz Steiner, 1949–72, vol. VII, ed. Iḥsān ʿAbbās. Wiesbaden, Franz Steiner, 1969.

al-Sakhāwī, Muḥammad b. ʿAbd al-Raḥmān (d. 902/1497). *Al-Maqāṣid al-ḥasana fī bayān kathīr min al-aḥādīth al-mushtahira ʿalā'l-alsina*, ed. ʿAbd Allāh Muḥammad al-Ṣiddīq. Beirut, Dār al-Kutub al-ʿIlmiyya, 1979.

al-Sanāmī, ʿUmar b. Muḥammad (d. 734/1334). *Niṣāb al-iḥtisāb*. Mecca, Maktabat al-Ṭālib al-Jāmiʿī, 1986.

al-Ṣanʿānī, ʿAbd al-Razzāq (d. 211/827). *Muṣannaf*, ed. Naẓīr al-Sāʿidī, 11 vols. Beirut, Dār Iḥyā' al-Turāth al-ʿArabī, 2002.

al-Shāfiʿī, Muḥammad b. Idrīs (d. 204/820). *The Epistle on Legal Theory*, ed. and tr. Joseph Lowry. New York, New York University Press, 2013.

al-Shahrastānī, Abū'l-Fatḥ Muḥammad b. ʿAbd al-Karīm (d. 548/1153). *Al-Milal wa'l-niḥal*, ed. Muḥammad Sayyid al-Kaylānī, 2 vols. Cairo, Muṣṭafā al-Bābī al-Ḥalabī, 1961, I, 157–9.

al-Shammākhī, Abū'l-ʿAbbās Aḥmad b. Saʿīd (d. 928/1522). *Kitāb al-Siyar*, 2 vols. Muscat, Wizārat al-Turāth al-Qawmī, 1987.

al-Shaybānī, Muḥammad b. al-Ḥasan (d. seventh/thirteenth century).[1] *Nahj al-bayān ʿan kashf maʿānī al-Qur'ān*, ed. Ḥusayn Dargāhī, 5 vols. Qumm, Nashr al-Hādī, 1998.

Shaykhzāda, Muḥyī al-Dīn Muḥammad b. Muṣṭafā (d. *c.* 951/1544). *Ḥāshiyat Muḥyī al-Dīn Shaykhzāda ʿalā tafsīr al-qāḍī al-Bayḍāwī*, ed. Muḥammad ʿAbd al-Qādir Shāhīn, 8 vols. Beirut, Dār al-Kutub al-ʿIlmiyya, 1999.

al-Shiblī, Abū Bakr (d. 334/945). *Ādāb al-mulūk*, ed. B. Radtke. Beirut, Franz Steiner Verlag, 1991.

[1] Note that this author has been confused with the more famous Muḥammad b. al-Ḥasan al-Shaybānī (student of Abū Ḥanīfa) in several university catalogues, which give the death date of 804–5 for this author; however, this Muḥammad b. al-Ḥasan actually lived centuries later.

——. *Dīwān*, ed. K.M. al-Shaybī. Baghdad, Dār al-Taḍāmun, 1967.

al-Shīrāzī, al-Muʾayyad fīʾl-Dīn (d. 470/1078). *Al-Majālis al-Muʾayyadiyya*, ed. Ḥātim Ḥamīd al-Dīn. Mumbai, 1975; 2nd edn, Mumbai, Leaders Press, 2002.

al-Sulamī, Abū ʿAbd al-Raḥmān (d. 412/1021). *Ḥaqāʾiq al-tafsīr*, ed. Sayyid ʿImrān, 2 vols. Beirut, Dār al-Kutub al-ʿIlmiyya, 2001.

al-Suyūṭī, Jalāl al-Dīn (d. 911/1505). *Al-Durr al-manthūr fīʾl-tafsīr biʾl-maʾthūr*, 6 vols. Beirut, Dār al-Maʿrifa, [197–?].

——. *Ḥusn al-Muḥāḍara fī akhbār Miṣr waʾl-Qāhira*, 2 vols. Cairo, Būlāq, 1880–1.

——. *Al-Muzhir fī ʿulūm al-lugha wa-anwāʿihā*, ed. Muḥammad Aḥmad Jād al-Mawlā *et al.*, 2 vols. Cairo, ʿĪsā al-Bābī al-Ḥalabī, n.d.

al-Ṭabarānī, Sulaymān b. Aḥmad (d. 360/971). *Al-Muʿjam al-kabīr*, ed. Ḥamdī ʿAbd al-Majīd al-Salafī, 11 vols. Baghdad, Wizārat al-Awqāf waʾl-Shuʾūn al-Dīniyya, 1984.

al-Ṭabarī, Abū Jaʿfar Muḥammad b. Jarīr (d. 310/923). *Jāmiʿ al-bayān fī taʾwīl āy al-Qurʾān*, ed. Muḥammad Shākir and Aḥmad Shākir, 30 vols. Cairo, al-Hayʾa al-Miṣriyya al-ʿĀmma liʾl-Kitāb, 1954–69; partial English tr. [up to Q. 2:103] John Cooper, Wilferd Madelung and Alan Jones, eds., *The Commentary on the Qurʾān by Abū Jaʿfar Muḥammad b. Jarīr al-Ṭabarī*, 1 vol. Oxford, Oxford University Press, 1987.

——. *Taʾrīkh al-rusul waʾl-mulūk*, ed. Michael Jan de Goeje *et al.* Leiden, Brill, 1879–1901. In English this work has been translated as *The History of al-Ṭabarī*, gen. ed. Ehsan Yarshater, 39 vols. Albany, State University of New York Press, 1989–98. For the individual translations, *see* secondary sources: I tr. Rosenthal; II tr. Brinner; XXXIX (*Dhayl al-mudhayyal*) tr. Landau-Tasseron.

Ṭabāṭabāʾī, ʿAllāma Muḥammad Ḥusayn (d. 1360/1981). *Al-Mīzān fī tafsīr al-Qurʾān*, 20 vols. Beirut, Muʾassasat al-Aʿlamī liʾl-Maṭbūʿāt, 1973–4; tr. Sayyid Saʿīd Akhtar Rizwī, *Al-Mīzān: An Exegesis of the Qurʾān*, 8 vols. Tehran, World Organisation for Islamic Services, 1983–92.

al-Ṭabrisī (al-Ṭabarsī), al-Faḍl b. al-Ḥasan (d. 548/1154). *Jawāmiʿ al-jāmiʿ fī tafsīr al-Qurʾān al-majīd*, 2 vols. Beirut, Dār al-Aḍwāʾ, 1985.

——. *Majmaʿ al-bayān fī tafsīr al-Qurʾān*, ed. Hāshim al-Rasūlī and Faḍl Allāh al-Ṭabāṭabāʾī al-Yazdī, 10 pts. in 5 vols. Mashhad, al-Maʿārif al-Islāmiyya, 1976.

Tāshköprülüzāde, Aḥmad Muṣṭafā (d. 968/1561). *Al-Shaqāʾiq al-nuʿmāniyya*, tr. Mecdī Efendi as *Ḥaqāʾiq ush-sharāʾiʿ*. Istanbul, 1296/1878.

Tirmidhī, Muḥammad b. ʿĪsā (d. 279/892). *Sunan* [*al-Jāmiʿ al-ṣaḥīḥ*], ed. Aḥmad Muḥammad Shākir, 5 vols. Cairo, Muṣṭafā al-Bābī al-Ḥalabī, 1937–56.

al-Ṭūsī, Shaykh al-Ṭāʾifa Abū Jaʿfar Muḥammad b. al-Ḥasan (d. 460/1067). *Fihrist*, ed. Muḥammad Ṣādiq Āl Baḥr al-ʿUlūm. Najaf, al-Maṭbaʿa al-Ḥaydariyya, 1960.

——. *Al-Tibyān fī tafsīr al-Qurʾān*, ed. Āghā Buzurg al-Ṭihrānī, 10 vols. Najaf, al-Maṭbaʿa al-ʿIlmiyya, 1957–63.

al-Yaghmūrī, Yūsuf (d. 673/1274). *Nūr al-qabas fī akhbār al-najāt waʾl-udabāʾ waʾl-shuʿarāʾ*, ed. R. Sellheim. Wiesbaden, Franz Steiner, 1964.

Yāqūt al-Ḥamawī (d. 626/1229). *Muʿjam al-udabāʾ aw irshād al-adīb ilā maʿrifat al-adīb*, ed. Iḥsān ʿAbbās, 7 vols. Beirut, Dār al-Gharb al-Islāmī, 1993.

al-Zajjāj, Ibrāhīm b. al-Sarī. *Maʿānī al-Qurʾān wa iʿrābuh*, ed. ʿAbd al-Jalīl ʿAbduh Shalabī. Beirut, al-Maktaba al-ʿAṣriyya, 1973.

al-Zamakhsharī, Jār Allāh Maḥmūd b. ʿUmar (d. 538/1144). *Al-Kashshāf ʿan ḥaqāʾiq al-tanzīl wa ʿuyūn al-aqāwīl fī wujūh al-taʾwīl*, 4 vols. Beirut, Dār al-Maʿrifa, 1987.

Interview Subjects Cited

Alasvand, Fariba. Personal interview with Karen Bauer. Qumm, Iran, 8 June 2011. Follow-up email correspondence 10 June, 2014 and throughout May, 2021.

Ghorbannia, Nasser. Personal interview with Karen Bauer. Qumm, Iran, 29 May 2011.

Mehrizi, Mehdi. Personal interview with Karen Bauer. Qumm, Iran, 9 June 2011.

Saanei, Yusuf. Personal interview with Karen Bauer. Qumm, Iran, 13 June 2011. Follow-up correspondence 1 July 2014.

Shaikh, Sa'diyya. Personal interview with Karen Bauer and Feras Hamza. Zoom, 22 October 2020.

wadud, amina. Personal interview with Karen Bauer and Feras Hamza. Zoom, 15 October 2020.

SECONDARY SOURCES

Abbott, Nabia. *Studies in Arabic Literary Papyri*, 3 vols. Chicago, IL, Chicago University Press, 1957–72.

Abdel Haleem, Muhammad. '*Sūrat Maryam* (Q. 19): Comforting Muḥammad'. *Journal of Qur'anic Studies* 22.2 (2020), 60–85.

Abdul, Musa A.O. *The Qur'an: Shaykh Tabarsi's Commentary.* Lahore, Sh. Muhammad Ashraf, 1977.

Abou-Taleb, Amira. 'Constructing the Image of the Model Muslim Woman: Gender Discourse in Ibn Saʿd's *Kitāb al-ṭabaqāt al-kubrā*' in *Islamic Interpretive Tradition and Gender Justice: Processes of Canonization, Subversion, and Change*, ed. Nevin Reda and Yasmin Amin. Montreal, McGill-Queen's University Press, 2020, 179–208.

Abu-Lughod, Lila. *Veiled Sentiments: Honor and Poetry in a Bedouin Society.* Berkeley, University of California Press, 1999.

——. *Do Muslim Women Need Saving?* Cambridge, MA, Harvard University Press, 2013.

Abū'l-Naṣr, M.A. *ʿAbd Allāh b. ʿAbbās: Ḥibr al-umma wa tarjumān al-Qur'ān*. Beirut, Mu'assasat al-Risāla, 1992.

Abu-Rabiʿ, Ibrahim M. *Intellectual Origins of Islamic Resurgence in the Modern Arab World.* Albany, State University of New York Press, 1996.

Abu Wandi, Riyad and Yusuf Qazma Khuri. *ʿĪsā wa Maryam fī'l-Qur'ān wa'l-tafāsīr.* Amman, Dār al-Shurūq, 1996.

Abū Zahra, Muḥammad. *Ibn Ḥanbal: Ḥayātuhu wa ʿaṣruhu, ārā'uhu wa fiqhuhu.* Cairo, Dār al-Fikr al-ʿArabī, 1947.

Abū Zayd, Naṣr Ḥāmid. *Falsafat al-ta'wīl: Dirāsa fī ta'wīl al-Qur'ān ʿinda Muḥyī al-Dīn Ibn ʿArabī*. Beirut, Dār al-Tanwīr, 1983.

Abun-Nasr, Jamil M. *A History of the Maghrib in the Islamic Period.* Cambridge, Cambridge University Press, 1987.

Adamson, Peter. 'Creation and the God of Abraham'. *Journal of Islamic Studies* 23 (2012), 89–91.

Adamson, Peter and Robert Wisnovsky. 'Yaḥyā Ibn ʿAdī on a *Kalām* Argument for Creation' in *Oxford Studies in Medieval Philosophy*, vol. I, ed. Robert Pasnau. Oxford, Oxford University Press, 2013, 205–28.

Addas, Claude. *Quest for the Red Sulphur: The Life of Ibn ʿArabī*, tr. Peter Kingsley. Cambridge, Islamic Texts Society, 1993 (orig. pub. as *Ibn ʿArabī, ou, La quête du soufre rouge*. Paris, Gallimard, 1989).

Agha, Saleh Said. 'A Viewpoint of the Murjiʾa in the Umayyad Period: Evolution Through Application'. *Journal of Islamic Studies* 8.1 (1997), 1–42.

Ahmad, Saiyad Nizamuddin. 'Twelver Šīʿī *Hadīṯ*: From Tradition to Contemporary Evaluations'. *Oriente Moderno* 82 (2002), 125–45.

Ahmed, Leila. *Women and Gender in Islam*. New Haven, CT, Yale University Press, 1992.

——. *A Quiet Revolution: The Veil's Resurgence, from the Middle East to America*. New Haven, CT, Yale University Press, 2012.

Ahmed, Shahab. *What is Islam? The Importance of Being Islamic*. Princeton, NJ, Princeton University Press, 2016.

Akhtar, Syed Waheed. *The Early Shīʿite Imāmiyyah Thinkers*. New Delhi, Ashish Publishing House, 1988.

Alhassen, Leyla Ozgur. 'A Structural Analysis of *Sūrat Maryam*, Verses 1–58'. *Journal of Qurʾanic Studies* 18.1 (2016), 92–116.

Ali, Kecia. '"The Best of You Will Not Strike": Al-Shāfiʿī on Qurʾan, Sunnah, and Wife-Beating'. *Journal of Comparative Islamic Studies* 2.2 (2006), 143–55.

——. *Sexual Ethics and Islam: Feminist Reflections on Qurʾān, Hadith, and Jurisprudence*. London, Oneworld, 2006.

——. *Marriage and Slavery in Early Islam*. Cambridge, MA, Harvard University Press, 2010.

——. *Imām Shāfiʿī: Scholar and Saint*, London, Oneworld Academic, 2011.

——. 'The Omnipresent Male Scholar'. *Critical Muslim* 8 (September 2013), 61–73.

——. 'Destabilizing Gender, Reproducing Maternity: Mary in the Qurʾān'. *Journal of the International Qurʾanic Studies Association (JIQSA)* 2 (2017), 89–109.

Alshech, Eli. '"Do Not Enter Houses Other than Your Own": The Evolution of the Notion of a Private Domestic Sphere in Early Sunnī Islamic Thought'. *Islamic Law and Society* 11.3 (2004), 291–332.

——. 'Out of Sight and Therefore Out of Mind: Early Sunnī Islamic Modesty Regulations and the Creation of Spheres of Privacy'. *Journal of Near Eastern Studies* 66.4 (2007), 267–90.

Altorki, Soraya. 'Milk-Kinship in Arab Society: An Unexplored Problem in the Ethnography of Marriage'. *Ethnology* 19.2 (1980), 233–44.

al-ʿĀmilī, Muḥsin al-Amīn. *Aʿyān al-shīʿa*, ed. Ḥasan al-Amīn, 11 vols. Beirut, Dār al-Taʿāruf, 1986.

Amin, Yasmin. 'Umm Salama and her Ḥadīth'. Unpublished MA thesis, American University of Cairo, 2011. http://dar.aucegypt.edu/handle/10526/1524.

——. 'Umm Salama's Contributions: Qur'an, Hadith, and Early Muslim History as Sources for Gender Justice' in *Muslim Women and Gender Justice: Concepts, Sources, and Histories*, ed. Dina el Omari, Juliane Hammer and Mouhanad Khorchide. London, Routledge, 2019, 185–203.

——. 'Umm Salamah: A Female Authority Legitimating the Authorities' in *Female Religious Authority in Shiʿi Islam: Past and Present*, ed. Mirjam Künkler and Devin Stewart. Edinburgh, Edinburgh University Press, 2021, 47–77.

Amir-Moezzi, Mohammad Ali and Sabine Schmidtke. 'Twelver-Shīʿite Resources in Europe. The Shīʿite Collection at the Oriental Department of the University of Cologne, The *Fonds* Henry Corbin and the *Fonds* Shaykhī at the École Pratique des Hautes Études (EPHE), Paris. With a Catalogue of the *Fonds* Shaykhī'. *Journal Asiatique* 285.1 (1997), 73–122.

Anawati, Georges C. 'Fakhr al-Dīn al-Rāzī: Tamhīd li-dirāsāt ḥayātih wa muʾallafātih' in *Ilā Ṭāhā Ḥusayn fī ʿīd mīlādihi al-khamsīn/Mélanges Taha Husain*, ed. ʿAbd al-Raḥmān al-Badawī. Cairo, al-Hayʾa al-Miṣriyya al-ʿĀmma, 1962, 193–234.

Anchassi, Omar. 'Status Distinctions and Sartorial Difference: Slavery, Sexual Ethics and the Social Logic of Veiling in Islamic Law'. *Islamic Law and Society* (2021), 1–31.

Anthony, Sean. *Muhammad and the Empires of Faith: The Making of the Prophet of Islam*. Berkeley, University of California Press, 2020.

Anthony, Sean and Catherine Bronson. 'Did Ḥafṣah Edit the Qurʾān? A Response with Notes on the Codices of the Prophet's Wives'. *Journal of the International Qurʾanic Studies Association* 1 (2016), 93–125.

Arberry, Arthur John. *Muslim Saints and Mystics: Extracts from Attār's Tadhkīrat al-auliyāʾ*. London, Routledge, 1979.

van Arendonk, Cornelis. *Les debuts de l'imāmat zaidite au Yemen*, tr. Jacques Ryckmans. Leiden, Brill, 1960 (orig. pub. 1919 as *De opkomst van het Zaidietische Imamaat* in Yemen).

Arnaldez, Roger. 'L'oeuvre de Fakhr al-Dîn al-Râzî commentateur du Coran et philosophe'. *Cahiers de civilization médiévale, Xme–XIIme siècles* 3 (1960), 307–23.

——. 'Trouvailles philosophiques dans le commentaire coranique de Fakhr al-Dīn al-Rāzī'. *Études Orientales* 4 (1989), 17–26.

——. *Fakhr al-Dîn al-Rāzī: Commentateur du Coran et philosophe*. Paris, Vrin, 2002.

Asad, Talal. *Formations of the Secular: Christianity, Islam and Modernity*. Stanford, CA, Stanford University Press, 2003.

Asad, Talal, Wendy Brown, Judith P. Butler and Saba Mahmood. *Is Critique Secular: Blasphemy, Injury and Free Speech*. New York, Fordham University Press, 2013.

Ateş, Süleyman. *Sülemî ve Tasavvufî Tefsirî*. Sönmez, Cağaloğlu, 1969.

——. 'Üç müfessir bir tefsir'. *Ankara Üniversitesi İlahiyat Fakültesi Dergisi* 18 (1970), 85–104.

ʿAthāmina, Khalīl. 'The Early Murjiʾa: Some Notes'. *Journal of Semitic Studies* 35 (1990), 109–30.

Ayāzī, Muḥammad ʿAlī. *Al-Mufassirūn: Ḥāyatuhum wa manhajuhum*. Tehran, Wizārat-i Farhang wa Irshād-i Islāmī, 1373 Sh./1994.

Ayni, Mehmet Ali. *Ismaïl Hakki, philosophe mystique, 1653–1725*. Paris, Paul Geuthner, 1933.

Ayoub, Mahmoud. 'The Speaking Qurʾān and the Silent Qurʾān: A Study of the Principles and Development of Imāmī Shīʿī Tafsīr' in *Approaches to the History of the Interpretation of the Qurʾān*, ed. Andrew Rippin. Berlin, de Gruyter, 1988. Repr. Piscataway, NJ, Gorgias Press, 2012.

Ayubi, Zahra. *Gendered Morality: Classical Islamic Ethics of the Self, Family, and Society*. New York, Columbia University Press, 2019.

Azam, Hina. 'Competing Approaches to Rape in Islamic Law' in *Feminism, Law, and Religion*, ed. Marie Fallinger, Elizabeth Schiltz and Susan Stabile. Burlington, VT, Ashgate, 2013, 327–44.

——. *Sexual Violation in Islamic Law: Substance, Evidence, and Procedure*. Cambridge, Cambridge University Press, 2015.

Azami, M.M. *Studies in Early Hadith Literature*. Indianapolis, IN, American Trust Publications, 1978.

Azani, Eitan. *Hezbollah: The Story of the Party of God, from Revolution to Institutionalization*. New York, Palgrave MacMillan, 2009.
Aziz, Talib M. 'The Islamic Political Theory of Muhammad Baqir al-Sadr of Iraq'. Unpublished PhD dissertation, University of Utah, 1991.
——. 'Fadlallah and the Remaking of the *Marjaʿiya*' in *The Most Learned of the Shiʿa: The Institution of the Marjaʿ Taqlid*, ed. Linda S. Walbridge. New York, Oxford University Press, 2001, 205–15.
Baalbaki, Ramzi. *Grammarians and Grammatical Theory in the Medieval Arabic Tradition*. Ashgate, Variorum, 2004.
Bābāʿammī, Muḥammad b. Mūsā *et al. Muʿjam aʿlām al-Ibāḍiyya min al-qarn al-awwal al-hijrī ilāʾl-ʿaṣr al-ḥāḍir*, 2 vols. Beirut, Dār al-Gharb al-Islāmī, 2000–2006.
Babayan, Kathryn and Afsaneh Najmabadi, eds. *Islamicate Sexualities: Translations across Temporal Geographies of Desire*. Cambridge, MA, Harvard University Press, 2008.
El-Badawi, Emran Iqbal. *The Qurʾān and the Aramaic Gospel Traditions*. Abingdon, Routledge, 2014.
al-Baḥrānī, Jaʿfar. *Marjaʿiyyat al-marḥala wa ghubār al-taghyīr liʾl-Sayyid Muḥammad Faḍl Allāh*. Beirut, Dār al-Amīr, 1998.
Bano, Masooda and Hilary Kalmbach, eds. *Women, Leadership, and Mosques: Changes in Contemporary Islamic Authority*. Leiden, Brill, 2016.
Bar-Asher, Meir M. *Scripture and Exegesis in Early Imāmī Shiism*. Leiden, Brill, 1999.
Barazangi, Nimat Hafez. *Woman's Identity and the Qur'an: A New Reading*. Tallahassee, University Press of Florida, 2004.
Barlas, Asma. *Believing Women in Islam: Unreading Patriarchal Interpretations of the Qur'an*. Austin, University of Texas Press, 2002.
Bauer, Karen. '"Traditional" Interpretations of Q. 4:34'. *Comparative Islamic Studies* 2.2 (2006), 129–42.
——. 'Room for Interpretation: Qur'anic Exegesis and Gender'. Unpublished PhD dissertation, Princeton University, 2008.
——. '"The Male is Not Like the Female" (Q 3:36): The Question of Gender Egalitarianism in the Qurʾān'. *Religion Compass* 3.4 (2009), 637–54.
——. 'Debates on Women's Status as Judges and Witnesses in Post-formative Islamic Law'. *Journal of the American Oriental Society* 130.1 (2010), 1–30.
——. '"I Have Seen the People's Antipathy to this Knowledge": The Muslim Exegete and His Audience, 5th/11th–7th/13th Centuries' in *The Islamic Scholarly Tradition: Studies in History, Law, and Thought in Honor of Professor Michael Allan Cook*, ed. Asad Q. Ahmed, Behnam Sadeghi and Michael Bonner. Leiden, Brill, 2011, 293–315.
——. 'Spiritual Hierarchy and Gender Hierarchy in Fāṭimid Ismāʿīlī Interpretations of the Qurʾān'. *Journal of Qur'anic Studies* 14.2 (2012), 29–46.
——, ed. *Aims, Methods and Contexts of Qur'anic Exegesis (2nd/8th–9th/15th C.)*. Oxford, Oxford University Press in association with the Institute of Ismaili Studies, 2013.
——. 'Justifying the Genre: A Study of Introductions to Classical Works of *Tafsīr*' in eadem, ed., *Aims, Methods and Contexts of Qur'anic Exegesis (2nd/8th–9th/15th C.)*. Oxford, Oxford University Press in association with the Institute of Ismaili Studies, 2013, 39–66.
——. *Gender Hierarchy in the Qurʾān: Medieval Interpretations, Modern Responses*. Cambridge, Cambridge University Press, 2015.

——. 'Emotion in the Qur'an: An Overview'. *Journal of Qur'anic Studies* 19.2 (2017), 1–30.
——. 'The Emotions of Conversion and Kinship in the Qur'ān and the *Sīra* of Ibn Isḥāq'. *Cultural History* 8.2 (2019), 137–63.
Bausani, Alessandro. *La Persia Religiosa: Da Zaratustra a Bahâ'u'llâh*. Milan, Il Saggiatore, 1959.
Beck, Edmund, ed. and tr. *Des heiligen Ephraem des Syrers Sermones I–IV*, 8 vols. Peeters, Secrétariat du Corpus SCO, 1970–73.
Bedjan, Paul, ed. *Homiliae selectae Mar Jacobi Sarugensis*, 5 vols. Leipzig, Harrassowitz, 1905–10.
Bernheimer, Teresa. *The 'Alids: The First Family of Islam, 750–1200*. Edinburgh, Edinburgh University Press, 2013.
Bertucci, Paola and Giuliano Pancaldi, eds. *Electric Bodies: Episodes in the History of Medical Electricity*. Bologna, Bologna University, 2001.
Blatherwick, Helen. 'Textual Silences and Literary Choices in al-Kisā'ī's Account of the Annunciation and the Birth of Jesus'. *Arabica* 66.1–2 (2019), 1–42.
Booth, Marilyn. *Classes of Ladies of Cloistered Spaces: Writing Feminist History through Biography in Fin-de-Siècle Egypt*. Edinburgh, Edinburgh University Press, 2015.
Bostani, Ghasem. 'Ibn Abī Al-Awja: His Historical Existence and the Evaluations of the Claims about Him'. *Quranic Sciences and Tradition* 50.1 (2017), 9–31. doi: 10.22059/jqst.2017.224588.668787.
Böwering, Gerhard. 'The Scriptural "Senses" in Medieval Ṣūfī Qur'an Exegesis' in *With Reverence for the Word: Medieval Scriptural Exegesis in Judaism, Christianity, and Islam*, ed. Jane Dammen McAuliffe *et al.* Oxford, Oxford University Press, 2003, 346–65.
Boyarin, Daniel. 'Gender' in *Critical Terms for Religious Studies*, ed. Mark C. Taylor. Chicago, IL, University of Chicago Press, 1998.
Brandl, Marco. 'Reading the Qur'ān in the Light of al-Manār'. Unpublished PhD dissertation, Oxford University, 2019.
Brinner, William, tr. *The History of al-Ṭabarī*, vol. III: *The Children of Israel*. New York, State University of New York Press, 1991.
Brockelmann, Carl. *Geschichte der arabischen Literatur*, [*GAL*], 5 vols. Leiden, Brill, 1898–1949.
Bronson, Catherine. 'Eve in the Formative Period of Islamic Exegesis: Intertextual Boundaries and Hermeneutic Demarcations' in *Tafsīr and Islamic Intellectual History: Exploring the Boundaries of a Genre*, ed. Andreas Görke and Johanna Pink. Oxford, Oxford University Press in association with the Institute of Ismaili Studies, 2014, 27–61.
Brown, Jonathan A.C. *Hadith: Muhammad's Legacy in the Medieval and Modern World*. Oxford, Oneworld, 2009.
Burrell, David B. 'Creation' in *The Cambridge Companion to Classical Islamic Theology*, ed. Tim Winter. Cambridge, Cambridge University Press, 2008, 141–79.
Burton, John. *An Introduction to the Hadith*. Edinburgh, Edinburgh University Press, 1994.
Busool, Assad Nimer. 'Shaykh Muḥammad Rashīd Riḍā's Relations with Jamāl al-Dīn Afghānī and Muḥammad 'Abduh'. *Muslim World* 66 (1976), 272–86.
Cairns, Douglas L. 'The Meaning of the Veil in Ancient Greek Culture' in *Women's Dress in the Ancient Greek World*, ed. Lloyd Llewellyn-Jones. London, Duckworth and the Classical Press of Wales, 2002, 73–93.

Calder, Norman. '*Tafsīr* from Ṭabarī to Ibn Kathīr: Problems in the Description of a Genre, Illustrated with Reference to the Story of Abraham' in *Approaches to the Qur'ān*, ed. Gerald R. Hawting and Abdul-Kader A. Shareef. London, Routledge, 1993, 101–40.

——. *Islamic Jurisprudence in the Classical Era*, ed. Colin Imber. Cambridge, Cambridge University Press, 2010.

Caspar, Robert. 'Un aspect de la pensée musulmane moderne: Le renouveau du moʿtazilisme'. *Mélanges de l'Institut Dominicain d'études orientales du Caire* 4 (1957), 141–202.

Ceylan, Yasin. *Theology and Tafsīr in the Major Works of Fakhr al-Dīn al-Rāzī*. Kuala Lumpur, International Institute of Islamic Thought and Civilisation, 1996.

Chamas, Sophie. 'Sayyid Muhammad Hussein Fadlallah: Muslim Cleric and Islamic Feminist'. *Journal of Alternative Perspectives in Social Sciences*, 1.2 (2009), 246–57.

Chaudhry, Ayesha S. *Domestic Violence and the Islamic Tradition: Ethics, Law, and the Muslim Discourse on Gender*. Oxford, Oxford University Press, 2013.

Chittick, William C. *The Sufi Path of Knowledge: Ibn al-ʿArabi's Metaphysics of Imagination*. Albany, State University of New York Press, 1989.

——. 'On Sufi Psychology: A Debate between the Soul and the Spirit' in *Consciousness and Reality: Studies in Memory of Toshihiko Izutsu*, ed. Sayyid Jalāl al-Dīn Āshtiyānī, Hideichi Matsubara, Takashi Iwami and Akira Matsumoto. Leiden, Brill, 2000, 341–66.

——. 'Worship' in *The Cambridge Companion to Classical Islamic Theology*, ed. Tim Winter. Cambridge, Cambridge University Press, 2008, 218–36.

Chrysostomides, Anna. 'Ties that Bind: The Role of Family Dynamics in the Islamization of the Central Islamic Lands, 700–900 CE'. Unpublished PhD dissertation, University of Oxford, 2017.

Clark, Gillian. *Women in Late Antiquity: Pagan and Christian Lifestyles*. New York, Oxford University Press USA, 1993.

Clarke, Morgan. 'After the Ayatollah: Institutionalisation and Succession in the *marjaʿiyya* of Sayyid Muḥammad Ḥusayn Faḍl Allāh'. *Die Welt des Islams* 56.2 (2016), 153–86.

Commins, David. *Islamic Reform: Politics and Social Change in Late Ottoman Syria*. New York, Oxford University Press, 1990.

Cook, Michael. *Early Muslim Dogma: A Source-Critical Study*. Cambridge, Cambridge University Press, 1981.

——. 'The Opponents of the Writing of Tradition in Early Islam'. *Arabica* 44.4 (1997), 437–530.

——. *Commanding Right and Forbidding Wrong in Islamic Thought*. Cambridge, Cambridge University Press, 2000.

Cooper, John. *The Commentary on the Qur'ān by Abū Jaʿfar Muḥammad b. Jarīr al-Ṭabarī being an abridged translation of Jāmiʿ al-bayān fī ta'wīl āy al-Qur'ān, Volume I*, ed. Wilferd Madelung and Alan Jones. Oxford, Oxford University Press, 1987.

Corbin, Henry. *En Islam iranien: Aspects spirituals et philosophiques*. I: *Le shīʿisme duodécimain*; II: *Suhrawardī et les Platoniciens de Perse*; III: *Les fidèles d'amour, shīʿisme st soufisme*; IV: *L'école d'Ispahan, l'école shaykhie, le douziéme imam*. Paris, Gallimard, 1971–2.

——. *The Man of Light in Iranian Sufism*, tr. Nancy Pearson. Boulder, CO, Shambala, 1978 (orig. pub. as *L'Homme de lumière dans le soufisme iranien*, Paris, Librairie de Médicis, 1971).

Crone, Patricia. *Meccan Trade and the Rise of Islam*. Princeton, NJ, Princeton University Press, 1987.

——. *Roman, Provincial and Islamic Law: The Origins of the Islamic Patronate*. Cambridge, Cambridge University Press, 1987.

——. 'A Note on Muqātil b. Ḥayyān and Muqātil b. Sulaymān'. *Der Islam* 74 (1997), 238–50.

——. *Medieval Islamic Political Thought*. Edinburgh, Edinburgh University Press, 2005.

——. 'The Religion of the Qur'ānic Pagans: God and the Lesser Deities' in *The Qur'ānic Pagans and Related Matters: Collected Studies in Three Volumes, Volume I*, idem, ed. Hanna Siurua. Leiden, Brill, 2016, 52–101.

Crone, Patricia and Fritz W. Zimmermann. *The Epistle of Sālim ibn Dakhwān*. Oxford, Oxford University Press, 2001.

Daftary, Farhad. *The Ismailis: Their Histories and Doctrines*. Cambridge, Cambridge University Press, 1990.

Darling, Linda T. *A History of Social Justice and Political Power in the Middle East: The Circle of Justice from Mesopotamia to Globalization*. London, Routledge, 2013.

Das, Veena. 'Ordinary Ethics' in *A Companion to Moral Anthropology*, ed. Didier Fassin. New York, Wiley Blackwell, 2012, 133–49.

Dawānī, ʿAlī, ed. *Hazāra-yi Shaykh Ṭūsī*, 2 vols. Tehran, Dār al-Tablīgh-i Islāmī, 1362 Sh./1983 (orig. pub. Tehran, Amīr Kabīr, 1349 Sh./1970).

Deeb, Lara. 'Sayyid Muhammad Husayn Fadlallah and Lebanese Shiʿi Youth'. *Journal of Shiʿa Islamic Studies* 3.1 (2010), 405–26.

Dessing, Nathal M. *Rituals of Birth, Circumcision, Marriage, and Death among Muslims in the Netherlands*. Leuven, Peeters, 2001.

al-Dhahabī, Muḥammad Ḥusayn (d. 1418/1977). *Al-Tafsīr wa'l-mufassirūn*, 3 vols. Repr. Cairo, Dār al-Kutub al-Ḥadītha, 1976–89 (orig. pub. 1381/1961–2).

Dixon, Suzanne. 'Infirmitas Sexus: Womanly Weakness in Roman Law'. *Legal History Review* 52.4 (1984), 343–71.

Donner, Fred. *Muhammad and the Believers: At the Origins of Islam*. Cambridge, MA, Belknap Press of Harvard University Press, 2010.

Dost, Suleiman. 'An Arabian Qur'ān'. Unpublished PhD dissertation, University of Chicago, 2017.

Dutton, Yasin. *The Origins of Islamic Law: The Qur'an, the Muwaṭṭa' and the Madinan ʿAmal*. Surrey, Curzon, 1999.

Eliade, Mircea. *A History of Religious Ideas*, vol I: *From the Stone Age to the Eleusinian Mysteries*. London, Collins, 1979.

Elias, Jamal J. *The Throne Carrier of God: The Life and Thought of ʿAlā' ad-Dawla as-Simnānī*. Albany, State University of New York Press, 1995.

Elsaidi, Murad H. 'Human Rights and Islamic Law: A Legal Analysis Challenging the Husband's Authority to Punish "Rebellious" Wives'. *Muslim World Journal of Human Rights* 7.2 (2011), 1–25.

Elshakry, Marwa. *Reading Darwin in Arabic, 1860–1950*. Chicago, IL, University of Chicago Press, 2013.

Enayat, Hamid. *Modern Islamic Political Thought*. Austin, University of Texas Press, 1982.

Ernst, Carl. *Rūzbihān Baqlī: Mysticism and the Rhetoric of Sainthood in Persian Sufism*. Richmond, Surrey, Curzon Press, 1996.

Esack, Farid. *On Being a Muslim: Finding a Religious Path in the World Today*. London, Oneworld, 2009.

Esposito, John. *The Oxford Dictionary of Islam*. Oxford, Oxford University Press, 2003.

van Ess, Josef. 'Das *Kitāb al-irǧā'* des Ḥasan b. Muḥammad b. al-Ḥanafiyya'. *Arabica* 21 (1974), 20–52.

——. 'Untersuchungen zu einigen ibāḍitischen Handschriften'. *Zeitschrift der Deutsche Morgenländische Gesellschaft* 126.1 (1976), 25–63.

——. *Theologie und Gesellschaft im 2. Und 3. Jahrhundret Hidschra: Eine Geschichte des religiösen Denkens im frühen Islam*, [*TG*], 4 vols. Berlin, New York, de Gruyter, 1991–7.

Fadel, Mohammad. 'Two Women, One Man: Knowledge, Power, and Gender in Medieval Sunni Legal Thought'. *International Journal of Middle East Studies* 29.2 (1997), 185–204.

——. '*Istaftī qalbaka wa in aftāka al-nāsu wa aftūka*: The Ethical Obligations of the *Muqallid* between Autonomy and Trust' in *Islamic Law in Theory: Studies on Jurisprudence in Honor of Bernard Weiss*, ed. A. Kevin Reinhart and Robert Gleave. Leiden, Brill, 2014, 105–26.

Fadil, Nadia and Mayanthi Fernando. 'Rediscovering the "Everyday" Muslim: Notes on an Anthropological Divide'. *HAU Journal of Ethnographic Theory* 5.2 (2015), 59–88.

Fierro, Maribel. 'Women as Prophets in Islam' in *Writing the Feminine: Women in Arab Sources*, ed. Manuela Marín and Randi Deguilhem. London, I.B. Tauris, 183–98.

Frank, Richard M. *Al-Ghazālī and the Ashʿarite School*. Durham, NC, Duke University Press, 1994, 36–9.

Fudge, Bruce. *Qur'ānic Hermeneutics: Al-Ṭabrisī and the Craft of Commentary*. London, Routledge, 2011.

Fyzee, A.A.A. *Outlines of Muhammadan Law*. Oxford, Oxford University Press, 1976.

Gadamer, Hans-Georg. *Truth and Method*, 2nd rev. edn, tr. John Weinsheimer and Donald G. Marshall. New York, Continuum, 2004.

Geissinger, Aisha/Ash. 'The Exegetical Traditions of 'Ā'isha: Notes on Their Impact and Significance', *Journal of Qur'anic Studies* 6.1 (2004), 1–20.

——. 'Mary in the Qur'ān: Rereading Subversive Births' in *Sacred Tropes: Tanakh, New Testament, and Qur'an as Literature and Culture*, ed. Roberta Sterman Sabbath. Leiden, Brill, 2009, 379–92.

——. "A'isha bint Abi Bakr and Her Contributions to the Formation of Islamic Tradition', *Religion Compass* 5.1 (2011), 37–49.

——. *Gender and Muslim Constructions of Exegetical Authority: A Rereading of the Classical Genre of Qur'ān Commentary*. Leiden, Brill, 2015.

Gesink, Indira Falk. 'Intersex Bodies in Premodern Islamic Discourse: Complicating the Binary'. *Journal of Middle East Women's Studies* 14.2 (2018), 152–73.

Ghaffār, 'Abd al-Rasūl. *Al-Kulaynī wa'l-Kāfī*. Qumm, Mu'assasat al-Nashr al-Islāmī, 1995.

Giddens, Anthony. *The Transformation of Intimacy: Sexuality, Love, and Eroticism in Modern Societies*. Palo Alto, CA, Stanford University Press, 1992.

Gilliot, Claude. 'Portrait "mythique" d'Ibn ʿAbbās'. *Arabica* 32 (1985), 127–84.
——. *Éxègese, langue, et théologie en Islam: L'exégèse coranique de Tabarī (m. 311/923)*. Paris, Vrin, 1990.
——. 'Muqātil, grande exégète, traditionist et théologian maudit'. *Journal Asiatique* (Paris) 279 (1991), 39–92.
——. 'Le commentaire coranique de Hūd b. Muḥakkam/Muḥkim', *Arabica* 44 (1997), 179–233.
——. 'The Beginnings of Qur'ānic Exegesis' in *The Qur'an: Formative Interpretation*, ed. Andrew Rippin. Aldershot, Ashgate Variorum, 1999.
Gimaret, Daniel. *Une lecture Muʿtazilite du Coran: Le Tafsīr d'Abū ʿAlī al-Djubbāʾī (m. 303/915) partiellement reconstitute à partir de ses citeurs*. Louvain-Paris, École Pratique des Hautes Études, Peeters, 1996.
Giolfo, Manuela E.B. '*Fa-*' in *The Subjunctive Mood in Arabic Grammatical Thought*, ed. Arik Sadan. Leiden, Brill, 2012, 127–71.
——. '*Yaqūm* vs *Qāma* in the Conditional Context: A Relativistic Interpretation of the Frontier Between the Prefixed and the Suffixed Conjugations of the Arabic Language' in *The Foundations of Arabic Linguistics: Sībawayhi and Early Arabic Grammatical Theory*, ed. Amal E. Marogy. Leiden, Brill, 2012, 135–60.
Gleave, Robert. 'Between *Ḥadīth* and *Fiqh*: The "Canonical" Imāmī Collections of *Akhbār*'. *Islamic Law and Society* 8.3 (2001), 350–82.
——. *Scripturalist Islam: The History and Doctrines of the Akhbārī Shīʿī School*. Leiden, Brill, 2007.
——. 'Early Shiʿi Hermeneutics: Some Exegetical Techniques Attributed to the Shiʿi Imams' in *Aims, Methods and Contexts of Qur'anic Exegesis (2nd/8th–9th/15th C.)*, ed. Karen Bauer. Oxford, Oxford University Press in association with the Institute of Ismaili Studies, 2013, 141–72.
Gledhill, Paul. 'The Development of Systematic Thought in Early Mālikī Jurisprudence'. Unpublished PhD thesis, Oxford University, 2014.
Goldfield, Isaiah. 'The "Tafsīr" of ʿAbdallāh b. ʿAbbās'. *Der Islam* 58 (1981), 125–35.
Goldziher, Ignaz. *Muslim Studies, Volume II*, ed. S.M. Stern, tr. C. R. Barber and S. Stern, with an introduction by Hamid Dabashi. London, Aldine Transaction, 2006.
Gouda, Moamen and Niklas Potrafke. 'Gender Equality in Muslim-Majority Countries'. *Economic Systems* 40.4 (2016), 683–98.
Gray, Louis. 'Zoroastrian Elements in Muhammedan Eschatology'. *Le Muséon*, New Series, 3 (1902), 153–84.
El Guindi, Fadwa. *Veil: Modesty, Privacy and Resistance*. Oxford, Berg, 1999.
Gully, Adrian. *Grammar and Semantics in Medieval Arabic: The Study of Ibn Hisham's 'Mughni l-Labib'*. London, Routledge, 2013 (orig. pub. Surrey, Curzon Press, 1995).
Hādīzādah, Majīd. 'Kāshānī-nāma' in *Majmūʿa-yi rasāʾil wa muṣannafāt taʾlīf ʿAbd al-Razzāq Kāshānī*, ed. Majīd Hādīzāda. Tehran, Mīrāth-i Maktūb, 1380 Sh./2000, 23–126.
Haeri, Shahla. *Law of Desire: Temporary Marriage in Shiʿi Iran*. Syracuse, NY, Syracuse University Press, 1989.
Hamza, Feras. 'To Hell and Back: A Study of the Concepts of Hell and Intercession in Early Islam'. Unpublished PhD dissertation, University of Oxford, 2002.
——. '*Tafsīr* and Unlocking the Historical Qur'an: Back to Basics?' in *Aims, Methods and Contexts of Qur'anic Exegesis (2nd/8th–9th/15th C.)*, ed. Karen Bauer. Oxford, Oxford University Press in association with the Institute of Ismaili Studies, 2013, 19–37.

Hamza, Feras and Sajjad Rizvi, with Farhana Mayer, eds. *An Anthology of Qur'anic Commentaries*, vol. I: *On the Nature of the Divine*. Oxford, Oxford University Press in association with the Institute of Ismaili Studies, 2008.

Hamzić, Vanja. *Sexual and Gender Diversity in the Muslim World: History, Law and Vernacular Knowledge*. London, I.B. Tauris, 2017.

Harding, Sandra. *Objectivity and Diversity: Another Logic of Scientific Research*. Chicago, IL, University of Chicago Press, 2015.

Hassan, Rifaat. 'Equal before Allah?' *Harvard Divinity Bulletin* (The Divinity School, Harvard University) 17.2 (January–May 1987), 2–14.

Hawting, Gerald. *The Idea of Idolatry and the Emergence of Islam: From Polemic to History*. Cambridge, Cambridge University Press, 1999.

Haydūs, Maḥmūd. *Ḥawl Tafsīr al-Qummī: Dirāsa taḥqīqiyya*. Qumm, Dār al-Kitāb, 2001.

El-Hibri, Tayeb. *Reinterpreting Islamic Historiography: Hārūn al-Rashīd and the Narrative of the 'Abbāsid Caliphate*. Cambridge, Cambridge University Press, 1999.

Hidayatullah, Aysha. *Feminist Edges of the Qur'ān*. Oxford, Oxford University Press, 2014.

Hildebrandt, Thomas. 'Waren Ǧamāl al-Dīn al-Afġānī und Muḥammad 'Abduh Neo-Muʿtaziliten?' *Die Welt des Islams* 42 (2002), 207–62.

Hodgson, Marshall. *The Venture of Islam: Conscience and History in a World Civilization*, 3 vols. Chicago, IL, University of Chicago Press, 1974.

Hoffman, Valerie J. *The Essentials of Ibāḍī Islam*. Syracuse, NY, Syracuse University Press, 2012.

Hourani, Albert. *Arabic Thought in the Liberal Age, 1798–1939*. Cambridge, Cambridge University Press, 1983.

Howes, Moira. 'Objectivity, Intellectual Virtue, and Community' in *Objectivity in Science: New Perspectives from Science and Technology Studies*, ed. Flavia Padovani, Alan Richardson and Jonathan Y. Tsou. New York, Springer, 2015, 173–88.

Hoyland, Robert. *Seeing Islam as Others Saw It: A Survey and Evaluation of Christian, Jewish and Zoroastrian Writings on Early Islam*. Princeton, NJ, Darwin Press, 1997.

——. *Arabia and the Arabs: From the Bronze Age to the Coming of Islam*. London, Routledge, 2001.

al-Ḥusaynī, Muḥammad. *Al-Imām al-shahīd al-sayyid Muḥammad Bāqir al-Ṣadr: Dirāsa fī sīratihi wa manhajihi*. Beirut, Dār al-Furāt, 1989.

Ibish, Yusuf. 'The Life and Works of al-Bāqillānī', *Islamic Studies* 4.3 (1965), 225–36.

Ibrahim, Celine. *Women and Gender in the Qur'ān*. Oxford, Oxford University Press, 2020.

ISESCO (Islamic Educational, Scientific and Cultural Organisation). *Al-Imām al-Ṭabarī fī dhikrā murūr aḥad 'asharat qarnan 'alā wafātih, 310H–1410H*, 2 vols. Rabat, al-Munaẓẓama al-Islāmiyya li'l-Tarbiyya wa'l-ʿUlūm wa'l-Thaqāfa (ISESCO); Damascus, Maṭbaʿat al-Kātib al-ʿArabī, 1992.

İskenderoğlu, Muammer. *Fakhr al-Dīn al-Rāzī and Thomas Aquinas on the Question of the Eternity of the World*. Leiden, Brill, 2002.

Ismāʿīl, Muḥammad Ḥasan. *Kitāb al-Radd 'alā al-manṭiqiyyūn*. Beirut, Dār al-Kutub al-ʿIlmiyya, 1998.

Izutsu, Toshihiko. *Ethico-Religious Concepts in the Qur'ān*. Montreal, McGill-Queen's University Press, 2002.

Jackson, Sherman A. *Islamic Law and the State: The Constitutional Jurisprudence of 'Shihāb al-Dīn al-Qarafī'*. Leiden, Brill, 1996.

Jaffer, Tariq. 'Fakhr al-Dīn al-Rāzī's System of Inquiry' in *Aims, Methods and Contexts of Qur'anic Exegesis (2nd/8th–9th/15th C.)*, ed. Karen Bauer. Oxford, Oxford University Press in association with the Institute of Ismaili Studies, 2013, 241–61.

——. *Rāzī: Master of Qur'ānic Interpretation and Theological Reasoning*. New York, Oxford University Press USA, 2015.

al-Jalālī, Muḥammad Ḥusayn, ed. *Al-Tafsīr al-mansūb ilā'l-Imām Abī Muḥammad al-Ḥasan b. ʿAlī al-ʿAskarī*. Qumm, Mu'assasat al-Imām al-Mahdī, 1409/1988.

Jeffery, Arthur. *Materials for the History of the Text of the Qur'ān: The Old Codices*. Leiden, Brill, 1937.

Johansen, Baber. 'Dissent and Uncertainty in the Process of Legal Norm Construction in Muslim Sunnī Law' in *Law and Tradition in Classical Islamic Thought: Studies in Honor of Professor Hossein Modarressi*, ed. Michael Cook, Najam Haider, Intisar Rabb and Asma Sayeed. New York, Palgrave Macmillan, 2013, 127–44.

Jomier, Jacques. *Le commentaire coranique du Manâr; tendances modernes de l'éxegèse coranique en Égypte*. Paris, G.-P. Maisonneuve, 1954.

Juynboll, G.H.A. *Muslim Tradition: Studies in Chronology, Provenance and Authorship of Early Ḥadīth*. Cambridge, Cambridge University Press, 1983.

Kaegi, Walter E. *Byzantium and the Early Islamic Conquests*. Cambridge, Cambridge University Press, 1992.

Kaḥḥāla, ʿUmar Riḍā. *Muʿjam al-mu'allifīn: Tarājim muṣannifī al-kutub al-ʿArabiyya*, 15 vols. Damascus, al-Maktaba al-ʿArabiyya fī Dimashq, 1376–81/1957–61.

Kaltner, John. 'Mary' in *Ishmael Instructs Isaac: An Introduction to the Qur'an for Bible Readers*. Collegeville, MN, Liturgical Press, 1999, 207–39.

Katz, Marion Holmes. *Body of Text: The Emergence of the Sunni Law of Ritual Purity*. Albany, State University of New York Press, 2002.

——. *Prayer in Islamic Thought and Practice*. Cambridge, Cambridge University Press, 2013.

——. *Women in the Mosque: A History of Legal Thought and Social Practice*. New York, Columbia University Press, 2014.

——. 'Beyond *Ḥalāl* and *Ḥarām*: *Ghayra* ('Jealousy') as a Masculine Virtue in the Work of Ibn Qayyim al-Jawziyya'. *Cultural History* 8.2 (2019), 202–25.

Keddie, Nikki. *An Islamic Response to Imperialism: Political and Religious Writings of Sayyid Jamāl ad-Dīn 'al-Afghānī'*. Berkeley, University of California Press, 1968.

——. *Sayyid Jamāl ad-Dīn 'al-Afghānī': A Political Biography*. Berkeley, University of California Press, 1972.

Keeler, Annabel. *Sufi Hermeneutics: The Qur'an Commentary of Rashīd al-Dīn Maybudī*. Oxford, Oxford University Press in association with the Institute of Ismaili Studies, 2007.

Keeler, Annabel and Sajjad Rizvi, eds. *The Spirit and the Letter: Approaches to the Esoteric Interpretation of the Qur'an*. Oxford, Oxford University Press in association with the Institute of Ismaili Studies, 2016.

Kennedy, Philip F. *Abu Nuwas: A Genius of Poetry*. Oxford, Oneworld, 2005.

Kerr, Malcolm. *Islamic Reform: The Political and Legal Theories of Muḥammad ʿAbduh and Rashīd Riḍā*. Berkeley, University of California Press, 1966.

Khalid, Detlev. 'Some Aspects of Neo-Muʿtazilism'. *Islamic Studies* (Islamabad) 8 (1969), 319–47.

Khan, Ruqayya. 'Did a Woman Edit the Qur'ān? Hafṣa [sic] and Her Famed "Codex"'. *Journal of the American Academy of Religion* 82.1 (2014), 174–216.

Kholeif, Fathalla. *A Study on Fakhr al-Dīn al-Rāzī and His Controversies in Transoxiana*. Beirut, Dar el-Machreq, 1966.

Kinberg, Naphtali. *A Lexicon of al-Farrā's Terminology in His Qur'ān Commentary, with Full Definitions, English Summaries, and Extensive Citations*. Leiden, Brill, 1996.

Kirmānī, Sayyid Muḥammad-Riḍā Ghiyāthī. *Barrasī-ye ārā' wa naẓarāt-i tafsīrī-yi Abū Muslim Muḥammad b. Baḥr al-Iṣfahānī*. Qumm, Intishārāt-i Ḥuḍūr, 1378 Sh./1999.

Kister, M.J. '*Ḥaddithū ʿan Banī Isrā'īla wa-lā ḥaraja*'. *Israel Oriental Studies* 2 (1972), 215–39.

Klopfer, Helmut. *Das Dogma des Imâm al-Ḥaramain al-Djuwainî und sein Werk al-ʿAqîdat an-Niẓâmîyya*. Cairo, Salaheddine Boustany; Wiesbaden, Otto Harrassowitz, 1958.

Kohlberg, Etan. *A Medieval Muslim Scholar at Work: Ibn Ṭāwūs and His Library*. Leiden, Brill, 1992.

Kohlberg, Etan and Mohammad Ali Amir-Moezzi. *Revelation and Falsification: The Kitāb al-Qirā'āt of Aḥmad b. Muḥammad al-Sayyārī*. Leiden, Brill, 2009.

Kraus, Paul. 'The Controversies of Fakhr al-Dīn al-Rāzī'. *Islamic Culture* 12 (1938), 131–53.

Krone, Susanne. *Die Altarabische Gottheit al-Lat*. Frankfurt am Main, Peter Lang, 1992.

Kugle, Scott. *Homosexuality in Islam: Critical Reflections on Gay, Lesbian, and Transgender Muslims*. London, Oneworld, 2010.

——. *Living Out Islam: Voices of Gay, Lesbian, and Transgender Muslims*. New York, New York University Press, 2014.

Kulinich, Alena. 'Beyond Theology: Muʿtazilite Scholars and Their Authority in al-Rummānī's Tafsīr'. *Bulletin of the School of Oriental and African Studies* 78.1 (2015), 135–48.

——. 'Rethinking Muʿtazilite *Tafsīr*: From Essence to History'. *Religion and Culture, Seoul National University* 29 (2015), 227–62.

Künkler, Mirjam and Devin Stewart, eds. *Women's Religious Authority in Shiʿi Islam: Past and Present*. Edinburgh, Edinburgh University Press, 2020.

Künkler, Mirjam and Roja Fazaeli. 'The Life of Two *Mujtahidas*: Female Religious Authority in Twentieth Century Iran' in *Women, Leadership, and Mosques: Changes in Contemporary Islamic Authority*, ed. Masooda Bano and Hilary Kalmbach. Leiden, Brill, 2016, 127–60.

Laidlaw, James. *The Subject of Virtue: An Anthropology of Ethics and Freedom*. Cambridge, Cambridge University Press, 2014.

Lalani, Arzina. *Early Shīʿī Thought: The Teachings of Imam Muḥammad al-Bāqir*. London, I.B. Tauris in association with the Institute of Ismaili Studies, 2000.

Lambek, Michael. *Ordinary Ethics: Anthropology, Language and Action*. New York, Fordham University Press, 2010.

Landau-Tasseron, Ella, tr. *The History of al-Ṭabarī*, vol. XXXIX: *Biographies of the Prophet's Companions and their Successors*. Albany, State University of New York Press, 1998.

Landolt, Hermann. 'Der Briefwechsel zwischen Kāšānī und Simnānī über Waḥdat al-Wuǧūd'. *Der Islam* 50 (1973), 29–81.

Lane, Andrew. *A Traditional Muʿtazilite Qur'ān Commentary: The Kashshāf of Jār Allāh al-Zamakhsharī (d. 538/1144)*. Leiden, Brill, 2006.

Lane, Edward William. *Arabic–English Lexicon*. Repr. Cambridge, The Islamic Texts Society, 1984.

Lange, Christian. *Paradise and Hell in Islamic Traditions*. Cambridge, Cambridge University Press, 2016.

Laoust, Henri. *Le califat dans la doctrine de Raŝīd Riḍā*: Traduction annotée d'*al-Ḫilafa au al-Imama al-ʿuẓmā* (Le Califat ou l'Imāma suprême). Beirut, Institut Français de Damas, 1938.

Lecker, Michael. 'Biographical Notes on Abū 'Ubayda Maʿmar b. al-Muthannā', *Studia Islamica* 81 (1995), 71–100.

——. 'Biographical Notes on Ibn Shihāb al-Zuhrī'. *Journal of Semitic Studies* 41 (1996), 21–63.

Lecomte, Gérard. 'Sufyān al-Thawrī: Quelques remarques sur le personnage et son oeuvre'. *Bulletin d'études orientales de l'Institut Français de Damas* 30 (1978), 51–60.

Leemhuis, F. 'MS 1075 *tafsīr* of the Cairene Dār al-Kutub and Mujāhid's *tafsīr*' in *Proceedings of the Ninth Congress of the Union Européene des Arabisants et Islamisants*, ed. R. Peters. Leiden, Brill, 1981, 169–81.

Levitt, Matthew. *Hezbollah: The Global Footprint of Lebanon's Party of God*. Washington, DC, Georgetown University Press, 2015.

Lory, Pierre. *Les commentaires ésoteriques du Coran d'après ʿAbd al-Razzāq al-Qāshānī*. Paris, Les Deux Océans, 1980; 2nd rev. edn, 1990.

Lowry, Joseph E. *Early Islamic Legal Theory: The Risāla of Muḥammad Ibn Idrīs al-Shāfiʿī*. Leiden, Brill, 2007.

MacLeod, Arlene E. 'Hegemonic Relations and Gender Resistance: The New Veiling as Accommodating Protest in Cairo'. *Signs: Journal of Women in Culture and Society* 17.3 (1992), 533–57.

Madelung, Wilferd. 'Early Sunni Doctrine Concerning Faith as Reflected in the *Kitāb al-Īmān* by Abū 'Ubayd al-Qāsim b. Sallām (d. 224/838)'. *Studia Islamica* 32 (1970), 233–54.

——. 'Ar-Rāghib al-Iṣfahānī und die Ethik al-Ghazālīs' in *Islamwissenschaftliche Abhandlungen Fritz Meier zum 60sten Geburtstag*, ed. R. Gramlich. Wiesbaden, Steiner, 1974, 152–63.

——. 'The Early Murji'a in Khurāsān and Transoxania and the Spread of Ḥanafism'. *Der Islam* 59 (1982), 32–9.

——. 'The Theology of al-Zamakhsharī' in *Actas del XII Congreso de la U.E.A.I. (Malaga, 1984)*. Madrid, Union Européene d'Arabistants et d'Islamisants, 1986, 485–95.

——. *Religious and Ethnic Movements in Medieval Islam*. London, Routledge, 1992.

——. 'Abd Allāh b. 'Abbās and Shīʿite Law' in *Law, Christianity and Modernism in Islamic Society: Proceedings of the Eighteenth Congress of the Union Européene des Arabisants et Islamisants*, ed. U. Vermeulen and J.M.F. van Reeth. Leuven, Peeters, 1998, 13–25.

Maghen, Ze'ev. 'See No Evil: Morality and Methodology in Ibn al-Qaṭṭān al-Fāsī's *Aḥkām al-Naẓar bi-Ḥāssat al-Baṣar*'. *Islamic Law and Society* 14.3 (2007), 342–90.

Mahdawī, Aṣghar, and Iraj Afshar, eds. *Majmūʿa-yi asnād wa madārik-i chap-nashūda dar bāra-yi Sayyid Jamāl al-Dīn mashhūr bi-Afghānī/Documents inédits concernant Seyyed Jamāl al-Dīn Afghānī*. Tehran, Dānishgāh-i Tehran; Institut Français de Recherches en Iran, 1342 Sh./1963.

Mahmoud, Mohamed A. *Quest for Divinity: A Critical Examination of the Thought of Mahmud Muhammad Taha*. New York, Syracuse University Press, 2007.

Malka, Orit. 'Disqualified Witnesses Between Tannaitic Halakha and Roman Law: The Archaeology of a Legal Institution'. *Law and History Review* 37.4 (2019), 903–36.

Mallat, Chibli. *The Renewal of Islamic Law: Muhammad Baqer as-Sadr, Najaf and the Shi'i International*. Cambridge, Cambridge University Press, 1993.

Marcinkowski, Muhammad I. 'A Glance on the First of the Four Canonical *Ḥadīth* Collections of the Twelver-Shīʿites: *Al-Kāfī* by al-Kulaynī (d. 328 or 329 AH/940 or 941 C.E.)'. *Hamdard Islamicus*, 24.2 (2001), 13–30.

——. 'Rapprochement and Fealty during the Būyids and Early Saljūqs: The Life and Times of Muḥammad ibn al-Ḥasan al-Ṭūsī'. *Islamic Studies* (Islamabad) 40.2 (2001), 273–96.

Marcotte, Roxanne. 'The Qur'ān in Egypt, 1: Bint al-Shāti' on Women's Emancipation' in *Coming to Terms with the Qur'ān: A Volume in Honor of Professor Issa Boullata, McGill University*, ed. Khaleel Mohammad and Andrew Rippin. New Jersey, Islamic Publications International, 2008, 179–208.

Maʿrifat, Muḥammad Hādī. *Al-Tafsīr wa'l-Mufassirūn fī thawbihi'l-qashīb*, 2 vols. Mashhad, al-Jāmiʿa al-Raḍawiyya li'l-ʿUlūm al-Islāmiyya, 1997–8.

Marín, Manuela. 'Des emigrations forcées: Les *ʿulamā'* d'al-Andalus face a la conquête chrétienne' in *L'Occident musulman et l'Occident chrétien au Moyen Âge*, ed. Mohammed Hammam. Rabat, La Faculté des lettres et des Sciences Humaines, Université Mohammed V, 1995, 43–59.

——. 'Disciplining Wives: A Historical Reading of Qur'ân 4:34'. *Studia Islamica* 97 (2003), 5–40.

Marín, Manuela and Randi Deguilhem, eds. *Writing the Feminine: Women in Arab Sources*. London, I.B. Tauris, 2002.

Marlow, Louise. *Hierarchy and Egalitarianism in Islamic Thought*. Cambridge, Cambridge University Press, 1997.

Marmura, Michael E. 'Some Aspects of Avicenna's Theory of God's Knowledge of Particulars'. *Journal of the American Oriental Society* 82.3 (1962), 299–312.

Marogy, Amal. *Kitāb Sībawayhi: Syntax and Pragmatics*. Leiden, Brill, 2010.

Martin, Richard C., Mark R. Woodward and Dwi S. Atmaja. *Defenders of Reason in Islam: Muʿtazilism from Medieval School to Modern Symbol*. Oxford, Oneworld, 1997.

Mashannī, Muṣṭafā Ibrāhīm. *Madrasat al-Tafsīr fī'l-Andalus*. Beirut, Mu'assasat al-Risāla, 1986.

Maʿṣūmī, M. Ṣaghīr Ḥasan. 'Imām Fakhr al-Dīn al-Rāzī and His Critics'. *Islamic Studies* (Islamabad) 6 (1967), 355–74.

Mayer, Farhana. Review of *The Women of Madina*, by Muḥammad Ibn Saʿd (tr. Aisha Bewley), *Journal of Qur'anic Studies* 2.1 (2000), 139–41.

Mayer, Toby, tr. *Keys to the Arcana: Shahrastānī's Esoteric Commentary on the Qur'an*. Oxford, Oxford University Press in association with the Institute of Ismaili Studies, 2009.

McAuliffe, Jane Dammen. 'Qur'ānic Hermeneutics: The Views of al-Ṭabarī and Ibn Kathīr' in *Approaches to the History of the Interpretation of the Qur'ān*, ed. Andrew Rippin. Oxford, Clarendon Press, 1988, 46–62.

——. 'Fakhr al-Dīn al-Rāzī on God as al-Khāliq' in *God and Creation: An Ecumenical Symposium*, ed. David B. Burrell and Bernard McGinn. Notre Dame, IN, University of Notre Dame Press, 1990, 276–96.

McAuliffe, Jane Dammen, Barry D. Walfish and Joseph W. Goering, eds. *With Reverence for the Word: Medieval Scriptural Exegesis in Judaism, Christianity, and Islam*. Oxford, Oxford University Press, 2003.

Meier, Fritz. 'Stambuler Handschriften dreier persischer Mystiker: 'Ain al-quḍāt al-Hamadānī, Naǧm ad-dīn al-Kubrā, Naǧm ad-dīn ad-Dāja'. *Der Islam* 24 (1937), 1–39.

Melchert, Christopher. 'Ibn Mujāhid and the Establishment of Seven Qur'anic Readings'. *Studia Islamica* 91 (2000), 5–22.

Mir-Hosseini, Ziba. *Marriage on Trial: Islamic Family Law in Iran and Morocco*. London, I.B. Tauris, 1993.

——. *Islam and Gender: The Religious Debate in Contemporary Iran*. Princeton, NJ, Princeton University Press, 1999.

——. 'Islamic Law and the Question of Gender Equality' in *Routledge Handbook of Islamic Law*, ed. Khaled Abou El Fadl, Ahmad Atif Ahmad and Said Fares Hassan. Abingdon, Routledge, 2019, 340–54.

Mir-Hosseini, Ziba, Mulki al-Sharmani and Jana Rumminger, eds. *Men in Charge? Rethinking Authority in Muslim Legal Tradition*. London, Oneworld, 2015.

Mirza, Younus. 'Ishmael as Abraham's Sacrifice: Ibn Taymiyya and Ibn Kathīr on the Intended Victim'. *Islam and Muslim-Christian Relations* 24.3 (2013), 277–98.

——. 'Was Ibn Kathīr the "Spokesperson" for Ibn Taymiyya? Jonah as a Prophet of Obedience'. *Journal of Qur'anic Studies* 16.1 (2014), 1–19.

Modarressi, Hossein. *Crisis and Consolidation in the Formative Period of Shi'ite Islam: Abū Ja'far ibn Qiba al-Rāzī and His Contribution to Imāmite Shī'ite Thought*. Princeton, NJ, Darwin Press, 1993.

——. *Tradition and Survival: A Bibliographical Survey of Early Shī'ite Literature*. Oxford, Oneworld, 2003.

Mookherjee, Monica. 'Affective Citizenship: Feminism, Postcolonialism and the Politics of Recognition'. *Critical Review of International Social and Political Philosophy* 8.1 (2005), 31–50.

Morony, Michael G. *Iraq After the Muslim Conquest*. Princeton, NJ, Princeton University Press, 1984.

Motzki, Harald. '*The Muṣannaf* of 'Abd al-Razzāq al-Ṣan'ānī as a Source of Authentic *aḥādīth* of the First Century AH', *Journal of Near Eastern Studies* 50 (1991), 1–21.

——, ed. *The Biography of Muḥammad: The Issue of the Sources*. Leiden, Brill, 2000.

——. *The Origins of Islamic Jurisprudence: Meccan Fiqh Before the Classical Schools*. Leiden, Brill, 2002.

Mourad, Suleiman. 'Review of Andrew Lane, *A Traditional Mu'tazilite Qur'ān Commentary: The Kashshāf of Jār Allāh al-Zamakhsharī (d. 538/1144)*'. *Journal of Semitic Studies* 52.2 (2007), 409–11.

——. 'The Survival of the Mu'tazila Tradition of Qur'anic Exegesis in Shī'ī and Sunnī *tafāsīr*'. *Journal of Qur'anic Studies* 12 (2010), 83–100.

——. 'The Revealed Text and the Intended Subtext: Notes on the Hermeneutics of the Qur'ān in Mu'tazilah Discourse as Reflected in the *Tahdhīb* of al-Ḥākim al-Jishumī (d. 494/1101)' in *Islamic Philosophy, Science, Culture, and Religion: Studies in Honor of Dimitri Gutas*, ed. Felicitas Opwis and David Reisman. Leiden, Brill, 2012, 367–95.

——. 'The Mu'tazila and their *Tafsīr* Tradition: A Comparative Study of Five Exegetical Glosses on Qur'an 3:178' in *Tafsīr: Interpreting the Qur'an. Critical Concepts in Islamic Studies*, ed. Mustafa Shah. Abingdon, Routledge, 2012, III, 267–83.

——. 'Towards a Reconstruction of the Muʿtazilī Tradition of Qur'anic Exegesis: Reading the Introduction to the *Tahdhīb* of al-Ḥākim al-Jishumī (d. 494/1101) and Its Application' in *Aims, Methods and Contexts of Qur'ānic Exegesis (2nd/8th–9th/15th C.)*, ed. Karen Bauer. Oxford, Oxford University Press in association with the Institute of Ismaili Studies, 2013, 101–40.

Moussavi, Ahmed Kazemi. *Religious Authority in Shiʿite Islam: From the Office of Mufti to the Institution of Marjaʿ*. Kuala Lumpur, International Institute of Islamic Thought and Civilization, 1996.

Mubarak, Hadia. 'Breaking the Interpretive Monopoly: A Re-examination of Verse 4:34'. *Hawwa* 2.3 (2004), 261–89.

al-Muftāḥ, Fareed Y.Y.M. 'The Sources of al-Ṭabarī's *Tafsīr*'. Unpublished PhD dissertation, University of Edinburgh, 1998.

Munt, Harry. 'What did Conversion to Islam Mean in Seventh-Century Arabia?' in *Islamisation: Comparative Perspectives from History*, ed. Andrew Peacock. Edinburgh, Edinburgh University Press, 2017, 83–101.

Murata, Sachiko. *Mutʿa: Temporary Marriage in Islamic Law*. London, Mohammadi Press, 1987.

——. *The Tao of Islam: A Sourcebook on Gender Relationships in Islamic Thought*. Albany, State University of New York Press, 1992.

Murray, Stephen O. and Will Roscoe, eds. *Islamic Homosexualities: Culture, History, and Literature*. New York, New York University Press, 1997.

Musa'ad, Ishaq and Kenneth Cragg, tr. *The Theology of Unity: The First Translation of a Work by the Father of 20th Century Muslim Thought* [translation of Muḥammad 'Abduh's *Risālat al-Tawḥīd*]. London, Allen and Unwin, 1966.

Mutahhari, Murtada. *Woman and Her Rights*. CreateSpace Independent Publishing Platform, 2015.

Naguib, Shuruq. 'Bint al-Shāṭi''s Approach to *tafsīr*: An Egyptian Exegete's Journey from Hermeneutics to Humanity'. *Journal of Qur'anic Studies* 17.1 (2015), 45–84.

Najmabadi, Afsaneh. *Women with Mustaches and Men without Beards: Gender and Sexual Anxieties of Iranian Modernity*. Berkeley, University of California Press, 2005.

——. *Professing Selves: Transsexuality and Same-Sex Desire in Contemporary Iran*. Durham, NC, Duke University Press, 2014.

Naʿnaʿa, Ramzī. *Al-Isrāʾīliyyāt wa āthāruhā fī kutub al-tafsīr*. Damascus, Dār al-Qalam; Beirut, Dār al-Ḍiyāʾ, 1970.

Nasser, Shady. *The Transmission of the Variant Readings of the Qur'ān: The Problem of Tawātur and the Emergence of Shawādhdh*. Leiden, Brill, 2012.

——. 'Revisiting Ibn Mujāhid's Position on the Seven Canonical Readings: Ibn ʿĀmir's Problematic Reading of *kun fa-yakūna*'. *Journal of Qur'anic Studies* 17.1 (2015), 85–113.

——. *The Second Canonisation of the Qur'ān (324/936): Ibn Mujāhid and the Founding of the Seven Readings*. Leiden, Brill, 2020.

Neuwirth, Angelika. *Der Koran*, vol. I: *Poetische Prophetie. Frühmekkanische Suren*. Berlin, Verlag der Weltreligionen, 2011.

——. 'From Tribal Genealogy to Divine Covenant: Qur'ānic Re-figurations of Pagan Arab Ideals Based on Biblical Models' in eadem, *Scripture, Poetry and the Making of a Community: Reading the Qur'an as a Literary Text*. Oxford, Oxford University Press in association with the Institute of Ismaili Studies, 2014, 53–75.

——. 'Imagining Mary, Disputing Jesus: Reading *Sūrat Maryam* (Q. 19) and Related Meccan Texts in the Context of the Qur'ānic Communication Process' in eadem, *Scripture Poetry, and the Making of a Community: Reading the Qur'ān as a Literary Text*. Oxford, Oxford University Press in association with the Institute of Ismaili Studies, 2014, 328–58.

——. 'Mary and Jesus: Counterbalancing the Biblical Patriarchs. A Re-Reading of *Sūrat Maryam* (Q. 19) in *Sūrat Āl 'Imrān* (Q. 3)' in eadem, *Scripture, Poetry, and the Making of a Community: Reading the Qur'ān as a Literary Text*. Oxford, Oxford University Press in association with the Institute of Ismaili Studies, 2014, 359–84.

Newman, Andrew. *The Formative Period of Twelver Shīʿism: Ḥadīth as Discourse Between Qum and Baghdad*. Richmond, Surrey, Curzon Press, 2000.

Nguyen, Martin. *Sufi Master and Qur'an Scholar: Abū'l-Qāsim al-Qushayrī and the Laṭā'if al-Ishārāt*. Oxford, Oxford University Press in association with the Institute of Ismaili Studies, 2012.

Nöldeke, Theodor and Friedrich Schwally *et al. The History of the Qur'an*. Edited and translated by Wolfgang H. Behn. Leiden, Brill, 2013.

Norton, Angus. *Hezbollah: A Short History*. Princeton, NJ, Princeton University Press, 2014.

al-Nuʿmānī, Muḥammad Riḍā. *Al-Shahīd al-Ṣadr: Sanawāt al-miḥna wa-ayyām al-ḥisār*. Beirut, Dār al-Hādī, 1997.

Nwyia, Paul. *Exégèse coranique et langage mystique: Nouvel essai sur le lexique technique des mystiques musulmans*. Beirut, Dar el-Machreq, 1970.

Nyazee, Imran A.K. *Outlines of Islamic Jurisprudence*. Islamabad, Center for Excellence in Research, 1998; 6th edn, 2016.

Ohlander, Erik S. 'Fear of God (*taqwā*) in the Qur'ān: Some Notes on Semantic Shift and Thematic Context'. *Journal of Semitic Studies* 50.1 (2005), 137–52.

Ouzagane, Lahoucine, ed. *Islamic Masculinities*. London, Zed Books, 2006.

Pakkala, Maria. '"Take not Jews and Christians as Intimates!" Depictions of Jews and Christians in Modern Shīʿī Qur'ānic Exegesis'. Unpublished PhD dissertation, University of Helsinki, 2019.

Pease, Allan and Barbara Pease. *Why Men Don't Listen and Women Can't Read Maps*. London, Orion, 2001.

Pierce, Leslie. 'Writing Histories of Sexuality in the Middle East'. *American Historical Review* 114.5 (2009), 1325–39.

Pink, Johanna. 'Modern and Contemporary Interpretation of the Qur'ān' in *The Wiley Blackwell Companion to the Qur'ān*, 2nd edn, ed. Andrew Rippin and Jawid Mojaddedi. Oxford, Wiley, 2017, 479–91.

——. *Muslim Qur'ānic Interpretation Today: Media, Genealogies and Interpretive Communities*. Sheffield, Equinox, 2019.

Pregill, Michael. 'Isrā'īliyyāt, Myth, and Pseudepigraphy: Wahb B. Munabbih and the Early Islamic Versions of the Fall of Adam and Eve'. *Jerusalem Studies in Arabic and Islam* 34 (2008), 215–83.

——. 'Exegesis' in *The Routledge Handbook on Early Islam*, ed. Herbert Berg. Abingdon, Routledge, 2018, 98–125.

Qāba, ʿAbd al-Ḥalīm b. Muḥammad al-Hādī. *Al-Qirā'āt al-Qur'āniyya: Tārīkhuhā thubūtuhā ḥujiyyatuhā wa-aḥkāmuhā*. Beirut, Dār al-Gharb al-Islāmī, 1999.

al-Qadi, Wadad. 'The Development of the Term *Ghulāt* in Muslim Literature with Special Reference to the Kaysāniyya' in *Akten des VII. Kongresses für Arabistik und Islamwissenschaft, Göttingen, 15. bis 22. August 1974*, ed. Albert Dietrich. Göttingen, Vandenhoeck and Ruprecht, 1976, 302–9.

Qāsimzādah, Muḥammad, ed. *Yādnāma-yi Ṭabarī: Shaykh al-mu'arrikhīn Abū Ja'far Muḥammad b. Jarīr Ṭabarī 225–310 hijrī qamarī*. Tehran, Sāzmān-i Chāp wa Intishārāt-i Wizārat-i Farhang wa Irshād-i Islāmī, Markaz-i Taḥqīqāt-i 'Ilmī-yi Kishwar-i Wizārat-i Farhang va Āmūzish-i 'Ālī, 1369 Sh./1991.

Quraishi, Asifa and Frank Vogel, eds. *The Islamic Marriage Contract: Case Studies in Islamic Family Law*. Cambridge, MA, Harvard University Press, 2008.

Rabīʿ, Āmāl 'Abd al-Raḥmān. *Al-Isrā'īliyyāt fī tafsīr al-Ṭabarī: Dirāsa fī'l-lugha wa'l-maṣādir al-ʿibriyya*. Cairo, Dār al-Thaqāfa al-'Arabiyya, 2000.

Radle, Gabriel. 'The Veiling of Women in Byzantium: Liturgy, Hair, and Identity in a Medieval Rite of Passage'. *Speculum: A Journal of Medieval Studies* 94.4 (2019), 1070–1115.

Raghib, Yusuf. *Actes de vente d'esclaves et d'animaux en Égypte médiévale*, 2 vols. Paris, Institut français d'archéologie orientale, 2002.

Rahman, Fazlur. *Islam and Modernity: Transformation of an Intellectual Tradition*. Chicago, IL, University of Chicago Press, 1982.

Ra'ūf, 'Ādil. *Muḥammad Bāqir al-Ṣadr bayna diktātūriyyatayn*. Damascus, Markaz al-'Irāqī li'l-Iʿlām wa'l-Dirāsāt, 2001.

Reynolds, Gabriel Said. *The Qur'an and the Bible: Text and Commentary*. New Haven, CT, Yale University Press, 2018.

Riḍā, Muḥammad Rashīd. *Ta'rīkh al-Ustādh al-Imām al-Shaykh Muḥammad 'Abduh*, 3 vols. Cairo, Maṭba'at al-Manār, 1906–31.

Rippin, Andrew. 'Al-Zuhrī, *naskh al-Qur'ān* and the Problem of Early *Tafsīr* Texts'. *Bulletin of the School of Oriental and African Studies* 47 (1984), 22–43.

——, ed. *Approaches to the History of the Interpretation of the Qur'ān*. Oxford, Oxford University Press, 1988.

——. '*Tafsīr Ibn 'Abbās* and Criteria for Dating Early *tafsīr* Texts'. *Jerusalem Studies in Arabic and Islam* 18 (1994), 38–83.

Rippin, Andrew and Roberto Tottoli, eds. *Books and Written Culture of the Islamic World: Studies Presented to Claude Gilliot on the Occasion of His 75th Birthday*. Leiden, Brill, 2014.

Ritchie, Stuart. *Science Fictions: How Fraud, Bias, Negligence, and Hype Undermine the Search for Truth*. New York, Metropolitan Books, 2020.

Rizvi, Sajjad H. *Mullā Ṣadrā Shīrāzī: His Life and Works and the Sources for Safavid Philosophy*. Oxford, Oxford University Press for Manchester University, 2007.

——. *Mulla Sadra and Metaphysics: Modulation of Being*. Abingdon, Routledge, 2009.

Robinson, Chase F. *Islamic Historiography*. Cambridge, Cambridge University Press, 2003.

Robinson, Neal. *Discovering the Qur'an: A Contemporary Approach to a Veiled Text*, 2nd edn. Washington, DC, Georgetown University Press, 2003.

Rosenthal, Franz, tr. *The History of al-Ṭabarī*, vol. I: *General Introduction and From the Creation to the Flood*. Albany, State University of New York Press, 1989.

El-Rouayheb, Khaled. *Before Homosexuality in the Islamic World, 1500–1800*. Chicago, IL, University of Chicago Press, 2005.

Rowson, Everett. 'The Categorization of Gender and Sexual Irregularity in Medieval Arabic Vice Lists' in *Body Guards: The Cultural Politics of Gender Ambiguity*, ed. Julia Epstein and Kristina Straub. New York, Routledge, 1991, 50–79.

——. 'The Effeminates of Early Medina'. *Journal of the American Oriental Society* 111 (1991), 671–93.
——. 'Two Homoerotic Narratives from Mamluk Literature: Al-Safadi's *Law'at al-shaki* and Ibn Daniyal's *al-Mutayyam*' in *Homoeroticism in Classical Arabic Literature*, ed. J.W. Wright, Jr. and Everett K. Rowson. New York, Columbia University Press, 1997, 158–91.
——. 'Gender Irregularity as Entertainment: Institutionalized Transvestism at the Caliphal Court in Medieval Baghdad' in *Gender and Difference in the Middle Ages*, ed. Sharon Farmer and Carol Braun Pasternack. Minneapolis, University of Minnesota Press, 2003, 45–72.
Rubin, Uri. 'Exegesis and *Ḥadīth*: The Case of the Seven *Mathānī*' in *Approaches to the Qur'ān*, ed. G.R. Hawting and Abdel-Kader A. Shareef. London, Routledge, 1993, 141–56.
——. '*Al-walad li'l-firāsh* and the Islamic Campaign against *Zinā*'. *Studia Islamica* 78 (1993), 5–26.
——. *The Eye of the Beholder: The Life of Muḥammad as Viewed by the Early Muslims*. Princeton, NJ, Darwin Press, 1995.
——. *Between Bible and Qur'ān: The Children of Israel and the Islamic Self-Image*. Princeton, NJ, Darwin Press, 1999.
Rutner, Maryam. 'Religious Authority, Gendered Recognition, and Instrumentalization of Nusrat Amin in Life and After Death'. *Journal of Middle East Women's Studies*, 11.1 (2015), 21–41.
Saad-Ghorayeb, Amal. *Hizbu'llah: Politics and Religion*. London, Pluto Press, 2002.
Sachedina, Abdulaziz, tr. *The Prolegomena to the Qur'ān*. New York, Oxford University Press, 1998 (for his translation of Khū'ī's *al-Bayān*, *see* primary sources).
Sadan, Arik. 'The Meaning of the Technical Term *Jawāb* in Arabic Grammar'. *Jerusalem Studies in Arabic and Islam* 37 (2010), 129–37.
Sadeghi, Behnam. 'The Chronology of the Qur'ān: A Stylometric Research Program'. *Arabica* 58 (2011), 210–99.
Safi, Omid, ed. *Progressive Muslims: On Justice, Gender, and Pluralism (Islam in the Twenty-First Century)*. London, Oneworld, 2003.
Saflo, Mohammad Moslem Adel. *Al-Juwaynī's Thought and Methodology, with a Translation and Commentary of Luma' al-Adilla*. Berlin, Klaus Swartz, 2000.
Saleh, Walid. *The Formation of the Classical Tafsīr Tradition: The Qur'ān Commentary of al-Tha'labī (d. 427/1035)*. Leiden, Brill, 2004.
——. 'The Last of the Nishapuri School of Tafsir: Al-Wahidi and his Significance in the History of Quranic Exegesis'. *Journal of the American Oriental Society* 126.2 (2006), 223–43.
——. 'Ibn Taymiyya and the Rise of Radical Hermeneutics: An Analysis of *An Introduction to the Foundations of Qurānic Exegesis*' in *Ibn Taymiyya and His Times*, ed. Yossef Rapoport and Shahab Ahmed. Karachi, Oxford University Press Pakistan, 2010, 123–62.
——. 'Preliminary Remarks on the Historiography of *Tafsīr* in Arabic: A History of the Book Approach'. *Journal of Qur'anic Studies* 12 (2010), 6–40.
——. 'Marginalia and the Periphery: A Tunisian Modern Historian and the History of Qur'anic Exegesis'. *Numen* 58.2–3 (2011), 284–313.
——. 'Rereading al-Ṭabarī through al-Māturīdī: New Light on the Third Century Hijrī'. *Journal of Qur'anic Studies* 18.2 (2016), 180–209.

——. 'The Qur'ān Commentary of al-Bayḍāwī: A History of *Anwār al-Tanzīl*'. *Journal of Qur'anic Studies* 23.1 (2021), 71–102.

al-Sāmarrā'ī, Ḥabīb. 'Rashīd Riḍā al-mufassir'. Unpublished PhD dissertation, al-Azhar University, Cairo, 1978.

Sammoud, Hamadi. 'Un exégète oriental en Ifriqiya: Yaḥyâ Ibn Sallâm (742–815)', *Institut des belles-lettres arabes* 126 (1970), 227–42.

Sartain, Elizabeth M. *Jalāl al-Dīn al-Suyūṭī: Biography and Background*. Cambridge, Cambridge University Press, 1975.

Savage, Elizabeth. *A Gateway to Hell, a Gateway to Paradise: The North African Response to the Arab Conquests*. Princeton, NJ, Darwin Press, 1997.

Savant, Sarah. *The New Muslims of Post-Conquest Iran: Tradition, Memory, and Conversion*. Cambridge, Cambridge University Press, 2013.

al-Sawwāf, M.M. 'Muqātil b. Sulaymān: An Early Zaydī Theologian, with Special Reference to his *Tafsīr al-khams mi'at āya*'. Unpublished PhD dissertation, University of Oxford, 1969.

Schacht, Joseph. *An Introduction to Islamic Law*. Oxford, Clarendon Press, 1964.

Schöller, Marco. '*Sīra* and *tafsīr*: Muḥammad al-Kalbī on the Jews of Medina' in *The Biography of Muḥammad: The Issue of Sources*, ed. H. Motzki. Leiden, Brill, 2000, 18–48.

Sergeant, R.B. 'Early Arabic Prose' in *Arabic Literature to the End of the Umayyad Period (The Cambridge History of Arabic Literature)*, ed. A.F.L. Beeston, T.M. Johnstone, R.B. Serjeant and G.R. Smith. Cambridge, Cambridge University Press, 1983, 114–53.

Shah, Mustafa. 'Exploring the Genesis of Early Arabic Linguistic Thought: Qur'anic Readers and Grammarians of the Kūfan Tradition (Part I)'. *Journal of Qur'anic Studies* 5.1 (2003), 47–78.

——. 'Exploring the Genesis of Early Arabic Linguistic Thought: Qur'anic Readers and Grammarians of the Basran Tradition (Part II)'. *Journal of Qur'anic Studies* 5.2 (2003), 1–47.

Shaham, Ron. 'Women as Expert Witnesses in Pre-Modern Islamic Courts' in *Law, Custom, and Statute in the Muslim World: Studies in Honor of Aharon Layish*, ed. Ron Shaham. Leiden, Brill, 2007, 41–65.

Shaikh, Sa'diyya. 'Exegetical Violence: *Nushūz* in Qur'ānic Gender Ideology'. *Journal for Islamic Studies* 17 (1997), 49–73.

——. 'A *Tafsir* of Praxis: Gender, Marital Violence, and Resistance in a South African Muslim Community' in *Violence against Women in Contemporary World Religions: Roots and Cures*, ed. Daniel C. Maguire and Sa'diyya Shaikh. Cleveland, OH, Pilgrim Press, 2007, 66–89.

——. *Sufi Narratives of Intimacy: Ibn 'Arabi, Gender, and Sexuality*. Chapel Hill, University of North Carolina Press, 2012.

al-Shāmī, Sayyid Ḥusayn. *Al-Marjaʿiyya al-dīniyya min al-dhāt ilā'l-mu'assasa*. London, Dar al-Islam Foundation, 1999.

El Shamsy, Ahmed. *The Canonization of Islamic Law: A Social and Intellectual History*. Cambridge, Cambridge University Press, 2013.

——. 'Shame, Sin, and Virtue: Islamic Notions of Privacy' in *Public and Private in Ancient Mediterranean Law and Religion*, ed. Clifford Ando and Jörg Rüpke. Berlin, de Gruyter, 2015, 237–49.

Sharaf, M.A. *Jalāl al-Dīn al-Suyūṭī: Manhajuhu wa ārā'uhu al-kalāmiyya*. Beirut, Dār al-Nahḍa al-ʿArabiyya, 1981.

al-Shawābika, Aḥmad Fahd Barakāt. *Muḥammad Rashīd Riḍā wa dawruhu fī'l-ḥayāt al-fikriyya wa'l-siyāsiyya*. Amman, Dār ʿAmmār, 1989.

Shihadeh, Ayman. *The Teleological Ethics of Fakhr al-Dīn al-Rāzī*. Leiden, Brill, 2006.

Shpall, William. 'A Note on Najm al-Dīn al-Rāzī and the *Baḥr al-ḥaqāʾiq*'. *Folia Orientalia* 22 (1981–4), 69–80.

al-Shuaily, Sulaiman. 'Ibāḍī Tafsīr: A Comparison Between the Tafsīrs of Hūd al-Huwwārī and Saʿīd al-Kindī'. Unpublished PhD dissertation, University of Edinburgh, 2001.

al-Shushtarī, Muḥammad Taqī. *Qāmūs al-rijāl*, 14 vols. Tehran, Markaz Nashr al-Kitāb, 1968.

Silvers, Laury. '"In the Book We Have Left out Nothing": The Ethical Problem of the Existence of Verse 4:34 in the Qur'an'. *Comparative Islamic Studies* 2.2 (2008), 171–80.

Sinai, Nicolai. 'An Interpretation of *Sūrat al-Najm* (Q. 53)'. *Journal of Qur'anic Studies* 13.2 (2011), 1–28.

——. 'The Qur'anic Commentary of Muqātil b. Sulaymān and the Evolution of Early *Tafsīr* Literature' in *Tafsīr and Islamic Intellectual History: Exploring the Boundaries of a Genre*, ed. Andreas Görke and Johanna Pink. Oxford, Oxford University Press in association with the Institute of Ismaili Studies, 2014, 113–43.

——. 'The Unknown Known: Some Groundwork for Interpreting the Medinan Qur'an'. *Mélanges de l'Université Saint-Joseph* 66 (2015–16), 47–96.

——. 'The Eschatological Kerygma of the Early Qur'an' in *Apocalypticism and Eschatology in Late Antiquity: Encounters in the Abrahamic Religions, 6th–8th Centuries*, ed. Hagit Amirav, Emmanouela Grypeou and Guy Stroumsa. Leuven, Peeters, 2017, 219–66.

——. *The Qur'an: A Historical-Critical Introduction*. Edinburgh, Edinburgh University Press, 2017.

Sindawi, Khaled. *Temporary Marriage in Sunni and Shiʿite Islam: A Comparative Study*. Wiesbaden, Harrassowitz Verlag, 2013.

Sirry, Mun'im. 'Muqātil b. Sulaymān and Anthropomorphism'. *Studia Islamica* 107.1 (2012), 38–64.

Smerdjian, Elyse. *Off the Straight Path: Illicit Sex, Law, and Community in Ottoman Aleppo*. Albany, State University of New York Press, 2016.

Smith, Jane and Yvonne Haddad. 'Women in the Afterlife: The Islamic View as Seen from the Qurʾān and Tradition'. *Journal of the American Academy of Religion* 43.1 (1975), 39–50.

——. 'The Virgin Mary in Islamic Tradition and Commentary'. *Muslim World* 79.3–4 (1989), 161–87.

De Sondy, Amanullah. *The Crisis of Islamic Masculinities*. London, Bloomsbury Academic, 2013.

Speidel, Bianca. *Islam as Power: Shiʿi Revivalism in the Oeuvre of Muḥammad Ḥusayn Faḍlallāh*. Abingdon, Routledge, 2021.

Spellberg, Denise A. *Politics, Gender, and the Islamic Past: The Legacy of 'A'isha Bint Abi Bakr*, rev. edn. New York, Columbia University Press, 1996.

——. 'Writing the Unwritten Life of the Islamic Eve: Menstruation and the Demonization of Motherhood'. *International Journal of Middle East Studies* 28 (1996), 305–24.

Stewart, Devin. 'Divine Epithets and the Dibacchius: Clausulae and Qur'anic Rhythm'. *Journal of Qur'anic Studies* 15.2 (2013), 22–64.

——. 'Introductory Oaths and the Question of Composite Sūras' in *Structural Dividers in the Qur'ān*, ed. Marianna Klar. Abingdon, Routledge, 2021, 267–337.

Stillman, Yedida K. *Arab Dress, A Short History: From the Dawn of Islam to Modern Times*, 2nd rev. edn, ed. Norman A. Stillman. Leiden, Brill, 2003.

Stowasser, Barbara Freyer. *Women in the Qur'an, Traditions, and Interpretation*. Oxford, Oxford University Press, 1994.

Street, Tony. 'Concerning the Life and Works of Fakhr al-Dīn al-Rāzī' in *Islam: Essays on Scripture, Thought and Society. A Festschrift in Honour of Antony H. Johns*, ed. Peter G. Riddell and Tony Street. Leiden, Brill, 1997, 135–46.

Subḥānī, Jafar. *Manshūr-i ʿaqāʾid-i Imāmiyyah*, ed. and tr. R.S. Kazemi as *Doctrines of Shiʿi Islam: A Compendium of Imami Beliefs and Practices*. London, I.B. Tauris, 2001.

Sukar, ʿAzmī. *Muʿjam al-Shuʿarāʾ fī tārīkh al-Ṭabarī*. Sidon, al-Maktaba al-ʿAṣriyya li'l-Ṭibāʿa wa'l-Nashr, 1999.

Sundermann, W. 'Die Jungfrau der guten Taten' in *Recurrent Patterns in Iranian Religions: From Mazdaism to Sufism*, ed. Philippe Gignoux. Paris, Association pour l'Avancement des Études Iraniennes, 1992, 159–73.

Taji-Farouki, Suha, ed. *Modern Muslim Intellectuals and the Qur'an*. Oxford, Oxford University Press in association with the Institute of Ismaili Studies, 2006.

Throckmorton, Burton H., Jr. *Gospel Parallels: A Comparison of the Synoptic Gospels, New Revised Standard Version*. Nashville, TN, Thomas Nelson, 1992 (orig. pub. 1949).

al-Ṭihrānī, Āghā Buzurg Muḥammad Muḥsin. *Al-Dharīʿa ilā taṣānīf al-shīʿa*, 25 vols. Najaf, Maṭbaʿat al-Gharāʾ, 1936–78.

——. *Ṭabaqāt aʿlām al-shīʿa*, ed. ʿAlī-Naqī Munzawī, 5 vols. Beirut, Dār al-Kitāb al-ʿArabī, 1971.

——. *Zindagī-nāma-yi Shaykh Ṭūsī*. Tehran, Farhangistān-i Adab wa Hunar-i Īrān, 1981.

Toorawa, Shawkat. '*Sūrat Maryam* (Q. 19): Lexicon, Lexical Echoes, English Translation'. *Journal of Qur'anic Studies* 13.1 (2011), 25–78.

Tottoli, Roberto. 'New Material on the Use and Meaning of the Term *Isrāʾīliyyāt*'. *Jerusalem Studies in Arabic and Islam* 50 (2021), 1–43.

Tourage, Mahdi. 'Affective Entanglements with the Sexual Imagery of Paradise in the Qur'an'. *Body and Religion* 3.1 (2019), 52–70.

Tucker, Judith. *Women, Family, and Gender in Islamic Law*. Cambridge, Cambridge University Press, 2008.

Ullah, Kifayat. *Al-Kashshāf: al-Zamakhsharī's Muʿtazilite Exegesis of the Qur'ān*. Berlin, de Gruyter, 2017.

ʿUmar, Aḥmad Mukhtār and ʿAbd al-ʿĀl Sālim Mukarram, eds. *Muʿjam al-qirāʾāt al-Qurʾāniyya: Maʿa muqaddima fī'l-qirāʾāt wa ashhar al-qurrāʾ*, 8 vols. Kuwait, Dhāt al-Salāsil (vols. III, V, VI, VIII, Kuwait, Maṭbūʿāt Jāmiʿat al-Kuwayt), 1982–.

Versteegh, Cornelis ["Kees"] H.M. 'Grammar and Exegesis: The Origins of Kufan Grammar and the *Tafsīr Muqātil*'. *Der Islam* 67.2 (1990), 206–42.

——. *Arabic Grammar and Qurʾānic Exegesis in Early Islam*. Leiden, Brill, 1993.

——. *The Arabic Language*. Edinburgh, Edinburgh University Press, 1997.

wadud, amina. *Qur'an and Woman: Rereading the Sacred Text from a Woman's Perspective*, 2nd edn. Oxford, Oxford University Press, 1999.

——. *Inside the Gender Jihad: Women's Reform in Islam*. Oxford, Oneworld, 2006.

Walbridge, Linda S., ed. *The Most Learned of the Shi'a: The Institution of the Marja' Taqlīd*. Oxford, Oxford University Press, 2001.

Walbridge, John. 'Muhammad Baqir al-Sadr: The Search for New Foundations' in *The Most Learned of the Shi'a: The Institution of the Marja' Taqlid*, ed. Linda S. Walbridge. New York, Oxford University Press, 2001, 131–9.

Walker, Paul. *A Guide to Conclusive Proofs for the Principles of Beliefs*. (See al-Juwaynī, *Kitāb al-Irshād*).

Wansbrough, John. *Quranic Studies*. London, Oxford University Press, 1977.

Watt, W. M. *Muhammad at Mecca*. Oxford, Clarendon Press, 1960.

Watt, W.M. and R. Bell. *Introduction to the Qur'an*. Edinburgh, Edinburgh University Press, 1970.

Wikan, Unni. 'Man Becomes Woman: Transsexualism in Oman as a Key to Gender Roles'. *Man* 12.2 (1977), 304–19.

——. 'The Omani *Xanith*: A Third Gender Role?' *Man* 13.3 (1978), 473–5.

——. *Behind the Veil in Arabia: Women in Oman*. Chicago, IL, University of Chicago Press, 1982.

Wild, Stefan. 'Lost in Philology? The Virgins of Paradise and the Luxenberg Hypothesis' in *The Qur'ān in Context: Historical and Literary Investigations into the Qur'ānic Milieu*, ed. Angelika Neuwirth, Nicolai Sinai and Michael Marx. Leiden, Brill, 2010, 625–47.

Wilkinson, John C. *Ibâḍism: Origins and Early Development in Oman*. Oxford, Oxford University Press, 2010.

Winter, Tim. 'Mary in Islam' in *Mary: The Complete Resource*, ed. Sara Jane Boss. Oxford, Oxford University Press, 2007, 479–502.

Wittig, Monique. 'The Category of Sex'. *Feminist Issues* 2.2 (1982), 63–8.

Yahya, Osman. *Historie et classification de l'œuvre d'Ibn 'Arabī: Étude critique*, 2 vols. Damascus, Institut Français de Damas, 1964.

Zahniser, A.H. Matthias. 'The Word of God and the Apostleship of 'Īsā: A Narrative Analysis of Āl 'Imrān (3): 33–62'. *Journal of Semitic Studies* 37.1 (Spring 1991), 77–112.

Zellentin, Holger. *The Qur'ān's Legal Culture: The Didascalia Apostolorum as a Point of Departure*. Tübingen, Mohr Siebeck, 2013.

Zempi, Irene. '"It's part of me, I feel naked without it": Choice, Agency and Identity for Muslim Women who Wear the Niqab'. *Ethnic and Racial Studies* 39.10 (2016), 1738–54.

al-Ziriklī, Khayr al-Dīn (d. 1396/1976). *Al-A'lām: Qāmūs tarājim li-ashhar al-rijāl wa'l-nisā' min al-'Arab wa'l-musta'ribīn wa'l-mustashriqīn*, 4th edn, 10 vols. Beirut, Dār al-'Ilm li'l-Malāyīn, 1979.

al-Zuḥaylī, Muḥammad Muṣṭafā. *Al-Imām al-Ṭabarī: Shaykh al-mufassirīn wa 'umdat al-mu'arrikhīn wa muqaddam al-fuqahā' al-muḥaddithīn*. Damascus, Dār al-Qalam, 1990.

Online Reports/Articles

'Boris Johnson Faces Criticism over Burka "Letter Box" Jibe'. BBC News, 6 August 2018. https://www.bbc.co.uk/news/uk-politics-45083275.

Freedom House. 'Hard-won Progress and a Long Road Ahead: Women's Rights in the Middle East and North Africa'. Accessed 31 May 2021. https://freedomhouse.org/sites/default/files/270.pdf.

'The Islamic Veil across Europe'. BBC News, 31 May 2018. https://www.bbc.com/news/world-europe-13038095.
Saritoprak, Zeki. 'Mary in Islam'. *Oxford Bibliographies* (2015). https://www.oxford-bibliographies.com/
UN Economic and Social Commission for Western Asia. 'Against Wind and Tides: A Review of the Status of Women and Gender Equality in the Arab Region (Beijing +20)' (7 January 2016), p. 56, n. 256. Accessed 1 July 2019. https://sustainabledevelopment.un.org/content/documents/2283ESCWA_Women%20and%20Gender%20Equality%20in%20the%20Arab%20Region_Beijing20.pdf.

Websites

Critical Muslim. https://criticalmuslim.com/
Musawah. https://www.musawah.org/
Oxford Bibliographies (2015). https://www.oxfordbibliographies.com/
The website of Muḥammad Ḥusayn Faḍl Allāh. http://www.bayynat.org

Blogs

Ali, Kecia. 'The Politics of Citation'. *Gender Avenger* blog, 31 May 2019. Accessed 21 September 2020. https://www.genderavenger.com/blog/politics-of-citation.
——. 'No Manthology is an Island'. *Journal of Feminist Studies in Religion* blog, 4 June 2019. Accessed 21 September 2020. https://www.fsrinc.org/no-manthology-is-an-island/
El Shamsy, Ahmed. 'How Not to Reform the Study of Islamic Law: A Response to Ayesha Chaudhry'. *Islamic Law Blog*, 14 December 2020. https://islamiclaw.blog/2020/12/14/how-not-to-reform-the-study-of-islamic-law-a-response-to-ayesha-chaudhry/
Katz, Marion. 'Who are We Writing for When We Translate Classical Texts?' *Islamic Law Blog*, 6 December 2019. https://islamiclaw.blog/2019/12/06/muwaṭṭa'-roundtable-who-are-we-writing-for-when-we-translate-classical-texts/

Index of Qur'anic Citations

Index of Qur'anic Citations

Index of Qur'anic Citations

Index of Qur'anic Citations

Index